Dale Turner
Yale Divinity School
November 12, 1941

Dale Turner
Yale Divinity School
November 12, 1941

CONCISE BIOGRAPHICAL DICTIONARY

★

CONCISE

BIOGRAPHICAL

DICTIONARY

★

BY HARRIET LLOYD FITZHUGH AND

PERCY K. FITZHUGH

GROSSET & DUNLAP · PUBLISHERS

NEW YORK

*Manufactured in the United States of America
by H. Wolff Book M'f'g. Co., Inc., New York*

FOREWORD

It is not necessary to tell the reader of this book that there have been other Biographical Dictionaries which have preceded it. There have been volumes set up in eye-straining agate type boasting of their thousands of "little Somebodies and great Nobodies," including assassins, knaves, madmen, traitors, spies and other "tagrag and bobtail."

Frankly, this volume cannot compete with works of such heterogeneous scope. But, when all is said and done, how many really famous people have stood out head and shoulders above their fellows in their various fields of activity in the long chain of centuries that make up the history of the world? Of all the great Kings and Queens, Presidents, Warriors, Statesmen, Scientists, Writers, Actors, Poets, Orators, Explorers, Clerics, Adventurers, Philosophers, Artists, Engineers, Composers, Inventors, Humanitarians—how many does the average citizen, the average student in pursuit of his studies, really need to know?

The authors of CONCISE BIOGRAPHICAL DICTIONARY believe that out of the thousands of mere *names* which Time has uncovered it is really necessary to be thoroughly familiar with the lives of only 500 great men and women of the present and the past. They have tried to see how many could be left out instead of trying to see how many they could include in a thoroughly useful reference volume of this character. They have tried also to do what few editors of such a work have succeeded in doing in the past—to treat each life without national bias. They have not skimped on the "foreigners" in order to pad the Americans. In the conclave of the truly great there are no "foreigners."

Before beginning their heroic task of selection which preceded the compilation of this volume the authors collected from teachers and pupils of High Schools lists of the names of the outstanding personalities with whom they would come in contact during the course of their studies throughout the entire High School curriculum. From these lists the "500 Indispensables" were selected. CONCISE BIOGRAPHICAL DICTIONARY becomes, therefore, of particular value and significance to the young student, although it will be found to be quite as useful as a volume of reference in the home and the business office.

You will note that our volume gives the approximate pronunciation of difficult and un-English names in accordance with the latest dicta of the best authorities, and that it includes a very complete and scholarly index at the rear of the book.

THE PUBLISHERS

October 1, 1935

CONCISE·BIOGRAPHICAL DICTIONARY

KEY TO PRONUNCIATION

ā as in fate
â as in senate
â as in care and as e in there
ă as in am
ä as in arm, father
ȧ as in ant
ạ as in all

ē as in eve
ê as in elate
ĕ as in end
ẽ as in fern and as i in sir

ī as in ice
ĭ as in ill

ō as in old
ô as in obey
ô as in nor
ŏ as in not
o͞o as in food and as u in rude

ū as in use
ů as in unite
ŭ as in cut
ṷ as in full, and as oo in foot
û as in burn

EDWIN AUSTIN ABBEY was one of the foremost of modern American painters.

He was born in Philadelphia, Penn., on April 1, 1852. After studying drawing and painting at the schools of the Pennsylvania Academy of Fine Arts, at the age of nineteen he entered the art department of the publishing house of Harper and Brothers in New York City. He had there the advantage of association with such men as Howard Pyle, Charles Stanley Reinhart, Joseph Pennell and Alfred Parsons, and became very successful as an illustrator. In 1878 he was sent to England to gather material for illustrating the poems of Robert Herrick. These were published in 1882 and attracted much public attention to Abbey's genuine artistic gifts. He next illustrated Goldsmith's comedy, *She Stoops to Conquer,* published in 1887, after which he made the drawing for a book of *Old Songs* (1889), and for the comedies and some of the tragedies of Shakespeare. In addition to his pen and ink drawings he worked in water colors and pastels with marked success.

In 1883 Abbey was elected to the Royal Institute of Painters in Water-Colours, London, and thereafter he was closely identified with the art life of England, where he spent much of his time. Among his most notable water colors are "The Evil Eye" (1877); "The Rose in October" (1879); "An Old Song" (1886); "The Visitors" (1890); and "The Jongleur" (1892). Among the best known of his pastels are those entitled "Beatrice," "Phyllis," and "Two Noble Kinsmen." Abbey did not undertake oil paintings to any extent until 1890. His first oil, exhibited at the London Royal Academy, was "A May Day Morn" (1890). In 1896 he exhibited there his "Richard, Duke of Gloucester and the Lady Anne." In that year he was elected A.R.A., becoming a full R.A. two years later. He also became a member of the National Academy of Design in New York and an honorary member of the Royal Bavarian Society, the Société Nationale des Beaux Arts, Paris, the American Water Color Society, and other art institutions. His fame was now secure and increased with the years, for he was an industrious worker and continually advanced in artistic stature. He was celebrated for the warmth and vividness of his coloring and for his ability to depict highly dramatic subjects. All of his paintings possessed a pronounced individuality that distinguished them from the work of his contemporaries.

Outstanding among his works are the frescoes on "The Quest of the Holy Grail," executed for the Boston Public Library, upon which he was engaged for a number of years. Multitudes of visitors to Boston make a pilgrimage to the Public Library to see these frescoes and reproductions of them have been widely distributed. In 1901 King Edward VII commissioned Abbey to paint a picture commemorating his coronation. This contained many portraits elaborately grouped and attracted wide attention.

The last years of Abbey's life were devoted to a series of mural paintings for the State Capitol Building at Harrisburg, Penn., one for the House of Representatives' Chamber, one for the Senate Room, and another for the ceiling of the dome. The decoration of the Peers' Corridor of the Houses of Parliament at Westminster was completed under his direction in 1910, a short time before his death. He received many medals; at the International Art Exhibition of Vienna in 1898; at Philadelphia in 1898; at the Paris Exhibitions of 1889 and 1900, and at Berlin in 1903. France made him a Chevalier of the Legion of Honor. The Metropolitan Museum of New York City has a number of fine specimens of his work, as has the Boston Museum of Fine Arts, the London National Gallery, and other art institutions. He died in London on August 1, 1911.

PETER ABELARD—(Abelard and Heloise)   1079–1142

PETER ABELARD (ăb'ē lärd) was a medieval French theologian and philosopher and probably the most enlightened thinker of his century. But to the great mass of people in modern times he is more familiar as a participant in one of the most celebrated and romantic love stories of history, and the names of Abelard and Heloise are as inseparably linked as the names of Romeo and Juliet.

He was born near Nantes, Brittany, in 1079, in the small village of Palet. He early exhibited a thirst for knowledge and a propensity for disputation in which he was aided by extraordinary facility in the field of logic. He went to Paris to prosecute his studies under William of Champeaux, but soon confounded his teacher with his fine spun argument and as a consequence of jealousy and dislike thus incurred he found it expedient to withdraw from the scene of acrimonious debate.

He went to Melun and later to Corbeil where his controversial activities aroused the keenest interest. He was not without devoted admirers but his originality of thought and boldness of expression condemned him to persecution. He was never physically robust and the wear and tear of controversy made it necessary for him to lay down his intellectual labors and return home in the interest of his health. He later returned to Paris where his influence as a lecturer soon became potent and some of the most distinguished thinkers of the time were among his supporters.

It was at the height of his triumphs that fate crossed his path with that of Heloise, the beautiful, seventeen year old niece of Fulbert, Canon of the Cathedral of Paris, a maiden no less remarkable for her talents and accomplishments than for her feminine charms. Notwithstanding that Abelard was then in his 38th year, he fell hopelessly in love with the girl whose admiration for him was soon kindled into passion. In the relation of teacher and pupil this romantic affair grew until the girl's uncle became aware of it through the discovery of the lovers' impassioned verses.

The Canon's attempt to separate them was unavailing; they fled into the country where Heloise gave birth to a child. That event no doubt had its influence in conciliating her uncle who gave his consent to their marriage. Soon afterward, however, Heloise returned to his home and denied the marriage in the hope of safeguarding her lover's ecclesiastical ambitions. A second elopement so aroused Fulbert that he procured the emasculation of Abelard in order to prejudice his chances of preferment in the church. The sequel of this unhappy love was that Abelard, in deepest mortification, became a monk in the Abbey of St. Denis and at his urgent request Heloise took the veil.

Persecution because of his enlightened views continued to pursue Abelard. His opinions in regard to the Trinity were declared heretical and he withdrew from St. Denis to build a chapel and hermitage which he called the Paraclete and which he later gave to Heloise and her sister nuns as a retreat.

Still haunted by the love which he could not overcome and by the hatred of his less enlightened brethren, he was finally imprisoned by order of the Pope. Later, through the influence of Peter the Venerable, Abbot of Clugny, he recanted certain of his liberal pronouncements and a reconciliation was effected between him and his powerful persecutors. He died April 21, 1142, in the Abbey of St. Marcel and was, at the request of Heloise, buried at the Paraclete where it was her fond hope to lie with him in death. She survived him by twenty years and seven centuries later the ashes of these unhappy lovers were interred in one sepulchre in Pere la Chaise Cemetery in Paris.

The outstanding principle of Abelard's writing and preaching was that no form of belief should be regarded as compulsory until it has first been comprehended. It was this refreshingly modern view, so opposed to the theological thought of his time, that incurred the bitter enmity of the exponents of orthodox doctrine. The letters of Abelard and Heloise, in which the tragic story of their love is so touchingly revealed, are better known to the world today than are all his masterly theological and philosophical writings.

JOHN ADAMS   1735–1826

JOHN ADAMS, second president of the United States, was born in Braintree, Mass., Oct. 19, 1735. He was of good old Puritan stock. His father was a shoemaker and a man of some importance in his town, being a selectman and a church deacon. John was sent to Harvard and later taught school in Worcester. He thought of the army as a profession, considered also the church and decided on a legal career.

In 1764 he married Abigail Smith, daughter of a minister in Weymouth. He was soon plunged into the turbulent field of politics, casting his lot with the patriots who were opposed to the Stamp Act and other oppressive measures of the mother country. He was selected as one of the three councillors of Boston to present a protest to the governor against the Stamp Act but the repeal of that obnoxious measure put an end to the plan. He became a contributor to the *Boston Gazette* and some of his articles were published in the English press.

In 1770 he was elected to the General Court of Massachusetts where he promptly became a leader of the patriot party. Resigning from the Court, he continued to write articles, some of them dealing with the impropriety of judges being paid by the Crown.

The Congress of 1774 convened amid the excitement following the Boston Tea Party and Adams was one of the five members from Massachusetts. He took active part in the discussions about colonial independence and when a declaration was agreed upon he was chosen to embody the resolutions in proper form.

Upon his return from this momentous session he was sent to the Provincial Congress then in session, which had practically declared war by seizing the provincial revenues and beginning military preparations. Meantime he was busy, as ever, with articles dealing with the crisis and its causes. The Battle of Lexington brought affairs to a climax and Adams proceeded at once to Philadelphia to sit in the councils of the congress which soon became the supreme authority in the colonies. He was resolute in his opposition to attempts at reconciliation which he thought to be impossible. His career in Congress was one of great activity. He served on committees, notably the committee on naval affairs, and the rules which he laid down became the basis of our present naval code. Late in 1775 he was appointed chief justice of Massachusetts, but shortly resigned without assuming his judicial duties. In 1777 he was appointed commissioner to France, superseding Silas Deane, and returned home in 1779. He was made a member of the Massachusetts constitutional convention and immediately thereafter was appointed minister to Great Britain to treat for peace, returning to Europe on the same frigate that had brought him home. While in Europe he secured a loan of $2,000,000 from Holland and was made American minister to that country. Upon the establishment of peace with Great Britain he was appointed British ambassador and returned to London in May, 1785. But the English were not yet of a mood to extend cordial welcome to a United States representative; he found his life in London uncomfortable and shortly asked to be recalled.

Returning to America in 1788 he became vice-president and supported Washington in many important measures. He differed sharply from Jefferson about the French Revolution, which he denounced as a great evil. The differences between the sturdy conservative and the unqualified democrat became acute and in the second presidential election the friends of Jefferson nominated George Clinton for vice-president against Adams, who, however, was reelected.

Washington's refusal to run for a third time precipitated the first typical partisan campaign for the presidency, with Adams, Hamilton, Jay, Jefferson and Thomas Pinckney more or less in the field. Adams was elected. But the democratic party became more and more vigorous in its opposition to his conservative policies, charging him with selecting his cabinet under British influence and causing him endless difficulty because of his avowed attitude toward the revolution in France. Many baseless charges and insinuations were made against him by his political enemies, his private correspondence was exposed in a futile attempt to prejudice his reputation with the public which honored him, all of which culminated in his defeat in 1801 by Jefferson who was elected by the narrow margin of one vote.

Adams, much embittered by the ruthless attacks of his political enemies, withdrew to his estate in Quincy, near Boston, where he lived in distinguished retirement, attending to his farm, and receiving guests who were anxious to visit a man so illustrious as a patriot and public servant. At the age of 85 he served as a member of the convention appointed to revise the constitution of his state. He died on the 4th of July, 1826.

JOHN QUINCY ADAMS   1767–1848

JOHN QUINCY ADAMS was the sixth president of the United States and son of the illustrious patriot and statesman, John Adams, the second president. He was born in Braintree, Mass., July 11, 1767. When a youth he accompanied his father on one of the latter's diplomatic missions, visiting London and Paris. In 1788 he graduated from Harvard College and was admitted to the bar in 1791. In 1794 Washington appointed him minister to the Hague. Three years later he married the daughter of Joshua Johnson, formerly a merchant at Nantes. Acting upon the recommendation of Washington, young Adams' father, then president, appointed him minister to Berlin. While in Europe he wrote and traveled much; indeed, throughout his life he indulged his literary bent and was one of the most broadly cultured men of his time.

When Jefferson became president it was hardly to be expected that he would continue in office the son of his bitter political opponent and Adams was recalled. In 1802 he was a member of the Massachusetts state legislature and the following year, when he was but 36, he was elected to the United States Senate. In 1806 he was professor of rhetoric and belles lettres at Harvard, but the turmoil of politics was irresistible to him and he again entered the arena of public life, becoming a leader of the federal party. In 1809 President Madison appointed him minister to Russia, in which post he became very influential; it was at his urgent request that the Russian emperor offered to act as mediator between the United States and Great Britain in the War of 1812 and in 1813 Adams was one of the commissioners appointed to negotiate peace with Great Britain.

In 1815 he went to England as minister, holding that post until the newly-elected President Monroe recalled him to become secretary of state in his cabinet, an office which he filled with great distinction. The presidential contest of 1824 found four democratic candidates in the field— Adams, Jackson, Crawford and Clay—and after a desperately fought campaign Adams was elevated to the highest office in the land, the only instance in the nation's history of father and son both receiving this signal honor. During his incumbency he was not supported by the members of his party, the several factions rallying about Jackson. He had, moreover, an unfriendly congress and, like his distinguished parent, he was made the subject of bitter and unwarranted attacks which must have gone far to disillusion this accomplished gentleman and scholar as to the desirability of a political career. In his second campaign Jackson defeated him with 178 votes against his 83 and he retired to Quincy.

He did not long enjoy the repose to which his many years of distinguished public service entitled him. He was drafted by a new political party, the anti-masons, and for nearly a score of years represented his district in congress. In 1834 he was defeated for the governorship of Massachusetts by John Davis, and later was defeated by the same opponent in a contest for the United States senatorship.

He was wholly free from the political taint which sets office above country. He was preeminently honest with himself and fair to others. After he had thrown off the cares of office, he filled with dignity the unofficial post of citizen extraordinary—distinguished member of a distinguished family. In 1837 his independence and disregard of clamor and self-interest were strikingly exhibited when he arose in congress and presented a petition from a group of slaves, forcing its reception in spite of the astonishment which his act produced. He was sympathetic with the abolitionists and always a sturdy champion of the right to petition the governing power, from whatever source it came. The series of rules adopted by the House of Representatives to prohibit the reading of anti-slavery petitions, which were known as the "gag rules" and which were aimed against the tendency to debates on this dangerous subject, had little of his sympathy and it was through his efforts that these shameful restrictions of the people's rights were abolished. He was the great champion of free speech, espousing it on principle without regard to the matter involved.

He died on Feb. 23, 1848, from a stroke of paralysis while attending congress. Like his father, he was a Unitarian in religion. He found time in his distinguished public career to indulge his literary inclinations and wrote many poems and other works, besides keeping a voluminous diary.

JOSEPH ADDISON   1672–1719

JOSEPH ADDISON was one of the most engaging writers of English prose and his style has always been regarded as a model of grace, purity, wit and elegance. He is, par excellence, a master to whom the youthful aspirant may safely turn for guidance and his influence on other writers, stronger and more vital than himself, is incalculable.

He was born at Milston, in Wiltshire, May 1, 1672, son of a clergyman of some prominence, and after preliminary studies entered Oxford at the age of 15. It was probably the flattering interest which Dryden showed in him which turned his thoughts from a church career and directed his ambitions into the more appropriate channels of literature. His prospects in this direction were also advanced by the patronage of Lord Somers to whom he dedicated some verses.

After a continental tour in 1699, made possible by a pension, he returned home to find his cherished hopes of political preferment blasted by the defeat of the Whig party. It chanced, however, that in the following year the ministry desired the recent great victory of Blenheim to be commemorated poetically and he was given this piece of glorified hack work to perform. The result so pleased his employers that he was rewarded with the office of Appeals Commissioner and found himself knee-deep in politics.

In 1706 he became Under-Secretary of State and three years later accompanied the Lord-Lieutenant to Ireland in the capacity of secretary, where he obtained the office of Keeper of the Records at a salary of 300 pounds a year. He might have lived and died a politician with a mild literary flavor had not his friend, Richard Steele, started a periodical, the *Tatler,* to which he soon became a contributor.

In 1711 appeared *The Spectator,* famous in literary annals, with which the name of Addison is inseparably linked. Famous forever among periodicals, it was the vehicle of the winsome and sprightly essays which made their author's name a household word.

In 1713 appeared *The Tragedy of Cato,* a piece wholly lacking in dramatic quality but which, singularly enough, created a minor sensation and elicited the enthusiastic praise of eminent contemporaries. Not the least among these was Voltaire who placed Addison above Shakespeare with certain scathing references which the bard of Avon has managed to survive. The tragedy, having strutted its little hour upon the stage, is quite forgotten now and the episode invokes dubious thoughts as to the value of contemporaneous estimates, however highly sponsored.

In 1711 Addison married the Dowager Countess of Warwick and it is commonly alleged that the gentle and sweet-tempered essayist found the pomp and circumstance of his wedded life and the chilling dignity of his lady a prejudicial influence to his peace and contentment. Certain it is, the marriage was not "made in heaven."

Equally inauspicious was his appointment in 1717 to the office of Secretary of State, a post in which the timid and retiring writer was singularly out of his element; he was indeed peculiarly ill-fitted to the hurly-burly of politics and the necessary contact with larger assemblies. He resigned this post in 1718. His health had for some time been uncertain and, after an illness of several months, he died in Kensington on June 17, 1719.

Addison's writings were numerous and on a variety of subjects, but the famous *Sir Roger de Coverly Papers,* which originally appeared in

The Spectator, over-shadow all the rest. The charming Sir Roger, one of the most lovable and realistic of fictional creations, is closely rivalled by the other figures in this immortal series, Sir Andrew Freeport and Will Honeycomb. And the gentle satire, quaint raillery and buoyant humor of these sketches, couched in the purest and most exquisite style, make them one of the rarest treasures of English literature. Dr. Johnson has well said that "whoever wishes to attain an English style, familiar but not coarse, and elegant but not ostentatious, must give his days and nights to the volumes of Addison."

It remains only to be said that Addison exemplifies the familiar dictum that "style is the man." The simplicity and crystal purity of his English, his good humor and kindly playfulness are essentially the expression of his genial, generous and kindly nature.

ÆSCHYLUS   525 B.C.–455 B.C.

ÆSCHYLUS (ĕs′kĭ lŭs), one of the greatest of Greek dramatists, has been called the father of Greek tragedy, for he was the first to introduce second and third characters into Greek poetic drama.

He was born at Eleusis, the town of the Mysteries, near Athens, in 525 B.C., of an ancient aristocratic family. It is related that while he was still a boy the god Dionysus appeared to him and commanded him to write dramas—a legend to which his later life might easily have given rise. In his twenty-fifth year (499 B.C.) Æschylus first appeared as a competitor for the tragic·prize, which he was not to win until 485 B.C., but thereafter he took thirteen first prizes at the competitions, being defeated by Sophocles in 458 B.C. The total number of his plays is said by Suidas to have been ninety. The seven extant plays, together with fragments and plays namable, number about eighty, so that Suidas' statement is probably correct.

Æschylus saw military service in the Persian wars, having been present at the battles of Marathon and Salamis and, according to some accounts, at Artemisium and Platæa. Some time between the years 478 and 467 B.C. he visited Sicily with Pindar, Bacchylides, Simonides and other famous poets, and was royally entertained by Hieron, tyrant of Syracuse. Plutarch in his life of Cimon gives as the reason for Æschylus' departure from Athens the fact that the young Sophocles had just gained the victory in the tragic competitions and that wounded vanity led to the elder dramatist's self-imposed exile. This may be but another legend and his trial before the Areopagus on the charge of having revealed the Mysteries is also cited as a cause for his leaving Athens. While in Sicily he exhibited his play, *The Persians,* and wrote *The Aetneans* to celebrate the foundation of Etna by his patron. According to Diodorus, this was in 476 B.C., which would indicate his presence in Sicily six years before the date given by Plutarch. The poet was probably in Sicily at the time of the eruption of Etna in 479—the year of the battle of Platæa—allusion to which is made in his masterpiece, *Prometheus Bound,* thus placing the writing of that work not earlier than his forty-seventh year, the period of full maturity of his powers.

It seems fairly certain that Æschylus gained the tragic prize at the 78th Olympiad with his tetralogy of *Laius, Œdipus, The Seven Against Thebes,* and *The Sphynx* (467 B.C.). The trilogy of the *Oresteiae*—three plays on the fate of Orestes, comprising *Agamemnon, Choephori* and *Eumenides*—was exhibited, according to the argument of *Agamemnon,* in the year of the archonship of Philocles (458 B.C.). Many critics regard *Agamemnon* as not only its author's greatest work, but as the greatest Greek play that has survived.

Two years later (456) the poet died in Gela, Sicily, in his sixty-ninth year. His final retirement to the island was probably due to political differences arising between him and the Athenian populace, which had been steadily turning toward a democracy while Æschylus was an aristocrat by birth and by sympathies. In addition to this the reception given by democratic spectators to his eulogy of the aristocratic Court of the Areopagus in *Eumenides* may have caused him to take flight both for his own comfort and for his safety.

After his death Athens awarded him the extraordinary honor of decreeing that his dramas might be exhibited at the great Dionysiac festivals and the people of Gela, proud that the ashes of the great dramatist rested in their soil, erected a monument to his memory. Besides increasing dramatic action by introducing a number of characters, Æschylus greatly improved the whole machinery of stage presentation. Many traditions have clustered about his name since his death.

JEAN LOUIS RODOLPHE AGASSIZ   1807–1873

JEAN LOUIS RODOLPHE AGASSIZ (ag'à sē or à găs'ĭz) was one of the world's outstanding naturalists and geologists, and was the first to make a detailed and comprehensive study of fishes, fish fossils and glaciers.

He was born May 20, 1807, at Motier on the shore of Lake Morat, Switzerland, where his father was a preacher. After four years of study in the gymnasium at Bienne he entered the Academy of Lausanne, later attending the Universities of Zurich, Heidelberg and Munich. At Erlangen he took his Doctor of Philosophy degree, and at Zurich the degree of Doctor of Medicine. As a mere youth he developed a keen interest in the brook fishes of western Switzerland, but his lifelong interest in ichthyology arose from his being selected to study the fishes of Brazil (1819–20), along with two eminent scientists of Munich. He classified the large collection of specimens brought back from the Amazon (*Selected Genera et Species Piscium,* published in 1829) and the study of fish forms was ever afterwards a passion with him. In 1830 he issued his prospectus of a *History of the Fresh Water Fishes of Central Europe,* which was printed in parts from 1839 to 1842.

In 1832 Agassiz went to Paris and Neuchâtel, pursuing his studies and supporting himself meanwhile. Humboldt was instrumental in having him appointed Professor at Neuchâtel, and Cuvier and other eminent scientists of the day helped him. As early as 1829 he had planned a study of fish fossils in Europe, and his epoch-making work on that subject *Recherches sur les Poissons Fossiles,* appeared in parts from 1833 to 1844. In 1839–40 he published two volumes on the fossil echinoderms of Switzerland and from 1840 to 1845 his *Études Critiques sur les Mollusques Fossiles.* In the meantime he held the chair of Natural History at the University of Neuchâtel (1832–46) and during part of the time acted as his own publisher. He now began his *Nomenclator Zoologicus,* a catalogue, with references, of all the names applied to genera of animals from the beginning of scientific nomenclature. In 1836 he began a new line of studies—that of the movements and effects of glaciers—and four years later published *Études sur les glaciers,* in some respects the most important of his works.

In 1846 he visited the United States to study natural history and geology, and was at once engaged to give courses of lectures at Lowell Institute, Boston, in Charleston and later in other cities. Two years after his arrival he was appointed professor of zoology at Harvard University (1848) and spent the rest of his scientific career in America, becoming more enthusiastically American with the passing years. His chief scientific works published in America are *Lake Superior* (1850); *Contributions to the Natural History of the United States* (1857–63); *A Journey in Brazil* (1868), written in collaboration with his wife; and numerous articles for magazines. The trip to Brazil was made in 1865; another to California, by boat around South America, in 1871.

Agassiz established a museum of zoological research at Harvard

(1859), which grew into the University's present splendid museum. He was extraordinarily successful as a teacher of science, and was personally devoted to his pupils. He organized the Anderson school at Penikese, an island in Buzzard's Bay, which, although short-lived, had a profound effect upon the teaching of science in America and was the precursor of all American summer schools. He has been called the ablest, wisest and best informed geologist of his time. Of a religious temperament, he was nevertheless out of sympathy with sects and creeds. He was twice married: first to Cecile Braun, and second (in 1850) to Elizabeth Cabot Cary of Boston. He died on Dec. 12, 1873, and was buried in Auburn Cemetery, Cambridge, Mass.

LOUISA M. ALCOTT   1832–1888

LOUISA MAY ALCOTT, one of America's most popular writers for the young, was born in Germantown, Penn., on Nov. 29, 1832. Her father was A. Bronson Alcott, pedagogue and philosopher, and it was out of her experience of the privations and trials of the family due to his impracticality that she evolved her definition of a philosopher: "A man up in a balloon, with his family and friends holding the ropes which confine him to earth and trying to haul him down."

As a girl she confided to her journal her determination to earn money with which to make her family comfortable—a purpose which she amply fulfilled in later life. Outdoor life had given her a strong, healthy body, and she possessed an active mind and imagination. Her first attempt at earning money was as a doll's dressmaker, but she was soon turning her hand to anything that she could find—teaching, sewing, and for a time she tried even domestic service. Her earliest stories were of a rather sensational character, but the occasional five and ten dollars which she earned by her pen helped to furnish the necessities of life and to pay family debts, and when in 1860 she sold a story to the *Atlantic Monthly* for fifty dollars it seemed to her a fortune.

Miss Alcott's first book, *Flower Fables* (1854), was written for Ralph Waldo Emerson's little daughter, Ellen. Emerson was a neighbor in Concord, Mass., to which town Miss Alcott's father had taken his family, and where he established his school of philosophy in an old barn. Nathaniel Hawthorne lived in Concord, and Henry Thoreau was near by at Walden Pond, so that Louisa did not lack for literary companionship and inspiration. She won her first real popularity with the book of *Hospital Sketches* which was an elaboration of the letters she had written home during the six weeks when she was acting as a nurse in the Union hospital at Georgetown, D. C., during the Civil War (1862–63).

At that time she gave of her energy and strength so tirelessly to the nursing of sick and wounded soldiers that her own health was shattered, never to be completely restored. Her early poverty and her later nervous restlessness, as well as her ready generosity, kept her hard at the task of writing, however, despite the state of her health, and few calls upon her generosity went unanswered. A fairly accurate account of her own life may be gleaned from her books, particularly from *Little Women,* in which she figures as *Jo March.* This book was published in 1868 and remains today one of the most popular girls' books ever written by an American author. Events of her later life are reflected in *Jo's Boys,* published in 1886, as well as in *An Old-Fashioned Girl (1870),* and in *Aunt Jo's Scrap-Bag* (6 volumes, published from 1871 to 1879). *Little Men,* another favorite with children, published in 1871, was modeled about the personalities of her nephews.

Aside from her books for children, Miss Alcott wrote three novels which made but little impression at the time and are now all but forgotten. The first was *Moods,* which appeared in 1864, followed by *Work* in 1873, and *A Modern Mephistopheles,* all experimental in technique and hence lacking in general appeal. It was her children's books which made her name a household word and her home in Concord a literary shrine which still attracts many visitors. Her cheery wholesomeness and truthfulness to boy and girl nature contributed much to her success.

Her artist sister, May, upon her death bequeathed her little daughter to Louisa, and it was for this niece that she named the book *Lulu's Library* (3 volumes, 1885–89).

Miss Alcott was an ardent abolitionist and was one of the early advocates of woman suffrage. She died in Boston, March 6, 1888, two days after her father's death, and was buried in Sleepy Hollow Cemetery, Concord.

ALEXANDER THE GREAT   356 B.C.–323 B.C.

ALEXANDER THE GREAT, son of Philip of Macedon, was born at Pella in 356 B.C. His father had built his small principality into a powerful kingdom, uniting Greece with it and was driving the Persians out of Asia

Minor, which achievements caused young Alexander to make the dubious comment, "My father will leave nothing for me to do."

After studying under Leonidas and Lysimachus, his education was entrusted to Aristotle who removed him from the beguilements of the court and subjected him to a thorough course of training and study. Assuredly, he needed all the knowledge of government which his great teacher could impart for he was but 16 years of age when his father set forth on an expedition against Byzantium, leaving the cares of government to his son. At 18 he distinguished himself at the battle of Chæronea, receiving affectionate tribute from his proud father, but upon the latter's repudiation of his wife, Olympias, the son took sides with his mother and fled the consequent parental wrath, but returned and was forgiven. He assisted in an expedition against the Triballi and saved his father's life on the field. In 336 B.C., Philip was assassinated and Alexander ascended the throne. He proceeded against Persia (a plan of Philip's interrupted by his death) and on his return found the Illyrians and Triballi up in arms, marched against them and forced his way through Thrace, triumphing everywhere.

He next destroyed Thebes, crossed the Hellespont in 334 B.C. at the head of 35,000 troops and vanquished the Persians. Most of the cities of Asia Minor bowed to the conqueror. He reestablished democracy in all the Greek cities and proceeded to the conquest of Lycia, Ionia, Caria, Pamphylia and Cappadocia. While his triumphant career was interrupted by illness he was advised by letter that his physician, bribed by the vanquished Persian, Darius, intended to poison him. He confounded the physician by handing him the incriminating letter as he drank the potion prepared for him. This act, which might have cost his life, had no ill effect and he soon was advancing toward Cilicia where a Persian army of half a million men was thrown into confusion in the neighborhood of Issus and fled in dismay. Darius was treated with consideration, but Alexander would consider no overtures of peace which did not acknowledge him lord of all Asia. The victory at Issus opened the whole country to the conqueror. He next turned toward Syria and Phœnicia, occupied Damascus, appropriating its rich treasures, and subjugated all the cities bordering the Mediterranean. Tyre resisted bravely but was finally destroyed, after which he made a triumphal progress through Palestine, victorious everywhere. Gaza alone resisted, but was able only to defer surrender. Egypt, chafing under Persian domination, received the deliverer with open arms and here he founded Alexandria. He next marched through the Libyan Desert to consult the oracle of Jupiter Ammon and the following spring (October, 331 B.C.) on the plains of Arbela he vanquished Darius who had recruited a vast army in Assyria. Babylon and Susa, with their princely treasures, soon fell and Alexander made a triumphal entry into the Persian capital, Persepolis.

But he showed signs of collapsing under the weight of his own glory. He became a prey to dissolute habits and his reason at times seemed affected. In a cruel fit of caprice he set fire to Persepolis at the request of Thais, a courtesan, and was stricken with remorse when he saw it in ruins. In 329 he penetrated northern Asia, overthrew the Sythians and in the following year subdued the whole of Sogdiana and married Roxana, daughter of one of the enemy captains, having first made her a prisoner. In 327 B.C. he set out to conquer India, pressing his way through to the region now called Punjab and establishing Greek colonies, but he found it prudent to heed the murmurings of his weary troops and retreated to the Hydaspes where he built a fleet and sent one division of his army down the river while the other followed by land, in continuous battle with the natives. Reaching the coast he despatched his ships to the Persian Gulf and led a land force through the region which is now Beloochistan, crossing vast deserts where his weary soldiers suffered pitifully from heat and thirst, only a fourth of them reaching Persia. At Susa occurred his marriage to Stateira, daughter of the Persian, Darius, who was promptly murdered by Roxana.

As he was returning from Ecbatana to Babylon the Magi predicted that the latter city would spell his fate. Heedless of the warning, he proceeded triumphantly, met and attended and fawned upon by ambassadors from many lands, and full of mighty plans for the future. In Babylon he was suddenly stricken ill after a sumptuous banquet, and after lingering for eleven days he died on or about the 11th of May or June, 323 B.C. at the age of 32, having reigned for twelve years of unprecedented conquest.

ALFRED THE GREAT   849–901

ALFRED THE GREAT of England, commonly called "good King Alfred," was one of the wisest and most enlightened of all early rulers; a singular anachronism in a barbarous age. He was born in Wantage in 849, son of Ethelwolf whose father was Egbert, king of the West Saxons. Before Alfred's accession at the age of 23 he had already distinguished himself in repulsing the Danes, those dreaded invaders whose incessant raids kept the Saxons forever on the defensive.

Notwithstanding that he was the youngest of four brothers, he succeeded to the throne on the death of his brother Ethelred and, as monarch, proceeded with skill and vigilance to rid his kingdom of these predatory warriors from the north. His early efforts were discouraging, the invaders continued to swarm into his territory, and the Anglo-Saxons either fled or subjected themselves to the rule of the conquerors. By 878 the Danes had extended their sway over the whole kingdom and Alfred, unable to recruit an army to combat them, took refuge in the wilderness. It was during this time that the familiar episode of the disguised monarch set to baking cakes by a peasant's wife is supposed to have occurred, a pretty story with strong foundation of fact.

But Alfred was by no means daunted by the plight of his kingdom. He kept in touch with his loyal supporters and in time saw his people regain some measure of their wonted pride and resolution. He built a fortress in the marshland of Somersetshire where his followers rallied about him and from this spot raids were made against the Danes. He was soon in command of an imposing legion with which he moved against the enemy, completely defeated them near Edington, and after a siege of their stronghold, received their capitulation and exacted from them a promise, secured by hostages, to withdraw from his land. Guthrun, their leader, was baptized into the Christian faith at his instigation, and henceforth proved faithful in his allegiance to the Saxon king.

This outstanding triumph was the turning point of Alfred's fortunes. He built a navy, primitive craft indeed, but with it he repulsed the Danes again and again, and routed them on land until their possessions on the island were restricted to a narrow strip of northern coast.

In 886 he was tacitly accepted as the sovereign of the whole English country, of which his former dominions had been only a part. Peace at last prevailed and he proved himself quite as great in the arts of peaceful administration as he had been in the field of war. He reconditioned towns, built fortresses, had his people drilled in the use of arms, and generally put his kingdom in a posture of defence against future invasion.

Nor was this all. His peacetime activities were remarkable considering the dark and barbarous age in which he lived. He restored the war-torn London and set it on its career as a thriving city. He made laws, established courts, encouraged agriculture and scrupulously maintained justice among his subjects. Such was his enlightened rule, and so potent the influence of his character, that he has become a kind of legend and there is a tendency to give him credit for many reforms which he did not in fact originate. But making full allowance for this tendency, his rule was phenomenal and raised him both morally and intellectually far above the long line of sovereigns who followed after him.

He divided England into counties and so efficiently established the rule of law that William of Malmesbury said "a purse of money . . . might in Alfred's day be exposed for weeks in complete safety on the public highways." Some authorities credit him with the origination of trial by jury. He was trusted and beloved as few rulers have been. In that darkest period when feudalism was spreading over all Europe, and art and learning had gone down in the collapse of the western Roman Empire, this head of the little barbarous Saxon kingdom was an accomplished scholar, a devotee of culture, a patron of arts. He consecrated himself to the education and welfare of his people. Under his direction manuscripts were translated from Latin into Anglo-Saxon; other translations he made himself. He found time also to write several original works among which are *Laws of the West Saxons, Meditations* and *Chronicles,* all revealing his original and reflective mind and high ideals. His translations are often interspersed with pithy commentaries of his own. He made maps of different regions in Europe which are singularly accurate, considering the very limited materials with which he was obliged to work.

In 993 a fresh invasion from the north under Haesten put an end to these peaceful occupations, but Alfred, fully prepared for such a contingency, fought the enemy with such vigor and persistence that they were beaten again and again and finally completely overcome.

Alfred died Oct. 27, 901, leaving a name beloved by all later generations of English. No cruel and inhuman punishments, such as stain the reign of practically all his royal followers up to modern times, are reported in the life of this wise and humane ruler. He was an enlightened administrator in a benighted age, a great and good man.

HANS CHRISTIAN ANDERSEN 1805–1875

HANS CHRISTIAN ANDERSEN, beloved of millions of children for his folk tales and fairy stories which have been translated into almost every language, was born at Odense, in the Island of Fünen, Denmark, on April 2, 1805. His early life was somewhat unfortunate. He was the son of a shoemaker who made but a precarious living and who died while Hans was still young so that the boy was forced to go to work in a factory. He was an unattractive boy outwardly and showed early eccentricities of temperament which doubtless handicapped him and stood in the way of his success for a considerable time. He had a fine singing voice, however, which soon brought him many friends and patrons, and he had early shown a talent for writing poetry.

After a time he went to Copenhagen in the hope of getting an engagement in a theatre there but was refused a chance because of his lack of education. He next tried to find an engagement as a singer. His physical qualifications for a theatrical or singing career were against him but friends came to his assistance and application for aid was made to the King, which resulted in his being placed in an advanced school where he continued his studies with the objective of perfecting himself as a writer. He had already had a number of poems published which had attracted favorable attention, among them *The Dying Child,* and now he wrote a literary satire, *Walk to Amak,* a humorous narrative that made him somewhat widely known in Danish literary circles.

His first collected volume of poems was published in 1830, and a second collection, *Fantasies and Sketches,* appeared the following year. In 1833 the King granted him a traveling pension and he visited Germany, Switzerland, Rome and Naples. These travels bore fruit in *Travelling Sketches,* an account of his wanderings on a tour of northern Germany. In Switzerland he completed *Agnes and the Merman* and his trip to Italy inspired his *Improvisatore.* His novel, *O.T.,* which vividly depicted the manners and the scenery of the North, was published in 1836 and in the following year appeared a new story from his pen, *Only a Fiddler,* which enjoyed a wide success and is generally rated as the best of his novels.

Andersen's *Fairy Tales* were not very highly regarded by their author, who was more ambitious to shine as a novelist and playwright; yet it is for those fairy stories that he is remembered and loved throughout the world. The first volume of the tales appeared in 1835 and attained no great degree of popularity. A second series was published the following year, and a third in 1837. Gradually their fame spread; a new series appeared in 1838 and still another in 1845. Andersen was now becoming famous throughout Europe, except in his native Denmark, which did not yet recognize the quality of his genius, nor apparently did he himself, for he still hoped to win laurels as a novelist and playwright. He visited England in 1847 and upon leaving was accompanied to the pier by Charles Dickens. Still disdaining his fairy tales, he next wrote a romance, *To Be or Not To Be;* a travel book, *In Spain,* and his egotistic *Story of My Life,* but the ever-growing success of the fairy stories caused him to publish a new volume of them in 1847, another the following year and others at intervals, up to 1872. His world-wide fame now rests almost entirely upon these stories, which he regarded as of small importance except for the income they brought him. Among the best known of the tales are *The Tin Soldier, The Emperor's New Clothes* and *The Ugly Duckling,* which last is perhaps the most famous of all his writings and is said to somewhat symbolize the experiences of his own life.

Although to the end of his life he himself possessed much of the child's outlook, he had little liking for children and was not personally attractive to them. Singularly also, he fancied himself distinctive looking while to others he appeared as an awkward, loose hung man, with large hands and feet, a long nose and generally unattractive features.

In the spring of 1872 Andersen suffered a serious injury from falling out of bed and remained in ill health until his death near Copenhagen on Aug. 4, 1875.

His own *Correspondence with the Grand Duke of Saxe-Weimar* contains the best available information about his life.

GABRIELE D'ANNUNZIO   1863–

GABRIELE D'ANNUNZIO (à nōōn'dzĕ ō), Italian dramatist, novelist and patriot, was born at Pescara in Central Italy, in 1863. He began to write early in life, published a volume of verse while still a school boy (1879) and later on, in Rome, devoted himself to a literary career. In 1882 he published *Canto Nuovo; Terra Virgine,* the following year; *L'Intermezzo di Rime* in 1884; *Il Libro delle Virgini* in 1884, as well as the majority of the short stories later published under the title of *San Pantaleone* (1886).

He was hailed by critics as an infant prodigy, rejected by other critics as a perverter of public morals, proclaimed by still others as the bringer of a new vitality into Italian literature. The controversy raged about him for years. He joined the staff of the *Tribuna,* to which he contributed much brilliant work under the name of "Duca Minimo," including *Il Libro d'Isotta,* 1886. His first novel, *Il Piacere,* was published in 1889 (translated into English in 1898 as *The Child of Pleasure*); in 1892 his second novel, *L'Innocente* (in English, *The Intruder*) appeared; followed by a third, *Giovanni Episcopo,* the same year. These three books won for their author a wide reputation. Later novels include *Il Trionfo della Morte* (1894) (translated into English in 1896 as *The Triumph of Death*); *Le Virgini delle Rocce* (1896) and *Il Fuoco,* a glorification of Venice (1900).

He continued his poetical work and in 1897 began to write for the stage. Outstanding among his books of verse during this period are *Il Poema Paradisiaco* of 1893; *Odo Navali* of the same year, and *Laudi* of 1900. His first play was *Il Sogno de un mattino di primavera,* a lyric fantasia in one act. In 1898 he wrote for Sarah Bernhardt the play, *Città Morta.* This was produced in the United States by Eleonore Duse, who also found one of her best vehicles in d'Annunzio's *La Gioconda*. The same year (1898) he wrote *Sogno d'un tramonto d'autunno;* in 1899 *La Gloria;* in 1902 *Francesca da Rimini; La Figlia di Jorio* in 1904; *La Nave,* picturing the early history of Venice as a sea power, in 1908; *Fedra,* a classical drama, in 1909; *Le martyre de St. Sebastian,* a mystery play written in French verse with musical interludes by Debussy, in 1911; *La Pisanella ou la mort parfumée,* also written in French, in 1914; and *Parisina,* with music by Massenet, 1914. He published two novels during these years, *Forse che si, forse che no* (1910) and *La Leda senza cigno* (1913), as well as a volume of verse, *Canzoni della gesta d'Oltremara* (1912).

At the outbreak of the World War he was living in France, having had to leave Italy on account of financial difficulties. Convinced of the necessity of his country's participation to establish her sovereignty over the Adriatic, he returned to Italy to urge her making common cause with the Allies. The dreamer, the mystic, the æsthete, became the man of action when Italy declared war. He served first in the cavalry, then in the infantry, the navy, and finally in the air service. His exploits as an airplane pilot were of a fantastic nature; he lost an eye on one of his flights, was shot in the wrist at another time and his plane was frequently riddled by bullets.

After the war the attitude of the Allied Powers (and especially that of President Wilson) toward Italy aroused his bitter antagonism. Anti-French riots in Fiume led to the decision to reduce the Italian garrison and police the town with Maltese or United States troops. On Sept. 9, 1919, d'Annunzio entered Fiume with a small force and took possession of the town which he occupied and ruled for some fifteen months thereafter, in defiance of the Allied Powers and the home government alike. He refused to recognize the Treaty of Rapallo, signed Nov. 12, 1920, by which Fiume was created a Free State, but he was removed by force and went to live at Gardone on the Lake of Garda, where he wrote *Notturno* and *La faville del Maglio.*

He was an ardent supporter of the Fascist movement and in 1924 the King made him Prince of Monte Novoso. In 1927 the Italian government undertook the publication of a collected edition of his writings.

MARK ANTONY   83 B.C.–30 B.C.

MARCUS ANTONIUS, or Mark Antony, as this famous Roman soldier and orator is more widely known, was born about 83 B.C. On his mother's side he was related to Julius Caesar.

As a young man he was dissipated and being pressed by his creditors he fled from Rome to Athens in 58 B.C. He became popular with the army in Palestine and Egypt, aided Caesar in his campaigning in Gaul, and in 50 B.C. returned to Rome as a representative of Caesar, was appointed quæstor, augur and tribune of the plebs. The following year he was expelled from the curia and fled to Caesar, furnishing the latter with a pretext for his war against Pompey.

As commander-in-chief of Caesar's army in Italy, Mark Antony commanded the left wing at the battle of Pharsalia. Caesar appointed him master of the horse in 47 B.C. and left him to govern Italy while he journeyed to Egypt. Through his unfortunate habits, the divorcing of his wife and marriage to an actress, Antony was soon in disgrace again. In 44 B.C. he attempted to induce the Romans to receive Caesar as emperor.

Following the assassination of Caesar at the hands of Brutus and other conspirators, Antony, through his famous funeral oration (immortalized in Shakespeare's play of *Julius Caesar*) and his display of Caesar's blood-stained garment, made such a profound impression upon the populace that the conspirators (or "Liberators" as they styled themselves) were obliged to take flight from Rome and Mark Antony for a time held almost absolute sway.

His dispute with Octavian (later known as Caesar Augustus) and his besieging of Mutina called forth bitter denunciation from Cicero. Defeated at Mutina (43 B.C.), Antony crossed the Alps, won favor with the troops of Lepidus and was soon in command of the army. Plancus and Pollio joined him and with seventeen legions of foot soldiers and 10,000 horsemen, he marched upon Rome. Conflict was avoided when Octavian met Antony and Lepidus at Bononia and proposed that they three, as triumvirs, should govern the whole of the Roman Empire.

Proscription and plunder then began in Rome. Cicero was one of the first victims, thus placing the responsibility for one of the greatest crimes of history on Antony's shoulders. It is recorded that some 300 senators and about 2000 equites lost their lives in this slaughter.

Italy was soon won over and Antony and Octavian led their army into Macedonia and at Philippi defeated Brutus and Cassius.

After going to Athens, Antony sailed for Asia in an effort to compose a dispute with Cleopatra, Queen of Egypt, who was pure Greek by extraction. He fell a victim to her beauty and her wiles and followed her to Egypt where for several years he led an idle, luxurious life. Difficulties arose in Rome between his own kinsmen and Octavian, and Antony at length set out for Italy but the short war resulting from the quarrel was over before he arrived. The three triumvirs arranged a new division of territory during Antony's stay in Rome, and to him was given the eastern part of the Empire, to Octavian the western part, leaving Africa for Lepidus' share.

Although Antony had married Octavia, sister of Octavian, following the death of his wife, Fulvia, he returned to Egypt, drawn by his infatuation for Cleopatra, and the old life of idleness was resumed. He was guilty of many acts of injustice and cruelty, tales of which reached Octavian who was quick to seize his advantage and aroused the Roman people against the absent triumvir. A fleet was sent against Antony who was defeated in the naval battle of Actium, 31 B.C. He returned to Egypt but was deserted by the Egyptian fleet and by his own army. He had sacrificed an empire to his lawless love and the drama drew to a swift close.

Upon receipt of a baseless report that Cleopatra had taken her life, Antony killed himself by falling upon his own sword. Octavian completed his revenge by putting to death Mark Antony's son by Fulvia and Caesarion who was Cleopatra's son by Julius Caesar. Cleopatra herself was taken prisoner but rather than grace Octavian's triumphal reentry into Rome she killed herself, tradition says by placing an asp in her bosom.

THOMAS AQUINAS   1224–1274

THOMAS AQUINAS (à kwi′nàs) was an Italian scholar and theologian, born sometime during the year 1224 at the castle of Rocca Secca, near Aquino, in the kingdom of Naples. He came of a noble family, was educated first by the Benedictine monks and later at the university of Naples. Of a studious and philosophical turn of mind, he determined while still a youth, and greatly against the wishes of his family, to enter a religious order. It is said that in order to forestall any attempt on the part of his family and friends to win him back to a secular life, the Dominican friars to whom he entrusted himself arranged to send him to a convent of their order in France, but the boy's older brothers, learning of the plan, intercepted the expedition, wrested him from his religious guardians and took him to his father's castle where he was kept under guard for some two years. There are conflicting tales as to whether the monks finally helped him to escape or whether his father was persuaded to release him at the instance of the pope. Be that as it may, he went to Cologne in order that he might there receive instruction from the famous scholar, Albertus Magnus, who is said to have been so impressed with his qualities of mind that when his fellow students, in derision of his habit of solitude and silence, termed him a "dumb ox," Albertus uttered the prophecy that the dumb ox would yet fill the world with his bellowing.

After a few years the student emerged as a teacher in Paris and acquired a reputation as a lecturer and theologian. In 1257 he received his doctor's degree from the Sorbonne and four years later Pope Urban IV, before whom he had already appeared with an argument in connection with the condemnation of certain books, summoned him to teach philosophy in the Italian cities. He thus returned to Naples where he took up his abode in the convent, and the remainder of his life was spent in lecturing and writing, chiefly in the interest of the Dominican order. He declined to accept the office of archbishop and many other honors that he might devote himself more exclusively to his studies. His death occurred suddenly at Fossanuova, near Naples, on March 7, 1274, while he was on his way to the general council at Lyons to which he had been summoned by Pope Gregory X. He was buried in the convent at Toulouse.

He left many important ecclesiastical writings, mostly in Latin, and his application of the method of philosophy of Aristotle to the problems of theology, together with his clear and definite setting forth of his views and doctrines, gave him first rank among the scholars of his day. He was accorded wide recognition during his lifetime and came to be known as the father of moral philosophy. Pope Pius V, who arranged for the publication of Aquinas' complete works, ranks him as one of the greatest teachers the church has ever known and Pope Leo XIII in his encyclical issued in 1879 instructed that his teachings be used as the basis of theological instruction. In 1323 he was canonized by Pope John XXII. His most important works are *A Commentary on the Four Books of Sentences of Peter Lombard, quaestiones Disputatae et Quodlibetales, Opuscula Theologica;* his *Summa contra Gentiles* in which he seeks to make clear the distinction between the sphere of natural reason and that of faith; and, chief of all, his *Summa Theologica,* comprising a complete theological system in which he intended to embody the sum of all known learning. This was incompleted at his death.

ARISTOPHANES   circa 444 B.C.

VERY little is known about the personal history of Aristophanes, (ăr'ĭs tŏf' à nēz), the greatest writer of comedy in ancient times. He was a master caricaturist, mercilessly ridiculing the affectations of his day; neither statesmen nor philosophers were exempt from his raillery and satire. He was the son of one Philippus and was born about 444 B.C. in Athens. Notwithstanding that he was of a merry temper and, according to Plato, devoted to the pleasures of life, it seems quite likely that he had in him much of the serious reformer and the vigor of his caricatures and his sturdy independence bespeak the earnestness of purpose which underlies his work. In 427 B.C. he produced *Daitaleis (The Banqueters)* in which he ridicules the follies of extravagance. This was followed in the succeeding year by the *Babylonians,* the stinging satire of which so aroused the ire of Cleon, target of the dramatist's shafts, that he retaliated with an attempt to have Aristophanes deprived of his citizenship. We have only fragments of these two plays. In 425 B.C. appeared his *Acharnians,* written in the interest of the Athenian peace party in the war with Sparta then waging. It set forth the absurdity of the conflict and was awarded a first prize. This is one of the plays that has come down to us intact.

In the year following appeared *Hippeis,* the *Knights* or *Horsemen,* the first play to be produced under the author's own name, a striking act of boldness in view of its scathing shafts against Cleon whom he scruples not to depict as a shallow and vulgar demagogue. Nor is he more considerate of the public over which Cleon held sway, depicting it as an ignorant mob, easily duped and influenced. So merciless was the characterization of Cleon in this piece that it is said no actor could be found with sufficient hardihood to play the part, whereupon the author himself essayed the rôle. It should be said that these caricatures often ran into misrepresentation and it would be dangerous to accept too fully the dramatist's estimate of Cleon or any of his famous contemporaries.

Another outstanding comedy was *The Clouds,* produced in 423 B.C., which abounded in wit and satire and the richest fancy. In the following year appeared *The Wasps,* a sprightly attack on the courts of justice. Three years later in *Peace* the satirist revived his favorite theme, the Peloponnesian War, again launching his ridicule against the alleged madness of that conflict. The Sicilian expedition at that time projected was caricatured in *Amphiaraus* and in *The Birds,* and the utter failure of the undertaking gave point to the author's lively and biting ridicule. The comedy *Lysistrata,* produced in 411 B.C., deals with a civil war of the sexes. It is best known to the public of today by reason of elaborate revivals which attracted much interest.

Plutus appeared in 408 B.C.; *Ecclesiazusoe* in 392 B.C., both characteristic of Aristophanes in ridiculing innovations, of which he was always impatient and intolerant. Even Plato is treated to the author's shafts of ridicule in these plays. In *The Frogs,* which appeared in 405 B.C., the poet Euripides is not spared.

Of the 54 comedies of Aristophanes only eleven are in existence, but those show him to have been the preeminent master in his field, abounding in richest fancy and poetic beauty. His wizardry in verse construction has never been equaled, and he was a master of grotesque effects. He did not escape the perils of the caricaturist. He swung his weapon ruthlessly and sometimes struck unjustly. Moreover, his arrows were often poisoned with vulgarities and indecencies. In *The Clouds* he ridicules the new sophisticated school and reveals his inability to grapple with things profound. His depiction of Socrates as the type of a sophist was most unhappy. Even the gods were not spared and he scrupled not to handle them with a levity which often made them appear ridiculous. These are the inevitable effects of the transcendant power of caricature and comic delineation which he possessed. Few great caricaturists have escaped such tendencies and they are often to be met with in writers who lack utterly the supreme art which goes far to palliate the fault in Aristophanes.

ARISTOTLE   384 B.C.–322 B.C.

AMONG the students who flocked to study under the aged Plato in the Academy at Athens was a youth from the Greek colonial town of Stageira. He was the son of the court physician in Macedonia and his name was Aristotle (ăr′ĭs totl). He was never able to write in the finished style of his master, but acquired a prodigious amount of knowledge on every subject and is famed as one of the world's greatest teachers and philosophers. He was born in 384 B.C. While still a child his parents died and he was brought up by Proxenus, a citizen of Stageira. At 18 he went to Athens, then the intellectual centre of the world, and in the temporary absence of Plato, studied under other masters. On Plato's return he pursued his studies under the great man's guidance and it was not long before Plato became deeply impressed by the grasp and versatility of his intellect. He had come of a family of physicians and it is probable that his early interest lay along the line of that profession. He never ceased to have a lively interest in the science of physics; toward the end of his career we find him engaged in dissecting animals. But no single line of study could attract him to the exclusion of miscellaneous inquiry. He was "the intellect of the school." He remained in Athens for about 20 years, established a class in rhetoric rivaling that of Isocrates, and was by no means reticent in his criticism of that celebrated orator. It seems probable that his contempt for Isocrates was an expression of his contempt for all schools which regarded the teaching of mere linguistic proficiency as an end in itself. Such a devotee of solid knowledge and wisdom would look askance at these schools of rhetoric, so popular in Athens, in which elegance took precedence over substance. One of Isocrates' pupils, defending his master against Aristotle, referred to a work of Aristotle's on proverbs. It was probably his first published work but no other knowledge of it has come down to us.

The death of Plato in 347 B.C. was a keen blow to the younger philosopher. He must have been chagrined that his instructor designated his nephew, Spensippus, to preside over the Academy; a strange decision, for surely no man was so well qualified as Aristotle to fill that place, and no man knew better than Plato of the vast knowledge of this favorite pupil, a knowledge and wisdom which have given his name outstanding distinction in the history of the world. He departed from Athens and went to the town of Atarneus in Asia Minor. There he lived in the home of a former pupil, Hermeias, a man of some distinction who was chief of the town and who cherished a deep affection for him. Hermeias had wrested his dominion from the Persians who at that time dominated all Asia Minor and the two led a peaceful, scholastic life for three years until an officer in the Persian service captured Hermeias, put him to death and seized his possessions. Bereft of his friend, Aristotle took refuge in Mitylene on the island of Lesbos and commemorated in a poem the loss of this devoted pupil, host and friend. By his wife, Pythias, daughter of Hermeias, he had a daughter, named after her mother. A son by a concubine was born some years later, to whom he dedicated his principal work on ethics.

In 342 B.C. he was invited to take charge of the education of Philip of Macedon's young heir, a stripling of 14, destined to be known in history as Alexander the Great. For three years the boy listened and obeyed, acquiring a strong affection for his instructor. In 334 B.C. he laid aside his books to take up the sword and Aristotle returned to Athens. He was then 50 years of age, touched with sorrow, mellowed by long experience, wise and learned beyond all living men. He started a school which he called the Lyceum because of its proximity to the temple of Apollo Lyceius. Here he wandered to and fro in the garden delivering his lectures and answering questions; hence the familiar name of Peripatetic by which his famous school and sect are known. It was his custom to lecture to selected pupils each morning, dealing with profound and difficult subjects, and again in lighter vein in the evening to miscellaneous audiences. Thus he dominated the field of Athenian learning and letters for a dozen years while his former pupil, Alexander, was subjugating kingdoms and empires. After the illustrious warrior died and the anti-Macedonian party had come into power in Athens, a charge of impiety was made against Aristotle. Recalling the fate of Socrates, he stood not upon the order of his going and in 322 B.C. fled to Chalcis in Eubœa where he died later in the same year in the 63rd year of his age.

MATTHEW ARNOLD   1822–1888

MATTHEW ARNOLD, English poet, literary critic, essayist and educator, and prominent figure among the literary men of his time, was born at Laleham, near Staines, England, on December 24, 1822, and was the son of the famous Dr. Arnold of Rugby. He received his education at Winchester, Rugby and Balliol College, Oxford. He began to write and print verses while at Rugby (1837). *Alaric at Rome,* his first publication (1840), was a Rugby prize poem. The poem of *Cromwell* won the Newdigate prize at Oxford (1844). The following year he was graduated with second class honors, and in 1845 he was elected fellow of Oriel College. Among his colleagues was A. H. Clough whose memory Arnold commemorated in his elegy, *Thyrsis.* From 1847 to 1851 Arnold acted as private secretary to Lord Lansdowne. For a short time in the latter year he was an assistant master at Rugby, and was then appointed an inspector of schools, a position he continued to hold until within two years of his death. He married Lucy Wightman in 1851.

His first published volume of verse, *The Strayed Reveller, and Other Poems, by A,* appeared in 1849 and won a good deal of notice. It was followed in 1852 by another volume of poems "by A" entitled *Empedocles on Etna and Other Poems.* While undramatic, *Empedocles* contained many gems of poetic phrasing. In 1853 a volume of *Poems* appeared under his own name, with a second series in 1855. These made a great impression in academic circles and in 1857 Arnold was elected professor of poetry at Oxford, holding the chair for ten years. A classical tragedy, *Merope,* was published in 1858 and nine years later another collection under the title of *New Poems* (1867). During his Oxford professorship he published several series of lectures which greatly advanced his scholastic and critical reputation. Of these the lectures on *Translating Homer* and *On the Study of Celtic Literature* were brilliant criticisms, as were his two series of *Essays in Criticism*.

His poetical activity was intermittent and almost ceased after he left the chair of poetry at Oxford. His official duties as inspector of schools occupied much of his time, and the government sent him to France, Germany, Holland and other countries to study the educational systems and facilities of foreign nations. He devoted great energy to the prosecution of his investigations, as his painstaking reports indicate, and left a profound impress upon the development of education in England, especially in the elementary schools and on the department of education. More than twenty of his annual reports were published in 1889. In 1859, as foreign assistant commissioner, he prepared for the Duke of Newcastle's commission a report, printed in 1860 as *The Popular Education of France, with notices of that of Holland and Switzerland*. As assistant commissioner under Lord Taunton in 1865 he published *On Secondary Education in Foreign Countries* (1866), reprinted two years later as *Schools and Universities on the Continent*. His *Special Report on certain points connected with Elementary Education in Germany, Switzerland and France* was written twenty years later for the education department, after he had made a number of special investigations.

Arnold is best known to the present generation for such books of critical essays as *Culture and Anarchy* (1869), *St. Paul and Protestantism* (1871), *Friendship's Garland* (1871), *Literature and Dogma* (1873), *God and the Bible* (1875), *Last Essays on Church and Religion* (1877), *Mixed Essays* (1879), *Irish Essays and Others* (1882) and *Discourses in America* (1885). The contemporary public was somewhat startled by his rationalizing criticism, though the spirituality of his outlook and his ethical purposes were not questioned.

He died suddenly of heart failure in Liverpool, April 15, 1888.

CHESTER A. ARTHUR   1830–1886

CHESTER ALAN ARTHUR, twenty-first president of the United States, was elevated to that exalted post by the death of President Garfield at the hand of an assassin. The habit of American thought (influenced, no doubt, by the instance of President Johnson) is to regard a president thus inaugurated as inferior, and Arthur has suffered under this handicap in American history. But he rose to the solemn dignity of the presidential office and graced it with distinguished, if not with outstanding, abilities. He was born at Fairfield, Vt., on the 5th of October, 1830. At the age of 18 he graduated from Union College and at 23 began the practice of law, establishing himself in New York City where he soon became a distinguished member of his profession. His reputation was considerably enhanced by his participation in the Lemmon Case, famous in pre-Civil War slavery agitation. The case involved interpretation of the Fugitive Slave Law and through his skilful handling a decision was secured from the highest New York State court to the effect that a slave passing through that state en route from one slave state to another was in fact free during the period of transit through the free state. The case aroused keen interest and its issue conferred distinction upon Arthur.

During the Civil War he served with marked efficiency as inspector general and as quartermaster general in his state and was active in the recruiting and preparation of the troops for service. During the administration of President Grant his services and good republican standing were recognized in his appointment as Collector of the Port of New York, always a desirable plum on the political tree; he was reappointed four years later. Differences with President Hayes caused the termination of his incumbency. In 1880 he was nominated for the vice-presidency on the ticket with James A. Garfield and upon taking office carried his political activities into the halls of Congress to an extent prejudicial to his official dignity. In the bitter factional broils over New York State patronage he took an active part. On the death of Garfield, however, he assumed the presidential office with a high sense of its obligations and dignity. He was not the first, nor the last, incumbent to be sobered and uplifted by that exalted position. No unseemly partisan activities marred his incumbency and though he at no time revealed (nor indeed was called on to exert) the high qualities of statesmanship, his administration was vigorous and honest.

He supported the Pendleton law for civil service reform; vetoed the act prohibiting Chinese immigration for twenty years in contravention of the treaty of 1880; supported the Tariff Act of 1883 and the Edmunds law prohibiting polygamy in the territories. During his administration three great transcontinental railways were completed—the Southern Pacific, the Northern Pacific and the Atchison, Topeka and Santa Fe. During his term also letter postage was reduced to two cents and many other radical betterments in the mail service were effected, such as the speeding up of fast mails and the establishment of the free delivery and special delivery systems. A commercial treaty was made with Mexico and a treaty negotiated with Nicaragua empowering the United States to construct a canal across that country, which the Senate, however, failed to ratify.

Arthur was defeated for renomination but nevertheless supported his opponent, Blaine, who received the nomination. He died in New York on Nov. 18, 1886.

JOHN JAMES AUDUBON   1780–1851

JOHN JAMES AUDUBON, American naturalist, was born at Mandeville, Louisiana, in 1780 (or perhaps a few years earlier), son of a French naval officer and a Spanish creole. While still a child he was taken to France, where he was educated and studied drawing under the painter, David. His natural talent and instruction in art sufficed for his extensive work as a naturalist, but he never acquired preeminence as an artist. In his restricted field, however, his numerous drawings have had immense popularity and their instructive influence has been widespread. In 1798 he returned to the United States and made his home on a farm given to him by his father, in the neighborhood of Philadelphia. Here the next ten years of his life were devoted to collecting and sketching the bird life of the neighborhood. He was neither proficient nor interested in farming, but his inherent strain had imparted to him a love of recreation and social intercourse which doubtless had its part in the loss of his property and his failure as a man of business.

In 1808 he married Lucy Bakewell, a young Englishwoman of the neighborhood, and they sought their fortune in the west. But his temperamental qualities, however engaging, still stood in his way. In Kentucky, then in Louisiana, he was unsuccessful and eked out a poor living by giving dancing and fencing lessons, in which arts he was highly skilled. He was, as he readily admitted, wholly disqualified for orderly and systematic pursuits; he chafed at the humdrum round of business and preferred to follow the gypsy trail, fishing, hunting and roaming aimlessly in the woods and fields. He never long neglected the chief ambition of his life, the study of birds, and he continued to make his drawings despite adversity.

He returned to Philadelphia in 1824 where for the first time his talents were recognized and he soon became known to a widening circle of admirers throughout the country. He had now a large collection of drawings representing every variety of bird life, and in 1826 he went to England and arranged for the subscription publication of folio parts of his *Birds of*

America. These colored reproductions of his work were brought out over a period of years until 87 parts had been published, showing more than a thousand birds. At a later date reading matter was added to enliven this collection and a new edition was published in Edinburgh, completed in five volumes and called *Ornithological Biography.* Cheaper editions of this great work with smaller pictures were later published, the best known of which is the publication of 1844 called *Birds of America.* The success of these works spurred him to redoubled energy and the ensuing years were spent in extensive travel in every nook and corner of his own country and Canada. Business requirements incidental to publication called him again to Europe and by 1842 he was able to regain in some measure the ease which he loved. He was now able to settle in a permanent home and purchased an estate along the Hudson River in a section which is now within the confines of New York City. Again, however, he went forth in quest of material and penetrated to the upper reaches of the Missouri (a very considerable adventure at that time).

Assisted by his sons, Victor and John, who with their families made their homes on his estate, he prepared a work on American mammals, with scientific matter contributed by John Bachman. This was published under the name of *Quadrupeds of America.*

A mental breakdown preceded his death which occurred on Jan. 27, 1851, and he was buried in Trinity Cemetery, New York. His memory and his great work are beautifully and appropriately commemorated by the city park which bears his name.

MARCUS AURELIUS   121–180

MARCUS AURELIUS (a̲ rē'lyŭs) (surnamed ANTONINUS), Roman emperor, was born in Rome, April 20, 121 A.D. He was given a thorough education by his grandfather who adopted him after the death of his father. His unusual qualities of intellect and character so aroused the admiration of the Emperor Hadrian that he bestowed many favors on the infant scholar. At 17 he was adopted by Antoninus Pius, successor to Hadrian, who gave him his daughter in marriage and made him consul when he was but 20 years old. This was the first of many high offices which he filled with honor and distinction, retaining the affectionate regard of the emperor until the latter's death when he gave signal evidence of his generous character by insisting that Commodus, who had been adopted at the same time as himself, should reign jointly with him, notwithstanding that the

Senate had conferred the ruling power on him alone. He gave his daughter Lucilla in marriage to Commodus who later departed to the frontiers of the empire to check the barbarian hordes, but proved a weak leader, fell into habits of licentiousness and returned to Rome to receive the plaudits to which his vigorous subordinates were entitled.

Marcus Aurelius, meanwhile, ruled the state with wisdom and energy, contending with the devastating effects of earthquakes and of widespread pestilence said to have been brought to Rome by the returning soldiers. These calamities aggravated the panic of the citizens caused by the inroads of the barbarians and Marcus decided to go forth to check these invasions and put down insurrection in the outlying provinces. He subdued the Marcomanni and other rebellious tribes in the north but their insurrections were renewed two years later and continued to harass the peace loving emperor during the whole of his reign. His legions, depleted by pestilence, were recruited by the addition of slaves and gladiators and he carried on his military program under the most discouraging difficulties. He drove the Marcomanni out of Pannonia and proceeded with the same characteristic vigor and success against the Iazyges. Famed in history is his extraordinary victory in 174 over the Quadi, who inhabited Germania, when the Roman legions were perishing from thirst and a providential downpour came to their relief. In the grateful interval of refreshment the barbarians attacked and were on the point of victory when a storm of rain and fire confounded their efforts. The emperor himself is authority for the truth of this phenomenal occurrence and his voracity has never been questioned. That something extraordinary occurred all historians agree and the Germanic tribes were so appalled that they hastened to make submission. This great triumph was neutralized by an outbreak in the east, caused partly by the treachery of the emperor's wife, and he was obliged to proceed to this new theatre of rebellion. Avidius Cassius, his trusted governor, who had seized the whole of Asia Minor, was murdered and here again was shown the lofty character of Marcus Aurelius who regretted that the assassin had deprived him of the opportunity to pardon the conspirator, whose head (when proffered to him according to custom) he turned from in disgust and sorrow, and even burned the private papers of the traitor so that no others might be incriminated. With a magnanimity hardly credible, he treated the rebellious provinces with mercy and gave kindly reassurance to instigators of the rebellion. History shows few instances of such loftiness of soul as that displayed by this pagan ruler and lover of humanity.

While he was restoring order in the rebellious province, his wife Faustina died in an obscure village and the dishonored husband paid the most extravagant tributes to her memory; a circumstance which many historians have found it difficult to applaud. But Marcus Aurelius, like Lincoln, was without malice.

He visited Greece and Egypt, showing affectionate regard for all the people of his vast empire and was received everywhere with admiration and devotion. He founded chairs of philosophy at Athens and encouraged learning and education wherever he went. In 176 A.D. he returned to Rome where his unsanguinary triumph in the east was duly celebrated but he was not long to enjoy the rest which his failing health required and soon departed for Germany where he was again successful in subduing the barbarous hordes. His strength, which had been sorely strained by sorrow and care and continuous military activities, gave way and he died on March 17, 180 A.D., having reigned for 20 years. The place of his death was probably either Vienna or Sirmium.

Marcus Aurelius' love of study was insatiable. He cultivated the most learned men of his time, wrote much, was a profound thinker, and was proficient in metaphysics, mathematics, government and all the arts. His studies ennobled his life and outlook, adding the dignity of learning and wisdom to one of the purest characters that history reveals.

JOHANN SEBASTIAN BACH *very good*   1685–1750

JOHANN SEBASTIAN BACH, German composer and master of the organ, whose name is one of the most illustrious in musical history, was born at Eisenbach in upper Saxony, March 31, 1685, and there are few instances in history exhibiting as he does the potent influence of heredity. The family of which he was the most gifted member included in its seven recorded generations 49 musicians, half of whom achieved distinction. Johann's father was a master of the violin and played in the town band. His mother was Elizabeth Lämmerhirt, daughter of a furrier in Erfurt. He studied the violin under his father who died when he was 10 years old, and he then made his home with his elder brother, Johann Christoph, also a musician. The Bachs were in humble circumstances, but their home life was so permeated with music that it is difficult to perceive how any member of the extraordinary family could fail to be musical. By way of family reunions they held musical festivals annually, merry and fraternal affairs which must have rivaled a modern choral society. A well authenticated story is told that the youthful Sebastian's brother withheld from him a book containing certain musical works which the resolute young genius procured stealthily and copied by moonlight. The jealous brother discovered and deprived him even of his copy, but nothing could check the career of such a devotee. It was the custom in the schools of that time to train the pupils in choir singing and young Bach sang also at occasional weddings and funerals.

The death of his brother when he was 18 left him destitute and he secured employment in the choir of St. Michael's, Lüneberg, meanwhile continuing his schooling. It was in this formative period of his life that he walked 150 miles to Lübeck to study the organ under the great organist Buxtehude. In 1703 he was a member of the court band at Weimar for a few months. During a visit to Arnstadt he casually tried an organ in a new church which resulted in his being given a position as organist in that town where his grand uncle had previously filled a similar position. In 1708 the reigning duke appointed him court organist at Weimar, an exacting position, but its arduous duties did not prevent him from laboring incessantly to acquire mastery in every department of music. In 1717 he was made director of concerts and six years later director of music and cantor to St. Thomas' school in Leipzig which position he held for the remainder of his life. In 1718 he received the honorary post of kapellmeister to the Duke of Weissenfels and court composer to the king of Poland. In 1747 he visited Potsdam where one of his sons was in the service of Frederick the Great. He journeyed to the court with none of the pomp and circumstance which several years later characterized the arrival of a more flamboyant visitor of distinction, Voltaire. On being told of his arrival, His Majesty is reported to have exclaimed, "Gentlemen, old Bach is here!" and forthwith he had the composer summoned to his presence clad in his dusty and somewhat shabby traveling attire. The king, who did nothing by halves, had 15 pianos in the palace and on these his visitor was invited to experiment with a musical theme of the royal selection. He was treated with great distinction and left the court on the most cordial terms with his illustrious host, in contrast with the departure of the philosopher of France. His *Musical Offering* was written as a souvenir of this visit.

Years of continuous application at last affected his eyesight and total blindness put an end to his active labors. A brief and seemingly miraculous restoration of sight occurred a short time prior to his death on July 28, 1750. Notwithstanding his long and distinguished career and a genius which had been recognized and honored in a royal court, his death caused hardly a ripple in the town where he lived; the town council, which had always failed to appreciate him and had often thwarted him in his work, merely entered in its records a perfunctory note of his passing and his widow died in penury.

As an organist Bach stands alone, the only performer on this instrument to approach him being Handel. As a composer of organ music he may be said also to stand supreme. His compositions are, however, very elaborate and therefore the fullest appreciation of his genius is reserved to those who are highly educated in music. Some of his better known compositions are his *D minor Toccata and Fugue, Chromatic Fantasia and Fugue;* his *Well-tempered Clavichord,* published 50 years after his death; and among lighter pieces the *French Suites* and *English Suites.* His genius was versatile; he left some light and humorous pieces which were composed for the Bach family festivals and many religious works which are highly esteemed among musicians.

He was twice happily married; his children numbered 20 and the two eldest achieved distinction as musicians. The second marriage, to a singer, proved one of the few ideally happy artistic unions which history records.

FRANCIS BACON   1561–1626

FRANCIS BACON, LORD VERULAM, VISCOUNT ST. ALBANS, was one of the most illustrious of modern philosophers. He was born in London, England, January 22, 1561, son of Sir Nicholas Bacon and Anne Cooke. Both parents were distinguished for their talents, Sir Nicholas serving in responsible offices and showing high qualities of statesmanship during the reigns of Henry VIII, Edward VI and Elizabeth.

Young Bacon's thirst for knowledge began very early and was accompanied by a youthful sedateness which must have seemed somewhat priggish. Queen Elizabeth was so amused by his juvenile dignity that she called him her "young lord keeper." At 13 he entered Cambridge but was somewhat critical of its facilities and left after three years. He then went to Paris in the service of the British ambassador where he studied diplomacy, later embodying his observations in a work called *Of the State of Europe.* In 1579 the death of his father recalled him to England where, after failing to secure government financing for his projected scientific studies, he took up the study of law.

His uncle, Lord Burleigh, was then high in the royal favor and Bacon indulged the hope that his prospects might be advanced through this influence, but Burleigh's son, jealous of his cousin's all too apparent abilities, stood in the way and Bacon sought favor with the Earl of Essex, who assisted him under the handicap of Burleigh's rivalry and presented him with an estate (Twickenham). This signal act of generosity toward a

young protege was repaid with the grossest ingratitude. When the unhappy Essex came to grief and was brought to trial for conspiracy, no
voice was so loud against him as Bacon's; nor was he satisfied merely to
condemn, but used all his great talents to procure the conviction of his
former patron. To the apologists who say that Bacon's sense of right and
duty took precedence over friendship, it need only be observed that
this champion of the right was ere long himself to stand convicted of
corruption.

In 1590 he became council extraordinary to Elizabeth and later member of Parliament for Middlesex. Upon the accession of James I he rapidly
rose to the highest posts. In 1603 he was knighted and soon appointed
council to the Crown, then attorney general, in which office he committed
one of the acts which puts a stain on his illustrious name; he used the rack
to extort a confession of treason from an old clergyman. In 1617 he became
keeper of the great seal; two years later was elevated to the lord chancellorship with the title of Lord Verulam and made Viscount St. Albans in the
following year. His conduct in office had always been characterized by a
cynical subordination of honor to expediency. He had favored the monarch
and his favorites at the expense of right and justice and he now, in the
high office of chancellor, augmented his considerable revenues by accepting bribes from litigants. When the scandal was aired it was urged by his
friends that the custom of accepting "presents" from suitors at court was
not uncommon and some historians have thus sought to palliate Bacon's
corrupt acts. His exalted position, together with a natural taste for a
pretentious way of life, led him into a habit of extravagance which his
large income, augmented by that of his wife (daughter of a wealthy
alderman) did not suffice to support; in consequence he was deeply in
debt. He believed, or affected to believe, that the receipt of gifts would not
necessarily affect his judicial decisions. And indeed many of these decisions were made without regard to the "presents" from hopeful suitors.
It was just this fact which caused the exposé, for one of these disappointed
suitors in his court, not receiving value for his gift, denounced the recipient. If this illustrous philosopher had known as much about human
nature as his great compatriot, Shakespeare, he might have apprehended
such an issue.

On his own written confession Bacon was convicted of 23 acts of
corruption. He was honest enough not to condone his crimes after a
searching self-analysis. He was condemned to pay a fine of 40,000 pounds
and to be confined in the Tower during the king's pleasure; he was also
banished from court and disqualified from holding office. But the only
punishment which he actually suffered was the shame which besmirched
his great name. The fine was remitted, the "king's pleasure" terminated

his imprisonment at the end of two days and he was even encouraged to sit in Parliament and to appear at court, but he withdrew into private life with a government pension and thereafter devoted himself to literature and science.

It is in the field of philosophy that this "greatest, wisest and meanest of mankind" shines with resplendent lustre. The first edition of his essays appeared in 1597 and in 1605 his two great works on the *Advancement of Learning* and *Wisdom of the Ancients* in 1610. Several editions of essays, with additional matter, were published at different times and his two books of the *Novum Organum* in 1620. He was the author of numerous other works in English and Latin; his writings treat of a great variety of subjects, jurisprudence, morality, medicine, history.

His death occurred April 9, 1626, and is said to have been caused by the effects of a chill which he suffered after an experiment made to determine the value of snow as a preservative of flesh.

ROGER BACON   1214–1294

ROGER BACON, inventor of the magnifying glass, was an English monk who, by reason of his enlightenment and intellectual achievement, towers above the rude age in which he lived. Against the dark background of feudal barbarism he shines with a lustre hardly less extraordinary than does King Alfred. He was born at Ilchester in Somerset in 1214 and had such educational advantages as the young university of Oxford afforded. In was in the year of his birth that a group of existing schools were consolidated to form the educational centre now famous throughout the world as Oxford University; at the time of Roger Bacon its facilities were limited enough. He later went to Paris, which, by contrast with English towns, was a cultural centre, and there received his degree of doctor of theology.

Returning to England, he became a Franciscan monk and made his home in the primitive university town. But theology did not furnish sufficient scope for his inquiring mind. He interested himself in physics and his investigations of the secrets of nature (then a profound mystery) produced a singular reaction on the feudal ignorance which surrounded him. He was reputed to be in league with Satan and his difficulties were not lessened by his ecclesiastical colleagues whose ignorance was tinged with jealousy and envy. Moreover, Bacon denounced their dissolute habits to the pope, demanding reforms, and this act was answered by an accusation which resulted in a papal interdict forbidding him to teach in the university. He was also cast into prison and all but starved. He had, however, one enlightened sympathizer in the person of Sabina, cardinal-bishop and papal legate in England, whose friendly curiosity about Bacon was discouraged by the monks and they refused to show any of his writings. Bacon's opportunity came when Sabina became pope under the name of Clement IV. Disdaining the rule of the Franciscans, Clement demanded to see his writings and the way being cleared Bacon sent to Rome a favorite pupil, John of London, bearing several of his works and a more exhaustive indictment against his brethren, with a repetition of his demands for reforms. Clement soon died but for some time Bacon remained free from persecution.

In 1278, however, he was again in trouble. The head of the Franciscan order, Jerome of Esculo, denounced his activities and had him sent to prison with the approval of the pope, his incarceration lasting for ten years. Jerome, then on the papal throne as Nicholas IV, turned a deaf ear to the representations made by the now aged monk in the hope of gaining his freedom. But through the friendly intercession of several Englishmen the pope at last relented. Bacon returned to Oxford and busied himself with writing a compendium of theology, his last work. He died about 1294, being then in the neighborhood of 80 years old.

Like most enlightened individuals whose lots have been cast in ignorant and barbarous times, Roger Bacon presents a strange mixture of modern intelligence and medieval credulity. He was a chemist of no mean attainments and made important discoveries in this field, outstanding among which was his demonstration of the fact that lightning may be simulated with charcoal, saltpetre and sulphur, and that with this combination explosions can be produced. He was proficient in mathematics and had a fluent familiarity with several languages. His writings show a knowledge of optical science and a remarkable knowledge of astronomy. His outstanding achievement was his invention of the magnifying glass which has proved of such incalculable benefit to science. His astute and inquiring mind was not free from the superstitions of his time; he believed in astrology and ghosts and magic charms, but taking him by and large his varied interests and intellectual activities show him to have been a man strikingly in advance of his age, a brilliant light shining in the dense feudal darkness of the Middle Ages.

HONORÉ DE BALZAC   1799–1850

HONORÉ DE BALZAC (bål'zak') is one of the greatest names in fictional literature. No sweeping statement about his work could give as good an idea of his purpose as he has given himself in the preface to that vast reproduction of life called *La Comédie Humaine*. He would classify human nature, as the zoologist classifies animals, dividing mankind into species, each exhibiting its individual characteristics; he would give a whole, rounded out picture of life. To do this, he observes, would require several thousand characters. He set himself to this colossal task; that he succeeded is the almost unanimous verdict of historians and critics. His human comedy is not simply a collection of novels, it is a panorama of human life, worked out according to a preconceived formula.

He was born in the French town of Tours, May 20, 1799, and was first of the four children of his prosperous middle-class parents. His father held a civil office in the town. At the age of 12 he entered the college of Vendome, completing his education at the Pension Lepitre at Paris. By this time the family had suffered reverses, owing to the father's loss of employment, and the future novelist was placed in a notary's office where he served as a clerk. But he had what his sister called an "intuition of renown," and he found the humdrum round of duties intolerable. He gave up this employment and soon was launched on his literary career, writing under the name of "St. Aubin M. de Veillergré." For a while he was unsuccessful, but struggled on persistently, suffering poverty, harassed by debts, but applying to his work a concentration rarely equaled in literary annals. No amount of failure discouraged him, nor relaxed his rule to work with the most painstaking care. He is said to have spent hours in the selection of one word and to have emerged from his sanctum at nightfall utterly exhausted by the labors of composition.

In 1826, in this period of unrequited effort, he formed a partnership with the printer Barbier and became his own publisher, but the enterprise failed leaving him more deeply in debt and no nearer recognition than before. With persistence hardly less than heroic, he continued to write and at last in 1829 produced *Les Chouans,* a story of Brittany which is one of the best of his historical novels. All his previous work he now disregarded; *Les Chouans* inaugurated his career. If he had worked with extraordinary energy before he now labored with a zeal incredible. He found time, however, to fall in love with a Polish lady, Madame Evelina Hanska, and the path to marriage was at last cleared by the death of her husband in 1842. Illness and other causes, however, prevented the marriage until a few months before his death, when they were finally united at her Russian estate.

His courtship of this lady, the distance at which she lived, and for a time the obstacle presented by her married state, combined to diminish his superhuman productivity; but his energy was not spent, merely suspended. His entire output was enormous; he wrote about 70 novels, more than half of which constitute the *Comédie Humaine*. Among his best works are the *Physiologie du Mariage* and *Scènes de la Vie Privée* (1831); *Scènes de la Vie de Provence* and *Scènes de la Vie Parisienne* (1832); *Le Médicin de Compagne, La Père Goroit, La Peau de Chagrin, La Recherche de l'Absolu*. Of all his novels two only may be called symmetrical works—the *Histoire Intellectuelle de Louis Lambert* and *Eugène Grandet*. His last years saw the publication of four great works which completed the *Human Comedy; La Cousine Bette, Cousin Pons, Les Splendeurs et Misères des Courtisanes* and *L'en Vers de l'Histoire Contemporaine*.

As is inevitable with long works containing multitudes of characters, most of his novels lack proportion; it is in the scope and magnitude of his work that he stands unrivaled. Many critics place him second only to Shakespeare in his knowledge of human life and his skill as a delineator of character. Taine said of him that he was "the greatest storehouse of documents that we have on human nature." He died in Paris Aug. 18, 1850 at the age of 51.

PHINEAS T. BARNUM   1810–1891

PHINEAS TAYLOR BARNUM was one of the world's most astute showmen and out of his ability to interest and entertain the public he made a fortune.

He was born at Bethel, Conn., July 5, 1810, the son of a tavern-keeper, and his formal education was obtained in the local public schools. At the age of thirteen he became a clerk in a country store. There and also in his father's tavern, he listened to the strange stories told by travelers, played practical jokes with, and on, his father's customers, and when he was eighteen years old he went into the lottery business. A year later he was secretly married and moved to Danbury, Conn., where he edited the *Herald of Freedom*. He was not always accurate in the statements made in his paper and was at one time imprisoned for sixty days for libel.

In 1834 he went to New York City and hearing there of the negro slave, Joyce Heth, who was alleged to have been George Washington's nurse, he saw a chance to capitalize public curiosity concerning the old woman and bought her for $1000. With questionable documents supporting her claim as Washington's former nurse and with much publicity and ballyhoo, he exhibited her in New York and elsewhere, and for a time made a good deal of money. He was spending freely, however, and before very long he was reduced to poverty. He then turned his hand to various pursuits; sold Bibles, exhibited Negro dancers and wrote for newspapers, among other activities.

Fortune smiled on him again when he bought the old American museum in New York, which gave him the opportunity to capitalize his genius as a provider of entertainment, and as he was a born showman and publicity getter, he made the old Museum pay handsomely. He exhibited there a Japanese mermaid, fashioned from a fish and a monkey; a white negress, a woolly horse, and later the famous dwarf, General Tom Thumb. He gathered together all sorts of curiosities, real and otherwise, which could coax small coin out of the pockets of the sightseer and the curious-minded. He toured Europe with Tom Thumb in 1844, meeting with much success.

His first bold bid for a great fortune was successfully made in 1847 when he offered the Swedish opera singer, Jenny Lind, then the world's greatest singer, $1000 a night for a series of one hundred and fifty concerts in America. Tickets were sold at auction, one bringing as much as $650, and the public flocked to hear her. Gross receipts from ninety-five concerts amounted to $700,000, and Barnum, then probably with more money than he had ever dreamed of having, built a villa at Bridgeport, Conn., in imitation of Brighton Palace.

Many speculative enterprises followed. One of these was a clock factory which completed what some of his other undertakings had started and carried him steadily toward bankruptcy. He settled with his creditors in 1857 and started in new audacious enterprises, made another fortune and acquired two museums in New York (1865–68), both of which were later burned with tremendous losses.

Barnum, however, was not yet finished. He made his greatest challenge to Dame Fortune in 1871 by organizing the much advertised "Greatest Show on Earth," a traveling circus and menagerie with sideshows. Taking every advantage of what his museum experiences had taught him, that money was to be won by arousing public curiosity and then satisfying it, whether legitimately or not, he built up the circus until it was unrivaled, in reality the greatest show on earth. He later entered into partnership with James A. Bailey, and Barnum & Bailey's Circus became famous throughout the world, successfully touring Europe on four different occasions. This really great enterprise was continued long after the death of both men and after it was eventually bought by the rival Ringling Brothers it was billed as "Ringling Bros. and Barnum & Bailey's Circus."

At one time in his career Barnum had political ambitions. Connecticut elected him to its Legislature four times and he ran for Congress in 1866 but was defeated.

He published his *Autobiography* in 1854, *The Humbugs of the World,* in 1865, *Struggles and Triumphs* in 1869, and *Money-Getting* in 1883.

Barnum died on April 7, 1891, leaving an estate valued at about $5,000,000, though many times that amount had probably slipped through his fingers during the course of his life. Many pithy sayings have been ascribed to him, perhaps the best known of which was his statement that "there is a sucker born every minute." It would seem that he based his career on the truth of this observation.

JAMES MATTHEW BARRIE   1860–

Sir James Matthew Barrie won fame both as novelist and dramatist. He is preeminent in that category of writers whose abiding place in literature rests upon elusive charm rather than upon strength and vigor of substance. He was born at Kirriemuir, Scotland, May 9, 1860, and was educated at Edinburgh University. Soon after his graduation he began to write and the quaint, whimsical quality revealed in his early sketches of Scottish country life promptly won him recognition by the British public. At 25 he went to London where he thereafter lived and came to be much beloved by the distinguished literary group of which he became a member. In 1888 he published *Auld Licht Idylls,* a collection of brief sketches of Scottish village life, full of the quaint flavor and delicate touches of sentiment which were later to raise him to the heights of literary fame in more pretentious works. With the publication in the following year of *A Window in Thrums* his unique position in the field of letters was assured. In 1892 appeared *The Little White Bird,* followed shortly by *Sentimental Tommy* in which, perhaps, his distinctive charm reached its highest point. If not a profound character study, it is assuredly a most delicate and skilful delineation of a delightful conception. Soul-searching, Barrie may never have been, but none could vie with him in the gossamer fineness and sparkling delicacy with which the incredible Tommy was set forth. The tale (it is almost too whimsical to call a novel) is replete with that wistful fantasy and tender sentiment, always well clear of the sentimental, which have given Barrie a place apart among modern writers.

In 1891 appeared *My Lady Nicotine* and in the same year *The Little Minister* which, chiefly for its charm, no doubt, but also because of its sensational success as a play, is the work by which he is best known. In 1900 appeared *Tommy and Grizel,* continuing the story of the pair made famous in *Sentimental Tommy.* As a writer of fiction Barrie was now one of the most widely read and beloved of his time. He was to become equally famous as a playwright and to carry to the stage the same whimsical humor and poetic fantasy which made him unique in the purely literary field. In 1893 he married an actress who had played in his farce, *Walker, London,* and from whom he was divorced in 1909. His play *The Professor's Love Story* was produced in 1895. Like all his subsequent plays, it charmed by its tender sentiment and few stage climaxes have been more effective than that in which the preoccupied and crusty scholar awakens to the realization that his infant ward has grown to womanhood while he has been sending her toys. The stage version of *The Little Minister,* produced in 1897, was followed in 1903 by *Quality Street, Little Mary* and *The Admirable Crichton,* all pronounced successes which brought a refreshing breeze of wholesomeness and sentiment to the stage in England and America. In the following year was produced the beautiful fantasy *Peter Pan,* a dramatic fairy tale which proved a delight to children and adults alike. Independent as it is of human manners and customs and changing standards, it seems less likely to "date" as the years go by. In 1905 was produced *Alice-Sit-By-The-Fire,* the very name of which suggests Barrie's whimsical quality, and in 1908 *What Every Woman Knows.* In 1914 *The Legend of Leonora,* setting forth the charm of feminism against the harsh background of law and reason, was produced with marked success.

These plays and stories, together with many other lesser works, have touched a responsive chord in multitudes of readers and theatregoers. Barrie never manifested any interest in "sounding the depths," or in solving problems. There is a fairy tale atmosphere about all of his work and its indescribable charm makes it well nigh unique. The casual mood which impelled Shakespeare to give to the world a *Midsummer Night's Dream* was Barrie's characteristic humor. It pervades his realistic works (if any of them can be branded by so crude a term); it is joyously and tenderly expressed in fable and fairy tale. And this elusive quality, this quaintness of fantasy, will probably act as a bulwark to safeguard him against the modern rush of materialism and sophistication while stronger writers may fall by the wayside.

In 1913 he was made a baronet; in 1922 he received the Order of

Merit and became Rector of St. Andrews University. His later writings include *A Kiss for Cinderella, The Old Lady Shows her Medals, Dear Brutus, Echoes of the War, Representative Plays.*

FRANCIS BEAUMONT   1584–1616
JOHN FLETCHER   1579–1625

THE names of Beaumont and Fletcher, English poet-dramatists, are inseparably linked; they formed one of the most famous collaborations in literary history. They were of that coterie of poets and dramatists who gave lustre to the age of Elizabeth and would shine with a greater brilliance save for the dazzling and pervasive radiance of Shakespeare.

FRANCIS BEAUMONT was born at Grace-Dieu in Leicestershire in 1584, son of a common pleas justice. At the age of 12 he became a student at Oxford, leaving the university without taking a degree, and at 16 he was admitted to the Inner Temple. At 18 he made translations of Ovid which were published but without much advancing him in the field of letters. At that time the theatre was the arena in which the literati met and it offered the most inviting and immediately lucrative returns for creative effort. Here Beaumont met "rare Ben Jonson," whom he must have greatly admired judging by the laudatory verses he wrote for several of the latter's plays. Here, also, he encountered John Fletcher, who had been attracted to that field by the same inducements as himself. It was an auspicious meeting. They worked together and lived together until the domestic partnership was terminated by Beaumont's marriage in 1613 to Ursula Isley of Sundridge, in Kent, by whom he had two children. His death occurred at about the age of 30 and he was buried in Westminster Abbey.

JOHN FLETCHER was born in 1579, son of a clergyman of distinguished attainments in the ecclesiastical profession. He was Dean of Peterborough and is reported to have had the gloomy distinction of accompanying Mary, Queen of Scots, to the block and beguiling her last moments with such vehement spiritual consolation as to cause her annoyance. The son entered Cambridge at the age of 12, but whether he completed his studies there is not known. A play, probably of his exclusive authorship, called *The Woman-Hater,* was produced in 1606; he was then 27 years old. After the death of Beaumont he continued to write, producing a number of plays. His death, which occurred in 1625, is thought to have been caused by the plague.

Nothing more is definitely known about these two conspicuous figures of the Elizabethan stage, and even the catalogue of their joint works presents the same doubts and difficulties which scholars have had to contend with in the case of Shakespeare and others of that period. It was the custom to keep plays, new and old, in the theatrical archives and these plays were often freely overhauled by others than their authors. There was no copyright law and a play, more peculiarly that any other form of literary product, was public property. The magic touch of Shakespeare in another's play is usually readily discernible; not so, when writers of smaller creative stature revised and supplemented each other's work.

Literary scholars accord to Beaumont and Fletcher 52 plays, several poems and a masque, which was a sort of mythical and spectacular conception usually dealing with the supernatural. In one of their best known plays, *The Two Noble Kinsmen,* some scholars have found the characteristic touch of Shakespeare; and it is not unlikely that these prolific collaborators themselves introduced passages into the Shakespearean plays which are now recognized as not having the true ring of gold. Of the 52 accepted plays, 17 are believed to be joint products. Outstanding among them are *Philaster, The Maid's Tragedy* and *The Two Noble Kinsmen.* In *The Maid's Tragedy,* a play of great power, it is commonly thought that Beaumont's handiwork predominates. Another play, *The Faithful Shepherdess,* is believed to have been written mostly by Fletcher. The generally accepted critical thought is that Beaumont was the deeper and more serious genius and Fletcher the more idyllic, and most of the tragic parts of their joint work are ascribed to the former. Morally, they are equally offensive to modern taste which, notwithstanding its tolerant bent, would find their plays shocking. There is tragic power in them and here and there a sweet lyric strain. The authors were always clever, but never profound nor creative in the sense of depicting character.

THOMAS À. BECKET   1119–1170

THOMAS À BECKET, archbishop of Canterbury, was the central figure and victim in one of the most tragic episodes of the Middle Ages. He was born in London in 1119, studied theology at Oxford and at Paris, then law at Bologna and at Auxerre in Burgundy. The recital of such educational background is apt to create a false impression in the modern reader's mind about the period treated. It is well to remember that London was then hardly more than a clustering of primitive abodes and Oxford University a group of ill-housed schools which had not yet been consolidated under that name.

On the recommendation of Theobald, archbishop of Canterbury, Becket was made chancellor by Henry II which office he filled with vigorous efficiency. He maintained an extravagant feudal hospitality rivaling that of the king himself and his domestic establishment with its army of retainers was an imposing spectacle of the pomp and circumstance of office. He conceived that all this was proper enough for a high lay dignitary, but when, in 1162, he was created archbishop of Canterbury an extraordinary change of habit and policy became apparent. This great office had never before been held by any save a churchman and Becket seemed overwhelmed and exalted by its spiritual responsibilities. He straightway resigned the chancellorship, renounced his luxurious way of life and assumed the austerity which he thought to be in keeping with his religious duties. His lavish expenditures were turned into the channels of charity and he soon appeared as a zealous champion of the church against the aggressions of the king and the barons. Henry II, who had not apprehended such a sequel to his appointment, found his own position difficult in the extreme. He had always striven to keep the clergy in subordination to the state and he now witnessed the spectacle of his favorite using an iron hand with his nobles. The terrible punishment of excommunication (wholly outside the king's authority) was pronounced against several laymen for their alienation of church property.

Henry soon realized that Becket's policy was wholly antagonistic to his own and that the power which the prelate exercised was perilous to the royal prerogatives and dignity. He made known his displeasure in a manner so threatening and emphatic that Becket, apprehensive for his safety, tried to leave the country, which the king construed as a breach of allegiance and confiscated his property. A claim was also made upon Becket for a large sum represented to be due to the Crown when he ceased to be chancellor. He could not meet this demand which was probably unjustified; his private life and personal honor had always been above reproach. He appealed to the pope and meanwhile fled in disguise to France where he spent two years in retirement. Supported by the French king, he journeyed to Rome where his representations won him reinstatement. This was a hollow triumph but at last, in 1170, an understanding was reached with the British monarch and Becket returned to Canterbury amid the rejoicings of the people who had always (with dubious reason) counted him their friend and defender of their liberties. If Henry had expected that the archbishop would now "lie down like a lamb" he was soon disillusioned. The prelate abated none of his former vigor and jealousy for the welfare and authority of the church. This was a difficulty which all the feudal kings of Britain encountered but the vast influence and rigorous policy of Becket made it peculiarly intolerable to Henry. At last the king expressed impatience that none of his loyal subjects would rid him of this thorn in his side. It was an ill-considered remark and soon bore fatal consequences. Henry, perhaps innocent of any evil intent, was in Normandy at the time. Four barons who were with him took the hint and proceeded immediately to carry out what they construed to be the king's desire. They proceeded to England by four separate routes and on the night of Dec. 29, 1170, entered the cathedral at Canterbury where, after attempting to drag Becket from his devotions, they murdered him before the altar of St. Benedict in the transept.

The king affected grief and consternation; historians differ as to the measure of his culpability, but he paid a heavy price for the relief he enjoyed and submitted to the most humiliating papal requirements in order to avert the threat of excommunication. The assassins made a penitential journey to Rome where they were sentenced to make a pilgrimage to Palestine, not an unwelcome punishment in an age when the crusades were regarded in the light of high adventure. Shortly afterwards Becket was canonized by Pope Alexander III and in 1220 Henry III had his bones taken from a crypt where they had been thrown by the assassins and deposited in a shrine which became the destination of pilgrims and furnished the inspiration for Chaucer's Canterbury Tales.

As a gesture to show the supremacy of the government over all ecclesiastic authority, Henry VIII destroyed the shrine and had the bones of the great prelate burned and the ashes scattered in the air.

HENRY WARD BEECHER   1813–1887

HENRY WARD BEECHER, American pulpit orator, was an outstanding member of a distinguished family. His father, Rev. Lyman Beecher, was married three times and had thirteen children; all of his seven sons became clergymen. Equally famous with Henry was his sister, Harriet Beecher Stowe. He was born in Litchfield, Conn., June 24, 1813. At 17 he entered Amherst College and later attended Lane Theological Seminary where he experienced a spiritual conflict between skepticism and religious devotion, resulting in a conception of God as the embodiment of infinite love and pity, and in his consecration to christianity which he thereafter preached with commanding eloquence and in a broad spirit of humanity.

His first pastorate was of a Presbyterian church at Lawrenceburg, Ind.;

its modest membership of 40 made it necessary for him to act in the dual capacity of pastor and sexton. After two years he became the pastor of a Presbyterian church in Indianapolis, which he held for eight years. In 1847 the Congregational society of Plymouth Church was organized in Brooklyn, N. Y., and two years later was housed in the spacious structure which was destined to become famous the world over as "Beecher's Church." To this church he accepted a call and thus inaugurated a pastorate lasting for nearly 40 years during which time he rose to be a national figure. Year after year his heroic mien and melodious and stirring voice thrilled congregations ranging from 2000 to 3000. His voice was always loud in the cause of freedom and in sympathy with the slave, and Plymouth Church, always sturdy in its support of its leader, was the scene of more than one stirring and touching incident born of Beecher's eloquence.

A feature of his pastorate was his series of "Lecture Room Talks," and these (as also many of his sermons) were published and eagerly read throughout the country. In 1855 he edited the *Plymouth Collection,* a hymnal which became famous as the repository of hymns which, under his inspiration, were associated with the congregational singing which was a feature in his church.

He often appeared as a lecturer and spoke on many subjects. In 1863 he visited England where he swayed multitudes with his oratory, and was successful in winning many sympathizers to the northern cause in the Civil War which was then waging. His handling and subduing of unfriendly mobs was a thrilling spectacle. He was a liberal, or "modernist" at a time when the old orthodoxy was universal, an enthusiastic student of science and a convert to the theory of evolution which he found no difficulty in reconciling with an essential christianity.

He became editor of a new publication, the *Independent,* but resigned the post to his friend, Theodore Tilton, who was later to figure sensationally in his life. In 1870 he became editor of the new *Christian Union,* and shortly thereafter Tilton publicly charged Beecher with adulterous relations with Mrs. Tilton. The trial resulting from these charges was one of the most prolonged and famous in legal history. It lasted six months, ending in a disagreement of the jury with nine voting for acquittal. Friends and admirers of Beecher have generally accepted this as an exoneration. Plymouth Church stood by him with staunch loyalty and complete confidence in him was later unanimously expressed by a great council of Congregational churches. It is perhaps significant that in a public tribute held eight years later to celebrate his 70th birthday, the justice who had presided at his trial presided also at this vast outpouring of citizens in his honor.

As an orator Beecher ranks with the greatest. In his later years, when his fame had become world-wide, he was a noble figure, his massive head with its flowing white locks completing an imposing picture which fulfilled every physical requirement of the great orator. He was not of the flowery or sensational school but had always a wholesome regard for facts. So potent is the tradition of his oratory that his great erudition is sometimes overlooked. He carried a vast store of learning which was always readily available and it was customary for him to answer questions on every variety of subject at the termination of his addresses. He was intensely human with an irrepressible sense of humor and love of fun.

He was married in 1837 to Eunice White Bullard. He died on March 8, 1887, survived by his wife, three sons and a daughter.

LUDWIG VAN BEETHOVEN   1770–1827

LUDWIG VAN BEETHOVEN (bā′tō vän) was one of the world's greatest composers. He invented and introduced many new devices for giving depth, beauty and richness to musical composition and the production of music.

Of Flemish descent, he was born at Bonn, in Prussia, on Dec. 16, 1770, the son of a tenor singer in the band of the Elector of Cologne, who supervised the boy's early musical education. He made his début as a piano virtuoso in Holland in 1781; two years later he joined the band of the Elector of Cologne as accompanist, later becoming organist and afterwards playing the viola in the same organization. He became one of the most accomplished extemporaneous players of his time. In 1792 the Elector sent him to Vienna to study under Hayden and Albrechtsberger, and Vienna thereafter became his home although he made a number of extended tours in various parts of Europe. He had no official appointments as had a number of other composers of the period, but spent his time working on his own compositions, in Vienna during the winters and in some nearby village during the summers.

Beethoven at first composed along the standard lines of the period and critics assert that many of his early compositions resemble Mozart's so closely that they can scarcely be distinguished from each other. He gradually found that he needed more freedom, more life, vigor and richness for his musical genius to find full play, and he introduced many innovations. He enlarged the introduction and the coda, introduced episodes in developing a composition, changed the minuet into the scherzo, multiplied the key-relations of the movements, and introduced the chorus into the finale of the symphony. He first introduced the song-cycle in music and gave new value and authority to variations of theme, which have since been carried to still greater lengths. The initiation of modern program-music is due to his musical inventiveness. He brought to his musical composition a seriousness and a profound appreciation of tonal beauty that have given his works a permanent place in the library of the world's greatest music—a place of security such as few composers have achieved. Critics have found Beethoven's music broader, richer, more deeply colored than that of his predecessors, with more beauty of tone than music had possessed before, and more varied, due to innovations and new arrangements.

In 1798 the composer's hearing became affected and not long afterward he became totally deaf. He had no court position to pay him a regular income and his extreme poverty together with family troubles, largely due to an ungrateful nephew whom he had educated, depressed him greatly. These afflictions, however, brought a peculiar quality into his musical themes that have helped to make of them a rich heritage to succeeding generations. His last years were solitary and sad; he became brusque in manner, and a victim of hypochondria. He died of dropsy on March 26, 1827. His remains were transferred in 1888 to the Central Cemetery in Vienna.

Beethoven's numbered works total 138, exclusive of the many compositions which bear no opus number. About sixteen of his numbered works belong to his first period, before his individual genius had begun to find expression in his compositions. Included in these are his first three trios, and the symphonies in C and D. His second period embraces the numbered compositions from about 16 to 80, including such famous ones as the third, fourth, fifth and sixth symphonies, *Egmont, The Ruins of Athens,* his only opera, *Fidelio,* and many chamber pieces. To the great composer's third and most hauntingly beautiful style belong his last symphony (the ninth), the *Missa Solennis,* the later sonatas for the piano and for the string quartette. The so-called *Moonlight Sonata* for the piano is one of his most popular compositions, and is probably the most widely known of all his works.

ALEXANDER GRAHAM BELL   1847–1922

ALEXANDER GRAHAM BELL, a Scottish-American scientist, best known as the inventor of the telephone, was born in Edinburgh, Scotland, on March 3, 1847. His father, Alexander Melville Bell, was a distinguished teacher of elocution, and inventor of a system of so-called "visible speech" used in the instruction of deaf-mutes, and the son became deeply interested in his father's work. While a student at London University his health failed, and in 1870 father and son emigrated to Ontario, Canada, where they took up their residence in the town of Brantford.

Two years later the son became professor of vocal physiology in Boston University where he remained for four years. He had already, while in Canada, experimented with and partly constructed an instrument for the transmission of the human voice by electricity and in July, 1875, he completed the first speaking telephone, the basic construction of which was much like that of the telephone in common use today. It was first exhibited in June of 1876 at the Centennial Exposition in Philadelphia, and aroused great interest in scientists from many countries who studied it carefully.

The principle of the telephone had been recognized as early as 1860 by Reis of Frankfort, and various others besides Dr. Bell had been working with the idea, notably Gray of Chicago, but Dr. Bell was granted a patent in February of 1876 for the construction of the first workable instrument. Improvements were speedily made and a company was shortly organized to handle the operation of the telephone and Dr. Bell throughout his life was the recipient of large sums of money in royalties on his invention.

During the next ten years his active mind was busy with numerous other inventions, among them the photophone by means of which speech may be transmitted by a beam of light; the audiometer, phonographic apparatus, and an instrument by which bullets or other metallic objects in the human body may be located. He was interested in many lines of scientific research and did much to further geographical and aeronautical investigations. Eugenics and the promotion of longevity interested him and throughout his life he maintained his keen interest in the education of the deaf. It was through his suggestion that in 1887 Miss Anne Sullivan was sent from the Perkins Institution for the Blind in Boston (in which institution he had always been interested) to Tuscumbia, Ala., to teach the blind deaf girl, Helen Keller. Through his life, the genial, kindly man remained a devoted and valued friend to these two women.

In 1887 with prize money given him by the French government for his great invention he established and endowed the Volta Bureau in Washington for the study and dissemination of knowledge regarding the deaf, to which knowledge his own published researches have been an important contribution. He was a member of the National Academy of Sciences; president of the National Geographic Society; president and founder of the Association to Promote Teaching of Speech to the Deaf;

and regent of the Smithsonian Institution. He was the recipient of the degree of LL.D. from Dartmouth College, and of other honors. One of his early publications was a *Memoir on the Formation of a Deaf Variety of the Human Race.*

He married Mabel Gardiner of Cambridge, Mass. His death occurred in Nova Scotia on Aug. 2, 1922, and the hour of his burial was marked by the suspension of all telephone communication in North America.

ARNOLD BENNETT   1867–1931

ENOCH ARNOLD BENNETT, one of the most popular and prolific of British novelists during the first quarter of the 20th century, was born at Hanley, Staffordshire, on May 27, 1867. He studied law with the purpose of devoting himself to that profession, but the call of literature and journalism proved stronger than that of the law and after having a number of stories and articles published in magazines he decided to embark upon a literary career. He settled in London as an assistant editor on the magazine, *Woman,* succeeding to the editorship three years later. His first novel, *A Man from the North,* was published in 1898 when he was thirty years old, and met with sufficient success to embolden him to resign his magazine editorship and trust entirely to his writings.

He became intensely interested in the development of the modern hotel, and one of his early novels, *The Grand Babylon Hotel* (1902), and his last one, *Imperial Palace,* dealt with great hostelries and their place in the life of a large city. *Anna of the Five Towns* (1904) introduced the places and the material which he was to make famous in a number of his later books. The Five Towns occupied his imagination; he knew them and the life of their people, and he wrote of them realistically, whimsically, often impudently, so that they occupy much the same place in the affections of his readers as does Thrums in the minds of J. M. Barrie's admirers.

In his realistic descriptions Bennett often mingled the fantastic with a fresh humor and accurate observation of oddities of character and situation that escaped the majority of contemporary writers. In 1903 he published *The Truth About Authorship,* but it was not until he was forty years of age that he achieved a masterpiece which revealed the true bent of his genius, and which remains one of the remarkable and most powerful novels of his generation—the *Old Wives' Tale,* published in 1908. Its high quality was sustained in a number of his succeeding novels and short stories, notably in *Clayhanger* (1910) and *The Card* (1911). In the latter year he published also *Hilda Lessways,* the story of the heroine of *Clay-hanger,* the earlier book having dealt with the life of one *Edwin Clay-hanger.* A third book about these two characters, entitled *These Twain,* was published in 1916, and while not reaching quite so high a literary level as *Clayhanger,* it contains much that is in the author's best vein. In 1912 he wrote *The Matador of the Five Towns,* and the successful play, *Milestones. What the Public Wants,* a comedy of 1909, was fairly successful. *Sacred and Profane Love* (1919) and *The Love Match* (1922) were others of his plays.

Bennett remained a rapid and fecund writer throughout his life, but only once afterward did he reach the high level of his *Old Wives' Tale,* and the *Clayhanger* trilogy. That was in his study of miserliness, *Ricey-man Steps,* (1923), in which he again caught the realism and strangeness of daily life. *The Pretty Lady* of 1918 and *Mr. Prohack* of 1922 are enter-taining without achieving greatness. During the World War Bennett wrote many political articles. He published a number of common sense books on living, *How To Live on Twenty-four Hours a Day, Mental Efficiency* and others. His memory was prodigious; he absorbed books, music, painting and ideas easily and wrote of them all with equal facility. His last novel, *Imperial Palace,* was published in 1931.

While still at the height of his powers, he died in March of that year and his body rests in Burslem Cemetery, Staffordshire. Late in life he had married a French woman, from whom he afterwards separated and who published *My Arnold Bennett* shortly after his death. The two vol-umes of Bennett's *Journal* were issued from the press in 1932 and 1933 and were received with great acclaim by literary editors as presenting with absolute truthfulness the man Bennett, himself.

SARAH BERNHARDT   1845–1923

SARAH BERNHARDT is generally regarded as the first actress of her time. She outlived the emotional style of acting in which she won fame, and by her matchless technical skill prolonged her vogue, defying age and chang-ing standards of art. She was born in Paris in 1845 (the exact date is uncertain) of French and Dutch parentage and, although of Jewish ex-traction, she received Christian baptism and was educated in a convent by her father's desire. She later attended the Conservatoire, winning prizes for comedy and tragedy, and made her début in 1862, playing minor rôles; shortly afterward she played in burlesque. At 22 she triumphed as the queen in Hugo's *Ruy Blas* and also as Cordelia in a French version of *King Lear*. At 24 her creation of the rôle of Zanetto in Coppée's *Le Passant* was a sensational success.

She was now fairly launched upon her great career, one triumph following another. Notable among these early successes was her brilliant portrayal of Berthe de Savigney in *Le Sphinx* and her portrayal of *Phèdre* by Racine. Her performance of Dona Sol in Hugo's *Hermani* notably advanced her steadily increasing fame. She was first seen by English-speaking audiences in 1879 when she appeared in London, receiving the enthusiastic plaudits of multitudes who did not understand her language but were none the less thrilled by her acting. She always disdained obstacles which might have proved fatal, or at least prejudicial, to a lesser artist. In her tours she would play in a barn or a tent when she could not find a theatre; her genius always triumphed. Shortly after her return to Paris a characteristic outburst of temperament resulted in her withdrawal from the cast of *L'Aventurière* after one performance and she reappeared in London in *Froufrou* and *Adrienne Lecouvreur,* following which she toured in Russia and Denmark and achieved a series of signal triumphs in America.

In 1882 she married Jaques Damala, a Greek actor, but the union was of short duration. At about that time she began to appear in plays written especially for her by Sardou, among which *La Tosca* remained one of her most popular vehicles. In 1890 she appeared as Joan of Arc. The plays of this period were produced in her own theatre, the Porte Saint-Martin. She frequently visited America and in 1891–1903 made a tour of the world. Returning to Paris she became proprietress of the Théâtre de la Renaissance and there produced some of her greatest successes; *Les Rois, Sylvestre, Izeyl, Gismonde* and others. In 1899 she established the Théâtre Sarah-Bernhardt in Paris where, among other notable undertakings, she appeared in *L'Aiglon* by Rostand and in a French version of *Hamlet.* Her portrayal of the son of Napoleon in the former of these was a piece of exquisite acting, but her playing of the melancholy Dane was not a major triumph.

Bernhardt, in all the glory of her genius, was last seen in America in 1911 when she revived several of her greatest rôles. When she visited America again in 1913 she was crippled from an accident to one of her limbs and could not stand alone. But she triumphed over the grotesque spectacle of such assistance on the stage and gave a series of performances consisting of single acts from plays which she had made famous. The accident from which she suffered later necessitated amputation of part of the limb and it was supposed that she would not again appear upon the stage. Indomitable, however, she returned to America during the World

War (1915) under the auspices of the French government and gave a series of performances which aroused not only the customary enthusiasm for her genius but everywhere the strongest feelings of admiration for her unquenchable courage and patriotic ardor. These performances were little more than recitations, so far as she was concerned, but her golden voice thrilled her audiences as ever, and such freedom of movement as was left to her had the old magic, notwithstanding her 70 years.

In her long and necessarily busy career she found time to study painting and sculpture and showed talent in both of these arts. She also wrote much, including her memoirs. At the time of her death she was preparing for her appearance on the screen and the apparatus for making a photo play had been set up in her home in Paris, where she died on March 8, 1923.

BISMARCK   1815–1898

OTTO EDUARD LEOPOLD, PRINCE VON BISMARCK-SCHOENHAUSEN, chancellor of the German Empire, was born April 1, 1815, at Brandenburg in Prussia, of a noble family of which various members attained prominence as statesmen and soldiers. He was educated at Göttingen, Berlin and Greifswald, where he studied law. At the conclusion of his studies he lived for a time on his estates. In 1847 he married Johanna von Putkamer. Notwithstanding his learning and distinguished qualities, he had been little heard of prior to this time but he now began to attract attention in the Prussian parliament as an ultra-royalist and an advocate of extreme absolutism. He was one of those opposed to the project of a German empire, proposed by the parliament of 1849.

His diplomatic career began in 1851, when he was appointed chief secretary of the Prussian legation in the resuscitated German diet at Frankfort. Here he began to manifest that zeal for the interests and aggrandizement of Prussia which was to win him the name of "the iron chancellor" and which thereafter guided him, often regardless of the means he employed. In the diet, he gave open expression to the long felt discontent with the predominance of Austria and demanded equal rights for Prussia. In St. Petersburg, whither he was sent in 1859, he is said to have tried to bring about an alliance between France, Prussia and Russia, but without success. By this time he had acquired the special regard and confidence of the king who sent him in 1862 as ambassador to Paris in order to give him an insight into French politics and diplomacy before he assumed the direction of affairs at home.

When the German ruler's government could not obtain the consent of the lower house to the new military organization Bismarck was recalled from France and made minister of foreign affairs and president of the cabinet. Upon the refusal of the Reichstag to pass the reorganization bill and the budget, he closed the chambers (1862) with the announcement that the king's government would take the necessary action without the sanction of the deputies. Accordingly, the army reorganization went on and the next four sessions of parliament were closed or dissolved in the same way without the government's obtaining the sanction of the house. The people were now aroused almost to the point of revolution. At this crisis the death of the king of Denmark opened again the Schleswig-Holstein question and excited a fever of nationalistic feeling, which Bismarck adroitly worked upon so as to aggrandize Prussia by the acquisition of these duchies and reconcile his opponents to his high-handed policy by pointing to the success of the newly-formed army.

Throughout the events which culminated in the humiliation of Austria and the complete reorganization of Germany under the stern leadership of Prussia, Bismarck was the guiding spirit; and such was the magic of success that from being universally disliked he became the hero of Germany. Nay, this iron apostle of absolutism, pursuing his ruthless course without regard to public opinion, received in 1871 the thanks and congratulations of the extreme democrats of Great Britain for giving to North Germany a constitution based on universal suffrage. In 1867 he negotiated the neutralization of the Luxemburg territory. The action of France in regard to the candidacy of Prince Leopold of Hohenzollern for the throne of Spain gave Bismarck the opportunity of converting into action the intensified feeling of unity among the German people and precipitated the Franco-Prussian war (1870–71) resulting in the humiliation of France under terms dictated by Bismarck.

He was soon created a prince or chancellor of the German Empire. A striking feature of his administration was the contest with the Catholic Church in which the expulsion of the Jesuits (1872) and the application of the new ecclesiastical laws were the most notable events. In 1874 an attempt was made upon his life. Two years later he presided at the Berlin congress. Upon the ascension of William II, Bismarck lost favor and resigned from the chancellorship in March, 1890. Notwithstanding his stern and uncompromising nature and his devotion to the dubious policy that might makes right, he was, in his private life, kindly, witty and genial. He died at Friedrichsruhe on July 30, 1898.

WILLIAM BLAKE   1757–1827

WILLIAM BLAKE, English poet and engraver, was born in London, Nov. 28, 1757, the son of a hosier. Neglected and unknown to the vast majority of people in his lifetime, he has come to be regarded as one of the great figures in English art and poetry. Much of his work shows great originality and is of the purest poetic quality, though he lived and worked in the realm of mysticism and imagination rather than in that of reality and he came to believe that he was in actual communication with the shades of Moses, Homer, Dante and others of the departed great.

Early in life he showed artistic promise. He attended Par's drawing school, was apprenticed to an engraver for whom he made drawings of the monuments in Westminster Abbey; studied Burke, Locke and Bacon, but his early creative impulse found its best expression in a volume of verse, *Poetical Sketches,* published in 1783, which showed strongly the influence of the Elizabethans.

At 21 he became a professional engraver and in 1782 married Catherine Boucher, who survived him four years and who learned to draw and paint sufficiently well to be of considerable assistance to her husband. He earned his livelihood by making engravings for the publishers and in 1787 began to experiment with a new method of printing from etched copper plates. First results of this process are found in his *There is No Natural Religion,* and in *All Religions Are One.* It was developed still further in *Songs of Innocence,* lyrical poems etched on copper with hand-colored decorations. He later moved to Lambeth and there completed *The Book of Thel* (1789); *The Marriage of Heaven and Hell* (1793); *Songs of Experience* (1794); *America* (1793); *Visions of the Daughters of Albion* (1793) *Europe* (1794) *Urizen* (1794) *The Book of Los* (1795); *The Book of Ahania* (1795) and *The Song of Los* (1795). Mysticism and philosophy began to gain the upper hand. He often employed an irregular verse form, a forerunner of the *vers libre* of a later day.

He produced later a series of large color prints and a series of 537 water color designs to illustrate Young's *Night Thoughts.* He worked for a long time on a long mystical poem, *Vala, or the Four Zoas,* which, although never properly translated, was of great value to the student of his work. He labored with tremendous energy, with periods of mental and physical exhaustion. Three years were spent at Felpham while executing copper plates for Hayley's *Life of Cowper,* but later he returned to London where he painted much in water color and continued to write mystical poetry, much of which is embodied in his *Milton.*

In 1804 on a trumped-up charge by a soldier whom he had forcibly turned out of his garden, Blake was tried for treason, but acquitted. In 1805 he agreed to make copper plates for Blair's *Grave* for the publisher Cromer, who paid him a small sum for the designs and then employed another engraver. Blake became embittered, suffered fits of depression and many persons thought him insane.

In 1809 he held an exhibition of sixteen of his works, including a large painting of Chaucer's Canterbury Pilgrims, but the only public notice this received was a spiteful and unfair criticism in Leigh Hunt's *Examiner*. From 1810 to 1817 Blake lived in retirement. In 1812 he showed some of his work at the last exhibition of the Associated Artists in Water Color. From 1818 until his death in poverty and obscurity, his life was somewhat happier, due chiefly to his friendship with the painter, John Linnell, and during this period he executed his greatest creative canvases illustrating the *Book of Job*. Linnell commissioned him to illustrate Dante's *Divine Comedy* for which Blake completed 100 water color designs and had engraved seven of these when he died on Aug. 12, 1827 of an internal ailment from which he had suffered for some three years. His body was placed in Bunhill Fields, but it was not until 1927 that a marker was placed on the approximate spot of his burial.

GIOVANNI BOCCACCIO   1313-1375

GIOVANNI BOCCACCIO (bŏk kät' chŏ), Italian poet and novelist, author of the *Decameron* and one of the greatest figures in Italian literature, was born at Paris in 1313, the exact date being uncertain. His father was a wealthy merchant of Florence, his mother of the French nobility. He was sometimes called Il Certaldese because his family sprang from Certaldo, a village in the Florentine territory. He was reared in Florence. From early childhood he was interested in letters, especially poetry, a taste which his father endeavored to discourage. At about the age of 10 he was sent to Naples where he studied accountancy, but discovering no enthusiasm for that work, he turned to canon law which he also deserted for literature. On reaching his majority he pursued more freely the bent which he had not dared openly to indulge, writing poetry in Latin and Italian, but without encouraging results. At that time the court of King Robert of Naples was a centre of culture and here Boccaccio enjoyed the friendship of the most learned and talented persons of his day. Amid these surroundings he soon found his forte in the gay and sparkling prose of which he became a master. He was an ardent student of Dante, but an equally ardent student of life and was one of the gayest of scholars.

At about the age of 37 he formed an intimate friendship with the poet, Petrarch, and following his friend's example he collected many books and copies of rare manuscripts which he could not afford to buy. He is said to have been the first Italian to procure from Greece a copy of the *Iliad* and the *Odyssey*. He also wrote a *Genealogy of the Gods* in 15 books which was unquestionably the most exhaustive work on mythology published up to that time. He is so universally known for his justly famous collection of tales that his character as an exceptionally liberal-minded scholar has been somewhat overlooked, but his influence was very considerable in his time. He helped to give a freer direction to knowledge and made learning attractive by his light and charming style.

While in Naples he had fallen passionately in love with a young woman who was generally thought to be an illegitimate daughter of King Robert, and to please her he wrote *Il Filocopo,* a prose romance, and afterwards the epic poem, *La Teseide.* In 1342 he went to Florence, soon, however, returning to Naples where he wrote his *Amorosa Fiammetta Il Filostrato* and *L'Amorosa Visione.* Here also he wrote his famous *Decameron,* the work by which he is best known. He is said to have written it to entertain Joanna, the daughter and successor of King Robert. It consists of one hundred stories, ten of which are told each day by seven ladies and three gentlemen who are supposed to have fled from Florence during the plague which was then raging there, and to have sought refuge in a country villa where they beguiled their leisure with pleasure and story telling.

It would be difficult to overstate the influence of this book in the field of dramatic and fictional literature. Shakespeare drew from it; its plots have been recast and used by writers and dramatists throughout the intervening centuries. In wealth and variety of incident it is well nigh inexhaustible. That this matchless repository of sprightly fiction should be stained by the grossest impurity is, unhappily, not fully accounted for by the freedom of the age in which it was written. The reader is surfeited with plots and situations hinging on the sex relation.

About 1350 Boccaccio returned finally to Florence where he was honored with several diplomatic appointments and enjoyed the highest esteem of the citizens. The memory of his early indiscretions haunted him and he seriously contemplated taking holy orders as a penance for his dissolute gaiety at the court of Naples and elsewhere. His devoted friend, Petrarch, dissuaded him from such a gesture, suggesting that the renunciation of his vices would afford a more sensible solution to his difficulties. In 1373 he was appointed Dantean professor at Florence, a position devoted exclusively to interpretation of the *Divine Comedy* and its great author. When failing health forced him to resign this congenial post he retired to his quiet retreat at Certaldo where he died on the 16th of December, 1375.

SIMON BOLIVAR   1783–1830

SIMON BOLIVAR, a South American statesman, was born on July 23, 1783 at Caracas in what is now the state of Venezuela, but at that time was a Spanish colony. He came of a noble and wealthy Spanish family and was sent in his early life to Madrid where the educational facilities were greater than in his native country. There he studied law, spent some time in European travel, married and returned with his young wife to Venezuela. He traveled in Europe again after his wife's early death and about 1809 visited the United States. Presumably his observation of its institutions, the freedom of its life and of its general system of government played its part in arousing within him a desire to see his country freed from the despotic yoke of Spain. Be that as it may, he returned to Venezuela and joined the patriot, Francisco Miranda, who several years earlier, after serving with the French forces in the struggle of the American colonies for independence, had attempted to bring about a revolt among the Spanish troops in South America. Undiscouraged by his failure, he was at this time again seeking to arouse his countrymen and welcomed the aid of Bolivar who, in April, 1810, undertook a mission to England to enlist support. Unable to shake the British from their position of neutrality, he returned and distinguished himself in several successful battles under Miranda. The royalists finally gained the ascendency, however; Miranda was forced to surrender and sent to Spain where he later died in prison, and Bolivar fled to the island of Curaçao.

Encouraged by the officials of New Granada (later Colombia), he raised a small army of volunteers and after several victories over the Spaniards (each of which brought reinforcements for his army) he made his way to Caracas and in August, 1813, took possession of the city. He was hailed as The Liberator and became a virtual dictator; but his triumph was short-lived. He found himself forced to engage in continual battles with the Spaniards who at one time plotted his assassination, but the man who was hired to commit the fatal act, having tracked him to Jamaica, made the mistake of murdering his secretary. Gathering together certain refugees who had reached the island of Haiti, Bolivar led them to the small island of Margarita, off the Venezuelan coast, where he established a sort of government having as one of its features the abolition of slavery. For two years he engaged in conflicts with the Spanish General Morillo who had been sent out at the head of an army of 12,000 to subdue the rebellious provinces and who was finally vanquished. Following a congress at Angostura in February, 1819, Bolivar led his troops across the Cordilleras and after victories in the Magdalena Valley consummated the union of the two provinces of New Granada and Venezuela into the republic of Colombia, of which he became president. A constitution was adopted in August, 1821, and the following year saw the last of the royalist troops in Colombia, but The Liberator was called upon to aid Peru in her struggle against the Spaniards. He was constituted dictator of that country and after two years succeeded in freeing it from Spanish domination.

He made a sort of triumphal tour through the southern sections, received a gift of $1,000,000, which he devoted to purchasing the freedom of 1000 slaves, and was named president for life under the Bolivian code adopted in December, 1826. Returning to Colombia, he was reelected despite some dissatisfied elements, but about 1828 he was forced to suppress a conspiracy against his life by the execution and banishment of its leaders. The following year the Bolivian code was repudiated in Peru and he was ousted from the presidency; opposing factions had risen in Colombia; Venezuela withdrew from the republic and Bolivar, in failing health, resigned and retired to Cartagena despite the insistence of the mass of the people that he remain.

This great patriot has often been referred to as the Washington of South America. The exigencies of the times doubtless necessitated his assuming arbitrary powers, but his sincerity in the cause of liberty was evident and he devoted nearly all of his personal fortune to the service of his country. Not long before his death he wrote a farewell message complaining of ingratitude and defending himself against charges of personal ambition. He died at San Pedro on Dec. 17, 1830. In 1842 his remains were taken to Caracas where a triumphal arch commemorates the life of "El Libertador."

ROSA BONHEUR   1822–1899

MARIE ROSALIE (ROSA) BONHEUR (bǒ nĕr′), was one of the most eminent of women artists, her fame resting principally upon her paintings of animals, of which the "Horse Fair" is probably the most widely known.

She was born at Bordeaux, France, Oct. 22, 1822, the daughter of Raymond Bonheur, a drawing teacher who became director of a Free School of Design for Girls in Paris. Her father wished her to become a dressmaker, but her distaste for the work and the unusual ability which she demonstrated with pencil and crayon led him to take her as a pupil in his own school. She later studied under Coignet, but developed her ability and her own peculiar style through the painting of animals in their natural environment. She was nineteen years old when she first exhibited at a Salon in 1840. The two pictures on view on that occasion were "Goats and Sheep" and "Two Rabbits," but thereafter she was an annual exhibitor at the Salon until 1855. In 1845 she received a gold medal of the third class and in 1848 a first class medal.

Her first great picture, and one that many of her admirers consider her greatest, was "Ploughing in the Nivernais," exhibited in 1849, which was commissioned by the State and is now in the Luxembourg Gallery. The summer of 1850, spent in the Pyrenees, resulted in a number of outstanding animal canvases.

Miss Bonheur first adopted masculine garb while painting studies in the abattoirs on the outskirts of Paris, impelled thereto by the unwelcome attentions of men. She wore a costume somewhat similar to that of Breton peasants and found it so convenient that she continued its use. In 1853 she exhibited her "Horse Fair," which has been reproduced probably more often than any of her other work. It attracted great attention at the Salon and she offered it to her native city of Bordeaux for 15,000 francs. The offer was rejected and she sold the canvas to England for 40,000 francs. It was later bought by Cornelius Vanderbilt for the Metropolitan Museum, New York City, for 268,000 francs. "Hay Harvest in Auvergne" was another of her important early works.

In 1856 Miss Bonheur bought a Gothic château at By, near Fontainebleau, where she spent nearly all the rest of her life. She was visited there by Napoleon III and the Empress Eugenie in 1864 and the following year the Empress returned in person to present to the artist the cross of the Legion of Honor. Rosa Bonheur was the first woman ever to receive this coveted decoration.

In 1867 she visited Scotland and did a number of Scottish subjects, "Ponies of the Isle of Skye," "Sheep in a Boat," etc. Among her notable later pictures may be mentioned "Cattle and Sheep in a Pasture" (1867), "Wagon with Six Horses" and "Foulaison" (a troop of galloping horses).

The Metropolitan Museum in New York, besides the famous "Horse Fair," has "Deer in Park," "A Limier-Briquet Hound" (painted in 1877), and "Weaning of the Calves" (1879), while the public library of New York City has her "Deer Drinking."

Bonheur canvases are noteworthy for their sound and wholesome feeling, their spirited action and their faithfulness to nature. Her drawing is considered by art critics to have been good, but they find her color hard. The public, however, has not found that hardness of color any drawback to its appreciation of her great animal pictures and has accorded her a reputation which few women painters have ever achieved. Rosa Bonheur created no school of painting and followed none. She was individual in her treatment of her subjects and ranks close to Landseer among the notable painters of animals. She died in Paris, on May 25, 1899, at the age of seventy-seven.

DANIEL BOONE 1735–1820

TRAPPER, hunter and backwoodsman, trailmaker and pioneer, ever restive and adventurous, DANIEL BOONE stands out as one of the most picturesque figures in American history. The charm which makes Robinson Crusoe perennial casts its romantic glamour over this resourceful and solitary explorer and denizen of the wilderness. In the coterie of hardy scouts he stands supreme. He was born in Bucks County, Penn., in 1735; the exact date is uncertain. While he was still a youth his family migrated to Yadkin in North Carolina where his long career as a hunter and trapper may be said to have begun. Legends and traditions of his exploits prior to this are engaging but ill-founded. Here he attended school and must have been sufficiently restless under its restrictions and in proximity to its numerous attendants.

At about that time there visited the region along the Kentucky River one John Finley, a kindred spirit, loquacious as to his stirring adventures in the forest, and to him young Boone listened enraptured. With several comrades he entered the wilderness and for about two years explored its fastnesses; hunting, trapping and engaging in numerous conflicts with Indians. Boone would have been the solitary survivor of the party, all his companions being either captured or killed, had he not been joined by his brother, and these two, never disillusioned about the joys of forest life, lived on amid these perilous environments, having many hair's breadth escapes and such a variety of adventures as would suffice for any tale of fiction.

In 1773 he set out with five families for eastern Kentucky but a concerted attack by Indians compelled the abandonment of this migration. In the following year he fought the Indians along the frontier in that savage warfare which originated in the killing of the Mingo chief, Logan, and his family, and which was known as Lord Dunmore's war. In the following year Boone was engaged by a land company in North Carolina to represent it in the purchase of land along the Kentucky river where he built a fort. Here, with his family, he started the settlement which became the town of Boonsboro, Kentucky. In 1777 this fort was the scene of an unsuccessful attack by Indians. Early the next year Boone penetrated into the country along Licking River at the head of a small group of followers to secure a supply of salt, much needed in the settlement, and was taken prisoner in a surprise attack by the Indians who took him to their stronghold and, finding him friendly and courageous (he was utterly without fear), adopted him into their tribe. He lived among them for several months, then escaped, returning through the forest to Boonsboro. His arrival was most timely, for almost immediately a fresh Indian assault occurred which his leadership was instrumental in repulsing.

Boone could never remain long in one place. He now returned to North Carolina, but his restless habit took him back to the Boonsboro settlement, where in 1782 he again participated in the Indian warfare which was intermittent at that sequestered post. About 1790 he explored the region which is now West Virginia and for five years lived in this unpeopled wilderness. He then sought adventure in the Femme Osage settlement west of St. Louis where he remained for about four years, becoming commandant of the district which was under Spanish rule.

His death occurred on Sept. 26, 1820. In 1845 his bones were disinterred and buried at Frankfort, Ky. His wife, who had been a faithful companion in his many wanderings, was buried beside him. The many exploits of this redoubtable woodsman are too numerous for individual mention. Interest in his romantic career has been considerably revived by the latterday outdoor movement and he is the great hero of scouts the country over. Phenomenally courageous and resourceful, rivaling the Indians themselves in woods wisdom, he was gentle and kindly, with a modesty about his heroic adventures which stands in the way of historical treatment of his unique career.

EDWIN BOOTH   1833–1893

EDWIN BOOTH, distinguished American actor, was born at Belair, Md., Nov. 13, 1833. Like most of the outstanding figures of the stage, he inherited his dramatic bent. He was the son of Junius Brutus Booth, an actor hardly less famous than himself, whose acting was characterized by such intensity that it was said to be perilous to stand against him in a stage duel. Edwin received a rigorous training at the hands of this talented but eccentric parent and became familiar with classical rôles while he was still very young. His first appearance was at the age of 16 in Boston. Two years later in New York he played Richard III as understudy for his father. The following season their tour took them to the Pacific Coast where they separated, the young Booth remaining in the West and also visiting the Hawaiian Islands and Australia. Returning, he made a tour of the southern states. Decided triumphs followed in Boston and New York in his characterization of Sir Giles Overreach.

In 1860 Booth married Mary Devlin of New York whose death three years later cast a shadow over his subsequent life. After a successful trip abroad where he was received with marked favor, he engaged the Winter Garden in New York and enjoyed a series of triumphs in Shakespearean rôles, outstanding among which was that of Hamlet which became his great part and with which his name is peculiarly associated in dramatic history. He was deeply affected by the assassination of President Lincoln and felt keenly the stigma attaching to the family name by the insane act of his brother. In sorrow and mortification he withdrew from the stage, although no resentment was visited upon this gentle and kindly spirit except by a few fanatics. In 1866 he returned to the theatre and was enthusiastically welcomed by his large following. In 1869 he married Mary McViker, but the marriage was not a happy one. In that same year Booth's Theatre in New York City was erected and became the scene of a new series of triumphs and memorable portrayals; Lear, Othello, Macbeth, Richard, Hamlet and other rôles which he made famous. This splendid artistic enterprise continued until the financial panic of 1873 forced him into bankruptcy and he resumed his touring, triumphant wherever he went. Twice he visited Europe (1880–1882) where his success was both financial and artistic and where he achieved a distinction seldom accorded to dramatic stars.

He later appeared as co-star with Lawrence Barrett, a well-known actor who had formerly supported him, and this partnership (one of the most famous in dramatic history) continued until Barrett's death in 1891. Barrett lacked the spark of genius which was evidenced in all Booth's acting, but he was a player of great conscientiousness, always capable, and a writer and manager of undoubted ability. Booth retired shortly after Barrett's death. His last appearance was at the old Academy of Music in Brooklyn, N. Y., where he gave a memorable performance of Hamlet. His last years were spent in the beautiful home of The Players (erroneously called the Players Club) in Gramercy Square, New York

City, which he had founded and whose first president he became. The name was suggested by the phrase in *Hamlet,* "The Players." Here he died on June 7, 1893.

As an actor Booth occupies a unique place and is generally regarded as the greatest American tragedian. Latterday thought in regard to dramatic art and certain original experiments in the field of Shakespearean interpretation have maneuvered him into a position where his art seems old-fashioned. But great genius does not "date," and Booth was most decidedly a genius. He is commonly thought to represent the line of demarkation between the old bombastic, elocutionary school and the modern intellectual method of interpretation. This is true if he is to be regarded as standing on the hither side of the line. He was the first of the modern exponents and discarded the rant and thunder which had always been thought inseparable from tragic portrayals. A wistful melancholy, ingrained in his nature, made his playing of Hamlet exquisitely effective. He was not of imposing physique but he was lithe and graceful and his magic voice was capable of every shade of feeling. He was deeply loved by all the members of his profession and highly esteemed by the public for his sterling qualities as a man.

WILLIAM BOOTH

1829–1912

WILLIAM BOOTH, founder of the Salvation Army and its first "general," was born at Nottingham, England, on April 10, 1829. His father was a speculative builder who apprenticed his son, at an early age, to a pawnbroker. Of a serious disposition and a religious cast of mind, young Booth was converted at the age of fifteen and soon thereafter became a revivalist preacher. He went to London in 1849 and worked in a pawnbroker's shop at Walworth. He disliked the work intensely, but the money he could earn was needed at home and he continued at it for some time. In 1855 he married Catherine Mumford, having in the meantime become a regular preacher of the Methodist New Connection. After nine years with that sect he left it to become an independent revivalist.

Booth was possessed of a profound sympathy and pity for the outcast from society, for the sick and the suffering, and had a deep hatred of squalor, dirt and sin. He believed that eternal punishment would be the fate of those unconverted to the Christian religion. Back in London in 1864 he continued his revivalist meetings in halls, in tents, even in the open air, establishing the brief street service which is a characteristic expression of the Salvation Army organization. He founded his first regular mission in Whitechapel under the name of the Christian Mission and this was the nucleus of the organization which in 1878 took the name of Salvation Army.

The "Orders and Regulations" of his Army Booth modeled on those of the regular British Army. Its revival meetings were "campaigns," and these campaigns aroused violent opposition in London. A "Skeleton Army" was formed to break up the meetings. For many years Booth and his followers were repeatedly fined and imprisoned as breakers of the peace. The opposition continued sporadically and with decreasing force until about 1889.

The Salvation Army operations had been extended to America in 1880; the following year to Australia; and spread throughout Europe, to India, Ceylon and elsewhere. General Booth was a great traveler, visiting many countries to organize branches of his Army. His wife began to preach in 1860 at Gateshead where Booth was circuit minister, thus beginning the women's ministry which has become a notable feature of the work of the organization. She shared her husband's work until her death in 1890.

In Darkest England, and the Way Out (1890) prepared by Booth with the aid of the journalist, W. T. Stead, urged the remedying of pauperism and vice by the organization of the city colony, the farm colony, the oversea colony, the household salvage brigade, rescue homes for fallen women, deliverance for the drunkard, the prison-gate brigade to meet and help and encourage released prisoners, the formation of a poor man's bank, the appointment of a poor man's lawyer and the establishment of Whitechapel-by-the-Sea.

Toward the end of the nineteenth century, opposition gave way to a widespread admiration and respect for Booth and his work, which included the establishment of so many charities and social reforms. Plans which had been partly put into execution by liberal financial subscriptions were now more nearly realized. In 1902 he was officially invited to attend the coronation of Edward VII, which marked the definite end of hostility toward him and his Army. His progress through England in 1905 was almost in the nature of a triumphal procession. Meanwhile his work in the United States and elsewhere had been greatly extended and was encouraged by the authorities.

He died on August 20, 1912, after several years of failing eyesight and poor health.

JAMES BOSWELL   1740–1795

JAMES BOSWELL is best known for his famous life of Samuel Johnson, but he was more than a chronicler of a great man's doings; he was a masterly writer of English. Born at Edinburgh, on Oct. 18, 1740, he was the eldest son of Lord Auchinleck, a judge in the Court of Sessions. Young Boswell received his education in the Edinburgh High School and then in the Universities of Edinburgh and Glasgow. The desire for a literary career was manifested early in his life, and at the age of eighteen he kept an "exact journal," and wrote poems and prologues. He was but twenty-three when his first book was published, a series of letters in which the future biographer sought to display his wit. It was on his second visit to London, in 1763, that he met the great Samuel Johnson, shining literary figure of the times, who bestowed a warm friendship upon his worshipping young disciple.

Boswell spent a winter in study (combined with considerable dissipation) at Utrecht and made a tour through Germany, France and Italy, during which he met Voltaire and Rousseau. The latter gave him a letter of introduction to Paoli, the Corsican patriot, and Boswell set off for that island. His visit there is chronicled in his *Account of Corsica,* published in 1768, which developed into one of the best sellers of its day.

Soon after his return from his travels he became an advocate (1766), and three years later married his cousin, who bore him seven children. Lord Auchinleck gave his son an allowance of 300 pounds a year and frequently, with much grumbling and many threats, paid his debts. Boswell was never prosperous, and he liked to enjoy the good things life had to offer. He made many visits to London, and in 1773 was elected to membership in the famous Literary Club of that city. With the great Johnson he made the memorable voyage to the Hebrides which he has so minutely chronicled. Croker has estimated that Boswell was with the great man not more than 276 days, including the Hebrides tour, but his biography indicates that he could not have known the great Doctor better had he spent a lifetime in his society.

Boswell entered the Inner Temple in 1775 and was called to the English bar in 1786. Upon his father's death he succeeded to an estate of 1600 pounds a year. He had some inclination for a political career but did not advance beyond the recordership of Carlisle, which he resigned after a year. Following the death of his wife in 1789, his intemperance grew upon him; he became a hypochondriac and was always in financial straits. It was at this period that he wrote the *Life of Samuel Johnson,* in which he found some relief from his difficulties. The book was hailed with the greatest enthusiasm upon its publication in 1791, and a second edition was called for within two years. Its success had little effect on Boswell's pecuniary troubles, however, as his intemperance was too deeply rooted to be shaken off. His health gave way and he died in London on May 19, 1795.

Of weak character, a prey to vanity, intemperance and other follies, Boswell proved himself nevertheless the greatest biographer who has written in the English language. His reverence for the great Doctor, the minuteness and loving care which he displayed in the writing of the famous *Life,* prove that he had mental gifts of a superior order and which might have carried him to high honor had he been able to master his appetites and overcome his weaknesses. His book has become an English classic and has won the lasting admiration of the literary world for its vivid, dramatic revelations of Johnson's character, and the simplicity and subtlety of the means by which those revelations are made.

THE BRONTËS:
CHARLOTTE   1816–1855
EMILY   1818–1848

CHARLOTTE BRONTË was born at Thornton, Yorkshire, April 21, 1816, and Emily on August 20, 1818. They were the daughters of an austere Irish clergyman whose name had been originally Patrick Prunty and who had married a Cornish woman.

The life of the sisters was one of continuous struggle against adversity. Their mother died in 1822, a year after the family had moved to Haworth in the Yorkshire moors; the household was dismal, the father unapproachable in his gloomy austerity, and poverty dogged their footsteps. At the age of seven Charlotte was sent to Cowan's Bridge School (the original of the dark and forbidding "Lowood School" in her novel of *Jane Eyre*). Two of her sisters died and Charlotte herself suffered a breakdown in health so that she was taken out of school and remained at Haworth until 1831. In that year she entered a school at Roehead kept by one Miss Wooler who became her lifelong friend. Poverty forced Charlotte and her sisters, Emily and Anne, to seek some means of livelihood and they became governesses. Dissatisfied with that life they sought to fit themselves for higher and better paid teaching positions, and with that end in view the two elder ones went to Brussels in 1842 where they remained for two years. In 1846, the three sisters published a volume of verse—*Poems by*

Currer, Ellis and Acton Bell—which made no great impression upon the literary world. Its lack of success caused the authors to turn to prose writing. Charlotte wrote *The Professor;* Anne, *Agnes Gray* and Emily the weirdly romantic *Wuthering Heights,* which has kept her name alive along with that of her more famous sister. Publishers rejected *The Professor* on the ground that it lacked plot interest, and Charlotte set to work upon *Jane Eyre,* the most widely read and the most compelling of her novels. This was published in 1847 and met with a mixed reception, but gradually won the approval of the reading public and in the estimation of later critics it has placed its author in the ranks of the major novelists. *The Professor* was published subsequently but its chief claim to attention is that it was written by the same hand that penned *Jane Eyre.*

The year 1848 was one of bereavement for the young novelist; her brother Branwell died in September, and on December 19th Emily followed him. The next year Anne died and Charlotte was left alone in the parsonage with her gloomy father. Her third novel, *Shirley,* was published in 1849, and three years later *Villette,* which was her own favorite. A few months of happiness were in store for her before her death. In 1854 she married her father's curate, Arthur B. Nicholls, and their brief married life was one of joy for Charlotte, who had always craved the love about which she wrote with such deep understanding. Her husband would have preferred that she give up her writing, but he does not seem to have insisted upon it, as she was working upon a new novel, *Emma,* when death put an end to a literary career that was just in its prime, and to a happiness which was just in its budding after much sorrow and suffering.

She died at Haworth on March 31, 1855. By sheer native genius she had made a niche for herself in English literature against the odds of poor health, few advantages and much suffering. The manuscript of an early, immature novel by her hand was discovered in Holland and printed in 1931.

Many biographies of Charlotte Brontë have been written, of which that by Mrs. Gaskell, published within two years of the author's death, remains one of the best.

JOHN BROWN   1800–1859

JOHN BROWN, the famous abolitionist whose "soul goes marching on," was one of the picturesque characters in American history. He was of an extremely radical type and was undoubtedly a fanatic, but it must be conceded that his moral influence was great and few will deny his memory the tribute of respect. It is worthy of comment that two influences, wholly unofficial and both highly romantic, contributed in marked degree to the abolition of slavery in the United States; one, the publication of *Uncle Tom's Cabin;* the other, the bizarre exploits of John Brown.

Independence and the love of freedom ran in his blood, inherited no doubt from his Puritan ancestors. He was born at Torrington, Conn., on May 9, 1800, and was deterred from an evangelical career only by his defective eyesight. He was twice married and had 20 children, of whom eight sons died in early manhood. With his large family he moved to Ohio where he worked in a tannery and later engaged unsuccessfully in the wool trade. He then moved to Essex County, in the northern part of New York State, and lived on a sequestered farm where his grave is now pointed out to tourists, and which was alleged to have been used by him as a station on the so-called "underground railway," by which fugitive slaves were spirited to the Canadian border. Four of his sons settled in Kansas, then a scene of bitter strife where the sentiment for slavery was strong, and they endured much persecution because of their abolitionist views. Their father could not refrain from joining them and casting his lot with those opposed to slavery. When the free state advocates engaged in conflict with the pro-slavery element from Missouri, Brown took an active part and the killing of one of his sons in this factional warfare greatly intensified his hatred of the southerners. His heroic defence against a greatly superior force at Osawatomie won him national fame and has linked his name to that place in American history.

But he dreamed of more spectacular efforts in the cause of freedom; he conceived the project of instigating rebellion among the slaves of the South in the hope of thus achieving their liberation. In Iowa, during the winter of 1857, he recruited and drilled a band of followers and later drafted a provisional constitution for the states under authority of which he was to be made commander-in-chief. He next set about the rescue of some slaves in Missouri and in the fighting which ensued one of the slave owners was killed.

The exploit which finally cost him his life was rash to the last degree, but was momentarily successful. At Harper's Ferry in Virginia (now West Virginia) the government maintained a large arsenal. Brown planned to capture this and to take hostages whom he might later exchange for slaves. It was his hope that the slaves thereabouts would rally to his support and that his spectacular attack would be the signal for a general uprising of the blacks. On Sunday night, Oct. 16, 1859, he marched to the town with a band of seventeen white men and five negroes and seized the arsenal with little difficulty. A few citizens were captured and a number of houses searched before the people realized what was happening. They soon rallied, however, and some fighting occurred in which one negro was killed by Brown's men; the mayor of the town and one of Brown's sons received slight injuries. The expected uprising of the blacks did not occur and Brown and his followers found themselves in a perilous position. His chance of escaping to the mountains with his prisoners, where he might have negotiated for their release, passed and he confronted an increasing band of enraged citizens. In his extremity he sent out a flag of truce from the arsenal, the bearer of which was instantly killed, and in reprisal Brown killed one of his prisoners. By Monday night, his situation was desperate; only three of his white followers remained unwounded and the few negroes who had joined him were of no assistance. One of his sons was dead, another wounded. The arrival of a force of marines the next morning precipitated the end for the forlorn little band. Fighting desperately, Brown was captured after being thrice wounded. He and all his party were promptly indicted for conspiracy, murder and treason. At his trial, which lasted three days, he was unable to stand because of his injuries. He was sentenced to be hanged within 48 hours and met his death with calm fortitude on Dec. 2, 1859.

He was a man of stern principles and inflexible character and his deeds, however illegal and fanatical, were undertaken with the one aim of hastening the end of slavery. By many he was regarded as a martyr to that cause; to others his activities seemed those of an ordinary criminal.

CHARLES FARRAR BROWNE (*Artemus Ward*)   1834–1867

CHARLES FARRAR BROWNE (better known as ARTEMUS WARD) was an American humorist, born in Waterford, Maine, on April 26, 1834. As a boy he entered the printing office of the *Clarion* at Skowhegan, Maine, and at 15 he went to Boston as a compositor for the comic weekly journal, *The Carpet Bag*. His first writings were in the form of contributions to that publication. Later he became a reporter on the *Cleveland* (Ohio) *Plain Dealer* and while on that paper he published in its columns a series of *Artemus Ward's Sayings,* in which, to gain his humorous effects, he relied partly on the most atrocious spelling. The *Sayings* appear to have struck a popular note, were reprinted in other newspapers throughout the country and he became known as a humorist.

On the strength of this reputation he went to New York in 1860 and joined the staff of *Vanity Fair,* a newly established comic journal. The publication had but a short life and he turned to lecturing, probably as a stop-gap, but his first lecture, *The Babes in the Wood,* delivered in Brooklyn, proved so popular that he abandoned journalism and decided to devote his efforts to the lecture platform where he continued to use the style of humor to which he had accustomed his public in his newspaper work. He continued to use the name "Artemus Ward" throughout his life, and probably started the fad of literary *nom de plumes* which continued for some time and which was some years later adopted by the more famous humorist, "Mark Twain." His practice of misspelling for humorous effect was also at times used by Twain and was adopted by Josh Billings and other humorous writers of the period.

In 1862 he visited California and Utah where he gathered material for a series of humorous lectures on the Mormons "whose religion is singular but their wives are plural." These proved popular and Artemus Ward had become almost a national institution when he was attacked by tuberculosis in 1864 and compelled to retire from public life for a period of two years. By 1866 his health was much improved and he went to England on a lecture tour, opening with a panorama in the Egyptian Hall. His unconventional style of humor was new to the English and his efforts were received with enthusiasm. So successful were his lectures that he continued them over a period of three months, greatly overtaxing his strength, and on March 6, 1867 he died at Southampton.

In 1865 he had collected his humorous writings in one volume published under the title of *Artemus Ward, His Book,* which was so well received that he followed it the same year with *Artemus Ward, His Travels,* and in 1866 with *Artemus Ward, His Travels Among the Mormons.* In the year of his untimely death appeared *Artemus Ward in London.* A complete edition of his works was published in 1875 and there have been numerous later editions. His reputation endured for many years after his death, but to readers of today he is little more than a name and the vogue of extracting humor from grotesque spellings and ungrammatical sentences has long since passed.

ROBERT BROWNING   1812–1889
ELIZABETH BARRETT BROWNING   1806–1861

EQUALLY distinguished in the field of poetry, and peculiarly interesting because of their life together, the Brownings are most appropriately to be considered under one heading. Highly intellectual and profoundly learned as Robert Browning was, his poetry is characterized by a subtlety of thought which gives him a place apart among modern poets. Elizabeth Barrett was England's greatest poetess and one of the foremost of the world.

ROBERT BROWNING was born in the London suburb of Camberwell on May 7, 1812, and was educated at London University, after which he spent some time in continental travel, familiarizing himself with the literature of other lands. Proficient both as a musician and as an artist, it was thought that the significant performance of his life would lie along one or other of those lines, but he soon manifested a greater interest in letters and began the series of works which were to give him his distinctive place in modern literature. His first book, *Pauline,* written while he was still groping for an expressional form, but still a poem of rare beauty, was published anonymously in 1833. A sojourn, studiously spent, in Russia was followed in 1835 by a drama, *Paracelsus,* which first brought him into public notice. This was followed the next year by his tragedy of *Strafford,* dedicated to the actor, Macready. In 1838 he visited Italy, a country which always lured him, but returned to London where he made his home. His plays, *Sordello,* and *The Blot in the 'Scutcheon,* were not effective on the stage because of the lack of vivid and impressive incident. His lyrical drama, *Pippa Passes,* was accorded a greater measure of popular approbation. In 1855 he published *Men and Women,* one of his greatest works, containing poems which, for depth and subtlety of conception, profound analysis of the human mind and speculative insight, are unsurpassed in the English language. Inferior to Tennyson and others in melody of versification and beauty of style, his brilliancy and vigor of thought make him superior, in that respect at least, to any of his poetic brethren. Like Meredith and Henry James, he is often obscure (sometimes seeming purposely so), but he frequently exhibits a force and brevity of expression, a condensation and compactness of thought comparable only to Shakespeare. Some of his dramatic lyrics are faultless.

Among his other poems and collections are *The Ring and the Book, Balaustion's Adventure, Red Cotton Nightcap Country, Aristophanes' Apology, The Inn Album, Pacchiarotto and other Poems, La Saisiaz, The Two Poets of Croisic, Dramatic Idylls, Agamemnon* and *Ferishtah's Fancies. The Pied Piper of Hamelin* and *How They Brought The Good News* are the most familiar and popular of his poems in the public mind.

When the book containing *Pippa Passes* was published it was highly praised by Elizabeth Barrett, already known as a poetess of the first order. She was destined to join the poet she so much admired in a marriage hardly less than ideal and the beauty of their united lives is as famous as their poetry. She was born near Durham, England, on March 6, 1806.

In 1835 the family moved to London where she lived until after her marriage. The education which she received in early life was broad and thorough. Classics, philosophy and science were studied and she read incessantly. To a mind so sensitive and impressionable, self-expression was inevitable. At an early age she became a contributor to periodicals, and a series of articles on the Greek Christian poets showed her to possess both learning and poetic insight. Her first important essay in authorship was a translation of the *Prometheus* of Æschylus in 1833. Five years later appeared *Seraphim and Other Poems.*

Delicate health enforced on Miss Barrett a life of seclusion for a long time, but at length, with her health partially restored, in 1846 she married Robert Browning and went with him to Italy where they thereafter made their home. In 1850 Mrs. Browning published her collected works, together with several new poems among which was *Lady Geraldine's Courtship.* The next year appeared the *Casa Guidi Windows,* a poem the theme of which was the struggle for freedom made by the Tuscans in 1849. *Aurora Leigh,* her longest production, was published in 1856.

Mrs. Browning's poetry is distinguished by its depth of feeling, its true pathos, and its generous and noble sentiments. She poured forth her verse with ready facility and some of her poems show the defects of this free outpouring. She died in Florence, Italy, on June 20, 1861. Her husband survived her for 28 years and died in Venice on Dec. 12, 1889. One son was born to them who became known as an artist.

ROBERT BRUCE   1274–1329

ROBERT BRUCE was the great hero of the Scottish war for independence and king of Scotland from 1306 to 1329.

He was born in 1274, the son of Robert Bruce, Lord of Annandale and claimant to the Scottish throne, and was a descendant of one Robert de Bruis, a Norman knight who had accompanied William the Conqueror on his invasion of England.

Robert swore fealty to Edward I of England in 1296 at Berwick, and the following year renewed his oath of allegiance at Carlisle. Soon after this, however, he joined the Scottish revolt under Wallace. Later he made peace with Edward, but by 1298 he was again in revolt. After the battle of Falkirk his lands were laid waste by the English army. The following year he became one of the four regents of Scotland and maintained peace with Edward until the final Scottish uprising of 1306.

He is believed to have made some sort of an agreement with John Comyn (nephew of John de Baliol) who also laid claim to the throne of Scotland. A violent quarrel broke out between the two in the church of the Minorite Friars in Dumfries, and Bruce stabbed "Red Comyn" who was thereupon despatched by Kirkpatrick. Bruce proclaimed himself king, assembled his vassals, and two months later was crowned at Scone. The English, under command of the Earl of Pembroke, captured Perth, and Bruce retreated into the wilds of Athole. He later sought refuge off the north coast of Ireland. In 1307 he returned to Carrick, surprised the English garrison in his own castle of Turnberry, and defeated Pembroke's army at Loudon Hill.

King Edward died that year and Bruce rapidly cleared the English out of Scotland. The battle of Bannockburn, the decisive point of the rebellion and one of the world's outstanding battles, took place on June 24, 1314. Bruce with an army of 30,000 is said to have defeated 100,000 English under Edward II. In 1317 Bruce went to Ireland to aid his brother, Edward, to whom the Ulster chieftains two years previously had tendered the Irish crown, and defeated an English and Irish army at Slane.

At the head of his Scottish army, he made many forays into England until the truce of 1323. Hostilities broke out anew upon the accession of Edward III to the English throne, but in April of 1328 a final peace was made by the Treaty of Northampton, in which Edward recognized the independence of Scotland and Bruce's right to the throne. The following year Bruce died of leprosy at Cardross Castle on the Firth of Clyde. In fulfillment of his own desire, Sir James Douglas set out for Palestine to bury the heart of the deceased king in Jerusalem, but he was killed in Spain fighting against the Moors. The embalmed heart was taken back to Scotland and buried in Melrose Abbey while the body of Bruce was interred in the Abbey of Dunfermline where his bones were discovered in 1818 during the progress of some excavation work.

Bruce's immediate successor on the Scottish throne was his son David, born of his second wife, daughter of the Earl of Ulster, but the son of his daughter Marjory, born of his first wife, daughter of the Earl of Mar, subsequently ascended the throne as Robert II.

Robert Bruce remains one of Scotland's greatest national heroes and his life and achievements have passed into legend and song as well as into history.

WILLIAM JENNINGS BRYAN   1860–1925

WILLIAM JENNINGS BRYAN, American orator and political leader, was born in Salem, Illinois, March 19, 1860. After graduating from Illinois College in 1881 he studied at Union College of Law in Chicago and practiced law for a time at Jacksonville, Illinois. In 1887 he moved to Lincoln, Nebraska, practiced law there, served from 1891 to 1895 in the house of representatives in Washington and soon became known as a democrat of uncompromisingly liberal proclivities and an orator of outstanding qualities. In his congressional career his eloquent voice was always raised against the protective tariff and in favor of the free coinage of silver. In 1893, and again the following year, he was defeated for the United States senatorship. He then became editor of the *Omaha World-Herald,* remaining active as a political speaker and stirring thousands with his oratory on his favorite subject of free silver.

In July 1896, at the democratic national convention in Chicago he was a delegate and leader of the free silver faction. Twenty thousand spectators crowded the great hall; excitement ran high. The silver delegation was seated after furious opposition by the "sound money" delegates, pledged to the gold standard, who charged the silver men with repudiation. The silver men retorted with denunciations of Wall Street and the capitalistic power in the eastern part of the country. Debate was long and acrimonious and many outstanding democrats tried in vain to make themselves heard amid the clamor. Few political conventions and few intra-party strifes have been characterized by such bitterness.

Amid this scene of confusion Bryan's melodious voice rose, winning silence and holding the vast audience enthralled with the speech which made him a national figure and won him the nomination for the presidency. In his long career he was often the subject of criticism for his views but few failed to fall captive to the magic of his oratory. The ending of that speech has become classic: "You shall not press down upon the brow of labor this crown of thorns; you shall not crucify mankind upon a cross of gold." He was nominated by a majority of ninety delegates. The National Silver Party and the Populist Party also nominated him. His opponent on the republican ticket was William McKinley. Prejudicial to his chances was the nomination by the sound money democrats of Gen. John M. Palmer, representing the conservative element of the party. An exciting campaign ended in Bryan's defeat.

But he by no means became the shadowy figure which is the common fate of unsuccessful presidential candidates. In 1900 a more united democracy paid him the great tribute of nomination by acclamation at Kansas City and he was again defeated by McKinley in a campaign in which his free silver doctrine was not featured. In 1904 he again sought nomination but the conservative element was now dominant and chose Judge Alton B. Parker of New York, whom Bryan rather reluctantly supported. Still again, in 1908, he was nominated but defeated by the republican, William Howard Taft. This ended his active aspiration to the presidency but he remained a potent force in his party's councils and in 1912 was instrumental in bringing about the nomination of Woodrow Wilson who won the election against Taft in a campaign complicated by the entrance of Theodore Roosevelt as nominee of the new Progressive Party. Bryan was appointed secretary of state by Wilson and, always an ardent advocate of peace, he availed himself of this opportunity to negotiate peace treaties with 30 foreign powers. Because of Wilson's resolute attitude in regard to the sinking of the *Lusitania* in 1915 by German submarines, he resigned his post in the cabinet.

Although his immense following gave him continued power in his party, he never again ran for office nor occupied any appointive post. Through his newspaper, *The Commoner,* he continued to disseminate his views and policies, among which was his uncompromising stand in favor of national prohibition and he came himself to be known as "the commoner." His eloquent voice was often heard on the lecture platform; deeply religious, he lent his tremendous influence to the cause of orthodox Christianity and his last public appearance was in connection with the case of an obscure teacher in Dayton, Tenn., who ran foul of the state law by teaching evolution in his classroom. The case attracted national attention because of the principles involved and Bryan appeared as the champion of the "fundamentalists" who construed evolution to be subversive of religious truth and Christian doctrine. The trial resulted in the conviction of the teacher, one Scopes, and a nominal sentence. More tragic, it resulted also in the death of Mr. Bryan whose exertions, coupled with the intense heat and the equally intense ardor of his pleading, aggravated a cardiac disorder and he was found dead in bed near the scene of this tempest in a teapot on June 26, 1925.

He had married in 1884 Mary Elizabeth Baird of Perry, Ill., and his daughter, Mrs. Ruth Bryan Owen, after serving as representative in Congress from Florida, was appointed minister to Denmark, the first American woman to be given a diplomatic post.

WILLIAM CULLEN BRYANT   1794–1878

WILLIAM CULLEN BRYANT, American poet and editor, was born in Cum-
mington, Mass., on Nov. 3, 1794. His father was Peter Bryant, a physician
and surgeon. The family was of Puritan stock on both sides, and the
poet's early moral training is reflected in his writings. His education was
limited but after attending the village school he received a year of excellent
training in Latin under his mother's brother, the Rev. Dr. Thomas Snell,
of Brookfield, and a year of Greek under Rev. Moses Hallock, of Plainfield. At 16 he entered the sophomore class of Williams College and
remained through two sessions. Fond of books and an industrious student,
he made good use of this short period. He had hoped to enter Yale but
his father's circumstances forbade. He studied classics and mathematics
for a year; then law at Worthington and at Bridgewater, Mass., and at
the age of 21 he was admitted to the bar and opened an office in Plainfield.
A short time later he removed to Great Barrington, Mass., where he
practiced law for nine years.

Bryant's first volume of verse, *The Embargo or Sketches of the Times:
A Satire by a Youth of Thirteen,* was printed in Boston in 1808. *Thana-
topsis,* written in his eighteenth year, was published in 1817 in the *North
American Review,* and with it, said Richard Henry Stoddard, "American
poetry may be said to have commenced." This poem, undoubtedly the
best known of all his work, has been included in many school readers and
ranks high for its beauty and graceful appreciation of nature's moods.
Inscription was written in his nineteenth year and *To a Water-Fowl* two
years later. He published a volume of *Poems* in 1821 at Cambridge, and
an expanded volume at New York in 1832.

Bryant had been married in 1820 at Great Barrington to Miss Frances
Fairchild, who was to be his constant companion for nearly half a century.
In 1825 he removed to New York City to assume a literary editorship, and
in the following year became one of the editors of the *Evening Post.* In
1829 he became sole editor and chief owner of that newspaper which was
strongly democratic but which, because of its anti-slavery view, aided
greatly in forming the republican party in 1856. The editor made a
number of public addresses, and on his visits to Europe and the West
Indies he wrote letters for his journal which were later collected and
published in volume form. The last collection of his poetry during his
lifetime was the *Poetical Works* of 1876. Among his various volumes of
verse were *The Fountain and Other Poems* (1842); *The White-Footed
Deer and Other Poems* (1844); *Thirty Poems* (1864); his blank verse

translation of Homer's *Iliad* (1870), which he began at the age of 72; and *The Odyssey of Homer* (1871). His *Poetical Works* and his *Complete Prose Writings,* edited by his son-in-law and biographer, Parke Godwin, appeared in 1883–84.

Bryant's poetical gifts were of the contemplative, quietly appreciative sort. He depicted beauty, both physical and moral, but never sought to find it under any sort of mask. His *Robert of Lincoln* is the closest approach to humor in his poems and in *The Death of the Flowers* (commemorating his young sister) he comes nearest to the translation of sorrow into poetry. His poems still have a wide appeal for their moral and descriptive beauty.

Bryant died in New York on June 12, 1878—the month he would doubtless have chosen for his passing, as indicated in his poem of *June*. He was buried at Roslyn, Long Island, which had been the home of his later years.

JAMES BUCHANAN   1791–1868

JAMES BUCHANAN (bŭ kăn'ăn), the fifteenth president of the United States, was born at Stony Batter in Franklin County, Penn., April 22, 1791, the son of an Irish father. He studied law and was admitted to the bar in 1812 but his practicing was interrupted by his military service in the war with England which occurred that year. After serving in his state legislature he was elected to congress (1820) where he served for five terms. He was then sent by President Jackson (whose candidacy he had supported) to Russia where, as minister, he negotiated an important commercial treaty. In 1833 he entered the United States senate where he took the position that the question of slavery should be left to the slave-holding states and that the congress had no authority in the matter. He favored independence from Mexico for Texas and its annexation to the United States.

He was appointed secretary of state by President Polk and during his incumbency the important northwestern boundary question arose between the United States and England, both nations claiming the territory between the Rocky Mountains and the Pacific. It was in connection with this dispute that the phrase "54–40 or fight," became current. The line of 49 degrees north latitude was finally agreed upon as the boundary. In 1853 Buchanan was appointed minister to Great Britain by President Pierce. In 1856 the democratic party nominated him for the presidency. Southern sentiment supported him and he entered office with the vote of every slave-holding state except Maryland. His executive policy in regard to this increasingly bitter question of slavery was not firm. He sought to stifle the agitation, appeared not to recognize the imminence and significance of the conflagration. He has been severely dealt with by historians for his weakness and his alleged southern sympathies. In the brief period of his term following the election of Lincoln he became still more decided in his policy of suppressing the slavery question, and in his final message to congress blamed northern agitation for the threatening condition of affairs, stating that this "produced its malign influence on the slaves and inspired them with a vague idea of freedom." When South Carolina seceded he professed himself unable to cope with this menacing and crucial matter, protesting that he could not employ force except upon the demand of the authorities in that state, a demand which he knew would not be made. He declared that there was no power in the constitution to prevent secession, although he also maintained that the state had no right to secede. Shortly thereafter he was waited upon by a commission from the seceding state which demanded the surrender to it of all public property and sought to effect an arrangement for the continuance of peace and amity between that state and the government at Washington. Receiving these "private gentlemen of the highest character" with utmost consideration, he could find no better solution to his dilemma than to refer them to the congress. He did, however, refuse their demand for the withdrawal of federal troops from the harbor of Charleston. His secretary of state, General Cass, resigned upon the president's refusal to order reinforcements to Charleston. The secretaries of war, of the treasury and the interior also resigned. It was amid such tense conditions that Buchanan's term ended and Abraham Lincoln took office.

The last official act of President Buchanan was typical of his weak and inept policy in dealing with these portentous matters. He had his secretary of war (Holt) dispatch a letter to the governor of South Carolina stating that it was the presidential policy to protect the forts and arsenals of the United States wherever located, adding, however, that it was not the purpose to garrison these defences as he "considered them entirely safe under the protection of the law-abiding sentiment for which the people of South Carolina had ever been distinguished; but should they be attacked or menaced, with danger of being seized or taken from the possession of the United States he could not escape from his constitutional obligations to defend and preserve them."

At the expiration of his term Buchanan retired to private life. After the close of the war he published a defence of his administration, with an account of the measures he had adopted for the maintenance of peace. He never married. His death occurred June 1, 1868.

BUDDHA   Sixth or Seventh Century B.C.

THE BUDDHA (bōōd'à) who founded the religion of Buddhism, which still holds sway over many millions of the eastern peoples, was born in the late sixth or early seventh century B.C., in a small community in Bengal in the north of India. His name was Siddhattha Gautama (or Gôtama). Most of our knowledge of his life is gleaned from translations of the Pali language, as India had no written language at the time Gautama lived.

He was a young man of fortune and at 19 was married to a beautiful cousin. He had great natural gifts and the life of luxury and idle amusement which was the ordinary life of his class became to him very far from satisfying. Driving one day with his charioteer, Channa, so the story goes, Gautama saw successively a poor, feeble old man; one afflicted with a terrible disease; and an unburied body. "Such is the way of life," said Channa at each of these spectacles; "to that we must all come." Then Gautama met one of the wandering ascetics who were very numerous in India. These men spent their time in religious meditation and in seeking some deeper meaning in life. Gautama conceived a desire to become one of them.

While this longing held possession of his mind, and some ten years after his marriage, his wife was delivered of a son. The event was celebrated with dancing and feasting and that night as his wife slept Gautama went to her chamber and quietly looked at her and at his son. Then he mounted his chariot and was driven away by Channa. In the morning, by a river bank, he cut off his long hair and removed all of his ornaments which he sent back to his house by Channa. Thus he broke away entirely from his old life. He exchanged clothes with a beggar and made his way to a retreat in the mountains where a number of wise men lived as hermits and teachers. These men taught that power and knowledge could be attained by fasting and a rigorously ascetic life, coupled with all sorts of self torments.

Gautama spent a considerable time with these men, but at length, weakened and exhausted by his fasts and his severe penances, he one day fell unconscious and when he recovered the realization came to him that knowledge and truth could not be achieved in any such way. He gave up ascetic practices and wandered, a lonely outcast, seeking the light of truth. He was sitting one day under a large tree beside a river when a conviction came to him that he saw life plainly. (This was the famous Bo Tree from which a cutting planted in Ceylon still exists, the oldest historical tree in the world.) For a day and a night, it is said, Gautama sat under the tree deep in thought. Then he arose and went forth to share his new-found wisdom with the world.

In the town of Benares he won five followers who, convinced of his wisdom, accepted him as the Buddha. The word means "the enlightened one," and it was believed in India that at long intervals wisdom was revealed to the world through such an enlightened man, who was thenceforth known as the Buddha.

Gautama and his disciples built themselves huts in a park in Benares and there they taught and discussed and gathered many adherents who went about spreading the teachings of the Buddha by word of mouth in aphorisms, short verses, lists of "points," etc.

Buddha ascribed all the unhappiness and miseries of life to selfishness, the three principal forms of which he described as man's craving to gratify the senses, the desire for personal immortality, and the desire for prosperity. He taught that when all of these are overcome so that the individual no longer lives for himself, he has reached the higher wisdom, Nirvana, serenity of soul. His teachings are opposed alike to the "immortality religions," and to asceticism.

Gautama Buddha died at the age of 80, at Oudh in northern India. He was undoubtedly one of the great spiritual leaders of the age. The gentleness and purity of his own life and the sincerity of his teachings led many thousands to accept his simple creed.

BULWER-LYTTON   1803–1873

EDWARD GEORGE EARLE, first Lord Lytton, was born in London, May 25, 1803. He was the son of William Earle Bulwer (by which surname he is best known) and Elizabeth Barbara Lytton. He was educated at Cambridge from which he was graduated in 1826, and thereupon began his distinguished career in the field of letters and of politics. It is as a novelist that he is best known. He began to write poetry while a schoolboy and published a volume at the age of 17. An early poem on *Sculpture* was awarded the chancellor's prize at Cambridge when he was but 22. The following year he published a collection of miscellaneous verse entitled *Weeds and Wildflowers,* which was shortly followed by a tale in verse, *O'Neill, or The Rebel.* In 1827 he married Rosina Doyle Wheeler, an Irish girl, of which his aristocratic mother so strongly disapproved that she withdrew financial assistance from her son who was thereby, perhaps fortunately, compelled to seek his living in the field of literature. The marriage ended in a legal separation ten years later.

Meanwhile Bulwer had begun the series of novels which brought him both profit and popularity and won him his place among the little group of leading writers of his time. His star was already in the ascendant when, by his mother's death, he inherited the very considerable estate of Knebworth. In 1827 his first novel, *Falkland,* was published anonymously, followed the next year by *Pelham* which astonished the critics by its cynicism and icy glitter of epigram; it is counted one of his most delightful stories. Followed in rapid succession *The Disowned, Devereux* and *Paul Clifford,* the latter a romantic treatment of the gallant highwayman, outdoing the story of Robin Hood in glamorous incident. In 1831 appeared the sombre story, *Eugene Aram,* based upon the same well-known murder case which inspired the poetic muse of Thomas Hood. About this time Bulwer became editor of *The New Monthly Magazine* and contributed to it a series of papers which were later collected under the title of *The Student.* In 1833 appeared his book, *England and the English,* and he returned to fiction the next year with *The Pilgrims of the Rhine* which was shortly followed by the most familiar of his works and the one which has enjoyed a more abiding fame than all the others, *The Last Days of Pompeii.* Following this appeared *Rienzi* and then a five-act play entitled *The Duchess of La Valliere,* which failed dismally upon the stage.

In 1837 appeared *Ernest Maltravers,* a romantic and highly interesting tale to which he later wrote the sequel *Alice, or the Mysteries.* His facile genius next turned to the purely historical treatment of subject in *Athens, its Rise and Fall,* a work which was never completed. *Leila* and *Calderon* appeared in 1838. Again he essayed the drama, this time with pronounced success; the romantic comedy of *The Lady of Lyons* and the glamorous poetic melodrama of *Richelieu* held their place in the repertoires of histrionic stars for many years. *The Lady of Lyons* is a little too sentimental to stand against latter-day realism, but Cardinal Richelieu still threatens to pronounce the curse of Rome and seldom fails to thrill his audiences. *Money,* a splendid comedy, has not stood the test of time.

Still more novels, in every variety of stylistic treatment, came from Bulwer's facile pen; *Zanoni* in 1842, and in the same year a poem entitled *Eva.* Other poems, *The New Timon* and *King Arthur,* shortly followed. His next novels were *The Last of the Barons, Harold, the Last of the Saxon Kings* and *Lucretia.* Following these came *The Caxtons,* a domestic novel, vividly demonstrating (if any proof were needed) his amazing versatility. Next appeared *My Novel, or Varieties in English Life,* his longest work of fiction, to be followed shortly by *What Will He Do With it?* and a clever poem entitled *St. Stephen's.* Other works were *A Strange*

Story, a series of essays entitled *Caxtonia, The Lost Tale of Miletus,* a translation of Horace's *Odes* and a comedy entitled *Walpole.* In 1871 he published anonymously *The Coming Race,* the scene of which is set in the future. In 1873 *Kenelm Chillingly and The Parisians* appeared. He was then 70 years of age with his versatility and productiveness unabated. He died in Devonshire on Jan. 18 of that year.

JOHN BUNYAN   1628–1688

"The perfect allegory," known as *Pilgrim's Progress,* which is one of the famous books of the world, was written by an illiterate tinker, John Bunyan. This humble and inspired man was born at Elstow in England in 1628. The trade of tinker, which he learned from his father, was hardly respectable; its votaries were held in lower esteem than gypsies and strolling players. Macaulay thought the father of Bunyan somewhat better than his fellows because he had a fixed residence. Be that as it may, the tinkers of that day were regarded as thieving vagabonds. Working at this dubious calling Bunyan passed the early years of his life. It has been commonly thought that his youth was largely given to debauchery, but latter-day inquiries seem to prove that this supposition had its origin in his own Puritan propensity for exaggerating his misdeeds and that his early vices were largely apocryphal. In a fervor of self-accusation he later denounced his youthful indulgence in dancing and bell ringing (one of the popular recreations of his time) and a guilty conscience haunted him throughout his life.

In 1644, or thereabouts, he joined the forces under Cromwell and for about two years served in the parliamentary army. Many writers have found material in the theatre of war; Bunyan found it replete with suggestions for allegory, the channel in which his mind always ran. A battle suggested a conflict with sin; a long march, the arduous journey of a devout pilgrim; he saw everything in its figurative aspect. More than any other writer of symbolic representations, his thoughts ran naturally to such analogies. He saw nothing in its limited, literal meaning and this inborn propensity evolved at last the matchless tale which has made his name immortal.

Returning from military service he married in 1648 a woman who, with her "godly books," was to influence him deeply in the brief period of their union; they removed to Bedford (1655) where she soon died. In this interval Bunyan became deeply religious and joined the nonconformist sect to which his wife belonged, but his spiritual fervor was intermingled with haunting doubts and morbid fancies. He suffered the lashings of conscience for imaginary or trifling sins, combated temptations with maniac frenzy, saw visions of his own lost soul, until his health nearly collapsed under the strain of his unhappy visions and spiritual struggles.

Emerging somewhat from this valley of the shadow, he began to preach (1657) and his crude, homely discourses soon won him a reputation in his section of the country. He became somewhat of a novelty, like the rustic Burns in Edinburgh, and hundreds flocked to hear and tremble at his powerful but illiterate exhortations. After the Restoration, Charles II endeavored to throttle free speech and decreed that only ministers of the established church should be allowed to preach. Bunyan was not a man to be discouraged by human interdict; he preached with redoubled vehemence and in consequence was thrown into Bedford jail where he languished for twelve years, although he was allowed a certain measure of liberty throughout the period. During this time he supported his children and his second wife by his handiwork and found solace in the perusal of the Bible and Fox's *Martyrs,* the only books he had at hand. His release in 1672 was followed in 1675 by a second brief period of imprisonment.

It was while he was in prison that he wrote *Pilgrim's Progress* which, though hardly noticed at the time of its publication, steadily gained favor and the second edition in 1678 was eagerly bought up by an enthusiastic public which found delight in noting its multitudes of palpable analogies and in seeking out the less obvious ones which gave the book all the charm of a puzzle. In the modern trend toward liberalism this unique drama of the soul's progress toward the celestial city has lost something of popular favor, yet it is still a living book and its characters, allusions and analogies abide. Christian, Greatheart, Giant Despair, the Slough of Despond, are as firmly fixed in our language as any quotation from Shakespeare or Scripture. Feelings, impulses, predicaments, are spoken of by the figurative names that Bunyan gave them. The book ran through ten editions during his life and the editions since his death are almost unnumbered. He wrote much besides *Pilgrim's Progress,* but he is remembered only by this famous allegory. His other works, all of a religious character, include *The Life and Death of Mr. Badman, Grace Abounding,* which is an interpretation of his own spiritual experience, and a beautiful allegory, *The Holy War.* He died in London on August 31, 1688.

EDMUND BURKE 1729–1797

EDMUND BURKE, one of the foremost of English political writers and orators, is regarded with veneration in America because of his sympathy for the American colonists at the time of the Revolution.

The son of a Dublin (Ireland) attorney, Burke was born in that city on Jan. 12, 1729. He was educated at Trinity College, and in 1750 entered Middle Temple, London. For a short time thereafter he practiced law, but his eager reading at Trinity had aroused an interest in literature and he entered the world of letters in 1756 with his anonymous *Vindication of Natural Society,* an ironical refutation of Bolingbroke's social views. Later that year he published *Philosophical Inquiry into Our Ideas of the Sublime and Beautiful,* and in the same year married the daughter of Dr. Nugent, a Bath physician. From 1759 until within a decade of his death he was a frequent contributor to the *Annual Register.* In 1761 he returned to Dublin for two years as private secretary to "Single-Speech" Hamilton, Secretary for Ireland, after which he acted as secretary to the Marquis of Rockingham, then Premier (1765), and soon thereafter was elected to Parliament from the borough of Wendover. His eloquence soon won for him a great influence in the Whig party, but with Rockingham's retirement within the year Burke ceased his political activities until after the fall of the North régime. His interest in public activities, however, never abated.

Burke was a clear thinker with a quick imagination and ready sympathy, and his eloquence, strong character and political knowledge kept him in the centre of political affairs. Lord North was in power from 1770 to 1782, during which time the American colonies rebelled at the Stamp Act and other injustices and Burke made frequent and vigorous protest against the North policy toward the colonies. The best of his speeches and writings date from this period. His defence of sound constitutional government and his attacks on misgovernment, especially in the colonies, won him the respect and admiration of Americans. In 1769 appeared his *Observations on the Present State of the Nation,* while his article *On the Causes of the Present Discontents* followed in 1670. Among his ablest speeches were those on *American Taxation* (1774), *Conciliation with America* (1775) and *The Letter to the Sheriffs of Bristol* (1777), in which he advocated liberal measures toward the colonies which, had they been successful, probably would have kept the British flag flying over the thirteen provinces and ultimately over all of North America.

Burke visited Paris in 1773, and in the following year had to retire from his Parliamentary seat for Wendover, but was elected from Bristol which seat he lost in 1870 because of his support of the proposals to relax the restrictions on the trade between Ireland and Great Britain and to lessen the discriminations against Catholics. From that date until 1794 he represented Malton in Parliament. When Lord North's administration came to an end with the triumph of the American colonies Burke was Paymaster of the Forces under Rockingham (1782) and under Portland (1783). In the latter year the Whigs were defeated and Burke never afterwards held political office. He opposed Pitt's measures for free trade with Ireland, and the Commercial Treaty with Paris.

Perhaps the greatest effort of his career was the speech with which he opened the trial of Warren Hastings. In 1790 appeared his *"Reflections on the French Revolution,"* which ran through eleven editions during the year, and encouraged European opposition to the Revolution; and although his opinions alienated him from Fox and the Whigs he continued his opposition to the turn affairs had taken in France.

Burke was often in financial distress and was often forced to borrow money. Two pensions were granted him in 1794 when the proposal to raise him to the Peerage as Lord Beaconsfield was dropped, upon the death of his only son. He died on July 9, 1797, and was buried in the little church at Beaconsfield where he had lived for the last thirty years of his life.

ROBERT BURNS   1759–1796

Robert Burns was born Jan. 25, 1759, in a humble cottage near the town of Ayr in Scotland. His father was a farmer who, notwithstanding his desperate struggle with poverty, contrived to give his children a fairly good education. Burns read everything that was available, which was rather more than usually falls to the lot of young people of the peasant class, and acquired some knowledge of French and Latin. How much his miscellaneous reading was responsible for his poetic inspiration is questionable; he was par excellence a born poet and it is probable that his lyrical genius would still have found expression if he had never seen a book. He attended the country school and worked on his father's farm and at about the age of 16 began to write verses in his native dialect which attracted much attention in the countryside. A youth who could write so tenderly, with such natural humor and touching pathos, could hardly hope to escape the perils of rustic popularity and young Burns became the neighborhood gallant. His protestations of love proved irresistible to several of the peasant maidens. These amours have been exhaustively treated by historians, and such is the spell over those who worship at his shrine that much has been written to palliate, condone and even deny these well authenticated affairs.

In 1781 Robert and his brother undertook a small farm but the enterprise proved a failure and the young poet, much discouraged and embittered, resolved on a journey to the island of Jamaica. Some of his best poems, including *The Cottar's Saturday Night,* had been written during this period. He had tasted some of the bitters as well as the sweets along the primrose path and these difficulties no less than his financial predicament determined his course. In the hope of financing the trip he published (1786) a collection of poems which met with a reception quite beyond his fondest dreams. It attracted notice in Edinburgh where there soon was much curiosity to see this inspired son of the soil. He abandoned his plan to go to Jamaica and made his famous visit to Edinburgh which proved the turning point in his career. During his stay there he met the most distinguished people in the world of fashion and art who regarded him with great interest and with increasing respect. The young peasant conducted himself throughout this period with simple dignity and natural pride which did credit to his nature. There was no drop of snobbishness nor vanity in the blood of this ardent lover of humanity. He returned to his rustic neighborhood somewhat the better financially for a new edition of his poems and settled on a farm near Dumfries (1788) after making public declaration of his marriage to Jean Armour to whom he had previously, in an impulse of honor, given written acknowledgment of their union. She had borne him twins, notwithstanding which her people had discountenanced so poor a match and she had destroyed the paper. In the interval prior to this public acknowledgment he had participated in a tender affair with Mary Campbell (Highland Mary) whose early death was commemorated in one of the most touching of his poems. During the period at Dumfries he wrote his well known *Tam O'Shanter* and other poems.

The Armours, who had disdained the plowman, were reconciled to the darling of Edinburgh's elite and Burns settled down with his family to life on the farm, but the marriage was neither suitable nor happy. His admirers in Edinburgh had procured him appointment as an exciseman and the small salary from this office eked out the failing profits from his farm. Within several years he had given up farming altogether and for the balance of his unhappy life this great lyric poet lived in a sordid way in a wretched cottage in Dumfries quarrelling with his superiors, drinking and lounging in taverns. The fire of his old spirit was in some degree rekindled by the French Revolution, but he curbed his enthusiastic expression in the cause of human rights for fear of antagonizing the government. On one occasion certain imprudent remarks of his all but lost him his humble office. Embittered, unproductive, seized with occasional fits of remorse and broken in health, he died on the 21st of July, 1796 in the 37th year of his age. The 100th anniversary of his birth and death were celebrated with tremendous enthusiasm throughout English-speaking countries.

SIR EDWARD BURNE-JONES   1833–1898

SIR EDWARD COLY BURNE-JONES is said to occupy the same position among artists that Keats occupied among poets. He was of the Pre-Raphaelites, though not an original member of that artistic brotherhood started in England by Dante Gabriel Rossetti and others in protest against modern artistic tendencies, which they considered a corrupting influence, and in favor of the clearness and sincerity of an earlier school. He was born in Birmingham, England, August 28, 1833, entered Exeter College, Oxford, intending to prepare for the church, and in 1856 went to live in London. He early fell under the influence of Ruskin whom he studied assiduously and thus became interested in the Pre-Raphaelites. At college he had formed an intimate friendship with William Morris and they worked in close association until the latter's marriage in 1859. During this period Burne-Jones studied under Rossetti whom he much admired. In 1859 he visited Italy and the following year was married to Georgianna McDonald. Followed a second trip to Italy in 1862 with his wife and John Ruskin. He then settled in the London suburb of Fulham, in a picturesque home which he called The Grange, where most of his work was done.

At the opening of the Grosvenor Gallery in 1877 his three pictures, "Beguiling of Merwin," "Mirror of Venus," and "Days of Creation," attracted much critical attention and aroused the keenest interest on the part of the general public to whom he had previously been but slightly known. Thereafter his paintings had a sensational effect wherever they were exhibited. Notable among his works are "Chant d'Amour," "Garden of Pan," "Briar Rose," "Star of Bethlehem," "The Wheel of Fortune," "King Cophetua and The Beggar Maid," "Dies Domini," "Laus Veneris," "The Golden Stairs," "Depths of the Sea," "Love Among the Roses," "Spring, Summer, Autumn and Winter," "Wine of Circe," "Pan and Psyche," "Pygmalion Series," and illustrations for the fairy tale, "The

Sleeping Beauty." He also painted many portraits. As a designer his standing is hardly less unique and many of the most beautiful conceptions for stained glass cathedral windows are his. The Birmingham Museum has an extensive collection of his works and in the British Museum is a series of his drawings for pictures which he never completed. He made the illustrations for numerous books, notable among which is the series for an elaborate edition of Chaucer.

Many tributes were paid to his genius. He was made an honorary D.C.L. of Oxford, was given the Cross of the Legion of Honor, and was knighted in 1894. He died quite suddenly from an attack of influenza in London, June 17, 1898.

JOHN BURROUGHS 1837–1921

To THE great public John Burroughs was known as a naturalist. He was an essayist and a discerning critic of literature; but it was as a student of bird life that his name became familiar in his generation. Thousands found in him the inspiration to begin the restful and delightful study of the birds; thousands more, who did not study them, have observed them with a keener interest because of John Burroughs. He was born on a farm at Roxbury, N. Y., April 3, 1837, and his boyhood was spent attending to the humdrum work incident to farm life. Many years afterward he quaintly observed that he had enjoyed the advantages of growing up among people who had no interest in books. He was but 14 years of age when he began to write essays and in most of his critical work throughout life he used this literary form, making the brief essay always a delightful vehicle of his thought. He was much influenced by Emerson whose works he read eagerly.

At 19 he was encouraged by the acceptance of one of his essays (*Expressions*) by the *Atlantic Monthly*. In 1867 he published *Walt Whitman as Poet and Person*. That was a time when the country was beginning to recover from the staggering impact of Whitman's startling freedom and originality; Burroughs, like his favorite Emerson, had felt the refreshing, humanizing influence of the new voice. In 1863, after some experience in the field of journalism and teaching, he became associated with the Treasury Department at Washington where he remained for about ten years, and for some years thereafter he was a special national bank examiner. For several years during this period of commercial occupation, however, he engaged in fruit culture on a farm at Esopus, N. Y., where he also availed himself of the opportunity for literary study and keen observation of nature and its wild life. A list of his works, most of which achieved great and lasting popularity, follows in the order of their appearance covering the period from 1870 to 1913, during which time he wrote also many articles for periodicals: *Wake Robin, Winter Sunshine, Birds and Poets, Locusts and Wild Honey, Pepacton, Fresh Fields, Signs and Seasons, Sharp Eyes, Indoor Studies, Riverby, A Study, The Light of Day, Squirrels and Other Fur-Bearers, Literary Values, Far and Near, Ways of Nature, Bird and Bough, Camping and Tramping with Roosevelt, Leaf and Tendril, Time and Change, The Summit of the Years.*

In 1904 this sincere writer and keen observer was moved to raise his voice against a kind of writing which had been appearing chiefly in magazines, in which natural history was subjected to popular treatment by writers who in fact knew little or nothing about animals and birds, and who came to be called "nature fakers." He had, indeed, little patience with slipshod writing and cursory observation; the dominant note in all his work was sincerity, and his prestige as a naturalist went far to put an end to this expression of latter-day superficiality and cheapness. And the quality which moved him to disgust with this journalistic treatment of birds and flowers was apparent in the charming literary essays in which he seems to talk, rather than write, about his favorite authors, making the reader see them and understand them as he makes them see and understand robins and squirrels, and even insects. In his charming book of essays called *Literary Values* he says that all that is artificial and insincere about a writer will only impede him and finally kill him. If that be true, the writings of John Burroughs should assuredly stand the test of time. Among naturalists who have addressed themselves to the great public he is preeminent and outstanding. Perhaps not more keenly observant of forest life than Thoreau, he is quite free from the New Englander's opinionated and intolerant style.

Burroughs was appropriately honored by election to the American Academy of Arts and Letters. He died in 1921.

RICHARD E. BYRD, JR. 1888–

Richard Evelyn Byrd, Jr., American aviator and explorer and the first man to fly to the North Pole, was born on Oct. 25, 1888, in Winchester, Va. His father was a prominent lawyer and held various public offices. He attended the Shenandoah Valley Military Academy, the Virginia Military

Institute and the University of Georgia. From his boyhood the spirit of adventure was strong within him and when only about 12 years old he made a trip alone around the world. Following his graduation from the U. S. Naval Academy at Annapolis at the age of 24, he was assigned to service on various naval vessels; later studied for a year at Harvard and then entered the service of the State of Rhode Island as inspector of naval militia and commander of naval forces. At about this time he married Marie D. Ames of Boston who became the mother of his four children. He retained his commission in the federal navy and upon the entrance of the United States into the World War, organized and became secretary of the navy department commission on training camp activities. He later transferred his interests to aviation and was placed in charge of the U.S. air forces in Canada at a time when it was essential that a sharp watch be kept for enemy submarines.

In 1919 as navigator of the NC–3 he went as far as Newfoundland with the three seaplanes, NC–1, NC–3 and NC–4, on their flight to Europe, for which he had made all the preparations. He was instrumental in bringing about the creation of the naval bureau of aeronautics and invented various instruments of value in the development of air navigation. In 1921 he went to England to help navigate the ZR–2 to America, but it was destroyed by an explosion. His first Arctic trip was in 1925 when he accompanied the MacMillan expedition to the polar seas. The following year he headed an expedition and at midnight on May 9, with his pilot, Floyd Bennett, who had flown with him on the previous trip, he left Spitzbergen in the Fokker monoplane *Josephine Todd,* flew to the North Pole which he circled several times, taking observations, and at the end of 15 hours and a half he was back at King's Bay, Spitzbergen, having covered 1500 miles. He was awarded the Congressional Medal of Honor, the National Geographic Society's Hubbard Medal and various other honors and was given the rank of commander.

In 1927 he attempted a non-stop flight from New York to Paris. On June 29 he took off from Roosevelt Field, L.I., in the *America,* accompanied by two pilots, Bert Acosta and Bernt Balchen, and Lieut. George O. Noville as radio operator. The weather was unfortunate and for nearly 20 hours they flew blindly through a dense fog. As they neared the French coast a severe storm burst and for several hours they floundered in darkness over France, unable to locate Paris or even to see the earth below. As if to make disaster sure, their radio and compass refused to function properly. At length, with their fuel nearly exhausted, they descended in the sea 135 miles from Paris. Although they had failed to fly to Paris, they were acclaimed on both sides of the Atlantic for their skill and bravery and Commander Byrd was made an officer of the French Legion of Honor.

The following year he set out for the South Pole with an elaborately prepared expedition which had taken more than $1,000,000 to equip. It was planned to spend two years on the Antarctic Continent, where he established his base at Little America. On Nov. 29, 1929, with Bernt Balchen and two other companions, he flew over the South Pole and returned safely to his base. The expedition gathered much valuable scientific data and upon his return to America Byrd was given the rank of rear admiral in recognition of his achievement. In the fall of 1933 he set forth on his second Antarctic expedition, again elaborately equipped and accompanied by a large staff of scientists, photographers, etc., prepared for another two-year stay at Little America and with the primary object of gathering further scientific data about the vast unexplored South Polar regions.

These two expeditions stand apart from all former explorations of the kind because of the invaluable aid, sometimes dramatic in a high degree, of scientific facilities which had never before been available. It does not dim the glory of the intrepid leader's spirit and achievement that by means of the radio he was able to keep in touch with civilization and that the world did not have to wait for him to emerge from icy unknown regions to know that his party was safe and to hear the stirring tale of their adventures. Some thirty years had to elapse before the ghastly sequel of the ill-fated Andre attempt was revealed. The frozen bodies of Scott and his companions lay for many months in the vast wastes from which Commander Byrd was able to talk over the air to thousands in his home country. In order to make scientific observations, he lived alone for some months in a shack several hundred miles distant from his base and here his comrades, after a difficult journey, found him ill and well-nigh exhausted from his lonely vigil.

LORD BYRON   1788–1824

GEORGE GORDON, LORD BYRON, was an English poet whose fame endures for the romance of his brief, tempestuous life as well as for the intrinsic merit of his poetry.

He was born Jan. 22, 1788, in Holles Street, London, the only son of Captain John Byron and his wife, Catherine, who was the heiress of George Gordon of Gight, Scotland. His extravagant and dissolute father died in 1791 leaving his family destitute, but upon the death of his grand-uncle, the fifth Lord Byron, in 1798 the future poet succeeded to the title and removed with his mother from Aberdeen to Newstead Abbey, Nottinghamshire, which had been the Gordon estate from the days of Henry VIII.

In 1799 the boy was sent to Dr. Glennie's school in Dulwich and two years later to Eton, which he quitted in 1805 for Trinity College, Cambridge, where he neglected his studies and rebelled against the college authority. He was a spirited and active boy, despite a congenital lameness in one foot, and although at first unpopular he soon became a favorite with his fellow students.

Love for a cousin prompted his first attempt at poetry (1800). A privately printed volume (1806) was withdrawn and toned down because of the licentiousness of some of the verse. *The Hours of Idleness* (1807) met with caustic criticism from the *Edinburgh Review* and Byron replied with his famous *English Bards and Scotch Reviewers.* Following this he traveled extensively abroad, visiting Portugal, Spain, Malta, Albania, Turkey, Greece and Asia Minor. Upon his return to England in 1811 he published the first two cantos of *Childe Harold's Pilgrimage,* and "awoke the next morning to find myself famous," as he confided to his journal.

In May, 1813, his wildly poetic fragment, *The Giaour,* appeared, quickly followed by *The Bride of Abydos* which was written in one week, and *The Corsair,* a poem of higher merit and popularity which took him but ten days to produce.

On January 2, 1815, Byron married Annabelle Milbanke, heiress of Sir Ralph Milbanke, who had rejected his suit in 1813. A daughter, Augusta Ada, was born to them, but the marriage was apparently without deep attachment on either side, and in January, 1816, they parted, after which Lady Byron instituted an inquiry into her husband's sanity and asked for a legal separation which Byron at first refused but to which he later consented.

In the spring of 1816 he published *The Siege of Corinth* and *Parisina* and some verses relative to his separation from his wife, which caused society to turn against him and, stung by the attitude of the public, he left England, never to see it again.

He wandered to Geneva, where some of his most powerful poems were written—the third canto of *Childe Harold, The Prisoner of Chillon, Darkness,* part of *Manfred,* and others—to Venice, which he made his home for the most part until 1819. During this period he wrote *The Lament of Tasso, Beppo, The Foscari, Mazeppa,* canto four of *Childe Harold,* and part of *Don Juan.* In April of that year began his *liaison* with the young and beautiful Countess Guiccoli, which was countenanced by her elderly husband and, after the Count's separation from his wife, by her father. While living with the Countess in Ravenna, Byron wrote (1819–1821) part of *Don Juan, the Prophecy of Dante, Sardanapalus, Heaven and Earth* and *Cain*.

Early in 1823 he became greatly interested in the Greek struggle for independence and went to Greece to lend his aid against the Turks. He displayed great skill in organizing the poorly disciplined Greek army and received a commission as commander of an expedition against Lepanto, but was taken ill in February and died on April 19, 1824. Greece paid public honors to his memory and his body was taken to England and placed in the family vault in the parish church of Hucknell, near Newstead.

JOHN CABOT (GIOVANNI CABOTO) 1450–1498

JOHN CABOT, discoverer of the mainland of North America, was born in Genoa, Italy, in 1450, but later became a naturalized citizen of Venice. He made a number of trading voyages to eastern Mediterranean ports, going on one occasion as far as Mecca, which was then the central trading mart between the East and West. He believed that it would be easier and quicker to transport oriental goods to Europe by sea rather than overland if a sea route to Asia could be discovered. It was with this idea in mind that, about 1484, he took his family to England and established his home in Bristol where he interested prominent merchants in his plan.

It was decided that an attempt should be made to reach the "Island of Brazil," which it was believed lay to the west of Ireland, as the first stop on the westward way to Asia. Vessels were dispatched during a period of several years to find this island, but when news reached England in 1493 that another Genoese, Christopher Columbus, had reached the Indies, search for the island was given up and it was decided that Cabot should push on straight westward for Asia. Letters patent for this purpose were issued by King Henry VII in March, 1496, to John Cabot and his three sons, with the stipulation that the expedition was to return to Bristol and that one-fifth of any profit which resulted was to go to the King.

On May 2, 1497, Cabot and his sons set sail from Bristol on board the ship *Mathew,* manned by eighteen men. They went around Ireland, headed north and then west, and after fifty-two days, at five o'clock on Saturday morning, June 24, 1497, they reached the northern extremity of Cape Breton Island. Unfurling the royal banner, Cabot took possession of the country in the name of King Henry VII. The mildness of the climate and the fertility of the soil confirmed him in the belief that he had reached the northeastern coast of Asia. After exploring the mainland for some distance the party set sail for home. They reached Bristol on Sunday, August 6, and reported that 700 leagues beyond Ireland they had reached the land of the Grand Khan. Cabot received ten pounds from the King for having found the "new isle" and honors were heaped upon him. He proposed on his next voyage to follow the coast southward to Cipangu (Japan), and the king promised him a fleet of ten ships the following spring and granted him a pension of 20 pounds. In April, 1498, he put forth again from Bristol. In June he reached the east coast of Greenland which he named Labrador's Land, and then explored part of the coast of North America. Trouble with a mutinous crew and lack of stores forced him to turn homeward in the autumn. It seems established that he reached England, but nothing is known of his subsequent history.

JOHN C. CALHOUN   1782–1850

JOHN CALDWELL CALHOUN, (kăl hoon'), a distinguished American statesman, was born at Abbeville, S. C., on March 18, 1782. He was of Scotch-Irish descent and was the third son of Patrick Calhoun, descendant of an Irish family which had emigrated to America and started the Calhoun settlement in that state. Although he had little teaching in his early years, he was of a thoughtful habit of mind and took up the study of law at 18. His private study and reading enabled him to enter Yale college as a junior at 20 and he graduated two years later with high honors. He was admitted to the bar in 1807 and gained some distinction in his legal practice. In 1808 he was sent to the state legislature and in 1811 was elected to congress by South Carolina. He soon became a leader in the party which favored war with England because of that country's arbitrary attitude toward American shipping and impressment of American seamen into the British service. This agitation culminated in the War of 1812. He was the author of the tariff of 1816 which was very favorable to his state, and the following year was appointed secretary of war by President Monroe. In this post he rendered valuable service by bringing the affairs of the army into a more orderly state, and materially cutting down the expense of that department, although maintaining its high level of efficiency.

In 1824 he was elected to the vice presidency and reelected in 1828. Although in the early years of his public career he had shown himself to be actuated by broad and patriotic motives, he now became an ardent advocate of States' rights, and his predilection for southern interests became manifest. In 1828 when a tariff law was passed which was not favorable to the southern states, he attacked it vigorously with voice and pen, hoping that President Jackson would veto the measure. This hope failing, he declared that the act was not binding on the states, and going back to South Carolina in 1829 he succeeded in getting through the legislature a resolution that any state might declare null and void an act of the Federal government. The acquiescence of three other states, Virginia, Georgia and Alabama, was speedily given, and constituted a threat to the integrity of the Union. Jackson denounced the resolution and made the famous declaration, "The Union must and shall be preserved." Calhoun's relations with the president became strained. He lost popularity and was forced to abandon the hope he had cherished for himself reaching the presidential chair, and he shortly resigned the vice presidency. Soon afterward, however, he was elected to the senate and in 1838 he made his famous speech on slavery, in opposition to the abolitionist movement which was at that time growing under the powerful leadership of Wendell Phillips, William Lloyd Garrison and others. Throughout the remainder of his life Calhoun was active in behalf of the slave-holding interests and in advocating the dissolution of the Union.

In 1844 he was appointed secretary of state by President Tyler and while occupying that post he was instrumental in bringing about, after a long controversy over slavery, the annexation to the United States in 1845 of Texas, which had for some ten years been an independent republic, following its separation from Mexico. This precipitated the war of 1846–48 with Mexico.

In his private life Calhoun was of the highest character. In his public career he proved himself an able and thoroughly honest administrator and his political enemies as well as his friends admitted his sincerity and his remarkable powers, but he unquestionably implanted in the minds of many of his adherents those views which later brought about the War of the Rebellion. He died in Washington on March 31, 1850. For some time before his death he had been occupied with the writing of his book, *The Disquisition on Government,* in which he set forth his views as to the doctrine of state sovereignty. This, as well as his *Discussion on the Constitution and Government of the United States,* and some other works, was published after his death. In 1811 he had married his cousin, Floride Calhoun.

JOHN CALVIN   1509–1564

JOHN CALVIN, a leading spirit in the Reformation of the sixteenth century, was one of the six children of Gérard Caulvin, or Cauvin, secretary of the diocese of Noyon in Picardy, and was born in Noyon on July 10, 1509. He had many early advantages, educational and otherwise. His great mental activity and natural studiousness and gravity enabled him to acquire a wonderful mastery of Latin under one of the most learned teachers of the day. In 1528 his father, having previously intended him for the church, sent him to the University of Orleans to study law. While there he became interested in a translation of the Scriptures which a relative was making, and his religious instinct was aroused so that the study of the Bible soon became his absorbing passion. Later, while studying Greek at Bourges, he began the preaching of the reformed doctrines which were to change the face of Europe and to bring new and disturbing elements into religion and politics. The death of his father in 1631 freed him from that tie to the old religion and he gradually passed definitely into the ranks of Protestantism.

Persecution of the Protestants later became so intense that he was forced to flee and for three years he led a wandering life. In 1536 at Basel, he issued his *Institutes of the Christian Religion,* with the preface addressed to Francis I, which has become one of the most famous documents having to do with the Reformation.

Calvin later returned to Noyon, sold his father's estate, and set out for Strassburg. Stopping in Geneva, he was induced to remain in that city to help in furthering the cause of the Reformation. The citizens of Geneva had rebelled against the Duke of Saxony and they eagerly joined the reformers, but the latter's moral severity soon quenched their zeal and, under the leadership of the "Libertines," they rebelled against the new leaders and Calvin and others were compelled to leave the city (1538). During their régime in Geneva the Protestant Confession of Faith had been promulgated.

Calvin now went to Strassburg and began his critical writings on the New Testament. In 1539 he married a widow with whom he appears to have lived happily. Two years later the Genevans, tired of "Libertine" license, invited him to return to their city and resume control. After some hesitation he accepted and formed a theocracy which, through his College of Pastors and Doctors and his Consistorial Court of Discipline, directed the entire affairs of the city and prescribed the social and individual life of the citizens. His struggle against the "Libertines" lasted for fourteen years, but resulted in placing him in supreme control of the city in 1555. His controversies with Castello, Bolsec and Servetus during that period occupied much of his time and energy. Servetus' speculations on the Trinity outraged Calvin's religious susceptibilities and he forwarded incriminating documents to the Catholic authorities in Vienna where Servetus was arrested and sentenced to be burned but escaped, only to be recaptured in Geneva on his way to Italy. Calvin subjected him to a new trial and he was condemned and burned at the stake in 1553, the other leaders of the Reformation concurring in Calvin's harsh intolerance.

Despite his responsibility for this great crime, John Calvin stands forth as a man of intellectual brilliance, who rendered inestimable services to the cause of Protestantism throughout Europe. He systematized its doctrines and formulated its ecclesiastical discipline which alone was a great contribution to the cause. Stern and arbitrary and even cruel as he was at times, he was always actuated by the highest moral purpose. He was a master in the writing of graceful French and his commentaries on the Scriptures embraced the greater part of the Old Testament and all of the New except Revelations. The libraries of Geneva and Zurich contain 3000 of his manuscript sermons and other writings.

His physical and mental energy began to decline in 1561 and three years later, on May 27, 1564, he died. His body was buried in Plain-palais, the common burial ground of Geneva.

THOMAS CARLYLE   1795–1881

THOMAS CARLYLE, Scottish writer and philosopher, was born at Ecclefechan, Dumfriesshire, Scotland, Dec. 4, 1795. After attending lower schools he entered Edinburgh University where his extraordinary capacity for study was soon apparent. He was insatiable in his reading with a memory rivaling Macaulay's. He had entered college with a view to preparing for the church, but abandoned this ambition in favor of a literary career. After a brief period of teaching at Dysart he began to contribute to *Brewster's Encyclopedia*. His translation of Legendre's *Geometry,* with his original essay on proportion, was published in 1824. At about the same time his *Life of Schiller* and his translation of Goethe's *Wilhelm Meister* appeared in the *London Magazine*. These three very considerable works were written before his 28th year.

In 1827 he married Jane Welch and went to live at Craigenputtoch in Dumfriesshire, a small property belonging to his wife. This abode he described in a letter to Goethe as "the loneliest nook in Britain, fifteen miles northwest of Dumfries among the granite hills and the black morasses which stretch westward through Galloway almost to the Irish Sea." Here it was that Emerson, having hired a wagon to take him 16 miles over wild and rocky moorland, first saw the shaggy visage of the sardonic philosopher and talked with him about philosophy and literature. In the first year of his residence at this remote spot appeared his *Specimens of German Romance* in four volumes, and later the series of critical and biographical essays which opened the riches of modern German thought to English readers.

In 1828 the *Edinburgh Review* published his famous essay on Robert Burns, which has taken its place in literature as the standard exposition of Burns' genius; comprehensive, understanding, illuminating, it leaves nothing to be said. But his most notable production of this period was *Sartor Resartus* ("The Tailor Re-tailored"). Declined by many publishers, it was finally brought out in 1833–34 in *Fraser's Magazine*. In this extraordinary work the author appears under the guise of one Professor Teufelsdröckh whose various opinions and experiences make up the substance of the book.

In 1834 Carlyle moved to London. Three years later his great work, *The French Revolution,* was published. This vivid and panoramic picture of a great historic event stands unique in literature. It has justly been called a "prose epic." Dramatic and picturesque, it throws a floodlight on the period treated; some of its descriptions, such as that of the storming of the Bastille, are masterpieces of graphic descriptive writing. He never lost his interest in German thought and culture and to him more than to any other, English-speaking peoples are beholden for countless treasures which prior to his time had been unknown to them. In 1838 he delivered a series of lectures on German literature, also a series on *The History of Literature,* treating of the successive periods of European culture, and in the year following another series on *The Revolutions of Modern Europe.* The lectures later published under the name of *Heroes and Hero Worship* were delivered in 1840. This group has had a wide circulation and furnished inspiration to thousands seeking to know and understand Dante, Shakespeare, Cromwell, Napoleon and other outstanding figures in literature and history. In 1838 a collection of various contributions to magazines was published under the title of *Miscellanies*; in the following year appeared *Chartism*; in 1848 *Past and Present.* These were followed in 1845 by *Oliver Cromwell's Letters and Speeches with Elucidations and a Connecting Narative,* certainly one of Carlyle's major works and by many considered his masterpiece. His admiration for Cromwell, as for all masterful characters, was profound. Prior to the time of this publication the Protector's fame had been passing into eclipse and Carlyle's comprehensive work restored the great commoner to his exalted place in the nation's history and established him as one of the great heroic leaders of all time. Miscellaneous writings and a *Life of John Sterling* followed this epochal work and in 1858–60 was published his *History of Frederick the Great*. *Early Kings of Norway* and *The Portraits of John Knox* were published in 1875.

In 1873 Carlyle had received the Prussian royal order "Pour le Merite" and two years later he declined the Order of the Bath. His domestic life was reputed to be a somewhat stormy one, due no doubt at least partly to his own sardonic and gloomy temperament and his uncertain temper, but there unquestionably existed a genuine affection between himself and his wife and after her sudden death in 1866 he was overwhelmed with grief and became more secluded than ever in his habits. He died in London Feb. 4, 1881.

ANDREW CARNEGIE   1835–1919

ANDREW CARNEGIE (kär nĕ′g ĭ) was an outstanding example of a self-made man. He began as a workman in a cotton mill and died one of America's multi-millionaires. With his vast fortune he became one of the most munificent philanthropists of his era. His achievement was great, but it is as a liberal dispenser of well-considered charities and public benefits that his name abides. He was born at Dunfermline, Scotland, on Nov. 25, 1835, and emigrated to the United States when he was 13 years old. In Allegheny, Penn., he secured employment as a weaver's assistant and earned in the neighborhood of one dollar a week. After about a year at this work he went to Pittsburgh. If this canny little Scotch boy had then been told of the colossal interests he would one day have in this manufacturing Bedlam, he would probably have thought it a fairy tale. He secured a position as a messenger boy in the local office of the Ohio Telegraph Company, but was not long content to run on errands. Like the young Edison, he studied telegraphy and went to work as an operator for the Pennsylvania Railroad. His advancement rivals that of the most fortunate hero of an Alger book. By rapid steps he rose to be divisional superintendent, acquired an interest in the Woodruff Sleeping Car Company, and invested money in Pennsylvania oil lands. He was head of the military railroads during the Civil War, after which he became actively interested in iron and steel manufacture, organizing at Pittsburgh the Union Iron

Works and the Keystone Bridge Works. Shortly prior to this time the English engineer, Sir Henry Bessemer, had devised an economical means of converting pig iron into steel, known as the Bessemer process, and this Mr. Carnegie introduced into his manufacturing works. He acquired a controlling interest in the great Homestead Steel Works and other large plants and the merging of these in 1899 made him the chief owner and presiding genius of the Carnegie Steel Company.

In 1901 he retired to set about the laborious and grateful labor of giving away a very large part of his immense fortune. At that time the Carnegie Steel Company was consolidated with the United States Steel Corporation. Mr. Carnegie made his home thereafter in his beautiful residence adjacent to Central Park, in New York City, maintaining also Skibo Castle, a home which he had acquired in Scotland. In his retirement he gave as rapidly as he had earned, and became one of the greatest of philanthropists. There are varying estimates of his gifts, some of which, of course, have never been recorded. By the most conservative estimates the total sum was immense. He gave $10,000,000 to the Carnegie Institute for the Advancement of Teaching, a corporation chartered in 1906 to provide retirement allowances for educators. He gave $15,000,000 to found and equip the Carnegie libraries, making educational and recreational facilities available to millions. His method in establishing these libraries, which sprang up in many cities and towns throughout the United States and in England, was to furnish the building and equipment, if the local authorities would provide the site and assume maintenance costs.

He gave $10,000,000 to the universities of Scotland, $5,000,000 for the benefit of the employees of the Carnegie Steel Company; about $15,000,-000 to found the Carnegie Institute at Washington, and established the Carnegie Hero Fund with $5,000,000 to supply financial aid to those, and their dependents and survivors, who suffered in heroic effort to save human life. The Tuskegee Institute for negro education, in Alabama, benefited greatly from his generosity, as well as many other educational institutions. Such lavish, though judicial, giving enabled him to declare in 1912 that he had disbursed all but $25,000 of his princely fortune. He established in 1910 the Carnegie Endowment for International Peace and built for the International Court of Arbitration a Palace of Peace at the Hague.

He was the author of several books: *Triumphant Democracy, The Gospel of Wealth, Problems of Today, James Watt,* and others. He was married in 1887 to Louise Whitfield and had one daughter. On Aug. 11, 1919, he died at Lenox, Mass.

ENRICO CARUSO   1873–1921

ENRICO CARUSO (kä rōō′zŏ), one of the world's most famous tenor singers, was born in Naples, on Feb. 25, 1873. His voice developed early and he sang in choirs at the age of eleven. He was apprenticed to a mechanical engineer, but the call of music proved irresistible and at eighteen he began the serious study of singing under Guglielmo Vergine, who recognized the remarkable gifts of the youth and aided him in developing his voice. It was at the Teatro Nuovo in Naples that Caruso made his operatic début in 1894 in the opera *L'Amico Francesco*. His first great success was won four years later at Milan as *Marcello* in *La Bohème*.

The summer of 1899 he spent in Buenos Aires and the winter in St. Petersburg (Leningrad) singing the rôles of his increasing repertory. During the three following years he divided his time between those two cities with briefer appearances in London, Paris, Rome, Moscow, Warsaw and Egypt. His first appearance in America was made at the Metropolitan Opera House, New York City, in 1903, and for the next eighteen years he was the leading tenor in the Metropolitan Opera Company. His triumphs were world-wide, his personality engaging and his voice powerful and tender. He was unsurpassed in his generation and perhaps in all the history of opera in his rendering of the most famous tenor parts in the French and Italian schools of opera to which he largely confined his rôles. He mastered the English language fairly well and sang numerous ballads in that language, particularly for the making of phonograph records.

Holding high place in his repertory were *Rodolfo* in *La Bohème* (with the great Melba singing *Mimi*); *Rhadames* in *Aida,* the *Duke* in *Rigoletto, Samson* in *Samson and Delilah*; *Carmen, Les Huguenots, L'Elisir d'Amore, I Pagliacci, La Juive, Il Trovatore, La Tosca, Traviata, Manon, Martha, La Gioconda, L'Africane, The Pearl Fishers* and others.

The development of the phonograph aided enormously in bringing about Caruso's extraordinary popularity. It spread his reputation throughout the world until his name became known even in the most out-of-the way places, not one of whose inhabitants, in all probability, had ever heard him sing in person. The list of his phonograph records contains all the more important tenor songs from his extensive grand opera repertory, a long list of Neapolitan and other Italian folk songs, the *Largo* of Handel, many sacred songs, a few popular semi-classical numbers, and a dozen or so duets and quartettes in which his voice was heard with those of de Gorgoza, Galli-Curci, de Luca, Frances Alda, Journet, de Segurola, Titto

Ruffo, Alma Gluck, Schumann-Heink, Geraldine Farrar, Antonio Scotti and other popular opera singers.

During the later years of his life Caruso's income from his phonograph work was enormous, and the sale continued steadily after his death, despite the fact that very soon after that time the new electrical system of recording the voice displaced entirely the old acoustical method.

Caruso married Dorothy Benjamin of New York a few years before his death and one daughter, Gloria, was born to them. He was also the father of a son, Enrico Caruso, Jr., born in Italy. He was taken ill on the stage of the Metropolitan Opera House in New York in 1920, at the height of his career, and after a desperate illness in a New York hotel lasting for some months, he went to Naples where he suffered a relapse and died of pleurisy on Aug. 2, 1921. His body, preserved in alcohol, was buried in his native city.

CATHERINE THE GREAT   1729–1796

CATHERINE II of Russia, daughter of Christian Augustus, Prince of Anhalt-Zerbst, was one of Russia's ablest rulers. She was born at Stettin, Prussia, on May 2, 1729. Her baptismal name was Sophia Augusta Frederica.

In 1744 she was betrothed to the Grand Duke Peter, nephew of the Russian Empress Elizabeth and heir to the throne. Frederick the Great of Prussia favored the alliance as a means of strengthening friendship between the two countries and weakening the power of Austria. The Russian Empress took a strong liking to her nephew's future bride, who was received into the Greek Orthodox Church on June 28, 1744, and renamed Catherine Alexeyevna.

The marriage took place on Aug. 21 of the following year at St. Petersburg and Catherine adjusted herself readily to the atmosphere of intrigue of the Russian court. Peter was weak mentally and physically and Catherine's contempt for him gradually became hatred. She solaced herself with many lovers.

The Empress Elizabeth died in January of 1762 and Peter III was crowned Emperor. He committed many follies; he grovelled before Frederick the Great and threatened to divorce Catherine, disinherit her son (the future Czar Paul) and marry one of his favorites. He aroused the hostility of the Russian people largely because of his admiration for everything German. Catherine meantime became more and more identified with the Russians.

In July of 1762 Peter was removed from the throne and it is thought that he met his death at the hands of Gregory Orloff who was Catherine's favorite lover at the time. She thereupon became Empress and ruled for 34 years. She was always the Empress and never allowed herself to be dominated by any of her favorites. A woman of intellectual brilliancy and force of character, she devoted herself tirelessly to the work of the government and despite the immorality of her private life she made her court one of the most prominent in Europe. It was her custom to arise at five in the morning, make her own fire and work sometimes as much as fifteen hours a day. She was generally kind, reasonable and not revengeful to her husband's advisers, although to her son Paul she showed little favor.

She did much to develop the resources of Russia and to give it a place of power. She introduced many sanitary and other reforms, established schools and generally encouraged Russian scholars and artists. She read widely, made a digest of Blackstone's *Commentaries,* wrote some comedies, proverbs and tales, and began a history of Russia. She came much under the influence of Voltaire, D'Alembert and other French thinkers and strove to model the culture of Russia upon that of France until the French Revolution somewhat checked her enthusiasm in that direction.

Having to depend upon the support of the nobility, she obtained it by increasing their number and privileges. The down-trodden serfs rebelled at different times, supporting various claimants to the throne, and in 1773–1775 a serious revolt spread throughout the Volga region which, however, Catherine was able to suppress.

At the outbreak of the French Revolution she resorted to repression and exile and conducted her own foreign policy, sharing in the partition of Poland and engaging in war with Turkey, which gave the Crimea to Russia and secured an access to Black Sea ports.

She understood men and through her wise selection of ministers she was well served, but toward the end of her reign the extravagance and immorality of her court alienated not only Russia but sovereigns of other European countries. She died of apoplexy on Nov. 10, 1796.

CAMILLO BENSO DI CAVOUR 1810–1861

COUNT CAMILLO BENSO DI CAVOUR (kå vōōr'), Italian patriot and states-man, was born in Turin, Aug. 10, 1810, of an old Piedmontese family. His early life was devoted to agriculture and journalism.

After the close of the Middle Ages Italy had been a group of more or less independent cities and states and had been the scene of fierce wars for supremacy between the Spanish, French, Austrians and others. Cavour became fired with enthusiasm for the idea of a free and united Italy, under one central government, which was then gaining ground. In 1847 with Count Cesare Balbo, he founded a newspaper, *Il Resorgimento,* as an organ for his political opinions, and advocated a representative system of government. It was at his suggestion that the King was petitioned for a constitution, which was granted in 1848.

In 1851 Cavour was made Minister of Finance and later President of the Council and gradually became a dominating factor in the govern-ment. He was the originator of the Sardinian policy in Italian politics and its chief advocate. Not only was he Premier, but he also superintended finance, commerce, agriculture, the work of the home office and of foreign affairs. He improved the financial condition of Italy, introduced measures of free trade, furthered the cause of constitutionalism, and greatly weak-ened the power of the Catholic church in Italian politics.

When the Crimean war started, despite great opposition, he success-fully maneuvered to have 15,000 Piedmontese troops sent to the field of conflict as a means of later bringing the whole Italian question before a conference of the powers, and by his diplomatic skill at the Congress of Paris he obtained recognition of Piedmont as one of the great powers, succeeded in isolating Austria, indirectly got Napoleon III compromised in the Italian question, and brought the wretched condition of Italy to the attention of all Europe. War with Austria was inevitable and Cavour prepared for it. England was sympathetic, but did not want to fight; Napoleon hesitated to declare war jointly with Piedmont against Austria. Cavour secretly arranged with Garibaldi to organize a volunteer corps so that troops of all Italy (and not of Piedmont alone) would be involved. A military convention was signed with Napoleon III, but the latter accepted Russia's proposal of a Congress on Italian affairs. Cavour then manipulated matters so that Austria sent an ultimatum demanding the disarmament of Piedmont and finally declared war against her. France allied herself with Italy and Cavour became virtual dictator of his country.

After much strife and many negotiations Napoleon agreed to the union of Tuscany and Piedmont in northern Italy, Savoy and Nice were ceded to France, and by the early part of 1861 all Italy except Venice and Turin was united. On Feb. 8 the first parliament was held, which proclaimed Victor Emmanuel king of United Italy. Cavour continued to work for the establishment of Rome as the Italian capital, a goal which he did not live to see.

His death at Turin on June 6, 1861, was a serious loss to the new kingdom at this crucial time. Throughout his life he had been an ardent advocate of civil liberty and constitutional government, actuated only by his desire for the good of the state, had adopted a wide and far-sighted policy, and was trusted and beloved by the common people. He never married although an early romance is said to have furnished much of his inspiration and incentive. Many of his political writings and speeches were published.

BENVENUTO CELLINI　　　　　　　　　　　　　　　1500–1571

BENVENUTO CELLINI (chĕl lē′nĭ), one of the most arresting characters of the Italian Renaissance, was preeminent as a goldsmith and his intricate and exquisite designs, worked out with superb craftsmanship, have assured him enduring fame. He was equally notable as a sculptor, although his work in this field was somewhat marred by the elaboration and bizarre effects which were more appropriate in the field of metal work, where he excelled. If his work as a goldsmith made him famous, his autobiography has made him familiar and throws a floodlight, not only on his own checkered and adventurous career, but on the turbulent period in which he lived. From it we learn that he could use a sword as well as design one. It is a curious and interesting work, presenting a vivid picture of his life and character. He was born in Florence on November 1, 1500, and early became a pupil of the goldsmith, Bandinelli. It was not long before his propensity for quarreling led to an "affray" which made it imperative for him to leave Florence and after seeking diversion in various cities he finally appeared in Rome where he found employment by many distinguished patrons of art. He was later allowed to return to Florence where another affray resulted in a second sojourn in Rome during which he enjoyed the favor of Pope Clement VII.

His vagabond existence and romantic escapades seemed not prejudicial to his increasing fame as a designer in precious metals and he came to be widely recognized for his mastery in that department of art. He appears never to have lacked commissions for jewel settings and similar designings and his highly decorative sword handles, vases, personal and household ornaments, were in great demand in that age of gorgeous and bizarre adornment. Not content with his unique preeminence in his chosen field, this reckless devotee of pleasure and adventure studied art in all its branches. He was not, however, too preoccupied to participate in the siege of Rome by the Constable de Bourbon for whose death, by his own account, he was personally responsible. He boasted, also, that he killed the Prince of Orange. Returning again to his native city, he appears to have been kept busy, but his restless spirit (unless it was another affray) took him again to Rome where we find him designing coins for the Pope and associating himself with Michelangelo. His valued labors were interrupted by suspicions of murder and he fled to France. Again he returned, was imprisoned on a charge of embezzlement, escaped, and was soon back in France where he remained for several years under the patronage of the king (Francis I), executing many beautiful designs for him and receiving a pension. But his quarrelsome nature intervened to terminate this advantageous arrangement and he departed on bad terms with his courtly friends and patrons. Florence was again the scene of his activities and here he won the favor of Duke Cosimo de' Medici who must have been sorely tried by the continued misadventures which colored the artist's life from beginning to end. That he occasionally experienced the pangs of remorse is evidenced by his entering a monastery; two years of its peaceful life, however, was quite sufficient for him and he was about 60 years of age when he resumed his adventurous career. It was in this latter period of his life that he felt moved to embody his dubious exploits in the astonishing autobiography which has survived most of the exquisite specimens of his metal work, which have been melted down. He died in Florence, Feb. 25, 1571.

The object which is considered the most beautiful of all his smaller works and most expressive of his peculiar genius is fortunately preserved in the Museum of Vienna. This is the salt holder which he wrought for Francis I, a superbly beautiful ornament with figures of Cybele and Neptune in relief. In the Metropolitan Museum in New York City are several specimens of his work. A gold button which he executed for Pope Clement, for use on an ecclesiastical robe, is said to have contained among other gems the second largest diamond in the world. Outstanding among his sculptural work is the famous bronze statue of "Perseus" holding the head of "Medusa," which is still on exhibition in his native city. The niches about its base, holding small figures of gods, are marvels of exquisite detail and show the hand of the master metal worker, but are somewhat too ornate for a work of sculpture and detract from the beauty of the main conception.

CERVANTES   1547–1616

MIGUEL DE CERVANTES SAAVEDRA (sẽr văn'tēz), one of the greatest imaginative writers of Spain and author of the immortal *Don Quixote,* was born of an old Galician family at Alcalá de Henares, Oct. 9, 1547. He studied at Salamanca, and later at Madrid, where he was placed under the care of a learned theologian, Juan López de Hoyos, who was a professor in the university. His imaginative and poetic temperament, however, proved rebellious to general studies and he spent most of his time in writing poems and romances, none of which early efforts were at all significant. When he was 22 years old he served for some time as valet de chambre to a cardinal of Rome. In 1570, as a volunteer under the command of the papal admiral, Marco Antonio Colonna, he fought gallantly against the Turks. At the battle of Lepanto he was maimed for life by a gunshot wound in the left hand. He was made a prisoner on an Algerine ship, kept in slavery and ransomed after four years. Returing to Spain, he joined the army sent by King Philip into Portugal and distinguished himself in the expedition to the Azores.

In 1584 he settled down to a well-earned retirement in his native country, married and turned his attention to literature. His romance, *Galatea,* was published in 1584. He wrote many plays, among which was his tragedy of *La Numancia.* But all this work brought him no substantial returns and he was reduced to poverty. In 1605, he discovered his true forte in the field of humor and satire and the first part of *Don Quixote* was given to the world. Considering its originality, freshness and broad satire, it seems incredible that this work, one of the greatest humorous productions of all time, should have been received with indifference by a public that must have appreciated its matchless ridicule even if it failed to feel its poetry. It made its way, however, and in a short time its author's name was a household word in his native land. Slowly the book became known throughout Europe and took its place as a typical product of universal genius, appealing alike to the cultural and the unlettered. Time has affected its early popularity, but its high place in world literature seems secure.

Don Quixote was written to burlesque and put an end to the artificial romances of chivalry which were so widely read in Cervantes' day. It makes that kind of writing sufficiently ridiculous, but if that were all the work would probably not have stood the test of time, for mere ridicule, as such, has no character of permanence. The abiding quality of *Don Quixote* lies much deeper. Though written with a satirical purpose, it is throughout pervaded by the true spirit of poetry. With that universality which alone belongs to the highest genius, Cervantes connected a universal interest with descriptions of local and temporary characteristics and imparts the salutory truth that the high soul, however simple and guileless, can obtain a triumph which misfortune cannot tarnish. It is because the famous knight, though the "sweet bells of his intellect are jangled out of tune," is still generous, kindly and disinterested, that he gains a lasting hold on our affections.

Much has been written, and a great deal of time wasted, in speculation about an underlying meaning in this preeminently original work. Such speculations have been indulged also with regard to *Alice in Wonderland* which is nothing save what it obviously appears. The work of Cervantes has been called an allegory, which it is not, and it cannot be too strongly emphasized that it is not because of its superficial character of burlesque and its glowing ridicule (negative qualities at best) that it is counted one of the world's great books. Thousands have loved and pitied the benighted hero, as thousands have loved and pitied King Lear.

Following *Don Quixote* Cervantes wrote other works, all of them overshadowed by the great masterpiece. In 1613 he published twelve novels under the title of *Exemplary Tales* and in the year following his *Viage al Parnaso (Journey to Parnassus)* appeared, followed by another group of plays. In 1614 a certain Alonso Fernandez de Avellaneda published a spurious continuation of *Don Quixote,* containing vicious abuse of Cervantes, which deeply wounded him; but the ill wind blew much good for he shortly thereafter published the true continuation of his great work.

Notwithstanding his fame, he lived in poverty and the condition of his family was sometimes perilously near to destitution. Near the close of his life, however, he found a sympathetic patron in the Count of Lemos who afforded him a measure of relief from this continued strain. During the closing years of his life he lived at Madrid.

On April 23, 1616, at Stratford-on-Avon, Shakespeare died in comfortable retirement in the "fair home" which he had built for himself. On that same day died Cervantes, the recipient of charity, after a prolonged and bitter struggle with poverty.

CHARLES SPENCER CHAPLIN   1889–

"CHARLIE" CHAPLIN, a great pantomimic artist, whose motion picture comedies have carried his fame into practically every country on the globe, was born in London, the son of Charles and Hannah Chaplin, both well known English stage performers. His father died while Charles was a child. He made his first stage appearance as a baby in his mother's arms. While still a youngster he became a member of the juvenile dancers known as the "Eight Lancashire Lads" and a few years later played the rôle of *Billy*, the page boy, in an English production of *Sherlock Holmes*. Even at that time he was a skillful impersonator and the imitations of noted stage stars of the day which he gave for the benefit of his fellow players led to his being called upon for similar appearances at actors' club entertainments. Returning to vaudeville, he played for a number of years in the English music halls.

It was in 1910 that Chaplin first came to the United States as leading comedian with the Fred Karno Comedy Company, in a repertoire of pantomime acts which included "A Night in a London Music Hall." He toured both the United States and Canada with this company until the spring of 1912, when he returned to England, but before the year had ended he was back with the same company for another tour of American vaudeville theaters. While playing in Philadelphia he received a telegram from the old Keystone Film Company of New York offering him $150 a week to act in Keystone comedies for a year. He accepted the offer and made an enormous success in silent pictures with his comedy tramp, with Derby hat, big shoes, flapping trousers, slender cane and tiny moustache, which have remained characteristics of his motion picture rôles ever since. His short comedies became the rage in America, later in England and on the Continent; in fact, all over the world. No actor in motion pictures has enjoyed such a vogue. Sober critics of things theatrical who eschewed motion pictures found him a master of the art of pantomime; he was hailed as a genius, and his financial success was enormous. In 1912 he formed the Charlie Chaplin Film Company with a studio of his own in Hollywood—the first screen star to have his own studio—and began to produce his own comedies as well as act in them. A short time later, in association with Douglas Fairbanks, Mary Pickford and D. W. Griffith, the director, he formed the United Artists Corporation, an independent organization of stars and producers.

Among famous Chaplin screen comedies are *A Dog's Life, Shoulder Arms, Pay Day, The Immigrant,* and the longer pictures, *The Pilgrim* and

The Kid, in which his extraordinary success was aided by the inspired acting of the five or six year old Jackie Coogan. *The Kid* and the following feature picture, *The Gold Rush,* demonstrated that Chaplin had a great gift for dramatic acting and the ability to combine drama and comedy in satisfying proportions. He writes his own stories, having written and directed, without himself appearing in, *A Woman of Paris,* a dramatic photoplay that achieved much success. His later productions are *The Circus,* and *City Lights,* in the latter of which he employed sound effects without the use of dialogue.

Chaplin has been twice married; first to Mildred Harris, screen actress, and second to Lita Grey, who later became a screen and vaudeville player, and who is the mother of his two sons.

CHARLEMAGNE   742–814

CHARLEMAGNE (shär'lå mān) (CHARLES THE GREAT) was king of the Franks (768–814) and Roman emperor (800–814). He was born April 2, 742, probably at Aix-la-Chapelle. His father was the Frankish king Pepin the Short, who was son of the great Charles Martel. On Pepin's death in 768, Charlemagne and his brother Carloman jointly succeeded to the throne. When Carloman died his sons were excluded from succession and Charlemagne became sole king. It will be helpful to the student to bear in mind that the Franks, or freemen, made up the confederation of Germanic tribes along the lower Rhine and half a century prior to Charlemagne's time they overthrew the Roman dominion in Gaul (now France). In 772 it was resolved to make war against the Saxons, for the security of the frontiers (which their habit of exploration and invasion was continually threatening), and also to carry Christianity to them. Charlemagne advanced as far as the Weser river. Pope Adrian I then asked his assistance against Desiderius, king of the Lombards (the northern part of Italy, then called Lombardy). Charlemagne had married the daughter of this king, but repudiated her because she bore him no children, and married Hildegarde, daughter of the Swabian duke, Godfrey. Angered by this treatment of his daughter, Desiderius had urged the pope to crown Charlemagne's nephews (the sons of Carloman, mentioned above) and upon the pope's refusal had laid waste the papal territory. It was in this predicament that the pope sought Charlemagne's aid.

Charlemagne thereupon crossed the Alps (774), overthrew the Lombards, was acknowledged as their king and confirmed these triumphs with the pope's approval. In 775 he turned his attention to the north, completely subjugating the Saxons, and in the following year suppressed an insurrection in Italy. He then proceeded again against the Saxons whose nobles acknowledged him as their sovereign. His great power was now exerted in the wars of the Moors and Arabs in Spain, whither he led his army (778) and added to his dominions the regions between the Ebro River and the Pyrenees. An uprising among the Saxons recalled him to the north and he was soon successful in driving them back from the neighborhood of Cologne to which they had advanced.

In 781 he again went to Italy where the pope crowned his second son, Pepin, king of Italy and his infant son, Louis, king of Aquitaine. The Saxons, again in revolt, annihilated a Frankish army but their triumph was short-lived. Charlemagne, after a signal victory, executed 4500 of them as rebels. A more general uprising followed, but in 783–5 he succeeded in reducing them completely to subjection and in persuading their principal chiefs to submit to baptism. He was equally successful against the Huns and the Bulgarians. In 800 he went to Italy to aid Pope Leo III in his struggle with the rebellious Romans, a journey which was to have a dramatic sequel for him. The well-authenticated story runs that on Christmas day he was at his devotions in St. Peters', Rome, when to his surprise the pope approached and, calling him Carolus Augustus, placed the Roman crown upon his head. Great enthusiasm attended the impromptu ceremony. It was hoped that the Western Empire and the Empire of the East might now be consolidated by the marriage of Charlemagne with the Byzantine empress, Irene, but her overthrow confounded this plan. Still success succeeded success with this man of destiny. His conquests in Germany and Spain were extended, he instituted a missionary campaign among the Saxons, establishing churches and encouraging Christian teaching.

Though preeminently a warrior and continually forced into military activity by recurrent insurrections, he governed all his vast acquisitions with humane and enlightened policy. He was an anachronism in an age of enshrouding darkness. He patronized such art as there was, encouraged education, was keenly interested in commerce and manufactures. Not the least astonishing was his recognition of civil rights and of the wisdom of restricting the monarchical power. He planned a canal to connect the Danube and the Rhine and carried through many important public works. With paternal solicitude he concerned himself with ways and means of life among his people; no measure looking to the public welfare was too small for his consideration. In the royal palace he maintained a school for the children of his servants. His court was the rendezvous of the learned and cultivated, a limited enough company in that benighted age.

He understood both Greek and Latin and, like his great contemporary, King Alfred, delighted in writing and studying.

He is said to have been of an imposing presence, fond of games and outdoor sports, abstemious in his habits (in an age of gluttony); his noble character stained by only one vice, an amorous propensity. The execution of 4500 prisoners (which he probably deemed a salutory and needful act) seems to be the one real stain on his career. His renown was carried to every corner of the known world. Peace and good health attended his ripe old age; he died, honored and mourned by all his subjects, on Jan. 28, 814.

CHARLES I   1600–1649

CHARLES I, king of Great Britain and Ireland from 1625 to 1649, was born at Dunfermline, Scotland, Nov. 19, 1600. He was the second son of James VI of Scotland who became also James I of England. On the death of his elder brother in 1612, he became Prince of Wales (the title, however, being withheld for several years) and heir to his father's throne, to which he succeeded in 1625. From his father he inherited indifferent health; he had a disorder of the joints, was tongue-tied and stuttered. More portentous, he inherited also the strictest views of royal prerogatives, amounting to an obsession which was ultimately to prove his ruin. He early discovered impatience, often carried to the point of intolerance, about matters of personal preference. His strong predilection in favor of the Episcopal church moved him to inaugurate persecutions of the Puritans in England and the Presbyterians in Scotland. He never sensed the great undercurrents of thought among his people, invariably ascribing their manifestations to petty factional activities. He married a Roman Catholic, Maria Henrietta of France, which greatly displeased his subjects and their displeasure was intensified by his elevation of the Duke of Buckingham to the post of prime minister.

The parliament which he convened in 1625 promptly evinced a spirit to safeguard English liberties, withholding money from the king, and in the following year resolved on the impeachment of Buckingham, whereupon the king imprisoned two of the boldest members, dissolved the parliament and had recourse to arbitrary taxation to replenish his coffers; all of which had the effect of alienating his people and increasing his unpopularity. The parliament summoned in 1628, instead of granting his demands, presented the famous Petition of Rights. In high anger Charles again dissolved the body, threw some of its members into prison and for eleven years governed without a parliament. His measures, particularly in the matter of raising money, were necessarily illegal and arbitrary, and the people were increasingly dissatisfied. Steadily the love of liberty deepened and republican principles of government were widely and ominously discussed. Still Charles could not read the handwriting on the wall.

In 1638 the first signs of the gathering storm were apparent in armed resistance to his policies in Scotland, inspired mainly by the vexed question of church government. The Scots advanced to the border and the English people applauded. Alarmed at last, Charles made concessions and civil war was for the time averted. In 1640 the desperate need of supplies, which his arbitrary measures had not brought him, forced him to assemble another parliament which, instead of meeting his demands, promptly issued a statement of public grievances. Again he dissolved the parliament, prepared to meet the reassembled Scottish troops, and was defeated by them at Newburn-on-Tyne. The victorious army advanced into England, encouraged by the English generally.

Charles now called another parliament, memorable in history, which disregarded his demands, impeached several of his ministers and declared his measures null and void. A bill was passed in favor of triennial parliaments, to which the king reluctantly consented, agreeing also not to dissolve the existing body without its consent. He then attempted conciliatory measures by a friendly visit to Scotland, during which an uprising occurred in Ireland with the massacre of many Protestants, an event highly prejudicial to the king's hope of peace. Meanwhile parliament increased its demands. On Jan. 4, 1642, the king appeared before the Commons and made accusations of treason against five of its members—Pym, Hampden, Hollis, Hazelrig and Stroud—demanding that they be delivered to him. Both houses refused, resolved to protect their members by arms. The long-threatened conflict now seemed inevitable. The king and his household withdrew from London; parliament declared the nation in peril.

Thus civil war began. The king's army had initial successes, but public sentiment supported the parliament. On the 14th of June, 1645, at the battle of Naseby the royal army was nearly annihilated by the troops under Cromwell and Fairfax, and Charles sought refuge in the Scottish camp. After an unsuccessful effort to effect negotiations he was delivered to Cromwell's army. Still he sought to make terms but nothing was accomplished. He escaped and was recaptured. Even in his pitiful extremity he would not accede to the demands of his captors. An act of parliament was then passed making it treasonable to negotiate with him and a court composed of representatives of the army, the House of Commons, and the city of London, was appointed to sit in judgment of him. This solemn assembly of about 70 members convened in Westminster Hall, Jan. 20, 1649. Seven days later Charles was condemned to death as a tyrant, murderer and national enemy. The Scots, moved by religious misgivings, protested. The French court and the States-General of the Netherlands vainly interceded. On Jan. 30, 1649, he was beheaded at the block before the palace of Whitehall.

He went to his death with kingly demeanor. "Nothing in his life became him like the leaving it." In his private life he was a man of cultivated tastes and of stainless character. He believed in the absolute authority of kings and he died the victim of his own incurable obsession.

THOMAS CHATTERTON   1752–1770

THOMAS CHATTERTON, "the marvellous boy" of England, was a poetic genius of the first order; one of the greatest prodigies in literary history. Doubtless the tragic story of his short life has given color to the enthusiastic estimates of his work, and what he might have accomplished had he lived is purely conjectural. Unquestionably he gave promise of the highest achievement; what he actually did is sufficiently remarkable. He was born in Bristol, England, Nov. 20, 1752, the posthumous child of a father who had been a schoolmaster and singer in the Bristol Cathedral. His education was limited to that afforded by the parish school. It is said that a perusal of his mother's Bible first kindled the poetic fire which was not apparent in school, where he was regarded as dull. He early showed a susceptibility to all things old; medieval writings, musty manuscripts, old ruins, attracted him strangely. He seemed to live in the past and to visualize it accurately. This is significant in the light of his astounding story.

At 14 he was apprenticed to a local attorney who governed him rigorously, sparing not the rod and compelling him to eat with the servants. At this time the apprentice's mind was probably engrossed with matters other than his duties. The occasion of the opening of a new bridge at Bristol was seized by him as an appropriate moment for sending to a newspaper a very ingenious account, in antique phraseology, of the opening, several centuries earlier, of the old bridge which the new one now replaced. He explained that this quaint report had been culled from an old manuscript. In point of fact, he was himself its author. Encouraged by the success of this fraud, he circulated among his townspeople copies of medieval poems alleged to be the product of a 15th century monk, Thomas Rowley. The good people of Bristol were so edified by these specimens of antique literature that Chatterton, then 16, resolved to operate on a larger scale. He sent to Horace Walpole, wit, antiquarian and critic, several pages of antique writing about medieval artists which he suggested that Walpole would find useful in his *Anecdotes of Painting*. Walpole made enthusiastic acknowledgment begging that such other rare specimens as the sender had might also be forwarded. Chatterton replied with a generous batch of fraudulent material in verse and prose and a gratuitous account of himself, which aroused Walpole's suspicions. His friend, Thomas Gray, to whom he showed the poems, pronounced them spurious. A kindly letter from Walpole giving the misguided boy some good advice was answered by an angry demand for the manuscripts.

Dismissed from the attorney's office because of certain scurrilous writings, his thoughts turned to London whither he went, taking with him all his Rowley manuscripts and some of his acknowledged poems, and took lodgings in Shoreditch, but being shortly in financial extremities he found shelter in a wretched attic from which he sent glowing letters home as to his rosy prospects. With astonishing fertility he turned out poems, political essays, satiric sketches, some of which were published and favorably noticed. But what he needed was ready cash and this was not forthcoming. He had expected to "set the Thames on fire," but it did not ignite. In despair, with the spectre of starvation haunting him, he sought employment in a ship sailing for Africa but was refused. On the morning of Aug. 25, 1770 his landlady found him lying across his bed, the attic strewn with torn manuscripts. He had taken a fatal dose of arsenic. He was not yet 18 years old. A grim, ironic touch is given to this tragic sequel of his disillusionment by the fact that a distinguished scholar of Oxford was about to go to Bristol to make inquiries about the youthful genius. It was by the narrowest margin that Chatterton's literary forgeries did not get into Walpole's scholarly work. It was by the narrowest margin that he missed his chance of recognition and sympathetic guidance.

The poems which he circulated as his own were extraordinary, considering his age, and some of them are superb without regard to the author's age. Notable among them is *Kew Gardens*. His lyrics and short ballads have a distinctive charm. His acknowledged prose shows him to have been thoroughly sophisticated; his last will and testament, a piece of irreverent and bitter mockery written when he was barely 16, is disturbingly cynical with its bequests of his personal attributes of modesty, etc., to certain damsels of his acquaintance.

But it is in the forgeries, so-called, that his genius found its highest expression. He seemed able to project himself into the past, to absorb its thought and master its quaint expression. And in this antique phraseology he wrote some of the tenderest, most stirring, most beautiful passages in English literature.

GEOFFREY CHAUCER   Circa 1340–1400

GEOFFREY CHAUCER (chạ'sẽr), known as the father of English poetry, was the son of John Chaucer, vintner and tavern-keeper of London. He was born about 1340. The early events of his life are not known with much certainty. He may have attended Cambridge or Oxford. There is record of his serving as valet and later as squire in the King's household and of his accompanying Edward III on his invasion of France in 1359, during which he was taken prisoner and later released upon payment of ransom by the King.

On the death of his patron, Prince Lionel, Duke of Clarence, in 1368, Chaucer's services were transferred to Lionel's brother, John of Gaunt, Duke of Lancaster. From 1370 to 1386 he was attached to the court and was frequently employed on diplomatic missions to Italy, France and other countries. He held various official positions, such as Comptroller of the Petty Customs and Clerk of the Works at Westminster, and was later put on a commission to repair the banks of the Thames. Most of these offices he lost through political changes. In 1386 he was elected a knight of the shire for Kent in the Parliament held at Westminster.

Chaucer's wife, Philippa, whose surname is not known and whom he evidently married prior to 1374, died in 1387. In 1391 he wrote his treatise on the Astrolabe for his little son Lewis, of whom nothing more is known. In 1394 the King granted him a pension of twenty pounds a year for life. When Henry IV became King, Chaucer addressed to him a complaint as to his own poverty and the sovereign ordered that his pension be doubled. Chaucer died on Oct. 25, 1400, probably in a house in the garden of the Chapel of St. Mary, Westminster, which he had leased. He was buried in that section of Westminster Abbey which later became known as the Poets' Corner.

Chaucer's début as a poet was probably in 1369 with his *Death of Blanche the Duchess* (wife of John of Gaunt). To the years between that date and 1387 belong such writings as *The Assembly of Fowls, The House of Fame, Troilus and Cressida* and *The Legend of Good Women,* and probably a part of his great work, *The Canterbury Tales*.

During his visits to Italy Chaucer came under the literary influence of Dante and Petrarch and Boccaccio, but he imitated the spirit rather than the letter of the Italian masters. He found in the heptastich (or 7-line stanza), and later in the heroic couplet, the metrical measures suited to his genius. *Troilus and Cressida* is the crowning glory of his middle period, but even that pales before *The Canterbury Tales,* which is one of the chief glories of English literature, but so monumental in design that the poet did not live to complete it. The *Prologue* to the *Tales,* written in 1387, is generally considered his greatest achievement because of its humor, grace, reality and comprehensiveness.

ANTON CHEKHOV   1860–1904

ANTON CHEKHOV (chĕ′kŏf), one of Russia's greatest dramatists, was born Jan. 17, 1860, in the old Black Sea port of Taganrog. His father, the son of a serf, had married a merchant's daughter and settled in Taganrog where he carried on an unsuccessful trade in provisions during Anton's boyhood. The family was large and its income meagre and the youthful Chekhov was impressed into his father's business at an early age. He worked cheerfully and, being a close and sympathetic observer of the customers and idlers who collected in the store, he gathered many droll stories which he was fond of whispering to his schoolfellows. His grandfather had become manager of an estate near Taganrog, in the wild steppe country of the Don Cossacks, and young Chekhov spent many of his summers there, hunting and fishing.

When Anton was about fourteen his father moved to Moscow, but the son was left behind and, having time now to devote to study, his progress in school was remarkable. At the age of seventeen he wrote a long tragedy which he later destroyed. He was graduated from the high school in Taganrog with honors and while studying medicine at the University of Moscow began to write short stories as a means of aiding his struggling family. His first literary effort to be published appeared in a Moscow newspaper in 1880 and was followed by many brief stories in several of the smaller publications in the city. He also wrote a melodramatic play which the censor suppressed and of which nothing more is heard. He received his degree of Doctor of Medicine in 1884 and practiced that profession for a time. In 1887 two volumes of his collected stories were published both of which met with immediate success and ran through several editions. About this time the light-hearted humor which was one of the principal characteristics of his writing began to be overcast with the sadness and dark brooding that marked much of his later work, due probably to the ill health which now overtook him.

An obstinate cough manifested itself and Chekhov went south in 1888 to a little cottage on the banks of a river where he continued to practice medicine among the villagers and peasants. The stage had always fascinated him and the following year, although he was troubled by heart attacks, he wrote the play of *Ivanoff* in two and a half weeks, and then a one-act playlet, *The Swan Song. Ivanoff,* produced in Moscow, was a failure. He rewrote the play and it was put on at St. Petersburg with great success. There followed a farce written in a single evening, *The Boor,* which had a measure of success. The next play, *The Demon,* was a failure, but ten years later this also was rewritten under the title of *Uncle Vanya* and it ranks as an excellent play although not one of his best. In 1890 he made a journey by stage-coach across Siberia to the island of Saghalien, which he describes in his only long story, *The Steppe,* a series of sketches strung together on a slender thread.

Tuberculosis, which had long threatened, now declared itself and he spent the last ten years of his life in the Crimea, rather unhappily because of the ill health which prevented him from doing all of the literary work he wished to undertake and also because of a separation from his wife, Olga Knipper, who was one of the artistes of the Moscow Art Theater. *The Sea-Gull,* one of his more important plays, was presented at this theater in 1895, scoring an immediate success. *The Three Sisters,* produced in 1901, is the most gloomy of Chekhov's plays. *Uncle Vanya* came next and then his last and greatest play, *The Cherry Orchard.* This was produced at the Moscow Theater shortly before its author's death, and he was feted as one of Russia's greatest dramatists.

He died in the little village of Badenweiler in the Black Forest on July 2, 1904, and his body was taken to Moscow for burial.

FRÉDÉRIC FRANÇOIS CHOPIN   1810–1849

FRÉDÉRIC FRANÇOIS CHOPIN (shŏ'păn'), the great composer and pianist, was born near Warsaw, Poland, on Feb. 22, 1810. He early showed the precocity which is usual in musical geniuses and which was so conspicuously manifested in Mendelssohn and Mozart. His parents were prosperous and of refined taste and he enjoyed, from childhood, every facility for the development of the powers that raised him to a high, almost a unique, place among the great musical figures of history. He studied under Zwyny and Elsner, and first appeared in public when he was nine years old. Reared in an atmosphere of fashion and culture, he retained through his brief life an aristocratic habit and delighted in exclusive society. Like Mozart, his health was frail, but he was of a buoyant and lively nature and was thought by his intimates to possess the qualities which insure success in the theatrical field. He was but 19 when he played his own compositions before a distinguished company at Vienna, and the following year gave several concerts at Warsaw, winning in both places the highest praise. At about this time occurred his love affair with Constantia Gladowska, a young singer. The occupation of Warsaw by the Russians in 1831 caused him to leave his native land and he made his home thereafter in Paris. One of his greatest pieces, popularly called the *Revolution*, was inspired by the fall of Warsaw.

In Paris he was in his element, being welcomed by the most distinguished musical and literary celebrities of that city, among whom was the artist Ary Scheffer, who painted his portrait. Here he enjoyed the friendship of Liszt, Heine, Balzac, Mendelssohn and others; particularly that of the female novelist famous under the name of George Sand, who had left her husband for a glamorous bohemian career in the metropolis. His performances at public concerts during this period were numerous and his playing was hailed with enthusiasm. In 1835 he visited Dresden where he fell desperately in love with Marie Wodzinska. Followed an interval at Leipzig where he visited Mendelssohn, and then he returned to Paris. But his love lured him back to Dresden and after receiving the young lady's promise of marriage he returned again to Paris shortly to learn that she had married another. Overcome with grief and disappointment, he accepted the tender sympathies of Madam Sand who found it the easier to bestow them because of her admiration of his genius and an increasing passion for the wistful and disappointed lover. Thus was inaugurated one of the most familiar romances of musical or literary history. The composer's passion, though belated, became intense; and finding himself unable to part with his mistress he accompanied her to Majorca whither she went because of the illness of one of her two children. Chopin's health, always precarious, suffered from the inclement weather during this sojourn and Madam Sand proved a devoted nurse. When he was able to work he found her his inspiration and it was during this period that some of his wonderful preludes were composed. From 1839 to 1847 he and Madam Sand remained devoted, spending the summers at her country estate and the winters at Paris. Here he performed constantly in public and had a large number of pupils. He found teaching both agreeable and profitable. His published compositions also brought him large returns and his income enabled him to enjoy what he most craved, the society of brilliant and intellectual people and many of the luxuries of life. But his health was frail and he was compelled always to battle with this handicap. The death of his father in 1844 cast a shadow over his active and pleasurable life and he lapsed into a mood of melancholy to which has been ascribed his break with the woman who had been for so long his helpful and devoted companion. His wasting malady (tuberculosis) made him nervous and distraught and the separation only tended to increase his ill-temper and distraction. In February, 1848, debilitated from his incessant labors, he appeared for the last time at a public concert where the enthusiasm of his audience was so great that for a while he was aroused to continued effort. He went to London where every appearance brought him an ovation. But his strength was ebbing and he was compelled to indulge himself with an unavailing rest in Scotland at the beautiful estate of a former pupil. Still again he sought the stimulus of applause in London and in Paris where he made a desperate effort to continue his teaching, but he sank rapidly and died on Oct. 17, 1849.

He composed a great number of songs, polonaises, etudes, ballads, sonatas, preludes and many other forms of music.

CICERO   106 B.C.–43 B.C.

MARCUS TULLIUS CICERO (sĭs'ē rō), Roman orator and one of the most illustrious characters in ancient history, was born at Arpinum in southern Italy, Jan. 3, 106 B.C. His father, a man of much learning and ambitious for his son, sent him to Rome where the boy was prompt in applying the theory which he later pronounced as an educational dictum; that an orator's knowledge should be complete and various, embracing all subjects. Under the guidance of the learned Crassus, he studied assiduously, familiarizing himself with the Grecian language, with Roman law and oratory, and with philosophy. He acquired a breadth of culture hardly equaled by that of any of his contemporaries, excelling as a writer as well as an orator; he was a man of preeminent distinction, singularly human and vivid to the modern student of Roman history. When he was about 25 years old he emerged into active life as a pleader, but his passion for learning and professional perfection, as also his indifferent health, impelled him to visit the cultural centres of Asia and Greece where he made a particular study of elocution. After occupying several offices, including a governorship in Sicily where he ruled with wisdom and was highly popular with the people, he was elected chief magistrate, or consul, and it was during his occupancy of this post that the conspiracy of the infamous and profligate Catiline occurred. Revealed to Cicero by the mistress of one of the conspirators, he was enabled to confound the traitor and to frustrate the plan which comprehended not only the disruption of the state, but his own murder. For his prompt and skilful exposure of this plot a public festival of thanksgiving was held.

Cicero's enemies, however, were busy; he was charged with executing the conspirators without legal process, and for some months he lived in Thessalonica under sentence of banishment. Recalled, however, he was received with plaudits by the multitude on his arrival in Rome. Ever patriotic, he now tried to cooperate with the better element in the senate but this policy was made difficult by the proffered friendship of Caesar and Pompey, whom he hesitated to antagonize. A course of expediency, common enough in politics, seemed necessary which must have galled his soul. He was not free to defy the Triumvirs and must perforce be held measurably responsible for the fall of the republic. When civil war was threatened he joined the army of the Senate, but after the battle of Pharsalia he left his friends, ignominiously it must be admitted, and threw himself on the mercy of the victorious Caesar, who received him kindly.

He now lived in retirement and it was during this period that some of his greatest works were written. After the murder of Caesar he was at first inclined to cast his lot with the conspirators, but when Octavian returned to Rome after Caesar's death and discovered that Caesar had made him his heir, Cicero decided to join with numerous others who espoused his cause. Not content with passive support of Octavian, he delivered the orations against Antony, known as the *Philippics,* which are famous in history, but which were later to put him in a very embarrassing position, in which he must have felt himself the victim of an ironic and cruel fate. Octavian, Lepidus and Antony united in a triumvirate; Cicero was soon after proscribed and stood in peril of his life. If the world cannot forget those matchless orations, Antony could not forget them either.

Cicero was now infirm and old. His only hope lay in escape. While being borne from his home to Caieta where he intended to embark, he was intercepted by a military band sent by Antony. Beseeching his attendants to offer no resistance, he submitted to execution by sword as he lay peacefully in his litter, while those who had been carrying him stood close at hand. This tragic event occurred Dec. 7, 43 B.C.

As an orator Cicero is second to none, unless it be Demosthenes. In his writings, which are in a style of rare purity and beauty, he has left us many pictures of his time and country; pictures which enable the modern reader to visualize the familiar lives of the Roman people. As a statesman he had great ability and his handling of the Catiline conspiracy shows him capable of firmness. Yet there was little of the heroic in his make-up and when all is said he shines more in the field of letters than in the turmoil of politics. He seems deficient in resolution and courage, given to expediency and to a hesitant and cautious attitude of mind which stood in the way of decisive action. His orations are characterized not only by the highest order of eloquence, but by consummate art which was the result of unwearied industry. These have carried his name down through the ages and made him, in the estimation of all mankind, one of the very few supreme orators in history.

HENRY CLAY   1777–1852

HENRY CLAY, distinguished American statesman, was born in Hanover County, Virginia, April 12, 1777. He was the son of a poor Baptist minister, father of seven children, who died when Henry, the fifth child, was five years of age. His mother later remarried and removed to Kentucky. Meantime, Henry worked in a store in Richmond and later was employed in a clerical capacity in the chancery court of his state, which was the deciding influence in his resolve to become a lawyer. Admitted to practice in 1797, he opened an office in Lexington, Kentucky, then a sparsely settled region whither his mother had preceded him. Here he practiced among the rough frontiersmen, making his way rapidly and becoming immensely popular. He possessed a magnetic personality which was always a potent factor in winning him preferment.

In 1799 he participated in the revision of the state constitution and was thereupon launched upon his distinguished political career. In that same year he married Lucretia Hart, inaugurating a singularly happy married life which brought him eleven children. His wife was a lady of moderate wealth and their extensive estate, Ashland, near Lexington, was for many years the scene of a gracious hospitality. He early achieved marked success as a criminal lawyer and is said never to have lost a murder case, a recollection which afforded him scant satisfaction in later years when he regretted that he had been instrumental in the acquittal of many undoubted criminals. He was glad to abandon his criminal practice, and after serving for a period as public prosecutor, was elected to the state legislature in 1803. Three years later he entered the United States Senate to fill an unexpired term, which brought his abilities and his great personal charm to the attention of the nation. Declining the nomination for the ensuing congress, he resumed the practice of law in Kentucky. He was again elected to the state legislature in 1808 and presided as speaker. The session was notable for its attempt to exclude all English court decisions and precedents from state practice, an ill-considered measure which Clay in a memorable speech assailed. To him belongs the honor of "saving for Kentucky the treasures of English jurisprudence."

He returned to the U. S. Senate in 1809 to fill another unexpired term and two years later became speaker of the House of Representatives where he vigorously advocated the War of 1812 and all measures requisite to its prosecution, which course made him immensely popular throughout the country. He was later one of the commissioners to negotiate peace, and received a flattering ovation on his return from England. Declining a mission to Russia, he again entered the House of Representatives and was speaker throughout two sessions. He is best known as the author of the famous "Missouri Compromise," which restricted slavery in the territory comprised in the Louisiana Purchase to that part lying south of 36° 30′ north latitude, except in the new state of Missouri.

Declining another nomination to Congress, he resumed his lucrative legal practice but in 1823 was plunged anew into the turmoil of politics and again became speaker of the House. In 1824 he was a candidate for the presidency, his competitors being Andrew Jackson, William Crawford and John Quincy Adams. The election was thrown into the House and Clay, who ran fourth, was excluded by constitutional requirement. He thereupon supported Adams who made him secretary of state, an appointment which aroused much groundless comment about a bargain between these two men of the highest honor. It was such a remark by the eccentric John Randolph which precipitated the pistol duel between himself and Clay in which each missed his mark and no second shots were fired. In 1829 he was once more elected to the Senate and in 1832 again ran for the presidency against Jackson by whom he was defeated. Continuing in the Senate, he consistently opposed the measures of Jackson and followed a policy of moderation on the slavery question. In 1844 he ran for the presidency against James K. Polk, but was again defeated, owing largely to his failure to take a decided stand against the annexation of Texas. In 1848 he was again doomed to disappointment when the convention nominated General Taylor for the high office to which Clay had so long aspired. He was again sent to the Senate, however, in that year and did what he could to stem the rising tide of animosity between the North and South which culminated in the Civil War. It was he who uttered the familiar saying, "I would rather be right than be president." He was unqualifiedly and zealously in favor of the preservation of the Union, considering this ultimate purpose the keynote of all his acts, and did much to postpone the inevitable conflict. He has been criticized for his tendency to compromise, but there was never any question as to his ardent patriotism which shone out in glowing splendor in the difficult period succeeding the conflagration. He died in Washington June 29, 1852 at the age of 76.

GEORGES CLÉMENCEAU 1841-1929

GEORGES BENJAMIN EUGÈNE CLÉMENCEAU (klä'män sö'), French statesman and writer, was born on Sept. 28, 1841, at Mouillerou-en-Pareds, in western France. He studied medicine, but in his young manhood became more interested in politics and gave up the idea of being a physician. He was especially interested in the writings of John Stuart Mill and in 1866 he journeyed to America in order to study for himself the application of progressive theories in the American democracy. For three years he remained in New York and New England, teaching French for a time in a girls' school in Connecticut and writing, for the Paris *Temps,* articles on post-war conditions in America.

He was elected republican member of the Chamber of Deputies in 1876 where he vigorously opposed the royalists. Independent and outspoken, a brilliant speaker, with ready wit and telling epigrams which his political opponents learned to fear as much as they dreaded his keen arguments, he made his public influence still greater by founding and editing in 1880 a daily paper, *La Justice,* in which to expound his radical views. Some years later, during the famous Dreyfuss trial, he established another daily, *L'Aurore,* for the purpose of championing the cause of Capt. Alfred Dreyfuss, who had been accused of selling military information to a hostile country and of whose innocence he was firmly convinced. It was in *L'Aurore* that the famous letter of Emile Zola, *J'accuse,* was published which caused its writer to be sent to prison.

About 1893 reports were circulated that Clémenceau had been concerned in a scandal connected with Panama, but although he lost his seat in the Chamber of Deputies as a consequence, he was in 1902 elected to the Senate, became minister of the interior four years later and shortly thereafter was made premier, an office which he held until 1909, accomplishing during his incumbency many social reforms and making effective the complete separation of church and state. He used prompt measures to quell rioting in connection with a serious miners' strike organized by the socialists who, relying upon his well-known radical views, had believed that they could count on his sympathy; and again to put down an uprising of wine growers in the south of France, which almost assumed the proportions of a revolution.

He lost the premiership in 1909 but continued a power in politics and in 1913 overthrew the Briand ministry. He had established a third paper, *L'Homme Libre,* in which as well as in public utterances he had long urged preparation for war which he believed was threatening, and in September, 1914, *L'Homme Libre* was suppressed because of his criticisms of the army medical department. Nothing daunted, he immediately issued *L'Homme Enchaîné,* continuing his opposition. He was president of the Foreign Affairs Committee when the World War actually started and soon thereafter became president of the Army Committee. In November, 1917, he again became prime minister and formed his "Victory Cabinet." His policy was to prosecute the war to a finish, a policy which was vigorously opposed by the former prime minister, Joseph Cailleaux, who advocated making not only peace but an alliance with Germany, and whose activities in that direction led in 1917 to his arrest, imprisonment and exile from France.

Clémenceau adopted drastic measures to turn all the resources of the country toward the prosecution of the war and was supported by the people as long as hostilities continued. Although he lost something of public confidence after the signing of the Armistice, he was the chief delegate of his country to the Peace Conference at Versailles in 1919 and presided over the conference. The following year he resigned and retired from public life. In 1919 an attempt upon his life was made by Emile Cottin, a young anarchist. Besides his journalistic work, he was a versatile writer of novels, plays and essays on philosophic and other subjects. He was a member of the French Academy and was honored by a doctor's degree from Oxford in 1921. In 1922 on the occasion of a visit to the United States he was received with marked honor. He died in 1929.

SAMUEL LANGHORNE CLEMENS (*Mark Twain*)   1835–1910

SAMUEL LANGHORNE CLEMENS, American humorist and novelist (better known under his pen name of Mark Twain) was born in Nov. 30, 1835 in Florida, Mo. His father removed to Hannibal, Mo., when the boy was four years old and died four years later. Young Clemens learned to set type on the Hannibal *Journal* as assistant to his brother, became a journeyman printer and worked in St. Louis, New York and Philadelphia. In 1851 he left his trade to become a pilot on the Mississippi River. At the outbreak of the Civil War he went to Nevada with his brother who had been given a political appointment there, prospected for gold, made a trip to the Sandwich Islands, and joined the staff of the Virginia City *Enterprise,* writing under the name of Mark Twain, which was a call used by the Mississippi pilots in taking soundings. He soon went to San Francisco and became a shining light among the group of writers gathered about the *Golden Era;* Bret Harte, Artemus Ward, Charles Warren Stoddard and others. His publication of *The Jumping Frog of Calaveras County* made the rounds of the newspapers of the country and brought fame to its author. He went East soon afterwards, gave his lecture on the Sandwich Islands at Cooper Institute in New York, and then made a trip to the Mediterranean and the Orient on a commission from the *Alta Californian* of San Francisco. This resulted in the writing of his first book, *Innocents Abroad,* which brought him fame on both sides of the Atlantic. In 1870 he married Olivia L. Langdon, settled in Elmira, N. Y., for a time, then in Buffalo and later moved to Hartford, Conn., where he lived for many years.

Roughing it, his second book of pioneering adventure, told in humorous fashion, was published in 1872. Two years later came a novel, *The Gilded Age,* written in collaboration with Charles Dudley Warner. *The Adventures of Tom Sawyer,* one of his most famous books, was published in 1875 and *A Tramp Abroad* was the result of a second trip to Europe in 1880. In 1882 appeared his story of early England, *The Prince and the Pauper,* followed by *Life on the Mississippi* and *The Adventures of Huckleberry Finn,* which is a sequel to *Tom Sawyer* and probably his most enduring book. In 1884 he became a partner and chief owner in the publishing house of Charles L. Webster & Co., and persuaded General Grant to write his memoirs, a work which made a fortune for the publishing firm and for Grant's family. Twain spent years of time and a vast amount of money and impoverished himself in an attempt to perfect a linotype machine. In 1889 appeared *A Connecticut Yankee in King Arthur's Court; The American Claimant* followed in 1892; *Pudd'nhead Wilson* two years later. He went abroad in 1891, living in Berlin and Florence, and in the latter city he wrote his *Personal Recollections of Joan of Arc.* After two years at home he set out on a lecture trip around the world, by means of which he was able to pay off the debts incurred by the failure of his publishing house and to reestablish his fortune. His experiences during this tour were embodied in *Following the Equator* (1897). He returned home in 1900 and lived in New York until 1906 when he removed to a country house, "Stormfield," which he had built at Reading, Conn.

His later books include *How to Tell a Story, The Man that Corrupted Hadleyburg, The Double-Barrelled Detective Story, Adam's Diary, What is Man, Christian Science, Captain Stormfield's Visit to Heaven, Is Shakespeare Dead* and *The Mysterious Stranger,* published after his death which took place at Reading April 2, 1910. He was buried at Elmira, N. Y., and was survived by one of his four daughters, Clara, who a short time before his death married Ossip Gabrilowitsch, famous Russian musician. Twain was honored with degrees by Yale, Oxford and other universities. His letters and portions of his *Autobiography* were published several years after his death.

Although best known for his exaggeratedly humorous writings, he showed a more serious side in his articles and speeches on various public questions during his later years.

CLEOPATRA   (?) 68 B. C.–30 B. C.

THE name of CLEOPATRA (klē ō pā'trà) is universally associated with the daughter of the Egyptian king Ptolemy Auletes, though there were other Egyptian queens of that name. She it was who became Cleopatra VI and is famed in history, story and song for her voluptuous beauty and undying charm. She was born about 68 B. C. and by the will of her father inherited the throne jointly with her brother, Ptolemy Dionysus (Ptolemy XIV), to whom she was promised in marriage, a custom not repugnant to the ancient Egyptians. At the time of her accession to the throne she was 17 and her brother some five or six years younger. Neither the marriage nor the royal partnership proved auspicious, for the youthful king drove his sister from the throne. Recruiting an army in Syria, she prepared to battle for her rights, but accomplished nothing by military means. A more potent instrumentality, however, intervened.

Julius Caesar, arriving propitiously at Alexandria, fell victim to her charms and readily gave her the benefit of his power and prestige, with the result that the young Egyptian king lost his life in the war which followed and Cleopatra was enthroned. She now married her brother, Ptolemy XV (a union said to have been limited to their governmental partnership) and went to Rome as the mistress of Caesar, to whom she bore a son, Caesarion. She remained in Rome until after Caesar was assassinated (44 B. C.) It is believed that she procured the death of her Egyptian husband and brother by poison. In any event, he died and she resumed her throne, conferring much authority on Caesarion. In the civil war ensuing upon the death of Caesar, Cleopatra maintained a tactful neutrality and Mark Antony required her to appear before him at Tarsus in Cilicia to explain her attitude. Her response was most effective. In a vessel sumptuously bedecked, she appeared garbed as the Venus Anadyomene and so captivated Antony that he was glad to be her willing slave thereafter. He accompanied her to Egypt where she lived as his mistress and bore him twins, Cleopatra Selene and Alexandria Helois. Duties of state required Antony to interrupt this prolonged armour; he returned to Rome and in the course of his sojourn there took to wife Octavia, sister of the emperor Augustus, but her beauty and unquestioned virtue did not suffice to alienate him permanently from his Egyptian charmer. In 36 B. C. he led an expedition into Parthia and asked Cleopatra to join him an Antioch. He was at first defeated, but finally triumphed and repaired to Alexandria where a festive celebration was held and he remained there with the Egyptian queen. He bestowed upon her and her children great estates which he had no right to dispose of. Upon this, and other accounts, he became the object of enmity in Rome, the disaffection culminating in a declaration of war against Cleopatra whose ally and adviser he was now thought to be. At her instigation he risked the great naval battle of Actium and when she fled with 60 ships he forgot all else and hastened after her.

When Octavianus appeared before Alexandria, Cleopatra surreptitiously entered into negotiations with him for her own safety. Enraged at her perfidy, Antony vowed revenge, but upon a report that she had killed herself, his infatuation set all other considerations at naught and he fell upon his own sword. Mortally wounded, he was still able to comprehend the news that the report of her death was false and he demanded to be carried into her presence and died in her arms. Octavianus, by artifice, took her prisoner. Again she invoked the charms which had proved so potent, but Octavianus was not susceptible. Fearing that he spared her life only that she might be taken to Rome as a trophy of his victory, she ended her glamorous career by taking poison. The world has accepted the fairly well-authenticated story that she caused an asp to bite her arm. She died in August, 30 B. C. Her body was buried beside that of Antony, and his divorced wife reared the children whom the Egyptian queen had borne him.

Much curiosity has been manifested in modern times about the beauty of this extraordinary woman; but there is only the circumstantial evidence of its effect. No authentic picture of her exists unless it be that upon the ancient coins of her realm, which is not enlightening. The consensus of thought is that she was large and of an imposing presence, but even for this there seems to be no dependable authority.

GROVER CLEVELAND   1837–1908

(STEPHEN) GROVER CLEVELAND, the twenty-second and twenty-fourth president of the United States, was born in Caldwell, N. J., March 18, 1837. When he was three years old his father, a Presbyterian minister, was called to Fayeteville, N. Y., where the son was educated in the village school, later attending an academy in Clinton. Left to his own resources by the death of his father, he became a bookkeeper and assistant teacher in the New York Institution for the Blind. Two years later, at the instance of his uncle, he settled in Buffalo, N. Y., studied law, and in 1859 was admitted to practice. In 1863 he became assistant district attorney for Erie County, in 1870 was elected sheriff, and later resumed his private practice. In 1881 he was nominated by the democratic party for mayor of Buffalo, and notwithstanding that the city was a republican stronghold, the reaction against long-continued political corruption carried him into office. He was bluntly honest and uncompromising and soon disclosed qualities which were to make him an outstanding figure in national politics. He reorganized the municipal government, put an end to corruption and made liberal use of the veto, to the consternation of interested politicians.

His fine character in public service was widely recognized and in 1882 he was elected governor, defeating his republican opponent, Charles J. Folger, by a majority of 192,850. His gubernatorial term was characterized by the same independence and zeal for good government and reform, but these qualities proved prejudicial to him with certain elements in his own party. It was characteristic of him to see his goal clearly and to proceed with a certain forthright heedlessness which caused dismay even among his friends and supporters. But no political influence could stem the tide which was bringing him into national prominence. When the democratic national convention met at Chicago in July 1884 he was the leading candidate on the first ballot, and in spite of the efforts of a minority of the delegates from his own state he received the nomination. His opponent was the brilliant republican leader, James G. Blaine, who was unacceptable to many in his own party and a large number of republican votes were thereby thrown to Cleveland. After a bitter contest he was elected, receiving 219 electoral votes against 182 for Blaine.

In June of the year following his inauguration he was married at the White House to Miss Frances Folsom. His uncompromising honesty and courageous independence soon became a byword. He gave his personal attention to the minutest details and accepted full responsibility for every official act. He refused to remove republicans from office without cause, an innovation in political policy which was not taken complacently by office seekers in his own party. Nor did the Grand Army take kindly his measures for correcting abuses in the pension system and its entire organization was aligned against him. His stand in favor of a low tariff antagonized the large manufacturers. In face of these prejudicial influences he applied his policies with unwavering firmness. He suppressed an insurrection in Panama and prevented a Mormon uprising in Utah, using the army in both emergencies. In the Canadian fisheries difficulty he threatened to prevent traffic from crossing the border and entering the United States except by American carriers. During his term the Interstate Commerce Commission was established and various other noteworthy measures were enacted, including the Chinese exclusion act, the anti-polygamy bill and the presidential succession bill. Four new states were admitted to the Union.

He was renominated in June 1888 but was defeated by the republican, General Benjamin Harrison, and took up his residence in New York City, where he resumed his legal practice. His national reputation and prestige did not subside, however, and he was again nominated at Chicago in June, 1892, amid scenes of the greatest excitement, constituting a glowing tribute to an ex-president who had reluctantly answered the second call of his party as well as that of multitudes of independent voters throughout the nation. His electoral vote was 277 against 145 for Harrison. In his second administration he revealed still more strikingly his courage and independence, but he frequently incurred the charge of stubbornness. He could not compromise, and few presidents have encountered stronger opposition to measures honestly conceived. He suffered the unpopularity which accrues from tactlessness and a certain arrogant disregard of the opinions of others. Instead of carrying out the policy of his predecessor for the annexation of Hawaii, he endeavored to restore its dethroned queen to power, a decidedly unpopular move, which failed. Much of his attention was given to the vexed question of national credit and to foreign relations, notably the Venezuelan boundary dispute with Great Britain looking to the safeguarding of American territorial rights, in which his courage and vigor in almost threatening war were successful in effecting a satisfactory adjustment. An income tax law, passed during his administration, was declared unconstitutional by the Supreme Court. In 1894 a railway strike affected the whole country and he applied his customary drastic policy of sending troops to crush the disorders. His administration, indeed, was crowded with matters of the keenest public interest, and his strong hand and unswerving resolve were continually manifested. At the expiration of his term he made his home in Princeton, N. J., occasionally lecturing at the university, of which he was a trustee. He became a trustee also of the Equitable Life Assurance Society. Until his death, on June 24, 1908, he maintained with gracious dignity the position of an ex-president, respected and beloved by the entire nation.

SAMUEL TAYLOR COLERIDGE   1772–1834

SAMUEL TAYLOR COLERIDGE (kōle'rĭj) won popular fame as the author of *The Ancient Mariner,* one of the most familiar poems in the English language. He was a scholar, poet, philosopher and critic; and the world is indebted to him for his profound and illuminating critical writings about Shakespeare which have made it all but impossible for the student and lover of the supreme dramatist to proceed with his study without the searching and guiding light of Coleridge. He has been called the father of modern literary criticism.

He was born at Ottery St. Mary, in Devonshire, England, where his father was a vicar, and was educated at Christ's Hospital where the daily companionship of the lovable Charles Lamb furnished beguilement during his arduous studies in classical literature and metaphysics. His devotion to study and his prodigious capacity for miscellaneous reading was not motivated by any special purpose in life and he is said to have been on the point of apprenticing himself to a shoemaker, an impulse which was happily checked by his teacher. By such a narrow margin was this splendid intellect saved for the cause of scholarship and literature. In 1791 he entered Jesus College, Cambridge, devoting himself to the study of classical literature and winning a prize for a Greek ode. His course at the university was cut short by a period of despondency caused by an inauspicious love affair and he indulged his mood by going to London and enlisting in the army under an assumed name. His intellectual character attracting the attention of a superior officer, his identity was revealed and his discharge was procured by his friends. He then went to Bristol where, falling in with kindred spirits of an adventurous and liberal bent, he participated in an enterprise for seeking pastoral ease and social peace in the wilds of America. The plan fell through for lack of money and Coleridge solaced himself by the publication of a volume of poems. In 1795 he and his friend, Robert Southey, married sisters and went to live in Somersetshire where Wordsworth made his home. Here, amid beautiful surroundings, he wrote *The Ancient Mariner* and the first part of *Christabel,* and occasionally preached to Unitarian congregations of which sect he was a member. In 1798 he visited Germany and studied at Gottingen, and on his return lived in the "lake country" where he and his two friends, Wordsworth and Southey, came to be known as the "lake poets." Notable among his works of that period was his translation of Schiller's *Wallenstein.* He also became associated with the *Morning Post,* contributing to it many essays on literature and politics. In 1804 he was appointed secretary to the governor of Malta and held this position for over a year. Returning to the more congenial field of letters, he delivered lectures on poetry and literature at the Royal Institute in London and was widely acclaimed as a critic and commentator. But he had, unhappily, acquired a taste for opium which his splendid mind was not able to overcome and it sapped his character and loosened his moral fibre. Leaving his wife and children in the care of the loyal Southey, he went to London where the balance of his life was passed with occasional visits to his beloved lake country.

Through the mire of German metaphysics, in which he was always interested, his noble genius gleamed with increasing fitfulness and his impressive plan for "reducing all knowledge into harmony" never reached the point of execution. His failing will power obstructed every noble conception until at last he ceased to write. But his conversational brilliance (requiring little concentration) continued to charm and edify his friends and he discoursed easily "on every subject human and divine." These colloquial treats became a sort of institution in his literary circle and the young flocked to hear him as they had flocked to listen to Socrates. To him they brought questions covering almost the whole range of human thought and listened, enthralled, to his casual commentary. His pitiful life ended April 25, 1834.

Coleridge's noble intellect found expression in numerous ways. *The Ancient Mariner* and *Kubla Khan* are marvels of haunting melody. No poet ever evolved more superb fantasies nor wrought our language into more exquisite forms of beauty. As a critic he stands almost supreme, differing from others by the flavor of philosophy which characterized all his critical writings. He dominated and influenced every Shakespearian commentator and some of his observations about the plays are classical in Shakespearian literature. He was the first to introduce German philosophy and literature to English-speaking countries and shares with Carlyle the distinction of exploring and popularizing this vast intellectual field.

CHRISTOPHER COLUMBUS   (?) 1451–1506

CHRISTOPHER COLUMBUS (the Latinized form of the Italian Colombo and the Spanish Colon) was born at or near Genoa in Italy. There has been much research and controversy in the attempt to fix the exact date of his birth—important only because everything is important about a name so illustrious. So high an authority as John Fiske fixes the limits at 1436–1446, but the year 1451 seems to be more generally accepted. There are few historical characters about whose early lives there have been such conflicting accounts. His father was a wool-comber; his mother's name was Susanna Fontanarosa. He is said to have attended school in Pavia where he discovered a taste for astronomy and cosmography. While still a youth he probably sailed on the Mediterranean, although some authorities deny this, as also his early education. He is known to have made, with others, a voyage to Chios about 1475. The following year he embarked for England on a merchantman, but the vessel was attacked and failed to reach its destination. Later he sailed to England and into the North Seas. He engaged in trade in Lisbon (1477) and visited Genoa two years later where he declared himself a citizen of that city and gave his age as 27. He is next heard of in Lisbon where (probably in 1480) he married Filipa Moniz Perestrello; within a year was born Diego, the only child of that marriage. Among the numerous legends of his early life which perplex the student, these are the bare facts.

At that time Lisbon was the centre of maritime activity, its water front filled with sailors, its learned circles engrossed with the study of maps, geography and the science of navigation. It is said that Columbus made maps for the support of his family. Here tradition has been busy, but one authentic fact is outstanding; his wife's mother gave him certain interesting papers which directed his thoughts to maritime exploration. He is thought to have made several short voyages, to the Azores and elsewhere. We know that at that time the dream of a western route to the Indies was in his mind. About 1482 he laid his scheme before John II of Portugal who rejected it on the report of scientific and nautical advisers. Making dishonest use of Columbus' detailed plan, however, he sent a ship to survey the proposed route, but its timid pilots were soon back in Lisbon ridiculing the project. Sometime during the progress of these activities, or perhaps later, Columbus' wife died and (probably 1484) he left Lisbon in disgust. He is believed by some authorities to have unsuccessfully presented his plan in the Republic of Genoa. Certain it is that he went to Spain. In 1485 he paused, weary and hungry it is said, at the gate of the Franciscan monastery, La Rabida, where the monks showed keen interest in his enterprise. Here he left his little son and went forth encouraged by the suggestions of his kindly hosts. It is related that the superior of the monastery, Juan Perez de Marchena, used his influence to procure for the hapless wayfarer favorable consideration by the Spanish sovereigns.

His success with Ferdinand and Isabella and the outfitting of the three little vessels famed in the world's history (the Santa María, the Pinta and the Niña) is well known. It was not achieved without discouraging delays. Only one of the ships had a deck; they were manned by 120 men. Columbus claimed as his reward that he be made high admiral and viceroy over all the lands he should discover, with a tenth part of the revenues which should accrue therefrom. On the 3rd of August, 1492, the little flotilla set sail from the bar of Saltes, near Palos. Pausing for a month at the Canary Islands he then started on Sept. 6 for unknown seas. His crew soon began to grow fearful and when their protests were unavailing, became sullen and threatening. But the intrepid explorer sailed on. On the 12th of October his perseverance was rewarded by the sight of land which proved to be one of the Bahama Islands. Here he reverently planted the cross, giving the island the name of San Salvador. Soon thereafter he discovered the islands of San Domingo and Cuba, on the former of which he started a colony which he called Hispaniola. Taking several Indians with him, he turned his prows homeward and reached Spain March 15, 1493, where he was received with the wildest joy. It would be impossible to exaggerate the sensation caused by his return and his report. He believed, of course, that he had discovered the Indies, little dreaming that two vast continents intervened.

In September of the same year he sailed from Cadiz on a second expedition with 17 ships and 1500 men. This resulted in the discovery of the Caribee Islands and Jamaica. He returned to Spain in 1496 to answer calumnies and charges which were easily disproved before his sovereigns and in 1498 sailed on his third voyage. Directing his course to the southward he discovered Trinidad and the mouth of the Orinoco river in South America. He then sailed for Hispaniola, where he found affairs in a state of disorder. The king's mind had again been poisoned against him; an officer named Bovadilla had been sent to supersede him and the unspeakable spectacle occurred of the discoverer of a new hemisphere being sent home in chains. There is no personal affront in recorded annals comparable with this outrage. Alarmed at the righteous anger of his subjects, Ferdinand disclaimed responsibility, but he made no amends to the illustrious adventurer.

Humiliated and disillusioned though he was, the spirit of adventure still triumphed and on May 9, 1502, with four ships and 150 men, the old navigator sailed on his fourth and last voyage, to seek a passage which he believed united the Atlantic and Pacific Oceans. The mutinous attitude of his men finally compelled the abandonment of this quest, and after many difficulties he returned to Spain. Isabella, his gracious patron, was dead and he could hope for nothing from Ferdinand. He died at Valladolid, Spain, in comparative poverty, on the 20th of May, 1506.

CONFUCIUS   551 B.C.–478 B.C.

CONFUCIUS (kŏn fū' shĭ ŭs) (K'ung-Fu-Tsze), the great moral teacher of China, was born in 551 B.C. at Ch'üeh village in the State of Lû, a part of the present province of Shan-tung. His father, who was a distinguished soldier, died when Confucius was three years old. The family lineage is traced through the dukes of Sung to the kings of the Shang, or Yin, dynasty. At the age of 19 Confucius married and a son Li and two daughters were born to him. At about the time of his marriage he was in charge of the public stores of grain and the public herds. It was not until 531 B.C. when he was 30 that he began to teach and thereafter instruction became his life work. He soon came to occupy a place of honor and his advice was often sought by princes of his own and neighboring provinces.

In 501 B.C. the Duke of Lû appointed Confucius governor of the town of Chung-tû, where his teachings soon brought about a miraculous reformation in the lives of the people. A year later he was made minister of works and soon afterwards minister of crime. For three years he was the idol of his people, but the prosperity of the state under his administration awoke the jealousy of neighboring provinces, which brought about a breach between Confucius and the Duke of Lû and resulted in his leaving the state in 497 B.C., not to return until 485 or 484. During his long absence he traveled through China, visiting many states, teaching in many temples, accompanied everywhere by a body of his disciples. He was recalled to Lû by a new duke, but instead of interesting himself again in politics, he spent his last years in collecting the ancient Chinese writings and in reforming the music to which the old Chinese odes were sung.

It was probably at this period of his retirement from public life that Confucius wrote the only classical work ascribed to him, the *Ch'un Ch'iû,* a history of the province of Lû, from 722 to 481 B.C. He died in his native province in 478 B.C., five years after his recall. Not long after his death his disciples collected many of his sayings and his rules of living, which are preserved in the *Confucian Analects*.

To the occidental and Christian mode of thought, Confucius was a teacher of a system of philosophy and conduct rather than the founder of a religion. His teachings often have the sanction of the Christian religion, however, even paralleling those of Christ, as in Confucius' maxim, "What you do not wish done to yourself, do not do to others." He did not teach belief in a personal God, but laid great stress upon obedience to parents and veneration of ancestors, and insisted upon the cultivation of the five virtues of politeness, truthfulness, integrity, kindliness and sagacity.

Confucianism has become the religion of countless millions of the yellow race and its teaching of practical morality helps them to live their lives with more justice and charity to their fellow-men than would have been likely without the Master's rules of conduct.

A temple was erected in his honor by Duke Ai (who was not a follower of Confucius' teachings) in order that sacrifices or offerings might be presented to China's great sage from generation to generation. Succeeding dynasties paid honor to him in titles and offerings and his lineal descendants, with the title of *kung* or duke, ranked next to the members of the imperial house. Under the Chinese Republic Confucianism is not a state religion but it nevertheless remains the foundation of the nation's ethical teaching. His disciples recorded that the Master's frequent themes of discourse were the Odes, the Book of History, and the maintenance of the rules of propriety.

CALVIN COOLIDGE 1872–1933

CALVIN COOLIDGE, the 30th president of the United States, was born at Plymouth, Vt., on July 4, 1872. He was descended from John Coolidge, an Englishman who settled at Watertown, Mass., about 1630, and whose numerous descendants, mostly farmers, spread into various parts of New England. About the time of the Revolution one branch of the family established itself in the little village of Plymouth Notch, in the Green Mountains of Vermont, and here five generations of the family were reared. John Coolidge, the father of the future president, was a farmer and general store-keeper besides holding various local offices, and was a colonel on the military staff of Gov. Stickney.

The son was reared in the simplest of surroundings. He spent much of his time in the ordinary work of the farm, but at eight years of age entered the district school and later attended academies in the towns of Ludlow and St. Johnsbury. His mother died when he was 12 years old. At 19 he entered Amherst College, graduating with high honors in 1895 in a class numbering several members who attained eminence. He was a serious-minded youth who cared little for athletics and the lighter side of college life, but his great interest in the history of his country and the long hours spent in absorbing its traditions served him well in later years. During his senior year he won a gold medal for an essay on *Principles Underlying the American Revolution*. He studied law, was admitted to the bar in 1897 and established a practice in Northampton, Mass. His sterling qualities led him to be chosen for various local offices including after a few years that of mayor where he was singularly successful in reducing taxes and the huge city debt. In 1912 he was sent to the state senate and served for four terms, rendering valuable service as a member of important committees and later as president of the body. During his first years in the senate he was able almost single-handed to adjust prolonged and violent labor troubles in the mill town of Lawrence and the state of Massachusetts owes to him much of its existing social and other reform legislation. In 1916 he was elected lieutenant-governor and in 1919 governor of his state.

He first came into national prominence through his prompt and vigorous handling of the Boston police strike in 1919, which had caused serious disorders and violence. Declaring that no right existed to strike against the public safety and that the striking officers were deserters from their duty, he called out the state troops to end the strike. Public opinion was strong in approval and he was reelected by a huge majority, including many democratic votes, due no doubt partly to President Wilson's publicly expressed commendation of his act. Popular admiration for this champion of law and order was shown by an attempt to nominate him for the presidency in 1920. Although this failed he was elected vice president and, contrary to precedent, was made an ex-officio member of the president's cabinet. On the death of President Harding in 1923, he succeeded to the presidency. The news of Harding's death in San Francisco reached him in the little farmhouse in Vermont where he was born and there, by the light of kerosene lamps, he took the oath of office at 2:47 A. M. on August 3rd, administered by his aged father who was a notary.

He carried on the general policies of his predecessor and exhibited great ability and courage in dealing with public questions. A marked feature of his administration was economy. He forced material reductions in income and other taxes, brought about drastic retrenchments in expenditures in all departments of the government; came into conflict with congress over a soldiers' bonus bill which was passed over his veto, and also with regard to immigration and other legislation. The famous "Teapot Dome" oil and other scandals which arose toward the end of 1923 embarrassed his administration but he was reelected in 1924 and continued his policy of thrift, conservatism, wise legislation and the fostering of amicable diplomatic relations.

He refused to consider renomination in 1927 and at the conclusion of his term retired to his home in Northampton where he spent the remaining years of his life in literary pursuits and in attention to various business and philanthropic interests, in addition to his private law business. He was given the degree of LL.D. by a number of colleges, was a trustee of Dartmouth College and member of a committee to administer a $6,000,000 fund bequeathed to hospitals and other institutions. He wrote his autobiography in 1929 and published *Have Faith in Massachusetts* (1919) and *The Price of Freedom* (1924) which is a collection of his own articles and addresses.

He died at his home in Northampton on Jan. 5, 1933. In 1905 he had married Grace A. Goodhue. Of their two sons, John and Calvin, the younger died in 1924, at the age of 16.

JAMES FENIMORE COOPER   1789–1851

JAMES FENIMORE COOPER, author of the famous *Leatherstocking Tales,* was born at Burlington, N. J., Sept. 15, 1789, the eleventh child in a family of twelve. Having studied under a private tutor in his early youth, he entered Yale University at the age of 13, but neglected his studies in favor of outdoor pursuits and was expelled during his third year. As a preparation for a naval career, he next enlisted in the merchant marine service as a sailor before the mast. West Point Academy was not then in existence, but he was later granted a midshipman's commission and remained for several years at sea, absorbing the romance of nautical life which afterward played no inconsiderable part in his lusty stories of adventure. In 1811 he married a young woman of a Tory family which event, occurring almost simultaneously with his resignation from the navy on the eve of a naval war, subjected him to unfavorable comment at a time when the name of Tory signified disloyalty. For one reason or another, caustic criticism pursued this independent and outspoken man throughout his life and was prejudicial to his justly won fame as an author.

The first few years of his decidedly happy married life were passed at his wife's home in Westchester County, N. Y., where his six children were born and where he devoted himself to farming. A familiar and accepted story of his entering the field of authorship is that while listening to his wife's reading of a novel he casually observed that he could write a better one himself, and was thereupon encouraged to try. The outcome was *Precaution,* a work of indifferent merit, published in 1821. In the following year appeared *The Spy* and his reputation was assured. In quick succession followed *The Pioneers, The Pilot, The Last of the Mohicans* (considered his masterpiece), *The Red Rover, The Prairie, Water Witch, The Pathfinder, The Deerslayer, The Two Admirals, Wing and Wing,* a history of the American navy and other less important works.

In 1826 he visited Europe and, during his seven years residence there, was much honored in distinguished circles. It was a time when the utmost tact was required by prominent Americans on their foreign travels; and Cooper was without tact. The grace and humor by which Washington Irving charmed the sensitive English were unknown to him. He proclaimed the glories of democracy rather too freely and to his own prejudice. Shortly after returning to the United States in 1838 he went to live at Cooperstown, near Lake Otsego in New York, where his father had built a "manor house" on his extensive estate. In that same beautiful country young Fenimore had lived in a simpler abode when a boy. The region is still reminiscent of the noted author who henceforth made it his home and there he died on Sept. 14, 1851.

Personally Cooper was blunt and pugnacious. As he had scrupled not to extoll American institutions while in Europe, so also he scrupled not to denounce the faults of his countrymen. In consequence he aroused antagonism. He was unsparing in his criticism of New England; his predilection for the Episcopal church exceeded the bounds of discretion in his speech and writings, and he was much given to expressing his opinions and preferences in the superlative degree. He quarreled with publishers and others and engaged in numerous lawsuits, appearing as his own attorney. It must be admitted that in these contests, which he seemed to relish, he frequently came off triumphant. People were amused or annoyed at the exhibitions, according to their own natures. Unquestionably his popularity as a novelist was affected.

He has been called "the American Scott" with an appropriateness not usual in that somewhat overdone form of compliment to American writers. Like the author of Waverly, he was amazingly prolific, but his works are loosely constructed and carelessly written. Of art, in the latter-day conception of that word, he had none. He was distressingly leisurely and discursive. But the substance was there and it was enough to carry him to literary triumph despite his defects. The strongest qualities contributing to his success were his graphic descriptive powers and his thorough knowledge of the life and scenes which he depicted, whether it were the boundless ocean or the wide prairie, together with a very real skill (not always apparent) in the delineation of character. Leather-stocking, Harvey Birch, Long Tom Coffin and Natty Bumppo stand as vivid proofs of this. His numerous Indian characters have fared rather poorly at the hands of critics, but it has been urged that students of that race give a better account of his keenness of observation and accuracy of depiction.

NICHOLAS COPERNICUS   1473–1543

Nicolaus Koppernigk or Nicholas Copernicus (kō pēr' nĭ kŭs), who originated the modern theory of astronomy, was born on Feb. 19, 1473, at Thorn, in Prussian Poland, the son of a wholesale trader, a Germanized Slav, and of a German woman. He was brought up by his uncle, Lucas Watzelrode, who later became Bishop of Ermeland. In 1491 he became a student at Cracow University, studying mathematics, optics and perspective, and acquired some skill in painting. At the age of 23 he went to Bologna to study canon law and also attended lectures on astronomy given by Domenico Maria Novara. In 1497 he was appointed canon at Frauenberg, the cathedral city of Ermeland. At Rome in 1500 he gave lectures on astronomy and observed an eclipse of the moon. Obtaining further leave of absence from his duties at Frauenberg, he took up the study of medicine at Padua, remaining there until 1505. Returning to Poland then, he became physician to his uncle, the Prince-Bishop of Ermeland, at the episcopal palace of Heilsberg, and following the death of the Bishop in 1512, Copernicus returned to Frauenberg. He never took orders, but during the administrative and political upheavals that followed he acted as commissary of the diocese, bailiff, military governor, judge, and his medical skill was always at the service of the poor. In 1522 he laid before the Diet of Graudenz a plan for the reform of the currency.

Amid his many civil, religious and political duties, Copernicus found time to elaborate the system of astronomy which came to be known as the Copernican system; that is, that the earth and other planets revolve about the sun. Earlier astronomers (notably Pythagoras) had formed some general idea of this fact, but it remained for Copernicus to produce definite calculations to demonstrate the truth of the theory.

He outlined his great work at Heilsberg, and at Frauenberg, with such scanty means and instruments as were at his disposal, he tested his theory by observation. He had returned from Italy with a strong conviction of the correctness of the heliocentric theory of the universe. The book in which he set forth his arguments and proofs was completed in 1530, and his theory began to be circulated through the manuscript of a *Commentariolus,* or brief summary, written by Copernicus himself in that year.

Johann Albrecht Widmanstadt lectured upon it in Rome; Clement VII approved of it and Cardinal Schönberg sent to Copernicus a formal demand for its publication in full. The author did not consent to this until 1540, and then only after the prolonged importunities of friends and of his chief disciple, George Joachim Rheticus, who printed a preliminary account of the Copernican theory in the *Narratio Prima* (Danzig, 1540), at the same time sending to the press Copernicus' complete exposition in a treatise entitled *De Revolutionibus Orbium Coelestium* (1543). The first printed copy of the book reached Frauenberg only a short time before the death of Copernicus. Toward the end of 1542 he had suffered a stroke of apoplexy and paralysis and he died on May 24, 1543.

Copernicus had dedicated his book to Paul III. An anonymous preface had been slipped into the work by Andreas Osiander, for the purpose of disarming prejudice, insisting upon the purely theoretical character of Copernicus' reasonings and observations, but Copernicus does not seem to have been aware of this. The trigonometrical section of the book had been published as a separate treatise in 1542, under the direction of Rheticus. Copernicus published but one work of his own accord—a Latin version of the Greek epistles of Theophylact, in 1509.

HERNANDO CORTÉS   1485–1547

HERNANDO CORTÉS (kôr tās'), a brilliant Spanish soldier who conquered and despoiled Mexico and won many new provinces for his king in the new world, was born sometime in the year 1485 in Medellín, Estremadura. After studying law at the University of Salamanca, he became bent upon a career of adventure, sailed for San Domingo in 1504 and accompanied

Velásquez on his expedition to Cuba, where he was made alcalde (or chief judge) of Santiago. Velásquez placed him in command of an expedition to conquer Mexico and in November of 1518 he set sail with ten ships, 600 foot soldiers, 18 horsemen and some artillery. Velásquez wished to cancel his appointment almost at once, but Cortés refused to obey the orders superseding him.

He reached Mexico on March 4, 1519, and took possession of the town of Tabasco. The natives regarded the Spaniards as gods and sent them presents. Cortés founded Vera Cruz, had himself elected captain-general of the new colony, and scuttled his ships in order to prevent his dissatisfied force from returning to Cuba. He then set out for the interior of the country and subdued the warlike inhabitants of Tlascala, who thenceforth became his faithful allies, sending 600 of their native soldiers with him against their enemy, Montezuma, the Aztec chief.

His forces escaped an ambuscade at Cholula, and on Nov. 8, 1519, he reached Montezuma's capital, situated in a great salt lake with three long causeways leading to it, equipped with drawbridges. Tales of his might had preceded him and, believing the newcomer to be a descendant of the sun, Montezuma received him with great honor and Cortés fortified himself in one of the palaces. A small band of Spaniards had been left in Vera Cruz and were attacked by Aztecs there under one of Montezuma's men. The white men were victorious but several of their number were killed and the head of one of them was sent to Mexico, Montezuma's capital. This was sufficient to destroy the belief of the natives in the immortality of the white men and Cortés, finding his position dangerous, went to the palace, seized Montezuma, demanded that the men who had attacked Vera Cruz be turned over to him and had them burned before the palace gate. Montezuma, in irons, was forced to acknowledge the sovereignty of Charles V and to ransom himself for 100,000 ducats in gold and jewels.

Learning that Velásquez had sent a force under Pánfilo de Narvaez to deprive him of his command, Cortés left 200 men in Mexico and marched against Narvaez whom he defeated. During his absence the Mexicans had revolted and he returned to find a demoralized city. At his order Montezuma attempted to quiet the people and was killed. Cortés was forced to withdraw from the city which he did with the loss of most of his men and all of his artillery.

He did not, however, relinquish his determination to conquer Mexico. After six days of retreat, enduring great hardships, he was attacked on the plains of Otumba. He defeated the Mexicans decisively, recruited more natives from Tlascala, subdued the neighboring provinces and marched back against Mexico City. It was stubbornly defended, but capitulated on Aug. 13, 1521, after having been practically destroyed; some 50,000 natives had been killed.

Cortés' fame caused Charles V, in deference to public opinion, to appoint him governor of Mexico and name him Marquis of Oaxaca (1529). His harsh rule led to a new revolt, which he crushed with great cruelty. Jealous of his fame and popularity, the court at Madrid seized his property and imprisoned his retainers. Cortés returned to Spain to appeal to the Emperor. He was received with honor, but went back to Mexico with diminished authority and this division of powers frustrated his later enterprises. He discovered Lower California, returned again to Spain, where he was received coldly, accompanied the forces sent against the pirates of Algiers (1541) and died neglected near Seville on Dec. 2, 1547. His body was taken to Mexico in 1562 and finally deposited in Mexico City.

THOMAS CRANMER   1489–1556

THOMAS CRANMER, reformer in the English church, and the first Archbishop of Canterbury to embrace protestantism, was born on July 2, 1489, at Aslacton in Nottinghamshire. At 14 he entered Jesus College, Cambridge, where he obtained a fellowship in 1510. He was a diligent student and from early youth was particularly interested in the ancient languages, the Scriptures and the writings of Erasmus, Luther and other theologians. He sacrificed his fellowship at the age of 23 in order to marry, but upon the death of his wife a year later it was restored to him and in 1523 he took orders and became a lecturer on theology. Some six years later when the plague was raging in Cambridge he took refuge with two of his pupils at Waltham. While there he met Fox and Gardiner (afterwards bishops of Hereford and Winchester) and through them became interested in the desire of King Henry VIII to be freed from Catherine of Aragon. Henry eagerly welcomed his suggestion to submit the question of the legality of this marriage to the universities instead of relying upon churchly authority. He instructed Cranmer to write a treatise embodying his views for presentation to the European universities, made him a royal chaplain and archdeacon of Taunton and in 1530 he was sent on a special mission to Rome in connection with the divorce. Two years later he went to Germany on an embassy to the emperor. While there he married a niece of the German reformer, Osiander. He was summoned back to England to become archbishop of Canterbury on the death of Warham, a post which he accepted with reluctance. Shortly thereafter, in May,

1533, he declared the marriage with Catherine null and void and proclaimed the validity of the king's union with Anne Boleyn, which had already taken place. In September he stood as godfather to Anne's child, the future Queen Elizabeth.

In the swift marital changes which followed he played a part not very creditable. He annulled the marriage to Anne in 1536, but did not favor her condemnation and interceded with the king for her and for others. His share in the divorce of Anne of Cleves four years later was less prominent, although he presided over an assemblage of church dignitaries who gave their approval to the marriage. In matters of religious reform, also, he was subservient to the king to whom he too often subordinated his own judgment and convictions. He aided Henry in restricting the powers of the pope in England and, less actively in suppressing the monasteries. Both were drifting toward protestantism and after Henry's death in 1547 Cranmer advanced more swiftly in that direction. He encouraged the translation of the Bible and ordered a copy of it placed in every church; substituted the communion for the mass and instituted many other reforms. He officiated at the coronation of Henry's ten year old son, Edward VI, being himself one of a council of 16 regents, designated by Henry, of whom the Duke of Somerset became lord protector and actual ruler during the young king's short reign. Henry had provided for his daughter Mary's accession in the event of Edward's death and Cranmer had pledged his support, but at the death of Edward in 1553 he was persuaded to consent to the raising of Lady Jane Grey to the throne. Public support lacking for this usurpation, the catholic Mary became queen, whereupon Cranmer was ordered to confine himself to his palace at Lambeth. Realizing her personal as well as religious enmity toward him because of his share in the disgrace of her mother (Catherine of Aragon) friends urged him to flee, but he refused and in September was ordered to the Tower, the immediate pretext being his pronouncement against the mass which had been reestablished after the accession of Mary. He was tried on a charge of heresy, condemned to death, excommunicated and deposed from his high office with humiliating ceremonies. In the hope of saving his life he was persuaded to recant, but his courage returned and at the time when he was to proclaim his recantation publicly, he avowed his repentance for his cowardice and restated his true beliefs. In March, 1556, he was burned at the stake, meeting death with more resolution and fortitude than had characterized his life.

Although weak in moral purpose, he nevertheless rendered valuable service to the cause of the Reformation. He was a master of English prose and the 42 Articles of Edward VI were almost entirely his work. He revised the creed, prepared a litany and a catechism and published

A Defense of the True and Catholic Doctrine of the Sacrament. Although naturally tolerant according to the standards of that age, and opposed to persecution, he admitted that persecution and even death were justified for heretics, and himself condemned more than one person to the flames.

OLIVER CROMWELL   1599–1658

OLIVER CROMWELL, Lord Protector of England, was born at Huntingdon, England, April 25, 1599. His father was a country gentleman in good circumstances—son of Sir Henry Cromwell of Hinchinbrook. Many authorities disregard the persistent allegation that the great protector was distantly related on his mother's side to the house of Stuart; an ironical fact if true, considering the fate of Charles I at Cromwell's hands. So dependable an authority as Hume gives some credence to this report. Of the early life of Cromwell little is known. We know he attended Cambridge and that upon the death of his father he returned home to assume the management of family affairs. The numerous tales of his dissolute habits in early life are probably unwarranted, certainly exaggerated. It is probable, also, that this great Puritan protested too much about his sins. He was always the victim of slander by royalists. In August, 1620, he married the daughter of Sir James Bourchier, of London, which somewhat discredits the reports as to his vulgar origin and lowly social status which were circulated by his detractors during his life and have been perpetuated by some historians. He soon associated himself with the Puritans and became influential among them.

In 1628 he was elected to parliament, where his outspoken denunciations of "popery" were instrumental in bringing about his dismissal, with others, at the instance of the intolerant monarch. For ten years he devoted himself to farming, manifesting meanwhile a lively interest in public affairs. Naturally devout, he became progressively more religious, although not intolerant. In 1640 he was sent to parliament for the town of Cambridge. A glimpse of him at that time, afforded by Sir Philip Warwick, is interesting. He wore "a plain cloth suit which seemed to have been made by an ill country tailor; his linen was plain and not very clean . . . His hat was without a hatband; his stature was of good size; his sword stuck close to his side; his countenance swollen and reddish; his voice sharp and untunable; and his eloquence full of fervor." Sir Philip adds significantly, "It lessened much my reverence unto that great council, for this gentleman was very much hearkened unto." The great pro-

faithlessness

tector was not prepossessing, but he was commanding and forceful; people listened to him and respected him.

When the king's perfidy had destroyed the last hope of peaceable adjustment with parliament, Cromwell was among the first to offer his aid in defence of the state. In 1642 he moved in parliament for permission to raise two companies of volunteers in Cambridge, having previously at his own expense procured the necessary arms. In the following month he seized the magazine in Cambridgeshire and prevented the royalists from carrying off the valuable plate which it contained. As captain of a troop of horse, he soon revealed military genius of the first order. Promoted to the rank of colonel, and then to lieutenant-general, he distinguished himself on the bloody field of Marston (July 2, 1644) and in the second battle of Newbury (Oct. 27, 1644). His outspoken complaint in parliament helped to bring about the reorganization of the army with Fairfax as general and himself commanding the right wing. It was largely because of his military vigor and efficiency that the king's forces were routed at the battle of Naseby (June, 1645). The royalists in the West were now speedily reduced, Bristol was stormed and Charles, in his extremity, escaped, was recaptured and fell into the hands of the parliamentary commissioners, by whom on Cromwell's order he was, given in custody of the army in June, 1647. Again he escaped (November, 1647) and was again retaken. At this time the country was in a critical condition. The Welch had risen in insurrection, a Scotch army threatened in the North, the royalist element in Ireland was active. Firm and prompt action alone could avert anarchy, and Cromwell was not afraid to employ it. Everywhere his strong arm was successful; at Preston Moor the Scotch were badly defeated and upon his return to London the Presbyterians, who were still blindly temporizing with the king, were driven out.

In Cromwell's thought but one measure afforded hope of peace, and he did not scruple to act firmly for Enlgand's safety. In January, 1649, the king was tried, condemned and executed. The House of Lords was then speedily abolished. Cromwell now became a prominent member of the new council of state; and in the army, although only a lieutenant-general, he had greater influence than the commander-in-chief. Proceeding to Ireland, he subdued an uprising there and then turned his attention to Scotland. The Long Parliament had degenerated into the "Rump Parliament" with but a few members and its conduct of the government, in that time of stress and peril, was necessarily unsatisfactory. Cromwell therefore dissolved it (April, 1653) and although, with the cooperation of the non-conformist churches, another body was assembled, known as the Nominated or "Barebones" Parliament, it was so radical and extreme in its measures that it was shortly overthrown and in December of that year, under the authority of the "Instrument of Government," he became the sole ruler of the Commonwealth with the title of Lord Protector. From time to time he summoned parliaments, dismissing them at pleasure and they were uniformly subject to his will. His domestic policy, however, was just and liberal and conducive to national prosperity, while his foreign policy secured for England a position more commanding than she had ever before known. Few rulers have been so feared and respected in other lands. Under his rule swift retribution followed any injury to British subjects, wherever perpetrated, and religious persecutors on the Continent stayed their work of bigotry and bloodshed under stern warning from the Lord Protector.

He died on the 3rd of September, 1658, and was appropriately laid to rest in Westminster Abbey. On the anniversary of the birth of Charles I in 1661, however, Cromwell's and other graves were violated and the mouldering bodies were dragged forth and hanged at Tyburn.

MARY ANN EVANS CROSS (*George Eliot*)   1819–1880

GEORGE ELIOT was the pen name of Mary Ann (or Marian) Evans, novelist and one of the most intellectual of English women. She was the youngest daughter of Robert Evans, a Warwickshire land-agent of Welsh ancestry, and was born near Nuneaton, Warwickshire, on Nov. 22, 1819. The family moved to the farm of Griff four months after her birth and here she passed twenty-one years. At the age of five she was sent to school at Attleboro and later to Nuneaton. From her thirteenth to her sixteenth year she spent at Coventry and became deeply religious. In 1836 she lost her mother to whom she was devotedly attached. The following year her elder sister married and she then took entire charge of her father's household, studying German, Italian and music under a tutor. Following the marriage of her brother Isaac in 1841 and his taking over of the Griff farm, she went with her father to Coventry. Here she became acquainted with Charles Bray, a philosophical writer of the time, and his brother-in-law, Charles Hennell, author of *An Enquiry Concerning the Origin of Christianity*. She became a convert to their views and her relations with her father were nearly broken off because of what he regarded as her renunciation of Christianity. In 1844 she took over from Mrs. Hennell the task of translating Strauss' *Life of Christ* which was published in 1846.

After her father's death in 1849 she went abroad with Mr. and Mrs. Bray and upon her return to London in March, 1850, began to write for the *Westminster Review,* becoming assistant editor late in 1851, and shortly afterwards translated Feuerbach's *Essence of Christianity,* which was published under her own name as translator. Through this connection she became acquainted with Herbert Spencer, George Henry Lewes and others. There followed an increasing intimacy with Lewes who was separated from his wife although circumstances made a divorce impossible, and from 1854 until his death Miss Evans and Lewes lived together in what both regarded as a true, although not a legal, marriage.

They went to Weimar, where Lewes wrote his *Life of Goethe,* and then after visiting Berlin returned to London. It was largely due to the urging of Lewes that Miss Evans entered the field of novel writing. In 1857 she first adopted the name of "George Eliot" in connection with the publication of *The Sad Fortunes of the Rev. Amos Barton* in *Blackwood's Magazine.* Its unusual merit aroused immediate attention and the *nom de plume* was used throughout the rest of her life. There followed *Mr. Gilfill's Love Story* and *Janet's Repentance* which were afterwards published in a single volume as *Scenes of Clerical Life;* and then the first of her great novels, *Adam Bede* (1859) which met with instant success and has held its place as one of her most popular tales. *The Mill on the Floss* followed in 1860; then *Silas Marner,* which is perhaps her most artistic work; *Romola,* a story of Savonarola and his times, in 1863; *Felix Holt* in 1866, and George Eliot had come to be ranked among the greatest novelists of the age.

Several poems of high merit were published about this time; *The Spanish Gypsy, Agatha, The Legend of Jubal* and *Armgart,* which attracted considerable critical and popular attention. In 1871–72 appeared *Middlemarch, A Study of Provincial Life,* which ranks high among British novels of the nineteenth century. *Daniel Deronda* followed in 1876, but failed to arouse the public response that had been evoked by the earlier novels. *The Impressions of Theophrastus Such* (1879) was a collection of her earlier miscellaneous essays.

Following the death of Lewes on Nov. 28, 1878, George Eliot became a prey to melancholy, having for so long a time been dependent wholly upon him for affection and support, but on May 6, 1880, she married John Walter Cross, a merchant some years her junior and an old friend of her own and of Lewes. Their married life lasted only a few months. George Eliot died in Cheyne Walk, Chelsea, on Dec. 22, 1880, and was buried in Highgate Cemetery, next to the grave of Lewes.

Throughout her work is seen the evidence of her great store of scientific knowledge, her close study of the everyday life about her, and her deep understanding of human nature. Her delineations of country life and people show great insight and sympathy. In 1885 Cross published a *Life* of George Eliot as unfolded in her letters and journals.

PIERRE AND MARIE CURIE   1859–1906   1867–1934

PIERRE AND MARIE CURIE (kụ′ rē′) were co-discoverers of radium.

Pierre Curie was born in Paris in 1859, the son of a well-known physician and scientist. Becoming a physician himself he early developed a penchant for independent research and contributed much to the existing knowledge of physical science. In 1895 he became professor of physics at the university in Paris and later in that year married Marie Sklodowska who had been one of his pupils. She was eight years his junior and was the youngest of the five children of Ladislas Sklodowska, a professor of physics and mathematics in Warsaw, Poland, where she was born on Nov. 7, 1867. Her mother was the head of a high school for girls. The intellectual heritage of the family bore abundant fruit. A sister and brother achieved distinction in the field of medicine and Marie became probably the world's most famous woman scientist. Although of the landed proprietor class of Poland, the family circumstances were such that soon after her graduation at 15 from a girl's school she became governess in a private family, but continued her studies although she had not decided to what career she wished to devote her life. Poland was then under Russian rule which provided no system of education for the Polish children and she organized a class for them to which she gave much time. Becoming convinced that her greatest interests lay in physics and mathematics, she devoted herself to those subjects, working in a small laboratory in Warsaw and always encouraged and inspired by her father. In 1891 she entered the university at Paris from which she was graduated two years later.

The brief married life of Dr. and Mme. Curie was singularly happy and was devoted chiefly to the scientific studies in which both were so keenly interested. In 1896, after watching the work of Henri Becquerel who discovered the rays radiating from uranium, they undertook scientific investigations of various minerals, particularly pitchblende, and in 1898 discovered a new radioactive element which they named polonium in honor of Mme. Curie's native land. In December of the same year they made their much more startling discovery of radium. Important as this was, there remained years of study and toil before the new element could be put to practical use and its properties ascertained. Working with meagre equipment and under tremendous handicaps, the devoted pair gave themselves to this labor with the result that in 1902 much valuable information as to the character of radium was made public. A year later the Nobel prize in physics was awarded jointly to Dr. and Mme. Curie and Becquerel. In 1903 Mme. Curie, who had taught in a normal school for girls at Sèvres, became a doctor of physical science and later lecturer in the university at Paris. The following year a chair of physics was created at the Sorbonne for Dr. Curie and he was made a member of the Institute of France. In April, 1906, he was killed by an accident on a Paris street.

Despite this crushing blow, Mme. Curie soon resumed her scientific work and in 1908 she was appointed to succeed her husband at the Sorbonne. No other woman in France had ever been honored with a professorship at the university and the occasion of her first lecture was marked by a distinguished gathering which included the president of France, the members of the French cabinet and many leading scientists and notables from other lands. In 1911 she was herself the recipient of a second Nobel prize. Numerous other honors were accorded her by many countries and she was elected a member of the Academy of Sciences in Paris—the first woman to be so honored. She made many other valuable contributions to scientific knowledge and during the World War devised a radiograph apparatus for the examination of wounds, which saved countless lives through the prompt location of bullets and fragments of shell. In 1921 she visited the United States and was presented with a gram of radium which had been purchased by a popular subscription of $200,000 raised by the women of America as it had been learned that her work was greatly hampered by the lack of sufficient radium to carry on her experiments. In 1929 she again visited America and a second gram of radium was given her to be presented to the Radium Institute which had been established in her native city of Warsaw.

Almost to the end of her life she continued her work, despite a malady which she knew was being aggravated by the prolonged and arduous hours of work in her laboratory while she sought new discoveries. She died on July 4, 1934, in a sanitarium in the Alps where she had spent the last week of her life.

She had two daughters, one of whom, Mme. Irene Curie-Joliet, had collaborated with her mother during the later years as co-director of the Curie Laboratory in Paris.

DANTE ALIGHIERI   1265–1321

DANTE ALIGHIERI (dän'tä ä lē gǐ ä'rǐ), author of the *Divine Comedy,*
was incomparably the greatest Italian poet; his is one of the outstanding
names in the literature of the world. A solemn and lonely figure he was,
standing in awful solitude in the surrounding darkness of the Middle
Ages. Out of his sad soul came one immortal song of indescribable power
and beauty. In the category of poetic genius he stands almost supreme.
He was born in Florence, in the year 1265. There is much uncertainty
about his early years. By his own account his family was of high standing
in the city. He was still a child when his father died and his mother, who
was deeply concerned for his education, sought counsel of the great statesman and poet, Brunetto Latini, who directed the youth's training. He is
thought to have later studied philosophy at Bologna and Padua, and
theology at Paris. According to Boccaccio, he visited England. Whatever
his studious pursuits, we know that he served in the Florentine army
and was present at the taking of the fortress of Caprona in 1290. It is
known that he occupied several government posts and was finally chosen
one of the Priori, a position of the highest dignity.

Intense factional strife was rampant in Florence owing to the bitter
differences of the two elements in the Guelph party (i.e., the Neri and
the Bianchi). The question of Italian independence and home rule was
involved, but it is impossible to set forth briefly the intimate details of
these bitter contests. In connection with this turmoil Dante was sent,
probably in 1301, to intercede with Pope Boniface VIII in an effort to
terminate the high-handed policy of Charles of Naples in Florence, and
to counteract the representatives of the ultra-Guelph partisans (the
"blacks"), who had flocked to the Vatican with their complaints and protestations. The final outcome of these complicated disturbances and pleas
to the Pope was that the Bianchi, of which Dante was a member, were
completely subjugated, their property confiscated and many of them
banished. Among these was Dante; he went forth and never again visited
his native city. Carlyle says there is a record in the Florence archives doom-
ing Dante, wheresoever caught, to be burned alive.

From that time he was a lonely wanderer, visiting many places and
availing himself of the hospitality of many who pitied him and were glad
to patronize his sombre genius. He visited Arezzo, Padua, Verona. His
sad face, "the mournfullest face ever painted," was seen in many places,
in ducal palaces where he sat brooding, in highways and byways, dreaming and preoccupied. It was in these wanderings that he conceived and

worked out his transcendent work, The *Divine Comedy*. Another circumstance contributed to the pensiveness and sorrow of his great soul. At a festive party, early in life, he had seen Beatrice Portinaci, then but eight years old, daughter of a wealthy citizen. Though he was himself but a year or two older than she, there entered his heart a love for her, pure, chaste and tender, which thereafter colored and softened his whole existence. Beatrice married a nobleman, Simone de Bardi, and died while she was still young. Dante himself later married a young woman named Gemma Donita, by whom he is thought to have had four children. She is not known to have accompanied him in his long exile.

The closing years of his life were passed at Ravenna under the protection of Guido Novello da Polenta, where he is said to have been treated with great consideration. While on a mission to Venice for his princely host, he was taken ill and became progressively worse upon his return. He died on the 14th of September, 1321.

The *Divine Comedy,* although not his only work, is his masterpiece. A full consciousness of its miraculous power and of the innumerable problems, material and spiritual, with which it grapples is hardly to be derived by a first reading. There are no words to describe its greatness as an intellectual and imaginative achievement. The work depicts a vision with such completeness of detail and burning intensity of imagination as can hardly be duplicated in all literature. In this vision the poet is conducted first by Virgil (as the personification of human reason) through hell and purgatory. He is then led by the beloved Beatrice (personifying revealed truth) and finally by St. Bernard, through the several heavens, where he beholds the triune God. The work first appeared under the simple title of *Commedia;* the word *Divina,* added by an admiring world, is to be understood as complimentary rather than descriptive.

Half a century after Dante's death the Florentine republic set apart an annual sum for public lectures intended to elucidate the great work of the world poet whom she had so shamefully banished.

CHARLES DARWIN   1809–1882

CHARLES ROBERT DARWIN, the great English naturalist whose fame has become universal because of the theory of evolution with which his name is associated, was born at Shrewsbury, England, on the 12th of February, 1809. No attempt can here be made to give even the most cursory outline of Darwinism, so-called, which has revolutionized scientific and religious thought, and this sketch must be limited to the facts in the life of this outstanding figure of the 19th century. He was the son of Dr. Robert W. Darwin, F.R.S., and grandson of Erasmus Darwin, natural philosopher, physician and poet. His mother was a daughter of Josiah Wedgewood, manufacturer of the famous pottery so highly prized by collectors. He attended the public school in his native town, and after two terms at Edinburgh university became a student at Christ's College, Cambridge, where, in 1831, he took his degree of B.A. At that time the British government was preparing to send a vessel (H.M.S. *Beagle;* Captain Fitzroy R.N.) into South American waters and thence around the world, on a cruise of scientific exploration. Henslow, the distinguished mineralogist and botanist, who had been one of Darwin's instructors, urged his appointment as naturalist on the expedition, and in this capacity the future discoverer of the principle of natural selection became one of the party whose exhaustive and prolonged survey on the ship now famed in scientific annals lasted from 1831 to 1836.

He returned with an immense amount of data, part of which was embodied in his work published in 1839, *Journal of Researches into the Geology and Natural History of the Various Countries visited by H.M.S. Beagle.* His next work, *Zoology of the Voyage of H.M.S. Beagle,* with many notes and introduction, was published in 1843. Other works resulting from this cruise were *The Structure and Distribution of Coral Reefs; Geological Observations on Volcanic Islands; Geological Observations on South America,* and his *Monograph of the Cirripedia,* published in 1851–53. These works won for him high standing in scientific circles, but no one dreamed (perhaps least of all himself) that within a comparatively short time his name would be a household word, that the whole scientific fraternity would hail him as the most original thinker and investigator of his time, while multitudes of others would speak of him with indignation and protest.

In his quiet country home near Beckenham, in Kent, he was deeply engrossed with the study of the principles of natural selection, by which he accounted for the infinite variety of species. In 1844 he prepared a preliminary treatise on this tremendous theme, intending later to expand it into a more exhaustive work. Meanwhile, in 1858, he received from the explorer, Alfred R. Wallace, a paper sent from Malay with the request that it be presented to the Linnæan Society. The similarity of some of its contents to certain matters treated in his own paper impelled Darwin to accept the advice of scientific friends that he make public his own conclusions and this he accordingly did on the occasion of the reading of Wallace's paper before the society. Moreover, he accelerated the preparation of his more comprehensive work which, in 1859, was given to the world under the title of *The Origin of Species By Means of Natural Selection, or The Preservation of Favored Races in the Struggle of Life.* In this great work he set forth that the numerous species in animal and plant life, instead of being each specially created and immutable, are continually in process of change through natural adaptation. His conclusion, inevitable from these findings, was that a species survives and multiplies according to its fitness, and that in the measure that a species lacks such fitness, it does not persist, but dies off. In brief, it is the doctrine of the survival of the fittest.

This epoch-making work, with its unavoidable implications as to the origin of the human race, produced a staggering effect upon the world. It was followed by *Fertilization of Orchids; Variation of Plants and Animals Under Domestication;* his great work, *The Descent of Man; Expression of the Emotions in Man and Animals; Insectivorous Plants; Climbing Plants; The Effects of Cross and Self Fertilization in the Vegetable Kingdom; Different Forms of Flowers in Plants of the Same Species; The Power of Movement in Plants;* and *The Formation of Vegetable Mold through the Action of Worms.*

In 1830 Darwin had married his cousin, Emma Wedgewood, whose devoted care enabled him to carry on his work despite the ill health against which he had to struggle through the last 40 years of his life, and which made it impossible for him to attend scientific gatherings or to mingle except rarely with the intellectuals of his time. He was a brilliant conversationalist, kindly and gentle in manner and his lovable qualities won him many friends. He personally attended to his voluminous correspondence, generously answering even the most unimportant requests. He died April 19, 1882, survived by two daughters and five sons, four of whom became eminent in scientific circles.

JEFFERSON DAVIS   1808–1889

JEFFERSON DAVIS, American statesman, soldier and president of the Confederate States of America, was born on June 3, 1808, in Christian County, Kentucky, of Welsh and Scotch-Irish ancestry. At an early age he was taken with his family to Mississippi with which state he was thereafter identified. His education was acquired at various schools and at the age of 16 he left the Transylvania University in Kentucky to enter West Point. Following his graduation in 1828, he entered the army and spent the next seven years along the northwestern frontier, a period during which he had ample opportunity to manifest his soldierly qualities. Ill health then caused him to retire from the army. During the same year (1835) he married, but his wife, who was a daughter of Zachary Taylor, died after a few months and he then journeyed to Cuba in search of health. Upon his return after a short stay in Washington he became a cotton planter in Mississippi and for several years lived in retirement, devoting himself to agriculture and study. He interested himself in local politics and appeared in public as an ardent advocate of the States' rights theories promulgated by John C. Calhoun. In 1845 he married a Miss Howell and in that year he was elected to Congress where his voice was often heard in speeches of dignity and power. He was one of those who advocated the annexation of Texas.

At the beginning of the Mexican War in 1846 he resigned his office to take command of the First Mississippi Volunteers and served with gallantry and distinction, particularly at Buena Vista and Monterey. He was badly wounded and retired from the army. From 1847 to 1851 he served as U. S. Senator from Mississippi, resigning from office in order to run for governor of the state. He was defeated, but in 1853 President Pierce, who was his friend, appointed him secretary of war, an office which he filled conscientiously and capably. Four years later he was again elected to the Senate. In the turbulent days preceding the Civil War he became the recognized leader of the South; he had always been a pro-slavery man, had vigorously opposed the Compromise Measure of 1850, and contended that congress had no right to interfere with the institution of slavery, and he now maintained the right of individual states to secede from the Union. When Mississippi seceded in 1861 he delivered a farewell speech to a large and respectful audience in which he set forth his views and his real regret at what he felt to be this necessary course.

He was later elected president of the Confederacy and for a time he tried to avert actual warfare, but becoming convinced that it was unavoidable he set about military preparations. After the surrender of Lee and Johnson in April, 1865, and the fall of the Confederacy, he was captured at Irwinsville, Ga., while on his way to join his wife, and was imprisoned for two years, and subjected to needless indignities. An unwarranted charge was made that he had been involved in the assassination of President Lincoln and he tried to obtain a public trial in order to clear himself. He was indicted for treason but was admitted to bail through the efforts of Horace Greeley and other Northerners who went on his bond, and was finally released in February, 1869.

After visiting England and Canada, he engaged in business in Memphis, Tenn., and some ten years later retired to Beauvoir, Miss., and refused again to enter politics. He enjoyed the confidence and respect of the South and spent his remaining years in study and writing, publishing in 1881 his *Rise and Fall of the Confederate Government,* a full and able account of the four years' struggle and of his connection with it.

He died on Dec. 6, 1889, at New Orleans, where he was buried with an imposing ceremony, but his body was removed in 1893 to Richmond, Va.

DANIEL DEFOE 1660–1731

ALTHOUGH a prolific and versatile writer, DANIEL DEFOE is known to the world only as the author of Robinson Crusoe, one of the most celebrated of all stories of adventure. He was born in London probably in 1660, the exact date being uncertain, and was the son of a butcher whose name was James Foe. Daniel added the prefix De to his name after reaching manhood. The father was a dissenter (one whose religious beliefs are opposed to those of the established church) and Daniel was sent to a dissenting academy at Newington Green where he remained until his 19th year. His career as an author began when he was about 22 with the publication of a pamphlet in which he criticized the clergy. This was shortly followed by another pamphlet entitled *A Treatise Against the Turks.* In 1685 he became involved with the rebellious element under the Duke of Monmouth and narrowly escaped punishment. In 1688 he was active in supporting the plan to call William of Orange (son-in-law of the reigning king, James II) to the English throne. James' misgovernment and catholic prejudices had alienated his people and upon the arrival of his daughter and her husband he fled to France.

In 1701 Defoe published his famous satirical poem, *The True-Born Englishman,* in defense of William and retorting to attacks upon "the foreigners," as William and Mary had been called in certain quarters. This poem was immensely popular because of the political agitation and was sold in the streets to eager purchasers. In 1702 he published a pamphlet entitled *The Shortest Way With Dissenters,* the ironical concept of which was unhappily misunderstood and he was arrested, convicted and put in the pillory besides being fined and imprisoned. This drastic punishment for an offense which he had not intentionally committed furnished the inspiration for his *Hymn to the Pillory* which he wrote in prison. Upon his release he started a periodical called *The Review,*

which he conducted for nine years. In 1706, at the instance of Lord
Godolphin, he was appointed to a commission which had been organized
to negotiate terms for the union of England and Scotland, and his practical knowledge of affairs proved so valuable in these conferences that
he is said (though proof is lacking) to have received a life pension for
this service. He did not miss the literary opportunity of the occasion and
a by-product of his sojourn in Scotland was *A History of the Union.*
Followed a period of ease and inactivity, but in 1713 his caustic pen was
busy in denunciation of the Jacobite party, resulting in a second arrest,
fine, and imprisonment in Newgate. This experience is said to have
disillusioned him as to the desirability of a political career and he withdrew from participation in a field which had made him many enemies
and had been attended with heavy cost and ignominy. Fortunately for
the world, he now devoted himself to purely literary work and in 1719
appeared *Robinson Crusoe,* perhaps the most familiar fictional title in
all literature. The old story of repeated refusals by publishers is told
of this masterpiece and if the tale is true, they must have been sufficiently
chagrined by the instant and tremendous success of the work when it
was finally published. The story is credibly thought to be based on the
adventure of one Alexander Selkirk, master on a privateersman, who in
consequence of an altercation with his captain was put ashore on an
island off the west coast of South America about 1703, where he lived
for some time in solitude until taken aboard a passing ship. The book
was followed by a continuation of Crusoe's adventures.

It is difficult to overpraise *Robinson Crusoe;* it is the adventure story
par excellence. Devotees of the modern realistic school of fiction may
well take note of its author's discriminating use of minute detail to give
the illusion of reality and achieve dramatic effects. It has been often said
that the discovery of the footprint in the sand is one of the most effective
touches in fictional literature. The story is, of all things, convincing;
every trifling incident is telling and illuminating.

Still other works followed this great masterpiece. In 1721 appeared
Moll Flanders. Journal of the Plague, also made vivid by artistic use of
realistic detail, was published in 1722, and is a graphic picture of the
dread pestilence that swept Europe. Other works were *Colonel Jack,
Adventures of Roxana* and *Memoirs of a Cavalier.* He wrote steadily
almost to the day of his death, pouring forth fiction, biographies, works
on economics and on occult subjects. Many of his works were published
anonymously.

In 1864 he married Mary Tuffley who bore him several children.
He died in 1731 in London.

DEMOSTHENES
circa 383 B.C.–322 B.C.

DEMOSTHENES (dē mŏs'thē nēz), Athenian patriot and the most famous orator of the ancient world, was born at Athens about the year 383 B.C. He was early left an orphan, inheriting a considerable fortune from his father, of which his guardians deprived him, possibly through neglect though more probably by fraud. When he became of age, Demosthenes prosecuted them and won his case but his father's fortune had in the meantime been dissipated and he got little financial satisfaction.

In order to prosecute the case he was obliged to study law and that study awoke in him sufficient interest to impell him to adopt the profession as his own. He became a constitutional lawyer and made few if any speeches in court before he was thirty, usually arranging to have the speeches which he wrote delivered by others. He did, however, in the case of Ctesippus against Leptines, in 354 B.C., deliver one speech in person. At about this time his interest in politics was awakened and occupied much of his time although he continued to prepare court addresses until the age of forty when he retired to devote himself to politics, having by that time earned a comfortable fortune.

Philip of Macedon meanwhile had cast covetous eyes on Greece and was a constant menace. Demosthenes wrote and spoke against the designs of Philip from the very start of his political career, but his policy was not adopted by the Athenians until developments proved him to be right and it was then too late. Philip attacked the state of Olynthus, calling forth those speeches of Demosthenes' known as *Olynthiacs*. Together with his *Philippics,* his addresses against Philip, the *Olynthiacs* are generally regarded as his greatest orations—probably the greatest that either ancient or modern times have produced. They have given him an enduring reputation as an orator and writer, and have served as models for succeeding generations of lawyers and politicians. Athens, meanwhile, having fought vainly to save Olynthus from Philip, was forced to conclude peace with him. From 346 to 340 B.C., Demosthenes devoted himself to the formation of a strong anti-Macedonian party in Greece, and to bringing Æschines to trial on a charge of having betrayed Athens to Philip. The year 340 saw the renewal of war with Philip, which eventually ended disastrously for Athens and Greece in the battle of Chæronea in 338. The Athenians still had faith in Demosthenes, but the Macedonian party plotted to present him with a public crown and thus to seize the opportunity of destroying him politically. The trial of Æschines took place in 330, and was the occasion of Demosthenes' famous speech, *On the Crown,* which vindicated his indictment of Æschines and his own conduct, and which is regarded as one of the world's greatest masterpieces of oratory.

In 324 Harpalus, treasurer of Alexander the Great, absconded with a large sum of money and Demosthenes was convicted (whether rightly or wrongly) of having taken a bribe from him. He escaped from prison and fled into exile, but after the death of Alexander in 323, he was recalled to Athens to prepare for and to head a revolt against Macedonian control. This revolt was crushed at the battle of Crannon, and Demosthenes fled to the island of Calaurea where he took shelter in the ancient temple of Poseidon. He was pursued by the actor, Archias, with a body of Thracian spearmen. Archias, hesitating to violate so sacred a sanctuary, stood at the open door and urged Demosthenes to come out and surrender, promising him pardon. Demosthenes asked for a few moments' delay and died within the temple, tradition says from biting a poisoned pen.

Demosthenes was of the highest personal character, of singular purity as to his public and private life, of outstanding bravery and patriotism and his record as administrator and statesman (save *possibly* in the instance of his relations with Harpalus) entitled him to a place in the foremost ranks of the world's great men.

THOMAS DE QUINCEY   1785–1859

THOMAS DE QUINCY, author of that classic of English prose, *The Confessions of an English Opium Eater,* was the son of a linen merchant of the same name and was born at Greenhay, Manchester, on Aug. 15, 1785. His father died in 1792, leaving the family a comfortable income of 1600 pounds a year. The elder De Quincey had good literary taste and his wife was a woman of culture and refinement. An event that made a deep impression upon young De Quincey's mind in childhood was the death of an infant sister.

Thomas received his early education at Salford, Bath, Winkfield in Wiltshire, and at the grammar school of Manchester. He was a brilliant pupil and at the age of 15 could speak Greek fluently. His health failed and in 1802 he ran away from school and tramped about Wales, doing some desultory studying, with a weekly allowance from home of one guinea. Restlessness finally took him to London where he tried to raise money on his expectations. Failing in this, he underwent much privation, but was finally sent to Worcester College, Oxford, being allowed 100 pounds a year. In order to allay the physical pain which he suffered, due to privations, he began to use opium while still at Oxford and this habit clung to him intermittently throughout his life and led ultimately to the writing of the book which gave him his place in literature.

His mother had settled near Bath and De Quincey spent some time there. In Bristol he met Coleridge and his family and through them made a visit to Wordsworth and Southey at the Lakes. After revisiting Oxford in 1808 he went again to London, where he came into close contact with Lamb, Hazlitt, Knight and other literary notables. The following year he took up his abode in Grasmere, determined upon a literary career. There, in 1816, he married Margaret Simpson, who bore him three daughters and five sons, two of whom later achieved reputations as soldiers. De Quincey contributed articles and essays of an indifferent literary quality to *Blackwood's Magazine,* the *Quarterly* and other journals, and for about a year (1819) he edited the *Westmoreland Gazette.* Soon after his return to London in 1821 the *Confessions* began to appear in the London Magazine. They were written in a simple, smooth and flowing style that few authors have equaled and attracted an unusual amount of attention and curiosity. De Quincey became famous. Brought out in book form later on, the *Confessions* had a large sale. The novelty of the subject matter, the distinguished quality of the prose, the personal and confessional element that entered into them, gave the work a unique place in English literature.

After spending some time in Grasmere again, De Quincey formed an editorial association with *Blackwood's Magazine* (1828) and lived in Edinburgh for twelve years, contributing occasionally to the *Edinburgh Literary Gazette.* His wife died in 1837 and the family afterwards settled at Lasswade, but De Quincey himself stayed in lodgings, moving from time to time when the accumulation of papers filled his rooms. After his wife's death he again turned to opium but by 1844 he had reduced the daily dose to a small amount and he never again exceeded this self-imposed limit.

For fifty years De Quincey lived chiefly by his pen, aided by the income from his father's estate. In his later years he continued to contribute to *Blackwood's, Tait's Magazine* and *Hogg's Instructor*—articles on a variety of subjects, often witty, sometimes long drawn out and tiresome. He published two other books after the *Confessions*—*The Logic of Political Economy* in 1844, and in 1839 his only and unsuccessful attempt at a novel, *Klosterheim.* Diffuse and discursive as his writings often are, De Quincey was a wit, scholar, man of the world and a philosopher. He died in Edinburgh on Dec. 8, 1859 and his body lies in the West Churchyard.

RENÉ DESCARTES   1596–1650

RENÉ DESCARTES (dä'kärt'), French philosopher and mathematician, was born at La Haye, near Tours, France, March 31, 1596. At the Jesuit college of La Flèche, despite a delicate physique, he early gave promise of a brilliant career, but found the scholastic methods and doctrines far from satisfying to his keen intellect and immediately upon leaving school he sought to forget all that he had been taught in order that he might have an open mind to search for truth without prejudice or preconceived opinion.

Although he had graduated in law at the University of Poitiers in 1616, he seems to have embraced a military career in 1618 in Holland. He was more concerned with problems of the mind, however, than with military matters, and spent much time brooding over questions of philosophy and human knowledge, assailed by many doubts and indecisions. He had originated the system of analytical geometry and he later applied this same method to philosophy and other studies.

In 1620 Descartes visited Austria and Bohemia where he is reported to have served in the army of the Duke of Bavaria, as a volunteer, and to have fought against the Protestant princes. Some of his biographers, however, deny this. In 1622–23 he was back in France and for some years he lived partly in Paris, where contact with the learned men of the age stimulated his interest and his ambition and he carried on research work in optics with a lens-maker. In 1628 he went to Holland to escape the distractions of Parisian life and to be free to devote himself to study and writing. He spent nearly all the remaining years of his life there where many disciples gathered about him.

During this period he wrote his *Rules for the Direction of the Mind* and worked on a treatise called *The World* in which he adopted the Copernican theory, but learning that Galileo had been condemned by the Inquisition for similar teachings, he sought a more orthodox form of Copernicanism which he later found in his vortex theory. He published also his *Meditations on First Philosophy* and a *Discourse on Method* which involved him in controversy with mathematicians of Holland, France and Belgium. In 1643 a published reply to a violent attack which had been made upon him by Voetius led to his being summoned before a magistrate, but he refused to appear and judgment was passed against him by default. Influential friends eventually persuaded the magistrate to drop the matter.

His writings made an important impress upon philosophical thought, but perhaps his greatest contributions were to the science of mathematics. He did much to develop the theory of equations.

In 1649 he was invited to visit Stockholm to instruct Queen Christina in philosophy. He died there on Feb. 11, 1650. Sixteen years later his body was taken to Paris for burial in the churchyard of Ste. Geneviève-du-Mont, but in 1819 it was transferred to St. Germain-des-Prés.

ADMIRAL GEORGE DEWEY   1837–1917

GEORGE DEWEY, American naval officer and hero of the Spanish-American War, was born at Montpelier, Vermont, on Dec. 26, 1837. He attended Norwich University and the United States Naval Academy at Annapolis, from which he was graduated in 1858. He received his commission as lieutenant in April, 1861, and during the Civil War served under Admiral Farragut at the passage of the forts below New Orleans, and elsewhere. He later was with the North Atlantic squadron that enforced the blockade against the Confederate States, taking part in several naval engagements.

In 1897, having risen to the rank of commodore in the meantime, at his own request he was assigned to sea service and placed in command of the Asiatic squadron. While at Hong Kong with his fleet in April, 1898, he received orders to capture or destroy the Spanish fleet then in the neighborhood of the Philippines. With the protected cruisers *Olympia* (his flagship), *Baltimore, Raleigh* and *Boston,* an unprotected cruiser, a gunboat, an armed revenue cutter and a purchased supply ship and collier, he left Mirs Bay in China on April 27 and arrived off Luzon in the Philippines on April 30. Admiral Montojo, in command of the Spanish fleet, had anchored off the spit on which are the village and arsenal of Cavite, in a general east and west line, keeping his broadside to the northward. His fleet was not the equal of that commanded by Dewey although it was manned by a somewhat larger force, comprising 1875 men to 1748 under Dewey's command.

Dewey steamed into the Boca Grande, paying no heed to the report of torpedoes, passed El Fraile at midnight and, sighting the Spanish squadron to the south, steamed down in column with his ships at 400-yard intervals, and at a distance of 5000 yards he opened fire at 5:41 A. M. He gradually decreased his distance to 2000 yards. At 7:35 he withdrew and his men breakfasted, re-engaging the Spanish fleet at 11:16. The Spanish ships, *Christina* and *Castilla,* had broken into flames and the remainder of Dewey's task was the silencing of the Cavite batteries and the destruction of the smaller Spanish vessels. Every ship was sunk or destroyed without the loss of a single man on the American side, and Dewey took possession of Cavite.

Congress passed a joint resolution of thanks to Commodore Dewey and authorized the presentation of a sword of honor to him and bronze medals commemorating the battle of Manila Bay to his officers and men, and he was made a read admiral. In August following, his fleet aided General Merritt in the capture of the City of Manila and he was ordered to remain in the Philippines to maintain control. On March 3, 1899 he was given the rank of admiral, a title that had been granted to but two men before him, Farragut and Porter.

Upon his return to America in October, 1899, he was given a magnificent reception at New York. He was made a member of the Schurman Philippine Commission appointed that year and in 1901 acted as president of the court of inquiry asked for by Commander Schley. By special provision he was not retired but continued in service until his death and for the last seven years of his life he served as president of the General Board of the Navy. In 1900 his name was prominently mentioned for the presidential candidacy, but he did not receive the nomination.

Dewey was twice married; in 1867 to a daughter of Governor Goodwin of New Hampshire, and in 1899 to Mrs. Mildred McLean Hazen of Washington. He published his *Autobiography* in 1913 and upon his death in Washington on Jan. 16, 1917, he was given burial in Arlington National Cemetery.

CHARLES DICKENS   1812–1870

CHARLES DICKENS, English novelist, whose fame was the sensation of his time, was born at Landport, England, Feb. 7, 1812. So great was this fame that he became, in a peculiar sense, a public character and the facts of his unprecedented career are all available. His father, who was in the navy pay office, was pensioned after some years of service and worked thereafter as a parliamentary reporter. He was the original of the immortal Micawber and the novelist's mother was the original of Mrs. Nickleby. The numerous "difficulties" of Mr. Micawber had ample inspiration in the trials and adversities of the Dickens family; the novelist's father was imprisoned for debt in the Marshalsea (made famous in *Little Dorrit*) and for a time his wife and children shared his residence in this wretched theatre of sorrow. While Charles was still a boy the hapless family drifted to London—destined to furnish inspiration for innumerable graphic scenes and pictures in the fictions which were to make his name a household work. A sudden windfall, in the form of an unexpected legacy, enabled the impecunious father to send the boy for a short period to a private school, although it is probable that his youthful experiences in a blacking warehouse were just as valuable in his career.

Broadly speaking, Dickens had no education; he read and he observed—and he learned shorthand. For a time he was a parliamentary reporter. Soon his faculty of keen observation and his abounding humor found expression in the *Sketches by Boz,* a pseudonym suggested by his younger brother's pronunciation of the name of Goldsmith's character of Moses, while the boy was suffering from a cold (i.e., Bozes). The sketches appeared in the *Monthly Magazine* and the *Evening Chronicle* and in 1836 were published in book form. They contain only the germ of his genius, but their pronounced success brought an invitation to write the letterpress for a series of humorous sketches by the artist, Robert Seymour. Their rollicking humor, and particularly the character of Sam Weller, completely eclipsed the drawings and *Pickwick Papers* remains the most characteristic of its author's works. As a novel it violates every rule of continuity and construction; it has no plot, nor even a central idea, but is simply a rambling narrative of humorous scenes and episodes and of characters who dwell in the heart of the reader. Such abounding fun and animal spirits had never before been imparted to fiction. The work contains the keynote of Dickens' amazing genius. At his best (and he was unhappily not always at his best) he is not to be regarded as a novelist at all, but rather as a great spontaneous natural force, owing no allegiance to any fictional school, joyously heedless of art, a veritable wellspring of humorous invention. In the measure that he departed, as he too frequently did, from the application of this transcendent gift he was unsuccessful.

Not content to work within the bounds of his preeminent quality and with a passion for exposing wrongs, he next published *Oliver Twist,* dealing with workhouse conditions and picturing the more dubious side of life in terms of melodrama. Like most of his serious works, it is redeemed by its humorous characters and interludes of merriment. It should be said that all of his works were first published in monthly parts which were eagerly awaited by increasing multitudes. In 1839 appeared *Nicholas Nickleby,* a dramatic indictment of the sordid boarding schools in Yorkshire, its sombre scenes abundantly relieved by a wealth of humor and grotesque characterization. No attempt can here be made to analyze his many lengthy works. In 1840 appeared *The Old Curiosity Shop,* full of humor and pathos, and tender sentiment. Next came *Barnaby Rudge* and *The Tale of Two Cities,* unquestionably his best work from the constructive and artistic viewpoint, but the least characteristic of his unique genius. In 1858 came the *Christmas Stories,* overflowing with good cheer; he has been quaintly said to have invented Christmas. Prior to this he had visited America, where he was a sensation, but his *American Notes,* published on his return, aroused much anger in the country which had extended him the hand of hospitality. The American chapters of *Martin Chuzzlewit,* containing misleading ridicule and caricature, proved prejudicial to his standing on this side of the ocean and aroused an antagonism which a later conciliatory visit did not entirely dispel. Thousands, however, attended his public readings which added a new item to his fame.

In 1848 appeared *Dombey and Son,* followed by *David Copperfield,* commonly regarded as his masterpiece. *Bleak House, Hard Times, Little Dorrit, Great Expectations* are also outstanding, not to mention a variety of tales and lesser works. His last completed novel was *Our Mutual Friend.* He wrote also a *Child's History of England* and, exclusively for his own children, a life of Christ which was published in 1934 under the title of *The Life of Our Lord,* although it had been his expressed intention that this work should never be published. The writing of *The Mystery of Edwin Drood* was interrupted by his death at his home at Gadshill on June 9, 1870. He was buried in Westminster Abbey.

On April 2, 1836 he had married Catherine Hogarth by whom he had several children. The marriage was not happy and for the last few years of his life Mr. and Mrs. Dickens lived apart, his home being cared for by his wife's sister.

BENJAMIN DISRAELI   1804–1881

BENJAMIN DISRAELI (dĭz rā'lĭ), novelist and one of the most brilliant of English statesmen, was born in London, Dec. 21, 1804, the eldest son of Isaac D'Israeli. Although of the Hebrew race, he received Christian baptism at St. Andrew's, Holborn, in 1817, thus gaining many privileges still barred to Jews in England. He was educated partly at the private school of a Unitarian clergyman at Walthamstow. In 1821 he was articled to a solicitor and three years later entered Lincoln's Inn, which he attended for nine terms. In 1826 he published the first part of the novel, *Vivian Gray,* which quickly became the talk of London, but the second part, issued the following year, was little read. *Captain Popanilla* and *The Young Duke* followed in quick succession.

Returning from a year's holiday on the Mediterranean, in Spain and Jerusalem, Disraeli stood twice for the House of Commons for Wycombe as an advanced Radical, but failed of election both times as he did again in 1835 when he stood for Taunton. He finally entered Parliament as the member for Maidstone in the first year of Queen Victoria's reign, 1837. His maiden speech, on the Irish election petition, raised laughter in the House, but nine years later as the real leader of the Tory Protectionists, he was listened to respectfully enough. In the meantime, he had written *Contarini Fleming* (1832), *The Wondrous Tale of Alroy* (1833), *The Revolutionary Epick* (1834), *Vindication of the English Constitution* (1835), *Henrietta Temple* and *Venetia* (1837), *Coningsby* (1844) *Sybil* (1845), *Tancred* (1847), and other books.

In the Derby administration of 1852, as Chancellor of the Exchequer and leader of the House of Commons, Disraeli discarded protection and his budget failed through an attack on it by Gladstone, who succeeded him in the Aberdeen ministry. In 1858 he was back in power with Lord Derby, but upon the rejection of a Parliamentary reform measure he resigned, and for seven years was on the opposition bench while the Liberals were in power. He became Chancellor again in the third Derby administration in 1866, and the following year carried his Reform Act, which was more sweeping and democratic than the one the Conservatives had rejected. In February, 1868, he succeeded Lord Derby as Premier.

In 1874 Disraeli entered upon his second premiership, during which church patronage in Scotland was abolished, an act to put down ritualistic practices was passed, and measures to protect British seamen were enacted into law. Disraeli, however, found a more fertile field for his genius in foreign affairs and it was due to his political acumen that England, in 1875, obtained a half ownership in the Suez Canal, and that Victoria, in the following year, was crowned Empress of India. He was later created Earl of Beaconsfield and called to the Upper House, sitting for Buckinghamshire thereafter. In the Balkan insurrection he championed Turkey against Russia. In 1878, with Lord Salisbury, he attended the Berlin Congress which gave back to Russia all she had lost in the Crimean War, but they obtained Cyprus for England. The Afghan and Zulu wars, together with economic depression and troubles in England, returned the Liberals to power in 1880, and Disraeli retired to private life.

In 1839 he had married the rich widow of his first colleague, Mrs. Wyndham Lewis. Although many years his senior, upon her death some nine years later he characterized her as "the perfect wife."

In 1870 he had published the popular novel, *Lothair; Endymion,* one of his best tales, was published shortly before his death, which took place at his Curzon Street residence in London on April 19, 1881. He was buried at Hughenden, near Wycombe, where he had lived for thirty years.

Disraeli's novels are perhaps little read today, but they contributed much to preserve his reputation, brilliant as were his achievements in statesmanship. His marvelous mastery of wit and satire was one of the outstanding characteristics of both his writing and his political speeches. Some of his best work appears in *Coningsby* and *Sybil.*

CHARLES LUTWIDGE DODGSON (*Lewis Carroll*)   1832–1898

LEWIS CARROLL, author of Alice in Wonderland, that juvenile classic which makes an equally strong appeal to the adult mind, was also a mathematician of high standing and a clergyman.

He was born on Jan. 27, 1832, in Daresbury, Cheshire, where his father, the Rev. Charles Dodgson, was vicar. The boy attended Rugby for four years and then entered Christ Church, Oxford, in May, 1850. He won such high honors in mathematics that on finishing his course in 1854, he was appointed mathematical lecturer at Christ Church, a post which he held for 26 years. His earliest published writings had to do with that science; *A Syllabus of Plane Algebraical Geometry* (1860) and the following year *The Formulae of Plane Trigonometry.*

Four years later he published a book of very different character—so different that he would not lend to it his own name but formed the pseudonym of "Lewis Carroll" from his two given names, and this pseudonym has come to be a household name not only in English, but in world, literature, while the name of Charles Lutwidge Dodgson is almost unknown save to students of mathematical history and delvers into biography.

This book was *Alice's Adventures in Wonderland.* The original of *Alice* was the daughter of Dean Liddell for whose amusement Dodgson was accustomed to invent stories which he later enlarged into the famous nursery classic.

Lewis Carroll continued to write fantasies for children. *Phantasmagoria* appeared in 1869; *Through the Looking-Glass* in 1871; *The Hunting of the Snark* in 1876; *Rhyme and Reason* (1883); *A Tangled Tale* (1885); *Sylvia and Bruno*, in two parts, in 1889 and 1893; but of these not even *Through the Looking-Glass* (which continues Alice's adventures) attained the popularity of the first book.

Dodgson's authorship of the *Alice* books was well known, but it was his custom to state when the subject came up that "Mr. Dodgson neither claimed nor acknowledged any connection with the books not published under his name."

He wrote skits occasionally on subjects dealing with Oxford. *The Dynamics of a Particle* followed a contest between Gladstone and Gathorne Hardy, later Earl of Cranbrook, and *The New Belfry* ridiculed the erection of a belfry at Christ Church for the bells that were removed from the cathedral tower. Under the name of C. L. Dodgson he published in 1867 *An Elementary Treatise on Determinants; Euclid, Book V, Proved Algebraically* (1874); *Euclid and His Modern Rivals* (1879); and in 1888 the work upon which his reputation as a mathematician largely rests— *Curiosa Mathematica.*

Lewis Carroll lived until Jan. 14, 1898. As a memorial to him after his death a cot in the Children's Hospital in London was endowed perpetually by public subscription. The original manuscript of *Alice in Wonderland*, as written out for Dean Liddell's daughter, in small, neat handwriting, was sold by the original *Alice* in 1928 for 15,400 pounds and eventually found its way into the hands of an American collector. In 1932 the anniversary of Carroll's birth was celebrated in England and America, where the names of *Alice*, the *Mad Hatter*, the *March Hare*, the *Duchess*, the *King, Queen* and *Knave of Hearts*, have become household words with old and young.

DONATELLO   circa 1386–1466

DONATELLO (DONATO DI BETTO BARDI), an Italian sculptor of the early Renaissance period, was born in Florence about 1386 of a family in humble circumstances. Little is known of his youth or of his early studies. Among his first great works were the statues of "St. Peter" and "St. Mark" for the church of Or San Michele in Florence, and a figure of

"St. George," completed in 1416 (now in the National Museum in Florence) which is perhaps the most beautiful of his early works. During this period he executed several statues for the cathedral in his native city and in a more realistic style the figures of "Joshua," "John the Baptist," "Jeremiah," and the famous "Zuccone" (or Baldhead) which was said to be his own favorite.

Mention can be made of but a few of his works. About 1425 he became associated with the architect Michelozzo and the first product of this union was the monument to Pope John XXIII for the baptistery of Florence, which shows an effigy of the pope in bronze lying under a marble canopy. On the beautiful marble base are three statutes of "Faith," "Hope" and "Charity." Much other work in bronze was executed during this period, Michelozzo doing the casting in which he was experienced. In 1433 he left Florence for Venice in the train of Cosimo de' Medici and the partnership ceased. Donatello about the same time went to Rome. He had become adept in the art of decoration; assisted the sculptor Simone in preparations for the coronation of Emperor Sigismund and executed several works which show the influence of his study of classical art in Rome. A year later he returned to Florence and designed eight medallions for the decoration of the Medici palace, entrusting the execution of them, however, to his pupils. Other notable works were the nude bronze statue of "David" (National Museum) and a relief of the "Annunciation" carved in sandstone, in a chapel in Santa Croce. He did many bas-reliefs and decorative pieces for church interiors and several representations of John the Baptist which seems to have been his favorite subject.

In 1443 at Padua after a bronze crucifix for the church of Sant' Antonio, he undertook a series of bronze statues which were later combined to form an altar, but much of the execution in these was the work of pupils. Of a different order is the great bronze equestrian statue of "Erasmo di' Narni" or "Gattemelata," begun in 1446 and completed seven years later. The commanding figure of the rider astride his spirited war horse forms a noble monument to the genius of its creator. Soon after its erection in Padua's public square, Donatello, never long happy away from Florence, returned visiting Venice and other cities by the way. His last years produced several important works, among them "Judith Bearing the Head of Holofernes" and a "Magdalen" in wood. At the time of his death on Dec. 13, 1466, he was engaged in designs for the pulpits of San Lorenzo, founded by the Medici family and in which, before his departure for Padua, he had executed a beautiful bronze sepulchral statue and other decorations. Although his unfinished pulpit designs were imperfectly executed after his death, they show his marvelous powers to have been undiminished to the end.

Donatello never married. The later Italian architect and writer, Vasari, whose writings give us much valuable information about the Renaissance period, pictures him as a lovable, generous and charming man. Critics find in his work many reminders of the marvels of ancient Greece, but he broke away from the antique influence in his devotion to realism. His works are full of dramatic action and character, the quality of beauty being sometimes sacrificed. He was a master technician and his grasp of perspective in sculpture made possible his wonderful effects in relief work. Through his many pupils his influence dominated Italian art down to the time of Michelangelo and he stands as one of the greatest sculptors of all time.

GUSTAVE PAUL DORÉ   1833–1883

Louis Christophe Gustave Paul Doré (dō'rā'), was a French artist, born at Strasburg on Jan. 6, 1833, the son of an engineer. Although his illustrations have familiarized his name to nearly every household, his versatile genius also made him notable as a painter, etcher and sculptor. He was educated in Paris. As a boy his sketches attracted attention and he was only 15 when he was employed as illustrator by the *Journal pour Rire*. At about the same time he exhibited a series of sketches in the salons. Although his training in art had been slight and he lacked the technical fundamentals which he had thereafter no time to acquire, he soon turned from caricature to the illustrating of books. In this field he was amazingly productive. His illustrations for Rabelais' works, produced in 1854, attracted wide notice and were speedily followed by others, among which may be mentioned Dante's *Divine Comedy,* (1861) Balzac's *Contes Drolatiques* (Droll Stories) (1856), *Don Quixote* (1863), *The Ancient Mariner,* Tennyson's works, Poe's *Raven,* the *Atala, Paradise Lost* and, perhaps best known of all to the general public, his Bible pictures produced from 1865–1867. In all of these his grotesque imagination was allowed full play.

He soon found himself famous in other lands and his work brought him large monetary returns. In London there was established the Doré Gallery where his work was exhibited for many years. Among his paintings the first to be shown was his "Battle of the Alma" (1855) and "Battle of Inkerman" (1857). He was fond of historical subjects which he liked to portray on huge canvases, but in his paintings more than in his illustrations his lack of technical training was evident in defects of drawing and other faults. Nevertheless his real genius, both as artist and poet, is always apparent. Among the best of his paintings are the "Neophyte," "Francisca da Rimini" and the large works, "Christ Leaving the Praetorium" and "Christ's Entry into Jerusalem." He did some landscape work but was never at his best in that field, betraying a too conscious striving after his effects, but revealing a lack of real sympathy and understanding of nature. His paintings nevertheless were popular in England and he frequently reproduced many of his designs and exhibited them both in Paris and in London.

In sculpture also he was handicapped by his lack of training, but he executed a monument to Alexandre Dumas, which stands in the Place Malesherbes in Paris and which is probably his best known work in this field. In the Golden Gate Park in San Francisco there stands a huge vase which is gracefully decorated with many small fancicul figures of animals and genii, the whole representing the "Vintage." In this his poetic fancy is given full freedom of expression. The vase was first exhibited at the Exposition Universelle in 1878.

In 1861 Doré was decorated by the Legion of Honor. He died in Paris on Jan. 23, 1883.

STEPHEN A. DOUGLAS   1813--1861

STEPHEN ARNOLD DOUGLAS, American statesman, was born on April 23, 1813 at Brandon, Vt., and was the son of a physician who died during his infancy. Much of his boyhood was spent on a farm with an interval of apprenticeship to a cabinet maker. At about the age of 20 he drifted to Illinois where he taught school for a short time, continuing the study of law which had previously engaged his attention, and in 1834 he was admitted to the bar. So conspicuous were his abilities that a year later he was made state's attorney and this public office marked the beginning of his rapid rise to prominence. He next served a term in the state legislature of Illinois, was appointed register of the U. S. land office in Springfield and in 1838 narrowly missed being elected to Congress. For a brief period he was secretary of state in Illinois and then for two years judge of the supreme court. Successful in 1843 in his race for Congress, he served for three terms as a representative and then was elected senator for a six-year period.

His voice was often heard in political debate. He actively favored the annexation of Texas, supported President Polk and the Mexican

War, and in the controversy with Great Britain over Oregon he was insistent in claiming the whole area for the United States up to latitude 54°40'. He vigorously fought measures to restrict the extension of slavery in the new territories, including the "Wilmot Proviso," and earnestly upheld the principle of popular or "squatter" sovereignty which claimed the right of settlers in each territory to decide for themselves whether they would permit slavery without interference by the federal government. He had by this time become a national figure and much bitter controversy was aroused in 1854 over the Kansas-Nebraska bill drawn by him. The Missouri Compromise of 1820 had provided for freedom from slavery in those territories, but Douglas' bill repudiated that provision and opened the way for the extension of slavery. It was passed by Congress and bitter denunciations were heaped upon its author throughout the northern states.

In 1852 and again in 1856 he had vainly sought nomination as presidential candidate. In 1858 occurred the famous series of debates between Douglas and Abraham Lincoln which brought the latter into national prominence and afforded opportunity for a brilliant display of Douglas' oratorical powers. He desired reelection to the U. S. Senate and Lincoln was the opposing republican candidate for that office. Throughout Illinois they spoke from the same platform, discussing slavery in all its phases. Douglas was elected and in 1860 he received the democratic nomination for the presidency although much of his prestige in the South had been lost by his break with President Buchanan. Again his republican opponent was Abraham Lincoln who was elected president. After the outbreak of the war Douglas threw his strong influence in support of Lincoln, denounced secession and declared it the duty of every man to maintain the integrity of the Union. At the request of the president, he started on a tour of the outlying states in an effort to arouse loyalty to the Union and after speaking in Ohio, West Virginia and Illinois, he died at Chicago on June 3, 1861.

Although he was a man of small stature, his vigorous physique and the impression of power which he always gave had gained for him the nickname of "Little Giant." In 1847 he had married Martha Martin who bore him three children. His second wife, who was childless, was Adele Cutts of Washington. His eldest son, Robert Martin Douglas, became secretary to President Grant.

SIR FRANCIS DRAKE   circa 1539–1596

SIR FRANCIS DRAKE was the most romantic and redoubtable of the hardy mariners who, in the 16th century, made the name of England terrible on the seas. Spaniards called him "the dragon," and fittingly enough, for by his own account he "singed the bearde of the king of Spayne and annoyde him in his Indyes." He was indeed a buccaneer of the first order, but his dubious exploits were somewhat redeemed by a fine personal honor and an inspiring patriotism. He was the first commanding explorer to circumnavigate the globe, since his great predecessor, Magellan, lost his life before his expedition completed its amazing cruise. He was born in a humble cottage on the banks of the river Tavy in Devonshire, England, about the year 1539; was one of 12 sons of a yeoman whose strong Protestant proclivities laid him in peril of the persecuting Queen Mary and he fled into Kent where his large family was reared. Here he held a clerical post in connection with maritime enterprises and it has been assumed that young Drake thereby encountered many "mariners of the sea" and imbibed much of the salty romance which he always relished. In reading of his predatory exploits one feels that he made a most favorable impression and was immensely liked by his many captives who scrupled not to sing his praises.

Great mariners, like great actors, have usually grown up in their profession. Drake was still a youth when he was apprenticed to a seafaring neighbor who made short voyages and when he died young Drake took over the vessel and continued the trading voyages on his own account. While thus engaged he heard of the deeds of the adventurous Hawkins who was forcing the West Indian planters to buy his cargoes of slaves. He sought out this enterprising commander and cast his lot with him. They were a kindred pair. The ensuing voyage was not successful and Drake returned with only adventures in lieu of profits. He rallied a group of boisterous spirits who, for one reason or another, sought a life on the ocean wave, and led them on several trips to the West Indies. Queen Elizabeth was glad to sanction his plundering designs with a commission and he found these expeditions decidedly profitable. One of his notable achievements was the sacking of Nombré de Dios in Mexico after which he crossed the isthmus of Panama and, gazing upon the vast expanse of the Pacific, prayed that he might sail an English ship upon those waters. It is reported that on his arrival in England on a Sunday, enthusiastic multitudes deserted their churches to do him honor.

In 1577, by authority of the queen, he set sail with five vessels on the cruise which was destined to exalt him far above the level of an ordinary buccaneer. His little 100-ton flagship, the *Golden Hind,* was outfitted in a manner to awe and edify all who should see it and be a constant reminder and salutary warning of the greatness of England. An orchestra of "musitians," destined to astonish many savage tribes, was taken to beguile the weary hours of cruising while the redoubtable commander in a gorgeous chair dined from a gold and silver service. Nor did he forget to carry a huge Bible from which he read regularly to his crew, who loved him loyally, for his rigid discipline was tempered with consideration and justice. In the autumn he sailed through the straits of Magellan, losing one of his ships, and indeed when he eventually sailed into Plymouth harbor in England the little *Golden Hind* was quite alone. He continued up the coast of South America, sacking Spanish towns and spreading terror among the settlers of Chile and Peru. He captured a great galleon laden with gold and silver, whose captain was lavish in his praise of Drake's generosity and hospitality. He then tried to find a northwest passage and touched at what is now San Francisco. Prevented by the cold from cruising farther north, he sailed across the Pacific, visiting various islands, including Java, from which he directed his course to the Cape of Good Hope and sailing up the African coast came at last to England on the 26th of September, 1579. The honor of knighthood, which Elizabeth conferred upon him, seems but a paltry recognition of the untold booty which he laid at her feet.

In 1585 he commanded a fleet of 21 ships against Philip of Spain, spreading terror in the West Indies and along the South American coast. At that time the great Spanish Armada was in preparation for the invasion of British waters and Drake was sent to harass the vessels of this flotilla in their several harbors. In April, 1587, he passed the batteries at Cadiz, destroyed about 100 ships, sailed into the Tagus creating havoc with a number of galleys moored there, collected as usual a great amount of booty, and sailed away to the Azores taking possession of a large Spanish vessel on the way. Again he sailed triumphantly into Plymouth and was lavish in his generosity to the town, contributing liberally to public works. He was vice admiral in the fleet under Lord Howard which finally scattered the Armada and terminated Spanish naval supremacy. An interlude in parliament as member from Plymouth afforded this insatiable adventurer but a short breathing space and he was off again to America. At Nombré de Dios an epidemic broke out among his crews and Drake himself was one of the victims. He died on the 27th of December, 1596 and was buried at sea, while his fleet lay anchored off Puerto Bello.

THEODORE DREISER   1871–

THEODORE DREISER, American novelist, was born in Terre Haute, Ind., Aug. 27, 1871. He attended the public schools of Warsaw, Ind., and for a short time the Indiana University. He gained his knowledge and experience of life largely in the newspaper business, as reporter on the old *Chicago Globe,* then on the staff of the *St. Louis Globe-Democrat,* and later as dramatic critic and traveling correspondent for the *St. Louis Republic,* 1893–94. For the three years following he edited *Every Month,* a literary and musical magazine.

In 1898 he married Sarah Osborne White of St. Louis, and at about that time he began to contribute and do special work for many of the magazines—*Century, Harper's, McClure's, Cosmopolitan.* He was editor of *Smith's Magazine* in 1905–06; managing editor of *Broadway Magazine,* 1906–07; editor-in-chief of the Butterick publications, 1907–10. In November, 1907, he organized the National Child Rescue Campaign.

Dreiser's first novel, *Sister Carrie,* published in 1900, was suppressed but nevertheless gained for its author something of a reputation in English and American literary circles. Frank Norris, H. G. Wells, Arnold Bennett and Hugh Walpole expressed their admiration for its unsparing realism. The next novel, *Jennie Gerhardt,* was published in 1911, just after Dreiser's retirement from his editorial labors. It had been written as a diversion from those duties and thereafter he devoted himself entirely to literary pursuits. In 1912 he published *The Financier,* based upon the career of a well-known traction magnate, continuing the same central character two years later in *The Titan.* Between those two novels he had published an autobiographical volume, *A Traveller at Forty;* in 1915 there appeared *The Genius,* a detailed depiction of the artistic temperament; and within the next few years, *Plays of the Natural and Supernatural,* his first attempt at drama; *A Hoosier Holiday,* inspired by a visit to his native state; *The Hand of the Potter,* a tragedy; *Twelve Men; Hey, Rub-a-Dub; A Book about Myself* and *The Color of a Great City.*

Dreiser's next novel, *An American Tragedy,* based upon an actual crime, published in 1925, outsold all his previous books and brought him great popularity. Dramatized by Patrick Kearney, the play had a considerable run in New York City and was produced as a talking motion picture in 1931, over the protests of the author who sued to stop its distribution on the ground that his story had been garbled and emasculated. In 1929 Dreiser published *A Gallery of Women* in two volumes, character studies of women of various temperaments.

Dreiser ranks high among American novelists and his work is esteemed in critical circles for its rugged sincerity and undoubted power. It lacks form and harmony and his style is crude. But, like Scott, he triumphs over those defects by the sheer force of his overmastering earnestness and the essential truth of his delineations. His realism, the dominant quality of his work, is achieved by the cumulative method rather than by artistic suggestion and his categorical enumeration of small details is sometimes felt to be tedious, but his psychology is generally recognized as accurate and he has presented some of the most significant aspects of modern American life to be found in fiction. His literary reputation grew slowly and Europe first recognized him as a novelist of the first rank.

JOHN DRYDEN 1631–1700

JOHN DRYDEN, English dramatist and poet, was born at Aldwinckle, in Northamptonshire, August 9, 1631, and was the son of Erasmus Driden, Bart. After rudimentary training at Tichmarch, he entered Westminster School and while a student there tried his hand at some poetry which was of indifferent merit. It was published, however, in 1650, he being then 19 years of age, and perhaps it helped to win him the scholarship at Trinity College, Cambridge, which he was granted in that year. Here he took his B.A. degree and three years later his degree of M.A. While he was still at college he inherited a small estate by his father's death and upon the completion of his studies went to London where, under the patronage and influence of Sir Gilbert Pickering, he is thought to have absorbed some of the sympathy with the Commonwealth which that distinguished friend retained. His admiration of the great Protector was given expression in his *Heroic Stanzas on the Death of Cromwell,* but did not deter him from hailing Charles II and the Restoration with equal enthusiasm in two poems, *Astræa Redux* and *Panegyric on the Coronation.* This led to a breach with Sir Gilbert and his family and Dryden was forced to seek at the hands of the public the favors withdrawn by his patron.

He first turned his attention to the stage and wrote *The Wild Gallant,* a play which was not successful in the theatre. In 1663 he married Elizabeth Howard, a sister of his friend, Sir Robert Howard, himself a poet. Besides her considerable marriage portion, the lady brought a rather dubious reputation which doubtless had its influence in producing a decidedly unhappy wedded life. In 1670 he was appointed poet laureate with a salary of 200 pounds a year. Shortly thereafter he entered into an agreement with the theatres to supply them with three plays each annually, for which he was to receive from 300 to 400 pounds, a contract which he did not fulfill. In 1671 the duke of Buckingham produced on the stage a satirical play of which he was himself the author; it was called *The Rehearsal* and was an amusing satire on the heroic drama of the day, of which Dryden was the chief exponent. Amid the hilarity which greeted this dramatic lampoon, Dryden maintained an ominous silence. But the profligate and talented duke was soon to find that he had inspired a genius for satire which would more than repay his own efforts. Dryden was indeed a satirist of the first order and his poem of *Absalom and Achitophel,* published shortly thereafter, had potent effects. The political complications and conditions with which it dealt are of little interest now, and in the perspective of time this satirical masterpiece seems a rather large hammer applied to a small nail. Briefly, it defended the king (Charles II) against the whigs; several notables of the time, including Buckingham, appeared as characters. In consequence of its publication, Shaftsbury was arrested for treason, although later discharged, and bitterness ran high against the poet whose blasting lines had caused such political commotion. In the same year he published another poetic satire, *The Medal,* to which Elkanah Settle, one of his bitterest foes, replied with some effect. Settle was sufficiently chastened the following year (1682) by the publication of *Mac Flecknoe* and the second part of *Absalom and Achitophel,* two withering satires which crushed Dryden's enemies completely. Thereafter this terrible warrier of the pen lived and wrote unmolested, the undisputed literary monarch of his time.

It seems astonishing that throughout these acrimonious literary and political conflicts he was not called upon to settle such weighty questions in a duel, for in that time and for many years thereafter a poet often laid aside his pen to wield that more potent weapon, the sword; all of which seems strange in an age when writers and their critics dine genially together in their clubs.

After the death of Charles II, Dryden (who was always rather fickle in his convictions) became a Roman Catholic, a circumstance which he proclaimed in *The Hind and Panther,* published in 1657. Because of this change of faith, Macaulay (who would have proved his equal in debate) calls him an illustrious renegade. Others have defended his course. In any case, he was deprived of his laureateship and, being thereby thrown into financial difficulties, resumed his writing for the stage. For three years he was busy with a translation of Virgil; in 1696 he published his famous *Ode on Alexander's Feast* and two years later his *Fables*. His last work was a mask with prologue and epilogue. He died in London on the 1st of May, 1700, and was buried in Westminster Abbey.

ALEXANDRE DUMAS 1802–1870

ALEXANDRE DUMAS (dü'mä') was one of the greatest and most popular of story tellers. As an artist his standing is not high, but his glowing romances have fascinated multitudes of readers and *Monte Cristo* and *The Three Musketeers* have an abiding charm in the realm of make-believe. He was the son of a general in the French republican army whose parents were a marquis and a Haitian negress. His crisp hair and thick lips bore all too conclusive evidence of his negro strain and a certain barbaric taste, expressed in a flamboyant, sometimes almost savage, habit of life, lends confirmation to this influence in his blood. He was born at Villers-Cotterets on July 24, 1802. The death of his father while he was still a child necessitated a very limited education and at the age of 20 he went to Paris, with a capital of twenty francs, to seek his fortune. After a brief period he secured employment with the duc d'Orleans.

In 1826 he first appeared as an author with a volume of *Nouvelles* and three years later the presentation of his historical drama, *Henri III et sa Cour,* brought him sensational recognition. Produced at a time when romanticism was gaining favor, it was received with such applause as only the French can give and the author awoke to find himself locally heralded as a genius. The duc d'Orleans rewarded him with the post of librarian and under the impetus of this auspicious beginning he continued to supply the voracious appetite of his increasing public and to enjoy meantime the company of the elite, among whom he disported with all the glittering appurtenances of his prosperity. In 1846 he accompanied the duc de Montpensier to Spain, visited Africa, returned somewhat embarrassed financially and, to maintain his princely scale of living, started a theatre of his own in Paris.

His attempts to achieve a political career were not successful. The nation which delighted to read him balked at accepting him as a leader. In 1853 financial difficulties caused him to withdraw to Belgium and after recovering from this setback he visited the East and later lent his aid to the cause of Garibaldi who had lately conquered Sicily, but here again he was not encouraged to play the rôle of leader.

He is said to have written a hundred romances. It is quite impossible here to enumerate them, nor is it desirable for he actually wrote but a small number of them. He it was who introduced the "sweating system" into literature and inaugurated what has since been called "ghost writing." He employed a number of poor writers to whom he supplied outlines of his gorgeous conceptions and then paid them for composing the narratives which were subjected to revision by himself and to the final introduction of that glamorous quality and sense of incident, adventure and suspense which he unquestionably possessed in a superlative degree. This method more than once involved him in a too liberal use of the ideas of others and in charges of plagiarism (accusations which did not in the least embarrass him, although on one occasion, at least, he found it expedient to absent himself from the scene of his labors). In his work, as in his life, he was quite without ideals. But no assistance or collaboration could dim the glory of his matchless power to evolve a breathless narrative. He had little skill in delineating character and his narratives are carried along by lively dialogue rather than by description. After his first historical novel, *Isabelle de Bavière,* he conceived the idea of presenting the whole history of France in this form and the resulting *Chroniques de France* are probably his best work. These include *Le Bâtard de Mauléon, Duguesclin, La reine Margot, La Dame de Montsoreau, Les Quarante-cinq, Les Trois Mousquetaires, Vingt ans après, Le vicomte de Bragelonne, La chevalier d'Hermantel, Une fille du régent, Joseph Balsamo, Le collier de la reine, Ange-Pitou, La comtesse de Charny, Le chevalier de Maison-Rouge, Les blancs et las bleus, Les compagnons de Jéhu, La rose rouge.*

The works in which he held proprietary rights brought him returns beyond the dreams of avarice and it was only by reason of his reckless extravagance that he occasionally found himself in need of funds. The pomp of his life verged on the vulgar and he was continually involved in lawsuits. He built a castle for himself, only to desert it before an army of creditors, and went roaming over Europe for literary material at a time when he might have been living in opulent retirement. His son, a noted dramatist and author of *Camille,* whom he had persistently neglected, came to his rescue when poverty and old age had broken him down, and took him to Puys, in the neighborhood of Dieppe, where he died on Dec. 5, 1870.

ELEONORA DUSE 1859–1924

In the estimation of eminent critics and the most distinguished members of her own profession, Eleonora Duse, (doo'za), was one of the greatest actresses of all time. She was born at Vigevano, near Milan, Italy, and, like so many who have risen to distinction in the theatre, she came of theatrical stock and may be said to have been born in the profession. Her birth occurred on Oct. 3, 1859, while the family was on a theatrical tour and it is said that she was carried to her christening in a gilt property box. Her grandfather was the founder of the famous Garibaldi Theatre in Padua. She was only four years old when she first set foot on the stage, appearing as Cosette in *Les Misérables,* and her health, which was never robust, is thought to have been permanently impaired by the rigors and hardships which she endured in her life of strolling player during girlhood, particularly when she was cast on her own resources at about the age of 14 after the death of her mother, which was a severe blow to her. At about that time she played Juliet and for several years she struggled with dire poverty, traveling about with one company after another. Such transcendent genius as hers, coupled with her capacity for sheer hard work and her beautiful speaking voice, could hardly fail to win early recognition, and before she was twenty-six she was acclaimed by the Italian people as the foremost actress of her country. Thenceforth, despite intervals of retirement, she continued preeminent and her career was a series of triumphs.

In 1884 she appeared in Paris and in 1892 in Vienna, arousing the greatest enthusiasm. Thereafter she played in all the principal European cities. Perhaps her greatest triumph was in the part of Camille which she essayed after seeing Sarah Bernhardt play it in 1882. Visiting America in 1893 she won a tremendous success in the part and was warmly received in London during the same year. In 1897 she appeared again in Paris and her Camille took the town by storm, Bernhardt herself being loud in her praise. Her repertoire included Juliet, Francesca da Rimini, Marguerite, Fernande, Magda and many other rôles, covering a wide range and showing a versatility running from light comedy to deep tragedy. It is said that Ibsen was not altogether pleased with her presentation of his famous character, Hedda Gabler, contending that she wrongly portrayed the latter as a neurotic. Some of her most successful plays were written for her by the Italian poet, Gabriele d'Annunzio, with whom she was intimately associated in an affair which terminated in a quarrel in 1899, although she continued to appear in his plays and during her

American tour of 1902–3 she would appear only in his works, refusing to play the old favorite roles. In 1909 ill health caused her to retire from the stage at the height of her career, giving her last performance in Berlin in Ibsen's *Lady from the Sea*. Financial misfortunes arising from the World War made it necessary for her to return some 12 years later and she chose for her first performance the same play and scored a new success. She toured Italy, appeared in London in 1923, acting to even more crowded houses than in her earlier period, and the same year she returned to America where her appearance at the Metropolitan Opera House in New York was an event in stage history never to be forgotten. Her acting aroused the wildest enthusiasm from the multitude which crowded to see her. An audience accustomed to the illusions and artificialities of the stage was astonished to behold a frail, elderly, gray-haired woman, utterly without make-up, disdaining theatrical accessories and depending only upon her magic intensity and power of interpretation. This notable reappearance was followed by a tour through the states which heavily taxed her strength and she broke down in Pittsburgh, Penn., where she died on April 21, 1924. She had been pathetically loth to die so far away from Italy and almost with her last breath begged her attendants to pack up and take her home. Her sudden passing elicited expressions of deepest regret from distinguished Americans both in and out of her profession and her body was conveyed to Italy where she was mourned as a national figure and the greatest artist of her time.

Duse was a woman of wide culture and deeply religious. She shunned personal publicity as assiduously as her only rival, Bernhardt, coveted it. Consequently, the world knows little of her intimate history. She married a Signor Checchi, but her wedded life was not happy and ended in a separation. Mrs. Fiske, one of the great ladies of the stage in America, said of her, "When I remember Duse, I cannot think of her degree of success in this or that impersonation. I cannot think of her variations. I think only of the essential thing, the style, the quality, that was Duse."

MARY BAKER G. EDDY   1821–1910

MARY BAKER GLOVER EDDY, founder and leader of Christian Science, was born at Bow, near Concord, N. H., on July 16, 1821, the youngest daughter of Mark Baker, justice of the peace and Congregational deacon. In 1843 she married George W. Glover, a builder then living in Charleston, S. C., but a native of Concord, who died within a year after their marriage. Her only child, George W. Glover, was born after his father's death. For nine years Mrs. Glover lived at Tilton, N. H., with her father or her sister, Mrs. Abigail Tilton, teaching, but always in delicate health and suffering from nervous disorder. In 1853 she married Dr. Daniel Patterson, a dentist, of Franklin, N. H., whom she divorced some twenty years later, and resumed the name of Glover. In 1877 she married Dr. Asa G. Eddy, of Lynn, who died in 1882.

In her younger days Mrs. Eddy attended public school, the Academy at Tilton, received instruction from tutors, and read widely. She wrote some verse and prose which appeared in several New England periodicals, and showed much interest in religious subjects during her youth. Her interest in mental or Christian healing, ultimately leading to the Christian Science movement, dated from 1866 when, following severe injuries from a fall on an icy sidewalk, she discovered and applied to herself what she afterwards presented to the world as the principle of Christian Science. From that time on she devoted herself to the study and teaching of the principles of mental healing.

Her first published writing on the subject was a pamphlet, *The Science of Man,* which appeared in 1870; followed in 1875 by *Science and Health with Key to the Scriptures,* which throughout her life was frequently revised and reissued, has been translated into many languages, and remains the foundation stone of Christian Science. Among later books were *The People's Idea of God, Christian Healing, Unity of Good, Rudimental Divine Science, Church Manual, Christian Science versus Pantheism, Messages to the Mother Church.*

In 1879 Mrs. Eddy established a church in Boston, later reorganized as the First Church of Christ, Scientist, which was to become known throughout the world as the "Mother Church." Branch churches or local congregations were later organized throughout the country and the movement rapidly spread until it gained adherents in nearly every country of the world. In 1881 she established the Metaphysical College in Boston, under a state charter. In 1893 she formed the Christian Science Publishing Society as an agency of her church. She founded, and edited for eleven years, the *Christian Science Journal* and the *Christian Science Sentinel.* In 1908 she founded the *Christian Science Monitor,* a daily newspaper, which has attained a large circulation.

Mrs. Eddy lived a secluded life in Lynn until 1882 and then after seven years spent in Boston she established a home at Pleasant View, near Concord, N. H. In 1908 she took up her residence at Newton, Mass., living in virtual retirement. She died there on Dec. 3, 1910, and was buried in Mt. Auburn Cemetery, Cambridge.

Few characters in modern life have been the subject of more varying comment than has Mrs. Eddy. To her vast following she was a saintly leader and beloved spiritual guide, and she had certainly the power to arouse the spirit of veneration and a devotion amounting almost to worship. She has not fared equally well at the hands of all her biographers, some of whom have charged that she maintained too close personal control over the spiritual edifice which she erected. Some, indeed, have denied her the original inspiration on which her cult is founded. But that she was a great leader and an executive genius none can doubt.

THOMAS ALVA EDISON 1847–1931

Among great inventors THOMAS ALVA EDISON was unique in the popular fame which he achieved. In America he became an institution and was affectionately known as the Wizard. He was a great benefactor of humanity, and humanity in turn not only enriched him but paid him the tribute of unceasing interest in his life and work. He was born at Milan, Ohio, Feb. 11, 1847 and was still a child when his parents moved to Port Huron, Mich. He, indeed, was an authentic instance of a great man starting as a newsboy for he sold papers on the Grand Trunk Railway, devoting his spare time to experiments in electricity. Not long satisfied with selling, he was soon printing a paper of his own on a press installed in a freight car, which served as combination editorial office and experimental laboratory. As a reward for saving a child from being run over, he was given a sort of scholarship in a telegraph office at Mount Clemens, where he learned telegraphy. His inquiring mind could not long be satisfied with the routine duties of an operator, and he began to experiment, with the result that he shortly perfected a repeating instrument which automatically transmitted messages on a second line without the aid of an operator. He became known as an expert telegrapher, and filled positions at Stratford, Canada and Adrian, Mich. After wandering about the West and South, he appeared in Boston where he had no difficulty in obtaining employment and here he supplemented his regular work as a telegrapher by setting up a shop for scientific experiments. He devised a vote-recording machine which, though practical, was not put to use. In 1870, when he was but 23, he tested out, between Boston and Rochester, his invention of duplex telegraphy, which was not successful. For a while he was employed by the Gold and Stock Telegraph Company, of New York, and during this connection he brought out several new inventions and introduced improved apparatus. On his own account, meanwhile, he started a plant at Newark, N. J., for manufacturing his devices, but discontinued it and in 1886 established a plant and laboratories at Menlo Park in West Orange, N. J., where he also made his home. The group of buildings erected there and the neighboring spacious residence of the inventor became a center of interest to the public. Here, working early and late (for he seemed to require scarcely any sleep), he grudgingly paused, counting the precious moments, as he received the tributes of notables from every land. Here he grew into a mellow and illustrious old age, forever toiling to gratify his insatiable curiosity about the secrets of science and nature.

His inventions numbered over 1000 and only the most important can be mentioned. Among his many telegraphic improvements was an automatic system by which greater speed became possible, and a quadruplex system which was revolutionary in its effect. He invented the microphone, the mimeograph and the carbon transmitter for the telephone. In 1878 appeared the first crude model of the phonograph, developed later to such marvelous perfection. Destined to equal universality of use was the megaphone. These and other triumphs were sufficient to place him in the first rank of inventive benefactors. But the device which has given his name the brightest lustre and by which he conferred the greatest blessing on mankind was the incandescent lamp. The steps from the tallow candle to kerosene, and from kerosene to gas, were as nothing to the giant stride which marked the advent of this new, efficient and convenient form of illumination. The years of patient research and experiment required for its practical development constitute one of the treasured tales of indomitable persistence in the annals of invention. Not only did this epoch-making invention light the world, but the story of it throws a floodlight on the unique character of Edison's genius. There shines here with resplendent radiance the homely moral to try and try again. He knew not the meaning of defeat. Added to his unconquerable curiosity about every conceivable phenomenon was an attention to detail which was not the least factor in carrying him to the dizzy heights of fame. He would send to the farthest corner of the earth for some unfamiliar growth of which he had become cognizant, with which to experiment. In this way the filament for his lamp was finally discovered. The incandescent bulb has been greatly improved, but every improvement only adds to the glory of its original inventor. It was first exhibited in 1880.

Less successful were his experiments in the field of electric traction. He developed also a plan for the electrical treatment of iron ore. The kinetoscope, with its sensational potentialities, overshadows all his other inventions except the lighting bulb and the phonograph. From it was developed the modern motion picture and, having improved the phonograph with the disc record and a diamond-point reproducer, he synchronized it with the kinetoscope and achieved the "talking movies." Among other outstanding inventions must be mentioned the nickel-iron storage battery, produced after years of patient experiment. He labored incessantly, despite the handicap of almost total deafness, even through the early stages of the illness which caused his death, and was so keenly curious about its cause and manifestations that it was said he knew as much about it as the physicians who attended him. One of his last achievements was a process for manufacturing rubber from golden rod.

He was the recipient of innumerable honors from governments, universities and scientific institutions, and in his old age came to be regarded as a sage from whom advice was sought on every conceivable subject. He was simple and kindly and without ostentation. His death on Oct. 17, 1931, was the occasion of many tributes of profound respect for his great genius, through all of which was apparent an affectionate regard which seemed to make his passage, in a peculiar sense, a personal and heartfelt loss. He had been twice married, in 1873 to Miss Mary Stillwell and after her death to Miss Nina Miller in 1886, and was the father of five children.

EDWARD III OF ENGLAND   1312–1377

EDWARD III, King of England from 1327 to 1377, was born at Windsor, Nov. 13, 1312. He was crowned king on Nov. 29, 1327, after his father, Edward II, had been deposed. During his minority, although the country was nominally governed by a council, his mother, Queen Isabella, and her lover, Mortimer, were the real rulers.

A year after his coronation Edward III married Philippa of Hainault. In 1330 he put Mortimer to death and banished his mother to Castle Rising. He invaded Scotland soon afterward to aid Edward Baliol, who had been crowned at Scone after the death of Robert Bruce. The Scots were defeated at Halidon Hill and Baliol paid homage to Edward, but a few months afterwards was forced to flee from Scotland. Edward invaded Scotland for three successive years with large armies, each time overcoming the Scots who rallied again as soon as the English armies were withdrawn.

Following the death of the childless Charles IV of France, who was the brother of Queen Isabella, Edward claimed the throne through his mother, although the law of France excluded women from the crown. Philip of Valois, nearest heir in the male line, ascended the French throne as Philip VI and Edward declared war against him in 1337. That was the beginning of the Hundred Years' War. He raised money by the imposition of taxes, by forced loans and the seizure of wool, and won a brilliant naval victory at Sluys in 1340. He purchased grants of money to continue the war by selling concessions of privileges, which he evaded when possible. In 1346 he again invaded France, accompanied by his son, Edward, the Black Prince, who was only 16 at the time, and inflicted upon the French a severe defeat at Crécy. Calais fell after a year's siege and a truce was declared, which was from time to time renewed.

The rebellious Scots had been defeated in 1346 at Neville's Cross, and King David II imprisoned. In 1349 the Black Death ravaged England, carrying off a third of the population and relations between master and laborer were permanently changed as a result of the depopulation.

The war with France was continued in 1355 and the Black Prince won a brilliant victory at Poitiers, where King John of France was captured by the English. In 1357 Edward released King David II of Scotland under promise of a ransom of 100,000 pounds. King John, released in 1360, when a peace was concluded with France, went to Paris to raise money for his ransom but finding himself unable to do so he returned to London and was held a prisoner until his death in 1364. By the treaty of Calais in 1360 Edward renounced his claim to the French throne in return for the cession to him of the whole of Aquitaine, a province in Southern France. A short time before this David of Scotland had made a secret agreement with Edward by which if he died without a male heir, his kingdom was to revert to the King of England. After a victory at Navarette and the sacking of Limoges, the Black Prince was obliged to conclude a three years' truce, so that Edward failed to realize his ambition in either Scotland or France, despite his many brilliant victories.

Affairs in England were in an equally unsatisfactory condition during the final years of Edward's reign. He had taken Alice Perrers as his mistress in 1366, and came more and more under her rapacious influence; he quarreled with Parliament, the financial condition of the country became deplorable and discontent grew throughout England. Edward had never won the love of his subjects and now he let affairs of state slip from his grasp into the hands of his fourth son, John of Gaunt, who was thought to be aiming at the crown for himself, but if so he was unsuccessful. The Black Prince, who toward the end of his father's life, headed the party opposed to Edward's policies, died in June, 1376, and

Edward survived him but a year, dying on June 21, 1377. He was an excellent tactician, a leader in knightly chivalry, with great vigor and energy of temperament, but selfish, extravagant, often faithless and in his public life governed only by self-interest.

JONATHAN EDWARDS   1703–1758

JONATHAN EDWARDS, an eminent New England divine and metaphysician, was born at East Windsor, Conn., Oct. 5, 1703, the son of one clergyman and grandson of another. He was a precocious child and at the age of 10 wrote a tract on *The Nature of the Soul,* and at 12 a paper on *The Habits of Spiders.* At 13 he entered Yale College, graduating at the head of his class when 17. Two years were spent in theological study in New Haven and eight months as acting pastor of a small Presbyterian church in New York, and then after tutoring at Yale for two years he was made assistant to his mother's father, the Rev. Solomon Stoddard, in Northampton, Mass.

The same year he married Sarah Pierrepont, then 17, who bore him 12 children and who survived him but a few months. On the death of his grandfather in 1727 Edwards became pastor of his church which was one of the largest and wealthiest in Massachusetts.

During these years he had come to accept the doctrine of divine sovereignty (which he had earlier rejected), and the doctrine of "unconditional election" (that is, the election of certain souls for eternal life and the election of certain others for damnation) became a belief to him "exceedingly pleasant, bright and sweet."

Edwards is said to have had more love for books and abstract ideas than for people and life; he often shut himself up in his library for 13 hours a day, visiting his parishioners only in extreme cases. He found intellectual satisfaction in upholding the Calvinistic doctrines and in attacking Arminianism. His first public attack on the latter was published in 1731 as *God Glorified in Man's Dependance.* He was an exceptionally profound thinker and a preacher of marvelous power, holding the rapt attention of his hearers sometimes for hours. The membership of his church increased by more than 300 within six months. One sermon on the *Reality of Spiritual Light,* in which the Calvinistic ideas and the spirit of mysticism were remarkably blended, led to a revival in Northampton, which later spread into the so-called "Great Awakening," of 1740 and the years following, in which he was a leader. But his severe

Calvinism, his strict interpretation of its doctrines and his rigorous opposition to the "half-way covenant," by which persons of exemplary life and character but not consciously "converted," were admitted to the sacraments of the church, alienated many of his people and in 1750 he was dismissed from his congregation.

He refused a subsequent call from a Virginia church and from another in Scotland, but accepted a pastorate in Stockbridge, Mass., and became a missionary to the Housatonic Indians. He also entered upon the period of his greatest literary labors, finding time to write *Original Sin*, *The Nature of True Virtue*, the *Essay Concerning the End for which God Created the World*, a profoundly speculative philosophical work; and spent four months writing *The Freedom of the Will*, which is one of the most famous of American theological works. He was contemplating a *History of the Work of Redemption* when, in 1757, after some hesitation he accepted the presidency of the College of New Jersey (now Princeton University), but the period of his service was short; small-pox was epidemic and Edwards, with others, submitted to a physician's advice and was inoculated. He was apparently recovering when he suffered a sudden change and died on March 22, 1758.

He was unquestionably a man of tremendous intellect; his great fame, not only throughout New England but across the seas, rested largely upon his theological work in the defense and development of the evangelical system. His brilliant treatises have less appeal to well-informed minds of today. He was unquestionably sincere in his religious thought and life and while often the center of theological controversy, he always commanded respect by his calmness, his justice and his fair methods of conducting discussion, as well as by the serenity and modesty which he always exhibited.

ALBERT EINSTEIN 1879–

Albert Einstein, German-Swiss scientist, is best known to the world as the author of the theory of relativity. He was born on March 14, 1879, of Jewish parentage at Ulm, Württemberg, in southwest Germany, where his father was the owner of electro-technical works. Most of his early life was spent in the city of Munich. While attending the University of Zurich, he taught in the high school in that city and later in a school at Schaffhausen. About 1901 (having then become a naturalized citizen of Switzerland) he obtained a position in the government patent office at Berne, but he continued to study the subjects which interested him and later took a doctorate at Zurich. He had followed with great interest the experiments undertaken by the American physicist, Albert Michelson, in conjunction with Professor Morley, designed to measure the relative motion of matter and ether, and in 1905 he wrote a thesis on his special theory of relativity in which he showed that light must travel in all directions with equal speed whatever the motion of the observer. He demonstrated that since motion depends upon the observer no one point can be considered the zero of motion; that time is relative and depends upon the observer. While his theory was at first considered fantastic, it gradually gained ground in Germany and eventually brought him recognition in the scientific world.

At the age of 30 he became a teacher of physics at the University of Zurich and later held a professorship at Prague. In 1913 an address which he delivered before the Prussian Academy of Science led to his appointment as director of the Kaiser Wilhelm Physical Institute at the University of Berlin, a position especially created for him, and he was given an income which freed him from financial cares and enabled him to devote his entire time to research. Meantime he had been elaborating and generalizing his theory and applying it in the field of gravitation. In 1919 by its use he was able to make certain mathematical calculations in the field of astronomy which were so much more accurate than the earlier calculations based on the theory of Sir Isaac Newton, that he became famous throughout the world and was hailed as a second Newton. Upon visiting the United States and European countries he was accorded many honors. In 1920 he published his famous work, *The Special and General Theory of Relativity,* followed in 1922 by *Sidelights on Relativity.* He had in the meantime during a stay in America delivered a series of lectures at Princeton University which were published under the title, *The Meaning of Relativity.*

He has made important contributions in other branches of physics, his work being by no means confined to abstract questions. He developed a formula for the Brownian motions (having to do with the movement of heat particles) which had been a baffling subject to scientists for nearly a century. He developed a law of radiation and his light-quantum theory and law of photo-electric effect, and conducted research in magnetism. He is a member of the Royal Society; received the Nobel prize for physics in 1921, and many other honors and awards have been accorded him.

In 1930 he made a second visit to America conducting further researches at Mt. Wilson Observatory and the California Institute of Technology. He was at this time much interested in the cause of the

Jewish Zionists and later published *About Zionism*. He returned to Europe early in the following year and located for a time at Oxford. During the later political unrest in Germany and the excesses against the Jews under the National Socialist Party, headed by Adolf Hitler, he suffered from persecutions and threats were made against his life. It eventually became necessary for him to leave his native land and he took up his residence in America.

Few men distinguished for achievement in fields of abstruse science have been so familiar to the general public as Einstein. Thousands who are baffled by the difficult theme of relativity have felt drawn toward this man of kindly human impulses and simple tastes. His burning interest in the cause of universal peace, his love of music and the familiar picture of him with his violin, his shyness and his unostentatious habit, have made him a peculiarly human figure.

QUEEN ELIZABETH   1533–1603

ELIZABETH, one of England's most picturesque rulers, is generally regarded as one of the greatest queens of history. She was born at Greenwich Palace on Sept. 7, 1533, the daughter of Henry VIII by his second wife, Anne Boleyn, for whose sake he had divorced Catherine of Aragon. In Elizabeth's third year her mother was beheaded and her father married Jane Seymour. Most of her early life was spent in seclusion in the country, her sister Mary or her brother Edward sometimes being with her. She received splendid intellectual training from devotees of the "new learning," some of whom were Protestants. At thirteen her father died and during the reign of her brother Edward VI her life was quiet and uneventful. After his death her Protestant inclinations aroused the hostility of her half-sister, Queen Mary, and although she outwardly accepted the Catholic religion, Mary's uneasiness continued and when Elizabeth became implicated in Wyatt's Rebellion (1554) the Queen ordered her imprisoned in London Tower.

Mary died in November, 1558, and Elizabeth, at the age of 25, was proclaimed Queen with the support of Catholics and Protestants alike. Deciding that her part in European affairs was to be that of a Protestant sovereign, she ordered that all church services be conducted in English; England took its place as a Protestant country and renounced allegiance to Rome, and the establishment of the Church of England followed.

One of Elizabeth's first acts after her accession was the securing of peace with France and Scotland. Her policy was to avoid open warfare but to prevent foreign interference in English affairs. She strengthened her own throne, however, by secretly aiding the Protestants of Scotland, France and the Low Countries. Her cousin, the Catholic Mary Queen of Scots, fell into her power and Elizabeth, unwilling to yield to the wishes of her ministers that Mary should be executed, held her prisoner for years, thus affording English Catholics grounds for entering into various conspiracies having for their object the assassination of Elizabeth and the placing of Mary on the English throne. The discovery of Babington's conspiracy and the demands by Walsingham, Cecil and others for her execution at length prevailed and Elizabeth signed her death warrant. Mary was beheaded on Feb. 8, 1587, at Fotheringay Castle.

Elizabeth never married, but conducted many flirtations, some of which scandalized her subjects. Leicester was for a long time her favorite, and her relations with him somewhat compromised her. She refused the hand of Philip II of Spain after holding out hopes to him for a time, as she did to some of his Austrian cousins whenever France or Mary Stuart seemed to threaten.

Philip had long meditated vengeance upon England for inciting rebellion in The Netherlands, capturing Spanish ships, and challenging Spanish supremacy in the New World. These considerations, strengthened by the wish to restore the Catholic faith in England, and his resentment toward Elizabeth after her refusal of his suit, led him to attack England. He gathered together the great Armada, which sailed from the Tagus in 1588 with 8000 sailors and 20,000 soldiers, while simultaneously the Duke of Parma was to transport an army of 100,000 from The Netherlands. This expedition, however, was decisively defeated and routed by the English under Howard, Drake, Frobisher and Hawkins.

Upon the death of Leicester, Robert Devereux, the twenty-one year old Earl of Essex, became the chief favorite of Elizabeth who was then sixty. He fell under her displeasure upon his marriage to the widow of Sir Philip Sidney (1590), but was restored to her regard and sent on various expeditions, succeeding Burleigh as Chancellor in 1598. He lost the Queen's favor again in the Irish campaign, was ordered imprisoned, and after making a demonstration in London was finally executed (after much wavering on Elizabeth's part) on Feb. 25, 1601, a blot on her reign which she afterwards passionately regretted.

Elizabeth died at Richmond, March 24, 1603, the last of her line. Her reign of forty-five years was noteworthy for development in literature, the arts and commerce. She lived in an age of splendor, cruelty and coarseness, and reflected the characteristics of her times, but although there was much in her character that was capricious and vain, she possessed great personal courage and displayed on occasion a stately and regal demeanor and gained for herself the name of "Good Queen Bess."

RALPH WALDO EMERSON   1803–1882

RALPH WALDO EMERSON was one of the most distinguished figures in American literature. In the field of letters he was, perhaps, our most original and independent genius and his influence is of wide scope. He was born in Boston, Mass., May 25, 1803. His father, who died while he was still a child, was the seventh in an unbroken line of Puritan ministers. After preliminary training in the public Latin School of Boston, he entered Harvard, was graduated in 1821, and several years thereafter was engaged with his brother in teaching school in Boston. Meanwhile he studied for the ministry, was ordained in 1829 and became associate pastor in the Second Unitarian Church of Boston. In the same year he married Ellen Louisa Tucker, who died three years later. The death of his colleague left him pastor of the church, but his pastorate was brief for he was shortly beset with scruples as to church ordinances and he could not support the custom of the communion. As a consequence he resigned his pulpit and shortly withdrew from the ministry, which occasioned some consternation among the Unitarians as well as those of other denominations.

He next went to Europe where he sought out several of the notables whose work he admired and received a rather lukewarm welcome from Carlyle and Coleridge, neither of whom apprehended the distinctive qualities of mind which were to bring him international fame. Upon his return in 1833 he began his distinguished career as a lecturer, including among his topics Michelangelo, Milton, Luther, George Fox and Edmund Burke. Thenceforth he was in constant demand on the lecture platform, traveling extensively and attracting large audiences from the most thoughtful and intellectual element in the country. In 1835 he married Lydia Jackson, and took up his residence in Concord, Mass., in a house which, later improved and enlarged, was to become one of the literary shrines of America. Here, with intervals of travel, he lived for the remainder of his life, venerated by his distinguished townsmen, Hawthorne, Thoreau, Alcott, and others; honored and beloved by all. As he grew older his tall figure and intellectual face, surmounted by silvery locks, was a familiar sight in the quiet, shaded streets of that village peculiarly distinguished in literary annals. His benign countenance bespoke his mellowed wisdom; graciously and fittingly he filled the role of kindly sage and philosopher, casting a spell which still lingers in Concord.

The subjects of his many lectures delivered in Boston and elsewhere are too numerous and varied for particular mention. He spoke on English literature, the philosophy of history, various branches of life and culture, and on many timely themes. In 1838 he delivered an address before the senior class of the Cambridge Divinity School which created no little stir in the literary and theological world. His first book, entitled *Nature*, appeared in 1836 and contains the essential features of his philosophy, extolling the idealistic as against the materialistic concept of life. In 1841 appeared his *Method of Nature*, developing more fully his distinctive quality of mind and way of thinking, and its freshness and beauty greatly increased his already large audience. His was now a "name to conjure with" in Europe as well as in America and he was recognized as a pre-eminent leader of thought. The "transcendental" movement, so-called, received much impetus from his work. For four years (1840–44) he was associated with a quarterly magazine called *The Dial*, with which his friends, Parker, Ripley, Channing, Alcott, and others were also affiliated and he was its editor during the last two years of its existence. In 1841 appeared his first volume of essays, to be followed by another two years later; and in 1846 by his collected poems. The following year he visited England and this time was enthusiastically received in intellectual circles as well as by the general public which flocked to hear his lectures. In 1850 appeared his *Representative Men*, essays on Plato, Swedenborg, Montaigne, Shakespeare, Napoleon, Goethe and others; profound and illuminating biographical studies, somewhat after the manner of Carlyle's *Heroes and Hero Worship*, but infinitely more graceful in style. He assisted in preparing the *Memoirs of Margaret Fuller* in 1852 and in the year following published his *English Traits*, containing observations on English life and character under the several headings of *Race, Ability, Manners, Truth, Religion*, etc., showing his power of keen penetration and understanding, but always kindly and gently humorous. Next appeared (1860) *The Conduct of Life*, a work which brings clearly to view the lofty spiritual and ethical principles which motivated his thought and pervaded all his writings. A second volume of poems was published in 1867 entitled *May Day and Other Pieces*, and in 1869 a complete edition of his prose works to date.

Although throughout his entire life his health was far from robust, he lived to be 79 years old and died at his home in Concord, on April 27, 1882, after a brief illness.

EPICURUS   340 B.C.–270 B.C.

EPICURUS (ĕp'ĭ kū'rŭs), whose name furnishes us with the familiar word, *epicure,* and whose teachings are known as Epicureanism, was a Greek philosopher, born on the island of Samos about 340 B.C. His mother is thought to have practiced the arts of magic while his father followed the more prosaic occupation of schoolmaster. While he was still a youth he went to Athens and is thought to have studied under the philosophers, Xenocrates and Theophrastus, but he did not scruple later to declare that what he knew he learned by himself. At 32 he opened a school on the island of Mitylene (anciently Lesbos), which was then a center of culture and is famed as the home of the Greek poetess, Sappho. After a period of about five years he returned to Athens where he purchased a garden and cultivated it as a fragrant and appropriate scene for imparting his philosophy. Here the studious youths flocked to him and, in this soft environment, became imbued with his theory that pleasure, rightly conceived, is the chief aim and end in life. They were not led astray by this engaging doctrine, and their lives were characterized by a temperate habit and the utmost simplicity. They came to be known as "the philosophers of the garden." The modern epicure would scorn their frugal diet with its limited accompaniment of one cup of wine, and would turn away from the menu, posted on the garden gate, of barley cakes and water. Nor was the abstemiousness of the teacher and his followers limited to food alone; chastity was their rule, so uniformly observed, at least, by Epicurus himself, as to inspire the comment that little merit was to be ascribed to this form of abstinence since he was without sexual impulses. In any event, his success as a teacher was great and his unique school came to be widely known and highly esteemed throughout Greece and Asia Minor. Hundreds flocked thither and became not only converted to his views, but warmly attached to him, and he enjoyed a loyalty and affection on the part of his pupils which can only be accounted for by assuming a most magnetic and lovable personality on the part of their instructor. From all we can learn of him he was tolerant, kindly and benevolent. He died in 270 B.C. at the age of 72.

Of his numerous writings, estimated to have filled about 300 volumes, only three letters have come down to us. But in the account of him by Diogenes Laertius, who wrote a history of the Greek philosophers, are numerous sayings of his which throw a vivid light upon his thought and personal life. For an account of his philosophy we are indebted chiefly to Seneca and Cicero, and to the great didactic poem of the Roman

Lucretius, *On the Nature of Things,* which Cicero revised and which treats largely of the doctrines of Epicurus.

Of the philosophy of this illustrious teacher, only a cursory outline can be here given. He believed that the greatest bar to human peace and contentment was fear—fear of death and of the gods. To dissipate this fear was the broad aim of all his speculations. He was, in modern phrase, a materialist, believing that the soul is a bodily substance composed of particles, and somewhat comparable to the breath. Hence it dissolves with the body. He did not question the existence of gods, but maintained that they have no connection with the affairs of man, and therefore need give him no concern. Nor should we, he thought, be concerned with death. "When we *are,* death is *not;* and when death *is, we* are *not.*" Logically, his philosophy removes the fear of death.

It is the positive side of his philosophy by which he is best known to people generally. He held that pleasure was the chief good, but the universal error as to the meaning he gave to the word is the reason for loosely regarding him as a devotee of license and unbridled appetite. The true Epicurean would be far from that. He did, however, believe that true *feeling* is the test of ethical quality. If we replace the word *pleasure* with the word *happiness,* we come nearer to his underlying thought. According to him, the two strongest feelings are pleasure and pain. Instinctively we seek one and avoid the other. Hence, any kind of excess is the negation of true pleasure. The bloated sensualist finds no support in the philosophy of this ancient practitioner of common sense. Ethical and moral determinations hinge upon a balancing of pleasures and pains, and out of this philosophy, so astonishingly modern in its trend, emerges the requisite of *prudence* in all human action. So, also, injustice is bad because of its inevitable reactions. He did not, as certain modern sects do, venerate spirit as the only reality. He believed in the beneficence of sensation: Freedom of the body from pain, of the spirit from fear or anxiety, the quest of wholesome benefit, from thought, from the wine cup, from the table, from all the joys of life—this is the rational philosophy which, misunderstood, has linked the name of this great thinker and guide to illconsidered debauchery and gluttony, in all subsequent ages.

DESIDERIUS ERASMUS   1466–1536

DESIDERIUS ERASMUS (ĕ răz'mŭs), scholar and theologian, was one of the outstanding figures produced by the Reformation. He was born, probably at Rotterdam, on Oct. 28, 1466, the illegitimate son of a Dutchman named Gheraerd (or Garrit) and the daughter of a physician. The name by which he is known in history was chosen by himself. When a child he sang in the choir in the cathedral at Utrecht, and was later sent to school at Daventer, where his talents and studious habits inspired the prediction that he would one day be the most learned man of his time. The death of both his parents when he was 14 left him in the care of guardians who placed him at 17 in a monastery with the purpose of appropriating his patrimony and compensating him with the blessings of religion. But his vigorous spirit remained not long in the shadow of monastic restraint; he was released by the Bishop of Cambray and, having taken priest's orders in 1492, he went to Paris to complete his theological studies in the glamor of that metropolis. Here he devoted himself to science and theology, gave private lectures and led a somewhat precarious existence until 1497 when he accompanied a group of young Englishmen, who had found him a congenial teacher, to England where his accomplishments are said to have won him a gracious reception in the court of Henry VII. Returning shortly to Paris, his studious and inquiring mind presently took him to Italy, where he increased his generous store of knowledge and, at Turin, took the degree of D.D. At about this time the pope, at his request, granted him a dispensation from his holy vows. He visited Parma, Venice and Rome, accompanied by his pupil, Alexander Stuart, who was an illegitimate son of the Scottish king, James IV. At Rome he was affectionately received and signally honored by the celebrated Cardinal Grimani and by John de' Medici who later was elevated to the papacy as Leo X. Pope Julius II offered him high preferments which, many years later, the reformer wistfully regretted having renounced.

In 1509, when he was 43 years old, he made good his promise to return to England where, also, his learning and ingratiating qualities had won him many admiring friends. By that time Henry VIII had ascended the throne and the scene was set for the English Reformation. Erasmus' journey thither was interrupted by visits in various cities where, as usual, he was highly honored and besought by friends to fix his permanent residence among them. But he had been led to hope for major favors at the hands of the British sovereign, with whom he had maintained a correspondence, and he pinned his faith to the dubious stability of that royal patron. Arriving in London, he accepted the hospitality of the ill-fated Sir Thomas More in whose home he wrote his *Encomium Moriœ,* or Praise of Folly, exposing fools, with special regard to ecclesiastical fools, not excepting the occupant of the papal throne. His high hopes for preferments and dignities from the burly king were soon dissipated and, after nursing his chagrin in a poorly paid professorship at Oxford, he repaired, disillusioned, to the continent and died at Basel on the 12th of July, 1536, in the seventieth year of his age.

The early prediction that he would be the most learned man of his time was probably fulfilled; and his profound and varied erudition was set off by a sprightly wit and engaging personality which his intimates found highly captivating. He had about him a disarming frankness and in an age of heroic martyrdom readily admitted that he had "no inclination to die for the sake of truth." He was a charming compound of the man of the world and the scholar. He had not Luther's militant power, nor had Luther his sense of humor, and the great hero of the Reformation reproached Erasmus for his alleged cowardice. His service in the cause of science was great and his various writings are even now held in highest regard not only for their substance but for the purity and beauty of his literary style. It was he who prepared the earliest edition of the Greek Testament (1516), a masterly labor which by many scholars is regarded as the greatest of his writings. The most familiar of his works, however, is his *Colloquia,* first published in 1522, written as he declared "to make youths better Latinists and better men." Notwithstanding its subsequent wide influence, it was at the time burned in Spain, prohibited in France, and generally condemned because of its bitter and satirical treatment of monks, monastic life, religious pilgrimages and church customs generally. It has been translated into many languages and has always been widely read.

EURIPIDES   480 B.C.–406 B.C.

EURIPIDES (ů rǐp′ ǐ dēz) was one of the great tragic poets of Greece. There are conflicting versions of his life, but the prevailing thought is that he was born on the island of Salamis, off the Greek coast, in 480 B.C. According to an accepted tradition, his birth occurred on the very day (Sept. 23) of the great victory won by the Greeks over the Persians on that island. Despite the humble station of his parents, who were probably petty tradespeople (though about this point also there has been considerable controversy), the son had a good education. The prediction of an oracle that he would be "crowned with silver garlands" moved him to prepare for his destiny, not only by study, but by the practice of gymnastic exercises. He also took up painting and later studied philosophy under Anaxagoras and rhetoric under Prodicus. He is thought to have enjoyed the intimate friendship of Socrates by whom he was certainly much influenced, and many of the ideas embodied in his works were derived from this source. He, of all the Greek dramatists, is the one who deals most particularly with human motives uninfluenced by religion and by this measure he seems more modern than any of his colleagues. His first play, *Peliades,* was produced in 456 B.C. Several years later (it is not certain what he produced in the meantime) he was awarded the first prize for tragedy and continued thereafter to write plays for production in Athens. From the beginning he appears to have been held in high esteem by the more intellectual element; the long speeches in his plays had a strong appeal to those who had studied oratory, and he was highly praised by Cicero.

Of his personal life little is known, and much that is contradictory has been published about him. He is thought to have been twice married and to have been deceived by both his wives. The rational and philosophical tenor of his works caused charges of impiety to be made against him and the fate of his friend Socrates seemed likely to befall him. Whether he was exiled or found it the part of discretion to withdraw from Athens, is not known. The prevailing version of his departure is that about 408 B.C. the king of Macedonia invited him to sojourn at that court where after several years he met with a strange and tragic fate. About 406 B.C. professional rivals, jealous of his success, drove a pack of furious hounds upon him and he died from wounds inflicted in their vicious attack. He was then over 70 years of age. The Athenians requested that his body be returned to them, but he was buried at Pella in Macedonia. A cenotaph erected to his memory in Athens contains an epitaph to the effect that although Macedonia covers his bones all Greece is his monument.

Of the 90 or more plays which he is believed to have written, only 18 have been preserved. These entitle him to a very high place among the dramatic poets of all time and he stands second only to his great contemporary, Sophocles. Unfortunately, from the standpoint of art and popularity, he held strong convictions which are always prejudicial to the artist. His liberal tendencies in the matter of religion colored his work and the witty champion of orthodoxy, Aristophanes, found him an easy target for his ridicule. The plays which have survived are *Alcestis, Medea, Hippolytus, Hecuba, Heracleidæ, Supplices, Ion, Herecules, Furens, Andromache, Troades, Electra, Helena, Iphigeneia in Tauris, Orestes, Phœnissæ, Bacchœ, Iphigeneia in Aulis* and *Cyclops. Rhesus,* sometimes attributed to him, is of doubtful authenticity. No better estimate of Euripides can be given than that of Schlegel, the eminent German translator and critic: "Of few authors can so much good and evil be predicated with equal truth. He was a man of infinite talent, skilled in the most varied intellectual arts; but although abounding in brilliant and amiable qualities, he wanted the sublime earnestness and artistic skill which we admire in Æschulus and Sophocles. He aspires only to please, no matter by what means. For this reason he is so frequently unequal to himself; producing at times passages of exquisite beauty, and frequently sinking into positive vulgarity."

MICHAEL FARADAY   1791–1867

MICHAEL FARADAY was a distinguished chemist and experimenter in the realm of physics and electricity. To him, indeed, the world owes much that has been accomplished in the field of electricity for the pioneering experimental work which he carried on with such meticulous care and which he carefully recorded in his *Experimental Researches in Electricity,* published in more than 20 different series from 1839–55, furnished a basis for the later work of the Scottish physicist, James Maxwell, and others.

He was born at Newington, in Surrey, Sept. 22, 1791. His father was a blacksmith and although at an early age he was apprenticed to a bookbinder and had apparently little opportunity for education, he nevertheless triumphed over these early handicaps. In his spare time he studied such scientific works as he could obtain and by the time he was 20 he had made an electrical machine of his own with which he experimented. At about this time he attended four lectures given by the eminent chemist, Sir Humphrey Davy, of the Royal Institution, who was so impressed by the notes which the young man had taken and which he sent to Sir Humphrey in the hope of thereby obtaining some more suitable employment, that he engaged Faraday as his own assistant. On their return to London after some time spent in travel on the continent, Faraday was allowed to conduct experiments for his chief which resulted in the liquefying of certain gases under pressure. In the course of this work he evinced such keenness and originality of mind that his name began to be known and in 1824 he was elected a member of the Royal Society and three years later he succeeded Davy as professor of chemistry in the Royal Institution.

His discoveries and researches in chemistry were many and important. He developed a number of new compounds, one of which resulted in the discovery of benzol which forms the basis of aniline dyes. Alloys of steel, decomposition of hydrocarbons and a number of valuable experiments leading to the manufacture of optical glass having a higher power of refraction, were other subjects that engaged his fertile mind. His earliest discoveries of importance had to do with the revolution of a magnetic needle around an electric current and the effect of one such current on another. These led to the publication in 1821 of his work on magneto-electricity and induction, and to the development of magnetos, dynamos and other important inventions. He investigated the subject of electrolysis, originated the electrical terms "anode" and "cathode," and "specific inductive capacity;" made clear the separation of electricity from magnetism. In short, his work laid the foundation of the modern science of electricity, but an enumeration of his many investigations and discoveries could be of interest only to the technically trained.

When in middle age he was granted a life pension of 300 pounds a year, was made scientific adviser to Trinity House and given the use of a house in Hampton Court. He declined the presidency of the Royal Society. He was of a generous and kindly nature and very religious, being a member of a small sect of Christians known as "Sandemanians." Toward the close of his life his mental and bodily powers waned, although some of his best work was done shortly before his death which occurred at Hampton Court on Aug. 25, 1867.

DAVID GLASGOW FARRAGUT 1801–1870

DAVID GLASGOW FARRAGUT, American naval officer, whose brilliant career in the Civil War gave him lasting fame, was born on July 5, 1801 at Campbell's Station, near Knoxville, Tenn. He was the son of George Farragut, a Spaniard from the island of Minorca who had aided in the American war for independence. At the age of 11 the boy became a midshipman and was placed under Captain David Porter on the *Essex,* of which his father had earlier been master. He was present at several engagements during the War of 1812 and took a gallant part in the battle with the two English ships, *Cherub* and *Phoebe,* in March of 1814. When only 12 he was placed in charge of a naval prize taken in battle. From 1815–17 he served in the Mediterranean waters on the *Independence* and the *Macedonian,* studied for nearly a year with the American consul at Tunis, was transferred to the *Shark* and later to the *Ferret* and then to the *Brandywine* in 1825. By this time he had risen to the rank of lieutenant and had acquired a considerable degree of education and culture, including a knowledge of French, Italian and Arabic, and was very accomplished. He was a man of marked religious faith, kindly and gentle in his bearing and possessed of great physical strength although under the medium height. In short, he was the traditional officer and gentleman.

The next several years were spent in various capacities on a number of different vessels and he was sent to many parts of the world. He was in command of the *Erie* in 1838 and during the Mexican War with the sloop of war *Saratoga* under his command he maintained a blockade of the port of Tuxpan. There followed a period at the Norfolk Navy Yard in Virginia and after some time in Washington helping to formulate a new code of regulations for the navy he was sent to the Pacific Coast to superintend the construction of a navy yard in San Francisco Bay. Four years later he was given command of the sloop of war Brooklyn and the outbreak of the Civil War found him again stationed at Norfolk. Although a southerner he was loyal to the Union and when Virginia seceded he immediately started for the North and in December 1861 was given command of a squadron of 17 vessels and despatched to the Gulf of Mexico to blockade the Gulf ports. On the 24th of April 1862, after a bombardment by Commander Porter of the Confederate forts Jackson and St. Philip, which faced each other across the mouth of the Mississippi, Farragut in his flagship *Hartford* made a daring run by the forts and completely destroyed the Confederate fleet of 15 boats. It was one of the most brilliant of recorded naval achievements. In the engagement three of his own boats were forced to put back and one was lost. New Orleans surrendered and Farragut sailed into the Mississippi River in obedience to instructions, although against his own judgment. The trip was futile but the following year when Gen. Grant with his troops was outside of Vicksburg Farragut rendered valuable assistance in taking the city and securing Federal control of the river.

He was raised to the rank of rear admiral and toward the close of the war, with a fleet of 25 vessels, he entered Mobile Bay and after a terrific engagement with the Confederate forts and vessels in which his ship, the *Tecumseh,* was sunk by a torpedo from the enemy, he succeeded in demolishing the forts and captured the city of Mobile. Ill health forced his withdrawal from active life and in December, 1864, the rank of vice admiral was created for him by Congress. Two years later the rank of admiral was similarly given him. After a cruise in European waters and a visit to California, he went to Portsmouth, N. H., where he died on Aug. 15, 1870. His biography was published by his son Loyall.

FERDINAND V OF SPAIN
and ISABELLA

1452–1516;
1451–1504

FERDINAND and ISABELLA were joint sovereigns of Spain at the period of her highest development and power.

Ferdinand the Catholic was born March 10, 1452, at Sos in Aragon, son of John II, King of Navarre and Aragon. He became Ferdinand V of Castile, II of Aragon and III of Naples. In 1469 he married his cousin, Isabella, sister and heiress of Henry IV of Castile. Henry's nobles, at his death, refused to recognize the legitimacy of his daughter, Juana, and in 1474 proclaimed Ferdinand and Isabella joint sovereigns of Castile. Civil war followed lasting until 1479, when the rebellious subjects surrendered and, following the death of Ferdinand's father, the crowns of Aragon and Castile were united. Isabella retained full control in Castile throughout her life, while Ferdinand was occupied largely in pursuing successful warfare. In order to suppress the bandits in Aragon who were very troublesome, he reorganized the "Holy Brotherhood," a sort of militia-police of which he also made use in breaking up feudalism among the aristocracy and depriving them of many of their privileges. The influence of that class was greatly lessened also through the establishment of the Inquisition, organized in 1478–80.

Ferdinand's campaign against the Moors succeeded in 1492 with the fall of Grenada, which had long withstood Spanish arms. The Jews were thereupon expelled from the conquered territory and a short time later all the rights which had been secured to the Moors by the treaty of surrender were abrogated. They were given their choice of baptism into the Catholic religion or exile. Both Jews and Moors were industrious, with a high degree of civilization and their exile left Spain that much the poorer.

The year 1492 was also memorable for the sailing of Christopher Columbus on a voyage which had been made possible by the support of the Spanish monarchs, particularly of Queen Isabella, and which ended in the discovery of the West Indies. The prestige resulting from this discovery and the acquisition of colonies across the Atlantic made Spain the leading nation of Europe for a time.

Ferdinand and Isabella recovered from France by treaty the territory now known as the Pyrénées-Orientales. In 1485 Ferdinand, with the Pope, the head of the Holy Roman Empire, with Milan and Venice and later England, formed the Holy League. Under Gonsalvo de Cordova the League drove the French out of Naples on two occasions. After the second

French defeat, in 1503, Ferdinand maintained permanently his authority over Naples.

Isabella, who was born in 1451, died in 1504. The following year Ferdinand married Germaine de Foix, a niece of Louis XII of France. Financial troubles followed. He was compelled to buy off French claims on Naples, and he experienced difficulty in raising money for the dowry of his daughter Catharine, whose marriage with the Prince of Wales, afterwards Henry VIII of England, was then under negotiation.

In 1508 Ferdinand joined the League of Cambrai in a campaign against Venice. The next year he conquered Oran, and in 1512 the Kingdom of Navarre, so that now for the first time there was a united Spain, from the Pyrénées to Gibraltar, under one ruler. His passion for dominion and political power was gratified, but not without deceit and treachery on his part. He is said to have boasted that he had deceived Louis XII of France twelve times. His treaties were frequently found to contain provisions of advantage to himself about which the other party to the treaty remained in ignorance. He distrusted the famous Cardinal Ximenes, who had been of incalculable help to him in the early part of his reign, and distrusted also Columbus, jealous lest they become too independent and attach to themselves a little of the authority which he coveted. Some of his acts were illegal, but usually the good of Spain and the security of his own position was served by them. He died at Madrigalejo, in Estremadura, Feb. 23, 1516.

EUGENE FIELD   1850–1895

EUGENE FIELD, favorite minor American poet, was born in St. Louis, Mo., and was the son of Roswell M. Field, a lawyer who attained prominence in the Dred Scott case. His mother died while he was but a child and most of his boyhood was spent with relatives in Amherst, Mass. His early education was obtained in private schools; later he attended Williams and Knox Colleges and the University of Missouri, although his stay in each was short.

His gift for lyrical expression was manifest in his youth and that facility probably kept him from going upon the stage as was his early inclination. He had a gift also for satire which proved an open sesame to a newspaper career. His journalistic experience was obtained first in St. Louis, continued in St. Joseph and Kansas City, Mo., in Denver and Chicago. He contributed to the various newspapers upon which he was employed satirical shafts, short bursts of lyric poetry, brilliant sayings, witty observations. Some of his unprinted poems made the rounds of newspaper offices throughout the country, and his published writings were reprinted in many dailies, often with credit to their author so that he quickly established a reputation.

Field joined the editorial staff of the *Chicago Daily News* in 1883 and continued as a regular contributor to that paper until his death. His daily column came to be one of the most popular features of that journal. He was one of the first, as well as one of the best, of newspaper columnists. He wrote about anything that interested him at the moment—light verse, serious articles, satirical pieces, literary gossip, prose sketches, fanciful conceits. A ready humor and caustic wit characterized many of his early contributions to the *News,* particularly in his grotesque inventions about well-known personages of the day for whom he invented a whole list of preposterous actions. He struck a new note in journalism and became one of the most quoted of newspaper writers. A collection of his writings, taken from his column in the *News,* was published in book form in Boston in 1887 under the title of *Culture's Garland*. It attracted favorable reviews and won enough popular success to encourage him to attempt more serious literary work.

He turned his lyrical gift to the writing of poems for and about children and many of his later books were chiefly for the young. They became instantly popular and he became known as "The Children's Poet." Many of his poems were set to music; others appear in most collections of nursery rhymes. In 1889 he published privately in Chicago two volumes, *A Little Book of Western Verse* and *A Little Book of Profitable Tales*. The following year both volumes were issued by a publishing house in New York and enjoyed a wider sale. In 1892 appeared *A Second Book of Verse* and *With Trumpet and Drum,* one of his most popular collections of poems for children, followed the next year by *Love Songs of Childhood*. In 1892 he had published privately rhymed translations from Horace, written in collaboration with his brother, Roswell Field, under the title of *Echoes from a Sabine Farm*. Soon after his death a complete edition of his published works was issued in ten volumes; in 1901 two more volumes collected from fugitive newspaper contributions and some hitherto unpublished material were added to his collected works.

He was the owner of an extensive library notable for the number of first editions and rare volumes it contained. Some of his experiences as a collector were recounted in *The Love Affairs of a Bibliophile,* which contains much of his best light prose work. The final chapter of this book was written the night before his death which occurred on Nov. 4,

1895. In 1926 his body was transferred to the church in Kenilworth, a suburb of Chicago. He had married in 1873 Julia S. Comstock of St. Louis.

HENRY FIELDING   1707–1754

To the general public of today HENRY FIELDING is known as the author of *Tom Jones,* a novel which stands high in the category of English fiction, but he wrote several other works as well. He has been called the father of the modern novel. He was born in the neighborhood of Glastonbury, England, on April 22, 1707, son of Gen. Edmund Fielding, and was educated at Eton and later at the university of Leyden where he also studied law. On his return to England he made his home in London and wrote for the stage, working with such industry that in ten years he produced about 20 comedies and farces of indifferent value, which were forgotten as rapidly as they were produced.

In 1736 he married and, falling heir to a small estate, he withdrew with his young wife from London. But the rôle of country gentleman which he essayed could not long continue on his wife's diminishing means, and within three years he returned to London where he resumed his legal studies at the Temple. He found himself unable to practice, however, by reason of a rheumatic affliction and again had recourse to creative composition, this time in the field of fiction. Richardson's novel *Pamela* had lately been published and the public found its priggish morality highly palatable. It is hardly possible to exaggerate the silly and platitudinous prudery of all of Richardson's works, and one there was whose high disgust of *Virtue Rewarded* found an outlet in satire—and that was Fielding. He conceived and published a sort of sequel to *Pamela,* purporting to be the adventures of Pamela's brother, under the title of *Joseph Andrews.* The conventional Richardson was quite without the saving grace of humor and he never forgave Fielding for this parody which, lightly conceived, developed into a narrative replete with originality and humorous adventure. It is in this story that the exquisite Parson Adams appears —a masterpiece of delineation. Encouraged by this success, Fielding next wrote *Jonathan Wild,* published in 1743, a masterpiece of irony which deserves a better fate than it has received at the hands of subsequent generations, and which is thought to have furnished to Thackeray the inspiration for his equally neglected work of *Barry Lyndon.*

In 1745 he undertook the editorship of the *Jacobite Journal* in support of the Hanoverian succession; and shortly afterward, as a reward for his loyalty, his friend Lord Lyttelton secured him a pension and the post of justice of the peace of Middlesex and Westminster, which he filled with marked efficiency for the remainder of his life. It was in seeking relaxation from his magisterial duties that he wrote *Tom Jones,* the novel on which his fame chiefly rests, though indeed much of his finest work is to be found in his other fictions. But critical, as well as popular, opinion has been all but unanimous in accepting *Tom Jones* as one of the few great novels of the world. It is a marvel of wit, invention and skilful depiction of character; full of the most amusing scenes and adventures in high and low life and abounding in sparkling satire. Fielding was quite too fine an artist to make his work the vehicle of his own whims, convictions and prejudices; he had not, as Dickens had, the flair for reform. But there is apparent in these pages the kind of revealing quality which is noticeable in Shakespeare; a broad and tolerant mind, a shrewd sense and sympathetic understanding, a robust scorn of meanness and hypocrisy. His fine humanity, indeed, is said to have been abundantly proved in his capacity of magistrate. The defects of his great work are familiar and so often commented upon as to make a reference to them all but superfluous, its coarseness often running close to the line of indecency. This propensity of Fielding, which cannot adequately be explained by the literary habit of his time, was expressed not only in his language, but in the shocking grossness of plot and episode. Yet the thoughtful reader feels that this marring quality is to be ascribed to a certain straightforwardness and impatience with cant, rather than to a morbid tendency. In any event, *Tom Jones* has triumphed over its defects.

His next work was *Amelia* (1751), less striking and masterly than its predecessor, but quieter in style and enriched with scenes of domestic tenderness. Shortly after its publication he was attacked by a complication of disorders and sought relief in a journey to Lisbon where he died on the 8th of October, 1754.

MILLARD FILLMORE   1800–1874

MILLARD FILLMORE, 13th president of the United States, was born at Summer Hill in Cayuga County, N. Y., on Feb. 7, 1800. His parents were English, and being in rather straitened circumstances they were able to give him only such education as could be had at the country school. At 15 he went to a neighboring county to learn the drapery business and then spent four years as apprentice to a wool carder in his home town. Meanwhile, he devoted his spare time to study and toward the end of his apprenticeship a lawyer by the name of Wood became interested in him to the extent of taking him into his own office and helping him financially to pursue his studies. He was admitted to the bar in 1823 and began the practice of his profession in Buffalo, where his industry immediately began to bear fruit. Having acquired some means and local reputation, he was elected to the state legislature in 1828 and twice reelected. It was largely due to his efforts during this period that New York State abolished the practice of imprisonment for debt. In 1832 he was sent to Congress as a representative by the whigs where, with a brief interruption (1835–37), he served until 1843. He became prominent as a public speaker, served as chairman of the Ways and Means Committee and practically drew up the Tariff Act of 1842. In 1844 he resumed the practice of law in Buffalo, made an unsuccessful attempt to win the presidential nomination and also ran unsuccessfully for governor of New York State. Three years later he was elected comptroller of the state; the following year became vice-president of the United States and upon the sudden death of President Taylor in July, 1850, he succeeded to the presidency.

During his administration some very beneficial laws were passed. One of his first acts was to press through the Compromise Measures of 1850, which permitted the extension of slavery in certain parts of the territory covered by the Louisiana Purchase. His support of these measures and of the Fugitive Slave Law lost him the approval of many voters in the North. During his term of office diplomatic relations with Japan were established. His vigorous domestic and foreign policy and his personal dignity and integrity commanded universal esteem and respect. He sought renomination by the whigs in 1852, but failed to receive it. In 1856, after returning from a trip to Europe, he was nominated by the short-lived party called the "Know-Nothings" or American party, but although he had the support also of the conservative element among the whigs (notably of the statesman and senator, Edward Everett, who had held the post of secretary of state during Fillmore's term as president), he carried only the one state of Maryland.

His political career thus ended, he returned to his law practice at Buffalo where he spent the remainder of his life. Although he was on the side of the Union in the Civil War, he took no active part in that conflict. He died at Buffalo on March 8, 1874. In 1836 he had married Abigail Powers who died in 1853 leaving two children, and some five years later he married Mrs. Caroline McIntosh.

MINNIE MADDERN FISKE   1865–1932

MARY AUGUSTA DAVEY, more familiarly known as Minnie Maddern, and who rose to the zenith of her fame as Mrs. Fiske, was one of the most sparkling and intellectual actresses of all time and occupied a unique place in the American theatre.

She was born in New Orleans Dec. 19, 1865, the daughter of Thomas Davey and his wife Elizabeth Maddern, a pair of theatrical troupers who billed their domestic group under the name of the "Maddern Family." The future interpreter of Ibsen was not three years old when she made her first stage appearance in Little Rock, Ark., as the little Duke of York in Richard III.

She early took her mother's maiden name, calling herself Minnie Maddern. Until she was fourteen she acted in a wide variety of plays, showing extraordinary talent and versatility. She played old women's parts when she was a young girl and as a middle-aged woman played the rôle of a fourteen year old girl. Her juvenile career was interrupted for brief periods when she attended convents in New Orleans, St. Louis, Cincinnati and Montreal, her education being supervised by her mother who was a woman of cultivated tastes.

Minnie Maddern made her first appearance in New York at the age of five at Wallack's Theatre as Fritz in *Fritz, our German Cousin,* and that city first saw her as a star at the old Park Theatre, May 20, 1882, when she appeared as Chip, in *Foggs' Ferry,* and a year later she played the lead in the musical play, *Caprice.*

In 1890 she married Harrison Gray Fiske, journalist and playwright, who was for years editor of the *Dramatic Mirror* and who was thenceforth to be her manager, and cooperator in her distinguished career. Years later, when she had successfully defied time and changing tastes, she protested that she would long since have been obliterated but for his invaluable guidance. Her marriage was followed by four years of retirement, devoted largely to study, and when she again appeared upon the stage it was as Mrs. Fiske in a play of her husband's authorship, *Hester Crew.*

Soon followed her sensational success as Tess in a dramatization of Thomas Hardy's *Tess of the D'Urbervilles,* a triumph of restrained emotional acting revealing her uncanny power, the despair of imitators, to convey emotional effects by the merest gestures. It was in reference to her acting of this rôle that William Dean Howells spoke of her "eloquent silences." She could, indeed, express more with the flick of an eyelash than another actress could by an emotional tirade.

It was her acting in this play which caused her to be acclaimed the greatest of English-speaking actresses. It was followed by another triumph, a dramatization of Thackeray's *Vanity Fair* produced under the name of *Becky Sharp,* and her impersonation of the novelist's famous character was perhaps the most notable, certainly the most sensational, in her long career. It stands as one of the great characterizations of dramatic history.

It was in the nineties that she was first seen in an Ibsen play, *A Doll's House,* introducing the great Norwegian dramatist to America. From time to time she appeared in other Ibsen plays, *Rosmersholm, The Pillars of Society, Ghosts,* and scored a notable success in *Hedda Gabler.* Among other plays in which she appeared in that period were *Frou Frou, The Queen of Liars, A Bit of Old Chelsea* and *Cesarine;* also a play of her own authorship, *A Light from St. Agnes.* She was often credited with extreme revision of the plays she selected, a recurrent declaration which she often denied.

In 1906 she appeared in another of her major triumphs, *The New York Idea,* written by Langdon Mitchell, who had dramatized *Vanity Fair* for her. Still other outstanding successes were *Salvation Nell,* and *Erstwhile Susan.*

Her later career was given over to parts in lighter vein, showing her incomparable qualities as a comedienne and putting less strain upon her increasing years. She quaintly observed that she had retired but that no one knew it. Approached by a playwright with a play that "ran the gamut of all the emotions," she observed that she had run all the gamuts that she intended to. She was deeply interested in the cause of animal welfare and fought a gallant fight against the cruel trapping of fur-bearing animals.

In the later years of her career she found it not always easy to secure a suitable play and appeared in many vehicles quite unworthy of her genius. But certain outstanding successes graced these final years. Notable among them were *Miss Nell of N'Orleans; Wake up, Jonathan;* a revival of *The Rivals;* the *Merry Wives of Windsor* and *Mary, Mary, Quite Contrary,* in which she appeared under the management of Belasco, fulfilling the long-cherished dream of that wizard producer "to have the great honor of being associated with her."

She died in Queens Village, L. I., Feb. 15, 1932.

GUSTAVE FLAUBERT 1821–1880

GUSTAVE FLAUBERT (flŏ'bâr'), French novelist, was born at Rouen on Dec. 12, 1821, the son of a surgeon. He was educated in Rouen until 1840 when he went to Paris to study law. He had already begun to write for his own gratification and, lacking any real interest in law even at the outset, the meeting of Victor Hugo, Louise Colet, Maxime du Camp and other literary figures encouraged his interests in that direction. His stay at Paris was cut short by the appearance of a malady which recurred throughout his life and which necessitated his return to his home in Rouen.

In 1846 Flaubert and his mother (his father and his sister Caroline having died) settled at Croisset, near Rouen, where he made his home for the rest of his life, with occasional visits to Paris. About this time began a *liaison* with Louise Colet which lasted until 1855.

He traveled in Brittany with du Camp in 1847 and in 1849 they set out for the Mediterranean. It seems to have been on this tour that the story of *Madame Bovary* was planned. Flaubert had already written two volumes, neither of which had been published; *Education sentimentale* between 1843 and 1845, and *Tentation de Saint Antoine,* 1848–49. The actual writing of *Madame Bovary* required more than four years (1852–56). In October of the latter year it began to appear serially in the *Revue de Paris*. It has been the centre of discussion on the art of the novel ever since. The French government brought a charge of immorality against both Flaubert and his publisher. Both were acquitted and the novel was published in book form in 1857. He had returned to the *Tentation de Saint Antoine* but laid it aside for the time being when *Madame Bovary* raised such a literary storm. His mind had been working at *Salammbô* for some time and he now devoted himself to that novel of the war of the mercenaries against Carthage. It was published in 1862 and condemned by the critics of the period but the younger generation of writers applauded it. Flaubert next devoted seven years to getting his *L'Education sentimentale* into shape for publication. It appeared in 1869 but failed to win the approbation of most of the critics.

Flaubert was greatly distressed by the Franco-German War, which may have helped to cause the breakdown of his health and the increase of his nervous malady. He lost some of his best friends; some through death, others through quarrels. His mother died in 1872, and he was thereafter cared for by his niece. His friendship with George Sand was of long duration and he saw Zola, Daudet, Turgeniev and the Goncourts occasionally in Paris, but his later years were lonely and desolate and he became something of a recluse.

La Tentation de Saint Antoine, at which Flaubert had worked intermittently for years, was at last completed to his satisfaction and published in 1874. In 1877 he published three short stories in one volume—*Trois Contes,* including *Un Coeur Simple, La Légend de Saint-Julien-l'Hospitalier* and *Hérodias.* These placed him among the great masters of the short story. The rest of his life he spent on *Bouvard et Pécuchet,* a satire on the futility of human knowledge which was published in a fragmentary state after the author's death. He died of apoplexy on May 8, 1880, at Croisset, and was buried in the family vault in the cemetery of Rouen. A monument to him by Chapu was unveiled at the museum of Rouen in 1890.

Flaubert brought a new note into fiction—that of exact reality, expressed in words which conveyed the exact shade of his meaning and his faultless style was attained by his practice of spending years on each production. He has probably had more influence on the development of the art of the novelist than any other writer of his century and he did much to develop the talent and mould the style of Guy de Maupassant, one of the younger of French writers, who became his literary disciple. Many of Flaubert's works have been translated into most of the important languages.

FERDINAND FOCH   1851–1929

FERDINAND FOCH, French marshal and commander of the Allied forces in the World War, was born at Tarbes, France, on Oct. 2, 1851. He received his education at the Lycées at Tarbes and Rodez, the seminary at Polignan, the Jesuit college at St. Étienne and at St. Clément's College at Metz, where he prepared for the École Polytechnique. He enlisted during the war of 1870, but saw no fighting. Returning to Metz, he made an excellent record at the École Polytechnique. In 1873 he was commissioned and rose rapidly to important posts, spending four years in command of the École de Guerre, and in the summer of 1914, while in command of the 20th Corps at Nancy and on leave at his small estate in Brittany, he was recalled by Germany's declaration of war. He was then 63, but a man of physical and intellectual vigor and of great will power.

The 20th Corps was part of the 2nd Army and Foch was one of the commanders of Castelanu's army which was thrown into Lorraine on Aug. 19, 1914. Defeated at Morhange, he retreated to Couronne de Nancy from which he resumed the offensive, defeated the Germans and prepared the victory in Lorraine. Marshal Joffre called him to headquarters and assigned him to command a new army, the 9th, to fill the widening gap between the 4th and 5th Armies retreating from Belgium into the Ardennes. He established himself at Fère Champenoise and, when the German right was turned, had to support the main strain of battle with numerically inferior troops. He forced the enemy back. His part in the victory of the Marne won him citations in general orders. On Oct. 4, Joffre sent him to the North as "deputy to the commander-in-chief" to direct the operations of the French troops and coordinate them with the British and Belgian troops in heading off the German drive toward the sea, which was to split the Allied forces. His resoluteness and his dispatching of reinforcements as needed by British and Belgians resulted, after the battle of Flanders and the fighting of the Yser and Ypres, in checking the German invasion for the year 1914.

Foch remained as general commanding the group of Armies of the North for two years; was in charge of the two Artois offensives of May and September, 1915, and the battle of the Somme in the summer of 1916 which the German attack on Verdun prevented from attaining the decisive nature desired. General Pétain, called to the chief command in May, 1917, suggested Foch as chief of general staff (after Foch had been relegated to Senlis on a mission of inspection).

When, in March, 1918, the Germans launched their first grand offensive, the necessity of a supreme commander of all the Allied forces was recognized and Foch was given the post. He stopped the Germans at the gates of Amiens, ending their effort to break through to the Channel. He checked the German offensive of the Aisne and of the second battle of the Marne. His victorious attack on the enemy's flanks on July 18 was the signal for the Allied grand offensive. The great offensive of August 8 on the Somme spread and forced the Germans back to the Hindenberg line. On September 3, Foch launched his famous "directive," culminating in the German general retreat of November 5, the Armistice of Nov. 11, the terms of which he drafted, and Allied occupation of the left bank of the Rhine. He was later censured for not continuing his offensive instead of allowing the war to come to a close, but he contended that to prolong hostilities would have meant useless sacrifice of life.

He was honored by many countries, was made a British Field Marshal in 1919, an honor never before extended to a foreigner; received the Distinguished Service Medal of the United States, the Grand Croix of the Legion of Honor and the Croix de Guerre. He was president of the Allied Military Commission at Versailles. His only son was one of the early victims of the war.

Upon his death on March 20, 1929, Marshal Foch was buried with great pomp beside Napoleon in the Dome of the Invalides, Premier Poincaré of France delivering the funeral oration and representatives of all the Allied nations participating in the ceremony.

HENRY FORD   1863–

HENRY FORD, American automobile manufacturer and one of the world's wealthiest men, was born on a farm near Dearborn, Mich., July 30, 1863. He attended the public school in Greenfield, working on the farm after school hours and during vacations and at 16 he went to work in a Detroit machine shop at $2.50 a week, working evenings for a jeweler to make living expenses. After two years in an engine shop he secured employment with a company which manufactured small steam engines for the farm, his work being to install and repair the engines. He spent two years at this work after which he returned to the farm and fitted up a workshop where he built a single-cylinder steam farm tractor, but was unable to devise a boiler with pressure enough to keep the tractor plowing.

In 1884 his father offered him forty acres of wooded land to divert him from mechanics and the son set up a sawmill on the property and sold off the lumber. In 1887 he married Clara Bryant and went to Detroit to live working as engineer and machinist with the Detroit Edison Company. He set about building a two-cylinder gasoline motor car, completed it in 1892 and after running it for 1000 miles sold it for $200 using the proceeds to build a lighter and stronger car. In 1899 he began to manufacture automobiles for the Detroit Automobile Company of which he was chief engineer. The directors wanted to make cars to order but Ford wished to manufacture them in large quantities. In 1902 he resigned from the company, continued to experiment and built several cars, two of them for speed, the "999" and the "Arrow." On the reputation for speed of the "999" Ford in 1903 formed the Ford Motor Company, capitalized at $100,000, but with only $28,000 in stock subscribed. It was enormously successful and in 1926 this company had assets of about $1,000,000,000, was the largest motor car company in the world, and the third largest industry in the United States, comprising about 50 other industries—coal, ore and forest lands, railroads, a fleet of lake ships, etc., for Ford rapidly acquired the sources from which the materials that went into his car were obtained and turned his profits back into construction. The company has never issued bonds nor borrowed money and is entirely owned by Ford and his son, Edsel B. Ford, who bought out the minority stockholders in 1919 for $70,000,000.

During its first year the company built 1708 two-cylinder, 8 horse-power cars. In its second year it made three models and during five years various models of four and six-cylinder cars. Ford was working to produce a light car of great strength which would require a minimum of care and cost in upkeep. He experimented with vanadium steel and with it designed the famous Model T—made to fit the needs of the largest possible number of consumers in both quality and price. In 1914 he startled the industrial world by raising the wages of his employees to a minimum of five dollars for an eight hour day (double the usual nine hour a day wage) and in 1926 still further increased his wage minimum to six dollars a day. By mass production and keeping the selling price of its cars within the means of all, the company continued to expand and in December, 1915, produced its millionth car. By 1926 it was producing at the rate of 2,000,000 cars a year. In the spring of 1928 the fifteen millionth Ford car was sent out and in that year Ford shut down his plant for six months while producing his new Model T four-cylinder car at an initial cost of $200,000,000. In 1932 he produced an eight-cylinder, as well as an improved four-cylinder, car.

He established the Henry Ford Hospital in Detroit, open to all on a fixed schedule of payment, with physicians, surgeons, nurses, etc., on salaries. In 1915 he chartered a "peace ship" and went to Europe with a company of distinguished persons (bearing the entire expense himself) in the hope of inducing the warring nations to stop the war, but his attempt proved futile. In 1918 he was nominated for the United States Senate but was defeated. He wrote *My Life and Work* and in collaboration with Samuel Crowther, *Today and Tomorrow*. The Ford home is at Dearborn, Mich.

GEORGE FOX   1624–1691

GEORGE FOX was a famous religious leader and founder of the Society of Friends, popularly known as the Quakers, a name first used contemptuously in ridicule of their habit of trembling, in speech and otherwise, in moments of religious exaltation. The appellation is said to have originated with an English magistrate, one Bennett, whom Fox, when arraigned before him, had adjured to "tremble at the word of the Lord." He was born at Drayton in Leicestershire, England, in July, 1624, and had little, if any, schooling. During his youth he is said to have been employed as a shepherd. Certain it is that he was apprenticed to a shoemaker and that his progress in this trade was interrupted by the consciousness of his divine mission; he believed that he heard a call and, obedient to it, he renounced his worldly toil and wandered forth seeking in solitude the opportunity for religious meditation. He roamed through the country in lowly raiment of his own manufacture and was a familiar sight in his rough leather doublet, absorbed in continual reverie as he indulged his spiritual visions. He was, in a measure, dissuaded from his unproductive life of exaltation by friends at whose instigation he returned to his home. But the intensity of his religious convictions did not long suffer him to live on the plane of work-a-day and uninspired folk, and he soon went forth again resolved to be an itinerant preacher and reformer.

He was 22 years old when he renounced the church, but he was by no means to become a stranger to it for it was his resolute custom to interrupt divine service whenever he felt moved to do so and to proclaim his unwelcome conception of Christianity, to the consternation of its accredited exponents—"professors," as he called them. This custom of forcing their testimony on unwilling listeners in hallowed precincts was always prejudicial to the early Quakers, who were gentle, kindly and long-suffering, and it bore its serious, and sometimes tragic, consequences, particularly in the New England colonies where they became a major problem to the Puritan authorities. Fox's career may be said to have started in Manchester, England, where his proselyting was so intense as to cause much trouble, the upshot of which was that he was thrown into prison on a charge of disturbing the peace. Every such logical consequence was conceived by Fox and his followers to be persecution, but the impartial student of history must distinguish between persecution of the sect (of which there was much) and the obvious duty of authorities to maintain law and order. Undaunted by his imprisonment, he made a tour of the country exhorting the people to follow the basic Christian virtues, denouncing drunkenness and every kind of vice. His creed, as far as he may be said to have had any, was simple. He recognized no affinity between learning and religion, abhorred form and ceremony, went straight to the very heart of essential Christianity, denounced and refused any participation in war, refused to take an oath, and exalted the guidance of the Holy Spirit. In 1655 his activities had become so conspicuous that Oliver Cromwell ordered him brought to London for questioning. But the great Puritan, always fair and tolerant, found nothing dangerous or contaminating in Fox's teaching and dismissed him without reproach. The Puritan authorities generally, however, were not so friendly and for years his path was difficult. His simple faith, without dogmatism and clear as crystal, could hardly be comprehended by the devotees of a doctrinal church which, with all its obvious merits, bred up a race of fanatics. He was persecuted continuously and often imprisoned by country magistrates, which only stimulated his zeal. In a sense the Quakers may be said peculiarly to have thrived on persecution. Even ridicule of their grotesque simplicity was welcomed by them as a tribute.

In 1669 Fox married a widow, ten years his senior, and soon visited America where he remained for several years, winning many converts and encountering, as usual, strong opposition which was sometimes carried to the point of persecution. He returned to England in 1673 and almost immediately had the familiar experience of being cast into jail, this time in Worcester, for "terrifying the king's subjects," an ironical charge in view of the gentle and pacifist character of his sect. He thereafter visited Holland and several cities of the Continent, preaching unceasingly and endeavoring to persuade men to listen to the voice of Christ within him. He was not a man of broad culture and was incapable of reasoned disputation. He spoke in homely phrase, but his preaching had all the force of thought concentrated on a single strongly held belief. He died in London Jan. 13, 1691.

ANATOLE FRANCE   1844–1924

ANATOLE FRANCE, French critic and novelist, whose real name was Jacques Anatole Thibault, was born on April 16, 1844, in Paris, the son of a bookseller. Naturally studious and fond of books, he became a very learned man and ranks high among the writers of his day for his wit, his graceful humor and his pure style. Among his first writings were the "blurbs" which publishers print on the jackets of their books and in their advertising. He contributed a weekly article under the name of Gérôme to the *Universe Illustré.* His first books were collections of his poems; *Poèmes dorés* (1875) and *Les noces corinthiennes* (1876). In 1879 he published a volume of short stories, *Jocaste et le chat maigre,* followed two years later by the very successful novel, *Le crime de Sylvestre Bonnard,* which still retains its popularity. In 1883 he met Mme. Arman de Caillavet, a clever and charming woman who became his lifelong friend and gave him much encouragement in his work. Her receptions were attended by the chief literary and artistic figures of France and she used them and her social position to forward the career of Anatole France.

For thirty of the forty years of his writing life France dominated

French letters. He wrote many books, short stories, novels and political satires. He was a skeptic—witty and profound—who played with ideas. He has been called the spiritual son of Voltaire. He showed little pity for the weaknesses and pettinesses of mankind, whether in the past or the present, and portrayed them in a spirit of witty malice. Among his books are *Balthasar* (1889); *L'étui de nacre* (1892) and *Le puits de Sainte-Claire* (1895); volumes of short stories; the critical *Opinions de M. l'Abbe Jérôme Coignard* (1893) and *La vie littéraire* (4 vols., 1883–92); *La rôtisserie de la reine Pédauque,* a philosophical novel (1893); *Thais* (1890); *Les dieux ont soif* (1912), a story of the French Revolution and the Terror; *Le lys rouge* (1894), a study of jealousy; *Sur la pierre blanches* (1903); *L'Ile des Pingouins* (1908) and *La révolte des anges* (1914), the last three novels of revolutionary tendencies. His four volumes of political satires include, under the general title of *L'Histoire contemporaine, L'Orme du mail, Le mannequin d'osier, L'Anneau d'améthyste* and *M. Bergeret à Paris,* portraying society before and during the famous Dreyfus trial. His biography of Jeanne d'Arc was published in 1909–10. Two volumes of his reminiscences, *Le petit Pierre* and *La vie en fleur,* contain much of charm and were widely popular.

In 1896 he was elected to the Academy and most of his work has been translated into English and German. A true skeptic, he observed and reported indulgently upon an imperfect universe. He absorbed what he read, adapted and transformed it into his own uses, giving it a grace and limpidity that was all his own. His intelligence was perhaps too keen and critical to allow of ardour and enthusiasm and his appeal as a creative artist is to the intelligently skeptical. His knowledge of antiquity and of classical literature was great, and the wisdom he acquired from the ancients and from his own observations was set forth in magical, if simple, French. With the political crisis of 1900 his temper underwent a change; his sympathies were with the progressives, finally leading him to support the revolutionary parties. He was an opponent of both Church and State, with his faith resting in the people. Too old to serve in the World War, he asked to be employed in a Tours office. Late in life he married his housekeeper. He died in Tours Oct. 13, 1924.

FRANCIS OF ASSISI   circa 1182–1226

SAINT FRANCIS OF ASSISI (äs sĕ′ zĕ), founder of the Franciscan order, was one of the most extraordinary men of his age, illustrating in his career all the most remarkable characteristics of the religious life of the Middle Ages. He was born in Assisi, Italy, about 1182, of the family called Bernardini and was the son of a rich tradesman in that small town. His baptismal name was John, but he early acquired the name of Il Francesco (the little Frenchman) because of his familiarity with the Romance, or language of the troubadours, and perhaps also because of his father's extensive trade with France. In his youth he was of a gay and carefree nature, and of a prodigal habit from which, it is said, the poor of his neighborhood reaped much benefit. He was also of a romantic and adventurous turn and his participation in one of the petty feuds of his time resulted in his imprisonment for a year. The mind's picture of him, deduced from these early escapades and habits, is that of a very winning and picturesque character. While he was ill in prison, however, his thoughts turned to serious matters and a subsequent illness, suffered during military service, convinced him of his holy mission and he was thereafter wedded to his "bride" of poverty. He took a vow never to refuse alms to a beggar, made a pilgrimage to Rome, and there humbly offered to God his possessions and his life. Returning to his native town, he exchanged his raiment with a mendicant and thereafter, in defiance of ridicule, he wore always the meanest attire. He sold his horse to help build a church and attempted even to consecrate the money of his father to these purposes, which so aroused the parental anger that he found it expedient to take refuge in a cave whence he returned after a month, his resolution stimulated by his continuous prayer in solitude. Incarceration in the parental abode followed, which only strengthened his purpose, and he was taken before a magistrate whose jurisdiction in such matters he so successfully contested that he was then taken before the bishop where he readily renounced both his father and his inheritance, adopting the "father that is in Heaven." He now consecrated his life in the utmost humility, begging at the gates of monasteries, ministering to lepers in the hospitals, working as a common laborer on church edifices, discarding his wallet and even his shoes and retaining as his only possession his brown tunic and his girdle of hempen rope.

Such enthusiasm and renunciation by one so young (he was then 26) soon bore fruit and two of his townsmen, Bernard of Quintavalle and Peter of Catala, joined him. They were followed by others, yet at the end of two years only eleven had elected to submit to the rigorous and beggarly life which their leader's habits and principles imposed. For this little brotherhood he drew up a rule by three times opening the gospels upon the altar at random and selecting the passages thus indicated as the basis of their government. The little group then repaired to Rome and received a sort of tentative sanction from Pope Innocent III, after which they devoted their time to wandering through the countryside, exhorting and preaching and setting a noble example of lowly piety. In 1212 Francis settled the simple constitution of his order (then known as the Friars Minor), which took up its abode in quarters adjoining the chapel of Saint Mary of the Angels, at Assisi. Thus was established the famous Franciscan Order, founded upon the three vows of obedience, poverty and chastity. Its emphasis of the vow of poverty sets it apart from other orders, in which poverty is merely an inevitable incidental to a life of simple piety and devotion. Such orders may hold property in common and a certain opulence has not been uncommon among them. It was such worldly possessions of the monasteries that attracted the covetous eye of Henry VIII in England. But the Franciscan Order is founded upon the absolute renunciation of temporal possessions and the vow to live upon alms. This is a positive principle and applies to the order as a whole, as well as to its individual members. The very tunics which they wore, nay, the very breviaries which they used, were not their own in the fine conception of their lowly life and mission.

Many flocked to the standard of this lowly devotee who represented so vividly the simple teachings of Jesus. He sent parties of them into various parts of Italy; five visited Morocco and paid with their lives for their courageous project of converting the Moors. In 1206 the papal approval was solemnly ratified and from that time the order increased rapidly. In 1219 it numbered 5000 members. In 1223 the founder set the example and inaugurated the missionary character of his brotherhood by journeying to the East, achieving the bizarre purpose of exhorting the sultan and winning his promise of indulgent treatment of Christian captives. He also secured for his order the privilege which it has since enjoyed of guarding the church of the Holy Sepulchre. He died at Assisi, Oct. 4, 1226, and two years later was canonized by Pope Gregory IX.

BENJAMIN FRANKLIN   1706–1790

BENJAMIN FRANKLIN, American statesman and scientist, was the son of Josiah Franklin, a Boston tallow chandler. He was born in that city, Jan. 17, 1706, and was the 15th of his father's 17 children. At the age of 11, after working at candlemaking with his father for a year, he was apprenticed to his half-brother James, a printer and later the founder of one of New England's earliest newspapers, the *New England Courant*. Following fraternal quarrels, Franklin betook himself to New York. Unsuccessful in his search for work there, he went on to Philadelphia where he arrived almost penniless in October, 1723. He was a good workman and quickly secured employment and made friends. In 1724 Gov. William Keith offered to set him up in a print shop of his own and sent him to England for supplies but neglected to provide the promised funds and the stranded youth found work in London print shops.

Soon after his return in 1726 he rejoined Samuel Keimer, a printer for whom he had worked in Philadelphia, but later established a shop of his own with Hugh Meredith. He bought the *Philadelphia Gazette* and made a success of it; was appointed public printer for the State; wrote and sold, in 1732, the first *Poor Richard's Almanack,* which he continued to issue and which brought him fame and fortune. In 1730 he married Deborah Read who survived him and who, in addition to caring for his natural son, bore him two children, a son who died at the age of four and a daughter Sarah who married Richard Bache.

Franklin became Philadelphia's leading citizen and founded in 1731 the Library Club which grew into the first circulating library in America; was made Grand Master of the Freemasons (1732); was clerk of the Pennsylvania Assembly (1736–51); organized the city's first fire company (1736); was appointed postmaster the following year; contributed many philosophical and scientific essays to his own and his half-brother's newspapers; discovered and proved the relation of lightning with electricity and conducted much research work which added greatly to the understanding of electricity; invented the Franklin stove; organized Braddock's transport system; organized the Northwest Territory against Indian raids; was instrumental in obtaining paved streets, a hospital, street lamps, founded the Academy of Philadelphia, later the University of Pennsylvania.

In 1753 he was appointed Postmaster-General for the Colonies. Sent to London later to urge the King to take over the province from the Penn family, he remained to fight the Stamp Act which was repealed in 1766 chiefly through his efforts. He continued to fight for the rights of the colonists but in 1775, realizing that war was unavoidable he returned to America and was at once sent as a representative to Congress. He presided over the Constitutional Convention of Pennsylvania; was elected one of the Committee to frame the Declaration of Independence and was one of its signers.

Sent to France in 1776 as one of three Commissioners seeking food, money, arms, ammunition and a military alliance with that country he met with signal success. In 1781 he was appointed a member of the commission to negotiate a treaty of peace with England. After his return in 1785 he was four times elected President of the Commonwealth of Pennsylvania. Late in life he wrote part of a projected *Autobiography* and was named a delegate to the Constitutional Convention. He died on April 17, 1790 and was buried in Christ Church Cemetery, Philadelphia. The impressive funeral in which the entire city paid homage was a befitting tribute to Philadelphia's first citizen and one of the world's great men. Congress passed resolutions of mourning and the French National Assembly went into mourning for three days.

FREDERICK THE GREAT   1712–1786

FREDERICK II, of Prussia, known as Frederick the Great, was born in January, 1712, the exact date being uncertain. He was the son of Frederick-William I and the Princess Sophia-Dorothea, daughter of the British king, George I. Frederick-William was both eccentric and ignorant and his policy of maintaining a large army recruited by giants amounted to a mania. Wholly deficient in all the arts which his famous son later encouraged, he maintained such a rigorous discipline both within and without the palace that citizens in the public streets were not exempt from the vigorous chastisements of his cane. Under the shadow of this stern paternalism the young Frederick read and studied and solaced himself with his flute. Seized in the act of attempting to escape to England, he was severely chastised, kept in confinement and brutally required to witness the execution of a lieutenant who was his sympathizer and friend. It is related that the rulers of Sweden and Poland were moved to exert their kindly influence in behalf of the wretched prince who was finally liberated from this insane household tyranny and permitted to live in Ruppin, a princely possession, where he gathered about him the most interesting and cultured people of his day and maintained a correspondence with Voltaire whom, as king, he was destined later to entertain. Here he remained until his accession to the throne in 1740. Among other arbitrary acts, his father had compelled him to marry Elizabeth of Brunswick-Bevern, who commanded his respect but never his love. He never relinquished his interest in the arts and amid the turmoil of his military activities and his busy concerns about the affairs of his people, he found time always to pay his respects to genius, and to write innumerable verses of indifferent merit. He was glad to receive the great composer Bach and to furnish him with a dozen pianos on which to practice hymns in praise of Prussian glory.

His extraordinary military career was inaugurated by his victory over the Austrians at Mollwitz (1741). His seizure of Silesia (one of the most unwarranted acts in history) involved him in bitter warfare with the Austrian queen, Maria Theresa, and resulted in his mastery of upper and lower Silesia. A second Silesian war, ending in 1745, augmented his territories and won him the reputation of a military genius of the first order. Followed a peaceful period of eleven years, during which this never-ceasing fountain of nervous energy set his national house in order. He overhauled all his governmental departments, organized and systematized a vast army, and was assiduous in devising means to promote the domestic welfare of his subjects. Few rulers have been so intimately paternal. He kept a weather eye on the procreative tendencies of his people, gave much gratuitous and sage advice about household economy and in a hundred ways improved his kingdom; and continued to play the flute. This "piping time of peace" came to an end with the beginning of the third Silesian, or Seven Years' War in which almost all of Europe became embroiled and which had its echo in America in the French and Indian War. It began with Frederick's invasion of Saxony in anticipation of the action of France, Austria, Saxony and Russia which he feared would deprive him of Silesia. Great Britain aligned herself with Prussia and hence the conflict between the French and English possessions in the new world (See Montcalm). This remarkable contest in the European theatre left the balance of power practically unchanged though it crippled the numerous powers engaged. It very much increased the prestige of Frederick and raised him to an exalted position as a military genius in the eyes of all Europe.

Upon the establishment of peace he lost no time in repairing the damage which the prolonged conflict had wrought. In 1772 he shared in the partition of Poland, obtaining as his share all of Polish Russia and a part of Great Poland, and by the treaty of Teschen (1779) Austria was obliged to accede to the consolidation of the Franconian provinces with Prussia. His kingdom was now one-half larger than at his accession; in sound financial condition despite the heavy strain of war, and he had an army of 200,000 men. This relentless warrior never forgot, either in war or peace, the comfort and welfare of his people, and the people of his conquered dependencies. He declared a moratorium of tax payments in Silesia, Pomerania and New Brandenburg to give the inhabitants the opportunity to recover from the stresses of war and invasion. He set an example of thrift and rigid economy and simplicity of life. His reign was free of ostentation. Persecution of every sort was unknown, the press was free, prosperity and contentment prevailed in his well-ordered kingdom. He was himself a prolific writer and ever indulged his musical and poetical proclivities. The famous visit of Voltaire to the palace of this versatile and erratic genius who was one of his most ardent admirers, is one of the amusing incidents of history. They quarrelled (as two such natures were pretty sure to do) and Voltaire left Berlin, only to be arrested by Frederick's order on his way to France on the pretext that he had taken away with him a volume of the king's poems, and he was subjected to various indignities.

Frederick left no children. He died at the chateau of Sans Souci, Aug. 17, 1786.

JOHN C. FRÉMONT
1813–1890

John Charles Frémont, American explorer and soldier, was born in Savannah, Ga., in 1813, the son of a French father and a Virginia mother. He was educated in the College of Charleston, receiving his degree in 1836, and spent three years teaching mathematics on the sloop of war, *Natchez*. Declining then an appointment as professor of mathematics in the United States Navy, he turned his attention to railroad surveying and in 1838 was made a second lieutenant in the Topographical Corps, U.S.A., and assisted John Nicholas Nicollet, who had been employed by the War Department to survey and map the territory between the Mississippi and Missouri Rivers.

Frémont later devoted several years to exploring the West. In 1842 he surveyed the Oregon Trail from the Mississippi to South Pass in Wyoming. The following year he continued the survey to the mouth of the Columbia River, where he turned southward to Nevada, the Truckee and Carson Rivers, hitherto unexplored territory. He then led his expedition across the Sierra Nevada mountains in mid-winter—a bold and rash undertaking which added much to his increasing fame. He wintered on the Sacramento and rounded the southern end of the Sierra Nevada range on the return.

In 1845 when war with Mexico was imminent, Frémont was sent on a third expedition, ostensibly to explore the Great Basin and the Pacific Coast, but with secret orders to be followed if war were declared. He reached the valley of the Humboldt in January, 1846. Mexican authorities ordered him out of California (which then belonged to Mexico), and he at first refused to leave but later reconsidered and led his force toward the Oregon border until he was overtaken by Lieutenant Gillespie, a messenger from the government, when he turned back to California. While his men were in camp the American settlers in the Sacramento Valley revolted, seized some government horses, captured the town of

Sonoma and proclaimed the "Republic of California." Captain Frémont took no actual part in this "Bear Flag Revolt," but he now took command, thus establishing an American military occupation. Commodore Stockton presently took over the chief command, appointed Frémont major of a battalion and by January, 1847, the American flag was floating over Southern California.

General Stephen W. Kearny had in the meantime arrived with orders to conquer the territory and conflict of authority arose between Kearny and Stockton. Frémont had been appointed Governor of California by Stockton whose authority he continued to recognize. Kearny, however, secretly given full authority, refused to recognize the appointment and ordered Frémont's arrest on charges of mutiny and disobedience. He was court-martialed in Washington, found guilty and sentenced to dismissal from the service, but President Polk immediately remitted the sentence. Frémont was embittered and resigned in March, 1848.

He later led a fourth expedition to survey routes for a railroad to the Pacific, the expedition being financed by himself and Senator Thomas Hart Benton, with whose daughter Jessie he had eloped in 1841. After many hardships and the loss of a number of men from exposure he reached California by a southern route in the spring of 1849, to find that gold had been discovered. Through the development of mines on a 40,000 acre tract which he had bought in 1847, he became a multi-millionaire.

In 1850 he was elected Senator from California; was defeated by James Buchanan for the presidency in 1856; and during the Civil War served as major-general in charge of the Western Department with headquarters at St. Louis. On August 30, 1861, he issued a proclamation confiscating the property of Missouri rebels and emancipating their slaves, but the action was annulled by President Lincoln who feared it would drive neutral states (whose loyalty he still hoped to preserve) into the Confederacy, and Frémont was transferred to another command, but resigned in 1864.

In that year also he was nominated for the presidency by the radical Republicans, but he withdrew his name and turned his attention to building a railroad to the Pacific by a southern route. Unsound financing led to the collapse of this enterprise in 1870 and Frémont lost his entire fortune. In 1878 he was appointed Governor of Arizona, serving until 1882.

He died in New York City on July 13, 1890, and was laid to rest in Rockland Cemetery, Piermont, N. Y.

SIGMUND FREUD   1856–

SIGMUND FREUD (froit), Austrian psychiatrist and founder of psycho-analysis, was born on May 6, 1856, at Freiberg, Moravia, of Jewish extraction. At the age of four he was taken to Vienna which has been his home throughout his life. Although as a youth he was principally interested in scientific research, he determined upon a medical career under the influence of Goethe's essay, *Die Natur*. His chief interests, even during his early medical studies, were in botany and chemistry. He spent six years in the physiological laboratory conducted by Brücke, and then studied under Meynert at the Institute for Cerebral Anatomy, completing his medical course in 1881. Lack of means compelled him to give up his research work and he determined to become a clinical neurologist. His interest in what later came to be known as psycho-analysis began in 1884 when Dr. Breuer related to him an incident in which symptoms of hysteria were cured by getting a patient to recollect and tell, while in a state of hypnosis, the causes of the hysteria. This was the starting point of Freud's psycho-analytic treatment for nervous disorders. In 1885 he visited Paris and spent a year studying under Charcot, the eminent French neurologist, who encouraged his determination to investigate hysteria from a psychological point of view. His pathological and clinical investigations won for him a Docent Pathology, but his fellow-workers disapproved of his psychological investigations. Two of his important works were published about this time—one on aphasia and the other on cerebral paralysis in children.

In 1893 Freud and Breuer collaborated on *Studien über Hysterie*, but before its publication two years later the two men had gone their separate ways and Freud began to replace hypnotism as a means of recalling to his patients long buried memories with the use of the "free association" method which has continued to be the method of specialists in psycho-analysis. He continued his research as to the nature of psycho-neuroses and to the extending of them to the normal mind. His three most important discoveries were the existence of the "unconscious" and its active influence upon consciousness; the splitting of the mind into layers due to an intra-psychical conflict between different sets of forces, to one of which he gave the name of "repression"; and the existence of infantile sexuality and its importance. He came to hold the belief that the unconscious conflicts in the young child's attitude toward its parents were the central factor in the neuroses and also a factor in the formation of character. He demonstrated the mechanism of neuroses in many other spheres—dreams, literary product, art, mythology and religion.

In 1902 he was made associate professor of neuropathology in the University of Vienna. About 1906 Adler, Brill, Ferenczi, Ernest Jones, Jung, Adger, Stekel and other famous neurologists became convinced of the truth of his discoveries and joined him in their study and application. In 1908 they called the first International Congress of Psycho-Analysis. The International Association of Psycho-Analysis, founded in 1910, has branches in nearly all countries. Freud has continued his investigations into the subject of psychoneuroses far in advance of his colleagues. He has met with active opposition in the application of his fundamental theories although it is generally conceded that he has greatly advanced the study of psychology and the field of mental ailments. He is the author of many books dealing with the subjects which he has made a life-long study.

On his seventieth birthday he received the congratulations of many learned societies throughout the world.

FRIEDRICH WILHELM AUGUST FROEBEL   1782–1852

FRIEDRICH WILHELM AUGUST FROEBEL, German philosopher, educational reformer and the father of the modern kindergarten, was born at Oberweissbach, Thuringia, April 21, 1782. He was considered a backward child and was apprenticed to a forester. In the great woods of Thuringia the mystical side of his nature developed and he became imbued with a desire to study the natural sciences and the laws of the universe. At the age of 17 he left the forest for the university at Jena where his career was cut short by lack of funds. He returned home and found employment of various kinds—surveyor, accountant, private secretary—and at length while studying architecture at Frankfort-on-Main, he met the director of a model school who was using some of Pestalozzi's methods, and who offered him a post. After a time in this work he became connected with Pestalozzi's famous school at Yverdon, near Neuchâtel (1807–09). In 1811 he went to Göttingen to study but although not a Prussian he answered the call of the King of Prussia to the colors and served in the campaign of 1813 in Lützow's corps.

In the army he met two young men whose names later became linked with his in the educational reforms he was to undertake. Their names were Langethal and Middendorff, and they sacrificed their prospects to help Froebel carry out his ideas. After the peace of 1814 he became curator of the museum of mineralogy at Berlin, giving up this work, however, after a short time to devote himself to the education of children. In 1816 he established a school at Griesheim to promulgate his own ideas of teaching, but two years later removed it to Keilhau in Thuringia where he and his two colleagues were joined by one Barop, a relative of Middendorff. With their wives they formed an educational community and for fourteen years they worked, their school increasing gradually in the number of its pupils and in prestige though they were often lacking both money and food.

In 1830 Froebel opened another school in a castle at Wartense, Lucerne, offered by a friend, but the Catholic clergy resented the experiment as a Protestant invasion and in 1833 the school was removed to Willisau in the same canton where its fortunes were not much better. The Swiss government sent young teachers to Froebel's school to profit from his instruction and finally he moved to Burgdorf (where Pestalozzi had conducted his educational experiments 30 years earlier) and established a public orphanage. There he superintended a course for schoolmasters, young instructors coming for three months every alternate year to compare experiences and listen to lectures by Froebel, Bitzius and others. From these conferences Froebel decided that the schools suffered because the children, prior to school age, were neglected. He came to attach primary importance to training in the earliest years of a child's life. His great book, *The Education of Man* (1826) deals almost entirely with the child up to the age of seven and for these young children he evolved a graduated course of exercises, based on the games which he observed to interest them most. He believed that the function of education was to develop the faculties by arousing voluntary activity.

In 1837 he established at Blankenburg, near Keilhau, the first "kindergarten" (or garden of children). Lack of funds compelled him to give it up but he carried on the courses at Keilhau and, from 1848 to 1852, at Liebenstein and in the Duchy of Meiningen. In 1848 he presented to Parliament an address on the Kindergarten, but his nephew, Professor Karl Froebel of Zurich, had published books which were considered to be socialistic and the uncle's name unfortunately becoming associated with the nephew's, he was forbidden to establish schools in Prussia. This was a heavy blow and doubtless his grief over the palpably untrue charges which had been made hastened his death which occurred on June 21, 1852, less than a month after his 70th birthday had been celebrated with great acclaim.

JEAN FROISSART   circa 1338 – circa 1410

JEAN FROISSART (frwä'sär'), French writer and one of the greatest historians of his age, was born at Valenciennes about the year 1338. His father is believed to have been a painter of armorial bearings. The boy was educated for the church but very early manifested his love for poetry and for tales of chivalry in which the region of Valenciennes abounded. At 20 he began to write a history of the wars of his time and traveled somewhat extensively for three years gathering material for this work. In 1361 he went to England which he had previously visited, and was received with great favor by Philippa, wife of King Edward III, to whom he presented a long account in verse of the recent war between England and France. The queen designated him her secretary and gave him much encouragement in his writing. Two years later he visited the Scottish court; in 1366 he traveled in the train of the young Prince Edward (the Black Prince) to Aquitaine and Bordeaux and later went with the Duke of Clarence to Italy. Everywhere this gay and attractive and much-traveled Frenchman was popular and was received with honors.

After the death of Philippa in 1369 he returned to Valenciennes, but he shortly found new admirers and patrons and after many adventures became secretary in 1370 to Wenceslas, Duke of Brabant, who was himself a poet. Froissart made a collection of the duke's verses, adding some of his own, and published it under the title of *Meliador, or the Knight of the Golden Sea*. Although it contains interesting and beautiful passages, this long poem as a whole is verbose and tedious to modern taste. For some ten years he lived a quiet life, working much upon his *Chronicles*, the work for which he is chiefly famous. About 1383 he was appointed chaplain to Guy of Blois, and for 15 years thereafter he traveled much, visiting various courts of Europe, seeking always men from whom he might learn at first hand of the wars in which they had taken part. He lived for a time at the court of Gaston Phoebus at Béarn, of whom he has given us a remarkable account.

The four books of the *Chronicles* cover the events and wars of the period from 1326–1400. Through 40 years of his life they engaged Froissart's attention and they have been published in many editions and translated into Latin as well as into English and other modern languages. They first appeared in Paris under the title, *Chroniques de France, d'Angleterre, d'Ecosse, d'Espagne, de Bretagne, de Gascoyne, Flanders et lieux d'alentour*. The whole is a delightful and masterly presentation of the events of which he writes and a valuable record of the manners and characteristics of his age. Having visited most of the places mentioned, he was able to give faithful descriptions and his wide intercourse with the actual actors in the dramas he describes gave his work a realistic note. He was a master hand in the art of making people tell him all they knew. He was keenly interested in every detail and never forgot anything. The gorgeous feasts and spectacles and pageantry of the feudal age in which he so delighted are set forth in rich detail. Lacking somewhat in critical ability, despite his powers of shrewd observation, he includes many supernatural tales which tax the credulity of the modern reader, although he apparently accepted them at their face value. His sole object was to please. He had little sense of historical responsibility and was too much influenced by his personal prejudices to preserve the strict impartiality proper to the historian. In the earlier forms of his work his friendliness toward England is clearly shown. In a later revision, prepared after the murder of Richard II, grandson of Queen Philippa, his grief and resentment led him to omit much that was favorable to England and even to cast reflections on the English nation.

Among his poetical works worthy of mention besides the *Meliador* are *L'Epinette amoreuse* (The Little Thorn of Love), an account of his boyhood love affair, which was his first published work, and the *Dit du Florin,* which is partly autobiographical.

Little is known of Froissart's life after his second visit to England in 1395, when he was royally entertained by Richard II. He is said to have died in dire poverty. The place and date of his death are uncertain, but it was probably in the year 1410 and the church of St. Monegunda at Chimay is believed to be his resting place.

ROBERT FULTON   1765–1815

ROBERT FULTON, inventor of the first steamboat to move under its own power, was born in 1765 at Little Britain (now Fulton), Penn., of Irish parentage. The family being poor, Robert's only education was to be taught reading and writing and at an early age he was apprenticed to a jeweler in Philadelphia, where Benjamin Franklin later became his friend. He spent his spare time in study and in experimenting and at the age of 13 he had constructed paddle-wheels and applied them successfully to a fishing boat. He learned to paint and by the sale of his miniatures and landscapes he was able to buy a small farm on which he established his widowed mother.

In 1786 he went to London and was received into the family of the artist, Benjamin West, with whom he studied painting for several years and then settled in Devonshire and practiced the art for a time under the patronage of the Duke of Bridgewater, Lord Stanhope and other wealthy men. It was through this association that his interest in mechanics and boats was reawakened. Bridgewater was famous for the canal he had constructed from Wrosley to Manchester and Stanhope was the inventor of the Stanhope printing press. In 1793 Fulton began to experiment for the purpose of improving canal navigation and the following year he obtained a British patent on a double-inclined plane for raising and lowering ships from one level to another. He patented many other inventions and from his plans a great cast-iron aqueduct was built across the River Dee, and bridges were erected in various parts of Surrey.

In 1794 he had become a member of the family of Joel Barlow in Paris, and there he experimented on the Seine with a boat built for submarine navigation to be used in torpedo warfare. He conducted experiments with this submarine at Brest in 1801 under the auspices of the French government, which lost interest when he failed to blow up British ships sailing along the coast. At Lord Stanhope's instance, Great Britain arranged to obtain Fulton's services and, after a short stay in Holland, he proceeded to London in May, 1804. His submarine was finally found impracticable, but possibilities were seen in his torpedoes and he was taken out to sea to test them against French ships off Boulogne. The torpedoes burst harmlessly near the ships but the following year he succeeded in blowing up a 200-ton ship provided for the purpose by the government. In 1806 he returned to the United States and continued his experiments; invented a machine for cutting the cables of ships at anchor, and in 1813 patented "several improvements in maritime warfare, and means of injuring ships by igniting gunpowder under water."

He had first turned his attention to steam navigation in 1793. Ten years later he launched a small steamboat on the Seine, but, faultily constructed, it sank at once. Another was built of the old machinery and this one worked but with no great speed. He was sufficiently encouraged, however, to return to America and continue his work and in the spring of 1807 he completed at a shipyard on the East River, New York, a new boat, the *Clermont,* the engine for which he had imported from London. On Aug. 11, 1807, in the presence of an astonished crowd, the boat was launched and steamed up the Hudson River to Albany, making the trip from New York in 32 hours. The success of the *Clermont* aroused much jealousy and several persons who had been experimenting along the same line disputed Fulton's claim to originality so that litigation and competitions threatened to rob him of all profits on his invention. He was, however, unquestionably the first man to apply steam to navigation with any degree of success and was awarded patents for steamboat construction.

Steamers thereafter multiplied rapidly and shortly came into general use for river navigation. Fulton's reputation was made and the United States government employed him in connection with various canals and other projects. In 1814 he constructed a steam warship to carry 44 guns, which was launched the following year. His last work was a modification of his submarine, *Nautilus*, only the hull of which was completed before his death, which occurred in New York, Feb. 24, 1815. The entire country paid tribute in demonstrations of mourning and a monument was later erected to his memory in upper New York City, overlooking the Hudson River.

THOMAS GAINSBOROUGH   1727–1788

THOMAS GAINSBOROUGH, one of the most famous of English landscape and portrait painters, was born in Sudbury, Suffolk, early in 1727. He early showed a talent for drawing and at the age of 14 obtained his father's permission to go to London where he studied etching under Hugh Gravelot, and painting at the Academy in St. Martin's Lane under Francis Hayman. Returning to Suffolk, at 19 he married Margaret Burr, a lady of great charm who contributed much happiness to his life, and settled at Ipswich, painted portraits and landscapes, joined a musical club, and learned to play several instruments. Philip Thicknesse, governor of the Landquart fort and later his biographer, introduced Gainsborough among his own friends, secured commissions for him and persuaded him to go to Bath (1759), then the centre of wealth and fashion, where he painted many portraits and at the estates of some of his patrons he had opportunities of studying the work of Van Dyck and other painters.

He developed his art chiefly by himself in the study of nature though early in his career he copied masterpieces by Rembrandt, Van Dyck, Murillo, Velazquez and Wynants. His early landscapes were painted with the thorough minutiae of the Dutch masters. Those of his Bath period are accounted his finest and it was in these portrayals of the scenery of his native country that his genius found much of its best expression. It has been said that "nature was his teacher and the woods his academy." In 1774, having become prosperous, he removed to London and settled at Schomberg House, Pall Mall. George III summoned him to the palace and he painted eight different portraits of that monarch. The Queen and other members of the royal family sat to him as did such famous men and women of the day as Sheridan, Burke, Johnson, Mrs. Siddons, Canning, Pitt, Clive and Blackstone. In 1768 he had been elected one of the original 36 members of the Royal Academy, where he showed both landscapes and portraits at the annual exhibitions until 1783. In that year, being dissatisfied with the position given a portrait of the three princesses, he withdrew all his pictures and later arranged an exhibition in his own home. He died on Aug. 2, 1788.

"The Blue Boy" (now in the Huntington collection, California) is the most celebrated of his work. Of his more than 500 pictures, including over 200 portraits, some of the finest productions are "The Shepherd's Boy," "The Woodman in the Storm," "The Fight Between Little Boys and Dogs," "The Morning Walk," "Mrs. Sheridan," "The Baillie Family." His "Lizbeth, Duchess of Devonshire," was stolen in 1876, taken to New York and Chicago, but recovered in 1901 because the thieves were unable to dispose of so valuable a painting, and was later sold to J. Pierpont Morgan. H. C. Frick, G. J. Gould and other American collectors have also acquired valuable Gainsboroughs. His portraits, while remarkable as likenesses, lack something of careful finish and rank less high than his landscape work. The best of the portraits are those of the royal family. He frequently posed his sitters against a harmonizing landscape background and is accounted the forerunner of impressionism.

GALILEO (GALILEO GALILEI)   1564–1642

THE name of GALILEO is one of the most illustrious in the annals of science. He was born at Pisa, Italy, on the 15th of February, 1564, of a family in moderate circumstances which had earlier changed its surname from Bonajuti to Galilei. By his father's wish he early studied medicine and philosophy, but his mind was not of a type for purely intellectual speculation and he is said to have entertained a robust dislike of dogma of every sort. At the age of 18 he took note of a swaying lamp in the cathedral and, testing the regularity of its swinging movement by the beating of his pulse, he decided that this steady oscillation might be utilized for the measurement of time. Thus was evolved the pendulum which he first used in a clock of his own construction. He studied mathematics with such enthusiasm that his father at length sanctioned his abandonment of medicine and he soon made good his preference for experimental science by the invention of a hydrostatic balance for determining the specific gravity of solids. In 1589 the Grand Duke of Tuscany, impressed by his learning and achievements, made him professor of mathematics in the university of Pisa. Besides the many innovations in physical science which he there introduced, he made experiments that resulted in his formulating the law governing falling bodies. These interesting tests, made from the summit of the famous leaning tower, so aroused the anger of professional dissenters that he found it expedient to resign his professorship and he went to Padua where, for several years, he lectured to enthusiastic audiences at the university, and might have continued to do so but for his desire to return to his native city where the authorities were now glad enough to restore to him his former post.

In 1592 he devised the first thermometer and in 1609 exhibited his microscope to astonished beholders. In this same year, from the tower of St. Mark, he pointed his newly invented telescope at the starry depths of heaven. Thus was opened to him a new and fascinating field of investigation. He discovered that the moon shone by reflected light, took note of its topography, explored the Milky Way, discovered the four satellites of Jupiter, and examined the spots on the sun. In 1611 he made a triumphal visit to Rome where he was made a member of the Lincei Academy and was the recipient of many honors. His subsequent declaration in favor of the Copernican system of astronomy was the cause of a much cooler reception on his second visit when he was denounced as a heretic. He had the hardihood to defend his views in face of ecclesiastical censure and was probably only saved from paying the penalty of his courage and independence by the tactful interference of influential friends at home who reminded him, in effect, that discretion was the better part of valor. His friend and patron, the Grand Duke of Tuscany, shrewdly required his presence in Pisa, and none too soon in view of the papal warning that he desist from uttering heresies.

He now found it necessary to negotiate with the authorities of the church for license to publish his theories and discoveries, but these privileges, after being granted, were capriciously revoked. He contrived, however, to publish his opinions only to see his work consigned to the gentle mercies of the Grand Inquisitor. Pope Urban, moreover, conceiving that he had been satirized in certain of the scientist's writings, had Galileo summoned before the Inquisition. Then 70 years of age and in failing health, he was subjected to the rigors of an absurd and interminable trial and held in close confinement meanwhile. He was finally required to recant the opinions whose truth he had so abundantly proved, and which have since made his name illustrious. Weak and exhausted, and in peril of excruciating torture, he took an oath renouncing the truths which his genius had so gloriously established. A prison sentence for an unspecified time was promptly commuted by the pope, who took great credit to himself for this gracious act, and the aged scientist was permitted to withdraw into peaceful retirement, thanks to his loyal champion, the Grand Duke of Tuscany. The last years of his life were spent at his retreat at Arcetri, where his continued, indefatigable researches were handicapped, but not relinquished, as his sight failed until complete blindness supervened. He died on the 8th of January, 1642, in his 78th year, and was buried in the cathedral of Santa Croce where an imposing monument was erected in his honor.

He had never married, but three children were born to him by a Venetian woman, a son who married and left descendants and two daughters, both of whom became nuns.

DOM VASCO DA GAMA 1450–1524

Dom Vasco Da Gama (gä'mà), discoverer of the maritime route from Europe to India, was born in the small Portuguese seaport town of Sines in 1450, the exact date being uncertain. He was descended from an ancient family, said to have been an illegitimate branch in a royal stock. He early distinguished himself as an intrepid mariner and about 1487 was selected by King João to undertake the discovery of a southern passage to India. The sovereign's plans were frustrated by death, but his successor, Manoel the Fortunate, fitted out four vessels, manned by 160 men, and entrusted them to the command of da Gama, presenting him with letters to all the potentates whom it was thought likely he might visit. One of these notes of introduction was to the mythical Prester John, supposed by Europeans to be reigning in fabulous splendor somewhere in the east of Africa.

The little fleet sailed from Lisbon on July 8, 1496, and after many delays, caused by storms and contrary winds, arrived on the 16th of November at the haven now known as Table Bay in the neighborhood of the Cape of Good Hope. Here, while at anchor in a frightful storm, the terrified crew mutinied, demanding that their venturesome leader return to Portugal. Three days later, having suppressed this uprising, da Gama set sail and rounded the southern extremity of Africa, touching at various points along the hitherto unknown eastern coast. At Melinda, where he found the people far more civilized than he expected, he obtained the services of a pilot who, to his astonishment, was familiar with the astrolabe, the compass and the quadrant. Under his guidance, da Gama struck out to sea, crossed the Indian Ocean and arrived at Calicut, on the southwestern coast of India, toward the end of May, 1498. His reception by the Indian ruler was not very favorable; the Arab merchants residing there were jealous of the newcomers and incited the Hindus against them. Other complications also arose with the result that da Gama had difficulty in escaping from the scene. Fighting his way out of the harbor, he turned his course homeward, reaching Lisbon in September, 1499, where he was received with the greatest enthusiasm, and honored with the privilege of prefixing Dom to his name, besides being promised a share in the profits from the trade about to be opened with India.

The Portuguese sovereign lost no time in despatching a squadron of 13 ships under Pedro Alvarez Cabral to India to plant settlements there, but the enterprise was vigorously resisted by the natives, and at Calicut a number of the Portuguese were murdered. To avenge this and to establish commerce, the king fitted out a new squadron of 20 ships, which set sail under command of da Gama in 1502. This fleet reached the east coast of Africa, founded the Portuguese colonies of Mozambique and Sofala, and sailed to Travancore, in the south of India. On his way he captured a richly laden vessel filled with pilgrims from all parts of Asia on their way to Mecca. He barbarously set it on fire and the entire crew of some 300 were burned or slain. It is said that this bloody stain on da Gama's character was due to his confounding the wretched victims with the Moors who were the hereditary enemies of his nation. On reaching Calicut, he opened a bombardment, destroyed the native fleet and completely humiliated the rajah. In December, 1503, he sailed again into Lisbon harbor, was again wildly acclaimed and honored with distinguished titles. It appears, however, that save for these empty acknowledgments, the king neglected to compensate his doughty adventurer and da Gama remained unemployed for about 20 years, while a profitable trade with India continued under the supervision of several despotic Portuguese viceroys. The last of these was so unfortunate in his barbarous administration of affairs that the king (now João III) found it expedient to fall back on the neglected hero and in 1525 appointed him viceroy, and da Gama sailed once again for the scene of his discoveries and early triumphs. As he approached the Indian coast, a strange agitation of the water was noted and his worthy followers were greatly dismayed at the phenomenon. But their redoubtable commander assured them that the sea was merely trembling before its conquerors, one of the very few instances on record of the ocean's proving cowardly.

Da Gama's firmness and courage soon availed to reestablish respect, or at least fear, among the hapless natives. But while he was engaged in enforcing submission by his rigorous policies, a greater conqueror, in the form of death, intervened to put an end to his colorful career. He died at

Cochin, India, in December, 1524, and his body was conveyed to Portugal where a tardy testimonial to his valued services was given in a funeral of great pomp and splendor. It should be stated that in addition to his courage and patriotic despotism, he was of a deeply religious nature. There is no doubt that his discovery of a passage to India almost vies, in importance, with the discovery of America by Columbus.

JAMES A. GARFIELD   1831–1881

JAMES ABRAM GARFIELD, 20th president of the United States, was born on Nov. 19, 1831, in a log cabin in the frontier town of Orange, Ohio. Two years later his father died leaving him the youngest of four children. His youth was filled with hard work on the family farm and in various country employments. At one time he drove mules along the Ohio Canal. Again he was employed as a boat hand. He nevertheless acquired sufficient education to enable him to teach a country school for a time and at 18 he was attending a seminary at Chester, Ohio; at 20 he entered an institution at Hiram (now Hiram College), and in 1854 he was able to go to Williams College in Massachusetts, from which he was graduated with honors two years later. From 1857 to 1859 he was president of the Hiram Institute to which he had returned as a teacher of ancient languages and very soon thereafter was admitted to the bar in Ohio after a period of studying law almost by himself.

His political career began with a short period in the Ohio senate. At the outbreak of the Civil War he was made lieutenant-colonel, and shortly colonel, of volunteers and served with distinction in various engagements under Buell, Sherman and Rosencrans. In 1863 as chief of staff under Gen. Rosencrans, he was largely responsible for the advance on Chickamauga and after the reverses of the Union army he made a daring ride under fire across open country which resulted in saving the situation. In recognition of his important services and his heroism President Lincoln promoted him to the rank of major-general. He resigned from the army upon his election to Congress and represented Ohio for the next 17 years in that body, where as one of the radical element in the republican party he took an active part in the important legislation of the post-war period. When the terrible tidings of Lincoln's assassination reached New York, Garfield, who was there on government business, quelled the excitement of an angry mob with his calm and historic reminder that "God reigns and the government at Washington still lives."

He served on important committees, fought against post-war inflation of the currency, opposed President Johnson's attitude toward the South and favored the impeachment proceedings which were instituted against him. He headed an investigation into the cause of the financial panic of 1869 and framed and introduced a number of reform bills. Despite charges of corruption (apparently unfounded) which were made, the confidence of his state was shown by his repeated reelections to Congress and in 1880 to the U. S. Senate. In the republican national convention of that year, after prolonged and fruitless balloting in which the advocates of Gen. Grant, James G. Blaine, John Sherman and others were unable to reach a decision, Garfield, whose able speeches on behalf of Sherman had excited much admiration, was put forward as a compromise, received the nomination and was elected by 214 votes, his opponent, Gen. Hancock, receiving 155.

He appointed Blaine his secretary of state, the son of the murdered President Lincoln secretary of war and made an earnest effort to bring about harmony in his party which was disrupted by strife between his own adherents and the faction known as the "Stalwarts," from which the vice-president, Chester A. Arthur, was drawn. Dissension arose over some of his appointments, giving rise to bitter hostility on the part of Senators Conkling and Platt and others. On July 2, 1881, as he was starting for the commencement exercises at Williams College, the president was shot in a railway station in Washington by Charles Jules Guiteau, who had unsuccessfully sought appointment and whose mind was doubtless unbalanced. For weeks he lay in a precarious condition, his party and the entire nation united in indignation at the crime, and at Elberon, N. J., on Sept. 19 he breathed his last. The assassin was captured and executed several months later.

In 1858 Garfield had married Lucretia Randolph. Of their seven children at least two rose to prominence, one son becoming president of Williams College and another serving as secretary of the interior in the cabinet of Theodore Roosevelt.

GIUSEPPE GARIBALDI   1807–1882

GIUSEPPE GARIBALDI (gä'rĕ bäl'dĕ), great Italian patriot and liberator, was born at Nice, July 22, 1807. Following in his father's steps, he became a sailor and at the age of 23 was in command of a brig. His interest became aroused in the national movement of the Young Italy party to free their country from Austrian supremacy and establish a republican form of government, and he made the acquaintance of Mazzini and other leaders of the movement, which had the result of strengthening his interest until the cause of universal freedom became the great dominating passion of his life.

In 1834 he took part in an outbreak at Genoa which came to nothing, but he was condemned to death for his share in the uprising. Before the sentence was pronounced, however, he had escaped to French territory and later taking ship to South America he gave valuable assistance to the young republic of Uruguay, then engaged in a struggle against the Argentine dictator, Manuel Rosas. He developed such powers of leadership that he was given command over all military operations by land and sea, but in 1848 when the liberals of northern Italy rose against Austria, he hurried home to join in the struggle. In command of volunteer forces, he gave effective assistance and in the following summer for four weeks he defended Rome against repeated attacks by the French under General Oudinot. The vastly superior numbers of the French army, however, at length proved victorious and he was forced to retreat. With great difficulty he made his way through a section occupied by Austrian troops and with his Brazilian wife, Anita, who had faithfully shared his hardships, embarked on a small fishing boat, hoping to get to Venice. His flight was discovered and to avoid capture he was forced to land wherever he could. His wife, exhausted, died and he at length made his way to Genoa from which point he was able to sail to Tunis and afterward to America. For a time he lived quietly on Staten Island, N. Y., then visited South America and later commanded a trading vessel on the Pacific.

He returned to Europe about 1854 and was active in the war of 1859, terminated by the unsatisfactory peace of Villafranca, following which revolutionary activities were resumed, centering in the island of Sicily. Garibaldi, who in the interim since the disturbances of 1848 had provisionally accepted monarchy as represented by the Sardinian government, gathered together at Genoa about 1000 men with whom he landed on the island and on May 15, 1860, routed a much larger force of Neapolitans. He fought his way to Palermo which he entered after a second terrific battle, and after a bombardment lasting several days the Neapolitan fleet at length withdrew. In a brilliant campaign lasting through the summer and extending over into the mainland, he won repeated victories against superior numbers and made his famous march to Naples, his forces constantly augmented until by the middle of September they numbered more than 25,000. Reaching Naples, from which the king, Francis II, had withdrawn the previous day, he entered the city not as a conqueror but as a liberator with only one or two companions. Although acting as the representative of the Sardinian government, he assumed temporarily the title and powers of a dictator. On October 1 he was forced to resist a terrific attack by royalist troops and for a time it seemed that the patriot cause would be lost just on the eve of success, but the tide finally turned and Garibaldi was again victorious.

This was the climax of his great career. On the arrival of Victor Emmanuel he turned over to that sovereign his army and all the conquered territory and retired to Caprera. His later attempt to add Rome to his conquests was checked by Victor Emmanuel who was fearful that this might bring about foreign complications and jeopardize such measure of Italian unity as had been achieved. In 1866 Garibaldi was again active against the Austrians in the Tyrol and the following year he organized an invasion of the papal states. He was taken prisoner but escaped and the year 1870 found him fighting for the French in the Franco-Prussian war. He declined a seat in the National Assembly at Bordeaux in 1871, retired again to his home at Caprera and later entered the Italian parliament. Some years previously he had contracted an unfortunate marriage with the Countess Raimondi, which was annulled in 1874 and he afterwards married a woman of peasant origin who had been in the service of his family for many years. He died at Caprera on June 2, 1882, and was mourned by all Italy.

DAVID GARRICK   1717–1779

ACTOR, author, playwright, Shakespearian scholar and manager of the famous Drury Lane Theatre in London, DAVID GARRICK is one of the most notable figures in the history of the stage. He was born at Hereford, England, Feb. 19, 1717, and attended school at Lichfield where his mother's people lived and where a school was maintained by another man destined to fame, Dr. Samuel Johnson. After a brief residence at the home of an uncle who was a wine merchant at Lisbon, he returned to Lichfield and for a few months continued to enjoy the benefits of association with Johnson who was his senior by nine years. The latter had already experienced many unprosperous vicissitudes and the school also proving unsuccessful he and Garrick resolved to seek their fortunes in the metropolis where, as the whole world knows, Dr. Johnson became the presiding spirit of the group (including Boswell, Goldsmith, Garrick and others) which is famous in literary annals.

At first Garrick studied law; abandoning that he engaged for a brief period as a wine merchant, using a legacy which had been left him by his uncle. But there had persisted in him since childhood an irresistible longing for the stage and this he was now bent on gratifying. It may be observed in passing that he was one of the comparatively few who have risen to prominence in the theatre who were not born to the profession. After such training as was afforded by amateur theatricals, he made his début at Ipswich in 1741 as Aboan in a play entitled *Oroonoka* which was, in modern theatrical parlance, a hit. Encouraged by this success, he cast his eye on the metropolis and ventured before a London audience in 1741 in the difficult rôle of Richard III. Wholly unknown and but 24 years old, his playing caused a sensation and he was greeted with tremendous applause. He awoke to find himself famous; the fashionable theatres were deserted while their wonted patrons flocked to see the new star. It is reported that Quin and Cibber, stage celebrities of the day, could not repress their chagrin and jealousy.

The career inaugurated so triumphantly continued on a level of high distinction. In the following year he went to Dublin where the generous and susceptible Irish received him with enthusiasm. The theatre, it is said, was so crowded and the applause so vociferous "that a very mortal fever was produced, which was called Garrick fever." In 1747 he became one of the partners of the Drury Lane Theatre; two years later, we are told, a minor sensation among the female members of his company was caused by his marriage to Mademoiselle Violette, an Austrian dancer. He had previously fallen in love with the famous Peg Woffington at a time when his obscurity saved him from any practical complications. Apprehending ridicule and criticism of his subsequent choice, he persuaded a poetic friend to write a poem in commendation of his marriage. But the tide of disaffection could not be stemmed and he witnessed the withdrawal of many of his fair associates and their sympathizers, who forthwith entered the ranks of the Covent Garden Theatre and there ensued a sort of professional war between the rival companies who chose the immortal love poem, *Romeo and Juliet,* as their vehicle in this bitter competition. It is only fair to say that the Romeo of Garrick achieved a complete victory after a few performances and Covent Garden retreated from the field.

In 1763 Garrick paid a visit to Italy where he was well received and met many distinguished people. In 1769 he conceived and was the moving spirit of the memorable Shakespearian Jubilee at Stratford-on-Avon, and wrote a ballad for the occasion. At another time he wrote certain witty pamphlets in criticism of his own acting. He accumulated a considerable fortune from his acting. His status in the field of dramatic interpretation is very high and he is commonly regarded as his country's greatest actor. There is no way to form an adequate judgment of this for a player's art dies with him; but his range was great, running from farce to tragedy, and there can be no doubt that as an interpreter of the great Shakesperian roles he revealed a universal quality which is the essence of greatness in an actor.

He died in London on Jan. 20, 1779.

THÉOPHILE GAUTIER   1811–1872

THÉOPHILE GAUTIER (gŏ tyȧ'), French critical writer, poet and novelist, was born at Tarbes, France, on August 31, 1811. He attended public school in his native town, and thereafter went to Paris where he studied at the college Charlemagne. He early became interested in the French literature of an earlier period, and his familiarity with sixteenth century prose and poetry became apparent in his own work and qualified him to participate in the romantic movement of his day. With a group of young writers and artists he formed a romantic clique whose members indulged a taste for Bohemian picturesqueness of apparel which caused dismay even in unconventional circles. Gautier himself affected a flamboyance running to absurdity, disporting in a flaming crimson waistcoat, his head surmounted with a luxurious mass of waving hair. Seldom has artistic affectation been carried so far as by these devotees of the romantic, who performed mocking dances around the harmless bust of Racine as an expression of contempt for his classical renown. But if true genius can redeem such childish display, Gautier is sufficiently redeemed. In his papers, collected and published under the title of *Histoire du romantisme,* he gives us very delightful pictures of his comrades, Gerard, Petrus, Borel, Corot and other less noted figures, who participated in these esthetic gambols. His first considerable poem, *Albertus,* published in 1830, was somewhat marred by extravagance, but was full of imagery and rare descriptive power. In 1832 appeared his poem, *Comedie de la Mort,* followed thereafter by various shorter poems, all exhibiting a rare command of poetic form and expression. In 1856 appeared the *Émaux et Camées,* revised and republished in 1872. All of these poems revealed, in varying degree, the author's keen susceptibility to beauty in art and nature.

But it was not as a poet, original and distinctive as his muse was, that he achieved his highest fame. Experimental and restless in temperament, he tried every literary form. He wrote for the theatre, but here he did not excell. He was, for a brief period, secretary to the great Balzac and must have been sufficiently distressed by the methodical habits of that prodigious worker. Perhaps it was this experience which turned his thoughts to the novel as a literary medium; he was certainly mildly influenced by the master. His first important novel (1835), esteemed by many his greatest work, was *Mademoiselle de Maupin,* a work which shocked even the liberal-minded French. From this period on he produced novels and short stories in large number. In *Le Jeune France* he found it possible to satirize the romantic group of which he had been such a conspicuous member. A note of pathos characterizes his splendid short story, *Jettatura.* Other fictions of this form were *Arria Marcella, Avatar* and *Roman de la momie,* the latter a study of life in ancient Egypt. One of his most remarkable books was *Le capitaine Fracasse,* a novel after the manner of Dumas, planned early in life but not published until 1861.

Notwithstanding his achievement in the field of poetry and in novels and shorter fictions, it is as a critic that he has a unique fame. His *Histoire du romantisme,* above mentioned, is a splendid work in this field and his essays on Lamartine and Baudelaire are exquisite and discerning masterpieces of critical writing. He was for some time associated with the *Moniteur,* and in this capacity was a recognized critical authority, writing numerous pieces which were characterized by keen penetration and a facile and witty style. He found time to travel extensively and his observations and experiences are delightfully set forth in *Voyage en Espagne, Italia, Constantinople, La Russie* and other works.

Master of a faultless style, flexibly employed in a variety of ways, supreme critic of his time, he never overcame in all his long life at Paris a touch of that affectation which characterized him and made him somewhat absurd while young. After it ceased to be apparent in his dress, it persisted in his manner. He wore a languid mein and affected a theatrically dubious air, when his distinction should have impelled him to scorn this claptrap of the amateur.

He died in Paris where for years he had been a conspicuous figure of the artistic set, on Oct. 23, 1872. His biography *Théophile Gautier,* prepared by his son-in-law, was published in 1879.

HENRY GEORGE   1839–1897

HENRY GEORGE was an American writer and political economist who became most widely known as the exponent of a proposed Single Tax, and the author of *Progress and Poverty,* in which his theory is fully set forth. He was born in Philadelphia on Sept. 2, 1839. Circumstances cut short his formal education at the early age of 14 and he worked his way on a ship to India and Australia and then back to California. He was 19 years old when he returned to American shores. Gold had just been discovered in British Columbia and excitement ran high. Caught by the fever, the young traveler shipped again on a vessel bound for Victoria, B. C., but after many difficulties and hardships he returned again to San Francisco and went to work in a printing office, having somehow learned this trade between his various voyages. For a time he shifted about from one line of work to another, at one time working in a rice mill. With a group of other printers he started a daily newspaper, the *Evening Journal,* but was unable to make it a success. At about the age of 25 he began to write and, securing employment as a reporter for the San Francisco *Times,* he rapidly rose to an editorial position, and occasionally was moved to write to New York papers on subjects which aroused his interest, such as the monopolistic practices of certain large companies. An article written for the New York *Tribune* in 1869 on the Chinese question attracted some attention in the East. In that same year he went to New York and attempted to establish a telegraphic news bureau, but this enterprise also was a failure, and once again he returned to San Francisco.

There had been growing in his mind a deepening realization of the evils arising from the unequal distribution of property and of the deprivations imposed upon the poor of the land through the amassing of great fortunes by a favored few. He resolved to dedicate himself to finding a remedy for the conditions of poverty which prevailed among so great a share of the people. The first result of this determination was a little volume published in 1871, entitled *Our Land Policy,* in which he advocated the concentrating of all taxes into one tax on land, thus freeing labor and the products of labor and destroying the land monopoly which he believed prevented equal opportunities for all. A thousand copies of this little book were sold, but its author saw that to accomplish his object the subject must be presented more thoroughly and convincingly. Six years later appeared *Progress and Poverty,* his famous exposition of the doctrine of the Single Tax. The book had been written during a year and a half of financial stress and privation. He sent it to various New York publishers, some of whom thought it visionary and some thought it revolutionary. All agreed that it would not sell sufficiently to make its publication profitable. But at length a publisher was found who agreed to bring it out if Mr. George would stand the major part of the cost. Not much attention was paid to it at first, but presently it was noticed abroad and hailed as an important and remarkable work, especially in England where the Irish land question was a burning issue. Interest increased until Mr. George came to be regarded as the preacher of a new social creed, although indeed he was not the originator of the fundamental doctrine of the equal right of all men to the use of the earth, but his lucid explanation of a method by which this could be accomplished brought it within the comprehension of all.

Although he has often been termed a socialist, that is by no means a true designation. He held that economic progress should not be marked by increasing extremes of wealth and poverty, but that increase of population should bring greater plenty for all, and that his single tax on land would make possible equality of opportunity and more widespread prosperity. He was thereafter called upon to lecture, both in America and in Great Britain and he wrote many articles on various political and economic questions, as well as on his favorite subject. Although his book was eventually translated into most of the important languages and had a vast sale, he never reaped large pecuniary returns and was in straitened circumstances throughout his life. He had no political ambitions, but in 1886 he ran for mayor of New York City as an independent candidate and was so popular that it was only by a union of the two major parties that he was defeated. In 1897 he was again a candidate, but before the election was held he died suddenly on Oct. 29. His death was followed by an enormous demonstration of popular esteem.

His own words in the dedication of his famous book might well serve as his epitaph for he was one of "those who, seeing the vice and misery that spring from the unequal distribution of wealth and privilege, feel the possibility of a higher social state and would strive for its attainment."

EDWARD GIBBON   1737–1794

"IT WAS at Rome on the 15th of October, 1764, as I sat musing amidst the ruins of the Capitol, while the barefooted friars were singing vespers in the temple of Jupiter, that the idea of writing the decline and fall of the city first started in my mind." Thus wrote EDWARD GIBBON, and the idea thus inspired resulted in *The Decline and Fall of the Roman Empire,* one of the greatest historical works and repositories of learning in the world. It was his life work; there is little in his life beside it. This great scholar and writer was born at Putney, England, on the 27th of April, 1737, son of Edward Gibbon and his wife, Judith Porten. He was the first of seven children, all of whom save himself died during childhood. Our chief source of information about him is his own autobiography in which the plain facts of his unadventurous life are set forth with a charm and interest which is astonishing considering the undramatic material of his career. Like the much shorter autobiography of David Hume, it captivates by its obvious truthfulness and candor. In it he says, "My name may hereafter be placed among the thousand articles of a Biographia Britannica; and I must be conscious that no one is so well qualified as myself to describe the series of my thoughts and actions." But it was not until his fifty-second year that he proceeded to do this, and before that time his colossal history had been completed.

During a childhood of indifferent health he received the rudiments of education from his maternal aunt whom he calls "the mother of my mind" and whose instruction and devotion he never forgot. At the age of 15 he entered Magdalen College, Oxford, but the informal and affectionate tutelage he had received at home proved prejudicial to his progress in college where he did little but read theology, with the result that at the age of 16 he became a Roman Catholic. This precluded him from Oxford and his father placed him under the care of the poet Mallet, whose liberal views did not suffice to shake his newly acquired faith, and he was thereupon sent to Switzerland to board in the home of a Calvinist minister where it was hoped that the atmosphere and teaching would recall the youthful convert back from "popery." This task of conversion was carried on with the greatest tact and caution by the good minister with the result that his protégé, after his theological excursion of a year and a half, was reestablished in the Protestant faith and baptized on Christmas Day, 1754. The devout wish of Gibbon's father being thus fulfilled, the youth continued to live in the home of his clerical adviser, devoting himself to study, and we are told that the amount of historical and other data which he stored in his prodigious memory during that period was miraculous. This independent and unguided way of learning made him the greatest scholar of his day. He found time, however, to fall in love with a highly accomplished young woman, Susanne Curchod, but here again parental meddling interfered; his father disapproved, evidently without good reason, and the son abandoned his fond hopes. The girl, who was the daughter of a clergyman, later married the distinguished French financier, M. Necker, and became the mother of Madame de Staël, while Gibbon remained single for life.

In 1761, having returned to England three years previously, he published a book under the title of *Essai sur l'Étude de la Littérature* and about that time he became captain in the Hampshire militia. When this was disbanded he traveled in Italy where he was inspired to write the great work which made him famous. On his return he sat for eight years in parliament where, he tells us, the great speakers filled him with despair, the bad ones with terror, and he is said never to have made a speech himself. In 1776, when he was 39, the first volume of *The Decline and Fall* was published and received with the greatest enthusiasm. After his retirement from parliament he went to Lausanne, the scene of his former residence and blighted romance; and here, withdrawn from every distraction, he completed his great task on the 27th of June, 1787. In his memoirs he records the emotions which he felt when, close to midnight, he finally laid aside his pen after his prolonged and tremendous labors. The last three volumes of the work were published in 1788. In 1793 he returned to England, and died quite suddenly in London on the 16th of January, 1794.

SIR WILLIAM SCHWENCK GILBERT   1836–1911
SIR ARTHUR SEYMOUR SULLIVAN   1842–1900

ONE of the most auspicious partnerships in literary history was that of Gilbert and Sullivan. Each was separately distinguished; one for his music, the other for his plays and whimsical verse. Together they produced a series of light operas, hauntingly tuneful and with a humor as delicate and airy as gossamer. Time, and the vulgarizing of theatrical taste, have not sullied their jaunty charm; they are truly classics and recur each season like "the flowers that bloom in the spring."

GILBERT, a descendant of the explorer, Sir Humphrey Gilbert, was born in London in Nov. 18, 1836, son of William Gilbert, a prolific writer of fiction. He attended London University where he took his degree of B.A. and was then employed for about five years in the privy council office, after which he began the practice of law. His experience in this profession later served him well in his inimitable humorous portrayals; he delighted to depict legal dignitaries (not excepting the Lord Chancellor) in ludicrous aspect. His libretto of *Trial by Jury* is excrutiatingly funny by reason of his ridiculous treatment of legal procedure. He became a contributor to various English magazines and was on the staff of *Fun,* the humorous periodical in which most of his famous *Bab Ballads* first appeared. These versified drolleries exhibit an amazing faculty in rhyme and meter; the unusual verse forms have often been copied, but no one has ever succeeded in capturing that elusive quality of humor which has come to be called Gilbertian. It consists, chiefly, in the perfectly sober treatment of utter absurdities. The point of view is never lost, and the nonsense proceeds with the utmost circumspection and dignity. In 1866 appeared his burlesque *Dulcamara,* followed by numerous other burlesques and fantastic comedies, among which may be mentioned *The*

Palace of Truth, Pygmalion and Galatea and *The Wicked World*. Notable among his plays are *Engaged, Sweethearts, Charity, Gretchen, Comedy and Tragedy, Randall's Thumb, Fogerty's Fairy* and *The Hooligan*. All of them are characterized by whimsical conception and delicacy of treatment. But it was not until he fell in with the composer, Sir Arthur Sullivan, that his unique qualities as a humorist and librettist were sufficiently emphasized to give him the status of a classic in the field of humorous literature. Here he reigns with Lewis Carroll in the very small circle of writers who have been able to use the nonsensical as material for literature. After a conspicuously successful career as a collaborator in the production of the famous operas, he died at his home, Grim's Duke, near Harrow, May 29, 1911, in the 75th year of his age. His end was heroic; he was bathing in the company of two young women in the private lake on his estate. One of them was in difficulties and he went to her rescue, but sank under her, the circumstances pointing to heart failure and not to actual drowning.

The gifted composer, SULLIVAN, was born in Lambeth, London, on May 13, 1842. He was the son of an Irish musician and through his mother inherited an Italian strain. He was brought up to music from childhood and at eight years old had learned to play every wind instrument in his father's band. He sang as a choir boy in St. James chapel, in London, and then studied music in Germany. After his return to England he devoted himself to composition. His attractive personality and unquestioned genius quickly won him many friends and he was admired and loved in all circles of society. His music to Shakespeare's *Tempest* and his songs and sacred music, notably *The Lost Chord* and *Onward, Christian Soldiers,* have given him an enduring place among composers. He cooperated with F. C. Bernard in a highly successful extravaganza, *Cox and Box,* and other pieces. In 1873 his oratorio, *The Light of the World,* was produced; he wrote music to *Henry VIII,* a sacred cantata, and in 1886 what is perhaps his masterpiece, *The Golden Legend*. He was conductor of the Leeds Festivals for 20 years and in 1885 of the Philharmonic. As a conductor his efforts did much to raise the standard of orchestral playing in England. He liked to have his name associated with patriotic movements and the last of his work to be produced during his life was his musical setting of Kipling's *Absent-Minded Beggar*. It is, however, as composer of the delicate and singularly appropriate melodies to accompany Gilbert's elfin conceits that he is best known to the world. He died in London, Nov. 22, 1900, in the 58th year of his age, and was buried in St. Paul's Cathedral.

The famous partnership between the two began in 1871 and after a short period of joint control at the Royalty Theatre they settled at the

Savoye which became famous the world over as the scene of original production for the series of pieces which have made their names a household word. Their first collaborative effort was *Thespis* which was only moderately successful and has not survived as an acting piece. It was followed, in 1875, by *Trial by Jury,* in which a breach of promise suit is tunefully treated in rich burlesque. *The Sorcerer* followed in 1877 and the next year was produced the immortal *Pinafore.* The operettas appeared at the rate of about one a year and were, in the order of their production, *The Pirates of Penzance, Patience* (a burlesque of the esthetic craze which then prevailed), *Iolanthe, Princess Ida, The Mikado, Ruddigore, The Yeoman of the Guard, The Gondoliers, Utopia Limited* and *The Grand Duke.*

WILLIAM EWART GLADSTONE   1809–1898

WILLIAM EWART GLADSTONE, British statesman and four times prime minister of England, was born Dec. 29, 1809 at Liverpool and was the fourth son of Sir John Gladstone, a wealthy merchant of Scottish parentage who sat in parliament from 1818 to 1827. In 1821 he was sent to Eton and in 1828 to Christ Church, Oxford, where he was a brilliant student, notable for his religious interests and love of outdoor life, and where he already gave evidence of his powers of oratory by a remarkable speech against the Reform Bill which was introduced in the House of Commons in 1831. Leaving college with high honors at the age of 23, he wished to enter the church but after returning from a trip to Italy, he acceded to his father's desire and entered parliament, representing the borough of Newark. In June, 1833, he made his first speech in defense of his father against whom charges had been made in connection with the treatment of slaves on his South American plantation. In the Peel government in 1835 he was appointed lord of the treasury and afterward under-secretary for the colonies, and in 1843 during the second Peel government he became president of the Board of Trade. He took a leading part in the revision of the tariff, that being his first work in finance in which direction he showed unmistakable genius.

In 1839 he had published *The State in its Relations with the Church,* and in 1845 he resigned his office rather than compromise his own convictions by supporting a bill providing for an increased grant to Waymooth college, which he considered opposed to his published views. Later in the year he was appointed colonial secretary and rendered valuable assistance to Peel in formulating the free trade measures leading to the repeal of the Corn Laws. In 1847 and for 18 years thereafter he represented Oxford University in parliament. While on a trip to Italy in 1850 his sympathies were aroused by the plight of the many political prisoners confined there and a letter which he wrote to the Earl of Aberdeen had the result of arousing all Europe to their indignities and wrongs. He thereafter made many eloquent speeches in behalf of Italian independence. He was Chancellor of the Exchequer in the Aberdeen government (1852–55) and again under Palmerston (1859–65) and two years later became leader of the Liberal party toward which he had been gradually tending.

From 1868 to 1874 he was prime minister and carried on a vigorous campaign for reform in Irish affairs. A bitter struggle in the House of Lords in 1869 brought about the disestablishment of the Irish church and he next gave his attention to the Irish land system and a measure to lessen the oppression of the tenant farmers by the landlords, which was carried in 1870. Superseded by Disraeli four years later, he retired to private life in order to devote himself to classical and ecclesiastical studies, for he still maintained his strong interest in the church, but a year later he emerged to attack the government in connection with the Bulgarian atrocities and throughout the Russo-Turkish War he opposed Disraeli's pro-Turkish policy, again taking the leadership of the Liberal party and becoming prime minister in 1880 on Disraeli's downfall. Irish questions were prominent during this period; the famous Phoenix Park murders occurred, followed by some repressive government measures which lost Gladstone the support of the Irish leaders. After the defeat at Majuba Hill in 1881 he made generous terms with the Boers which were not to the liking of the English people. The failure to rescue Gen. Gordon at Khartoum was another blow to his ministry and in 1885 he resigned. The following year he again became premier, but his party was split over the Irish Home Rule bill and badly defeated in the elections, and in July he again resigned. He became premier for the fourth time in 1892 and presented a new Home Rule bill which he carried through the House of Commons, but the Lords rejected it and, wearied of public life, he laid down his office in March, 1894.

He continued his interest in public affairs and made many stirring speeches, his last public appearances being in connection with the Armenian massacres of 1896. He died on May 19, 1898, and was buried in the Statesman's Corner in Westminster Abbey. In 1839 he had married Catherine, the daughter of Sir Stephen Glynne, who survived him. Four daughters and four sons were born, two of the sons later becoming members of parliament.

Gladstone was a greater financier than statesman. Among the far-reaching reforms which he carried through were the establishment of a new educational system, voting by ballot, and the extension of suffrage. He represented the highest type of English gentleman rather than the astute politician. Generous, with high moral qualities which were lacking in his brilliant rival, Disraeli, he acted always in what he conceived to be the public interest, never in the interest of his own private ambitions. He cared little for office and remained in the public arena through a high sense of duty rather than from love of power. He was perhaps weakest in his foreign policies, his great interest lying in domestic questions and in the safeguarding of the liberties of all the English people. A scholar of high attainment, he published a number of books, among them, *Studies in Homer* and *Gleanings from Past Years* (1879–90) containing articles on political and literary subjects which had originally appeared in the *Quarterly Review*.

JOHANN WOLFGANG VON GOETHE   1749–1832

JOHANN WOLFGANG VON GOETHE (gẽ tå), the most distinguished figure in German literature, and one of the most highly gifted and variously accomplished men of the 18th century, was born at Frankfort-on-the-Main, Aug. 14, 1749. His father, a man in good circumstances, was an imperial chancellor, whose wife, Katherine Elisabeth Textor, bore him four children, of whom only Johann and a sister survived childhood. At the age of 16 he went to the university of Leipzig to study law, but his dominant interest was in the wide domain of literature and philosophy to which he devoted his time, laying the foundations of that all-inclusive culture which was to make him a marvel among the literary men of all time. At 21, after an interval of illness in Frankfort, he went to Strassburg to complete his legal studies, but found time to familiarize himself with chemistry, anatomy and architecture, and to continue his studies in classical literature. Here transpired one of those love affairs so conspicuous in his early life and about the extent of which there has been much speculation. Frederica Brion was the 19-year old daughter of a minister. He is thought to have loved her deeply, but not sufficiently to impel him to relinquish his freedom at the altar. This man of noble mind and character appears to have been peculiarly human in his romantic susceptibilities. In his several love affairs there is no suggestion of the libertine, but on the other hand it cannot be denied that for many years, at least, he indulged his honest emotions while shrinking from the golden clasp of matrimony.

At 22 he took his degree of Doctor of Laws and lived for a short time at Wetzlar, then the seat of the imperial chamber of the German Empire, which afforded exceptional facilities for his continued study of law. Here, however, as in other places, his knowledge of the human heart and his interest in character overshadowed his professional studies, and Wetzlar became to him the scene of his famous *Sorrows of Werther,* published in 1774, a glowing leaf from the life of the human soul, full of interest and beauty, which was to stir the literary mind of Europe. A few years now spent in his native city were filled with creative work. His first great work was *Götz von Berlichingen,* published in 1773, and translated into English by Sir Walter Scott. At about this time he began his great poem of *Faust* on which he worked at intervals for many years. In 1775, at the instigation of his friend and admirer, the Grand Duke of Saxe-Weimar, he settled at Weimar, where he presided as a sort of little statesman and literary oracle, the center of a devoted and admiring group augmented by literary celebrities and aspirants who flocked thither to bask in the influence of his all-inclusive intellect and to pay him homage. He was, indeed, a kind of intellectual monarch and few men, during their lifetime, have enjoyed such prestige and wielded such influence as he. In 1782 he received a patent of nobility. From about this time he traveled for several years, visiting Switzerland and Italy, the literary results of which sojourns appeared in his *Iphigenia, Egmont, Tasso* and his *Venetian and Roman Elegies.* Of this last work the heroine was Christiane Vulpius, a woman who was the mother of his eldest son, born in 1789. He lived with her in extra-marital relationship prior to their formal marriage in 1806. In 1792 he participated in the German campaign against France about which he later wrote a memoir. In 1815 he was made minister of state. The death of his munificent patron, in 1828, left him disinclined to public activities and he thereafter lived withdrawn from social and political distractions, devoting himself wholly to literary pursuits. He died on March 22, 1832, in the 84th year of his age.

Goethe is universally esteemed one of the great ornaments of literature. It is impossible to give in this restricted space even the most cursory notice of his numerous works, covering such an extensive range in theme and treatment. There was scarcely a subject of interest to the enlightened mind that did not engage his attention, and what he touched he adorned. In English-speaking countries it is as a poet that he is best known and to the European and American public he is most familiar as the author of the great philosophical poem, *Faust,* the operatic version of which has, of course, greatly widened its popular appeal. In him the poet, critic, naturalist, scientist, and even statesman, were combined in peculiar harmony, and though he was unquestionably a poet of the first order, it is still his amazing versatility that gives him a place apart and raises him to a position of impressive isolation. He was not universal, in the sense that Shakespeare was, nor had he the uncanny and inspired wisdom, much less the godlike melody, of the greatest dramatist and poet. What Shakespeare knew, he knew; what Goethe knew (and the sum total was vast), he learned. But there is hardly to be found in literary history any intellect that presents such rounded completeness; so much profound thought and speculation combined with so much luxuriant imagination, so much science with so much fancy. It is hardly saying too much to call him a phenomenon and let that suffice for the numerous adjectives which crowd for utterance at the mention of his name.

OLIVER GOLDSMITH   1728–1774

OLIVER GOLDSMITH, beloved among English writers, was born at Pallas, a small village in Ireland, on Nov. 10, 1728, son of a clergyman. In his sixth year he was put in charge of the village schoolmaster, but his studies were interrupted by an attack of smallpox, the marks of which disfigured him through life. In 1745 he entered Trinity College, Dublin, at the expense of his uncle but gave no sign of the talents which were to make him famous. His premature departure from college was precipitated by some irregularity in which he became involved. Of an impecunious habit, he tarried in Dublin until his money was spent, then wandered forth and reaching Cork was glad to accept a handful of peas from a sympathizing maiden, an incident which he said remained ever a tender memory. The irresponsible wanderer was returned to college by his brother Henry where in 1749 he received the degree of B.A. The generous uncle, himself a clergyman, desired Oliver to enter the church but the bishop rejected the happy-go-lucky applicant who with fifty pounds, gift of the devoted uncle, set forth again to Dublin to study law. But the gaming table, ever a potent temptation to him, intervened and he lost the wherewithal for his legal studies. His patient relative advanced a further sum which carried him to Edinburgh where he studied medicine but did not take a degree. He is next found in Leyden still wooing the goddess of chance; but his ill luck in this dubious field prompted him in February, 1755 to set forth upon a vagabond journey through the continent, armed with his beloved flute. His equipment for the enterprise was singularly deficient, but he carried what is ever an asset in such a pilgrimage, one of the kindliest and most lovable and simple natures that ever man was blessed with.

In 1756 he returned to England, having taken his degree either at Louvain or Padua. He now set up as a physician but was not successful and tried his luck as an usher in a private school during which time he contributed to the *Monthly Review*. An effort to obtain a medical appointment was unsuccessful and his failure was complicated by the fact that his sponsor, the editor of the *Monthly,* threatened him with the law for pawning the clothes which he had supplied in order that the aspirant might fittingly appear for his examination. This was the lowest ebb before the turn of the tide for Goldsmith. He was soon launched in the field of authorship. His *Inquiry into the State of Polite Learning in Europe* was published in 1759. In the following year his *Chinese Letters* (later brought out under the name of *The Citizen of the World*) were published in a new periodical, the *Public Ledger*. Other works were *A Life of Beau Nash* and *A History of England*. But more interesting than any of these earlier works was his meeting with Dr. Johnson who promptly made him one of the figures of the famous Literary Club where Goldsmith's childlike, guileless nature and general clumsiness soon established him as the butt of friendly raillery, albeit he was much beloved. In 1767 appeared his poem *The Traveller,* which established his reputation, and this was followed in 1766 by that gem of English prose, the *Vicar of Wakefield*. Its quaint humor and style of simple purity have raised this work to the status of a classic and the lovable Vicar is one of the familiar characters of fiction. Success had come to the charming ne'er-do-well and there followed in rapid order other works which have added to his abiding fame. His comedy, *The Good Natured Man,* was produced in 1767 and in the following year his *Roman History*. In 1770 appeared *The Deserted Village,* the most familiar and beautiful of his poems. Three years later his comedy *She Stoops to Conquer,* was produced before an enthusiastic audience. In 1774 appeared his *Grecian History* and his versatile talent was busy with a *History of Animated Nature* (filled with astonishing errors but delightful like all his work) when his death occurred.

Success and fame did not free Goldsmith from financial difficulties. He never overcame his weakness for the gaming table and he had a childlike love of finery which, together with the ill-considered generosity of his guileless nature, kept him always poor. He died April 4, 1774, greatly in debt and deeply mourned by his distinguished colleagues whose incessant banter and ridicule of his awkward body and simple mind had never disguised their love for the writer who "wrote like an angel and talked like poor Poll." Goldsmith never married. He was buried in Temple Church.

A monument bearing an epitaph by Dr. Johnson was later erected to him in Westminster Abbey.

ULYSSES S. GRANT   1822–1885

ULYSSES SIMPSON GRANT, the distinguished soldier who brought the American Civil War to a triumphant end and was twice president of the nation, was born at Point Pleasant, Clermont County, Ohio, on April 27, 1822. He was of Scottish ancestry, descended from Matthew Grant, a man of considerable distinction in the early Massachusetts and Connecticut colonies. His father was Jesse R. Grant, a farmer and tanner, who married Hannah Simpson, and their famous son was the oldest of six children. His early life was spent on the farm with attendance at the primitive district school of the neighborhood. At 17 he went to the military academy at West Point, and after his graduation four years later was assigned to Jefferson Barracks, Missouri, with the commission of brevet second lieutenant. As a subordinate officer he served creditably in the war with Mexico, participating in all the battles of General Scott's campaign. Returning with his regiment in 1848, he married Julia T. Dent, by whom he had a daughter and three sons. In 1854 he resigned his commission, being then a captain, and entered upon an inconspicuous career as a farmer in the neighborhood of St. Louis, abandoning this to become a leather merchant in Galena, Ill.

He did not prosper and one would have been discerning indeed to predict for him at that time the glorious career and world-wide fame which became his. Yet that quality of dogged persistence and the shrewd common sense which became so conspicuous in his military career were noticed by his intimates. When the rebellion broke out he lost no time in offering his services and accompanied the 21st Infantry to Missouri with the rank of colonel. He was soon made brigadier-general of volunteers, commanded at the battle of Belmont and in February, 1862, captured Forts Henry and Donelson, taking some 14,000 prisoners. These victories brought him the rank of major-general of volunteers. On April 6–7, 1862, he commanded the Army of the Tennessee in the sanguinary battle of Shiloh, in which he was driven back, but recovered all lost ground on the following day and achieved a victory. In April of the following year he forced the enemy within their entrenchments at Vicksburg and laid siege to that place, which resulted in its surrender with about 31,000 prisoners and the opening of the Mississippi River. In October he fought the battle of Chattanooga and cleared Tennessee of the rebel forces. In March, 1864, he was given the rank of lieutenant-general, and made supreme commander of all the union forces. As such he directed the operations of the several armies which were involved in the great final struggle in Virginia. His quiet confidence in himself was sustained by the hearty devotion of the armies, and the people of the North took courage after a season of the gravest misgivings. This laureled soldier seemed invincible. While Sherman made his devastating march toward Atlanta, Grant directed the army of the Potomac against Richmond. On May 5–6, 1864, he fought the terrible and indecisive battle of the Wilderness in the hope of opening the road to his objective and, beginning May 8, the battle of Spottsylvania Court House, where he captured a whole division of the enemy's forces, but failed to dislodge the rebels. Those were days of dreadful suspense in the North, but the tension was somewhat lessened by Grant's famous message, "I purpose to fight it out on this line if it takes all summer." At last he drove the enemy within the defences about Richmond and after a few days more of desperate fighting, on April 9, 1865, General Lee surrendered his entire army of 27,000 men at Appomattox Courthouse. To the vanquished confederate chief, Grant was magnanimous and considerate; his noble qualities shone here with resplendent lustre.

This virtually ended the war and Grant was the hero of the nation. He was made full general and Congress ordered a gold medal struck in his honor. In May, 1868, the republican party nominated him for president and he was elected with 214 electoral votes against his opponent, Horatio Seymour's, 80. In 1872 he was again elected, defeating Horace Greeley with 286 votes. Notable among the events of his administration was the adoption of the 15th constitutional amendment, assuring suffrage to all races under American citizenship. At the close of his second term in 1877 he made a tour of the world and was honored as a great soldier in all the countries which he visited. On his return, in 1880, an attempt was made to nominate him again for the presidency, but the movement was defeated because of the national prejudice against a third presidential term. He made his home in New York where he and his two sons became partners in a financial house which traded on his great name, and the result was financial ruin to himself. For the great soldier who had been deceived and used by unscrupulous friends, the whole nation felt the deepest sympathy. The last months of his life were spent in suffering from the ravages of a malignant disease, during which time he resolutely and bravely labored on his memoirs, a noble work, and one of the finest autobiographies ever written. He died at Mt. MacGregor, N. Y., on July 23, 1885, and his body rests in an impressive granite mausoleum on Riverside Drive in New York City.

HORACE GREELEY 1811–1872

HORACE GREELEY, founder of the *New York Tribune,* and a leader in the anti-slavery movement, was born at Amherst, N. H. on Feb. 3, 1811. His people were farmers of small means and at the age of 14 he became an apprentice in the print shop of the *Northern Spectator* at East Poultney, Vt. He was intensely interested in politics and within a short time became practically an editor of the paper which, however, suspended publication in 1830 and Greeley went to New York City, where, in January, 1833, he formed a partnership with Francis V. Story and began publication of *The Morning Post.* It failed within three weeks' time, but the firm had the printing to do for the *Bank Note Reporter,* and soon got the printing of the tri-weekly *Constitutionalist.* James Gordon Bennett proposed that Greeley go into partnership with him to start the *New York Herald.* Greeley refused and in 1834, with a new partner, he inaugurated *the New Yorker,* a weekly literary and news journal. Its publication was continued for seven years and while it was never profitable it brought Greeley into prominence as an able editor and was admitted to be the best literary newspaper in America at that time.

In 1838 he was selected by Whig leaders to edit *The Jeffersonian,* a campaign newspaper in Albany. This was very successful and after the nomination of William Henry Harrison for the presidency Greeley began publication of *The Log Cabin,* a weekly campaign paper, which was a political, although not a financial, success. In September, 1841, *The Log Cabin* and *The New Yorker* were merged into *The Weekly Tribune,* which soon had a circulation of 225,000 copies. In April of the same year Greeley had begun publication of the daily *Tribune* and it was through this newspaper that he acquired fame as one of the ablest of American editors and journalists.

His income from the *Tribune* was large but he lacked business and financial ability and was frequently in difficulties. To better his finances he sold interests in his newspaper to several individuals at various times. As editor of the paper he gave space to new ideas. He advocated a high protective tariff, opposed woman suffrage and the theatre, attacked easy divorce, denounced the repudiation by the states of their debts, supported the Irish aim of independence. He practiced and advocated total abstinence. He was a staunch opponent of slavery; quickly became a leader in the abolitionist movement and issued the *Appeal of Twenty Millions* to President Lincoln advocating the freeing of the slaves. He opposed the Mexican war as a scheme to get more slave territory.

A staunch Whig, he became one of the founders of the Republican party and was a militant advocate of its principles and platforms. He served in Congress for three months (1848–49) filling a vacancy, and introduced the first bill providing small tracts of free government land for settlers. He was active in bringing about the nomination of Lincoln and in defeating Seward's ambitions. He was defeated as a candidate for the Senate in 1861 and again in 1867. He encouraged vigorous prosecution of the Civil War, but in 1864 urged peace negotiations with Confederate representatives in Canada and was appointed a member of the committee by President Lincoln. At the end of the war he urged universal amnesty. His signing of Jefferson Davis' bail bond brought upon him a torrent of abuse.

Dissatisfied with General Grant's administration, he opposed him for a second term in 1872 and was himself nominated for the presidency by the Liberal Republicans, but when the Democrats also nominated him, feeling turned against him and he was defeated. He rushed from the campaign to the bedside of his dying wife. He had taxed his powers of endurance for many months and during the campaign had gone without sleep for weeks. A disorder of the brain developed and he died on Nov. 28, 1872, and was buried in Greenwood Cemetery, New York.

GUSTAVUS ADOLPHUS   1594–1632

GUSTAVUS II (ADOLPHUS), King of Sweden from 1611 until his death, and one of the greatest generals of modern times, was the eldest son of Charles IX, and was born at Stockholm on Dec. 9, 1594. The family were Lutherans and Gustavus was carefully educated and trained in preparation for his accession to the throne. Well versed in the classics, he spoke half a dozen modern languages, was accomplished in music and proficient in military matters.

He was introduced to public life at the age of nine and at thirteen received petitions and gave audiences to the foreign ministers. At fifteen he administered the Duchy of Vestmanland. In 1611 on the death of his father he succeeded to the throne and showed superior power and ability from the beginning of his reign. The country was torn by internal disorders and involved in wars abroad. He at once set himself to secure the loyalty of the nobles and bring about a more orderly form of government. He then turned his attention to the war with Denmark, bringing it to an end on terms which restored to Sweden access to the Baltic Sea. In 1617 he concluded peace also with Russia, thereby extending the Swedish dominion over territory to the east of the Baltic, as far as what later became St. Petersburg. A nine-year war with Poland followed, ending in 1629 with a treaty which secured freedom of trade and religion to both countries and gave Gustavus control over part of East Prussia.

The following year, leaving his infant daughter Christina in the care of the able Axel Oxenstierna, whom he had appointed Chancellor early in his reign, he set sail for Germany with some 13,000 men. Conceiving himself as divinely appointed to deliver the German Protestants, who were engaged in a bitter struggle against the Catholic League, he plunged into the Thirty Years' War which had been steadily going against the Protestant forces. The Swedish army disembarked at Peenermünde and occupied Stettin, the capital of Pomerania. Repeated victories over the imperialists followed and Gustavus with his army undoubtedly saved the cause of Protestantism in Germany, but on Nov. 6, 1632, he fell during the battle of Lutzen (southwest of Leipzig) just as his forces were on the eve of victory. It was not until after many hours of hard fighting that his mangled body was recovered. His men remained masters of the field, however. The spot where he fell was marked by the "Swede's Stone," erected by his body servant, Jacob Ericsson, during the following night. Two hundred years later this was replaced by a monument erected by the German people.

Although primarily a great soldier, Gustavus was a deeply religious man, of the highest personal character, and much of his success in battle was doubtless due to his better methods of warfare and to the high moral influence which he exerted over his men. Under his training the Swedish troops became known as the best and most efficient in all Europe and a number of brilliant commanders were developed who carried on his policies after his death. He raised Sweden to the position of the great power of the North, a prestige which she maintained for a century. He did much to improve the internal government of the country and to promote its commerce and manufactures.

He was succeeded by his daughter, Christina.

JOHANN GUTENBERG   circa 1398–1468

JOHANN GUTENBERG (gōō′tĕn bĕrg) (or GENSFLEISCH), German inventor of the process of printing from movable type, was born about 1398 at Mainz of an aristocratic family which took the names of Gensfleisch and

Gutenberg from two of their estates. Little is known of his early life. The family settled in Strassburg, apparently having been expelled from Mainz. In 1434 Gutenberg is said to have seized and imprisoned the town clerk of Strassburg for a debt due him by the city, but to have freed him and relinquished his claims at the plea of the mayor and councilors. In 1438 he entered into a partnership with Andreas Dritzehn and Andreas and Anton Heilmann, and it would appear from the word "drucken" used in the lawsuit that speedily grew out of the arrangement that it had to do with printing. Records show that he was still in Strassburg in 1441 and 1442, but after March, 1444, he disappears from sight until October, 1448.

In 1450 he entered another partnership, this time with Johann Fust who agreed to advance him 800 guilders on the security of the tools he was to make and to advance 300 guilders a year for expenses. The latter condition appears not to have been fulfilled, nor was Gutenberg's agreement to return the 800 guilders if he and Fust should dissolve partnership, as they did in 1455. During the intervening years he is believed to have printed a number of small books, a letter of indulgence issued by Pope Nicholas V (1451) to King John II of Cyprus, and to have begun a large folio Latin Bible. He and Fust printed from wooden blocks a vocabulary (or dictionary) called *Catholicon* which appears to have been lost. The Mazarin Bible (so-called because the first copy described was found in the library of the French Cardinal Mazarin), a Latin Bible, printed with two columns to the page and with spaces for illuminated initials, finished before August 15, 1456, is claimed by German bibliographers as the work of Gutenberg, but is generally ascribed to Peter Schöffer, who had been employed by Gutenberg and Fust and who afterwards became Fust's partner.

In 1452 Fust contributed another 800 guilders to keep the business from collapsing, but a few years later, before November, 1455, he demanded payment and brought a lawsuit against Gutenberg, who apparently was forced to give up to him all his printing material and paraphernalia, which Fust took to his home in Mainz and continued to print books with them aided by Schöffer until 1462 when Adolphus II sacked the city and work was suspended until 1465.

Little is known of Gutenberg's life and activities after parting from Fust. A document of 1457 shows that he was then in Mainz. He apparently never achieved much commercial success and in 1465 he accepted the post of salaried courtier from the Archbishop Adolf of Nassau, receiving a suit of livery and an allowance of corn and wine. He appears to have been printing books in the meantime as in February, 1468, Dr. Conrad Homery of Mainz claimed, and obtained, certain forms, types, tools and instruments which he had furnished to him.

His death took place early in 1468 at Mainz. A number of German cities have erected statues to his memory and in 1901 a Gutenberg Museum was opened in his native city.

DOUGLAS HAIG 1861–1928

Sir Douglas Haig, English general and commander-in-chief of the British Army in France during the World War, was born at Edinburgh on June 19, 1861. He was educated at Oxford, joined the Seventh Hussars in 1885, was promoted to a captaincy in 1891, served with the Egyptian Army during the Nile campaign of 1898, and the following year went to South Africa where he was present at the engagements near Ladysmith. During Lord Roberts' advance into the Transvaal he was chief staff officer of the cavalry division and was promoted to the rank of brevet lieutenant-colonel. At the close of the Boer War he was appointed A.D.C. to the king, made brevet colonel and given the C.B. After a year in command of the 17th Lancers, he was inspector-general of cavalry in India. In 1905 he married the Hon. Dorothy Vivian. Recalled from India in 1906, he served as director of the War Office for three years and then returned to India where he was chief of the general staff from 1909 to 1912. In 1910 he became a lieutenant-general and two years later was called home to take command in Aldershot.

As commander of the first army of the British Expeditionary Force in the World War, he distinguished himself in the Mons, Marne and Aisne operations, at the first battle of Ypres and at Neuve Chapelle. In November, 1914, he was made a full general. The following year he succeeded Sir John French in chief command of all the British armies in France and Flanders. He combined the remnants of the British forces in France, the new armies created by Kitchener and the Territorial Army into a well-disciplined and organized whole. During the German attack on Verdun early in 1916 he relieved French troops at the front and prepared for the battle of the Somme which convinced General Joffre as well as himself that the Germans were becoming exhausted and that the battle should be renewed early in 1917. Joffre was succeeded by Nivelle, who was given general direction of the British army, and friction developed between the French high command and Haig, although the latter was not opposed to a unified command. Nivelle's campaign failed and Pétain, placed in command, appealed to Haig to keep the Germans occupied while he restored the morale of the French troops.

When the collapse of Russia and the German-Austrian attacks on the Italians at Caporetto resulted in the formation of the Supreme War Council in November, 1917, Haig took over more territory. Foreseeing a German offensive, he asked for reinforcements, but the British Prime Minister was eager for a Palestine campaign and refused his request. The German offensive occurred in the spring of 1918. Haig induced the British Government to send Lord Milner to France, resulting in the unified Allied command under Foch of France. Haig then persuaded General Foch to extend the battle northwards, which was followed by the breaking of the Hindenberg line and the armistice of November, 1918.

Haig was raised to the peerage as Earl Haig and Baron Haig of Bemersyde, given a grant of 100,000 pounds and received the Order of Merit. The Haig home at Bemersyde was purchased by national subscription and presented to him. After the close of the war he interested himself in the welfare of the ex-service men, founded the British Legion and the British Empire Service League. In 1919–20 he was field-marshal commander-in-chief of the army in Great Britain. He died on January 29, 1928 and was buried at Dryburgh Abbey, Scotland.

NATHAN HALE   1755–1776

NATHAN HALE, one of the heroes of the American Revolution, who was executed by the British as a spy, was born on a farm near Covington, Conn., June 6, 1755, the fifth son of Richard and Elizabeth Hale, and was descended from the knighted Hales of Sussex, England, through Robert who was the first of the family to emigrate to America.

He received the customary local school training, followed the customary pursuits of a farm boy of the time, and at the age of fourteen, two years after his mother's death, entered Yale University with his next older brother, Enoch. His health was not very robust in his early years but he was often referred to as the "flower of the family." He was very popular at Yale and was a good student. He became scribe or secretary of the Linonia debating society, founded in 1753, and was a frequent speaker at its meetings. He was graduated with honors on Sept. 3, 1773, and after a visit with his uncle Samuel Hale, who conducted a school at Portsmouth, N. H., he returned to Connecticut and taught in the school at East Haddam on the Connecticut River. He seems to have been a successful teacher for in February, 1774, he was engaged to take charge of the Union School at New London for one quarter at a salary of $200 a year. He loved the work, made many friends, and expressed the desire to continue teaching, but resigned in July, 1775, when he was made a first lieutenant in the newly-created 7th Regiment. His company was sent to join Washington's army which was besieging the British at Winter Hill, near Boston. When the British evacuated Boston and sailed for New York, the first unit of the American army which started for that city in the attempt to reach it ahead of the British was Webb's 19th Regiment, which included Hale's company. For a short time in April or May his regiment was stationed on Long Island. Gen. Howe arrived on July 28 with 25,000 men, but did not offer battle until August. The two armies were engaged on August 27 in the battle of Long Island, but Hale's regiment did not participate.

When George Washington asked for a volunteer to enter the British lines and bring back information as to the enemy's strength and plans, Hale (then a captain) answered the call. He first proceeded to Norwalk, Conn., and arranged with Captain Charles Pond to take him across Long Island Sound to Huntington. His movements for the following week are not recorded. It is known that he succeeded in getting within the British lines disguised as a Dutch schoolmaster, but whether or not he was able to send back any information is not known. The next fact which comes to light concerning him was contained in the regular daily orders issued in New York by the British on September 22, 1776, a part of which read: "A spy from the enemy (by his own full confession) apprehended last night was this day executed at 11 o'clock in front of the Artillery Park." It was reported that he was denied the use of a Bible and was not allowed to see a minister and that letters which he had written to his mother and his fiancée were destroyed before his eyes.

It has been alleged, whether with truth or not is now impossible of proof, that he was betrayed to the British by a relative. However that may be, the name and fame of Captain Nathan Hale have loomed large in the history of the American Revolution; his youth, his accomplishments, his bravery and devotion to duty, together with the pity awakened by that tragic end to so young and promising a life, have endeared him to all Americans. He met his death with dignity and courage, his last words being, "I only regret that I have but one life to give for my country." Many states have erected memorials to his memory; among them are a monument at South Coventry, Conn., a memorial column and fountain at Huntington, Long Island, and a statue of him by Frederick MacMonnies in City Hall Park, New York.

FRANS HALS circa 1584–1666

Frans Hals, considered second to Rembrandt among Dutch painters, was born in Antwerp about 1584. He probably studied painting first under van Noort at Antwerp and after removing to Haarlem became a pupil of van Mander who was both painter and historian. None of the work of his early period has come down to posterity save one engraving by Jan van der Velde of Hals' lost portrait of Johannes Bogardus. The earliest of his works which we now possess are the "Two Boys Playing and Singing" (Cassel Gallery) and the "Banquet of the Officers of the 'St. Joris Doele' " (Haarlem Museum). These show careful drawing and excellent finish though the flesh tints lacked the clearness that he later attained in his portraits. With the years he developed a freer style and a greater command of effect.

Among the masterpieces of his second decade as a painter are the beautiful full-length portrait of "Madame van Beresteyn" (Louvre), "Willem van Heythuysen" (Lichtenstein collection, Vienna), and several other banquet scenes which are among his most interesting work.

About 1637, according to art critics, the influence of Rembrandt became apparent, seen in such paintings as "Regents of the Company of St. Elizabeth" and the portrait of "Maria Voogt." Gradually, however, Hals drew away from the Rembrandt influence and gave himself up to the silver and gray harmonies of tone found in many of his canvases. Two of his paintings of 1664—"The Regents and Regentesses of the Oudemannenhuis"—are considered masterpieces of color although done in monochromes. After 1641 he showed this tendency to suggest color rather than to express it, as may be seen in the graying of his flesh tints until finally, in shadow, they became almost black. As this tendency occurred during the period of his greatest poverty, it has been suggested that the free use of black and white was due to the cheapness of those pigments in comparison with the more costly and more vivid colors.

His large family and his own improvidence reduced him to absolute penury and in 1654 his pictures, furniture and household utensils were sold in order to pay his debts. For a time the city paid for his rent and fuel and in 1664 gave him an annuity of 200 florins which he enjoyed but a short time as he died in Haarlem in 1666.

As a portrait painter Hals is not considered quite the equal of Rembrandt and Velazquez, his pictures lacking the psychological insight into character displayed by those two great masters. Several of his group portraits, however, reveal evidences of searching character analysis, and he possessed an uncanny facility in translating to canvas the fleeting expressions of character found in a smile, a glance of the eye, a turn of the head. He had no great reputation during his life, and for two centuries after his death was held in little esteem. The earliest recorded sale of a Frans Hals in Great Britain was in 1769 when "A Music Conversation" was bought by Lord Byron for 28 pounds sterling. In 1908 the London National Gallery paid 25,000 pounds for a family group while the small "Portrait of Cozmans" sold for nearly 27,000 pounds in 1919. Examples of his work are to be found in nearly every leading public and private art collection.

ALEXANDER HAMILTON   1757–1804

ALEXANDER HAMILTON, American soldier and statesman, was one of the foremost figures in establishing American nationalism. He organized the national finances and left his imprint on the administrative organization of the nation.

He was born on the island of Nevis in the West Indies on Jan. 11, 1757. His father was a Scottish merchant, his mother of French Huguenot extraction. His father failed in business and in his twelfth year Hamilton entered a counting-house in St. Croix. Without the advantages of systematic schooling, he read and studied by himself and early displayed a poise and maturity of mind that were exceptional. In 1772 friends made it possible for him to enter a preparatory school at Elizabethtown, N. J., and two years later he went to King's College (now Columbia University), but his studies were interrupted by the Revolutionary War into which he threw himself with ardor on the side of the colonists.

Although barely 18 he wrote a series of articles defending the rights of the colonies which showed remarkable controversial ability, attracted wide attention and were at first thought to be the work of the statesman, John Jay.

He organized an artillery company, was appointed captain, won the interest of Nathaniel Greene and George Washington by his ability and bravery in the campaign of 1776 around New York City; became a lieutenant-colonel in 1777 and for four years served as Washington's private secretary and confidential aide. Ambitious for independent action and military glory, he resigned and Washington later obtained for him a field command. He won renown at Yorktown by conducting the American column that captured the first redoubt of the British works.

In 1780 he married Elizabeth, daughter of Gen. Philip Schuyler of

New York. As early as 1779–80 he had urged the need of centralization of the governmental powers of the rebelling colonies. He served in the Continental Congress for a year (1782–83) and then settled in New York where he practiced law, soon becoming one of the most eminent men in his profession. As delegate from New York to the Annapolis Convention in 1787, he supported Madison in inducing the Convention to exceed its powers and summon the Federal Convention which met in Philadelphia during the same year to revise the articles of confederation. He was a delegate to that convention and had an important share in drawing up the Constitution which was later adopted. He upheld the British government as a model and favored an executive who should be elected for a life tenure of office and who should hold an absolute veto on national legislation. His series of essays (afterward collected and published under the title of *The Federalist*) urging the adoption of the Constitution have become classics on American constitutional law and the principles of government.

In 1789 Hamilton became Secretary of the Treasury in Washington's cabinet—a position of peculiar difficulty and importance owing to the disordered state of the country's financial system. His reports on public credit and his speeches advocating a protective tariff to encourage American manufacturing still serve as a basis for argument. He advocated a national bank; brought order and efficiency to the national financial structure and successfully withstood congressional opponents who instigated an investigation of his official accounts. His advice on domestic questions, particularly in the realm of finance, was accepted if not sought by Washington. He differed radically on domestic policies with Thomas Jefferson and their conflicting opinions formed the basis of the opposing political parties, Republicans and Whigs.

In 1795 Hamilton resigned his office and resumed the practice of law in New York, but a few years later he took an active part, under Washington, in organizing an army for threatened war with France, and after Washington's death he was appointed commander-in-chief, but the war was averted. He later became involved in political intrigues and his influence in government ceased. Hostilities arose between himself and Aaron Burr, a leader of the Democratic party, and Burr, embittered by his failure to be elected to office, partly through Hamilton's efforts, seized upon some personal pretext and challenged the latter to a duel. The two men met on July 11, 1804 at Weehawken, N. J., on the bank of the Hudson River under the Palisades and at the first shot Hamilton was mortally wounded. His death the following day aroused a widespread sentiment against dueling.

On Nov. 30, 1880 there was unveiled in Central Park, New York, in the presence of many distinguished spectators, a granite statue of Hamil-

ton which had been presented to the City of New York by his son, John
C. Hamilton.

HANNIBAL   247 B.C.–183 B.C.

HANNIBAL, the Carthaginian general who precipitated the second Punic
War and led the long and bitter struggle of Carthage against Rome for
world dominance, was one of the world's greatest military geniuses. He
was the son of Hamilcar Barca and was born in 247 B.C. At the age of
nine he accompanied his father on an expedition into Spain, and before
starting he was made to take an oath of eternal hatred toward the Romans,
an oath which dominated his entire life.

His father, who had instructed him in the science of warfare, died in
Spain and at the age of 29, following the death of his brother-in-law, Hasdrubal, he succeeded the latter as commander-in-chief of the army in
Spain. He deliberately started the second Punic War in 219 B.C. by besieging and capturing Saguntum, a city which was allied with Rome.
Leaving his younger brother (also named Hasdrubal) in charge of Spain,
Hannibal with a vast army set out for northern Italy, crossing the Alps
into the valley of the Susa. Although he lost two-thirds of his troops en
route, he defeated one Roman army after another and his offensive was
so rapid that Publius Cornelius Scipio withdrew the Roman forces south
of the Po. Encamping on the left bank of that river, Hannibal was attacked by four Roman legions, but so brilliant were his tactics that the
battle resulted in an overwhelming victory and soon all of northern Italy
except Placentia and Cremona was abandoned to him.

In 217 B.C. he crossed the Apennines, ravaged Etruria, surprised and
overwhelmed the Roman commander, Servilius, at Lake Thrasimeme, as
the latter sought to join forces with Flaminius. He then ravaged the
Adriatic coast as far as Apulia, where he went into winter quarters. Early
the next year he captured the fortress of Cannae with its huge depot of
supplies, and utterly routed 50,000 Romans under the consuls, Lucius
Æmilius Paulus and Gaius Terentius Varro. This victory made him master of northern Italy. He later marched against Naples, but failing to take
that city he occupied Capua, then the second largest Roman city, and
there he spent the winter. Fabius, the Delayer, was now put in command
of the Roman legions and their accustomed method of warfare gave place
to a more desultory kind. Fabius avoided all proffered battles, never offered battle on equal terms, but sought to harass the Carthaginians on

all sides, and Hannibal's military genius under those conditions was somewhat nullified. He won no more great victories. In 211 B.C., Capua was besieged and Hannibal, to draw the besiegers out of their entrenchments, played one of his boldest strokes. He left his main army and with part of his force marched towards Rome. When within three miles of the capital a new Roman army marched out of the walled city and he was forced to retreat. Syracuse, then Capua, and in 209 B.C., Tarentum, capitulated to the Romans. Hasdrubal marched into Italy to his brother's aid, but was defeated at Metaurus and beheaded. The war was lost, but for four years longer Hannibal contested the advance of the Romans, until Scipio carried the warfare into Africa, whereupon Hannibal returned to defend Carthage. For some sixteen years he had been able to maintain his army in Italy.

His native city had already accepted an armistice when he arrived, but it then determined to continue the struggle. In 202 B.C., at Zama Regio, facing a greatly superior force, Hannibal asked for peace, but the terms offered were so severe that he gave battle instead and was badly defeated. He then advocated the submission of Carthage and after peace had been declared in 201 B.C. he was placed in charge of the government. His hatred of Rome persisted and he set himself to prepare for renewing the struggle at some later day. His immediate task was to make political reforms and put the finances of Carthage in better shape in which he succeeded so brilliantly that Carthage was soon able to offer Rome full payment of the war indemnity. Rome, however, could not afford to permit her rival to recover her old standing and accused Hannibal of conspiring against peace. He fled to the court of Antiochus at Ephesus, but when the latter made peace with Rome with the surrender of Hannibal as one of the conditions, he escaped to the court of Prusias, King of Bithynia. In 183 B.C., Prusias in turn was at the mercy of Rome which again demanded Hannibal. The latter, seeing no hope of escape, swallowed poison, a supply of which he had carried with him for such an emergency. He is said to have been married to a Spanish woman of Castulo but appears to have had no children.

WARREN G. HARDING   1865–1923

WARREN GAMALIEL HARDING, 29th president of the United States, was born Nov. 2, 1865, at Corsica (then Blooming Grove), Ohio, and was the son of a farmer and country doctor. After attending Ohio Central College at Iberia, he taught a country school, studied law, worked in a newspaper office, becoming in 1884 editor and owner of the *Marion Star,* and in 1891 married Florence Kling.

He served for two terms (1900–1904) in the Ohio State Senate and from 1904 to 1906 was lieutenant-governor of the state. He was defeated when nominated for governor in 1910 but in 1914 was elected to the United States Senate. In the Senate he advocated naval preparedness in 1915, supported the declaration of war against Germany, the selective draft, espionage bills and other war measures, excepting the federal control of food and fuel. Favoring prohibition, he voted for the Volstead Act over Wilson's veto, and for exemption of American shipping from Panama Canal tolls. He opposed the covenant of the League of Nations and voted for the ratification of the Treaty of Versailles with reservations.

In 1920 he was elected president of the United States, defeating James M. Cox who had been President Wilson's choice. He was the sixth president to come from the state of Ohio. Among his cabinet appointments were Charles E. Hughes, Secretary of State; Herbert C. Hoover, Secretary of Commerce; Andrew Mellon, Secretary of the Treasury; Harry M. Daugherty, Attorney General; Albert B. Fall, Secretary of the Interior and Will H. Hays, Postmaster-General. The appointment of Fall and Daugherty later brought severe criticism and discredit upon Harding and the Republican party when the Teapot Dome and other oil leases were investigated.

During his term of office he signed a bill providing for a Budget Bureau and appointed Charles G. Dawes its director. His administration refused to resume trade relations with Russia, denied Japan's claim to a mandate over the island of Yap and rejected the League of Nations covenant. Peace treaties were signed with Germany, Austria and Hungary, including most of the Versailles peace stipulations, but repudiating adherence to the League of Nations. In August, 1921, he formally invited the principal naval powers to a Conference on the Limitation of Armaments, which was held in Washington. This was one of the most outstanding acts of his administration and he advocated succeeding conferences as a means of obtaining international association for the promotion of peace.

Harding himself was not involved in the political dishonesty which later investigation disclosed to have taken place in Washington during his administration, but it appeared evident that his kindly and genial nature had led him to repose too great trust in his friends.

In the summer of 1923, while returning from a speaking tour of the United States and Alaska, which had been undertaken for the purpose of fostering support for his administration, he became ill in Oregon and was taken to San Francisco where he died on Aug. 2, 1923. His body was buried at Marion, Ohio, where an impressive monument was later erected to his memory.

THOMAS HARDY   1840–1928

THOMAS HARDY, one of the greatest of English novelists in the generation following that of Thackeray and Dickens, was born in Dorsetshire, England, June 2, 1840, a descendant of the Dorset Hardys. Educated in the local schools (1848–64) and then privately, he was articled to John Hicks, ecclesiastical architect of Dorchester, in 1856. Three years later he began to write verse and essays, but continued his work on old Dorset churches preliminary to their repair. In London in 1862 he became assistant to Sir Arthur Blomfield and the following year won the medal of the Royal Society of British Architecture for a paper on *Coloured Brick and Terra-Cotta Architecture. Chambers' Journal* published his first article, *How I Built My House,* in 1865 and for several years thereafter he varied his architectural work by writing verse. In 1867–68 he wrote a novel under the title of *The Poor Man and the Lady,* which George Meredith advised him not to print but to write another with more plot.

In 1871 he published *Desperate Remedies,* his first crude novel, followed the next year by *Under the Greenwood Tree* which was more successful, a story of rural life in the depiction of which he was unsurpassed. The tragic and ironic novel, *A Pair of Blue Eyes* (1873), was followed by *Far From the Madding Crowd,* published anonymously in the *Cornhill Magazine,* and attributed by many to George Eliot. This remains one of his finest novels. *The Hand of Ethelberta* was published in 1876 and in 1878 *The Return of the Native,* a sombre and powerful story which was surpassed by only one other of his novels. Then followed in rapid succession *The Trumpet-Major, A Laodicean, Two on a Tower, The Mayor of Casterbridge, The Woodlanders, Wessex Tales, A Group of Noble Dames, Tess of the D'Urbervilles,* probably the best known of all his works and one which aroused a storm of criticism; *Life's Little Ironies* and *Jude the Obscure.* The latter was his most thoughtful, yet perhaps his least popular book. The early struggles of its hero to gain an education were said to be drawn largely from his own experience. The bitter attacks on *Tess* and *Jude* caused the author to abandon the writing of novels. The American actress, Minnie Maddern Fiske, achieved one of her greatest successes in a dramatization of *Tess of the D'Urbervilles,* which was later also produced as a motion picture.

From 1904 to 1908 Hardy worked upon his epic drama, *The Dynasts,* a chronicle of England's struggle against Napoleon, which has been characterized as one of the greatest works in English literature. It was produced, in part, during the World War at the Kingsway Theatre, London, and again at Oxford in 1930. He devoted the rest of his literary life to poetry, publishing from 1914 to 1927 *Satires of Circumstance, Selected Poems, Moments of Vision, Collected Poems, Late Lyrics and Earlier, Human Shows, Far Phantasies. Winter Words* was published after his death in 1928. Many of the poems dealt with the World War.

In 1874 he had married Emma Lavinia Gifford who died in 1912 and two years later he married Florence Emily Dugdale, herself a writer of children's books. The Order of Merit was conferred upon him in 1910 and he was made a Doctor of Literature of Oxford and of Cambridge. On the occasion of his 70th, and again on his 80th, birthday he received at his home delegations bringing to him the homage of the English-speaking world. He died on Jan. 12, 1928; his ashes were interred in Westminster Abbey, but his heart was buried in the yard of his parish church, in deference to his affection for his native Wessex.

Generally considered the "last of the great Victorians," Hardy was one of the most pessimistic of England's writers, yet possessed a tragic power that few have equaled. Despite his lack of university education, he possessed great erudition and his writings evince a wide knowledge of both classical and modern literature.

EDWARD H. HARRIMAN   1848–1909

EDWARD HENRY HARRIMAN, American financier and railway magnate, was born at Hempstead, L. I., Feb. 20, 1848. Three years later the family moved to Jersey City where he attended public schools, entering Trinity School in New York City in 1860. Two years later he became a messenger boy for a brokerage firm and in 1870 opened his own brokerage office. His first venture in the transportation line was the acquisition of the Steamer *Twilight* in 1877. Two years later, following his marriage to Mary W. Averell of Ogdensburg, N. Y. he was elected a director of the Ogdensburg & Lake Champlain Railway, and in 1881 he acquired an interest in the Lake Ontario & Southern which he reorganized and sold to the Pennsylvania System. He then became a director of the Illinois Central, and in

1885 retired from his New York brokerage firm, bought property in Orange County, N. Y., and began to build his famous Arden home.

During the next 20 years he interested himself principally in railroad properties, acquiring controlling interests and directorships in many of the roads throughout the United States and doing much to reorganize and improve and extend them. His activities from time to time brought him into conflict with J. Pierpont Morgan and other financiers. As a traction genius he has probably had no equal.

In 1901 he gained control of the Southern Pacific, became its president, and brought $79,000,000 of stock in the Northern Pacific in an attempt to secure control of that road, creating the famous Union Pacific "corner" and bringing about one of the most serious financial crises in the history of Wall Street.

He visited Mexico and got a concession from President Diaz to build a railroad to Mazatlan and beyond. In 1904 he became a member of the Frick Committee which investigated the Equitable Life Insurance scandal. He made a trip to the Orient to obtain railroads in Manchuria and Siberia for his proposed around-the-world transportation system, and obtained the consent of the Japanese government which, however, was later rescinded. In 1906 he invested $130,000,000 of Union Pacific money in the stocks of various railroads. During that year occurred the great fire and earthquake in San Francisco and Harriman went to the rescue on a magnificent scale. His lines carried 224,000 refugees out of the city and took 1600 carloads of food and supplies into the city, all free of charge.

In 1907, at the request of President Theodore Roosevelt, he set his Southern Pacific engineers at work to fill the crevasse which the Colorado River had made into Salton Basin, imperilling the entire Imperial Valley. The crevasse was filled with 2,000,000 cubic feet of rock brought from distances of from 60 to 485 miles at a cost of $3,000,000, but Congress refused to reimburse him for the expense. In 1908 he saved the Erie Railroad from bankruptcy by taking $4,500,000 of its notes, and planned extensive reorganization and rehabilitation of the road, but after returning from a visit to Europe for his health he died on Sept. 9, 1909 at Arden where he was buried.

Following his wishes his widow and their son Averell presented $1,000,000 and 10,000 acres of land to New York State for the extension of the Palisades Interstate Park northwards along the Hudson.

BENJAMIN HARRISON 1833–1901

BENJAMIN HARRISON, the 23rd president of the United States, was born at North Bend, Ohio, Aug. 20, 1833, grandson of President William Henry Harrison, and great-grandson of Benjamin Harrison of Virginia, who was a signer of the Declaration of Independence. His father, John Scott Harrison, was a member of Congress from 1853 to 1857. His youth was passed on a farm. He was graduated from Miami University in 1852, studied law in Cincinnati, being admitted to the bar in 1853, and began the practice of his profession in Indianapolis where he soon came to be known as one of the city's ablest lawyers. He married the daughter of the Rev. J. W. Scott.

He was strongly abolitionist in sentiment and at the outbreak of the Civil War he offered his services to the governor who appointed him a second-lieutenant. He raised a regiment of volunteers and was commissioned its colonel in which capacity he served throughout the war. On Jan. 23, 1865, he was breveted Brigadier-General of Volunteers. He served in Buell's Kentucky and Tennessee campaigns in 1862–63 and was with Sherman's march on Atlanta in 1864. The same year he was in the Nashville campaign and was then transferred to Sherman's army in its march through the Carolinas. He served with distinction at the battles of Kenesaw Mountain, Peach Tree Creek and Nashville (1864).

Following the war he returned to his law practice. He was a staunch Republican, though not a professional politician. He took part in the campaign which elected Garfield to the presidency and was offered a post in the latter's cabinet, but declined it as he had just been elected to the Senate in which he took his seat on March 4, 1881. In 1887 he failed of reelection to the Senate but the following year was elected president against Grover Cleveland who was a candidate for reelection.

During Harrison's term as president the Pan-American Congress met in Washington; the McKinley tariff bill and the Sherman silver bill were passed; the Louisiana lottery was suppressed, the navy enlarged and civil service reform furthered. Commercial reciprocity was established with many European countries, an international monetary conference was called by the United States; controversies with Chile, Germany and Great Britain were settled peacefully; North and South Dakota, Idaho, Washington and Montana were admitted to the Union as states. His policies included a general program for the revival of American industries and governmental efficiency leading to the reduction of the public debt. He was renominated and ran against Cleveland for a second time, but was defeated, partly owing t6 the labor unions which were arrayed against him.

He resumed the practice of law, accepted a lectureship in international law at Leland Stanford Jr. University, and in 1898 was retained by Venezuela as leading counsel in its boundary dispute with Great Britain. He appeared before the international tribunal in Paris (1899) and was a representative of the United States at the Hague Conference in the same year. In 1897 he published *This Country of Ours,* treating of the American government, and after his death a collection of his essays appeared under the title of *Views of an Ex-president.* He died in Indianapolis March 13, 1901.

WILLIAM HENRY HARRISON   1773–1841

WILLIAM HENRY HARRISON, the ninth president of the United States, was the son of Benjamin Harrison, governor of Virginia, who was one of the signers of the Declaration of Independence. He was born at Berkeley, Va., Feb. 9, 1773, received a classical education at Hampden-Sidney College and began the study of medicine in Philadelphia. Upon the death of his father in 1791 he left college and enlisted in the 10th Regiment at Fort Washington, Cincinnati. He later served with gallantry under Gen. Anthony Wayne in his campaign against the Indians. He resigned from the army in 1797; was appointed secretary of the Northwest Territory and represented that territory in Congress in 1799. The following year President Adams appointed him governor of the newly created Territory of Indiana and he served in that capacity until 1812, handling the troublesome Indian tribes with great skill. He obtained the passage of more effective land laws and of legislation for better treatment of the Indians and for the prevention of the sale of liquor to them. In 1803 he became a special commissioner to treat with the tribes regarding lands and boundaries and negotiated a number of treaties by which portions of the states of Indiana, Illinois, Wisconsin and Missouri were opened to settlement by the whites. For a short time in 1804 he acted as governor of the Territory of Louisiana.

When the hostility of the Indian chief, Tecumseh, and others was aroused by cessions of land along the Wabash River, Harrison held conferences with the tribes who had combined under Tecumseh and his brother, the "Prophet," to prevent the encroachment of the whites. The conference proving fruitless, he advanced against them with a force of militia and regulars and won a decisive victory at the Tippecanoe River on Nov. 7, 1811. This victory established his military reputation and was partly responsible for his later nomination to the presidency.

The Indian warfare developed into the War of 1812 and became also war against the English in Canada. Harrison, as Brigadier-General in command of the army in the Northwest, showed great military talent. He checked the British under Proctor and, following Perry's victory on Lake Erie, pursued the invaders into Canada where at the battle of the Thames on Oct. 5 he administered a crushing defeat to the British general. He resigned his commission in 1814, and negotiated the treaty of Greenville with the Indians of the Northwest by which they were to become the allies of the United States. From 1816 to 1819 as a representative in Congress he worked for more liberal pension laws and better militia organization and in 1824 was elected to the United States Senate. In 1828 he was appointed first minister of the United States to Colombia, but was recalled a year later and retired to North Bend, Ohio.

In 1836 he ran for the presidency as a Whig candidate but was defeated by Van Buren, whom he in turn defeated in 1840, but he lived only one month after his inauguration as president. He appointed Daniel Webster as his Secretary of State, with Thomas Ewing as Secretary of the Treasury and John Bell Secretary of War. His death occurred on April 4, 1841 from pneumonia, aggravated by excitement and the demands of office seekers. He was buried temporarily in Washington and later taken to the tomb at North Bend, Ohio, where his body still lies.

WILLIAM HARVEY   1578–1657

WILLIAM HARVEY, an English physician who discovered the circulation of the blood, was born at Folkestone, England, April 1, 1578. His entire life was devoted to the study and practice of medicine with particular reference to the heart and the circulatory system which had never before been understood. He studied at Cambridge and later at the University of Padua, then the world's most celebrated medical school, where he attended the lectures of Fabricius, Julius Casserius and other eminent men. He received his degree in April, 1602 and returned home to settle in London. In June, 1607, he was admitted as a fellow of the Royal College of Physicians and in 1609 became physician to St. Bartholomew's Hospital. In 1616 as Lumleian lecturer at the College of Physicians he began a course of lectures in which he first enunciated his theories as to the heart and the blood. In 1617 he was appointed physician-extraordinary to James I and in 1630 was chosen as physician to Charles I.

In 1628 he published his book on the circulation of the blood, *Exercitatio-Anatomica de Motu Cordis et Sanguinis,* which revolutionized the study of physiology and did much for the advance of the science of medicine. Aristotle had taught that the blood was elaborated from the food in the liver, carried to the heart and sent through the veins over the body. Erasistratus and Herophilus taught that while the veins carried the blood from the heart, the arteries carried a subtle kind of air or spirit. Galen discovered that the arteries contained blood as well as vital air or spirit. Physicians of the 16th century made some advances. They believed that the blood moved in the body, but slowly and irregularly. They supposed that one kind of blood flowed from the liver to the right ventricle of the heart and thence to the lungs and the general system through the veins, and that another kind flowed from the left ventricle through the arteries. They supposed that blood could pass directly from the right to the left side of the heart. Fabricius had set forth the system of valves in the veins. Harvey had not only studied all the books on the subject, but had made extensive experiments on dogs, pigs, fishes, snakes, oysters, the transparent shrimp and the chick while still in the egg. He described his experiments on the ventricles, auricles, the arteries and the veins. His explanation of the circulation of the blood was generally accepted and was complete except for one detail,—that of the capillary channels which take the blood from the arteries into the veins. This added detail was supplied some 80 years later by the Italian anatomist, Marcello Malpighi.

Between 1629 and 1632 Harvey traveled with James Stewart, afterwards Duke of Richmond, in Italy and elsewhere. Four years later he accompanied the Earl of Arundel on his embassy to Ferdinand II. Returning to his London practice for a time, he accompanied Charles I on various expeditions and was in attendance on him at the battle of Edgehill (October 1642). He was later made warden of Merton College, Oxford, but when Oxford was surrendered to the Parliament in 1646 he returned to London. Being now 68 years of age, he gave up his practice and lived in retirement with one or another of his brothers who were men of wealth and standing. Dr. George Ent visited him at Combe in 1650 and after some difficulty obtained from him the manuscript of a work on the generation of animals, which he later published under the title of *Exercitationes de Generatione Animalism*. The book showed Dr. Harvey's patient and extensive observations, but because of the need of a fine microscope to aid his studies it lacked the scientific value of the earlier work on the blood.

In 1654 Harvey had been elected president of the College of Physicians, but declined the honor because of his age. He died in London on June 3, 1657 and was buried at Hempstead in Essex.

WARREN HASTINGS   1732–1818

WARREN HASTINGS, English statesman and administrator, was born at Churchill in Oxfordshire, England, on Dec. 6, 1732. The glory had departed from his ancient line and the ancestral estate at Daylesford had passed from the possession of the family when he who was destined to be its most distinguished representative was born. Warren's grandfather continued in the neighborhood as a poor clergyman. His second son, Pynaston, was a roving and irresponsible youth who married at the age of 16, drifted to the West Indies and died. His young wife also died early, leaving the care of the orphaned Warren to his grandfather who was already sufficiently burdened with debts, lawsuits and other perplexities incidental to the loss of the ancestral domain. It is significant of the towering ambition of the future empire builder that at the age of seven he declared his intention to recover this estate. His grandfather sent him to school where it is reported he gave promise of being "one of the greatest scholars of the age."

At 17 he was sent out to India as a clerk in the East India Company's service and rose steadily to posts of responsibility. He assisted Colonel Clive in reestablishing British authority in Calcutta and was later made a member of the Calcutta Council in which he served with credit and distinction. He returned to England in 1764 in possession of a moderate fortune. Three years later he was appointed a member of the council at Madras, again took up his residence in India and was promoted, in 1772, to the presidency of the Supreme Council of Bengal. By parliamentary enactment, a year later, the incumbent of this post was given the title of governor-general of India, and thus Hastings became the first governor-general of that vast empire. He was not long in disclosing a capacity for ruthless and unscrupulous practices. The unceasing demands of the East India Company for money, and the involved state of the government finances, impelled his to seize certain rich provinces from the Great Mogul and sell them to the Nawab of Oudh. He even rented the company's army to the Nawab for the maintenance of order among the people, who were justly angered by this arbitrary transfer of their allegiance. The great Brahman, Nuncomar, was put to death by his influence in order to strike terror to the native population. He exacted vast sums from the Rajah of

Benares and finally seized all his belongings. He formed a treaty with Asaph-ud-Dowlah under which the mother and grandmother of the Nawab were to be stripped of their possessions for the benefit of the company. These were the chief blemishes on his administration, and they are sufficiently odious. That his reputation survived or was in a measure restored, after the sequel, seems conclusive proof of the high character of his services and abilities. Macaulay observes that the splendor of his fame would bear many dark spots. When war with France broke out he acted with vigor and did much to achieve an orderly administration of justice among the Indian people. It has been urged that his administration was made difficult by too much meddling on the part of the home government. Unquestionably his administrative course was complicated by a powerful and overbearing council with which he had to contend. But these influences seem insufficient to account for the ruthlessness and despotic cruelty which bespeak the essence of tyranny and a cold heart.

In 1785 he resigned his office and returned to England, where his administration promptly received the royal approval and a unanimous vote of appreciation was given him by the directors of the company. Amid the clamor, however, were heard voices condemning his conduct in office, the Whig opposition was loud in denunciation of his acts and this rising tide of disapproval was crystalized in a successful motion in the House of Commons for his impeachment before the House of Lords. The trial, which dragged out for seven years, became one of the most celebrated in history. It was marked by the stirring oratory of Burke, Sheridan, Fox and others and is made familiar to the public of a later time by the matchless eloquence and graphic pictures of Macaulay's famous narrative. Hastings was finally acquitted and passed the remainder of his life at Daylesford, the ancestral home which he had so early coveted, beguiling his increasing years with literature and the care of his estate until he was 86 years old. He died August 22, 1818. While in India he had married a Mrs. Buchanan. Of their two children one died in infancy shortly before her mother and the other died soon after his father's return to England.

NATHANIEL HAWTHORNE   1804–1864

NATHANIEL HAWTHORNE, one of America's greatest novelists, was born July 4, 1804, at Salem, Mass., where his father was a merchant captain. The elder Hawthorne died in 1808, leaving his family in straitened circumstances. When the son was eighteen Mrs. Hawthorne removed to a lonely farm near Raymond, Maine, where the life he necessarily lived doubtless aggravated his habit of solitariness. He attended Bowdoin College and after graduating in 1825 returned to Salem and devoted himself to writing, living much in seclusion. His first novel, *Fanshawe,* published anonymously in 1828, gave little promise of his future greatness. He earned a scanty living for several years by contributing tales and verses to various magazines which he later collected and published under the title of *Twice-Told Tales* (1837). The stories attracted considerable attention and created some demand for more work from the same pen, although not sufficient to relieve the author from financial worries.

In 1839 George Bancroft, the historian, then Collector of the Port of Boston, appointed him weigher and gauger in the Boston Custom House, a post which he occupied for two years and then returned to Salem, later joining a semi-socialistic colony at Brook Farm. In 1842 he married Sophia Peabody and took up his residence in Concord, Mass., where Emerson and Louisa M. Alcott lived. His home there (which had been formerly occupied by Emerson and is now preserved as a Hawthorne museum) was the "Old Manse" immortalized in the volume of tales and sketches published in 1840 under the title of *Mosses from an Old Manse.* A second volume of *Twice-Told Tales* had appeared in 1845 and he had also published his *Biographical Sketches, Grandfather's Chair* and other tales for children. The loss of some money in the Brook Farm experiment led him to accept the post of surveyor in the Salem Custom House where he remained until 1850. In that year he published his first important romance, *The Scarlet Letter,* which met with immediate success both in Europe and America, as did also *The House of the Seven Gables,* published in 1851, both of which have become classics of English literature. *The Wonder Book,* tales for children, appeared the same year, and in 1852 *The Snow Image* and *The Blithedale Romance,* the latter based upon the Brook Farm experiment.

In 1852 he wrote a *Life of Franklin Pierce* who had been a schoolmate at Bowdoin College, followed by *The Tanglewood Tales* in 1853, a continuation of the *Wonder Book.* After Pierce's inauguration as President he appointed Hawthorne as consul at Liverpool and the novelist lived in that English city from 1853 to 1857. The following year he went to Italy for the benefit of his health and while there gathered material for *The Marble Faun,* published in 1860. After his return to Concord he wrote the papers on English life for the *Atlantic Monthly,* which were collected and published in 1863 as *Our Old Home.* He began a new romance, *Dr. Grimshaw's Secret,* based on the idea of the discovery of an elixir of eternal life, but death intervened on May 18, 1864, at Plymouth, N. H., where he had gone to recover his health. He was buried in Sleepy

Hollow cemetery, Concord, Mass. His daughter, Una, published a version of the unfinished romance in 1872 under the title of *Septimius Felton,* and his son, Julian, who later became well known as a journalist and novelist, published another version under the title of *Dr. Grimshaw's Secret.* His *American Note-Books, English Note-Books* and *French and Italian Note-Books* were published by his widow after his death.

In his sombre field Hawthorne stands supreme, unique not only in American literature, but in all literature. He was, par excellence, an artist and his best works are models of form and color. Not even Hardy surpasses him in the wizardry by which he infuses into his theme the mood and atmosphere in which the narrative moves. Conrad was able to "weave this purple spell," but he was not the equal of this Puritan brooder. So eminent a critic as Henry James regarded *The House of the Seven Gables* as the outstanding work of fiction produced in America, and few will question its supremacy as a work of art.

It is unfortunate, and perhaps significant of the naive character of American critical writing at the end of the 19th century, that Hawthorne was so commonly likened to Poe between whose work and his own there is little resemblance except in point of gloom. Hawthorne never invoked the horrible simply for dramatic effect; there was always a deep underlying significance to his haunting pictures. It is just this quality which makes his work hopeless for the screen or stage. His stories cannot be dissociated from the rich and flexible style in which they are clothed.

RUTHERFORD B. HAYES   1822–1893

RUTHERFORD BIRCHARD HAYES, the 19th president of the United States, was born on Oct. 4, 1822, in Delaware, Ohio, and was descended on both sides from Scottish chieftains who had fought with Robert Bruce. Late in the 17th century certain of his ancestors had emigrated to Connecticut, but the father of the future president, although born in Vermont, had moved to Ohio where he died shortly before the boy was born. To a bachelor uncle, who was a well-to-do banker, he owed his education at Kenyon College from which he was graduated with honors at the age of 20. He studied law in Columbus and later for two years in Cambridge, Mass.; was admitted to the bar in 1845, practicing in Fremont, Ohio, and then in Cincinnati, where he became most successful in his profession and was one of a literary group which included Salmon P. Chase, Gen.

John Pope and other distinguished men. At about this time he married Lucy Ware Webb who died in 1889.

At the outbreak of the Civil War he laid down his lucrative practice and enlisted for the period of the war. He was at once commissioned major and throughout the four years of struggle acquitted himself with bravery and distinction. He led a number of important expeditions, and his coolness and courage in the face of the gravest dangers often saved his men from demoralization. He was several times wounded and narrowly escaped death on a number of occasions. In the attack on Lynchburg in June, 1864, his skill covered the retreat of the Union forces in a hazardous situation. He took a conspicuous part in the famous attack on the Virginia and Tennessee Railroad and in the battle of Winchester under Sheridan, on which occasion he was badly injured when his horse, galloping at full speed, suddenly fell dead. In March, 1865 he was breveted major-general in recognition of his distinguished services.

His war record had given him great prestige in his native state and he was urged to retire from the service and assist in a political campaign in order to bring about his own election to Congress as a republican representative. In a scathing reply he refused and denounced any man who would leave the war at that juncture to electioneer for Congress, but he did consent to his nomination with the understanding that if elected he would not take his seat until the war was over. When he finally entered Congress after hostilities had ceased, he immediately attracted countrywide attention by his outstanding ability. He was reelected in 1866, but the following year the republicans elected him governor of Ohio in which post he put through some important financial reforms. Nine years later while serving his third term, he was elected president of the United States, defeating Samuel J. Tilden by one electoral vote after a close and bitterly disputed contest. In fact, there were those who never conceded that Hayes was actually elected.

His administration was recognized as generally fair and honorable. He opposed the party politicians in his endeavor to discontinue the practice of making official appointments serve as rewards for political services; used his veto power courageously to kill certain bills which would have delayed the financial rehabilitation of the country, and also to prevent the repeal of certain existing laws which had been designed to safeguard the honesty of national elections. At the expiration of his term he retired to private life and throughout the remainder of his life devoted himself largely to philanthropic and educational enterprises. He died on Jan. 17, 1893, at Fremont, Ohio.

WILLIAM HAZLITT   1778–1830

WILLIAM HAZLITT, English critic and essayist, who is remembered for his style, his epigrams and his lively wit, was born at Maidstone, England, on April 10, 1778. His father, a Unitarian minister, took his family to America in 1783, but returned to England in 1787, settling in Shropshire. When his son was 15 he was sent to Hackney to study for the ministry but theology did not appeal to him and a meeting with the poet, Coleridge, in 1798, awakened his literary ambition. Coleridge recognized the young man's latent literary ability and under his encouragement Hazlitt set to work upon his *Principles of Human Action,* published in 1805. For a time he turned his attention to art and painted a number of portraits. His bent, however, was literature, and the following year he published *Free Thoughts on Public Affairs,* and in 1807 his *Reply to Malthus.* In 1812 he went up to London from Winterslow and most of the remainder of his life was spent in that city. He first found work on the *Morning Chronicle* and later on the *Examiner.* His wit, his mastery of the pungent epigram and of the arts of controversy soon won a reputation for him and two years after arriving in London he became a contributor to the famous *Edinburgh Review* for which he continued to write until his death.

Two books appeared in 1817; *Round Table Essays* and *Characters of Shakespeare's Plays,* which added greatly to his growing reputation. For three years following he delivered at the Surrey Institute lectures which when published under the titles, *The English Poets, English Comic Writers* and *Dramatic Literature of the Age of Elizabeth,* established his fame as a scholarly critic.

He had married in 1808 Sarah Stoddart from whom he was divorced in 1822 and he then appears to have fallen in love with the daughter of a tailor at whose house he lodged; the *Liber Amoris* poems published in 1823 were addressed to her. Two years previously he had republished the essays written for the *London Magazine* under the title of *Table Talk,* a collection that still ranks among the greatest of English essays. Another collection of articles made its appearance in 1826 under the title of *Plain Speaker.* In 1825 he published *Spirit of the Age, or Contemporary Portraits,* brilliant appreciations and criticisms of many notables of the period.

Politically, Hazlitt's sympathies were with the unpopular side and he was outspoken to the point of vehemence so that attacks on him in the *Quarterly Review* and *Blackwood's Magazine* almost stopped the sale of his books for a time and made publishers chary of undertaking a new volume by him. After recovering from his passion for his landlord's daughter, he married a widow, Mrs. Bridgewater, but separated from her after a year's travel on the Continent. During his travels in Italy he wrote a series of letters to the London *Morning Chronicle* on the great Italian painters. This led to his intimacy with the cynical painter, James Northcote, whose book, *The Conversations of James Northcote, R.A.,* he helped to prepare for the press (1830). Following his return from the Continent, he undertook what he hoped would be his crowning literary work, a *Life of Napoleon Bonaparte* (published from 1828 to 1830 in four volumes.) Unfortunately, the work not only did not enhance his literary reputation, but brought him little financial return as his publishers failed soon after bringing it out.

Charles Lamb, from whom Hazlitt had been estranged by his political beliefs, became reconciled to him and was with him at his death, Sept. 18, 1830. His fame rests upon his remarkable essays. His prose style is notable for its vigor and simplicity.

LAFCADIO HEARN   1850–1904

LAFCADIO HEARN, Irish-Greek writer and one of the most picturesque of literary men, was born in 1850 in Leucadia, one of the Ionian islands, the son of Surgeon-Major Charles Hearn, an Irishman stationed there during the British occupation who had married a Greek wife. Hearn himself adopted the name Lafcadio from the name of the island upon which he was born and which is pronounced Lefcadia.

He early developed artistic and Bohemian impulses. His education was haphazard, acquired partly in England and partly in France, but at the age of 19 he was thrown upon his own resources and emigrated to the United States where he engaged in newspaper work, chiefly in Cincinnati and New Orleans. In the latter city while employed on the *Times-Democrat* the colorfulness of his prose and his unique powers of description began to attract attention. The newspaper sent him to the West Indies as its correspondent and his life there furnished material for his book, *Two Years in the French West Indies.*

In 1891 he went to Japan as a newspaper correspondent and while the newspaper connection soon ceased he found in Japan something that appealed to the artist in him, that aroused his literary sympathy and satisfied his yearning for the colorful and beautiful. He became a teacher of English at the University of Tokyo, studied Japanese manners, customs, legends and scenery and began to write of his adopted country with an insight and sympathy remarkable in a foreigner. He became so imbued with Japanese ideas and so satisfied with the life about him that he became a naturalized Japanese citizen, adopted the name of Yakumo Koisumi, married a Japanese wife and became a professed Buddhist. He had early broken away from the Catholic religion and his children were raised as Japanese in the Buddhist faith.

He suffered most of his life from a serious eye trouble and that is perhaps a partial explanation of the curious light of the mystical and strange that pervades his descriptions of nature. His health began to fail in 1902 and he was deprived of his position as teacher of English at the Tokyo University.

His books about Japan are unique and authoritative, with a fascination that is lacking in most books written by others than native Japanese. He developed a sympathy and understanding of Japanese culture that few except genuine members of that race possess. The books he had written in America had given him a certain reputation, mostly among writers, but his works on the East made him known to the world at large. Originality of subject matter, power of description, sympathy with his subject, and the literary charm which he possessed in a high degree, combined to make the volumes unique in literary annals. In 1894 he published *Glimpses of Unfamiliar Japan;* the following year *Out of the East;* followed by *Kokoro, Gleanings in Buddha Fields, Exotics and Retrospections, In Ghostly Japan, Shadowings, A Japanese Miscellany, Kotto, Japanese Fairy Tales* and *Kwaidan.* He died on Sept. 26, 1904 and later that year appeared his last book, *Japan, an Attempt at Interpretation,* which is generally considered one of the most enlightening books that has been written on that fascinating country.

HEINRICH HEINE   1797–1856

HEINRICH HEINE (hī′nĕ), one of the greatest of German lyric poets, was born at Düsseldorf, in Rhenish Prussia, Dec. 13, 1797, of Jewish parentage. His early education was of a desultory sort, derived largely from Roman Catholic monks and from the reading of French writers. He was a precocious boy and early became a skeptic. With the thought of pursuing a mercantile career, he studied foreign languages and during this period, under the inspiration of his love for one "Veronica," he wrote many of his earlier poems. He conceived also a passion for a maiden named Josepha, the daughter of a public executioner, and to her he addressed several of his most beautiful poems. In 1816 he went to Hamburg and there he fell in love with his cousin Amalie, who under many different names figures in a number of his beautiful songs. He tried to establish himself in business in Hamburg but failed, and failed also to win the lady's affection. Her father, however, who was his generous friend throughout his life, made it possible for him to enter the University of Bonn in 1819 with the purpose of studying law, but he found the study of modern and ancient German literature more to his taste, and these interests were made the more delightful to him by the affectionate super-vision of his teacher and friend, August Wilhelm Schlegel. He subse-quently studied at Berlin and at Göttingen, to which latter place he returned in 1825 and took his degree of Doctor of Laws. At about this time he abandoned Judaism and was baptized in the Lutheran Church of Heiligenstadt, apparently in order that he might obtain a license as an advocate, rather than from any genuine religious feeling. He had earlier published *Gedichte,* a notable volume of poems, and *Lyrisches Intermezzo* (1823) which contains some of his best lyrics, besides his tragedies, *Almansor* and *Ratcliff.*

A visit to the Harz Mountains and to the North Sea supplied him with material for his *Reisebilder* (Picturesque Travel) which attained on its first appearance in 1826 an extraordinarily brilliant success. The youth of Germany, in particular, acclaimed it with keen enthusiasm. Contained in this volume is the best known of his prose work, the *Harzreise,* spark-ling with graceful wit and humor. His famous *Buch der Lieder,* or Book of Songs, (1827), received an equally favorable reception. Many of those songs are of the most exquisite and ethereal beauty and are unmatched in German literature except by the early lyrics of Goethe. He had in the meantime made a short visit to England which he found uncongenial; had tried journalism in Munich, where he also tried to secure a professor-ship in German literature, and vented his disappointment in some unfair attacks upon his successful rival and upon the king. He next visited Italy in 1828 and described his journey in *Die Bäder von Lucca,* a brilliant but revolutionary and atheistic work which served to increase the number of enemies his uncontrolled, bitter and often coarse satires had created. The government prohibited the circulation of the third book of his *Reisebilder* (1830) and he found his presence in Prussia unwelcome. This fact and his democratic fervor made it expedient in 1831 for him to leave Germany, and he went to Paris where he spent the remainder of his life, cultivating belles-lettres with a facility and brilliance of wit hardly equaled in the annals of literature.

With the professed object of promoting better understanding between France and Germany, he wrote many articles, some of which were refused publication in Germany, and in 1833 he published in the *Revue des Deux Mondes* his *History of Religion and Philosophy since Luther,* a brilliant work which afterward appeared in German.

In 1835 he married Mathilde Mirat who figures in many of his writings, and to whom he was thereafter devoted. In 1843 he visited his native land to see his mother, to whom throughout his life he was deeply attached, and on his return he published *Deutschland, ein Wintermarchen* (Germany, A Winter's Tale), in which he recounts imaginary adventures and burlesque episodes, and in which a great number of his countrymen, kings, statesmen, professors, authors, artists, etc., are mercilessly satirized and abused. He was stricken with a disease of the spine in 1847 and was thenceforth almost constantly bedridden. He suffered the most acute pain, together with loss of eyesight, with the most remarkable equanimity until the day of his death which occurred at Paris, Feb. 17, 1856. In his will he stipulated that there should be no religious ceremony at his funeral. Through these final years of suffering this brilliant but unprincipled man presented a nobler picture than at any other time in his life. As long as he could hear and speak he continued to work; he produced the tender, exquisite poems of the *Romanzero; The White Elephant* and other humorous pieces; fervid political songs, and a great variety of poems, as well as his *Memoirs,* which he continued almost to the day of his death.

HENRY II OF ENGLAND   1133–1189

HENRY II, King of England from 1154 to 1189, was born March 5, 1133, at Le Mans, France, the son of Matilda (daughter of Henry I) and her second husband, Geoffrey Plantagenet. At 18 he was invested with his mother's heritage, the duchy of Normandy. A year later by his father's death he became Count of Anjou. The domains of Poitou and Guienne were added to his realm in 1152 by his marriage with Eleanor of Aquitaine, divorced wife of Louis VII of France.

From his birth he had been looked upon as the successor of his grandfather on the throne of England, but upon the death of the latter Stephen of Blois had seized the throne and a civil war followed. Henry went to England in January, 1153 and the following November by the Treaty of Wallingford it was arranged that he should succeed Stephen. The latter died the following year and Henry was crowned king.

He confirmed the laws put into effect by his grandfather, strengthened the finances of the country and banished the mercenaries. He demolished hundreds of castles built during the reign of Stephen, and recaptured the royal estates. He spent the year 1156 in France fighting his brother, Geoffrey of Nantes, for his possessions. Having won Geoffrey's territories, he spent some five years fighting for and organizing his continental realm, building up the royal power at the expense of the barons and the Church.

Returning to England, he appointed Thomas à Becket Archbishop of Canterbury to help him in his struggle to compel the Church to submit to his power. Becket, however, was loyal to the Church and opposed Henry with such sturdiness that the monarch at length had him killed. Henry did penance at Becket's tomb in 1174, allowing himself to be scourged by the monks, but he had accomplished his end and made valid his authority in civil matters as against that of the Church.

In 1155 Pope Adrian IV gave Henry authority over the whole of Ireland which was then inhabited by various tribes. In 1166 Leinster, one of the petty Irish kings, appealed to England for help. Several of Henry's nobles responded, including Richard de Clare, Earl of Pembroke (known as "Strongbow") who, following the subduing of the Irish coast region, married the heiress of Leinster and assumed rule as the Earl of Leinster. In 1171 Henry went over himself to complete the conquest of Ireland, all of which except Connaught submitted for a time. In 1185 Prince John was appointed King of Ireland, but was driven out of the island the following year. Henry's queen, Eleanor, alienated from him by his faithlessness, incited his sons to organize a rebellion against him and the kings of France and Scotland gave them aid. William the Lion of Scotland ravaged the north of England, but in 1174 was taken prisoner at Alnwick. To regain his liberty he paid homage to Henry, who was successful also in reestablishing his authority throughout all of his domains in France.

Prince Henry died during a second rebellion against his father in 1183 and Geoffrey, the next brother, was killed in a tournament in Paris in 1185. The third son, Richard (Coeur de Lion) joined King Philip of France, with whom Henry was again at war, and in 1189 Henry, who had lost most of Anjou and Maine and was deserted by his troops, was forced to make peace and grant indemnity to the followers of Richard, in the list of whom he found the name of Prince John. The defection of this favorite son is said to have broken his heart and he died at Chinon on July 6, 1189. He was buried at Fontevraud.

Judged by the standards of the age in which he lived, Henry II was an enlightened sovereign. In politics he was clear-headed, though unprincipled. In the field of battle he proved himself an able general, and in domestic affairs he instituted many legal reforms in addition to wresting the civil power from the Church. Despite his furious outbursts of rage, in the main he ruled justly and well. He read widely and was a lover of learning. He had three illegitimate children, two of whom are remembered; William Longsword, Earl of Salisbury, and Geoffrey, who became Archbishop of York and who remained faithful to him when his four legitimate sons opposed him.

HENRY IV OF FRANCE   1553–1610

HENRY IV, King of France (1589–1610) and of Navarre, was born Dec. 13, 1553. He was the third son of Antoine de Bourbon and Jeanne d'Albret, heiress of Henry II, King of Navarre and Béarn, and was the first of the Bourbon kings. His mother was an adherent of Calvinism and after the death of his father in 1562 Henry was carefully trained in that faith. At La Rochelle where he and his mother joined the Huguenot army on the outbreak of the third Civil War, he was proclaimed head of the Protestant party in France.

After the peace of St. Germain in 1570 and the death of his mother in 1572, by which he became King of Navarre under the title of Henry III, he married Margaret of Valois, sister of King Charles IX. There had been much opposition to the match on the part of both Catholics and Protestants, but the occasion was celebrated with great pomp and less than a week later occurred the terrible Massacre of St. Bartholomew, in which some 50,000 Huguenots were killed in France. Henry's life was spared upon his promise to embrace the Catholic faith, but he was held virtually a prisoner at the French court for three years. He escaped to Alençon in 1576, recanted his compulsory conversion to Catholicism, resumed his leadership of the Huguenot army, won a number of victories and at length effected a favorable peace. In 1584 he became presumptive heir to the throne upon the death of the Duke of Anjou. In 1589 his cousin, Henry III, who reigned following Charles IX, was murdered and because Philip II of Spain and the Dukes of Lorraine and Savoy disputed the Protestant Henry's accession to the throne he retired to the south of France to gather troops and raise money to fight for his royal heritage.

Dissension developed in the Catholic League, which had been formed some years previously, thus strengthening Henry's cause, which he effectively established by the defeat of the Duke of Mayenne at Ivry in 1590. Three years later, upon his again formally professing his adherence to the Catholic faith, the great cities of France, including Paris, quickly surrendered and peace between France and Spain was brought about by the treaty of Vervins in 1598. On April 13 of that year Henry IV signed the famous Edict of Nantes, by which liberty of conscience and impartial administration of justice was promised to all Protestants in France.

Henry furthered reforms during his reign. The provinces were at the mercy of governors and landed proprietors who levied taxes to suit themselves and forced compulsory service upon the peasants, a practice which he speedily stopped. He ordered the building of many roads which opened up the kingdom to new commercial prosperity and added to the nation's wealth. Finances were placed in the capable hands of his minister, Sully, whose energetic and resourceful measures resulted in decreasing the French national debt from 330,000,000 livres to 50,000,000 livres within ten years' time. Colonization in America received some attention; in 1604 and again in 1608 he sent Champlain to Canada in attempts to plant a French colony. During his reign the army was reorganized, its pay raised, and a school for cadets formed to supply it with officers. He did much to add to the beauty of Paris, built the great gallery of the Louvre, finished the Tuileries, built the Pont Neuf, the Hôtel-de-Ville, and the Place Royale.

In 1610 Marie de' Medici, Henry's second wife, was crowned Queen of France. Just as he was about to set out for war upon Germany the following day he was assassinated by one Ravaillac, a tool of the Jesuits. Nineteen previous attempts had been made upon his life.

Often called "Henry the Great," he was probably the most popular of all French monarchs. Kindly, quick-witted and generous by nature, he showed great sympathy for the common people, was skilled in reading character and possessed a reckless courage that made him the idol of his soldiers. Although never considered a good strategist, his genius as a general partly compensated for that lack. His greatest weakness was his passion for women. He had many love affairs, the most famous being those with Gabrielle d'Estreés and Henriette d'Entragues. Marie de' Medici bore him five children, one of whom became Louis XIII, and his illegitimate children by Gabrielle d'Estreés were raised to high honors.

HENRY VIII OF ENGLAND 1491–1547

HENRY VIII, King of England from 1509 to 1547, was born at Greenwich, June 28, 1491. He was the second son of Henry VII and Elizabeth of York. In June, 1509, seven weeks after he became king, he married Catharine of Aragon, widow of his elder brother Arthur. The marriage was a happy one for many years.

A man of learning, a good linguist, handsome, accomplished in many directions and fond of sport, Henry cared little for politics at first but took a keen interest in the navy. He supported the anti-French policy of Cardinal Wolsey and Ferdinand of Spain. Much of his time during the first half of his reign was spent in foreign expeditions and in 1513 he took part in a successful campaign in northern France by which the French were defeated at the battle of Guinegate and forced to surrender Thérouanne and Tourney. Learning that both Ferdinand and Maximilian of Germany had deserted him, he made peace with the French but hostilities were later resumed upon the accession of Francis I to the throne. After the death of Ferdinand in 1516 and the succession of his grandson, Charles V, Henry and Cardinal Wolsey played France against Spain and vice versa until English influence on the continent was lost by Charles' capture of Francis I of France (1525), the sack of Rome (1527) and the peace of Cambrai (1529).

Having now become keenly interested in politics, the King grew critical of Wolsey's expensive foreign policy; a Parliament called to grant subsidies for purposes of warfare refused them; Henry, desiring a male heir, wished to obtain a divorce from Catharine, whose only living child was her daughter, Mary; Wolsey failed to obtain the consent of the papal court to such a divorce and the Cardinal's power was broken.

Henry, staunch in the Catholic faith, in 1521 had written a book defending the papacy against Luther which gained for him from the Pope the title of "Defender of the Faith," a title which all English sovereigns have since borne. Intent upon procuring a male heir, however, but with no intention of introducing Protestantism, to which he was opposed, he seized the papal authority and revenues in England and forced his own recognition as head of the church in his country, divorced Catharine and married Anne Boleyn who bore him a daughter, Elizabeth, but failed to produce a male heir. Three years later she was charged with adultery, convicted on very slight evidence, and beheaded. Ten days later Henry married Jane Seymour who died in giving birth to a son, later Edward VI. In order to carry out his purposes he had dissolved many monasteries and added their wealth to the crown and had indulged in acts of despotism, ruthlessly beheading or burning as traitors many who dared oppose him, among them Sir Thomas More who had been his friend and close companion.

In 1537 he authorized an English translation of the Bible and advanced toward Protestant doctrine with the Ten Articles. He married Ann of Cleves to attach the Protestants of Germany to England, but very quickly turned against her, divorced her, beheaded Thomas Cromwell who had arranged the marriage, and ten days afterward married Catharine Howard. In 1542 he caused her to be put to death and married his sixth wife, Catharine Parr, who survived him.

He attempted to placate Ireland, of which he was made King and head of the Irish Church in 1540, but used more forceful means in trying to establish his old claim to suzerainty over Scotland. From 1542 to 1546 he was at war with Scotland and France. James V of Scotland was defeated at Solway Moss and died leaving his throne to his infant daughter, Mary Stuart, whose hand Henry obtained for his son. Probably to prevent French intervention in his struggle with Scotland, he joined Charles V of Spain in invading France and capturing Boulogne (1546), but upon Charles' making peace with France, Henry was left to bear the brunt of a French invasion of the Isle of Wight.

He died Jan. 28, 1547, and was buried in St. George's Chapel, Windsor. By Act of Parliament in 1544 he had secured the succession following his son to Mary, his daughter by Catharine of Aragon, and then to Anne Boleyn's daughter, Elizabeth. The three reigned in that order, all dying without offspring.

Despotic, greedy of power and devoid of moral sense as Henry was, it must be said of him that he had a passion for efficiency and the greatness of England.

PATRICK HENRY 1736–1799

PATRICK HENRY was an American orator and patriot, born on May 29, 1736 in Hanover county, Virginia. His Scottish father was a near relative of the historian, Robertson, and in his mother's family was a Welsh strain known for its musical and conversational accomplishments. As a child, Patrick gave no indication of having inherited any capacity for the use of words. In fact, he was so disappointing as a student that at 15 he was taken from school and put to work with a tradesman and after a year's training was started in a small business with his older brother. He showed as little aptitude for business as for study. He was careless about his personal appearance; fishing, hunting, lounging about, telling stories, and desultory playing of the violin seemed to be his only interests, and within a year the business was given up. He tried farming and was equally unsuccessful through lack of knowledge and lack of the necessary application. A small store which he opened speedily added to the list of his failures. At some time during these years when his fortunes were at their lowest ebb, he married a Miss Shelton, daughter of a farmer. He had, however, at length developed an interest in reading, particularly history, not only of the American colonies but of England, Greece and Rome, and had somehow gained a knowledge of the Greek and Latin languages to add to his apparently intuitive and limitless knowledge of human nature.

At about the age of 24 he was inspired to take up the reading of law and after a very brief period of study was granted a license to practice. Meanwhile he had been giving occasional assistance to his wife's father, a small tavern-keeper on whom fell the burden of supporting Henry and his family. It is said that when he was about 14 he had been greatly stirred by the eloquent preaching of the famous Presbyterian divine, Samuel Davis. A germ of oratory was probably thus implanted in his mind which had been lying dormant through all the years of his outward failures and when in 1763 he was entrusted with the defense in the famous case known as the "Parsons' Cause," involving an unpopular tax, the seed burst into immediate flower and he made a speech so unexpectedly brilliant that it held the audience spellbound for two hours, at the end of which the excited people bore him triumphantly on their shoulders. Thus at a bound he leaped into the position he has ever since held in the front rank of American orators. There was no lack of clients thereafter and his prosperity was assured. Not satisfied with the narrow bounds of the legal profession, he became in 1765 a member of the Virginia House of Burgesses where, by his historic and impassioned speech against the Stamp Act and other taxes levied by the British, he at once became a leader and a power. Meanwhile he continued his highly successful legal career. He was active in the agitation which years later resulted in the Religious Freedom Act, disestablishing the Church of England in Virginia.

In 1774 he was a leader in those acts of defiance toward England which led the governor, Lord Dunmore, to dissolve the House of Burgesses. He was a member of the first Revolutionary Convention in Virginia and a delegate to the first Continental Congress where he was acclaimed as the champion of constitutional liberty and his wonderful eloquence was displayed to the utmost. In the Provincial Convention in Richmond he was the moving spirit and here was delivered that impassioned plea to the people to prepare for resistance, ending with the memorable words, "Give me liberty or give me death!" He helped to frame the first constitution of Virginia and served as governor from 1776–79 and again from 1784–86. In 1788 as a member of the state convention he opposed ratification of the federal constitution, believing that it reposed too great power in the federal government, but with the powerful opposition of Madison he voted for ratification with amendments. He refused a place in the National Senate in 1794, the post of secretary of state the following year; also declined the chief justiceship of the Supreme Court and an offer of a special mission to France, and in 1796 refused to be a candidate for governor. In 1799 he was elected to the House of Delegates, but before he could take his seat he died, on June 6, 1799.

HERODOTUS   circa 484–425 B.C.

HERODOTUS (hĕ rŏd'ŏ tŭs), a Greek historian who has been called the "father of history," was born at Halicarnassus in Asia Minor about 484 B.C., of a family belonging to the upper rank of citizens. At that time Halicarnassus was under the dominion of Persia so that Herodotus was a Persian citizen by birth and until he was about 30 years old. He seems to have been exiled, or to have fled, from the city following the execution of his uncle (or cousin) Panyasis, an epic poet of power who was suspected of conspiring against the tyrant Lygdamis, and whose political beliefs Herodotus is believed to have shared.

Judging from his own writings he must have begun at an early age the wide course of reading, traveling and observation which makes him one of the most instructive and entertaining of historians. He became acquainted with all the Greek poets and prose writers. His travels seem to have taken place between his 20th and 37th year and were remarkably far-reaching for the age. He not only traveled throughout Greece and all the most important islands under her authority, but made the perilous journey from Sardis to Susa, the Persian capital, visited Babylon, Colchis, the western shores of the Black Sea, Scythia, Thrace, Zante and Magna Graecia, Tyre, Palestine and Egypt—nearly all of the then known world. It has been estimated that his travels covered 31 degrees of longitude and 24 of latitude. They were not mere sight-seeing journeys; he lingered at the various points of interest, studying, making measurements, gathering material for his great history of the Persian war of invasion.

He had lived for seven or eight years in the island of Samos when he returned to his native city of Halicarnassus. Lygdamis had become so tyrannical that he was expelled and Herodotus was apparently one of the leaders in the rebellion against him. The city then became a voluntary member of the Athenian confederacy, but Herodotus soon departed (about 447 B.C.) for Athens where he found ample appreciation of his historical work as may be inferred from the fact that in 445 a certain Anytus proposed that he be voted the sum of ten talents (about $12,000) by decree of the people. That sum was granted to him by Athens, but the jealously guarded franchise of the Athenian citizen was withheld and in the spring of 444 he sailed with a group of men who left Athens to found the colony of Thurii in southern Italy. He became a citizen of that new town at about the age of 40, and little is known about his life thenceforth. He apparently made a number of journeys—to Crotona, to Metapontum and possibly to Athens about 430 B.C. According to Pliny, Herodotus occupied himself at Thurii in revising and elaborating his great history. He may also have written the history of Assyria to which he twice refers in his first book and from which Aristotle quotes. He died about the year 425 B.C., according to most ancient authorities at Thurii where in later ages his tomb was exhibited to visitors.

Herodotus' work has been inaccurately called a "universal history." His purpose was to tell the story of the Persian invasion of Greece and the great battles that followed, but he took occasion in his introduction (which comprises two-thirds of the work) to set before his readers the previous history of the two nations concerned. In this historical survey he brought in some account of nearly all the nations of the then known world, describing their geography, manners, customs, antiquities, climate, natural productions, etc., in a manner which made his book a narrative of sustained interest, of literary charm and fullness of thought. He has been termed the "most Homeric of historians" and his work with its introductory historical survey remains one of the finest books of its kind. A Latin translation of his history was made in 1450; the first complete translation into a modern language was that by Littlebury into English in 1737.

ROBERT HERRICK   1591–1674

ROBERT HERRICK, English poet, was born in Cheapside, London, Aug. 24, 1591, a descendant of an old Leicestershire family. His father, Nicholas Herrick, was a goldsmith who died a year after the birth of his seventh child. A brother, Sir William Herrick, took charge of Nicholas' children and in 1607 Robert was bound to him as an apprentice. The future poet's early education was probably obtained at the Westminster school and in 1614 he entered Cambridge. During his apprenticeship he had become acquainted with men of wit and literary distinction in the city, and seems to have attended the first performance of Ben Jonson's play, *The Alchemist,* Jonson later adopting him as his "poetical son." That he suffered from lack of funds while at the University is shown by existing letters to his uncle asking for money. He received his M.A. degree in 1620. All trace of his activities for the next seven years is lost. He may have been studying for the ministry in Cambridge or living the life of the average young man of the day in London.

In 1629 the King presented him with a "living" at Dean Prior in Devonshire and in this remote and quiet village, cut off from all literary and social companionship, he lived until 1648 when, having been deprived of his parish by the Long Parliament, he returned to London. He seems to have found a certain pleasure, if not recompense for his rural sequestration, in the customs and manners of the people of the village, to judge by the poems he wrote during this period having to do with such customs as the morris-dance, quintains and wakes.

He never married. His vicarage was cared for by a faithful old servant named Prudence Baldwin, and he surrounded himself with various pets. There is authority for the statement that he had a favorite pig which he taught to drink out of a tankard. His sermons were florid and witty but he seems to have been given to outbursts of wrath and it is reported that on one occasion he threw his sermon at the congregation, cursing the people for their inattention. He was popular with the gentry of the neighborhood and a staunch supporter of the King in the Civil War which was the reason for his ejection from the living at Dean Prior. It is reported that he was reduced to great poverty following his return to London. In 1662 he was reinstated at Dean Prior supplanting Dr. John Syms, who had been given the living upon his own expulsion.

Herrick's first appearance in print was in 1635 when he contributed some verses to *A Description of the King and Queen of Fairies*. Sixty-two small poems appeared in *Wit's Recreations* in 1650 although they were not acknowledged by him until reprinted in *Hesperides; or the Works Both Human and Divine of Robert Herrick*. The "divine works" of the title referred to a section of the book called *Noble Numbers* while the *Hesperides* section contained his love poems, pastorals, etc. He published no other volume of verse but contributed in 1649 to *Lachrymae Musarum* and to *Wit's Recreations*. Although his genius was limited in scope, his love poems possess a charm and sweetness that have immortalized his name and his pastoral lyrics have a glow and simple beauty that is unsurpassed among English poets. He died Oct. 15, 1674, in his 84th year, at Dean Prior, where a monument to his memory was erected in the parish church in 1857.

JAMES J. HILL   1836–1916

JAMES JEROME HILL was one of the two most notable American railway magnates. He was born Sept. 16, 1836, near Guelph, Ontario, of Scotch-Irish ancestry and was educated at the Rockwood Academy, a Quaker school. His father was a small hotel keeper and upon his death in 1852, young James, who had planned to study medicine, left school in order not to burden his mother, and went to work in a country store, continuing his studies by himself at night. In 1856 he removed to Minnesota to seek his fortune and became a clerk in the office of the St. Paul agents for the Dubuque & St. Paul Packet Company's Mississippi boats, later changing to another line of river packets. In 1865 he was appointed agent for the Northwest Packet Company and the Dunleith Packet line of river steamboats; also for the Chicago & Northwestern, the Milwaukee & Prairie du Chien and the Illinois Central railways. The following year he contracted to supply the St. Paul & Pacific Railroad with fuel and, after shipping in wood for some time, introduced coal into the St. Paul market. He later entered into partnership with Egbert S. Litchfield under the firm name of J. J. Hill & Company, continuing in the shipping and forwarding business. The firm prospered and in 1875 he and others formed the Northwestern Fuel Company.

In 1873 the St. Paul & Pacific Railroad went into bankruptcy and Hill with several associates raised funds to buy the defaulted bonds, thus obtaining control of the road in 1878. From that early beginning in railroading developed the Great Northern System which brought settlers and prosperity to the Northwestern states, giving their produce access to eastern markets. Associated with Hill in the reorganization of the St. Paul & Pacific as the St. Paul, Minneapolis & Manitoba Railway were Sir Donald A. Smith (Lord Strathcona), George Stephen (Lord Mount Stephen) and other Canadian capitalists whom he had interested in the road and in the wheat country of the Red River Valley. Hill was general manager of the road from 1879 to 1881; then vice president and later president until 1890 when he made it a part of his Great Northern System. The main line of the Great Northern, from Lake Superior to Puget Sound, with north and south branches and with direct steamship connections to the Orient, was constructed between 1888 and 1893 with Hill as the principal promoter. He became president of the System and in 1907 chairman of its board of directors, from which post he retired in 1912.

The Hill interest obtained control of the Northern Pacific (which E. H. Harriman tried to secure in 1901 by buying $79,000,000 of its stock and bringing on the Northern Pacific "corner" and panic) and of the Chicago, Burlington & Quincy, and proposed the building of another northern route. With E. H. Harriman and J. Pierpont Morgan, he organized the famous Northwestern Securities Company and was its president until 1904 when the United States Supreme Court ordered its dissolution.

In 1867 he married Mary Theresa Mohegan; became a naturalized citizen of the United States in 1880; published *Highway of Progress* in 1910. Among his benefactions were a contribution of $500,000 to establish a Catholic Theological Seminary in St. Paul and $1,500,000 to the Roman Catholic Cathedral in that city. He acquired a valuable collection of paintings, particularly of the modern French masters. His death occurred on May 29, 1916, and he was buried on a knoll at his North Oaks home.

PAUL VON HINDENBERG   1847–1934

PAUL LUDWIG HANS VON BENECKENDORF UND VON HINDENBERG, German general and one of the heroes of the World War, was born in Posen, Poland, Oct. 21, 1847, the son of a Prussian officer. He was educated at military schools in Silesia and Berlin. At 18 he entered the Foot Guards at Danzig as second lieutenant and at the battle of Königgrätz in the war with Austria he stormed an Austrian battery under fire. He won distinction in the Franco-German war of 1870–71; spent several years at the staff college in Berlin where he became an instructor; served on the general staff and in the Prussian War Office; was commander of the 91st Infantry at Oldenberg (1893–96); rose to the rank of Major-General, and for four years was chief of the general staff of the Eighth Army Corps at Coblentz. Later he commanded the 28th Division at Karlsruhe, and in 1903 became general in command of the Fourth Army Corps at Magdeburg. In 1911, at the age of 65, he was placed on the retired list.

At the outbreak of the World War he was called from seclusion in Hanover on Aug. 22, 1914, and placed in command of the Eighth German Army, with Major-General Ludendorff as his chief of staff. With an inferior army, he twice encircled and practically annihilated Samsonov's Russian army at the battle of Tannenberg (Aug. 26–31, 1914). Going to the aid of the Austrian army, he withdrew before a superior Russian force at the Vistula and maneuvered it into position for the battle of Lódz where he forced the enemy to withdraw behind the Bzura and Rawka rivers. As Marshal and Commander-in-Chief of all the German forces in the

East, he annihilated the Tenth Russian Army on the Upper Bobr and captured the fortress of Kovno. When Rumania joined the Entente, Hindenberg, as Chief of the General Staff, was faced with the task of organizing a Rumanian offensive, forcing Russia to make a separate peace and standing meanwhile on the defensive on the western front. After a forced peace had been signed with Russia and Rumania, he prepared to attack the English and French and deal them a decisive blow in Flanders before the American troops could reach the battlefront.

His great offensive was intended to break through on either side of St. Quentin and drive the British force northward to the coast. The first blow at Amiens was a brilliant tactical success but without results. The attack upon the Lys front failed to break through and diverting attacks at Chemin des Dames and on both sides of Rheims failed to withdraw British troops from Flanders. Marshal Foch of France now assumed the offensive and attacked the German Marne position. American troops arrived and Hindenberg was forced to abandon the Marne salient. The advantage remained in the hands of the French; the German reserves melted steadily away and Hindenberg adopted a strategic defensive hoping to obtain a peace compatible with the dignity of the German people. On Sept. 28, 1914, the famous Hindenberg Line was broken. Turkey and Austria had made peace with the Allies; revolution was taking place in Germany; the war was lost; the Kaiser abdicated and an armistice was signed, leading to the peace treaty of Versailles.

Hindenberg thereafter lived in retirement, taking no part in political life, until 1925 when upon the death of President Ebert the anti-socialist parties in Germany induced him to stand for the presidency of the German Republic, and although a monarchist in his sympathies he was elected its second president on April 26, 1925 and remained in office until his death, which occurred in his sleep on Aug. 2, 1934, at his summer home at Neudeck in East Prussia.

HIPPOCRATES   460 B.C.–377 B.C.

HIPPOCRATES (hĭp pŏk′rȧ tēz), called the father of medicine, was a Greek physician, son of Heraclides, who was also distinguished in the same profession, and was said to have been a descendant of Æsculapius, the god of medicine who is portrayed as a human being by Homer, and was subsequently defied. His mother, Phænarete, is said to have been descended from Hercules. He was born about 460 B.C. on the small island of Cos, in the Grecian archipelago, which at the time was sacred to the worship of Æsculapius. Its modern name is Stanko or Stanchio. Here he is believed to have studied medicine under his father's supervision, and philosophy under the illustrious philosopher, Democritus, whom he is supposed later to have cured of a mental affliction. Little is known of his life more than that he traveled after completing his studies and finally returned to his island home where he practiced his profession.

Notwithstanding the abhorrence which the Greeks felt for dissecting the human body, they acquired an astonishing knowledge of its anatomy and Hippocrates appears to have carried this knowledge to the most extreme point that was possible in his day. He abandoned superstition absolutely, convinced that all morbid processes followed natural laws and were not due to evil spirits. Hence he may be said to have been among the first to emancipate medical science from superstition, opening the way for experiment and discovery. He classified the causes of diseases, first, as seasonal and climatic, including in this category ailments arising from conditions of water; and, second, the personal causes, such as errors in eating, lack of exercise, etc. He seemed fully aware of what is now universally known,—the influence of climate and locality on the condition of the body; and he noted the differences between the Asiatics and the strong and resistant Greeks. He believed that the seat of disease was in either the phlegm, the blood, or the black or green bile, and that a proper relation of these elements was requisite to normal health. He understood the instance of crisis in the progress of a malady and called it the "critical day." He was so modern in some of his theories of practice that the medical science of today may, in some respects at least, be said to have caught up with him. He had more faith in diet and regimen than he had in drugs and his supervision of a case of illness consisted chiefly in attention to these details, which laid him under the frequent charge of neglecting his patient. There is evidence, however, that in many cases he employed powerful medicines and also resorted to bloodletting. He appears to have enjoyed the highest standing in his profession and indeed was preeminent in his day. Plato often quoted him as a medical authority; Aristotle also quoted his opinions, and numerous stories of doubtful authenticity about him have been handed down through the ages. The Athenians generally held him in the highest esteem and it is evident from the tone of his writings which have been preserved that he was a man of the highest standards of honor and the purest morality.

His works, embodied in what is called the Hippocratic collection, are numerous and include many treatises by his sons, Thessalas and Draco, his son-in-law, Polybus, and others. Among these may be mentioned a few which scholars generally agree to be authentic works of Hippocrates; *Epidemics; Regimen in Acute Diseases; On Air, Water and Places; On Wounds in the Head; The Duty of the Physician,* etc. To him is ascribed the origin of the famous Hippocratic oath, a noble creed for a noble profession, which in abridged form is administered to graduating classes in many medical colleges today. Its most familiar clause is the one, "I will not give to a woman an instrument to procure abortion."

Hippocrates is believed to have lived to a very old age; some authorities place it at 90, some at 104 or thereabouts; one account gives it as 109 years. He evidently died about 377 B.C. at Larissa in Thessaly.

WILLIAM HOGARTH   1697–1764

WILLIAM HOGARTH, English artist, was born in London on Nov. 10, 1697. His father was an unsuccessful schoolmaster and a little known writer. As a youth he was apprenticed to a silversmith and at about the age of 21 he began to engrave on his own account coats of arms, crests, bills for shopkeepers, etc., soon branching out into the designing of plates for booksellers. Between 1721 and 1726 he designed a number of engravings, among them "Masquerades and Operas" in which he struck the satirical note which was to be the chief feature of his later work; and a series of illustrations for Gray's edition of "Hudibras." He had first intended to devote himself to line engraving, but in 1724 entered an art school conducted by Sir James Thornhill and turned his attention to painting portraits, but although he did not lack for sitters he achieved no great reputation as a portrait painter. In 1729 he was secretly married to Jane Thornhill, the daughter of his former instructor, who proved herself an excellent wife.

One of the most famous of his early series of drawings, which he engraved himself, was "A Harlot's Progress," consisting of six pictures, executed in 1730–31. He followed this moral dissertation in pictures with others of the kind, indulging his gift for satire in many of them. Among them were "A Midnight Modern Conversation," "Southwark Fair," "A Rake's Progress," "The Distressed Poet," "The Four Times of the Day," and "Strolling Actresses Dressing in a Barn." These satirical engravings, portraying commonplace English life, met with a great degree of success.

He next painted some large canvases for St. Bartholomew's Hospital, where they still may be seen—"Pool of Bethesda" and "The Good Samaritan"—which are generally regarded as less successful efforts than his engravings. He also painted a number of portraits but did not meanwhile neglect the vein of ore he had struck in his graphic satires. These were continued in "The Enraged Musician"; "Marriage à la Mode," a series of six pictures which critics consider his masterpiece and which are now in the National Gallery, London; "Calais Gate," the "March to Finchley," and the plates of "Beer Street," "Gin Lane," and "The Progress of Cruelty." In 1752 he published a treatise on *The Analysis of Beauty* and during the three years from 1755 to 1758 he produced four prints known as the "Election Series." He was appointed sergeant-painter to the King in 1757 and soon thereafter he made an ill-starred venture in politics, resulting in a quarrel with his two friends, John Wilkes and Churchill, the poet, both of whom he caricatured in portraits. Upon the accession of George III he was reappointed sergeant-painter and made but one more print after his quarrel with Wilkes and Churchill—the "Finis, or The Bathos," (1764) intended as a tailpiece to his collected prints.

He died at his home in Leicester Square on Oct. 26, 1764 and was buried in Chiswick Churchyard. In 1771 a tomb was erected by his friends with an epitaph by David Garrick whose portrait he had painted. The red brick Georgian villa in Chiswick Gardens where he spent the summers of his later life was purchased in 1902 by Lieut.-Colonel Shipway of Chiswick who turned it into a Hogarth Museum.

Hogarth liked to regard himself as an author rather than as an artist and considered in that light he ranks among the great satirists. His engravings told a tale vigorously and plainly, with humor and satire, and in his field he remains unequaled. He has been termed the Molière of painting. It was his constant effort to portray the vices and weaknesses of society with the hope of bringing about their reform. Finish and beauty of line were often sacrificed for vigor and quick intelligibility. He found a ready market for his engravings, but was not quite as successful with his dramas on canvas. One of the best examples of his portrait work is that of himself and his dog Trump, which is in the Tate Gallery, London. The Metropolitan Museum in New York has his portrait of Peg Woffington.

OLIVER WENDELL HOLMES   1809–1894

DR. OLIVER WENDELL HOLMES, familiarly called "the autocrat," was an American physician, author and poet, born at Cambridge, Mass., Aug. 29, 1809, son of the Rev. Abiel Holmes, a Congregational minister of that city. He was educated at Andover, Mass., and later at Harvard where he began to study law but abandoned it for medicine in which profession he achieved a distinction overshadowed only by his distinguished career in the field of letters. His earliest verses were written for the *Collegian,* an undergraduate periodical, and many of his minor poems were inspired by anniversaries of the class of 1829, which numbered many names destined to become famous. In 1830 the government's proposal to scrap the famous old frigate, *Constitution,* aroused him to write the stirring protest in verse, *Old Ironsides,* which thrilled the public to patriotic ardor and resulted in the abandonment of the project. After leaving college he continued his studies in Europe and in 1836 began to practice medicine in Boston, in connection with which he made the declaration "smallest fevers thankfully received." He wrote many papers on scientific subjects, including a critical denunciation of the new school of homeopathy, and discussed the interdependence of mind and matter in his scholarly *Currents and Countercurrents of Medical Science.* He wrote also *Mechanism in Thought and Morals* and an essay on certain contagious fevers. Throughout his long career he retained his high standing in the scientific field, but it is as a poet and essayist that his name is enshrined in American literature.

After occupying for two years the chair of anatomy at Dartmouth College, he returned to his practice in Boston, which he christened "the hub of the universe"; and remained its most distinguished citizen throughout his long life. In 1840 he married Amelia Lee Jackson of that city. He had already published a volume of fugitive poems many of which linger in the public memory and have found a place in school readers. His gay and prolific pen did not, however, deter him from filling the chair of anatomy and physiology in Harvard Medical School (1847–82). In 1857 the *Atlantic Monthly* was started with James Russell Lowell as editor. Some 20 years earlier Dr. Holmes had published in another magazine two papers of a charmingly informal character and he now began in the new *Atlantic* a series in the opening sentence of which whimsical reference was made to that earlier discontinued project—"I was just going to say when I was interrupted . . ." What he had to say, on an endless variety of subjects, was carried through many numbers of the *Atlantic* and launched that periodical on its distinguished career. The reader was invited to attend a group of docile listeners gathered about the breakfast table of a Boston boarding house while the "autocrat" poured forth his views, occasionally (but not too often) permitting others to speak. The deluge of humor and versatility took the reading public by storm as the irrepressible "autocrat" continued his observations, until the series ended in a charming romance when the "autocrat" and the school mistress "take the long road" through life. *The Autocrat of the Breakfast Table* shortly appeared in book form, firmly establishing its author in the hallowed circle with Montaigne and Lamb and Hood, whom he even rivaled as a punster. This rare American classic was followed by *The Professor at the Breakfast Table, The Poet at the Breakfast Table* and *Over the Teacups,* a work of the same general character. All three are only less delightful than *The Autocrat.*

The psychological problems in which he was so much interested were treated artistically in his novel, *Elsie Venner,* which is not without power and originality, but shows all too conclusively that fiction in this form was not his forte. *The Guardian Angel,* a meritorious novel of 1867, has not greatly added to his fame.

Songs in Many Keys appeared in 1861, followed by *Humorous Poems* and a prose collection, *Soundings from the Atlantic.* His collected poems are published in a single volume, covering a great variety of themes, both humorous and serious. Among them should be mentioned *The Deacon's Masterpiece; or The Wonderful "One-Hoss Shay";* the beautiful uplifting verses, *The Chambered Nautilus* and that favorite of Abraham Lincoln, *The Last Leaf.*

The genial autocrat lived to the age of 86 and died on Oct. 7, 1894 in the city which he loved and playfully ridiculed.

OLIVER WENDELL HOLMES, JR.   1841–1935

OLIVER WENDELL HOLMES, Associate Justice of the United States Supreme Court for more than twenty years, and son of the American poet of the same name, was born in Boston, Mass., March 8, 1841. Shortly after his graduation from Harvard University in 1861 he answered President Lincoln's call for troops, enlisting in the 20th Massachusetts Volunteers. He served three years with that unit, became its Lieutenant-Colonel, was wounded three times, at the battles of Ball's Bluff, Antietam and Fredericksburg; and was made aide-de-camp on the staff of the 6th Division. After the close of the Civil War he returned to Harvard to study law, received his LL.B. degree in 1866 and in March of the following year was admitted to the bar in Suffolk, Mass. He practiced law in Boston and in 1870 was appointed instructor in constitutional law and then lecturer on jurisprudence at his alma mater. Coincident with his appointment in 1870 he became editor of *The American Law Review* in which capacity his name was brought prominently before the practising members of his profession for the three following years.

He edited in 1873 the twelfth edition of Kent's *Commentaries,* which has since become the standard edition of that work. In the same year he became a member of the Boston law firm of Shattuck, Holmes and Munroe and soon had a large and lucrative practice. In 1880 he was appointed lecturer on common law at Lowell Institute, using as the basis for his lectures the articles on that subject which he had published in *The American Law Review,* and which the following year he collected, enlarged and published under the title of *The Common Law.* This book enhanced his reputation abroad and he was thereafter an international figure in legal circles. In the volume he presented the origin and history of common law, not only with profound learning but with a breadth of view and clarity of language rarely to be found in any legal work.

In 1882 he accepted the chair of law at the Harvard Law School, but resigned in December of the same year upon being appointed associate justice of the Massachusetts Supreme Court. His opinions during the next seventeen years established him as one of the wisest and most unbiased of American judges. On August 2, 1899 he was appointed Chief Justice of the Massachusetts Supreme Court.

During the first administration of Theodore Roosevelt, Holmes was nominated as an associate justice of the United States Supreme Court and on Dec. 4, 1902 he took his place in that body where he continued to serve until 1931 when, at the age of 90 but with his mental vigor unimpaired he retired to private life. Throughout his term Justice Holmes was one of the more liberal members of the Supreme Court and his opinions were written with the same clarity of thought, comprehension of the fine legal points and command of a lucid, vigorous and often epigrammatic English style which had won him his reputation many years earlier. In 1924 he was awarded the Roosevelt Memorial Association's medal for the development of public law. A volume of his *Speeches,* originally published in 1891, was reissued with additions in 1913 and his *Collected Legal Papers* were published in 1920.

He died in Washington, D. C., on March 6, 1935.

HOMER   Probably about 850 B.C.

HOMER, the earliest name in European literature, reputed to be a Greek poet and the author of the *Iliad* and the *Odyssey,* two Greek classics, next to the Bible probably the finest examples of literary art to be found in the world.

Whether Homer ever actually lived is not definitely known. Herodotus believed that he lived about 850 B.C., although other historians have placed his date as early as 1200 B.C. Nothing of the man nor of his life is known. Such a poet may have existed, and he may have written the *Iliad* and the *Odyssey;* certainly a tradition of him existed in ancient Greece and seven cities claimed the honor of being his birthplace—Smyrna, Rhodes, Colophon, Salamis, Chios, Argos and Athens. There is more or less agreement among modern philological and literary students that he was born in a Greek colony in Asia Minor. Tradition pictures him as a blind poet who wandered about from city to city in ancient Greece, earning his bread by singing his lays to the populace, accompanying himself on a lyre.

The theory advanced in 1795 by the German classical scholar, Friedrich August Wolf, that the *Odyssey* and *Iliad* were ballads composed and sung by various minstrels, collected by later editors and strung together on a thread of narrative, is now pretty generally believed. Wolf held that the two Greek classics were not written by the same person and that both had their origin in the lays recited by Homer and his followers (the Homeridae) in Chios; that professional "rhapsodists" changed them and chanted them for centuries and that about 540 the Athenian Pisistratus finally put them into the form in which they have come down to us.

The character and personality of Homer, if indeed he existed, are puzzles that can never be solved. The so-called *Homeric Hymns* and the *Batrachomyomachia (Battle of the Frogs and Mice)*, according to modern philologists, belong to a later age in Greek history than the period in which the *Iliad* and the *Odyssey* had their origin. Those two great works have been translated into most of the languages of the civilized world. Many English translations have been made in verse, notably those by Pope and Cowper, but the great poems lose much by translation and rather free adaptation into English verse and the student who does not read Greek can get much closer to the feel and rhythm of the sonorous originals by reading the prose translation of the *Iliad* by Lang, Leaf and Myers, and Butcher and Lang's translation of the *Odyssey*.

The critical study of Homer began in Greece almost with the beginning of prose writing. Theagenes of Rhegium in the sixth century B.C. and his pupil, Metrodorus, were probably among the first to begin such investigation and study. By the next century numerous educated men from impoverished cities and islands made their living by teaching literature—which meant specifically Homer. Many Greeks of culture knew the *Iliad* by heart and audiences numbering thousands listened eagerly to the recitals of both the *Iliad* and the *Odyssey* by the rhapsodists. About 150 B.C. Aristarchus of Samothrace, head of the Alexandrian library, published two successive editions of the text of Homer which were recognized as authoritative. It is not clear whether he created much of the text or whether he used some old text, perhaps of Pisistratus or of Homer himself. Zenodotus of Ephesus was the first great Alexandrian scholar who set himself the task of coping with the confusion in the Papyri texts of Homer, rejecting many passages which he thought spurious and preserving many ancient readings. His text was shorter than that of Aristarchus and was of great value to the latter in his own exegesis.

THOMAS HOOD   1799–1845

THE whimsical humor and rollicking fun of THOMAS HOOD emanated from a soul stricken by adversity and a body wracked with pain. He wrote several of the saddest and most touching poems in our language, and numerous fantastic drolleries, exhibiting a kind of verbal sleight-of-hand. The son of a London publisher and bookseller, he was born in that city on May 23, 1799. His mother, brother and two sisters died of consumption and he waged a prolonged and losing fight against that malady. He was early apprenticed to his uncle, an engraver, but this occupation proving ill suited to his poor health, he went to Scotland and remained with his father's relatives for about five years, during which he wrote some boyish papers that were published in local periodicals. At 21 he was resettled in London, improved in health and busy with his former work of engraving. Shortly he began to act as a sort of sub-editor for the *London Magazine*. He it was who originated the humorous column and his excrutiatingly funny answers to imaginary correspondents strike the keynote of the jesting humor and ludicrous twists of thought and words for which he became famous. In 1825 he collaborated on *Odes and Addresses on Great People,* and the following year published *Whims and Oddities,* the success of which called forth a second series two years later. Meanwhile he had married Miss Jane Reynolds who remained to the end unwearied in the care and attention made necessary by her husband's misfortunes and failing strength. In 1830 he began to publish his *Comic Annual* which continued for nine years. Simultaneously he edited another annual, *The Gem*, in which appeared one of the most celebrated of his narrative poems, the sombre and gripping *Dream of Eugene Aram,* based upon the historic murder which inspired Bulwer's famous novel.

In his unpretentious home at Wanstead, tragedy and misfortune pursued him. His first child died at birth, an event immortalized by Charles Lamb in his beautiful verses *On an Infant Dying as Soon as Born*. Here he did some writing for the theatre and wrote his novel, *Tynley Hall*. And here financial disaster complicated his sufferings. A publishing house with which he was affiliated failed, leaving him with a burden of debt, and, refusing to avail himself of any legal immunities, he resolved to labor and pay off his obligations in full. For two years he lived on the Continent, first at Coblentz, then at Ostend, where he continued his comic annuals, prepared another humorous collection called *Hood's Own,* and wrote *Up the Rhine*. Returning to England in 1840, much weakened, he continued his work in his room, often in his bed, in the several homes where he and his family struggled with ill health and poverty. In the *New Monthly Magazine* appeared *Rhymes for the Times* and, among other compositions, the longest and best of his humorous poems, *Miss Kilmansegg and Her Precious Leg,* a riotous series of verbal perversions, whimsical linguistic feats, drolleries and puns. In 1841 he became editor of that periodical with an annual salary of £300 which brought a measure of ease to his ebbing life. In 1843 appeared, anonymously, in *Punch,* the heart-rending poem, *Song of the Shirt,* a blasting indictment of sweatshop practices, which aroused the public indignation. On this triumphant wave he resigned his editorship and started *Hood's Magazine,* but his failing health was not equal to the exacting task, though *The Haunted House* and various other poems made notable its brief career.

His last days were somewhat cheered by a government pension of £100, in tendering which Sir Robert Peel took occasion to express his high appreciation of the poet's works. On May 3, 1845 this master of tears and laughter died and was buried in Kensal Green Cemetery. Some years later there was erected above his grave a monument upon which is inscribed, "He sang the Song of the Shirt."

This wizard of the ludicrous often doffed the cap and bells to touch the heart with wistful fancies, such as,

"I remember, I remember, the house where I was born";
and sometimes to *wring* the heart with the pathos of *The Bridge of Sighs*. In his finest serious pieces there is no jarring note, but his irrepressible impulse to play on words and to present grotesque and ludicrous contrasts, occasionally found its way into places where it would seem to suggest a doubtful taste. Great poet Hood certainly was, but his exuberance and whimsicality imposed a handicap which no other great poet has ever found it necessary to hold in check.

HERBERT C. HOOVER   1874–

HERBERT CLARK HOOVER, 31st president of the United States, was born on Aug. 10, 1874, at West Branch, Iowa. His father was Jesse Hoover, a blacksmith, and his mother was a Quaker preacher. He was orphaned at 10 years of age and for the next few years was cared for by relatives in Iowa and later in Oregon. At 14 he was working as a clerk in Portland, Ore., and attending a night school, and in 1891 he entered the newly opened Leland Stanford University in Palo Alto, Cal., where he specialized in geology and mining, paying his expenses by running a laundry and by various employments during the summers. He received his B.A. degree in 1895 and went to work as an ordinary miner. Becoming associated with Mr. Louis Janin, a leading mining engineer, he gained much valuable experience among the mines of the West and South, and in 1897 was engaged by an English company to develop mines in Australia. Two years later he became director-general of mines for the Chinese government, taking with him his bride, Lou Henry, who had been a fellow college student. At the time of the Boxer uprising in 1900 he was in the besieged city of Tientsin and organized not only the foreigners, but many Chinese refugees, for their own protection, establishing a system of food relief which helped them to withstand the siege. Changes following the revolution ended his official duties and for the next several years he engaged in mining and engineering activities in various parts of the world, gradually gaining wide repute and a large fortune. By 1907 he was established as an independent engineer with headquarters in New York and San Francisco and with connections in many foreign countries. Through his enormous industry and skill, numerous mines, railways and industrial plants were developed and made productive with American money, methods and machinery.

At the outbreak of the World War, being in London, he was called upon to aid in the relief of the many thousands of Americans stranded in Europe. He then took charge of relief work in Belgium where starvation threatened after the German occupation and the blocking of imports of food supplies. He organized the American Commission for Relief in Belgium, which developed into a great economic machine, and his able management not only proved the salvation of that country but made his name a household word throughout the world. Upon America's entry into the war in 1917 he returned home and was appointed United States food administrator where his task was to prevent profiteering and to conserve food supplies so that America might ship vast quantities to the suffering people of the allied nations. After the Armistice of 1918 he returned to Europe to confer with foreign powers on measures for relief of those in the devastated areas. A supreme economic council was created of which he became chief executive. Space does not permit an enumeration of the beneficent activities which engaged the attention of this indefatigable and public-spirited man; the care provided for millions of outcast children; the stamping out of a typhus epidemic in Poland and Rumania; the establishment of some 20,000 feeding stations to overcome the Russian famine of 1921 and the organizing of prompt and vigorous measures to fight the pestilence which followed; the opening of blocked ports and removal of frontier barriers. For nine years he gave himself unsparingly to this work without compensation; indeed, devoting much of his personal fortune to the cause of humanity.

In 1921 he was made secretary of commerce in Pres. Harding's cabinet and utilized his administrative and organizing genius to the full to counteract the demoralizing effect of the war on American business. He was continued in the office by Pres. Coolidge and during his eight years' incumbency developed the department into one of the most useful of governmental departments. In November, 1928, he was elected president of the United States with 444 electoral votes against 87 for his democratic opponent, Alfred E. Smith. His unprecedented victory included the carrying of many southern states for the republican party. Shortly after inauguration he opened negotiations for the limitation of armaments; appointed a national commission to study law enforcement (known as the Wickersham Commission), and created a federal farm board. In July, 1929, he announced the ratification of the Kellogg-Briand treaty to renounce war and entered into negotiations with Great Britain for further limitation of armaments. He appointed a federal power commission, a federal radio commission and, after the financial panic of 1929 with its serious economic consequences, he created the Reconstruction Finance Corporation, initiated a series of measures for national relief, launched a campaign to prevent hoarding of money and brought about a one-year moratorium on European debts.

In 1932 he was defeated for reelection by Franklin D. Roosevelt and retired to his home at Palo Alto, Cal. He has been the recipient of honors and degrees from almost countless universities and societies and has been offered decorations by a number of foreign countries.

HORACE   65 B.C.–8 B.C.

HORACE (QUINTUS HORATIUS FLACCUS), celebrated Roman poet and satirist, was born at Venusia, Italy, on the 8th of December, 65 B.C. His father had been born a slave, but had become a freedman, and as collector of taxes and of other accounts he had by his thrift acquired a modest competence which enabled him to give his son the best education which the times afforded. He early recognized the boy's intellectual promise and took him to Rome in order that he might have every advantage. Between the years of 18 and 20 the youth went to Athens to continue his studies in philosophy under the Athenian masters. This congenial employment was harshly interrupted by news of the assassination of Julius Caesar in 44 B.C., and the arrival of Brutus in Athens to enlist recruits for the republican cause. Brutus, who was himself a student of philosophy, immediately appointed the brilliant young scholar a tribune and Horace thus became involved in the civil war which followed Caesar's death

After the defeat of Brutus by the triumvirs, Antony and Octavian, at Philippi in the year 42 B.C., and the suicide of Brutus, Horace left the republican cause and returned to Rome only to find that his father's estate had been confiscated. Impoverished, he secured employment as a public scribe and turned his attention to literary creation. It was during this dark period of his life that he wrote the first of his epodes and satires. He soon made the acquaintance of Virgil who introduced him to the nobleman, Maecenas, and it was as the protégé of this wealthy patron of arts and letters that he was able to devote himself to literature. He was at this time about 26 years old. Through Maecenas he gained the friendship of Augustus and of other prominent persons and through the remainder of his life he was honored and respected as a man of genius. His first volume of *Satires* appeared about 35 B.C., containing 10 articles, and was followed some six years later by a second volume containing eight satires, which are among the best of his work in this field. At about this time Maecenas presented him with a small estate in the Sabine Hills and in this quiet retreat most of his later work was accomplished. The intense love of nature which is so strongly evidenced through all his work found gratification among those peaceful hills which he has immortalized in his poems.

The work by which he is best known is his *Odes*. The first three books, published in one small volume in 23 B.C., comprise 88 lyrics which had occupied him for some seven years, and which had undoubtedly been privately circulated among his friends before their publication. In form these follow in the main the style of the older Greek lyric poets, the study of whom had absorbed so much of Horace's earlier attention. He treats of simple themes but clothes his thoughts in expressions of surpassing beauty and charm. A few years later appeared his book of *Epistles*.

In the year 19 B.C. the death of Virgil left Horace the greatest living poet. Two years later he was commissioned by the Emperor Augustus to write a hymn for a religious festival. This, with two odes written to celebrate victories of the emperor's stepsons, Tiberius and Drusus, two others written in praise of certain acts of the emperor, and 11 shorter poems, was published in 17 B.C. as the fourth book of the *Odes*.

Little is known of his later years. Death came to him on Nov. 27, in the year 8 B.C., and he was buried near the tomb of his friend and benefactor, Maecenas, whose death earlier in the same year had been a severe blow to him.

From casual allusions in his poems it is easy to visualize Horace with his small rotund figure, his careless dress, his gray hair. He was sensual and not ashamed of his sensuality; he was kindly and honorable. He was so much a man of the world, so witty and philosophical, and so much given to moralizing, that some modern critics have inclined to regard him as philosopher rather than as poet. But the poetic charm of the famous *Odes* is irresistible; their delicacy and elusive touch, their imaginative power and lyrical quality, give them a high place as works of art. Wordsworth, who was certainly a poet rather than a thinker, found their exquisite form and construction acceptable models and they deeply influenced his own inspirations. But his *Satires* and *Epistles* rank even higher. Here was his chosen field, in which he ridiculed the follies of his time with an exquisite touch and a vivacity which has never been rivaled in satirical literature. They abound in epigrams which have become a part of our modern speech.

SAM HOUSTON   1793–1863

SAM HOUSTON, American soldier, was born on March 2, 1793, near Lexington, Va., of Scotch-Irish descent. His father was a Revolutionary soldier and died in 1806. His mother took her family to the frontier in Blount County, Tennessee, and Sam, after attending an academy for a short time and working in a trader's store, ran away and for three years lived with the Cherokee Indians in East Tennessee. After returning home he taught school for a time and in 1813 enlisted as a private in the army, serving under Andrew Jackson in his campaign against the Creek Indians.

In 1817 he was appointed sub-agent to aid in overseeing the removal of the Cherokees from East Tennessee to a reservation set apart for them in what is now Arkansas. His activities in attempting to prevent the smuggling of Negroes from Florida into the United States brought criticism upon him from the War Department, of which John C. Calhoun was Secretary, and when Calhoun administered a sharp rebuke because Houston appeared before him in Indian garments, and an inquiry was ordered into his official integrity, the latter resigned his commission and went to Nashville where he studied law and was admitted to the bar. From 1823 to 1827 he represented Tennessee in Congress and then was elected Governor of the state. Two years later he married Eliza Allen. The union lasted only three months when Houston resigned his office without giving his reasons, took refuge with the Cherokees and was formally adopted into their tribe.

He later visited Washington twice (1830 and 1832) to expose the frauds practised upon the Indians by government agents. In 1832 President Jackson sent him to Texas (then with Coahuila a part of Mexico) to negotiate treaties with the Indian tribes for the protection of American traders. He decided to remain in Texas and was appointed delegate to a convention which met at San Felipe in April, 1883, to draw up a constitution and attempt to have Texas made a separate state from Coahuila where the people were almost wholly anti-American. Their plea was rejected by the Mexican Congress which attempted to disarm the Americans and the War for Texan Independence developed in 1835. Houston was made Commander-in-Chief of the army and in April, 1836, with 743 raw soldiers in his command he met Santa Anna with 1600 Mexican veterans on the San Jacinto and utterly routed them. The following day Santa Anna himself was captured. This victory won the war and Houston was elected president of Texas on Sept. 1, 1836, succeeding David G. Burnett, the first president. He served for two years and in 1841 was elected for a second term.

During his first term as president the newly founded city of Houston was named in his honor and became the seat of the government. Texas was admitted into the United States as a state in 1845 and Houston was elected as one of its first two senators. He was a Union Democrat and served his state in the Senate from 1846 to 1859. In one of his ablest speeches he opposed the Kansas-Nebraska bill which was to nullify the Missouri Compromise, and his voice was often raised in Congress on behalf of the Indians whose rights he felt were being trampled upon.

In 1859 he was elected Governor of Texas. Two years later he attempted to prevent the secession of the state from the Union but failed and upon his refusal to swear allegiance to the Confederacy he was deposted as Governor in March, 1861.

He was one of the picturesque figures in American history; a soldier of ability, resolute and intrepid, cool, fearless and candid in public as in private life, and in winning Texas' War for Independence he won for his country an empire exceeding in square mileage some of the great countries of Europe.

He died at Huntsville, Texas, on July 26, 1863.

HENRY HUDSON   ?–1611

HENRY HUDSON was an English navigator and explorer. Nothing is known of his birth or early history. The first record which we have of him tells of a voyage which he made in the year 1607 for an English company with one small vessel, the "Hopeful," and a handful of sailors in an attempt to discover a northeast passage which would provide a shorter route to China and the Spice (or Molucca) Islands in the East Indies. Some four months after setting out the expedition returned to England having skirted the coasts of Greenland and Spitzbergen but found it impossible to force a way through the great ice barrier to the north. The following year Hudson set forth again and reached Nova Zembla. His third voyage was made on behalf of the Dutch East India Company in 1609. In his ship "Half Moon" with about 20 men he sailed from Amsterdam in March or April and again reached Nova Zembla intending to cross the Kara Sea which he believed would enable him to reach the Pacific Ocean. The intense cold discouraged his crew who became discontented and mutinous and turning about he crossed the Atlantic heading for Davis Strait where it was believed from the reports of Captain John Smith and other earlier explorers that only a narrow strip of land separated the two great oceans. Whether because of change of plan or by accident he went considerably to the southward of this course and reached land probably somewhere along the Nova Scotia shore and followed the shore line as far to the south as latitude 35. It is supposed that he had a rough map of the coast showing Capt. Smith's earlier explorations in Virginia.

Turning north he entered what we know as the Hudson River which he explored as far north as the present city of Albany, surveying the coasts and trading with the Indians as he went. Four weeks spent in this way convinced him that he could not reach the Pacific Ocean by that route and he returned across the Atlantic. It is said that he was seized by the English and he and his men cast for a time into prison because of their Dutch affiliations, being later released with the admonition to work for the English thereafter.

Undismayed, he made another attempt in April, 1610, in his little ship, the "Discovery," this time again financed by an English company. Still searching for a northwest passage, he reached Greenland in June and sailing through the strait later named for him came to the great inland sea now known as Hudson Bay. He spent some months in exploring this vast expanse and determined to spend the winter there in order to pursue his explorations farther in the spring. In November his ship became locked in the ice; the winter was long and cold; provisions were insufficient and his men became quarrelsome. When the ship broke out of the ice in the spring a mutiny occurred and Hudson with his son and a few of his crew who remained loyal to him (including also some sick men) were put into a small boat and set adrift. This was in June of 1611. Nothing further was ever heard of them.

Of the mutinous crew some were killed in difficulties with the Eskimos; some died of starvation. A few succeeded in reaching England and it was through one of these men that the fate of the intrepid Hudson was learned. An expedition was sent from England to search for the abandoned men but no trace of them could be found.

Although it is known that before Hudson's day most of the points which he reached had been discovered by earlier voyages, great credit is due to him for pushing his explorations and he was largely instrumental in developing the rich fisheries of Spitzbergen and the enormous fur industry which grew up about the Hudson Bay Territory.

CHARLES EVANS HUGHES   1862–

CHARLES EVANS HUGHES, American lawyer and jurist, whose distinguished and varied career in the service of his state and country has been rivaled by few public characters of his time, is one of the outstanding intellectual ornaments of the nation. A mere enumeration of his activities and honors forms an imposing catalogue of achievement. He was born at Glens Falls, N. Y., on April 11, 1862, son of Rev. David Charles Hughes. At 14 he entered Madison University and later Brown University, from which he graduated in 1881; taught school for a short period, attended law school at Columbia, and after graduating with high honors in 1884 began the practice of his profession in New York City. In 1888 he married Miss Antoinette Carter, by whom he had three daughters and a son, Charles Evans, Jr., who also achieved distinction in the legal profession.

From 1891 to 1893 he was professor of law at Cornell University, returning to private practice in New York where, in 1905, he was attorney for the Armstrong Committee, a body appointed by the state legislature to investigate the practices and conditions of the great insurance companies, against which the gravest charges of maladministration and extravagance had been made. In this difficult and complicated undertaking his inquisitorial skill became known throughout the country and he was popularly called "the man of the rising inflection"; terrible, indeed, was the ordeal which official after official underwent in submitting to his quiet, persistent and revealing interrogations. Sweeping reforms in the conduct of the insurance companies resulted from his masterly inquiry and illuminating report. It was natural that this outstanding figure should be selected for political preferment, a career which he never sought, and he declined the nomination tendered to him by the republican party for mayor of New York City. In 1906 he was nominated for Governor, defeating his opponent, William Randolph Hearst, by 60,000 votes. Two years later he was reelected after an unsuccessful effort of the New York delegation to the national convention to nominate him for president. His administration of the affairs of his state was characterized by complete independence of political influence and a rigorous policy of reform legislation and law enforcement which in some quarters laid him open to the charge of being puritanical. Always clear about his duty and with the highest conception of public trust, he proceeded with unwavering resolution and achieved an imposing record of reform, including a new public service commission law, the direct primary, laws for the protection of women and children in factories, and revised election laws. Pool selling and bookmaking at race tracks were, by new legislation, relegated to the category of common gambling and treated as such, resulting in the discontinuance of horse racing in the state.

In October, 1916, he was appointed by President Taft associate justice of the Supreme Court and resigned his gubernatorial office to accept this high judicial post for which he was eminently fitted. In the presidential campaign which resulted in the reelection of President Wilson he was persuaded to run on the republican ticket and resigned his judicial office (1916) to make a vigorous campaign. For a few days the result of this exciting contest hung in the balance, but the vote from California determined the election of Wilson. Mr. Hughes then returned to private practice in New York where his prestige as a lawyer was almost ·unprece. dented. In 1919 President Wilson appointed him to investigate charges of corruption in the building of army and navy airplanes, and in 1921 his professional practice was again interrupted by a summons to Washington to serve as secretary of state in the cabinet of President Harding, a post which he filled with the highest distinction, handling with tact and skill the difficult international problems arising from the war and presiding at the disarmament conference which the president called. He continued as secretary of state after the inauguration of President Coolidge, by whom he was appointed to sit in the Permanent Court of Arbitration at The Hague. He held this post until 1930, but returned to America in 1928 to become chairman of the U. S. delegation in the Pan-American Conference at Havana, Cuba, and was also a delegate in the Pan-American Conference on Arbitration and Conciliation held in Washington in 1928–29. In 1928 he was elected by the council and assembly of the League of Nations as Judge of the Permanent Court of International Justice, resigning this high office also in 1930. Again he resumed his private practice in New York where he cheerfully rendered semi-public service in a variety of capacities, and was often heard in public, always in the furtherance of civic and reform movements, education and cultural activities. His honorary degrees and the positions he filled in the interest of public welfare are too numerous to mention and suggest the query how any individual can render so much service in the limited span of a lifetime.

In February, 1930, Mr. Hughes' voice as a public speaker, always illuminating and interesting, was stilled by his appointment by President Hoover to fill the office of chief justice of the United States, left vacant by the death of William Howard Taft. In this august post he has held himself aloof from public activities.

VICTOR HUGO   1802–1885

VICTOR MARIE HUGO, French novelist and poet and distinguished also as essayist, dramatist and politician, is best known as the author of that great masterpiece of French fiction, Les Misérables. He was born at Besançon, France, on Feb. 26, 1802. His father was an officer in Napoleon's army (later a general and a count) and was long estranged from his son, whose childhood was spent in Elba, Corsica, Naples, Madrid, and largely in Paris where he attended the boarding school of Cordier and Decotte for three years. At 15 he competed for the prize in poetry offered by the French Academy and received honorable mention. In 1819 he took three prizes in a poetic competition in Toulouse and with his brother founded

Le Conservateur Littéraire, a fortnightly publication for which he did most of the writing during the next three years. The royalist sentiment of some of his odes in that journal won him the favor of the King and a grant of 500 francs. In 1819 he became a suitor for the hand of Adele Foucher, but both families objected and it was not until after the death of his mother (1821) and the publication of his *Odes et Poésies Divers* (1822) that he was able to marry. A son was born in 1823. Following the publication of *Hans d'Islande* his pension was increased to 2000 francs. Two daughters and a second and third son were born before 1830 but three years later, notwithstanding a happy domestic life, he began his famous *liaison* with Juliette Drouet. He had been steadily writing—*Bug Jargal,* a weirdly powerful story of Haiti; *Cromwell, Amy Robsart, Les Orientals, Hernani, Notre Dame de Paris, Le Roi s'Amuse,* and many other novels, plays and poems.

He offered himself as a candidate for the French Academy in 1836 and three times subsequently, being elected in 1841. He was elevated to the peerage in 1845; elected to the Constituent Assembly in 1848, and to the Legislative Assembly the following May. At first favorable to Louis Napoleon, he later became violently opposed to him and after the *coup d'etat* of 1851, by which Napoleon overthrew the Republic and proclaimed himself Emperor, Hugo attempted to organize opposition to him. The uprising was unsuccessful and he fled to Brussels in 1851 and did not see Paris again until after the downfall of Napoleon. His long exile was spent partly in Jersey and partly in Guernsey. He visited the Continent frequently, presiding at the peace conference at Lausanne in September, 1869, but refused to revisit France as long as Napoleon III was in power. His chief literary works during his exile were *Napoléon le Petit, Les Châtiments, Les Contemplations, La Légende des Siècles, Les Misérables,* which was published in 1862 simultaneously in ten languages; *William Shakespeare, Les Travailleurs de la Mer, Paris, L'Homme qui rit.*

Madame Hugo died in 1868 while in exile with her husband. Hugo returned to Paris Sept. 5, 1870 and remained during the siege. He was elected to the National Assembly in February, 1871, but resigned on March 8. Five days later his son Charles died. His public utterances on the Commune drew such a demonstration of hostility in Brussels, where he went after the burial of his son, that the government expelled him. He was an unsuccessful candidate for the National Assembly in 1871 and again in 1872. The last of his sons, François Victor, died the following year and Hugo began to feel the loneliness of old age despite the enormous popularity which came to him at about the time of his election to the Senate in 1876, and which continued until the end of his life. Neither political interests nor domestic sorrows interrupted the steady flow from his pen. Among the books of his later period are *L'Année Terrible, Quatre-vingt treize, L'Histoire d'un Crime, Le Pape, La Pitié Supreme, Religions et Religion, Les Quatre Vents de l'Esprit, Torquemada,* and *La Fin de Satan,* begun in 1851 and published after his death, which occurred on May 22, 1885. He was buried in the Pantheon after his body had lain in state under the Arc de Triomphe.

FRIEDRICH HEINRICH HUMBOLDT   1769–1859

FRIEDRICH HEINRICH ALEXANDER, BARON VON HUMBOLDT, German naturalist, was born in Berlin on Sept. 14, 1769, the son of a chamberlain to the King of Prussia. He attended the Universities at Frankfort-on-the-Oder, Berlin and Gottingen, showing special aptitude in the natural sciences. His first publication was a book on the basalts of the Rhine (1790) and the following year he went to Freiberg to study under the celebrated mineralogist, Werner, in the Mining Academy. Soon after the publication of his essays, *Flora Subterranea Fribergensis,* he was appointed superintendent of mines in Upper Franconia, where he continued his studies in natural science and devoted time to the study of muscular and nervous force, upon which subject he published a book in 1797. He was not satisfied with the more or less humdrum work of his official position and resigned that he might have freedom for travel and exploration. He had already in 1790 toured through Holland, France and England with the scientist, Georg Forster, and later had made exploratory trips among the Alps. He now spent about three months at Jena in close association with Goethe and Schiller, and then went to Paris, where with Aimé Bonpland, a young botanist, he planned an exploring expedition in northern South America to enlarge their knowledge of the flora and fauna, and the geography and geology of the tropics. In June, 1799, the two sailed from the Spanish port of Corunna.

The expedition lasted for five years and much territory was explored about which little had previously been known. They traveled through much of Venezuela, Colombia, Ecuador, Peru, Mexico and the island of Cuba. The monumental work which resulted from the five years of exploration was published in thirty volumes (1807–1827) under the general title of *Voyage aux Régions Équinoxiales du Nouveau Continent,* and is a landmark in scientific history.

In 1807 he returned to Paris, this time on a diplomatic mission with Frederick Wilhelm, and remained in that city much of the time for the next twenty years, until after the publication of his books of travel. Besides preparing these from the voluminous material he had collected (much of which, however, had been lost by shipwreck) he constantly conducted valuable and fruitful experiments in conjunction with Gay-Lussac and other eminent scientists in many branches of chemistry. He returned to Berlin to live in 1827 in response to the demand of Frederick Wilhelm and gave a series of brilliant lectures on scientific subjects. Two years later Emperor Nicholas of Russia invited him to explore the Ural and Altai Mountains of Central Asia and the region about the Caspian Sea. He was accompanied on the expedition by Ehrenberg and Gustav Rose. While much of their attention was devoted to geological formation, they took magnetic observations, made botanical and geological collections, and observed the general character of the country. The most spectacular feature of the journey was the fulfilment of Humboldt's prediction that diamonds would be found in the Ural Mountains. He published the results of this journey in *Asie Centrale* in 1843, Rose in the meantime having published an independent account.

The year 1830 brought about many political changes in Europe and Humboldt was employed on various political missions and other activities. He was a visitor at the French capital frequently during the next twelve years and there he published, from 1835 to 1838, his *Géographie du Nouveau Continent*. Most of his later life was spent in Berlin, where he held an important position at the Prussian Court. From 1845 until his death he was engaged upon his greatest scientific work, *Cosmos,* in which he gave elaborate detail of the many natural sciences and their relation to each other. Four volumes were finished and published from 1845 to 1858. They made a profound impression on the scientific world and were translated into many languages as fast as issued. Other volumes were published after his death which took place on May 6, 1859. He was buried with royal honors at Tegel, near Berlin. In addition to his great scientific works he published volumes on geography, geology, zoology, botany and physics. His work added something to human knowledge in almost every branch of science.

DAVID HUME 1711–1776

DAVID HUME, Scottish historian and philosopher, was born at Edinburgh on the 26th of April, 1711, second son of the laird (master) of a considerable estate in Berwickshire. His mother was the daughter of Sir David

Falconer, a judge. "My family, however, was not rich," he says in his autobiography, "and being myself a younger brother, my patrimony, according to the mode of my country, was of course very slender." While his brother presided at the ancestral estate, David proceeded to make up in learning what he lacked in property and it was he who made the family name famous. The rudiments of education having been given him at home, he was sent to the college of Edinburgh with the law as his ultimate goal, "but while my family fancied I was poring upon Voet and Vinnius, Cicero and Virgil were the authors which I was secretly devouring." With an insurmountable craving for literature and philosophy, he soon abandoned the thought of a legal career. A few months in a commercial house in Bristol were followed by a trip to France where, he says, "I laid that plan of life which I have steadily and successfully pursued. I resolved to make a very rigid frugality supply my deficiency of fortune . . and to regard every object as contemptible except the improvement of my talents in literature." Here, at 28, he wrote his *Treatise on Human Nature* which he published after his return to London in 1737. This profound work which contains the essence of his philosophy "fell dead-born from the press." *Essays Moral and Political* (1741–42) aroused a degree of interest that went far to neutralize his previous disappointment.

While living with his mother and brother on the ancestral estate and studying Greek, he was invited to make his home with the Marquis of Annandale whose family counted on his intellectual and friendly influence to help restore that young nobleman's health and allay his mental affliction. This difficult and profitable position he held until in 1747 he found more agreeable employment as secretary to Gen. St. Clair, with whom he traveled, taking notes of his impressions which were later published as *Life and Correspondence*. In 1751 he published his *Inquiry into the Principles of Morals,* a lucid exposition of the utilitarian system (briefly, the line of moral reasoning of which the principle is the greatest good for the greatest number). *Dialogues Concerning Natural Religion* he was deterred from publishing at about this time by cautious advisers who thought them rather too liberal for the current taste and they were brought out after his death. Soon after the publication of *Political Discourses* (1752) he was made librarian of the Advocates' Library at Edinburgh, a position from which, he says, "I received little or no emolument, but which gave me the command of a large library." This post, hardly more than menial to one of such distinguished attainments, was secured only after he had been refused the chair of moral philosophy in Edinburgh University and the chair of logic in Glasgow, both of which positions he would have filled with distinction. A philosopher in life as well as in theory, he adjusted himself to his new labors and availed himself of the large reference library in preparation for a colossal task, the work by which he is best known to general readers, his comprehensive *History of England*. This great work was not written in chronological sequence. In 1754 he published the part first written, covering the reigns of James I and Charles I. In a second volume he carried his narrative down to the Revolution. He then went back to the dawn of English history and brought the work up through the Norman Conquest and the feudal ages (published 1762). Meanwhile he wrote a work brought out in 1757 under the title of *Four Dissertations: the Natural History of Religion; of Tragedy; of the Passions; of the Standard of Taste. On Suicide* and *The Immortality of the Soul* were published after his death.

These profound works would seem sufficient to bring unqualified distinction to their author. Yet fame was slow to cast her mantle on this great writer and philosopher whose even temper enabled him to live on a level above disappointment and comparative adversity. He seemed untouched by public neglect and ill-considered criticism and censure. But visiting France in 1763 as ambassadorial secretary, he found himself the centre of an intellectual group which was proud to honor him. Returning to England three years later, he was appointed under-secretary of state for the Home Department and was at length in receipt of an income from his writings which, to his modest taste, seemed large. He died in Edinburgh on Aug. 25, 1776. He had never married.

JOHN HUSS   circa 1370–1415

JOHN HUSS (or HUS), Bohemian religious reformer, was born at Husinec, Bohemia, of Czech peasant parentage. The exact date of his birth is unknown. He was educated at the University of Prague where he was a brilliant student, took his M.A. degree in 1396 and two years later began to lecture on theology and philosophy. He became a priest in 1401 and shortly thereafter rector of the university. He was deeply interested in the writings of the English reformer, John Wycliffe (who had died in 1384) and not only made the liberal views of the latter the theme of many of his lectures and sermons, but translated Wycliffe's writings into Bohemian, with the result that he has often been given credit for views and opinions which were merely translations from the English theologian.

His championship of the teachings of Wycliffe brought him into difficulties. In 1403 the university authorities forbade him to lecture on certain of the latter's theses, and a few years later complaints were made to the archbishop of some of Huss' pulpit utterances in which he denounced corruption in the church, and he was forbidden to exercise the functions of a priest. He was reelected rector of the university, but in 1409 while the charges against him were being investigated Pope Alexander V issued a bull against the teachings of Wycliffe and ordered his writings publicly burned. A few months later Huss and his followers were excommunicated. He continued to preach in defiance of the church authorities; there were many demonstrations of popular admiration and loyalty, and in 1411 a papal interdict was pronounced against the city of Prague. In the following year his voice was raised still more boldly in condemnation of the practice of the church in granting indulgences. One result of this was the alienating of some of those who had been his supporters, including the university authorities, and after he wrote his book, *On the Church,* which was a reply to the papal interdict, his position at Prague appeared precarious and at the instance of King Wenceslas, who was friendly toward him, he took refuge in the castles of certain noblemen.

In 1414 a general council was convened at Constance, to which Huss was summoned. Provided with a safe-conduct from the Emperor Sigismund, he journeyed to that city, which he reached on November 3rd. Three weeks later he was arrested on the pretext that he had attempted to leave the city and was imprisoned despite a vigorous protest on the part of many noblemen. Charges of heresy were placed against him, but not until June of the following year did his trial begin. Of the 29 charges presented, a number were absolute misrepresentations of his teachings. He was required to recant his "errors" and to promise not to preach or teach his doctrines. He refused to recant unless they were proved to be errors; asserted that he had not renounced Catholic doctrine, but reiterated his admiration for Wycliffe. On July 6th he was condemned to be burned at the stake as a heretic and the sentence was carried out the same day and his ashes thrown into the Rhine.

The indignation and sorrow aroused throughout Bohemia by the martyrdom of Huss led to demonstrations and disorders in which many ecclesiastics were murdered by the people. About 450 nobles formed a league to maintain liberty of preaching in Bohemia, declared their confidence in Huss and condemned the action of the council which had caused his death. The culmination came in the Hussite War against Emperor Sigismund who had allowed Huss to be put to death despite the safe conduct he had given.

In his books *On the Church* and *On the Six Errors,* Huss upheld the authority of the Bible and attacked such doctrines of the church as belief in the saints, in the efficacy of priestly absolution, transubstantiation and obedience to the pope.

THOMAS HENRY HUXLEY 1825–1895

THOMAS HENRY HUXLEY, eminent English naturalist, and one of the out-standing figures in the scientific field of the 19th century, was born at Ealing, near London, on May 4, 1825. He was of a middle class family and his father was a schoolmaster. He was educated at the Medical School of Charing Cross Hospital. After his graduation later from the University of London, he became a surgeon in the Royal navy and while his ship was on an extensive cruise in the waters about Australia, he made independent studies of the marine animals in that region. These investigations, which discovered facts of the highest importance, were embodied in papers which he sent to England and which were published prior to his return, arousing keen interest in scientific circles. Notable among his discoveries was the peculiar construction of the jelly-fish known as the Medusæ, which he found to have an inner and outer membrane, a fact of the greatest significance to philosophical zoologists. On the return of his ship, the *Rattlesnake,* in 1850, he published at his own expense many of his notes, together with accompanying pictures, after the Admiralty had declined to cooperate with him in this undertaking. The work appeared in the following year under the title of *Philosophical Transactions,* and in the same year he was elected a fellow of the Royal Society, receiving shortly thereafter, in recognition of the scientific value of his papers, one of the two royal medals given annually.

About this time, when he was almost entirely without means, he became engaged to Miss H. A. Heathorn, whom he married in 1855 and who lived to see him the recipient of world-wide honors. In 1854 he was appointed professor of natural history in the Royal School of Mines and this high honor was followed, in 1855, by appointment as professor of comparative anatomy at the Royal Institute. In 1868 he became president of the Ethnological Society, and in the year following accepted the presidency of the Geological Society. In 1870 he became president of the British Association for the Advancement of Science and in 1883 president of the Royal Society. In 1872 he was made lord rector of Aberdeen University and held besides many other posts of honor and educational influence.

In all of these high positions he delivered many lectures and, though he made no concession to popular taste nor was one of those scientists who seek to make abstruse matters palatable for public consumption, he was nevertheless most engaging on the platform and his addresses were heard by multitudes with eager interest. His famous paper, *Origin of the Verte-*

brate Skull, delivered as a lecture in 1858, disproved the prior conception of the skull as merely an expanded section of the spinal column.

The publication of Darwin's epoch-making work, *The Origin of the Species* (1859) found Huxley in full accord with its arguments and implications and he became an enthusiastic supporter of the Darwinian theory. In 1860 he delivered a series of learned but delightful lectures on this great subject, addressed to the working men of London and later (1863) expanded the substance of these discourses into his famous book, *Man's Place in Nature.* In 1876 he visited America where he delivered, in New York, several lectures on evolution and accepted an invitation to deliver an address at the opening of the Johns Hopkins University.

But it was not only as a scientist that Professor Huxley became an outstanding figure of his epoch. His fame and influence as a publicist was only second to his tremendous prestige as an expounder of the facts of evolution. He was deeply interested in the cause of education generally and gave his services liberally in the furtherance of every sort of reform and of cultural undertakings. His great charm on the lecture platform, and his rare faculty of lucid statement made him ever in demand by educational authorities and his generous and patriotic interest in such a variety of movements and causes, together with his incessant scientific researches, put a heavy strain upon his health, which was never robust. Besides the familiar book already mentioned he was the author of the following works: *Elementary Physiology, Lay Sermons, Anatomy of Vertebrated Animals, Critiques and Addresses, Physiography, Hume, An Introduction to the Study of Zoology and Collected Essays,* besides numerous magazine articles on scientific themes.

He died at Eastbourne, June 29, 1895.

HENRIK IBSEN 1828–1906

HENRIK IBSEN, Norwegian poet and dramatist whose work marks the most conspicuous turning-point in the history of modern drama, was born in the small Norwegian town of Skien on the 20th of March, 1828. He was descended from hardy, sea faring stock. His father, a man of some means and position, suffered reverses while the son was still a child, and was compelled to relinquish his home and take refuge on a farm where the family lived on a very reduced scale for several years, finally moving back to Skien. One of our first glimpses of the youthful Henrik is in the gloomy attic of his home, poring over old books and practicing painting, for which he possessed some talent. Circumstances prevented the gratification of this bent and on leaving school he became apprentice to an apothecary, but soon began to write poetry and developed literary ambitions which led him in his 22nd year to leave home and seek his fortune at Christiania where he engaged in newspaper work.

Meanwhile he published (1850) his tragedy, Catalina, a youthful effort which was not a success. For five years he was employed as literary attaché of a theatre in Bergen during which time he produced several plays of indifferent merit. He returned to Christiania to become artistic director of a new theatre which soon failed and he was glad to accept employment with the rival house. Those were dark days for Ibsen; his literary plans did not thrive, he was often in distress, his hope of securing employment by the government was prejudiced by his satirical treatment of officialdom. He was independent and pugnacious and suffered the natural sequel of this temper and attitude. At length, when he was 38, he found it desirable to withdraw entirely from a scene so hopeless of preferment and success, and for 25 years he remained a voluntary exile from his country. His sojourns in Germany and Italy brought out the latent genius of which his countrymen had not dreamed. In Italy he wrote his poetical dramas, *Peer Gynt* and *Brand,* the former a masterpiece of characterization. These plays aroused the greatest enthusiasm in his own country; his cutting satire was forgotten and a pension was granted him which thereafter assured him comparative comfort.

He was 49 years old when the first of his famous satirical dramas was written, *The League of Youth.* Prior to that he had published the double drama, *Emperor and Galilean,* which has been called his most extensive work, although it was never even moderately successful on the stage. In 1877 the *Pillars of Society* was published and shortly thereafter produced in Copenhagen, where its success was instantaneous. In less than a month it was playing at half a dozen European theatres. In 1879 *A Doll's House* was produced, which remains one of his most popular plays. Like most of his work it aroused discussion. Its theme is that of a young wife leaving her husband and family in the cause of individuality and self-development, and the occasion of its production did not pass without acrimonious debate about the emancipation of woman from the limits of her conventional duties, a controversy which seems now singularly naive. *Ghosts,* sometimes called the perfect play, dealing powerfully with the unpleasant theme of inherited disease and insanity, was produced in 1881, followed by *An Enemy of the People, The Wild Duck, Rosmersholm, The Lady from the Sea, Hedda Gabler, The Master Builder, Little Eyolf, John Gabriel Borkman, When We Dead Awaken* (1900).

In 1891 Ibsen returned to his native country and settled in Christiania.

He was indeed the ugly duckling who had spread his wings and flown away to find himself a swan. His countrymen received him with pride and enthusiasm and were glad to pay their tribute to the dramatist who had sounded a new note and won a reputation throughout Europe. He contemplated this rather provincial adulation with a certain grim disdain but submitted to a public celebration of his 70th birthday in which the encomiums were quite sufficient to obliterate all memory of early neglect and repudiation of his budding powers. The following year a statue was erected outside the theatre where he had striven unavailingly and had all but starved. He died on May 23rd, 1906, and was given an impressive public funeral.

Controversy (latterly somewhat less acrimonious) has always raged about Ibsen. Most of his dramas deal with social problems in a large and powerful way, and are to be distinguished from the type of play which merely castigates the unsympathetic husband, the corrupt official, or the heartless capitalist. He was, par excellence, an artist and his theme is always pervasive and comprehensive. Hence the problems suggested by his characters and situations have always aroused discussion. He was not a reformer and he had no panaceas. He has been called unwholesome, sordid, pessimistic. He was certainly skeptical about the condition of society in his time. He never overlooked his mission as a dramatic artist; his situations and climaxes are worked out with rare skill, and the dialogue is always illuminating and realistic. There is little humor in his works. The march of time has made some of his themes obsolete but on the whole it may be said that his work does not date. More than any other writer, perhaps—certainly more than any other dramatist—he has been able to lay bare political and social corruption without taking toll of his artistic instinct. The theme seems to underlie the play; it is never obtrusive, but the reader or beholder becomes aware of the inevitable outcome and is left with the often staggering realization that the matter dealt with is greater than the play itself. Eminent stage stars of the more intellectual type have usually been attracted to the work of Ibsen, by reason of his power to dissect a widespread social condition with truly dramatic force, and often a poetic touch, no less than by the opportunities for skillful interpretation which his significant characters afford.

ST. IGNATIUS OF LOYOLA 1491–1556

INIGO LOPEZ DE RECALDE (ST. IGNATIUS OF LOYOLA), founder of the Jesuits, was born Dec. 24, 1491 of a noble family at the castle of Loyola in the Spanish province of Guipuzcoa. A page at the court of Ferdinand and Isabella, and later a soldier of fortune under the Duke of Nagera, he was severely wounded at the French attack on Pampeluna in 1521. During a long convalescence, lacking other reading matter, he read *The Life of Christ,* by Ludolphus of Saxony, and the lives of some of the saints, and became so impressed with the beauty of the spiritual life that he renounced his career as a soldier, gave away his possessions and adopted a life of the utmost austerity, serving the sick and the poor and living for a time in a cave.

In 1523 he set out on a pilgrimage to Jerusalem and would have stayed in the Holy Land but was forbidden by the authorities. He returned to Barcelona and, realizing that to carry out his purpose of doing good he must have more knowledge, he took up elementary studies, Latin and two years later philosophy at the University of Alcalá. He had in the meantime written his *Spiritual Exercises* and because of his showing these and of his attempting to instruct others with what was thought to be insufficient training, he was censured by the ecclesiastical authorities and forbidden to teach until he had studied for four years. Incurring similar censure at the University of Salamanca in 1527 he went to Paris to study at the University there, gaining a living by begging. Toward the end of 1529 he came into contact with two of the men who, with himself, became the fathers of the Society of Jesus (or Jesuits)—Pierre Lefèvre and Francis Xavier. They were later joined by Diego Laynez, Alfonso Salmeron, Simon Rodriguez and Nicholas Bobadilla. On Aug. 15, 1534, at the Feast of the Assumption, the seven consecrated their union in the crypt of the church of the Martyrs on Montmartre by vows of poverty and chastity.

They started to go to Palestine as missionaries but war between Christians and Turks made it impossible to proceed beyond Venice, so they put themselves at the disposition of the Pope, Paul III, who welcomed them and assigned them to various churches. Lefèvre and Laynez were to teach in the University of Sapienza, while Loyola himself was to continue his spiritual work. A profound impression was made by their godly lives and their earnest preaching, particularly by the plain, soldierlike, but impassioned utterances of Loyola. On the road to Rome he had had his vision of God associating him with Christ. The Society of Jesus began to take form, modeled on the military ideal, and in 1539 Ignatius asked official recognition for it. The Pope had opposed the formation of another religious order, but upon reading its proposed constitution he said, "The finger of God is here," and gave his approval in September, 1541. Ignatius was made its first superior. He now devoted himself to completing the *Spiritual Exercises*. This little book of hardly 100 pages is one of the most spiritually influential books the world has known, and upon its teachings the spiritual training of the Jesuits was molded.

Loyola gave much time to the care of Jesuit converts, established orphan asylums, homes for unfortunate women, and acquired an influence so great that he was later able to prevent a serious religious break between the Pope and King John of Portugal. In 1547 he tried to resign the generalship of the order, but the fathers opposed. He did relinquish active leadership in 1556, died suddenly in Rome on July 31 of that year and was buried under the altar in the north transept of the Gesu in Rome. He was beatified in 1609 by Pope Paul V and canonized in 1628 by Gregory XV.

ROBERT G. INGERSOLL   1833–1899

ROBERT GREEN INGERSOLL, brilliant American lawyer and orator, was born in Dresden, N. Y., on August 11, 1833, the son of a Congregational clergyman. He received a common school education in several towns in Ohio and Illinois where his father was stationed; studied law, was admitted to the bar in Mt. Vernon, Ill., in 1854 and soon became prominent in the courts and in democratic politics.

When war was declared against the seceding southern states he recruited the Eleventh Illinois Cavalry and entered the army as its colonel. He commanded the regiment in the battle of Shiloh and saw considerable fighting in various parts of Tennessee. On Dec. 18, 1862 he was ordered to intercept a Confederate raiding party and set out with 600 men. The raiding party proved to be an army of 10,000 men and Ingersoll was captured and held prisoner for a time but was soon paroled and later placed in command of a camp at St. Louis. He resigned shortly afterwards and resumed the practice of law. After the war ended he changed his political faith, became a republican and in 1867 was made Attorney-General of Illinois. His law practice increased and his political fortunes prospered. In 1876 he was a delegate to the Republican National Convention and in his speech nominating James G. Blaine for the presidency he used the phrase that has ever since been associated with the name of Blaine—"the plumed knight." So vigorous, sustained and flowery was this speech that it carried Ingersoll's fame as an orator throughout the land.

He remained active in politics for several years and might undoubtedly have won high political honors had it not been for the agnostic views which he never hesitated to proclaim, but he was not eager for a political career and refused diplomatic posts that were offered to him. In 1882 he removed to New York where he became the most noted trial lawyer of his time.

His national reputation was won, not through the law, but by the lectures which he delivered to immense audiences throughout the country, in which he attacked the Bible and Christian beliefs in general, arousing widespread opposition, hatred, vituperation and personal abuse from the clergy and others. His oratorical flights, his power of expressing his thoughts in language which often rose to poetic levels, the timbre of his voice and his mastery of the arts of oratory were sufficient to assure him of great audiences everywhere and had a profound effect on the thinking of the day. His oratorical style was rhythmic and its lilt and flow, especially in his perorations, was readily transposable into blank verse. His conversation and table talk often rose to an unusual degree of eloquence. But unlike most sentimentalists in the field of oratory, the force and power of his utterances was never prejudiced by his word painting and in the field of argument his logic was devastating. He engaged in many notable controversies on the subject of religion, outstanding among which was his famous debate with Gladstone published in the *North American Review* in which his liberal views were set forth with matchless power.

Among the most famous of his lectures were *Some Mistakes of Moses, The Family, The Liberty of Man, Woman and Child, The Gods* and *Ghosts.* The addresses have been published and are interesting reading although in print they make far less impression than they did upon listeners who came under the spell of his presence.

His *Lectures Complete* was published in 1886 and his *Prose Poems and Selections* in 1888. After his death appeared *Famous Speeches, Political Speeches* and a collection of his complete works.

He died at his home in Dobb's Ferry, near New York City, on July 21, 1899. His body was cremated and his wife kept the ashes with her until her death. In May, 1931 they were interred in Arlington National Cemetery.

SIR HENRY IRVING   1838–1905

SIR HENRY IRVING, distinguished English actor, was born Feb. 6, 1838, at Keinton, Mandeville, Somersetshire, England. His name was originally John Brodribb, but upon his first appearance on the professional stage, after a short experience in commercial work, he was billed as Henry Irving, and in 1887 the name became his legally by royal license. This first appearance was on Sept. 29, 1856, at Sunderland, where he took the rôle of Gaston, Duke of Orléans, in the play of *Richelieu*. It is said that in the next ten years of stock acting in the English provinces he played more than 500 rôles—a laborious and thorough training in the art of acting. In 1866 he made his first appearance in London as Doricourt in *The Belle's Stratagem*, at St. James's Theater. The new Queen's Theater was opened the year following and Irving joined the company which included Ellen Terry and other well known actors. He became popular in light comedy parts and in the rôle of "heavy villain," but his first conspicuous success was as Digby Grant in *The Two Roses* at the Vaudeville Theater in June, 1870, in which he appeared for 300 consecutive performances.

In 1871 he became associated with the Lyceum Theater, then under the management of Bateman, his first play in that house being *The Bells*, with which his name remained closely associated for the rest of his life, and which he frequently revived. At the same theater he appeared in *Charles I, Eugene Aram, Richelieu*, and in 1874 in *Hamlet*, which had a run of 200 nights and established Irving as one of the leading players of his generation. His portrayal of Hamlet was unconventional, done in the theatrical style of the period and aroused much discussion among the critics. Miss Bateman appeared with him in these productions and also in *Macbeth, Othello*, Tennyson's *Queen Mary, Richard III* and *The Lyons Mail*. In 1878 he took over the management of the Lyceum and engaged Ellen Terry as his leading lady, who played Ophelia in his revival of *Hamlet* and Portia to his Shylock in *The Merchant of Venice*. His interpretation of Shylock was as unconventional as his Hamlet and aroused as much controversy. After playing in Tennyson's drama, *The Cup*, he acted Iago to the Othello of the American actor, Edwin Booth, who was appearing in London. This was followed by *Romeo and Juliet, Much Ado About Nothing, Twelfth Night, Olivia*, adapted from Goldsmith's *Vicar of Wakefield; Faust*, a revival of *Macbeth, The Dead Heart* and Ravenswood from Scott's *Bride of Lammermoor*. Among the conspicuous successes of his later career were his Cardinal Wolsey in *Henry*

VIII (1892), *King Lear* (1893) and Tennyson's *Becket.* Under his management the Lyceum became the foremost of London theaters for the brilliancy of its productions and the perfection of its stage settings.

He made several tours of the United States with his entire company, where his popularity was as great as in England. The Lyceum passed into the hands of a limited liability company in 1899 but remained under his direction and he appeared in Sardou's *Robespierre* and in a revival of *Coriolanus.* His last London appearance was in Sardou's *Dante* in 1903 at Drury Lane. He married in 1869 Miss Florence O'Callaghan and had two sons, Henry Brodribb and Lawrence, both of whom attained some fame as actors. In 1895 he was knighted, being the first actor ever to be accorded that honor; and he received honorary degrees from Dublin, Cambridge and Glasgow. He died suddenly while touring the British provinces, at Bradford, Oct. 13, 1905, after giving an unusually brilliant performance of Becket. His ashes were placed in Westminster Abbey near the Shakespeare statue and beside those of Garrick.

He possessed a strongly marked personality and mannerisms that provoked much adverse criticism, but his versatility was extraordinary and he devoted all of his energies to his profession.

WASHINGTON IRVING   1783–1859

WASHINGTON IRVING, American writer, was born in New York City on April 3, 1783, the son of an English mother and a Scottish father who had become a successful merchant and intended to have his son embrace the legal profession, but illness compelled the son to abandon his studies for a time and he journeyed to Europe for the benefit of his health. He was admitted to the bar after his return but a literary career had a stronger appeal for him. His first writing of note was *Salmagundi,* written in collaboration with his brother William and J. K. Paulding, which displayed the young author's bent toward humor. In 1809 appeared *Knickerbocker's History of New York,* which had been intended as a burlesque on Dr. Samuel Mitchell's loquacious and pretentious guide to New York City. Irving expanded his idea as he wrote with the result that *A History of New York from the Beginning of the World to the End of the Dutch Dynasty by Diederich Knickerbocker* became one of the first of American humorous classics.

He became a partner of his brother William, following the death of their father, and proceeded to England in 1815 to superintend the

Liverpool branch of the business which, however, became bankrupt in a few years and he returned to the pen as a source of livelihood. He was a man of polished manners and amiable character; those qualities, together with the literary reputation which had preceded him, enabled him to mingle in the best literary circles of London. Scott, Moore, Jeffrey and Campbell were among his friends. Scott recommended him to the publisher, Murray, who brought out in 1819–20 *The Sketch-Book of Geoffrey Crayon, Gent*. Besides the sketches of English scenes and manners which it contained were a number of American tales—notably *Rip Van Winkle* and *The Legend of Sleepy Hollow,* the two stories by which Irving is perhaps best known. *Rip Van Winkle* was later dramatized and became one of the most famous rôles of the actor, Joseph Jefferson. *The Sketch-Book* sprang into popularity in both America and England, and was followed by *Bracebridge Hall, or the Humorists* in 1822. *Tales of a Traveler* appeared in 1824 in Philadelphia after its author had lived for a while in Paris and on the Rhine. He was now in comfortable financial circumstances and again visited Europe, settling in Madrid where he wrote his *History of the Life and Voyages of Christopher Columbus* in four volumes, published in 1828. Three years later he published *The Voyages and Discoveries of the Companions of Columbus*. From material gathered in Spain he prepared also two picturesque volumes, *A Chronicle of the Conquest of Granada* and *The Alhambra*.

He returned to America in 1832 after 17 years abroad to find himself famous and honored as the first American to win literary renown for his own country. In 1836 he published *Astoria,* a chronicle of John Jacob Astor's venture in founding that trading port on the Pacific Coast. *The Adventures of Captain Bonneville* (1837) was based upon the unpublished memoirs of a veteran explorer. In 1841 he was appointed Ambassador to Spain in which post he spent four years. After returning home he wrote his *Life of Oliver Goldsmith* and *The Lives of Mahomet and his Successors*. The later years of his life were devoted to his five-volume *Life of George Washington,* an exhaustive work which to his more devoted admirers is sometimes disappointing because it does not afford the same play for his poetic fancy as the more romantic historical and biographical subjects which he essayed. It is notwithstanding an authoritative and highly interesting work.

Irving never married but remained throughout his life faithful to the memory of an early love. He died on Nov. 28, 1859 at Sunnyside, the picturesque Dutch cottage at Tarrytown, N. Y., which was his home, and was buried in the little Sleepy Hollow Cemetery in the very heart of the scenes which his magic pen immortalized. He was without affectation or ostentation, but brought to his literary endeavors the exquisite good taste which characterized his personal life. It is safe to say that hardly another American author has been so heartily loved as he and he was quite as popular in England as at home. A simple, genial personality shines through all his works and infuses into them an indescribable charm. His literary style was a model of ease, refinement and grace.

IVAN III OF RUSSIA 1440–1505

IVAN III of Russia was born in 1440, the son of Vasily Vasilievich the Blind, Grand Duke of Moscow. During the latter years of his father's life Ivan was co-regent, succeeding to the dukedom in 1462. Eight years later he seized an opportunity of attacking the Republic of Novgorod (which with its possessions included all of northern Russia from Lapland to the Urals). The pretext for war was Novgorod's alliance with Casimir IV, King of Poland, out of fear of Muscovy's growing dominance, an alliance that Ivan chose to regard as contrary to "orthodoxy." He took the field in 1470 and in the following summer forced Novgorod to sue for peace, the terms of which included the breaking off of the Polish alliance, the cession of parts of her northern colonies to Ivan and the payment of a war indemnity of 15,500 rubles. A long-sought pretext for destroying Novgorod Ivan found in 1477 when the Novgorodian ambassadors addressed him in public audience as "Sovereign," instead of the customary "Sir" and were therefore repudiated by Novgorod. Ivan alleged that his sovereignty had been acknowledged and then repudiated. He took the field again with a large Muscovite army, aided by a Tatar contingent, and the republic, deserted by Casimir IV, surrendered in January, 1478 and acknowledged Ivan as autocrat. Revolts against his power occurred during the next ten years but were subdued and punished by the removal *en masse* of many of the richest and most ancient families to Moscow and other cities in central Russia.

The Republic of Pskov, which aided him in his struggles against Novgorod, purchased its continued independence, but Ivan gradually extended his sway over other Russian principalities; Yaroslav surrendered in 1463, Rostov in 1474, and Tver in 1485. He refused to share his conquests with his brothers and a number of civil wars resulted in which he was victorious despite the assistance Lithuania gave to his opponents. He determined to annex Lithuania, then ruled by his son-in-law Alexander whose forces he routed at Vedrosha in July, 1500, but Alexander obtained peace in 1503 by ceding to his father-in-law 20 Lithuanian towns.

Ivan's greatest contribution to the formation and growth of the later Russian Empire was in throwing off the yoke of the Golden Horde, a great body of Tatars who for centuries had held sway in eastern Europe. In 1480 he refused longer to pay the customary tribute to the Tatar Grand Khan Ahmed, who thereupon gathered an army and faced the Muscovite troops across the Ugra throughout the autumn, retiring in November into the Siberian steppes. He was preparing a second great expedition against his rebellious vassal the following year when he was suddenly attacked and slain and his army put to rout by Ivak, the Khan of the Nogai Tatars, after which the Golden Horde crumbled away.

In 1487 Ivan reduced the Khanate of Kazan to the status of a vassal state from which dependency it freed itself in his later years. His relations with the Sultan of Turkey and the Khan of Crimea were peaceful; indeed the latter aided him against Lithuania and in the opening of diplomatic relations with Constantinople to which he sent an embassy in 1495. Under Ivan the government of Muscovy became an autocracy. Men learned in the law of orthodoxy, after the fall of Constantinople saw in the Muscovite Grand Duke the legitimate successor of the Byzantine emperors.

Following the death of his first wife in 1467, Ivan had married Zoe (Sophia) Paleologa, daughter of Thomas, despot of Morea, who claimed the throne of Constantinople. She introduced into Muscovy the etiquette and the double-headed imperial eagle of Constantinople; the old patriarchal system of government vanished; the power of the boyars (or landed, privileged classes) was broken, and her son Vasily was crowned co-regent with his father on April 14, 1502. Ivan died in 1505. The first Russian law book was compiled during his reign.

IVAN IV OF RUSSIA   1530–1584

IVAN IV, son of Vasily III, Grand Duke of Muscovy, was born Aug. 25, 1530, proclaimed grand duke three years later on the death of his father and took the reins of government into his own hands at the age of 14. He was brought up in a brutal and degrading environment, so ill-treated by the boyars placed at the head of affairs by successive revolutions that he came to hate all boyars (the landed proprietors who held positions of great power) and to like their natural enemies, the merchants. He is said to have thrown the last of the boyar tyrants to his dogs and boldly announced that he intended to assume the title of Tsar. He was crowned first Russian Tsar on Jan. 16, 1547, and on February 3rd of that year selected for his wife Anastasia Zakharina-Koshkina of an ancient and noble family, later known as the Romanovs. His private life had been brutal and licentious, but in 1550 he summoned the first national assembly of the realm, made public confession of his youthful sins and promised to govern Russia justly and mercifully. In 1551 he submitted to a synod of 100 prelates certain questions as to the best methods of remedying evils in the kingdom and surrounded himself with good men from the common people, notably Alexis Adashev and the monk Sylvester, whose advice he sought and often followed.

In 1552 the Khanate of Kazan was conquered—the first territorial conquest Muscovy had ever made at the expense of the Tatars. The Volga now for the first time became a Russian river. Ivan continued to strike south and southwest and in 1556 Astrakhan fell to his arms. He even attacked the Crimea (which no Muscovite ruler had dared to do before) and Sylvester and Adashev advised him to seize the whole Khanate as he had done with Kazan and Astrakhan. He coveted Livonia and a seaboard, wishing to make Muscovy a nation equal to her neighbors, and intervened when Sweden, Poland and Denmark contested the possession of Livonia. He won a number of battles (1558–60) but discontinued his aggressions when Livonia put herself under the protection of Poland.

He had grown to distrust Sylvester and Adashev and by 1560 both disappeared; his wife and his son Demetrius died, his bosom friend, Prince Kurbsky, deserted him, and he entered upon ten years of furious struggle against the boyars. He left Moscow in 1564 and declared his intention of abdicating, but yielded to the plea of the common people that he return, making the condition that he should be free to deal with his enemies as he chose. He instituted the *oprichina* or "separate estate," by which certain Russian towns and estates were held apart, all their revenue going to the support of the Tsar and his court, among whom he thereafter lived exclusively.

Until his death twenty years later he devoted himself to depriving the boyars of their lands and their powers, transferred many princely families to outlying sections, distributed their estates among his friends and favorites, using every means to humiliate and degrade them. Many cruelties were perpetrated which gained for him the name of Ivan the Terrible.

From 1560 to 1582 he fought desultorily with Sweden and Poland for possession of Livonia and Esthonia and a seacoast, but despite many successes he was compelled by the peace of Zapoli (January, 1582) to abandon his claim to Livonia. In 1581 he began the conquest of Siberia. In 1584 commercial relations were entered into with England.

Some authorities have considered that Ivan showed strong evidences of insanity. It is reported that in a fit of fury he killed his best loved son Ivan and in remorse assumed the hood of the strictest order of hermits, dying as the monk Jonah on March 18, 1584. He had been married seven times, but left only two young sons.

ANDREW JACKSON   1767–1845

ANDREW JACKSON, seventh president of the United States, nicknamed "Old Hickory," for his sterling qualities, was born on March 15, 1767, but whether at the Waxhaw settlement in Lancaster, S. C., or in Union County, N. C., is not known with accuracy. He was the son of a Scotch-Irish immigrant who died a few days before his birth. He was wild, independent, quick-tempered in youth and in manhood, and received little formal education. At the call for soldiers to resist the British, he enrolled and at the age of 13 took part in the battle of Hanging Rock (Aug. 1, 1780). In the following year, while attempting to capture some British troops at Waxhaw Church, he and his older brother were taken prisoners and for refusing to blacken an officer's boots Andrew received a sabre slash which left him permanently marked.

In 1784 the death of his mother and his two brothers having left him alone in the world, he went to Salisbury, N. C., to study law, was admitted to the bar three years later and began to practise at Martinsville. The following year, being appointed prosecuting attorney for the western district of North Carolina (now Tennessee), he removed to Nashville and in 1791 married Mrs. Rachel Robards, daughter of a pioneer settler in that region. It was the belief of the two that Mrs. Robards and her former husband had been divorced by the courts of Virginia, but actually the divorce was not granted until two years later. Immediately thereupon Jackson had the marriage ceremony performed a second time, but the unfortunate circumstance was always a sensitive matter with him and he felt keenly the adverse comment which it had aroused.

In 1796 he helped to frame the constitution of Tennessee, became a congressman and the following year was elected to the Senate, but resigned in 1798 and became judge of the Supreme Court of Tennessee for a period of six years. Of a combative nature, he fought a number of duels; one with Charles Dickinson whom he killed, and a later one with Thomas Hart Benton and Jesse Benton. In both of these he received wounds which troubled him throughout his life.

He commanded in the campaign against the Creek Indians in 1813–14, defeating them at Talladega and Tohopeka, and as a Major-General in the regular army he captured Pensacola, a Spanish town used as a base of operations by the English. On Jan. 9, 1815, he successfully defended New Orleans against an attack by the British, repulsing them with the loss of their commander and some 2000 men, while his own loss was only eight men. This was the greatest American land victory during the War of 1812, and it made Jackson a national hero. He proclaimed martial law in New Orleans but came into conflict with civil authorities over some of his acts. In 1821 he was appointed military governor of the Territory of Florida, and during his short term again had some difficulties with the authorities.

In 1823 he was elected to the United States Senate from Tennessee. In 1824 he ran for the presidency but although he received the largest number of electoral votes he did not have a majority, and when the House of Representatives chose a president from the three candidates having the largest number of electoral votes, John Quincy Adams was elected. Jackson believed he had been defrauded and that Henry Clay had agreed to support Adams in return for appointment as Secretary of State. Under his banner opposition to Adams' administrative policies was organized and in 1828 he was elected president over Adams by 178 votes to 83. There were two factions in the administration, one led by Martin Van Buren, the other by John C. Calhoun, the latter of whom Jackson came to regard as a personal enemy, and in 1832 he was re-elected to the presidency defeating Clay.

During his eight years in office a more thoroughly democratic régime was inaugurated. Springing from the common people, his sympathies were with them and many of them were appointed to high offices. One important event was his prompt crushing of the attempt of South Carolina to nullify the high tariff which was in effect and his insistence upon the existing law being enforced although he himself was opposed to the tariff. During his term the national debt was entirely paid off; Federal authority over the states was strengthened; the United States Bank was discontinued after a somewhat prolonged "bank war."

After the completion of his second term he supported the cause of slavery, which he believed to be in danger. He died at Nashville, June 8, 1845.

THOMAS JONATHAN JACKSON   1824–1863
(STONEWALL JACKSON)

THOMAS JONATHAN JACKSON, a Confederate general known as "Stonewall" Jackson, was born at Clarkson, Va. (now West Virginia), Jan. 21, 1824. He was orphaned early in life but was given some business training by an uncle. At 18 he was sheriff of his county and by industry and hard study won a nomination to West Point, receiving his commission as second-lieutenant of artillery in 1846, after which he served in the war with Mexico. In 1851 he was appointed professor of artillery tactics and natural philosophy at the Virginia military institute. He was deeply religious and although not a good teacher his influence on his pupils was great. At the beginning of the Civil War he was named Colonel of Virginia Volunteers, and sent to Harper's Ferry, Va. He commanded the first brigade of General Johnston's force opposing the first invasion of Virginia by the Union army and united with Beauregard's forces at the first battle of Bull Run, where the speed of the Federal attack brought confusion to the Confederates. It was reported that General Lee, to encourage his South Carolina troops, called to them, "Look, there is Jackson standing like a stone wall." The retreating soldiers rallied, the Federal troops were repulsed, and Jackson was thenceforth known as "Stonewall" Jackson.

While McClellan was moving part of his force by sea to Yorktown for an advance against Richmond, Jackson, in the valley of the Shenandoah, attacked a force of 7000 Federals at Winchester with his command of 3000 men. He was repulsed, but the boldness of his attack caused great alarm in Washington. McClellan landed at Yorktown while two other Union armies were converging on Richmond, opposed by weaker Confederate forces. General Robert E. Lee, military adviser to Jefferson Davis, seeing that the only way to save Richmond was to keep the Federals at a distance, suggested that Jackson unite the Confederate detachments and fall upon General Banks, who commanded the Union forces in the Shenandoah Valley. Jackson first drove the Federals who were threatening his flank into the mountains of western Virginia, and then attacked Banks' 10,000 men with his own force of 17,000. By the middle of May, McClellan was within sight of Richmond, but Jackson, feinting at Strasburg, advanced down the North Fork, defeated Kenley, caught Banks on his retreat at Winchester, defeated him and drove him back to the Potomac, thus drawing away so many of McClellan's troops that he hesitated to attack Richmond.

Johnston being wounded, Lee succeeded to the command of the

Confederates and with the help of Jackson achieved a decisive victory at the second battle of Bull Run. Jackson next captured Harper's Ferry, taking 11,000 prisoners and a quantity of supplies, reached Antietam in time to avert a Confederate disaster, and as Lieutenant-General in command of the Confederate right at Fredericksburg, checked Burnside's advance. In April Hooker attempted to turn the Confederate position on the Rappahannock with 120,000 men opposed to Lee's 60,000. On the night of May 1–2 Lee and Jackson planed a bold stroke, Lee keeping 10,000 men to make demonstration against Hooker and sending Jackson with his whole corps to move secretly around Hooker's right with the aim of surrounding his force in the woods of Chancellorsville. The move was successful, and on the evening of May 2 Jackson rolled up the Federal flank. Riding forward in the dusk to organize a pursuit, he was shot down and mortally wounded in a misdirected charge by his own men who mistook his party for the enemy. He died on May 10, 1863. The spot where he received his fatal wound is marked by a granite shaft and in the city of Richmond is a monument erected to his memory by English admirers.

He was twice married; to Eleanor Junkin who died in 1854 and later to Mary A. Morrison.

HENRY JAMES 1843–1916

HENRY JAMES, American novelist, essayist and critic, was the son of the distinguished theologian, Henry James, and brother of the psychologist, William James, and was born in New York City on April 15, 1843. His education was acquired under his father's close supervision in New York, Switzerland, England and France. At 19 he entered Harvard Law School, but literature interested him more than legal studies, and he presently began to write magazine articles and short stories with sufficient success to embolden him to trust to writing for his career. In 1869 he took up his residence in England where most of his subsequent life was spent, with periods of European travel and for a time he lived in Italy.

His first novel, *Roderick Hudson,* was published in 1875, followed by *The American;* the exquisite gem of characterization, *Daisy Miller,* and *The Portrait of a Lady* (1881). His style was simple and natural and in these earlier works he dealt chiefly with the lives of American travelers abroad. The development of his characters interested him more than dramatic action and he presented in subtle and masterly fashion the contrasts afforded by the meeting of representatives of a rather new civilization with those of the older and more sophisticated races. His cosmopolitan training and his familiarity with modern French literature are evidenced in his portrayals and also in his clever studies of *French Poets and Novelists* (1878) and *Partial Portraits* (1888). During a period of 30 years he published more than 40 volumes, including some collections of essays, but mostly fiction. His theme continued to be most often the presentation of the American character against a continental or English background although, notably in *What Maisie Knew* (1897), *The Awkward Age* (1899) and *The Wings of the Dove* (1902), he treats of the marked changes taking place in England tending toward greater freedom and unconventionality in life and manners.

It is probable that few writers since the day of Washington Irving have contributed as greatly to mutual understanding between the people of Europe and America than has James through his international and society novels, which not only portrayed with faithful realism the various types of American character, but introduced Americans to aristocatic English and continental life by their equally truthful delineations of society abroad. Gradually, however, his style changed, growing more complex and involved and analytical, until in some of his later works, the interest of the plot is almost lost in a sea of obscurity and verbosity and mystification. The quality becomes apparent in *The Sacred Fount* (1901), and is perhaps exemplified best of all in *The American Scene,* published after a trip to America in 1905. He was a man of the widest culture, and of intellectual delicacy and refinement, with acute powers of observation and insight, but lacking in the force and vigor necessary to create virile characters and handle strong situations.

His works, besides those already mentioned, include *Watch and Ward* (1871); *An International Episode* (1879); *A Bundle of Letters* (1879) in which some of his best short stories appear; *A Life of Hawthorne* (1879); *Washington Square* (1881); *Portraits of Places* (1884); *The Bostonians* (1886); *The Tragic Muse* (1890); *Essays in London* (1893); *The Two Magics* (1898); *The Ambassadors* (1903); *The Golden Bowl* (1904); *English Hours* (1905); *The High Bid* (1909); *Italian Hours* (1909); *Notes on Novelists* (1914); *A Small Boy and Others* and *Notes of a Son and Brother,* both of which are autobiographical; and numerous others. *The Middle Years* was left uncompleted at his death.

After living for the greater part of his life in England, his sympathies were so aroused after the outbreak of the World War that he decided to become a citizen of that country and was naturalized in 1915; the following year he received the Order of Merit. On his 70th birthday he was presented by admirers with a portrait of himself by John Sargent, which was hung in the Royal Gallery and was later mutilated by a militant suffragette. He died in London on Feb. 28, 1916. In 1919 was published *Within the Rim,* giving his impressions of the World War.

JOHN JAY 1745–1829

JOHN JAY, American patriot and jurist, was born of Huguenot ancestry in New York City, Dec. 12, 1745, and was graduated from King's College (now Columbia University) in 1764, admitted to the bar in 1768 and became a successful lawyer. His father was a wealthy merchant and John, through his marriage in 1774 to Sarah Livingston, became connected with one of the most prominent American families.

When trouble arose with England leading up to the Revolution he sided with the colonists but took a conservative attitude. Though at first reluctant to advocate the actual separation of the colonies from England, he became one of the staunchest supporters of the Revolutionary cause, was a member of the First Continental Congress (1774), drew up addresses to the people of Great Britain, Canada, Ireland and Jamaica. Although a delegate also to the Second Continental Congress, in 1776 when the Declaration of Independence was signed he was absent attending the Provincial Congress of New York where he drafted resolutions authorizing the New York delegation to sign that instrument. He was chairman of the committee that drafted the New York State constitution and, returning to the Continental Congress, became its president on Dec. 10, 1778.

The following July he was sent to Spain to negotiate a military alliance and to seek a subsidy of $5,000,000. Spain, although an ally of France and at war with England, hesitated to imperil her colonial interests by direct aid to Britain's rebelling colonies and withheld recognition of the United States. Jay was able to accomplish little and after a disappointing and fruitless stay of two years he joined Benjamin Franklin in Paris in the summer of 1782, where he gave valuable service in negotiating the peace treaty with Great Britain. They were instructed not to act without the knowledge and concurrence of the French government, but Jay suspected the good faith of France and induced the commission to treat independently with England. The treaty was signed Nov. 30, 1782 and adopted without important change Sept. 3, 1783. Upon his return to America in July, 1784, Jay was elected to the Continental Congress, resigning in December to become Secretary of Foreign Affairs. His proposal to Congress that matters still in dispute with Great Britain be adjusted by a mixed commission constituted the first important step in the history of the country toward arbitration of international disputes.

Jay was an aristocrat by temperament, conservative and nationalistic, and advocated a strongly centralized government. He played an active part in the campaign to get the Federal Constitution ratified. Under the name of "Publius" he wrote a number of the issues of *The Federalist* (Nos. 2, 3, 4, 5, and 64) of which Hamilton was the guiding spirit. He wrote and published anonymously *An Address to the People of New York,* a pamphlet advocating adoption of the Constitution, and aided Hamilton in securing ratification by the state at the Poughkeepsie convention. After Washington was inaugurated as President, he appointed Jay as Chief Justice of the United States Supreme Court in which capacity he served from 1789 to 1795. He negotiated the famous Jay Treaty with Great Britain in 1794 and served as Governor of New York from 1795 to 1801 when he retired from public life.

He died May 17, 1829 and was buried in the family cemetery at Rye, N. Y.

JOSEPH JEFFERSON   1829–1905

JOSEPH JEFFERSON, a distinguished American actor, was born in Philadelphia on Feb. 20, 1829. Like so many others who have attained eminence on the stage, he came of a theatrical family and was the third in line of the same name to become well known to the American public. His mother was a popular singer who, before her marriage to the elder Jefferson, was a Mrs. Burke. He made his first appearance on the stage at the age of three and appeared in various juvenile parts during his childhood. In 1842, after four years of traveling and playing in various southern and western cities, his father died of yellow fever in Mobile, Ala., and the boy thereafter spent several years in the hard life of a strolling player, appearing in such small parts as he could get. His wanderings took him into many cities of the United States, into Mexico and back to Philadelphia. In 1849 he married Miss Margaret Lockyer, an actress then playing in New York, and at about that time his talents began to be recognized; he had several fairly prosperous years touring the east and south and in 1856 visited England where he made the acquaintance of many well-known theatrical people.

The following year, after a short stay in Paris, he returned to New

York and as a member of Laura Keene's company made successful appearances as Dr. Pangloss in *The Heir-at-Law,* Caleb Plummer in *The Cricket on the Hearth,* and in other parts. His portrayal of Asa Trenchard in *Our American Cousin* was received with great enthusiasm and was an instance of excellent character acting of a new sort peculiar to Jefferson, who presented the keen, shrewd Yankee in a far more natural manner than the caricatures which had theretofore been made familiar to the theatre-going public. So popular did this become that he took the play on tour. In 1860 he went to California and thence to Australia, where he met with great success in *The Ticket-of-Leave Man.*

In London five years later he appeared in Dion Boucicault's version of *Rip Van Winkle,* the rôle in which he achieved his greatest fame and which has come to be closely associated with his name. He had played the part earlier in Washington in a less satisfactory dramatization without any very great success, but the new version gave him full opportunity for the expression of humor and pathos. This is perhaps the most notable instance in American theatrical history of the identification of an actor with a particular rôle. Rip Van Winkle was Jefferson, and Jefferson was Rip Van Winkle. Yet he disdained any of the appurtenances which a less skilful artist might have used to achieve his realistic effects. Rip's famous dog did not appear upon the stage; no dog was necessary to Jefferson's matchless art. When asked about this omission he explained that he could give a better impression of the companionship without the physical presence of the animal, a device which he regarded as claptrap. His conception in this matter illumined the very essence of his art and might well be taken to heart by latterday actors and playwrights.

After a successful run in London and other cities he returned to New York, to meet with equal success, and throughout the remainder of his stage career the character of Rip Van Winkle and that of Bob Acres in *The Rivals* were the principal ones in his repertoire. Some 10 years later he made a third visit to England and Paris and also played his favorite rôles in Scotland and Ireland. In 1867 he married his second wife, Miss Sarah Warren, and a few years later purchased a plantation in Louisiana where he made his winter home, spending many of his summers on his farm in New Jersey. He was an enthusiastic lover of nature and of fishing. He also displayed conspicuous talent as a painter, particularly of landscapes in oil.

Probably no actor has been more loved and honored than Joseph Jefferson, both for his achievements and for his personal character. His acting was characterized by simplicity and by the utmost fidelity to the types which he portrayed. He was a member of the American Academy of Arts and Letters. His autobiograpy, published in 1889–90, is an entertaining work, full of interesting allusions to well-known members of his profession. He died in 1905.

THOMAS JEFFERSON   1743–1826

THOMAS JEFFERSON, third President of the United States, was born April 13, 1743, at Shadwell, Va., the son of Peter Jefferson, civil engineer, justice of the peace and colonel of militia. He attended the College of William and Mary in Williamsburg, leaving it at the age of 20 with a good knowledge of Latin, Greek and French, later acquiring Spanish and Italian, and becoming proficient in higher mathematics and the natural sciences. He was a good violinist, singer and dancer, and was fond of horses and all outdoor sports. He never gambled, played cards, used tobacco, or engaged in a personal quarrel. He was admitted to the bar in 1767. After the death of his father, he had the income from an estate of 1900 acres, and in 1772 married Mrs. Martha Wayles Skelton, who bore him six children, four of whom died in infancy.

His first public service was as a justice of the peace. In 1789 he became a member of the Virginia House of Burgesses. Prevented by illness from attending the Virginia convention of 1774 to select delegates to the Continental Congress, he wrote out a set of resolutions which, although too strong for the convention, were published as "A Summary View of the Rights of British America" and greatly influenced public opinion. In 1775 he entered the Continental Congress, was reappointed to the next Congress and drafted the Declaration of Independence. Again reappointed, he resigned and in October, 1776, reentered the Virginia Legislature, aided in revising the state laws making education by the state a fundamental of democratic faith, and advocated the gradual emancipation of all slaves. He was Governor of Virginia from 1779 to 1781. His wife, to whom he had been deeply devoted, died shortly before his retirement from office.

Again in Congress in 1783, he headed the committee to consider the treaty of peace, advocated the establishment of the monetary system which had been proposed by Gouverneur Morris and won the ceding by Virginia to the United States of its vast territory northwest of the Ohio River. His resolution that slavery should not exist in the Northwest Territory after 1800, rejected in 1784, was adopted in 1787. In 1784 he was sent to Europe with Franklin and Adams to negotiate commercial treaties and in 1785 became Minister to France, succeeding Franklin. Upon his return Washington offered him the secretaryship of State, which he reluctantly accepted. He clashed with Alexander Hamilton, Secretary of the Treasury, on financial measures and on questions relating to France and England, Jefferson's sympathies being with France. The Democratic party was formed about him, the Federalist about Hamilton. He repeatedly sought to resign and receiving Washington's reluctant consent in December, 1793, he retired to his home at Monticello, Va., where he remained until elected Vice-President in 1796. After the passage of the Alien and Sedition Laws, Jefferson, together with Madison, drew up the Kentucky and Virginia Resolutions which acquired great prominence later in connection with the doctrine of States' Rights.

In the presidential election of 1800 Jefferson and Burr received equal electoral votes and it devolved upon the House of Representatives to make one of them President, the other Vice-President. Hamilton used his influence in favor of Jefferson as the more dependable of the two men and he was declared President, to which office he was reelected in 1804. He eschewed all pomp and ceremony in his inauguration, recognized no social distinctions and, following his lead, simplicity became the order of the day both in dress and in official etiquette. Important events of his first term were the purchase of Louisiana from the French and the sending of Lewis and Clark on their great exploring expedition across the continent. In 1806 he recommended to Congress the prohibition of the slave trade. Prosperity marked his years in office although troubles arose with France and more particularly with England because of the failure of those two nations, which were at war with each other, to respect the neutrality of American shipping. He refused to consider a third term and retired to his plantation at Monticello, Va., withdrawing from public life although his writings thereafter exerted a marked influence. In debt at the expiration of his term, his financial embarrassments increased through his generous hospitality and in 1814 he sold to the nation 13,000 volumes of his own library. In 1826 a popular subscription of some $16,000 was raised for him. He died on July 4 of that year. His last years were devoted to establishing the University of Virginia. He was a man of much personal charm, a great political manager with faith in the people and one of the most influential men of his day. His ideas regarding slavery and many other matters were far in advance of his day.

JENGHIZ (OR GENGHIS) KHAN   1162–1227

JENGHIZ (OR GENGHIS) KHAN (jĕn'gĭz kän') was a Mongol conqueror who, by force of arms, extended his sway over most of the Orient and as far west as the Dneiper River. He was born in 1162 near the northern bend of the Hoang-ho River, and was the son of Yesukai Bahâdûr, ruler of some forty clans known as the tribe of Neyrun, who lived between the great wall of China and the Amur River to the north and paid tribute to the khan of East Tartary. He ascended the Mongol throne at his father's death, when he was but 13 and through the sagacity of his mother held his ground against much plotting and many rebellions until 1206 when he declared himself ruler of an empire, summoned a conference of his nobles on the banks of the Onon and assumed the name and title of Jenghiz Khan (greatest of khans). Until this time he had been known as Temuchin, after a chief whom his father had defeated in battle.

He claimed to be divinely inspired to conquer the whole world and led his troops against his one remaining Mongolian enemy, Polo, the Naiman Khan, whom he defeated and killed in battle, forcing Kushlek, his successor, to flee to the river Irtysh. Next he invaded the province of Hia in northern China and captured many strongholds (1208). Learning that Kushlek was preparing for war, he advanced to the Irtysh and defeated him, after which he returned to more conquests in Hia. The following year he sent three armies to overrun China; one commanded by three of his sons, Juji, Jagatai and Ogotai, marched south; the second, under his two brothers, headed for the sea; while the third, commanded by Jenghiz himself and his son Tulē, marched southeasterly, all three armies meeting with success. He crossed the great wall of China and after long and bloody warfare conquered the city of Peking.

By chicanery and trickery, Kushlek, aided by Mohammed, Shah of Khwārizm, defeated the Khitan Khan, who had afforded him refuge, appropriated his kingdom, and now prepared for another conflict with Jenghiz, but the latter defeated him, took him prisoner and added Kushlek's stolen kingdom to his own possessions. Jenghiz then sent envoys offering peace to Mohammed, who accepted the presents and the offer, but a party of Jenghiz' traders in Transoxiana were executed as spies by the governor of Otrar, and when Jenghiz demanded extradition of the offending governor his chief envoy was killed and the others sent back with their beards shaved off, an insult that Jenghiz was prompt to avenge. He sent four armies into Mohammed's territory; one army took Otrar by assault after a siege of five months, slaughtered the governor and his followers and razed the city; another army, led by Juji, routed Mohammed's force of 400,000, killing 160,000, but Mohammed himself made good his escape to Samarcand; a third army besieged and captured Khojent on the Jaxartes, while Jenghiz and his son Tulē, with the fourth army, took Samarcand, Bokhara (destroying its valuable library) and other important cities. Two columns pursued Mohammed to Nishapur and defeated him, but he again escaped, this time to the Caspian Sea, where he died.

During the next several years Jenghiz and his Mongol armies spread devastation throughout Persia and the Caucasus, and penetrated into Russia, plundering the land as far west as the Dneiper River. He returned to Mongolia in 1224. His generals meanwhile had been pursuing successful warfare to the eastward and he, still eager for conquest, led his forces across the great Gobi desert and besieged the city of Min-hai in northwest China, but before the siege was ended he died on Aug. 24, 1227.

He is said to have left a large number of children among three of whom he divided his possessions. It is estimated that in the course of his wars and ravaging expeditions he must have destroyed at least 5,000,000 people. Although his conquests were accompanied with the utmost barbarity and cruelty, he nevertheless showed many statesmanlike qualities. He was tolerant in religion, established rigid laws against crime and so ably organized a crude sort of civil authority that it was said one might travel throughout his domains without fear of molestation. He also seems to have had great respect for learning and culture.

EDWARD JENNER   1749–1823

EDWARD JENNER, an English physician whose discovery of vaccination as a preventative of smallpox constituted him a benefactor of mankind, was born in Berkeley, Gloucestershire, England, May 17, 1749, the son of a clergyman. He began the study of medicine under Daniel Ludlow, a surgeon of Sodbury, but later went to St. George's Hospital in London. During his period of study he helped Sir Joseph Banks catalogue the zoological specimens which Captain James Cook had brought back from his first voyage. Declining a position as naturalist on Cook's second voyage, he returned to his native city to practice medicine. In a paper which he read before a local medical society he seems to have anticipated later discoveries on rheumatic inflammations of the heart. Something of a musician, and poet, he was popular in society, studied local ornithology and geology and constructed the first balloon seen in that part of England. He was married in 1788 to Catharine Kingscote.

About 1775 he began his study of smallpox and cowpox which led him to the conclusion that the latter could be introduced into human beings and act as a protection against smallpox. He spent many years in investigation before actually putting his theory to the test and then inoculated his own son and demonstrated that the boy was immune to smallpox. His first public inoculation was performed in 1796 and two years later he published his *Inquiry into the Cause and Effects of the Variolae Vaccinae,* in which he announced his discovery and presented his proofs; and went to London but was unable to prevail upon the medical profession to adopt the practice of vaccination. He was strenuously opposed by both physicians and clergymen, but within a year he was able to inspire confidence in his discovery to such an extent that a large number of the leading physicians of London gave it their public and written approval. Henry Cline, surgeon of St. Thomas' Hospital, made a number of inoculations with much success and advocated the practice before the British medical profession.

A meeting with members of the royal family helped Jenner to spread the use of vaccine throughout England. He devoted almost his entire time to the demonstration of his theory and in 1803 the Royal Jennerian Society of London was established. During its first 18 months 12,000 persons were inoculated, and the annual death rate from smallpox was reduced from 2018 to 600. The Society died in 1808, due to dissensions, and a national vaccine establishment was founded. The practice was adopted in the British Army and Navy and rapidly spread to most of the other countries of the civilized world. Parliament voted Jenner a grant of 10,000 pounds in 1802 in recognition of his great service to humanity, and in 1806, at the instance of Lord Lansdowne, a further sum of 20,000 pounds. He continued to vaccinate the poor, sometimes as many as 300 in a day. His fame spread and he was honored by many foreign as well as English scientific societies.

The Empress of Russia sent him a diamond ring as a mark of her admiration; he was presented with a gold medal upon the adoption of vaccination in the British Army; in India public subscriptions of some 7000 pounds were raised for him.

His strenuous labor and the death of his eldest son in 1810 undermined his health and after the death of his wife in 1814 he retired from public life, although he continued to practice as a physician, became a magistrate, continued his studies as a naturalist and published in 1822 his work *On the Influence of Artificial Eruptions in Certain Diseases.* He died in Berkeley on Jan. 24, 1823, of apoplexy.

JOAN OF ARC (JEANNE D'ARC) 1412–1431

JOAN OF ARC, the Maid of Orleans, was the daughter of a laborer in the little village of Domrémy on the borders of Lorraine and Champagne. The humble cottage in which she was born in 1412 was shadowed by the great woods of the Vosges; here the peasant children played, conjuring the wind in the tree-tops into fairy voices, spelling supernatural terror into the distant calls of beasts, and seeing goblins and evil spirits in the lurking shadows. These intangible influences were very potent in the childhood of this dreamy and spiritual girl, and they are to be borne in mind in estimating the sincerity of her visions. In her limited rustic life, without any of the diverting facilities of modern times, there was but a hazy line between romance and reality. There seems little doubt of the deep and moving power of her spiritual convictions. In accordance with the peasant custom, she learned to spin but not to read and write. The most searching and even antagonistic inquiry has revealed her as modest, dutiful, industrious and pious. In her whole brief and tragic career no lapse has ever been discovered to tarnish the simple purity of her life.

She was still but a child when she was conscious of a supernatural voice adjuring her to virtue and religious devotion. The world is familiar with the beautiful fanciful picture of Joan leaning against a tree in the woodland absorbed in spiritual meditation. As she grew up she was deeply moved by the distress of her country, which was subjugated and overrun by the English soldiery, and her patriotic ardor conceived the voices which she believed she heard as summoning her to the defense of the Dauphin (eldest son of the king of France). Notwithstanding charges of insanity and wilful deception, she succeeded finally in achieving an audience with the Dauphin and convincing him of the reality of her visions. Persuaded of her divine mission, and perhaps estimating the contagious value of her ardor, he authorized her to assume military attire and with a sword and white banner she put herself at the head of the French troops which were soon heartened and inspired by the conviction of her heavenly authority. During a period of service at an inn she had become familiar with horses and acquired skill in riding them and there seems little doubt that she possessed some genuine military skill (such as it was in that rude time) and remarkable powers of leadership. But much nonsense has been written about her martial genius. From first to last she was guided and directed by those who realized the value of exploiting her and playing on the credulity of the troops. The belief in her supernatural power went far toward shattering morale in the British forces.

On April 29, 1428, at the head of an army of 10,000 men, she threw herself, amply provisioned, into Orleans, then closely besieged by the English, and for several days thereafter made remarkably successful raids against the enemy, forcing them at last to abandon the siege. The effect of this great triumph was electrical; the French army took courage, the English became demoralized and hopeless in the face of this supposed demonstration of the divine will. She now conducted the Dauphin to Rheims where he was crowned as Charles VII, and she tearfully but joyously besought him to allow her to return to her rustic home. But the monarch was in no mood to relinquish such a potent influence and she consented to remain with the army, thereafter participating in numerous conflicts. On the 24th of May, 1430, she led a body of troops into the besieged town of Compiègne where she was driven back in a sally and made a prisoner. The Burgundians, who invested the place, sold her to their English allies for 16,000 francs, and to the commanding officer (one of her own race) who negotiated this shameful bargain accrues an ignominy hardly palliated by military custom and exigency. She was forthwith conveyed to the English headquarters at Rouen and brought before the spiritual tribunal of the Bishop of Beauvais as a heretic and sorceress. After a prolonged trial, which abundantly revealed the ignorance, corruption and superstitution of the time, she was condemned to be burned at the stake. The ungrateful Charles appears to have shown no interest whatever in her fate after her capture. In the face of death she recanted her alleged wrongdoing, expressing penitence for sins wholly imaginary, in the desperate hope that her dreadful sentence might be reconsidered and a lesser punishment imposed. But nothing less than agonizing death would satisfy her persecutors and she was consumed by flames on the public street of Rouen on May 30, 1431, and her ashes cast into the Seine.

In 1440 the family of "the Maid," which had been ennobled because of her, was granted the hollow satisfaction of a review of her shameful trial and 16 years later with all legal rigmarole, she was declared to have been innocent. In 1920 she was canonized by Pope Benedict XV.

JOSEPH JACQUES CÉSAIRE JOFFRE 1852–1931

JOSEPH JACQUES CÉSAIRE JOFFRE (zhŏ'fr'), French general and hero of the World War, was born Jan. 12, 1852, at Rivesaltes in southern France. He left the Ecole Polytechnique at the beginning of the Franco-German war and took part in the defense of Paris (1870). Later he joined the engineers, helped build the fortifications of Paris, and was made a captain in 1876. After the death of his wife he was transferred at his request to Indo-China where he remained for three years as chief of engineers. Returning to Paris, he was assigned in 1889 to the railway regiment and in 1892 was sent to Senegal, Africa, to build a railroad. He took a prominent part in the French occupation of Timbuktu and later in the fortifying of Madagascar. In 1900 he became General of Brigade and five years later General of Division. He was called to the Conseil Supérieur de Guerre in 1910 and entrusted with the lines of communication and the following year was made vice president of the Conseil and chief of staff; for three years he exercised complete authority over the French army.

When Germany declared war on France in August, 1914, he became Commander-in-Chief of the French army. He tried to stop the advancing Germans by throwing French troops on their flank, but was compelled to fall back. Early in September he resumed the offensive and at the battle of the Marne forced the Germans back upon the Aisne. He next tried to turn the German right wing, a vain maneuver which left both armies resting at the sea. In November the Germans tried to break the Allied lines on the Yser, but failed, as did the French in an attempt to break the German front in Champagne, in the Woevre and in Artois. Public alarm at these checks resulted in a campaign against Joffre in military and political circles by the friends of General Galliéni and General Serrail whom Joffre had relieved of his command. Joffre was accused of rejecting all superior authority and of organizing a regular government at Chantilly. The Minister of War, Millerand, who upheld Joffre, was replaced by Galliéni in October, 1915. Rivalry between the general staffs of the two commanders was keen but, in December, Joffre was given supreme command of all the French armies, including that of the Orient, commanded by General Serrail.

After the German advance before Verdun in February, 1916, Galliéni's suggestions to the council of ministers on the necessity of reforming the high command were rejected and he resigned. His successor, General Rocques, was friendly to Joffre, but the campaign against him was continued throughout 1916, partly due to the indecisive outcome of the battle of the Somme, partly to the personal quarrel between Joffre and Serrail. General Nivelle, having taken the fort of Douamont before Verdun, now appeared as a possible successor to Joffre and a decree of December, 1916, conferred upon the latter the title of technical adviser to the government concerning the direction of the war. He continued to hold the title of Commander-in-Chief, however, and Nivelle was appointed to the French front, while the army of the Orient became independent of general headquarters. Both armies were free to proceed independently of Joffre. When General Lyautey became Minister of War in December, 1916, he considered the posts of Commander-in-Chief and technical adviser incompatible with his own authority, so the two offices were abolished and Joffre was made a Marshal of France (the first to receive that honor since 1870).

In the spring of 1917 he visited the United States on behalf of the Allies, and later undertook diplomatic missions to other countries. He was made a member of the Académie Française in 1918, and awarded the British Order of Merit in 1919. He died on Jan. 2, 1931.

KING JOHN OF ENGLAND   1167–1216

JOHN, King of England from 1199 to 1216, the youngest son of Henry II of England, was born Dec. 24, 1167 at Oxford. His elder brothers received continental possessions but John had none; hence his nickname of John Lackland. His mother was Eleanor of Aquitaine, second wife of Henry II. He was betrothed while a child to the heiress of Maurienne and Savoy, but the arrangement was abandoned and he was given grants of revenues, castles and lands in England and in France so that he was no longer "Lackland," although the name has clung to him. The earldom of Cornwall, then vacant, was reserved for him in 1175 and he was betrothed to Isabella, heiress of the Earl of Gloucester in 1176. The following year he was made Lord of Ireland. His father, in 1183, attempted to transfer to him from his brother Richard Coeur de Lion the duchy of Aquitaine, which brought about a civil war. John failed to distinguish himself in the fighting but in 1185 he was sent over to govern Ireland, which he did so badly that in a few months he was recalled to England having aroused the hostility of the loyal Irish chiefs by his arrogance and insolence and failure to protect the settlers. In 1189 he joined his brother Richard and the French king, Philip Augustus, in a conspiracy against his father and when Henry learned that his favorite son had proved a traitor he was broken-hearted.

After Richard became king he confirmed John in his possessions, pushed through his marriage with Isabella, gave him the revenues from six English shires and other grants, but excluded him from participation in the regency during his own absence on crusade. Soon after Richard's departure when it became known that he had designated his young nephew, Arthur of Brittany, as his successor, John intrigued to gain the throne for himself and turned to Philip of France for aid. Richard was captured by Leopold of Austria while returning from the crusade, and John and Philip planned to divide his possessions but were unable to win either English or Norman support. Upon his return to England in 1194, Richard pardoned John's perfidy and on his death-bed in 1199 persuaded his barons to swear fealty to John, passing over Arthur of Brittany whose claim to the throne was superior. Anjou and Brittany were defeated in their attempt to uphold Arthur's rights and the young prince was taken prisoner. Forced by political necessity to accept John as their sovereign, the barons and the people soon came to despise him for his cowardice, his fits of rage, his vices, his sloth and his ferocity towards his enemies. He was treacherous in his dealings with his supporters, unscrupulous and untrustworthy.

He faced many difficulties in the feud with France, dissensions among his continental possessions, discontent at home and lack of interest in foreign conquest. His divorce from Isabella in 1200 further alienated his barons and his marriage to Isabella of Angoulême, who was engaged to Hugh LeBrun, led to a new revolt against him and he lost his French possessions. His quarrel with Pope Innocent III, his plundering of the clergy, severity to the barons and misgovernment estranged most of his subjects. In 1212 the Pope formally declared him deposed and encouraged the French king to invade England. His fleet was destroyed but in a later battle John was defeated (1214) and the English barons seized the opportunity to end his tyranny. They drew up and forced him to sign at Runnymede on June 15, 1215, the Magna Charta, which secured certain liberties to the people, prohibited unjust taxation and punishment without lawful trial, and provided for other reforms, putting the crown under control of an oligarchical committee. The Pope soon after annulled the charter and war broke out again during which John died on Oct. 19, 1216, but the Magna Charta remained in force and has been confirmed by subsequent English monarchs.

ANDREW JOHNSON   1808–1875

ANDREW JOHNSON, the 17th president of the United States, was born Dec. 29, 1808, at Raleigh, N. C. When he was only four years old his father died, leaving little provision for the family, and at 10 he was apprenticed to a tailor. Even at that early age, he seems to have realized the handicap under which his lack of education would place him and, having by his own efforts learned to read, he spent as much time as he could call his own in study. He worked at his trade in various places and when barely 20, in Greeneville, Tenn., he married Eliza McCardle who thereupon undertook to teach him writing and arithmetic. At about this time he was instrumental in forming an organization of workingmen against the planters; at 22 he was elected mayor of the town, and five years later was sent to the state legislature where he took an active part in framing a new state constitution. In 1841 he was elected to the state senate; two years later to the national House of Representatives where he served for five consecutive terms, and in 1853 he was elected governor of Tennessee, reelected two years later and then sent to the United States Senate. He possessed some skill as a public speaker, having in his early Greeneville days joined a debating society composed mostly of college students. He tried to discourage agitation of the slavery question and although he was himself a slave-owner he strongly opposed secession and worked hard to maintain the integrity of the Union, thereby arousing so much personal hostility that at one time his family was turned out of the house and his own life was endangered. In 1862, after the expiration of his Senate term, he was made military governor of Tennessee and in that capacity continued his efforts to have the state return to the Union.

Two years afterward, he was elected vice president of the United States on the ticket with Abraham Lincoln, becoming president after Lincoln was shot six weeks later. With his well-known attitude toward the secessionists, the radical republicans were confident that he would adopt severe measures toward the South, an expectation which was encouraged by the tenor of his first speech after taking office. His attitude quickly changed, however; he welcomed Virginia back to the Union, opened the way for trading freely with the states which had seceded, and declared an amnesty to all (with a few special groups excepted) who would take an oath of allegiance to the government. All this precipitated a bitter struggle with Congress, which passed several bills over the president's veto, arousing his denunciation; three members of his cabinet resigned and there was general disaffection. He vetoed a resolution that every seceding state must ratify the 14th Amendment before being readmitted to the Union; also acts giving the vote to negroes in new territories, all of which were passed over his veto. In 1867 he was accused of illegally removing Secretary of War Stanton, the only member of his cabinet who failed to support him in his opposition to the radical element. The Senate refused to confirm the removal and Stanton was restored, only to be again removed early in the following year. By this time Congress had shorn the president of practically all his powers and impeachment proceedings were instituted in the House of Representatives. Johnson's defence was that he was attempting to carry out a plan of reconstruction that had been determined upon by President Lincoln. In the trial before the Senate he was acquitted. His last official act as president was to extend, on Christmas Day, 1868, a general pardon to all who had been concerned in secession.

He failed to receive the nomination for reelection and retired to his home in Greeneville. In January, 1875, he was elected United States senator, but on July 31st of that year he died. It is the verdict of history that Johnson was a man of ability and political wisdom who displayed courage in a difficult period, and his exoneration by the Senate is now generally commended.

SAMUEL JOHNSON   1709–1784

THE fame of DR. JOHNSON has outlived his works. His *Rasselas,* written as he tells us, "in the evenings of a week" to pay his mother's funeral expenses, is quite forgotten. His dictionary is only a relic; his *Lives of the Poets* is unknown except to scholars, who usually "damn it with faint praise" or no praise at all. But Dr. Johnson stands a robust figure in the history and literature of his country. DeFoe is known by *Robinson Crusoe;* Cervantes by *Don Quixote* and Bunyan by *Pilgrim's Progress.* But sturdy old Dr. Johnson stands without a prop. It has been urged that the *Life* by Boswell has functioned as a life preserver, but few people read it. Yet Dr. Johnson stands secure unswayed by the winds of time. Such personal fame gives every evidence of permanency.

He was born at Litchfield, England, Sept. 18, 1709, and received his early education in that town under a master who urged him along "the flowery path of knowledge" with the rod, for which the redoubtable old doctor was ever grateful. "He beat me very well," he tells us, adding that without this stimulus "I should have done nothing." The rudiments being thus instilled, he spent about two years learning his father's business of bookseller, which probably included bookbinding for it is stated in a local history that specimens of his work in this craft are still in existence. He probably read more books than he bound and a retentive memory made his intellect a veritable library. At 19 he entered Pembroke College, Oxford, where progress was made difficult by the haunting religious doubts from which so many people suffered in those days. Moreover, his exaggeration of the importance of these questions was complicated by debts and other difficulties. When he was 22 his father died a bankrupt and he was forced to relinquish his hope of taking a degree. He became an usher in a school at Bosworth but, unable to bear the monotony of the life, he went to work for a bookseller in Birmingham where miscellaneous reading took the place of formal education. He was one of those to whom culture was more easily available along this haphazard road.

At 27 he married a widow, a Mrs. Porter, and with the moderate fortune which she brought him he started a school. This proving unprofitable, he sought his fortune in London, accompanied by one of his pupils, also destined to fame, the talented David Garrick. Here he contributed to the *Gentleman's Magazine* and later to *Clive's Magazine,* but his path was not easy, poverty stalked in his wake and it is thought that he often suffered hunger. In 1744 he published his interesting life of the English poet, Richard Savage, whose dramatic career might have been expected to furnish lively reading for the public, but it met with only indifferent success. In 1749 he published what is generally considered the best of his poems, *The Vanity of Human Wishes,* and in the year following started a periodical called *The Rambler,* the contents of which was mostly of his own composition; it lasted but two years. For many weary years amid his adversity he had worked assiduously on a dictionary which was published in 1755 and for many years retained its prestige as an authority. Another periodical, *The Idler,* begun in 1758, also lasted but two years. During its life the story of *Rasselas* was written under the bitter stress of grief and need, an incident which has been more than once used to spur the lagging muse of writers and whip them into a state of laborious concentration.

It was the dark hour before the dawn for Johnson. Through the friendly influence of Lord Bote, the government granted him a pension of 300 pounds a year, and James Boswell, with observant eye and a notebook, entered his life and by continued association with his hero was able to produce that biographical masterpiece which throws a floodlight on the life of Johnson. Mention must be made of the famous Literary Club which included the interesting characters of his time, among whom he reigned a beloved mentor. In 1764 appeared his edition of Shakespeare from which scholars still cull his wise and pithy commentaries. In 1773 he journeyed to the Highlands, accompanied by the indefatigable Boswell and his notebook. In 1781 appeared his splendid work, the *Lives of the Poets*. He died on the 13th of December, 1784, and was appropriately buried in Westminster Abbey.

JOHN PAUL JONES   1747–1792

JOHN PAUL JONES, the earliest of American naval heroes, was born in the parish of Kirkbean, Kirkcudbright, Scotland, in 1747, the son of a landscape gardener named John Paul. At the age of 10 he was apprenticed to a shipmaster. One of his first voyages was to Virginia, following which he was acting midshipman in the royal navy, third mate on a slave ship and first mate on another slaver. Becoming disgusted with the slave trade, he returned to England at the age of 21 on the ship *John* of which he had taken command after the captain and first mate had died on the voyage. He was made master and supercargo of the vessel on which he made two voyages to Tobago and then he purchased the ship *Betsey* and sailed to Tobago on his own account, intending to delay payment to his crew until he had sold the cargo he carried. The crew mutinied, but Jones killed the ringleader and escaped from the ship. There was no admiralty court in Tobago and he fled from the island to escape imprisonment while awaiting trial.

In 1773 his brother, who was a planter in Virginia, died and he inherited the estate and gave his attention to it for a time, taking the surname of Jones, for what reason is not clear. In 1775 at the outbreak of the Revolution he aided the Naval Committee of Congress with advice and was commissioned senior lieutenant of the flagship *Alfred* which he commanded under Commander Hopkins in a successful expedition against New Providence in the Bahama Islands. In May, 1776, he was given command of the *Providence,* convoying supplies for the defence of New York, and in August he received a captain's commission with orders to proceed against British shipping. In seven weeks cruising between Bermuda and Nova Scotia, he took six brigantines, one ship and one sloop, and destroyed six schooners, a ship and a brigantine. Returning from an unsuccessful attempt to free the Americans imprisoned on the Isle Royale, he captured a 16-gun privateer from Liverpool and ran down an army transport with food and clothing for Burgoyne's army.

In 1777 he was given command of the newly built *Ranger* and sailed for France with dispatches for the American commissioners, capturing two prizes on the way. Balked by Britain and France from gaining a ship then building for the colonies in New Amsterdam, Jones at the suggestion of Benjamin Franklin (then in France) sailed again on the *Ranger* with a free hand to follow his own judgment. He surprised the two forts commanding the harbor of Whitehaven, spiked their guns and made an unsuccessful attempt to fire the shipping in the harbor. Four days later he forced the British sloop-of-war *Drake* to strike her colors after an hour's fighting and took the ship as a prize to France where during several months of inactivity he was forced to support himself and his men. Franklin finally obtained an old French ship which Jones refitted and renamed the *Bon Homme Richard*. With the *Alliance,* a new continental frigate, three small French ships and several privateers, he set sail for the Scottish coast in August, 1779. Some of the ships deserted and the commander of the *Alliance* was insubordinate, but an attack was made on Leith which was foiled by contrary winds, although several prizes were taken. Returning to France he encountered the British man-of-war *Serapis* and the ensuing fight, one of the most famous naval battles in history, lasted three and a half hours, when the *Serapis* asked for quarter. The two ships had been lashed together during the battle. The *Bon Homme Richard* sank two days later and Jones took the *Serapis* back to France where Louis XVI presented him with a gold mounted sword and made him a Chevalier of France. His exploits had created great excitement in America and upon his return in 1781 he received a gold medal from Congress which also proposed to create for him the rank of rear admiral. In 1788 Catherine the Great offered him command of the Russian navy, then fighting against the Turks, but because of jealousies and intrigues among the Russian officers he resigned and retired to Paris, where he died in 1792. In 1905, after a long search, his burial place was discovered and his body taken by an American squadron to Annapolis, Md., where it was buried with naval honors.

BEN JONSON   1573–1637

BEN (christened Benjamin) JONSON, English dramatist, was born probably in 1573, in Westminster, of North Country gentry stock. His father died a month before Ben's birth and his mother shortly afterwards married a London master bricklayer. Although Jonson tells us he was "poorly brought up," he attended a Westminster school apparently at the expense of William Camden, a man of great learning who was second master there and under whom he gained a good knowledge of the classics. He was taken from school to work in a bricklayer's yard near Charing Cross, but after a short time joined the English troops who were fighting against Spain in the Netherlands, and returned to London probably in 1592. Little is known of his life in the following years save that he married a woman whom he later described as "a shrew but honest," and from whom he was separated for five years. She bore him a son who died of the plague at the age of seven. He emerged from obscurity in 1597 as player and one of the hack playwrights at the Fortune Theatre, managed by Philip Henslowe.

He first appeared as a master poet-dramatist with *"Every Man in His Humor,"* which scored a triumph in 1598 at the Globe Theatre, with Shakespeare playing in the cast. Soon afterward Jonson became involved in a duel with an actor, Gabriel Spencer, whom he killed and for this he was imprisoned and "brought almost to the gallows." While in prison he fell under the influence of a Catholic priest and embraced Catholicism at a time when to be an adherent of that faith was heresy, but Ben Jonson never lacked courage. Soon after his release from prison *"Every Man Out of His Humor"* was produced with brilliant success. His third play was *Cynthia's Revels,* which was followed by *The Poetaster,* a satire on a one-time friend and collaborator, John Marston, with whom he was later reconciled. His first tragedy, *Sejanus,* a drama of political adventure, was produced in 1603 without much popular approval, although it still holds attraction for the student of English drama. *Volpone, or The Fox,* a comedy, followed in 1605 and met with much success. Jonson was frequently called upon to write court masques, particularly for the weddings of royalty, and in that capacity he was equaled by none. Some of these are of great beauty, notably *The Masque of Hymen,* the *Hue and Cry After Cupid* and *The Masque of Queens.*

Epicoene, or The Silent Woman, produced in 1609, is perhaps the best of his comedies. This was followed by *The Alchemist; Catiline,* a tragedy which aroused the universal admiration of students and classical scholars; and the series of great comedies was brought to a close by his *Bartholomew Fair* in 1614. Although he continued to write for many years, the old vigor and boldness is lacking in such plays as *The Devil is an Ass, The Staple of News, The New Inn, The Magnetic Lady, The Tale of a Tub,* which are the chief among his later works, except for the final delightful pastoral fragment, *The Sad Shepherd.* He was finally ousted from court favor through Inigo Jones, who had assisted him in the mechanics of the production of the court masques, but he continued his many friendships among writers, the great and the learned. He wrote many letters, epigrams, love poems and songs, one of the best known of which is the lyric, *Drink to Me Only with Thine Eyes.*

In 1613 he traveled abroad with the son of Sir Walter Raleigh and wrote an account of the Punic Wars for the latter's *History of the World.* A volume of essays published as *Discoveries,* revealed his graver prose style. He was of a convivial temperament and was usually the center of festivities at the inns where the literati of the day gathered. Poverty and disease were his lot toward the end; he was compelled at times to sell his books; once he lost them in a fire; his insatiable curiosity in every field of learning never left him. He died Aug. 6, 1637, was buried in Westminster Abbey, and the slab over his grave is inscribed "O rare Ben Jonson."

FLAVIUS JOSEPHUS

37 circa–100

FLAVIUS JOSEPHUS (jō sē'fŭs) was a Jewish historian, born at Jerusalem in the year 37 A. D. He was of priestly lineage on his father's side, but his mother was of royal descent. Such knowledge as we have of his life is derived solely from his own autobiography and his other writings. He was well educated, both in Greek and Hebrew literature, and displayed brilliant powers at an early age. Before he was 19 he had made a study of the three Jewish sects, Pharisees, Sadducees and Essenes, and after attending religious lectures for a time he betook himself into the desert and was associated for three years with a certain Banos, who is believed to have been either a disciple of John the Baptist or one of the esthetic sect of Essenes. Returning to Jerusalem he became a member of the Pharisees; at 26 was sent as a delegate to Nero, and was appointed governor of Galilee at the time of the Jewish insurrection against the Romans. He fulfilled his office with wisdom and courage but in the year 67 he was forced to withdraw into the city of Jotapata before the advance of the Roman general Vespasian, and after a desperate struggle lasting some six weeks the city fell. Josephus with a few followers took refuge in a cave but was captured and brought before Vespasian. He tells us that it was only by the ruse of predicting that his captor would one day become emperor of Rome that he escaped being sent to Nero. He was kept under surveillance for three years, and being with the Roman forces when Jerusalem was besieged and taken by Titus he was able to save some of his own relatives from death.

Thereafter he evidently lived in Rome and devoted himself chiefly to study and writing. His *History of the Jewish War* was written both in Hebrew and Greek. The voluminous *Jewish Antiquities* in 20 books gives a detailed history of his race from the earliest times to the end of Nero's reign. *Antiquity of the Jews* is a treatise rich in extracts from earlier historians. His *Autobiography* covers the events of his own life up to the year 90. The date of his death is not known, but there is evidence that he outlived Herod Agrippa II who died about the year 97. Numerous other works which have been attributed to this historian, including a description of Christ which aroused much discussion, are now believed to be the work of other hands.

The writings of Josephus have served as a well of information and reference for later historians and his easy, flowing style has sometimes caused him to be termed the Greek Livy. He had great pride in the history of his race and a genuine love for his people, but he evidently realized the futility of trying to oppose the powerful Romans, and he therefore to some extent became one of them, although in this he may have been actuated partly by the hope that in so doing he might be in a position to be of service to his race. His familiarity with the Greek philosophy and learning is shown in all his work, and doubtless contributed to his almost modern skepticism toward the miracles described in the Old Testament, such as the story of Jonah and the whale, the parting of the Red Sea in order that the Israelites might cross dry shod, and so forth. He evidently regarded Moses as a wise lawgiver, but not as divinely inspired, and in general he appears to have discounted the theory that his people were under the care of a special Providence.

He was three times married and had children by his second and third wives.

JULIUS CAESAR   100 B.C.–44 B.C.

CAIUS (OR GAIUS) JULIUS CAESAR, Roman general and statesman, was the son of a Roman praetor of the same name and was born July 12, 100 B.C. In 83 B.C. he allied himself with the popular party by marrying Cornelia, daughter of Cinna, thus incurring the wrath of the dictator, Sulla, who was Cinna's enemy, and Caesar thereupon withdrew to Asia where he remained until Sulla's death in 78. He was elected pontifex in 74 B.C., and threw himself wholeheartedly into public life.

His aunt, Julia, and his wife, Cornelia, died shortly before he went to Spain in 69 as quaestor, and upon his return to Rome in 67 he married Pompeia, a relative of Pompey. As curile aedile in 65 B.C. he spent great sums on public buildings and games, thus increasing his already great popularity, and in 63 he was made pontifex maximum and then praetor. He is believed to have taken part in Cataline's conspiracy. In 61 he was given charge of the province of Hispania Ulterior, which he quickly pacified, and upon returning to Rome he became consul and succeeded in reconciling Pompey and Crassus, forming with them the First Triumvirate (60 B.C.). He gave his daughter Julia to be Pompey's wife, and himself married Calpurnia.

The Triumvirate assigned to Caesar the provinces of Cisalpine Gaul, Transalpine Gaul and Illyricum, and in 58 he set out on a nine-year campaign devoted to the subjugation and Romanizing of the barbarian hordes inhabiting those provinces. He conquered the Helvetii and Ariovistus, the Belgic confederacy in 57, and the Nervii, Brittany and Normandy in 56, drove two German tribes across the Rhine, and invaded Britain in 55 and again in 54, crossing the Thames and forcing the southeastern part of the island into submission. Returning to Gaul, he faced one insurrection and then another which he finally crushed and exacted a terrible vengeance upon the leaders. He then returned to Italy but in the dead of winter he received word that the whole of Gaul was rising in rebellion under a young warrior named Vercingetorix. He hurried thither, gathered his scattered forces, and by a series of brilliant victories crushed the rebellion and made himself the undisputed master of all Gaul.

Affairs in Rome were troubled; Crassus had fallen in Asia in 53, and Pompey had deserted the democrats and gone over to the aristocratic party. At his bidding the Senate sent an order to Caesar to disband his army, resign his command, and return to Rome. However, supported by his victorious troops, Caesar crossed the Rubicon (a small stream separating Gaul from Italy) and moved on to Rome. Pompey fled to Greece (49 B.C.) and in three months' time Caesar had won all of Italy, and after subduing Pompey's legates in Spain was made dictator. He crossed the Adriatic to meet the greatly superior force of Pompey at Dyrrhachium, where he suffered a severe defeat but this was retrieved on Aug. 9, 48 at Pharsalia, where he utterly routed Pompey's much larger force. Pompey fled to Egypt where he was later murdered.

Caesar was again appointed dictator for one year and consul for five. He went to Egypt where he fell under the spell of Cleopatra (who bore him a son, called Caesarion), and out of love for her he entered upon the Alexandrine War in 47, which placed her on the throne of the Ptolemies. He defeated Scipio and Cato, two of Pompey's generals, in Africa in 46; put down an insurrection in Spain led by Pompey's sons, and received the title "Father of His Country" and "Imperator." He was made dictator for life and consul for ten years, his person was declared divine, his image struck on Roman coins, his statue placed in the temples, and the name of the month of Quintilis was changed to Julius in his honor.

In the midst of far-reaching plans for internal improvements (the founding of libraries, draining of the Pontine marshes, enlarging the harbor of Ostia, etc.), he was stabbed to death in the public square on the Ides (15th) of March, 44 B.C., by a group of aristocratic conspirators led by Brutus and Cassius and including a number of his friends who had been persuaded that he proposed to establish a hereditary monarchy.

Besides being a brilliant general, Caesar excelled as an orator and historian. *His Commentaries on the Gallic and Civil Wars* form an invaluable historical document.

JUSTINIAN I   483–565

JUSTINIAN I (FLAVIUS ANICIUS JUSTINIANUS), popularly known as Justinian the Great, was emperor of the eastern half of the Roman Empire from 527 to 565, succeeding his uncle, the emperor Justin I. He was born of peasant stock (the date of his birth probably May 11, 483), in the village of Tauresium, on the site of which is built the present city of Constantza on the Black Sea. His name is believed to have been originally Uprauda. At an early age he went to Constantinople, the capital of the Byzantine (or eastern Roman) Empire, which was at that time the center of the trade and culture of the East. There he was educated and became accomplished in music, poetry and the arts as well as learned in philosophy, theology and law. After his uncle became emperor, Justinian, declining the post of commander-in-chief of the army, was made consul, and from this influential position in 527 he was raised to be the joint ruler with the emperor, who was then about 75 years old. The aged man died a few months later and Justinian succeeded him as sole ruler. His reign was long and brilliant.

Although his own tastes were not military, he selected the most able generals, notably Belisarius and Narses, and with his army under their command he carried on a successful war with Persia; but hardly had the general rejoicing over its termination ceased when there arose political dissensions among the factions known as the Blue and Green, which almost caused a revolution. Justinian, learning that a rival emperor Hypatius, had been elected, determined to flee the country, but his queen Theodora (a former dancer of obscure origin), a woman of great energy and resolution, persuaded him to stay and fight for his throne. It was due to her spirit and determination that the revolt was put down, although with the sacrifice of many thousands of lives. Through the valiant work of Belisarius the Vandals in Africa were overthrown and their kingdom regained for the empire, which for a time assumed much of its earlier power, not only in Rome and northern Italy but extending into a large part of Spain.

Justinian caused to be erected a large number of public buildings in the various cities of his realm and had a vast amount of effort put into the rebuilding and strengthening of a formidable system of fortifications which extended along the southern and eastern boundaries of his empire. But his greatest claim to fame was in his legislative work. One of his first acts after his accession was to recodify the constitutions of all previous rulers. This code with his own constitution added was published in 528–29. He next caused to be prepared a digest of the existing laws of the realm, with an exhaustive study of judicial opinions and commentaries, so as to simplify and bring into a single treatise all the statutes, which were in a very confused state. This great work consumed four years in preparation and was published from 529 to 533 in 50 volumes (*Digesta Pandecta*). He also undertook and published under the title of *Institutes* a methodical treatise on the laws, intended for the instruction of lawyers and students.

He was an able and enlightened ruler, his personal character commanding the utmost respect, and although his program of public works necessitated a heavy burden of taxation on the people, it is believed that his administration was conducted with a high degree of integrity and justice. The one blot on his record appears to have been his arbitrary attitude of interference in ecclesiastical affairs.

He died on Nov. 14, 565 at the age of 83.

JUVENAL   circa 60–140

JUVENAL (jū′vĕnäl) (DECIMUS JUNIUS JUVENALIS) was a Roman satirist and poet, born at Aquinam in the Volscian country on the estate of his father who was a free Roman citizen. The exact year of his birth is not known, but it was evidently during the reign of the tyrant, Nero, who became emperor in 54 A.D., and there is evidence that he was grown to manhood and writing and practicing declamation during the time of the equally cruel emperor, Domitian. Little is known of his life but he practiced in Rome as an advocate and filled important public posts in his native town. He may have served also as a tribune in the Roman army. He was evidently a man of independent means and is believed to have visited Egypt at some time in his career. Among his friends were Martial, the Roman poet renowned for his wit; Status and probably the rhetorician, Quintilian.

His interest for the modern world lies in the fact that he was the author of sixteen poetic satires which are not only of inestimable value because of the vivid pictures they present of the Roman life of the day, but they are of the highest rank in satirical literature of all time. His style contrasts with that of Horace, the great master in the satire of ridicule, Juvenal being often described as the satirist of indignation. He used his masterly power as a means of attacking the corrupt practices, the crimes and follies and extravagances which were prevalent in that rich and luxurious civilization, and above all the tyrannies and cruelties of those in power which raged unchecked.

Some of the satires were evidently read by the author in public to appreciative audiences. Not until many years after they were written were they published, in five books. The first volume contained five satires, perhaps the most caustic and scathing of all, showing his powers at their highest. It appeared shortly after the accession of Trajan as emperor in 98, but the verses were quite obviously penned during or immediately after the murder, some years previously, of the tyrant Domitian whose reign had been characterized by cruelties and brutalities of the most extravagant kind, often resulting in the execution of innocent citizens, and who was finally killed by a freedman at the instigation of Domitian's wife.

The second book contains one satire directed at women in general. The third and fourth and fifth books appeared after the accession in 117 of Trajan's nephew Hadrian. Seven of the satires constitute moral essays of a general character rather than attacks upon existing evils.

Many translations have been made of Juvenal's work into English. Five of the satires translated by John Dryden were among his best work and Dr. Samuel Johnson paraphrased, or imitated, the third and tenth which are perhaps the best known, for his *London* and *Vanity of Human Wishes*. A complete and faithful edition of the whole sixteen was published by Gifford in 1802. They are rich in pungent epigrams many of which have become household words.

It is reported that certain verses written on an actor by the name of Paris who was a favorite with the emperor Domitian, and which later formed a part of the seventh satire, so aroused the anger of influential persons that when Juvenal was about eighty years of age the emperor was persuaded to banish him to Egypt under the guise of giving him a military appointment in that country. It is believed that Juvenal died of grief shortly afterward.

IMMANUEL KANT   1724–1804

IMMANUEL KANT (känt), one of the greatest philosophers that Germany has ever produced, whose metaphysical and other writings have exerted a profound influence on modern thought, was born on April 22, 1724, at Königsberg, in Prussia, where his father was a saddler. He was of Scottish descent. He attended the university of Königsberg where he was a brilliant student, his interests lying chiefly in such studies as philosophy, theology, mathematics. Indeed, in his early years he intended to enter the church. He took his degree in 1775, having in the meantime spent several years as tutor in various private families, an occupation which he disliked but to which he was forced to resort by financial embarrassment after the death of his father in 1746. Then followed a period of lecturing at the university, his lectures embracing logic, metaphysics, mathematics, politics, anthropology, physical geography, mineralogy; indeed, there seemed hardly any subject too profound to engage his attention. He felt constrained, however, to decline the first real salaried position offered him, that of the chair of poetry in 1762, for which he did not consider himself fitted, but the following year he was glad to accept a moderate salary as assistant librarian.

It was not until he had reached the age of 46 and had acquired a wide reputation for his learning that he was finally appointed professor of logic and metaphysics, and although he received offers from the University at Jena and from other places, he chose to remain at Königsberg throughout the rest of his life. In 1781 appeared his great work, *Critique of Pure Reason,* which occupies a high place in the literature of philosophy. It was followed by *Metaphysics of Ethics, Critque of Practical Reason, Philosophy of Law, Principles of Politics, Critique of Judgment, Cosmogony,* and other works too numerous for mention here, dealing with an infinite variety of subjects.

He developed a system of religion founded upon reason, experience and moral law, which brought him into conflict with the government and the constituted authorities of orthodox religion. After the publication in the *Berlin Journal* of the early part of his book, *On Religion Within the Limits of Reason Alone,* the government forbade publication of the remainder. Kant, however, published it locally with the consent of the Königsberg authorities. Thereafter he was threatened with the displeasure of the king, Frederick William II, and ordered to cease either writing or lecturing on religious subjects, a mandate with which he complied until after the death of the king in 1797, by which time he had practically ceased to lecture on any subject. The following year he issued, *Strife of the Faculties,* recapitulating his earlier religious writings.

He never married and cared little for travel or for the beauties of nature. Although in his earlier years of a social habit and a brilliant conversationalist, he more and more withdrew from the society of friends and devoted himself to his studies and his philosophic speculations, living quietly at Königsberg and ordering his life with a strict regimen amounting almost to asceticism. He was a rapid reader with a prodigious power of absorbing what he read and was well versed in the literature of England and France as well as of his own country. As a lecturer he was popular and injected into his addresses a wit and lightness which were foreign to his written work. Toward his pupils he was kindly but he devoted his greatest efforts to those who were of moderate intellect, believing that those who possessed genius did not need his help and those who were stupid would not profit by it. He was a man of the highest personal character, of simple tastes, an ardent advocate of progress and of personal liberty. His sympathies were with the American colonists in their struggle to throw off the yoke of England, and with the revolutionaries of France. He was small of stature and of delicate physique but the regularity of his life protected him from serious illness despite his long hours of study. After his retirement in 1797 from public work his health and his mental powers began to fail and he died on Feb. 12, 1804, in his 80th year. On the 100th anniversary of his death, a Kantian society was formed to promote the study of his works.

JOHN KEATS · 1795–1821

JOHN KEATS, one of the greatest of English poets despite his short life, was born in London on Oct. 29 or 31, 1795. He was the oldest of the three sons of Thomas Keats, a livery stable keeper. At about eight years old he was placed at a school in Enfield kept by one John Clarke, whose son Charles became his friend and helped to turn his interest toward literature. Thereafter he read widely, particularly Greek mythology, although he never learned the Greek language. While at school he began to write in Latin a prose version of the Æneid, which he finished after leaving school. Except for his absorbing interest in literature he was not particularly studious, but was fond of sports, popular, courageous, of lively disposition and with marked physical beauty. His father died when he was nine years old and his mother, who had married a second stable keeper, died six years later, after which he was taken from school and apprenticed to a surgeon at Edmonton whom he left in 1814 and went to London. Although during the Edmonton period he had become fascinated by Spenser's *Faerie Queen,* and had tried his own hand at writing verse, he continued his medical studies at the London hospitals and for a few years practiced in London.

He had made the acquaintance of Gray and Moore and he now met Shelley, Leigh Hunt and other writers, and the painter Haydon, all of whom gave him added stimulus toward the pursuit of beauty in literature. He lived for a time with Hunt and soon abandoned medicine to devote himself to writing. In 1816 appeared in Hunt's *Examiner* his first published sonnet, beginning, "O, Solitude, if I with thee must dwell," followed by a second, *On First Looking into Chapman's Homer.* Four others quickly followed and in 1817 he published a volume, *Poems by John Keats,* with a dedication to Leigh Hunt. The reading public at that time was under the spell of Scott, Moore and Byron and the new poet's volume attracted little attention. The following year he published his long poem, *Endymion,* dedicated to the memory of Thomas Chatterton. His youngest brother, Thomas, had developed consumption and in March, 1818, he went to Teignmouth to care for him, replacing in the capacity of nurse the third brother, George, who had recently married and was about to sail for America. Nevertheless, a few months later he started on a walking tour with a friend through the lake section of England and into Scotland which proved too fatiguing for him and he was obliged to abandon the trip and return home by boat. The rigors and exposure which he had experienced resulted in his contracting the throat trouble which was the beginning of his declining health, but he nevertheless resumed the care of the sick brother who died in the following December. Certain bitter attacks on his poem appeared in *Blackwood's Magazine* and the *Quarterly Review* shortly after his return to London, and despite the efforts of Shelley and Byron who defended him loyally, his sensitive nature was deeply hurt.

Despite his failing health, poverty and an unfortunate love affair with Miss Fanny Brawne, a seventeen-year old girl with whom he had fallen passionately in love, he continued to write, hoping still to make his living by his poetry, and in 1820 published his third volume, *Lamia and Other Poems,* containing some of the most exquisite of his verse. These poems are free from the affectations which marred his earlier work. The beautiful odes, *On A Grecian Urn, To a Nightingale* and *To Autumn,* are all included in this volume, as well as *Isabel, The Eve of St. Agnes,* and the fragment of *Hyperion.* In September of that year his malady had made such ravages that he sailed for Italy, accompanied by his loyal friend, the artist Joseph Severn, who had undertaken to care for him, and in Rome on Feb. 23, 1821, he died of consumption and was laid to rest near the grave of Shelley in the old Protestant cemetery.

Keats was an artist in the truest sense, and the world lost much by his untimely death. His work abounds with romantic charm, tender pathos and haunting melody. Although he did not live to produce much, his influence upon later English poetry has been greater than that of almost any other one poet. His longer poems, despite their defects, yet contain many passages of rare beauty, and his influence is discernible in the work of Rossetti and Tennyson, as well as Swinburne and perhaps even Browning.

HELEN ADAMS KELLER 1880–

HELEN ADAMS KELLER, whose name is known the world over because of her remarkable intellectual accomplishments despite the handicap of being totally blind and deaf from infancy, was born in Tuscumbia, Ala., on June 27, 1880. Her father was of the family of a colonial governor of Virginia (Alexander Spotswood) and was connected with several other old southern families. Her mother was related to the Hales, Everetts and Adamses of New England. Before the end of her second year an attack of scarlet fever left her deprived of the senses of sight and hearing. When she was eight years old Miss Anne Sullivan (later Mrs. John Macy), a teacher trained at the Perkins Institution for the Blind in Boston, undertook the difficult task of educating this unfortunate child, and through many years of constant companionship this devoted woman accomplished a seeming miracle. Miss Sullivan had herself been partially blind from early childhood. She came of an obscure Irish family in Massachusetts and after an unfortunate and neglected childhood had been sent in 1880, the year of Helen Keller's birth, to the Perkins school, where Dr. Samuel G. Howe was accomplishing such marvelous results with the deaf blind girl, Laura Bridgman.

Arriving at Tuscumbia, Miss Sullivan took charge of her little pupil, a headstrong, rebellious child whose disabilities had made it impossible to give her any training. Gradually she gained the child's love; the slow and laborious process of learning the finger language was accomplished, the Braille system of reading at length mastered, and the girl learned to write. She then resolved that she would also learn to talk. She and her teacher had spent much time during the years between 1888 and 1893 at the Perkins Institution and she was now placed under Miss Sarah Fuller at the Horace Mann school where, in an incredibly short space of time, she became able to speak intelligibly. The ability to enunciate was gained largely through feeling the vocal cords of her teacher. She spent several years at the Wright-Humason and Cambridge schools and at the age of 20 was able to enter Radcliffe College fom which she was graduated after the usual period of four years.

In the years following she turned to literature and became widely known as a writer and lecturer, her principal theme being her own life experience and the possibilities for a full and rich life for others similarly handicapped. She attained a high degree of culture, mastered several languages, and is an outstanding instance of the remarkable progress that can be achieved against apparently unsurmountable obstacles. One of the first occasions on which she spoke in public was before a group of physicians in Boston in 1912 when to their amazement she addressed them intelligibly in three different languages. She thereafter took a course of instruction at the Boston Conservatory of Music.

She served as a member of the Massachusetts Commission for the Blind and on various other committees. Her autobiography, *The Story of My Life,* is an inspiring account of her struggle and achievement. Other writings are *Optimism* (1903); *The World I Live In* (1908) *The Song of the Stone Wall* (1910); *Out of the Dark* (1913); *Midstream* and *My Religion;* and many contributions to magazines. Always on her lecture tours and on her foreign travels she has been accompanied by her inseparable friend and teacher, Mrs. Macy.

THOMAS À KEMPIS   circa 1380–1471

THOMAS HEMERKEN (OR HAMMERCHEN), known as Thomas à Kempis (Thomas of Kempen), was a German monk and religious writer, born about 1380 in Kempen near Düsseldorf, Germany. His father was a peasant and his mother conducted a school for the younger children of Kempen. At the age of 12 he was sent to a school in the Dutch city of Deventer, where he was educated in an atmosphere of mystical theology and practical benevolence. Gerhard Groot, founder of the school, and Florentius Radewyn, his teacher, were his heroes but he was a quiet, bookish person and did not, like them, become a man of affairs or an educational reformer. When through a dream he was convicted of sin and convinced of God's grace, Radewyn advised him to embrace a monkish life and sent him to Zwolle, where Thomas' brother John was prior of the new convent of Mount St. Agnes. He entered the convent in 1399, took the vows, was ordained a priest and in 1425 was made sub-prior. Almost all of his quiet life was spent in this convent where he died on Aug. 8, 1471. After two or three removals his remains found a final resting place in 1897 beneath a beautiful monument in St. Michael's Church at Zwolle.

The monks of Mount St. Agnes gained a livelihood by copying missals, books of devotions and other manuscripts, and Thomas à Kempis spent many arduous years in that work during which he copied a famous manuscript Bible. He did much original writing, the work upon which his fame principally rests being *The Imitation of Christ*. This book is one of the most famous in theological history and is said to have been translated into more languages than any other work save the Bible. It has appeared in over 2000 editions. The first English translation was published in London in 1502. There has been much controversy over its authorship but scholars now generally recognize it as the work of à Kempis.

During his 72 years in the convent of Mount St. Agnes he wrote biographies of his Deventer school heroes, Radewyn and Groot, of Groot's original disciples, and of the Flemish Ste. Louise. He wrote also many tracts on the monastic life, several collections of sermons, some letters and hymns and tracts for children. Among his works are *The Monks' Alphabet, The Discipline of the Cloisters, A Dialogue of Novices, The Life of the Good Monk, On Poverty, Humility and Patience, A Manual of Doctrine for the Young, The Garden of Roses, The Soul's Soliloquy.*

He was a small, ruddy-faced man, a true mystic, rather helpless outside of his cubiculum at the convent, absent-minded and simple in regard to worldly affairs but devoted in his duties as sub-prior and excelled by none in his devotion to the godly life.

JOHANN KEPLER 1571–1630

JOHANN KEPLER, German astronomer, was born at Weil, Württemberg, Dec. 27, 1571, son of a soldier of fortune. An attack of smallpox in his fourth year left him with crippled hands and permanently injured eyesight, despite which he devoted his life to researches which led to great advances in astronomical science. In 1584 he was sent to the seminary of Adelberg, with a view to a theological career; two years later to the academy of Maulbronn, and in 1589 he was admitted to the University of Tübingen where he studied the Copernican principles of astronomy. From 1594 to 1600 he held the chair of astronomy at Gratz, where his duties were mostly of an astrological nature and where he acquired belief in an abstract intelligible reason for the existence of the universe, believing that he had found the cause in the relation of the "five regular solids," and in the number and distances of the planets. The publication of his views at Tübingen in 1596 brought him into correspondence with Tycho Brahe and Galileo, the two most famous astronomers of the age.

He left Gratz not long after this due to religious difficulties and became assistant to Brahe in his observatory near Prague. Emperor Rudolph II made him imperial mathematician following Brahe's sudden death in 1601, and entrusted him with the task of completing Brahe's "Rudolphine" tables. He published a few treatises on astrology to preserve a grain of truth he thought to have discovered in it, and to please the Emperor, but did not neglect the chief purpose of his life—the foundation of a new astronomy based upon physical causes and not upon hypotheses. With this end in view he made a study of optics and made public in 1604 important discoveries in the theory of vision and an approach to the true law of refraction. His investigation of the orbit of Mars was published in 1609 in *Astronomia Nova,* in which two of the main principles of modern astronomy were set forth—the laws of elliptical orbits and of equal areas —as well as new truths in regard to gravity, and the ascribing of tides to lunar attraction. He also originated a theory of vortices, similar to that later adopted by Descartes. In 1610 he obtained one of Galileo's telescopes and in his *Dioptrice* (1611) he explained the theory of refraction by lenses, and suggested the principle of the "astronomical" or inverting telescope.

He was retained as court astronomer and became mathematician to the states of Upper Austria. He published several essays to prove that the birth of Christ had taken place five years earlier than the accepted date. Later publications include *Nova Stereometria Dolorium,* which gives him rank as one of the discoverers of the infinitesimal calculus; *De Cometis, De Harmonice Mundi,* in which he announced the discovery of the "third law"—the connection between planetary periods and distances; *Epitome Astronomiae Copernicanae,* in which great prominence was given to "physical astronomy;" and *Chilias Logarithorum.* In 1627 he published the *Rudolphine Tables,* which for a century ranked as the best aid to astronomy.

In 1597 he had married an heiress, Barbara von Mühleck, who died fourteen years later and he afterward married Susanna Reutlinger, who outlived him. He died at Ratisbon on Nov. 15, 1630.

RUDYARD KIPLING 1865–

RUDYARD KIPLING, English writer who won distinction at an early age by his stories of India and by his poetry, and who became one of the most popular authors of the 19th century, was born in Bombay on Dec. 30, 1865, the son of John Lockwood Kipling, a well known artist. He was educated in England and upon his return to India he became sub-editor, at the age of 17, of the Lahore *Civil and Military Gazette*. His first published book was a volume of verse, *Departmental Ditties,* issued in 1886. The following year appeared a volume of short stories, *Plain Tales from the Hills,* collected, as was the book of verse, chiefly from his contributions to the paper on which he worked. In 1888–89 he published six paper-covered volumes in Wheeler's *Railway Library; Soldiers Three, The Story of the Gadsbys, In Black and White, Under the Deodars, The Phantom 'Rickshaw* and *Wee Willie Winkie.* These tales were written before he had reached the age of 24 and among them is some of his best work, notably in *Soldiers Three,* introducing *Terence Mulvaney* who has become one of the outstanding characters in fiction and carried Kipling's name around the world.

During the years 1887 to 1889 he traveled in India, China, Japan and America, sending letters back to his old newspaper in Lahore which were later published in book form under the title *From Sea to Sea.* Reaching London in 1890 he suddenly found himself famous. Another volume of stories, *Life's Handicap* (1891) contained some of the best of his Indian tales. His first novel, *The Light that Failed,* was published in the same year, after having first appeared with a different ending in *Lippincott's Magazine.* It was dramatized in 1905 and acted by Johnston Forbes-Robertson in England and America. Kipling, however, showed a greater mastery of the short story and the ballad than of the novel. He was an outspoken Imperialist and his poetry at times took on a political and controversial tone that marred its popularity somewhat. In his prose he became more consciously literary and studied, with the result that his later tales lacked the popularity accorded to all of his earlier work.

To the *National Observer* he contributed a series of *Barrack Room Ballads,* published in book form in 1892, which made him outstanding among younger English poets. In several of these he introduced the note that was to dominate much of his verse and some of his fiction for several years—the ocean and the engine room. Two of his most famous poems, however, are *The Recessional,* written for Queen Victoria's Diamond Jubilee in 1897, and *The White Man's Burden.*

For four years he lived in the United States where he married in 1892 Caroline Starr Balestier, with whose brother, Wolcott, he collaborated on the Indian novel, *The Naulahka. Many Inventions* (1893) contains some of his finest short stories. Perhaps his widest popularity was won with *The Jungle Book* and *The Other Jungle Book* (1894–95) which introduced him as a prince of story-tellers to English-speaking youth throughout the world. A volume of poems, *The Seven Seas* (1896) was followed by *Captains Courageous,* a novel of the Newfoundland fishing banks; *The Day's Work,* short stories; *Stalky & Co.,* stories of life in a boys' school; *The Five Nations,* poems; *Kim,* a study of India in novel form, and probably the best picture of India ever written; *Just So Stories* for young children; *Traffics and Discoveries, Puck of Pook's Hill, Actions and Reactions, Rewards and Fairies, Debits and Credits,* all collections of short stories.

He refused the offer of a baronetcy, but accepted the Nobel award for literature in 1907. *The Irish Guards in the Great War* was published in 1925.

EARL KITCHENER   1850–1916

HORATIO HERBERT KITCHENER, one of the most brilliant military men of England, was born at Bally Longford, Kerry, Ireland, June 24, 1850, the son of Lieut.-Col. H. H. Kitchener. He entered the Royal Military Academy at Woolwich in 1868 and became second lieutenant of the Royal Engineers in 1871. While his parents were living in Dinan in France, he had volunteered in 1870 for service in the army of the Loire in the Franco-German War. In 1883 he was promoted to a captaincy and attached to the Egyptian army then being reorganized under British officers. He served in the force on the Nile, was breveted Major and Lieutenant-Colonel, and was Governor-General of the Eastern Sudan from 1886 to 1888, and Adjutant-General of the army from 1889 to 1892 when he became Sirdar (commander) of the Egyptian army. After three years devoted to reorganizing the Egyptian army, he proceeded against the Mahdists in the Sudan, breaking their power and ending the River War by the victory of Omdurman, Sept. 2, 1898, for which he was raised to the peerage as

Baron Kitchener of Khartoum, received the thanks of Parliament, the K.C.B., and a grant of 30,000 pounds.

While still Sirdar, he was appointed chief-of-staff to Lord Roberts in South Africa and promoted to Lieutenant-General. He served in the campaign of Paardeberg, the advance on Bloemfontein and the advance to Pretoria. Upon Roberts' being recalled to England in December, 1900, he became commander-in-chief, receiving the local rank of General. He was largely responsible for the successful outcome of the war with the Boers and the acceptance of the peace terms in May, 1902. On returning to England he received an enthusiastic welcome, was made a Viscount, received the Order of Merit and a grant of 50,000 pounds. He then went to India as Commander-in-Chief of the Army of the East Indies and carried out many administrative reforms. Leaving India in 1909, he was made Field-Marshal and succeeded the Duke of Connaught as Commander-in-Chief and High Commissioner in the Mediterranean. He visited Japan, Australia and New Zealand, helping to formulate plans for defence of the two latter islands. In 1911 he became British agent and consul-general in Egypt and helped that country safely through the Tripoli and Balkan Wars, developing it commercially and financially.

He visited England in 1914, was created Earl by King George and was on board a Channel boat to return when the Prime Minister asked him to stay in England. Three days later he took over the seals of the War Office. Believing that the World War, then beginning, would last for at least three years, he laid plans for an army of 70 divisions. In June, 1915, he established the Ministry of Munitions to keep the British army supplied with guns and ammunition. His extraordinary organizing ability and his prestige with the people enabled him to develop the military power of England; his long friendship for France helped greatly in establishing friendly relationships between the armies of the two countries; and he supplied the almost weaponless Russian forces with British guns and ammunitions. His influence in Russia was amazing. In May, 1916, the Czar urged him to visit Russia, promising that his advice would be followed in full, even if it included the transfer of certain controls into British hands.

On June 5, 1916, at Scapa Flow in the Orkney Islands he embarked on H.M.S. Hampshire, bound for Archangel, only to meet a tragic death when the cruiser struck a mine and went down with practically all on board. On Dec. 15, 1925, a memorial chapter in St. Paul's Cathedral was dedicated to Earl Kitchener and to all who laid down their lives in the World War. Kitchener never married.

JOHN KNOX   1505?–1572

John Knox, leading spirit of the Reformation in Scotland, was born at or near Haddington, Scotland, in 1505 or a few years later. He attended the Haddington schools and then probably the Glasgow University. He was originally of the Roman Catholic faith, but while acting as a tutor in 1544 he became acquainted with the preacher, George Wishart, who was full of zeal for the Lutheran reformation, and allied himself to Wishart and his cause. In March, 1545, Wishart was arrested and burned and in May Cardinal Beaton, who had been largely responsible for his arrest, was assassinated in his own castle of St. Andrews. There Knox took refuge and devoted himself to the preaching of Protestant doctrines. The castle was surrendered to the French a few months later; Knox was taken prisoner and for 18 months served in the French galleys. That experience undermined his health but not his zeal. He was liberated in 1549 at the intercession of King Edward VI and made his home in England for the next four years, taking a prominent part in the Reformation as one of Edward's six chaplains and in close intercourse with Archbishop Cranmer of Canterbury and other reformers. He was associated with Cranmer in the drawing up of the 42 Articles and was influential in obtaining the adoption of the 38th Article which committed the Church of England to the Genevan doctrine of the Eucharist. He preached in many places.

Upon the accession of Queen Mary, he fled to Geneva where he was pastor of an English congregation of refugees. He went back to Scotland in 1555, made various preaching journeys and returned to Geneva in July of the following year. There he fell under the influence of John Calvin. His *First Blast of the Trumpet against the Monstrous Regiment of Women* was published in 1558. The previous year the advocates of the new faith in Scotland had bound themselves together by the First Covenant and in 1558 they summoned Knox to help them in the struggle in Scotland. He soon made himself leader of the party and won Perth and St. Andrews as well as a strong following in Edinburgh. The regent, Mary of Guise, subsidized by France, was able to keep the reformers from gaining a stronghold, and the Scottish Protestants, chiefly through the influence of Knox, got help from England against the French invasion. The treaty of Leith and the death of the Regent gave them the upper hand and Parliament ordered the ministers to draw up a Confession of Faith which established Protestantism in Scotland. The first *Book of Discipline,* with liberal suggestions for the religious and educational organization of the country, and the *Confession of Faith of the Reformed Kirk* were largely formulated by Knox.

Strife broke out afresh in 1561 with the return of the Catholic Mary Queen of Scots and Knox became an uncompromising antagonist of the young queen throughout the six years of her reign. Aroused to wrath by the celebration of mass in Holyrood Chapel, he delivered a sermon in St. Giles which led to the first of his interviews with the Queen. He was so bitter and unyielding in his opposition to her that he alienated even many of the Protestant leaders and for a time he retired from preaching. After Mary's marriage to Darnley, these breaches were healed and he again became active. The Protestant party gained control of the government following Darnley's murder, Mary's marriage to Bothwell and her flight and imprisonment in England. The acts of 1560 in favor of the Reformed religion were put into effect under the regency of Murray whose murder in 1570 and the formation of a strong party in favor of Mary again aroused hostility toward Knox who fled to St. Andrews for safety. Although suffering from a stroke of apoplexy his will and courage were indomitable. He preached a last sermon to his congregation at St. Giles on Nov. 9, 1572. On the 24th of that month he died and was buried in the churchyard of St. Giles.

He had married, probably in 1553, Margery Bowes who died in 1560 and four years later he married a 16 year old girl, Margaret Stewart. His *History of the Reformation of Religion in the Realm of Scotland* includes his own biography. He was a man of deep and stern convictions, fearless and violent in carrying out what he believed to be the right.

ROBERT KOCH   1843–1910

THE name of ROBERT KOCH (kŏk) is one of the most distinguished in the annals of bacteriological science. It was he who isolated the bacilli of tuberculosis, a momentous discovery which has given new direction to the treatment of that insidious malady. He was born at Clausthal, in the province of Hanover, in Germany, in 1843 and after studying medicine at the University of Göttingen, practiced his profession in several towns, settling finally at Wollstein, where he devoted his time increasingly to bacteriology. It is said that while he was still an unknown country doctor his thrifty wife, in order that he might pursue the studies which so interested him, saved enough money to buy him a microscope and thus enabled him to start on his great career.

In 1876 he published the results of his study of anthrax, a disease chiefly affecting animals, but sometimes also man. This, and his work on traumatic infections (1878) aroused keen interest in scientific circles and stimulated research in the bacteriological field. In 1880 he was appointed a member of the Imperial Health Board at Berlin, a post which facilitated his researches, and it was in 1882 that he succeeded in isolating the tubercle bacillus. To render visible these pernicious micro-organisms involved much ingenious preparation and patient experimentation, in which this resourceful scientist was the pioneer, and his discovery is one of the epoch-making achievements of medical science, making possible other discoveries and opening the way for a hopeful campaign against the enemies of suffering humanity. For some years the infectious nature of tuberculosis had been strongly suspected by scientists, but it remained for Koch to establish this beyond all doubt.

In 1883 as the head of a group of distinguished scientists sent by the German government to study cholera in Egypt and India, Koch was conspicuously instrumental in discovering the germ of that disease. Upon his return in the following year, he was rewarded with a grant of 100,000 marks and somewhat later received appointment as professor in the University of Berlin and director of the new Hygienic Institute. About 1890 he developed a "lymph" or "paratoloid," a substance prepared from the tubercle bacilli itself, which for a time it was thought would prove a prompt cure for the dread disease. Dr. Koch himself was very conservative in his estimates of its effectiveness, but news of the discovery leaked out through a too-sanguine student and many physicians as well as patients went to Berlin to take advantage of the new treatment, which subsequently was proved to be of aid in diagnosis although not of pronounced remedial benefit. This tuberculin found its greatest use in the testing of animals intended to be used for food. Dr. Koch held the belief that tuberculosis in cattle is an entirely different disease from tuberculosis in humans and that, therefore, humans are less likely to be infected from milk and meat than from association with other human beings who have the disease. A conference in London in 1901 at which he advanced this belief led to the formation of a British royal commission to study the subject.

In several visits to Africa during the years between 1896 and 1906 he made extensive studies of the cattle plague in South Africa, of the causes of malaria, so prevalent in German East Africa, and of the sleeping sickness, which had made alarming ravages in West Africa since the early part of the 19th century. His investigations demonstrated the fact that this disease is communicated by certain species of the African tsetse fly, which at the moment of biting transmits the parasites (trypanosomes) to human beings. Dr. Koch was awarded the Nobel prize for medicine in 1905 and was the recipient of many other honors. Throughout the years of his great work in behalf of humanity he published many scholarly works, chiefly on bacteriological and kindred subjects, which are too many to enumerate here, but which have been of inestimable value to the medical profession. Six weeks before his death his last article on *The Epidemiology of Tuberculosis* was read before the Berlin Academy of Sciences.

He died from heart disease on April 7, 1910, at Baden-Baden, and his body, at his own request, was cremated.

TADEUSZ KOSCIUSZKO   1746–1817

TADEUSZ ANDRZEJ BONAWENTURA KOSCIUSZKO, (kŏs chōōsh'kŏ), a great Polish patriot, was born Feb. 12, 1746 at Mereczowszczyzna, near Vovgorod in Western Russia. He was of an old and noble, but impoverished, family and his father was sword-bearer of the palatinate of Brzesc. He entered the corps of cadets at Warsaw and attracted the attention of Prince Adam Casimir Czartoryski, through whose influence he was sent to Germany, Italy and France to pursue his military education at the expense of the state. At Brest, he studied fortifications and naval tactics, returned to Poland in 1774 with the rank of captain of artillery and became tutor to the daughters of the Grand Hetman, Sosnowski of Sosnowica. He planned to elope with the youngest of the daughters but they were discovered and he was set upon and wounded by the father's servants. A little later in the same year (1776) he went to America and joined the colonies fighting for their independence from the British where he proved himself an excellent soldier and became colonel of artillery. He distinguished himself with General Gates' army near Saratoga, N. Y., where he was largely responsible for the strategic position taken at the Battle of Bemis Heights. He was chief engineer in constructing the West Point fortifications and later became adjutant to Washington. In reward for his services the United States in 1783 granted him American citizenship, an annual pension with landed estates, the rank of brigadier-general and the thanks of Congress.

He returned to Poland in 1786; three years later was made major-general in the army and gave valuable service in the war with Russia following that country's repudiation of the constitution of May, 1791. He was among the generals who resigned their commissions when the King surrendered and Poland was divided and for a time he lived in Leipzig with other Polish *emigrés*. In 1793 he went to Paris and endeavored to win France to the support of the Polish cause. Upon his return to Leipzig he became dictator and commander of the national armies. In April, 1794, with a force of some 4000 men, poorly equipped, he overwhelmed 6000 Russians who were marching against Cracow and established a temporary government. He was unprepared, however, for a sustained struggle; the country was poverty-stricken and he was placed almost immediately on the defensive. In June his army was defeated by the Russians, greatly aided by the Prussians, and retreated to Warsaw. Polish forces were defeated at Kholm the following week and the Prussians occupied Cracow. Meanwhile, the Warsaw jails were broken into by a mob and the political prisoners murdered. The ringleaders were summarily punished by Kosciuszko and 10,000 of the people were drafted into his army. Dissension in Polish governmental circles broke out; Warsaw was besieged and Kosciuszko defended it with energy and brilliancy, but his troops outside were attacked and defeated. In October of the same year at Maciejowice the Poles suffered defeat at the hands of an army three times their own strength, Kosciuszko was badly wounded, captured and held prisoner in Russia until 1796 when the new Czar Paul liberated him, gave him an estate and offered him his sword, but Kosciuszko refused it with the reply, "I have no more need of a sword as I have no longer a country." He afterward returned to the Czar the estate and a sum of money which had accompanied it.

He visited America and lived in Philadelphia until the passage by Congress of the Alien Act in 1798 after which he went to Paris. He emancipated the serfs on his estate in Poland shortly before a fall from his horse in Switzerland caused his death on Oct. 15, 1817. His body was buried at Cracow beside that of John Sobieski, who had been king of Poland in the 17th century.

Kosciuszko was a thorough democrat believing in absolute legal equality, but he was often forced to compromise because of the strong aristocratic prejudices which prevailed among his countrymen.

LOUIS KOSSUTH   1802–1894

Louis (Lajos) Kossuth, Hungarian patriot and leader of the revolution against Austria and the Hapsburgs, was born at Monok near Zemplin, Hungary, in 1802 and was the son of a poor Protestant family of noble rank. He studied law and practiced that profession for a time. In 1832 he was deputy in the Diet of Presburg and edited a Liberal newspaper which was not allowed to be printed under Austrian law, but had to be copied by hand. He afterwards lithographed a newspaper for circulation which caused his arrest and imprisonment in 1837. Upon his liberation in 1840 he became editor of the *Pesti Hirlap,* a journal through which he spread views too liberal for the nobles, but appealing strongly to the public. In 1847 he was returned by Pest to the Diet where he quickly became leader of the opposition and worked to do away with feudal privileges, and for the freedom of the press and the uplifting of the common people.

The French Revolution of 1848 spurred him on to demand an independent government for Hungary. As head of the Committee of National Defence he entered with characteristic energy upon measures to prepare the country for the war to which he was urging it. It was chiefly due to his influence and his standing throughout Hungary that the National Assembly at Debreczin in April, 1849, declared the end of the Hapsburg dynasty and the independence of Hungary.

He was elected governor of the new republic and sought by every means in his power to persuade the powers of western Europe to intervene in behalf of a free Hungary. His quest proved vain and feeling that disagreements between himself and Arthur Görgei, who had inflicted a series of defeats upon the Austrians, were damaging to the national cause, he resigned the dictatorship in favor of Görgei. Only a few days afterward the latter was forced to surrender with 24,000 troops to a greatly superior army under the Russian commander, Rüdiger, at Villagos, and the revolution collapsed. Kossuth himself fled to Turkey where he was held a prisoner by the Turkish authorities which, however, refused to extradite him although both Russia and Austria demanded it. Influential British and Americans went to his aid and Turkey liberated him in September 1851. He was received in England with hospitality and sympathy and then visited the United States where he was acclaimed as a hero and a fighter against oppression. From 1852 until 1859 he spent most of his time in England. At the beginning of the Franco-Italian war against Austria in 1859, he proposed to Louis Napoleon to instigate an uprising against Austria in Hungary. He bitterly resented the peace of Villafranca which ended his country's war against Austria. In 1861 and again in 1864 he attempted to arouse his countrymen against Austria but was unsuccessful.

Following the reconciliation of Hungary with the Hapsburg dynasty in 1867, he gave up all activity in political affairs, refused a seat in the Diet although elected to it and retired to Turin. A general amnesty was declared later that year, but he refused to avail himself of it, continued his self-imposed exile and devoted himself to writing an autobiography, "Memories of My Exile," three volumes of which appeared between 1880 and 1882, with subsequent volumes in 1890. In the later years of his life, he advocated a federation of Danubian nationalities, reversing the intolerance of his earlier views. The law of 1879, depriving of citizenship all Hungarians who had voluntarily been absent from the country for ten years, made his exile permanent. A completed manuscript history of Hungary was found among his effects following his death at Turin, March 20, 1894. His body was taken to Budapest where it was buried with solemnity amid the mourning of the entire nation.

PAUL KRUGER   1825–1904

STEPHANUS JOHANNES PAULUS KRUGER, later known as Paul Kruger (and more familiarly as "Oom Paul"), President of the South African Republic, was born in Colesberg, Cape Colony, Oct. 10, 1825, of Huguenot ancestry and was a member of the narrow and puritanical Dopper sect. At the age of 13, three years after the family had moved from Cape Colony to the territory north of the Orange River, he took part in the crushing of the Zulu king, Dingaan. Constantly trekking and hunting as a youth, he had little opportunity for education, his reading being confined chiefly to the Old Testament. When he was 14 the family settled north of the Vaal River and was among the founders of the South American Republic, later known as the Transvaal. At 20 he was a field cornet and at 27 had a command in an expedition against the Bechuana chief, Sechele. His hunting trips took him as far north as the Zambesi and in 1853 he was a member of the expedition against Montsioa. In 1852 the Transvaal obtained recognition of its independence from Great Britain and Kruger later joined forces with M. W. Pretorius in an attempt to abolish district governments, overthrow the Orange Free State and federate the two countries. The result was a fruitless raid into the Orange Free State.

The factional strife ended in 1864; Pretorius was elected president of the Transvaal, and Kruger was made commander-general of the republic's army. The boundary dispute with Great Britain, ended by the Keate award in 1871, was so unsatisfactory to the Transvaal that Pretorius and his party fell, and Thomas François Burgers was elected president. Kruger devoted his energies to undermining Burgers' authority and the dissension led to the annexation of the Transvaal by Great Britain in 1877. He accepted office under the British, but continued his agitation for the restoration of political independence and was a member of two deputations sent to London for that purpose. In 1878 he was dismissed from service by the

British administrator. Two years later came the Boer rebellion and after the defeat of the British at Majuba, Kruger with General Piet Joubert and M. W. Pretorius negotiated the terms of peace on which the Pretoria convention of 1881 was drafted. He was elected president of the Transvaal in 1883, and in November of that year visited England and worked for the London convention, granted in 1884 by Lord Derby on behalf of the British government. He was reelected in 1888 and devoted himself to obtaining political monopoly for the Boers by disenfranchising laws aimed against the Uitlander population.

In the election of 1893 his opponent, Joubert, charged the government with tampering with the ballots which returned Kruger to office by a majority of about 700, but his appeal to the Volksraad failed. Kruger continued his policy of enlarging the frontiers of the Transvaal at the expense of Great Britain, but in 1895 was checked in his endeavor to reach the sea at Delagoa Bay. The Jameson raid strengthened his hold over his people and his stand against the Uitlanders. He was elected president for the fourth time in 1898 by a great majority. The uncompromising attitude of the British and his refusal to yield led to the Boer War of 1899. After the British had occupied Bloemfontein and Pretoria in 1900 he went to Europe and tried in vain to induce the European powers to interfere in behalf of the Boers. He lived at Utrecht in the Netherlands for a time and there dictated his book, *The Memoirs of Paul Kruger,* published in 1902. He died at Clarens on Lake Geneva, July 14, 1904, and was buried in Pretoria the following year.

He had married a Miss Du Plessis, of a famous French family, and later married a niece of his first wife. Several children were born of the second union.

KUBLAI KHAN   1216–1294

Kublai Kahn (koo′blī kän′), Emperor and founder of the Mongol dynasty in China, was the most eminent of the descendants of Jenghiz Khan. He was born in 1216, the second son of Tulē, youngest of the four sons of Jenghiz. With his younger brother, Hulagu, he participated in Jenghiz's last campaign (1226–27) although then not yet in his teens. Jenghiz had conquered Cathay, or northern China, and in 1235 Kublai was named as his brother's lieutenant in the effort to subjugate that part of the Chinese Empire south of the Yangtsze-kiang River. He directed his first attack against the far western province of Yunnan. He captured

Tali Fu and then returned north, leaving the war to be carried on by one of his generals. Following the death of his brother, Mangu, then Khan, on a campaign in west China, Kublai assumed the succession (1259), which led to wars with his brother, Arikbugha, and his cousin, Kaidu, retarding the campaign against China.

In 1260 he drove the Tatars out of north China and took possession, selecting, to the northeast of the old city of Yenking, a rectangular plot 18 miles in circumference where he founded his new capital, Kaan-baligh or Kambalu ("city of Khan"). From this beginning grew the modern city of Peiping (Peking). In 1267, having established his capital, he renewed the war against south China, but his campaign was made difficult by the stubborn resistance of the defenders of the twin cities of Siang-yang and Fen-chēng, on opposite sides of the river Han, which commanded the approach to the valley of the Yangtsze-kiang. He besieged the two cities for five years, after which his lieutenant, Bayan, took command and forced their surrender in 1276. The young emperor and his mother were sent as prisoners to Kaan-baligh, but two younger princes who had been sent south before the fall of the capital were successively proclaimed emperor by their followers, their attempts to regain their empire continued until 1279, when they were finally defeated in the province of Kwang-tung. Kublai thus became the ruler of all China. His sway was disputed by princes of his house in Turkistan, but was acknowledged by princes on the Volga river, whose dominion extended to the Polish frontier, and by the family of his brother, Hulagu, whose territory extended from the Oxus to the Arabian desert. He was the nominal sovereign of more people than had ever before acknowledged the authority of one man.

He enlisted among his ministers, generals and scientists from many countries; from Venice that great traveler, Marco Polo, who spent several years at his court and left a vivid description of its splendor. Kublai Khan encouraged Chinese literature and culture which were far beyond that of his own people, and sent emissaries to the pope inviting the sending of Christian missionaries to educate his people in a higher form of religion, but failing in that, Buddhism, as it existed in Tibet, received his favor. He was an able organizer and administrator, encouraged commerce and agriculture, and put into effect a great paper currency system. His court was one of splendid entertainment, and he undertook great hunting expeditions. His repeated attempts to conquer Japan were unavailing and in 1281, after extensive preparations, resulted in a great disaster to his arms. His attack on Champa (Cochin China) failed, but he overran Burma as far as the Irrawaddy delta. In the last year of his reign he sent an expedition against Java. His envoy was sent back in ignominy and

Kublai equipped a great armament to seek vengeance; it met with some success but was compelled to sail for home after losing 3000 men.

He died at Peking in 1294; his empire fell into the hands of less capable rulers and in 1368 the Yuen dynasty, which he had founded, came to an end.

MARQUIS DE LAFAYETTE 1757–1834

MARIE JOSEPH PAUL ROCH YVES GILBERT DU MOTIER, MARQUIS DE LA-FAYETTE, French general and statesman whose name is held in grateful remembrance by all Americans for the part he played in the War of Independence, was born at the Château of Chavaniac in Auvergne, France, on Sept. 6, 1757. His father was killed in 1759 and his mother died in 1770, leaving him an orphan with a princely fortune. At 16 he married Marie Adrienne Françoise de Noailles and the same year entered the Guards, later becoming a captain of dragoons. At the outbreak of the American Revolution he determined to go to the aid of the colonists and in defiance of the king who forbade him to leave the country he fitted out a ship for the expedition. At the instance of the British, orders were issued to seize the ship and he was arrested. He had his ship sent to a Spanish port, escaped from prison in disguise and sailed in April, 1777, landing in Georgetown, S. C., with eleven supporters, among whom was the Baron de Kalb. Reaching Philadelphia, he presented himself before Congress with credentials from Silas Deane, American agent in France, and offered to serve as a simple volunteer, but Congress, on July 31, passed a resolution giving him the rank and commission of a major-general. He met Washington the following day and was soon attached to his staff, the two becoming lifelong friends.

His arrival did much to hearten the discouraged American colonists. He first saw action with the American army on Sept. 11, 1777, at Brandywine where he was wounded. In November, Washington asked that Lafayette be given the command of a division and early in 1778 he commanded troops detailed for a projected expedition to Canada, which was abandoned for lack of supplies and he again joined Washington's army at Valley Forge in April, 1778, distinguishing himself by his masterly retreat from Barren Hill where he was surprised by a force more than twice the size of his own. After the battle of Monmouth, Congress extended formal recognition of his services. Following England's declaration of war on France, he returned home and was instrumental in persuading

France to send a fleet as well as a land force to aid the colonists. Six months later he was back in America. He served as a member of the court-martial which decided the fate of Major John André and participated brilliantly in the battle of Yorktown in the summer of 1781. On the day after Cornwallis' surrender he received public thanks from Gen. Washington. In December he again sailed for home where he was made major-general in the French army. He visited the United States in 1784 after peace was declared and was given a tremendous ovation.

In France he threw himself into the cause of the French Protestants and became one of the leaders of the French Revolution. He was elected to the States-General, chosen vice-president of the National Assembly, and in July, 1789, presented a declaration of rights modeled on the American Declaration of Independence. By acclamation he was made Colonel-General of the new National Guard of Paris and for three years, until the end of constitutional monarchy in France, his career was bound up in that of the Revolution. He pleaded for the abolition of arbitrary imprisonment, for religious tolerance, popular representation, gradual emancipation of slaves, freedom of the press, and abolition of titles of nobility. In 1790 he refused supreme command of the National Guard which increased his popularity with the people. When Louis XVI fled to Varennes he ordered his arrest. He participated in proclaiming the constitution in 1791 and then resigned his command. When war broke out with Austria and Prussia he took an active part but after the storming of the Tuileries he left the army and returned to Paris to find his influence gone.

His attempts to restore a limited monarchy resulted in his being declared a traitor and he fled to Liège where he was arrested as a prisoner of state and held captive for five years in Prussia and Austria. Napoleon obtained his release in 1797. From 1818 to 1834 he was active in political life, his last public speech being made on behalf of the Polish political refugees. In 1824 he revisited America, received an enthusiastic welcome and a gift of $200,000 from the government. He died in Paris on May 20, 1834.

CHARLES LAMB   1775–1834

CHARLES LAMB, one of the most delightful and companionable of English essayists and men of letters, was born in London on Feb. 10, 1775. The pathetic circumstances of his life and a certain wistful quality which pervades his writings have endeared him to a world of readers. He was educated at Christ's Hospital, London; Coleridge was his schoolfellow and with this early friend and Wordsworth, Hazlitt, Hunt and other distinguished men he lived in affectionate intimacy. His lovable personality triumphed over an impediment in his speech, which, nevertheless, barred him from following his original inclination to teach in one of the universities, and he became a clerk in a department of the East India House from which post he retired with a pension in his 50th year. The shadow of insanity overhung his family; he was in early life confined for a brief period in an institution, and the taint took tragic form in his sister Mary, an accomplished woman who collaborated with him in his *Tales From Shakespeare,* one of the classics of nineteenth century literature. In one of her recurrent violent attacks she killed her mother who had been similarly afflicted; her devoted brother, renouncing all thought of marriage, consecrated his life to the unhappy sister's care. In her rational intervals she made her home with him, assisting in the work for which they are jointly famous, and the pathetic picture of his conducting her to a retreat at the threshold of each relapse is a vivid and touching episode in his blighted life. In several of his sonnets he mentioned "the gentle maid," (Ann Simmons) whose companionship he sacrificed because of this family spectre. This sadness in his life distilled into his writing a certain gentle charm, that wistful quality resulting from "the smile and the tear."

His first poems appeared in a small collection edited by Coleridge, *Poems on Various Subjects* (1796), followed by a second volume and a third entitled *Blank Verse* which included one of his most familiar and characteristic poems, concentrating that quality of pensiveness, so charming but so hard to describe:

All are gone—all the old, familiar faces.

In 1798 appeared his tale, *Rosamund Gray;* the play, *John Woodvil,* and the farce, *Mr. H.* followed, all of which had indifferent success. In 1807 he was invited to contribute to a *Juvenile Library,* then in course of publication. The result was the famous *Tales from Shakespeare.* Although told in story form suitable for young readers, these have been read with delight by multitudes of adults. Thousands, young and old, have entered through this golden gate into the enchanted realm. In this joint labor Lamb wrote the tragedies and his sister the comedies, although the whole work seems pervaded by his rare quality of style. He was a devoted lover of the great dramatist and his commentaries are classics in Shakespearian literature. The *Adventures of Ulysses* from *Homer* was followed by *Specimens of English Dramatic Poets,* which promptly won him recognition for his familiarity with the Elizabethan period treated and his rare critical discernment. After publishing a miscellaneous collection in 1818, he became associated with the *London Magazine* where appeared most of the essays and sketches written under the name of "Elia," later published in book form as *Essays of Elia* and *Last Essays of Elia*. These exquisite pieces, mostly in lighter vein, are unsurpassed in delicacy of style by anything in the English language. No writer has succeeded quite so well in infusing his own personality into his work. They are of a quality to engage the admiration and the affections of the reader. Of their great number may be mentioned the famous *Dissertation on Roast Pig,* a whimsical and highly characteristic description of the discovery of the luscious flavor of pork through a fire which consumed a number of unfortunate pigs. In 1826 appeared *Popular Fallacies,* ludicrously treating such familiar axioms as that "ill-gotten gains never prosper," that "enough is as good as a feast," that "handsome is as handsome does," and so forth, charmingly ironical and full of the most playful humor.

He died Dec. 27, 1834, his sister outliving him by 13 years.

SIR EDWIN HENRY LANDSEER   1802–1873

EDWIN HENRY LANDSEER, the most eminent member of a family of English painters and particularly distinguished for his paintings of animals, was born March 7, 1802 in London, the son of John Landseer, an engraver whose two other sons, Thomas and Charles, also became artists. He early showed a talent for drawing and was encouraged and trained by his father. At the age of 13 he sent two pictures to the Royal Academy and was named an "honorary exhibitor," because of his youth. He dissected the bodies of animals to learn their physiological structure and studied the live animals in the Tower of London and the Exeter Exchange. He was admitted as a student to the Royal Academy schools in 1816, and the following year exhibited a portrait of a favorite dog, "Old Brutus." In 1818 he exhibited his "Fighting Dogs Getting Wind." "The Cat's Paw" created something of a sensation at the British Institution in 1824. It was sold for 100 pounds and he used the money to move into new quarters at No. 1 St. John's Wood Road, where he lived for nearly fifty years. Other paintings of his early period are "The Cat Disturbed," "Alpine Mastiffs Reviving a Traveler in the Snow," "The Larder Invaded," "The Rat-catchers," etc.

He was elected an associate of the Royal Academy in 1826 and at about this time a change in his style is noticeable; a growth in largeness, but a decrease in the niceties of modeling and draughtmanship. The subject matter began to dominate the execution. This increased his popularity with the great public to whom his pictures had become familiar through engravings of some of them made by his father and brother. His sentiment charmed the people and although a certain lack of care in the technical qualities of his work grieved the critics, he was often able to inject a quality of humor into his pictures which added greatly to their appeal. In 1825 he had visited Scotland and thereafter used the mountain scenery for many of his backgrounds. He painted Sir Walter Scott with his dogs and from that time on his pictures show animals, and particularly dogs, in their relations to human beings rather than as purely animal studies, a characteristic which makes him compare unfavorably with really great animal painters such as Potter, Troyan and Snyder. Among his works of this period are "The Monkey who has Seen the World," "Taking a Buck," "High Life and Low Life," "The Highland Whiskey Still." He developed an amazing facility and could execute an entire composition in a few hours' time. He was made a Royal Academician in 1831.

Among the best of his later paintings are "Suspense," "A Distinguished Member of the Humane Society," "Dignity and Impudence," and "Monarch of the Glen," the only completed one of three pictures of the hunt which he was commissioned to paint in the Houses of Parliament; "A Piper and a Pair of Nutcrackers," "Man Proposes, God Disposes," "Peace," "War," and "The Chase." He refused the presidency of the Royal Academy in 1865.

Although at his best in portraying animals, he also did some portrait work worthy of note, and as a sculptor he designed four lions for the base of the Nelson monument in London. He was knighted in 1850 and in 1855 and in 1873 received gold medals in Paris and Vienna. He died Oct. 1, 1873 and was buried in St. Paul's Cathedral.

SIDNEY LANIER   1842–1881

SIDNEY LANIER, American poet and musician, was born at Macon, Georgia, Feb. 3, 1842, of Huguenot descent on his father's side while his mother was of Scotch ancestry. As a child he showed an unusual delight in music and learned to play, without instruction, on almost every kind of instrument. Playing the violin often left him in such rapture that he would sink to the floor in a trance. He was able later in life to coax almost violin-like effects from the flute. At 14 he entered the sophomore class in Oglethorpe College, Georgia, and after graduating was given a tutorship in the college, which he held until the beginning of the Civil War when he enlisted with the Macon volunteers of the Second Georgia Battalion. He was in the battle of Seven Pines, Drewry's Bluffs and the seven days' fighting around Richmond culminating in Malvern Hill, but managed to find time to study German, French and Spanish and to entertain himself and his comrades with music.

He was next transferred, with his brother, to the signal service and stationed for a short time at Petersburg. His military detachment was mounted in 1863 and did service in Virginia and North Carolina, following which he was put in charge of a vessel to run the blockade, was captured and spent five months in Point Lookout prison, being exchanged shortly before the close of the war. His experiences are given vivid expression in *Tiger Lilies,* a novel which he published two years later. Upon being released in February, 1865, he walked to his home in Macon which he reached in a state of exhaustion and was for six weeks desperately ill. The hardships and exposure which he had suffered caused him to develop tuberculosis, but he later went to Montgomery, Alabama, where he taught and acted as clerk in a shop. In September, 1867, he took charge of a country academy at Prattville, Ala., and married Miss Mary Day, but his poor health soon forced him to return to Macon, where he studied and practiced law with his father for a few years. He went to San Antonio, Tex., but the climate was unsuitable and he again returned to Macon determined, since the end was inevitable, to give himself up to music and literature. He visited New York, then settled in Baltimore as first flutist for the Peabody Symphony concerts.

One of the saddest and bravest struggles of genius against the ravages of tuberculosis followed, Lanier always forcing his strength beyond endurance to support his family and to give utterance to some of the beauty that he felt. His father and brother helped him, he visited Texas, Florida, Pennsylvania and North Carolina in search of relief, devoting himself to literature, studying and writing. In 1876 he was selected to write a cantata for the Centennial Exposition and a year later published a volume of poems. He gave a course of lectures on Shakespeare at Peabody Institute and was appointed lecturer on English literature at Johns Hopkins in 1879. Although his literary career was short, he was one of the most talented of American poets and it is a question whether his poetical or his musical genius was the greater. The quality of music pervades all his writings. Among his best known poems are *Corn, The Revenge of Hamish, The Song of the Chattahoochee, The Marshes of Glynn* and the uncompleted *Hymns of the Marshes*. He died at Lynn, N. C., Sept. 7, 1881. After his death his complete poems, edited by his widow, were published and also a volume of his letters.

PIERRE SIMON LAPLACE   1749–1827

PIERRE SIMON LAPLACE (MARQUIS DE), recognized as the greatest of French astronomers and mathematicians, was born on his father's farm at Beaumont, in Normandy, on March 28, 1749. Despite the humble circumstances of his family, he was able to study at the college of Caen and at the Beaumont Academy where for a time he taught mathematics. At 18 he went to Paris and through the influence of the scholar, D'Alembert, who was secretary of the Academy, and whose attention had been attracted by a remarkable paper on dynamics written by the youth, he was appointed professor of mathematics in the Royal Military School. His wonderful mastery of mathematical analysis, and some scholarly articles which he wrote soon attracted the attention of scientists and won him a membership in the august Academy of Sciences (1785). His application of mathematical science to practical astronomy resulting in his solution of what he called the "mechanical problem of the solar system," gave rise to the Three Laws of Laplace. He established the theory that what had been considered merely irregularities of movement in the solar system were all governed by exact laws. He was indefatigable in his pursuit of knowledge regarding the heavenly bodies, promulgated a theory regarding the satellites of Jupiter, studied the movements of tides, and made many valuable discoveries of an astronomical nature. In conjunction with Lavoisier, he conducted important experiments in physics. In pure mathematics his theory of probabilities was perhaps his most outstanding contribution. He embodied the results of his various researches in many scholarly treatises and has been termed "the Newton of France." In 1817 he became president of the Academy of Sciences.

In 1799 he was appointed Minister of the Interior by Napoleon Bonaparte, who however removed him from the post some six weeks later, it is said with a remark to the effect that Laplace was too much given to carrying the infinitesimal into his administration. He was given a seat in the Senate, however, of which he became vice-president and in 1803 he was made chancellor. The following year Napoleon created him a count. He seems not to have been very strong in his political convictions, which he was able to change with a changing régime, and we find him sufficiently in the favor of King Louis XVIII to be raised to the peerage by that monarch in 1815. Two years later he received the title of marquis.

He was president of the Bureau of Longitudes; president of a commission to reorganize the École Polytechnique; served on a commission to establish the metric system and was a member of many of the scientific societies of the world. Among his works may be mentioned *Exposition du Système du Monde* (1796); *Mécanique céleste* (1799–1825); *Théorie analytique des probabilitiés* (1812); *Théorie du Mouvement et de la Figure des Planetes*.

His realization of the fact that all his wonderful discoveries were but as nothing in the vastness of the universe was indicated by the remark he is said to have made during his last illness: "What we know is little, what we do not know is immense." He died at Arcueil, where he had a country home, on March 5, 1827, leaving a son who succeeded to his title and became a general in the artillery.

RENÉ ROBERT CAVELIER, SIEUR DE LA SALLE   1643–1687

RENÉ ROBERT CAVELIER, SIEUR DE LA SALLE, French explorer and the first man to sail down the Mississippi River, was born at Rouen, France, in 1643, of a wealthy merchant family. He received his education at the hands of the Jesuits and, joining himself to that organization, lost his right to inherit his father's wealth. He left France for Montreal in 1666 and was given a grant of land on the St. Lawrence River, some miles above Montreal. He spent much of his time in exploring the wilderness. In 1669–70 he traversed the region south of Lakes Ontario and Erie. Governor Frontenac sent him to France in 1674 to defend the building of Ft. Frontenac (now Kingston, Ont.), which the governor had undertaken on his own authority. La Salle succeeded in his mission and went to France again in 1677 to obtain trading privileges to the westward and permission to build other forts. He secured a monopoly of the fur trade in the Mississippi Valley and was given financial help. In 1679 his expedition boarded the *Griffon,* the first commercial ship to ply on Lake Erie, and proceeded to Green Bay, Wis., where a cargo of furs was obtained. He hoped to pay his creditors with the proceeds, but the vessel was lost on the return voyage and he traveled down the west shore of Lake Michigan to the mouth of the River St. Joseph where Ft. Miami was built. Then, with his lieutenant, Tonti, and 34 men, he ascended the river into the Illinois and built Ft. Crèvecoeur near Lake Peoria.

He now sent Michael Accault and Father Hennepin up the Mississippi beyond the Falls of St. Anthony, while he himself with a few companions returned to Ft. Frontenac for supplies and funds. Returning, he learned that Ft. Crèvecoeur had been abandoned and the men had deserted. He descended the Illinois to the Mississippi seeking Tonti and his men but not finding them returned again to Ft. Frontenac. The following spring, having raised funds, he set out again and was rejoined by Tonti who had been captured by the Indians and had escaped. The long journey to the mouth of the Mississippi was successfully undertaken. On April 9, 1682, having reached the mouth, he took possession of the region watered by it and its tributaries in the name of Louis XIV and named it Louisiana. He was thus the first man to trace the course of the great river and to link the discoveries of De Soto near its mouth with those of Joliet and Marquette along its upper waters.

He hoped to form a colony independent of Canada, and in December, 1682, he sailed up the Illinois River and built Fort St. Louis as a gathering place for the western Indian tribes whose cooperation he had secured and whom he had formed into a sort of league against the Iroquois. Some 20,000 of them settled in villages along the Illinois. His supporter, Frontenac, however, had been recalled to France and La Salle's jealous merchant rivals campaigned against him with the new governor, De la Barre, who seized Ft. Frontenac and ordered La Salle to return to Quebec. La Salle went to France and was able to convince the court that the establishment of a colony at the mouth of the Mississippi would be a strategic move against Spain with which France was at war. He was constituted governor of Louisiana, which was to include all the territory from Lake Michigan to the mouth of the Mississippi, the forts in the Illinois country were restored to him and with four ships and about 400 men he sailed from France to make the new settlement. The voyage was ill-fated. Captain Beaujeu, naval commander of the ships, refused to obey his orders and was responsible for the loss of the main supply ship to the Spanish. When they finally reached the Gulf of Mexico they found it difficult to locate the Mississippi delta and becoming convinced that Beaujeu was deliberately working against him La Salle finally landed his disorganized party at Matagorda Bay, thinking it the place he sought. Beaujeu returned to France and two of the ships were wrecked. Realizing his mistake and with but 45 men left, La Salle's task was hopeless. He made two attempts to reach Canada and after months of wandering a mutiny took place and he was treacherously shot by one of his own men.

WILLIAM LAUD, ARCHBISHOP OF CANTERBURY 1573–1645

WILLIAM LAUD, ARCHBISHOP OF CANTERBURY, was the son of a well-to-do clothier, and was born at Reading, England, on Oct. 7, 1573. He attended the free school at Reading, entered St. John's College at Oxford when he was 16 and later became a fellow of the college. He was ordained in 1601, but soon incurred the displeasure of the college authorities because of his openly expressed hostility toward the Puritanism then sweeping over England. He was an industrious and learned man, a sincere and devoted churchman and he soon won friends, among them Charles Blount, Earl of Devonshire (whom he married to the divorced Lady Rich despite the laws of the church), and the Duke of Buckingham to whom he became confessor in 1622. He mounted steadily in church preferment, obtaining five livings between 1607 and 1610. He received the D.D. degree in 1608 and three years later became president of St. John's College and King's chaplain. In 1614 he was made prebendary of Lincoln; in 1615 Archdeacon of Huntingdon; in 1616 Dean of Gloucester; in 1621 prebendary of Westminster and Bishop of St. David's; in 1626 Bishop of Bath and Wells, Dean of the Chapel Royal and a privy councillor; in 1628 Bishop of London; in 1630 Chancellor of Oxford; and in 1633 Archbishop of Canterbury, at the same time refusing two offers of a cardinal's hat in the Roman Church.

After the assassination of the Duke of Buckingham, he became virtually the first minister of the nation. He worked with Charles I and Strafford to make the church and the state absolute in England and Scotland. He was to raise the English Church to its rightful position as a branch of the Church Catholic, to destroy Presbyterianism in Scotland and Calvinism in England. Going about his task with vigor and resolution, he made a list of Orthodox and Puritan ministers in England and proceeded to separate them by all the means in his power. Freedom of worship was withdrawn from the Walloon and French refugees in England; an order was issued forbidding Englishmen abroad from attending Calvinistic meetings; and in England he attempted to supersede by elaborate ritual and by the doctrine of celibacy, confession and the "Book of Sports" the gospel preaching, justification by faith and the Sabbatarianism of the Puritans. The Court of High Commission and the Star Chamber rigorously enforced his orders.

In Scotland he attempted to Anglicise the Scottish church (1635–37), but his first attempt to have the liturgy read in St. Giles' Church, Edinburgh, caused a riot which led up to the Covenant, the Bishops' War, the meeting of the Long Parliament and the Revolution under Oliver Cromwell and the Puritans. He was impeached on a charge of treason by the Long Parliament on Dec. 16, 1640. Ten weeks later he was sent to the London Tower. Friends urged him to escape, but he refused to do so. He was tried before a handful of peers and after a long and tedious trial was found guilty, on Dec. 17, 1644, of "endeavoring to subvert the law, to overthrow the Protestant religion and to act as an enemy to Parliament." The judges declared that these charges did not constitute treason, but Laud was nevertheless beheaded in the Tower on Jan. 10, 1645. He was buried in the church of All-Hallows, Barking, and in 1663 his body was transferred to the chapel of St. John's at Oxford.

He had a high regard for learning, but wrote little for publication. His *Diary*, published in 1694, is regarded as the most interesting of his works. Many lives of the Archbishop have been written, the first by his chaplain, Peter Heylin, *Cyprianus Anglicanus*, in 1668.

ANTOINE LAURENT LAVOISIER 1743–1794

ANTOINE LAURENT LAVOISIER (lȧ vwȧ′ zyȧ′), known as the founder of the modern science of chemistry, was born in Paris on August 26, 1743. Being the son of a wealthy merchant, he received a good education at the Collège Mazarin and under the best masters of the time. He early developed an interest in mathematics and the physical sciences, particularly chemistry, and at the age of 23 wrote a paper which won a prize from the Academy of Sciences. A second paper led to his admission as a member of the Academy. He had already made an extended trip through France studying geological formations with J. E. Guettard, whom he assisted in compiling a mineralogical atlas. In 1769 he was appointed to the office of farmer-general of the revenue, a post which allowed him to devote a large share of his time to research work in his chosen field. Two years later he married the daughter of his colleague, Jacques Paulze.

About 1776 he developed a method which greatly improved the quality of gunpowder and made other discoveries valuable in the application of chemistry to agriculture. He held a number of important posts. While a member of the provincial assembly of Orleans he was instrumental in establishing various institutions which helped to improve the prevailing social and economic conditions. In 1788 he became a trustee of the Bank of Discount; as one of a commission to secure uniformity of weights and measures, he helped to formulate a new decimal system; and while commissary of the treasury he published an essay on the economic condition of the country which gave him high rank as a political economist. He interested himself in the most diverse subjects; from the theory of colors, mesmerism, analysis of water supply, to invalid chairs and the cultivation of crops. He established model farms to demonstrate scientific methods of cultivation, cattle breeding, etc.

His absorbing interest, however, was in chemistry. Following the lines of discoveries already made by Priestley, Cavendish and others, he made many experiments and discoveries which were of great value and published important essays on chemical subjects. It is an unfortunate, but apparently well established, fact that he at times published as his own observations which had been made by other workers in the scientific field, but his own achievements were of such undoubted brilliance and value that this can be forgiven him. Not the least important of his contributions to chemical advancement was the preparation in conjunction with three other chemists, Berthollet, Guyton de Morveau and Fourcroy, of a new and comprehensive system of nomenclature. This was published under the title of *Methode de Nomenclature Chimique,* and in its essential features is the system still used in chemistry. His other most important work was *Traité Elémentaire de Chimie.*

His lucrative office of farmer-general of the revenue proved the downfall of this illustrious man. This peculiar method of tax-gathering dated from ancient times and shortly before the French Revolution abuses of the most flagrant sort had crept into the system, which offered abundant opportunity for the accumulation of great wealth. During the Reign of Terror a popular outcry was raised against these officials; they were accused before the Revolutionary Tribunal of being enemies of their country and Lavoisier with 26 other farmers-general was condemned to die. The innocent suffered with the guilty. In vain did his friend and fellow worker, Antoine Fourcroy, plead his scientific achievements as an argument for sparing his life. He was met only with the reply that France needed no more scientists and Lavoisier perished by the guillotine on May 8, 1794.

ROBERT E. LEE   1807–1870

ROBERT EDWARD LEE, American general and commander-in-chief of the Confederate forces in the War of the Rebellion, was born on Jan. 19, 1807, at Stratford, Va., and was the son of "Lighthorse Harry" Lee, a cavalry officer distinguished in the Revolutionary War. The Lee family had emigrated to Virginia from Shropshire, England, in the reign of Charles I, received large grants of land between the Potomac and the Rappahannock Rivers, and had figured prominently in the Revolution, two of its members, Richard Henry Lee and Francis Lightfoot Lee, having been among the signers of the Declaration of Independence. At the age of 18 Robert entered the Military Academy at West Point, was graduated in 1829 as second in his class and received a commission in the army engineering service. In 1832 he married Mary Custis, the great-granddaughter of Martha Washington, who survived him three years.

At the outbreak of the Mexican War, Lee was appointed chief engineer with the central army in Mexico, took part in a number of engagements, and was wounded at the storming of Chapultepec. His remarkable record during that war caused Gen. Scott at its close to pronounce him "the greatest living soldier in America." In 1852 he was appointed commander of the National Military Academy at West Point where he made many improvements and added to the efficiency of the military instruction given there. Soon after leaving this post in 1855 he was sent to the Texas border as a cavalry officer and remained there until 1859. After the capture of the Harper's Ferry arsenal by the abolitionist, John Brown, and his supporters, Lee was sent to that point to effect the capture of Brown and his men, which he did in short order. In 1860 he was placed in command of the army in Texas, but the following year, after seven of the southern states had seceded and formed the Confederate States of America, he was recalled to Washington. President Lincoln offered him command of the Army of the United States, but although opposed to secession, he declined because he was unwilling to take any part in an invasion of the southern states.

On April 17 Virginia joined the seceding states and Lee, believing that his duty was to his state rather than to the government in whose army he was a high official, resigned his commission and went to Virginia where he was made commander-in-chief of the Virginia forces. He spent the spring and summer in Richmond overseeing preparations for the defense of that city. In the fall he went to West Virginia to oppose the advance of the Union general, Rosencrans. The spring of 1862 found him in Georgia superintending the coast fortifications of that state and also of South Carolina. When McClellan began his advance on the Confederate forces centered about Richmond, Lee was summoned back to the city and served in the defense until the wounding of Gen. J. E. Johnston, the Confederate commander-in-chief, when he was appointed to the supreme command of the army about Richmond. He now proved himself an able commander and a master of strategy and in seven days of fighting defeated McClellan's attempted advance on the Confederate capital. He frustrated Gen. Pope's campaign, defeating him decisively at the second battle of Bull Run, and succeeded in getting a Confederate army of invasion into the Union Territory in an advance upon Washington, but suffered a disastrous defeat at Gettysburg. He conducted the defensive campaign against Grant's gradual approach to the defenses of Richmond with great military skill, but was compelled to surrender his entire army of 28,231 men on April 9, 1865 at Appomatox Courthouse, thus bringing the war to an end.

The military genius which he displayed throughout the Civil War is recognized by all. His resourcefulness against enormous obstacles, his undaunted courage and gallantry, his humane conduct of the war and his magnanimity in the face of defeat inspired the greatest devotion on the part of his men and admiration from friend and foe alike. He urged the South to accept the result with loyalty, and to set about the task of reconstruction. He declined pecuniarily attractive offers and became president of Washington College at Lexington, Va. (now Washington and Lee University). During his five years of office he did much to restore the institution from the devastation caused by the war. He died on Oct. 12, 1870 and was buried in the university grounds. His eldest son, George Washington Custis Lee, aide-de-camp to Jefferson Davis, and a major-general, succeeded him as president of the university. Two other sons served in the Confederate Army. Lee's estate on the Potomac was purchased by the National government in 1864 and the Arlington National Cemetery established there.

NIKOLAI LENIN (VLADIMIR ILYICH ULYANOV)   1870–1924

NIKOLAI LENIN, leader of the Russian Bolsheviki and founder of the Soviet Republics and of the Communist International, was born April 22, 1870, in Simbirsk (now Ulyanovsk), Russia, where his father was a councilor of state. He studied law at Kazan University, and was banished to Siberia for taking part in a student gathering, but was allowed to return in the fall of 1889 when he took up the study of Karl Marx and became one of his most devoted disciples and a leader of the radical Social Democrats. In 1891 he began to practice law at Samara, but gave it up three years later and went to St. Petersburg (Leningrad) to begin his propaganda work, where he soon organized an illegal Union for the liberation of the working classes. In December, 1895, he was arrested, imprisoned for a year and in February, 1897, exiled to Siberia for three years. In 1898 he married N. K. Krupskaya, a comrade of his St. Petersburg union, who aided him in his later work. While in Siberia he wrote most of his *Development of Capitalism in Russia* and in 1900, upon the expiration of his term of exile, he went to Switzerland and arranged for the publication of a revolutionary paper, *Iskra (The Spark)*.

The second congress of the Russian Social Democrats held in London in 1903 accepted the program worked out by Plekhanov and Lenin, but ended in a split of the party into Bolsheviks and Mensheviks, with Lenin becoming the leader of the former. He saw in the peasantry the closest ally of the proletariat. The struggle with the Mensheviks led to a break with the Second International, the October Revolution, and the change of the name of the party from Social Democrat to Communist. Following the revolutionary situation in Russia created by the Russo-Japanese War of 1905, he began to urge the three policies which ultimately resulted in the Soviet State: the temporary seizure by the people of real political freedom, the creation of a new if only potential revolutionary power in the shape of soviets of workers, soldiers and peasants' deputies, and the use of force by the people against those who had used force against them. The abortive Moscow rising of December, 1905, with resultant exiles and executions, forced him to flee from Russia and for ten years he conducted his propaganda from abroad. In November, 1914, he denounced the World War as imperialistic and promulgated a program for a new International to organize the proletariat for revolutionary attack on capitalistic governments, and for civil war against the bourgeoisie of all countries. At the conference of European Socialists opposed to the war (September, 1915) his demand for the transformation of the imperialist war into a civil war was adopted and became the nucleus of the later Communist International.

He returned to Russia at the outbreak of the Revolution of February, 1917, but his far-reaching schemes aroused opposition among the Bolshevists and, as St. Petersburg (then Petrograd) was occupied by "reliable troops" which Kerensky had called back from the front, he had to work under cover, and did so to such good effect that the Bolshevists obtained a majority in the Soviets of Petrograd and Moscow, and declared the supreme authority to rest in the Soviets. The Soviet of People's Commissaries was appointed, with Lenin at the head, whereupon he dissolved the Constituent Assembly and established the dictatorship of the proletariat. He transferred the government to Moscow, and brought the country through the counter-revolution of 1918, the rising of Czechoslovaks on the Volga, and the British intervention in Archangel and in Baku. He was shot and wounded by a social-revolutionary in August, 1918, but quickly recovered. The counter-revolution was defeated in 1921 and the Soviet State increased in strength despite non-recognition by the other powers and the lack of international commerce. Late in 1921 he became ill, lost the power of speech and was obliged to let others rule in his name. He died at Gorky, near Moscow, Jan. 21, 1924. His body lies in the Kremlin in Moscow and his tomb has become a Soviet shrine.

LEONARDO DA VINCI   1452–1519

LEONARDO DA VINCI (lā'ȯ när'dō dȧ vēn'chĕ), Italian painter and sculptor of the Renaissance period, was also renowned as architect, engineer and scientist. He was born some time in 1452 at Vinci, between Pisa and Florence, and was the natural son of a wealthy Florentine notary who gave the boy the best education obtainable in Florence which was at that time the intellectual centre of Italy.

He seems early to have displayed a talent for drawing and painting and about the year 1470 became a pupil-apprentice of Andrea del Verrocchio, a celebrated Florentine sculptor and painter. In 1843 he settled at Milan where he attached himself to the Duke Lodovico Sforza. In 1498 on a commission from the Duke and the monks of Santa Maria delle Grazie, he executed the justly famous "Last Supper," painted on the walls of the refectory of the convent. Because of dampness and his use of a method unsuited to the plaster walls, the painting soon showed signs of deterioration. It remains, however, one of da Vinci's masterpieces despite the frequent restorations which have been necessary.

The years in Milan were fruitful ones but most of da Vinci's paintings during those years, including several portraits, have been lost. He acted as general factotum to the Duke, was called upon to direct the court pageants, and also employed his engineering skill in devising a system of hydraulic irrigation for the plains of Lombardy.

In 1501, after the fall of Duke Lodovico, he began work on a painting of the Madonna and child with St. Anne. The many studies and sketches made for this project created intense interest in Florence. The painting itself, which is now in the Louvre, was completed some years later with the help of several of his pupils. The next year da Vinci entered the service of Caesar Borgia, Duke of Romagna, in the capacity of architect and engineer, his duties taking him to different sections of Italy. After his return to Florence in 1503 he entered into a contest with Michelangelo for decorations for the Palazzo Vecchio, choosing as his subject "The Battle of Anghiari." The actual execution of this painting seems never to have been completed.

His most famous easel picture and perhaps the most famous painting of all time was "The Mona Lisa," known in France as "La Gioconda," the subject for which was long thought to be the third wife of Francisco del Giocondo, but recent exhaustive investigations on the part of an American scholar point to one Isabella d'Este, a celebrated beauty of the period, as the model for the famous picture. Leonardo spent four years on this work and then did not consider it finished. In August, 1911, this masterpiece disappeared from the Louvre and two years later was found in possession of Vincent Perugia, who claimed that he had been actuated by patriotic motives in stealing it and bringing it back to Florence. It was returned to the Louvre after being exhibited to multitudes in Italian cities.

In 1506 da Vinci became court painter to Louis XII of France, and ten years later Francis I gave him a yearly allowance and the use of the Château Cloux, near Amboise, France, where he died on May 2, 1519.

"The Virgin of the Rocks," now in the National Gallery, London, is one of his notable later works, of which the Louvre has a replica, as are also "St. John the Baptist" and "Saint Anne." He paid scant honor to the ancients in his work but relied upon his own marvelous observation of nature about him. He is justly regarded as one of the greatest masters of the art of painting, but few of his finished works still exist, although there are collections of his drawings, cartoons, and sketches in Milan, Paris, Florence, Vienna, at the British Museum in London and at Windsor. In scientific research he was outstanding; he wrote a celebrated treatise on the art of painting, *Trattato della Pittura,* which was published first in 1651, although in 1817 a more complete manuscript of the work was discovered in the Vatican and published. There exist many other manuscripts, some of which have been reproduced in facsimile. His literary works, edited by Richter, were published in 1883; his *Note Books,* edited by McCurdy, in 1906. Many biographies and monographs have been written on this celebrated artist.

FERDINAND DE LESSEPS   1805–1894

FERDINAND DE LESSEPS, French diplomat, builder of the Suez Canal, and the first man to attempt to cut a canal across the Isthmus of Panama, was born in Versailles, Nov. 19, 1805. He entered the consular service and served at Lisbon, Rotterdam, Malaga, Barcelona and Cairo. While at Alexandria in 1832 he became keenly interested in the possibility of a canal to connect the Mediterranean and Red Seas, through reading Lapere's memoir on the subject drawn up on the instructions of Napoleon. He made friends with Said Pasha who had wide influence in Egypt. From 1833 to 1837 while serving at Cairo he won wide popularity by his courage in combating an outbreak of the plague. In 1848–49 he was French minister at Madrid. In the latter year he was sent to Rome, but, the French elections resulting in a change of foreign policy, he was recalled and retired from the service.

Said Pasha had in the meantime become viceroy of Egypt and now invited de Lesseps to Cairo. The invitation reawakened the Frenchman's ambition to build a Suez Canal and on Nov. 30, 1854, Said Pasha granted him authority to undertake this great and important work. His plans for the project were drawn up by M. Linant Bey and Mougel Bey, and with but slight modification were adopted by an international commission of engineers in 1856. A company was organized to prosecute the work and de Lesseps succeeded in inducing the French people to subscribe more than half of the capital required. The work was begun at Port Said on April 25, 1859, and nearly ten and a half years later (Nov. 17, 1869) the Suez Canal was officially opened by the Khedive, Ismail Pasha. Meanwhile, through the efforts of Benjamin Disraeli, British Premier, a majority of the shares in the Suez Canal Company were acquired by the British government and de Lesseps cooperated with the British authorities in consolidating the various interests and pushing the project forward to fulfilment.

The successful completion and satisfactory operation of the Canal aroused much interest in the possibility of cutting through the Isthmus of Panama, to connect the Atlantic and Pacific Oceans, and when in 1879 the Geographical Society at Paris, with Admiral de la Roncière de Noury as president, voted to undertake the project, public opinion centered on de Lesseps as the man for the task despite the fact that he was then 74 years of age. He accepted the offer and work was begun in 1881 with the intention of building a sea level canal, but confronted with the Culebra and the Chagres, the mountain and river which made this impossible, de Lesseps determined to construct the canal with locks. He worked for fully eight years at the gigantic task but it became apparent that the work could not be carried to completion with the available capital. Scandals arose (doubtless to some extent justified by inefficient management) and in 1889 the company was found to be bankrupt and the work was abandoned. Many innocent persons suffered. Just how far de Lesseps was responsible has never been determined. He and his son, Charles, were later convicted of misappropriation of funds, but while the charge may have been technically warranted, it was established that they were innocent of any fraudulent intent.

De Lesseps died at La Chenaie on Dec. 7, 1894.

GOTTHOLD EPHRAIM LESSING 1729–1781

GOTTHOLD EPHRAIM LESSING, German dramatist and critic, was born Jan. 22, 1729, at Kamentz in Saxony, where his father was chief pastor. In 1746 he entered the University of Leipzig as a theological student but was later diverted from theology by philological lectures and philosophical disputes, and by his friendship for the dramatist, C. F. Weisse, and the journalist, Christlob Mylius. The theatre in Leipzig, directed by the actress Karoline Neuber, held a great fascination for him and a comedy which he had begun at school, *Der junge Gelehrte,* was produced there in 1748. His father, displeased with these activities, called his son home, but later he was allowed to return to the University on condition that he take up the study of medicine. He attended a few medical classes, but his great interest continued to centre in the Leipzig theatre, which broke up later in the year. Lessing had become surety for the debts of some of the players; to escape the creditors he fled to Wittenberg and at the end of the year joined his friend Mylius in Berlin. During his three years there he translated Charles Rollin's *Histoire ancienne,* wrote a number of plays and with Mylius in 1750 began the short-lived periodical *Beiträge zur Historie und Aufnahme des Theaters,* devoted mainly to discussions of the drama. For a few months he was literary critic of the *Vossiche Zeitung.*

The end of 1751 found him back in Wittenberg studying, and after receiving his master's degree he returned to Berlin, continuing his literary criticisms in the *Vossiche Zeitung,* publishing several numbers of the *Theatralische Bibliothek,* and making translations for the booksellers. Six volumes of his *Schriften* appeared in 1753, containing his earlier writings, and a new play, *Miss Sara Sampson,* based on Lillo's *Merchant of London,* a tragedy of common life, first performed at Frankfort-on-Oder in 1755. This met with great success and marked the breaking away of the German theatre from the French classic drama. In 1755 Lessing settled in Leipzig, writing criticisms and studying medieval literature. He published *Briefe, die neueste Literatur betreffend* and *Philotas,* a one-act prose tragedy. From 1760 to 1764 he was in Breslau as secretary to the governor, General Taunetzein. He collected a large library, studied early Christianity and the philosophy of Spinoza and planned his greatest play, *Minna von Barnhelm,* which he wrote after returning to Berlin in 1765. During the next two restless years appeared his greatest literary works, the famous *Laokoon,* an analysis of the limitations of poverty and the plastic arts; and *Minna von Barnhelm.* In 1767 he helped to establish a national theatre in Hamburg, which soon closed, and after the failure of a printing establishment in which he had invested some money, he accepted an offer from the Prince of Brunswick to become his librarian at Wolfenbüttel. His health was poor at the time and he was heavily in debt.

In 1772 and 1773 he published *Emilia Galotti,* a tragedy of common life based on a Roman legend; and *Zur Geschichte und Literatur.* His last play, *Nathan the Wise,* was an exposition of tolerance emphasizing the nobility to be found in men of whatever creeds. In 1776 he had married the widow of a Hamburg friend, who died with her infant son two years later. Three years afterward he suffered a stroke of apoplexy and died at Brunswick on Feb. 15, 1781.

Lessing's life was one devoted to the search for truth. Many of his writings were controversial in character and he was doubtless influenced by his friendship for Voltaire with whom he later quarreled. He was an ardent believer in free speech and held it better that error should be taught than that limitation should be put upon freedom of thought. He gave Germany a national drama; his writings marked a distinct advance in prose style and his theological essays gave a new direction to religious philosophy despite attacks by the orthodox and the skeptical alike.

MERIWETHER LEWIS
WILLIAM CLARK

1774--1809
1770–1838

MERIWETHER LEWIS and WILLIAM CLARK, American explorers whose names are inseparably linked, headed the first expedition to cross the American continent from St. Louis to the mouth of the Columbia River, 1804–1806.

Lewis was born near Charlottesville, Va., on Aug. 18, 1774. He was a militiaman in the "Whiskey Insurrection," an officer under Gen. Anthony Wayne and in 1801 became private secretary to President Jefferson, who later entrusted to him and to his old friend and army comrade, Lieut. William Clark, the leadership of an expedition which was to explore the Louisiana Territory, then comprising the vast section from the Mississippi River west to the Rocky Mountains and stretching from the Gulf of Mexico to Canada, which had just been purchased by the United States from France.

Clark was born in Carolina County, Va., in 1770, but removed to Kentucky at an early age. He entered the United States army as lieutenant of infantry in 1792 and served under Gen. Anthony Wayne against the Indians in 1794.

Late in 1803 Lewis and Clark and their subordinates went into winter camp near St. Louis, where they made preparations for the journey across the continent. The expedition got under way on May 14, 1804, and proceeded northwest along the Missouri River. By early November they had reached the site of the present town of Bismarck, S. D., and there they spent the winter among the Mandan Indians, starting in April, 1805 to follow the Missouri toward its headwaters. In July they came to the three forks of the river which they named Jefferson, Madison and Gallatin. They followed the Jefferson to its source in the southwestern part of the present state of Montana where they obtained horses and a guide from the Shoshone Indians and continued westward, crossing the Rocky Mountains in September. Reaching the Columbia River they embarked in canoes and floated down the river, reaching the Pacific Ocean in November. They had traveled more than 4000 miles mostly through territory inhabited by tribes of Indians who had never before seen a white man. They made many valuable scientific observations and collections along the route.

They spent the winter on the Pacific Coast and on March 23, 1806, set out on the return journey. After crossing the divide they separated, Lewis taking a part of the men and exploring Maria's River, while Clark explored the Yellowstone. They came together again near the confluence of the Yellowstone and Missouri Rivers, and reached St. Louis on September 23. But one member of the party died during the two years, while one other deserted. It was one of the greatest and most romantic of exploring achievements and has made the names of Lewis and Clark conspicuous in the annals of American pioneering. At times the party endured terrible sufferings and hardships and for more than a year were absolutely cut off from all communication with the world. The reports sent back to President Jefferson were published in his *Message from the President of the United States, Communicating Discoveries* (1806).

The explorers were rewarded for their achievement by grants of land from the public domain. In March, 1807, Lewis was made governor of Louisiana Territory. His death, which took place at Nashville, in October, 1809, is shrouded in mystery.

Clark became territorial governor of Missouri in 1813 and remained in that post until 1820. From 1822 until his death in 1838 he was superintendent of Indian affairs at St. Louis.

The original journals of the expedition were published in 1905, in which year the Lewis and Clark Centennial Exposition was held at Portland, Oregon, to commemorate the expedition.

ABRAHAM LINCOLN   1809–1865

ABRAHAM LINCOLN, sixteenth president of the United States, was born in Hardin County, Ky., Feb. 12, 1809, the son of pioneer parents. The family moved to Indiana in 1816 where Mrs. Lincoln died when Abraham was about eight years old and his father remarried. He grew up among the most primitive surroundings and attended a country school at intervals, but probably for not more than a year altogether. He developed a taste for reading and study, however, and managed to educate himself by means of the few books he could borrow.

At the age of 19 he took a cargo of goods by flatboat to New Orleans where he saw the slave-mart in operation. Two years later his father removed to central Illinois where Abraham helped him to clear and plant some 15 acres. After another boat trip to New Orleans he became clerk in a store at New Salem, Ill., and later ran for the Illinois Legislature, was defeated and bought a small store. Upon its failure he became postmaster of the village (where mail arrived only once a week) and deputy county surveyor, and continued his efforts to improve himself by studying grammar and law. He was elected to the Legislature by the Whigs in 1834 and served there until 1842 in which year he married Mary Todd in Springfield. In 1839 he had begun to practice law. In 1846 he was elected to Congress where he introduced a measure to free the slaves in the District of Columbia. He was gradually withdrawing from politics and becoming immersed in his law practice when Stephen A. Douglas succeeded in getting the Missouri Compromise Act of 1820 repealed, reopening the question of slavery in the territories. There was much resentment at the bill in the North. Douglas defended his position in a speech at Springfield and Lincoln's reply to that defense revealed his skill in public debate. He was a leader in the organization of the Republican party in Illinois in 1856 to oppose the extension of slavery, and made one of his most famous anti-slavery speeches. The delegates of Illinois presented him as their choice for the vice-presidency.

In 1856 Douglas sought reelection to the Senate from Illinois and canvassed the state, advocating "popular sovereignty." Lincoln's speeches and debates with Douglas attracted attention throughout the country and he was invited to New York where his speech in Cooper Union was well received and followed by other addresses throughout New England. In November, 1860 he was elected president by the Republicans, the Democratic party being divided on the question of slavery. In December South Carolina voted to secede from the Union and in February, 1861, with the six Gulf states, formed the Confederate States of America with Jefferson Davis as President. At his inauguration on March 4, Lincoln declared the Union indivisible, denied the right of any state to withdraw and announced his determination to execute the law in all of the states. The South interpreted this as a declaration of war and both North and South hurriedly prepared. On April 12, 1861, the Confederates fired upon Fort Sumter and the Civil War was begun. Lincoln called for 75,000 volunteers and the country responded wholeheartedly. On April 19 he declared a blockade of southern ports. He also called a special session of Congress which met on July 4 and granted his request for 400,000 men and $400,000,000. to carry on the war. Shortly afterward a resolution was passed, almost unanimously, pledging any amount of money and any number of men necessary to crush the Rebellion.

The Union forces were defeated at Bull Run, Va., on July 21 and again in August, but following McClellan's victory at Antietam in September Lincoln issued his Emancipation Proclamation freeing all slaves in the seceding states after Jan. 1, 1863. This was done as a war measure although it accorded with his personal views, and it had the effect of giving him stronger support from the abolitionists in the North and increasing the prestige of the government abroad. He planned and urged the adoption of the thirteenth amendment to the Constitution, abolishing slavery forever in the United States; it was passed in 1865. Grant's capture of Vicksburg in July, 1863, opened up the Mississippi territory to the Union forces and Meade's defeat of Lee at Gettysburg, Penn., destroyed the Confederate hope of carrying the war into northern territory. In March, 1864, Lincoln placed Gen. Grant in supreme command of the northern forces.

In November, 1864, Lincoln was reelected president and in his second inaugural address he explained the moral significance of the war, which Grant had brought to a close with the surrender of Lee and his army at Appomatox on April 9, and outlined his plans for the reconstruction of the country. On the 14th of April, 1865, while attending a performance at Ford's Theater, he was shot by John Wilkes Booth, a fanatical and dissipated actor and brother of the most famous of American actors, Edwin Booth. The ball entered the President's brain and he died on the morning of April 15 without regaining consciousness. He was buried in Springfield, Ill.

Lincoln's broad humanity, his keen political insight, his able statesmanship, his sense of justice and fair play have made him one of the greatest figures in our national life; while his wide sympathy, his many acts of mercy and his ability as a teller of droll stories have endeared him to the hearts of all Americans. His memory is held in greater veneration year by year.

CHARLES A. LINDBERGH   1902–

On May 20, 1927, CHARLES AUGUSTUS LINDBERGH, a competent young American aviator, but unknown to the general public, took off alone from Roosevelt Field, L. I., in a little plane called the *Spirit of St. Louis,* on a flight which was destined to bring him a fame unique in the annals of adventure. He was born in Detroit, Michigan, on Feb. 4, 1902, and was the grandson of a member of the Swedish parliament who had been secretary to the king of Sweden. His father, Charles A. Lindbergh, was a Minnesota lawyer and farmer, who had been a member of Congress and unsuccessful candidate for governor of his state. His mother was Evangeline Lodge (Land), an educator. His father had died prior to the exploit of his famous son. After his public school education the boy entered the University of Wisconsin, but interrupted his engineering course there and went to a flying school at Lincoln, Neb. After running an aerial taxi service at Lincoln for a time with his own plane, he entered the U. S. army air service and speedily became a skilful pilot. In 1925 he received the rank of second lieutenant in the air reserve corps and as pilot for the Robertson Aircraft Corporation he flew the first air mails between St. Louis and Chicago. For nearly two years he made regular night flights without serious misadventure.

Confident of his skill, he then undertook the transatlantic flight in competition for a prize of $25,000 offered some eight years earlier by Raymond Orteig of New York for the first non-stop flight from New York to Paris. He stepped into his plane at 6:52 A.M. and in the evening of the following day alighted at Le Bourget Field, near Paris, amid tremendous excitement from the crowds which had been watching for hours for his arrival. He had covered a distance of 3610 miles in little more than 33 hours. After brief flights to Brussels and London, where he was received with equal enthusiasm, he returned with his plane on a U. S. cruiser. This hitherto unknown young man, who as he started on his momentous flight is said to have modestly asked a friend to save for him any item which might appear in the newspapers about it, found himself suddenly world-famous. He was given an unprecedented welcome in New York; was received by the president and given the first Distinguished Flying Cross and a commission as colonel in the officers' reserve corps, and was the recipient of many other honors. He thereafter devoted himself to the advancement of aeronautics under the auspices of the government and of the Daniel Guggenheim Fund for the Promotion of Aeronautics, making a 22,000 mile aerial tour of the United States to stimulate popular interest.

Late in 1927 he made a "good will tour" to Mexico on the invitation of President Calles. Dwight W. Morrow had just been appointed ambassador to that country at a time when its relations with the United States were badly strained and Col. Lindbergh's visit helped to bring about a friendlier feeling and to cement the amicable adjustments made by Mr. Morrow. Entering the commercial field as technical adviser to certain large companies, he inaugurated a regular service between Mexico and Texas and in 1931 piloted the first plane from Miami to Panama and return.

In 1929 the famous flier married Anne Spencer Morrow, daughter of the ambassador, who became an ardent devotee of aeronautics and accompanied him on many subsequent flights, including a journey to China and Japan in 1931, in the course of which they suffered many hazards and gathered much data of value in the routing of future air services. An official reception was tendered them in Tokio and Japanese orders were conferred upon Colonel Lindbergh. In China their aerial surveys were of much aid to the government in flood relief work. In 1933 they made an extended survey for a proposed air route to Europe by way of Greenland, Iceland and the Hebrides. Col. Lindbergh has been the recipient of many medals and decorations, including the Congressional Medal of Honor, all of which were given into the care of the Missouri Historical Society, and his *Spirit of St. Louis,* in which he made his first memorable flight, was placed in the Smithsonian Institution. In March, 1932, his firstborn son was kidnaped for ransom from his home at Hopewell, N. J., and his lifeless body was found in the woods near by some two months later. A second son was born later in the same year. His book *We* (the title referring to himself and his plane) was published in 1927, describing his transatlantic flight and later trips.

JOSEPH LISTER
1827–1912

JOSEPH LISTER, English surgeon and the originator of modern aseptic methods of surgery, was born at Upton, Essex, England, April 5, 1827, the son of Joseph Jackson Lister, eminent in optical science, who sent his son to the Quaker schools at Hitchin and Tottenham and to University College, London, where he received training under two noted physiologists, Wharton Jones and William Sharpey. He later studied at the University of Edinburgh; became assistant surgeon to the famous Dr. James Syme at the Royal Infirmary, lectured on surgery and published his famous treatise on *The Early Stages of Inflammation.* In 1863 he lectured at the Royal Society on the closely allied subject of coagulation of the blood. He was appointed to the chair of surgery in Glasgow in 1860 and there continued his researches, reaching the conclusion that decomposition of blood in a wound was the cause of suppuration. Appreciating the significance of Pasteur's demonstration in France that putrefaction was due to microbes growing in the putrescible substance, he searched for a means of destroying germs before they might enter a wound. Until this time carelessness of sanitary precautions had been prevalent in all surgical wards, but Lister insisted upon scrupulous cleanliness, the use of antiseptics and the sterilization of instruments. He first used carbolic acid in 1865 upon a compound fracture. It was applied undiluted and, with the blood, formed a thick crust which was painted daily with the acid. After a first failure the results were successful and he wrote a paper for the *Lancet* on his method.

In 1869 he succeeded Dr. Syme, whose daughter he had married in 1856, in the chair of clinical surgery of Edinburgh. He continued his researches in bacteriology and the development of antiseptic dressings and instituted the use of a spray of a 1–20 watery solution of carbolic acid in an attempt to free the air of the surgery from microbes. This spray method came into general use throughout the continent for a time, but by 1880 Lister had begun to doubt its value and abandoned its use, becoming convinced that the air of a surgery during operations might safely be disregarded, experiments having proven to his satisfaction that the serum of the blood is unfavorable for the development of the bacteria in the air, and that the cells of blood clots have the power of disposing of microbes.

In 1877 he took the chair of surgery at King's College, London, which he held for 15 years, retiring in 1896 from active practice, but continuing his scientific researches. He was president of the Royal Society for five years and in 1896 became president of the British Association for the Advancement of Science. In 1883 he was created a baronet and four years later was raised to the peerage as Baron Lister of Lyme Regis. He was made an original member of the new Order of Merit in 1902 and in 1891 founded the British Institute of Preventive Medicine which later became the Lister Institute of Preventive Medicine. He wrote many important papers for medical magazines, delivered many lectures, introduced new and improved methods and surgical instruments, and his work and teachings undoubtedly revolutionized the practice of surgery. He died at Walmer, Kent, Feb. 10, 1912.

FRANZ LISZT

FRANZ LISZT (list), Hungarian pianist and composer, was born at Raiding, Hungary, on Oct. 22, 1811. His father was clerk to the agent of the Esterhazy estates and an amateur musician. The boy began to play in public at the age of 10 and his talent so attracted the attention of some Hungarians of influence that they furnished the means for him to continue his musical education at Vienna and Paris, although as a foreigner he was refused admittance to the Paris Conservatory. He played in Paris and in other French cities and in Switzerland and became known as the "ninth wonder of the world." His first operetta, *Don Sancho,* was produced in 1825 and performed three times at the Académie Royale. His father died in 1828 and young Liszt thereafter devoted himself largely to teaching, at which he was highly successful. He was extremely impressionistic, did much reading and was touched by the literary, religious and political aspirations of the times. Both Paganini and Chopin visited Paris in 1831 and their playing inspired him to hard and constant study and practice. He strove to transcribe to the piano the effects that Paganini achieved on the violin.

From 1835 to 1840 he lived in Switzerland and Italy with the Comtesse d'Agoult by whom he had three children, one of whom afterwards became the wife of Wagner. He continued to study and appeared in public on occasion in Geneva, Milan, Florence, Rome and Paris, his only serious rival as a pianist being the Genevan, Thalberg. In 1840 he received a patent of nobility from the Emperor of Austria, and a sword of honor from Hungary. During the next eight years he played in all the principal cities of Europe, acquiring a large fortune, much of which he gave away in charity. At his own expense he completed the monument to Beethoven at Bonn and aided Spohr in conducting the musical festival at its unveiling in 1845.

From 1848 to 1861 he lived at Weimar with Princess Karoline Sayn-Wittgenstein, acting as conductor at court concerts and on special occasions at the theatres, although the Princess had induced him to give up the career of a virtuoso. Their home became a musical center; he took a number of promising young pianists under his wing and gave them lessons; wrote many articles of a musical nature on the works of Berlioz, the early music dramas of Wagner. His efforts on behalf of Wagner, then in exile in Switzerland, resulted in the first performance of *Lohengrin* in August, 1850 and the popularizing of Wagner, with the ultimate establishment of the Bayreuth festivals. He produced other works by Wagner, compositions by Berlioz, Schumann, Schubert, Cornelius and others, writing explanatory articles on them which were gathered together in his *Gesamnelte Schriften.*

He went to Rome in 1861, and there in 1865 joined the Franciscan order. The Princess Wittgenstein is said to have been determined to marry him and as both her family and his were opposed to the marriage Cardinal Hohenlohe quietly had him ordained. After 1869 Abbé Liszt lived alternately in Rome and in Weimar where, during the summers, he continued to receive pupils gratis. From 1876 on he taught for several months each year at the Hungarian Conservatoire at Budapest and died at Bayreuth on July 31, 1886.

He composed much sacred music and won renown as a musical critic. Among his most important compositions are his thirteen *Symphonic Poems,* the oratorios, *Legend of St. Elizabeth and Christus, Hungarian Rhapsodies* and the *Faust* and *Dante* symphonies. As a pianist he has probably never been excelled.

DAVID LIVINGSTONE   1813–1873

DAVID LIVINGSTONE, Scottish missionary in Africa and world famous as an explorer of that continent, was born in Blantyre, Lanarkshire, Scotland, on March 19, 1813. He worked in a cotton factory while a young boy and until he was 24, acquiring his education by attending a night school. The desire to become a missionary was kindled in him by reading Dick's *Philosophy of a Future State.* He studied medicine in London and was attracted to Africa as a field for his future work by Dr. Robert Moffat, who had been a missionary in that country and whose daughter he later married. In November, 1840 he was ordained by the London Missionary Society and sailed for Africa, arriving in Bechuanaland in July, 1841, where he remained for several years studying the languages and the customs of the native tribes, making friends among them and establishing mission posts. He endeavored to introduce native missionaries into the Transvaal, but the Boers objected and he traveled northward, discovering Lake Ngami, and then made up his mind to explore the African continent from the Indian Ocean to the Atlantic.

He spent four years carrying out his plan. He was accompanied by his wife and children and by a small number of attendants and native bearers. The hardships and perils they endured were such as few men had known, but he learned much about the native tribes, about the country, its products, wild game, etc. He discovered the Victoria Falls, the greatest cataract in the eastern hemisphere, explored the Zambezi River, in 1854 reaching Loanda on the Atlantic Coast. He then turned back to the Zambezi and followed it to its mouth at the Indian Ocean, reaching Quilimane in 1856. Returning to England, he was welcomed with great enthusiasm and during fifteen months in England and Scotland he published his *Missionary Travels*.

Wishing to continue his explorations in Africa, he severed his connection with the London Missionary Society and the English government appointed him consul to Quilimane and also chief of an expedition to explore east and central Africa. Reaching Africa he set out on the new expedition in March, 1858, explored the waters of the Zambezi with its tributaries and discovered Lakes Shirwa and Nyassa. He decided that the Lake Nyassa district was the best field for commercial and missionary operations. The Portuguese authorities put difficulties in his path, and the discovery that the slave trade was being extended to that territory further hampered his projects. The British government recalled the expedition in July of the following year, and Livingstone, bearing all the expenses himself, continued his explorations of the northern banks of Lake Nyassa on foot. Afterwards he navigated his little ship to Bombay and returned to England in July, 1864. He published his second book, *The Zambezi and its Tributaries,* in 1865. He hoped to awaken interest in establishing a settlement for missionaries and commerce near the head of the Rovuma.

In 1865 he returned to Africa to settle for the Royal Geographical Society a disputed point regarding the watershed of central Africa and the sources of the Nile. Starting inland from Zanzibar in March, 1866, nothing was heard of him for two years. He again encountered innumerable hardships and perils, but he pressed on and discovered Lakes Mweru and Bangweolo and returned to Ujiji for a rest, after which he again struck westward and reached the river Lulaba which he thought to be the Nile or, as it proved, the Congo. He suffered a severe illness but managed to return to Ujiji where, in November, 1871, he found Henry M. Stanley who had been sent to Africa by the *New York Herald* to search for him. He was not yet ready to abandon the expedition and returned to Bangweolo where he again fell ill and died at the village of a friendly chief, on May 1, 1873. His native followers buried his heart under a tree at the spot where he died, carving a rude inscription on the tree trunk, but his body was embalmed and taken to England where it was buried in Westminster Abbey on April 18, 1874. His wife had died in 1862 and was buried in Africa. His *Last Journal* was published after his death.

DAVID LLOYD-GEORGE   1863–

DAVID LLOYD-GEORGE, British statesman and prime minister of England, was born on Jan. 17, 1863, in Manchester. His father, William George, was a poor and invalid Welsh schoolmaster who died when his child was a year old and, his mother being without means, he was taken to Llanystumdwy, Wales, and placed in the care of her brother, Richard Lloyd, who was a shoemaker and Baptist preacher. He made good progress in school and while still a youth became prominently connected with a group of Welshmen who were struggling for freedom from Church of England domination. He studied law, became well known through one of his early cases, organized the Welsh Farm Union, and at 27 years of age was elected to Parliament.

For ten years he held his seat without making any particular stir, being known merely as a hot-headed little Welsh lawyer. But with the outbreak of the Boer War in 1899 he became prominent in opposition to the government and throughout the three years of that struggle he fought vigorously for the cause of the Boers, arousing much bitter personal antagonism which at times placed him in danger from mob violence. His independence, his brilliant speeches and his ability forced public respect, however, and after the bitterness of the war had subsided he rapidly rose to a conspicuous place. In 1906 he was made president of the Board of Trade in the Liberal cabinet and his masterly handling of the British railway strike and other labor troubles and of disputes arising in connection with foreign patents won him high approval.

In 1908 he became Chancellor of the Exchequer. His able defense of the old-age pension bill resulted in its passage and he next promulgated the famous "Lloyd-George Budget," so revolutionary in some of its provisions that the financiers of the country were all arrayed against him and he found himself the center of a heated controversy, which he eventually won and secured passage of his bill. From that time on he remained one of the most conspicuous figures in English politics, advocating as his next great reform the National Insurance Bill (1911); and after the outbreak of the World War in 1914 it devolved upon him as Chancellor to arrange for the largest war loans in British history and to stabilize credit to meet the huge demands incident to the war. He became minister of the newly created department of munitions in the coalition cabinet and flung all his energies into the task of arousing England to the great need for increase in the output of munitions. He enlisted the cooperation of prominent men, traveled about to the great centers of trade where he conferred with union officials and with working men, obtaining their consent to abrogate many of their privileges for the sake of the great cause, and throughout the country plants were turned over to the making of munitions.

On the death of Earl Kitchener in 1916, Lloyd-George succeeded him as secretary of state for war, but before the close of the year he became prime minister, and until the end of the war practically dictated the policies of the government. Believing that the war committee of the cabinet was too large effectively to handle the grave situations which were constantly arising, he created a war cabinet of four members, giving them full powers, and in order to free himself for matters relating to the conduct of the war, Mr. Bonar Law was made leader of the House of Commons. After the Armistice, Lloyd-George was returned to power by an overwhelming majority and at the Peace Conference in Versailles in 1919 he was a leading figure and with Clemenceau and President Wilson, dominated the conference. His remarkable powers of conciliation, which had so often been demonstrated in his relations with the Allies and in labor disputes, were now repeatedly brought to bear on the conflicting points of view presented. President Wilson's plan for a league of nations appealed to him strongly, while at the same time he was in sympathy with the determination of Clémenceau to safeguard France. He had taken with him to Versailles representatives of India and of the dominions, thus establishing a new precedent. He signed the treaty on June 28 and it was promptly accepted by the House of Commons. Lloyd-George was strongly in favor of bringing to trial those responsible for the war and particularly the German Kaiser, whom he considered the chief offender.

His oratorical powers were brought into frequent play during the next few years in the many conferences looking to the rehabilitation of Europe and the stabilizing of social and political conditions and he made powerful appeals for brotherhood and understanding between nations and between classes. In 1920 he sponsored the Home Rule Bill and was largely instrumental in the establishment of the Irish Free State in 1921. His government fell in 1923 but he was returned to Parliament and remained leader of the Liberal party. He visited the United States in 1923. In 1888 he had married Margaret Owens who became the mother of his two sons and two daughters.

JOHN LOCKE   1632–1704

JOHN LOCKE, English philosopher and writer, was born Aug. 29, 1632, at Wrington, Somersetshire, the son of a country attorney. After attending Westminster he was sent in 1652 to Christ Church, Oxford, where he later lectured on Greek, rhetoric and philosophy. He studied and, for a time, practiced medicine although he was more concerned with problems of ethics, morals and philosophy. He was a pronounced advocate of religious toleration and keenly interested in the relations of church and state.

Through his medical practice he became acquainted with Lord Ashley (afterwards the first Earl of Shaftesbury), whose confidential secretary he became and with whom his fortunes later became intimately involved. In 1670–71, at a meeting of friends for the discussion of social and religious matters, Locke made the suggestion that they should first determine what questions the human mind was capable of dealing with, what were the limits of knowledge it was capable of acquiring and how the mind acquired knowledge. He devoted 17 years to the study of this problem and embodied the results of his long investigation in his famous *Essay Concerning Human Understanding,* published in 1690, which is still regarded as one of the finest treatises on this subject. In this famous essay he maintained that knowledge cannot be consciously innate in each man, but is a gradual growth depending upon fallible experience.

He was appointed Secretary to the Council of Trade in 1672 when the Earl of Shaftesbury became Chancellor, but three years later, when Shaftesbury fell, Locke retired to France and spent the years from 1675 to 1679 working on the philosophical problems that occupied his mind. He returned to Lord Shaftesbury in London in 1679, but upon the latter's flight to Holland, following the collapse of Monmouth's Rebellion, which he had fomented, Locke also came under suspicion and spent the next five years in exile in Holland, where he was known as Dr. Van der Linden. During this period his liberal tendencies in theology became greatly strengthened. The way for his return to England was opened up by the Revolution of 1688–89. In February of the latter year he declined an appointment as English Ambassador to Brandenburg, but accepted a Commissionership of Appeals. His first published work, *Epistle de Tolerantia,* appeared anonymously in Holland during that year and was translated into English by William Popple. In 1690 appeared another anonymous treatise on *Civil Government.*

From 1691 on he lived mostly at Oates in Essex, the country-seat of

Sir Francis Masham, publishing from time to time tracts on economics and the currency; his *Thoughts on Education,* an anonymous treatise on the *Reasonableness of Christianity* (1695), and adding chapters and emendations to his *Essay Concerning Human Understanding* which appeared in later editions of the work (1694, 1695, 1700). In 1696 he was appointed a Commissioner of the Council of Trade at a salary of 1000 pounds a year. He was occupied in writing defences of his philosophy, vindicating his letter on toleration, and working on a treatise on the *Conduct of the Understanding* until his death, which took place at Oates on Oct. 28, 1704. He was buried in High Laver Church. After his death his *Commentaries on St. Paul's Epistles* were found.

HENRY WADSWORTH LONGFELLOW   1807–1882

HENRY WADSWORTH LONGFELLOW, American poet, was born at Portland, Me., on Feb. 27, 1807, the second son of Stephen Longfellow, a well-to-do lawyer. He was educated at Bowdoin College and immediately after his graduation was appointed professor of modern languages and sent to Europe by the college trustees to qualify for the position. He spent nearly three years in France, Spain, Italy and Germany studying the languages of those countries. In 1831, soon after his return, he married Miss Mary Storer Potter who died in 1835 on a European tour.

He had begun to write poetry while at college or earlier and he published about this time a version of *The Coplas of Don Jorge Manrique.* An account of his travels abroad on his first European tour appeared in 1835 under the title of *Outre Mer; Hyperion,* a record of travels of a later date, appeared in 1839. In 1836 he became professor of modern languages and literature at Harvard College, a post which he filled for nearly eighteen years. His first book of original poems, published in 1839 under the title, *Voices of the Night,* met with favorable reviews and a cordial welcome from the public so that when his *Ballads* appeared in 1841 an appreciative audience was ready to greet it. Among the ballads in that collection were *The Skeleton in Armor, The Wreck of the Hesperus, The Village Blacksmith* and *Excelsior,* which are among the most popular of his short poems and have been used in many schoolbooks. His *Poems on Slavery* were published in 1842, followed the next year by a poetic drama, *The Spanish Student.* A third trip to Europe was made in 1842 and upon returning to Cambridge the following year he married Miss Frances

Appleton of Boston (the heroine of Hyperion), who was accidentally burned to death in 1861. Five children were born of the union.

In 1854 he resigned his office at Harvard and thenceforth devoted himself to writing, living a quiet life at his home, the Craigie House, in Cambridge, Mass. His poetry is distinguished for grace and refinement and for its reflection of the kindliness of his nature. His quick sympathies and the simplicity and directness of his verse, much of it celebrating the homelier virtues of mankind, largely account for his extraordinary popularity. His volume on *The Poets and Poetry of Europe* appeared in 1845; *The Belfry of Bruges and Other Poems* in 1846. Probably the most popular of his long poems was *Evangeline,* a story of the French exiles in Acadia. *The Building of the Ship,* another favorite, was included in the collection, *The Seaside and the Fireside* of 1850, followed by *The Golden Legend,* and in 1855 another long narrative poem, *Hiawatha,* an American Indian legend.

The Courtship of Miles Standish, another long narrative poem describing the early days of the Plymouth Colony, is known to nearly every public school pupil in the country. *Tales of a Wayside Inn* appearing in three parts, 1863, 1872 and 1874, enjoyed a good degree of popularity. Some of his most finely wrought and finished work appeared in *Flower-de-Luce* (1867). *The New England Tragedies,* blank verse tales of the Salem witchcraft, appeared in 1868 and for several years thereafter he worked on a translation of Dante's *Divine Comedy.* In 1872 appeared *Christus, A Mystery,* in blank verse, and *Three Books of Songs,* containing more of the *Wayside Inn Tales, Judas Maccabœus* and other poems. Works of his declining years were *Aftermath, The Masque of Pandora, Ultima Thule.* He died at his home in Cambridge on March 24, 1882 and was buried in Mt. Auburn Cemetery, Cambridge. He may be regarded as one of the most influential founders and one of the brightest ornaments of American literature.

LOUIS IX OF FRANCE   1214–1270

Louis IX of France, called Saint Louis, was born April 25, 1214, and succeeded to the throne on the death of his father, Louis VIII, in 1226. His mother, Queen Blanche of Castile, who acted as Regent during his minority, was a woman of great piety and he was given strict religious training. He married Margaret, daughter of Raymond Berenger, Count of Provence, in May. 1224.

A rising of the nobles under Hugh de Saintonge in the southwest was suppressed by the King in 1242. Henry III of England, who had come to the aid of de Saintonge, was defeated at Saintes. Raymond VIII, Count of Toulouse, yielded without a fight when faced by two royal armies in 1243 and thereafter Louis had his nobles well in hand. He was a head taller than any of his knights, energetic and firm, wise, just and naturally kindly, and enjoyed the trust and respect of his people. Of a devout temperament, he was given to fasting, listening to sermons and surrounded himself with priests. He built hospitals, tended the sick with his own hands and gave charity to more than 100 beggars daily. After his first crusade he wore woolen shirts in winter, skins in summer, and made presents of haircloth shirts to his friends.

At the end of 1244, during an illness, he vowed to go on a crusade. He bought from John of Brienne, Emperor of Constantinople, the crown of thorns, parts of the true cross, the holy lance and holy sponge and built the Sainte Chapelle in Paris to house the sacred relics. Quarrels between the Pope and the Emperor Frederick II and difficulties in preparing for his crusade postponed it until 1248 when he and his followers embarked in August for Cyprus, and the following spring went on to Egypt. In April, 1250, he was defeated by the Mohammedans, captured and held a prisoner in Syria. A treaty made with his captors called for the return of Damietta, which had surrendered to him without resistance, and the payment of a ransom of 800,000 pieces of gold. He was released upon paying half that sum and surrendering Damietta. He then proceeded to the Holy Land where he remained for four years, but accomplished little. He could get no help from France; the Shepherd's Crusade, started in answer to his request, became so anti-clerical that it was suppressed. In 1254 his mother died and he was forced to return home.

From 1254 to 1269, when he undertook a second crusade, he devoted himself to the affairs of France. He was able to bring about peace between the quarrelsome nobles, by moral force aided by public opinion. They did not dare rebel at the tight hand he held over them. By the treaty of Paris of May, 1258 he adjusted his differences with Henry III of England and in return for Henry's acknowledging him as liege suzerain and renouncing Normandy, Anjou, Touraine, Maine and Poitou, he received all the fiefs and domains of the King of France in the diocese of Limoges, Cahors and Perigueux and the expectation of Saintonge, south of the Charent, and Agenais, if they should fall to the crown of France by the death of Alphonse of Poitiers. The treaty was unpopular because it sacrificed a large part of France which Henry had not won, but Louis believed that absolute sovereignty over the northern provinces made up for the loss in the south. By a compromise with the King of Aragon in 1258 the latter gave up his claims to part of Provence and Languedoc (except Narbonne) while Louis gave up Rousillon and Barcelona.

On his second crusade he got as far as Tunis where his army was decimated by a plague which caused his own death on Aug. 25, 1270. He was canonized in 1297 by Pope Boniface VIII.

LOUIS XI OF FRANCE   1423–1483

Louis XI was born at Bourges, July 3, 1423, the eldest son of Charles VII and Marie of Anjou. At 13 he was married to Margaret, daughter of James I of Scotland. In 1439 he was sent by his father to defend Languedoc against the English and to put down the brigands of Poitou, but rebellious nobles induced him to join their cause. His father later forgave him for this rebellion, and he fought against the English in 1440, and three years later aided King Charles in suppressing the Count of Armagnac's revolt. In 1444 he led an army of mercenaries against the Swiss canton of Basle, and after an ineffectual campaign returned to find that his father had established his court at Nancy, and had fallen under the spell of Agnes Sorel. Louis' wife (a favorite of the King) died in 1445 and soon afterward Louis again conspired against his father. Charles, learning of the plot, banished his son (whom he never saw again) to Dauphiné where Louis dismissed the governor, made a secret treaty with the Duke of Savoye and married Charlotte, daughter of Duke Ludovico, despite his father's formal prohibition.

When Charles VII visited the Bourbonnais in 1456, Louis, fearing for his life, fled to Flanders leaving Dauphiné to be annexed to the crown of France. He waited in Brabant five years for his father's death after which he was anointed and crowned at Reims Aug. 15, 1461. He imprisoned some of his father's ministers and chose his advisers mostly from the middle class. He began his reigning with the high-handed methods he had used toward the nobles of Dauphiné; forced the clergy to pay feudal dues, intrigued against the great houses of Anjou and Orléans in Italy. Jean Dunois and John II, Duke of Bourbon, stirred up a revolt, and Francis II, Duke of Brittany, was soon at odds with Louis over the latter's attempt to assert his control of that almost independent duchy. The nobles rallied around Charles the Bold (later Duke of Burgundy) and in 1465 formed a "league of public welfare" which declared war on Louis XI, with Louis' brother Charles, Duke of Berry, as the nominal head of the revolt. The country was on the verge of anarchy, but the lesser gentry refused to rise and the citizen class was allied with the King who won some victories in the Bourbonnais, fought an indecisive battle with the Burgundians at Montlhéry (July 16, 1465), was besieged in Paris and made a truce with Charles the Bold on September 28, yielding on all points, giving up the Somme towns in Picardy (for which he had paid 200,000 gold crowns) to Philip of Burgundy, and Normandy to his own brother Charles. Two months later he found a pretext for retaking Normandy in a quarrel between Charles and the Duke of Brittany. Duke Philip of Burgundy died in 1467 and Charles the Bold had a free hand, but while he was in England for his marriage to Margaret, sister of Edward IV, Louis overran and reduced Normandy. A new revolt was planned in 1471 but the death of the King's brother Charles prevented a civil war and Charles the Bold was forced to make a lasting peace.

Louis then campaigned to overthrow him, bought off the King of England who had come to Charles' aid, and defeated Charles at Nancy in January, 1477, in which action Charles perished. By the treaty of Arras (1482) Louis received Picardy, Artois, the Boulonnais, Burgundy and French Compté. France was now united except for Brittany; upon the death of René of Anjou her borders were enlarged by acquisition of the duchies of Anjou and Bar, and in 1481 Maine and Provence were added.

Louis lived in isolation during his last years, died Aug. 30, 1483 and was buried in the church at Cléry. Although by nature cruel and tyrannical, he lived simply and devoutly, contributing largely to the church, was a skilful diplomat and did much to bring about orderly government in France by his warfare against the feudal lords. He encouraged the development of manufacturing, commerce and printing, the building of roads and established institutions of learning.

LOUIS XIV OF FRANCE   1638–1715

Louis XIV, called The Great, son of Louis XIII, was born at St. Germain-en-Laye on Sept. 16, 1638. His mother, Anne of Austria, became regent on his accession to the throne in 1643 following the death of his father, but left the management of the kingdom largely to Cardinal Mazarin, her chief minister, who was more ambitious for power than interested in the education of Louis. From 1648 to 1659 France was troubled by the civil wars of the Fronde, instigated by certain nobles who had been excluded from high offices; and by war with Spain, which was concluded by the Peace of the Pyrenees in 1659. In 1660 Louis married the Infanta Maria

Theresa of Spain. Mazarin died the next year and Louis took the rule of the realm into his own hands, governing as an absolute monarch until his death. He possessed indomitable perseverance and a clear head. He chose able ministers and although he ruled despotically, he gathered about him an exceptionally able group of men and under his influence the national life of France attained greater development than ever before. Colbert restored the ruined finances; Louvais raised the army to such a point of efficiency that it excelled any other in Europe. His court became the most magnificent on the Continent.

Continuous foreign wars marked his reign. On the death of Philip IV of Spain in 1665, Louis, as his son-in-law, claimed part of the Spanish Netherlands. In 1667, with Turenne, he made himself master of French Flanders and French Compté. England's alliance with Holland and Sweden ended his conquests and at the peace of Aix-le-Chapelle (1668) he surrendered French Compté. He made German alliances, bought the support of Charles II of England, seized Lorraine in 1670. Two years later he again entered the Netherlands with Condé and Turenne, and conquered half of the country in six weeks. The States-General of the Netherlands forming an alliance with Spain, he seized ten cities of the Empire in Alsace and in 1674 took the field with three armies and extended his conquests in the Netherlands, despite the deaths of Condé and Turenne. By the peace of 1678 he retained control of fortresses in the Spanish Netherlands and French Compté. He became more and more arrogant and ambitious, captured Strassburg and many other border towns. He was hated and feared by all of Europe. In France he ruled the courts of justice which were obedient to his whims. The nobles had been reduced to mere satellites of the King and even the church had been brought under his control. In 1685, the Queen having died, Louis married Madame de Maintenon under whose influence in 1685 he revoked the Edict of Nantes. The persecution of the Protestants that followed resulted in half a million of the better class of French subjects emigrating to other countries. Despite the Revocation, Louis called together a council of French clergy which declared that the Pope's power extended only to matters of faith.

Following the death of the Elector Palatine, Louis claimed part of the latter's territory for the Duchesse of Orléans, gathered an army and invaded the Palatinate which he laid waste by fire and sword the following year. The Grand Alliance was now formed against France, headed by William of Orange and including many of the countries of Europe. Louis' first successes gave way to defeat and the war dragged on for several years until the Peace of Ryswick in 1697. France had become exhausted with the long warfare and the people were impoverished.

The death of Charles II of Spain led to the long War of the Spanish Succession. Louis supported the claims of his grandson, Philip of Anjou, who finally became Philip V of Spain after years of contention with rival claimants, but Louis sacrificed valuable colonies. France was almost completely ruined and her power among the nations gone, but Louis' absolute sway continued until his death on Sept. 1, 1715, four years after the deaths of his son and his eldest grandson. His great-grandson, Louis XV, succeeded him.

LOUIS XV OF FRANCE   1710–1774

Louis XV, great-grandson of Louis XIV, was born at Versailles on Feb. 15, 1710, and succeeded to the throne in 1715. The Duke of Orléans, who was Regent during his minority, allowed the country to be nearly ruined through the financial schemes of the Scotsman, John Law, and all the capital that could be raised was pocketed by the financial cliques, the court and the state. Louis was married at the age of 15 to Maria Leszczynska, daughter of Stanislas, dethroned King of Poland. Upon the death of the Regent, he assumed the government of the country, under the advice of his wise and able teacher, Cardinal Fleury, who became his Prime Minister. Through his wife Louis became involved in the war of the Polish Succession and obtained the duchy of Lorraine for his father-in-law, with the proviso that upon the latter's death it should revert to France.

Through supporting the claims of the Elector of Bavaria to the Austrian crown against those of Maria Theresa, Queen of Hungary, Louis became embroiled in the War of the Austrian Succession in 1740. Success fell to the French arms almost uninterruptedly through the first year of the war, but in 1742 Louis was badly defeated and his able counselor, Cardinal Fleury, died the following year. Louis entered into an alliance with Frederick the Great of Prussia and together they defeated the English, the Austrians and the Dutch at Fontenoy in 1745, though at the cost of France's navy and her sea trade. Peace was made at Aix-le-Chapelle in 1748.

Louis was one of France's most dissolute monarchs. He lavished public funds upon his mistresses. To Madame de Pompadour, with whom he became infatuated toward the conclusion of the War of the Austrian Succession, he gave notes upon the treasury for enormous sums. He was soon involved in war with Great Britain over the Nova Scotia boundary. The Seven Years' War began in 1756 and France allied herself with

Austria against Prussia and England. The Franco-Austrian arms met with defeat after defeat; France was financially crippled, her people in the utmost misery, but Louis, under the influence of his mistresses, persisted in continuing the war. Britain had taken nearly all of France's possessions in both the East and the West Indies and the great Province of Canada had been lost. Peace was at last concluded in 1763.

The war over, Louis found himself beset by discontented subjects in the domestic sphere. The Paris Parliament was intent upon suppressing the Jesuits and a long contest ensued between the King and Parliament, with the latter winning the victory in 1764. Embolded by the suppression of the order, the Parliament now tried to restrict the powers and prerogatives of the monarch and refused to register the King's edicts of taxation but Louis asserted his authority, abolished the Parliament, banished its members to the provinces and formed a new and subservient Parliament which carried out his wishes. He continued to squander public moneys upon his favorites, giving to Madame du Barry, who had succeeded Madame de Pompadour in his affections, more than 100,000,000 livres in five years' time. His long life of profligacy finally had its natural result; his constitution was ruined and he fell an easy victim to smallpox from which he died on May 10, 1774, with few to mourn his passing. His indifference to the financial ruin which his extravagances had brought upon the country and to the sufferings and misery of his people sowed the seeds of the French Revolution.

LOUIS XVI OF FRANCE   1754–1793

Louis XVI, third son of the Dauphin Louis, only son of Louis XV, was born Aug. 23, 1754, and became Dauphin by the deaths of his father and two elder brothers. In 1770 he married Marie Antoinette, daughter of the Empress Maria Theresa of Austria. He ascended the throne in 1774 on the death of his grandfather, to find the treasury empty, the nation with a debt of 4,000,000,000 livres, his subjects crushed and miserable under heavy taxes. He restored to the Paris and provincial parliaments their rights. Certain reforms which he proposed, on the advice of Turgot, were rejected by court, church, parliament and the aristocracy, but Louis remitted some of the most hated taxes, reduced the expenses of the court and made some other reforms. He was by nature honest, temperate and moral and for a time was popular with his subjects, but he was weak and lacked the judgment to rule capably.

Necker was made Comptroller-General in 1777 and greatly improved the financial status of the nation, but France spent much money in aiding the American colonies to fight their war of independence and to make up for this Necker proposed taxing the aristocracy and the wealthy. They resisted so effectively that he resigned and was succeeded in 1783 by Calonne who renewed the lavish splendor of the court and advised the calling of the Assembly of Notables, made up of the aristocracy, the churchmen, councillors of parliament and municipal officers. When they had gathered they compelled Calonne to flee to London. Brienne succeeded him and obtained new taxes, the edict for which the parliament of Paris refused to register. The people demanded a meeting of the States-General. Louis himself registered the tax edicts and banished the councillors of parliament whom he was soon afterwards forced to recall.

In 1788 he dissolved all parliaments, establishing a Cour Plénière. In August an edict was promulgated that the treasury should make no cash payments except for the troops. Brienne now resigned and Necker again assumed the reins as chief minister. An Assembly of the States of the nation was resolved upon, and Necker advised calling the Third Estate in double number. The States-General met at Versailles in May, 1789. The Third Estate formed itself into a National Assembly, undertook to make a new constitution and called itself the Constituent Assembly, declaring that political independence, equal rights and universal freedom were inviolable rights. Louis' attempt to suppress this Assembly brought to a head all the political and social unrest and precipitated the long-brewing Revolution. He ordered the troops under arms, dissolved the ministry and banished Necker. On July 12, 1789 there were revolutionary outbreaks in Paris. The National Guard was called out the following day. On the 14th the people stormed the Bastille. The provinces followed the lead of Paris. The Assembly on August 4 abrogated feudal and manorial rights, declaring the equality of all human rights. The royal princes and many of the nobles fled from Paris. The royal family, prevented from following their example, failed to convince the people of their espousal of republican principles. On October 5, Versailles was attacked and Louis and his family were compelled to return to Paris. By his wavering and lack of decisive action he had lost the confidence of the people and the Royalists alike.

During the two following years he alternately made concessions to the republicans and conspired to escape from their hands. He and his family reached Varennes on one occasion but were captured and brought back. From that day his fall was inevitable. In August, 1792 a mob invaded the Tuileries, slaughtered the guards and imprisoned the King in the Temple after heaping insults on Marie Antoinette. In September

France was proclaimed a republic and in December the King was brought to trial on charges of treason, pronounced guilty and condemned to death. He was guillotined at the Place de la Revolution on Jan. 4, 1793.

JAMES RUSSELL LOWELL   1819–1891

JAMES RUSSELL LOWELL, American poet, essayist, critic and diplomat, was born at Cambridge, Mass., on Feb. 22, 1819, of a prominent Massachusetts family, his father being a Unitarian minister. He was a great reader of poetry and romance; a none too industrious student, but was graduated in 1838 from Harvard College where he had contributed a number of papers and poems to a college publication. He had studied law and was admitted to the bar in 1840 but found the profession uncongenial and soon turned to literature. His first volume of poems, *A Year's Life* (1841) was inspired principally by his engagement to Maria White, whom he later married. With a friend, Robert Carter, he started a literary journal, the *Pioneer,* to which he contributed poems and articles and for which he obtained contributions from Hawthorne, Emerson, Whittier, Poe, Story and others, but the magazine lived for only three months. At the end of 1843 he published a collection of his poems and *Conversations on Some of the Old Poets,* from contributions to his own and other magazines. He married and spent the winter and early spring of 1845 in Philadelphia where he was an editorial writer on the *Pennsylvania Freeman.*

In the spring he returned to Cambridge and made his home at his birthplace, Elmwood. Three daughters were born, two of whom died in infancy, and a son. He contributed poems, mostly on the slavery question, to the daily press, became correspondent for the London *Daily News* in 1846, and two years later agreed to contribute a weekly article or poem to the *National Anti-Slavery Standard* of New York. During this period he published a second collection of poems, *A Fable for Critics, The Vision of Sir Launfal* and the *Bigelow Papers.* The homely New England philosophy and humor of the last named won him wide fame. The *Papers* dealt satirically with the Mexican War to which he was strongly opposed. In 1851, following the death of his mother, he went to Europe with his wife and daughter and infant son Walter, who died in Rome a few months later. Returning in November, 1852, he wrote some travel papers which were collected and published in book form under the title of *Fireside Travels.* Mrs. Lowell died in 1853.

In the winter of 1855 he delivered a course of lectures on English poets before the Lowell Institute in Boston, following which he was offered the Smith Professorship of Modern Languages in Harvard, which Longfellow had but recently vacated. He accepted, spent a year abroad in study, entered upon his professorial duties in 1856 and continued in the post for twenty years. In 1856 he married Frances Dunlap, of Portland, who had cared for his daughter after the death of his first wife. From 1857 to 1861 he was the first editor of the *Atlantic Monthly* and thereafter continued his contributions to its pages, including the second or Civil War series of the *Bigelow Papers*, sharp satires against the slavery party. He also contributed political articles to the *North American Review*, of which he was joint editor from 1862 to 1872. Much of his best critical work appeared in these two magazines. His articles on great writers were republished in book form and his collected *Literary Essays* fill six volumes. Among his other works are *My Garden Acquaintance, A Good Word for Winter, On a Certain Condescension in Foreigners,* and a volume of poems, *Under the Willows and Other Poems*. His *Commemoration Ode,* delivered at a memorial service for Harvard students who had died in the Civil War, ranks as one of the best of American poems. Later works were *Impressions of Spain, Democracy and other Addresses, Political Essays, Heartsease and Rue.*

In 1847 President Hayes appointed him Minister to Spain and in 1880 he became Minister to England where his second wife died in 1885 shortly before his return home. He died at Elmwood on Aug. 12, 1891. He was perhaps the most scholarly of American writers and some of his works represent the highest American attainment in culture and style.

MARTIN LUTHER , 1483–1546

MARTIN LUTHER, German reformer and founder of Protestantism, was born at Eisleben, Germany, on Nov. 10, 1483, the son of a miner. He attended school at Magdeburg and Eisenach; entered the University of Erfurt in 1501 and after taking his degree he became a monk in the Augustinian friary at Erfurt. He was ordained a priest of the Catholic church in 1507; the following year taught philosophy at the new University of Wittenberg and then returned to Erfurt where he taught theology. His success as a preacher was already notable.

He was sent to Rome in 1511, and began his career as a reformer almost immediately after his return. The raising of money for Rome by the sale of indulgences had aroused his indignation, and the shameless way in which the traffic was carried on caused him to draw up 95 theses in which he questioned the Pope's right to forgive sins, and particularly condemned the practices used in selling such indulgences. These theses he nailed on the church door in Wittenberg on Oct. 31, 1517. They were written in Latin but German translations were made and published without his knowledge and caused widespread discussion. Many people had been opposed to the practice but this was the first public protest. The Church immediately ordered him to recant, which he refused to do. Pope Leo X summoned him to Rome to answer for his theses, but the Elector, Frederick HI of Saxony, interfered. Luther grew bolder and attacked the whole papal system, denying the supremacy of the Pope and defending the doctrines for which John Huss had been put to death as a heretic in 1415. He published a series of three pamphlets setting forth his views, upholding freedom of thought and the right of each individual to interpret the Bible for himself. His *Address to the Christian Nobility of Germany* called upon them to reform the abuses in the Church. The Pope issued a bill threatening him with excommunication which Luther burned before a crowd of doctors, students and citizens in Wittenberg.

In 1521 Charles V convened the first Diet of Worms before which Luther was summoned to appear. His journey to Worms was almost a triumphal progress, but he refused to recant and was put under the ban of the Empire. Upon returning to Wittenberg he was seized by the friendly Elector of Saxony and hidden in the castle of the Wartburg in the Thuringian forest. He spent a year in the Wartburg during which he translated the New Testament, wrote a treatise proclaiming that monastic vows were wrong and urging nuns and monks to renounce their vows, and did other literary work. Religious disorders arose in Wittenberg in 1522 and Luther returned there, restored order and organized a church, establishing a new form of church government and sacraments. His reply to Henry VIII of England on the seven sacraments was published during the year.

In the same year he married Catharine von Bora, one of the nine nuns who had withdrawn from a convent. A happy domestic life followed and in addition to his own six children he cared for several nephews and nieces and befriended many poor students. The year 1529 marked his disputes with Zwingli and other Swiss clergymen on the Real Presence in the Eucharist. The drawing up of the Augsburg Confession, at which Luther, an outlaw, was represented by Philip Melanchthon, was the culmination of the German Reformation which by 1530 had conquered the country. Luther's life thereafter was passed in comparative quiet. Despite increasing ill health he kept at the task of maintaining and vindicating his doctrines and continued to war against the Papacy as anti-Christian. In 1540 he reluctantly sanctioned the bigamous marriage of the Landgrave Philip of Hesse which caused a scandal in the new church. In his latter years he prepared a translation of the Old Testament, wrote a number of hymns and prepared two catechisms for instruction in the Reformed doctrines. He died at Eisleben on Feb. 18, 1546. Count Albrecht wished to bury him at Eisleben, but Elector John Frederick insisted on transferring his body to Wittenberg where it was interred on Feb. 22 in the Castle Church.

LORD MACAULAY 1800–1859

THOMAS BABINGTON MACAULAY was one of the most sparkling ornaments of English literature. He made his scholarship and learning charmingly available to vast multitudes who read him with all the delight associated with the reading of fiction. Whether as historian, essayist, or conversationalist, he was always interesting. He was born in Leicestershire, Oct. 25, 1800, son of Zachary Macaulay, a West Indian merchant, and grandson of Rev. John Macaulay, a Scottish minister of some attainment. His mother was the daughter of Thomas Mills, a bookseller of Bristol who was so zealous in the boy's training that when he entered an academy in his 13th year he astonished his comrades and teachers with the extent and variety of his achievements, his startling feats of memory and his easy familiarity with the classics and history. Sydney Smith later said of him that his conversation was illuminated by occasional flashes of silence and this quality was evidenced from early youth.

At 18 he entered Trinity College, Cambridge, and soon acquired a reputation as a scholar and debater. Intellectually, his career was so uniformly triumphant that no one achievement is outstanding. He won the chancellor's medal twice; first for a poem on Pompeii and again for one called *Evening*. In 1821 he was awarded a scholarship, took his degree of B.A. the following year, was elected a fellow of Trinity, and soon inaugurated his career in the field of letters by publishing in *Knight's Quarterly Magazine* a number of poems and critical essays. In 1825 he took the degree of M.A. and in the same year published in the *Edinburgh Review*, with which he was long identified, his essay on Milton, perhaps the finest specimen of his glowing eloquence and brilliant critical faculty. Its rich and flowing style has made it a model in its literary field and it is hardly possible to overpraise its brilliance.

In 1826 he was called to the bar, but never practiced, and it may be said that notwithstanding his captivating eloquence and a certain convincing character of statement, he was not profound and never achieved the highest distinction in the field of politics. In 1830 he entered Parliament and made several speeches in favor of reform measures. He was made secretary of the board of control for India, went to that country as a member of the supreme council, and drew up a penal code for the government of the province, characterized by a humane and understanding attitude toward the natives whose oppression he so eloquently and scathingly pictured in his splendid essay on the career of Warren Hastings. On his return to England he entered Parliament (1839) for the city of Edinburgh and in the following year was appointed war secretary. In 1842 appeared his *Lays of Ancient Rome,* including the familiar and stirring *Horatius.* He was in no sense a great poet but few readers have failed to be affected by these thrilling poems dealing with an historical period which he knew as well as he knew his own time. In 1843 appeared his collected essays in three volumes. Ever a staunch champion of religious freedom and personal rights, he spoke with convincing eloquence for the Roman Catholic relief bill and the bill to repeal the civil disabilities of the Jews.

In 1848 appeared the first two volumes of his famous *History of England* "from the accession of James II down to a time within the memory of men now living." It was received with an acclaim, and enjoyed a circulation, almost without precedent. The third and fourth volumes, published in 1855, were greeted with still greater enthusiasm. Never before had history been written with such a popular appeal, and its outstanding defect (the author's irrepressible propensity for conceiving his own strong convictions as settled facts) has not invalidated its generally authentic character. In 1857 the French Academy of Moral and Political Science made him a foreign associate and in the same year his own country honored him by raising him to the peerage. For some time his health had been failing and he died Dec. 28, 1859 at his residence, Holly Lodge, Kensington, London. He had never married.

Macaulay's learning was prodigious and seemed the greater for his amazing memory. He is at his best in his famous essays, most of them masterpieces of style and artistic construction. His review of a literary or historical work leaves the reader with nearly all the knowledge which he would have acquired by reading the book itself, and with a sense of esthetic satisfaction which the original author seldom affords. The essays on Macchiavelli, Bunyan, Barère, Frederick the Great, Chatham, Doctor Johnson, Bacon, Hastings, and many others are eminent specimens of critical and interpretive biography. The amount of knowledge which they include can be estimated only by those who have laboriously read the many volumes they so brilliantly condense. Multitudes have found in Macaulay a delightful short-cut to a knowledge of famous characters.

NICCOLÒ DEI MACHIAVELLI   1469–1527

NICCOLÒ DI BERNARDO DEI MACHIAVELLI (mä'kyà věl'lě), Italian states-man, historian, founder of the science of politics, was born at Florence, Italy, on May 3, 1469. His youth was passed in the troublous times of the French invasion and after the Medici had been expelled from Florence, he obtained a position in the new republican government established by Savonarola. In 1498 he was appointed First Secretary of the Ten and held that position until the fall of the Florentine Republic in 1512. He was sent on various diplomatic missions representing the government—one to Cesare Borgia, of which he gave an account in numerous letters; one to the Emperor Maximilian, and four to France. His dispatches from the various countries he visited form a valuable picture of the political con-ditions of the times.

The Medici were restored in 1512 and Machiavelli's patron, the Gon-faloniere Soderini, fell from power and was charged with conspiracy. Machiavelli was himself arrested in 1513, also charged with conspiracy, and was put to the torture and then acquitted. For several years he devoted himself to writing and was commissioned to write a history of Florence. In 1521 he again became engaged in diplomatic services and upon his return to Florence after one of his absences, he became ill and died on June 20, 1527. He had married in 1502 Marietta Corsini who bore him six children.

He was an astute observer and thinker but never a leader and was a poor man throughout his life. For many years he enjoyed positions of trust and responsibility and had unusual opportunities for studying the science of government and the methods of those who held political power. His letters and state papers contain much of political wisdom and sagacity, and he holds a high place for his writings on history, politics and diplo-macy. It was not until 1682 that the first great edition of his works was published, establishing his reputation as the founder of modern political science. His historical writings include *Florentine Histories, Discourses on the First Decade of Titus Livius,* the *Life of Castruccio Castracani* (which he left incomplete) and *History of the Affairs of Lucca.*

His purely literary writings embrace an imitation of the *Golden Ass* of Apuleius, an essay on the Italian language and several comedies which marked an epoch in the development of the Italian theatre, chief among them being *La Mandragola,* which is generally regarded as a masterpiece of the dramaturgic art, despite its shameless indecencies and its biting humor and satire. His reputation as a master of political science and for intellectual cunning and ability, rests largely upon one book, *De Principatibus* or *Il Principe* (rules for the education of a prince), published in Rome five years after its author's death. In that work he maintained that for the establishment and maintenance of authority all means may be employed, the worst and most treacherous as well as the best and most loyal. He held that treachery on the part of the ruler was justified by wickedness and treachery on the part of his subjects. His ardor for the liberation of Italy was unbounded; he became convinced that strong native governments, even though they were absolute, must be endured for the good of the country at large and, having accepted the rule of the Medici in Florence, he was willing to use any means at his command to make it secure. During his lifetime he was bitterly assailed by the clergy and it is due mainly to them that the word "Machiavellian" has become a synonym for the diabolic, for devilish cunning and trickery.

JAMES MADISON   1751–1836

JAMES MADISON, fourth president of the United States, was born in Port Conway, Va., on March 16, 1751, the son of a Virginia planter of independent means, also named James Madison. After graduating at 21 from Princeton (then known as the college of New Jersey), he studied law and taught his younger brothers and sisters, but his bent was toward politics and in 1776 he was a member of the Virginia convention which prepared the state constitution, having previously served on a committee of public safety in his own country. Although never a great orator (due perhaps to his own retiring nature) he became one of the most prominent and distinguished of American statesmen. He was a man of the highest character, of scholarly attainment, great erudition and breadth of view, opposed always to religious intolerance and to a state church, maintaining that all religions should be on an absolute equality.

In 1780, when he was not yet 30 years of age, he represented Virginia in the Continental Congress and after the capitulation of Yorktown the following year and the recognition of the independence of the colonies in 1782, he took a prominent part in framing the important legislative measures which were necessary to launch the new republic. Returning to his father's house in 1783, he pursued his legal studies, but the following year found him in the Virginia house of delegates and for the next few years he alternately devoted himself to his studies (natural history and philosophy engaging much of his attention) and to the service of his state. He performed most of the arduous work of codifying the laws of the state, was an active member of a convention of delegates from five of the original thirteen states, held at Annapolis in September, 1786, to consider political and commercial matters, and in the Virginia legislature the following month he brought about the passage of an act which led to the Philadelphia Convention in May, 1787. He was one of that body of able statesmen, including Washington and Patrick Henry, who there framed a new constitution to take the place of the Articles of Confederation which had been adopted in 1781, and his own views of government were so embodied in the document as to earn for him the title of Father of the Constitution. In order to combat opposition which developed, he joined with Alexander Hamilton and John Jay in writing a series of articles, the earlier ones of which were published in a New York paper under the signature of "Publius." Later essays were issued as separate numbers of *The Federalist*. The entire series consists of 85 essays, 29 of which were by Madison, and the whole is regarded as one of the most able compendiums of political commentary ever published. In his own state there developed strong opposition to approval of the constitution (led by Patrick Henry who was governor), but Madison by his lucid reasoning and convincing array of arguments, after a battle lasting several weeks during which he sometimes made as many as a dozen speeches in one day, turned the tide and Virginia became the ninth state to ratify the constitution, thus securing its adoption.

He was elected to the first congress assembled in New York in 1789 and served continuously and with distinction for the following eight years. During the first session he became the leader of the republican party, then for the first time distinct from the federalists, of whom Hamilton was the moving spirit. He later took issue with Hamilton (who was secretary of the treasury) on the latter's financial policies. In 1797 he retired to private life. He had long been an ardent admirer of Thomas Jefferson and upon the latter's election to the presidency in 1801, he became secretary of state, holding that post through Jefferson's eight years of office. In 1809 he succeeded Jefferson as president. His first term was largely occupied with the effort to establish satisfactory diplomatic and commercial relations with England and France, England's aggressive acts of interference with American ships and impressment of American seamen having brought the country to the verge of war. Madison made every effort to preserve peace, but in June, 1812, convinced that the national dignity could no longer tolerate England's arrogance, he signed a declaration of war. He was reelected and before the end of his second term had the satisfaction of seeing the war brought to a close by the treaty of Ghent in December, 1814.

In 1794 he had married the beautiful Mrs. Dorothea Payne Todd, who became known to the country as Dolly Madison, and who by her gracious presence, lively disposition and brilliant social gifts, was well fitted to be the first lady of the land. Through her wide circle of admirers she exercised much influence throughout her husband's administration. In March, 1817, Madison retired to his estate at Montpelier, Va., where he spent the remainder of his life in quiet pursuits, farming, social enjoyments and extensive writing on political matters. He was a rector of the university of Virginia and in 1829 rendered his last public service as a member of the constitutional convention of the state. He died at his home on Jan. 28, 1836, survived by his wife.

MAURICE MAETERLINCK   1862–

Maurice Maeterlinck (mä′tĕr lĭnk), Belgian poet, dramatist and essayist, was born at Ghent, Aug. 29, 1862, of Flemish extraction. He received his education at the Collège Sainte-Barbe and at the University of Ghent. In 1887 he settled in Paris and became acquainted with Villiers de l'Isle-Adam and other leaders of the symbolist school in French letters, by whom his work was greatly influenced. Upon the death of his father he returned to Belgium, living at Ghent in the winter and in summers on an estate at Oostacker. His literary career began in 1889 with the publication of a volume of poetry, *Serres chaudes,* and a play, *La Princesse Maleine.* In 1890 he published two plays in Brussels, *L'Intruse* and *Les Aveugles,* followed in 1891 by *Les sept princesses.*

In his early writings he leaned strongly toward the mystical and symbolical. His translation of the *Adornment of the Spiritual Marriage* by Ruysbroeck (1891) made clearer to the public the meaning of his mysticism. In 1892 appeared one of his major mystical dramas, *Peléas et Mélisande,* followed two years later by three powerful little dramas written to be played by marionettes—*Alladine et Palomides, Interieur* and *La Mort de Tintagiles.* In 1895 he published under the title of *Annabella* a translation of Ford's drama, *'Tis Pity She's a Whore.* Two philosophical works followed, a study of Novalis and *Le Trésor des Humbles;* another mystical drama, *Aglavaine et Sélysette,* and a volume of lyric verse, *Douze chansons.* In 1898 appeared *La Sagesse et la destinée,* a monograph on the ethics of mysticism, and a sort of commentary on his own mystical plays. *La Vie des abeilles* (1901), a mingling of philosophy, fancy and natural history, won wide popularity. He achieved the effect of mystery that underlies life by the simplicity of his diction and a realistic symbolism. The adventures of the soul interested him rather than the actions and intrigues of human beings that we daily come in contact with. Although their action is shadowy, their meaning metaphysical and illusive, yet his plays enjoyed wide popularity in most of the countries of Europe.

A radical change appeared in most of his later works, after he had again settled in France. The plays, *Monna Vanna* and *Mary Magdalene* (1909) deal with realities, with human beings caught in the mesh of bodily actions and emotions, their action being concentrated in a few powerful scenes. He won fame as a dramatist with *L'Oiseau bleau,* published in 1910 and produced the following year. This was produced in New York as *The Blue Bird,* had a very long run and was later revived and shown in motion pictures. It has much of the mysticism that characterized his early plays, but with a realism of fancy which gives it a stronger popular appeal.

He has published several volumes of essays; *The Buried Temple, The Double Garden, Life and Flowers, Death. The Betrothal,* produced in London and New York, dealing with some of the characters in *The Blue Bird,* met with a degree of success. His war play, *The Burgomaster of Stilemonde* (1920), dealing with the German occupation of Belgium, added to his reputation as a dramatist. In 1919 he published *The Miracle of St. Anthony* and *Mountain Paths,* and in 1923 two plays in a modern setting, *The Cloud that Lifted* and *The Power of the Dead.*

FERDINAND MAGELLAN 1480–1521

FERDINAND MAGELLAN (mȧ jĕl'lan) or FERNÃO DA MAGALHÃES, the illustrious Portuguese navigator who was the first to circumnavigate the globe, was born at Sabrosa about the year 1480. Nothing is known of his early years except that he went to Lisbon where his noble lineage made him acceptable at court and he is said to have lived for some time in the royal household. He served with distinction in maritime expeditions to the East Indies and had many adventures, but feeling that his services were ill-rewarded by his government he repaired to Spain in 1517 accompanied by his friend and countryman, Ruy Falero, an astronomer and geographer who had participated in many of his adventures. While awaiting the king's pleasure he resided with a Portuguese gentleman, Diego Barbosa, whose daughter Beatriz he married.

His plan for reaching the Moluccas by a western route was well received by the young king, Charles V, and his advisers, and after a year or more of preparation the little fleet of five small ships, destined to various and harrowing adventures, stood out to sea on Aug. 10, 1519. These ships, manned by about 280 men, were old and worn. Prior to their departure a note of intrigue and adventure was already sounded by the presence of a gang of ruffians, in the employ of the Portuguese sovereign, who lurked in the streets of Seville under instructions to waylay Magellan and terminate his high hopes with murder. After leaving the Canaries on Oct. 3, the little fleet was becalmed and made hardly any progress for a month. Food and water grew scarce, mutiny threatened, and only the rigorous conduct of Magellan averted disaster from this cause. On the 29th of November they reached the Brazilian coast which they explored and then sailed along the coast of Patagonia, battling with the intense cold and with the most violent storms. No sooner were they settled in winter quarters than the mutiny which had been smouldering broke out in all its fury; intrigue was rife among the several shipmasters, and the suppression of this uprising of the wearied and fearful mariners, representing many interests and several nationalities, was a masterful achievement of their inflexible commander. The story of that winter rivals the wildest narratives of imagined adventure.

With the earliest signs of spring they again set sail, encountering violent storms, and after two months reached the headland still known as Cape Virgins. Discovering the strait which bears his name, Magellan consumed five weeks in passing through its intricate windings, beset by demands that, the passage to the Spice Islands having been found, the expedition should turn back. This he firmly refused to do. As a consequence, one of the ships left the others and made its way back to Spain where its commander and his men circulated the grossest libels about Magellan. Meanwhile the intrepid mariner turned his prows westward across the vast and unknown expanse of the Pacific. Month after month they sailed over this mysterious waste of waters. On January 24, 1521, they came upon a small wooded islet where their longest plummet failed to touch bottom. Eleven days later they reached another desert speck of land, where neither food nor water could be obtained. They knew not when again they might touch land; in point of fact, 5000 miles were yet to be traversed before so much as a rock or tree would again meet their gaze. Famine and scurvy combined to render more terrible the uncertainty as to where they were sailing and whether, indeed, there was any end to this uncharted wilderness of water. Mutiny could be of no avail now. In desperation and with haunting fears, they could only press forward. At last, on March 6, 1521, they reached a group of islands inhabited by savages. Here the abundance of fruit and water put an end to their famished condition. On the 16th of March the three ships arrived at the islands subsequently named the Philippines, and to his astonishment Magellan found there Asiatic traders from Siam and China and soon learned the true greatness and significance of his adventure. He had accomplished the circumnavigation of the globe, and although his voyage was not yet completed, he knew that the rest of it lay through familiar waters.

But tragedy awaited this prince of explorers at this scene of the realization of his great achievement. In the rôle of a missionary he consecrated his religious fervor to converting the savage natives and fell a victim to their murderous spears and scimitars. The hero who had throttled mutiny, defied storm and famine, and challenged the unknown seas, was stabbed through and through and trampled under foot by these ferocious savages. The date of his death was April 27, 1521.

One of the three remaining ships, being found unseaworthy, was burned and the other two proceeded on their voyage. One of these sprang aleak and was left behind for repairs, and the only remaining ship, the *Victoria,* turned her prow toward the Cape of Good Hope. At last, on the 6th of September, 1521, after many adventures and delays, the little vessel sailed into Guadalquiver with 18 gaunt and haggard survivors to report, after an absence of two years, the proud story of the first circumnavigation of the earth.

RICHARD MANSFIELD 1857–1907

RICHARD MANSFIELD, American actor, son of Maurice Mansfield, a London wine merchant and Mme. Erminia Rudersdorff, his wife, an opera singer, was born on the island of Helgoland, May 24, 1857. While at school in England he played the rôle of Shylock at a class day production. His mother wished him to become an artist and he studied painting at Kensington but his father's business reverses caused him, at the age of 17, to enter a mercantile house in Boston, Mass., where his mother had established herself as a teacher of singing. He returned to England in 1875, taking with him a number of pictures he had painted while in Boston. His hope of selling them proved vain and he became a drawing room singer and entertainer. W. S. Gilbert heard him sing in 1878 and engaged him, at $15. a week, for a provincial company appearing in several Gilbert and Sullivan operas.

He returned to America and made his New York début at the old Standard Theatre in September, 1878, in *Les Manteaux Noires*. He sang Vedder in the light opera, *Rip Van Winkle* and appeared in Gilbert and Sullivan's *Iolanthe*. His legitimate stage career began in Baltimore when A. M. Palmer gave him the part of Baron Chevrial in *A Parisian Romance*. He won his first great success in that rôle in 1883 and played it frequently in later years. He supported Mrs. Fiske in *Andrea,* sang in *The Mikado,* and finally organized his own company. In 1887 he met with much success in *Dr. Jekyll and Mr. Hyde,* and in 1890 achieved one of his most popular characterizations as Beau Brummel. In 1892 he played Arthur Dimmesdale in his own dramatization of Hawthorne's *Scarlet Letter,* followed by Shylock in 1893. The next year he introduced George Bernard Shaw to the American public in a production of *Arms and the Man.* His success in that play led him to put on another Shaw play, *The Devil's Disciple,* three years later.

He achieved striking popularity in his 1898 production of Edmond Rostand's romantic play, *Cyrano de Bergerac*—a production that he abandoned at the height of its success because the claims of an American to the authorship of the play were upheld when Rostand contemptuously refused to fight them. Mansfield would not pay royalties to both authors and *Cyrano* remained unacted in America until Walter Hampden revived it about twenty years later when the American claimant to authorship of the play withdrew his demand for a share in the royalties. Mansfield acted one of Shakespeare's seldom performed histories, *Henry V,* in 1900, following by Booth Tarkington's *Monsieur Beaucaire* and Shakespeare's *Julius Caesar.* Later productions were *Ivan the Terrible, Don Carlos,* Molière's *Misanthrope,* Ibsen's *Peer Gynt.* Prince Karl in *Old Heidelberg* was another of his favorite rôles. He portrayed Richard III in London in 1889 and made a few other professional appearances there.

He was a man of high artistic ideals, but of a sarcastic, overbearing disposition. He worked hard at his profession and was exacting in his demands upon the members of his company. He married Beatrice Cameron, an actress in his company, and had one son, Gibbs, who died in young manhood, shortly after he had made his appearance on the stage under the name of Richard Mansfield, Jr.

Mansfield died on Aug. 30, 1907.

JEAN PAUL MARAT 1744–1793

JEAN PAUL MARAT (mä'rä'), a leader in the French Revolution, was the son of a Sardinian designer named Mara, born at Boudry near Neufchâtel, May 24, 1744. He studied medicine at Bordeaux, and practiced in Paris, Holland and London. In the latter city in 1773 he published his *Philosophical Essay on Man,* embracing the materialistic theory, and an essay in social philosophy, *The Chains of Slavery,* appeared the following year. Returning to Paris in 1777, he was appointed by the Comte d'Artois (later Charles X of France) as physician to his guards, a post which he held until 1786, finding time meanwhile to indulge in his scientific studies and experiments in optics and electricity. He published in 1780 his *Plan de Législation Crimenelle,* translated Newton's *Optics* (1787) and the following year his own *Découvertes sur le Lumière* appeared.

With the outbreak of the French Revolution Marat entered eagerly into a war of pamphlets on the side of the common people. He founded *L'Ami du Peuple,* one of the most famous papers of the period, which he made an organ for his venomous attacks. He denounced in turn Necker, Bailly, LaFayette, Louis XIV, Dumouriez and later, with extreme bitterness, the middle class political party known as the Girondists. Such virulence produced its natural result in hatred of himself on the part of many leaders of the Revolution, but he had made himself the idol of the lower classes in Paris who gave him a power which even his enemies respected and feared. He attacked the Constituent Assembly, the ministers, the corps municipal, and the Court of the Châtelet. He was arrested and imprisoned from October 8 to Nov. 5, 1789, and would have been arrested again in January, 1790, had he not fled to London where he wrote his *Dénonciation contre Necker.* In May he returned to Paris and continued to edit his paper, vehemently attacking everyone in power, even the King himself. He had to remain in hiding much of the time, in cellars, garrets, sometimes even in the sewers where he contracted a loathsome skin disease. In December, 1791, he fled again to London and there wrote his *École du citoyen.*

In 1792 he returned to Paris, became a member of the Commune and demanded a tribunal to try royalists then in prison. No such tribunal was formed but the September massacre of prisoners resulted, due largely to his influence. He was elected a member of the Convention, and upon the declaration of the Republic suspended *L'Ami du Peuple* and started the *Journal de la république française,* which was even more radical. He took no sides in the Assembly, refused power for himself, suspected and opposed those who took or were given power. After the execution of the King, Marat engaged in an unrelenting struggle against the Girondists, but they succeeded in having him tried for sedition before a Revolutionary Tribunal in April, 1793. He was acquitted and became more powerful than ever in the Convention. The fall of the Girondists on May 31 was a triumph for him.

On the evening of July 13, 1793, while in his bath, he heard a young woman begging to be admitted to see him and heard her say that she brought news from Caen where the escaped Girondists were trying to arouse Normandy. He ordered her to be admitted and assured her that the deputies whom she named to him would soon be guillotined, whereupon she plunged a dagger into his heart. It was thus that the name of Charlotte Corday came into the history of the French Revolution. His death aroused great excitement. His ashes were taken to the Panthéon with great pomp and a bust was later placed in the Hall of the Convention.

GUGLIELMO MARCONI   1874–

Guglielmo Marconi, Italian engineer and inventor of the wireless telegraph, was born at Bologna, Italy, April 25, 1874, the son of an Italian father and an Irish mother. He was educated privately and early showed a keen interest in physical and electrical science. In 1895 he conceived the idea of sending messages through the air by electromagnetic waves. Others had been experimenting along similar lines, but it remained for him to devise practical means which brought wireless telegraphy into general commercial use. He experimented at his father's country house at Pontecchio and established communication over a distance of a mile. Failing to interest the Italian government in his work, he went to England in 1896 and there took out the first patent ever issued for wireless telegraphy based on electric waves. He demonstrated his results for officials of the British post-office and representatives of different nations and obtained a nine mile range of communication. In June, 1897, Italy invited him to go to Spezia and attempt to communicate with Italian warships and he sent messages to vessels twelve miles off shore. Later successful tests were carried out in Rome.

In July, 1897, a company was formed in England to acquire the Marconi patents for all countries except Italy. Permanent stations were established at Alum Bay, Isle of Wight, and at Bournemouth (later removed to Poole) and Marconi's experiments continued. Within two years it was possible to exchange messages across the English Channel and the British and Italian navies were equipped with wireless apparatus. On March 3, 1899, the East Goodwin lightship was run down by a steamer, wireless calls for help were sent out and lifeboats proceeded to the rescue. During the same year wireless was used in naval maneuvers over a distance of 74 miles. Its first military application was in the South African War. In October, 1900, Marconi erected a long distance wireless station in Cornwall and preliminary test messages were carried over 200 miles. In 1901 he succeeded in sending a message across the Atlantic Ocean, from Poldhu in Cornwall to St. John's, Newfoundland. The following year he made a voyage on the American liner *Philadelphia* and received messages during the day up to a distance of 700 miles, while at night the distance was increased to 2000 miles, thus demonstrating that wireless is much more far-reaching at night.

He patented his magnetic detector in 1902 and three years later his horizontal directional aerial. In 1903 he inaugurated the sending of news messages from the United States to the London *Times* and found it possible to maintain communication with the steamship *Lucania* during her entire passage across the ocean. In 1910 he received messages at Beunos Aires from Clifden, Ireland, a distance of more than 6000 miles. A new wireless invention appeared in 1912, the "timed spark system" for generating continuous waves, which was employed for a number of years at long distance stations and by means of which he first sent a message from England to Australia (Sept. 22, 1918). During the World War, aside from serving in both the army and navy, he took charge of Italy's wireless and conducted experiments with short waves for the purpose of devising a directive, or beam, system of telegraphy which could be used in war times with a certain degree, at least, of secrecy. Important results were obtained later in England in association with G. S. Franklin by using 15-metre waves between London and Birmingham. They found that short waves, even with a minimum of power, could carry messages over any distance by night or by day.

Marconi was a member of the Italian War Commission to the United States and was the plenipotentiary delegate of his government to the Paris Peace Conference in 1919 and to other conferences on peace treaties. He was awarded the Nobel prize for physics in 1909 and has been the recipient of many medals and honors from England, the United States and other countries.

MARIA THERESA   1717–1780

MARIA THERESA, Empress of Austria, ranks among the great women rulers of the world. She was the eldest daughter of Emperor Charles VI, and was born at Vienna, May 13, 1717. Her father made her heir to his hereditary thrones by the "Pragmatic Sanction" for which the principal European powers became sureties. She was married in 1736 to Francis of Lorraine, afterwards Grand Duke of Tuscany. Charles VI died in 1740 and she became Queen of Hungary and Bohemia and Archduchess of Austria. When she ascended the throne, the country was nearly exhausted, the army weak, her subjects discontented, and she found herself beset by Prussia, Bavaria, Saxony and Sardinia (aided and abetted by France), all of which nations claimed portions of her dominions. Frederick II of Prussia claimed Silesia and made war upon her to obtain it. Spain laid claim to her dominions in Italy; the Bavarians, assisted by the French, invaded Bohemia and the Elector of Bavaria was crowned Emperor as Charles VII (1742). Before all this onslaught the young Queen would have been defeated and her possessions lost had it not been for the loyalty of her Hungarian subjects and the aid of Great Britain.

The war of the Austrian Succession, started in 1741, was ended in 1748 by the peace of Aix-la-Chapelle, but Maria Theresa had lost Silesia to Prussia, Parma and Piacenza to Spain, and some of her Milanese districts to Sardinia. By the peace treaty her rights were admitted and her husband was recognized as Emperor. In 1745 he had succeeded to the throne of Germany on the death of Charles VII. The Queen-Empress then devoted herself to internal affairs and financial reforms. Agriculture, manufactures and commerce began to flourish again under her fostering care, and the national revenues were doubled although taxes were lowered. She appointed Marshall Daun to reorganize her armies, and Kaunitz became her foreign minister. She never became reconciled to the loss of Silesia and her attempt, with France as her ally, to recover it from Frederick the Great resulted in the Seven Years' War (1756–63) and nearly brought about the downfall of Frederick, who, however, maintained his possession of Silesia by superior force of arms. After peace had been signed, the Empress again concerned herself with domestic problems, among the most pressing of which was amelioration of the condition of the peasantry. She softened to some extent the administration of the penal code; did what she could for the cause of popular education by establishing schools, and organized charitable societies to care for the poor and the suffering. After the death of her husband in 1765 she associated her son

Joseph with her in the government. In 1772 she joined with Russia and Prussia in the partition of Poland, obtaining for Austria and Hungary the Polish provinces of Galicia and Lodomeria. From the Porte, in 1777, she obtained Bukowina and later acquired several districts from Bavaria.

She was a woman of majestic figure and of undaunted spirit, possessing truly masculine energy which she combined with feminine tact and won and retained the admiration of her subjects. She raised Austria from the position of an impoverished, second-rate nation to a place of power in the comity of nations. She was a devout Roman Catholic, but interested herself in reforming some of the more flagrant abuses of the Church. She had ten children of whom the eldest son, Joseph II, succeeded her on the throne. Her daughter, Marie Antoinette, became the wife of Louis XVI of France and was guillotined in the French Revolution. Maria Theresa died on Nov. 29, 1780, in Vienna.

MARIE ANTOINETTE   1755-1793

MARIE ANTOINETTE (än twä nĕt'), wife of Louis XVI of France, was the daughter of the famous empress, Maria Theresa of Austria. She was born on Nov. 2, 1755, at Vienna and at the age of 15 was married to the Duc de Berri who became king in 1774 upon the death of his grandfather, the profligate Louis XV. The young queen was unpopular in France from the outset. Her gay and simple nature and her dislike of ceremonial shocked the court. She was frank and outspoken, heedless of the impression she made, fond of dress and pleasure, and with a lightness of disposition and tendency to extravagance which, in that time of growing restlessness and bitterness preceding the French Revolution, when the people were groaning under their burden of taxation, added to their general distrust of this foreign queen. One of those who most openly opposed her was Louis' younger brother, the Count of Provence, who was responsible for rumors accusing her of constant intrigues. She was blind to the misery and discontent of the common people and opposed many measures of reform instituted by the king. She did not attempt to disguise her love for her native land and used her influence with her husband to shape his foreign policies in the interests of Austria, which caused her to be suspected of being a spy and she came to be popularly known as "the Austrian woman." She was more resolute in character than Louis and often aroused that weak-willed monarch to spasmodic displays of authority.

In 1789 after a period of disorganization in the financial system of the country, the king called for an assembly of the states of the kingdom, a move which she strongly protested. One of the first acts taken by this states-general after its convening on May 5th was to declare the queen and her extravagances the cause of the financial distress of the country and the fanatical hatred of the populace was inflamed anew against her. On the morning of Oct. 6, 1789, an attempt upon her life was made at Versailles and, alarmed by the seriousness of her situation, she thereafter made some more or less sincere efforts to gain the popular good will. But it was too late; the people had no faith in her sincerity and she became convinced that her only safety lay in flight. She would not go without her husband and for a long time Louis who, despite his weaknesses and his lack of the decisive qualities needed at such a time, yet possessed some sense of royal honor and of duty to his country, refused to go. He at length consented, however, realizing that their position was becoming more and more precarious, and in June, 1791, an attempt was made to leave the country by night. The flight was discovered and the royal couple was captured at Varennes and imprisoned in the Tuileries which was invaded by a mob on the 20th and insults were heaped on the queen. On Aug. 10th the Tuileries was again stormed by the revolutionists, the guards were murdered and the king and queen were sent to the Temple as prisoners. Marie was separated from her family and subjected to the most humiliating indignities.

In January, 1793, Louis was brought to trial before the national assembly on a charge of attempting to conspire with foreign powers, was found guilty and put to death by the guillotine. Seven months later, the widowed queen was removed to the Conciergerie. Two attempts were made to bring about her escape but on Oct. 14 she was taken before the revolutionary tribunal and charged with inciting civil war and with giving council to foreign enemies of the country. After a trial lasting two days, in which her enemies sought to defame her character by false charges, she was found guilty of treason and on Oct. 16 met the same fate as her husband.

This unfortunate queen has been sometimes portrayed as an innocent victim and martyr of the Revolution and sometimes as the embodient of selfishness, heartlessness and extravagance. The truth probably lies somewhere between these two extremes. There is no doubt that during her imprisonment she had been in communication with her brother, Leopold II, in an attempt to have an Austrian army invade France and rescue the royal family.

DUKE OF MARLBOROUGH   1650–1722

JOHN CHURCHILL, first Duke of Marlborough, the foremost general of Europe in his day, and the second son of Sir Winston Churchill, an impoverished royalist, was born June 24, 1650, at the Manor House of Ashe in Devon. He was page to the Duke of York, an Ensign in the Guards, and in 1667 was sent to Tangier, perhaps because of the King's jealousy of his favor with the Duchess of Cleveland who had given the youth 5000 pounds. He was made a captain on his return and served in the Netherlands under the great French general, Turenne. His ability, and the influence of his sister, Arabella, mistress of the Duke of York, won him rapid promotion. In 1678 he married Sarah Jennings, a beautiful and wealthy lady in waiting and close friend of Princess Anne, and thus he secured the favor of Anne who later became Queen.

In 1682 he was created Baron Churchill of Eyemouth in Scotland, and three years later Baron Churchill in the English peerage. He became still more prominent when the Duke of York succeeded to the throne as James II in 1685 and fought for the Crown in Monmouth's Rebellion, but in 1688 he joined the invading William of Orange who rewarded him with the title of Earl of Marlborough. He rendered distinguished service in Ireland and against the French in the Netherlands, but in 1692 he plotted to overthrow William and aid in the restoration of James II. He was arrested and lodged in the Tower, but was later restored to favor and given command of the British army in the Netherlands. After the death of William and the accession of Queen Anne (second daughter of James II) Marlborough was made Knight of the Garter, Commander-in-Chief, and Master General of the Ordnance, while his wife was named Groom of the Stole, Mistress of the Robes, and Keeper of the Privy Purse. He was at this time practically the real ruler of England and as Commander-in-Chief of the British and Dutch forces he received 10,000 pounds a year.

His military triumphs in the Netherlands and his victories over the French won him a dukedom. In 1704, with Prince Eugene of Savoy, he defeated the French and Bavarians in the famous Battle of Blenheim. He was given the estate of Woodstock by Parliament, the Queen ordered Blenheim Park to be built for him, and the Emperor made him a Prince of the Holy Roman Empire. On May 23, 1706, he signally defeated the French at Ramillies and in 1708 repulsed Vendome's attempt to regain Flanders at Oudenarde, and took the cities of Lille and Ghent. Another great victory at Malplaquet in September, 1709 brought a brief cessation of the fighting, but he was in the field again in 1711, capturing town after town from the French until the Treaty of Utrecht brought Europe a thirty years' peace.

Meanwhile, the Queen had quarreled with Marlborough's wife, who had become tyrannical, and dismissed her. Marlborough was charged by his enemies with embezzling public money and was deprived of all his offices. Upon the accession to the throne of George I, he again came into favor but took little part in public affairs. A stroke of apoplexy in 1716 impaired his powers of speech, but he continued to attend Parliament until within six months of his death, which occurred on June 16, 1722. He was buried in Westminster Abbey after a funeral of great pomp and magnificence. He left a large fortune and the Duchess survived him for twenty years. His avarice and his lust for power and influence had made him unpopular, but his abilities were unquestioned and the lustre of his military achievements for England cannot be dimmed. He was one of the few generals of the world who never lost a battle.

CHRISTOPHER MARLOWE   1564–1593

CHRISTOPHER MARLOWE, the first of the great English poetic dramatists, was the son of John Marlowe, a shoemaker, and was born at Canterbury in February, 1564. He was educated at King's School, Canterbury, and at Benet College (now Corpus Christi), Cambridge, where he obtained his bachelor's degree in 1583. What his life was immediately thereafter has never been known. It has been stated that he became an actor and that, like Ben Jonson, he saw military service with Leicester and Sidney in the Low Countries, but these assertions are not supported by evidence. The first of his plays of which there is any record is *Tamburlaine the Great,* which was performed about the year 1588, with the famous actor Edward Alleyn in the lead, who also appeared in most of his later plays. This was the first of the early English plays to be written in the common speech as we know it today and was a great success. Marlowe brought a color, variety and sonorousness to the stage that previous dramas had lacked.

His second play, *The Tragical History of Doctor Faustus,* based upon the legend that had come down through the centuries, of a man who sold his soul to the devil, became immediately popular abroad as well as in England. *The Jew of Malta,* produced after 1588 and first published in 1633, shows a technical advance over *Doctor Faustus.* It was written in the transition period of Marlowe's life—between that of a young and most promising tragic poet and the mature and sensitive author of *Edward II,* which is considered his masterpiece and was produced about 1590. While it lacks the majestic poetry of *Doctor Faustus* and parts of *The Jew of Malta, Edward II* is technically far in advance of both and some critics have estimated it a greater historical drama than Shakespeare's *Richard III.* Just what the association may have been between Marlowe and Shakespeare we do not know, but Marlowe is considered to have had a share in the writing of the three parts of *Henry VI* and probably of *Titus Andronicus.* His *Massacre of Paris* has come down to us in mutilated form. *The Tragedy of Dido* was probably written in collaboration with Nash who completed and published it a year after Marlowe's death. Another fragment, the incompletion of which the world mourns, is the poem of *Hero and Leander,* generally considered one of his greatest works, without which the full range of his genius for poetic expression would not be known to us. Havelock Ellis has called it the "brightest flower of the English Renaissance," a "free, fresh and eager song." It was first published in 1598; a second edition, with Chapman's continuation, appeared during the same year.

Marlowe translated Ovid's *Amores* and the first book of Lucan's *Pharsalia,* neither of which adds to his reputation among moderns. His brief lyric, *Come, live with me and be my love,* is one of the treasures of English song which called forth an answer by Sir Walter Raleigh and was imitated by Herrick, Donne and others. Like Shakespear, Marlowe went to published books for the material of his plays, but brought his own vigorous, passionate imagination to play upon the events he selected.

In the spring of 1593 when the plague raged in London, Marlowe was among those who fled to the country. It is known that in May of that year he was in the little town of Deptford, near London, where he was killed by a dagger thrust in a tavern brawl; old accounts say in a quarrel with a serving man over a courtesan. The parish book of Deptford contains this entry: "Christopher Marlowe, slain by Ffrancis Archer, the 1 of June, 1593." Modern investigation puts the onus of the stabbing on one "Ingram Frizer, Gentleman," over a tavern bill. His body was buried in an unknown spot beneath the towers of St. Nicholas.

KARL MARX   1818–1883

HEINRICH KARL MARX, German economist and founder of modern socialism, was born on May 5, 1818, in Trèves, Germany, of Jewish parentage. His father, who was a lawyer, embraced Protestantism during the son's early boyhood, in which he was followed by all his family. He was educated at the universities of Bonn and Berlin, first studying law, but later turned his attention to philosophy and developed radical ideas which made it impossible for him to become a university professor.

At 24 he formed a connection with a radical paper which he edited for a short time and which was suppressed after his withdrawal from it the following year. He had in the meantime gone to Paris and associated himself with a group of French socialists. Here he met Friedrich Engels, a German socialist who became his close friend and who later collaborated with him in the famous *Communist Manifesto*. Some contributions which Marx made to a radical magazine in Paris caused him, with nearly all the other members of its staff, to be expelled from the city in 1845 and he went next to Brussels, where he spent three years in study and writing. There he was joined by Engels and together they engaged in various socialistic activities, finally becoming associated with the Communist League, which had branches in London and in Paris, Brussels and other continental cities. For this society they wrote in 1847 the *Communist Manifesto,* which practically embodies the creed of modern socialism. It was published in several languages and given wide circulation. Briefly, it advocates the abolition of landed property and inheritance rights; confiscation of the property of rebels and emigrants; centralizing credit in the hands of the state; state ownership of means of transportation and communication; the reclamation of waste lands; state management of productive enterprises; more even distribution of population, thereby eliminating great cities; compulsory labor and the combining of manufacturing with agriculture; abolition of child labor and free educational facilities.

The following year the two friends went to Cologne where they founded a political daily paper, so revolutionary in its tenor that it was suppressed within the year; Marx was tried for treason and although he was acquitted he was ordered to leave Germany. Returning to Paris, he found his presence still unwelcome and went to London where he spent the remainder of his life. He was unsuccessful in his efforts to reorganize the Communist League, which was finally dissolved altogether, and was unsuccessful also in his attempt to establish a literary review. In the six issues which were published, however, there appeared articles from his pen on the French Revolution, which were afterwards published in book form. With his devoted wife, Jenny von Westphalen, daughter of a Prussian government official, whom he had married in 1843, he lived during this period in very straitened circumstances, supporting himself and his family by such literary work as he could get. Three children died during these years. In 1864 he became correspondent for the *New York Tribune* and some of his articles were later printed in pamphlet form.

In 1864 he became the moving spirit of a great organization known as the International Working Men's Association, founded in London, in which he hoped to enlist for their own betterment the workers of all the civilized world. For a time the organization bade fair to be successful, but an anarchist element arose, and the Franco-Prussian war and the Paris Commune brought about a condition which it could not withstand. The headquarters was removed to New York in 1872, but four years later the association was forced to dissolve. Numerous socialistic movements in various countries have since been founded largely on the Marxian principles, although not conforming entirely to his conception of socialism which is set forth in a criticism (published in 1891 in the *Die neue Zeit*) of the program adopted by the German socialists in 1875. In 1867 Marx had published *Das Kapital* (Capital), a scholarly production intended as the first volume of a comprehensive work which should cover the whole field of political economy. The breaking up of the International gave him leisure to resume this work, but in order to make it as complete as he wished he found it necessary to spend much time in study and research, which was often interrupted by illness, and he died on March 14, 1883, fifteen months after the death of his wife.

MARY QUEEN OF SCOTS   1542–1587

MARY STUART, QUEEN OF SCOTS, was born at Linlithgow, Scotland, in December, 1542, the daughter of James V of Scotland by his second wife, Mary of Guise. She was but a week old when she was crowned Queen, following the death of her father. The Regent, Arran, promised her in marriage to Prince Edward of England, but the Scottish Parliament refused its sanction to the marriage and war with England resulted. It was later arranged that she should marry Francis, eldest son of Henry II of France and Catharine de'Medici. In 1548 she sailed for France where during the next ten years she was given a careful education at the French court. She was married to the Dauphin in 1588 after signing a secret agreement that if she died childless her Scottish kingdom and her right of succession to the English crown should pass to France. Her husband became king in 1559, but died the following year and Catharine de'Medici, who grasped the reins of government, being unfriendly to her, Mary returned to Scotland in 1561.

The Protestants were in the ascendency, but she stipulated that she herself should continue in her own religion. Many of her ministers were Protestants including her chief adviser, her illegitimate brother, James Stuart, whom she created Earl of Mar and later Earl of Moray. She was beset by royal suitors but suddenly, in 1565, she married her weak and vicious cousin, Henry Stewart, Lord Darnley, who had some claim to both the Scottish and English crowns. Moray and other Protestant nobles were alienated by the marriage and rebelled, but the revolt was soon quelled. Mary quickly became disgusted with Darnley, to whom she had given the title of king and who now demanded that the crown should be secured to him for life and to his heir if Mary died without issue. Believing that David Rizzio, an Italian confidential adviser of Mary's, was the obstacle to his desires, Darnley plotted his murder and he was assassinated on March 9, 1566. Mary hid her indignation and detached Darnley from Moray, Ruthven, Morton and other of the Protestant chiefs. He was held in contempt by both parties. Mary was apparently partly reconciled to him shortly before the birth of their son, the future James VI, but soon became more estranged than ever. He became ill with smallpox in January, 1567. Mary visited him frequently in the small house in Edinburgh where he was lodged. On the evening of Feb. 9, she was with him and early the next morning the house was blown up and Darnley killed. The Earl of Bothwell, Mary's favorite, was unquestionably the murderer and it is generally believed that Mary was privy to the plot. Bothwell was acquitted at a mock trial and carried the Queen off to Dunbar Castle. On May 7 he was divorced from his wife of a year; on the 12th Mary pardoned his seizure of her person and made him Duke of Orkney, and on the 15th, three months after Darnley's murder, she married him. The Scottish nobles were arrayed against her. Her army melted away at the field of Carberry where she surrendered on June 15. She was taken to Edinburgh, then to Lochleven where she was forced to abdicate the throne in favor of her son.

She escaped from her island prison on May 2, 1568, was defeated by the Regent, Moray, at Langside on May 13, crossed the Solway and threw herself upon the protection of Queen Elizabeth. She was immediately imprisoned and spent the rest of her life in various prisons. The Catholic minority espoused her cause and plot followed plot. After the conspiracy instigated by Anthony Babington, the object of which was the murder of Elizabeth and the deliverance of Mary, she was brought to trial in September, 1586, and although she denied all knowledge of the affair she was sentenced to death and beheaded on Feb. 8, 1587. Her body was buried at Peterborough and in 1612 was removed to Henry VII's Chapel at Westminster.

COTTON MATHER 1663–1728

COTTON MATHER, a celebrated New England colonial divine, was born in Boston, Feb. 12, 1663, son of the Rev. Increase Mather, Congregational minister and president of Harvard University, and grandson of Rev. Richard Mather, who emigrated to Boston from England in 1635. His mother was a daughter of the Rev. John Cotton. He was a precocious child, entered Harvard University at 11, graduated at 15 and the following year took up the study of medicine as it was thought that he was barred from the ministry by his stammering which, however, he was able to overcome and at the age of 17 he preached his first sermon. He married in 1686 and two years later became minister of the North Church in Boston where he remained until his death.

He was one of the leaders of the colonists who opposed Sir Edmund Andros, the royal governor, in 1688–89 and supported Sir William Phipps, as did his father who was then in London trying to regain the old colonial charter. Mather was widely known as a scholar and became quite influential in political matters for a time, waging war on intemperance and other evils, but he lacked the diplomatic temperament; he was fanatic, hot-tempered, eager in debate; his power began to wane and he lost much of his public influence after a disagreement with Governor Joseph Dudley in 1707.

He was made a fellow of Harvard in 1690, resigning the office after his father had been removed from the presidency of that institution. He had hoped to succeed his father but his dictatorial tone in public affairs aroused too much opposition. Harvard became less strict and Mather turned much of his attention to Yale, hoping that it would continue a stronghold of Congregationalism, and he seems to have declined its presidency in 1722. With his father he advocated inoculation against smallpox in 1721, and interested Dr. Zabdiel Boylston who urged acceptance of the practice by the medical profession. Mather was well known in Europe and was elected a member of the Royal Society in 1713. Three years previously Edinburgh University had made him a D.D. His reputation abroad was based largely upon his voluminous writings; he published at various times more than 450 works covering almost the entire field of human knowledge—history, science, biography, theology and religion. Probably the most important of all his works were the historical and biographical sketches on the church history of New England, published in 1702 under the title of *Magnalia Christi Americana,* the historical value of which exceeds its literary worth. He was a man of great learning and noted for his preaching ability and his knowledge of science.

His religious zeal led to his investigation of cases of supposed witchcraft in the colony. He believed firmly in diabolical possession and wrote several books on the subject, among them an account of the Salem witchcraft trials. For many years he was held to be largely responsible for the Salem persecutions of 1692 and doubtless his writings did stir up much popular agitation on the subject but modern investigators doubt that he can be considered responsible for the outbreak of persecution. He was doubtless sincere and not intentionally cruel.

In his later years he grew more tolerant of other religious sects; he helped ordain a Baptist minister in 1718; in 1726 he boasted that the Congregational church had admitted to communion members of other denominations and he worked unsparingly for what he believed to be for the general good of his fellow men. He married three times and was the father of fifteen children, nine of whom died in youth, and only two survived him. He died on Feb. 13, 1728.

GUY DE MAUPASSANT   1850–1893

Henri René Albert Guy De Maupassant (mŏ′pȧ sän′), French novelist and short story writer, was born at the Château of Miromesnil in Normandy on Aug. 5, 1850 and was the son of a Paris stock-broker. He received his education at Yvetot and at the Rouen lycée. He entered the ministry of marine in a clerical capacity, and was promoted to the Cabinet de l'Instruction Publique where he served without in any way distinguishing himself. He was athletic and extremely fond of rowing.

He attended many literary gatherings at the home of Gustave Flaubert, who was his mother's friend, and there he met many of the great writers of the day. His first literary attempt was an indecorous dramatic piece twice given at Étretat in 1873 before some of Flaubert's friends. Flaubert took the young author under his wing and for seven years criticised his stories and verse, urging him to write only of what he observed and to find just the right, simple word to convey a vivid picture. So well did he follow this advice that it was his later boast that he had no invention but wrote only of what he himself had seen.

In 1880 he published a volume of poetry, *Des Vers,* which was later withdrawn from circulation. In the same year he contributed to the *Soirées de Médan,* a collection of short stories by Zola, Huysmans and others. His tale, *Boule de Suif,* revealed him as an amazing master of the short story. It was followed in 1881 by *La Maison Tellier* which won the admiration even of those who were repelled by his subject matter. That year also saw the publication of another collection of short stories, *Mademoiselle Fifi,* and of his first novel, *Une Vie,* which is the realistic depiction of the disillusion in a woman's life. *Contes de la bécasse* is a collection of brilliant stories. This was followed by a travel book, *Au Soleil* (1884). Collections of stories published in 1883–84 were *Clair de lune, Miss Harriet, Les Soeurs Rondoli* and *Yvette.* The volumes published in 1885 show some falling off in Maupassant's power—*Contes et nouvelles, Monsieur Parent* and *Contes du jour et de la nuit.* A second novel, *Bel-Ami,* was published the same year. *Toine* and *La Petite Rogue* of 1886 are chiefly stories of the Norman peasants in whom his literary interest was great.

His work now began to show evidence of the mental ailment which for a time kept him in a sanitarium. *Le Horla,* published in 1887, is a study in the symptoms of approaching madness which he may have drawn from his own experience. He took a sea voyage (recorded in *Sur l'eau*) and then published more Rabelaisian short stories, *Le Rosier de Madame Husson* (1888) and the novel, *Pierre et Jean,* followed by another novel, *Fort comme la mort* in 1889, and still another, *Notre Coeur,* in 1890. In the latter year appeared another volume of tales, *Inutile beaute,* and a volume of travels, *La Vie errante.* He wrote little after that time, although *Musotte,* a dramatic piece written with Jacques Normand, was published in 1891.

As the end approached, Maupassant began to take an interest in religion and the *Imitation* was a constant companion. His malady increased, his great physique began to crumble from his excesses and the use of drugs. He attempted suicide in January, 1892, and was removed to Paris where he died on July 6, 1893, and his remains were buried in the cemetery of Montparnasse.

JULES MAZARIN   1602–1661

JULES MAZARIN (mà zà'răn') (Giulio Mazarini), Cardinal and Prime Minister of France, was born at Piscina in the Abruzzi, Italy, on July 14, 1602, the son of a Sicilian, Pietro Mazarini, intendant in the household of Philip Colonna. He went to Rome at an early age, studying there under the Jesuits and then to Alcala, Spain, where he continued his Jesuitical training. He first went to France with a papal legate to the French court.

In 1632 he negotiated the peace of Turin between France and Savoy. From 1634 to 1636 he was papal nuncio in Paris, after which he entered the service of Louis XIII, becoming a naturalized citizen of France in 1639. He quickly became a favorite with Cardinal Richelieu, who was at that time the virtual ruler of France, and through Richelieu's influence he received a cardinal's hat in 1641. Before his death in 1642 Richelieu recommended him to Louis XIII as his own successor. Louis died the following year, but Mazarin retained his power under the Queen-Regent, Anne of Austria, made himself invaluable to her and eventually gained her love. It is said that they were privately married although no definite proof on that point exists. As Mazarin had never taken more than the minor orders of the Catholic priesthood, marriage was quite possible for him.

He proved almost as able as his great predecessor; his power was almost as great and he possessed more urbanity and smoothness than Richelieu had shown. When the Parliament of Paris resisted registration of his edicts of taxation he ordered the arrest of the leaders of the opposition (1648). This led to the disturbances of the Fronde and Mazarin retired with the royal court to St. Germain. He was generally execrated throughout the country, but with the aid of Condé he triumphed over the Fronde and returned to Paris. At his instigation the Queen-Regent caused the arrest of Condé, Conti and Longueville in January, 1650, the popular anger at the Cardinal blazed forth anew and the Parisian and provincial press published satirical articles and issued pamphlets against him which were known as the *Mazarinades*.

He retained a strong influence, however, and set to work to form a new royal party. He won Gen. Turenne over to his support and in February, 1653 returned to Paris where he quickly regained all his former power and popularity. At the price of surrendering Dunkirk he won the alliance of Oliver Cromwell and recovered the northwestern cities of France. By arranging the marriage of Louis XIV to the Infanta Maria Theresa of Spain in 1659, he brought the succession to the Spanish throne within the range of possibilities. He brought from Italy to France his seven celebrated nieces, all of whom he succeeded in marrying to counts, dukes and princes, although some of them later died in poverty and obscurity. He weakened the power of the nobles, destroying the remains of feudalism and left France at peace with foreign nations, but the administration of justice became corrupt and the financial and commercial position of the country declined greatly. He was shrewd and avaricious, acquired an immense fortune and gathered a magnificent collection of books which he bequeathed to the Collége Mazarin. He died at Vincennes on March 9, 1661.

GIUSEPPE MAZZINI 1805-1872

GIUSEPPE MAZZINI (măt sē'nė), Italian patriot, was born at Genoa, June 22, 1805. He studied at the University of Genoa and at the age of 19 began the practice of law. He was a champion of liberalism and wrote in favor of the literary romantic movement. He joined the Carbonari in 1829 and the following year was betrayed to the Sardinian police, imprisoned for several months and released upon condition of his leaving Italy. From Marseilles he organized the Young Italy party with the purpose of uniting the entire peninsula under a republican government and of working for the general advancement of moral law and political equality throughout the world. In 1831 he sent an appeal to Charles Albert of Sardinia, urging him to place himself at the head of the Italian struggle for independence. This resulted in a sentence of perpetual banishment. He went to France from which he was expelled by the authorities in 1832. He became the greatest political agitator of his time, fervid and eloquent with conviction.

In 1834 he organized the abortive invasion of Savoy and then spent two years in Switzerland, spreading the seeds of republicanism throughout Europe. He was banished from Switzerland in 1837 and proceeded to London where he taught fellow Italians and continued his agitation. He charged that the British government opened his mail and disclosed the contents to the rulers of Italy—a charge which he substantiated in 1844, arousing much indignation against the British government. When Lombardy revolted in 1848 he projected himself into the thick of the struggle and after the capitulation of Milan to the Austrians he attempted to keep the war alive in the Italian Alps, aided by Garibaldi. When the republic was proclaimed at Rome he became one of the triumvirs with dictatorial powers. The French arrived in April and the republic fell. In June the triumvirate resigned and Mazzini returned to London.

In England he bitterly attacked the course of France and continued his agitation for Italian independence. He planned the attempted rising at Mantua in 1852; at Milan in 1853; at Genoa and at Leghorn in 1857. With Kossuth and Ledru-Rollin he founded the republican European Association, and organized the Society of the Friends of Italy. In 1858 he condemned the alliance between Piedmont and Napoleon III. When Garibaldi organized his expeditions against Sicily and Naples, he joined the movements and gave able support. He was defeated by Piedmont at Aspromonte in 1862 and taken prisoner. He now broke entirely with the Italian monarchical party and although Messina four times elected him to the Italian Parliament he refused to take his seat under a monarchical government. In 1870 he entered Italy but was arrested and imprisoned for two months at Gaeta.

Mazzini was an idealist, a dreamer, an ardent advocate of democratic and republican principles, a conspirator always eager for action. He possessed a remarkable organizing ability; was impatient of all moderates and opportunists. He disliked and distrusted Cavour. Always sincere and disinterested in his struggles, he planted the seeds of that Italian independence and unity which Garibaldi brought to actual fruition and which Cavour organized. His private life was above reproach. Nearly all of his writings were of a political nature. *On the Duties of Man* is an outline of ethical theory; *Thoughts Upon Democracy in Europe,* a discussion of economics and socialism. His complete writings were published in 16 volumes in 1861. He died at Pisa on March 10, 1872 and was buried in the cemetery of Staglieno, Genoa.

WILLIAM McKINLEY   1843–1901

WILLIAM McKINLEY, 25th President of the United States, was born at Niles, Ohio, Jan. 29, 1843, of Scotch-Irish stock. He received a public school education and entered Allegheny College at Meadville, Pa., but his health failing he left college, taught in a country school at Poland, Ohio, and at the outbreak of the Civil War enlisted as a private. He was in the West Virginia campaign, at South Mountain and Antietam, and in 1861 was breveted major of volunteers for gallantry in action. He was on the staff of Gen. George Crook and later on the staff of Gen. Rutherford B. Hayes.

After the war he studied law, was admitted to the bar at Warren, Ohio, in 1867, and began to practice in Canton, Ohio. In 1876 he was elected to Congress and except for the election of 1882, which he lost, he retained the post for 20 years despite the fact that his Congressional district was democratic. In 1880 he succeeded Garfield on the Ways and Means Committee in Congress and helped to defeat the democratic Morrison tariff bill in 1884. Defeated by Thomas B. Reed for speaker in 1889, he became Chairman of the Ways and Means Committee and in April, 1890, sponsored what became known as the McKinley tariff bill. He was elected Governor of Ohio in 1891, and reelected in 1893.

When James G. Blaine withdrew his name for the presidential nomination at the Republican Convention of 1888, there was a movement to nominate McKinley but, being a delegate pledged to John Sherman, he refused to become a candidate. At the convention in 1892 which nominated Benjamin Harrison, McKinley received considerable support and in 1896 he became the presidential candidate. His democratic opponent was William J. Bryan, running on a "16 to 1" silver platform. The gold standard plank of the republican platform became the rallying cry of the campaign, instead of the protective tariff as had been expected, and McKinley was elected. He called a special session of Congress, which passed the Dingley tariff bill.

After the blowing up of the U. S. Battleship *Maine* in Havana Harbor, McKinley sent an ultimatum to Spain on March 23, 1898, and on April 25, at his recommendation, Congress declared war, in which the United States was shortly victorious. Peace was signed in Paris on Dec. 10, 1898, by the terms of which Porto Rico, the Philippines and Guam were ceded by Spain to the United States, and Cuba was to come under American authority while an independent government was being set up there. The Filipino insurrection under Emilio Aguinaldo was put down; friendly relations with Great Britain were cemented; the Hawaiian Islands were annexed to the United States (1898) and formed into the Territory of Hawaii; the Samoan Islands were annexed by tri-partite treaty with England, Germany and France, and American forces participated in the march of foreign troops into Pekin.

McKinley was reelected in 1900 against Bryan. The first Congress after his second election arranged for the termination of American military occupation of Cuba and William H. Taft was appointed governor general of the Philippines. The country was prosperous and free from foreign complications. Accompanied by most of his cabinet members, McKinley made a tour of the country, through the South to the Pacific coast, and on his return attended the Pan-American exposition in Buffalo, where he delivered an address. The following day, Sept. 6, 1901, at a reception in one of the public buildings, he was shot by Leon Czolgosz, an anarchist. After appearing well on the road to recovery, he suffered a collapse and died on the 14th. He was buried at Canton, Ohio.

He had enjoyed to an unusual degree throughout his term of office the confidence and esteem of the people whose admiration for him was the greater because of his unceasing devotion to his wife, Ida Saxton, who was an invalid and who survived him. He had married in 1871.

LORENZO DE'MEDICI   1449–1492

LORENZO DE'MEDICI (mä'dĕ chē) (Lorenzo the Magnificent), one of the famous de Medici family which rose to first rank in the Florentine Republic, was born in 1449, probably in Florence. He had the literary talent of his grandfather, Cosimo, who had ruled Italy for 34 years, and like him was a liberal patron of the arts and sciences, although he had not his grandfather's genius. He seized the reins of power firmly and carried on the policy of Cosimo with less caution and more tyranny. When the Pazzi clan, who were among his greatest enemies, were on the point of inheriting a large property, Lorenzo succeeded in getting the law of succession changed. The Pazzi enlisted the support of Pope Sixtus IV and, aided by the pontiff's nephews and Archbishop Salviati, they attacked Lorenzo and his younger, gentler brother while they were attending mass in the Cathedral of Florence (April 26, 1478) and mortally stabbed Giuliano who was able to beat off his assailants and escape into the sacristy. The vengeance executed by Lorenzo was a terrible one; several of the Pazzi were hanged from the palace windows along with their followers; others were hacked to pieces and cast into the Arno; others were condemned to death or sent into exile. Pope Sixtus IV excommunicated Lorenzo, issued an interdict against Florence and, with the aid of the King of Naples, made war against the Florentine Republic. Lorenzo proceeded to the court of King Ferdinand of Aragon, at Naples, and obtained a peace to which the Pope soon agreed, bringing about a reconciliation with Lorenzo.

In 1480 Lorenzo succeeded in having a new *Balia,* or magistracy, of seventy of his adherents placed in authority. They were made a permanent *balia,* elected the chief magistrates and had charge of numerous affairs of state. Thus Lorenzo, while nominally the head of the Republic of Florence, was in reality an absolute ruler, a virtual tyrant. He succeeded in having intelligent, capable men appointed to power; raised men of low station to high office, often causing dissatisfaction, but they were usually men of ability who helped to give Florence its standing among the Italian states. Under his rule Florence prospered greatly in commerce and industry; great public works were undertaken, and civil equality was more firmly established than in any other medieval nation. His authority and influence were widespread throughout Italy; he cemented friendly relations with Pope Innocent VIII and induced the latter to bestow a cardinalate upon his son, Giovanni de'Medici, when the boy was but fourteen. Giovanni later became pope himself under the title of Leo X. After the death of Sixtus IV, Lorenzo sought to bring about a union of Florence and Rome.

Although a capable ruler, adding to the power and influence of Florence and the civil rights of her people, Lorenzo's greatest claim to remembrance (and to his title of Il Magnifico) rests upon his interest in, and advancement of, the cause of art, literature and learning in general. He was the instigator of the revival of literature in the native Italian tongue. He took the youthful Michelangelo into his home and transferred him from his apprenticeship to a painter to the school of sculpture which he had established in the Medici gardens. His palace became the resort of the distinguished men of the time and a gathering place for the members of the Platonic Academy; not only Leo X but the later Pope, Clement VII, also of the Medici family, was trained there. Lorenzo was of brilliant intellect, an excellent talker, keenly interested in painting, sculpture, music, philosophy, poetry, and the lesser arts, and himself wrote both prose and poetry with much skill. He died on April 8, 1492.

His great granddaughter was the famous Catherine de'Medici who became Queen of France and ruled that country for many years during the minority of her sons.

HERMAN MELVILLE   1819–1891

HERMAN MELVILLE, American novelist, was born in New York City on Aug. 1, 1819, of a New England family. His grandfather is said to have been the original of Oliver Wendell Holmes' poem, *The Last Leaf*. His father was a merchant of some importance who died while Herman was still a boy. The son received his education at the Albany Classical School and in New York City. In 1837, at the age of 18, he shipped as a cabin boy and thus made his first trip to England. At 24 he shipped on a New Bedford whaler bound for the Pacific, but after a year and a half, because of the cruelty of the captain, he deserted the ship in the Marquesas Islands of the South Pacific and was captured by a tribe of cannibals on the island of Nukahiva who kept him with them for four months, but without harming him. He was rescued by an Australian whaler, joined its crew and two years later was back in New York City. That was the last of his sea voyaging except for a trip as passenger around the world in 1860. He devoted the rest of his life to literature and to his duties as a government employee in the New York custom house.

His first book was *Typee: A Peep at Polynesian Life, or Four Months'*

Residence in a Valley of the Marquesas, an account of his captivity with the cannibals of Nukahiva, published in 1846. It met with success and he at once set to work on his second book, *Omoo, a Narrative of Adventure in the South Seas,* published in 1847. In that year he married a daughter of Justice Lemuel Shaw of Massachusetts. In 1850 he published *White Jacket, or the World in a Man-of-War,* which is credited with having brought about the abandonment of flogging in the United States Navy; and took up his residence in Pittsfield, Mass., where he made his home until 1863. *Moby Dick, or the White Whale,* the most original and vigorous, as well as the most popular of his stories, appeared in 1851. *Pierre, or the Ambiguities,* followed and enjoyed a fair degree of popularity. With the publication of these volumes he seems to have worked out his vein of adventure and his remaining books were mostly "philosophical romances," eccentric, opinionative, so loosely constructed and written that they bore little resemblance to any of his masterly books of the sea. They met with little success and have been almost forgotten.

Melville's knowledge of the sea is perhaps greater than that of others who have chosen salt water as the locale of their stories. John Masefield has said that *Moby Dick* speaks the whole secret of the sea. Hawthorne wrote to Melville in praise and admiration; Stevenson paid his tribute; Barrie confessed that he owed his Captain Hook to Melville. From 1866 to 1885 he was employed in the custom house in New York City from which he retired because of ill health. He published several small volumes of verse, the best of which is to be found in his *Battle Pieces, and Aspects of the War.* Among his other books are *Mardi, and a Voyage Thither; Redburn, his First Voyage; Israel Potter, Piazza Tales, The Confidence Man in Masquerade* and *The Refugee.*

He died in New York City, Sept. 28, 1891. His fame was in eclipse for a time, but later years saw a Melville revival, due in part to a motion picture based on *Moby Dick,* partly to a number of biographies of him (by R. M. Weaver, John Freeman and Lewis Mumford), and to the publication of his complete works in 1924.

MENDELSSOHN-BARTHOLDY   1809–1847

Jakob Ludwig Felix Mendelssohn-Bartholdy (měn'děl sōn bär tŏl'dĭ), eminent German composer and pianist, was born at Hamburg on Feb. 3, 1809. He was the son of Abraham Mendelssohn-Bartholdy, a prominent banker, and grandson of the philosopher, Moses Mendelssohn. In lieu of an individual sketch of his distinguished forebear, a brief account of him is appropriate. Moses Mendelssohn was born at Dessau, Sept. 7, 1729, son of a Jewish schoolmaster. At 13 he went to Berlin, studied languages and philosophy, and, after a prolonged period of poverty, became the tutor of the children of a wealthy silk manufacturer, which resulted in a business partnership between the merchant and the philosopher. He was active in efforts to dissipate the prejudice against the Jews in his country and to procure repeal of the discriminatory laws against them. So influential was he among his people that he was called another Moses. He died on the 4th of January, 1786.

The father of the famous composer was converted to Christianity and the son was educated in that faith. The advantages under which he was reared presented a striking contrast to the early difficulties over which his grandfather triumphed. He was educated with the greatest care and solicitude. His musical genius very soon became apparent, and he was placed in the care of Zelter for instruction in composition and studied the piano under Ludwig Berger. As in the case of Mozart, his first public appearance occurred so early in his life as to suggest marvelous precocity. He was but nine years old when he gave a public concert in Berlin and the following year he performed in Paris. He had already written numerous compositions and continued to produce pieces for the violin, violoncello and piano, and in 1824 he published several of these. Up to this time his father seems to have entertained some misgivings as to the desirability of a professional musical career for his son, but the great success of the youthful performer converted him and he gave his approval.

Mendelssohn traveled thereafter in England and on the Continent, and was everywhere enthusiastically received. His beautiful overture to Shakespeare's *Midsummer Night's Dream* was, in particular, highly praised and has always been regarded as a masterpiece. In it the composer captures the elusive charm of that matchless poetic fairy tale and seems to have partaken of the poet's own inspiration. He later composed music for the entire play. A visit to the wild highlands of Scotland inspired his *Isles of Fingal*. At Düsseldorf he made an unsuccessful attempt to conduct a permanent theatre for the encouragement of musical taste. Shortly thereafter (1835) he was appointed director of the Leipzig Concerts, an influential musical institution, and here, in the musical centre of the world, he became an outstanding figure and the recipient of numerous honors. It was during this period that his finest work was done. It was in England, however, that he enjoyed the most enthusiastic response to his genius. Here, at the Birmingham Festival in September, 1837, his oratorio of *St. Paul* caused something approximating to a sensation. In 1846 another masterpiece, the oratorio of *Elijah,* was produced under the same auspices.

These two noble compositions represent his genius at its highest. Among other famous works are the music of Goethe's *Walpurgisnacht,* the *Antigone* and *Œdipus* of Sophocles, *Athalie,* and numerous trios, concertos and sonatas. In his *Lieder ohne Worte* (Songs without Words) he achieves a distinctive triumph.

Mendelssohn was a man of great charm, with a sweet and winning personality and of notable beauty of character. These qualities are abundantly revealed in his delightful letters which were translated into English and published in London in 1862. He died at Leipzig on Nov. 4, 1847.

He had married in 1837 Cécile Jean-Renaud, the daughter of a Frankfort clergyman, and his married life was most happy.

GEORGE MEREDITH   1828–1909

GEORGE MEREDITH, English novelist and poet, was born in Portsmouth, Hampshire, on Feb. 12, 1828, the grandson of a tailor who was the prototype of the Great Mel in his novel, *Evan Harrington.* His father was a naval outfitter. He received an excellent education at Neuheim on the Rhine, remaining there until he was 16. Returning home, he studied law for a time but soon turned his attention to literature. His first appearance as a poet was in *Chambers' Journal* for July, 1849, with *Chillianwallah,* followed in 1851 by a thin volume of *Poems.* His first attempt at fiction, *The Shaving of Shagpat,* a burlesque on the Eastern story, was published in 1855. *Farina: a Legend of Cologne,* was a satire on the German romantic tale. *The Ordeal of Richard Feverel,* one of his greatest novels, appeared two years later and stamped him as among the most gifted and intellectual of English novelists. It is a tragic romance dealing mainly with the problem of educating the young. *Evan Harrington* (1861) dealt with social ambitions.

His next volume was one of poetry and contains some of the finest passages to be found in English verse; *Modern Love, and Poems of the English Roadside, with Poems and Ballads.* Always a lover of nature, he was a keen observer of it and celebrated it in crisp, fresh and often fragmentary phrases. Both his poetry and his novels offer many difficulties to the casual reader, which was the cause for his many years of non-recognition by the general public although he won the critics and intelligent readers. *Emilia in England* (1864; renamed *Sandra Belloni* in 1886) was a story of the Italian rising in 1848 and was continued two years later in *Vittoria.* His tragic and gripping *Rhoda Fleming* was followed by the romantic *Adventures of Harry Richmond. Beauchamp's Career* is one of the more easily readable and more popular of his novels. *The Egoist* (1879), a remorseless, satirical comedy of male egoism and selfishness, worked out in a vein of high comedy, is generally regarded as his greatest work. *The Tragic Comedians* treats of the German, Ferdinand Lassalle. *Diana of the Crossways* was the first of his novels to enjoy a fairly wide popularity and is ranked by critics as one of his best.

He continued to publish small volumes of verse. In 1883 appeared *Poems and Lyrics of the Joy of Earth,* followed by *Poems of Tragedy* and *A Reading of Earth;* and three other novels, *One of Our Conquerors, Lord Ormont and his Aminta,* which achieved popular success, and *The Amazing Marriage,* one of the characters in which, Gower Woodseer, is said to have been based on the personality of Robert Louis Stevenson, between whom and Meredith a close, if long distance, friendship existed. He left an unfinished novel, *Celt and Saxon,* which was published after his death.

Critics rank Meredith as one of the most invigorating and stimulative writers of his age. They find among the elements contributing to his power his accurate and sympathetic observation of nature and life, his great inventive resource, his mastery of words, his power of verbal description, his feeling for the higher moods of comedy, the variety and vividness of the moods he conjures in the reader, and his keenly analytical mind. His plots are usually quite intricate, his allusions often unexplained. He died on May 18, 1909, at Box Hill, Surrey. His body was cremated and his ashes interred at Dorking beside the grave of his second wife.

PRINCE METTERNICH 1773–1859

Clemens Wenzel Nepomuk Lothar, Prince Metternich (mĕt tĕr nĭk), an Austrian statesman, was born at Coblenz, May 15, 1773, the son of the diplomat, Count Franz George Karl von Metternich-Winneburg zu Beilstein. He was educated at the University of Strasbourg, studied law at the University at Mainz and then went to the Netherlands and England for a time. In 1795 he married the Countess Eleanore von Kaunitz, granddaughter of the Austrian statesman, Kaunitz. The marriage brought him great estates in Austria and introduced him into the most exalted circles in Vienna. In 1801 he was appointed Austrian envoy at Dresden and two years later ambassador to Berlin where in 1805 he brought about an alliance of Austria, Prussia and Russia against France. The following year he went to Paris as ambassador. His influence in European politics grew rapidly. In the war between France and Austria in 1808 he was arrested by Napoleon in reprisal for Austria's interning two members of the French embassy in Hungary, but upon Napoleon's capture of Vienna he was exchanged for the French diplomats. He became Austrian Minister of State, completed the treaty of Schönbrunn with France by which Austria was relegated to the position of a second-rate power, and helped to bring about the marriage of Marie Louise to Napoleon. He formed an alliance with Napoleon in March, 1813, gaining some concessions, but Napoleon's arrogance later led him to extricate Austria from her alliance and maneuver his country into the position of arbiter in European affairs. In 1814 he negotiated the Quadruple Alliance against France and for some fifteen years thereafter he was the leading statesman of Europe. Presiding at the Congress of Vienna, he succeeded in imposing his policies upon the allies and in giving Austria a foremost position among the European powers.

Following the battle of Leipzig he was created a hereditary prince of the Austrian Empire and was made Count of Daruvar. His policy as Minister of Foreign Affairs (to which post he had been appointed in 1809 and which he held for forty years) was to use the concert of powers to ensure the stability of Europe by suppressing any revolutionary movements, whether in Germany, Italy, Austria or remoter countries. The Berlin Convention of 1833, which reaffirmed the divine right of intervention, was the last conspicuous triumph of his diplomacy. He struggled against growing nationalism in Germany and Italy, believing it fatal to Austria's position. He miscalculated its strength and the work of his later years failed to obtain the stability he sought. Although for many years Chancellor of Austria, he was not primarily interested in internal reform and when a violent revolutionary movement took place in 1848 he fled from Vienna to Belgium and England. He returned in 1851 and was honored by the Emperor but occupied no official position, and died in Vienna, June 11, 1859.

MICHELANGELO   1475–1564

Michelangelo Buonarroti (mē kĕl än'jȧ lō), known to the world for his wonderful paintings, but also a poet of powerful imagination, an architect, and a military engineer, was born on March 6, 1475, the son of a Florentine who was governor of Caprese and Chiusi. His chief interest while in school was in drawing, and at 13 he was apprenticed to the painter, Ghirlandajo. The latter interested Lorenzo de Medici who took the youth under his protection, gave him a room at his home and a seat at his table. *The Battle of the Centaurs,* one of the works of this early period, shows the straining muscles that are a characteristic of his later work. An early *Madonna,* however, is more in the classical style of Donatello. Lorenzo died in 1492 and his son Piero took less interest in the young artist. Michelangelo spent a few years in Bologna, returned to Florence in 1495 and executed a marble statue of *Cupid* which so impressed Cardinal San Giorgio that he called the artist to Rome the following year.

The *Bacchus,* in the National Museum of Florence, shows the influence of the artist's experiences and associations in Rome. Another *Cupid* of this period is in the London South Kensington Museum, while the Pieta, showing a realism that early Italian art had not before evidenced, is now in St. Peter's. After four years in Rome, Michelangelo returned to Florence and was occupied for many months in carving out of a gigantic block of marble his noble and majestic David, a piece of statuary with a touch of grandeur seldom attained by any artist. To this stage of his development belong the *Holy Family of the Tribune* and the *Manchester Madonna,* in the English National Gallery. His great interest was in sculpture as form held a stronger appeal for him than color. Julius II, becoming Pope in 1503, summoned him to Rome. Both being of haughty spirit and unable to brook opposition, many quarrels occurred between them but he was commissioned to execute a tomb for His Holiness, and for forty years he lived in the hope of completing that work, but he had made many enemies and intrigue and spite prevented its completion. The great statue of Moses is a magnificent fragment of it. Vasari states that Bramante poisoned the Pope's mind against Michelangelo, and instead of being allowed the leisure to finish the tomb, which he hoped to make his great life work, he was ordered to decorate the ceiling of the Sistine Chapel, although he protested in vain that he was a sculptor and not a painter, and that Raphael was the more suitable man for that work.

From 1508 to 1512 he worked on the Sistine ceiling and achieved a masterpiece of decorative design, with an inventiveness and variety that are the marvel of artists to this day. He was then permitted to return to his work on the tomb of the Pope, but in 1513 Julius II died and the Cardinals who were his executors demanded a more modest design. Pope Leo I then commissioned him to rebuild the façade of the church of San Lorenzo in Florence, and Michelangelo set out for Carrara to quarry marble. Practically nothing is known of his life from 1514 to 1522; rebuilding the façade of the church, however, was abandoned. In 1528–29 he superintended the building of fortifications for Florence, which was threatened by its enemies. After the city's surrender he completed his great monument to Giuliano and Lorenzo de Medici. Another agreement was made for the completion of the tomb of Pope Julius, but the sculptor was again commissioned to decorate the Sistine Chapel with frescoes. In 1537 he began to paint *The Last Judgment* which he finished in 1541. The next year he was appointed architect of St. Peter's and performed his duties faithfully until his death on Feb. 18, 1564. He was buried at Santa Croce, the Parthenon of Florence. He was unquestionably the supreme artist, the most brilliant figure of the Italian Renaissance.

JOHN STUART MILL   1806–1873

JOHN STUART MILL was an English philosopher and economist. He was born in London on May 20, 1806, the eldest son of James Mill, a distinguished Scottish writer and philosopher of radical views, a profound and original thinker, among whose writings were a masterly *History of British India* and a work on *Elements of Political Economy,* the latter written primarily as an aid in the training of his precocious son. The child was educated at home and is said to have begun the study of Greek at the age of three. Under his father's careful tutelage he became proficient in that language and in calculus before his 10th year. The intellectual stimulus imparted by the elder Mill bore abundant fruit, not only in his son but also in a number of other youths, several of whom became eminent in various fields.

The boy was never permitted to indulge in the games of childhood, but at 14 he went to France and there, away from his father, he learned for the first time the pleasures of fencing and other physical exercise. He made himself thoroughly familiar with the French language, met many distinguished men, and became imbued with an interest in French literature and politics which later led to a thorough study of those subjects. He spent considerable time in Paris in the home of the economist, Jean Baptiste Say, and for a time lived in the household of Sir Samuel Bentham, brother of Jeremy Bentham, the distinguished utilitarian philosopher whose friendship with the elder Mill had been of great value. During his stay in France also he acquired an intense interest in travel and remained throughout his life an ardent lover of mountain scenery. On his return to London he read law, history and philosophy and became a clerk in the Examiner's office of the India House, with which his father was also identified. During the 33 years of this connection he rose through various positions until he became head of the department having to do with the transactions of the company with the native states. In 1858, having vigorously opposed the transfer of the Indian government to the crown, he refused a seat in the new Indian council on the plea of failing health and retired from office.

From his early years he had written much, contributing his first articles to the *Westminster Review,* and from 1835–1840 was editor and joint owner of the *London and Westminster Review,* for which he wrote many articles. He participated in the discussion following the French upheaval in 1830 and in other political reforms. His *System of Logic,* published in 1843, established him as one of the foremost thinkers of his time. For many years this work was regarded as a standard authority by those who shared his general views on philosophy, although it was severely attacked by others who held opposing views. It is still considered a great work, despite its now acknowledged errors. Other publications were *Principles of Political Economy;* an essay on *Liberty; Discussions and Dissertations; Utilitarianism.*

From 1865 to 1868, representing Westminster in parliament, he was identified with the advanced liberal party and urged extension of suffrage to women. He was rector of St. Andrews University in 1867. During these years he continued to write, publishing in 1865 *Comte and Positivism,* followed by an *Examination of Sir William Hamilton's Philosophy; England and Ireland; The Subjection of Women.*

In 1851 he had married Mrs. John Taylor, the widow of a very old friend. Her death occurred eight years later, but throughout his life he was devoted to her memory and ascribed his most cherished ideals to her influence. He died on May 8, 1873, at Avignon, where his last years had been spent. His *Autobiography,* published shortly after his death, was received with much interest and was followed by *Three Essays on Religion* (1874) and a second volume of *Discussions and Dissertations* (1875).

Although radical in his philosophy like his father, John Stuart Mill was broadly humanitarian. His fame has been somewhat dimmed in the years since his death by the modern trend away from individualistic standards, but upon his own generation his influence was enormous.

JOHN MILTON   1608–1674

WHEN he was a comparatively young man John Milton declared, in one of his numerous tracts, that he intended to write a poem which would be acknowledged as one of the literary glories of his country. For many years he did not make good his boast for he was beset by cares and official duties. Then, in old age, blindness and neglect, he redeemed his pledge with one of the noblest poems in the English language. It was the outpouring not only of transcendent genius, but of a character, austere no doubt, but crystal pure. "He is," says Emerson, "rightly dear to mankind." He conceived eloquence, with which he was abundantly endowed, "to be none but the serious and hearty love of truth." He is one of the most majestic figures in the history of literature.

He was born in London on Dec. 9, 1608, descendant of a Catholic family which had disowned his father because of his Protestant convictions. The elder Milton was a scrivener who amassed a considerable estate from his trade and was also a man of great musical accomplishment. The boy was educated first at the hands of a private tutor, then at St. Paul's School in London and finally at Christ's College, Cambridge, where he took the degree of M.A. Abandoning his original intention of a legal or church career, he went to live at his parents' home in Buckinghamshire for several years, devoting his time to study, contemplation and literary composition. In 1637, following the death of his mother, he traveled on the Continent, visited the centres of learning in Italy and became acquainted with many distinguished leaders of thought, including Grotius and Galileo. In 1639 he returned to England where the difficulties of Charles I with his subjects were beginning to assume a portentous aspect, and was soon engaged in the bitter controversies arising from these conditions. Notable among his works at this time are *Of Reformation, The Reason of Church Government Urged Against Prelacy* and *An Apology for Smectymnuus.*

In 1643 he married Mary Powell, daughter of an active royalist, whose delight to "dance with the king's officers" probably had its part in preventing the marriage from being happy. The austerity and studious habit of her husband were prejudicial to her gay proclivities and she refused to return from a visit to her fashionable relatives to the more sober environment of her domestic life. Her husband's high ideals of conjugal duty caused him to repudiate her, but after a reconciliation they lived together until her death in 1652. Three daughters were born, Ann, Mary and Deborah, and the world is familiar with the famous picture of the blind poet dictating *Paradise Lost* to one of them while the others listen enraptured. It is reported, however, that they were undutiful and ungrateful. No doubt the problem presented by the disparity of tastes in this first marriage prompted the great Puritan's several treatises on divorce, in which he took a singularly modern and liberal view of the subject. In 1644 were published his learned *Tractate on Education* and his eloquent *Areopagitica*. After the execution of Charles I he became secretary to the council of state and his pen, wholly dedicated to the cause of the people, was quite as potent as was the sword of Cromwell.

In 1656 he married a Miss Woodcock who died in childbirth two years later. In a beautiful sonnet he perpetuated his brief happiness and untimely bereavement. Already the long night of blindness had fallen upon him, caused by excessive study, and the accession of Charles II left him without preferment or influence. It is reported that in those unhappy days he was once held in custody of the law. The Act of Oblivion, however, saved him and his country from any further such disgrace. Still again he married (Elizabeth Minshull) and retired to a quiet home in Artillery Walk, where he lived withdrawn from the turmoil of life and politics. Here his great poem of *Paradise Lost* was written. This poetic account of the Fall of Man was published in 1667. Milton is said to have received five pounds for the manuscript. Its range, imaginative power and miraculous eloquence have raised him to a position in English literature second only to Shakespeare. There is a stateliness, a kind of glory, in the poem which makes it awe-inspiring. It has been aptly likened to organ music, solemn and sublime. Yet to the general public of today it is hardly more than a name. It was followed the next year by *Paradise Regained* and *Samson Agonistes*.

Milton died on Nov. 8, 1674 and was buried in the chancel of St. Giles at Cripplegate.

MOHAMMED · circa 570–632

MOHAMMED (The Praised One) was founder of one of the world's greatest religions, Mohammedanism, which has countless millions of adherents in Asia and Africa. He was born at Mecca, in Arabia, about 570 A.D., the son of a poor merchant, Abdallah, of the powerful tribe of the Koreish, who died shortly before his birth. After the death of his mother he was adopted by an uncle, Abu Talib, and became a sheepherder. In his 25th year he became the servant of the rich widow, Khadija, who is said to have been 15 years his senior, and soon afterwards he married her. She bore him two sons who died at an early age, and four daughters. Until he was 40 he lived a commonplace life in Mecca, perhaps becoming a partner in an agricultural business. Both Judaism and Christianity had penetrated into Arabia by 600 A.D. and attacks on the old pagan gods had been made by earnest adherents of those two sects.

In Mohammed's 40th year, it is said that the angel Gabriel appeared to him at Mt. Hira, near Mecca, where he went each year to pray, declared him the chosen prophet of God and commanded him to preach the true religion. He communicated the revelation to his family and to his friend Abu Bekr and later to acquaintances, and at the end of four years had made 40 humble proselytes. He then revealed some verses involving the assertion of the unity of God, certain generalizations about the righteous life, the obtaining of mercy through prayer, fasting and almsgiving. These verses constituted the beginning of the Koran. Under the influence of Judaism, he prohibited certain kinds of food and later issued prohibitions against wine, gambling and usury. He made many converts and the Meccans, fearing for the sacredness of their city, opposed his teachings, punishing severely many of his followers. His wife died; then his uncle, and his protector, Abu Talib, and he was left in utter poverty. In June, 622 he emigrated with some 150 followers to Medina, among the pilgrims from which city he had made some converts, and there he became a judge, lawgiver, ruler of the city and of two powerful tribes. This journey (known as the Hegira) has been regarded as a flight from persecution, but it seems to have been rather a voluntary removal and marked the real beginning of organized Mohammedanism.

The Jews of Medina aroused his enemity by refusing to support him, and in the first year of the Hegira he permitted his followers to war with the enemies of Islam in the name of God. This permission was specifically aimed at Mecca and in December, 623, at Badr, came the first armed conflict in which 314 of his embattled followers defeated 600 Meccans, taking many prisoners. Expeditions against the Koreish and the Jewish colonies were successful, but he was defeated and dangerously wounded by the Meccans at Ohod in January, 625. Two years later, the Meccans, 10,000 strong, advanced on Medina, but the wall and ditch which Mohammed had built frustrated their attack, and in 628 Mecca made peace with the Prophet and permitted him to send his missionaries throughout Arabia. His doctrines were carried to foreign countries, and he wrote letters (by amanuenses, for he was unable to write, it is said) to various rulers demanding that they accept him as the true prophet.

In 630 the Meccans made war against a tribe of Mohammedans, and the Prophet marched against them with an army of 10,000, whereupon the city surrendered and recognized him as its chief prophet. Deputations from various parts of Arabia arrived to honor him as God's prophet and as Prince of Arabia, and he prepared for a war on Syria which was never carried out. In 632 he made his last pilgrimage to Mecca, and there upon Mount Arafet he drew up the ceremonies for all future pilgrimages. He was taken ill soon after returning to Medina, and went to the house of his ninth wife, Ayesha, daughter of Abu Bekr, where he died on June 8, 632.

MOLIÈRE (JEAN-BAPTISTE POQUELIN) 1622–1673

JEAN-BAPTISTE POQUELIN (who took the name of Molière) (mǒ′lyâr′), was a French dramatist and actor, born in Paris, Jan. 15, 1622, the son of Jean-Baptiste Poquelin, a well-to-do tradesman and valet de chambre to King Louis XIII. He was educated at the Jesuit college of Clermont, where he studied philosophy and law, although it is not known that he ever practiced law. His mother died when he was ten and at his coming of age he inherited a share of her property. He refused to enter his father's business, and in 1643 engaged in a theatrical venture with the Béjart family and others at L'Illustre Théâtre in Paris. After three years this enterprise failed, but the company toured the provinces with some success for twelve years. For a time they were under the protection of the Prince de Conti, and later under that of Phillipe d'Orléans, brother of the King. Molière played before the King in October, 1658, and organized a theatre, first in the Petit Bourbon and later in the Palais Royale. During his years on tour, besides acting, he had written many farces in the old style and other plays, two of which, L'Étourdi and Le Dépit Amoureux, are among his published works. He opened his theatre in Paris with Corneille's Nicomède, which was a failure.

He was no more fortunate in his association with the other great tragic poet of the time, Racine, a personal friend, and was forced to fall back upon his own genius as a comic writer to keep his theatre open. In 1659 was published his Les Précieuse Ridicules and from that date until his death a new play from his pen was produced each year; comedies which are appraised as among the world's greatest examples of the playwright's art. Early in 1662 he married Armande Béjart, the youngest of the Béjart family and an actress in his company.

In 1665 the King adopted Molière's players as his own servants, but two years later symptoms of tuberculosis manifested themselves and the great playwright died on Feb. 17, 1673. His last play, Le Malade Imaginaire, was on the boards at the time; he refused to remain out of the cast and while on the stage a fit of coughing caused the bursting of a blood vessel. He died in his own house a half hour later and was buried in the cemetery of St. Eustace, in Paris.

During the last fourteen years of his life, Molière wrote thirty plays, each a masterpiece of dramatic art, although many of them seem artificial to audiences familiar with the gentler humor, the wider variety of character and incident, and the more human sympathy of Shakespeare. He was amiable and generous in disposition and helped many budding playwrights. His plays satirized the follies and foibles of the time, ranging from farce to high comedy, and portrayed living, breathing human beings of his own time. Among his best known plays are *Sganarelle, L'École des Maris, L'École des Femmes, Le Mariage Forcé, Le Festin de Pierre, Le Misanthrope, Le Médecin Malgre Lui, Tartuffe, L'Avare, Monsieur de Pourceaugnac, Le Bourgeois Gentilhomme, Les Fourberies de Scapin, Les Femmes Savantes* and *Le Malade Imaginaire.* In collaboration with Quinault and Corneille he wrote *Psyche* and was also the author of a number of court masques and poems.

HELMUTH CARL BERNHARD VON MOLTKE   1800–1891

HELMUTH CARL BERNHARD, COUNT VON MOLTKE (mŏlt′kä), famous Prussian general and strategist, was born at Parchim, Mecklenberg, Oct. 26, 1800, of a German family settled in the Danish province. He attended the cadet school at Copenhagen and later entered the Danish army, but at 21 decided to join the Prussian army. He attended the war academy, for a year had charge of a cadet school at Frankfort-on-Oder, and was then employed for three years on the military survey of Silesia and Posen. He was transferred to the Berlin staff in 1833, and in 1835 (promoted to captain and on leave) was offered a post in the Turkish military service which, with the consent of Berlin, he accepted. He surveyed Constantinople, the Bosphorus and the Dardanelles for the Sultan, learned the Turkish language, and in 1838 was sent as adviser to the Turkish general in Armenia who was to lead a command against Mehement Ali of Egypt. Little attention was paid to his advice; he resigned as staff officer, took charge of the artillery in the battle of Nisib where the Turks were defeated, and then made his way back to Constantinople, after great hardship, broken in health, to find Sultan Mahmud dead, whereupon he returned to Berlin.

In 1841 he married Mary Burt, stepdaughter of his sister who had married an English widower. He published his *Russo-Turkish Campaign in Europe* in 1845, became a director in the Hamburg-Berlin railway, and personal adjutant to Prince Henry of Prussia, spent much time in Rome of which he published a map in 1852. Prince Henry died in 1846 and

Moltke was appointed to the staff of the 8th army corps at Coblenz, later became chief of staff of the 4th army corps, and in 1855 was named first adjutant to Prince Frederick Wilhelm, afterwards Emperor. When the Prince became regent he appointed Moltke chief of the general staff of the army. In that post he studied European politics and adapted tactical and strategical methods to the changes in armaments. In 1862 he was consulted as to the military aspect of Prussia's quarrel with Denmark, but his advice was not followed and the beleaguered Danish army escaped. In April he was sent to be chief of staff to the commander of the allied forces and soon thereafter the Danes were forced to accept the German peace terms.

His plans were adopted at the beginning of the campaign against Austria in 1866 and the Seven Weeks' War was brought to a triumphant conclusion at the battle of Königgratz on July 2nd, called the greatest battle of the century. His conduct of that campaign has been termed Napoleonic. When he advanced on Vienna, Austria sued for peace. After the treaty had been signed the Prussian Diet voted him $150,000 with which he bought the estate of Creisau in Silesia. *The Campaign of 1866 in Germany,* prepared under his supervision, was published in 1867.

For years Moltke had studied preparations for a possible attack on France and when war was declared in 1870 his plans were at once adopted and he was appointed chief of the general staff of the army at the headquarters of the King, so that his orders were equivalent to royal commands. Bazaine was defeated, Aug. 16; the French army surrounded and forced to capitulate at Sedan, Sept. 1; Metz forced to surrender, Oct. 27, and the armistice was signed Jan. 28, 1871. In October, 1870, Moltke had been created Graf and in June, 1871, he was made Field-Marshal. He then superintended the preparation of the history of the Franco-German war, published from 1874 to 1881. He resigned as chief of staff in 1888; died suddenly April 24, 1891, was given a magnificent funeral in Berlin and buried beside his wife at Creisau.

JAMES MONROE 1758–1831

JAMES MONROE, the fifth president of the United States and author of the Monroe Doctrine, was born on April 28, 1758, in Westmoreland County, Va. He was a descendant of one Captain Monroe who had fought in the army of Charles I of England and who later emigrated to Virginia. A student at William and Mary College when the Revolutionary War began, he left college to become a lieutenant in a Virginia regiment. He was present at several engagements, was wounded at the battle of Trenton in 1776; served as aide on the staff of Lord Stirling in the campaign of 1777–78 and two years later he left the military service and took up the study of law with Thomas Jefferson. In 1782 he was elected to the Virginia legislature and the following year to the congress of the new confederation where he took an active part in the discussions looking toward the framing of a new constitution. He was an advocate of States' rights and, fearing that the document as it was finally drawn, placed too much power in the federal government, he joined with Patrick Henry and others in opposing ratification. Due largely to the efforts of James Madison, the opposition failed and Virginia became the ninth state to ratify.

After a period of practicing law, Monroe was elected to the United States Senate, where he sat from 1790 to 1794, when he was appointed minister to France. He was enthusiastically received in that country, but a feeling that his sympathies were too decidedly with the French led to his recall two years later, over which there raged a heated controversy and much party feeling and he retired to private life, from which he was summoned to become governor of Virginia in 1799. Four years later he was again sent on a mission to France by Pres. Jefferson and in conjunction with Robert R. Livingston, U. S. minister to that country, he conducted negotiations for the purchase of the great territory known as Louisiana for $15,000,000. For the next few years he was engaged in diplomatic errands in England and Spain, negotiating with the latter country for the purchase of Florida. In 1811 after the election of James Madison to the presidency, Monroe was appointed secretary of state. In 1816 he was himself elected president by a very large vote and served for two terms.

His administration was popular and covered a period of general prosperity and absence of political strife. Vast internal improvements were initiated, and the western migration of the people became marked. Five states were admitted to the Union; Mississippi, Alabama, Illinois, Maine and Missouri, and the Missouri Compromise was adopted. The independence of Mexico and the South American republics was recognized, and what has come to be called the "Monroe Doctrine" was promulgated by the president in his message to Congress in December, 1823. This doctrine lays down the policy of the United States to regard as a hostile act any effort on the part of any foreign power to make further conquests or colonizations in either North or South America, viewing such attempts as dangerous to its own peace and safety; and declares it contrary to the policy of the United States to become entangled in the "broils of Europe" or to allow "the powers of the old world to interfere with the affairs of the new." No official action was taken by Congress on this doctrine, but it was generally accepted and the acquiescence of most of the foreign powers served to give it strength throughout subsequent years. It has been invoked on many occasions by successive administrations; notably in the shape of a warning to Spain against her transferring Cuba to a European power; a demand to France in 1865 to withdraw her forces from Mexico; a protest to Great Britain in 1895 in connection with the Venezuelan boundary dispute; and Pres. Theodore Roosevelt's protest against forcible collection of debts in the South American republics.

At the close of his second term Monroe retired to his estate at Oak Hill in Virginia. He retained his interest in public affairs and served in some local offices. The hospitable life of a southern country gentleman unfortunately involved him in heavy debts and toward the close of his life he left his native state and took up his abode with relatives in New York, where he died on July 4, 1831.

MICHEL EYQUEM DE MONTAIGNE   1533–1592

"READER, thou hast here an honest book," was the prefatory warning with which Montaigne began the immortal collection of essays on which his fame rests. By ignoring all the customary rules of book writing, he turned out a precious book. He was as self-revealing and unabashed as Walt Whitman, and indescribably companionable. The familiar query of what single work an exile to a desert island might select for his life of solitude, suggests the *Essays* of Montaigne. This old Gascon lives always in his famous book. "Cut these words and they would bleed," said Emerson.

He was born at the château of St. Michel de Montaigne, in the old province of Gascony in March, 1533. In this paternal home he studied Latin and Greek under the rigorous rule of his father and became so proficient that when, in his tenth year, he entered the college of Bordeaux his masters are said to have stood in awe of him. On the completion of his course he studied law and in 1554 was appointed councillor in the Parliament of Bordeaux. About 1560 began his romantic friendship with Etienne de la Boetie, whom he had met by chance at a festive gathering. They immediately felt an irresistible attraction for each other and for six years or more this alliance was foremost in the heart of Montaigne, as it was in his memory after her death. In 1566 he married Françoise de Chassaigne, daughter of a councillor in the Parliament of Bordeaux. He held the title of Gentleman-in-Ordinary to the king, spent much time at court and was highly esteemed for his learning and character. Several passages in the *Essays* indicate that he was in military service. What is significant is that in his 38th year he resolved to renounce society and politics and devote the remainder of his life to contemplation and study. Being possessed of ample means, he was able to indulge his bent and he withdrew to his ancestral château on one of the walls of which he caused a Latin inscription to be placed announcing his consecration to these congenial pursuits.

He was an omnivorous reader, an acute observer, and of a whimsically reflective turn, and he soon acquired the habit of setting down his random thoughts just as they occurred to him. He was sometimes gross, often playful, serious at times, quaint and familiar—always honest. He talked (for his essays read like talks) about his domestic affairs, his aches and pains, love, friendship, women, the rearing of children, the most intimate matters, with a frankness which is captivating. He never dissembles, he has no reserve. He is willing that the reader should know all his experiences, thoughts, doubts and temptations. He discourses about drink, and passion, and cannibals, and prayer; there is hardly a subject that he does not touch. He establishes a personal intercourse with his reader and writes about matters which no other writer has dreamed of treating in a published work. He set out to perpetuate his personality, and he did it abundantly. This book, which was to confer immortality on the writer, appeared in Bordeaux in 1580. He had for sometime suffered from a painful disorder; and it was with the thought of distracting his thoughts from his malady that he made an Italian tour. He traveled, just as he wrote, completely at his ease and without the least constraint. The good inns, the soft beds, all the familiar details of his journey, are set forth in an account which he wrote and which was published separately from his essays. While on his travels he learned by letter that he had been elected mayor of Bordeaux and his doubts about accepting this honor were soon resolved by a letter from King Henry III in which, having complimented Montaigne in the highest terms, he intimated that he would not take No for an answer. This interruption to his leisurely and congenial life was not altogether grateful to the philosopher, but he filled the post with credit and dignity and at the end of four years withdrew again to his beloved countryside and found much solace in revising and adding to his essays. It is chiefly by these delightful rambling discourses that we know him, and he gives the impression of being democratic, genial, friendly, generous and considerate to his retainers. He must have been a good neighbor, if indeed there were any neighbors in his sequestered retreat.

But the malady which tormented him, and about which he was able to talk so philosophically, grew steadily worse, the while he spent his time in reading and speculation and the care of his estate. Until almost the end he continued to jot down his miscellaneous reflections. When he died, on the 13th of September, 1592, he had succeeded in embalming so much of himself in his unique book that, in a sense, he may be said hardly to have died at all.

LOUIS JOSEPH MONTCALM DE SAINT-VERAN
MARQUIS DE MONTCALM   1712–1759

LOUIS JOSEPH DE MONTCALM-GOZON, Marquis de Montcalm, a distinguished French general, was born near Nîmes, France, Feb. 29, 1712, and received a good classical education under the tutorship of his kinsman, Louis Dumas. At the age of 15 he entered the army and saw active service in the war of the Polish succession. Having succeeded in 1735 to his father's titles and estate, he married Algelique-Louise Talon du Boulay by whom he had ten children. He was promoted to a colonelcy in the war of the Austrian Succession in 1743. At the battle of Poacenza, Italy, in 1746, he was wounded five times and taken prisoner. He was made brigadier-general in 1747 and after the war ended was given command of a cavalry regiment. For several years he resided at Candiac with his family, but in 1756 was assigned to the command of the French troops in Canada and commissioned brigadier-general.

He arrived at Quebec on May 13, 1756, and almost at once came into conflict with the Marquis de Vaudreuil, the governor-general who was his superior and who proved to be jealous and unfair in his dealings with Montcalm. Aside from the incompatibility of the tempers of the two men, Montcalm was hampered by some of the government officials who were engaged in corrupt practices and were headed by the Intendant, François Bigot. In the summer of 1756, probably at the suggestion of Vaudreuil, he proceeded against the English fort at Oswego, N. Y., which he besieged vigorously and forced to surrender, thus regaining French control of Lake Ontario. On Aug. 4, 1757, he laid siege to Fort William Henry which the English and Americans had built at the head of Lake George. After five days the fort surrendered with its garrison of 2000 men, many of whom were murdered by Montcalm's Indian allies despite his vigorous protests. Under his direction the French had hastily thrown up earthworks at Ticonderoga in July, 1758, when they were attacked by an army of 15,000 under the English general, Abercromby. Although Montcalm had but 3800 men, he repulsed them. This was the greatest success in his campaign against the English, but his victory had been held due as much to Abercromby's lack of generalship as to his own skill and Vaudreuil criticized him severely for not following up his victory which was the last defeat he administered to the English on their own ground.

The English sent James Wolfe to carry the war into Canada. He took up a position across the St. Lawrence from Quebec, while Montcalm, with superior numbers but inferior troops, placed his men along the opposite side of the St. Lawrence from the Charles River to the Montmorency. For two months he remained on the defensive in his entrenched lines. On July 31 Wolfe made an attack on the French position near the Mont-morency Falls and was severely defeated. Montcalm's final defeat on the Heights of Abraham might not have been so utterly disastrous had not Vaudreuil frustrated his purpose of strengthening the French defense at the point where Wolfe's men scaled the Heights of Abraham in the night of Sept. 11–12. The battle that took place on the plains on the 13th decided the fate of Canada which thereafter became British territory. Montcalm showed great courage and bravery but was mortally wounded while try-ing to rally his troops which had broken under the charge of the British. Wolfe died on the field of battle in the moment of victory; Montcalm lived until the next day, Sept. 14, when he died in Quebec. He was buried in the chapel of the Ursuline Convent where a monument was later erected to his memory.

MARIA MONTESSORI   1870–

Maria Montessori (mŏn'tĕs sō'rĕ), an Italian educator, was born in 1870 at Chiarvalle, near Ancona, Italy. She studied medicine at the University of Rome and was the first woman to secure a medical degree in Italy. Almost immediately she interested herself in the education of defective children, experimenting with such children, from the age of three to six years, at the Case dei Bambini (the "Children's Houses") of Rome, in certain rooms set apart for children in the courtyards of large tenement buildings which were a part of the reformed dwelling scheme instituted by E. Talamo. She followed the lines which Dr. Séguin, a French physician, had laid down, and met with remarkable success. Under her system of instruction, even idot children became capable of passing the state examination in reading and writing prepared for normal children. She next applied the system to the education of normal children and met with such remarkable success that her schools became famous throughout the world and attracted educators from all countries.

She had studied the educational system of the Continental schools before starting her experiment at the Case dei Bambini in Rome and was amazed at the stolidity of the children under a strict discipline which she believed "annihilated" instead of disciplining them. She compared the children of Europe's schools to "rows of butterflies transfixed with a pin," and when she undertook her first experiments she departed widely from the established methods. She instituted what is now known as "free discipline"; freedom of movement among the children was permitted, moving about the school room as they liked as long as good manners and harmony were maintained. She found the children worked happily together and that an astonishing degree of discipline could be kept up along with their independence of movement. Her idea of "free discipline" has permeated most of the schools of the world in a greater or lesser degree. She aroused a good deal of opposition from teachers of the ordinary methods who believed her "free" methods were subversive of authority and discipline alike. Certain educators, however, rallied to her support. From 1900 to 1907 she lectured on pedagogical anthropology at the University of Rome, and in 1912 published *The Montessori System,* which sets forth and explains her theories of education.

Perhaps a more important aspect of her work is to be found in the "educational apparatus," built upon the work of Dr. Séguin, which she provided for her pupils. She devised simple yet exact objects which aroused attention and concentration on the part of young children; even the youngest would repeat an exercise (despite the distraction of the movements of other children) with all the concentration that could be brought to bear by a well-trained adult. The period of concentration might last from a quarter of an hour to a full hour, when the child would seek other work which aroused the same concentration, without any evidence of fatigue. Within the course of a year or two discipline became almost self-regulatory and Dr. Montessori was free to give individual instruction in more exacting studies. By her method the teacher shows the pupil the exact and precise manner in which a movement is made, a task performed, so that no imperfect method is formed. Her children learned to read, write, count, scrub the table without spilling a drop of water, wait on the table, and other simple tasks. Later she applied similar methods and worked out material for older children in such subjects as grammar, geometry, music, art work, etc. The system is set forth in her *Advanced Montessori Method.* She has also evolved methods for religious instruction, for nursery schools and kindergartens.

THOMAS MOORE   1779–1852

"The harp that once through Tara's halls the soul of music shed" was
not able to perpetuate its strains in the succeeding century. The art of
Thomas Moore was like that of an actor and died when his own voice
was stilled. He is to be regarded rather as a minstrel than as a poet.
A few of his contagiously musical sentimental ballads are still familiar,
their lilt seeming likely to give them enduring fame, but most of his
songs have experienced harsh treatment at the hands of critics who are
deprived of the rare delight of hearing them sung by the Irish composer
to the accompaniment of his harp. Yet Moore was a man of no inconsiderable literary talent and his life of Lord Byron is one of the finest
biographies in our language.

He was born in Dublin, May 28, 1779, the child of a poor tradesman,
and was educated at Dublin University where he took a B.A. degree.
Here, in addition to his regular studies, he indulged his taste for music
and became proficient at the piano which, with the harp, was later to
prove so useful to him in interpreting his poetic melodies. He also in
his college years translated the *Odes of Anacreon* and on the completion
of his course he took the manuscript to London whither he went to study
law, and it was published in 1800. His legal studies at the Middle
Temple did not suppress his muse and he published in 1802 *The Poetical
Works of the Late Thomas Little* (by himself), a collection of verse
which had a brief popularity for no better reason than because of its
licentious character. The following year he secured a government position
in Bermuda, but finding the life there not to his liking he delegated his
duties to a substitute and traveled in America. On his return to England
he published *Odes and Epistles*. Conceiving his honor to be involved
by a denunciatory article in the famous *Edinburgh Review*, he fought a
duel with Jeffrey, editor of the periodical. Like so many literary duels,
it resulted only in the lasting friendship of the combatants. In 1807 he
began, and for many years continued, to publish his *Irish Melodies* which
he was wont to sing with musical accompaniment at social gatherings.
Though published and commonly regarded as poems, they are really
songs and few of them are characterized by imaginative power and
intensity, or even by lofty poetic imagery. They are highly sentimental,
although some of them contain much pure sentiment. They are readily
committed to memory and *Go Where Glory Waits Thee; There is Not in
this Wide World a Valley So Sweet; Come, Rest in this Bosom; Lesbia
Hath a Beaming Eye; Oft in the Stilly Night; Oh, Ever Thus From*

Childhood's Hour and *The Last Rose of Summer* are not easily forgotten while memory gropes in vain for the lines of more pretentious poems.

In 1811 Moore married and settled in Derbyshire where he soon began the writing of *Lalla Rookh,* a long poem which he was moved to undertake because of the success of his poetic contemporaries in this sort of composition. But the poem of sustained interest was not his forte; he was the minstrel par excellence, and *Lalla Rookh,* though as gorgeous as a bespangled dancer, is tedious and artificial. In 1818 after a trip to Paris he published *The Fudge Family.* The neglect of his official duties in Bermuda now produced complications and he became liable for a large sum of money which his substitute had appropriated. His good friend, Lord Landsdowne, paid an acceptable amount to settle the claim and was later reimbursed by Moore. In 1819 he traveled on the Continent, visited Byron in his retreat in Venice and then settled with his family in Paris where he wrote *The Loves of the Angels* (1823) and a prose romance, *The Epicurean* (1827). Returning to England, he lived in a cottage in the neighborhood of Bowood where he wrote the life of his brilliant Irish contemporary, Richard Brinsley Sheridan, published in 1825. His outstanding prose work was his famous *Life of Lord Byron,* highly commended by Macaulay, and indeed the basis of Macaulay's glowing narrative of the unhappy genius who was Moore's admirer and friend. Several other works of considerable merit should be mentioned; the *Memoirs of Captain Rock,* a *Life of Lord Edward Fitzgerald* and *A History of Ireland.* For several years preceding his death he was affected with softening of the brain which brought his varied career to an end on Feb. 25, 1852.

J. PIERPONT MORGAN   1837–1913

JOHN PIERPONT MORGAN, American financier, was born in Hartford, Conn., April 17, 1837, a son of Junius Spencer Morgan, founder of the English firm of J. S. Morgan & Co. The younger Morgan was educated in the English High School in Boston and at the University of Göttingen. His first banking experience was with the New York firm of Duncan, Sherman & Co., in 1857–60; for the next four years he was agent and attorney in New York for George Peabody & Co., of London, and its successor, J. S. Morgan & Co., of which he became the head. In 1864 he organized the firm of Dabney, Morgan & Co., of which he was a member until 1871, when he entered the firm of Drexel, Morgan & Co., which, in 1895, became J. P. Morgan & Co. He headed this company until his death and under his direction it became an extraordinarily powerful and influential banking house with a hand in many great financial and commercial undertakings throughout the world. The firm had close connections with Drexel & Co., of Philadelphia, Morgan Harjes & Co. (originally, Drexel, Harjes & Co.) of Paris, and Morgan, Grenfell & Co. (the former J. S. Morgan & Co.) of London.

The Morgan house effected the formation of the United States Steel Corporation (the "Steel Trust"), and brought about harmony and cooperation between the coal and railway interests in Pennsylvania. In 1902 the firm purchased the Leyland and other British lines of Atlantic steamships, creating the Atlantic shipping "combine" known as the International Mercantile Marine. Many of its ships flew the British flag, but with the passing years it has become increasingly American in character. Morgan had extensive railroad interests and several times came into conflict with E. H. Harriman over the control of various systems. His firm reorganized the Chesapeake & Ohio, the Erie, the Reading, the Northern Pacific, and the Baltimore and Ohio railroad companies. With Harriman and J. J. Hill he formed the Northern Securities Company, later ordered dissolved by the United States Supreme Court. In 1895 his banking house supplied the United States government with $62,000,000 in gold to restore the Treasury gold reserve to $100,000,000.

He was a collector of old and rare books and other objects of art, and was an enthusiastic yachtsman. He built the yacht *Columbus* which defeated Sir Thomas Lipton's *Shamrock* in 1899 and again in 1901 for the *America's* cup. He served as president of the New York City Metropolitan Museum of Art, gave to it many pieces from his own collections and also gave liberally to the support of the Museum of Natural History in New York City, to the Harvard Medical School, to Yale, to the Lying-in Hospital of New York and to many other public institutions. His books and collections of art objects were left to his son, J. P. Morgan (who succeeded him as head of the Morgan firm), but with a notation in his will that he desired and had intended to make some disposition of them which would make them available for the instruction and pleasure of the American people. Carrying out these intentions the son, in 1917, presented an art collection of 3000 pieces to the Metropolitan Museum of Art, and a new wing was added to the Museum to house it. In 1923, by public charter, he made his father's library, appraised at $7,500,000 and consisting of 25,000 volumes, an institution of research for scholars and endowed it liberally.

J. Pierpont Morgan died in Rome, March 31, 1913, leaving an estate valued at many millions.

WILLIAM MORRIS   1834–1896

WILLIAM MORRIS was first of all a poet, but also a painter, printer, designer and manufacturer of stained glass, wallpaper, furniture and other household decorations. He was born in Walthamstow, England, March 24, 1834, received his early education at Marlborough and then attended Exeter College, Oxford. He became a close friend of the painter, Burne-Jones, and tried his own hand as an artist, but literature proved to hold the stronger appeal and in 1858 he published *The Defence of Guinevere and Other Poems,* followed in 1867 by *The Life and Death of Jason.* These two works gave him high standing among contemporary English poets, a reputation which was greatly heightened by the appearance in 1868–70 of his best known book, *The Earthly Paradise,* in three volumes, containing 24 legendary poems representing stories told by hardy Norsemen on their westward quest. In 1873 he published *Love is Enough,* the most elaborate of his poems; three years later his translation of the *Æneid,* also *Sigurd the Volsung,* and the following year, *The Fall of the Niblungs.* He translated a number of sagas from the Icelandic tongue in collaboration with Magnusson. These include *Grettir the Strong, The Story of the Volsungs and Niblungs* and *Three Northern Stories.*

His translation of Homer's *Odyssey,* published in 1887, had a much larger sale than his *Æneid.* He next turned to an archaic prose style which he affected for some years and wrote *The House of the Wolfings, The Roots of the Mountains,* a story of primitive life in the northland; *The Glittering Plain* and *News from Nowhere.* In 1891 he published his last volume of original poetry, *Poems by the Way. The Wood Beyond the World* appeared in 1895, and *Child Christopher,* his verse translation of the old English poem, *Beowulf. The Well at World's End* was published in 1896, the year of his death; *The Water of the Wondrous Isles* in 1897 and *Sundering Floods* in 1898.

Morris was a many-sided man; in 1861, in association with several others, he established a factory for the manufacture of wallpaper, stained glass, tiles, chairs, tables and other artistic household utensils and decorations—among them the Morris chair—and in 1881 a tapestry industry at Merton, in Surrey. These enterprises played a large part in the reformation of English taste in color and design. In later years he became a pronounced socialist and wrote and lectured much in the cause of the poor and downtrodden. For a time he contributed to and edited the *Commonweal,* a journal of socialistic proclivities. A volume of his lectures was published in 1892 under the title, *Hopes and Fears for Art.*

Much of his time and energy in his later life were devoted to the Kelmscott Press which, between 1891 and 1897, brought out many sumptuous books, noted for their beautiful printing, in type especially designed for his shop. They were beautifully bound and embellished, exquisite specimens of the book printer's art. Among them were translations of early French romances, editions of such famous English poets as Keats, Shelley, Rossetti, Herrick, Chaucer, parts of Shakespeare's works, and Morris' own *Beowulf.* His collected works, edited by his daughter, May, and published from 1910 to 1915, fill 24 volumes. He lived at Kelmscott in an old house in which Rossetti had previously lived; died there on Oct. 3, 1896, and was buried in Kelmscott churchyard near his home.

Swineburne, who was a close friend of Morris, said of him that he was always more truly inspired by literature than by life. His poetry, while dealing with the human passions, is concerned more with the attitude of a group than with the reactions of individuals. He did much to advance the theory that all visible things should be beautiful and devoted much of his time and talents to the dissemination of fine and generous ideals. He had married in 1859 Jane Burden, a famous beauty who had sat as a model for his paintings.

SAMUEL F. B. MORSE   1791–1872

SAMUEL FINLAY BREESE MORSE, American inventor of the telegraph, was born at Charlestown, Mass., on April 27, 1791. While a student at Yale, from which he was graduated in 1810, he became interested in electrical studies, influenced in that direction by two of his instructors, Jeremiah Day and Benjamin Silliman. He early showed an inclination for art and in 1811 became a pupil of the American painter, Washington Allston, and accompanied him to England where he continued his studies. He was one of the founders of the American National Academy of Design in 1825 and was its first president, holding that office until 1845. His interest in electrical investigation and development was reawakened in 1827, but it was not yet strong enough to turn him from the pursuit of an artistic career for in 1829 he made another trip to Europe to study the master painters.

After his return to the United States in 1832 his interest in electrical science began to overshadow his artistic pursuits, and he set to work upon rough drafts of an apparatus for sending messages by electrical impulse over wires. The result was the foundation of telegraphy, the modern sending instrument being substantially the same as that sketched by Morse. He spent twelve years perfecting the instrument, making his own models, moulds and castings. By 1836 he had completed an instrument which would work and exhibited it at the University of the City of New York on Sept. 2, 1837. Its success was sufficient to arouse the interest of Messrs. Vail, iron and brass workers of New Jersey, who put money into the invention and became associated with Morse in its further development and commercialization. The inventor filed his application for a patent and petitioned Congress for an appropriation to pay the expenses of putting the instrument into actual experiment to demonstrate its value and its possibilities. Congress adjourned without having made the necessary appropriations and Morse took ship for England for the purpose of taking out patents there.

His application in England was refused and he went to France where he obtained a patent, but later the French government took over his invention without paying him any compensation, not even a royalty on the manufacture of the instruments. He journeyed to St. Petersburg, but failing to get any action from the Russian government, he returned to New York the following year and continued his efforts toward financial aid from his own government. Congress did not pass the necessary appropriation until 1843. As soon as the means were available Morse and his associates set about constructing a telegraph line from Baltimore to Washington. The line was used for the first time on May 24, 1844, when the famous message, "What hath God wrought," was sent over the wires. In 1847 he was compelled to go to court where he successfully defended his claim of being the original inventor of the electro-magnetic recording telegraph.

Early in his study of telegraphy he had laid out the principles of the dot-dash-space code based on the duration or absence of the electrical impulse over the circuit—the famous Morse telegraph code. By 1851, fifty companies using the Morse patents were in operation in the United States and within the next ten years his apparatus was in operation generally in Europe. In 1858 representatives of Austria, Belgium, France, Holland, Piedmont, Russia, the Holy See, Sweden, Tuscany and Turkey made a monetary appropriation in recognition of the use of his instruments in those countries. He subsequently introduced in America Daguerre's process of photography and in 1842 he experimented with telegraphy by submarine cable.

He died April 2, 1872, in New York City and was buried in Greenwood Cemetery in Brooklyn.

WOLFGANG AMADEUS MOZART   1756–1791

THE musical career of WOLFGANG AMADEUS MOZART (mō'tsärt) began when he was three years old. He was not only one of the greatest of composers, but an infant prodigy of the first order. He was born at Salzburg, Austria, Jan. 27, 1756. His father, a talented violinist in the service of the archbishop of Salzburg, surrounded the child with every advantage to musical study and supervised his training with affectionate devotion. The musical field, so full of instances of juvenile precocity, can offer few parallels to the case of Mozart. At the age of four he played the clavichord and composed a number of minuets. When he was six years old his father took him with his sister (whose talents were only less extraordinary than his) to Munich and Vienna where they aroused the interest of the Elector of Bavaria and the Emperor Francis I who were quite ready to lend their valuable patronage to such genius. In the following year the children were taken to London and Paris where they created a sensation in musical circles. On one occasion during these sojourns, the boy, without any preparation, and to the consternation of his parent and others, picked up a stringed instrument and performed in a trio. When but nine or ten years old he composed symphonies which were played in public and several sonatas which were published. At 12 he composed music for the religious service and for a concert at the dedication of the Orphan House Church in Vienna and conducted it in the presence of the imperial court. At 13 he was appointed director of concerts given by the Prince Archbishop of Salzburg, a purely complimentary designation, however. In the same year he made an Italian tour in the care of his father, performing in various places and arousing the keenest enthusiasm. In 1770 (he was then 14) his opera *Mithridates* was given in Milan. Before he was 16 he had produced numerous hymns and offertories, four operas, a number of symphonies, 24 sonatas and a great number of concertos for various instruments. Such is the amazing record of his childhood and youth.

After a journey to Paris with his mother in 1777 he returned to

Salzburg and on being appointed composer to the imperial court in Vienna two years later he took up his residence in that city. About this time he seems to have fallen in love with a young singer named Aloysia Weber, the daughter of a penniless prompter at the theatre and it is said that the opera *Idomeneo* (1780) was composed in the hope of advancing his suit, which however did not prosper and in August of 1782 he married a younger sister, Constance Weber, a woman who was not his equal either in intellect or in prudence. The financial difficulties under which he struggled were increased and in less than a year the young couple were hopelessly in debt, for the position with which the court had honored him was more dignified than remunerative, and he was forced to have recourse to wearisome musical tours (for his health was not robust) and to instruction of private pupils. His condition, almost desperate at times, was somewhat relieved by a stipend which the emperor was virtually shamed into giving him after he had received a generous offer from the king of Prussia. It was thought that his two operas, produced at about that time, *The Marriage of Figaro* and *Don Giovanni,* also aroused his patrons to a tardy consciousness of responsibility to this great genius, so handicapped by haunting poverty and failing health. In 1791 was produced *The Magic Flute,* the reception of which was a disappointment to him, but it gained favor with subsequent renderings and came to occupy a high place among his compositions.

The story seems well authenticated that while he was at work on this opera he received a call from a stranger who in greatest secrecy desired him to compose the music for a requiem mass, saying that he would call for it on a certain date thereafter. This allegedly stealthy call has been surrounded with a pleasing atmosphere of romance, but the caller has been identified as the servant of a certain nobleman. His request, coinciding with Mozart's rapidly ebbing strength, moved the composer to observe that he felt as though he were writing his own requiem and it is sometimes said that he composed his own requiem, which is not quite true. Weak and suffering, he proceeded with the work, but on Dec. 5, 1791, he was too exhausted to participate, with several friends, in a rehearsal of the part which he had finished, and at midnight he died in the 35th year of his age. Some years before his marriage a sad blow had befallen him in the death of the archbishop who was his patron and whose successor, Hieronymous, a man without any appreciation of intellectual pursuits, not only placed many obstacles in his way but treated him with the utmost indignity.

JOACHIM MURAT   circa 1767–1815

JOACHIM MURAT (jō'ăkǐm mū'rä'), a French marshal, created king of
Naples by Napoleon Bonaparte, was born at La Bastide near Cahors in
France where his father kept an inn. The date of his birth is variously
given by historians as March 25 of 1767, 1768 and 1771. After his elementary education he took up the study of theology with the intention of
entering the priesthood, but being diverted from this object he later
entered the army where his career was not altogether satisfactory and
which he finally deserted when punishment threatened for some act of
insubordination. After a time at home and a period of work in some
menial capacity in Paris, he joined the king's guard. In 1795 he enlisted
in Napoleon's army and served with gallantry and distinction in the
latter's foreign campaigns. By 1799 he had risen to the rank of general
of division. Certain important services which he rendered were rewarded
by the hand of Napoleon's youngest sister Caroline in marriage. He was
in command of the cavalry at the defeat of the Austrians by Napoleon
in June, 1800, distinguished himself in a similar capacity at Austerlitz in
1805 and in many other battles. After the establishment of the French
Empire he received many honors and in August, 1808, he was proclaimed
king of Naples of which he thereupon took possession.
    Although preeminently a soldier and lacking in those qualities of
diplomacy and political skill requisite for a ruler, he nevertheless became
popular with his subjects. Indeed, so closely was he himself under the
sway of Bonaparte that little of kingship was actually his except its outward pomp and circumstance, in which he reveled, being by nature fond
of show and theatrical display. He commanded the cavalry during
Napoleon's advance into Russia in 1812 and after the disastrous retreat
from Moscow returned to Naples. The following year he again joined
the French army, but after the emperor's defeat in October at the hands
of the combined Russians, Austrians and Prussians he resolved to break
away from his allegiance to Napoleon under which he had long been
restive, and he made a treaty with Austria which was to guarantee his
possession of the throne of Naples. Despite his promised support to the
allied armies, however, he entered into secret communication with
Napoleon during his exile at Elba and when the latter returned to
France in March, 1815, Murat with an army of 40,000 men made a hastily
conceived attack on the Austrians, was defeated at Ferrara and Tolentino
and returned to Naples where disorder prevailed and Ferdinand IV
had resumed the throne. His wife and children took refuge with the

British fleet and he made his way to France. Napoleon spurned his offer of aid and he remained for a time in hiding, but after the emperor's final downfall at Waterloo Murat fled to Corsica, gathered a few followers and sailed for Naples where he intended to proclaim himself king and deliverer. His few ships became scattered and on Oct. 8 with only 30 men he reached Pizzo, but was at once taken captive, tried by court martial and shot on October 13, 1815.

Without doubt he was a brave and gallant soldier, loved by his men who never hesitated to follow him into positions of the greatest danger. It is said that Napoleon later regretted his scornful refusal of Murat's assistance whose presence at Waterloo and inspiring effect upon the French cavalry might have saved the day for the emperor.

His two sons later emigrated to the United States where the elder settled in Florida, published several works on political subjects and married a grandniece of Gen. Washington. The younger, after a series of misfortunes, returned to France, took part in the revolution of 1848, held a number of political posts and eventually received recognition by Napoleon III as Prince Murat.

BARTOLOMÉ ESTEBAN MURILLO   1617–1682

BARTOLOMÉ ESTEBAN MURILLO (mōō rēl'yŏ), Spanish painter, was born at Seville in 1617 and baptized on Jan. 1, 1618. He was orphaned at an early age and cared for by an uncle who placed him under the painter, Juan del Castillo. After the latter moved to Cadiz about 1640, Murillo earned a living by painting crude pictures for public fairs and unimportant churches, madonnas and saints to be sent to converts in Mexico and Peru, and other such work from which he acquired a certain dexterity and quickness. One of his early paintings, the *Madonna giving a rosary to St. Dominicus,* is now in the Archbishop's palace at Seville; another *Madonna* in the Seville Museum; and *Fray Lauterio before the Madonna* in the Fitzwilliam Museum, Cambridge, England. His work at this period was somewhat harsh and cold in color. In 1642 he decided to make a journey to Italy to improve his painting and placing his dependent sister with friends he went to Madrid. There a fellow townsman and painter, the great Velazquez, gave him lodgings in his own home and obtained admission for him to the royal galleries at Madrid, where he spent two years studying and copying the master paintings of Italian and Flemish artists. In 1644 Velazquez submitted some of Murillo's paintings to the King, and urged him to go to Rome, but Murillo preferred to return to his sister and his native city.

In 1648 he married Doña Beatriz de Cabrera y Sotomayor, a wealthy woman of rank, and his home soon became a favorite meeting place for artists and connoisseurs. The friars of the convent of San Francisco in Seville wished to decorate the walls of their cloister but lacked money and Murillo offered his services. He painted eleven large, beautiful and powerful pictures on the cloister walls, executed in what has become known as his *estilo frio* (cold style), but substantial in workmanship. His popular *Flight into Egypt* was painted at this period, followed in 1655 by San Leandro and San Isidoro, in his *estilo cálido,* or warm style, softer outlines, warmer colors. *The Nativity of the Virgin,* painted for the Cathedral, was taken to Paris by Marshal Soult and is now in the Louvre. In the following year he painted one of his most notable works, a *San Antonio de Padua,* which is still in the baptistery of the Seville Cathedral. In 1665 he produced two large pictures for the church of Santa Maria la Blanca which are in his third, or *vaporoso* (vapoury) style. In 1658 he established a public academy of art in Seville, which was opened in January, 1660 with himself as its president.

Eleven pictures which he produced for the restoration of the delapidated Hospital de la Caridad include eight of his masterpieces; *Abraham Receiving the Three Angels, Moses Striking the Rock, The Return of the Prodigal* (now in Stafford House); *The Charity of San Juan de Dios; Miracle of the Loaves and Fishes; Our Lord Healing the Paralytic* (now at Orwell Park); *St. Peter Released from Prison by the Angel* (Hermitage, Leningrad); and *St. Elizabeth of Hungary.* Following these he excuted eighteen paintings for the humble church of the Franciscans, the Convent de los Capuchins, most of which are preserved in the Museum of Seville; three pictures for the Hospital de los Venerables, —*The Mystery of the Immaculate Conception* (Louvre), *St. Peter Weeping,* and *The Blessed Virgin;* and a series for the Augustinian Convent at Seville.

In 1681, mounting a scaffolding in Cadiz, where he was painting the *Espousal of St. Catharine* for the Capuchins, he fell and suffered injuries from which he died in Seville on April 3, 1682. He was buried in the Church of Santa Cruz in his native city. Many fine examples of his work are to be found in the galleries of London, Paris and other European cities.

BENITO MUSSOLINI   1883–

BENITO MUSSOLINI (mōō′sō lē′nĭ), premier and dictator of Italy and organizer of the Fascist movement, was the son of a blacksmith of revolutionary opinions. He was born at Dovia, Province of Forli, Italy, on July 29, 1883, attended Salesan college, Faenza, and the normal school at Forlimpopoli, and then became a teacher at Gualtieri at the age of 18. He soon became interested in the Italian Socialist movement and later went to Switzerland where, supporting himself by manual labor, he took courses at the universities of Lausanne and Geneva, obtaining a diploma as a teacher of French. He organized labor unions among the Swiss working classes, was expelled from several cantons and finally from the country. After military service in the Bersaglieri, he resumed teaching, read widely in the classics, became involved in the political agrarian conflict in Romagna, was imprisoned for 10 days, and kept under police surveillance as a revolutionary.

In Trento in 1908 he joined the staff of the Socialist newspaper, *L'Avvenire,* but soon went over to the *Popolo.* He studied German literature, the philosophy of Nietzsche, became an Irredentist, founded and edited the Socialist paper, *La lotta di classe,* at Forli, supporting Socialist ideals but deploring bourgeois materialism. He opposed Giolitti's Tripoli campaign (1911), and organized a popular movement against it. In December, 1912, he became editor of *Avanti,* the official Socialist organ, but lost many of his Socialist illusions in the "Red Week" outbreak in Marche and Romagna (June, 1914). At first strongly opposed to his country's entry into the World War, he later realized the danger of Italy, unarmed and alone in the conflict, and gave his support to the government's military measures. In 1914 he founded a newspaper of his own, *Il Popolo D'Italia,* and was arrested the following year for advocating revolutionary measures at a public meeting. Ten days later he was slightly wounded in a duel with an orthodox Socialist. In September, 1915, after war was declared, he served in the trenches as a private Bersaglieri, was wounded by the explosion of a mortar in February, 1917, and after months in a hospital returned to editing his newspaper.

At the Peace Conference following the Armistice, he advocated a dignified foreign policy. In reply to the first manifestation of Bolshevism he founded the first Fascio di Combattimento at Milan on March 23, 1919, opposing Bolshevik doctrines, and supporting d'Annunzio's occupation of Fiume. He was now bitterly hated by the Socialists and was arrested by the Nitti government for supporting d'Annunzio's *coup,* but soon liberated and then followed a period of hard work on his paper while for relaxation he wrote plays, studied the violin and spent considerable time in motoring and aviation.

He did not disapprove the workers' seizure of factories in 1920, but when the Communists sponsored political murders at Bologna, Modena and Ferrara, his Fascists became the nucleus of the national anti-Bolshevik reaction which led to the downfall of the Communist-Socialist domination and in November, 1921, he organized Fascism into a national party. The Fascists broke the strike of August, 1922, and on September 29 Mussolini proclaimed his support of the monarchy, gaining adherents from the Army, and Non-Fascist Italians as well. He organized and directed a march on Rome, with the intention of seizing power. Refusing to cooperate with Salandra, he was given the mandate to form a ministry and did so in seven hours. He reformed the political administration of Italy, eliminated many abuses, took for himself the portfolios of Foreign Affairs and of the Interior, and later those of War, Marine and Air, which he consolidated into a department of National Defence, and became the virtual dictator of Italy.

He settled the 60-year old Roman question through a treaty with the Vatican which made the Pope sovereign of a newly created state, the City of the Vatican, and freed Italian politics from domination by the church. He organized an extensive program of public works, strengthened the army and secured for Italy an important position in post war European negotiations.

NAPOLEON BONAPARTE   1769–1821

NAPOLEON BONAPARTE, "Man of Destiny," conqueror of Europe, and one of the world's greatest generals, transformed the French Revolutionary Republic into an empire, and made it for a time the most powerful nation in Europe. He was the son of Charles Bonaparte, a French official at Ajaccio, Corsica, where he was born Aug. 15, 1769. He attended the military schools of Brienne and Paris, commanded artillery at the siege of Toulon (1793), and was given command of the army of Italy in February, 1794. Shortly after his marriage to Josephine Beauharnais in March, 1796, he proceeded to Italy which was at war with Sardinia and Austria. A series of brilliant campaigns resulted in the capitulation of both those countries and all of northern Italy. By the treaty of Campo-

Formi (1797) France acquired Lombardy, the Ionian Isles and Belgium, thus arousing the hostility of England, which could not afford to let the French have too extensive a seacoast.

Napoleon returned to France in 1797 a national hero and was given command of an expedition against Egypt with the intent of ultimately driving the British from India. He captured Alexandria, marched on to Cairo and was victorious in the bloody "Battle of the Pyramids," only to have his fleet destroyed by Admiral Nelson at the battle of the Nile. With his return to Italy thus cut off, he led his 13,000 men across the desert, vanquished the Turkish forces who were gathering against him in Syria and returned to Cairo where he left his armies in command of an aid and took ship secretly for France. There in November, 1799, he overthrew the Directory which was then administering the government, secured a new constitution and had himself made first consul for 10 years, with almost unlimited power. He restored order, regulated the administration of justice and reorganized finances. Upon Russia's withdrawal from the coalition against him, he offered a cessation of hostilities, which was refused by England, Austria and Turkey. Thinking to force England's agreement by a smashing blow on the Continent, he crossed the Alps with a vast army, defeated the Austrians at Marengo, Italy (June, 1800) and forced the treaty of Lunéville. After the fall of Pitt in England he renewed negotiations which resulted in the treaty of Amiens (1802) and Europe was temporarily at peace. In recognition of his accomplishments he was made first consul for life and on May 18, 1804, the Senate unanimously proclaimed him Emperor.

In 1805 war again broke out. Napoleon led his army through the German states and overthrew the third coalition against him by defeating Austria at Austerlitz and Prussia at Jena (October 1806). He entered Berlin and formed the Confederation of the Rhine, drove the Bourbons from Spain and placed his brother Joseph on the thrones of Spain and Naples, and made his brother Louis king of Holland and Bavaria. He divorced Josephine, who had given him no heir, and in April, 1810 married the daughter of the Emperor of Austria, Marie Louise, whose son was later named king of Rome.

In 1812 he invaded Russia with 600,000 men, defeated her armies at Borodino (September 7) and entered Moscow on the 10th only to find that most of the city had been burned the preceding day. The retreat from Moscow was accompanied by terrible suffering from cold and lack of food as well as from the pursuing Russians, and Napoleon crossed the Beresina with but a fragment of his army left. He reached Paris, raised a new army, and after a campaign in which Prussia and Austria joined Russia against him, he was defeated at Leipzig (October

1813) and forced to retreat. His enemies invaded France, attacked Paris and forced Napoleon to abdicate on April 11, 1814. He was exiled to the island of Elba but escaped and returned to France the following spring where he gathered an army and defeated the Prussian Blücher at Ligny, but failed to follow up the victory and was crushed by Wellington and Blücher at Waterloo on June 18. He fled to Paris, abdicated again and was sent by the British to the island of St. Helena in the South Atlantic, where he died of cancer of the stomach, May 5, 1821. His body was taken to Paris in 1840 and laid in the crypt of the Invalides.

LORD NELSON   1758–1805

HORATIO, VISCOUNT NELSON, British admiral, and one of England's greatest heroes, whose decisive defeat of the French fleet off Cape Trafalgar saved England from invasion by Napoleon, was born Sept. 29, 1758, at Burnham-Thorpe rectory, Norfolk; entered the British navy in 1770, served in the West Indies, in the Arctic expedition of 1773, and in the East Indies. He was invalided home in 1776, but a year later was active again as lieutenant of the frigate, *Lowestoft*. In 1779 he was transferred to the frigate, *Hinchingbrooke,* and a year later commanded the naval force against San Juan. Commissioned to the Albemarle in 1780, he joined Lord Hood's squadron in America, and in 1784 commanded the frigate *Boreas* in the West Indies, enforcing the English navigation act against the Americans. There he married a Mrs. Nisbet, after which he retired in 1787 to Burnham-Thorpe for five years, then reentered service in the Mediterranean under Hood, served in the blockade of Corsica, and commanded the naval brigade at the reduction of Bastia and Calvi, in the latter engagement losing the sight of one eye from gravel scattered by a shot.

As commodore, Nelson in 1797 was in the battle with the fleet of Spain (which had made common cause with France) off Cape St. Vincent, where his squadron for an hour withstood the assault of the combined enemy. The Cross of Bath was given him and in July he was made rear admiral and shortly afterward lost his right arm in an attack on a Spanish vessel at Santa Cruz. In 1798 while in command of a squadron keeping watch upon the French in the Mediterranean, in a gale his flagship, the *Vanguard,* was separated from the other vessels but later found them in Aboukir Bay where they had followed the French warships. In the engagement that followed Nelson destroyed the entire fleet except the two rearmost French vessels and two frigates which escaped. He returned in triumph to Naples and it was at this time that his relations began with the noted beauty, Lady Hamilton, wife of the British ambassador, who thereafter exercised a great influence upon his life.

He was raised to the peerage as Baron Nelson of the Nile; was voted a pension of 2000 pounds a year by Parliament, and 10,000 pounds by the East India Company, and the King of Naples conferred on him the title of Duke of Bronte, with an estate valued at 3000 pounds a year.

For refusing to obey an order from his commander-in-chief, Nelson was censured by the Admiralty, resigned his command, and returned home with Lady Hamilton and her complaisant husband in 1800. After an interview with his wife, they parted and never met again. In January, 1801, he was created vice-admiral and was second in command under Sir Hyde Parker in the Baltic expedition which resulted in a signal defeat for the enemy and an armistice which became peace upon the death of the Czar. He returned to England in ill health, but was speedily ordered to undertake the defence of the coast against a threatened French invasion by Napoleon. He failed to destroy the French fleet at Boulogne but at noon of Oct. 21, 1805, met the enemy under the command of Villeneuve, off Cape Trafalgar, and signally defeated it, thus ending the threat of invasion.

The battle of Trafalgar is one of the most famous in the history of naval warfare. Nelson had twenty-seven ships opposed to thirty-three French and Spanish warships. At noon of that notable day in British history, the lee of his fleet, under Collingwood, broke through the rear of the French-Spanish line, while Nelson, with the other division, sailed straight for the centre of the enemy line. As he passed astern of Ville-neuve's flagship, he came in range of the enemy's *Redoubtable* so that his quarter-deck was exposed to fire from the tops of the latter. Nelson was badly wounded and died three hours later as the engagement ended in complete victory for his fleet. By this famous battle he destroyed forever Napoleon's hope of creating a great naval power. His body was taken home and buried in St. Paul's Cathedral, London, with a great popular demonstration and in 1849 the famous Nelson Monument was erected to his memory in Trafalgar Square.

NERO   37–68 A.D.

NERO, sixth Roman emperor, was one of the most profligate and tyrannical of rulers, whose name stands in the popular mind as a synonym for cruelty and inhumanity. He was born at Antinum on Dec. 15, 37 A.D. His father was Domitius Ahenobarbus, and his mother was Agrippina, daughter of Germanicus. His mother becoming the wife of the Emperor Claudius, Nero was adopted by the latter in 50 A.D. Claudius died in 54, poisoned by Agrippina's orders, and the Praetorian Guards declared Nero, who was not quite 17, Emperor of Rome. He was a moral weakling, sensual, extravagant and tyrannical. In spite of these defects he made a promising start and his reign might have been a success had he not been so strongly under the influence of his mother. He caused the poisoning of Britannicus, son of his benefactor, Claudius, and a short time afterwards, in 59 A.D., in order to please his mistress, Poppaea Sabina, whom he wished to marry, he caused his mother to be murdered and had his wife Octavia, the sister of Britannicus, put to death, after divorcing her.

In 61 A.D. an insurrection against Rome took place in Britain, led by Queen Boadicea, but was suppressed by the Roman army under Suetonius Paulinus. The following year Nero's forces were engaged in a war with the Parthians in Armenia, in which the Parthians were the victors, and in 63 A.D. Pompeii was destroyed and Armenia evacuated. On July 18, 64 A.D., occurred the great fire in Rome with which Nero's name has always been infamously linked. Two-thirds of the then world capital was burned. The report has come down from antiquity that Nero himself started the conflagration simply because he wished to witness such a spectacle. He did witness it, we are told, from a distance, reciting verses meantime about the burning of Troy, and playing a musical instrument while the flames raged. If he was guilty of this enormity, as seems likely, he found a scapegoat in the Christians, many of whom were put to cruel and horrible deaths.

He set about the rebuilding of Rome at once in a spirit of magnificence and on the Palatine Hill he built for himself a great palace, the "Golden House." The splendor of the rebuilt city necessitated enormous amounts of money and he added the necessary funds to his treasury by plundering the rest of Italy and the Roman provinces. In 65 A.D. a conspiracy against his life was discovered and among those who lost their lives to satisfy his vengeance were Piso, Faenius Rufus, Seneca and the poet Lucan. Poppaea's end was even more tragic than that of Octavia, the wife she had succeeded, as in a fit of brutal passion Nero kicked her so violently that she died in consequence. He then offered himself in marriage to Antonia, daughter of Claudius, sister of his first wife and, upon being refused, he caused her to be murdered and married Statilia Messalina after he had murdered her husband. He also caused to be put to death many others of the leading citizens of Rome who fell under his displeasure.

Nero's vanity was as great as his tyranny and debauchery; he sought to achieve distinction as a poet, philosopher, actor, musician and as a charioteer. The end was an inevitable rising against his tyranny, his inhuman cruelty and sensuality. In 68 A.D. the Roman legions in France and Spain revolted against his authority; the Praetorian Guards rose against him to make Galba emperor and Nero fled from Rome, taking refuge in the house of a freedman four miles out of the city. He knew that execution awaited him if he were captured and to avoid that ignominy he died by his own hand on June 11, 68 A.D., in his thirty-first year, just as horsemen approached to take him prisoner. His remains were placed in the family tomb of the Domitti, on the Pincian Hill, Rome. His statues were broken, his name everywhere erased, and his "Golden House" demolished.

SIR ISAAC NEWTON   1642–1727

SIR ISAAC NEWTON, one of the most illustrious of natural philosophers, was born at Woolsthorpe, in Lincolnshire, England, on Dec. 25, 1642, the same year that his great compeer in the field of science, Galileo, died in Italy. His education was begun at the grammar school of Grantham, near his home, and continued at Trinity College, Cambridge, which he entered in his 19th year, matriculating as a sizar (one who was allowed free commons and other gratuities), and applied himself assiduously to the study of mathematics, thoroughly familiarizing himself with the literature of the subject. He was but 23 years old when he made exhaustive memorandums in connection with his discoveries of fluxions (the rate and variation in the flow of changing quantities), and it was at about that time that the celebrated incident occurred, so familiar to the world, of his observing the fall of an apple in the garden of his home, which was the basis of his epoch-making discovery of the law of gravitation. He was thus impelled to study the law controlling the movements of the moon and the planets, using the then accepted, but incorrect, estimate of the earth's radius, which was so prejudicial to the success of his investigations that he temporarily abandoned these studies.

He next interested himself in the study of the nature of light which led him to consider the construction of telescopes, and a series of experiments upon sunlight refracted through a prism brought him to the conclusion that the refrangibility of light rays varies according to their colors. This fact, once established, enabled him to explain certain imperfections of the telescope and led to the realization that a single lens could not produce a distinct image. His subsequent conclusion, made after some experimenting, that a combination of lenses was also incapable of producing a true image has since been proved erroneous, but nevertheless led him to devise a reflecting telescope which (later greatly improved) came into common use. These investigations and discoveries gave him prestige in scientific circles and he was but 29 years old when he was signally honored by election to membership in the Royal Society. In 1670 Jean Picard, the French astronomer, obtained a more accurate measure of the earth than that which had formerly obtained, and Newton was moved to renew his inquiries into the subject of gravitation. In this he was encouraged by Edmund Halley, whose computations of the orbit of Halley's comet (most recently appearing in 1910) have made his name familiar to the modern world. Newton, accordingly, prepared a treatise on these principles, entitled *De Motu Corporum,* which was further elaborated in his *Philosophiae Naturalis Principia Mathematica,* published in 1687.

At about that time the despotic meddling of King James II had begun to be felt in the English seats of learning and Newton was called from his studies to lend his ability and prestige to help check these unwarranted encroachments. His activities in this cause resulted in his being seated in Parliament in which he remained for about a year. In 1696 he was appointed warden of the mint and was later made its master, a position which he held until his death. In 1701 he again subordinated his scientific pursuits to represent his university in Parliament and was keen and active in the public welfare which seemed to him of paramount importance. He did not neglect the cause of science, however, and not only continued his experiments and mathematical computations, but sought official encouragement for inventors; and the development of the chronometer, devised by John Harrison, was very largely the consequence of his generous interest. In 1703 he was elected president of the Royal Society and was each year reelected as long as he lived. The distinction of this post, as well as his natural inclination, enabled him in many ways to advance the cause of science. He supervised the publication of the *Greenwich Observations* of the astronomer, John Flamsteed, and under the interested patronage of Prince George of Denmark was able to foster much experiment and research among others. To Newton belongs the honor for the discovery of differential calculus, the principles of which were also independently discovered by the German scientist, Leibnitz. There has been much controversy, unhappily characterized by some bitterness, about this matter, but the consensus of opinion among scientists and historians seems to be that, notwithstanding the priority of Newton's discovery a very great debt is owed to Leibnitz because of the advantages in method which he evolved.

Newton died on March 27, 1727, and rests in Westminster Abbey, where a monument was erected to his memory in 1731.

FRIEDRICH WILHELM NIETZSCHE 1844–1900

FRIEDRICH WILHELM NIETZSCHE (nēt'shå), German philosophic writer, was born at Röcken, near Leipzig, Oct. 15, 1844. His father, a Protestant clergyman, died when the boy was five years old. He was educated at Naumburg and at the state school at Pforta, later studying theology and classical philology at the universities of Bonn and Leipzig. He soon abandoned theology, and a little later Christianity, under the influence of Schopenhauer's writings. His love of music brought him into contact with Wagner at Triebschen on the Lake of Lucerne while Nietzsche himself, at the age of 25, was a professor at Basel. His *Die Geburt der Tragödie* (1870–71) combined Wagner's views with the results of his own studies of Greek artistic achievement. With Wagner he waged war against the German lack of culture and much of his early writing was devoted to the struggle to restore it.

Shortly, however, he began to have reservations on the value of Wagner's music which led to estrangement with the composer and finally to complete denial of the artistic value of Wagner's compositions, set forth in *Der Fall Wagner* and *Nietzsche contra Wagner* (1888). In Wagner, and then in Schopenhauer, he found tendencies toward Christian and Buddhistic negation. He broke with both men and became more independent and daring in his thinking. His emancipation from them finds expression in *Menschliches Allzu Menschliches* (1878), which began his negative critical period. Ill health forced him to resign his professorship in 1879. Thereafter he lived chiefly in Italy and the Engadine on a small pension granted him by the University of Basel and devoted himself wholly to philosophy. With improvement in his health he entered upon the most productive period of his life. He fought romanticism, whether in revealed religion, art or philosophy, as illusions invented by man, setting forth these views in his books *Morgenröte* and *Die Fröliche Wissenschaft,* which appeared from 1880 to 1882. His gospel of the superman is set forth in *Also Sprach Zarathustra,* written in Old Testament style. Parts of this are difficult to understand and Nietzsche provided something of an interpretation of the book in *Jenseits von Gut und Böse* (1885–86) and *Zur Genealogie der Moral* (1887). He planned a greater work, *Der Wille zu Macht: Versuch zur Umwertung aller Werte,* which he never completed. Three other stimulating books date from this period—*Götzendämmerung, Der Antichrist* and the autobiographical *Ecce Homo.*

His health broke again at the beginning of 1889 and his mind became seriously affected, due to overwork and loneliness, for he was the most misunderstood of philosophers and had few followers or friends. He lived twelve years longer, part of the time with his mother at Naumburg, and after her death with his widowed sister, Elizabeth Förster-Nietzsche, at Weimar where he died Aug. 25, 1900. He was buried in the churchyard of Röcken.

In his philosophy Nietzsche condemns the ruling values of our civilization—the good, the true, the beautiful—as life-arresting and illusory. He regarded the central value of life as the "will to power," the will to a stronger existence. The good, the true and the beautiful he traced to the "slave morality" of the Jews after they had been conquered and enslaved. The instinct of the will to power, thrusting aside everything that stood in its way, led him to the "master" philosophy of the "superman" to come, the rearing of a higher type of manhood, the creation of a new ruler class, dominated by ruthlessness, courage and pride. His rejection of all the values which had been held sacred for generations made him a great solitary whose teachings are but now beginning to be rightly understood. He has been held to be largely responsible for the war spirit which pervaded Germany and culminated in the World War. How far this charge is warranted is difficult to determine.

FLORENCE NIGHTINGALE   1820–1910

FLORENCE NIGHTINGALE, who laid the foundations of modern scientific nursing, was born in Florence, May 12, 1820, the daughter of William Edward Nightingale of Embley Park, Hampshire, England. She was named after the city of her birth, but her childhood was spent mostly in England. Not content to lead the ordinary social life of English girls of her class and under the influence of her mother, who was a woman of philanthropic interests, she became interested in hospital work, studied many such institutions in London, Edinburgh and on the Continent, took a course of training in nursing with the Sisters of St. Vincent de Paul in Paris and later at the Institute of Protestant Deaconesses at Kaiserswerth on the Rhine. In August, 1858 she became superintendent of the Hospital for Invalid Gentlewomen in London.

Shortly after the beginning of the Crimean War England was stirred by reports of the inadequate preparations to receive and care for the wounded, and of the methods used at the poorly equipped field and barrack hospitals. A royal commission of inquiry was appointed, a fund opened; Miss Nightingale offered her services to her childhood friend, Sidney Herbert, secretary of war, and was sent to the Crimea to supervise the whole army hospital problem, with complete authority over all the nurses and the promise of the fullest assistance and cooperation of the medical staff. With 38 nurses she reached Scutari (November, 1854) as the wounded came in from Balaklava. A few days later 600 wounded arrived from Inkerman. Her labors in the unsanitary barrack hospitals at Scutari carried her name over the English-speaking world. She devoted herself, body and soul, to her task, often spending 20 hours a day looking after the accommodations for the wounded and the sick, spending much time in the operating room to comfort and encourage; and made the rounds of the hospital at night.

With 10,000 men under her care, she was soon placed in charge of all the hospitals on the Bosphorus. She had to meet the resistance of the military authorities and the commissary department, who regarded her as a dangerous innovator and thwarted her efforts with military red tape, but in the end she won. In February, 1855, the death rate in the hospitals was 42 per cent; by June it had been reduced to 2 per cent. By her dominant personality, her firmness, often her anger, and by superhuman effort, with the backing of Sidney Herbert, she succeeded in getting sanitary measures adopted and general hospital conditions bettered. In the summer she went to Scutari to visit the hospitals at Balaklava, fell dangerously ill with the Crimean fever and was in hospital for twelve days, but refused to leave her posts at Balaklava and Scutari until Turkey was evacuated by the British in July, 1856. A man-of-war was ordered to bring her home, but she took a French ship and evaded the great reception prepared for her in London. In September she laid before the Queen a plan for urgent reforms needed in the military hospitals. With the 50,000 pounds raised in recognition of her services she founded the Nightingale

Home for training nurses at St. Thomas' Hospital. She wrote and lectured on army hospital work. Hospital schools of nursing in London were followed, at her suggestion, by the formation of a school at Liverpool Infirmary and other institutions for nursing. The Order of Merit was bestowed upon her in 1907. During the Civil War in America, the Indian Mutiny and the Franco-Prussian War she was often called upon for advice as to camp hospitals.

She died in London, Aug. 13, 1910, and was buried at East Wellow, Hampshire.

DANIEL O'CONNELL   1775–1847

DANIEL O'CONNELL, an Irish patriot and orator, often called "The Liberator," was born Aug. 9, 1775, near Cahirciveen, County Kerry, Ireland, the son of one Morgan O'Connell who came of an old Irish family, but was at this time in humble circumstances. The son received some training at the hands of a Catholic priest and at 15 was sent to the English college of St. Omer in France where his career was cut short by the outbreak of the Revolution. It is probable that his experiences in France, where on more than one occasion he was an eye-witness to the excesses of the Revolution, had an effect in forming his ideas and in directing the course of his later career.

In 1794 he took up the study of law at Lincoln's Inn and four years later was called to the bar, becoming immediately popular and successful, and within a very few years he had built up an enormous practice. It was not long before he was drawn into the turmoil of politics, always an active factor in Irish life. His first public speech was made at a meeting held in Dublin to protest against repeal of the Union with England, although in later years he was an ardent advocate of that repeal. He became a leader in the agitation for the rights of the Catholics, and in 1823 organized the Catholic Association which grew to such formidable proportions as to make it apparent to the government that some measure of relief must be afforded the Catholic body. He brought matters to a head by having himself elected to Parliament for Clare in 1828, notwithstanding that, being himself a Catholic, he could not subscribe to the oaths of abjuration and supremacy without which it was impossible for him to take his seat. This incident led to discussions which culminated in the spring of 1829 in the passage of the Catholic Emancipation Act, repealing the oath of abjuration, modifying the oath of supremacy and admitting

Catholics to Parliament. O'Connell was at once reelected, and from that time until his death he sat, representing at different times the county of Kerry, county of Cork, the city of Dublin and the town of Kilkenny.

He had entirely abandoned his law practice to devote himself to public affairs, but he was so idolized by the people that a huge fund was raised by voluntary subscription which supplied him with a large yearly income. The people were heart and soul with him in his fight for repeal of the Union with England, for disestablishment of the English church in Ireland and for other reforms. The movement for repeal of the Act of Union was renewed in 1841 and carried on by the circulation of a great amount of literature and by huge gatherings throughout the country. O'Connell traveled into every corner of Ireland, arousing the people by his impassioned oratory, his powerful voice making itself heard even by the vast multitude (said to number three-quarters of a million people) gathered on the Hill of Tara on Aug. 15, 1843. The agitation grew to such strength that early in 1844 he, with his son and five others, was tried on a charge of seditious conspiracy. After a lengthy trial he was convicted, sentenced to a year's imprisonment and a large fine. The judgment was reversed by the House of Lords in September and bonfires blazed from one end of Ireland to the other in celebration of the event.

He resumed his career, but dissensions arose in his party; he lost popularity by supporting the Whigs on their return to power in 1846, and eventually broke with the "Young Ireland" party, the Catholic clergy in the main standing with him. But his health was broken and in search of a milder climate he started for Rome, but died suddenly on the way at Genoa on May 15, 1847. In 1802 he had married his cousin, Mary O'Connell. Besides three daughters, she bore him four sons all of whom became members of Parliament.

He was well fitted for the part he played; a giant in size and strength, with energy which seemed inexhaustible, a vast capacity for work, a wonderful command of picturesque and telling language, and a ready sense of humor which, with his unsurpassed oratorical powers, never failed to give him control over the emotional Irish crowds.

EUGENE O'NEILL 1888–

EUGENE GLADSTONE O'NEILL, American dramatist, son of the actor James O'Neill, was born in New York City, Oct. 16, 1888. After his early education at Roman Catholic schools, he attended Princeton University in

1906–7 and then went to sea as a sailor before the mast for two years; engaged in various lines of business in the United States, Central and South America; became a vaudeville actor presenting a shortened version of his father's old play, *Monte Christo,* and then became a reporter on the *Telegraph* of New London, Conn. Indications of tuberculosis developed and while in a sanitarium he began to assimilate and digest his varied experiences. In 1914–15 he attended Harvard University.

In 1914 he published a volume, *Thirst and Other one-Act Plays,* followed in 1919 by *The Moon of the Caribbees and Six Other Plays of the Sea.* He spent the summer of 1916 on Cape Cod and became one of the "Provincetown group" of writers and actors who gave plays in the summer time in a barn-like theater in Provincetown, while in the winter they produced them at the Provincetown Theater in New York City. It was at the latter theater that O'Neill's first short plays, mostly of the sea, were introduced to the public. He rapidly became the most conspicuous of young American playwrights. *Beyond the Horizon* was the first to be performed of his full-length plays (published in 1920), while *Emperor Jones* (1921), the story of a negro railroad porter, emperor of an island, who reverted to type, and a remarkable study in the psychology of fear, was his first conspicuous success. In that year (1921) three other O'Neill plays were presented; *Diff'rent, The Straw* and *Gold.* Three more were produced the following year; *Anna Christie* (which won the Pulitzer prize for that year as had *Beyond the Horizon* in 1920), *The First Man* and *The Hairy Ape,* in which O'Neill, always an experimenter with dramatic technique, first made use of the mask which he later used with considerable success in *The Great God Brown* to indicate the appearance of his characters to others while the real person was shown without the mask.

In 1923 he was represented on the stage with *The Fountain,* which was not a popular success; in 1924 came *All God's Chilluns Got Wings, Welded* and *Desire Under the Elms,* which aroused considerable controversy. *The Great God Brown* (1926) was followed by *Marco Millions, Lazarus Laughed* and *Dynamo* (1929), produced by the Theatre Guild in New York City which since that date has produced all of his plays. His most successful work in point of popularity as well as financially is *Strange Interlude* which takes five hours to present. This play made its author the outstanding American dramatist of his time. In it he adopted the old theatrical device of the "aside" to present to the audience the real thoughts of the characters. It was the third of his plays to win the Pulitzer award and in 1932 was produced as a motion picture. In 1931 was produced his nine-act play *Mourning Becomes Electra* (a modern application of the old Greek tragedy of Clytemnestra, Agamemnon, Electra and

Orestes), really three plays in one, which also runs for about five hours.

In 1934 his comedy *Ah Wilderness* was produced with marked success, affording the distinguished American actor, George M. Cohan, the opportunity for an unprecedented triumph in its leading part. Many found the conventional construction and lighter quality of this charming piece, a refreshing relief from the very palpable straining after new methods and effects which characterize so much of O'Neill's work.

O'Neill has been married three times, first to Kathleen Jenkins of New York, then to Agnes Boulton Burton of London and later to the New York actress, Carlotta Monterey.

IGNACE JAN PADEREWSKI   1860–

IGNACE JAN PADEREWSKI (pä'dä rěf'skĕ), Polish composer, pianist and patriot, was born at Kurylovka, Podolia, in Russian Poland, Nov. 18, 1860. He studied music in Warsaw, Berlin and Vienna, showing such extraordinary musical ability that at the age of 12 he gave public recitals and from 1879 to 1881 he was a professor in the Warsaw Conservatory. He made his formal début as a pianist in Vienna in 1887 which at once placed him in the foremost rank of virtuosos. His marvelous playing in Paris and London in 1889–90 won him an enormous popularity and in 1891 he made the first of his many successful tours in America. In 1900 he established the Paderewski Fund to aid American musical composers, under which awards are made every three years. His first wife was Rose Hassal who died after a year in giving birth to a crippled son, and in 1899 he married the Baroness von Rosen, daughter of a Russian nobleman who became a devoted foster mother and whose wealth enabled him to continue with his work. After 1900 he appeared in but few public concerts until 1920 when he gave recitals in England and America. His opera, "Manru," was played at Dresden in May, 1901 and in New York the following year. He has written many compositions for the piano, among them the concerto for piano and orchestra in A minor. His symphony in B minor was played with success in Boston and in London in 1909.

Aside from his musical genius, he was an ardent patriot, devoted to the revival of an independent Poland, and a political orator of ability. In 1910, at the 500th anniversary of the victory of Grünwald over the Teutonic knights, he presented a memorial at Cracow. He was honorary president of a non-partisan group of Poles who met in the fall of 1914 to organize a committee for the relief of World War victims in Poland.

He established branches in Paris and London and then returned to the United States where he gave many concerts and collected large sums for the cause of Poland. A powerful pro-Polish movement was created in the United States through his efforts. His propaganda work found an echo in President Wilson's allusion, in January, 1917, to a "united, independent and autonomous Poland." The 4,000,000 Poles in America were guided by Paderewski until 1918. In 1917 on a gala occasion at the Metropolitan Opera House in New York City in honor of General Joffre, he made what he announced as his farewell appearance as a pianist. Believing that the United States would enter the war, he had induced the Polish National Alliance to found a preparatory school for Polish officers at Cambridge Springs. When the raising of a Polish army in France was authorized, he obtained permission from the American War Department to recruit volunteers. From the Canadian government he secured a great military camp at Niagara where 220,000 Polish volunteers were trained by Canadian officers. The Polish National Guard Committee, founded at Lausanne, in August, 1917, appointed him its representative in Washington.

After the armistice he returned to Poland and proclaimed his independence of all political parties. An unsuccessful attempt upon his life was made during the negotiations which resulted, in January, 1919, in the formation of the Polish Republic, of which he became prime minister and minister of foreign affairs. He obtained official recognition of the Polish nation by the various powers, suppressed the military groups which hindered national unity and was instrumental in the formation of a regular army. In April, 1919, he was Poland's first delegate to the Paris peace conference. Although the Diet twice afterward expressed its confidence in him, he was unable to achieve national unity and peace with the Soviet because of the violent opposition of the military party, and he resigned office on Nov. 27, 1919, broken in health, and retired to his estate in California, although he continued his efforts in behalf of Poland at the Conference of Ambassadors and at the League of Nations.

Having devoted most of his fortune to the cause of his country he was compelled to resume his public career as a pianist and upon his reappearance in New York in November, 1922, he was greeted with the wildest enthusiasm.

THOMAS PAINE   1737–1809

THOMAS PAINE, English-American writer, was born at Thetford, Norfolk, England, Jan. 29, 1737, the son of a Quaker. He had little schooling, spent several years at sea and tried his hand at various callings in England, eventually taking up his father's trade of staymaker in London. He obtained an appointment in the excise service in 1761 and was discharged three years later for alleged neglect of duty but was later reinstated and resumed the work in 1768. In the meantime he had supported himself in London by teaching and had also been a Methodist preacher. In 1759 he had married Mary Lambert who died the following year and in 1771 he married Eliza Ollive who with her mother kept a tobacco shop and later a grocer's shop with his assistance. They separated in 1774 and Paine, who was always in financial straits, was again discharged from his post.

He sailed for America with letters of introduction from Benjamin Franklin and shortly after his arrival in November, 1774, he was made editor of the *Pennsylvania Magazine.* He entered into the revolutionary spirit of the times and in January, 1776, published his famous *Common Sense,* the first of his powerful republican pamphlets in support of the growing desire for independence. He argued that government is at best a necessary evil and that the colonies owed no real allegiance to the British government. After war had been declared and the colonists had suffered reverses, Paine, then a volunteer aide-de-camp to General Greene, wrote *The Crisis,* a series of 16 pamphlets which greatly encouraged and inspirited the Americans. He was made secretary of a commission to treat with the Indians and then secretary of the congressional committee on foreign affairs. He was forced to resign that post in 1779, however, because of his publishing information which he had gained in his official capacity. He was afterwards made clerk of the Pennsylvania legislature, and then went to France with John Laurens on a successful mission to raise money. His great services by word and pen in aid of the colonists were later recognized; New York granted him an estate at New Rochelle and Congress voted him a goodly sum of money.

The financial ease thus gained gave him leisure to perfect the model of an iron bridge which he had designed and with which he returned to Europe in 1787. In that year he published *Prospects on the Rubicon,* an attack on Pitt's war policy. His pamphlet on *The Rights of Man,* written in reply to his former friend Burke's *Reflections on the Revolution in France,* appeared in 1791 and was widely circulated, bringing him into some disrepute. The British government regarded it as an attack on the constitution and declared Paine an outlaw. He had already departed for France, however, where he received an enthusiastic welcome and was made a "citizen" (along with Washington, Hamilton, and others). He was elected to the French Convention by the department of Calais and took his seat, but not knowing the French language nor entirely understanding the difficulties confronting the revolutionists, he quickly got himself into disfavor with the Jacobins by opposing the execution of the king and Robespierre ordered his arrest. He was imprisoned in December, 1793, but happily escaped the guillotine. Before his arrest he had completed the first part of his second great work, and the one by which he is chiefly remembered, *The Age of Reason*. He was a Quaker who did not believe in revealed religion; he held that all religions were "mild and benign" when not associated with political systems. He advocated with much eloquence a pure morality founded upon natural religion and he attacked superstition unsparingly.

His book, construed as an attack upon the Bible, caused great indignation both in England and America. During his ten months in the French prison he wrote the second part and after the fall of Robespierre he was restored to his seat in the National Convention, serving until its adjournment in October, 1795. In that year he published a letter to George Washington in which he attacked his policies as president of the United States and his integrity as a general. He returned to America in 1802 to find that his *Age of Reason* had lost him much of popular esteem. His health was poor and his last years were spent in loneliness. He died in New York on June 8, 1809 and was buried in New Rochelle where a monument was erected to him in 1839 although his body had been removed to England by William Cobbett in 1819.

FRANCIS PARKMAN   1823–1893

FRANCIS PARKMAN, American historian, was born in Boston, Mass., Sept. 16, 1823, the eldest of six children of Francis Parkman. His health was delicate and he spent much time in boyhood at the home of his mother's father in Medford, near the then wild and rocky woodland of Middlesex Fells. While a student at Harvard he became much interested in American history and during a journey through the woods of northern New Hampshire he determined to write a history of the war which had wrenched from France her colonial empire and bestowed it upon Great Britain. Later he expanded his subject to include the entire conflict between France and England in America. He became much absorbed by the theme, but he was not yet to begin his great task; illness in 1842 caused him to take a trip to Italy and it was not until 1844 that he was graduated from Harvard with high honors.

He had studied woodcraft, was adept with the rifle and an excellent horseman. His feats on horseback, whether the animal was tame or wild, aroused much attention. To study the forest and the Indians in their primitive state and gain understanding of the Indian character and the savage Indian background against which he wished to paint his picture of the great struggle, he went to the Black Hills with a friend and spent several months living with a tribe of Dakota Indians where his tact and courage were tested and brought him through unscathed. This experience formed the basis for his *California and the Oregon Trail*. The rigors of the life, however, so far from benefiting his health, resulted in a breakdown and he remained thereafter a semi-invalid afflicted with a nervous exhaustion which caused extreme sensitiveness to light so that he was obliged to spend much time in a darkened room. With indomitable courage he struggled against this difficulty. He devised a machine which supported his hand in such a manner that he could write legibly with his eyes shut. Books and documents were read to him while he took notes with this machine and then his notes were read while he arranged and stored the facts in his mind. His strength permitted only a half hour's work at a time and for a long time he could not write more than six lines a day. Under these conditions he completed between 1848 and 1851 *The Conspiracy of Pontiac*. He then set to work on his great book, *France and England in the New World*. He made a number of journeys to Europe in search of material for the new work, the first volume of which, entitled *Pioneers of France in the New World,* appeared in 1865 and recounts the history of the French in Florida and the story of Champlain and New France.

It was 27 years before the final volume of his great work was published, the year preceding the historian's death. Other volumes in the great history, in sequence, are *The Jesuits in North America, La Salle and the Discovery of the Great West, The Old Régime in Canada, Frontenac and New France under Louis XIV, Montcalm and Wolfe,* and *A Half Century of Conflict*.

Completing the individual steps of his history appeared to have an invigorating effect upon his condition. He worked with plants, became a skilled horticulturist and developed several new varieties of flowers, published some books on gardening and in 1871–72 was professor of horticulture at Harvard. He died at Jamaica Plain, Mass., Nov. 8, 1893.

Parkman was the first great writer who made an exhaustive study of the Indian character and was able to write of the tribes with sympathy and understanding. Despite the handicap of his ill health he worked indefatigably to secure a thorough knowledge of his subjects and visited and investigated most of the localities of which he wrote. As an historian he stands in the front rank.

CHARLES STEWART PARNELL   1846–1891

CHARLES STEWART PARNELL, Irish statesman, was born at Avondale, County Wicklow, on June 27, 1846. His father was of an old Protestant family which had bought land in Ireland under Charles II; his mother, the daughter of an American admiral. He attended Magdalen College, Cambridge, for four years but took no degree. In 1874 he was named high sheriff of County Wicklow and the following year was returned to Parliament from County Meath, after vainly contesting County Dublin. He was an ardent advocate of Home Rule and quickly became popular throughout Ireland for his address, his audacity, and his ability to obstruct parliamentary tactics. He was keenly interested in the Irish agrarian question in 1878 and was made president of the Irish National Land League. To further its purposes he visited the United States and raised a fund of $350,000. He was elected to Parliament by Meath, Mayo and the city of Cork in 1880, and chose to sit for the latter. As chairman of the Irish parliamentary party he formulated a method of boycotting and at the instance of the Gladstone cabinet he and other members of the Land League were placed on trial, but were discharged when the jury failed to agree.

With 34 of his followers he was ejected from the House of Commons in 1881 for opposing the government's Coercion Bill. He refused to accept Gladstone's Land Bill as a settlement of the matter; in October Gladstone caused his arrest and he was imprisoned in Kilmainham jail, from which he was released in May, 1882. The Land League had been pronounced illegal but Parnell and his followers revived it as the National League in 1884, a further gift of $175,000 having been sent to him by admirers in America. Unable to make terms with the Conservatives, he swung the 86 Irish votes to the Liberals, causing the fall of the first Salisbury ministry, but after Salisbury's subsequent victory at the election of 1886 he accepted alliance with Gladstone who was now committed to Home Rule for Ireland. In 1887 the London *Times* charged him with condoning the murder of Thomas Henry Burke, the Undersecretary for Ireland. A facsimile letter was shown purporting to have been written by him but it was later proved to be a forgery by one Richard Pigott who thereupon fled the country and took his own life in Madrid. A special government commission spent 128 days investigating the entire affair and cleared Parnell of actual participation in the organizing of the outrages, although his party was found guilty of inciting to crime. He brought a £100,000 libel suit against the *Times,* which was settled for £5000.

In July, 1889 he was given the freedom of the city of Edinburgh, but in that same year at the height of his prestige he became involved in a scandal which ruined his public career. He had been absent from Parliament on many occasions and his disappearances were explained when one Captain O'Shea named him as co-respondent in his divorce suit. The Gladstone ministry demanded his retirement as leader of the Irish party. The Irish members had in the meantime reappointed him but after some dissension they now elected Justin McCarthy as their chairman. Parnell and his followers carried the struggle into Ireland, but the church's condemnation and the defeat of his candidates in various parts of Ireland foreshadowed the collapse of his party. After the elections of 1892 but nine Parnellites were returned to Parliament as against 72 anti-Parnellites.

A short time before the elections he died suddenly, on Oct. 6, 1891, at Brighton, five months after his marriage to Mrs. O'Shea. He was buried in Glasnevin Cemetery, Dublin. Unquestionably one of Ireland's ablest and most earnest patriots, he has been the subject of many biographies and the central figure in a number of plays. He was often referred to as "the uncrowned king of Ireland."

LOUIS PASTEUR   1822–1895

LOUIS PASTEUR (pàs'tẽr'), one of the greatest figures in bacteriological science, was born at Dôle, in the department of Jura, France, Dec. 27, 1822. He was the son of a tanner. Unlike his distinguished compeer, Koch, who began as an obscure country doctor, he was early educated in chemistry and achieved distinction in other lines of research before turning his attention to the study of bacteria, in which field his name is resplendent. In 1847 he was graduated from the École Normale, in Paris, and in the following year became professor of physics at Dijon, shortly resigning this post to become professor of chemistry at Strassburg. He had already made important discoveries in chemistry and was at this time absorbed in his studies as to the nature, causes and effects of fermentation, particularly in relation to the "diseases" of beer and wine, a problem which

had long engaged the attention of chemists. He was always an indefatigable worker and after long and thorough experimenting he proved fermentation to be due to the presence and growth of tiny organisms, or
ferments, and set himself to find a way by which the formation of these
organisms might be prevented.

He had gone in 1854 from Strassburg to Lille and three years later to
Paris in the important position of director of the École Normale Su-
périeure. Here he continued his work, undiscouraged by the opposition
of friends who believed that he was carrying on a fruitless quest, and
eventually he was rewarded by finding it within his power to give to the
world specific knowledge which has proved of incalculable benefit to
mankind. One of the first practical results from his study of fermentation
was to revolutionize the industry of beer and wine manufacture, making
it possible to abandon the old uncertain methods and carry on the work
with assurance of definite results.

In 1865 (being at that time professor of chemistry at the École des
Beaux Arts) his help was sought in investigating a silkworm disease
which was making severe ravages and ruining the silk industry in the
south of France. Although he had never seen a silkworm, he attacked
the problem, at the insistence of his friend Dumas, and within a few
months was able to discover the origin of the disease and suggest means
for its cure. He also developed a method of inoculation of cattle to prevent the dreaded anthrax which took such heavy toll and occasioned
severe financial loss to cattle raisers all over the world.

His greatest gift to mankind, however, and the one which is inseparably linked with his name in the popular mind is his treatment for
hydrophobia, which was developed after long and patient experiments
in inoculating dogs with a virus from the spine of a rabid animal. The
treatment having proved successful with dogs, he tried it on human beings in 1885 with equal success and three years later the Pasteur Institute
was founded in Paris. All over the world, similar institutions have since
been established, to the ineffable benefit of mankind. Many thousands of
lives have been saved through the Pasteur treatment, and the death-rate
from this terrible disease has been reduced to less than one per cent.

It may be said that, so far from taking only an academic or scientific
satisfaction in the results he was able to achieve, Pasteur's gratification
was always immensely increased when his discoveries were put to some
immediate practical use, and certainly in this respect he had repeated rewards, as in the case of the beer and wine industry, the difficulty of the
silk growers and, greatest of all, in the saving of human life through his
hydrophobia treatment.

He was the author of many works dealing with chemical and kindred subjects. During his early years at Strassburg he had married one Mlle. Laurent, who was a devoted wife, and we may believe that her life with this simple, affectionate and great-hearted man was a singularly happy one. He was the recipient of many honors. From 1867 to 1889 he was professor of chemistry at the Sorbonne in Paris and he died at St. Cloud on Sept. 28, 1895.

WALTER PATER   1839–1894

WALTER HORATIO PATER, English essayist, was born at Shadwell, Aug. 4, 1839, the son of Dr. Richard Glode Pater, a physician of Dutch extraction, who had been born in New York City but had moved to England after his father's death. The ambition of the young Walter was to enter holy orders. He was educated at King's School, Canterbury, and at Oxford University, with which his life thenceforth was intimately concerned. After taking his degree he settled in Oxford as a private tutor and was elected to a fellowship at Brasenose College in 1864. His first appearance as an author was with an essay on Coleridge in the *Westminster Review* in 1866; his study of *Aesthetic Poetry* appeared in 1868 in the *Fortnightly Review* and was followed by papers on Michelangelo, Leonardo da Vinci, Sandro Botticelli, Pico della Mirandola and others. In 1878 he published a collection of essays which included much new material, under the title of *Studies in the History of the Renaissance*.

He had become the center of a small coterie at Oxford. Among his friends were the painters of the pre-Raphaelite school which Millais, Holman Hunt and Dante Gabriel Rossetti had founded. When his *Marius the Epicurean,* a fictional study of Greek art and life, appeared in 1885 it was hailed as a gospel of beauty and is one of his greatest contributions to English literature. It is written in the most polished and meticulous English and in it he elaborated his cult of the aesthetic life, of beauty in opposition to bare asceticism, and set forth the pursuit of beauty as in itself an ideal to be striven for. *Imaginary Portraits,* a series of essays in philosophical fiction, and perhaps his most delightful work, appeared in 1887 and two years later *Appreciations, with An Essay on Style,* an elaborate and penetrating study. *Plato and Platonism* was published in 1893 and the following year came *The Child in the House.* Two volumes of his collected miscellaneous writings, *Greek Studies* and *Miscellaneous Studies,* were published posthumously in 1895; the following year his romance of *Gaston de Latour* and a year later *Essays from the "Guardian"* were privately printed. The first complete collection of his works was published in 1901.

In his later years his interest in religion was renewed, his boyhood fervor for taking holy orders returned, and it is probable that had he not died in the prime of life, July 30, 1894, he would have carried out that early purpose.

One of the most painstaking of English writers, he worked over his sentences with zealous care and developed a style that is simple, crystal clear, sonorous in reading aloud, and burnished to a hard metallic surface. His influence upon young English writers who sought beauty of phrase, richness and colorfulness of words and sentence structure, was deep and was widening at his death. His appeal was necessarily limited and he never entered the "best seller" class; his reputation is primarily that of a stylist and a devotee of beauty.

ST. PATRICK

circa 389–461

St. Patrick, the traditional patron saint of Ireland, was born probably about the year 389, son of a deacon, Calpurnius, and grandson of a presbyter named Potitus, at Banneventa, the location of which is uncertain, but it was probably in southwestern Britain near the Severn River. His British name was Succat ("warlike"). His Latin name has survived in a Hibernicized form, Cothride. There is little definite information about his life; he was doubtless educated as a Christian and a subject of the Roman Empire. At about the age of 16 he was seized by a band of Irish marauders. Irish tradition has it that during his captivity he tended the herds of a chieftain named Miliucc near Slemish mountain in county Antrim, or perhaps in Connaught. He became subject to religious emotions and visions which encouraged him to escape from his captivity after six years and he succeeded in working his way to the Continent. At the end of three days he landed, presumably on the west coast of Gaul. After traveling for 38 days through a desolate country and suffering much from hunger, he left his sailor companions and took refuge in the monastery of Lerins, off the coast of Provence, where he probably remained for several years. He then seems to have returned home.

He is said to have conceived the idea of missionary work in Ireland from a vision in which a man named Victorious who bore many epistles gave him one beginning, "The Voice of the Irish." He recounts that as he read he seemed to hear the voice of the Irish among whom he had been a captive, asking him to come and live among them again. Against family opposition, he returned to Gaul to prepare himself as a missionary. At Auxerre he was ordained a deacon by Bishop Amator along with Fith (or Iserninus) and Auxilius who later went with him to Ireland. He is said to have spent at least 14 years at Auxerre. He was consecrated Bishop of Ireland in 432 and set sail immediately to convert the pagans of Ireland. He probably landed near Wicklow and proceeded north, beginning his work in county Down. Ireland consisted of a number of petty kingdoms. The high king, Loigaire, seems to have had a certain authority over the other kings and Patrick gained his favor and protection although he did not become a Christian. Later Patrick was probably invited by the king to help codify the *Senchus Mór* to protect the interests of Christian communities. He is said to have overthrown the idol, Cenn Cruaich, in county Cavan; to have founded churches in county Meath and in Ulster and Connaught, which he evidently visited on three occasions. Some traces of his mission work are found in South Ireland—in Leinster and Munster. There is evidence that he visited Rome about 441–443 where he gained the approval of Pope Leo. Returning to Ireland, he founded the church and monastery of Armagh on a site granted him by the king of Oriel, probably intending it as the seat of supreme ecclesiastical authority in the island. He resigned his position as Bishop of Armagh to his disciple, Benignus, some years before his death and retired to Saul in Dalaradia, county Down, where he probably died in 461.

Two documents purporting to have been written by him have come down to us. One, *The Confession,* probably written toward the end of his life, gives in crude, illiterate style, the story of his career. The other is a stern letter to Coroticus, a British king of Strathclyde, who had raided Ireland and carried off a number of Christian neophytes. Many legends have clustered about his name, the most widely known being the tale of his driving the snakes out of Ireland. He undoubtedly deserved veneration as a great Christian missionary and did much to Christianize Ireland and overthrow Druidism.

ROBERT EDWIN PEARY   1856–1920

Robert Edwin Peary (pē′rĭ) was an American explorer and discoverer of the North Pole. He was born on May 6, 1856, at Cresson, Penn., was educated at Bowdoin College, Maine, and became a civil engineer. He entered the U. S. Navy and in 1887 became chief engineer of the Nicara-

guan Canal Survey. The previous year he had made a trip to Greenland
to survey the inland ice cap and from this time on all his interests lay in
Arctic exploration. In 1891–92 he again visited Greenwich, made a remarkable trip of some 1300 miles over the inland ice, at an altitude of
5000 to 8000 feet above sea level, reaching Independence Bay at the northeast extremity of the island, proving the insularity of Greenland and recording much valuable scientific data. In 1893–95 he made a third trip to
make further studies among the Eskimos known as the Arctic Highland-
ers, journeyed a second time across the ice cap to Independence Bay and
near Melville Bay, on the west coast, discovered "Iron Mountain," the
existence of which had been known since 1818 and which proved to be
three huge meteorites. These he removed to New York in later voyages
in 1896 and 1897, where they were placed in the American Museum of
Natural History. The largest one weighs 90 tons and is the largest me-
teorite known.

In 1888 Peary had married Josephine Diebitsch who accompanied
him on his second and third voyages to Greenland, where was born to
them a daughter, Marie Ahnighito (snow baby), who was the first white
child to be born in those northern regions. In 1898 he started north again
on an expedition which occupied four years, during which he made surveys of the coast lines and the land masses to the north of Greenland and
made a number of hazardous sledge journeys among the northern channels. Early in 1902 he started from Cape Hecla, on the northern coast of
Grant Land, to the west of Greenland, in an ambitious attempt to reach
the North Pole, but was unable to get beyond latitude 84° 17'. Three years
later he again set out in a vessel which had been especially built for the
purpose (the *Roosevelt*), but after a year of effort he was able to pene-
trate only three degrees farther north.

At length, on July 6, 1908, at the age of 52, this intrepid man again set
forth from New York in the *Roosevelt* with a well-equipped expedition
and able assistants. At Etah on the northwest coast of Greenland they
were supplemented by 22 Eskimos and 246 dogs and pressed on to the
north where they made a winter camp and went about the work of establishing a chain of posts to aid them in their attempt to reach the pole in
the spring. Then, leaving the *Roosevelt*, Peary with seven of his companions, 17 Eskimos, 19 sledges and many dogs, reached Cape Columbia
and on March 1, 1909, he began the hazardous march over the Arctic ice.
At intervals detachments from the party were sent back to the base until
by the beginning of April the dauntless leader had with him only Matthew Henson, a negro, four Eskimos and about 40 dogs. The final dash
of 125 miles was made in forced marches occupying five days and on
April 6 Peary, almost at the point of exhaustion, was successful in reach-

ing the North Pole where he spent some thirty hours before starting back to his ship. The return journey to the *Roosevelt* was even more difficult than the march to the north and the little party suffered great hardship and danger, increased by violent storms.

On his return to the United States, Peary was the recipient of many honors and medals, was raised to the rank of rear admiral and received the thanks of Congress. He was later made an officer of the French Legion of Honor, was president of the American Geographical Society (1901–1906) and of the eighth International Geographical Congress in 1904. His various experiences are recorded in his published volumes, *Northward over the Great Ice, Snowland Folk, Nearest the Pole, The North Pole.*

He died on Feb. 20, 1920.

WILLIAM PENN   1644–1718

WILLIAM PENN, English Quaker writer and preacher, and the founder of the City of Philadelphia, was born in London, Oct. 14, 1644, the son of Admiral William Penn of the British navy. While attending Christ Church, Oxford, he became a zealous Quaker and was expelled from the college following some disorders with which he was connected.

Throughout his life he was repeatedly imprisoned because of his religion. Believing that the gaiety of French life might turn his son from his absorption in religion, Admiral Penn sent him to the Continent, where he served for a short time in the Dutch war. Visiting Cork on business for his father, he attended illegal Quaker meetings and renewed his allegiance to that faith which led to an estrangement from his father. In 1668 he was imprisoned in London Tower because of his book, *Sandy Foundation Shaken,* an attack on the doctrine of the Trinity and other orthodox doctrines. While in the Tower, he wrote two of his most popular books, *No Cross, No Crown* and *Innocency with her Open Face,* the latter an explanatory vindication of his beliefs and actions which probably helped to obtain his freedom, although the Duke of York who was friendly to his father was instrumental in bringing about his release.

He inherited 1500 pounds a year upon the death of his father in 1670, and during that year was imprisoned for preaching Quaker doctrines; in 1671 he was sent to Newgate for six months and following his release he visited Holland and Germany, still preaching the new faith. In 1681, in lieu of certain claims of his father's against the government, he obtained from the Crown the grant of territory in America which he named Pennsylvania in honor of his father. He arrived in America in 1682 with a shipload of fellow-religionists for the purpose of establishing a home where they would be free from persecution. They sailed up the Delaware river and in November Penn purchased from the Indians the site of the present city of Philadelphia. He laid out plans for the city and drew up a constitution for the government of the colony where he remained in person for two years governing with wisdom and benevolence. Card-playing, attending the theatre and other "evil sports," frowned upon by Puritanism, were forbidden. Persecuted members of other sects as well as Quakers sought refuge in the colony, where the spirit of toleration prevailed. Meanwhile persecutions of the Quakers in England continued and Penn returned there to do what he could in their behalf. He appears to have had a strong influence with James II and a belief that that monarch's intentions were good. It has been claimed that he was a tool in the hands of the wily James, but history fails to maintain this assertion.

Whatever the reasons, efforts in their behalf resulted in 1686 in the freeing of 1200 Quakers and many others who had been imprisoned for their religious beliefs. After the downfall of James and the accession of his son-in-law, William of Orange, as William III, Penn was several times accused of treasonable adhesion to James and was not finally acquitted of those charges until 1693. Affairs in the colony of Pennsylvania were running none too smoothly, and in 1699 he visited it in an effort to straighten out the troubles. Finding that the original constitution was displeasing to many of the colonists, and in some respects unworkable in practice, he assisted in altering many of its provisions. Like many other Quakers, he owned Negro slaves, but he was kind to them and contributed towards ameliorating the conditions of slavery.

In 1701 he returned to England and did not again visit the colony. Disputes about the boundary and with his son and his steward in Philadelphia troubled his later years, as well as financial reverses. Through false claims on the part of his agent in Philadelphia he was imprisoned in the Fleet for nine months in 1708, which undermined his health and he died at Ruscombe in Berkshire, July 30, 1718.

He was twice married, in 1672 to a daughter of Sir William Springett, and two years after her death to Hannah Callowhill. He left children by both marriages.

SAMUEL PEPYS   1633-1703

DURING the reigns of Charles II and James II of England, there lived in London a man of no particular distinction named SAMUEL PEPYS (pronounced pēēps), the intimate details of whose life are as familiar to the world today as are those of any celebrity that ever lived. He illuminated the whole era in which his life was passed by means of a diary which is a model of frankness and sincerity, utterly free of self-consciousness, full of the most delightful observations and confessions; betraying at no point the slightest hint of any expectation that it would one day be opened to the public gaze.

The facts of his life may be briefly told and seem commonplace enough beside the confidential narrative which is one of the treasures of seventeenth century literature. He was born on Feb. 23, 1633, son of a London tailor, and was educated at St. Paul's School and at Magdalen College, Cambridge. At 22 he married Elizabeth Marchant. Through his cousin, Sir Edward Montagu (the first earl of Sandwich) in his 27th year he was appointed clerk of the acts of the navy, later becoming secretary for naval affairs. He was a conscientious and competent official, diligent in the reforming of abuses, but his good repute did not save him from a charge of assisting in a conspiracy to dethrone the king and destroy the established religion. Nothing came of this charge and Pepys resumed his position in the Admiralty, holding it until James II fled his throne. He met a great many distinguished people in public life, attended innumerable fêtes and functions, always with a weather eye for feminine charm and beauty, and for the little idiosyncracies of the great which seldom find their way into the pages of history. All his observations he jotted down in shorthand, frequently finishing his gossipy entry with the phrase "and so to bed." For two years he was president of the Royal Society and he found time, among his multifarious semi-political and social activities, to write a very acceptable work, *Memoirs of the Royal Navy,* published in 1690. He was, in a conventional way, a man of taste and culture and amassed a large library, including many interesting manuscripts and prints and about 2000 ancient English ballads which he bequeathed to Magdalen College.

The famous diary was deciphered by the Rev. J. Smith from the original draft in shorthand in the Pepysian Library, Cambridge, and was first published in 1825. It begins on the 1st of January, 1659, and continues for nine years when the diarist was compelled to abandon it because of failing eyesight. It has always possessed the keenest interest for general readers, while for historians and those seeking special information about the manners and customs of the period treated, it has proved an invaluable repository. It is the unproclaimed authority for familiar detail in dramas and novels and has, moreover, been dramatized, or rather a play made of which it is the basis. For the literary artist it has proved a veritable well of local color. As a familiar picture of court life in the reign of the "Merry Monarch," it is vivid and accurate, detailing with the most illuminating touches the follies, vices, events and peculiarities of the age, and depicting the notable characters of the time in true and lively colors. The historian may record the address of a monarch or the machinations of a duke, but Samuel Pepys, in the privacy of his sanctum, takes note of the trivial realities dear to the hearts of the devotees of "human interest."

". . . . . we stayed and saw the king and queen set out toward Salisbury, and after them the Duke and Duchess, whose hands I did kiss. And it was the first time I did ever, or did see anybody else, kiss her hand, and it was a most fine white fat hand. But it was pretty to see the young ladies dressed like men, in velvet coats, caps with ribbands, and with laced bands, just like men. Only the Duchess herself it did not become."

This treasured work (if it may be called a work) throws a floodlight on the stiff and formal annals of the historic period it covers. It is thrilling to speculate on what we might have had if Samuel Pepys, the gossipy observer and greatest of diarists, had lived in the golden age of Queen Elizabeth. For then, perchance, we should know the color of Shakespeare's doublet and the sound of his voice and have an authoritative and appreciative comment on the manners of Sir Walter Raleigh, and the beauty of Mary Queen of Scots.

He died on May 26, 1703.

PERICLES   circa 490–429 B.C.

PERICLES (pĕr'ĭ klēz), was one of the greatest leaders of ancient Greece. He was born early in the fifth century B.C., in Athens. Descendant of a distinguished family, he was carefully educated, became a leader in the Athenian democracy and rose to the highest position of power. In 463 he dealt a forceful blow at the oligarchy which then ruled Athens by depriving the Areopagus (the chief court of the city) of its greatest political powers. He formed Greek colonies in various parts of the Mediterranean world; and built ships which brought the naval supremacy of the world to his native city. He strove to put an end to the destructive wars that had been waged between Athens and Sparta and other cities of Hellas through the formation of a Hellenic confederation and his plan might have succeeded had it not been for the open hostility of the Spartan aristocrats who were violently opposed to a democracy.

Athens and Sparta were both opposed to a confederation. Instead of an amicable settlement of their difficulties, they were drifting toward war. First difficulties were surmounted, however, and in 445 B.C. a thirty years' truce with Sparta was concluded. Cimon, the great aristocratic leader, had died and his successors sought in 444 to overthrow the authority of Pericles by attacking him in the popular assembly. They charged him, among other things, with squandering the public funds on great buildings, on festivals and popular amusements, but he was too strongly entrenched in the public estimation for their attack to succeed. In the Samian war of 439 he demonstrated great ability as a naval commander and Greece became supreme on the Mediterranean. Unable to reach Pericles, his enemies had to content themselves with attacking his friends, Phidias and Anaxagoras, and his mistress, Aspasia.

He was a patron of learning and of the arts. Under him architecture and sculpture reached their highest development; the Periclean age became one of the greatest in all the annals of Greece, and Athens the centre of literature and of the fine arts and the most magnificent city of the ancient world. Athens and posterity owe to him such triumphs of architecture as the Parthenon, the Erechtheum, the Propylaea, the Odeum, and numerous other public and sacred edifices. Music and the drama flourished; industry revived; commerce with other cities on the Mediterranean, the Adriatic, the Black Sea and other adjacent waters increased. He carried on Ephialtes' policy of making the Athenians self-governing and introduced the policy of paying from the state treasury for service to the State. He created a "theorikon" fund to enable poor citizens to attend the dramatic festivals. He was a great orator, of much dignity of presence and was often compared by his followers to Olympian Zeus. His sagacity, his eloquence and his patriotism won admiration from all and his freedom from superstition and his independent thinking raised him far above most of his contemporaries.

New wars troubled the later years of his life. In 433 in a conflict between Corinth and the colony of Corcyra, he took the part of the island of Corcyra which was on the western trade route to Sicily and Italy, and had a powerful fleet, thereby arousing the resentment of Sparta, head of the Peloponnesian League, which declared war on Athens. Hostilities began in 432. Pericles gathered the inhabitants of Athens within the walls and for two years they withstood the attacks of the enemy. In 430 a plague ravaged the city; Pericles was attacked by his enemies at home; his friends were arrested or obliged to flee. He was deposed from his magistracy, fined 50 talents on a charge of embezzlement and although he was soon reinstated with still greater powers, the plague which had carried off two of his sons and a sister left him so weakened that he died in the autumn of 429 B.C.

JOHN J. PERSHING   1860–

JOHN JOSEPH PERSHING, commander of the American Expeditionary Force in the World War, was born Sept. 13, 1860 in Laclede, Mo. By teaching school he earned money to attend the normal school at Kirksville, Mo., and later won an appointment to the United States Military Academy at West Point. Commissioned in the Sixth Cavalry (1886) he saw service within a short time in Arizona in the campaign against the Apache Indians; was in charge of Indian scouts in the Sioux uprising in the Dakotas in 1890 and the following year became military instructor in the University of Nebraska, where he studied law and received his degree, after which he was appointed instructor in tactics at West Point. In 1898 he served in Cuba through the Santiago campaign of the war with Spain, where he proved himself a cool, levelheaded and brave officer.

In 1903 he was sent to the Philippines where by his diplomacy and the proper use of force he was able to pacify the rebellious Moros at Mindanao and in 1905, during the Japanese campaign in Manchuria he was American military attaché in Japan. In recognition of his services in the Philippines he was jumped from the rank of captain to that of brigadier-general in 1906 by President Roosevelt, who passed him over 862 senior officers. He was again sent to the Philippines as commander of the department of Mindanao and governor of the Moro Province, but was recalled for duty in America in 1913. In 1915 his wife and three daughters were burned to death in a fire during his absence. In 1916 he was sent from San Francisco to take command of a punitive expedition into Mexico against the brigand, Francisco Villa, and on the death of Major General Funstan the following year Pershing succeeded him as commander on the Mexican border.

When the United States declared war against Germany in April, 1917, he was appointed to command the American troops and reached France with his staff on June 13, 1917. He insisted from the outset that the American army be preserved as a fighting unit instead of being put into action as shock troops or reserve forces for the various British and French armies, and maintained the integrity of his army against all the appeals and persuasiveness of French and English commanders and political leaders. He set about the task of training his men in France with the thoroughness that had characterized his previous military commands and built up and trained an army of 3,000,000 men, while the armies of the Allies continued to withstand the blows of the Germans, with great loss of life. The disasters to the Allies early in 1918 caused him to place his resources temporarily at the disposal of General Foch, reverting to his original policy, however, as soon as the crisis had passed. His contention for an integral American army was justified at the St. Mihiel fighting in September, 1918, which was the first entirely American operation, and resulted in a hard-won but important victory. He then commanded the American forces in the Meuse-Argonne battle, a battleground he had accepted in deference to the Allies against his own preference for a blow toward Metz. It was a slow and costly struggle, but it was won, and soon afterwards the Hindenberg line was reached and broken and the Armistice followed.

In recognition of his great contribution to the Allied victory and of his building up a huge army from almost nothing, the permanent rank of general was conferred upon him, Sept. 1, 1919; an honor that had been bestowed upon only four other officers, Washington, Grant, Sherman and Sheridan. In 1921 he was appointed chief of staff, and thereafter designed the framework of the present army organization. He was retired in September, 1924. The following year he went to Arica as United States representative and ex-officio head of a commission to supervise the plebiscite under the Tacna-Arica award, and has since served as head of a commission on American war memorials in France.

PETER THE GREAT   1672-1725

PETER I (ALEXEYEVITCH, CZAR OF RUSSIA) called PETER THE GREAT, was born in Moscow, May 30, 1672, son of the Czar Alexei Mikhailovitch and his second wife, Natalia Naryshkin. He received little formal education and until his tenth year went through many perils and miseries in which his family was involved; saw one of his uncles dragged from the palace and butchered; saw his best friend torn from his restraining arms and cut in pieces. Such experiences and his indulgence in unbridled passions doubtless were responsible for the convulsions to which he was later subject. His half-sister, Sophia, was regent from 1682 to 1689 and, although Peter and his feeble-minded brother, Ivan, had been crowned joint rulers, he occupied a subordinate position, being left much to himself and spending his time in childish games, sailing ships and sham fighting. He became friends with the Swiss adventurer, François Lefort, who introduced him to all the profligacies of the times but also taught him how to be a sovereign. His mother forced him to marry Eudoxia Lopukhina in 1689 to free him from Lefort's influence. He demanded that his sister resign her regentship which she did only after a struggle. In 1694 after his mother's death, Peter, free to follow his own inclinations, launched at Archangel a ship he had built the previous year. His interest in military and naval science was deep and long continued and his chief desire was to create a navy and develop overseas commerce.

In order to tap the riches of the Orient, he wished to get possession of the Caspian Sea. To do so it was necessary to fight the Crimean Khan and his suzerain, the Turkish sultan. He besieged the Turkish fortress of Azov from July to Sept. 1695, but the attack was a failure because he had no ships to drive away the fleet that came to the relief of the fortress. He sent to Austria and Prussia for shipbuilders and the following May approached Azov anew with two warships and many other vessels. Azov surrendered and Peter established Taganrog as a new naval station at the head of the Sea of Azov. To get aid in attacking Turkey he sent to the western powers an embassy which he accompanied as Peter Mikhailov and studied gunnery at Königsberg, shipbuilding at Saardam and Deptford, anatomy at Leyden, engraving at Amsterdam, but secured no help against Turkey. He was recalled to Moscow in 1698 by a revolt of the Streltsi, a troublesome organization of musketeers which had given him much trouble. The revolt was easily suppressed and he wreaked a terrible vengeance for its effect upon the reactionary majority of the nation. The organization was broken up, many of its members condemned to death and he divorced the Czarina whom he suspected of being concerned in the outbreak.

Realizing the value of western civilization, he had brought from England 500 engineers, artisans, surgeons, etc., and he set about introducing western customs. He ordered his chiefs to sacrifice their beards and national costumes and changed the calendar so that the year should start on January 1 instead of September 1. Numerous rebellions resulted from his reforms. In 1700, having concluded an advantageous peace with Turkey, he made an alliance with Denmark and Poland and embarked upon a long struggle to win from Sweden an ice-free seaboard on the Baltic. The war lasted for 21 years during which he met with many defeats but he laid the foundations of St. Petersburg, to which he later transferred the central government and by the peace of Nystad (1721) Sweden surrendered her best Baltic provinces, including Livonia, Esthonia and part of Finland, and Peter proclaimed himself Emperor of all the Russians. He had continued to institute internal reforms, opening institutions modeled after those of the West. He introduced the "Administrative Senate" in 1711, the "Holy Synod" in 1721. He passed over the rightful heir to the succession and by manifesto made his consort, the low-born Catharine, his successor. She was crowned May 7, 1724.

War with Persia (1722–23) gave him the towns of Baku and Derbent and opened the Caspian Sea for Russian commerce, but the monarch's health was broken. A fatiguing inspection of the Ladoga Canal, latest of his public works, brought on a new attack of his paroxysms and he died Jan. 28, 1725. He had welded the Russian nation into a modern state, created a navy, won an access to the sea and left a powerful impress on the political life of his country.

PETRARCH
1304–1374

FRANCESCO DI PETRACCO (or PETRARCA) Italian lyric poet, who later changed his name to Petrarch (pē'trärk), was born at Arezzo on July 30, 1304, the son of Ser Petracco, a notary who was expelled from Florence by the decree of January 27, 1302, which also banished Dante for life. In 1313 Ser Petracco removed to Avignon, France. The son studied the humanities at Carpentras and then for seven years studied law at Montpellier and Bologna. He returned to Avignon upon his father's death in 1326, took ecclesiastical orders and was befriended by Giacomo Colonna, afterwards Bishop of Lombez.

On April 6, 1327, at the church of St. Clara in Avignon, he met a beautiful woman with whom he fell deeply and lastingly in love. She has become known to the world only as Laura. The beautiful poems in which he commemorated his love for her indicate that she was a young married woman who accepted his homage but refused any closer relationship. In 1333 he left Avignon where he had many influential friends, on the first of his many long journeys, visiting Paris, Ghent, Liège and Cologne. In 1338 he withdrew to the valley of Vaucluse where for some years he spent his time almost alone with his books, reading Roman history and preparing for his great epic poem *Africa*. He wrote many of his odes and sonnets to Laura while at Vaucluse. There was born to him by a woman whose identity is not known, a son, Giovanni and daughter, Francesca, who were later legitimized by papal decree. His fame as a poet spread with the circulation of the first drafts of *Africa*. In 1341 King Robert of Naples invited him to visit that city and sent him with magnificent credentials to Rome, where in April was conferred upon him the great honor of the laurel wreath of the poet. He was the papal ambassador to Naples when King Robert died and it was probably at this time that he first met the poet, Boccaccio.

In 1347 he threw himself into the cause of the Roman republic. The same year he established his home at Parma. Within two years Laura and several of his friends died in rapid succession and he thought of leaving the world and establishing a humanistic convent. He did not carry out that intention, but a marked change came over his writings. His poems on *In Morte di Madonna Laura* are of a religious nature. He became a European celebrity and was entertained by many of the Italian despots. In 1350, en route to Rome on a pilgrimage, he stopped in Florence and there entered into a close friendship with Boccaccio who in 1351 obtained for him the restoration of his rights as a citizen of Florence and an invitation to become rector of the newly founded university of that city, which however he refused. At Vaucluse in 1351 he wrote his *Epistle to Posterity*. In 1353 he went to Milan and was employed on various diplomatic missions. After the death of his son by the plague, he settled in Padua (1362) and gave his library to the republic of St. Mark. In 1369 he retired to the little village of Arquà where he spent his last years quietly in study. One of his last writings was a Latin version of his friend Boccaccio's story of Griselda. His fame, however, rests chiefly upon the *Rime,* consisting of sonnets and poems to Laura composed throughout a period of some forty years.

He was found dead among his books on July 18, 1374.

PHIDIAS   Probably 500 B.C.–432 B.C.

PHIDIAS (fĭd'ĭ ŭs), (or PHEIDIAS) was born probably between 500 and 490 B.C. in Attica, the son of a certain Charmides. Such meagre information as we have about him is indefinite and often conflicting. He appears to have studied under the Athenian Hegias, famous for his statues of the gods and goddesses. There is not one original sculpture by Phidias remaining so far as is known, yet the world agrees in esteeming him the greatest sculptor of ancient Greece and one of the greatest of all time. Descriptions of his statues are held to warrant this estimation as do some marbles which are believed to be copies of his work. Some of the designs of the Parthenon are undoubtedly his. The testimony of the ancients and the evidence of monuments marks him as a typical artist of the best in Greek culture. He found the most congenial soil for his genius in the Athens of Pericles, and his sculptures are held to stand with the tragedies of Sophocles as the most perfect expression of the noblest ideals of Greece. He was a thorough master of technique and, while true to nature in his representations, sought to express the ideal beauty that lies behind reality.

He is thought to have drawn from Homer the inspiration for his colossal statue of Zeus at Olympia which showed the god seated, wearing an olive wreath, holding in his left hand a sceptre crowned with an eagle, while on his extended right hand stood a "Nike" (or Victory) holding a fillet; the throne was elaborately decorated with figures in relief and in the round. Representations of this statue are found on late coins of Elis. He attained his greatest fame in what is known as the chryselephantine technique, in which a core of wood is overlaid with ivory to represent the flesh, and gold, often inlaid with enamel, is used for the drapery. The *Zeus* and the *Athena* in the Parthenon were his most celebrated examples of this style. He was celebrated in all branches of sculpture. Among his bronze statues were the *Athena* of the Lemnians, and the colossal *Athena* (sometimes called the *Pronchos*) ascribed to him by ancient tradition. In marble were the *Aphrodite* in Athens, the face, hands and feet of an *Athena* at Platæa whose drapery was of gilded wood, forming a cheap substitute for the chryselephantine technique. The *Athena* in the Parthenon was a standing figure, lance in her left hand, shield at her left side, while on her extended right hand was a "Nike." The right hand may have been supported by a pillar. The shield, pedestal, helmet and sandals were decorated with scenes from Greek legends. The gold on this statue was detachable and was valued at 44 talents. It was erected in 438 B.C. and if Phidias supervised the work on the Parthenon, for which he is supposed to have drawn the designs, he must have been in Athens from about 437 to 433 B.C. when the building was completed.

The chronicles of his later life are conflicting. All accounts agree that he was tried in Athens on a charge of embezzling the gold appropriated for the statue of *Athena,* but they differ as to what followed. One account says that he died in prison; another states that he was banished to Elis, made the statue of *Zeus* at Olympia and was then accused of embezzling gold and was put to death by the Eleans. The latter account can hardly be true in the opinion of modern investigators, as his descendants enjoyed hereditary honors at Olympia. The more probable theory is that the *Zeus* was made just after the middle of the fifth century B.C. and that after this he remained in Athens. It is certain that he shared in the attacks made against the friends of Pericles, and one account states that he was acquitted of the embezzling charge but condemned for impiety in putting his own portrait on the shield of the Athena Parthenos.

PHILIP II OF SPAIN   1527–1598

PHILIP II of Spain was born May 21, 1527, at Valladolid, only son of the Emperor Charles V. He was married in 1543 to Maria of Portugal, who died three years later, after giving birth to a son, Don Carlos. The three years following his wife's death he spent with his father in the Low Countries. A marriage of policy was arranged with Mary Tudor, Queen of England, in 1554, and he remained in England for fourteen months thereafter, but failed to make himself popular with the English people. His father abdicated his throne the following year and Philip thus became one of the most powerful monarchs in Europe. In addition to Spain, Sicily, Milan, the Low Countries, French Compté, Mexico and Peru were under his sway. Spain was then at the zenith of her power, but the wars of Charles V had drained the national treasury of funds, and a dangerous alliance was being formed against Philip by King Henry II of France and the Pope, Paul IV. Philip sent the Duke of Alva to Italy who speedily overcame the papal resistance. Philip himself took the field against Henry's French army, which he defeated at St. Quentin in 1557 and again at Gravelines the following year. Henry sued for peace in 1559, soon after having captured Calais from the English.

Mary Tudor died in 1559 and Philip asked for the hand of Queen Elizabeth, but the Virgin Queen finally refused the alliance and Philip married Elizabeth of Valois. He was jealous of his authority and sought to concentrate all the power of his empire in himself. To accomplish this purpose he strove to destroy all the free institutions in the countries under his sway, put himself at the head of the Catholic party and employed the Inquisition to carry out his purpose, succeeding by its help in Spain, but the Low Countries rebelled, their revolt ending in 1579 with the Seven United Provinces independent of Spain. The war had been long and costly, Philip's treasury needed replenishing and he proceeded to exact enormous contributions. His son, Don Carlos, between whom and the King there was little love, died in prison in 1568. In 1570 he married his niece, Anne of Austria, who bore him a son (later Philip III).

In 1571 he attained his only great naval victory in the battle of Lepanto against the Turks, his half-brother, Don John of Austria, commanding the Spanish fleet. In 1580 he sent Alva to occupy Portugal, which he claimed upon the death of the last male heir to the throne. His hatred of England, perhaps due in part to the rejection of his offer of marriage by Elizabeth and his jealousy of England's increasing sea commerce and the number and prosperity of her American colonies, led him to the fitting out of the great Armada with which he expected to crush the British. It set sail in 1588, but when it reached the English Channel a great storm arose which, together with the ability of England's naval commanders and the bravery of her seamen, entirely destroyed the powerful fleet. Philip intrigued against Henry of Navarre, but his plottings failed of their object. Besides the long and costly struggle with Holland, Spain was put to great expense in trying to fight off the British ships which ravaged the islands of the Spanish Main, and his country was reduced to financial distress.

The cumulative effect of these reverses greatly embittered his final years. He was one of the most powerful monarchs of his age. Although a bigot, he was apparently something of an idealist and sincere in his belief that he was benefiting his country by his severe measures. While permitting and even encouraging the methods of the Inquisition, he was often sympathetic to appeals for mercy. As a ruler he possessed great abilities, but he scattered them and disrupted his finances through the number and magnitude of his many enterprises, most of which came to nothing. He crushed Spanish commerce by his monetary exactions and by his persecution of the Moriscos, his most industrious subjects. He died on Sept. 13, 1598.

FRANKLIN PIERCE   1804–1869

FRANKLIN PIERCE, fourteenth president of the United States, was born at Hillsboro, N. H., Nov. 23, 1804, the son of Benjamin Pierce, Revolutionary general and twice governor of the state. He attended Hancock, Francestown and Exeter Academies, entering Bowdoin College in 1820, where he formed a lifelong friendship with Nathaniel Hawthorne; then studied law and was admitted to the bar in 1827. Two years later he was elected to the New Hampshire House of Representatives where he served as speaker in 1831 and 1832. In 1833 he was sent to Congress where he supported President Jackson, opposed the re-charter of the Bank of the United States, and appropriations for the Military Academy at West Point; favored a volunteer-army. During his first term in Congress he married Jane Means Appleton, daughter of the president of Bowdoin College. In 1837 he was the youngest member of the United States Senate. He resigned his seat in 1842 and resumed the practice of law at Concord, N. H. In 1845 he refused the Democratic nomination for governor, an appointment to fill an unexpired term in the United States Senate, and the post of attorney general in President Polk's cabinet, on the ground that he had permanently retired from political life.

In 1846 he enlisted as a private for service in the Mexican War, became colonel of the 9th Regiment and later brigadier-general of volunteers. He was with General Scott in the advance on Mexico City and was injured by being thrown from his horse in the battle of Contreras. At the close of the war he returned to his law practice.

In 1852, factional rivalries having brought about a deadlock between Lewis Cass, Stephen A. Douglas and James Buchanan, Pierce was entered as a "dark horse" candidate and was elected to the presidency. He was the youngest man to have held the office and was brilliant, handsome and genial. For political and commercial reasons of expediency, the element of the Democratic party which supported him was pro-southern in regard to slavery and his cabinet was composed of eastern business men and southern planters. Jefferson Davis was his secretary of war. He held that his election was a mandate to maintain the Compromise of 1850 and to bury the anti-slavery controversy. He maintained that the acquisition of Cuba was necessary to the safety and commercial prosperity of the United States. Spain refused to sell the island and Pierre Soulé, American minister to Spain, after a conference with Buchanan, minister to Great Britain, and John Y. Mason, minister to France, issued the famous Ostend Manifesto that the United States, if unable to obtain Cuba peacefully, was justified in taking it by force. A storm of controversy arose and Pierce disclaimed responsibility for the manifesto. When William Walker's filibustering expedition into Central America to establish a pro-slavery government which could be brought into the United States, succeeded and he became military dictator and then president of Nicaragua, Pierce recognized his régime.

It was during his administration that Commodore Perry in 1853 induced Japan to open her doors to American trade. He effected a reorganization of the diplomatic and consular service and established the United States Court of Claims; favored the building of a transcontinental railroad and in order to open a southerly route purchased 50,000 square miles of territory from Mexico in 1853 (the Gadsden Purchase) at a cost of $10,000,000. He sanctioned the Kansas-Nebraska bill, reawakening the slavery agitation. After his term ended he lived in Concord, N. H., until his death on October 8, 1869.

WILLIAM PITT, EARL OF CHATHAM   1708–1778

WILLIAM PITT, first Earl of Chatham, was one of England's most brilliant orators and statesmen. He was born at Westminster, Nov. 15, 1708; attended Eton and Trinity College, Oxford, and studied law at the University of Utrecht. At the age of 20 he obtained a cornetcy in Lord Cobham's regiment of horse. In 1735 he entered the House of Commons representing Old Sarum and joined the opposition. He became one of the greatest orators the House has known, a master of invective and satire whose sting Horace Walpole often felt. He was instrumental in bringing about the fall of Walpole's government in 1742. Carteret, long one of Walpole's opponents, became secretary of state and Pitt devoted himself to accomplishing Carteret's downfall. Both were determined to overthrow the Bourbon power, but they differed in their method. Carteret wanted German support, a confederation of German states under the leadership of England, to support Maria Theresa of Austria in her struggle against France. Pitt held that England should devote herself entirely to her own duel with France in the proper English sphere, the sea. He denounced Carteret's secret methods, practically forcing his resignation in 1744.

Pitt had opposed the king, George II, who now refused to have him in the new ministry, but after the fall of Pelham in 1746, the ministry was recalled on its own terms and Pitt was named Vice-Treasurer for Ireland and became a member of the Privy Council. During the next seven years he supported the Pelham administration. In 1744 he had received a legacy of 10,000 pounds from the old Duchess of Marlborough. After Pelham's death in 1754 Pitt's opposition to the foreign policy of the Newcastle ministry caused his dismissal from office. Two years later, however, the king, in response to popular demand, called upon him to form a new cabinet, and he became virtually the ruler of England. The country had become involved in the Seven Years War and Pitt adopted vigorous measures. He got rid of the German mercenaries; "put England on board her fleet," fastening upon India and America as the main objects of his strategy. He won Canada from France; helped Clive and the East India Company in the struggle against the French East India Company; attacked France on her own coasts, in the West Indies, in

Africa and elsewhere. The Treaty of Paris, 1763, left England supreme in America and India.

George III, crowned in 1760, was determined to rule the country and to stop the "bloody and expensive war," and Pitt resigned in 1761, receiving a pension of 3000 pounds a year. For five years he remained out of office, actively opposing, however, the stamp tax and other taxes imposed on the American colonies. After the repeal of the stamp tax in 1766 and the resignation of Rockingham's cabinet, he formed a new ministry, but his health was failing and he took for himself the easy office of Privy Seal and was created Viscount Pitt and Earl of Chatham. His acceptance of the title caused loss of prestige with the people, who had named him the Great Commoner. His impaired health prevented his taking an active part in the government and he resigned in 1768 and did not again hold office. He continued his active interest in public matters and worked for an amicable settlement with the American colonies, declaring that England had no right to tax them.

At the end of a powerful address in the House of Lords, he collapsed and died a few days later, May 11, 1778, at his country house at Hayes, in Kent. He was buried in Westminster Abbey where a statue was erected to his memory.

WILLIAM PITT   1759–1806

WILLIAM PITT, English statesman and son of the first Earl of Chatham, was born at Hayes, England, May 28, 1759. He entered Pembroke Hall, Cambridge, at the age of 14; was admitted to the bar in 1780; and entered the House of Commons the following year for Appleby. He assailed the North ministry, which was tottering from the struggle with the American colonies, and later refused a post in Rockingham's ministry, but became Chancellor of the Exchequer under Shelburne at the age of 23. Peace negotiations with the United States, France and Spain were signed and a truce entered into with Holland. When Shelburne left office in 1783 King George III offered Pitt the premiership, but he declined, being doubtful of sufficient support. The Duke of Portland became premier and Pitt led the opposition and introduced bills for parliamentary reform which failed of enactment. The Commons passed, but the Lords rejected, his bill for the reform of abuses in public office. The King dismissed the ministry in December, 1783, and Pitt took office as Chancellor of the Exchequer and First Lord of the Treasury against tremendous opposition in the House of Commons. He fought against Burke, Fox, North and Sheridan. They failed to drive him from office and the majorities against him gradually grew smaller. Parliament was dissolved in March, 1784 and the following election was a great triumph for his administration. Although only 25 years old he was one of the most powerful men England had known and his ministry lasted almost unbroken for twenty years. He was popular with the king, with Parliament and with the people.

Under Pitt the House of Commons acquired new importance, the people a greater control over its proceedings; parliamentary corruption was put down and parliamentary rights established. He reformed revenue methods, did away with sinecures in public office and restored the financial system of the country which had been disorganized by the conflict with America. A commercial treaty with France was negotiated. During his ministry England became a greater power in European politics. Opposition arising to parliamentary reform and the abolition of the slave trade, he cast those measures aside. It has been said of him that he loved power more than measures. His Sinking Fund has been held thoroughly vicious in principle and results. His proposed free trade measure with Ireland failed through the jealousy of English manufacturers. He has been roundly blamed for his opposition to reformation of abuses in the Irish parliament and for his wavering policy toward the Irish Catholics. He was lavish in the creation of peerages and cared little for the development of literature, science and the arts. His policy regarding the French Revolution was one of rigid neutrality, but he was eventually forced into war by France's aggressive policy in Flanders and toward Holland. He believed the struggle with France would be a short one. He was lacking in the qualities of a great war minister and his military measures and plans were badly managed and executed. He adopted repressive measures at home through fear of a revolutionary movement and attempted to meet the famine prices of corn by relaxing the poor laws. In Ireland he attempted to win over the Catholics by measures of conciliation, but in this he was hampered by the king, by divided support at home and by his own vacillation. His recall from Ireland of a popular viceroy led to the Irish rebellion of 1798. He attempted to place Irish affairs on a sound basis by a legislative union (accomplished by corrupt means), but when he attempted to emancipate the Catholics, the king opposed the measure so forcefully that Pitt resigned office in February, 1801. He gave his loyal support to the succeeding ministry of Addington, but his health was poor and he withdrew from active life. In May, 1803, England declared war against France and he at once came to the aid of the country and again became prime minister in 1804, throwing himself vigorously into the struggle.

He died at Putney, Jan. 23, 1806, and was buried in Westminster Abbey. He contributed much to the final downfall of Napoleon and may perhaps be considered England's greatest prime minister.

FRANCISCO PIZARRO

circa 1470–1541

FRANCISCO PIZARRO (pĕ zär′rō), Spanish conqueror of Peru, was born at Trujillo, Spain, about 1470 and had his first experience of fighting in Italy under Gonsalvo di Cordova in whose army his father was a soldier. He was at Darien in 1509 and was a member of Balboa's party when that adventurer crossed the Isthmus of Panama and caught the first glimpse of the Pacific Ocean ever vouchsafed to a white man. About 1522, having lived in Panama for several years, he and the Spanish Almagro undertook to explore the country to the south of the Isthmus in quest of more information about the Incas of Peru and the enormous wealth which they were reputed to have. After several attempts, fraught with dangers, hardships and delays, they reached the territory about the Gulf of Guayaquil and as a result of the information which they had obtained Pizarro set sail for Spain to induce the Spanish king to send an expedition against the Empire of the Incas—an easy task after he had inflamed the court with his tales of the great wealth they possessed. He was given permission in 1529 to proceed against Peru, and was made governor and captain-general of the province of New Castile, with Almagro as marshal. Unable to raise the troops required, Pizarro and Almagro secretly took ship for Panama, where Pizarro gathered together a band of 183 men and 37 horse, and with this small force he sailed for Peru in December, 1531, leaving Almagro behind to raise reinforcements with which he was to follow and join forces with Pizarro in Peru. Included in Pizarro's company were his four brothers.

The expedition disembarked at Tumbez and, after some delay devoted to collecting information and making preparations for the projected conquest, began its journey inland in May, 1532, reaching Cajamarca, on the eastern side of the Andes, in November after long and arduous marches. By resorting to treachery, Pizarro got the Inca, Atahualpa, in his power near Cajamarca and demanded an enormous ransom of some $18,000,000 to spare his life, but after the ransom money had been paid he treacherously had the Inca put to death in August,

1533. In the meantime Almagro had arrived with his reinforcements and in November Pizarro entered Cuzco and there permitted Manco, son of the former ruler, Huayna Capac, to be crowned. Later while Almagro undertook an expedition into Chile, Pizarro founded Lima (the City of Kings) in January, 1535. A dispute arose soon afterwards between Pizarro, his brothers, Juan and Gonzalo, on the one hand, and Almagro on the other, as to the boundaries of the territories under their respective jurisdictions and this dispute resulted in an armed conflict near Cuzco in 1538 in which Almagro was defeated and executed.

The followers of Almagro recognized as his successor his half caste son known as Almagro the Lad and, bitter and resentful, the youth and his adherents formed a conspiracy against Francisco Pizarro which resulted in his assassination in June, 1541. But Charles V had appointed Vica de Castro as governor of the province of New Castile and sent him out with ships and men. Upon his arrival in Peru, Castro proceeded at once against Almagro the Lad, defeated him at Cuzco and ordered him beheaded.

Hernando Pizarro, upon returning to Spain, was imprisoned until 1560 for having beheaded Almagro. Gonzalo, another brother of the conqueror of Peru, retired to Charcas after the assassination and in 1544, upon the request of the Spaniards to protect them when the new governor, Vela, arrived, entered Lima in October, was proclaimed governor and defeated the Viceroy, Vela, who was killed in battle (1546). Pedro de la Gasco, an able ecclesiastic, was then sent out to restore order. Gonzalo defeated one force which was sent against him, but when faced by Gasco near Cuzco in April, 1548, deserted by his men, he surrendered and was beheaded.

PLATO   427 B.C.–347 B.C.

PLATO, Greek philosopher and writer (originally named Aristocles), was born about 427 B.C., probably in Athens. He received the usual education of a well-born Athenian youth, in music, literature and gymnastics, distinguished himself as an athlete and wrote poetry, but he evidently was not attracted to a political career as would have seemed natural to one of his position and culture. He became a disciple of Socrates when he was about 20 years old and studied with him for eight years. He says in the *Phaedo* that he was prevented by illness from being present at the last talk and the death of Socrates. After the death of his teacher he seems to have been absent from Athens for some ten years, studying with Euclid at Megara and traveling extensively. He visited Cyrene, Egypt, Italy and Sicily. About 388 he is said to have been captured by Dionysius of Syracuse as he returned from Sicily and to have been sold as a slave in Ægina, from which bondage he was ransomed by friends.

Shortly after this he established the famous Academy in Athens. In the grove of the Academy and in his own garden close by he taught philosophy for 40 years to a small band of disciples, mostly by means of conversation and discussion. He gathered about him a group of distinguished followers who became known as the philosophers of the Academy and carried on his work after his death. Numbered among them were Aristotle, Demosthenes, Lycurgus and many other eminent men.

Plato died in 347 B.C., in his eighty-first year, while at a wedding feast, esteemed and loved by his many pupils. He had never married and apparently possessed some independent means as there is no record of his having held any public office from which he could have received an income, and he was much opposed to receiving payment for his teaching. Some of his writings have been lost but a number of authenticated works as well as several of doubtful authenticity, have come down through the ages. The *Epistles* have been rejected by Greek scholars as not coming from his pen and his authorship of ten or more of the *Dialogues* is a matter of dispute. There are enough of his known works surviving, however, to make secure his place among the world's great thinkers. The *Apology* or *Defence of Socrates on his Trial* is probably accurate history, Plato by his own statement having been present at the trial. The short dialogues quoting Socrates' sayings are believed to be genuine. The *Phaedo,* the last conversation with Socrates on the immortality of the soul, was probably written after the latter's death. The great works which show Plato's literary and dialectical skill at their fullest devlopment were probably written after his fortieth year. These include *Phoedrus, Symposium, Gorgias, Republic* and *Phaedo.* The more metaphysical *Parmenides, Theoetetus, Sophist* and *Statesman* were probably written later.

Plato's philosophy developed from that of his teacher, Socrates, though evidences of the teachings of earlier Greek philosophers are also found in his writings. He maintained that one knows only when he has arrived at the reasons or causes of things, when he sees the facts connected in a chain of causation. In his philosophy both the permanent and the changing have a place, the former in the world of ideas with which science is concerned, the latter in the world of sense, of opinion. Ideas to him were not mere concepts of the mind, but "the most real existences." His theory underwent modification in his later years. He agreed neither with the Cyremaics that pleasure is the good, nor with the Cynics that pleasure is evil, but held that pleasures may be good or bad. The great work of his later years is the *Laws,* although his *Republic* is probably the most widely known of his writings. His influence on human thought in his own time and down through succeeding ages has been incalculable, even surpassing that of Aristotle. The study of his philosophy and writings was revived in the Italian and English Renaissance in the revolt against scholasticism and among later German students, and in present day scholarship his mastery is still supreme.

PLINY (THE ELDER AND THE YOUNGER)   23–79 and 62–113

THESE two eminent Roman authors, uncle and nephew, are commonly referred to as PLINY (plī′nĭ) the Elder and PLINY the Younger. Gaius Plinius Secundus, the elder, was the author of the celebrated *Natural History,* occupying 37 volumes, a monumental work on which his fame chiefly rests. He was born probably at Verona in 23 A.D. While still a youth he was sent to Rome where he was educated. At 23 he entered the army and fought in Germany under Pomponius Secundus. In the intervals of military service he devoted his time to authorship and wrote, among other things, the first part of his comprehensive history of the Germanic wars, later completed and published in 20 volumes. With his commander, Pomponius, of whom he afterward wrote a memoir, he returned to Rome in his 29th year and began the study of law, a profession for which he was not temperamentally fitted, and he abandoned it for the more congenial work of authorship which he prosecuted in retirement at his native home. Here, while the unspeakable Nero made a vicious spectacle in Rome, this engaging writer worked upon his treatise (*Studiosus*) on the training of a youth from childhood to his entrance in public life, a work intended particularly for the perusal of his nephew.

In 71 A.D., while he was visiting Spain on legal business, he was apprised of the death of his brother-in-law and his appointment as guardian to the boy whose name is so inseparably linked with his own. Returning to Rome, he was warmly received by the new emperor, Vespasian, with whom he enjoyed an intimate friendship and whom he assisted. We have a familiar picture of his method of work while living in Rome during this period of his life, which might well serve as a model of system and literary concentration to modern members of his craft. He would begin his labors at a late hour of the night, work by candlelight until dawn, then call upon the emperor (who must have been an early riser) to receive his commissions. These duties attended to, he would return to his writing, pausing only for a frugal meal and to allow himself the luxury of basking in the sunshine for a short while in the middle of the day. But even in this brief recess he was not idle and made copious notes from the books which an attendant would read to him. Indeed, it is difficult to see how he could have spared much time from his labors. The Roman history of Aufidius Bassus which he completed and brought up to his own day filled 31 books. His life's work seems incredible and presupposes an incalculable amount of reading. Even at his meals, books were read to him by a secretary. He is said to have studied at all times except when asleep and even while in his bath the faithful reader was in service, reading or taking dictation. It was by this method that he collected the vast amount of material for his great *Natural History,* published two years before his death. This is the only one of his numerous works that has come down to us and its title is misleading to the modern student for it includes astronomy, geography, mineralogy, zoology, botany and indeed is more an encyclopedia of universal knowledge than a natural history. His death was tragic. In 79 A.D. he was on a ship stationed off Misenum, in command of a Roman squadron, for this indefatigable author found time to engage in military and naval service. The great eruption which destroyed Pompeii and Herculaneum was then at its height, and he went ashore at Stabiæ for a closer view of the terrible spectacle, and was suffocated by the deadly vapors.

GAIUS PLINIUS CÆCILIUS SECUNDUS (Pliny the Younger) was nephew of the preceding and son of A. Cæcilius. He was born at Novum Comum (Como) in 62 A.D., and upon the death of his father was adopted by his uncle, under whose care he was educated. His mother, and also his tutor, were likewise devoted to his training, but it was the wisdom and affectionate solicitude of his distinguished uncle that guided him in the path of knowledge. At the age of 13 he wrote a Greek tragedy, later studied oratory under Quintilian and gave every promise of fulfilling the highest expectations of his guardian. In his 19th year he began speaking in the Forum, and soon was continually in demand as an advocate. He filled numerous official posts, served as a military tribune in Syria, was prætor about 93 A.D. and consul several years later. In 102 he was appointed proprætor of the province Pontica, and later was curator of the banks and channel of the Tiber. He was twice married but had no children.

The letters of Pliny the Younger fill ten books, and it is from these, collected and edited by himself, that most of our knowledge about him is derived. They are peculiarly interesting for their vivid pictures of contemporary Roman life and the personages of the time, with most of whom he was on friendly terms. Not the least engaging feature of these epistles are the very unstudied glimpses which they give us of their author who seems to have been of a sociable temper, decidedly likable, genial, tolerant, humorous, observant and studious. He was a man of fortune and took delight in the improvement of his house and gardens. To the numerous servants (slaves) on his estate he was a humane and considerate master. No doubt the most valuable matter, from the historical standpoint, contained in his epistles, are the references to the persecution of the Christians. He is known to have suffered from infirm health throughout his life and is thought to have died about 113 A.D.

PLUTARCH   circa 46–120 A.D.

PLUTARCH (plū'tärk), (or PLOUTARCHOS), Greek scholar and writer, was born about the year 46 A.D., at Chæronea in Bœotia. It is probable that he obtained his early education in that city but in 66 A.D. he went to Athens to pursue his studies; doubtless philosophy, history and the careers of great men of the past. He visited Rome a number of times, at least once officially as *chargé d'affaires* of his native city, and while there gave a course of public lectures in philosophy. Except for these few facts very little is known about his life, although most of his mature years were spent in his native town of Chæronea where he died about 120 A.D.

His name has been made immortal by his *Lives,* which are vivid character sketches of 46 famous heroes, generals and statesmen of previous ages. Founded as they were upon records and information which have since been lost, they give a valuable and probably for the most part authentic account of the lives of those of whom he wrote and form a treasure-trove for students of ancient biography. They were published in successive books, each volume containing two sketches, one of a Greek, the other of a Roman, in whose careers the author found some resemblance. Following most of the biographies are addendums, or sequels, comparing in detail the life of the subject with the lives of other noted men of his class. These sequels are generally regarded as having been written by another hand. Plutarch touches but lightly upon the famous events in which each person chosen for a sketch was concerned, or the actions for which he was noted, devoting most of his space to an analysis of the character of the man and the quality of his genius.

Aside from the *Lives,* a number of his writings are extant; some are grouped under the general head of *Opera Moralia* or *Moral Works,* which contains sixty or more short treatises upon various subjects— ethics, politics, history, love stories, philosophy, health, facetiæ, and on the *Isis* and *Osiris.* Some students find a Christian spirit running through several of the essays, but it is doubtful if Plutarch ever heard of Christ. It is generally accepted that not all of these *Moral Works* were written by him. Still a third collection of his works is the *Symposiaca* or *Table-Talks,* which reveal him in an amiable light as a charming friend and good companion, while his dialogue, *Gryllus,* shows a keen sense of humor. His knowledge of men and events was encyclopedic and his writings reveal a remarkable breadth of learning, if not great depth as a thinker.

Various complete editions of his works have been published within the past century and a half, including an edition edited by Reiske in 1774–79; Dübner-Dohner's, 1846–55; Clough and Goodwin's, 1914. Perhaps the best text of his parallel *Lives* is that of Sintenis, published in 1874–81; and of the *Opera Moralia,* that of G. N. Bernardake, 1888–95. Annotated editions of the *Lives* have been published in various countries, notably Germany and England; in England in the Loeb Classical Library, with translation by B. Perrin (10 volumes), and by Dr. Holden whose elaborate commentaries are a valuable feature of the edition. The Brothers Langhorne translated the *Lives* into English, as did Dryden and Sir Thomas North, the latter founding his translation upon the scholarly French translation made by Jacques Amyot (1559). Oakesmith published his *Religion of Plutarch* in 1902 and Dill's *Roman Society* (1905) and Mahaffy's *Age of the Greek World* (1911) contain interesting and informative material concerning the great biographer.

EDGAR ALLAN POE   1809–1849

EDGAR ALLEN POE, the most tragic figure in American literature, was born in Boston, Mass., Jan. 19, 1809, the son of David and Elizabeth Poe, who were strolling players. When he was but two years old his mother died shortly after her husband, leaving the family of three children penniless in Richmond, Va. Edgar was adopted by a wealthy merchant,

Mr. John Allan of Richmond. In 1822 he was sent to the University of Virginia but his habits of dissipation caused his dismissal and a subsequent quarrel with his foster father.

He left Richmond in 1827 and is next heard of in Boston where he managed to achieve the publication of *Tamarlane and Other Poems,* a small volume which attracted no attention. In the same year he enlisted in the army under the assumed name of Edgar A. Perry, made a creditable record and was honorably discharged two years later. In 1829 he published at Baltimore another small book of verse and later procured a cadetship to West Point where he had a brief and dubious career, culminating in his dismissal at the close of 1830.

In 1831 he published still another volume of verse, by means of subscriptions procured from his former military comrades. In October, 1833 his tale, *Manuscript Found in a Bottle,* won a prize of $100. offered by the *Baltimore Visitor*.

In 1834 he married Virginia Clemm, the daughter of an aunt in Baltimore. He was 26 years old and his bride 13. Thereafter this hapless trio lived together and Mrs. Clemm became the unfailing and sympathetic companion and prop of both husband and wife. For about two years Poe was literary editor of the *Southern Literary Messenger* in Richmond, contributing to it a number of stories and articles. In January, 1837 he moved to New York where Mrs. Clemm took boarders while "her Eddie" completed the *Narrative of A. Gordon Pym,* a part of which had been published in the *Messenger* and which was now brought out in book form.

During 1838 the little family moved to Philadelphia where they remained until 1844, Poe making many contributions to local publications. In 1839 he became a contributor to Burton's *Gentleman's Magazine* in which appeared his famous short story, *The Fall of the House of Usher,* commonly regarded as the most superb of all his prose works. In 1840 a collection of his various magazine contributions was published in two volumes. Although he had quarreled with his employer, the kindly William E. Burton stipulated for his employment when the *Gentleman's Magazine* was combined with *The Casket,* owned by George R. Graham, and Poe became editor of *Graham's Magazine* in which some of his best-known stories were published.

In 1843 he resigned this position and planned a periodical of his own, but the project was not carried out and he sought, but failed to receive, a government position. Unhappily his reputation for drinking stood ever in his way. During this year several of his best-known poems and stories appeared and he delivered a lecture in Philadelphia on *The Poets and Poetry of America*.

Moving again to New York, he took employment with the *Evening Mirror* and after his voluntarily terminating this editorial post his superior, the popular writer, N. P. Willis, gave a refreshingly favorable account of his character and conduct. It was in this periodical that Poe's most celebrated poem, *The Raven,* first appeared, which took the world by storm.

He next associated himself with *The Broadway Journal* in which he reprinted many of his formerly published tales and poems, but it came to an untimely end. He had now become something of a social lion, owing chiefly to his authorship of *The Raven,* but financial adversity ever haunted him and he was soon reduced to the most pitiful extremities of poverty in a tiny cottage at Fordham, above New York City. Here his young wife sank rapidly from the ravages of consumption, aggravated no doubt by poverty and consequent malnutrition, and died on January 30, 1847. For a time the stricken poet and the loyal Mrs. Clemm lived on in this scene of his bitter grief, but he was not able to write and these days constituted the dark prelude to the tragic fate which terminated his unhappy career.

In June, 1849 he started for Richmond, stopping at Philadelphia where his friend, John Sartain, noticed symptoms of mental disturbance. In Richmond he delivered a lecture with the proceeds of which ($1500) he started north.

What happened upon his arrival in Baltimore is not clearly established. It was an election day and it has been alleged that he was drugged and recruited as a "repeater." However that may be, on Wednesday, Oct. 3, he was taken to a hospital suffering from a violent brain fever and there, on Sunday morning, Oct. 7, he died. He rests under the Poe monument in Baltimore which was erected in 1875.

JAMES K. POLK 1795–1849

JAMES KNOX POLK, eleventh president of the United States, was born in Mecklenburg County, N. C., Nov. 2, 1795, of Irish ancestry. In 1806 he removed with his parents to Maury County, Tenn. He was graduated from the University of North Carolina in 1818, studied law at Nashville and began to practice at Columbia, Maury County, in 1820. From 1823–25 he served in the Tennessee House of Representatives and from 1825–39 in Congress. He sided with Jackson and Van Buren in the factional strife following the election of 1824, became leader of the

Democratic party and was speaker of the House from 1835 to 1839, when he retired to become governor of Tennessee. He was defeated for reelection in 1841 and again in 1843.

At the Democratic National Convention in Baltimore in 1844, Van Buren's followers being unable to nominate him for president under the two-thirds rule, Polk received the nomination as a compromise and was elected president, his opponent, Henry Clay, having lost support through his attitude toward the immediate annexation of Texas, which Polk and his party favored. The historian, Bancroft, who was Polk's secretary of the navy, has characterized him as "prudent, far-sighted, bold," and James Schouler, another historian, asserted that Polk, as president, was the framer of his own policies instead of being under the influence of the experienced statesmen and politicians in his cabinet.

His administration saw the establishment of the independent treasury system which the democrats had advocated during Van Buren's administration. By the Walker bill of 1846 he reduced the tariff in direct violation, according to the protectionists, of a pledge he had given. His message to Congress of Dec. 2, 1845, was a criticism of the protection theory and in it he urged the adoption of a tariff for revenue only. Another accomplishment of his administration was the settlement of the Oregon boundary dispute with England. He had favored 54° 40' as the northern boundary, but it was finally fixed at 49°. In 1846 a war with Mexico resulted in the acquisition of Texas and other territory in the West and Southwest.

The independent treasury system, the reduction of the tariff and the settlement of the Oregon boundary dispute were urged in his first message to Congress; he had already privately informed Bancroft of his intention of seizing California. He was an ardent expansionist; increase of territory was the overshadowing issue of the time. It has been contended that his desire for expansion was due to his desire to increase the slave territory of the country. This is refuted by his advocacy of 54° 40' as the Oregon boundary which would have added greatly to the free territory, and his opposition (as revealed in his manuscript diary) to the efforts of several members of his cabinet and others in the Senate to retain the whole of Mexico—territory in which slavery would undoubtedly have been instituted. He favored the acquisition of California, Utah and New Mexico, from which slavery would have been excluded by geographical and climatic conditions.

Polk retired to his home in Nashville at the end of his presidential term and died there on June 15, 1849. He was buried in a tomb before his home and his body later was removed to the state capitol. He left a detailed diary besides private papers and correspondence upon which

Bancroft, at the time of his death, was at work preparing a biography. These manuscripts are in the New York Public Library.

MARCO POLO

MARCO POLO, celebrated traveler of the early Middle Ages, was born sometime in 1254 at Venice, of a noble Venetian family. At the time of his birth his father and uncle were on a journey to Cathay where they were well received at the court of Kublai Khan, who commissioned them as envoys to the Pope with a request that 100 men from Europe, learned in arts and sciences, be sent to China to bring western knowledge and attainments to the East. Back in Italy in 1269, the Polos endeavored to fulfil their commission but were unable to do so and two years later they embarked on another trip to China, taking young Marco with them. They traveled across western Asia and the Desert of Gobi, arriving at Kublai Khan's court at Shangtu in 1275. The youthful Marco seems to have captured the fancy of the great Mongol prince, who sent him as an envoy to Yunnan, northern Burma, Cochin-China and southern India and later entrusted him with the government of a province for three years.

Kublai wished to keep the Polos at his court, but at length they obtained permission to return home and sailed in the train of a Mongol princess by way of Sumatra and southern India to Persia. It was not until 1295, twenty-four years after leaving Venice, that they again reached their native city bringing great wealth with them, mostly in precious stones and silks, only to have their identity scornfully denied. In the war between the Venetians and the Genoese in 1298, Marco Polo took part with his own galley in the battle of Curzola Island on September 7. The Venetians were defeated and he was taken prisoner and held in Genoa for a year during which period he began the famous narrative of his travels, dictating his account to a fellow prisoner. The prologue to the book contains his personal narrative, the body of the volume being devoted to descriptions of the notable sights he had seen, and manners and customs of the different courts and countries of Asia, with especial attention to Kublai Khan and his court, his battles and conquests, and a history of the civil wars of the house of Genghis Khan during the second half of the thirteenth century. The work is called *The Book of Marco Polo*. For several centuries it was believed to have been written in Latin, or in the Venetian dialect, but in 1827 Baldelli-Boni was able to prove that it had been written in French, and an old French text, published in 1824, is regarded as the most accurate transcription of his oral narrative of his adventures. It was translated into several languages and for some centuries was almost the only knowledge Europeans had of the Oriental countries. Many of his tales were so colorful that they were thought to be greatly exaggerated, but later knowledge has established their essential accuracy.

Polo was freed within a year of his captivity, returned to Venice in July or August, 1299, and little is definitely known of his life thereafter although it is a matter of record that on January 9, 1324 he sent for a notary and priest to make his will, and died on the same day. He was survived by his wife, Danata, and three daughters, Fantina, Bellela and Moreta. In accordance with his own wish he was buried in the church of St. Lorenzo. Venetian archives make a few mentions of the Polos, one document referring to some objects given by Polo to one of the Faliero family. A portion of the Ca' Polo—the mansion where the three travelers were at first denied entrance after their long absence— still stands and in the time of Ramusio, Polo's first biographer, the court where it is situated was known as the "Corte del millioni" (hence the nickname of Marco Millioni), and now is called Corte Sabbionera.

POMPEY THE GREAT   106 B.C.–48 B.C.

GNEIUS MAGNUS POMPEIUS, known in history as Pompey the Great, was a Roman general and statesman, born in 106 B.C. He received a military training and at the age of 17 fought in campaigns against the Italians under Marius and Cinna. He was an ardent supporter of the Roman dictator, Sulla, and, having given extraordinary proof of his valor and prowess, he was sent to Africa to destroy the remnants of the Marian faction there, which he did with signal success. He then proceeded against the followers of Lepidus in Italy, driving them out of the country, and was next sent to Spain where, in 76 to 71 B.C., he destroyed the Marian faction under Sertorius, and the remainder of Spartacus' army. His achievements in the field made him the idol of the populace and in 70 B.C. he was elected consul for the year. He had hitherto cast his lot with the aristocratic party but had latterly been weakening in that regard and at length espoused the cause of the people for whom he carried through a law restoring to them the tribunician power.

One of his first acts as consul was to clear the Mediterranean and adjacent waters from the pirates that had infested it for years. Having driven them from the seas he proceeded against Mithridates of Pontus, whom he conquered. Tigranes of Armenia was next to surrender to his military genius; Antiochus of Syria was subdued and Pompey then proceeded against the Jews, defeated them, captured their capital, Jerusalem, and his third great triumphal entry into Rome took place in 61 B.C. He wished the Senate to ratify his acts in Asia and to apportion certain lands among his soldiers but this the Senate refused to do. Pompey allied himself with Julius Caesar and a short time later, with the aid of the wealthy Crassus, they made themselves the ultimate power in Rome, forming the powerful First Triumvirate. Pompey now received the ratification of his acts in Asia and the requested fulfilment of his promises to his soldiers. Caesar gave his daughter Julia in marriage to Pompey as an additional pledge of their alliance.

Caesar left Rome with an army, invaded Gaul, and for nine years was engaged in subduing the Frankish tribes and making his incursions into Britain, rising higher in the esteem of the people while Pompey remained idle in Rome and his power began to wane. Jealousies arose, Julia died in 54 B.C., and Pompey returned to the aristocratic party who wished to strip Caesar of his power. He was ordered to surrender his office as triumvir which he agreed to do provided Pompey also laid down his office. The Senate demanded Caesar's unconditional surrender and the disbanding of his army on penalty of being declared a public enemy. Caesar then crossed the Rubicon into Italy, defying the Senate and its armies under Pompey's command. Civil war followed; Pompey's forces greatly outnumbered Caesar's but they were scattered over the Empire. Caesar's soldiers remained loyal to him and as they proceeded toward Rome, Pompey fled, took ship for Greece and gathered an imposing army in Greece, Egypt and the East, with a powerful fleet. Caesar crossed the Adriatic and met Pompey's army at Dyrrhachium, but was driven back with heavy losses.

Pompey, flushed with victory, met his opponents again at Pharsalia in August, 48 B.C., but in this encounter he was badly defeated and the senatorial army was almost completely destroyed. He escaped to Egypt where he was treacherously murdered by one of his own men. On Caesar's arrival in Egypt Pompey's head was presented to him, which he refused to accept and ordered the murderer executed.

WILLIAM SYDNEY PORTER (*O. Henry*)   1862–1910

O. HENRY was the pen-name of WILLIAM SYDNEY PORTER, a prolific American short story writer, who was born in Greensboro, N. C., on Sept. 11, 1862, the son of a physician. He attended school until he was 15 and then for five years acted as a clerk in his uncle's drug store. His health being not of the best, he went to Texas and spent two years on the ranch of a friend in La Salle County. There he absorbed much of the color and detail of ranch life which served him well in later years in the stories of western life which first brought him fame. He lived for a time in Austin, Tex., and in other southern cities, his roving tendencies enabling him to gather all sorts of journalistic material. He drifted to Central America where he spent considerable time and his experiences there are reflected in his book, *Cabbages and Kings*, published in 1904.

At about the time of his marriage in 1887 he began to send paragraphs and humorous sketches to the newspapers. In 1894 he embarked upon an editorial and literary venture which was not a financial success but which brought him to the attention of the public; he bought, edited, wrote for and illustrated Brann's *Iconoclast*, a satirical weekly which he transformed into a humorous publication. Following its failure he joined the staff of the Houston *Post*, to which he contributed a daily column of light verse and burlesque skits. In 1896 he was charged with having embezzled a small sum from a bank in Austin in which he had been employed in 1891; a matter that has never been satisfactorily cleared up, but he was convicted and sentenced to five years' imprisonment. While waiting for his trial he received from several important magazines acceptances of short stories which he had submitted. His prison term was reduced to three years and three months and during that time he worked steadily at his story writing. From 1902 until his death he lived in New York. He contributed a weekly story to the *New York World* at $100 each. *The Four Million* was published in 1906, followed in rapid succession over a period of some five years by *The Trimmed Lamp, Heart of the West, The Gentle Grafter, The Voice of the City, Roads of Destiny, Options, Whirligigs, Let Me Feel Your Pulse, The Two Women,* and *Strictly Business;* all collections of short stories. *The Gift of the Wise Men, Sixes and Sevens, Rolling Stones, Waifs and Strays, Letters to Lithopolis* and *Postscripts* were published after his death.

O. Henry, as he came to be universally known, was a quiet, reserved man who made few friends, but those admitted to intimacy with him found him a witty and cheerful companion. The cruel and probably unmerited experience which he had undergone had hurt his sensitive nature and increased his natural shyness. He came to love New York which he christened "Bagdad on the Subway." He liked to wander about the city in out-of-the-way places, observing the romance and picturesqueness of the life to be found there, picking up stray bits of knowledge of its life and its dwellers. Much of his best work is found in his sympathetic presentation of its derelicts, its shop girls and others in the humbler walks. It was said of him that he had "no talent, only genius," and the magic of his story telling, which triumphed over even the most journalistic of his tales, bears this out. He breathed new life into the short story and was a master of the unexpected and surprising, yet entirely logical, ending. Success and competence and fame came to him only toward the end of his life. The sale of his books has been very great and they have been translated into many foreign languages.

In 1907 a childhood friend, Sarah Coleman, became his second wife. He died in New York City on June 5, 1910, and was buried in Asheville, N. C.

WILLIAM HICKLING PRESCOTT   1796–1859

WILLIAM HICKLING PRESCOTT, American historian, was born in Salem, Mass., May 4, 1796, the son of a lawyer, and grandson of Col. William Prescott, who commanded the American troops at the battle of Bunker Hill. While attending Harvard University he was blinded in one eye by an accident, but continued his studies, was graduated in 1814 and entered his father's law office. Upon the advice of physicians who feared for the sight of his other eye, he abandoned the study of law and decided to devote himself to a literary career. His first published writing was a review of Byron's *Letters on Pope* in the *North American Review* (1821) to which he continued to contribute for many years. History had long been a favorite study on which he had written some early essays, and in 1826 he decided to take up the writing of history as a profession and selected Spain and her American conquests as his general field. He was compelled to spend much time in a darkened room with a noctograph (a sort of writing apparatus with an ivory stylus) with which he wrote out notes while an assistant read to him. His notes were read over to him until he had assimilated them sufficiently to work them into final shape in his mind. He trained himself so carefully that he was able to retain 50 pages of printed matter in his mind.

The actual writing of his *History of the Reign of Ferdinand and Isabella* began in October, 1829 and was finished in June, 1836. He spent another year revising it (during which his essay on *Cervantes* was published) and when it appeared it established his reputation as one of the ablest of American historians. He next undertook the *History of the Conquest of Mexico,* a subject which Washington Irving had already selected but from which he withdrew that Prescott might have the field alone. The preparation and writing of this book occupied him for five years, although during that period he wrote a number of reviews and prepared a shortened edition of *Ferdinand and Isabella. The Conquest of Mexico* was published in December, 1843, and is perhaps his most brilliant work.

Three months later he embarked upon his preparation for *The Conquest of Peru,* which was completed in November, 1846, published the following year and speedily translated into French, Spanish, German and Dutch. In 1845 he had been elected a corresponding member of the French Institute and of the Royal Society of Berlin. At the age of 50 he stood in the front rank of historians, but his sight was becoming worse and he hesitated to undertake the writing of his projected life of Philip II, for which he had been preparing material for a number of years. In March, 1848, however, he began the work, being aided by de Gayangos, Professor of Arabic literature at Madrid, who sent him much material from official Spanish archives, and the following year when the work did not advance as he wished he visited England. *Philip II* was never finished, but in 1855 the first two volumes were published and the sale exceeded that of any of his previous books. In 1856 he published a revision of Robertson's *Charles V.*

He suffered a slight stroke of apoplexy in February, 1858, but continued to work on the third volume of *Philip II* until January 28, 1859 when a second stroke caused his death. He had married Miss Susan Amory in 1820.

His histories have become household classics. He wrote in a style dignified, but picturesque and readable. It has been sometimes claimed that he was inclined to color his pictures too highly and to give rather too free play to his admiration for his heroes. The research of later scholars, also, has added new knowledge regarding the times and subjects of which he wrote, but in the main his works are dependable and valuable accounts.

PTOLEMY I   circa 367 B.C.–283 B.C.

PTOLEMY I (tŏl'ĕ mĭ), who founded the dynasty of Macedonian kings in Egypt, was the son of Lagus, a Macedonian nobleman, and was born about 367 B.C. He became one of the most trusted generals of Alexander the Great, played a large part in Alexander's campaigns in Afghanistan and India, and at the Susa marriage festival Alexander caused him to be married to Artacama, a Persian princess who thereupon disappears from history. Alexander died in 323 B.C. and the division of his empire among his generals is credited to the suggestion of Ptolemy who himself became satrap of Egypt and Libya under the nominal kings, Philip Arrhidæus and the young Alexander. He killed Cleomenes, the financial controller in Egypt appointed by Alexander the Great, got possession of Alexander's body which was to be buried with imperial pomp, and placed it temporarily in Memphis. This led to a rupture with Perdiccas, the imperial regent, who invaded Egypt in 321 and there met his death. A succession of wars with the Macedonian chiefs followed by which Ptolemy sought to make secure his possession of Egypt and to gain control of the Cyrenaïca, Cyprus and Palestine.

He occupied Palestine first in 318 B.C., established a protectorate over Cyprus and joined a coalition against Antigonus who became master of Asia in 315, but upon the outbreak of war he evacuated Palestine, reconquered Cyprus (313) and suppressed a revolt in Cyrene. In 312, aided by Seleucus, fugitive satrap of Babylonia, he invaded Palestine and defeated Demetrius, the son of Antigonus, at the great battle of Gaza, occupying the country, but was forced to evacuate it a short time later when Demetrius won a victory and Antigonus himself entered Syria in force. A peace was concluded in 311 B.C., and not long afterwards Alexander, the surviving king of Macedonia, was murdered, leaving Ptolemy supreme in Egypt, and ready to violate the peace with Antigonus from whose crown he detached certain towns. He then crossed to Greece and took possession of Corinth, Sicyon and Megara in 308. Demetrius attacked Cyprus with a great fleet, defeated and captured Ptolemy's brother, Menelaus, in the battle of Salamis and won the island. Antigonus and Demetrius now assumed the title of kings and Ptolemy, Cassander, Lysimachus and Seleucus took up the challenge and proclaimed themselves kings. In 306–5 Antigonus invaded Egypt but was held on the border by Ptolemy, who sent a force to the relief of Rhodes, besieged by Antigonus, and thereby won divine honors in Rhodes and the surname of Sotēr (savior).

He continued to engage constantly in wars and instituted two more invasions of Palestine, but governed Egypt ably and well and under his rule it became a power of foremost rank. His wise policies were able to reconcile the differences between his Egyptian and Greek subjects. His capital, Alexandria, became the greatest city of the world and the museum and library which he established there attracted scholars from many countries. He was a patron of letters and art and wrote a history of Alexander the Great.

At the end of his successful reign he abdicated in 285 in favor of Ptolemy II, one of his sons by Berenice, passing over his eldest legitimate son, Ptolemy Ceraunus, whom he had repudiated. Ptolemy I, Sotēr, died in 283 B.C. at the age of 84.

FRANÇOIS RABELAIS   circa 1495–1553

FRANÇOIS RABELAIS (ra'b'lä'), French satirist, was born about 1495 at Chinon, France. He was sent to the monastery of Seuilly when he was nine, and later to that of La Baumettes near Angers. After a novitiate in the Franciscan order he entered the monastery at Fontenay-le-Comte, in Poitou, where he acquired a knowledge of Greek, Hebrew, Arabic and Latin, studied the works of the old French writers, mathematics, astronomy, botany and medicine. He found a patron in Bishop Maillezais. The Franciscans, who were out of sympathy with the new as well as with the old learning, took away his books and he deserted the monastery. Through the intercession of Bishop Maillezais he obtained permission from the Pope, in 1524, to leave the Franciscan order and join that of the Benedictines. He remained with the Bishop for six years and in 1530 entered the University of Montpelier as a medical student. Two years later he went to Lyons where he became physician in the hospital and there his first books were published; translations of parts of Hippocrates and Galen.

Lyons was an intellectual centre of the time and many scholars and poets were attracted to it, partly by the presence of the printer Gryphius. They were men of broad minds and advanced thinking who derided the superstitions of Christianity and were agnostic in belief. Rabelais now began to produce the books that have given him high rank among the world's writers. In 1532 his *Great and Inestimable Chronicles of the Grand and Enormous Giant Gargantua* was published, a glorious if licentious burlesque. Its sequel, *Pantagruel,* lacked the heroic burlesque of the first book, but advanced serious ideas in a nonsensical setting. The two were prodigious literary labors and met with enormous success. About the same time he began the almanac which he continued for eighteen years, in which his humor found free expression in making game of the devotees of astrology. All but a few fragments of this have been lost. In 1534 he went to Rome with Cardinal du Bellay and visiting that city again in 1536, after new editions of his two books had been published, he received permission to enter any Benedectine monastery which would receive him, to hold ecclesiastical offices and to practice medicine. For his own amusement he collected plants and various curiosities and it was he who introduced into France the artichoke, the melon and the carnation.

He took his doctor's degree in 1537, and taught at Montpellier until 1539, then went to Lyons for a time but in 1540 removed to Paris, and obtained from the church permission to enter the Collegiate Chapter of St. Maur des Fossés instead of a convent. He arranged to have his first two books read to Francis I and the latter was so pleased with them that he granted a license for a third book (1546). But when the king died in 1547 the authorities attacked Rabelais. They found impieties in his books and had another printed which they asserted he had written. He took refuge in Metz where he again practiced medicine. Cardinal du Bellay, being suspected of liberal tendencies, left France for Rome and summoned Rabelais there. When King Henry's first son was born, Rabelais wrote an account of the rejoicings which took place in Rome and sent it to the Cardinal de Lorraine, whereupon Henry granted him permission to return to France and made him the curé of Meudon and Jainbet. His books aroused so much condemnation among Catholics and Protestants alike, who demanded their destruction and the burning of their author, that he discontinued the writing of his fourth book, resigned his living and went to Paris where he died April 9, 1553.

Ten years after his death was published *L'Isle Sonante,* which purported to be a continuation of his masterpieces. He was a writer of riotous mirth, restrained by neither reverence nor decency. *Gargantua* and *Pantagruel* are filled with broad humor and ironical reflections on moral and social questions. His genius expressed much social wisdom and political insight under the guise of nonsense.

JEAN RACINE   1639–1699

JEAN RACINE (rå sĕn'), one of the greatest of French dramatists, was born at La Ferté-Milon, Aisne, in December, 1639. Early left an orphan, he lived with his grandparents who sent him to the grammar school at Beauvais. In October, 1655, he was transferred to the school at Port Royal established by the "solitaires." He was a good student, wrote verses in both Latin and French and in 1658 entered the Collège d'Harcourt, having already resolved to be a writer. He wrote *Le nymphe de la Seine* upon the marriage of Louis XIV, earning 600 livres from it. After his graduation he spent some 15 months with an uncle in Languedoc. He was a diligent student of the Greek, Latin and Italian poets and historians, a brilliant scholar and filled with poetic and social ambition and upon his return to Paris in 1662 he became a fashionable poet. An ode on the recovery of Louis XIV from an illness won him another grant and is said to have brought him to the attention of Molière and Boileau whose advice and criticism greatly helped him. Molière's company acted the first of the plays for which Racine is famous, *La Thébaide,* at the Palais Royale, June 20, 1664, and also his second play *Alexandre le Grande,* on December 4, 1665. Two weeks later rival actors at the Hôtel de Bourgogne performed the play which led to an estrangement between Racine and Molière. The play, however, made Racine's reputation and he began to be considered a serious rival of the great Corneille. The Port-Royalists were bitter against the theatre; Nicole, their chief writer, published a diatribe in which he termed dramatic authors "poisoners of the public." Racine replied with a savage letter and was about to publish a second which Boileau persuaded him to withhold although it was published after his death. He later bitterly repented this unworthy satirizing of his former teachers, whose influence upon his youthful mind dominated his entire life.

Little is known of his next ten years. He evidently lived in intimate relations with at least one actress and was elected to the Academy in 1673. *Andromaque* began the series of his theatrical triumphs in 1667. It is held to vie with *Phèdre* and *Athalie* for the place of honor as his masterpiece. In 1668 his one comedy, *Les Plaideurs,* was produced, unsuccessfully at first, but when played at court a month later it provoked the king's laughter which brought it into favor. *Britannicus* (1669) held its own for but a few nights, but later gained popularity. The subject of Bérénice was proposed to Corneille and Racine at the same time by Henrietta of Orleans. Both wrote plays on the theme and both were successful, Racine's being perhaps the better. His *Bajazet,* performed in 1672, is regarded as having technical merit but little oriental atmosphere. The same criticism is applied to *Mithridate* (1673) which was very popular. *Iphigénie* was acted at court in 1674. The last of his tragedies, generally considered his finest, *Phèdre,* was played in January, 1677 at the Hôtel de Bourgogne. A week later an opposition theatre launched a *Phèdre* by Nicolas Pradon, employed to write it by Racine's enemies. Pradon's play almost drove the flower of Racine's genius—and of the French classical stage—from the boards. Perhaps because of his irritation at this incident, or perhaps because of dissatisfaction with his dramatic work, he stopped writing plays almost entirely, grew domestic and ostentatiously religious, and became reconciled with Port Royal. In June, 1677 he married Catherine de Romanet, a plain woman of means who bore him seven children and with whom he had a happy domestic life. He had an income from some well paid government offices, was appointed historiographer-royal at a salary of 2000 crowns, and received special presents from the king. He wrote two later plays, *Esther* (1689) and *Athalie* (1691), both of high rank. He died in Paris April 21, 1699 and was buried at Port Royal.

Racine's life offers puzzling contradictions. He was credulous and superstitious in his religion, vain, easily influenced, gentle and lovable, but with definite weaknesses of character. His keen, analytical mind possessed remarkable delicacy and his work, though simple, shows rare combinations of feeling, imagination, wit, self-restraint and eloquence. His plays have found their admirers among the most cultivated classes rather than among the plain people.

SIR WALTER RALEIGH   circa 1552–1618

SIR WALTER RALEIGH, English courtier and explorer, was born about 1552 at the farmhouse of Hayes near East Budleigh. He spent a year or two at Oriel College, Oxford, and in 1569 was one of a body of English volunteers who served with the French Huguenots. He apparently spent some five years in France. His half-brother, Sir Humphrey Gilbert, obtained a six years' patent in 1578 to explore and seize any foreign territory not the possession of a Christian prince or people, and Raleigh accompanied him on one or two expeditions of discovery, of which probably the real object was the capture of Spanish galleons. In 1580 he was twice arrested for fighting duels; and late in that year he served as captain of a company of foot soldiers in Munster, and took an active part in suppressing the rebellion of the Desmonds, advocating assassination of the Irish leaders. He was sent to England with despatches in 1581 and his handsome presence and gallantry won the favor of Queen Elizabeth. His rewards were out of all proportion to his services in Ireland and he became a wealthy courtier with official appointments and profitable grants of land. In 1584 he was knighted and became a member of Parliament from Devonshire and two years later was given 40,000 acres of the forfeited lands of the Desmonds in Ireland and made captain of the guard.

The patent given to his half-brother was renewed in Raleigh's favor after Gilbert's death and in April, 1584, he sent two captains on a voyage of exploration. They sailed along the coast of Florida northward to the inlet between Albemarle and Pamlico sounds. They named the territory Virginia, but did not sight the present state of Virginia. In 1585 he sent colonists to America who settled on Roanoke Island, off the Carolina coast, but the settlement was abandoned the following year. Two other attempts to colonize the island failed and Raleigh resigned his patent to a company of merchants three years later. The enterprise resulted, however, in his introduction of potatoes and tobacco into England.

Essex's rise as Elizabeth's favorite placed Raleigh in eclipse (1587–88). He visited Ireland where he formed a friendship with the poet Spenser. In July, 1592, he was about to sail in command of an expedition against the Spanish shipping when Elizabeth recalled him because of an intrigue with one of her maids of honor, Elizabeth Throgmorton. He was imprisoned in the Tower until September and although he married the young woman he was forbidden to appear at court. After his release he retired to an estate at Sherborne where a son was born (1594). The next year he sailed for South America in a search for El Dorado, bringing back the first mahogany seen in England. His gallant part in the capture of Cadiz (1596) restored him to the Queen's favor and in 1600 he was named governor of Jersey. He was unpopular in England because of his greed, his arrogance and his religious skepticism. After the accession of James I his properties were seized and he was charged with conspiracy, sent to the Tower and condemned to death. A reprieve was secured, but he was held a prisoner until 1616 when on his representations that he could discover gold for the needy king he was allowed to head another expedition to South America, with strict orders not to engage in any hostilities toward the Spanish. The voyage met with a series of disasters and failed of its purpose and upon his return to England he was arrested and executed under the old sentence on Oct. 29, 1618. His body was buried near the altar of St. Margaret's Church, Westminster, but his widow kept his embalmed head with her.

During his long imprisonment he had written his monumental

History of the World and he was also the author of essays on philosophy and religion and of several poems.

RAPHAEL   1483–1520

RAPHAEL SANTI (or SANZIO) (rä′fà ĕl), one of the world's greatest painters of religious subjects, was born in Urbino, Italy, April 6, 1483. His early training was received from his father who was also a painter and poet, but who died in 1494, and he entered the studio of Perugino (about 1499), but soon afterwards began to paint independently. Probably dating from this early period are the portrait of Tangino (Borghese Gallery, Rome); four pictures for the churches at Città di Castello and the Connestabile Madonna at St. Petersburg. In 1504 he removed to Florence, where he absorbed and made his own the artistic methods and knowledge of such great contemporaries as Michelangelo, Signorelli, da Vinci and Bartolommeo. His "Coronation of the Virgin" (Vatican) shows his transition from the Perugian to his Florentine style. Returning to Perugia in 1505, he painted his first fresco, the "Trinity and Saints," for the Carmoldi monks of San Severo, which was finished by Perugino after Raphael's death. The "Madonna of San Antonio" (Metropolitan Museum, New York) was finished about 1505. Back in Urbino in 1506 he painted for the Duke a picture of St. George, which was sent to England as a present for Henry VII, and returning to Florence the same year he produced some of his finest works, among them the "Madonna del Gran Duca" (Pitti Gallery), "Madonna del Giardino" (Vienna), "Holy Family with the Lamb" (Madrid), "Madonna del Cardellino" (Uffizi), "Tempi Madonna" (Munich).

In 1508 he went to Rome at the instance of his fellow-citizen, Bramante, who was erecting the new church of St. Peter, and there came in contact with the great painters of the age, among whom he took a leading place. Pope Julius II, as well as some of the city's rich bankers, became his friend and patron and commissioned him to redecorate a series of rooms in the Vatican. The matchless frescoes which resulted show his transition to his third, or Roman, period. Among the Vatican paintings are his "School of Athens," "Temptation of Eve," "Battle of Ostia," "Earthly Knowledge," and "Incendio del Borgio." To this period belong many of his Madonnas and other religious subjects as well as portraits of Pope Julius II, Castiglione, etc. For Pope Leo X he painted in 1513–14 the "Triumph of Galatea," designs for Apuleius' romance of *Cupid and*

Psyche, and "Sibyls in Santa Maria della Pace." For his friend Agostini Chigi he built and decorated a private chapel in Santa Maria del Popolo. One of his latest works, "St. Michael and the Devil," is in the Louvre. For Cardinal Giuliano de' Medici (1519) he undertook his famous "Transfiguration," which he did not live to complete, as an altar piece for the Cathedral of Norbonne. The Cardinal, regarding the unfinished work as too precious to send out of Rome, bequeathed it to the monks of San Pietro in Montorio, and it now hangs in the Vatican Gallery. Of all his many Madonnas the last and best known for its perfection of form, color and composition is the "Sistine Madonna," now in the Dresden Gallery. It was painted just before his death at the early age of 37.

Following the death of Bramante and at his request, Raphael was appointed chief architect of St. Peter's by Pope Leo X. After completing some of the designs of his predecessor, he designed the Palazzo dell' Aquila, destroyed in the 17th century when St. Peter's was extended. This was one of his chief architectural works. In 1515 Pope Leo made him inspector of all excavations of antiquities in and about Rome. No painter has been so universally admired as he. The greatest men of his day sought his favor. He lived like a prince and attended court accompanied by 50 artists. He died April 6, 1520, following an attack of fever. His body, after lying in state in his studio beside the unfinished "Transfiguration," was buried in the Pantheon. All Rome mourned his passing.

CHARLES READE   1814–1884

CHARLES READE, English novelist and dramatist, was born at Ipsden, Oxfordshire, June 8, 1814. He was graduated from Magdalen College, Oxford, in 1835, became a fellow of that college and later dean of arts and vice-president. He studied law at Lincoln's Inn and was admitted to the bar in 1843. While he kept the fellowship at Magdalen, he spent the greater part of his life in London and traveled much abroad. He began his literary career as a dramatist with *The Ladies' Battle,* performed at the Olympic Theater in May, 1851, and it was as a dramatist that he always preferred to be known. A second play, *Angelo,* followed the same year, with *The Village Tale* and *The Lost Husband* in 1852 and *Gold* in 1853. He came into prominence with *Masks and Faces,* written in collaboration with Tom Taylor and produced in November, 1852 at the Haymarket Theater. On the advice of the actress, Laura Seymour, the play was "novelized" and published in 1853 under the title of *Peg Wof-*

fington. Christie Johnstone was written soon afterward. With Tom Taylor he collaborated on *Two Loves and a Life* and *The King's Rival,* produced in 1854; alone he wrote *The Courier of Lyons* (later called *The Lyons Mail*) and *Peregrine Pickle.* A year later *Art* (afterwards called *Nance Oldfield*) was produced.

He gained public recognition as a novelist in 1856 with *It is Never Too Late to Mend,* written with the purpose of exposing abuses in prison discipline and the treatment of criminals. The following year he published *The Course of True Love Never Did Run Smooth,* followed by *Jack of All Trades, The Autobiography of a Thief, Love Me Little, Love Me Long* and *White Lies,* dramatized as *The Double Marriage* (1860). The following year appeared his masterpiece, *The Cloister and the Hearth,* which deals with the life and adventures of the father of Erasmus in the fifteenth century and is one of the finest historical novels ever written. In *Hard Cash* he drew much shocked public attention to the abuses in private insane asylums. *Foul Play* appeared in 1869; *Put Yourself in His Place,* published in 1870, dealt with the evils of the trades unions. *A Woman Hater* (1877) was concerned with evil and degrading conditions in village life. In 1875 appeared *The Wandering Heir,* suggested by the famous Tichborne trial, which he also dramatized.

Not all of Reade's later works were books with a purpose. He wrote three elaborate and well-sustained novels in which character rather than thesis or adventure played the prominent part; *Griffith Gaunt,* 1866; *A Terrible Temptation,* 1871, and *A Simpleton,* 1873. His greatest success as a playwright was won with his last bit of writing for the stage, a dramatization of Emile Zola's realistic novel, *L'Assommoir,* produced in 1879 under the title of *Drink.*

Reade never married but he formed a close platonic friendship with Laura Seymour who looked after his home from 1854 until her death in 1879. His own health began to fail soon afterwards; he died in London April 11, 1884 and was buried in Willisden churchyard. Among his papers was found the manuscript of a completed novel, *A Perilous Secret,* which contains as much suspense, as ingenious a plot as any of his previous writings. Also published after his death were *The Jilt and Other Tales* and *Good Stories of Man and Other Animals.* While not in the first rank of novelists and lacking in artistic sense, he always had a story of supreme interest to tell and his depictions of character development and his working out of his situations gave him a secure hold on the interest of his readers. In documentation of facts for fictional purposes he was a forerunner of Zola. He was a violinist of considerable skill and among his writings is a paper on Cremona violins, *A Lost Art Revived.* He was naturally combative and was involved in several lawsuits during his life.

He provided that his workshop and his accumulations of documents, notes, etc., should remain open for public inspection for two years after his death.

REMBRANDT 1606–1669

REMBRANDT HARMENS VAN RIJN (rĕm'brȧnt), one of the world's greatest painters, was born at Leyden, Holland, July 15, 1606, son of a well-to-do miller, who sent the boy to Latin school and then (1620) to the University of Leyden. He soon determined to become a painter, studied for three years under Swanenburgh and for a few months under Peter Lastmann in Amsterdam. In 1626 he returned to Leyden and there painted his earliest pictures; "St. Paul in Prison," "St. Jerome," "Samson in Prison," "Presentation in the Temple," and others, all in the prevailing tone of greenish-gray. Influential residents of Amsterdam persuaded him to remove to that city in 1631 and he began the long series of portraits upon which his fame chiefly rests. The first of these magnificent groups, "Lesson in Anatomy," showed Tulp, the anatomist, and his seven associates. He was a master of light and shadow, of unrivaled technical skill and mastery of expression and had the ability to transform a portrait, through grouping, expressiveness and lighting, into a picture, investing it with the sense of life.

In 1634 he married Saska van Uylenburgh, who brought him a large dowry and bore him four children, all but one of whom, Titus, died in infancy. His portraits of his wife are among his finest paintings. Outstanding in his work of 1634 are the portraits of Martin Daey and his wife (Rothschild collection) and "The Old Woman" (National Gallery, London). The "Marriage of Samson" and "Samson Menacing his Father-in-law" occupied much of his attention early in the Amsterdam period. His mastery in drawing the female figure is shown in the "Danae" of 1636 (Leningrad), though beauty of form was not aimed at in "The Bather" (National Gallery). The year 1640 marked the beginning of his more mature period. His tonal qualities changed and golden-browns prevailed in many canvases. He did fewer portraits but his dramatic expression was truer. He had many friends among the foremost men of his day, many pupils, numerous commissions. He bought a large house in the Breedstraat, where for 16 years he gathered his collection of pictures, armor, costumes and engravings. In 1642 came the great painting "Sortie of the Banning Cock Company" (usually called "The Night Watch"). He painted many pictures of the Holy Family and among other notable works of the period are "The Woman Taken in Adultery" (National, London); "Simeon," "Pilgrims at Emmaus," "Good Samaritan" (Louvre), and "Slaughtered Ox" (Louvre). Among his landscapes are "The River Scene," "Winter Scene," and "The Canal." Later works were "Joseph Accused by Potiphar's Wife," "Portrait of a Lady," "Venus and Cupid," "Portrait of Jan Stix," "John the Baptist Preaching," "Adoration of the Magi," "Christ Preaching," "Syndics of the Cloth Hall," etc. In his later period he used dull reds, yellows and grays in preference to the brilliant coloring of the second period. Rembrandt also excelled as an etcher.

After the death of his wife in 1642 and still more after he became involved in financial reverses, due partly to his own simplicity in money matters, his generosities, and to civil troubles and changing public taste, he withdrew from the world, and was forced to borrow money on his house which in 1656 was transferred to his son. In July, 1656, he was declared bankrupt and part of his great collection of art objects, including some of his own work, was sold the following year for a pitifully small sum. His son died in 1658 and Rembrandt himself died in poverty on Oct. 4, 1669.

He left the imprint of his genius on the art of the day and undoubtedly influenced many of the German and Dutch painters. The United States has many Rembrandts, both in public and private collections, 18 being in the Metropolitan Museum. It is estimated that he painted from 600 to 900 pictures. In 1906 the 300th anniversary of his birth was celebrated by a great exposition of his works in Amsterdam.

ERNEST RENAN   1823–1892

ERNEST RENAN (rǎ nän'), French religious writer, was born at Tréguier, Brittany, Feb. 27, 1823, and was trained for the church until his sixteenth year. He was one of a group of boys selected in 1836 by the Abbé Dupanloup for the Catholic Seminary of St. Nicholas du Chardonnet in Paris, and after spending three years there he was transferred to St. Sulpice and its branch at Issy. Through the study of Hebrew and of German biblical criticism, he became distrustful of the traditional views of Christianity and came to the conclusion that he could not continue in the career his relatives had chosen for him. He withdrew from St. Sulpice in 1845, abandoning all thoughts of a clerical career for a life of study unhampered by religious creeds, dogmas and formulae. His sister Henriette aided him and in 1850 he obtained a position in the Bibliothéque Nationale.

His papers on oriental subjects made a name for him, and in 1860 he was designated by the French government as one of a commission to study the remains of Phœnician civilization. The following year he was appointed professor of Hebrew in the Collège de France, but the clerical party opposed him because of his unorthodoxy and appealed to the emperor, who refused to ratify the appointment. Nine years passed before he was finally able to take the chair in 1870. In 1878 he was elected a member of the French Academy because of his eminence as a writer and scholar. His literary career had begun in 1847 with a paper which he later (1854) enlarged and published as *Histoire Générale des Langues Sémitiques*. In 1852 he published *Averroès et Averoïsme,* a study of life in the Middle Ages, and many essays written at this period of his career were collected and published in book form in 1856 under the title, *Études d'Histoire Religieuse.*

His European reputation began with the publication in 1863 of his *Vie de Jésus,* the first of a series of seven books which he regarded as his great life work—*Histoire des Origines de Christianisme.* The Life of Jesus was widely translated and aroused an extraordinary amount of interest, criticism and opposition, and directed toward him the animosity of the Catholic clergy. Some critics hold that Renan in this book exaggerated the weakness and strength of his own method into caricature, but nevertheless it had a profound influence upon the religious thinking of many persons during the latter half of the nineteenth century. Three years later he brought out his book on St. Paul, which also created a stir and as a literary production is considered superior to its predecessor. His volume on Marcus Aurelius, published in 1882, is another noteworthy literary work. To complete his life task of the history of the origins of Christianity, he wrote an exhaustive and learned chronicle of the Hebrew race in five volumes (1887–1894).

Besides devoting much of his time and efforts to the prosecution of the one great task he had set himself, he published many other books on various subjects; in 1858 a work on Job; in 1860 on the Song of Solomon; in 1882 on Ecclesiastes; in 1883, aside from the *Études d'Histoire Religieuse, Questions Contemporaines, La Réforme Intellectual et Morale, Dialogues Philosophiques, Drames Philosophiques, Souvenirs d'Enfance;* in 1885 *Le Prêtre de Nemi;* in 1888 *L'abbesse de Jouarre;* in 1890 *L'Avenir de Science. Ma Soeur Henriette* was published three years after his death, which took place on Oct. 2, 1892. He was buried in Montmartre cemetery.

In London, in 1890, he delivered the Hibbert Lectures, later published as *The Influence of Rome On Christianity*. Many of his books have been published in English and many wordy and bitter battles on the supposed conflict between science and religion grew out of his writings.

SIR JOSHUA REYNOLDS   1723–1792

SIR JOSHUA REYNOLDS, English portrait painter, was born at Plympton, Devonshire, July 16, 1723. His father, who was a clergyman and master of a free grammar school, intended him to be a physician, but yielded to the boy's strong desire to be a painter and at 17 he was placed with Thomas Hudson, a popular though somewhat mediocre portrait painter in London. After two years' study he returned to Devonshire, settling at Plymouth Dock (1743) where he painted a number of portraits. Back in London the following year, he renewed his association with Hudson, painted a portrait of Captain John Hamilton, and became acquainted with Captain (afterwards Viscount) Keppel, who took the young painter on his ship, the *Centurion,* to Algiers, Minorca, and then to Leghorn. He studied the Italian masters in Rome, Venice, Florence and other cities for three years and while in Rome caught a severe cold which resulted in deafness from which he never recovered. In 1752 he returned to London and almost immediately became one of the fashionable portrait painters of the day as well as a social favorite. His patron, Lord Edgcombe, obtained many commissions for him, his portrait of Keppel having attracted much attention. In 1755 he had 120 clients and in 1757 his sittings reached 667. He made the acquaintance of Samuel Johnson, Burke, Goldsmith, Garrick, Sterne and Bishop Percy, most of whom were members of the Literary Club which was established in 1764 at Reynolds' suggestion.

In 1760 he proposed that the Society of Artists hold a public exhibition of paintings by its members which exhibition, held in April, was very successful and was followed by many others. In 1765 the Society obtained a royal charter and became the Incorporated Society of Artists. Much jealousy was aroused among the younger painters and they appealed to George III, who promised them his patronage and help. In December, 1768 they founded the Royal Academy and after some hesitation Reynolds joined the new association and was elected its first president. He was knighted by King George and in 1784 was appointed painter to the king.

His presidential *Discourses* were published and attracted much attention for their literary style as well as for their subject matter. Although he was a kindly man, his relations with his fellow artists were not always friendly, usually caused by their jealousy, but in the case of Gainsborough, due to his own lack of appreciation of Gainsborough's ability. In the summer of 1789 he began to lose his sight, but did not entirely give up painting until the end of 1790 when, on December 10, he delivered his final address at the Royal Academy. He died Feb. 23, 1792 and was buried in St. Paul's, leaving an estate of about 150,000 pounds.

While not recognized as a painter of the very first rank, Reynolds was the head of the English school and was especially happy in his portrayals of women and children. The strong feature of his paintings was their color, but he made some unfortunate experiments which have prevented the preservation of some of his work. It is estimated that he must have painted well over 2000 portraits. While most of them are still in England, the United States has a fair representation in various collections, the Metropolitan Museum having 14. Among his famous canvases are "Johnson," "Goldsmith," "Gibbon," "Burke," "Fox," "Garrick," "Mrs. Siddons as the Tragic Muse," "Viscountess Crosbie," "Duchess of Devonshire and her Baby," "Three Ladies Decking a Figure of Hymen," and "Three Ladies Waldegrave." He contributed several essays on art subjects to magazines, and left two brilliant imaginary conversations with Dr. Johnson which were published after his death.

CECIL JOHN RHODES   1853–1902

CECIL JOHN RHODES, British and South African statesman, was born in Hertfordshire, July 5, 1853. A breakdown in health caused him in 1870 to join his eldest brother Herbert, then farming in Natal, South Africa. Diamonds were discovered in Kimberley that year and by the end of 1871 both brothers were successful diamond diggers. At the age of 19, Rhodes with his health completely restored found himself financially independent. An eight-months' ox-wagon trip through the almost unknown country north of the Orange and Vaal rivers—a territory rich in minerals and agricultural possibilities—gave him a life purpose and he set himself the task of extending the area of British sway in Africa. He returned to England and entered Oxford in 1873 but his health again failed and he went back to Africa the following year. From 1876 to 1881 he studied at Oxford, spending half of each year in Africa and thus finished his university course and took his degree. During these Oxford years he amalgamated a large number of the Kimberley diamond mines with the De Beers company, thus becoming a great financial power.

He entered the Cape Assembly in 1881, the year of the Majuba settlement, when Dutch and British settlers were in disagreement. Dutch opinion favored a United States of South Africa under its own flag. Rhodes proposed to British and Dutch alike a South African Federation governing itself within the British Empire. As Cape assemblyman he obtained formal cession of half of Bechuanaland to the British and in August, 1884, he was appointed resident deputy commissioner of the new territory. South Bechuanaland was later annexed and an English protectorate was declared over the northern regions up to the 22nd parallel. Rhodes wished to extend British influence still farther, but the discovery of gold on the Witwatersrand (1886) threatened his purpose. In 1887 he obtained from Lobengula, the Matabele potentate of the coveted territory, a charter for trading and mining purposes for the British South Africa Company over an immense area which came to be known as Rhodesia, and extended the territories of the company to the southern end of Lake Tanganyika and the British settlements in Nyasaland, hoping to "make Africa British from Cape to Cairo." The treaty of 1890 with Germany defeated that hope, but war with the Matabele in 1893 added 450,000 square miles to the British Empire. In 1890 Rhodes had become Prime Minister of the Cape in which capacity he conciliated the Dutch and afforded protection to the Kaffirs. The Jameson raid of 1895 ended the brilliant period of his Cape premiership. It was proven that he had aided the raiders with money, arms and influence, although a committee of the House of Commons acquitted him of responsibility in Dr. Jameson's final movements.

His political influence was gone; he was forced to resign as premier of Cape Colony and devoted himself to developing Rhodesia. In the Matabele rebellion of that year, when the natives had withdrawn to impregnable positions in the Matoppo Hills, he went alone to their councils and induced them to surrender. His cherished dream of a railroad from the Cape to Cairo had progressed as far as Bulawayo, with arrangements to extend it to Lake Tanganyika and a land telegraph line connecting with Cairo was arranged for when in 1899 the Boer war broke out. He had again entered Parliament and was regaining something of his former position of power. He was besieged at Kimberley but his old illness returned and he went to Egypt, later returning to Cape Colony where he died on March 26, 1902. He was buried on his estate in the Matoppo Hills.

He left most of his great fortune for the establishing of scholarships by which a certain number of British, American and German students would be maintained at Oxford, in the belief that such education would help to secure international understanding and the peace of the world.

RICHARD I OF ENGLAND   1157–1199

RICHARD, surnamed COEUR DE LION (Lion-hearted), was born at Oxford Sept. 8, 1157. He was the third son of Henry II and Eleanor of Aquitaine. While still a child he was invested with the duchy of Aquitaine, his mother's patrimony. It is said of him that he did not in all his life spend a full year in England and it is open to question whether or not he could even speak the English language. When he was but 16 he was induced by his mother to join his two older brothers, Henry and Geoffrey, in rebellion against their father (1173). He was again in rebellion and leagued with Philip Augustus of France in 1189, and in July of that year on his father's death he became king of England, Duke of Normandy and Count of Anjou. Before coming into the crown he had taken the Crusader's vows, and prepared for an expedition against the Turks in the Holy Land by selling everything that he could to raise funds to equip his army. The following year, in company with Philip, he set out for Palestine, spending the winter in Sicily which Tancred, the Norman, had but recently seized. While there he betrothed his nephew, Arthur, to Tancred's infant daughter.

As they proceeded toward Palestine in 1191 part of Richard's fleet was wrecked on the island of Cyprus and the crews given such an inhospitable reception by Isaac Commenus, the king of that island, that Richard later took ship at Rhodes and returned to Cyprus. He defeated the king and gave his crown to Guy de Lusignan. While in Cyprus he married Berengaria of Navarre whom he carried along with him. In July, 1191, he captured the seaport of Acre, marched to Joppa and twice advanced toward Jerusalem, but he was never able to see that city. His exploits in Palestine, however, spread his fame throughout the western world and he was hailed as a hero. In September he concluded a three years' peace with the Sultan, Saladin, by which Jerusalem was left in Saladin's possession, and set forth alone on the journey home. He had quarreled with Philip who had already returned home. Richard suffered shipwreck in the Adriatic and was compelled to travel through the domain of his enemy, Leopold, Duke of Austria. He made his way, disguised, part way through that country, but was at length seized in December, 1192, and turned over to Emperor Henry VI, who held him captive until a heavy ransom was raised by his subjects, and in March, 1194, he returned to England.

The secular taxation of movable property had its inception in raising the money to ransom this British king. He magnanimously forgave his brother John, who had treacherously usurped the government in his absence, but after a few weeks in England he returned to the Continent where his interests claimed his attention for the rest of his reign. He left Hubert Walter to govern England and seldom thereafter exercised his own authority except in demands for new subsidies. He was in the main successful in his war against the French and on the battlefield had proved himself the superior of Philip, but the difficulty of raising and paying armies to carry on the struggle increased yearly. He became embroiled with the Viscount of Limoges over a matter of treasure in 1199, laid siege to the castle of Chalus and while directing the assault was wounded in the shoulder by a crossbow from the result of which he died April 6, 1199. Following his wish he was buried at the feet of his father in the church of Fontevrault, where his effigy may still be seen.

He is chiefly remembered as the picturesque hero of the Crusade about whose name many romantic tales have gathered. He was a poet and an accomplished knight. As sovereign, he chose able ministers and left his administration largely to them, but he impoverished his people by the heavy burdens of taxation which he laid upon them.

RICHARD III OF ENGLAND   1452–1485

RICHARD III, youngest brother of Edward IV and son of Richard, Duke of York, was born at Fotheringay Castle on Oct. 2, 1452. His father was killed in 1460 and Richard and his brother George were taken by their mother to Utrecht for safety, returning to England the following year after their brother Edward had won the crown. Richard was made Duke of Gloucester and took part in the final stage of the Wars of the Roses, the struggle between the houses of York and Lancaster. He is believed to have had a hand in the murder of Prince Edward, Henry VI's son, and after the battle of Tewksbury, of the murder of Henry himself. In 1472 he married Anne, the youngest daughter of the Duke of Warwick (the famous "kingmaker") and sister-in-law of his brother, George, Duke of Clarence. The latter resented his brother's marriage into the same family, as he hoped to inherit all of Warwick's wealth and possessions. Clarence was shortly put to death in the Tower of London, a judicial murder in which Richard is believed to have played a prominent rôle. This supposition has never been proved, but it is plausible as a part of the trail of blood that paved his way to the throne of England.

He was an able statesman, high in the royal councils and in 1480 he was made the king's lieutenant-general in the North; commanded the army sent to invade Scotland in 1482, and captured Berwick in a successful campaign. King Edward died in April, 1483, naming Richard as administrator of his kingdom and guardian of his son, the thirteen-year-old King Edward V. Richard, then in Yorkshire, set out for London and en route caused Earl Rivers and Lord Richard Grey, uncle and step-brother respectively of the young king, to be arrested. He was able to rally the old nobles about himself and on May 4 took young Edward to London. On June 13 he accused Lord Hastings, one of the leading councillors, of treason, had him condemned and beheaded. Three days later he induced the Queen Dowager to give her young son, the little Duke of York, into his keeping. The boy was sent to the Tower, ostensibly to be company for his brother, the king. Rivers and Grey were executed on June 25. Parliament declared the marriage of Edward IV to be invalid and his children therefore illegitimate and Richard was crowned king of England on July 6. While he made a royal journey through the North the Duke of Buckingham, who had been one of his principal supporters, entered into a plot with the followers of Henry Tudor, Earl of Richmond, head of the Lancastrian faction, who later became Henry VII, to rescue the captive princes, overthrow Richard and proclaim Henry king. Their attempt to foment a rising against Richard was suppressed and Buckingham was seized and executed on November 2. It was believed that by Richard's orders, his two little nephews, still prisoners in the Tower, were murdered a short time before Buckingham's execution but the public did not learn of the deed until some time afterward.

Richard met his only Parliament in January, 1484, and is credited with wise intent in the legislation which he favored. It has been said that if he had been the rightful king he would probably have been a just and wise monarch. The country was disaffected, however, largely because of the general belief that he had murdered his nephews in order to gain the throne. His ministers were unpopular and his only legitimate son died in April of that year, further weakening his position. His queen died in March of the following year and Richard proposed to marry his niece, Elizabeth of York, to whom he had intended to marry his son in order to unite the Yorkist faction more closely to him. Public opinion opposed the match and turned more strongly against him and toward Henry Tudor. On Aug. 7, 1485, Henry landed at Milford Haven and advanced to meet Richard and his army at Bosworth Field on the 22nd. Richard's troops were half-hearted, the Stanleys deserted to the enemy and his cause was lost, but he died fighting. After the battle his body was slung across the back of a horse and taken to the church of the Greyfriars where it was buried without honor.

Unscrupulous as Richard was, he was probably not responsible for all of the murders ascribed to him. He is described as undersized and hunch-backed (which gained for him the nickname of "Crookback"), but it is doubtful if a hunchback could have shown the military prowess which he displayed at Tewksbury and Bosworth.

SAMUEL RICHARDSON   1689–1761

SAMUEL RICHARDSON has been called the first great English novelist; it is doubtful if anything more than an historical interest attaches to his name today. He was assuredly the originator and foremost exponent of senti-mental and prudish fiction and if the manners and customs he depicts existed, their interest is quite obliterated by the healthy realism of a later day. Yet he won and held a large and enthusiastic audience, which, like Mr. Micawber, could admire sterling virtues which it did not care to emulate. He was born in Derby, England, in 1689, the son of a carpenter who is said to have come from a social stratum somewhat above that of his trade. In any event, he entertained ambitions for his son whom he de-sired to become a clergyman and though his restricted means prevented the fulfilment of this desire, he at least had the satisfaction of knowing that young Richard would ever exert a salutary influence in the cause of religion and convention.

At 17, with nothing but his rustic schooling for capital, he went to London in quest of his fortune and became apprenticed to a printer, one John Wilde, who was so pleased with his services that at the expiration of his apprenticeship he employed him as foreman. He was ambitious and in course of time started a printing establishment of his own. Cautiously deferring matrimony until success was assured, he then married John Wilde's daughter, who bore him six children. She died in 1731 and he married a Miss Leake who also bore him six children. He was a man of great rectitude, both in domestic and business relations, but it was hardly to be expected that he would become a conspicuously successful author; he possessed the practical qualities which seemed to destine him to a pros-perous commercial career. He printed journals for the House of Com-mons, became interested in a stationers' company and was one of the king's printers.

It was not until he was 50 years old that his thoughts turned from printing books to writing them, and he became equally successful in that field. His career emphasizes a fact, exemplified also by Shakespeare, that practical sense and business shrewdness (alas, too rare among authors) is an invaluable ally to the muse. In 1740 this printer astonished the public with a novel, *Pamela*, which was immediately so successful that an unknown writer sought to benefit by its vogue and published an unauthorized sequel under the name of *Pamela's Conduct in High Life*. It was this first novel of Richardson's which inspired Fielding's satirical *Joseph Andrews*. In 1748 he published four volumes of *The History of Clarissa Harlowe*, commonly thought his masterpiece, and the enthusiastic public waited in suspense for the concluding part of the story. It is of great length, written like all his works in the minutest detail and marred by that obtrusive ostentation of virtue which tries the patience of latter-day readers. Yet the story possesses genuine interest. In 1753 he published *The History of Sir Charles Grandison*, inferior to its predecessors and marred by its unconvincing delineation of the higher classes with whom he was not sufficiently familiar; a defect, however, which he was able to triumph over. Perhaps the world has indulged in a too ready levity in regard to the homely virtues and beauties of domestic life; in any event, an understanding of the impulses of goodness and fidelity and the sentiments which move the heart has seldom failed to win a large audience, and Richardson's novels, are, par excellence, the proof of this.

He is said to have been the friend and adviser of many women whose problems and perplexities they did not scruple to divulge to this wholesome and kindly man who reigned so peacefully in his family circle, surrounded by admiring friends. One sunspot there was upon his shining fame, an inordinate vanity inspired by his great success and the knowledge that neither ridicule nor criticism affected his vogue. Other less important works were *An Edition of Æsop's Fables with Reflections, Familiar Letters to and from Several Persons on Business and Other Subjects*, and his published correspondence. He died on July 4, 1761.

CARDINAL RICHELIEU 1585–1642

ARMAND JEAN DU PLESSIS, CARDINAL DUC DE RICHELIEU (rĕsh′lyē′), one of the most eminent statesmen in the history of France, was born Sept. 5, 1585, near Chinon. He first adopted a military career but left it at the age of 22 and was consecrated bishop of Luçon to succeed his older brother and keep the bishopric in the family. By 1616 he had risen in politics until he was minister both of war and of foreign affairs, but the following year through a change in the government he was sent back to his diocese where his hard work had made him successful both as preacher and administrator. He was made a cardinal in 1622, and two years later Louis XIII made him minister of state, a post which he held until the end of his life and in which he was the real ruler of France.

His first great state stratagem was to bring about an alliance with England and the marriage of the king's sister Henrietta to Charles I in 1625—a blow aimed at Spain. He was then faced with the task of destroying the political power of the Huguenots. By 1628 he had starved La Rochelle into submission and then Montauban, the last refuge of Huguenot independence, was destroyed. In 1630 he entered Italy with a great army and reduced Savoy to submission. He next entered into intrigues against Austria with various Italian princes, the Pope and the Protestants of the North. He was instrumental in bringing the Swedish Gustavus Adolphus into Germany and took an active part in the later years of the Thirty Years War. The king reposed implicit trust in Richelieu who thus incurred the enmity of many of the nobles whose influence was thereby lost. The queen mother, the house of Guise and other powerful French families combined to overthrow his power, but he was able to triumph over them, and was made a duke and the governor of Brittany. Other rebellions against his growing power were fomented by various nobles, but he crushed them with ruthless severity, sending many of the conspirators to the block, and thus he eventually broke down the political power of the nobles and made the king absolute ruler. In foreign affairs his chief object was to break the power of Austria and Spain. In July 1632 he seized the Duchy of Lorraine and continued his intrigues with the Protestants against Ferdinand. In 1635, having made an alliance with Victor Amadeus of Savoy, Bernard of Saxe-Weimar, and the Dutch, he declared war against Spain. At first he was defeated and the enemy advanced dangerously near to Paris but Richelieu raised an army of 30,000 foot soldiers and 12,000 cavalry and drove them out of Picardy. Revolts developed in Catalonia; Portugal was detached from Spain; the Spanish forces and government were disorganized. The imperial forces were defeated at Wolfenbüttel and Kempten and by 1641 he had made the French party ascendant in Savoy. The hatred of the nobles for the powerful cardinal never weakened, and his downfall was prevented probably only by the fact that the king was helpless without him. Cinq-Mars headed the last great conspiracy against him. His intrigues with the Duke of Bouillon and the Spanish court developed into an espionage system that covered all of France. The cardinal discovered the conspiracy and caused Cinq-Mars and his confederates to be put to death.

Richelieu died on Dec. 4, 1642. Though proud and vindictive and often using unscrupulous means to attain his ends, he was nevertheless a great statesman and was actuated by what he believed to be the good of his country and his king. He built up the power of France through burdensome-taxation, the destruction of constitutional government and liberty of French citizens, but at his death France wielded a preponderance of power in Europe. He never hesitated to sacrifice his personal ambition for the good of the country. He was an able military commander, administrator and diplomat, and was also a patron of literature. He wrote several volumes himself, the most important of which are his *Mèmoires* which afford brilliant commentary on the times and are of value to students of history and politics.

JAMES WHITCOMB RILEY   1853–1916

JAMES WHITCOMB RILEY, the "poet of the common people," possessed a humor and simple charm that promise to keep his name alive among the best of America's minor poets. He was born of pioneer American stock in Greenfield, Ind., Oct. 7, 1853. After his happy boyhood he gave some attention to his father's profession of law, but it proved distasteful and he spent several years as a wandering sign-painter, entertainer and assistant with a patent-medicine show, becoming quite adept as an actor and writer, for he wrote songs and sketches for the show as well as performing in them. He was a good mimic and his ability delighted the country folk of Indiana in these days spent as a strolling player as it did his friends in later years. One of his first attempts at literature was a contribution to a newspaper and was in the nature of a hoax, a poem entitled *Leonainie,* purporting to have been written by Edgar Allen Poe. This was followed by a series of poems in the Hoosier dialect, supposely written by a farmer, "Benjamin F. Johnson of Boone," published in the Indianapolis *Daily Journal,* the staff of which he had joined in 1873. For a short time he was local editor of the *Democrat* of Anderson, Ind. His first published book was *The Old Swimmin' Hole and 'Leven More Poems by Benj. F. Johnson of Boone* (1883). The humorous and sentimental character of the verse appealed to the general public and the volume aroused a good deal of attention.

His second book was issued in 1886, *The Boss Girl* (republished in 1891 as *Sketches in Prose*), and after that scarcely a year passed without one, and occasionally two, volumes from his pen. *Character Sketches and Poems* and *Afterwhiles* were issued in 1887; *Old Fashioned Roses* and *Pipes o' Pan* in 1888; *Poems of Childhood* in 1890; *The Flying Islands of the Night* and *Neighborly Poems* in 1891. He had become by this time one of the more popular poets of the day, for he dealt always with the virtues, sentiments and foibles of the common people, whether his verse was in the Hoosier dialect or otherwise. His poetry was sincere, filled with humor, pathos and a quizzical kindliness that struck a responsive chord and made him one of the best loved of poets. His poems for and about children rank with those of Eugene Field and Robert Louis Stevenson, with an added quality of homeliness and sincerity. He was a genuine poet of childhood for he never outgrew the ability to seize upon the child's point of view. Among his books published in the 1890's are *Green Fields and Running Brooks, Poems Here at Home, Armazindy, A Child World, The Rubaiyat of Doc Sifers.*

He was elected a member of the American Academy of Arts and Letters and received the gold medal of the National Institute of Arts and Letters. Since 1915 his birthday has been observed as a holiday ("Riley Day") throughout Indiana. During his later life he made his home in Indianapolis and continued to write almost until the day of his death which took place in that city on July 22, 1916. Among his later works are *Home Folks, Book of Joyous Children, A Defective Santa Claus;* the favorite poem, *An Old Sweetheart of Mine; Out to Old Aunt Mary's* (which is perhaps one of the best known of all his collections of verse); *The Raggedy Man, The Little Orphant Annie Book, Old Schoolday Romances, When the Frost is on the Punkin, Knee Deep in June and Other Poems* and *Old Times,* published in 1915. That Riley's poems were not forgotten following his death, but continue to be read, admired and loved is proof that he understood the psychology of the average public, both juvenile and adult. He did not attempt to reach the trained intellect but was satisfied to touch the heart of the mass of the people.

NICOLAS ANDREIEVICH RIMSKI-KORSAKOV   1844–1908

NICOLAS ANDREIEVICH RIMSKI-KORSAKOV (kôr′så kŏv), one of the most original and colorful of Russian composers, was born at Tikhvin, Novgorod, Russia, March 18, 1844. After spending six years at the naval college in St. Petersburg (now Leningrad) he received his commission in 1862 and saw service aboard ship for the next three years. While a student at the naval college, however, he had shown considerable musical ability and was one of the amateurs—with Borodin, Cui and Mussorgsky—who did homage to Balakirev, the most popular composer of the day in Russia. While in the navy he composed a symphony in E minor which Balakirev performed in St. Petersburg. This is said to have been the first symphony written by a Russian composer, and its success was sufficient to impel him to retire from the navy and become a professor in the St. Petersburg Conservatoire (1873). At about this time he married Nadejda Pourgold, a pianist of ability, and his first grand opera, *Pskovitianka,* was performed.

Of his operas, *Sadko* and *Le Coq d'Or* are included in the repertory of most foreign grand opera companies and have served to give him world-wide standing among operatic composers. With the exception of *Mozart and Salieri,* his operas deal with Russian stories and Russian people and despite their vigor and colorfulness were not accorded as great popularity in foreign countries as his symphonies in which he used the Russian folk melodies with fine effect and proved himself a master of orchestral composition. His first, second and third symphonies take high rank among his orchestral works while his suites (*Scheherazade* and others), his overtures (*Russe,* etc.) are works that music lovers will refuse to let die. He wrote many notable songs, pieces for the pianoforte, etc. *The Berceuse* and *Song of India* from the opera *Sadko; Snow Maiden, Spanish Caprice, Oriental Romance, Festival at Bagdad, Chanson Arabe* and *Grande Pâque* are among his most popular compositions.

He was a well educated man who had studied music from all angles, and showed freshness and originality not only in subject matter but in his instrumentation. Through his book, *The Foundations of Instrumentation,* and also through personal contact he exerted a wide influence upon the younger Russian composers. His *History of My Musical Life* has been translated into English and is of first importance to students of his music. Stassov published a biography of him in 1890 and the importance of his work is considered in Rosa Newmarch's *Russian Opera* (1914) and in Montagu Nathan's *History of Russian Music.* He succeeded Balakirev as the leading conductor of St. Petersburg and was active in promoting appreciation of the Russian composers, particularly of Mussorgsky, although he has been criticised for tampering with the original text of Mussorgsky's opera, *Boris Godounov.* He died in St. Petersburg on June 20, 1908.

MAXIMILIEN DE ROBESPIERRE   1758–1794

Maximilien François Marie Isidore de Robespierre (rŏb'spě âr'), one of the chief figures of the French Revolution and the Reign of Terror, was born at Arras, May 6, 1758, of a family which was by tradition of Irish descent. He was sent to the college of Arras and the college of Louis-le-

Grand, Paris. In 1782 the Bishop of Arras appointed him criminal judge in the diocese, an office which he resigned in order to avoid pronouncing a sentence of death, and he then became a successful lawyer, interested in literature, and a social favorite. In 1789 he was elected fifth deputy of the Third Estate of Artois to the States-General. He was radical in his views and upheld the doctrines of Rousseau for the regeneration of France. He spoke frequently and successfully before the Constituent Assembly and became one of the leaders of the small body of the extreme left. Feeling that his doctrines would have no success in the Assembly, he turned to the Society of the Friends of the Constitution, known later as the Jacobins. The death of Mirabeau strengthened his influence in the Assembly.

In December, 1791, he made his great speech against war with Austria, which the queen and the Girondins were urging as a means of restoring Bourbon absolutism. He was violently attacked by the Girondins and in April, 1792, he resigned as public prosecutor of the tribunal of Paris and started a journal, *Le Defenseur de le Constitution*. He took no active part in overthrowing the Bourbon dynasty and was shocked at the shedding of blood by the Commune, yet was ready to take his seat on the Commune of Paris, which overthrew Louis XVI. On Aug. 16, 1792, he presented to the Legislative Assembly the petition of the Commune demanding the establishment of a revolutionary tribunal and the summoning of a convention. Despite his opposition to the September massacre of prisoners, he was elected first deputy for Paris to the National Convention and voted for the king's death, which he declared was necessary that France might live. The Girondins' attack on Robespierre drove other leaders to his side, and on May 31 and June 2, 1793, the Commune of Paris destroyed the Girondin party. In July he was elected to the new Committee of Public Safety and for a time was its most prominent member. He was not the originator of the "Terror," nor of its machinery, but lent his support to it as a necessary means of destroying the enemies of France and preparing the way for the reign of virtue which he hoped to establish through the idealism of Rousseau. With the aid of Danton he sent Hébert and other leaders to the guillotine after a trial which was a travesty of justice. Danton himself and other supporters who did not share Robespierre's fanatical views were the next victims and Robespierre now sought, through his influence over the Jacobin Club, to dominate the Commune and attempted to usurp the influence of the other members of the Committee over the army. He increased the pressure of the Terror and Couthon, his ally on the Committee, proposed and carried on June 10, 1794, an outrageous law by which even the appearance of justice was taken from the tribunal, which became a court of condemnation without witnesses and sent as many as 200 victims a week to the guillotine. Robespierre obtained from the Convention a decree inaugurating a new state religion and recognizing the existence of a Supreme Being. His position seemed secure; he believed himself able to impose his ideas on France and thus ensure the happiness of his fellow countrymen. He retired from the Convention for some weeks to prepare his plans, reappeared on July 26, declaring the Terror ought to be ended, and made one of his carefully prepared speeches intended to justify the execution of the few leaders who still remained to oppose him. His motion was first passed, then reconsidered. The men he had doomed to die rose against him. He was arrested and imprisoned, rescued by the National Guards and installed in the city hall, where he was attacked. The Convention reassembled, declared Robespierre and the members of the Commune outlaws and the following day he and 21 of his supporters were guillotined.

JOHN D. ROCKEFELLER   1839–

JOHN DAVISON ROCKEFELLER, American capitalist, was born at Richford, N. Y., July 8, 1839, moved to Cleveland with his family when he was 14 and after attending public school became assistant bookkeeper in a commission house at a small salary. In 1858 he became partner in a similar firm. In 1862 he and his partner invested $4,000 in Samuel Andrews' invention of a method for cleaning crude oil and in 1867 the firm became Rockefeller, Andrews and Flagler. In January, 1870, Rockefeller, with his brother William, Stephen V. Harkness and other associates, organized the Standard Oil Company, with a capitalization of $1,000,000, and within ten years the new company became the leader of the petroleum industry. It brought order and consolidation to the chaotic petroleum business and its success stimulated consolidation of the various oil refining businesses into groups in which Standard Oil held the lead.

The way to its domination of the industry was prepared through the South Improvement Company, an association of leading refiners, which induced the Pennsylvania, Erie and New York Central railways to grant rebates on all oil shipped by members of the association, and to give "drawbacks" on oil shipped for competitors. As a result 21 out of 26 refining companies in Cleveland sold out either for cash or for stock in Standard Oil. The railroads were forced by public opinion to withdraw their rebates within three months, but Rockefeller then had a monopoly of the oil refining business of Cleveland and about one-third of that of the country. By 1875 he had merged the larger refineries of New York,

Philadelphia and Pittsburgh with Standard Oil and three years later he controlled 90 per cent of the refineries of the United States. He then secured control of companies marketing oil, acquired oil terminals in the large cities and gained control of the pipe lines laid by competitors. A congressional investigation led to dissolution of the South Improvement Company in 1872. The Central Association of Oil Refiners was instituted in 1875, but Rockefeller proceeded to form a "trust," the organization of which was not made public until the New York State Senate investigation of 1888. That inquiry revealed that 39 corporations in many states had turned over their stock and right to control it to an organization having no legal existence—a "trust" consisting of nine trustees who could do things no incorporated company could do. The Standard Oil Trust was capitalized at $70,000,000, later increased to $102,233,700. The Ohio Supreme Court declared the Trust illegal in 1892 but it was not dissolved until 1899, when its interests were reorganized as the Standard Oil Company of New Jersey. In 1911 the Supreme Court declared this combination a violation of the Sherman Anti-Trust Act and ordered its dissolution.

In 1911 Rockefeller, having become the richest man in America, if not in the world, retired as president of Standard Oil, turned the management over to his son, John D. Rockefeller, Jr., and devoted himself to the disposal of his great fortune. He invested in iron ore and coal lands, in railway stocks, and spent huge sums in philanthropic enterprises. By the end of 1927 he had given more than $500,000,000 to philanthropic and charitable undertakings. He chartered the Rockefeller Foundation (1913) to promote the well-being of mankind throughout the world which in 1929 was consolidated with the Laura Spelman Rockefeller Memorial (founded in 1918). He founded the General Education Board, which up to 1928 had expended more than $176,000,000. The Rockefeller Institute for Medical Research was founded in 1901 and in 1928 the Spelman Fund of New York for charitable, educational and scientific purposes.

AUGUSTE RODIN   1840–1917

AUGUSTE RODIN (rŏ′dăn′), leading French sculptor of the nineteenth century and one of the greatest of all times, was born in Paris, Nov. 10, 1840, of a poor family and as a young man studied sculpture under Barye, but from 1864 to 1870, lacking means to pursue his studies, he was employed in the studio of Carrier-Belleuse where he came into familiar contact with the mechanical processes of casting, etc. The "Man with a

Broken Nose" (1864) was one of his early sculptures which reveals the artist's individual outlook. He served with the National Guard in the siege of Paris in 1870 and after the war was over went to Brussels where he worked with the Belgian artist, Van Rasbourg, until 1877 on the caryatids for the interior of the Bourse and on the exterior sculpture. He exhibited his "Portrait of Garnier" in 1875 and two years later was represented at the Salon by "The Bronze Age" (cast in bronze for the Salon of 1880 and now in the Luxembourg). His busts of Jean-Paul Laurens and of Carrier-Belleuse were exhibited in 1882, of Victor Hugo and Dalou in 1884 and of Antonin Proust in 1885.

He next began work on the "Portal of Hell," one of the largest and most elaborate of all his sculptures, which occupied him for twenty years. It was commissioned by the Musée des arts décoratifs, and was based upon the *Inferno* section of Dante's *Divine Comedy*. The artist did not devote his entire time to this great design, however, but executed various commissions. For the town of Damvillers he did a statue of Bastien-Lepage; for Nancy a "Monument to Claude de Lorrain" and for Calais "The Burgesses of Calais." He withdrew from the old Society of French Artists in 1890 and joined the seceding National Society of Fine Arts (New Salon), where in 1892 he exhibited his bust of Puvis de Chavannes, "Contemplation," and "Caryatid," both in marble, and the "Monument to Victor Hugo," showing the great poet nude, his right hand extended in a gesture of authority, and backed up by muses. In 1898 Rodin exhibited "The Kiss," a marble group representing Paolo and Francesca, one of the most delicate and beautiful of his statues. His "Statue of Balzac" was commissioned by the Society of Men of Letters who rejected it upon seeing the artist's rough sketch and gave the commission to Falguière, of whom Rodin made a bronze bust which he exhibited in 1899 at the salon which revealed Falguière's "Balzac." His bust of Henri Rochefort was in the same Salon. The original study for the magnificent head of Balzac is now in the Metropolitan Museum in New York.

A signal honor was paid to Rodin by the city of his birth in 1900 in the erection of a building close to the entrance to the Great Exhibition in which were collected nearly all of his works, the unfinished "Portal to Hell," the rejected "Statue of Balzac," other unfinished projects and sketches for past and future undertakings, water color sketches, etchings, etc. Of his etchings, the best known is probably the portrait of Victor Hugo. Two of his best known sculptures which have been often reproduced are "The Hand of God," exhibited in the New Gallery at London in 1905, and "The Thinker," which Lord Grimthorpe presented to the British nation in 1904, the year in which the artist became president of the International Society of Sculptors, Painters and Engravers in succession to James McNeill Whistler. Rodin continued active until almost the end of his life, executing portrait busts of many famous personages of the day. Examples of his work are to be found in nearly all the public galleries and in many private collections. Philadelphia opened a Rodin Museum in 1929; the Metropolitan Museum of New York has a number of his sculptures and drawings.

He died Nov. 17, 1917, and was buried at Meudon.

WILHELM KONRAD VON RÖNTGEN   1845–1923

WILHELM KONRAD VON RÖNTGEN OR ROENTGEN (rĕnt'gĕn), discoverer of the Röntgen ray (or X-ray) was born at Lennep, in Prussia, on March 27, 1845. He began his education in Holland, going afterwards to the University of Zurich where he pursued the study of physics and other material sciences. He showed aptitude for scientific research and later became assistant to the noted Professor Kundt at the university of Würzburg and afterwards at the university of Strasbourg where, in 1874, he became a teacher. Already he had made something of a name for himself in educational and scientific fields and in 1875 he became professor of mathematics and physics at the Agricultural Academy of Hohenheim, only to resign the post the next year and return to Strasbourg as extraordinary professor. Three years later he became professor of physics and director of the Physical Institute at Giessen, resigning this post in 1885 to return to Würzburg where he made the discovery for which he is noted and which bears his name, the Röntgen ray.

This was in 1895 while he was experimenting in passing an electric current through a glass bulb exhausted to the point where it contained only a trace of air. X-rays had unquestionably been produced before this time but had not been recognized. It is believed that one William Morgan, as far back as 1785, had actually produced similar rays. The recognition of the ray by Röntgen was partly accidental; he noticed that when he passed an electric discharge through the vacuum tube some crystals of barium platinocyanide near by became brilliantly fluorescent, although the visible light from the tube was completely screened by black paper. He placed various substances between the tube and a card on which barium platinocyanide crystals were spread and found that they cast a shadow. Further tests demonstrated that the radiation had the power of passing through certain substances which are opaque to ordinary light, and he was led to doubt whether what he had produced was actually light at all, particularly because of its curious behavior in respect to reflection and refraction. He suggested the theory that the radiation was due to longitudinal ether vibrations rather than to transverse ones as with ordinary light. Because of its unknown nature he termed his discovery X-ray. Its potential value in medicine was at once recognized and immediately after his announcement of his discovery X-rays were used in America to locate a bullet embedded in a patient's leg.

In 1896 Röntgen was awarded the Rumford Medal of the Royal Society jointly with the Hungarian physicist, Philip Lenard, who had made similar demonstrations. The tube with which Röntgen made his discovery (the common glass bulb usually called the Crookes tube) bears but little resemblance to the X-ray tube of today. Sir Herbert Jackson, who was among the first to experiment with the rays, introduced the "focus" or standard X-ray tube shortly after Röntgen's revelations. Following this discovery, so epoch-making in surgery, many other branches of physics and related subjects engaged Röntgen's attention and his researches into elasticity, capillarity, piezo-electricity, the ratio of specific heats and absorption of heat rays by different gases, electro-magnetic rotation of polarized light and so forth continued unflaggingly throughout the remaining years of his life and contributed much to scientific knowledge.

FRANKLIN D. ROOSEVELT   1882–

FRANKLIN DELANO ROOSEVELT (rō′z′vĕlt), 32nd president of the United States, was born on Jan. 30, 1882, at Hyde Park, N. Y. He was the son of James Roosevelt, a prominent New York lawyer and railroad president, and descendant of a Hollander who had settled in New York prior to 1636. He was educated at the Groton Boys' School in Massachusetts, at Harvard College and the Columbia Law School in New York, from which he was graduated in 1907, and was admitted to the bar in the same year. For some 20 years he practiced law in New York City. He served on the Hudson-Fulton Celebration Commission in 1909, the Plattsburg Centennial in 1913 and the national commission of the Panama-Pacific Exposition of 1915. He was active in politics and although a democrat was elected to the state senate in 1910 from the strongly republican district which included his home town of Hyde Park. He was reelected but resigned in 1913 when appointed assistant secretary of the navy by Pres. Wilson, of whom he had been one of the earliest supporters for president the preceding year. He held that post until 1920 and during the World War (1914–18) enormous responsibilities devolved upon him, which he discharged with wisdom and ability. He was inspector of American naval forces in European waters in 1918 and the following year took charge of demobilization in Europe.

He resigned in 1920 to become democratic nominee for vice president, but after a vigorous campaign he was defeated in a republican landslide and returned to private law practice in New York. In 1902 he was made president of the American Construction Council and thus became the recognized arbiter of one of the most vast industries in the country. As such he performed a valuable public service in coordinating and harmonizing the various elements in the building and allied industries, establishing more orderly conditions and a higher standard of ethics. In 1928 he was elected governor of New York State, running ahead of the national democratic ticket and succeeding Alfred E. Smith, whose name he had himself placed in nomination for the presidency in 1924 and again in 1928. In 1930 he was reelected by a large majority. As governor he continued the policies of his predecessor, advocating much social and reform legislation.

At the democratic national convention in Chicago in 1932 he was nominated for president. A spectacular feature of this event was the flight of Mr. Roosevelt by airplane from his home in Hyde Park to Chicago in order to receive official notification of his nomination before the convention adjourned. He was elected by a popular plurality of some 7,000,000 votes, and the country, which had been in the grip of a serious economic depression for three years, looked to him to inaugurate a new era. Many banks throughout the country had been forced to close and almost his first official act after taking office in March, 1933, was to declare a nation-wide bank closing of several days in order to save the financial situation. He called a special session of Congress and asked and received from it powers which were unprecedented in peace time and which enabled him to put into effect many new and vigorous measures designed to instill confidence and aid economic recovery. These included the temporary abandonment of the gold standard; a plan of agricultural relief; a huge program of public works to provide work for the millions of unemployed; passage of a home owners' bill with measures to protect the interests of owners of small homes who were threatened with foreclosure; and, most far-reaching of all, the passage of the National Industrial Recovery Act, providing, among other things, government control over hours and wages of labor, the elimination of child labor, and an elaborate system of codes designed to prevent unfair practices in the conduct of business. In May, 1935, the Roosevelt policies received a severe blow in a decision of the

U. S. Supreme Court which, in effect (after two years of its operation), held the National Industrial Recovery Act to be unconstitutional.

Late in 1933 the 21st amendment to the Constitution, which provided for repeal of the 18th (Prohibition) amendment, was adopted, "repeal" having been one of the chief issues of the campaign in which Mr. Roosevelt was elected.

In 1905 he married Anna Eleanor Roosevelt, a distant cousin and niece of Theodore Roosevelt, who was herself active in educational and political affairs, a teacher and writer of some note. She became the mother of his five children. In 1921 while in robust health he was stricken with infantile paralysis and for a long time was thought to be permanently crippled, but after a long fight, which won him universal admiration, he regained the use of his limbs. He thereafter established the Warm Springs Foundation in Georgia for the benefit of other sufferers from the disease who were without financial means. At Miami, Fla., in February, 1933, shortly before his inauguration as president, an unsuccessful attempt was made upon his life by a fanatic, the bullets costing the life of Mayor Anton Cermak of Chicago who was sitting beside him.

THEODORE ROOSEVELT 1858–1919

THEODORE ROOSEVELT, soldier, author, naturalist, explorer, and 26th president of the United States, was born on Oct. 27, 1858, in New York City, of a wealthy and aristocratic family of Dutch origin. He was educated at Harvard University and Columbia Law School, and early embarked on a political career, his first public office being that of republican assemblyman in New York State, to which he was elected at the age of 23 and twice reelected. Independent in means and independent in character, he quickly established his reputation as a fighter against political abuses and corruption. After 1884 he spent two years on a ranch in North Dakota, returning to New York to run for mayor in 1886, but was defeated by the democratic Abram S. Hewitt.

Then followed six years of service on the U. S. Civil Service Commission; two years as police commissioner of New York City, during which he adopted vigorous measures to stamp out corruption and to improve conditions among the poorer sections of the city; and in 1897 he was appointed Assistant Secretary of the Navy by President McKinley. In April of the following year at the beginning of the Spanish-American War, he resigned and organized the First U. S. Volunteer Cavalry. As colonel of this regiment, which was known as the "Rough Riders," he led the famous charge up San Juan Hill in Cuba, which made him something of a popular hero. After the close of the war, during the same year, he was elected governor of New York State and throughout his two years of office he actively fought corruption and fraud. Although he would have welcomed a second term in order to carry on the reform measures which he had started with such eagerness and energy, certain politicians and corporate interests which he had antagonized brought about his nomination to the vice-presidency in order to remove him from his position of power in the state. He was elected and on the death of President McKinley in September, 1901, he became president, and was elected for a second term in 1904, defeating the democratic candidate, Judge Alton B. Parker, by the largest majority then ever recorded.

His term of office was marked by many important events and legislative measures. He continued his vigorous attacks upon the methods of the powerful corporations and inspired widespread demand for legislation to dissolve the "trusts." He recognized the new Republic of Panama in 1903 and negotiated a treaty with that country under which the construction of the Panama Canal was begun the following year. He brought about the revision of the financial system of the country, and established the Census Bureau and the Department of Commerce and Labor. When the entire country was paralyzed in 1902 by a prolonged coal strike, he called together representatives of both sides and by the force of his personality and a judicious use of his "big stick" methods, brought them to agree to arbitration. In 1905 he was awarded a $40,000 Nobel peace prize for his diplomatic skill in bringing to a close the Russo-Japanese War, and with the money he endowed a Foundation for the Promotion of Industrial Peace. Pure food legislation was enacted and he urged the conservation of national resources.

He declined to run for a third term, used his great influence to secure the nomination of William Howard Taft to succeed him, and spent a year hunting big game in Africa, followed by a lecture tour through Europe, where he was everywhere received with honors seldom accorded a private citizen. In 1912 he was again a candidate for the nomination, but upon its being given to Taft, with whose administration he had become dissatisfied, he broke with the republicans and organized the Progressive (Bull Moose) party, thereby throwing the election to the democratic candidate, Woodrow Wilson. It was his first serious defeat. He had thrown his boundless energy into what was probably the hardest struggle of his life, and the result was a bitter humiliation to him. For years he had been a great force in American public life and he now felt that his public career was ended. He next went on an exploring expedition in

Brazil, during which he followed the course of a hitherto uncharted river for some 600 miles, in recognition of which the Brazilian government afterward named the river for him, Rio Teodoro. He endured many hardships and contracted the seeds of disease from which he never fully recovered.

After the outbreak of the World War he strongly criticised President Wilson's policy of strict neutrality and when the United States entered the war he offered to raise and lead a division of volunteers, but the offer was refused. His four sons fought in the war and the youngest, Quentin, was killed in an air battle.

Roosevelt's interests, outside of his official life, were varied, embracing literature, simplified spelling, opposition to race suicide and to "nature fakers." He was the author of many books on a wide variety of topics, political, historical, natural history, entertaining accounts of his travels, biographies, and many other subjects. He was twice married; in 1880 to Alice Hathaway, who died in 1884, and two years afterward in London he married Edith Kermit, daughter of Charles Carow of New York, who outlived him. He died in his sleep on Jan. 5, 1919, at his home in Oyster Bay, Long Island.

ELIHU ROOT   1845–

ELIHU ROOT, one of the most distinguished of American statesmen, was born at Clinton, N. Y., on Feb. 15, 1845, son of a professor in Hamilton College of that town. He was educated at this seat of learning, graduated in 1864, and studied law at New York University, taking his degree in 1867. Thereafter he practiced, chiefly as a corporation lawyer, in New York City and achieved nation-wide distinction in his profession. In 1883 he became federal attorney in New York, serving in that capacity for two years. In 1894 he was a delegate to the Constitutional Convention of New York State, and five years later was appointed secretary of war in the cabinet of President McKinley in which post he inaugurated many important reforms in the War Department, established the general staff and planned the War College, designed to afford advanced study in military science to officers of the army and navy. He drafted the so-called "Platt Amendment," which provides for the intervention of the United States in Cuban affairs under certain conditions. In 1903 he was a member of the Alaska Boundary Tribunal and the following year resigned his cabinet office.

From 1905 to 1909 he was secretary of state in the cabinet of President Theodore Roosevelt. In July, 1906, representing his country at the Pan-American Congress in Rio de Janeiro, he was constituted honorary president of the body and rendered valuable service in furthering commercial and political relations between the United States and her southern neighbors. Throughout his term of office he worked for international peace and concluded many arbitration treaties with foreign powers. In 1909 he was elected United States senator from New York and continued to hold various other public offices. In 1910 he helped to settle a long-standing dispute with England over the North Atlantic fisheries and became president of the Carnegie Endowment for International Peace, as well as a member of the Permanent Court of International Arbitration at The Hague. A staunch republican, he remained loyal to the party after the break in 1912 when Roosevelt formed his Progressive party, and an effort was made in 1916 to induce him to run for the presidency, but he declined to be a candidate for the nomination. The previous year, being then 70 years of age, he had presided over the New York State Constitutional Convention, and continued his distinguished career by going to Russia in 1917 at the head of a special diplomatic commission appointed by President Wilson. Three years later, with other eminent jurists, he formulated for the League of Nations a plan for the Permanent Court of International Justice, which was placed in operation in 1921. He was prominent in the disarmament conference held in Washington in that year and still later drafted a plan for the entry of his country into the World Court. At the advanced age of 86 he was called upon in 1931 to present to the Senate Foreign Relations committee an explanation of the World Court protocols.

The list of public bodies and organizations, in addition to those already mentioned, of which this public-spirited man has served as president and member throughout his long career is a long one. He has been the recipient of many honorary degrees and in 1912 was awarded the Nobel peace prize and devoted the entire amount to the promotion of the cause of peace. Though not outstanding as an orator, Mr. Root was the master of a style which for purity and eloquence has not been surpassed among American statesmen. Scholarly, witty and epigrammatic, his written and uttered prose is notable for its clarity and beauty. Many of his addresses on political as well as other subjects are masterpieces of perfect diction. He was the author of many books on political and economic subjects, international relations, etc.

In 1878 he married Clara Wales of New York, who died in 1928 leaving two sons and a daughter. The latter became the wife of a grandson of General Grant.

DANTE GABRIEL ROSSETTI 1828–1882

DANTE GABRIEL ROSSETTI (rŏ sĕt' tĕ), English poet and painter, son of the exiled Italian poet and liberal, Gabriele Rossetti, and of his English wife, was born in London, May 12, 1828. He was educated at King's College School, London, where his father was professor of Italian. In 1843 he attended Cary's Art Academy and three years later entered the Royal Academy Antique School, and then became a pupil of the painter, Ford Madox Brown. At a chance meeting in 1848 between Rossetti, Millais and Holman Hunt, Rossetti proposed the formation of the group which afterwards became famous as the Pre-Raphaelite Brotherhood. "The Girlhood of Mary Virgin" (1849) was Rossetti's first attempt at painting under the Pre-Raphaelite banner. "Ecce Ancilla Domini!" (Tate Gallery) of 1850 was a much finer picture, but was violently attacked by the critics. At 20 he had written his remarkable poem, *The Blessed Damosel.*

Critical attacks on the Pre-Raphaelites injured the sales of the paintings and Rossetti turned to water-color, executing in that medium "The Laboratory," "Hesterna Rosa," "Dante Drawing the Angel," and "Found," which was never completed. John Ruskin undertook the defence of the Pre-Raphaelites, but after a few years when it was on the point of success the Brotherhood was broken up. Ruskin, however, became the friend and patron of Rossetti. With William Morris and Burne-Jones, who were his enthusiastic disciples, he took part in the decoration of the Oxford Union (1857–68) and sent a number of paintings to the Pre-Raphaelite exhibition of 1857; "The Wedding of St. George and Princess Sabra," "Arthur's Tomb," "Bocca Baciata," "Dr. Johnson at the Mitre." In 1861 he published his translations of *The Early Italian Poets,* later revised as *Dante and His Circle.*

With William Morris, Rossetti took a keen interest in decorative art and was actively interested in the revival of the stained glass art. His imaginative powers and mastery of painting developed greatly and some of his finest work appeared in the following years; the triptych of the lives of Paolo and Francesca, "Beata Beatrix," "Prosperpina in Hades," "Sibylla Palmifera," "Venus Vertocordia," "Monna Vanna," "La Ghirlandata," "Aurea Cantna," "Pandora," "The Blessed Damosel," and "Dante's Dream." His literary career kept even pace with his development as a painter.

In 1860 he married the beautiful Elizabeth Siddall who had been painted many times by Hunt and Millais and who appears in many of Rossetti's best known pictures. She lived but two years and he never recovered from his grief at her loss. For a short time after her death he lived in Chelsea with Swinburne, Theodore Watts-Dunton and his brother, William Michael Rossetti. In his sorrow he had insisted upon placing the manuscripts of all his unpublished poems in his wife's coffin where they remained until in 1869 friends persuaded him to have them disinterred and they were published in 1870. Among these was the sonnet-sequence, *The House of Life,* containing some 100 magnificent sonnets, most of which were inspired by his great love for his wife. This volume of poems and *Ballads and Sonnets,* published in 1881, contain all of his poetical work except for *Dante and His Circle,* which consisted of translations from the Italian poets.

He continued to write poetry and to paint until his death. A victim of insomnia, with a nervous shrinking from meeting people, aggravated by the use of narcotics, he saw few persons except his family and Watts-Dunton in his later years. He died April 9, 1882 at Birchington. Many of his paintings are in private collections in America and Italy as well as in England.

EDMOND ROSTAND   1868–1920

EDMOND ROSTAND (rŏ'ständ') was a French poet and dramatist, born in Marseilles, on April 1, 1868, the son of Eugène Rostand, a journalist of some note. He went to Paris early in life and devoted himself to the writing of plays, producing *Les romanesques, La princesse lointaine* and *La Samaritaine,* all of which were moderately successful The great Bernhardt created the part of Mélissande in the second play and also appeared in the third, which was based on the biblical story of the woman of Samaria.

Rostand's first great success came with the presentation of *Cyrano de Bergerac,* a five-act drama based on the life of one Savinien Cyrano de Bergerac, a novelist and soldier of the early seventeenth century who was reputed to have engaged in more than a thousand duels, most of them precipitated by derogatory references to his enormous nose. The play was first produced in 1897 at the Porte Saint-Martin Theatre in Paris with the great French actor, Coquelin, in the title rôle. It was very shortly translated into several languages, including Russian, and the following year Richard Mansfield appeared as Cyrano in New York and scored a tremendous success. Some years later it was revived and again presented with great success in New York with Walter Hampden in the title rôle.

In 1900 appeared another successful play, *L'Aiglon* (The Eaglet), with Sarah Bernhardt in the title rôle in the character of Napoleon's unhappy son, the young Duke of Reichstadt. It was ten years before the dramatist's next effort appeared, the play of *Chanticler,* which had been long awaited and which the author had written for Coquelin. The actor unfortunately died before its completion and his part was taken by Lucien Guitry. This fantasy of bird and animal life contained many passages of great merit, but was less successful than its predecessors, much of its symbolism being marred in its presentation through the conversation of barnyard and woodland fowls. Madame Simone appeared as the pheasant, a part which was played in America by Maude Adams, who had previously appeared successfully in *L'Aiglon.*

Rostand also wrote *La journée d'une precieuse* and during the World War he produced much patriotic verse. Most of his works have been translated into English. In 1901 he was elected a member of the French Academy. He married Rosemonde Étienette Gérard, who was herself a well-known dramatist and poet. With their son, Maurice, she wrote in 1913 *Un bon petit diable,* which was produced later in New York by David Belasco under the name of *A Good Little Devil.* Edmond Rostand died in Paris on Dec. 2, 1920.

MAYER ANSELM ROTHSCHILD   1743–1812
NATHAN MAYER ROTHSCHILD   1777–1836

THE world-famous financial house of the Rothschilds was founded by Mayer Anselm Bauer (later Rothschild), but the financial genius of the family was his son, Nathan Mayer Rothschild.

MAYER ANSELM BAUER, son of Alselm Moses Bauer, a Jewish merchant of Frankfort-on-the-Main, was born in that city in 1743 and opened a money-lending business at the sign of the "Red Shield" (Rothschild, from whence came the name) in the Frankfort Judengasse. He soon became agent for William, ninth Landgrave and afterwards Elector of Hesse Cassel, and in 1802 negotiated his first government loan for the Danish government. When the French entered Hesse Cassel and the Landgrave was forced to flee he entrusted his funds and other treasure to Rothschild who is said to have buried it in a corner of his garden, digging up part of it at a time as an opportunity to dispose of it or to make an investment presented itself. So successful was he that he returned to the Elector every cent that had been entrusted to his keeping plus five per cent interest. He died in Frankfort on Sept. 19, 1812, leaving five sons and five daughters, with branches of the business in Vienna, London, Paris and Naples, each branch in charge of a son. In 1815 the sons were granted the privilege of hereditary landowners from Austria and in 1822 were created barons.

The eldest son, Mayer Anselm, had charge of the Frankfort office. The London branch was under the management of NATHAN MAYER who is generally considered the real genius of the family and it was he who raised the house to world-wide importance in finance. He was born on Sept. 16, 1777, and at the age of 21 opened a branch office in Manchester, England. Five years later he was in London, playing the financial game with great skill and boldness. He was at first regarded with suspicion by bankers and money merchants because of the extreme boldness of his transactions, but their suspicion soon turned to admiration and emulation. He had special sources of information lacking to many of his competitors and used fast boats and carrier pigeons to transport that information so that he could make use of it before it became known to his rivals. He became an adept in bringing about the rise or fall of stock values. When Wellington issued drafts on the British government which England was unable to honor, Rothschild successfully negotiated the drafts and from that occurrence dates the great influence of the house of Rothschild in Great Britain and throughout the world. He believed that Napoleon would ultimately be overthrown and risked his entire fortune in backing up that belief by handling loans for England and her allies in the coalition against the French Emperor.

He popularized French loans in England by fixing the interest rate in sterling money and making dividends payable in London instead of in the capital of the country which obtained the loan. In his later years he was the financial agent for most of the nations of the world, although he would never accept a contract for Spain or for any of the American countries. His transactions reached every quarter of the globe and were not confined to large loans for governments. He died July 28, 1836. His son Lionel, who succeeded him as manager of the London branch of Rothschild, represented London in Parliament from 1852 to 1874 and his name is associated with the removal of the political disabilities of the Jews in England. Lionel's son, Nathaniel Mayer Rothschild (1840–1915) became head of the London financial house, was a member of Parliament and was raised to the peerage by Gladstone in 1855 as first Baron Rothschild, the first of his faith to be admitted to the House of Lords.

JEAN JACQUES ROUSSEAU 1712–1778

JEAN JACQUES ROUSSEAU (rōō′sŏ′), French writer, was born in Geneva, June 28, 1712, of French Protestant parents. His mother died at his birth and his father fled from Geneva in 1722 leaving his ten-year-old son to the care of relatives. He was apprenticed to a notary at the age of 13, and then to an engraver who treated him so cruelly that in 1728 he ran away to the Duchy of Savoy where he was persuaded to change his religion and became a Catholic. There followed a period of strange wanderings and adventures. At times he had some lucrative employment, acting by turns as footman, lackey, household servant and secretary. He spent considerable time with a Madame de Warens who for some ten years exercised a strong influence upon him. In his *Confessions* he has given a delightful description of his life in her country house, Les Charmettes. During this period he improved himself so that he was able to take a position as a private tutor.

In 1741 he settled in Paris, hoping to make his living from a new system of writing music. This did not succeed and he became secretary to a Monsieur de Francueil. He had, however, gained access to the intellectual and musical circles of Paris and after a time wrote for the stage, remodeled one of Voltaire's plays for Louis XV (with the consent of Voltaire), and took a prominent part in the conflict between French and Italian music which was then raging Paris. While associating with the intellectuals—Diderot, Grimm, D'Alembert and others—he entered into an intrigue with a servant girl at the inn where he stayed, Thérèse Levassuer, a stupid, illiterate woman who bore him five children, each of whom Rousseau, by his own statement, promptly abandoned to a foundling hospital.

He drew public attention in 1749 by his *Discourses on Arts and Sciences,* in which he eloquently denounced all the arts, sciences and culture in general as proofs and causes of social corruption. In 1753 he composed an opera, *Devin du Village,* which was played before the court. The same year his *Discourse on the Origin of Inequality* established his fame as a serious writer. In this book he advanced the idea that all property is derived from confiscation; that all wealth is a crime, all government tyranny, all social laws unjust. To show his independence of society, he lived poorly and was churlish in his manners, although he accepted the hospitality of a cottage at Montmorency from Madame d'Épinay. He was of a suspicious nature, however, and soon quarreled with her as well as with Baron Grimm and Diderot. He left the cottage for Montlouis where he made friends with the Duke and Duchess of Luxemburg, and published in 1760 his romance, *The New Héloïse,* which won much commendation. This was followed two years later by *The Social Contract,* published in Amsterdam to escape the French censorship, and two months later *Émile* was published in the same city. The two books made him famous, but his views on monarchies and government made him obnoxious to the state while his deistic doctrines displeased the church. He fled to Motiers in Neuchâtel, where under the rule of Frederick the Great he studied botany, made lace, wrote his *Letters from the Mountains,* and made a powerful reply to ecclesiastical charges made by the Bishop of Paris. He had renounced Catholicism but the hostility of the authorities because of his too liberal religious views drove him in 1774 to the Lake of Bienne. Threat of prosecution by the government of Berne caused him to accept an offer from David Hume of a home in England (1766) and for 18 months he lived at Wooton, Staffordshire, writing his *Botanical Dictionary* and his *Confessions.* He quarreled with Hume and, becoming obsessed with the idea that he was being persecuted, in 1767 he crossed to France and took refuge with Marquis de Mirabeau and the Prince de Conti. In 1770 he returned to Paris where he lived for some two years and wrote *Rousseau juge de Jean Jacques,* vindicating his own character in a manner that cast doubt on his sanity. He also wrote the *Réveries du Promeneur Solitaire,* perhaps the calmest and most idyllic of his work. He sought shelter at a hospital, and retired in 1778 to a cottage at Ermenonville, where he died suddenly on July 2, 1778, in a manner which occasioned some suspicion of suicide. He was buried on an island in a lake, but 16 years later his body was taken to the national temple of great men.

PETER PAUL RUBENS   1577–1640

PETER PAUL RUBENS (rū'běnz), the most noted of Flemish painters, was born at Siegen, Westphalia, June 29, 1577, son of Jan Rubens, a Protestant lawyer of Antwerp who had been exiled to Cologne and later to Siegen. After the father's death his widow took her son to Antwerp where he studied painting under Tobias Verhaegt, Adam Van Noort and Otto van Veen. In 1600 he went to Vienna where his work so impressed Vincenzo Gonzaga, Duke of Mantua, that he took the painter into his household where he remained for eight years. He spent much time studying the work of the great Italian painters in Venice and Rome, copying some of

Raphael's works for his patron and painting several pictures for the church of Santa Croce, of which "St. Helena with the Cross," "The Crowning with Thorns" and "The Crucifixion" are now in the hospital at Grasse in Provence.

In 1603 he went to Spain as the Duke's emissary to Philip III, spent a year in Madrid familiarizing himself with Titian's masterpieces there and then went with the Duke to Genoa. To this period belong such paintings as "Heraclitus" and "Democritus" (Madrid Gallery); "Baptism of our Lord" (Antwerp Gallery); "The Transfiguration" (Mancy Museum); "Vincenzo and his Consort Kneeling before the Trinity" (in the library at Mantua); an altar piece, "The Circumcision" (St. Ambroglio, Genoa); the "Virgin in a Glory of Angels," and two groups of saints painted on the walls of the church of Santa Maria, Rome.

In 1608 he went from Rome to Antwerp because of his mother's illness, arriving after her death. The sovereigns, Albert and Isabella, persuaded him to remain in Antwerp and he was appointed court painter, in which capacity he painted in 1610 for the City Hall the large and colorful "Adoration of the Magi" (now in Madrid Gallery), containing 28 life-size figures. He completed the "Elevation of the Cross" and the following year began the celebrated companion piece, "Descent from the Cross," which was finished in 1614 and is generally considered his masterpiece. These two paintings are in the Antwerp Cathedral. Gothic churches now began to be decorated after the style of Titian, Veronese and Tintoretto in Italian churches, and Rubens, who liked to work with large canvases, delighted in undertakings of such great size. For Maria de' Medici he made a series of 24 pictures (now in the Louvre) illustrating episodes from her life, and took them to Paris in 1625. While there he painted "Felicity of the Regency," and "Triumph of Henry IV" (Uffizi Gallery), one of his greatest canvases. In 1626 he completed the "Assumption of the Virgin" at the high altar of Antwerp Cathedral.

After the death of Albert in 1621 Isabella employed him on various diplomatic missions and in 1627 he undertook negotiations to conclude peace between Spain and England. He went to Madrid in 1628 and then to London where upon the successful termination of the negotiations he was knighted by the king, Charles I, and later by Philip IV of Spain. In Madrid he had met Velazquez and painted portraits of the royal family. In London also he had painted many portraits. Until the death of Isabella in 1633 he was in favor both as an artist and political agent. Ferdinand of Austria, the new Spanish governor of the Netherlands, confirmed him in his official standing, and he continued to produce masterpieces until the very end of his life without apparent diminution of his powers. Between 1637 and 1639, 120 large paintings, intended to decorate the pavilion at the Pardo, were designed by him and completed by himself or under his direction. Unsurpassed fertility of imagination and mastery of color characterizes the work of his mature years.

In 1609 he had married Isabella Brant, of whom he painted many portraits and who died in 1626, leaving two sons. In 1630 he married 16-year old Helèna Fourment who appears in many of his later paintings. Two more sons and three daughters came to him. He died in Madrid, May 30, 1640 and was buried with great pomp in St. Jacques Churchyard, Antwerp.

He was one of the most prolific of painters. The number of his works is estimated at over 1200. Besides his many religious pictures and his portraits and landscapes, he was an animal painter of the highest rank, and much sought after as a teacher from the time of his first settling in Antwerp, Van Dyck being his most famous pupil.

ANTON GRIGOROVICH RUBINSTEIN   1829–1894

ANTON GRIGOROVICH RUBINSTEIN, Russian pianist and composer, was born of Jewish parentage in Wechwotynecz, Podolia, Nov. 28, 1829. His father was a pencil manufacturer who afterwards removed to Moscow; his mother, who was a pianist of some ability, undertook the musical education of her son when he was four years old. Two years later, when he had learned all that she could teach him, she placed him under the piano master, Alexander Villoing. In July, 1838, he appeared at the theatre of the Petrowski Park at Moscow and in other cities. In 1840 he entered the Paris Conservatory and remained in Paris for eighteen months, attracting the attention of Liszt, Chopin and Thalberg. After a number of very successful concert tours, upon the advice of Liszt, he went to Berlin where he studied composition and theory under the famous instructor Dehn. In 1846 his parents, who had accompanied him to Berlin, returned to Moscow and being thrown upon his own resources, he taught and studied for two years in Vienna and in 1848 returned to Russia, settling in St. Petersburg (Leningrad).

For the next eight years he studied and wrote assiduously, giving piano concerts to raise funds, and composed several operas and orchestral and piano works. His opera *Dmitri Donskoi* was performed in St. Petersburg in 1851, and *Toms der Narr* in 1853, while a third, *Die Sibirschen Jäger,* remained unproduced. In 1857 he toured Germany, France and England giving concerts. Returning to St. Petersburg in 1858 he was appointed Concert Director of the Royal Russian Musical Society and court pianist and conductor of the court concerts. In 1862, in association with Carl Schuberth, he founded the St. Petersburg Conservatory of which he was director until 1867, returning in the same capacity in 1887 for a period of three years. In 1870 he was engaged to direct the Philharmonic and Choral Societies of Vienna, and afterwards toured the principal cities of the world with the violinist Wieniawski, including the United States in his itinerary (1872). He made various prolonged concert tours during the twenty years from 1868 to 1888, visiting America a number of times. From 1890 to 1892 he lived chiefly in Berlin, and later in Dresden, afterwards returning to St. Petersburg where he died on Nov. 20, 1894. In 1889 he had been decorated with the order of Vladimir, which made him a Russian noble, and received the title of Imperial Russian State Councillor.

Rubinstein was ambitious to become a great composer, but it was as a pianist that he attained his greatest fame, being sometimes considered superior even to Liszt. There are many passages of beauty and grandeur in his compositions, but critics hold that he lacked the power of sustained inspiration and that he was unfortunate in being unable to criticise his own compositions. Among his best works are the *Ocean Symphony,* the *Dramatic Symphony, Ivan the Terrible* (a sketch for a grand orchestra), and among his operas, *Die Kinder der Haidi* (1861), *Feramors, oder Lall Roukh* (1863), *Die Nakkabäer* (1875), *Der Dämon* (1875) and *Nero* (1879). Considered the best of his oratorios are *Paradise Lost* (1858), *The Tower of Babel* (1872), and *Christus* (1888). He also composed much chamber music, many piano pieces and songs. His *Die Musik under ihre Meister* was published in 1892, and *Gedankenkorb* in 1897. He instituted two prizes of 5000 francs each for playing and composition. These are awarded once in five years upon competitions which are open to persons of any nationality and are held in Leningrad, Berlin, Vienna and Paris.

JOHN RUSKIN   1819–1900

JOHN RUSKIN, English art critic and writer, was the son of a well-to-do London wine merchant of Scottish descent and of his wife Margaret. He was born in London, Feb. 8, 1819, was brought up under a rigid system of training by his Calvinist mother and accompanied his parents on many travels through the lake country of England and in Scotland, Switzerland and the Black Forest, always searching for the beautiful in nature and in art. In childhood he began a systematic practice of composition, in both verse and prose; read the Bible through every year under his mother's tutelage; listened to the reading of great poems by his father; took lessons in drawing, painting, the classics and mathematics. He was lively, but docile and naive; was never able to learn to dance or to ride. At the age of 17 he fell in love with the daughter of his father's business partner and wrote innumerable poems, dramas and romances addressed to her, but she eventually married someone else. His father hoped one day to see his son at least a bishop, and entered him at Christ Church, Oxford, where his course was broken by two years of ill health and travel, but he was graduated after five years (1842).

He had written essays on art and architecture for various magazines and upon leaving Oxford he worked hard and steadily on the first volume of *Modern Painters,* an elaborate work designed to prove the superiority of modern landscape painters over the old masters, particularly defending the artist, Turner. Its revolutionary tone excited violent attacks from the conservatives. He visited Italy in 1845, working on the second volume of *Modern Painters* (published in 1846), studying the Italian painters and writing articles for magazines, and in 1849 published *The Seven Lamps of Architecture.* The previous year he had married Euphemia Chalmers Gray, a woman of great beauty. The marriage, which seems to have been arranged by his parents, proved uncongenial, was later annulled and the lady married Millais, one of the Pre-Raphaelite group whom Ruskin had defended against popular ridicule. He never painted pictures but made many drawings for his own use and for illustrations of his books on architecture. In 1851 he published his essay on *Pre-Raphaelitism* and the first volume of *The Stones of Venice,* which was completed in 1853, and he then began a long series of *Notes and Letters,* after which the fifth and final volume of *Modern Painters* appeared in 1860, closing his series of works strictly on art; works which later in life he grew to dislike and would have recalled from circulation had the public demand not made it impossible. He then devoted himself to the writing of essays, mostly on social and economic matters.

His father died in 1864, leaving him a comfortable fortune. His delightful Manchester lectures on literature and other subjects were published that year under the title of *Sesame and Lilies,* one of his most popular works. Other publications were *Ethics of the Dust, The Crown of Wild Olives, Time and Tide* and *The Queen of the Air.* In 1869 he was elected Slade professor of art at Oxford which occupied much of his time and energy until 1884. Soon after the death of his mother in 1871 he bought an old cottage (Brantwood) on Coniston Lake and in that year he began the publishing of *Fors Clavigera,* a series of letters which he continued to issue until 1884, although they were somewhat over the heads of the British workingmen to whom they were addressed. He was always the apostle of beauty and actively opposed the disfigurement of the English countryside by the building of factories and railways. He founded a museum of art and a drawing school at Oxford, financed largely out of his own funds. In 1884 he resigned from Oxford because of a brain malady which afflicted him at intervals throughout the rest of his life. In retirement at Brantwood, he began his autobiographical *Praeterita* which gives a charming account of his youth.

By 1887 he had spent and given away his inherited fortune and was dependent upon the sales of his books which brought him an income of some 4000 pounds. He was given many degrees and many Ruskin Societies were formed. He died after two days' illness Jan. 20, 1900, and was buried at his wish in Coniston churchyard although a grave in Westminster Abbey was offered.

CHARLES-AUGUSTIN SAINTE-BEUVE   1804–1869

CHARLES-AUGUSTIN SAINTE-BEUVE (sănt' bĕv'), French writer and critic, was born at Boulogne-sur-Mer, Dec. 23, 1804, the son of a commissioner of taxes who died three months before his son's birth. In his 14th year he was sent to the Collège Charlemagne in Paris and from 1824 to 1827 he pursued a course in medicine. He became a contributor to the *Globe,* a literary and political paper founded by one of his teachers at the Collège Charlemagne, and later published his collected articles under the title of *Premiers Lundis.* Through his review of Victor Hugo's *Odes et Ballades,* he and Hugo became friends, and for a time Sainte-Beuve was an ardent advocate of the French romantic movement in literature of which Hugo was the head and front. In 1828 he published *Tableaux de la Poésie Française au Seizième Siècle;* the following year *Les Consolations,* a volume of poems of a melancholy and somewhat morbid nature.

In 1829 he began the publication of his longer critical *Causeries* in the *Revue de Paris.* Following the Revolution of 1830 he again wrote for the *Globe,* which had passed into the control of the Saint-Simonians, but his sympathies were not with its new socialist doctrines and he soon joined the staff of Carrel's *National,* a radical republican publication. His novel, *Volupté,* published in 1835, gives some idea of the religious questionings which troubled his mind during these years. In 1837 he lectured at Lausanne on the history of Port-Royal, later collecting his lectures into a book. While at Lausanne he wrote his last volume of verse, *Pensées d'août*. After traveling in Italy for a time, he returned to Paris and became keeper of the famous Mazarin Library, contributing literary opinions and criticisms throughout the next eight years to the *Revue des Deux Mondes*. He was elected to the French Academy in 1845 and three years later left Paris on account of the political upheaval and became professor of French literature at Liege, lecturing on *Chateaubriand et son groupe littéraire*.

He returned to Paris in 1849 and began to write for the *Constitutionel* his *Causeries de Lundi,* upon which his fame as a critic chiefly rests. These articles on literary subjects appeared each Monday. In 1861 he began to contribute them to the *Moniteur,* but in 1867 took them back to the *Constitutionel* and from 1867 until his death in 1869 he contributed them to the *Temps*. In 1854 he was appointed by the Emperor Louis Napoleon to the Collège de France as professor of Latin poetry, but the anti-imperialist students refused to listen to his lectures and he was forced to give up the chair. Embodied in the lectures which he had prepared was his critical estimate of Virgil. He was selected a senator in 1865 and won popular applause by his speeches in favor of liberty of thought, which the Emperor was then striving to suppress. He died Oct. 13, 1869 and, at his request, was buried without any sort of religious ceremony.

In the opinion of scholars Sainte-Beuve has never been surpassed as a critic. He possessed the faculty of seizing upon the salient and significant features of an author's style and thought-content, and presenting them in an interesting and thought-provoking manner. His prose was delicate, subtle and precise. His literary criticisms are held to have marked an epoch in the intellectual history of Europe.

AUGUSTUS SAINT-GAUDENS 1848–1907

AUGUSTUS SAINT-GAUDENS (sânt gạ'dănz), a leading American sculptor, was born March 1, 1848 in Dublin, Ireland, the son of a French father and an Irish mother, and was taken to the United States while still an infant. Early in his youth he was apprenticed to a cameo cutter in New York and attended the Cooper Union schools (1861) and the National Academy of Design (1865–66). His first work in sculpture was a bronze bust of his father, executed just before he sailed for Paris in 1867 to study under Jouffroy in l'École des Beaux-Arts. After two years in Paris he went to Rome and during three years there he executed his "Hiawatha" and "Silence." Returning to New York in 1873, his first important work was a relief of kneeling angels surrounding a large cross. This was for St. Thomas' Episcopal Church in New York and was destroyed by fire in 1904.

In 1876 Saint-Gaudens was commissioned to make a statue of Admiral Farragut for Madison Square, New York. Exhibited at the Paris Salon in 1880 and unveiled in New York in 1881, it received much critical praise and stamped the sculptor as an art leader in the United States. During this period he executed the "Governor Randall" at the Sailors' Snug Harbor, in Staten Island, and the caryatides for the Vanderbilt fireplace, now in the Metropolitan Museum, New York. For relief from his more serious work, he made bas-relief models of friends and noted personages of the day, his medallion of Robert Louis Stevenson (1887) being one of the best known. Others were William M. Chase, the children of Jacob M. Schiff, Mrs. Stanford White, Kenyon Cox, Bastien-Lepage and Dr. Henry Schiff. He developed another form of sculpture in the high-reliefs of Dr. Henry Bellows, Dr. McCosh, and the "Amor Caritas," etc. One of his greatest accomplishments was the statue of Abraham Lincoln, unveiled in Lincoln Park, Chicago, in 1887, and generally regarded as one of the finest Lincoln statues ever made. The same year his "Deacon Chapin," known as "The Puritan," was unveiled in Springfield, Mass. A notable example of his work, and considered by some critics the greatest artistic achievement of the United States, is the beautiful "Peace of God" memorial in Rock Creek cemetery, Washington, D. C. (1891), with its mysterious draped figure generally known as "Grief," but more probably intended by its creator to represent Peace. In 1895 he completed his Garfield memorial in Fairmount Park, Philadelphia.

Another noteworthy memorial, considered by many critics to be his masterpiece, is that to Robert G. Shaw, colonel of a Negro regiment in the Civil War, which was in work intermittently for twelve years and was dedicated in Boston in 1897. This is a bronze relief, 15 by 11 feet, showing the officer on horseback leading his colored soldiers into action. During the same year the sculptor completed his mounted "General Logan" in Grant Park, Chicago. Perhaps his most famous equestrian statue is that of "General Sherman," begun in 1892 and dedicated in 1903, which stands at an entrance to Central Park, New York City. The golden figure of Sherman, mounted on a golden steed, is led by a winged Victory. This was shown at the Paris Exposition in 1900, where it received the highest honors and Saint-Gaudens was made an officer of the Legion of Honor, and corresponding member of the Institute of France. The French government bought a bronze copy of his "Amor Caritas."

New York also has Saint-Gaudens' Peter Cooper memorial; Boston his Phillips Brooks memorial (not quite completed at the time of his death); Dublin has his "Parnell."

Saint-Gaudens married Augusta F. Homer in 1877 and died at Cornish, N. H., Aug. 3, 1907. His son, Homer Saint-Gaudens, is director of fine arts at Carnegie Institute, Pittsburgh.

CHARLES CAMILLE SAINT-SAENS   1835–1921

CHARLES CAMILLE SAINT-SAËNS (săn säns'), one of the more important of modern composers, is perhaps best known for his grand opera of *Samson and Delilah*. He was born in Paris, Oct. 2, 1835 and early showing a gift for music was placed with Halévy with whom he studied composition for a short time. He competed for the Grand Prix de Rome in 1852 and again in 1864, unsuccessfully on both occasions. At the age of 18 he became organist at the church of St. Merry, and succeeded Lefébure-Wély as organist at the Madeline in 1861, holding that position for 16 years. In 1867 he won a prize at the International Exhibition with his cantata, *Les Noces de Prométhée.*Five years later he composed his first opera,*La Princess Jeune,* and in 1877 a second, *Le Timbre d'argent,* neither of which met with great popular success. The public at large was first attracted to his musical gifts through his "symphonic poems," *Le Rouet d'Omphale, La Danse Macabre, Phaéton,* and *La Jeunesse d'Hercule.*His ability as a pianist had long been recognized.

His operatic triumph was soon to come, and it was through the influence of Liszt that *Samson et Delila* was presented at Weimar in 1877. This Biblical opera upon which the composer had been at work since 1869, received the discerning praise of the Weimar critics, although thirteen years were to pass before France was to hear it sung. It was presented at Rouen in 1890 and has come to be regarded as his operatic masterpiece. One act of the opera had been given in 1875 at one of Calonne's concerts, and in the following year Paris had heard that act at the Eden Theatre, but it was not until 1892 that the French capital saw the entire opera produced at the Grand Opera House in the repertory of which it has since remained. In 1909 it was produced with great success at Covent Garden, London, and has long been one of the popular numbers in the repertoire of the Metropolitan Grand Opera Company in New York. The first act with its formal choruses is held by critics to reflect the influence of Bach and Handel, and to be done in the manner of an oratorio, while the influence of Meyerbeer and Gounod is found in the more dramatic portions of the opera. Saint-Saëns was an eclectic in musical matters, but stamped his own individuality upon all his work.

He is considered to have sacrificed something of possible popularity and musical success by hesitating between the traditional style of the French school of composition and the new Wagnerian methods. To this may be ascribed the lack of success of his later operas. His *Etienne Marcel* was produced at Lyons in 1879; *Henry VIII* at the Grand Opéra, Paris, 1883; *Proserpine* at the Opéra-Comique in 1887; *Ascanio* at the Grand Opéra in 1890; *Phryné* at the Opéra-Comique in 1893; *Las Barbares* at the Grand Opéra in 1901. He did not confine himself, however, to grand opera, but has left compositions in nearly every department of musical art. His oratorios and cantatas were popular; notably *Oratorio de Noël, Les Noces de Prométhée, Le Déluge, La Lyre et la Harpe*. Among his other compositions are three symphonies, five pianoforte concertos; three violin concertos; the ballet, *Zavotte,* chamber music, a mass, a requiem, piano and organ music and many songs. He published a number of literary works, *Rimes familières, Harmonie et mélodie, Portraits et souvenirs* and *Problemes et mysteres*. He died in Algiers on Dec. 16, 1921.

CLAUDE SAINT-SIMON 1760–1825

CLAUDE HENRI, COUNT DE SAINT-SIMON (săn' sĕ môn'), Founder of French socialism, was born in Paris, Oct. 17, 1760. As a young man he served under Cornwallis in the American Revolutionary War and upon his return to France he resigned from the military service and devoted himself to travel and study, having already become interested in plans for bettering civilization. He took little part in the French Revolution of 1789 but advocated the abolishing of titles of nobility, although he himself bore a title. He was imprisoned in the Luxembourg for a time and following his release entered into land speculation and acquired a small fortune. He was one of the earliest advocates of a canal to connect the Atlantic and Pacific Oceans and also laid plans for the construction of a waterway from Madrid to the sea. He entered into many experiments and extravagances which gradually exhausted the competence he had won from his investments and his later years were spent in poverty. It is recorded that he worked nine hours a day in order to earn $200 a year until relatives settled a small pension upon him. He was a prolific writer but neither a clear nor systematic thinker and although he gained same followers his writings attracted little attention during his lifetime. In 1823 he attempted suicide and died two years later, May 19, 1825, in Paris. He was married in 1801 but the union quickly ended in divorce.

After his death his doctrines were organized into a system which gave direction to much nineteenth century thinking, both in France and elsewhere. He suggested much of what was later elaborated and brought before the public as Comtism, although he parted with Auguste Comte (who with Augustin Thiery had been his follower) after a final quarrel over the cause of the poor, which with Saint-Simon took the form of a religion and was discussed and emphasized in his greatest work, *The New Christianity*. His simple socialistic teachings were a reaction against both the French Revolution and the militarism of Napoleon. He did not advocate a new social revolt, but appealed to Louis XVIII to inaugurate a new order of things. He was opposed to the feudal and military system and advocated control of society by industrial leaders, with the spiritual direction in the hands of men of science instead of in the medieval church; an industrial state controlled by modern science, with war suppressed by universal association and society organized for productive labor by the most competent men.

While earlier in life he had concerned himself little with theology, in his *New Christianity* he attempted to resolve Christianity into its essential elements, propounding the precept that "the whole of society ought to strive toward the amelioration of the moral and physical existence of the poorest class; society ought to organize itself in the way best adapted for attaining this end," which became the shibboleth of the entire school of Saint-Simon. Two of his disciples, Olinde Rodrigues and Barthélemy Prosper Enfantin, who had received his last instructions and who did much of the clarifying and propagating of his doctrines after his death, established a journal, *Le Producteur,* which was discontinued in 1826 but the teachings of the sect were attracting much attention, meetings were held in Paris and in various towns throughout France and in 1828 Amand Bazard delivered a series of well-attended lectures in Paris giving a "complete exposition of the Saint-Simonian faith," and later published his two-volume *Exposition de le doctrine de St. Simon.* The Revolution of July 1830 brought new freedom to the socialist reformers who issued a proclamation demanding community of goods, abolition of the right of inheritance, and the enfranchisement of women. They acquired the newspaper, *Globe,* and formed an association from which Bazard, Enfantin and some of the strongest supporters afterwards seceded, Enfantin establishing a sort of communistic settlement which was broken up by the authorities in 1832.

SALADIN   1137–1193

SALAH-ED-DIN YOSSUF IBN AYUB, or SALADIN (săl'à dĭn), (the convenient name given him by Western historians), was a picturesque figure in the third crusade and shares with his English contemporary, Richard of the Lion Heart, a reputation for courage and chivalry. He was sultan of Egypt and Syria and was born in the year 1137 at Tekrit, a town on the African river Tigris, of which his father was governor. He early entered military service under Noureddin, that Syrian prince who was the scourge of the Christians who had invaded Syria and Palestine; and accompanied his uncle, who was a general in Noureddin's army, in several expeditions to Egypt. At the head of a small detachment of the Syrian army he was beleaguered in Alexandria by the combined Christians and Egyptians and it was on this occasion that he first exhibited his military skill. On the death of his uncle he succeeded him as grand-vizier of the Fatimite caliph and received the title of "the victorious prince." This advancement caused great concern to the Christians of Palestine and Syria who organized an attack on the new vizier which he repulsed at Damietta. Following up his advantage in Palestine, he took some strongholds and won a signal victory at the Syrian city of Gaza where he sacked the citadel which had been erected by the crusaders.

His master, Noureddin, instead of being gratified at his lieutenant's triumphant career, became inflamed with jealousy and Saladin found it necessary to proceed with the greatest caution. On the death of Noureddin (1174) he began a struggle with his successor with the outcome that he became sultan of Egypt and Syria. There followed a period of about ten years in which he was chiefly occupied in warfare with the Christians, but he did not neglect the affairs of his extensive domains and the welfare of his subjects. The crusading Christians were not so intent upon their devotional enterprise as to neglect the opportunity of plundering a pilgrim caravan on its way to Mecca for which they suffered a signal defeat at the hands of Saladin, who assailed them at Tiberias in 1187, taking many prisoners. In the following October he successfully stormed Jerusalem and soon thereafter had taken almost every other fortified place in Palestine, a series of triumphs which aroused the crusading spirit in Europe to fever pitch. The news, slow to reach western countries, was followed by the recruiting of a great army led by the king of France and Richard I of England which, after an adventurous journey, reached the scenes of these infidel triumphs. Difficulties between Richard and the French king complicated the enterprise and Richard, with such followers as remained loyal to him, continued the war with success. Saladin was twice defeated, losing Cæsarea and Jaffa, and in 1192 agreed to a treaty by which the coast from the latter city to Tyre was given to the Christians.

Saladin died at Damascus on March 4, 1193, leaving a reputation not only for military skill of a high order, but for his enlightened administration of affairs, which often presented a strange contrast to that of the Christian monarchs of his time. He is said to have been much given to gambling and drinking in his early years, but to have abandoned these vices as he became more and more imbued with a consciousness of his responsibilities. He built canals, dikes and roads, was deeply interested in the education and welfare of his subjects, and enjoyed the respect even of his Christian enemies who took back with them to the darkness of feudal Europe tales of his noble chivalry, elevation of soul, courage, honor and wisdom. Of him the historian Hume says, ". . . this gallant emperor, in particular, displayed during the course of the war, a spirit and generosity, which even his bigoted enemies were obliged to acknowledge and admire. Richard, equally martial and brave, carried with him more of the barbarian character, and was guilty of acts of ferocity which threw a stain on his celebrated victories."

In his will Saladin made bequests to Mohammedans, Jews and Christians alike. He ordered that his winding sheet be carried through the streets of the city, while an accompanying crier proclaimed, "This is all that remains of the mighty Saladin, the conqueror of the East."

JOHN SINGER SARGENT   1856–1925

JOHN SINGER SARGENT, one of the most eminent of modern painters, was born of American parents in Florence, Italy, on Jan. 12, 1856. His childhood was spent in Nice, Rome, Dresden and Florence. He early showed a predilection for drawing and took desultory lessons which were interrupted by school and travel. His mother encouraged his artistic gifts and in 1873 he won a prize for drawing at the Academia in Florence. He entered the studio of Carolus Doran in Paris at the age of 18 and two years later made the first of his many visits to the United States. His first exhibited picture, "En route pour la Pêche," (Corcoran Gallery, Washington), won honorable mention at the Salon in 1878 and his portrait of Duran, shown in the following Salon, was recognized as holding great promise. After visiting Spain in 1879 he painted many charming and well-known pieces, among them "El Jaleo," exhibited in 1882 (Fenway Court,

Boston), and "The Children of E. D. Boit" (Boston Fine Arts Museum).

He absorbed from the great painters of the past such atmosphere, tradition and method as suited his particular genius and commissions came to him without effort on his part. In his portrait of Madame Gautreau, friend of Gambetta, exhibited at the Salon of 1884, he was accused of having caricatured his subject and French papers heaped abuse upon him, but he continued on his independent way, painting what he saw in his sitter, regardless of criticism, either friendly or hostile. After 1884 he made his home in London, opening a studio first in Kensington and afterwards in Chelsea. His childhood study, "Carnation Lily, Lily Rose," was bought for the Tate Gallery and the Luxembourg acquired "Carmencita," the Spanish dancer (1890), which was the most famous of his early portraits. He was soon in demand in London as a portrait painter and "The Duke of Marlborough and his Family," "Ladies Acheson," "Daughters of the Hon. Percy Wyndham," portraits of the Duke and Duchess of Connaught, the Duchess of Portland, Lord Russell, Countess of Warwick, etc., greatly increased his reputation. He became well known in the United States and painted many prominent Americans, among them Edwin Booth, Lawrence Barrett, Joseph Jefferson, President Theodore Roosevelt and Secretary Hay. In 1894 he was elected to associate membership in the Royal Academy and three years later to full membership. Universities bestowed degrees upon him, and he won medals at many exhibitions, and was made a member of nearly every society of artists. He was frequently accused of accentuating the displeasing features of his sitters, but he dismissed the charge by his, "I chronicle, I do not judge." His portraits were incisive, brilliant and uncompromising; his sense of realism and of humor often brought out deep-seated traits of those who sat to him. He is declared never to have repeated himself, to have been able to see and capture a new point of view, a new angle or expression in almost every picture he painted. His resource and freshness were regarded as unfailing.

After 1910 he practically gave up portrait work and devoted himself to water-color, with which he had done little since the beginning of his career. Eighty brilliant examples in that medium were purchased by the Brooklyn Fine Arts Museum and 45 by the Boston Museum. One of his greatest achievements was his "Pageant of Religion," a series of finely conceived and magnificently executed murals for the great hall (later named for him) in the Boston Public Library, to which the last 20 years of his life were devoted.

He was in Austria at the outbreak of the World War in 1914 and placed himself at the disposal of the government for which he painted several war pictures, among them his terrible "Gassed" (London War

Museum). During his lifetime a magnificent series of his portraits, bequeathed to the British nation by Asher Wertheim, were hung in the National Gallery (a rare honor to be paid a living artist), and they now occupy a wing in the Tate Gallery. New York and Boston Museums have many fine examples of his work. He died in his sleep on April 14, 1925 and was buried in Brookwood Cemetery, a memorial tablet being later placed in the crypt of St. Paul's.

GIROLAMO SAVONAROLA   1452–1498

GIROLAMO SAVONAROLA (sä′vŏ nà rō′là), Italian preacher and reformer, was born of a noble family at Ferrara, Sept. 21, 1452. He entered the Dominican order in Bologna in 1475. Tradition has it that he preached in Florence in 1482 but was a failure. He retired to a convent in Brescia and there his zeal attracted so much attention that he was recalled to Florence in 1489, making his second, and highly successful, appearance in the pulpit at San Marco. People soon flocked to hear his fervid, semi-prophetic utterances. He boldly denounced the corruption which was then prevalent among the great, and the worldliness of the clergy. His followers asserted that he was an inspired prophet and he became an object of suspicion to the Medici, then the reigning house of Florence, for his teachings were antagonistic to the semi-pagan influences in art and literature which, under Lorenzo the Magnificent, were superseding the influence of the great religious painters. His conception of spirituality and religious morality did not coincide with those of the times. In 1493 he proposed reforms in the Dominican order of Tuscany and received the sanction of the pope, who appointed him the first vicar-general.

Soon, however, his preaching began to point toward political revolution as the means ordained by God for the regeneration of morals and religion, and after Charles VIII of France invaded Italy with a large army and drove the Medici from the city Savonarola became for a time dominant in the government. The French were compelled to leave the city and a republic was established with Savonarola its guiding spirit as the head of the Piagnoni (the "Weepers"). His denunciations of existing abuses became still louder and a profound religious enthusiasm laid hold upon the people so that Florence became almost a city of Puritans. With so much power as he now had he began to display the intolerance of the Puritan phase of his Catholicism. He put his extravagant theories into practice and by his genius and fervor brought a majority of the citizens to his way of thinking. He proposed to make the Republic of Florence a Christian commonwealth, with God as the sole sovereign, and his Gospel the law. Strict ordinances were passed for the suppression of vice and the curbing of frivolity. Women flocked to the public square and flung their richest garments and their articles of adornment down for the "bonfire of vanities" which Savonarola's followers lighted.

His sway did not last long. The people wearied of his rigorous rule and a reaction set in. He had aroused hostility by his attacks on the pope and in 1495 he was forbidden to preach and was summoned to Rome, both of which orders he refused to obey. Difficulties increased in Florence; his system proved impracticable and certain disaffected persons conspired to recall the Medici. The plot was discovered and five of the conspirators were executed. The rigor with which this conspiracy was suppressed helped to hasten the end of the Republic. In 1497 the pope excommunicated Savonarola who refused to accept the decree and openly defied the pope. He devoted himself heroically to the care of the sick in the plague which shortly afterwards swept Florence, although he was not permitted to perform the sacred offices. In the city elections the Medici were returned to power and Savonarola was again ordered to stop preaching. He had lost prestige, there was a general revulsion of feeling against him and he was finally brought to trial on a charge of heresy and sedition. During the long trial he was put to the torture until he broke down and confessed his guilt—a confession which he withdrew when the torture was discontinued, but he was declared guilty and on May 23, 1498 he and two of his disciples were hanged and their bodies burned. In 1901 Florence erected a tablet in his memory. He left numerous religious writings.

JOHANN VON SCHILLER 1759–1805

JOHANN CHRISTOPH FRIEDRICH VON SCHILLER, one of the greatest of German poets, was born at Marbach, Württemberg, Nov. 10, 1759, son of Johann Kaspar von Schiller, a former army surgeon who was a sort of superintendent of the gardens at the country estate of the duke of Württemberg. The boy's early desire was to become a clergyman, but the duke insisted, against the desires of both father and son, that he attend a military academy founded by himself. Here the young protégé, in accordance with the wish of his patron, began the study of law but, making slight progress, abandoned it for medicine. Like his great contemporary, Goethe, his heart was in the field of literature and he soon turned from his studies to the muse. Nevertheless, he was graduated as a surgeon in 1780, having consigned to the flames several youthful poetic productions. But if the world had acquired a surgeon, it at least had not lost a poet. He had already completed the outline of his memorable drama, *Die Räuber* (The Robbers), in which he gave expression of his attitude of rebellion toward the political conditions of which he felt himself to be a victim. In 1790 it was published (at his own expense) and aroused unbounded enthusiasm in literary circles, especially among the youthful literati, but also the sternest condemnation by the older and more conservative element who found its unbridled fancy and glowing passion a rather heavy dose and were accordingly scandalized. Among these latter was the autocratic duke of Württemberg who took occasion to censure the young dramatist in no uncertain terms, and forbade him to publish anything further without his personal sanction. The soul of the poet (he was then 21) rebelled against this unsympathetic rule of censorship and the play was shortly produced upon the stage at Mannheim, and attended by the author, who discreetly concealed his visit from the knowledge of his patron. The upshot of this affair was that Schiller spent two unhappy weeks in jail and then escaped and fled the harsh authority of the duke, taking up his residence at Bauerbach where he found it expedient for the time being to live under an assumed name. Here he completed his *Fiesko* and *Kabale und Liebe* and began *Don Carlos*. In 1783 he ventured back to Mannheim and soon became identified with the theatrical life of that city.

What is called the first period of his dramatic and poetic career was now passing; the tempestuous passion, often finding its outlet in unbridled speech and a kind of ostentation of freedom and recklessness, subsided as the flush of youth gave way to a better sense of values. In 1785 he went to Leipzig and it was here that he wrote his beautiful *Lied an die Freude*. Soon we find him at Dresden where he wrote *Der Giesterseher* (The Ghost-Seer) and completed *Don Carlos*. At that time Weimar was the cultural centre of Germany and thither, in 1787, Schiller went on the invitation of the duke Karl August and others. Here he was welcomed by the witty and accomplished Wieland, who introduced Shakespeare to Germany; by Herder, the distinguished theologian and philosopher; and here he met the reigning monarch of letters, Goethe, although it was not until several years later that the two became friends. The friendship, once formed, was close and enduring and Goethe's influence on his later work is abundantly evident. Here, in this sympathetic and congenial environment, he lived, struggling against indifferent health, studying and doing some of his best work. He was appointed to the chair of history at the university of Jena following the publication in 1788 of his masterly history of the revolt of the Netherlands against Spain (*Defection of the Neth-*

erlands), but his health did not permit of his retaining this post. He wrote *Götter Griechenlands* (Gods of Greece) and *Kleine prosaischen Schriften,* a four volume collection of treatises inspired by his excursion into the field of philosophy, besides a history of the Thirty Years War under the title of *Geschichte des Dreissigjährigen Kriegs.*

In 1790 he married Charlotte von Lengefeld and at that time was made a privi-councillor by his admirer, the duke of Meiningen. In 1802 he was raised to the rank of nobility. During a prolonged visit to his relatives in Württemberg he wrote his exquisite *Briefe über æsthetische Erziehung* (Letters on Æsthetic Culture). Other works of his later years, besides many articles on history and philosophy, were *Der Spaziergang* and the *Lied der Glocke* (Song of the Bell); *Wallenstein, Maria Stuart, Die Jungfrau von Orléans, Braut von Messina,* and the drama which is best known of all his works, *Wilhelm Tell.*

Constant study and application exhausted his naturally weak constitution and he died on May 9, 1805. After his death he came to be regarded as second only to Goethe in the ranks of Germany's great poets.

ARTHUR SCHOPENHAUER   1788–1860

ARTHUR SCHOPENHAUER (shō′pĕn hou′ẽr), German philosopher of pessimism, was born at Danzig on Feb. 22, 1788, the son of a banker. His mother was a prolific writer of novels and short stories. Following the death of her husband, she removed to Weimar in 1806 with her son who thereafter attended a number of schools—Gotha, Weimar, Gottingen, Berlin and Jena. Upon his graduation from Jena he wrote his thesis *On the Fourfold Root of the Principle of Sufficient Reason.* This ambitious treatise in which he attempted to classify the principles of the four sciences of mathematics, physics, logic and ethics, showed the bent of his mind and attracted some attention. He possessed great bodily energy, with inherited free-thinking tendencies, was passionate in nature and of a suspicious disposition and found emotion and reason frequently in conflict. It is probably not stretching the point to say that this inner conflict gave direction to, if it was not the basis for, his later elaborated philosophical doctrines. He was both vain and ambitious; he believed that his philosophy was worthy of the mantle of Socrates himself; and yet his own generation passed by his doctrines and became enthusiastic over what seemed to him the fatuous delusions of Fichte, Schelling and Hegel.

The best of his writings, and the work which has chiefly kept his name alive, is *The World as Will and Idea,* published in 1819. According to his philosophy of subjective idealism, the objective world is nonexistent, an idea, the fantastic imaginings of the brain; he held that Kant had forever demolished the possibility of knowledge of the "thing-in-itself;" that the ideas of art are the result of the intuition of genius. Such intuitions he regarded as the only knowledge not subservient to the will and the practical needs of existence. Will, being the active side of human nature, he held to be the force by which man knows from directly inside himself and therefore the key to the understanding of all things. Will, according to this philosopher, is the creative, the primary force, while Idea is the receptive, or secondary factor of our knowledge of things.

From 1814 to 1818 he lived at Dresden and after a visit to Italy he became a lecturer at the University of Berlin. In 1831 he retired to Frankfort-on-the-Main where he lived until his death.

Embittered by the triumph of Hegelianism and the neglect of his own work, he became morbid and possessed of an inordinate fear of robbery and assassination. He searched continually for things that would confirm his opinions expressed in *Die Welt als Wille und Vostellung,* noting them down carefully for future use. All his later writings were explanations and commentaries on the main thesis, announced in his book on Will and Idea. In 1836 he published *Über den Willen in der Natur;* in 1841 *Die beiden Grundprobleme der Ethik,* consisting of two essays submitted in competition for prizes offered by the Norwegian and Danish academies of science. He won the Norwegian prize, but the Danish Academy refused him the award although he was the only competitor. In 1844 appeared a revised edition of *The World as Will and Idea,* in two volumes, with commentaries and new chapters on the primacy of the will, on death and sexual love. But 500 copies were printed which sold slowly but his philosophy had begun to find followers—Frauenstädt, Dr. E. O. Lindner and others, and Frauenstädt found a publisher for Schopenhauer's *Parega und Paralipomena* (1851) and in 1854 published his *Letters on the Schopenhauerian Philosophy.* Between 1847 and 1860 new editions of Schopenhauer's works were published and after his death at Frankfurt on Sept. 21, 1860, the fame he had so vainly desired during his life rapidly grew about his name.

FRANZ PETER SCHUBERT 1797–1828

FRANZ PETER SCHUBERT (shoo'bert), Austrian composer, was born in Vienna on Jan. 31, 1797. His father was a schoolmaster who entered his son at 11 in the choristers' school of the court chapel where he spent five years and throughout was busy writing at practically all kinds of musical composition. Upon leaving the court chapel in 1813 he became an instructor in his father's school, but the work was distasteful to him and he sought relief in composing music. As early as 1810 he had written a piano duet and in 1813 he composed a symphony and began his first opera, *Des Teufels Lustschloss*. Some of his best work was done before he reached the age of 20. At this period two of his most popular songs were written, *The Erlking* and *The Wanderer,* as well as his famous *Mass in F* and his *Tragic Symphony*.

Through Vogl, a popular baritone of the time who introduced Schubert's songs to Vienna, the youth began to acquire a reputation in his native city and his *Schläfers Klagelied,* performed at a concert in 1819, brought him into some prominence. In the summer of that year, in company with Vogl, he made an extended tour, but even while sight-seeing he found time to compose his pianoforte quintet (Opus 114). He next tried his hand at writing the music for comic opera and during 1820 his *Zwillings brüder* and the *Zauberharfe* were produced at the Kärnthnerthor theatre. Despite the popularity of his songs, he derived only a very moderate income from them and, being totally without business instinct, he was always short of funds. One friend found him lodging, another supplied appliances and his meals were paid for by various friends—Von Schober, Mayrhofer, Vogl, Anselm and Joseph Hüttenbrenner, Gahy and Sonnleithner. They arranged musicales for him which soon came to be known as "Schubertiaden." It was not until after Vogl had sung *Erlkönig* (February, 1821) that a music publisher, Diabelli, agreed with some hesitation to publish some of his compositions on commission, but the arrangement ended after seven songs had been published after which Schubert received a mere pittance for his compositions. For the next three years he directed his efforts toward the stage, only to meet with discouragement and disappointment. *Alfonso und Estrella* and *Fierrabras* were refused; the censor prohibited *Die Verschworenen* and *Rosamunde* was withdrawn after two nights because of a very halting libretto. The two latter works contain some of his most charming music. He composed his famous octet, *A Sketch for a Grand Symphony,* in 1824 and that summer went to Zelesz and wrote the *Divertissement à l'Hongroise,* the string quartet in A minor and his grand duo in C major (perhaps a sketch of the *Grand Symphony*). He is said by some of his biographers to have cherished a hopeless passion at this time for one of his pupils, Countess Caroline Esterházy.

His *Mass in A Flat* and the *Unfinished Symphony* were other works of this period. The *Müllerlieder* and others of his songs were written in 1825; *Trockne Blumen* and the two string quartets in E and E flat, somewhat earlier. A little prosperity now came to him; his compositions came from the press quite rapidly and he spent a pleasant holiday in Upper Austria, composing his *Songs from Sir Walter Scott* and his piano sonata in A minor. From 1826 to 1828 he lived in Vienna, writing steadily. He applied for a conductorship at the opera in 1826 which was refused because he declined to alter one of his songs. In 1828 he gave his first and only concert of his own works. He was one of the most talented and spontaneous of all composers and is unsurpassed as a writer of songs of which he has left us some 600, besides his many masterpieces of instrumental music, including symphonies, piano music, an oratorio *(Lazarus)*, six masses. Of his 17 operas none achieved lasting fame. Among the work of the final two years of his brief life were *Der Tod und das Madchen,* the string quartet in G major, *Rondeau brilliant, Hark! hark! the Lark, Who is Sylvia?* the *Winterreise* songs, the *Song of Miriam,* the C major symphony, *Tantum Ergo,* and many songs. He also set to music 70 of Goethe's poems and 60 of Schiller's.

On Nov. 19, 1828, he died of typhoid fever after a short illness and was buried in the Ortsfriedhof, in the village of Währing, near the grave of Beethoven.

ROBERT SCHUMANN   1810–1856

ROBERT ALEXANDER SCHUMANN, German composer, was born June 8, 1810, at Zwickau, Saxony, the son of a publisher. He received the usual youthful training, traveled a good deal, studied half-heartedly at law and philosophy, but at the age of 21 he definitely determined upon a musical career and placed himself under instruction in Leipzig. In his attempts to become proficient as a pianist he injured the sinews of one hand so that he was forced to give up playing and he then turned to composition. Within two years his first compositions for the piano, which included a Toccata, were published and he began to write on musical subjects. In 1834 with some other musicians he established a publication, *Neue Zeit-*

schrift für Musik, to which for the next ten years he contributed articles many of which are still regarded as authentic expressions of musical wisdom, although some of them are undoubtedly fantastic and are now looked upon as mere musical curiosities. His greatest compositions for the piano were written between 1836 and 1839, and include such various forms as Fantasia, Noveletten, Humoreskes, pieces for children, etc.

In 1841 he turned to compositions for other instruments and for orchestras, writing a romantic concerto in A minor, three symphonies and three quartets, which were followed in 1842 by the famous Quintet for piano and strings. The following year he produced the choral work, *Paradise and the Peri* and scenes from *Faust.* A breakdown in health, inducing mental trouble, caused him to retire to Dresden and for four years he was unable to work. He regained his health in 1847 and the following year began to compose with great rapidity and facility works of varied character. This feverish activity lasted for two years and during the period he wrote his only opera, *Genoveva,* music for the songs in Byron's *Manfred,* and many original songs and music for single and concerted instruments. After his appointment as musical director in Düsseldorf in 1850 he found himself in many difficulties. He was very absent-minded, his mental ailment returned and he developed eccentricities, but throughout these trying times he continued to compose. He retained his post of musical director until 1854, by which time his eccentricities had become so extreme that he was compelled to give up the work. His mind turned to the occult, and he became interested in spiritualism, believed that he heard supernatural voices and on one occasion, announcing that Schubert and Mendelssohn had sent him a theme that he must write down, he composed five variations for the piano on this theme, which proved his last work. On Feb. 27, 1854, in one of his periods of melancholy, he attempted suicide by throwing himself into the Rhine, but was rescued and taken to a private asylum near Bonn, in which he died on July 29, 1856.

Schumann is regarded by music critics as one of the most original of composers. There was a freshness, vigor and fertility to his work that have kept its appeal alive. He showed great resources in rhythm and harmony, obtaining a variety and vividness peculiarly his own and has hardly a rival as a composer of songs and ballads. His piano compositions are among the most popular and enduring for that instrument and rank with those of Chopin for beauty and musical content. In 1841 he married Clara Josephine Wieck, a pianist and daughter of his first music teacher at Leipzig, who had been the inspiration of much of his music. She survived him for forty years. The introduction and popularizing of many of his piano compositions was due to her untiring efforts. She played them in many of the great cities of Europe and after his death edited a complete edition of his works in 34 volumes. His musical criticisms were published in four volumes and translated into English. The *Life of Schumann told in his Letters* was published in 1890.

SIR WALTER SCOTT   1771–1832

TOWERING above his own literary defects, Sir Walter Scott, great man and great romancer, occupies a hallowed place in the history of his country and in the hearts of humanity. His magic wand invoked in prose and verse a historic panorama that makes the sophisticated and often barren fiction of a later day seem poverty-stricken by comparison. He was born in Edinburgh, Scotland, on Aug. 15, 1771, descendant of an old border family. He was a sickly child and lame throughout life, but he developed into a powerful man, appropriately suggesting the vitality and hardy life which he so stirringly depicted. His childhood was passed at Sandyknowe, a farm owned by his grandfather in Roxburghshire, where he absorbed the historic legends and romance of Scotland and became versed in the folklore of the wild Highlands. From his long habit of dwelling mentally in the past he was able to visualize and reproduce it with all the convincing background and coloring which make his work unique.

When 8 years old he went to the High School in Edinburgh; four years later entered the university where he remained for three years and after six years in his father's office he was admitted to the bar in 1792 and was fairly successful as a lawyer. In his 26th year he married Charlotte Margaret Carpenter, who was of French birth and parentage, a marriage blessed with several children and characterized by an ideal love and devotion. In 1799 he became deputy sheriff of Selkirkshire which permitted him much leisure and he tried his hand at writing. His first literary efforts (1796) were translations of Burger's ballads *Lenore* and *The Wild Huntsman*. Two years later he published his translation of Goethe's drama. *Goetz von Berlichingen*. His first wholly original work, the ballads *Glenfinlas, Eve of St. John* and the *Gray Brothers,* were published in 1799. In 1802–3 appeared *Border Minstrelsy* (3 vols.) a collection which was enthusiastically received. He had all the charm of novelty and freshness and with *The Lay of the Last Minstrel* (1805) he became unquestionably the most popular writer of his time.

It is impossible here to attempt an enumeration of the works in prose and verse which flowed from his prolific pen and won him a place in the hearts of English-speaking people. He wrote biographies of Swift and

Dryden and edited their works. In 1808 appeared his long poem *Marmion,* followed in 1810 by that beautiful rhymed story, *The Lady of the Lake,* crowded with gorgeous pictures with stirring ballads interspersed. It took the public by storm, combining the charm of poetry with the charm of fiction and was followed in 1811 by *The Vision of Don Roderick. Rokeby, The Bridal of Trierman, The Lord of the Isles* and *The Field of Waterloo* followed in successive years. In none of these did he reach the heights of poetic expression and it is questionable if that can be done in a long poem. The concentrated passion and fervor of Byron is said to have discouraged Scott from continuing the form of poem which he had made so popular and he fell back on prose, to achieve at once a new glory with a new medium in the *Waverly Novels.* In 1814 *Waverly* was anonymously published, followed in the next few years by that series of romances which have made their author's name a household word; *Guy Mannering, The Antiquary, The Black Dwarf, Old Mortality, Rob Roy, The Heart of Midlothian, Ivanhoe, Kenilworth, The Bride of Lammermoor, Quentin Durward, Redgauntlet, The Talisman* and numerous others. All appeared anonymously; their author came to be termed "the great unknown," and although gradually they were recognized as the work of Scott, the identity of the author was not disclosed until 1827.

In the border country which he so loved he built a palatial home, Abbotsford, where he dispensed a princely hospitality to the multitudes who came for a glimpse of a man so beloved and illustrious. In 1820 he was made a baronet. Simple, unaffected and rugged, the genial friend of rich and poor, he lived in luxury but not in ostentation in the country whose legends and minstrelsy and virile adventures were packed in his teeming mind. And then came tragedy. The printing and publishing business in Edinburgh in which he was interested with his old friend, James Ballantyne, collapsed and he found himself bankrupt. The world is familiar with the inspiring spectacle of the great writer setting to work with his pen to liquidate his enormous debt. Leaving Abbotsford, where his loyal wife lay mortally ill, he took lodging in Edinburgh where for some years, in failing health, he labored incessantly, pouring out story after story and completing an 8-volume life of Napoleon. Forty thousand pounds, earned in drudgery and suffering, was returned to his creditors. But he broke under the strain. In 1830 he suffered a paralytic stroke from which he never completely recovered. In the hope that foreign travel might restore him the government placed a frigate at his disposal in which he voyaged to Italy. But he pined for his "ain countree" and returned to Abbotsford where, surrounded by his children, he died on Sept. 21, 1832. Four days later he was laid to rest beside his wife in the old Abbey of Dryburgh.

SENECA   circa 4 B.C.–65 A.D.

ABOUT 60 B.C. there was born at Cordova, Spain, a child who was named
M. Annæus Seneca. In his youth he journeyed to Rome where his wealth
and talents procured him the regard of the most noted Romans of that
time. He was a rhetorician and is said to have had a phenominal memory.
Several incomplete works of his are still extant. Returning to Spain, he
married a woman named Helvia and had several children. One of these,
a boy, accompanied his father to Rome where he was educated. This celebrated son of a noted father was LUCIUS ANNÆUS SENECA, who became
one of the most eminent of Roman philosophers. The year of his birth
is not known. Being a master of rhetoric, it was natural that the elder
Seneca should desire his son to be skilled in the arts of eloquence, but
the boy was not long content with the study of language in its esthetic
sense. He became interested in philosophy and we soon find him studying under the noted teachers of his day. He traveled in Greece and Egypt,
became a pleader in the law courts, and was distinguished for his forensic
powers. He is said to have abandoned his legal career in fear of the jealousy of the odious Caligula, the emperor whose inhuman cruelties and
nauseating absurdities made him the terror of his time. He it was who
had victims murdered and tortured to amuse him while dining and who
expressed the genial wish that "all the Roman people had but one neck so
that I might behead Rome at a blow." A man, indeed, whose disfavor was
to be avoided. After his merited assassination, his uncle, Claudius I, who
succeeded him, took Seneca into his favor, honoring him with preferment, but his advancement in the state was brought to a sudden end by
the charge of adultery which was made against him involving Julia, the
daughter of Germanicus and wife of Vinicius. He was thereupon banished to Corsica where he pursued his favorite study of philosophy for
eight years.

It may be said that his philosophic temper did not suffice to reconcile
him to his lot and he continually and complainingly appealed to the ob-
durate emperor for pardon. It was not until Claudius married his second
wife, Agrippina, that a pardon was forthcoming, thanks to her sympathy
and intervention. The exile was then recalled and given the post of prætor,
or magistrate, and was also appointed to superintend the education of
Agrippina's son, Nero, a difficult task as the sequel proved. The death of
his military tutor was the signal for Nero to launch himself upon a course
of unbridled license and Seneca found it quite impossible to subdue his
depraved propensities. His disappointment in this was somewhat pal-

liated by the receipt of princely gifts from his extravagant pupil and patron and he is said to have accumulated a fortune beyond the dreams of most philosophers. Even the unstable Nero himself began to cast a covetous glance at the wealth which his munificense had created, and the philosopher tactfully offered to refund his reckless gifts and to retire on a modest pension; but Nero would not hear of this and Seneca withdrew into seclusion under pretense of illness. Enraged at this strategic move, Nero tried to have his tutor imprisoned, but the attempt came to nothing.

The troubles of Seneca were not over. A short time afterward Antonius Natalis, while on trial for his alleged part in the conspiracy of Piso, implicated Seneca as one of the conspirators and this declaration seems to have been thought sufficient to establish his guilt. He was thereupon condemned to end his own life, and he elected to do this by bleeding to death in a bath. His wife, Paullina, accompanied him to the scene of death, resolved to die with him, and was only deterred by orders from the emperor. Thus his life ebbed away; the date of his death is given as 65 A.D.

Only a part of Seneca's works are extant. They treat of such subjects as *Consolation, Anger, Tranquillity, Mind, Providence, Benefits, The Philosophical and the Happy Life,* and similar moral themes. A few plays have been credited to him, but there has been some disagreement among scholars as to their authorship. He was also the author of several speculations on physical science and is believed to have anticipated certain principles now universally accepted in this field.

MICHAEL SERVETUS 1511–1553

MICHAEL SERVETUS (sĕr vē'tus), (more properly Miguel Servete) was a scholar of Spanish blood, born at Villanueva in Aragon in 1511. At about the age of 19 he went to France and took up the study of law at Toulouse. Subsequently he became interested in theology and, abandoning his legal studies, he devoted his active and speculative mind to the intricacies of religious dogma and the doctrinal problems involved in the reformation movement. In 1530 his inquiries took him to Switzerland and after hearing the noted theologians in Basel, he visited Strassburg where he absorbed the teachings of Capito and Bucer. The upshot of his investigation and the deliberations thus inspired was that he repudiated the doctrine of the Trinity, a courageous and foolhardy act which so aroused the authorities of the church as to jeopardize his safety. They declared him a "wicked and cursed Spaniard," and he somewhat naively appealed from their threatening attitude and harsh judgment to the public in two notable works which, however, won him few partisans. His position became so precarious in the face of his influential detractors that he found it expedient to change his name to Michael de Villanueva. As an additional precaution he fled to Paris and being, no doubt, somewhat disillusioned, he took up the study of medicine. He had a restless and active mind to which study and inquiry were a necessity. In this field, at least, there were no complicating difficulties and he took his degree with honors. It is often said that he discovered the circulation of the blood, about which he certainly thought much and made some interesting observations; but the great honor for this discovery belongs to the English physician, William Harvey.

Unfortunately this restless, controversial soul was again drawn into the arena of theological debate. He met John Calvin with whom he had some conversations which resulted in arrangements for a public debate. Sober second thought, however, deterred the impulsive Servetus from such an encounter with the fanaticism which Calvin represented (with its possible sequel of arrest and persecution) and he withdrew from a scene so fraught with tragic potentialities.

For a period he lived at Lyon, Avignon and Charlieu, supporting himself in a precarious way by his writing. In 1541 he found a hospitable host in Pierre Paulmier, Archbishop of Vienne, in whose palace he remained for some years and wrote his famous *Christianismi Restitutio,* published in the year of his death. This work spelled his doom. After its publication he set forth on a journey which took him through Switzerland and at Geneva he was arrested by order of Calvin, and cast into prison. The author of *Christianismi Restitutio* could hope for small consideration at the hands of the church authorities and he realized too late the unwisdom of his passing through this region of fanaticism. After a prolonged trial, in which no end of theological absurdities were introduced, he was condemned to be burned at the stake, and this dreadful sentence was carried out amid his agonizing cries, on the 27th of October, 1553.

Thinkers antagonistic to Christianity have ever since found in his tragic fate an outstanding instance of the bigotry and merciless cruelty of the church. He has been often called a martyr, but so far from seeking the glory of martyrdom, he sought to escape the death which was the ruthless punishment of his independence and enlightenment. On the other hand, the comfortable argument that he was the victim of an ignorant and cruel age and that his dreadful end was an inevitable incident in the career of religious reform, is hardly tenable. The affair was quite as shocking to his intelligent contemporaries as it is to the world today. It is well to keep a clear vision in such matters; the killing of Servetus is a dark stain on the memory of John Calvin.

WILLIAM SHAKESPEARE 1564–1616

WILLIAM SHAKESPEARE, the outstanding literary glory of the world, was born in the village of Stratford-on-Avon, Warwickshire, on or about the 23rd of April, 1564. His father, John Shakespeare, was a glover (later alderman and bailiff) who married Mary, the daughter of Robert Arden, a comparatively wealthy farmer of the small village of Wilmecote, in the neighborhood of Stratford. Neither of the poet's parents could read or write. They lived in a house on Henley Street, a commodious and substantial residence for a provincial tradesman; and from this abode, on April 26, their third child (two daughters having previously died in infancy) was taken to his baptism and given the Christian name of William. In all, four sons and four daughters were born of the marriage. An apartment on the first floor of the house is still shown as the birthroom of the poet. Among the rustic and illiterate people of the village his childhood and youth were passed. It is a natural inference that he attended the free grammar school; if so, it was all the schooling he ever had. It is thought that he was duly apprenticed to a trade, and that of butcher seems to take precedence in this field of speculation on probabilities. What is definitely known, and is probably significant, is that when he was a little boy, and presumably later as well, strolling players visited Stratford, and it is a fair assumption that he, with all the other youngsters of the place, gazed wide-eyed at their tinseled accoutrements and enchanting paraphernalia. Perhaps the primal instinct of childhood to follow a circus lingered in his glowing fancy. The ingenuity of mankind has been well nigh exhausted in the quest for data about the material life of the possessor of an intellect so stupendous. But only a few precious crumbs have been collected, the official record of his birth, of his marriage, of the birth of his three children, Susanna and the twins, Hamnet and Judith; of his death and his will. When the scene changes to London we have casual allusions to him by his contemporaries, Ben Jonson and others, which make the conclusion inevitable that he was an honorable, genial, tolerant and friendly man; he was called "Sweet Will Shakespeare." From the bust in the church at Stratford (which was formerly in colors) and from a combination of other evidence, it appears that he was of medium height, compact in form, with hazel eyes and auburn hair.

At 18 he married Anne Hathaway who lived in a picturesque thatched-roof cottage in the tiny hamlet of Shottery, a mile or two from Stratford. Along the winding path to this sequestered home may still be seen "the bank where the wild thyme blows"; he probably passed it often. Much has been made of a famous poaching episode in the park of Sir Thomas Lucy, and some of his worshippers have thought it necessary to defend the poet's name against the charge of a form of misdoing only too prevalent among the rustic youth of that day. If Sir Thomas Lucy lost a few deer, he has at least gained immortality; he is thought to have been the original of the memorable Justice Shallow. The poaching incident probably occurred and may have been the reason for Shakespeare's leaving Stratford. Here, again, we are caught in the eddies of surmise and speculation. Much has been written about his prolonged absence from his family. First and last, he probably spent more time in the domestic circle than many of the renowned explorers of that time; and no one knows how often he may have visited Stratford. His wife was several years his senior and the date of his marriage, taken in connection with the birthday of his first child, permits the inference that the marriage may have been an act of honor rather than of devoted love. There is no reason to assume that he was not a good husband and father. He certainly remained an attentive and dutiful son to a father stricken in adversity.

In any event, when he was about 20 years old he went to London. What his first occupation was, is not known. In 1592 he emerges from the mist of obscurity as an actor and playwright who had aroused the jealousy of a fellow craftsman, Robert Greene, in whose curious *Groatsworth of Wit* he is lampooned in an ill-tempered tirade including a poor pun on his name, "the only Shake-scene in a countrie." Greene later died and the editor of his work, one Chettle, made humble apology for his part in this jealous outburst. What he said throws a floodlight on the new writer who was attracting attention. ". . . I am as sory as if the originall fault had beene my fault, because myselfe have seene his demeanor no lesse civill than he exelent in the qualitie he professes; besides, divers of worship have reported his uprightnes of dealing, which argues his honesty, and his facetious grace in writting that approoves his art."

His first essayed non-dramatic poetry was *Venus and Adonis,* published about 1593, and *The Rape of Lucrece* (1594); his sonnets were not made public until 1609. Besides the Shakespearian profusion of power and imagery, the two poems are of peculiar interest because of the epistolary dedications to the Earl of Southampton; these are the only letters of Shakespeare's that have come down to us. The sonnets (most of them superb models of this poetic form) are of peculiar interest because of the biographical hints which they are thought to contain. Some critics think the "dark lady" wholly imaginary. By 1594 he had become a leading member of the chamberlain's company of players, his name appearing among those who were paid for acting before the court. He is known to have played the ghost in Hamlet, and many years afterward his brother Gilbert is reported to have recalled seeing him as old Adam in *As You Like It*. He did not achieve unusual distinction as an actor. As a dramatist, he was the mainstay of this company for a dozen or more years, overhauling and injecting his mighty powers of characterization, his dictional witchery and incredible wisdom and insight into the mass of old manuscript which filled the theatrical archives and was public property. Under his wizard touch these dry bones sprang to life. He never took himself very seriously —"My nature is subdued to what it works in." Like most great poets, he had his formative and his transition periods, his period of highest power (and tremendous it was at its height), and the final period when his great soul sought peace in fair romance and honeyed poesy. This transcendent spirit went through the most terrific storm—*Hamlet, Lear, Macbeth, Othello*—and came safely to shore in *The Tempest, The Winter's Tale* and *Cymbeline*.

He had as much shrewdness as is consistent with a great poetic soul, a marvelous balance of faculties, and he prospered. He was part owner of the Globe Theatre. He made occasional visits to Stratford where his son Hamnet died in 1596 and where his father suffered reverses which were mitigated by his bounty. In 1597 he bought a house and gardens in Stratford, which he called New Place, and here about 1610 he settled down to quiet retirement; as James Russell Lowell said, to stand at his gate and chat with his neighbors. After the death of his parents he had become owner of his birthplace; in 1602 he had added to his possessions an estate of some hundred acres in the open fields of the town, and in 1605 had leased certain tithes in Stratford parish for £440. He wrote some, entertained his friends of the metropolis, was liked and respected. In the diary of the town clerk is an entry: "My cosen Shakespeare comying yesterday to town, I went to see him how he did." He was doubtless welcome. Drayton and Ben Jonson visited him. In March, 1616, he made a will full of well-considered and generous bequests. Much has been made of his single bequest to his wife of his "second best bed." She was probably adequately provided for in the bequest of his real estate to his daughter Susanna, who had married a Dr. John Hall. It has been thought that she may have been in some way afflicted and subject to their care. Some time in April, 1616, he was seized with a fever which terminated fatally on his birthday, April 23. The funeral was solemnized two days later when all that was mortal of the supreme voice of mankind was consigned to his final resting place in the beautiful parish church of his native town.

Washington Irving speaks of its spire as a "beacon towering amidst the gentle landscape to guide the literary pilgrim of every nation to his tomb."

A list of the plays is here given in the order in which they are thought to have been written:

Henry VI (Three parts)
Two Gentlemen of Verona
Comedy of Errors
Richard II
Richard III
Love's Labor's Lost
Merchant of Venice
A Midsummer Night's Dream
Romeo and Juliet
King John
Taming of the Shrew
Henry IV (Two parts)
Henry V
As You Like it
Much Ado About Nothing
Hamlet
Merry Wives of Windsor
Troilus and Cressida

Measure for Measure
Henry VIII
Othello
King Lear
All's Well That Ends Well
Macbeth
Julius Caesar
Twelfth Night
Antony and Cleopatra
Cymbeline
Timon of Athens
Coriolanus
Winter's Tale
The Tempest
Pericles
Titus Andronicus (authorship doubtful)

GEORGE BERNARD SHAW   1856–

GEORGE BERNARD SHAW, Irish dramatist and critic, was born in Dublin, Ireland, July 26, 1856, of impoverished Irish "gentry." His mother was a singer and the son fell early under the influence of music and the drama. He attended the Wesleyan Connexional School at Dublin until he was 15 and then became a clerk with a Dublin land agent, but in 1876 he determined upon a literary career and went to London where his mother had become a music teacher. For the next nine years he lived in poverty, with an overshadowing sense of failure, supported partly by his mother and partly by his father who had a small property in Ireland. His literary earnings in that period amounted to six pounds. Between 1879 and 1883 he wrote five novels, *Immaturity, The Irrational Knot, Love Among the Artists, Cashel Byron's Profession* and *An Unsocial Socialist,* four of which were published a number of years later in a socialistic magazine. Hearing Henry George lecture he determined to join in the single tax campaign, but a reading of Karl Marx's *Capital* converted him to socialism and in 1884 he joined the Fabian Society.

His fortunes took a turn for the better when he was engaged as book critic for the *Pall Mall Magazine* and art critic for the *World*. Later he became dramatic critic for the *Saturday Review,* still keeping up his political propaganda work, his services as a socialist speaker being in great demand. In 1891 he published *The Quintessence of Ibsenism;* in 1898 *The Perfect Wagnerite,* and between those dates he had written four plays which he published with long prefaces on social, political, biological and religious questions. From 1894 his rise to fame was rapid and he became recognized as the most brilliant man in British journalism and one of the best debaters in England. His plays, however, remained for the most part unacted. He was not accepted on the London stage until 1904 although his work had been produced in the United States and in Germany six years earlier. Richard Mansfield introduced him to America with *Arms and the Man,* followed by *The Devil's Disciple.* His first play was *Widowers' Houses,* followed by *Mrs. Warren's Profession,* one of his best plays, directed against the social evil, but it was refused a license and not acted until 1902. *Candida,* written in 1894, was given with much success in Germany and had a successful run in America. In 1898 he published his *Plays Pleasant and Unpleasant* in two volumes (a collection of his earlier plays). *John Bull's Other Island,* a satirical drama of Irish character, was the first of his plays to score a triumph in London. From the time of its production in 1904 his popularity as a dramatist was assured. Other plays were *Major Barbara, Captain Brassbound's Conversion,* written for Ellen Terry; *Fanny's First Play, The Doctor's Dilemma.*

After he had reached the age of 60 he wrote the three plays which are regarded as his masterpieces; *Saint Joan, Heartbreak House* and *Back to Methuselah.* Still later plays are *The Apple Cart,* and *Too True to be Good.* His other writings include *The Intelligent Woman's Guide to Socialism and Capitalism, Commonsense About the War, Peace Conference Proposals,* and many other works.

As a critic of art, music, the drama, and of society and social conventions he has been original and outspoken, often caustic, biased and extravagant, but always a brilliant writer and an independent thinker. By many people he is regarded as a sort of witty montebank, by others as a philosophic socialist interested in ideas rather than in dramatic action. During the World War, while staunch for the cause of the allies, his blunt criticisms of his government and adverse comments on the management of the war caused widespread resentment.

PERCY BYSSHE SHELLEY   1792–1822

PERCY BYSSHE SHELLEY, the great English lyric poet, was born Aug. 4, 1792 at Field Place, near Horsham, Sussex. His father had inherited a small landed estate and the title of baronet and Shelley was reared in comparative luxury. He was a handsome, imaginative and precocious boy. At the age of 10 he entered the Sion House Academy where he was so tormented by his schoolmates that his sensitive nature developed an intense hatred of all tyranny. Two years later he went to Eton and while there wrote two youthful romances. In 1810 he collaborated with a cousin on a poem, *The Wandering Jew,* and with his sister Elizabeth on a booklet *Original Poetry, by Victor and Cazire* (now lost). Later that year he entered University College, Oxford, from which he was expelled in 1811 with his intimate friend, Thomas Jefferson Hogg, because of a pamphlet he had published on *The Necessity for Atheism.*

The two friends went to London where Shelley met his sister's schoolmate, Harriet Westbrook. After a short acquaintance he eloped with this 16-year old girl to Edinburgh where they were married. His independence of thought and his revolutionary ideas and uncontrolled impulsiveness had led to differences and finally alienation from his family, who were conventional people although they had encouraged his early literary precocity. Two children were born to the young couple who, always in financial difficulties, lived in various places in England and in Ireland, where he went in 1812 and engaged in political agitation. On coming of age he received a small inheritance, but domestic troubles had arisen and in 1814, putting into practice his theories of liberty, he eloped with Mary Godwin. He made some financial provision for Harriet, but two years later she committed suicide by drowning herself in the Serpentine. Shelley was refused the custody of his two children on the ground that he was an atheist. Within a few weeks he married Mary who was the daughter of the radical William Godwin whose philosophy colors much of Shelley's later work. During this time of private stress he wrote *The Revolt of Islam,* a portion of *Rosalind and Helen,* and other poems.

Indications of pulmonary disease sent him, with Mary and their children, William and Clara, to Italy in 1818 where the remainder of his brief and stormy life was spent. His daughter died in Venice, his son in Rome and in 1819 in Florence another son was born who survived him (Sir Percy Florence Shelley). He finally settled near Pisa. In July, 1822, he and his friend Williams crossed the Bay of Spezzia to visit Leigh Hunt. On the return trip on July 8, their boat was lost in a sudden storm and both were drowned. Shelley's body, washed up near Viareggo on the 17th, was cremated and his ashes were interred in the Protestant burial ground in Rome, with the exception of his heart, which was not consumed.

As with Keats, Shelley's reputation as one of the greatest of English poets has increased with the passing of the years. In *Queen Mab,* written about 1813, his first important poem and one by which he became widely known, he presented a view of the world and society as he saw them. *The Revolt of Islam* is a more imaginative work which seeks to depict the moral revolution of the world. During 1818 in Venice he completed *Rosalind and Helen,* translated Plato's *Symposium,* wrote *Julian and Maddalo,* and at Este he wrote the first act of the lyric drama, *Prometheus Unbound.* Seeking a warmer climate, he went to Rome and then to Naples. *Prometheus Unbound* was completed during this period. In Leghorn he wrote most of his tragedy, *The Cenci,* and at Florence *The Mask of Anarchy* and a number of his finest lyrics and translated the *Cyclops* of Euripides. His writings in 1820–21 include *The Witch of Atlas* and *Oedipus Tyrannus,* the lyrical drama *Hellas,* the unfinished historical drama, *Charles I,* and the fragmentary *Triumph of Life.* A growing element of mystery characterizes his later work. He was a man of great personal charm, beloved by all who knew him, both men and women.

His widow, Mary Wollstonecraft Shelley, was herself a writer and after his death worked tirelessly at journalistic and other literary work in order to educate her son. Her best known work is the weird, romantic novel, *Frankenstein.*

GENERAL PHILIP HENRY SHERIDAN 1831–1888

PHILIP HENRY SHERIDAN, American general in the Civil War, was born in Albany, N. Y., March 6, 1831, of Irish parents who moved a year later to Perry County, Ohio. Winning an appointment to West Point, from which he was graduated in 1853, he served in the frontier army against the Indians and was a first lieutenant when the Civil War began. He won his captaincy soon afterwards, and in 1862 was made colonel of the Second Michigan Cavalry, serving under Halleck in Tennessee. His able strategy at the battle of Booneville (July 1) won him the rank of brigadier-general of volunteers. At the battle of Perryville (Oct. 8) he commanded the 11th Division of the Army of the Ohio under Buell; and, after the battle of Stone's River (Dec. 26) was promoted to the rank of major-general of volunteers. During the summer of 1863 he was engaged with

Rosencrans in forcing the Confederates under Bragg out of middle Tennessee. Rosencrans followed Bragg to Chickamauga where he suffered a decisive defeat (Sept. 20) and was driven back to Chattanooga, his retreat being covered by Sheridan's cavalry. The latter showed great ability in the subsequent actions around Chattanooga, especially in his charge up Missionary Ridge (Nov. 25). When Grant was placed in charge of the Army of the Potomac (March, 1864) he made Sheridan his cavalry commander.

His cavalry corps took part in the battles of the Wilderness and Spotsylvania Court House and he was sent on a raid in the direction of Richmond, destroying railroads and telegraph wires and cutting the Confederate line of communication. After participating in the battle of Cold Harbor, he led another raid toward Charlottesville (June 7–26), cooperating with Gen. David Hunter. In August, 1864, he was appointed to command the newly formed Army of the Shenandoah, whose objective was to clear the valley of Confederates. In a brilliant campaign he defeated General Early at Winchester (Sept. 19) and again at Fisher's Mill three days later and then proceeded to destroy all means of subsistence in the valley in order to make it useless to the Confederate army. He was commissioned brigadier-general in the regular army in September. On Oct. 19 during his absence the main body of his army was attacked and thrown into confusion by General Early at Cedar Creek and he made his famous 20-mile ride from Winchester to Cedar Creek, rallied his men and routed the enemy. On Nov. 8 he was commissioned major-general and from Feb. 27 to March 24 he made another raid from Winchester to Petersburg, laying waste the intervening country. In April he turned Lee's flank at Five Forks, showing great skill and courage, and forced him to retreat toward Appomattox where he surrendered to Grant on April 9, 1865.

In May, Sheridan was placed in command of troops along the Mexican border to watch the activities of Maximilian, whom Napoleon III had set up as Emperor of Mexico. His presence there was of aid in the negotiations with France and the final overthrow of Maximilian. In 1867 he was placed in command of the Fifth Military District, with headquarters in New Orleans. He advocated stringent measures in dealing with the conquered South; was recalled by President Johnson in the following September, and for 16 years was in command of the Department of the Missouri. In 1869 President Grant made him a lieutenant-general. In 1883 he was given chief command of the United States Army and five years later was made general, shortly before his death at Nonquitt, Mass., on Aug. 5, 1888. He was buried in the Arlington National Cemetery. In 1875 he had married Irene, daughter of Gen. D. H. Rucker.

RICHARD BRINSLEY SHERIDAN 1751–1816

RICHARD BRINSLEY SHERIDAN achieved fame both as a dramatist and as an orator and during his life his brilliant talents were set off by a personal charm and companionable quality which made him one of the most engaging figures of the distinguished literary group in which he moved. He possessed the ready wit, nay, all the human weakness of the lovable Irish. He was born in Dublin in September, 1751, and after attending a local public school, was sent to the famous school at Harrow in Middlesex, England, where the unanimous verdict of his instructors was that he was a hopeless dunce. His father, who was a teacher of oratory and elocution, appears to have had no plans for his son's future and young Sheridan was quite content to accept life as it unfolded from day to day. At the age of 22 he eloped with Mary Linley, a young singer of great charm and beauty, having first fought two duels for her favor. As a matter of pride he insisted that his bride relinquish her labors, with the accompanying income, and the two soon found themselves in the throes of adversity, a condition all too familiar to the impecunious Sheridan throughout his life. But his financial predicament proved a blessing to the cause of art for he betook himself to literature and in January, 1775, produced his first comedy, *The Rivals,* a play which has stood the test of time better than most of the plays of that early day, and has ever been a favorite with stars in the field of character acting, by reason of the delightful Bob Acres and the incomparable Mrs. Malaprop. It is said that there has never been a time since its original production when *The Rivals* has not been on the boards somewhere. In the course of the following year he wrote and produced a farce called *St. Patrick's Day* and a comedy called *The Duenna,* neither of which are ever now produced although, like all his work, they abound in sparkling dialogue and the latter contains several songs of merit. He next became part proprietor of the famous Drury Lane Theatre and here was produced, in 1777, the comedy which the public then and of subsequent generations has regarded as his masterpiece, the *School for Scandal.* This charming play instantly leaped into popularity and it has been many times revived by theatrical luminaries since its initial success. In 1779 his very clever farce, *The Critic,* was successfully produced but its appeal, like that of *The Stranger* and *Pizarro,* has not continued into the present century.

The versatile Sheridan meanwhile found time to engage in politics and to indulge his social inclinations in a round of diversion in fashionable and pleasure-seeking circles. He is said to have been a delightful companion when in proximity to the convivial bottle and his Irish wit scintillated in the drawing room and the public house as well as on the stage. He was returned to Parliament in 1780 for the borough of Stafford and proved not only a serviceable recruit to the Whig party but a source of lively entertainment to the entire house. His sparkling wit seemed inexhaustible and his likeable qualities made him a prime favorite but he was far from being a mere entertainer and could, on occasion, rise to stirring eloquence. His memorable speech urging the impeachment of Warren Hastings is regarded as a triumph of oratory. "It was without doubt," says Macaulay, "the most elaborately brilliant of all the productions of his ingenious mind. The impression which it produced was such as has never been equalled."

In 1792 his wife died and three years later he married a Miss Ogle whose considerable fortune did not suffice to liquidate the load of debt under which he staggered and it is questionable whether any amount of financial assistance could have corrected a condition to which the brilliant Sheridan seemed predestined by his heedless temperament. Advancing years found him sinking in pride and spirit, beset by creditors, deserted by friends who found his faltering wit and gaiety less diverting than in the days of his prosperity. It is pleasant to add that his compatriot, Tom Moore, remained loyal to him to the end and, in the poet's own words, the "moonlight of friendship consoled his decline." He died in London on July 7, 1816.

GENERAL WILLIAM T. SHERMAN   1820–1891

WILLIAM TECUMSEH SHERMAN was one of the great Union generals produced by the Civil War. He was of an English family which had emigrated to Massachusetts in 1634 and was born at Lancaster, Ohio, Feb. 8, 1820, the son of Judge Charles R. Sherman of the Ohio Supreme Court. His father died in 1829 and Thomas Ewing, a close friend of the family, adopted the boy. He entered West Point in 1836 and after graduation he saw service, as a second lieutenant, against the Seminole Indians, became familiar with much of the southern territory and at the beginning of the war with Mexico he was ordered to California as an executive in administering the local government. He married Ellen Boyle, daughter of his benefactor, Thomas Ewing, in 1850. Three years later he resigned from the army to manage the San Francisco branch of a St. Louis bank and four years later engaged in business in New York for a short time, but

1858 found him in Leavenworth, Kansas, practicing law which he had studied while in the army. The following year he was selected by the state of Louisiana to head its newly formed military college, a post which he resigned when the state seceded from the Union, although his opinions against slavery were not very pronounced, and offered his services to the government when the call for volunteers was issued.

He was appointed colonel of a new United States Infantry regiment in May, 1861, and a little later was given command of a brigade under McDowell. After the first battle of Bull Run he was made brigadier-general of volunteers and served in Kentucky under Gen. Robert Anderson, succeeding to the command of the department in October. He was relieved of this command, however, when he reported that 200,000 men would be needed for the Kentucky campaign, and was given a minor command. He served under Grant at Pittsburgh Landing and at the battle of Shiloh showed conspicuous ability which brought him a commission as major-general. He served at Corinth under Halleck; was in command of the right wing under Grant at the siege of Vicksburg; took part in the fighting against Johnston about Jackson, Miss., and was made a brigadier-general in the regular army in July, 1863. Grant was now placed in supreme command in the West and Sherman succeeded him as commander of the Army of the Tennessee and participated in the battle of Chattanooga. When Grant was placed at the head of the Union forces, Sherman was given command of the military division of the Mississippi, which included the armies of the Tennessee, the Cumberland and the Ohio. He gathered his armies, numbering 100,000 men, at Chattanooga, and in May, 1864, began his Georgian campaign. By September 1 Atlanta had fallen to him after several hard engagements in a brilliant tactical campaign and, leaving a force under Thomas and Schofield to confront Hood, who had retired to northern Mississippi, Sherman with 60,000 men began his famous march from Atlanta to the sea, destroying railroads and supplies as he went. Savannah, 300 miles from Atlanta, was reached in December, and the Confederate eastern states cut off from the western territory. In January, 1865, he abandoned his base and marched northward, defeated General Johnston and by April 13 had reached Raleigh, N. C., 500 miles from Savannah. Thomas and Schofield, who had defeated Hood, rejoined him and with 90,000 men he drove Johnston northwards, receiving his surrender on April 18th, after General Lee had surrendered at Appomattox Court House.

Sherman was promoted to be lieutenant-general in 1866 when Grant was made a full general and succeeded to the rank of general when Grant became president in 1869. After 15 years as general of the American army, he retired from service and died in New York City, Jan. 14, 1891. He was buried in Calvary Cemetery in St. Louis.

SARAH SIDDONS   1755–1831

SARAH KEMBLE SIDDONS, one of the greatest of English actresses, was born July 5, 1755, in the "Shoulder-of-Mutton" public house at Brecon, Wales, one of the twelve children of Roger Kemble, manager of a small traveling theatrical company of which she was a member from early childhood. At the age of 18 she married William Siddons, a fellow actor. While she was playing at Cheltenham in 1774 David Garrick heard praises of her work and sent his agent to see her in the rôle of Calista in Rowe's *Fair Penitent*. As a result she was offered a contract to play at Drury Lane, London, where she made her first appearance as Portia, her beauty and her fine presence making a greater impression than her acting. In 1778 she went to Bath and so great was her success in that fashionable watering place that she remained for several years. Returning to Drury Lane in October of 1782, her appearance as Isabella in Garrick's version of *The Fatal Marriage* scored such a triumph as London had witnessed but few times in the history of her stage—equaled perhaps only by Garrick's first night at that theatre in 1741 and that of Edmund Kean in 1814. From that time she enjoyed a series of triumphs.

She was probably best known for her Lady Macbeth, a tragic part which gave full scope to her genius and which seems to have fitted her personality perfectly. She was a tall woman, of great beauty of face and figure and with eyes that were expressive and impressive, while her dignity befitted the rôle. She played a large number of Shakespeare's heroines, Desdemona, Rosalind, Ophelia, Volumnia and others, in all of which she won the acclaim of the public. Next to her Lady Macbeth her greatest rôle was the part of Queen Catherine in Henry VIII, in her brother John Kemble's revival of the play in 1788. She was inevitably brought into comparison with her only rival as the world's greatest actress of that period, the French tragedienne, Rachel, who was a less finished artist, without her poise and dignity, but with a greater emotional fire. Mrs. Siddons was less successful in comedy than in tragic rôles.

Her private life appears to have been as happy and triumphant as her public career, and she enjoyed the warm regard and friendship of many of the noted personages of the day. Sir Joshua Reynolds painted her as the "Tragic Muse" (a canvas now in the Dulwich Gallery), and the famous Dr. Samuel Johnson wrote his name on the hem of her garment in the Reynolds painting. Sir Horace Walpole for a time held out against the chorus of praise that was everywhere showered upon her, but was finally won over. She made her last appearance upon the stage on June 9, 1819 as Lady Randolph in Home's *Douglas* at a benefit performance for Mr. and Mrs. Charles Kemble. She died in London twelve years later on June 8, 1831, and was buried in Paddington Churchyard. A marble statue, unveiled by Sir Henry Irving at Paddington Green in 1897, was made by Chavalliaud after the Reynolds portrait. A statue by Chantrey is in Westminster Abbey and the London National Gallery has portraits by Lawrence and Gainsborough. The Garrick Club, London, has three portraits, two showing her as Lady Macbeth by G. H. Harlow, and another which is ascribed to Gainsborough.

SIR PHILIP SIDNEY 1554–1586

PHILIP SIDNEY, English writer and soldier, was born Nov. 30, 1554, at Penshurst, Kent, the son of Sir Henry Sidney and Mary Dudley, daughter of the Duke of Northumberland. He entered Christ Church, Oxford, about 1568 and later traveled on the Continent. He was in Paris at the time of the St. Bartholomew Massacre; then visited Germany and Italy (1572–75) studying literature, languages, history and acquiring the culture and erudition of a finished English gentleman. Returning to England, he entered upon a career at court. He was not a politician, however, and did not win renown as a statesman. Early in his career he was a favorite with Queen Elizabeth who sent him in 1577 as ambassador to the Emperor Rudolph, and later to the Prince of Orange. He sacrificed the queen's favor for a time by writing in defence of his father, for whose services as Lord Deputy in Ireland Elizabeth had proved ungrateful, and he also addressed to her a "remonstrance" against her proposed marriage to the Duke of Anjou. His mother's brother, the Earl of Leicester, once one of the most powerful of English nobles, also fell under Elizabeth's displeasure and Sidney, in 1580, retired to Wilton where his sister Mary, Countess of Pembroke, lived.

In 1575 he had met Penelope Devereux, daughter of the first Earl of Essex, but he was not an ardent wooer and, in fact, seems not to have realized his love for her until 1581, a year after her marriage to the Puritan Lord Rich. The 108 love sonnets and 11 songs of *Astrophel and Stella* (1591) were probably inspired by the late awakening of his love. Perhaps for her entertainment, also, and for that of his sister he had written, while at Wilton, his pastoral romance, *Arcadia*. In 1583 he was knighted and the same year he married Frances, daughter of Sir Francis Walsingham. Two years later he arranged to accompany Drake on one of his exploring and buccaneering adventures, but a whim on the part of the queen and treachery on the part of Drake brought the plan to nothing. When Leicester was chosen by Queen Elizabeth to carry a mild English support to the Netherlands in its war against Spain, Sidney was ordered to accompany him. He saw little fighting, but conducted himself like the gallant gentleman he was in one great exploit, a successful raid on Axel in July, 1586, and a wound received in September under the walls of Zutphen, while intercepting a convoy of provisions, caused his death on Oct. 17 at Arnheim. His body was taken to England and buried in St. Paul's.

It is probable that the bulk of Sidney's literary work was produced between 1578 and 1582. Although not published until after his death, some of his sonnets and parts of his romance were known to many personages of the day. His mind was brilliant and cultivated; he had many high connections and fast friends among the great men of the time and was a generous patron of men of letters. His *Arcadia* was published in part in 1590, four years after his death. This work was never completed, but all of it that he had written was later published in 1698. It is a pastoral romance based upon the *Arcadia* of Sannazaro (1504), an involved love story with melodious poems, the euphemism and literary conceits of the time. He made of prose a fine art, with an elaborate melody that appealed to readers of the period. His *Apologie for Poetrie,* published in 1591 and afterwards called *Defence of Poesie,* was written in reply to Puritanical tirades and pamphlets against the poetic art. His *Psalmes of David,* a paraphrase in which he collaborated with his sister, remained in manuscript form until 1823, and was then published. He translated part of the *Divine Sepmaine* of G. Salluste du Bartos, but this has been lost. Sidney's death was felt as a personal loss by people of all classes and more than 200 elegies were written in his honor, the most famous of which is Edmund Spenser's *Astrophel, a Pastoral Elegie.*

ADAM SMITH   1723-1790

ADAM SMITH, British political economist, was born at Kirkcaldy, Scotland, June 5, 1723. His father who died before his birth was comptroller of customs. In 1737 he entered Glasgow University and there won a Snell exhibition which enabled him to go to Balliol College, Oxford, where he remained for seven years. In 1748 he lectured in Edinburgh where he came into contact with some of the most brilliant men of the day; among others the historian, David Hume, with whom he formed a lasting friendship. His ability was soon recognized and in 1751 he was appointed to the chair of logic at the University of Glasgow, a year later becoming professor of moral philosophy. His first book, published in 1759, was the *Theory of Moral Sentiments,* which established his reputation as a philosopher, and which is still well regarded in the field of ethics. He resigned the chair of moral philosophy to become tutor to the youthful Duke of Buccleuch, with whom he traveled on the Continent from 1763 to 1765, and in Paris he met many of the learned men of Louis XV's court; Turgot, Necker, Morellet, Helvetius, Quesnay and others. On his return he went to live with his mother at Kirkcaldy where he remained for ten years occupied with the preparation of his *Inquiry into the Nature and Causes of the Wealth of Nations,* the work by which he is best known. It first appeared in 1776; four later editions were published during his life and the work has been translated into many languages.

Soon after the death of Hume in 1776, Smith went to London where he spent most of the two following years in association with Gibbon, Sir Joshua Reynolds, Burke and other notables, but upon being appointed commissioner of customs for Scotland, he went to live in Edinburgh with his mother and a cousin. There he formed a club which was his favorite resort during the later years of his life and which with his small but excellent library, afforded his chief pleasure. His health began to decline in 1784, following the death of his mother, and after a lingering illness he died on July 7, 1790 in Edinburgh.

Most of the manuscripts which he left were destroyed in accordance with his instructions. One that he wished preserved was a paper on the history of astronomy, which he called "a fragment of a great work." His lectures on natural religion and jurisprudence were probably among the papers destroyed and perhaps the lectures on rhetoric delivered at Glasgow University, to which Hugh Blair referred in his own work on *Rhetoric and Belles-Lettres* in 1783. Smith's fundamental doctrine of moral philosophy, that "all our moral sentiments arise from sympathy, leading us to place ourselves in the position of others and partake of their feelings," did not win any very great acceptance. His fame rests on the breadth and justness and insight of his views as a political economist which he developed in his *Wealth of Nations.* Turgot had already considerably advanced the theory of political economy and Smith therefore was not the originator of the science, as he has sometimes been named, but he carried it a long step forward by the keen observation of social facts from which he drew his conclusions, discrediting the economic theories of the preceding centuries and helping to overthrow old institutions which were unsuited to society as constituted in his day.

CAPTAIN JOHN SMITH   1580–1631

JOHN SMITH, famous explorer, colonizer and soldier of fortune, was born at Willoughby, Lincolnshire, England, in 1580. Early left an orphan, he traveled on the Continent as page to the sons of a nobleman, leaving this position at the age of 16 to enlist in the French army then fighting the Spanish, and when France made peace in 1598 he joined the insurgents against Spanish rule in the Netherlands. He studied the theory of warfare and cavalry tactics and then embarked upon a career of marvelous adventures for which we have only the authority of his own narrative as proof. According to his statements he shipped from France for Italy, was thrown overboard because he was a Protestant, was rescued by a pirate ship and received a share of the booty for a Venetian prize; and then went through Italy and Dalmatia to Syria where he enlisted in the army of the Archduke of Austria against the Turks. He claimed to have invented a signaling system that enabled the army to communicate with the besieged garrison at Limbach which resulted in the raising of the siege; and later to have defeated three Turkish champions in duels before the assembled armies; then, being taken prisoner and sold as a slave, he made good his escape to Morocco and returned to England in a British warship. Investigation allows some measure of truth to these statements.

He became interested in American colonization schemes, and after the failure of a project to found a colony in Guiana, he sailed from Blackwell, Dec. 19, 1606, with 105 other emigrants, having a royal patent to establish a colony in Virginia. His name appeared on the passenger list as a planter, but when the sealed instructions were opened on sighting the Virginia coast, April 26, 1607, he was found to be named as one of the Council. He was not allowed to act in that capacity at first, however, because during the passage he had been placed under arrest on charges of sedition. On May 13 the party landed fifty miles up the James River and the settlement of Jamestown was made on a peninsula on the north bank of the river. Smith was active in the work of the colony and in June he was admitted to the Council. Fortifications were built and excursions made to procure food, mostly under his direction. He proved an excellent leader and soon became virtual dictator of the colony. In December, 1607, on one of his journeys, he was captured by Indians, but released upon his promise to pay a ransom of two guns and a grindstone. In his *Generalle Histoirie,* published in 1624, he says that he was saved from death on this occasion by the Indian princess Pocahontas, a statement at variance with the narrative in his tracts published at the time and the story is not now fully credited.

Wingfield, the first president of the colony, was deposed in September, 1608 (due partly to Smith's influence) and Ratcliffe was elected, but a year later Smith was himself formally made leader of the settlement, and in that position he enforced discipline and more thrifty methods, had a church built, strengthened the defenses and made provisions for agriculture and fishing. He made two voyages from the colony, covering about 3000 miles along the shores of Chesapeake Bay, which he mapped. In August, 1609, a new party of colonists arrived, the government was reorganized without full recognition of Smith's work and he returned to England, never to visit Virginia again.

In 1614 he made a voyage of exploration up the New England coast and prepared a map of the coast from Penobscot to Cape Cod. A storm frustrated another exploring expedition in 1615 and on a second attempt he was taken prisoner by the French. He tried again in 1617 but bad weather kept him in port, and he retired to London where he made maps and wrote pamphlets and where he died in June, 1631. He was a versatile and accomplished man whose adventurous exploits in America were the greatest of his career.

JOSEPH SMITH   1805–1844

JOSEPH SMITH, JR., founder of Mormonism, was born at Sharon, Vt., Dec. 23, 1805, removing to Palmyra, N. Y., with his parents when he was 10. Beginning at about 1820 the boy claimed to have visions and, led by one of these, so he stated, he unearthed in 1827, on a nearby hill, the golden plates on which was written, in a sort of hieroglyph, the *Book of Mormon, together with Urim and Thummim.* He published the book in 1830 after dictating a translation from behind a curtain to several secretaries. The preface contained the testimony of three witnesses who declared that they saw the golden plates and the inscriptions which Smith claimed to have translated, eight other witnesses testifying to the same thing. The Mormons accept as scriptures the Old and New Testament, the *Book of Mormon,*

The Doctrines and Covenants (revelations given chiefly to Joseph Smith), and *The Pearl of Great Price,* all of which are asserted to be fragments of the writings of Abraham and Moses, not found in the Bible but which were revealed to Smith.

In April, 1830, having obtained a number of converts, Smith founded the "Church of Jesus Christ of Latter Day Saints." The sect spread rapidly and in 1831 he established headquarters of the Mormon Church in Kirtland, Ohio, where its first Temple was built and its priesthood thoroughly organized. A first presidency was created, with Smith and two others as incumbents and twelve apostles were chosen with quorums of 70 to help them. In 1831 a Mormon colony was established in Jackson County, Missouri, on land bought from the government and consecrated by Smith as "The Land of Zion," the site of the New Jerusalem. Converts were chiefly from New England, mostly poverty-stricken abolitionists, who looked forward to possessing the country round about them, and they soon aroused the opposition of the older, slave-holding settlers who, by resorting to violence and terrorism, drove the Mormons to Clay, Caldwell and Davies Counties in Missouri (1833). The failure of the Kirtland, Ohio, bank, an unchartered Mormon institution, which closed its doors in 1837, led to a charge of evasion of the state law, aroused bitter feeling against the prophet and many converts fell away. The faithful followed Smith and Rigdon to Caldwell County, Missouri, where they joined the refugees from Jackson County and there founded the City of Far West (now Kerr), projected a temple and laid out other towns. Mormon settlers began to spread to other counties and at Gallatin an attempt was made to prevent them from voting. Armed bands of Mormons and Gentiles were soon stalking about the country and lawlessness and bloodshed prevailed. The governor ordered out the militia, the City of Far West surrendered, the Mormon leaders were captured, but on their way to trial they escaped and made their way into Illinois where they founded the city of Nauvoo (1838–39) on the east bank of the Mississippi. The church then had a membership of about 20,000, most of whom lived in Nauvoo, where Smith made his headquarters, ruling both in spiritual and temporal affairs. At this period the Mormons held the balance of political power in the state, were courted by both Whigs and Democrats and in 1844 Smith declared himself a candidate for the presidency of the United States. He had privately announced a revelation proclaiming the doctrine of polygamy and was reported to have secretly taken several wives, although this was later denied by his son. Some of the leaders revolted against polygamy; publicity was given the matter in the *Nauvoo Expositor,* and Smith had the print shop and press destroyed. The country was soon inflamed to mob fury and Governor Ford ordered Smith to surrender, pledging the honor of the state for his protection, but on June 27, 1844, a masked mob of 200 men stormed the Carthage jail where he was incarcerated and, with the connivance of the guards, shot Smith, his brother and other Mormon leaders to death.

TOBIAS GEORGE SMOLLETT 1721–1771

TOBIAS GEORGE SMOLLETT, British novelist, was born at Dumbarton, Scotland, in 1721, descendant of a family of some distinction in that region. But for his comparatively early death he would have inherited the ancestral estate in the beautiful valley of Leven. He received a good education and was afterwards apprenticed to a surgeon in Glasgow, but his studies did not so engross him as to prevent his early practice of the literary art, and at the age of 18 he went to London, taking with him an original tragedy with which he hoped to achieve success and fortune. He was promptly disillusioned and was glad to utilize his medical training in the capacity of surgeon's mate on shipboard, a position which served a valuable purpose in equipping him with the knowledge of life at sea so convincingly set forth in his famous *Roderick Random,* one of the first and best sea stories in our language. This tale, published in 1748, was immediately successful and won for its author a position second only to that of Fielding whom he nevertheless excelled in imaginative power.

In 1751 was published *Peregrine Pickle,* originating the suggestively humorous alliterative title which Dickens later adopted in *Nicholas Nickleby.* The story is more ambitious, in a literary sense, and was as successful as its predecessor. *Ferdinand Count Fathom,* somewhat inferior, but replete with lively adventure and convincing dialogue and description, appeared in 1753. In 1755 he published his translation of *Don Quixote* and shortly thereafter became editor of *The Critical Review,* a tory publication, which connection involved him in continual bickerings and political broils which must have been distasteful enough to one of his artistic temper. One ill-considered article in criticism of a naval officer resulted in his being fined and imprisoned. In 1758 he published his *History of England* from the Roman Conquest to the Seven Years War. This fairly authentic and very considerable work in four volumes is said to have been written in a little over a year, furnishing a record for rapid literary production. It partakes of the quality more or less evident in all his works of fiction, of interest sustained by clever characterization and lively writing. After a brief and unhappy excursion into politics he resumed his creative work and published *The Adventures of Sir Launcelot Greaves* followed by two volumes of travel, a political satire, *The Adventures of an Atom;* and two years later his last work, *The Expedition of Humphrey Clinker,* was brought out and haled as his masterpiece. Few now would deny it this distinction and many critics have been quite ready to agree with Thackeray who declared it one of the finest novels ever written. Weakened and disheartened by ill health and private misfortunes, he sought solace amid the Italian scenes which he loved so well and died in Leghorn on Oct. 21, 1771. In early life he had married Nancy Lascelles, daughter of a West Indian planter. Their only child, a daughter, died at the age of 15.

Smollett was the first of the early English novelists to adopt that style of writing which so differentiates the 18th and 19th century writers from those of today. His humor is not forced; his style is easy, natural and picturesque. He is comparatively free from the distressing habit of indulging in long and irrelevant digressions, but goes straight to his point and is seldom tedious or dull. If story interest and rigorous attention to it are one of the chief conditions of novel writing, then it must be conceded that he stands very high. He possessed a lively imagination and his character delineations offer convincing evidence of his creative faculty. In coarseness and sensuality it must be admitted that he rivaled Fielding, but both of these great novelists wrote in an age which was not noted for its squeamishness and it is only requisite that a writer moulded by the influences and standards of that time disclose some qualities which are independent of them to entitle him to a high place in literary history. Smollett was a great story-teller; he would have been a great story-teller in any age.

SOCRATES   circa 469 B.C.–399 B.C.

SOCRATES (sŏk′rȧ tēz), one of the most important of early Greek philosophers, was born probably in 469 B.C., although possibly a little earlier, in Athens. His father was Sophroniscus, a sculptor, and his mother, Phaenaretè, was a midwife. He received the customary education of a well-to-do Athenian youth of that period, studying geometry, astronomy, music and gymnastics. During his youth the Sophist philosophers were frequently in Athens and he mingled with them, familiarizing himself with their teachings and absorbing much of their knowledge. This association is held to have had a great influence in forming his character and determining his outlook on life. He saw service in the Athenian army in his younger days, distinguishing himself in three campaigns by his bravery and his great physical vigor. He is reported to have been indifferent to fatigue, cold or heat. Politics seems to have held no lure for him; he had found in philosophy the answer to his inner desires and satisfaction for his mental curiosity. He went to his fellow men for first hand knowledge about themselves, their actions, theories and feelings. It has been said that he was wiser than his fellow men only in acknowledging his ignorance and in always seeking to learn. He believed himself divinely called to devote himself to the education of the young.

In teaching his system of philosophy, he adopted the dialectic method, spending his time in the streets and market place, discoursing with friends and with any one interested enough to listen, propounding questions in ethics, morals, philosophy, and then aswering his own questions. He committed none of his discourses to writing, and what we know about him has been gleaned mostly from two of his disciples, Plato, the philosopher and author of *The Republic;* and the bluff soldier, Xenophon, who wrote the *Anabasis.* The latter is believed to have under estimated Socrates as a man and as a teacher, while Plato may have employed his imagination to heighten his recollections, without sufficient care for historical accuracy, yet Plato's is undoubtedly the more accurate presentation of the great thinker. He presents for us the habits and the conversation of Socrates in such a manner as to show us a man with a wide knowledge of mankind, born of his insatiable curiosity and his eternal questioning.

From the picture which we have from his friends, Socrates was ugly in appearance, indifferent to the ordinary comforts of life and lived the life of an ascetic, content with the most meager fare and wearing but a single garment. Xenophon records that Socrates' wife, Xanthippe, was of shrewish temper and that her husband bore her waspish tongue with patience as a means of self-discipline. He held public office only once, in 406 B.C., when he was one of the "Senate of Five Hundred," the members of which were chosen by lot. He referred on various occasions to the "divine sign," a supernatural voice which guided him. Probably this "divine sign" as well as his skepticism in regard to the gods and religious matters, made him unpopular with the Athenians, who considered him blasphemous. After the restoration of democracy he was charged (in 399 B.C.) with neglecting the gods, introducing new divinities, and corrupting the morals of youth, and was placed on trial. Plato gives what is in all likelihood Socrates' defense, in which the philosopher made a bold vindication of his entire life. He was found guilty, however, by a small majority, those voting against him probably being angered by what must have seemed to them insolence and obstinacy on the part of the philosopher. He spent his last day in talking with his friends and in the evening he drank the fatal hemlock.

Socrates' teaching was aimed chiefly against ignorance; he had sought always to base conduct on knowledge; he was chiefly preoccupied with ethics and his teachings have been well summed up in the formula, "Virtue is knowledge; vice is ignorance."

SOLON   circa 640 B.C.–559 B.C.

SOLON (sō'lŏn), enrolled as one of the seven wise men of Greece, was the most famous lawgiver of ancient times. He was born in Athens about 640 B.C. and was one of a distinguished family. His father, Execestides, is said to have squandered his resources almost to the point of penury, which made it necessary for the son to engage in trade. This, however, did not deter him from writing amatory poems, a pastime which he seems to have abandoned for the more practical pursuits of politics and arms. His earliest participation in public affairs was during the contest between Magara and Athens for the possession of Salamis, when at the head of a body of volunteers, he conquered the island. Henceforth his public career was conspicuously noble and honorable. He was outstanding as a wise and unselfish patriot, seeking always and wisely to compose the social and political distractions that rent his native city. In 594 B.C. he was chosen archon, or chief magistrate, and invested with almost dictatorial powers. The nature and extent of the legislation for which he was responsible has been the subject of much critical inquiry in modern times; for a sort of legend grew up about him and he has been deemed the father of all wise laws enacted in his time and country.

In order to alleviate the wretchedness arising from the existing relations of debtor and creditor, he proposed and carried out a noble measure, the "disburdening ordinance," designed to relieve the lower classes from the burden of debt which weighed so heavily upon them. From redressing the grievances of a particular class, he next proceeded, at the solicitation of his countrymen, to remodel the constitution, and here the qualities that are popularly associated with his name, shine out conspicuously. Abandoning the theory which regarded the nobles alone as worthy of citizenship, and of the honors of public preferment, he introduced the principle of classifying citizens according to their wealth and prosperity; the effect of which was not to wrest *all* power and dignity from the well-born classes, but only to give a portion of it to others who might be as wealthy, and therefore presumably as intelligent, as they. He distributed the citizens into four classes. The first embraced all those whose yearly income reached 500 medimni; the second, those of between 500 and 300 medimni; the third, those between 300 and 200; and the fourth, those whose incomes were below 200. The first three classes were liable to direct taxation; the remaining class was not. With regard to the boule, or deliberative assembly, of 400, it appears that he left it the strictly aristocratic body that he found it. Its power, however, was practically limited by a new ecclesia, or assembly of the four classes, whose ratification was necessary to all measures originating in the boule, or upper house. On the other hand, the ecclesia itself could originate nothing, and thus the members of the Attic aristocracy would check each other's assumptions.

That part of Solon's legislation relating to the industrial pursuits of the people appears to have been as excellent and well-considered as the rest, but the number of his special enactments is so great that it is quite impossible to enumerate them. They embraced almost every subject of social and political importance; and the best testimony of their wisdom and value lies in the fact that when Peisistratos violently overthrew the political constitution established by his kinsman, he allowed the latter's social legislation to stand.

After he had completed his prolonged labors as a lawgiver Solon is said to have left Athens and spent about ten years in foreign travel. During his absence the old dissensions among the Athenians broke out anew and after he returned he struggled in vain to repress them. A strong hand, as well as a wise head, was needed and the conspiracy of Peisistratus was quite as much one against anarchy as against the constitution. After Solon's defeat he withdrew into private life, but occasionally assisted with advice his bold, ambitious and able, if tyrannical, kinsman.

The date of his death is not known.

SOPHOCLES   circa 495 B.C.–406 B.C.

SOPHOCLES (sŏf'ō klēz), one of the greatest of Greek tragic poets, was born, probably in 495 or 496 B.C., at Colonus, not far from Athens. Little is definitely known about the events of his life. His father's name was Sophillus and he seems to have been a pupil of the musician Lamprus, and to have been chosen to lead the chorus of boys in the celebration of the victory of Salamis (480 B.C.). The probable date of his birth is deduced from this occurrence, and the date of his death from allusions to it in

Aristophanes' *Frogs,* and in a lost play of Phrynichus. At about the age of 28 he entered into competition with the great tragic poet, Æschylus, who was then 58, and was awarded the victory over him in 468 B.C. Æschylus, who had won in thirteen poetic contests, is reported to have been greatly chagrined at losing to this young rival for poetic honors.

Sophocles made his home in Athens, but was frequently sent on embassies to other Greek states. That he must have had considerable military ability is indicated by the fact that Pericles appointed him as one of his generals in the Samian war (440–439 B.C.). He was famed for his piety and played a conspicuous part in the civic life of Athens, serving as general, treasurer of the public funds and ambassador. His life must have been a full one, with many opportunities of meeting the great men of his day, not only in Athens, but in the other Grecian cities to which he was sent from time to time. Aristophanes bears witness to his amiability in his play of *The Frogs,* and his earliest known biographer states that Sophocles welcomed the release from the passions that old age brings. The story that his son Iophon accused him of being incompetent to manage his own affairs rests only on the very unsubstantial authority of Satyrus, although Cicero also quotes it.

Tradition has it that Sophocles, due to the weakness of his voice, was the first poet who ceased to act in his own plays. Many minor improvements in stage decoration and carpentry have been attributed to him. It is also stated that he wrote his plays with certain actors in mind for the important rôles, that he was the first of the Greek dramatists to introduce more than two characters on the stage, and Aristoxenus says that he was the first dramatist to use Phrygian melodies.

All of Sophocles' minor poems, elegies, etc., and many of his plays have perished. Of more than 100 dramas which he is said to have written, but seven remain complete although fragments and titles of 90 others have been traced. His first drama was *Triptolemus.* It is considered probable that preservation of the seven extant plays was due to their selection for educational purposes in Alexandria. *Antigone* is believed to have been the most popular of his plays in ancient times, with *Oedipus Coloneus* attracting a special, small group. *Ajax, Electra* and *Oedipus Tyrannus* were read chiefly by Byzantine students, and more copies of these exist than of his four other surviving plays. It is considered probable that *Ajax* may have preceded *Antigone* in time of composition, while the *Electra* is believed to have been a later product than *Oedipus Rex. The Trachinian Maidens* shows a transition to a milder mood. The *Philoctetes* was produced in the year 408 B.C. when Sophocles was 87, while *Oedipus Rex* is said to have been brought out by his grandson in 402 B.C. after the poet's death which occurred about 406 B.C.

HERBERT SPENCER 1820–1903

HERBERT SPENCER, outstanding among British philosophers, was born April 27, 1820, at Derby, England, the son of a nonconformist schoolmaster who interested him in entomology. He attended school at Hinton for several years but at the age of 17 became a railway engineer, surveyor and designer of railroad lines and bridges and remained in that occupation for eight years. He had contributed several articles to professional journals, and in 1842 wrote a series of essays on *The Proper Sphere of Government* for the *Nonconformist*. From 1848 to 1853 he was an assistant editor on the *Economist,* developing the ethical and social views which found expression in *Social Statistics* (1850) and in the essays and reviews which he contributed to various publications, such as *The Development Hypothesis* (1852), *Manners and Fashions* and *The Genesis of Science* (1854), *Progress: Its Laws and Cause* (1857). In his *Principles of Psychology* (1855) (several years before Darwin published the *Origin of Species*) he began to apply the doctrine of evolution to various fields of study. Until he was 30 he had no thought at all of philosophy, and one of his secretaries, Collier, tells us that he never finished reading any book of science. His information was gained mainly through observation. He had a curious and insatiable mind which stored away and classified the bits of knowledge thus acquired. He pumped Huxley and other friends until their minds ran dry of information.

Spencer made many inventions but none of them gained any commercial success. He was practical minded with no interest in poetry or art. Having an exceptionally logical mind, he was one of the clearest expositors of complex subjects that history can show. In 1860 he announced his proposed *System of Synthetic Philosophy,* which was to begin with the first principles of all knowledge and trace the law of evolution in life, society and morals; a tremendous task for a man nearing 40, in ill health after a complete breakdown, unable to endure more than an hour of mental work at a time, and without an income. He conceived the idea of getting advance subscriptions for his proposed books which would enable him to live from hand to mouth while he was writing them. He submitted his outline to Huxley, Lewes and other friends who obtained for him an imposing list of subscribers including Kingsley, Lyall, Tyndall, Buckle, Froude, Herschel and many others. The published prospectus brought him 440 subscriptions from Europe and 200 from America, which promised him an income of $1500 a year.

He then set to work upon his *First Principles,* but upon the publication of the book in 1862 many subscribers withdrew because of his attempt in Part I of that work to reconcile science and religion. A "battle of the books" raged over his *First Principles* and Darwin's *Origin of Species,* with Thomas Huxley leading the forces of evolution and agnosticism. John Stuart Mill offered to guarantee the publisher of Spencer's next book against loss, as a public service—an offer which Spencer rejected; but when his American admirers bought $7000 worth of securities, the income from which was to go to him, he accepted their gift and resumed his writing. His *Principles of Biology* was published in 1864–67; and *Principles of Psychology* in 1870–72; *Principles of Sociology* in 1876–96; *Principles of Ethics* in 1879–93. In the preface to the third volume of the *Principles of Sociology* (1896) he explained that a proposed fourth volume—Linguistic, Intellectual, Moral and Aesthetic—must remain unwritten due to his age and infirmity.

He died Dec. 8, 1903, and later in that year his *Autobiography* and a supplemental *Life* were published. He profoundly influenced scientists and philosophers of his own and succeeding generations through the application of the theory of evolution to every field of study.

BENEDICTUS DE SPINOZA   1632–1677

BENEDICT SPINOZA, Dutch philosopher, was born in Amsterdam, Nov. 24, 1632, of Portuguese-Jewish descent. His father had fled from Portugal to the Netherlands to escape Catholic persecution. The boy was carefully trained in Jewish theology, but he early developed an independence of thought and was soon won away from orthodox doctrines. Influenced by such Jewish scholars as Farrar, Acosta and Prado, he declared to other students that there was nothing in the Bible to support the teachings that God has no body, that angels exist as real beings, and that the soul is immortal; or that the supposed writer of the Pentateuch knew more of physics or theology than did the Amsterdam students. He was excommunicated by the Jewish authorities, who sought in vain to silence him by threats and bribes in order to free themselves of responsibility for his statements to the civil authorities in a country where the Jews were not yet citizens. He continued to attend the synagogue and addressed an *Apology* to the synagogue authorities, defending his views. At 24 he stood almost alone. His ex-Jesuit, ex-bookseller Christian friend, Francis van den Enden, took him into his home, engaged him to teach in his school and gave him an opportunity to improve his Latin and Greek and study philosophy. He learned to grind lenses by which work he supported himself during much of his life.

After his excommunication he was at Ouwerkerk for a time making his living by working on lenses and by tutoring. With some young theological students who wished to learn Hebrew, he formed a sort of reading or discussion club and made friends with them. They were opposed to Calvinism and were mostly adherents of the Cartesian philosophy. The period of his mental storm and stress subsided about 1660 and he retired to Rhynsburg, near Leyden, and there wrote his *Short Treatise on God, Man and his Well-being, Treatise on the Improvement of the Understanding,* part of his *Geometric Version of Descartes Principia* with the appendix on *Metaphysical Thoughts* and the first book of his *Ethics.* He remained in Rhynsburg for ten years, until 1670, with occasional visits to Amsterdam and a stay at Voorburg. He became acquainted with many noted thinkers of the day and sent parts of his writings to the study circle he had helped to form. His *Ethics* was nearing completion in 1665, but he put it aside to write a tract on the Scriptures (published anonymously in 1670), *Tractatus Theologico-Politicus,* written to pave the way for his *Ethics* by vindicating freedom of thought that would at the same time serve the interests of the Republic.

After the publication of the *Tractatus* he moved to the Hague to be near influential friends. His book created a stir, five editions being published in five years. In 1671 he went to stay with the Van der Spycks and made his home with them for the rest of his life. He began a *Hebrew Grammar* but broke off to resume work on his *Ethics.* In 1672 the French invaded unprepared Holland, which suffered many reverses. The populace, seeking a scapegoat, murdered the brothers Jan and Cornelius de Witt. Spinoza prepared a placard which he intended to post at the scene of the murder but was prevented by Van der Spyck, who locked him in and thus undoubtedly saved his life, for his *Tractatus* was denounced as "forged in hell by a renegade Jew and the devil, and issued with the knowledge of Mr. Jan de Witt."

Spinoza refused the invitation of the Elector Palatine to the chair of philosophy at the University of Heidelberg because he wished to have no restrictions upon his thinking, and scornfully declined to dedicate a work to Louis XIV in order to secure a pension. He preferred to live in the most straitened way rather than place himself under obligation. He died Feb. 20, 1677 and was buried in the New Church on the Spuy, at the Hague. His influence upon the thought of his own and succeeding generations has been wide and far-reaching.

MADAME DE STAËL   1766–1817

ANNE LOUISE GERMAINE NECKER, known as Madame de Staël (stä´ĕl), was the only child of Jacques Necker, banker and French Minister of Finance, and was born at Paris on April 22, 1766. Her literary ambitions were awakened early and even in her girlhood she wrote romantic plays and novels and a number of essays. Her first published work was *Lettres sur Rousseau* in 1789, three years after her marriage to Baron de Staël-Holstein, the Swedish ambassador to France.

She was prominent in French social and literary life, brilliant, vivacious, filled with enthusiasm and with a great capacity for affection. Her personality was compelling and she attracted to her Paris salon the great personages of the time. Her social reign in the capital was interrupted by the French Revolution with which she sympathized in the early days, but after the King's imprisonment and the fall of her father from power, her feeling changed and in 1792, being forced to leave Paris, she took up her abode in Coppet near Geneva. She traveled a great deal, however, and in England in 1793 she became the centre of a circle of *émigrés* which included Talleyrand. Her devotion to Marie Antoinette led to the writing and publishing, after her return to Coppet that same year, of her *Réflexions sur la Procès de la Reine,* in an attempt to save the life of that ill-fated queen.

In 1795 her husband was again Swedish Ambassador to France and she returned to Paris with him, anxious for active participation in politics. Her *Réflexions sur la Paix intérieure,* published that year, was with that end in view, but resulted in her receiving a strong hint that she should return to Coppet where she continued her writing and the following year published *Influence des Passions.* She was permitted by Napoleon to return to Paris in 1797, but he was one of the few men who did not fall under her influence, and her admiration for him turned to dislike if not to actual hatred. In 1798 she separated from her husband who was bankrupt, in order to protect her fortune for her three children.

Her *Littérature et ses Rapports avec les Institutions Sociales,* coming from the press in 1800, brought her still more into the public eye and upon returning to Paris in 1802 her salon was soon as popular as ever— a gathering place for the learned, the literati, artists, politicians and soldiers. Her father's *Dernière Vues* appeared about this time and that publication, together with her association with Constant, Moreau, Bernadotte and other disaffected men, led Napoleon in the autumn of 1803 to banish her from Paris and she was ordered to keep at a distance of forty leagues from the capital. Her husband was dead, and she took her children and went to Weimar, where her social and personal charms and her brilliant mind soon brought Goethe, Schiller and the whole court to her feet. She visited Berlin and met August Schlegel, the philosopher, and intended next to visit Vienna, but the death of her father called her back to Coppet where she wrote her eulogy *Du Caractère du M. Necker.* After a visit to Italy with Schlegel, von Humboldt and Bonstetten, she returned to Coppet and wrote her romance of *Corinne,* which established her literary fame throughout Europe.

Towards the end of 1807 Mme. de Staël again visited Germany and the religious side of her character began to gain ascendancy. She finished her book on *De l'Allemagne* in 1810; it was passed by the censor and was partly printed when the edition was seized and destroyed and she was ordered back to Coppet. In 1811 she was secretly married to Albert de Rocca, an Italian officer, after which she went to Berne, St. Petersburg, Stockholm and London. In 1814 Louis XVIII welcomed her to Paris, from which she was again driven by the return of Napoleon from Elba. She died in Paris, July 14, 1817, and was buried at her father's feet in Coppet.

Although not a great writer in a literary sense, Mme. de Staël, with her boundless enthusiasm and her confidence in human progress, was largely responsible for the romantic movement in French literature. Among her other published works were *Delphine, Lady Jane Gray* and many political pamphlets.

SIR HENRY M. STANLEY 1841–1904

SIR HENRY MORTON STANLEY, writer and African explorer, was born at Denbigh, Wales, June 10, 1841, the son of John Rowlands. He was left an orphan at two years old, lived in a workhouse for several years and then with various relatives, and at 18 he worked his way as cabin boy on a ship to New Orleans. There he obtained employment with a merchant named Stanley and eventually took his name. He enlisted in the Confederate army in 1861, was captured at the battle of Shiloh, and after two months' imprisonment at Camp Douglas, Chicago, was released and joined the Federal artillery, from which he was shortly discharged as unfit after a severe illness. He returned to Denbigh but was turned away from his mother's home. He next enlisted in the United States Navy (1864) and became a ship's writer. In 1867 he was employed by the *New York Herald* and as special correspondent for that newspaper he was sent with Lord Napier's British expedition to Abyssinia.

In 1869 James Gordon Bennett, the owner of the *Herald,* commissioned him to go to Africa to search for David Livingstone, British missionary and explorer who had been in the heart of the Dark Continent so long that fears were entertained throughout the world for his safety. Stanley first went to Suez for the opening of the Canal and then traveled through Palestine, Persia and India, reaching Zanzibar in January, 1871. In March he started into the heart of the African wilderness and in November he found Livingstone ill and helpless at Ujiji on Lake Tanganyika. He nursed the older man back to health and the two explored the northern end of the lake. Then, as Livingstone refused to leave Africa, Stanley left supplies with him and returned to England in 1872. The English Royal Geographic Society awarded him a medal and his book, *How I Found Livingstone,* had a large sale in all English-speaking countries. He followed the Ashanti campaign for the *Herald* and was then commissioned jointly by it and the London *Daily Telegraph* to take up the exploration of the interior of Africa where Livingstone had left off at his death. He set out from Zanzibar in November, 1874, making direct for Lake Victoria Nyanza. He traveled entirely around that lake; established friendly relations with the Uganda tribe through their king, Mtesa; explored Lake Tanganyika, went down the Lualaba to Nyangwé, and traced the course of the Congo all the way to the sea. His experiences on this ten-months' expedition are described in his book, *Through the Dark Continent.* The following year he was commissioned by the King of Belgium to return to Africa where he labored hard to establish what later became the Congo Free State. In 1884 he attended the Congo Congress at Berlin, and lectured on his travels in both England and America with great success.

In 1886 he was placed in command of an expedition to go to the relief of Emin Pasha (the Silesian Eduard Schnitzer, whom General Gorden had made governor of the Equatorial Province in the Egyptian Sudan, and who had been completely cut off there). In March Stanley landed at the mouth of the Congo and with 650 men pushed inland, reaching Yambuwa in the middle of June. Leaving nearly half of his men there, he pressed on and reached Lake Nyanza and Emin Pasha in April, 1887, after much hardship and the loss of many of his men. He then marched eastward to Bagamoyo, reaching it in December, 1889, having discovered Albert Edward Nyanza Lake and Mount Ruwenzori, and through these explorations paved the way for the British East African Protectorate. The following year he was awarded a gold medal by the Royal Geographic Society, received honorary degrees from several universities, and married

Miss Dorothy Tennant, an artist. He became a naturalized British subject in 1892 and sat in the House of Commons from Lambeth (1895–1900). He made another visit to Africa in 1897 and died in London on May 10, 1904.

He has given the world more knowledge of Africa than any other man. Besides the books mentioned he wrote *My Kalulu,* a novel (1873); *Coomassie and Magdala* (1874), *The Congo* (1885), *In Darkest Africa* (1890), *My Dark Companions and their Strange Stories* (1893), *My Early Travels in America and Asia* (1895), and his *Autobiography,* published in 1909.

SIR RICHARD STEELE   1672–1729

SIR RICHARD STEELE, English essayist and playwright, was born in Dublin, Ireland, in March, 1672. Early left an orphan, his uncle, Henry Gascoigne, secretary to the Duke of Ormonde, took charge of his education and sent him to the Charterhouse in 1684, where he met Joseph Addison. Later he entered Christ Church, Oxford, but soon changed to Merton. In 1694 he enlisted in the Life Guards and in the following year published *The Procession,* a poem on the death of Queen Mary. His dedication of this poem to Lord Cutts resulted in the latter's making him his secretary and getting him an ensignship in the Coldstream Guards. In 1701 he published *The Christian Hero,* a religious treatise supposedly called forth by his having severely wounded an opponent in a duel the previous year. He next wrote a comedy, *The Funeral; or Grief à la Mode,* which was performed at Drury Lane in December, 1701. This was followed by two other plays, *The Lying Lover* (1703) and *The Tender Husband* (1705), all of which are now practically forgotten except by the student of dramatic lore.

In the meantime he had been commissioned a captain in Lord Lucas' Regiment of Foot, and had engaged in researches for turning baser metals into gold. He married, in 1705, Margaret Stretch, a widow with property in Barbadoes, who died after about a year. The following year he became gentleman in waiting to Prince George of Denmark, consort of Queen Anne, and in 1707 he was appointed Gazeteer. He then secretly married Mary Scurlock, the "Prue" who figures in his correspondence.

In 1709 he founded *The Tatler* and upon its demise in 1711, *The Spectator,* which became one of the most famous of English literary publications of the century. To this paper both he and his friend Addison contributed many essays which became famous in their day and which are among the best specimens of good English style. The *Spectator* ceased publication in December, 1712, and was followed in March of the next year by the *Guardian,* with which Steele and Addison were both associated. Steele later started other shortlived publications. At about this time through his pamphlets he became involved in a partisan political quarrel with the satirist, Dean Swift. Steele supported the Hanoverian succession and in its behalf wrote his pamphlet, *The Importance of Dunkirk Considered,* to which Swift replied with the grimly vitriolic *Importance of the Guardian Considered.* When he was returned to Parliament for Stockbridge, Steele dropped the *Guardian* for the political *Englishmen,* and published his Hanoverian pamphlet, *The Crisis,* to which Swift replied with *The Public Spirit of the Whigs.* Some of Steele's utterances in *The Crisis* brought about an impeachment and he was expelled from the House. Following the death of Queen Anne, however, his party again came into power and he was returned to Parliament, knighted, made deputy lieutenant of Middlesex and governor of the royal company of comedians. Probably the best of his political pamphlets is *Mr. Steele's Apology for Himself. The Plebeian* involved him in an unpleasant controversy with his old friend, Addison. For two years, following the suppression of the Jacobite rebellion, he was in Scotland as commissioner of forfeited estates.

In 1722 he again turned to the writing of comedy and *The Conscious Lovers,* his best and most successful play, was performed at Drury Lane, of which he had now become one of the patentees. He also founded the Censorium, a music hall of the better class. His second wife had died in 1718 and he had been deprived of most of his offices following a difference with the government over the Peerage Bill, but when Horace Walpole became Chancellor of the Exchequer he was reinstated.

He was always improvident, generous and carefree, lived in ostentatious style far beyond his means, and was nearly always in debt. In 1724 he was obliged to retire to his second wife's estate of Llangunnor in Wales and he died on Sept. 1, 1729, at Carmarthen, where he was buried in St. Peter's Church.

STENDAHL   1783–1842

Henri-Marie Beyle, French novelist and essayist, who took the pseudonym of Stendahl (stän'däl'), was born at Grenoble, Jan. 23, 1783. He attended the École Centrale in Grenoble from 1796 to 1799, excelling in mathematics; then went to Paris and studied for a time for the École Polytechnique, but abandoned his intention when a relative, Pierre Daru, secured for him a place in the War Office, and later the same year sent him to Italy where he established himself at Novara and later at Milan. He became a sub-lieutenant in 1800 but resigned his commission in 1802 and returned to Paris. He later attempted a business life in Marseilles and in 1806 became a deputy to the *commissaire des guerres.* For two years he lived in Brunswick. Appointed editor to the *Conseil d'Etat* in 1810, he took part in the Russian campaign and became *intendant* at Sagan in 1813. After the fall of Napoleon he went again to Italy where he remained from 1814 to 1821, spending six years in Milan. There he became acquainted with Byron, Madame de Staël and with Pellico and other Italian literary notables.

Under the name of L. C. A. Bombet, he published in Paris in 1814 *Les Lettres acrite en Vienne,* a volume mostly on music. In 1817 he published *L'histoire de la peinture en Italie, par M.B.A. (Beyle, ancien auditeur)* and the same year appeared his *Rome, Naples et Florence,* containing impressions of Italian life, music, patriotism, etc. Suspected of espionage and of being one of the carbonieri, he returned to Paris in 1821, became friends with Mérimée and other literary figures and also traveled in England, contributing articles to various English and French publications.

He published his *Vie de Rossini* in 1823 and in 1829 *Les Promenades dans Rome,* a collection of anecdotes, descriptions of manners, customs and art, which met with small success. In 1838 appeared another book which had grown out of his many travels, *Les Mémoires d'un Touriste,* but he was also engaged at the time in work of a more original character. *De l'amour,* which was published in 1822, is a mingling of the physiology and the psychology of love with which his future novels were to be intimately concerned. The first of these, *Armance ou quelques scènes d'un salon de Paris en 1827,* was a study in his theory of the "crystallization," or birth and growth, of love. *Le Rouge et le Noir* (1830), a story of love and ambition, based upon a famous scandal of the time, is told with psychological insight, with characters that are full-blooded and with dramatic incidents developed in a most realistic manner.

In 1831 Stendahl was appointed French consul at Civitavecchia. He explored Naples thoroughly, made excavations in the papal territory, visited Rome and Paris, and in 1840 published his romance, *La Chartreuse de Parme.* This was highly praised by Balzac in the *Revue Parisienne,* which did much to establish Stendahl's fame as a writer of remarkable power, and he had just closed a contract to write for the

Revue des deux Mondes when he suffered an apoplectic attack and died on March 22, 1842. He was buried in the cemetery of Montmartre.

Stendahl himself believed that his writings would not be appreciated until long after his death, possibly not until fifty years had passed, but long before that time elapsed he had been accorded a high place among French writers of the nineteenth century. A number of his works were published as late as the 1890's; some of them of an autobiographical nature; *Le Vie d'Henri Brulard, Souvenirs d'Egotisme, Lucien Leuwen;* the *Journal d'Italie* appeared in 1911. His letters to his adored younger sister, *Lettres à Pauline,* contain a charm not to be found in his other works.

GEORGE STEPHENSON   1781–1848

GEORGE STEPHENSON, English inventor and one of the foremost engineers of the 19th century, was born at Wylam, near Newcastle, England, on June 9, 1781, the son of Robert Stephenson, fireman of a colliery engine. His early boyhood was spent in farm work and at 14 he became assistant to his father and was quickly advanced from one job to another in the colliery. Meantime he attended night school where he learned to read, studied hard and made rapid progress. He was interested in the inventions of James Watts and Boulton, and he also studied watch and clock making by which he was able to add to his meager wages.

The year 1804 found him at Killingworth, engaged in various jobs in the colliery there. In 1812 he was made engine-wright of the High Pit, having by that time acquired a thorough working knowledge of engines and pumping machinery. He still spent his spare time in scientific pursuits and in 1815 invented a miner's safety lamp which would not cause explosions of the mine gases. Sir Humphry Davy invented a similar lamp at about the same time and there was much controversy as to rights.

Stephenson's greatest contribution to the mechanics of the day had been begun before this date, but its fulfilment was yet in the future. He had persuaded the owners of the colliery to let him build an engine which would travel over the tramroad between the Killingworth colliery and the port of lading nine miles away. Such an engine had been experimented with at Wylam. On July 25, 1814, a trial of his engine, which was named the "Blucher," was made and it proved to be a success. In 1822 when the Stockton and Darlington railway was under construction, he prevailed upon the directors to use steam on the new line instead of horses, and was authorized to build an engine for that purpose. He set to work on a locomotive which he named the "Active," but subsequently renamed it "Locomotion." The new railway was opened on Sept. 27, 1825, and on that day for the first time in history a public passenger train was drawn by steam power instead of by animal traction.

His work for the Stockton and Darlington led to his engagement to build the Liverpool and Manchester railroad. He succeeded in laying the tracks across Chat Moss, a difficult engineering feat for that period. It had been intended to have the trains hauled by fixed engines, but Stephenson urged the use of the locomotive. A prize of 500 pounds was offered for an engine suitable for the purpose and Stephenson built the "Rocket" which won the award and an order was immediately placed for seven other engines. The principal features of the "Rocket" were an improved steam-blast for urging the combustion of coal and a boiler in which a large heating surface was gained by the use of many small tubes, through which passed the hot gases. The cylinders, instead of being vertical as in previous locomotives, were set at a slope and later on changed to a position more nearly horizontal. The Liverpool and Manchester railway was opened in 1830 with eight engines built at the works started at Newcastle in 1823 by Stephenson, his cousin, Thomas Richardson and Edward Pease.

Stephenson later made many improvements in the locomotive, was consulting engineer for all the new railway projects shortly started in England, and also was consulted regarding the construction of roads on the Continent which he visited in 1846, being received with great honors. In 1847 he founded the Institution of Mechanical Engineers and was its first president. His later years were spent at Tapton House, Chesterfield, in farming and horticulture, and there he died on Aug. 12, 1848.

ROBERT LOUIS STEVENSON   1850–1894

ROBERT LOUIS BALFOUR STEVENSON, Scottish novelist and poet, was one of the outstanding literary figures of his generation and one of the most beloved of authors. Born Nov. 13, 1850, the son of Thomas Stevenson, engineer and builder of lighthouses, the son was educated for the same profession and entered Edinburgh University in 1867, but three years later he decided to study law and was called to the bar in 1875, having in the meantime only partially recovered from a serious pulmonary trouble. His literary inclinations soon caused him to desert the legal profession.

His first books, *An Inland Voyage* (1878) and *Travels With a Donkey in the Cevennes* (1879), were the result of journeys afoot and by canoe in France. *Virginibus Puerisque* (1881) contains some of his most charming essays and *The New Arabian Nights* was a venture in grotesque and macabre story-telling.

His first great success was won with *Treasure Island,* a romance of pirates and hidden gold, which still remains a favorite and has been produced as a play and as a motion picture. *Prince Otto* appeared in 1885 and was later dramatized. *Kidnapped* (1886) is another masterpiece in his best romantic vein. *The Black Arrow* (1888) and *The Master of Ballantrae* (1889) were less successful. Of his poetry, *A Child's Garden of Verse* (1885) ranks as his best and most enduring. Other volumes of verse are *Underwoods* (1887) and *Ballads* (1891). *The Strange Case of Dr. Jekyll and Mr. Hyde* (1886), inspired by a dream, is probably, with *Treasure Island,* the most widely known and popular of his books. It was later dramatized and met with great success on the stage. Others of his books are *The Merry Men, Island Nights Entertainments;* three books written in collaboration with his step-son, Lloyd Osbourne, *The Wrong Box, The Wrecker* and *Ebb Tide; David Balfour* which was a continuation of *Kidnapped;* and the unfinished romances, *Weir of Hermiston,* a noble fragment which promised complete fulfilment of his genius (published in its incompleted form after his death); *St. Ives,* which was completed by A. T. Quiller-Couch, and *The Waif Woman* which was not published until 1916.

Always in delicate health, Stevenson's indomitable will and splendid courage, his happy spirit, his gifts as a conversationalist, the gaiety and charm which permeated his writings, won him the friendship of most of the great literary figures of his time. His correspondence was wide and his collected *Letters* rank among his most charming and graceful writings. He traveled extensively in search of health, but his first trip to the United States, made in 1879, was due to the illness in San Francisco of Mrs. Fanny Osbourne, whom he had first met in Paris in 1876. Because of his limited means he embarked on an emigrant ship and the long journey across the Atlantic as a steerage passenger and then across the American continent wrecked his own already shattered health. These experiences formed the basis of *The Amateur Emigrant* and *Across the Plains.* After a visit with Mrs. Osbourne in San Francisco he went to Monterey hoping there to regain his strength. Somewhat restored, he returned to San Francisco, and on May 19, 1880, married Mrs. Osbourne, who had in the meantime been divorced. They returned to England soon afterwards, but throughout his life they were almost incessantly traveling in search of a climate which would prove beneficial to his health, trying Switzerland,

France, the Riviera, the Scottish Highlands, and the Adirondack Mountains. They spent a winter at Saranac Lake in New York State where the house they occupied has been preserved as a Stevenson Museum. Finally he chartered a schooner and sailed among the islands of the Pacific, eventually settling in Samoa in 1890, where he built his island home, Vailima. There he spent the final years of his life, industriously writing and interesting himself in the politics of the island where he gained a position of influence. The natives named him Tusitala, the "teller of tales," looked upon him as a friend and honored him at his death, which took place suddenly on Dec. 3, 1894. By his own desire he was buried on a mountain top behind his Samoan home.

HARRIET BEECHER STOWE   1811–1896

HARRIET ELIZABETH BEECHER STOWE, American novelist, whose best known work, *Uncle Tom's Cabin,* was one of the most widely read and most influential novels in all literature, was born June 14, 1811 at Litchfield, Conn., the daughter of Rev. Lyman Beecher and sister of Henry Ward Beecher. After the death of her mother in 1815, she was cared for by her elder sister, Catherine, who a short time later established a school at Hartford, where Harriet was first a pupil and later a teacher. In 1832 her father gave up his six years' pastorate in Boston to become president of Lane Theological Seminary in Cincinnati. Catherine Beecher accompanied him, eager to establish a pioneer college for women in which Harriet was her assistant. The latter took an active part in the school and literary life of Cincinnati, contributed stories and sketches to local newspapers, and compiled a school geography. In 1836 she married Rev. Calvin Ellis Stowe, one of the professors in the theological seminary and an ardent abolitionist. She continued to write and in 1843 published *The Mayflower, or Sketches of Scenes and Characters among the Descendants of the Pilgrims.* For 18 years she lived in Cincinnati and during that time came into contact with some fugitive slaves and learned much about the slave system of the South. That experience, together with her own observations during visits in the southern states, made her a determined enemy of the slavery system.

In 1850 her husband was elected to a professorship in Bowdoin College, Brunswick, Maine, and there she began to write *Uncle Tom's Cabin, or Life Among the Lowly,* as a sort of religious message to her fellow countrymen. It was published serially in the *National Era,* an anti-slavery periodical of Washington, D. C., appeared in book form in March, 1852, and very quickly achieved wide popularity. It was later translated into 23 languages. No novel ever had a more timely publication and it became one of the contributing factors in the Civil War and the freeing of the slaves. In reply to many criticisms and some attacks she wrote *A Key to Uncle Tom's Cabin,* which reinforced her story with many documents and testimonials evidencing the evils of slavery. In 1853 she visited Europe, partly in an attempt to bring about a sympathetic understanding between English and American women on the question of slavery. Her next story, *Dred; A Tale of the Dismal Swamp,* published in 1856, was an attempt to show the deterioration of a society which tolerated slavery. Upon the founding of the *Atlantic Monthly* in 1857 she became a regular contributor to its pages and the *Independent* of New York and the *Christian Union,* under the editorship of her brother, Henry Ward Beecher, published much of her work. The best known of her later novels is *The Minister's Wooing,* published in 1859. *Pearl of Orr's Island* (1861) is a study of the country folk of New England, whom she knew so well, and is said to have influenced Sarah Orne Jewett in the choice of subject matter for much of her fiction. Mrs. Stowe wrote many stories, sketches and essays on social life, published a small volume of religious poems and several novels of quiet New England life, and in her later life gave a number of public readings from her works.

From 1852 to 1863 the Stowes lived at Andover, Mass., where Mr. Stowe was a professor in the theological seminary, and in 1863 they removed to Hartford. After the Civil War ended Mrs. Stowe bought an estate in Florida hoping that life there would benefit the health of her son, Captain Frederick Beecher Stowe, who had been wounded in the war, and they spent many winters thereafter in Florida. In 1868 she assisted Donald G. Mitchell in editing *Hearth and Home.* Her husband died in 1886 and from that time on the author of *Uncle Tom's Cabin* lived in seclusion at her Hartford home, where she died on July 1, 1896; she was buried beside her husband in Andover.

RICHARD STRAUSS   1864–

RICHARD STRAUSS, German composer, was born in Munich, June 11, 1864, the son of Franz Strauss, a popular hornist, who gave his son a thorough musical education. The boy played the piano when he was four years old, and wrote his first composition at the age of six. He studied music under the court conductor, F. W. Meyer, and received a liberal education at the gymnasium and the University of Munich. Bülow and Ritter helped to form his musical taste and inspire his interest in the modern development of music. He succeeded Bülow as conductor of the Meiningen orchestra in 1885, but resigned a few months later to travel in Italy. He was appointed third conductor of the Munich Opera under Hermann Levi in 1886 and four years later became court conductor at Weimar where he attained such fame as composer and conductor that he was recalled to Munich as first conductor in 1894, in which year also he married Pauline de Ahna, a popular singer. In 1898 the Royal Opera Company of Berlin offered him a ten-year contract and during this connection he made extensive concert tours through Europe and in the United States.

Strauss's reputation as a composer may be said to have begun in 1887 when his *Macbeth* was played, followed the next year by a slightly earlier composition, *Don Juan.* He aroused something of a sensation with his *Tod und Verklärung* in 1889. His first opera, *Guntram,* produced in 1894, brought him much fame but the work has failed to hold its place in operatic repertory. *Till Eulenspiegels Lustige Streiche,* of the same year, is considered a most brilliant example of the rondo form showing a sense of fun that has made it one of his most popular compositions. In 1895 he published his symphonic poem, *Also sprach Zarathustra* (inspired by Nietzsche's book of the same name) which aroused no little discussion and opposition. He is considered to have reached his greatest height as a musical realist in his next work, *Don Quixote* (1898). This was followed by *Ein Heldenleben* (1898) and *Symphonia domestica* (1904).

Although his first opera (written under the influence of Wagner) had little success, *Feuersnot* attracted some attention and was conducted by Sir Thomas Beecham in London in 1910, while his *Elektra* at Covent Garden played to crowded houses and aroused the most heated discussion because of the sensationalism of his treatment of the theme. *Salome* appeared on the operatic stage in Dresden in 1905 in a startlingly novel musical setting. Regarded as a more important work and one that is more frequently heard is *Der Rosenkavalier,* tenderly gay and romantic, which was first performed in Dresden in 1911 and has been included in the repertory of most grand opera companies since that time. *Ariadne auf Naxos,* originally forming part of a musical setting for Molière's *Le Bourgeois Gentilhomme,* but later rearranged as a work by itself, was his next composition. This was followed by the dramatic ballet, *The Legend of Joseph,* and *Die Frau Ohne Schatten* (The Woman Without a Shadow), performed for the first time in Vienna in 1910, which is considered to contain some of his finest music. He next wrote both text and score for his "comic play-opera," *Intermezzo,* and the ballet-pantomime, *Schlagobers* (Whipped Cream) which had their premières in Vienna in 1924. The *opera, Helen of Egypt,* was first performed in 1928.

Strauss has won perhaps his most widespread popularity by his many songs, which have securely established him as a great master of melody.

PETER STUYVESANT   1592–1672

PETER STUYVESANT (stī' vå sånt), one of the early Dutch governors of New York, was born in Holland in the year 1592. He entered the military serv-ice of the West India Company about 1625 and for ten years directed the company's colony at Curaçoa (1634–1644). In April of the latter year he was wounded in an attack on the Portuguese island of Saint Martin and compelled to return to Holland where his leg was amputated. The West India Company appointed him in 1645 to supersede William Kieft as director of New Netherland and he was received with great enthusiasm upon his arrival in New Amsterdam (later New York City) on May 11, 1647. He conducted the government well, made many improvements and conciliated the Indians who had been made antagonistic by their treatment under the former administration, and for a time held the confidence of the colonists.

In 1650 he settled boundary disputes with the New England colonies in a way which granted to them considerable territory which the Dutch burghers felt was rightly theirs. The people had been demanding a greater share in the government of the colony and a voice in the appoint-ment of local officers, but Stuyvesant, who was violent and despotic in temperament, opposed them, maintaining that his first duty was to the Company. In 1653 he arbitrarily ordered an assemblage of delegates to disperse. He thus estranged the more important of the burghers and further opposition was aroused among the citizens of New Amsterdam by his efforts to increase the revenues of the West India Company, to im-prove the city's defences, and by his attempt to prohibit the sale of liquor to the Indians which had been a source of much revenue to the merchants. His persecution of the Quakers and Lutherans also estranged so many citizens that the Company eventually ordered him to discontinue those activities.

He was more successful in his attack upon the Swedes who in 1654 seized Ft. Casimir (Newcastle) which had been built by the Dutch. He sailed up the Delaware in 1655, recaptured the fort, defeated the Swedes and brought an end to their influence in that region. He used great vigor in suppressing various uprisings on the part of the Indians, notably in the years 1655, 1658 and 1663.

In 1664, Charles II granted to his brother, the Duke of York, the territory between the Connecticut River and Delaware Bay, and an expedition was sent out to take possession. Stuyvesant believed, from instructions sent him from Holland, that the expedition was against New England and made no preparations for defence until the fleet of four ships with three or four thousand men was almost at the city's gates. Their commander, Col. Richard Nicolls, demanded the surrender of the city. Stuyvesant at first refused, but the burghers failed to support him and there was nothing for him to do but to surrender the city, which he did on Sept. 8, 1664.

Returning to Holland in the following year, he was made a scapegoat by the West India Company for its own failures in New Amsterdam. Following the treaty of Breda in 1667, he returned to New York, having obtained the right of free trade between New York and Holland, and settled on a large farm called the Bouwerie (from which the New York City street now called the Bowery, derives its name). There he died in February, 1672. He was buried in a chapel on the site of which St. Mark's church was built in 1799 and an inscribed stone which covered his grave was built into the wall of the church.

SUN YAT-SEN   1867–1925

DR. SUN YAT-SEN (more familiarly known in China as Sun Wen) was a Chinese revolutionary leader who became the father of the Chinese Republic. He was born in 1867 at Hsiang Shan near the island of Macao, where his father was a poor farmer. He was converted to Christianity at an early age. In 1891 he entered the newly established medical school in Hongkong, was its first graduate (1894) and then practiced medicine for a year. While at this school he had formed a friendship with Sir James Cantlie and had become interested in a project to overthrow the Manchu dynasty. In 1895 he narrowly escaped with his life when the first revolutionary plot in which he took an active part was discovered and its leaders arrested and executed. This was an attempt to incite a revolt at Canton which failed and only he escaped. He fled from China and became active in interesting Chinese throughout the world in his revolutionary plans. In 1898 he adopted the three fundamental principles of nationalism, democracy and socialism, to be worked out through governmental, legislative and judicial means and through civil examinations and a department of censorship; and in 1905 he publicly announced his adherence to those principles.

In 1900, following the Boxer outbreak, he made an unsuccessful attempt to form a democratic party in China for the overthrow of the Manchu régime. A Chinese Revolutionary League was formed in Europe in 1905, enlisting the support and financial aid of Chinese in Europe and America. With the money thus raised he conducted secret propaganda operations in China. The Manchu government finally put a price of $50,000 on his head, and he was seized in London and held prisoner in the Chinese Legation until a note smuggled out to his old friend, Cantlie, caused the British government to demand his release. The anti-Manchu feeling had developed considerable strength by 1911 and through the influence of Sun and his adherents this feeling was consolidated into a revolutionary force through the organization of the Kuo-min-tang (Republican or Nationalist) party. At the outbreak of the revolution in 1911 Sun left England and returned to his native land where he was elected provisional president of the new republic by the National Convention in Nanking. On Feb. 2, 1912, an imperial edict was promulgated, announcing the abdication of the emperor and the establishment of the republic. Dr. Sun called upon Yuan Shih-K'ai to carry through the political transformation, and a short time later resigned the presidency to Yuan, realizing that he himself could not unite the country under his own administration. He remained in the new government as Director-General of Transport and Trade, but his activities were mostly of a propagandist nature.

He became increasingly dissatisfied with Yuan's leadership and after the latter's *coup d'etat* and death in 1917, he put himself at the head of a movement for an independent Republic of South China. Unable to cooperate with the military leaders of Canton, however, he soon resigned. In 1921 Ch'en Ch'iung-ming drove out the Kwang Si troops and recalled Dr. Sun. Sun and Ch'en split on policy in the following year, Sun wishing to advance against the North with an army while Ch'en favored consolidating republican power in Kwang-tung, and Sun fled to Shanghai, but in 1923, with the aid of troops from Kwangsi and Yunnan, he met and defeated Ch'en. He was chief executive of the province until his death, although his sway did not extend much farther than Canton. He used violent methods, burning and looting a part of Canton in 1924, and attacking the Merchants Volunteer Corps. He lost much overseas support, but the mass of workers and the student class of his party supported him. When Feng Yü-hsiang and Chang Tso-ling combined to put Tuan Ch'-jui in power they invited Dr. Sun to Peking to join in calling a people's conference and there he died of cancer on March 12, 1925. Despite his having adhered to the Christian religion throughout his life, he was buried at his own request by the ancient Chinese rites.

EMANUEL SWEDENBORG   1688–1772

EMANUEL SWEDENBORG was a Swedish scientist, mystic and philosopher, born at Stockholm on Jan. 29, 1688, the son of Jasper Svedberg, who was later bishop of Skara. He was educated at Upsala University and traveled for several years in England and on the Continent, following which he was appointed to an official position at the College of Mines. During this period he did much scientific studying and writing, contributing greatly to the development of the science of geology, and placed his skill as a military engineer at the service of Charles XII. In 1719 his family was ennobled and took the name of Swedenborg. Up to the age of 55 he devoted himself to science and philosophy. Mathematics claimed much of his attention and he published several treatises on algebra; on decimal money and measures; on sluices and docks; and on various phases of astronomical observation; the movements of the planets; a method of determining longitude at sea by the position of the moon; on the depth of the ocean and the force of the tides; and also on certain chemical subjects. At 36 years of age he declined the offer of a professorship at Upsala because purely speculative science did not appeal to him and for some years following devoted himself to his duties as assessor of mines and to the preparation of a detailed description of mining and smelting which was published in Leipzig in 1734 in three large volumes, entitled *Opera Philosophica et Mineralis*. The formulation of a theory of the origin of creation had also engaged his mind during these years and was fully set forth in his treatise entitled, *The Infinite, and the Final Cause of Creation; and the Intercourse between the Soul and Body* (1734). That he might trace the soul to its inmost recesses in the human body, he took up the study of anatomy and physiology and published two exhaustive treatises embodying the results of his investigations; *Æconomia Regni Animalis* (1741) and *Regnum Animale* (1744–45).

In 1743 he claimed to receive a revelation and to have his spiritual senses opened and from that time he lived as a seer, spending his time in meditation and in the cultivation of his visions and dreams. The history of this transition period from worldly life to an existence of strange communings with the unseen world is contained in a diary which he kept during the year 1744 and which was discovered and made public more than a hundred years later. He resigned his assessorship in 1747 that he might have more leisure for his heavenly visions. He claimed to have free access to the "three heavens" and the "three hells" and to have made several journeys to those regions, associating freely with the people of the spiritual world, as if he himself had died. He disavowed any resurrection of the body and described a World of Spirits in which a sojourn is made after death where the good are cured of their infirmities and intellectual mistakes and the evil are relieved of any pretensions to good. He declared that in the other world "thought brings presence;" if one spirit wishes to see another, the desire instantly brings them together. The three heavens are peopled by three orders of angels, natural, spiritual and celestial, and man after death continues to grow and may advance from one heaven to another.

He spent his time between Stockholm, London and Amsterdam and published several works embodying his spiritual experiences and his views. The most notable, *Arcana Cælestia,* was published in London in 1749–56, in Latin like all his works. There followed *The New Jerusalem* and *The True Christian Religion.* In his later years he attacked Protestant theology, but he made no attempt to establish a new religious sect and it was not until 1788, some six years after his death, that The Church of the New Jerusalem (or Swedenborgians), founded on his writings, was organized as a separate body in London. Swedenborg never married. Except for his visions there was nothing peculiar about him. He was genial, shrewd in worldly matters and able in discussions of politics and public affairs. He enjoyed the confidence and love of all who knew him and his sincerity was so manifest that no word of ridicule ever reached him, even from those who disbelieved most strongly in his visions and his views. He was simple in his habits of life and a vegetarian in diet. It is said that he paid no attention to the difference between night and day and would sometimes lie in a seeming trance for days together, although at other times his intercourse with spirits seemed to be perfectly natural when he was wide awake with all his faculties alert.

He died in London on March 29, 1772. In 1908 at the request of the Swedish government his remains were removed to Stockholm from the Swedish church in Princes Square, London, where they had first been deposited.

Such intellectuals as the poet Coleridge, the Brownings, Henry Ward Beecher and Thomas Carlyle have been greatly influenced by the writings of Swedenborg and modern psychology is attaching significance to his theory of the relation of the membranes of the body to the elements of the universe.

JONATHAN SWIFT   1667–1745

JONATHAN SWIFT was the foremost of English satirists, a master of irony and ridicule and skilled in a style notable for its flexibility, simplicity and force. But his pen did not "run and laugh," as was said of that other master of ridicule, Voltaire; rather did it sneer. He casts a shadow in English literature and his misanthropy and scorn of erring human nature make him one of the most unpleasant figures in the category of great writers. By an ironic caprice of fate, he was born among (though not of) a race noted for generosity, kindly impulse and good cheer—the Irish— and he first saw the light of day in Dublin on Nov. 30, 1667. His parents were English and he was a posthumous child. It is said that the condition of almost squalid poverty in which he was reared by unfortunate relatives galled him and inspired the bitterness which he so powerfully expressed. After attending Kilkenny School he entered Trinity College, Dublin, where for about seven years he was an indifferent student. Through his mother's efforts he was later received into the household of Sir William Temple as a sort of secretary. Meantime he studied, preparing himself for a clerical career and at 27 secured a small living in Ireland, but two years later returned to his former employment, remaining until after Sir William's death in 1698. He then filled several church offices in Ireland, including the vicarage of Laracor secured through the influence of Lord Berkeley. From 1713 until the end of his life he was dean of St. Patrick's Cathedral in Dublin, and the association with his name has given this church an abiding interest for readers the world over. He had already written a number of poems and prose pieces, among them *The Tale of a Tub,* a highly satirical work replete with wit and fancy, regarded by many as his masterpiece.

He had a keen interest in politics which seems to have availed him little in the matter of preferment, and he put his blasting satire at the service of the Tory party, but his bitter lampooning of the Whigs is of little interest to subsequent generations and these pasquinades and satires have not the vital quality to stand without the original prop of their timeliness and local significance. Indeed, but little literature of an abiding appeal has emanated from such minor tempests in teapots. The death of Queen Anne demoralized Swift's party and he thenceforth showed less interest in English political affairs, but transferred his sympathies to the Irish and identified himself with their problems, resisting with his acid pen and otherwise the attempt by an English patentee to supply Ireland with copper money (Wood's copper coinage), which made him for a time a popular hero. In 1726 he went to London to arrange for the publication of *Gulliver's Travels,* the unique work which was to make his name resplendent in English literature. This satirical masterpiece has found a vast audience in the nursery (although in abridged form), as well as in the scholar's library, and to multitudes of children Lemuel Gulliver is an enchanting giant. In this elaborate satire the author's cutting lash descends upon current politics, the court of George I, and subjects the Royal Society and Sir Isaac Newton to ridicule. The relentless contrast between the wisdom and sensibility of the animal kingdom and the follies and vices of the human race is carried to an extreme which Sir Walter Scott describes as "severe, unjust and degrading." The work abounds in the richest irony, is full of wit, invention and analogy and establishes its author as a creative genius of the first order.

He participated, with Gay, Pope and others, in the publication of a book of *Miscellanies,* and then returned to Dublin where the rest of his unhappy life was spent. Although he never married, there was romance in his life which has been the subject of much inquiry and speculation. Two women, known as Stella and Vanessa, were in some way bound up with this gloomy misanthrope and although it is believed that neither knew the utmost intimacy with him there is no doubt that both suffered the pangs of humiliation and blighted hopes. This phase of his life has aroused much interest among latterday students who have viewed him as a psychological problem and inferred from his incomplete affairs some physical defect in himself. In any event, a complete mental breakdown brought his career to an end. Thwarted ambition and the natural recoil of his own heartless invective increased his bitter disgust with the world; the premature death of Stella (who was a Miss Esther Johnson) shortly after the publication of *Gulliver,* severed his only remaining tie of personal affection. Passing from mental weakness to violent lunacy, he died on Oct. 19, 1745 in his deanery in Dublin where he had for several years been under the care of professional keepers.

ALGERNON CHARLES SWINBURNE   1837–1909

ALGERNON CHARLES SWINBURNE, English poet, was born in London, April 5, 1837, the son of Admiral Charles Henry Swinburne. His childhood was passed at his father's estate in the Isle of Wight and at the Northumberland home of his grandfather. He attended Eton and then Balliol College, Oxford (1857). *The Queen Mother* and *Rosamond,* two poetic dramas from his pen, were published in the year that he left Oxford (1860) and attracted much attention for their verve and dramatic quality. In London soon afterward he began his memorable ten years' literary friendship with Dante Gabriel Rossetti and also became associated with other outstanding literary figures of the time. With a brilliant mind, a wide knowledge of ancient and modern literature, a memory that retained impressions and facts, he became an important figure in the literary world. In the fall of 1862 he lived at 16 Cheyne Walk with Rossetti and George Meredith. In 1864 he visited France and Italy and the following year was a fertile one for him. His lyrical tragedy, *Atalanta in Calydon,* appeared, quickly followed by *Chastelard* and *Poems and Ballads.* The latter volume was the subject of much criticism, but its lyric quality swept his contemporaries off their feet and won for its author a place at the head of English lyric poets—at the age of 30. To the moralists whose sensibilities were shocked by certain poems in the volume, he made a scornful reply in *Notes on Poems and Reviews.*

The death of a favorite daughter caused Admiral Swinburne to remove from the Isle of Wight to Holmwood, near Reading; and the poet entered upon a life of gaiety in London. In 1867 he published the *Song of Italy;* in 1871, *Songs Before Sunrise,* and in 1874 a new lyric drama, *Bothwell,* continuing the story of Mary, Queen of Scots, which had been begun in *Chastelard* and was completed in *Mary Stuart* (1881). In 1876 came *Erectheus,* inspired by Greek literature. His *Study of Shakespeare* appeared in 1879; a second series of *Poems and Ballads, The Modern Heptalogia,* an essay in parody; *Songs of the Springtides* and *Studies in Song* in 1880. At about this time he formed his most lasting friendship—that with Theodore Watts-Dunton, at whose home, The Pines, in Putney, he spent the last 30 years of his life. Watts-Dunton took the poet in charge at a time when he was seriously ill and in the peace and quiet of The Pines, under his friend's watchful care, Swinburne recovered his health and the remainder of his life was passed in peaceful literary pursuits.

Tristram of Lyonesse was published in 1882 and in successive years thereafter *A Century of Roundels, A Midsummer Holiday, Marino Faliero, Locrine. Astrophel* appeared in 1894, followed by *The Tale of Balin, Rosamund, Queen of the Lombards, Duke of Gandia* and a collected edition of his poems and dramas in eleven volumes. In his early career he had written a novel in letter form, *Love's Crosscurrents,* published serially in the *Tatler,* revised and published in book form in 1905. His last published work, *The Age of Shakespeare* (1909), was as vigorous and arresting as the product of his maturity.

The ardor and vehemence and the spirit of rebellion against the established social order which characterized much of his earlier work and often exposed him to criticism, gave place in his later quiet life to a gentler mood. Love of nature, of the sea, of children, became evident. He was an artist in verse, a master of rhythmic technique, and introduced many new forms into English prosody. His prose work also shows much of the rhythm and resonance and passion of his songs. He died of pneumonia at Putney on April 10, 1909.

WILLIAM HOWARD TAFT   1857–1930

WILLIAM HOWARD TAFT, 27th president and 10th chief justice of the United States, was born in Cincinnati, Ohio, Sept. 15, 1857. He graduated from Yale University in 1878, studied at the Cincinnati law school and was admitted to the Ohio bar in 1880. The following year he was assistant prosecuting attorney of Hamilton County, resigning in 1882 upon his appointment as United States collector of internal reveue for the first district of Ohio. He resumed his law practice in 1883, was assistant solicitor of Hamilton County from 1885 to 1887, and then filled a vacancy as judge of the Superior Court of Ohio until 1888 when he was elected to that office. In 1890 he became solicitor general of the United States and in 1892 United States circuit judge for the sixth district. From 1896 to 1900 he was also professor and dean of the law department of the University of Cincinnati.

The period of his political accomplishment began with his appointment by President McKinley as president of the Philippine Commission in 1900. On the establishment of civil government he became governor of the islands in 1901 and served until February, 1904. In a personal interview with Pope Leo XIII in 1902 he arranged a matter of confiscated church lands, and returned to the States in 1904 to become Secretary of War. When the United States took charge of the affairs of Cuba upon the downfall of its own government in 1906, Taft was placed in temporary charge of the island. The following year he inspected the Panama Canal, visited Cuba and Porto Rico, and then the Philippines where he opened the first legislative assembly in October, 1907. While Secretary of War, he reorganized plans for constructing the Panama Canal and appointed George W. Goethals as engineer in charge of the project.

Taft was Theodore Roosevelt's own choice for his successor as president of the United States and defeated William Jennings Bryan in 1908 by a popular vote of 1,269,000. As president he urged tariff revision to give greater protection to American business; a postal savings bank system, a strong navy and the adoption of a federal budget. He called a special session of Congress in March, 1909, to pass a new tariff bill, and signed the resulting Payne-Aldrich bill in August. He negotiated identical treaties with England and France in 1910, which he signed in August, 1913. He favored the free passage of American ships through the Panama Canal and a bill embodying his views was passed by Congress but later modified, removing the discrimination in favor of United States ships. Anti-trust laws were vigorously enforced during his administration and the dissolution of the Standard Oil monopoly and the tobacco trust was secured. He was an ardent advocate of peace with foreign countries.

A split in the Republican party in 1912 and the candidacy of Roosevelt on a third (Progressive) ticket lost him the following election to Woodrow Wilson, the Democratic nominee. Upon retiring from office, he became Kent professor of law at Yale (1913); was subsequently elected president of the American Bar Association, and became a promoter of the League to Enforce Peace. He supported the war policies of President Wilson by whom he was appointed a member of the National War Labor Board. In 1921 President Harding appointed him Chief Justice of the United States Supreme Court, which post he held until ill health forced his retirement on Feb. 3, 1930, and he died in Washington on the 8th of the following March.

In 1886 he had married Miss Helen Herron of Cincinnati who became the mother of his three children. He was the author of a considerable number of works on civic and legal subjects.

HIPPOLYTE ADOLPHE TAINE   1828–1893

HIPPOLYTE ADOLPHE TAINE, French critic and historian, was born at Vouziers, France, April 21, 1828, son of an attorney who, dying in 1840, left a modest competence to his widow and three children. He attended the College Bourbon and later the École Normale, where he was refused the fellowship in philosophy which it was generally believed that he deserved. Appointed to a professorship at Toulon in 1851, he exchanged it for one at Nevers, but because of his failure to express approval of Louis Napoleon's *coup d'etat,* he was removed to an inferior position, following which he obtained leave of absence and started to write the essays on La Fontaine and his *De personis Platonicis,* which decided his career. He received his doctor's degree in 1853 and at once set to work upon an essay on Livy in a competition offered by the Academy. His offering awoke much opposition and the competition was postponed until 1855 when Taine toned down passages which had been objected to and the work was crowned by the Academy. An illness in 1854 compelled him to abandon his cloistered existence of hard work, following which he lived with his mother on the Isle Saint-Louis, mingled with old friends and made many new ones. He began to contribute to the *Revue de l'Instruction publique* and the *Journal des Débats*. In the former he published a series of articles on 19th century French philosophers, later issued in book form, in which he attacked the theories of the philosopher Victor Cousin and sketched a system in which the methods of exact science were applied to psychological and metaphysical research. This book was a great success.

In 1856 his *Histoire de la Littérature Anglaise* was announced which was not published until 1863. The following year he sent the volume to the Academy to compete for the Prix Bordin; it was violently attacked and although defended by the historian, Guizot, it was finally decided to make no award of the Prix Bordin. In the meantime he had published in 1858 *Essais de Critique et d' Histoire,* and in 1860 *La Fontaine et ses Fables* and a second edition of *Philosophes Français*.

His employment as a professor in the École des Beaux Arts in 1864 gave him some leisure for travel and study. He published several volumes and his various series of lectures during this period on the history of art are considered models. In 1868 he married Mlle. Denuelle, made a long stay in England where he took copious notes, and in 1870 published *Théorie de l'Intelligence,* followed in 1872 by *Notes sur l'Angleterre*. In 1878 he was elected to the Academy.

During the Franco-German war he abandoned his critical and philosophical writings for politico-social pamphlets and essays. In 1871 he began to write *Les Origines de la France Contemporaine,* and in 1884 gave up his professorship that he might devote his entire time to that greatest of all his works, which he was destined, however, to leave unfinished. It consisted of three parts; *Ancien régime, La révolution and Régime moderne,* and constituted a careful inquiry into the reasons why individual initiative in France was subservient to centralization and why the central power (whether in one man or in the Assembly) was the sole power of the country. He asserted that the French Revolution did not establish liberty, but simply caused absolutism to change hands, and that France was already a centralized country in 1789 and from that time on grew increasingly centralized. He was the spokesman of the period following French romanticism. Many of his works have been translated into various languages. He died in Paris, March 9, 1893, and was buried in Savoy on a hill overlooking Boringe.

TALLEYRAND 1754–1838

CHARLES MAURICE, DUKE DE TALLEYRAND-PÉRIGORD, French statesman, was born Feb. 13, 1754, at Paris, the eldest son of Comte Talleyrand de Périgord. Owing to an accident in childhood which made him permanently lame, he was educated as a clergyman but although he was brilliant and talented and eventually became a bishop, he lacked moral purpose and a genuine interest in the church. In 1775 he became Abbott of St. Denis and in 1780 agent-general to the French clergy. While in this lucrative position he began to interest himself in the government and in public affairs and showed himself an astute administrator although given to excesses in his private life. In 1789 he became Bishop of Autun, was elected by the clergy of his diocese to the States-general and was made one of the Assembly Committee to draw up a constitution for the nation, having won the good will of the popular party. Although occupying the office of bishop he proposed the confiscation of the landed property of the church. Early in 1790 he was elected president of the National Assembly. Still asserting his attachment to the Holy See, he consecrated two bishops in 1791, but soon afterwards was himself excommunicated and compelled to resign from his bishopric.

He was responsible for some of the excellent changes made in the French educational system. With relations between France and England on the point of rupture, he was sent to London in 1792 in a vain attempt to win over the hostile minister, Pitt. Being suspected of royalist sympathies he was placed upon the list of *émigrés* and remained in England until the Alien Act was passed in January, 1794, when he fled to the United States.

The guillotining of Robespierre was the signal for him to return to Paris (1795). Two years later, largely through the influence of Madame de Staël, he was made foreign minister. He was among the first to recognize the genius of Napoleon and became his ally and supporter in the overthrow of the Directory and the establishment of Napoleon as first consul and later as Emperor. He was instrumental in breaking up the coalition against Napoleon formed by England and some of the European states in 1805, was of great aid to the Emperor in organizing the Confederation of the Rhine in the following year, and was created Prince de Bénévento by Napoleon. He later retired from the ministry. His services under the First Empire were of great value to France as well as to the Emperor and he played well the rôle of wise statesman. He later opposed Napoleon's invasion of Russia, thus paving the way for his desertion of the latter in 1814 and his heading of the opposing faction. He opened communication with the leaders of the European coalition against the Emperor as well as with the heads of the House of Bourbon, dictated to the Senate the terms of Napoleon's deposition, and was rewarded by being made minister of foreign affairs by Louis XVIII.

Talleyrand deserves credit for preserving France's boundaries in the treaties with the Allies (1792), and for upholding her right to be heard in the Congress of Vienna, although during the Hundred Days that followed Napoleon's escape from Elba he was of little help to Louis. After the second restoration, he became prime minister for a time, but he had become unpopular with the nobility and soon gave up the post. After the accession to the throne of Louis-Philippe he was sent as ambassador to London where he was able to compose the differences between France and the British court and brought about the Quadruple Alliance between England, France, Spain and Portugal. He returned to France in 1835 and died on May 17, 1838.

Talleyrand stands as one of the most skilful and unscrupulous politicians of his time, but is no longer regarded as a great statesman. He was brilliant, cynical and corrupt, a skeptic in religion and with a peculiar talent for working on the lower motives of his associates.

TAMERLANE (TIMŪR)   1336–1405

TAMERLANE (TIMŪR I LENG, TIMŪR THE LAME) a Mongol potentate and conqueror, was born in 1336 at Kesh, near Samarkand, in what is now southeastern Russia, but was at that time a part of the great region of Central Asia known as Turkestan. He was the son of Teragai, head of the tribe of Bėrlas. He became an adept in outdoor sports and by the time he was 20 had won a certain reputation as a reader of the Koran. By 1358, when he was 22, he was a leader of armies and most of the remaining years of his life were spent on the battlefield. In 1365 the Kalmucks, a nomadic people of the Mongol race who had overspread Turkestan some five years previously, were driven from the country and Tamerlane and his brother-in-law Hessain became joint rulers. They had shared many dangers and romantic adventures and now became rivals for power. In 1369 war broke out between them, Hessain was killed and Tamerlane became the sole sovereign and was crowned at Samarkand.

There was no cessation in the wars he waged; after overcoming domestic foes, he invaded the territory of neighboring potentates and added portions of their possessions to his own domain. To the west and northwest he reached the land of the Mongols at the Caspian, along the banks of the Ural and the Volga, while his conquests to the south and southwest included almost every province of Persia; even Baghdad, Kerbela and Kurdistan. In 1398, when he was past 60 years of age, he invaded India which was at that time disrupted by civil wars. On September 12 he arrived at the banks of the Indus, crossed the river and proceeded upward along its left bank, meeting little resistance, capturing and destroying towns, massacring the inhabitants. An attempt was made by the natives to halt him before Delhi, but Tamerlane defeated them as easily as he had captured the small towns and entered Delhi in triumph. In April, 1399, he was back in his own capital of Samarkand with an immense quantity of spoils which he used for the adornment of his capital. It is said that on one occasion when the number of prisoners taken had become so numerous as to constitute an embarrassment to him he slaughtered 100,000 of them.

Soon after returning from India, he devastated Georgia (1401) and then marched against the Turks to aid some of the deposed princes of Asia Minor who had appealed to him for help. Upon his request to the Sultan of Turkey to reinstate these princes, the Sultan (Bayezid) replied in such insulting terms that war was inevitable, and after his activities in Syria and Mesopotamia Tamerlane defeated the Turks and captured Bayezid in a great battle near Angora (1402). He possessed himself of the Sultan's treasure, captured many Turkish cities, took Smyrna, Aleppo, Baghdad and Damascus, and returned to Samarkand in 1405. He was preparing for a campaign against China and was encamped on the farther side of the Sihon when he was attacked by a fever and died at Atrār (Otrar) on Feb. 17, 1405. His body, embalmed in musk and rose water, was sent in an ebony coffin to Samarkand.

Despite his ruthlessness in warfare, he seems to have been a just and kindly ruler in time of peace and to have showed qualities of statesmanship. He did much to encourage interest in arts and science throughout his domain.

BOOTH TARKINGTON 1869–

Newton Booth Tarkington, American novelist and playwright, was born in Indianapolis, July 29, 1869, son of Hon. John Stevenson Tarkington. He studied at Phillips Academy in Massachusetts, then at Purdue University in Indiana, but later transferred to Princeton where he displayed his literary and artistic talents in the college magazine. He was graduated in 1893 and received an honorary A.M. degree in 1899 and Litt. D. in 1918.

His first published novel was *The Gentleman from Indiana* (1899) which had run serially in *McClure's Magazine* and which won him recognition as a promising writer. The charming romance, *Monsieur Beaucaire*, appeared in 1900 and after publishing *The Two Vanrevels* in 1902 he was elected to the Indiana House of Representatives where he served during 1902–03. *Cherry*, a tale of colonial life written somewhat earlier, was published in 1903 and *In the Arena* in 1905, consisting of realistic stories of political life, gained from his own experiences. A versatile writer with a vein of comedy running through his books and plays, most of his subjects are treated in the lighter vein although he has demonstrated his ability for accurate observation and serious writing in *The Turmoil*, the story of a modern American city (1915); in *Alice Adams*, perhaps his finest piece of writing, the realistic story of a young American girl of flirtatious tendencies; and in *The Magnificent Ambersons* (1918), a story of life in the Middle West in an earlier generation. The two latter were awarded the Pulitzer prize. Among his other novels are *The Conquest of Canaan, The Flirt, The Guest of Quesnay, The Beautiful Lady, His Own People* (short stories), *Beauty and the Jacobin, Ramsay Milholland, Gentle Julia, The Fascinating Stranger, The Midlander, Women*. This enumeration does not include the several books which quickly made the name of Booth Tarkington a household word wherever there are readers interested in the actions, the sayings and the psychology of the growing boy. He is unsurpassed in depicting the comedy of boyhood and youth. Penrod Schofield (almost as famous as Tom Sawyer and Huckleberry Finn) was born in book form in 1914, although he had been appearing in short stories in the magazines for a year previously. He is one of the most alive and believable, as well as most humorous, boys in American literature, perhaps not very deeply analyzed by his creator, but accurately observed, truthfully and humorously presented. Almost equally successful was the sequel, *Penrod and Sam* (1916). Tarkington showed an equal appreciation of the humors and inanities of youth in *Seventeen* in the character of Willie Baxter and others.

While less popular as a playwright than as novelist, he has had some very conspicuous successes in the theater. *Monsieur Beaucaire*, dramatized in association with E. G. Sutherland, was a success as a play, a musical comedy and later as a motion picture. *The Man from Home*, written in collaboration with Harry Leon Wilson (1906) was one of the biggest hits of the time. Other plays were *Cameo Kirby, Your Humble Servant, Springtime, Getting a Polish, Mister Antonio, The Country Cousin* (with Julian Street), *Up From Nowhere, Clarence, Poldekin, The Intimate Strangers, Tweedles, Magnolia.*

Despite a serious eye trouble which developed in his middle life, necessitating more than one operation, he continued to write without cessation, in his later years producing *The Plutocrat, The World Does Move, Young Mrs. Greeley, Mary's Neck* and the play *Penrod Jashber.*

He was elected a member of the National Institute of Arts and Letters, and was twice married, first to Laurel Louisa Fletcher of Indianapolis and second to Susanna Robinson of Dayton, Ohio.

TORQUATO TASSO   1544–1595

Torquato Tasso (täs'sō), one of the greatest of Italian poets, was born at Sorrento, in Naples, March 11, 1544, son of Bernardo Tasso, who was also a poet of distinction. The exile of his father left the boy entirely in the care of his mother who reared him with affectionate solicitude. His early education was received from the Jesuits. When he was ten years old his mother entered a convent and he never saw her again. He joined his father at Rome, and continued his studies in several Italian cities, meanwhile assisting his father by copying and revising, and is reported to have collaborated with him in the poem, *L'Amadigi,* when he was but 16 years old. Later he was sent to Padua to study law, but found time to woo the muse and wrote, in 1562, his poem of *Rinaldo* which is said to have so pleased his father that he forgave him for neglecting his legal studies. After a period at the university of Bologna, where he studied philosophy and acquired a reputation for eloquent disputations, he traveled for a brief period, returning to Padua to associate himself with a literary academy there.

His great work, the *Gerusalemme Liberata,* was planned at about this time. Conceived in a heroic view, it describes the crusade under Godfrey de Bouillon. Great was the joy of the elder Tasso upon learning of this noble undertaking and his perusal of the earlier portion of the work inspired the rather complacent compliment that his son was even a greater poet than himself. A more substantial encouragement of the young man's genius came in the form of his introduction to the Duke of Ferrara (Alfonso II) by the Cardinal Luigi d'Este, to whom he had dedicated the *Rinaldo.* For a time the young poet basked in the sunshine of the good duke's favor and enjoyed his bounteous hospitality. He is said to have possessed a winning personality together with the physical graces and romantic pensiveness of mood which are ever a fatal lure to susceptible maidens and he caused something approximating to havoc among the young women of the court. Nor did he confine his attentions to the aristocracy, for on one occasion at least he laid siege to the heart of a pretty waiting maid and (as if to run the whole social gamut) he is said to have aspired to the favors of the duke's sister, a matter about which authorities have been in conflict. In any event, he completed his great epic, above mentioned, in 1575, and despatched it to Rome for the approval of scholars and critics in the ecclesiastical coterie. He would have been better advised to make a short cut from producer to consumer with this momentous child of his genius, for he was one of those tender souls, like Keats, who wither under adverse criticism. The clerical authorities vigorously denounced the poem, largely because of its classical and mythical touches, and their carping criticism had a torturing effect upon the sensitive poet. It may be doubted whether the deepening melancholy which finally shattered his noble intellect can be ascribed to this cause, although that is the persistent legend. Pathological authorities of a more scientific age would probably seek elsewhere for the cause. He began to construe every bitter comment about his work as proceeding from personal rancor and believed that his literary detractors sought his ruin at the cruel hands of the Inquisition. He feared that he would be burned as a heretic.

Alarmed by his symptoms, the good duke went to the extreme of procuring a reassuring letter from Rome, but this did not soothe the troubled spirit of the poet, whose reason was tottering. On the 15th of June, 1577, he attempted to stab a servant at the court, moved by an hallucination that the harmless menial was a secret foe. His fearful host had now no alternative but to place him in confinement, and he was conveyed to a prison-hospital from which he escaped and fled to his birthplace, Sorrento, finding shelter with his devoted sister. But his apparent restoration to health found him yearning for the gay life which had been so potent a contributing cause to his breakdown, and the good duke consented, rather reluctantly, to receive him again at court, which precipitated another collapse and ended in another flight. At length he appeared, a pitiable, half naked spectre, at the door of his friend, the Marquis d'Este, in Turin, where he was kindly received. Somewhat restored, he sought again the diversions of the court, again broke down, and was placed in confinement where he remained for seven years, until released in July, 1586. His one hope of repose seemed to lie in removal from the social environment which had proved so disastrous, and the remainder of his life was passed in freedom at Naples. In 1595 he visited Rome, there to be honored by the authorities who had once so blightingly denounced his great epic. The strain proved too much for him. He sank into a fever and was conveyed to the convent of Santo Onotrio where his distracted and unhappy life came to an end on the 25th of April, 1595.

Tasso's other works include the tragedy, *Torrismonda,* and a pastoral drama, *Aminta.*

ZACHARY TAYLOR   1784–1850

ZACHARY TAYLOR, 12th president of the United States, was born in Orange County, Virginia, Sept. 24, 1784, son of Richard Taylor, an officer in the Revolutionary Army who was appointed by Washington collector of the port of Louisville, Ky., and there Zachary spent his youth, acquired some elementary schooling and volunteered in 1806 for military service during the disturbances caused by Aaron Burr's southwestern settlement schemes. Through the efforts of James Madison, to whom he was related, he was commissioned as lieutenant in the Seventh Infantry. He served in Harrison's Indian campaigns and in the War of 1812, resigning after the conclusion of peace because his rank was then lowered in the reduction of the army to peacetime strength. President Madison restored his old rank in 1816 and for the next 20 years Taylor was stationed at various posts throughout the country. He took part in the 1832 expedition against Black Hawk, spent three years fighting the Seminoles in the Everglades, was breveted brigadier-general after the battle of Kissimee on Lake Okeechobee and placed in command of operations, but met with little success against the Seminoles and in 1840 asked to be relieved.

While in command of the first department in Louisiana he bought a plantation in Baton Rouge, but with the acquisition of Texas in 1845 he was ordered to occupy the border and moved down to the mouth of the Rio Grande with 3000 men. He established Ft. Brown, across the river from the Mexican army, shortly before a skirmish on the American side led to the declaration of war with Mexico. To protect his base of supplies he fought and won two battles with the Mexican forces in May, 1846. The Mexicans withdrew across the river to Matamoras which Taylor occupied on May 18 after they had fled. He was placed in charge of the army invading Mexico, breveted major-general and later raised to the full rank. In August he went up the Rio Grande to Camargo and made toward Monterey. A series of skirmishes and a costly bayonet assault against the defenders of the town resulted in the surrender of the enemy. General Scott was later placed in command and took over most of Taylor's troops, but Taylor led the remnant back to Monterey and then moved southward. Meeting Santa Ana's advancing army of 20,000 men with but 5000 of his own he won the battle of Buena Vista in February, 1847, and held northern Mexico. At home it was felt that he had been stripped of his troops and unfairly treated by a jealous administration.

He was nominated for the presidency by the Whigs, was elected president and inaugurated on March 5, 1849. He was a better military than political leader and it was largely the wide popularity won by his victories in the Mexican war that carried him into the White House. With little political knowledge, he strove to be non-partisan and to execute the laws, leaving their making to Congress, but under Seward's tutelage he became convinced that it was his duty to build up the Whig party through patronage. He urged California and New Mexico to apply for statehood and, although a slave owner himself, he discouraged the establishment of that institution in the new states. When the South objected to California's prohibition of slavery, he warned its leaders that he would take the field if necessary to enforce the law. He opposed the Compromise measures of 1850. He was ruggedly honest and charges brought against three of his cabinet members deeply humiliated him. He died of a fever on July 9, 1850.

PETER ILYITCH TCHAIKOVSKY   1840–1893

PETER ILYITCH TCHAIKOVSKY (chī kŏf'skĭ), one of the greatest of Russian composers, whose genius was tardily recognized in his own country, was born at Votkinsk, in the province of Viatka, Russia, May 7, 1840, the son of a mining engineer who soon after his sons's birth moved to St. Petersburg (Leningrad). He studied at the school of jurisprudence and held office in the ministry of justice, but becoming deeply interested in music, entered the Conservatory of St. Petersburg under Zaremba and was encouraged by Anton Rubinstein, the director of the school, to devote himself to music as a profession. Rubinstein seems never to have fully appreciated his gifts, but his brother, Nicholas Rubinstein, invited the youth in 1866 to become first chief of the newly founded Moscow Conservatory. There Tchaikovsky wrote, among other compositions, his first opera, *The Vojevoda (The Chieftain)* which was a failure upon its production in 1869. He had in the meantime become acquainted with Rimsky-Korsakov, Balakirev and others of the Russian "advanced" school of music, with whom he had little sympathy, and had fallen desperately in love with the opera singer Désirée Artôt, who married another. He found some consolation in writing an opera, *The Oprischnik,* a brilliant pianoforte concerto in B flat minor, the third symphony and another opera, *Vakoula the Smith*. The two operas were produced in St. Petersburg (1874 and 1876) but without success. The piano concerto was condemned by Nicholas Rubinstein at first but after it had been taken up by Hans von Bülow and performed with great success, Rubinstein added it to his own repertory. In the late '70's Tchaikovsky composed the E flat quartet, *The Swan Lake* ballet and the *Francesca da Rimini* fantasia, and in 1877 began work on *Eugen Onegin* (most popular of his grand operas) which was first heard at the Moscow Conservatory in March, 1879. In 1876 he had aroused the interest of Mme. Nadezhda Filaretovna von Meck, a wealthy widow who gave him commissions for work and later made him an allowance of about $3000 a year until 1890 when he no longer needed her aid. In that same year occurred his disastrous marriage to Antonina Ivanovna Milyukova which lasted but three months, due to the composer's eccentricities of temperament, and which increased his tendency to melancholy and morbid introspection. After a trip abroad he returned to Russia in better health and composed the *Italian Capriccio* and the famous *1812* overture, among others. He wrote the opera, *Maid of Orleans,* and his first suite for orchestra in 1879 and in 1881 the pianoforte trio in A minor dedicated to the memory of Nicholas Rubinstein who died during that year.

Chief among his compositions during the next five years were *Manfred,* a symphonic poem; the *Hamlet* overture fantasia, the operas *Mazeppa* and *Charodaika,* the *Mozartian* suite, and the fifth symphony which is now recognized as one of his greatest works, but which failed to arouse any enthusiasm when first produced. *The Queen of Spades* (later to vie with *Eugen Onegin* in popularity) had a lukewarm reception as did *The Lake of Swans* ballet, *The Sleeping Beauty* and the *Casse-noisette* which are now considered to rank with the best of his compositions. In 1887 he gave concerts in Leipzig, Berlin, Prague, Hamburg, Paris and London and in 1891 in New York, Baltimore and Philadelphia, and was received with immense enthusiasm. In 1893 he sketched his *Pathetic* symphony which he considered his finest achievement. In October, 1893 it was produced, with an indifferent reception in St. Petersburg. The verdict was speedily reversed but not before the composer's death in that city from cholera on Nov. 6, 1893. The world now recognizes this symphony as the finest composition of its kind.

ALFRED TENNYSON   1809–1892

ALFRED TENNYSON, one of the most popular of English poets, was born on Aug. 6, 1809, at Somersby, Lincolnshire, where his father was rector. His early education was received from his father with a few years at the near-by school of Louth. At the age of 17 with his brother Charles he published *Poems by Two Brothers*. In 1828 he entered Trinity College, Cambridge, and the following year captured the university prize with his poem *Timbuctoo*. In 1830 he published *Poems, chiefly Lyrical,* and two years later another small volume which contained some of the best known of his shorter poems, although at the time of its publication it received little praise. A volume of collected poems published in 1842 contained, besides the best of his earlier work, many of the fine lyrics for which he is famous and these established his reputation among the poets of the age. His first sustained work was *The Princess* (1847), a romantic medley in blank verse. Three years later he was made poet laureate of England to succeed Wordsworth, a post which he held for 42 years, and in the same year he published his beautiful elegy on the death of his friend Arthur Hallam, *In Memoriam,* which contains some of the tenderest, most melodious lyrics in the English language. He was married in June of the same year (1850) to Emily Sarah Sellwood, and settled at Twicken-ham but after three years they took up their abode at Farringford, Fresh-water, on the Isle of Wight.

Maud: *A Melodrama* appeared in 1855 and showed further evidence of his easy command of that lyric melody which assures him of immor-tality. For several years following he was absorbed in the writing of the first four of the *Idylls of the King* (published in 1859), retellings in verse form of the legends of King Arthur's court on which he had previously written *The Lady of Shalott, Mort d'Arthur* and others. *The Idylls* grew gradually to twelve in number, the last of the series being published in 1885. They are perhaps his most popular work, and by many considered his best. *Enoch Arden* and *Aylmer's Field* (1864) show his art at its ripest, and probably from a purely artistic point of view they outrank the *Idylls*.

From 1867 to 1870 he was much occupied with the building of a home from his own plans at Aldworth, Sussex, between which and the Isle of Wight home he divided his time until his death. He wrote a number of dramatic plays in verse, beginning with *Queen Mary* in 1875 and in-cluding *Harold, The Cup, The Falcon, Becket, The Promise of May, The Foresters,* and a rendering of the Robin Hood legend. *The Cup* met with some success on the stage but Tennyson's plays are of the character known as "closet dramas," more enjoyable perhaps for firelight reading than when seen behind the footlights.

He continued the writing of lyrics, idylls and ballads for the remainder of his life, volumes appearing at intervals until 1890. His interests were wide and he embodied in his poems bits of history, dialect and classical pieces, problems in morals, etc. He was able to evoke all moods in his poetry with a singing melody that few could equal. If his poems did not evidence great depth of thought his command of melody attracted a wider reading public than the rugged stanzas of his contemporary, Browning. In his later years he published several additional volumes of verse, among them *Demeter and Other Poems,* which contained the well-known *Crossing the Bar,* and shortly after his death appeared *The Death of Œone and Other Poems.*

He died at Aldworth on Oct. 6, 1892 and was buried in Westminster Abbey, where many of England's great poets have their final resting place. In 1884 he had been raised to the peerage as Baron Tennyson of Freshwater and Aldworth and the title was inherited by his eldest son, Hallam, who wrote a biography of his father.

ELLEN TERRY   1848–1928

ELLEN ALICIA TERRY, one of the most distinguished of English actresses, was born Feb. 27, 1848, at Coventry, England, daughter of two players well known in the British provinces. She was one of five children all of whom showed theatrical talent. Her first appearance on the stage was in the rôle of the boy Mamilius in *The Winter's Tale,* at the Princess Theatre, London, in April, 1856. As Prince Arthur in *King John,* two years later, she evoked high critical praise. She appeared with various stock companies in the provinces between 1860 and 1868. Her first appearance with Henry Irving, whose name has become closely linked with her own in the annals of the English stage, took place in December, 1867, when she played Katharine to his Petruchio in Garrick's version of *The Taming of the Shrew* at the Queen's Theater. While a young girl she married the painter, G. F. Watts, but the union was soon dissolved and she later married E. A. Wardell, an actor known professionally as Charles Kelly, following which she retired from the stage in 1868, returning under the management of Charles Reade at the Queen's Theater in 1874. The following year she appeared under the management of the Bancrofts at the Prince of Wales' Theater in *The Merchant of Venice* and later in a number of productions at the Court Theater, achieving a high degree of success. Her interpretation of Olivia in the *Vicar of Wakefield* led to her engagement as leading lady for Henry Irving at the Lyceum Theater. The charm of her personality as well as her skill as an actress contributed much to the success of this long-continued partnership. She appeared in all of his Lyceum productions of Shakespeare's plays through the period from 1878 to 1901; as Ophelia in *Hamlet;* Portia in *The Merchant of Venice;* Desdemona in *Othello;* Juliet; Beatrice in *Much Ado about Nothing;* Viola in *Twelfth Night;* Lady Macbeth; Katharine in *Henry VIII;* Cordelia in *King Lear;* Imogen in *Cymbeline,* and Volumnia in *Coriolanus.* With Irving she also appeared in *Charles I;* as Camma in Tennyson's drama, *The Cup;* in Wills' *Faust;* in Charles Reade's one-act play, *Nance Oldfield;* as Rosamund in Tennyson's *Becket;* Madame Sans-Gene; and Clarisse in *Robespierre.*

Miss Terry made a number of tours of the United States with Irving's Lyceum Theater Company and appeared with Mrs. Kendal in Beerbohm Tree's revival of *The Merry Wives of Windsor* at His Majesty's Theater in 1902. After Irving's death she continued to act in various London theaters and appeared in Barrie's *Alice-Sit-By-the-Fire* in 1905, under the direction of the American manager, Charles Frohman, at the Duke of York's Theater. The following year she played in Bernard Shaw's *Captain Brassbound's Conversion* which was included in her repertory in 1907 on the first tour which she made of the United States after Irving's death. While on that tour she married her leading man, James Carew, a young American actor. They separated after a time but remained excellent friends. Miss Terry's stage jubilee was celebrated in London in 1906 when English and American admirers raised a fund of about $40,000 for her by popular subscription. Visiting the United States in 1915, she lectured on the heroines of Shakespeare. In 1922 she received the honorary degree of LL.D. from St. Andrews and in 1925 was awarded the Grand Cross of the Order of the British Empire. She died July 21, 1928 at Small Hythe, Kent. In 1908 she had published *The Story of my Life.*

WILLIAM MAKEPEACE THACKERAY   1811–1863

WILLIAM MAKEPEACE THACKERAY, English novelist, was born on July 18, 1811 in Calcutta, India. His father, Richmond Thackeray, who was in the East India service, died in 1816 and the boy was sent to an aunt in England. A few years later his mother returned to England with her second husband who was said to be the original of Thackeray's famous character, Colonel Newcome. After attending two small schools he was placed in the Charterhouse School, London. In 1829 while a student at Trinity College, Cambridge, he made his first appearance as an author with a humorous weekly, *The Snob,* which he carried on with a friend for a short time. In 1830–31 he studied in Weimar. He did not take a college degree but was ambitious to become an artist and studied art in Paris and Rome. On reaching his majority he inherited a considerable fortune which was reduced by losses due to the failure of a bank in India and in other ways, and he found it necessary to depend upon his own efforts for a livelihood.

He first became known to the reading public through *Fraser's Magazine,* to which he contributed for several years under the names of "Michael Angelo Titmarsh," "George Fitz-Boodle, Esq." "Charles Yellowplush," and other *noms de plume.* He wrote tales, sketches and poetry. One of his stories, *The Great Hoggarty Diamond,* attracted the attention of John Sterling, who ranked its author with Fielding and Goldsmith. Thackeray was an educated man of the world who had mingled much in society, traveled a great deal, and his writings contained much shrewd observation, philosophic reflection and biting satire. In 1836 he offered to illustrate Dickens' *Pickwick,* but his offer was refused. In the same year, with his step-father, Major Carmichael Smith, and others, he started the *Constitutional,* a daily newspaper which was continued for a year with loss to all concerned. He then took up the study of law at the Inner Temple, apparently with no intention of making it a career although he was called to the bar in 1848, for he continued to write, publishing *The Paris Sketch-Book* in 1840, *The Irish Sketch-Book* (1843), *Barry Lyndon* (1844). *Punch* was started in 1841 and Thackeray's writings and drawings appeared in its pages frequently, to the number of some 400 sketches.

In February, 1847, *Vanity Fair* began to appear in monthly parts under his own name and quickly placed him in the first rank of English novelists. A Christmas volume, *Our Street,* appeared in 1848 and his second major novel, *The History of Pendennis,* in monthly parts during 1849–50. He then republished some of his magazine articles and stories and in 1851 began to give his lectures on *The English Humorists of the Eighteenth Century,* which were very successful both in England and America. His next work, *Henry Esmond,* issued from the press in 1852, is a historical romantic novel of much charm, skill and insight which made an immediate success. *The Newcomes* (1855) is considered by many literary critics to be his masterpiece and one of the finest English novels ever written. During that year and the next he lectured on *The Four Georges* in both

England and the United States, and upon his return from America stood for Parliament for Oxford but was defeated.

Some of the characters of *Henry Esmond* appeared in his story of *The Virginians* (1857–59), which is a charming novel of life in the early days of Virginia, but it was not as popular as some of his other works. From 1860 to 1862 he conducted the *Cornhill Magazine,* in which appeared various essays and the two unimportant short novels, *Lovel the Widower* and *Philip on his Way Through the World.* Four monthly parts of a new novel, *Dennis Duval,* had been published and he had resigned his editorship in April, 1862. On December 24, 1863 he was found dead in bed. He was buried in Kensal Green and a bust to his memory was placed in Westminster Abbey. In 1836 he had married Isabella Shaw who bore him three daughters and who survived him.

Thackeray's work is largely descriptive of life in the English upper classes and he gives a vivid picture of middle nineteenth century conditions. He was a lovable, generous man with a scorn of all pretense and hypocrisy, which led him often to write so scathingly of human weaknesses that he was sometimes regarded as a cynic.

THEMISTOCLES   circa 514 B.C.–449 B.C.

THEMISTOCLES (thĕ mĭs′tō klēz), a soldier and statesman of ancient Greece, was born in Athens, probably in 514 B.C., the son of Neocles, an Athenian of moderate station who had married a Carian or Thracian woman and hence, by Periclean law, Themistocles could not have been a free Athenian citizen. Little is known of his early years, but he evidently displayed unusual ability and ambition. Plutarch mentions his great ambition for power for himself and for Greece and the unscrupulous, though able, manner in which he pursued his ends. After the battle of Marathon and the death of Miltiades, the two men in power were Themistocles and Aristides. The former was an advocate of a strong navy, which Athens unquestionably needed, while the latter opposed it. Themistocles persuaded the Athenians to begin the building of 200 triremes, and to fortify the natural harbors of Peiraeus, inducing them to set aside for this purpose the income obtained from the new silver mines at Laurium which it had been intended to distribute among the citizens. Actually about 100 triremes were built. In 482 Aristides was ostracized, his followers lost influence and Themistocles gained control and in 481 was made archon (the highest magistrate of Athens).

The Greek fleet was nominally under the command of the Spartan Eurybiades when the Persians under Xerxes invaded Greece in 480 B.C., but it was Themistocles who forced the indecisive battle of Artemisium in which the Grecians were put to flight. By his threat that he would lead the Athenian army to found a new home in the West (Italy) and by sending treacherous messages to Xerxes, he brought on the battle of Salamis in September, 480 B.C., in which Xerxes attacked the Greek fleet under unfavorable conditions, was defeated and forced to retire to Sardis. Freed from the Persian invasion, Themistocles, now the most influential man in Athens, set about restoring the ruined city, and despite the opposition to the rebuilding of its walls by Sparta, succeeded through a subterfuge in getting them built high enough for defensive purposes. He was able to carry out his original plan of making Peiraeus a harbor and fortress for Athens, thus causing that city to become the finest trading center in Greece. By remitting the tax on aliens he induced many foreign merchants and businessmen to settle in Athens.

The differences between Themistocles and Aristides appear to have been reconciled after the Persians had been repelled, and a short time afterwards Themistocles lost the esteem of the Athenians, through his boastfulness, no doubt, and his alleged acceptance of bribes, to which both Diodorus and Plutarch make some reference. He was ostracized in 471 and in 465, being charged with treason, he fled to Asia Minor where he appears to have been well treated by his recent enemies, the Persians, and permitted to settle at Magnesia on the Maeander where he died about 449 B.C., at the approximate age of 65. The residents of the city of his refuge raised a memorial to him but it was rumored that his bones had been secretly transferred to Attica. He appears to have been worshipped by the Magnesians as a god, for his image appears upon their coins.

Thucydides states that Themistocles possessed a marvelous power for analyzing a complex situation and for taking prompt action. Despite his lust for wealth and power he unquestionably rendered great service to Athens through the creation of her navy which led to the formation of the Delian League and later the Athenian empire.

THEODOSIUS THE GREAT

circa 346–395

THEODOSIUS I, Roman emperor, called "The Great," was the son of the Roman general Theodosius who saved Britain from the Picts in 368–69 and suppressed the revolt of Firmus in Mauretania in 372. He was born about the year 346 A.D., somewhere in Spain, was with his father in the struggle against the Picts in Britain in 368 and in 374 defeated the Sarmatians from southern Russia, who had invaded Moesia, an ancient Roman province corresponding approximately with modern Bulgaria and Serbia. His father was put to death in 376 and Theodosius retired to the place of his birth in Spain where he lived until the Roman emperor Gratian, after the battle of Adrianople in August, 378, summoned him to share the cares of the empire. He won some more engagements against the Sarmatians, after which he was made Augustus at Sirmium, Jan. 19, 379, and given the eastern provinces of the empire, including Illyricum. He reorganized the army of Thessalonica and carried on a campaign against the Gothic tribes along the Danube river, some of which swore allegiance to him.

In 381 Theodosius' realm was invaded by the Goths under Fritigern while the Ostrogoths swarmed into the Danube country under Alatheus and Safrax. Theodosius himself took the field against Fritigern and conquered the invaders only after their leader's death. The defence of the Danube country was entrusted to Promotus, one of Theodosius' generals, who succeeded in beating back Alatheus and Safrax before they had effected a crossing of the Danube. It was not as a general alone, however, that Theodosius won the name of "The Great;" he showed high qualities as a diplomat and statesman. By his diplomacy he won the allegiance of Athanaric, fugitive king of the Visigoths, who entered his service and enlisted 40,000 of his former enemies, making settlements for them in various parts of the Roman Empire. In 383 Maximus, in command of the Roman army in Britain, had headed a revolt and proclaimed himself emperor of Gaul, Britain and Spain. Theodosius accepted Maximus as his colleague in the government of the empire for five years at the end of which period Maximus invaded Italy, proposing to make himself master of the heart of the Empire. Theodosius gathered a great army and proceeded against the invading force which he severely defeated and at Aquileia on July 28, 388, he captured Maximus and ordered him beheaded. He then bestowed upon Valentinian II all that part of the empire which his father had held.

Theodosius celebrated his triumph at Rome in 389, where he remained for the two following years, making arrangements for the governing of Italy. The Greek historian, Zosimus, is authority for the statement that he then gave himself up to gluttony and luxurious living, but in May, 392, word reached him that Arbogastes had slain the young Emperor Valentinian in the western empire and had raised one Eugenius Augustus to power. Theodosius gathered an army and took the field against Eugenius whom he met at the river Frigidus, 36 miles from

Aquileia. The result of the first day's fighting went against him and he spent the night in prayer.

Toward dawn, the story goes, he beheld a vision in which St. John, mounted on a white steed, promised him victory. The issue was still in doubt on the second day of fighting until, as contemporary church historians tell us, the enemy's arrows were blown back upon themselves by a sudden gust of wind, when the tide of battle turned and Theodosius gained a decisive victory. Eugenius was slain by the soldiers and two days later Arbogastes committed suicide. Theodosius then proceeded southward to Rome and the two parts of the Empire were again united under one ruler until his death at Milan four months later, on Jan. 17, 395.

HENRY DAVID THOREAU 1817–1862

THE fame of HENRY DAVID THOREAU as a writer and naturalist has been much augmented by his positive and unusual character and his peculiar habit of life. He was so decidedly individualistic that this attribute dominated all his work and actions, and he appears in the annals of American literature as a curious personality. He was born at Concord, Mass., July 12, 1817 and spent most of his simple life there, claiming that everything of interest to the student of nature was there abundantly available to him who had eyes to see. His father was a maker of lead pencils in that town, which is famous as the home of Emerson, Hawthorne, the Alcotts, and other distinguished Americans, and for a while the son worked at that trade. His acuteness of sight and touch is indicated in the familiar story that he could quickly lift a dozen, or any given number, of pencils from a basket by a single casual plunge of his hand. It was the same hand that could reach gently into the depths of a pond and lift out a docile fish. He early developed an uncanny proficiency in everything he attempted and became an expert at pencil making, giving as his reason for abandoning that craft that he had no interest in continuing to do a thing after he had once done it well.

He was educated at Harvard and continued throughout his life to be a student of classical literature which he found much time to enjoy and comment upon in the leisurely—almost primitive—life that he chose for himself. He never acknowledged the value of his education, and was indeed always grudging in according credit to any human instrumentality for the vast and varied store of information which he acquired. For a while he taught school in partnership with his brother, but soon wearied of the restrictions it imposed. He did some private tutoring in his native town and in Staten Island, N. Y. Thereafter he led the life of a free lance, making his home in Concord and earning his living by various odd jobs which brought him just enough for his few simple wants; he was particular never to work steadily at anything, and by this means he was able to adjust his efforts to his immediate needs. He set out to demonstrate to himself, and ended by demonstrating to the world, how satisfactorily one may live and give his precious time to the improvement of his own soul without any of the usual pomp and circumstance of living. He was sincere with himself and without any of the ostentation of the rebel and the faddist.

He wandered about the woods and fields studying plant and animal life and became so much a part of this woodland existence that Emerson tells us a snake would familiarly wind itself about his sturdy limb. He became, in a word, miraculously acceptable to the denizens of the stream and the forest, and established a kind of fraternity with them. For a brief period he lived in the home of Emerson and the gentle sage was glad enough to let this competent and self-assured master plant trees, supervise his garden, mend his roof, discover rare plants on their rambles, build fences, and peradventure discuss philosophy and literature. From July, 1845, to September, 1847, Thoreau gave a picturesque demonstration of his theory of existence. He built a rough shack near the shore of Walden Pond in an outlying section of Concord where he lived quite alone, obtaining what little money he needed by odd jobs about the countryside and living on the products of his garden. On his long walks to and from his labors he was keenly observant of leaf and bud and insect, always entering the minutest details in his notebook. He would neither kill nor trap an animal and lived wholly on a vegetarian diet. The valuable time which this mode of existence released was spent in meditation, writing and study. He seemed averse to human company unless it brought him worthwhile knowledge and food for thought, and this seclusiveness and a certain flinty and impatient habit in his contacts have given currency to the fiction that he was without human feeling and scornful of the gentler sentiments. Later in his life his noble independence and love of freedom moved him to a quick, brief plunge into human affairs; he hired a hall in Concord and hurled defiance at the institution of slavery and the flabby tolerance of it, at the moment when John Brown's raid was being denounced throughout the country. Nor did he scruple to defend that misguided abolitionist. He refused to pay his poll tax to a government that sanctioned slavery and was at one time sent to jail in consequence.

His experiment at Walden (charmingly told in his book of that name) was followed by another sojourn at Emerson's spacious home.

Thereafter he lived with his parents and sister at Concord where he died May 6, 1862. He never married. Notable among his works are *The Maine Woods, Cape Cod, Early Spring in Massachusetts, Summer, Winter* and *A Week on the Concord and Merrimac Rivers.* His *Walden, or Life in the Woods,* has always been the most popular of his works. His literary style was like his character, emphatic, straightforward, vital, and he had a gift for striking and picturesque statement. His essays published under the title of *Miscellanies and Excursions* show him to have been a master with a truly classic flavor, scholarly and discerning. The *First and Last Journeys of Thoreau, Lately Discovered Among his Unpublished Journals and Manuscripts* is the title of a work not published until 1905, but received then with much interest.

TITIAN   circa 1477–1576

TIZIANO VICELLI, Italian painter, better known as TITIAN (tĭsh'ȧn), was born about 1477 near the old castle of Cadore in the mountains north of Venice. At the age of 10 he was sent to live with an uncle in that city where he studied mosaics under Zuccato and painting and drawing under Gentile and Giovanni Bellini. His development was somewhat slow. During his early years he painted many Madonnas and numerous other subjects, among them the well-known "Tribute Money," now in Dresden, representing Christ and the Pharisee; and "The Daughter of Herodius" for which his own daughter served as his model. The masterpiece of this early period was "Sacred and Profane Love," painted when he was about 23. His services as a portrait painter and worker in fresco were early in demand. He visited Padua in 1511 doing fresco work and five years later was in Ferrara. These years also produced the "Pesaro Altar Piece," (now at Antwerp); "Doge Marcello" (1508) in the Vatican.

Titian was married about 1524. Some years later the Emperor Charles V became so pleased with his portrait work that he made him a count palatine and a Knight of the Golden Spur. His reputation had spread throughout Christendom. To this period in his career belong "The Three Ages," and "Noli Me Tangere," both painted in 1518; "Bacchus and Ariadne" of 1520, now in the London National Gallery; "St. Peter the Martyr," which was destroyed in a fire in Venice in 1867; "The Repose in Egypt" (Louvre); and "A Summer Storm" (Buckingham Palace). In 1545 he paid his first visit to Rome where he was received with high honors by Pope Paul III, his portrait of whom is now at St. Petersburg.

He executed also an excellent portrait of the Pope and his two grandsons. The following year he was back in Venice, working industriously, producing more of his wonderfully colored masterpieces; "The Farnese Family Picture," "Venus and Adonis," now in the National Gallery, London; "Martyrdom of St. Lawrence," (Gesuiti, Venice); "Jupiter and Antiope' (Louvre); and a second "Peter Martyr." His "Battle of Cadore," done for the council chamber in Venice in 1537, was destroyed by fire in 1577. In 1548 and again in 1550–51 he went to Germany where he painted portraits of Charles V and his son Philip II. In 1566 he was elected to the Florentine Academy, soon after having designed decorations for the church at Pieve, among them the "Transfiguration" and an "Annunciation" which were partly executed by his pupils. Many celebrated religious and mythological pictures were the product of his later years, among them the well-known "Christ at Emmaus" "Christ Crowned with Thorns," "Diana and Actaeon," "Diana and Callisto," "Jupiter and Antiope," "The Last Supper," "The Entombment," and "St. Jerome." He executed also innumerable portraits including several of his daughter Lavinia.

He selected the Chapel of the Crucifix in the church of the Frari as his burial place and agreed, in return, to paint a picture of the "Pièta" for the Franciscans. Before the picture was completed he fell a victim to the plague then ravaging Venice, and died on Aug. 17, 1576 at about 99 years of age.

Lacking the universal genius of Michelangelo and Da Vinci, Titian yet carried his genius for painting and color to great heights. He was unquestionably the greatest painter of his time in Venice and one of the greatest of all times.

COUNT LEO TOLSTOY   1828–1910

COUNT LEO NIKOLAIEVITCH TOLSTOY (also spelled Tolstoi), famous Russian writer and social reformer, was born Sept. 9, 1828 at Yāsnaya Polyana, in the province of Tula. He had all the usual advantages of the youth of the nobility, studied at Kazan University (1844–47), and in 1851 joined the army of the Caucasus as a gentleman-volunteer, where he was attached to the staff of Prince Gortschakoff, in Turkey. His first story, *Childhood,* was completed in 1852, after which he served in the Crimean War and took part in the storming of Sebastopol in 1855. He had in the meantime published a number of poems and novels; *The Cossacks, The Incursion,*

The Morning of a Landed Proprietor; and had gained some distinction as a writer. His three *Sebastopol* sketches, vivid pictures of the horrors of war, immediately placed him in the front rank of writers. After the Crimean War he retired from the army and became for a time a member of the brilliant literary and social set of St. Petersburg. He traveled in Germany and Italy and in revolt against the social conditions of modern civilization he wrote *The Memoirs of Prince Mekhlyudov* and retired to his estate at Yāsnaya Polyana where he devoted himself to the welfare of the peasantry and the teaching of their children. *The Snow Storm* and *The Two Hussars,* written during his travels in Europe, were followed, after his return home, by *Family Happiness, The Three Deaths* and *Polikushka.*

In 1862 he married Sophie Behrs, who was 16 years his junior. *War and Peace,* the first of the great novels to bring him world-wide renown, published from 1865 to 1868, presents on a mighty canvas Napoleon's Russian campaign and Russia's defence. It is a long novel, with a multiplicity of characters and scenes presented with a vividness and a literary style which at once gave its author rank among the great novelists of the century. His most successful novel is *Anna Karenina* (1875–76), the tragic story of an ill-considered marriage which, according to his own statement, contains much material drawn from the experiences of his own life. At about this time he began to develop the religious mysticism and the feeling of social responsibility for the peasants upon his estate which became his absorbing passion throughout the rest of his long life. He turned in disgust from the fleshly life of a successful author and landed proprietor, adopted the costume and the manner of life of the peasants and devoted himself to their welfare. He could not accept the fasts and rites of the orthodox peasantry, however, and renouncing the Church he evolved a Christianity of his own based upon his own reading of the Gospels. Poverty, humility and non-resistance became the keynotes of the creed which gradually became known as "Tolstoyism." His religious experience is set forth in his own *Confession* (1879; published in 1884), which some critics hold worthy to rank with the *Confessions* of St. Augustine. It was in 1884, after a visit to the Moscow slums, that his religion became definitely social. It was organized into a sect and acquired proselytes. It is expounded in his *What I Believe In* and *A Short Exposition of the Gospels.* During the later years of his life his fame spread, he became greatly venerated and many pilgrimages were made to his home. His unorthodox utterances caused him to be excommunicated in 1901.

He eschewed fiction almost entirely during his later years, but published *Commentary on the Gospels, My Religion* and a number of other treatises on social, philosophical and religious subjects, and a brilliant discussion on *What is Art? The Death of Ivan Ilyitch* (1884) and *Master and Man* (1895) are based upon his own inner experiences. In *Resurrection* only (1899–1900) did he return to his former literary style. Other later works were *Father Sergius, The False Coupon; The Kreutzer Sonata* (1889), a much misunderstood novel which aroused adverse criticism in Russia and elsewhere. *The Powers of Darkness* and *The Living Corpse* (both plays) were his last works aside from *The Fruits of Enlightenment.* He had long planned to end his days in solitude and in 1910 he left his estate with this object in view, but was taken ill with pneumonia and died at a railroad station on Nov. 20, 1910. He was buried at Yāsnaya without Christian ceremony.

In 1905 and 1906 he had written to the Czar certain memorable addresses in which he pleaded for such reforms as universal suffrage and representative assemblies.

ANTHONY TROLLOPE   1815–1882

Anthony Trollope (trŏl′lŭp), English realistic novelist, was born in London, April 24, 1815, son of Thomas Anthony Trollope, a lawyer who devoted much time to an *Encyclopedia Ecclesiastica* and of Frances Milton Trollope, who journeyed to America with her husband and after returning to England wrote *Domestic Manners of the Americans,* a prejudiced and overdrawn picture of American life which aroused considerable resentment in the United States. She later wrote many novels and books of travel. Thomas Adolphus Trollope, Anthony's elder brother, was also a novelist. He was educated at Winchester and Harrow and then became "classical usher" in a private school in Brussels. In 1834 he became a clerk in the London General Post Office at a small salary and after seven years was transferred to Ireland (1841) as surveyor's clerk and traveling inspector. He developed a good deal of business ability under his new responsibilities, became widely acquainted with people of all classes, and in 1844 married Rose Haseltine.

Throughout these years he cherished the idea of writing and was prepared for it. He settled at Clonmel and wrote *The Macdermots of Ballycloran* (1847) and *The Kellys and the O'Kellys* (1848) both of which were failures. In 1850 he published a historical novel, *La Vendée,* which met with a similar fate. A visit to Salisbury Close gave him the idea which he elaborated in *The Warden* (1855), his first success and the first of his books of clerical life. Some of its characters appeared in his second book, *Barchester Towers* (1857). These two novels launched the *Barset-shire Chronicles,* a series of long, carefully written novels which brought their author increasing fame and eventually a good income. *The Three Clerks* (1858) was the first to be financially successful and was rapidly followed by *Dr. Thorne, Framley Parsonage, The Small House at Alling-ton* and *Last Chronicles of Barset, Orley Farm, Can You Forgive Her?, Phineas Finn, The Claverings, The Way We Live Now* and others. He had in the meantime become inspector of rural deliveries for the southwest of Ireland, and is said to have been the inventor of the pillar-box. His success in postal work led to his being sent to the West Indies in 1858 and the following year his first travel book, *The West Indies and the Spanish Main,* appeared. He visited Egypt (1858), the United States (1862), Australia and New Zealand (1871–72) and South Africa (1878) on official business and these trips furnished the basis for several books of travel. In 1859 he was transferred from Ireland to England and settled at Waltham Cross, retiring from the postal service in 1867.

He was one of the founders of the *Fortnightly Review* (1865), edited *St. Paul's Magazine* (1868) and contributed to *Cornhill, Blackwood's* and other magazines. He ran for Parliament for Beverly in 1868 but failed of election. He was methodical in his writing habits, calculating each book as so many days' work, rising at an early hour and writing steadily for a certain number of hours, turning out an exact number of pages each day. Bluff, honest, hearty and vociferous, he liked society and hunting and found ample time for both. He lived in London from 1872 to 1880 and then removed to Harting, Sussex, where he died of paralysis on Dec. 6, 1882.

Trollope's books are pictures of English life and society, showing minute powers of observation and written with humor and sympathy. He was particularly happy in his portrayals of the clergy and the life of cathedral towns. His best work is probably in *The Chronicles of Barset-shire.*

IVAN SERGEYEVICH TURGENEV   1818–1883

Ivan Sergeyevich Turgenev (tŭr gĕn'yĕf), Russian novelist, was born at Orel, Nov. 9, 1818, of a family of the provincial gentry. His early education was received at home and at 16 he entered the University of St. Petersburg and later studied in Berlin (1839–40) where he came under the influence of western ideas. He returnd to St. Petersburg in 1841 but his relations with his mother, which had long been strained because he opposed her treatment of the serfs, were broken off and he entered the civil service, but soon decided to devote himself to literature. In 1845 he published *Parasha,* a story in verse which had a favorable review by Belinsky. His infatuation for the singer, Pauline Garcia (Mme. Viardot) caused a further breach with his mother but upon her death in 1850 he became a wealthy man and was able to follow his own tastes. One of his first acts was to free all the serfs on his estate. In the meantime he had published the very successful *Kolosov* and *Khor and Kalinytch.* His lifelong affection for Mme. Viardot met with scant response but it left a marked impression on his life and work. He gave up the writing of poetry for drama and prose fiction and in the course of a short time abandoned the writing of plays (1852). *Annals of a Sportsman,* which he had begun in 1847, was published in book form in 1852. In this work he gave free rein to his great love for humanity and for the oppressed peasantry. It was quite successful and won him a certain reputation in his native country. In that year he wrote an obituary of the novelist Gogol which, with other too liberal utterances, brought him into disfavor with the Russian officials and he was exiled to his estate for a time.

He wrote a number of short stories; among them such masterpieces as *The Backwater, Asya, First Love,* etc., but his reputation outside of Russia was made by his novels. He published *Eydin* in 1856; *A Nest of Gentlefolks* two years later; *On the Eve* in 1860. In these novels he discussed current social questions and scored the life of idleness of the Russian upper classes at the expense of the serfs. Russian critics gave them long reviews and praised his literary skill and his presentation of character and social problems. He had become the most important literary figure in the country. He sought to portray a strong man in the agnostic nihilist Bazarov and when the radical press sneered at it as a caricature, the novelist, always sensitive to criticism, became embittered. He had left his native country and although he paid it occasional visits thereafter, he spent most of the remainder of his life in Paris where he came into contact with the social and literary life of the city and made friends with many noted French writers, particularly with Gustave Flaubert. Younger writers, like de Maupassant, looked up to the Russian as a master. Translations of his novels were published in English and other languages and his fame spread to England and America.

Although living away from his own country, Turgenev continued to write about Russia. Two of his later novels, *Smoke* (1867) and *Virgin Soil* (1877), considered among his finest works, showed him to be out of touch with Russian life and still in bitter mood. His last visit to Russia, in 1880, was in the nature of a triumphal progress, although the leading

Russian writers—Tolstoy, Dostoyevsky and others—were hostile to him.

Critics have traced in his writings the influence of the Russians, Pushkin and Lermontov, and of the French romantic novelist, George Sand, and pronounce him the most poetical of the great Russian realists, with his character drawing depending, not on psychology, but on a certain poetic aura with which he invests his characters. Generally speaking, he succeeded better with his women characters than with his men, most of whom suffered from the neurasthenia that marks Doystoyevsky's characters. In style, Turgenev is probably the simplest of the Russian novelists, his prose the most polished. Various English translations of his works have been made, by Isabel F. Hapgood, 1903; and by Constance Garnett, 1919–23. He died at Bougival, near Paris, Sept. 3, 1883.

J. M. W. TURNER 1775–1851

JOSEPH MALLORD WILLIAM TURNER, one of the greatest of English landscape artists, was born April 23, 1775, probably at Covent Garden, London. His father was a barber who could not afford to give his son much education, and Turner remained more or less illiterate throughout his life. When he was about 13 he entered the employ of an architect who was so impressed by the youth's ability that he urged him to become a pupil at the Royal Academy. His progress in painting was rapid; at the age of 15 he began to exhibit his landscapes and at 18 he received a commission from a publisher to visit four of the English counties and paint and draw the scenes that attracted him. He visited Wales and traveled in England, making architectural drawings of some of the most famous cathedrals. He was elected an Associate Royal Academician at the early age of 24, four years later was made a full Royal Academician and became professor of perspective at the Academy when he was but 33. He traveled much, visiting France, Switzerland and Italy, and one of his publications he named *Turner's Annual Tour*. He never married but was devoted wholly to his art and worked ceaselessly and unsparingly, cultivating his talent by long, hard labor and subordinating everything else to that one thing. He lived alone and in a secrecy that amounted almost to complete obscurity; society had no charms for him. He was so frugal in his living that he was often accused of miserliness, but he earned enough money to enable him to travel where and when he liked and he was generous on occasion and made some close friends.

His first great naval picture was "The Battle of the Nile" (1799).

His picture of Kilchurn Castle was painted in 1802 and the following year saw some Continental subjects committed to canvas; "Calais Pier," "The Vintage at Maçon" and a number of Alpine pictures. "The Garden of the Hesperides," one of his finely imaginative canvases, was painted in 1806, and "The Sun Rising in Mist" the following year. Among his many paintings between the years 1811 to 1844 were "Apollo and the Python," "The Frosty Morning," "Crossing the Brook," "Dido Building Carthage," "Bay of Baiae"; several paintings of Yorkshire; "The Rivers of England," "Provincial Antiquities of Scotland"; his series of paintings of "England and Wales"; Ulysses Deriding Polyphemus," "Childe Harold's Pilgrimage," vignettes illustrating Rogers' poems; "The Rivers of France," "The Golden Bough," "Phryne Going to the Bath as Venus," "The Temeraire," "Opening of the Valhalla," "The Approach to Venice" and "The Sun of Venice"; and "Rain, Steam and Speed."

He became an adept etcher and engraver, completing 71 of the contemplated 100 plates for his *Liber Studiorum* (1807–19). In his early work he followed the general style of the old masters, but later, as he matured, worked out a color system of his own in which he used pale general tones, with strong dark colors for contrast. His tendency was to beautify and make somewhat mysterious that which nature revealed to him.

He bequeathed his pictures and drawings to the London National Gallery to be kept together in rooms bearing his name and left his fortune of 140,000 pounds to found a home for sick and unfortunate artists, but as he was ignorant of legal forms his will was broken. He died in the Chelsea section of London on Dec. 19, 1851 and was buried in St. Paul's Cathedral.

JOHN TYLER   1790–1862

JOHN TYLER, tenth president of the United States, was born at Greenway, Va., March 29, 1790, son of John Tyler, governor of Virginia and United States District Judge. He attended the College of William and Mary in 1802–07, was admitted to the bar in 1809 and two years later was elected to the Virginia house of delegates where he supported the republicans and the war with Great Britain. He raised a company for the defense of Richmond in 1813, but the unit was not called into action. While a member of the national house of representatives from 1816 to 1821, he opposed internal improvements, a protective tariff, Clay's proposed recognition of the independence of Spain's South American colonies, and the Missouri Compromise legislation. Ill health caused him to decline reelection to the house in 1821, but he was again a member of the Virginia house of delegates, 1823–25, and governor of the state, 1825–27. In the latter year, after being reelected governor, he succeeded John Randolph in the United States senate where he was independent of party, voted against the tariffs of 1828 and 1832, believing them unconstitutional, but supported and helped to initiate the compromise tariff of 1833, following the hostility of South Carolina, although he condemned that state's nullification. In 1832 he supported Andrew Jackson for president as being the least objectionable of the candidates.

In 1833 he aligned himself with the Whigs, although in sympathy with the democrats as to states' rights. He sought to prohibit slavery in the District of Columbia, subject to the consent of Virginia and Maryland which had ceded the district to the United States. He upheld the Bank of United States in the controversy over removing the government funds from that depositary. In February, 1836, he resigned from the senate, was an unsuccessful candidate for the vice-presidency and became again a member of the Virginia house of delegates in 1838. In 1840 he was elected vice-president by the Whigs on the ticket with William Henry Harrison and became president on April 4, 1841, after Harrison's death. Although nominally the leader of his party, his policies were contrary to those of the Whigs. Clay was the real leader and forced a break with Tyler but the Whig majority was not large enough to pass any measure over his veto. The party repealed the sub-treasury law in 1841 and gained modified protection by the tariff bill of 1842. Tyler retained Harrison's cabinet until his veto of the bill for a fiscal corporation (which he held was opposed to states' rights) when all the members resigned except Daniel Webster who was just closing negotiations with England in the northeastern boundary controversy and who resigned a year later.

Tyler opposed the spoils system and retained in their posts abroad some able democrats. He had the support of neither party; Van Buren would not recognize him as a democrat and Clay, leading the Whigs, fought his policies in Congress. Cooperation was impossible and little was accomplished. Toward the close of his administration Texas was admitted to the union which led to his nomination for the presidency by an irregular democratic convention in Baltimore. The regular democrats nominated James K. Polk and in August, 1844, Tyler withdrew from the contest. He was in demand as a public speaker and took a firm stand for union when South Carolina adopted its secession ordinance. The Virginia legislature appointed him a commissioner to confer with President Buchanan regarding the *status quo* of Fort Sumter and he presided over the Peace Conference in Washington on Feb. 4, 1861. Upon its failure he threw himself into the Confederate cause. Elected to the Virginia convention, he advised secession and became a member of the provisional Confederate Congress. He died Jan. 18, 1862, in Richmond, before he could take his seat in the Confederate house of representatives to which he had been elected.

MARTIN VAN BUREN   1782–1862

MARTIN VAN BUREN, eighth president of the United States, was born of Dutch ancestry at Kinderhook, N. Y., Dec. 5, 1782, the son of a farmer and tavern-keeper. After attending the common schools and the Kinderhook Academy, he studied law, was admitted to the bar in New York City in 1803, became a successful lawyer and drifted into politics, becoming surrogate of Columbia county (1808–13), was twice elected to the state senate (1812–20) and served his state as attorney general (1815–19). He lived in Albany from 1816 to 1829. As a politician he was one of the "Albany regency" group which introduced the "spoils system" although he did not originate it. Elected to the United States senate in 1821, he proposed in 1824 a constitutional amendment authorizing internal improvements, but the following year he took an opposite position. He changed his attitude also on the tariff question, voting for it in 1824 and against it thereafter although he did vote for the "tariff of abominations" in 1828 under instructions from his state. Reelected to the senate in 1827, he became one of the managers of Andrew Jackson's campaign for the presidency, but resigned his seat when elected governor of New York the following year.

He had served as chief executive of his state for but two months when Jackson appointed him secretary of state. Throughout the latter's administration Van Buren stood high in his regard, particularly because of his attitude toward Mrs. John H. Eaton (Peggy O'Neill) wife of the secretary of war, who was ostracised by the wives of the other cabinet members. He did not oppose Jackson's use of the spoils system but did not himself participate in it; he supported Jackson against Calhoun in the controversy with the Bank of the United States, and after the break between the president and Calhoun he became the logical candidate for the vice-presidency. He resigned from the cabinet in 1831 on his appointment as minister to England, but learned after his arrival in that country that the senate had failed to confirm the appointment, Calhoun, the vice-president, having cast the deciding vote. The following May he was elected vice-president on the ticket with Jackson and in 1836 was elected to the presidency against Gen. William Henry Harrison.

The fever of land speculation and the order of July, 1836, notifying land agents to accept only gold or silver in payment for government land, brought about the great panic of 1837, which Van Buren held must right itself without government interference. However, when the government found its funds locked up in suspended banks, he called a special session of Congress to find some relief and after four years' effort he succeeded in getting an independent treasury system established, but neither his firmness nor his courage could overcome the hostility to him and he lost the following election to Gen. Harrison, being held largely responsible in the public mind for the continued financial distress of the country. At the democratic convention of 1844 he had a majority of the votes for the presidential nomination but not the necessary two-thirds, because of his opposition to the annexation of Texas, which lost him the votes of the southern democrats. In 1848 he was nominated by the "Barnburners" faction of the democrats and by the "Free Soilers," but did not win a single electoral vote. In 1860 he voted for the fusion ticket in New York— the ticket that opposed Lincoln—but he did not approve Buchanan's course in dealing with the seceding states and swung around to support Lincoln and his policies.

He died at Kinderhook on July 24, 1862. His election to the presidency has been considered a victory for Andrew Jackson rather than for Van Buren as shown by the smallness of his plurality of the popular vote. In 1867 his sons compiled from his unpublished writings an *Inquiry into the Origin and Course of Political Parties in the United States.*

CORNELIUS VANDERBILT 1794–1877

CORNELIUS VANDERBILT, American capitalist, was born near what is now Stapleton, Staten Island, on May 27, 1794. His father was a farmer and the boy's early life was spent in the usual farm tasks. He had little opportunity for acquiring education, but at the age of 16 he grasped an opportunity to buy a ferryboat and engaged in transporting passengers and farm products from Staten Island to Long Island and to New York City. Within two years he controlled three boats and his ferry service was well established. He expanded his business rapidly and soon came to be known as "Commodore," a title which clung to him as long as he lived. In 1813 he married and removed his residence to New York City, but continued to devote his time and energy to adding to his river and harbor craft. In 1817 he built a steamboat to run between New York and New Brunswick, N. J., and himself acted as its captain.

In 1827 he leased a ferry running to Elizabeth, N. J., and a short time later acquired an interest in steamboat lines which plied up and down the Hudson river and through Long Island Sound. His business prospered and he was rapidly becoming a wealthy man—rich enough by 1851 to establish a fast steamship line from New York to California. Passengers were carried down the east coast, across the Bay of Mexico to Central America and there transferred across the Isthmus of Nicaragua to the Pacific Coast where other vessels waited to carry them northward to California ports. It proved a profitable investment and was reported to have netted the "Commodore" $10,000,000. Another opportunity presented itself during the Crimean War when British shipping was off the seas, and Vanderbilt took advantage of that fact to establish a steamship line between New York and Havre, France, which also proved a paying proposition, but the "Commodore" about this time becoming interested in transportation by land, began to transfer his capital from water traffic to transportation by rail, and was soon entered upon a career of railroad financing and management that ended by building up one of the world's greatest fortunes. He had become president of the New York and Harlem Railway, and in 1864 acquired control of the Hudson River Railroad, which he speedily placed on a profitable basis and then acquired also the New York Central of which he became president in 1867.

During the Civil War he presented to the government the steamship *Vanderbilt* and received in recognition of that gift a gold medal which Congress ordered to be struck off. He managed the railroad lines under his control with great business sagacity, improved their organization and added to their service to the public. He consolidated the New York Central and the Hudson River Railways in 1869 and eventually extended the system to Chicago through the acquisition of a large interest in three intervening lines, the Lake Shore, the Canada Southern and the Michigan Central Railroads.

He was interested in various educational and philanthropic enterprises, and one of his chief benefactions was the gift of $1,000,000 to found Vanderbilt University in Nashville, Tenn., a charter for which had been granted in 1872 under the name of Central University. The name was changed to Vanderbilt the following year and the work of erecting the buildings was started in 1875. The "Commodore's" son, William H. Vanderbilt, and his grandsons have continued his benefactions to that institution.

Vanderbilt died in New York City on Jan. 4, 1877, leaving a fortune estimated at $100,000,000—one of the largest in the world at that time—the bulk of which went to his son William H. Vanderbilt, who had been a partner in all his huge railroad and financial interests, succeeded him as president of the New York Central and Hudson River lines, and continued to develop and expand that large system with its many connections.

ANTHONY VAN DYCK   1599–1641

ANTHONY VAN DYCK, Flemish portrait painter, was born in Antwerp, March 22, 1599, the son of a wealthy silk manufacturer. Having shown an early inclination for drawing and painting, he was sent in his 15th year to study under Rubens, and at 19 he was admitted a master to the Guild of St. Luke. He made his first visit to England in 1620 and it is considered probable that he then painted the portrait of James I which is now at Windsor. In 1623 he went to Italy, visited Venice, Genoa and Rome and remained for two years in the latter city. In Genoa he painted a number of portraits of the nobility and in Rome was commissioned to do a "Crucifixion" for Cardinal Bentivoglio and two paintings for the Pope, an "Ascension" and an "Adoration of the Magi." While in Italy he had studied the works of the old Italian masters and that of a number of his contemporaries and had improved his technique. He returned to Antwerp about 1628 and soon set to work on one of his finest paintings, "The Ecstasy of St. Augustine," for the Augustinian monastery. Another masterpiece of his early period is "Christ Crucified Between Thieves," painted for the church of the Récollets at Mechlin where the canvas may now be seen in the cathedral. Some of his best work was done during this period.

He was rapidly coming into prominence as a portrait painter and many notables among his contemporaries sat to him. These portraits were issued in 1641 as engravings, a large number of which were executed by Van Dyck himself with such skill that he ranks among the world's great engravers as well as among its most famous painters. He visited England again in 1629, but soon afterward was at the Hague engaged in painting portraits of the Prince of Orange, his family and other notables. Upon his third visit to England he was warmly received at court and knighted by Charles I who made him his painter in ordinary and granted him a pension of 200 pounds a year. He executed many portraits of the king and the royal family which are among his best known works, and numerous other paintings and in 1634 returned to the Netherlands where he painted the portrait of Ferdinand of Austria, now in Madrid, and other prominent personages.

Among other canvases executed during this period were "The Adoration of the Shepherds," now in the church at Termonde, and "The Deposition" which is in the Antwerp Museum. For the remaining six years of his life he made his home in England. He painted portraits of the king and queen and their two children and of many of the nobles at court. His reputation was second to none among his contemporaries and time has upheld it. He was a graceful painter, with a keen sense of beauty and of character, and a tenderness that is lacking in many of the masters of the art.

He married in 1640 an English woman, Lady Mary Ruthven, granddaughter of the Earl of Gowrie. He was a man of refined and aristocratic tastes, was fond of pleasure, spent freely and liked to live lavishly. Consequently he was nearly always in straitened financial circumstances, due in part also to difficulty in collecting payment for the royal commissions which he received. Examples of his work are to be found in most of the larger art museums, not only in England but on the Continent and in America. The National Gallery in London possesses seven. He made a last visit to Antwerp in 1640, spent some time in Paris and died at Blackfriars, soon after his return to London, on Dec. 9, 1641. He was buried in old St. Paul's Cathedral.

VELAZQUEZ   1599–1660

DIEGO RODRÍGUEZ DE SILVA Y VELAZQUEZ (vå läs'kåth), the greatest painter of Spain, was the son of Juan Rodríguez de Silva, a lawyer of noble Portuguese descent, and was born in Seville in 1599. Following a Spanish custom he was known by his mother's maiden name of Valazquez (usually spelled Velasquez in English and French). He was trained in languages and philosophy for a learned profession, but his bent was toward art and he studied under the painter, Herrera, then for five years in the school conducted by Pacheco. In 1618 he married Juana de Miranda, his master's daughter. Of his paintings in his Seville period are "El Aguador" (The Water Carrier), now at Apsley House, London; "Adoration of the Magi" at Madrid; "Christ and the Pilgrims of Emmaus," in the New York Metropolitan Museum of Art.

In 1622 he visited Madrid where he painted several portraits, the poet Gongora among them. The following year Olivarez, minister of Philip IV, summoned him back to Madrid and in 1624 he moved his family to the capital which became his home thereafter and he spent the remainder of his life in the service of the king. Two of his later portraits of Philip are in the Prado. In competition with three Italian painters in the king's service, he captured a prize offered for a picture on the expulsion of the Moors from Spain. When Rubens visited Madrid in 1628 the king appointed Velazquez to be his guide among the art treasures of the capital, and through Rubens' influence he obtained leave and financial assistance to visit Italy. Before going he painted his famous masterpiece, "Bacchus" (1629), now in the Madrid Gallery. In Rome he painted "Forge of Vulcan" (Madrid Gallery), "Joseph's Coat" (Escorial), and some landscapes. He visited Naples where he painted the Infanta Maria, sister of the king, and then returned to the court at Madrid where he made many portraits of the young prince, Don Baltasar Carlos, and of the Duke of Olivarez, two of which are in the collection of the Hispanic Society, New York, and one in the Madrid Gallery. Most famous of all are his equestrian portraits of the king and his retinue at the hunt with his marvelous representations of the horses and dogs. The "Boar Hunt" (National Gallery, London) and the "Stag Hunt" (Prado) are admirable examples. The sculptor Montañes made a bronze statue from one of Velazquez' equestrian portraits of King Philip which is now in the Plaza del Oriente, Madrid. Many portraits of this period are to be found in New York and Boston, as well as in continental cities. The greatest of his religious paintings is "Christ on the Cross" (1638) now in the Madrid Gallery.

He had received steady promotion in the royal household, both in increased pension and in responsibilities and was the recipient of many honors. His daughter had married the painter, del Mazo. In 1649 he made a second visit to Italy, visiting Genoa, Milan, Venice, Rome, where he bought paintings by Titian, Tintoretto and Veronese. His famous portrait of Pope Innocent X, painted in Rome, is in the Doria Palace in that city. A painting of his servant, Pareja, won his election to the Academy of St. Luke. He sailed for Spain in 1651, with many paintings and 300 pieces of statuary. He made many portraits of Philip's new wife, Mariana of Austria, and at about this period executed many of his most famous masterpieces, among which are "El Bobo del Coria," "El Niño de Vallegas," "Don Antonio del Inglés," "Æsop," "Menippus," (all in the Madrid Gallery), "Las Meniñas," "Venus and Cupid" (National Gallery, London), "Coronation of the Virgin" (Madrid), "St. Anthony the Abbot and St. Paul the Hermit" (Madrid), "Las Hilanderas," 1656 (Madrid).

He was stricken with fever in July 1660, died on August 6 following, and was buried in the Fuensalida vault of the church of San Juan, which was destroyed by the French in 1811. His place of interment is now unknown.

Velazquez' fame did not spread far beyond his native Spain until 150 years after his death. The impressionists have hailed him as their forerunner. His works display great dramatic force and realism and he was a consummate master of color and detail.

GIUSEPPE VERDI   1813–1901

GIUSEPPE FORTUNINO FRANCESCO VERDI (věr'dě), was one of the most famous Italian composers whose operas are still sung in all the great opera houses. Most popular of them are *Rigoletto, Aida, Il Trovatore, Otello* and *Falstaff*. He was born on Oct. 10, 1813, at Le Roncole, near Busseto, where his parents kept an inn. While a young boy he was apprenticed to Antonio Barezzi, a merchant of Busseto, who was a musician of ability and president of the Philharmonic Society of the town. There the boy began his musical education. He studied under Provesi, conductor of the municipal orchestra, for which organization he wrote many marches and other compositions. His first symphony was performed in 1828 and four years later he went to Milan to continue his studies. The Conservatory rejected him as a pupil on the ground of his lack of musical ability, but he studied under Vincenzo Lavigna. The death of Provesi in 1833 recalled him to Busseto where he succeeded Provesi as conductor of the municipal orchestra but not as cathedral organist, although he soon afterwards became organist of the church of San Bartolomeo. His first opera, *Oberto, Conte di San Bonifacio,* was performed upon his return to Milan in 1839. He next set to work on a comic opera, *Un Giorno di Regno* (or *Il Finto Stanislao*), but he was so affected by the death of his wife and two children that the work was a complete failure and in his disappointment he declared he would write nothing more for the stage, but in 1842 he produced a new opera, *Nabuccodonosor,* which was not only a success but placed him in the front rank of the composers of the day.

In 1843 he composed *I Lombardi,* and the following year *Ernani* which carried his reputation throughout Europe. Thenceforward the demand for his works was continuous and he composed rapidly, somewhat to the detriment of his style. His *Macbeth, Luisa Miller* and *I Masnadieri* proved disappointing, but with *Rigoletto* (1851) he reached the highwater mark of his second period. The two following operas, *Il Trovatore* and *La Traviata,* rank with it in musical worth although they have not retained quite the popularity of *Rigoletto*. In *Les Vêpres Siciliennes* of 1855 he attempted the grandiose style of French opera. *Un Ballo in Maschera* (1859), *La Forza del Destino* and *Don Carlos* are the only works of the next ten years that maintain any hold upon opera-goers of today and they are but infrequently sung. With *Aida,* however, written for Ismail Pasha, the Khedive of Egypt, and performed in Cairo in December, 1871, he achieved one of the most successful operas ever written. While retaining Italian characteristics in this composition, he broke away from the Donizetto tradition, perhaps coming under the influence of Wagner. His *Requiem* (1874) commemorating the death of Manzoni, was bitterly assailed by many critics because of his application of his new method to sacred music, but later critics have accepted it as a work of genius.

In 1887 Verdi produced his opera *Otello,* which is considered an advance both musically and dramatically over anything he had hitherto written. He was then 74 years old. He turned to Shakespeare again for his next subject, Falstaff, produced at Milan in 1893, when in his 80th year. It is held to have the dramatic and musical quality of *Otello,* with a fancifulness and humor in the true Mozartian mood. It was Verdi's last and perhaps his greatest opera. In 1898 he produced four sacred pieces, *Ave Maria* and *Laudi alla Virgine* for voices alone, and *Stabat Mater* and *Te Deum* for voices and orchestra, all of which are beautiful examples of the musical art. His non-dramatic compositions were few in number; among them a string quartet of 1873, a hymn written for the opening of the International Exhibition of 1862, two sets of songs, a Paternoster for a five-part chorus, and *Ave Maria* for soprano solo with string accompaniment.

In 1849 he had married a celebrated prima donna and his later years were spent in retirement near Busseto. He died in Milan Jan. 27, 1901. In 1898 he had presented a large sum of money to Milan to found a home for old and invalid musicians.

VERGIL (or VIRGIL) 70 B.C.–19 B.C.

PUBLIUS VERGILIUS MARO, greatest of the Latin poets, is renowned for romantic imagination and for the sweetness and rhythm of his poems. His Æneid is a world masterpiece known to every student of Latin. He was the son of a small property owner of Andes, near the ancient Roman town of Mantua, and was born Oct. 15, 70 B.C. The population of Cisalpine Gaul was chiefly Celtic, although the civilization of Rome had long since penetrated there, and the warmth of his temperament, his lively imagination, his melancholy, his romanticism, are convincing evidence that Celtic blood flowed in the great Latin poet's veins. That fact doubtless had much to do with his success as a poet and the harmony and singing quality with which he was able to invest the Latin tongue gave his work an appeal to the cultivated tastes of the age. He received his education at the schools of Cremona and Milan until he was 16, after which he was sent to Rome to pursue the study of rhetoric and philosophy. He was probably scribbling verse at this time, as some of the compositions accredited to him bear internal evidences of being juvenile work, such as the *Culex* and the *Moretum* which were written in hexameters, the *Copa,* and a number of elegiac poems. He was a diligent reader throughout his life and studied the literature of Greece as well as that of his own country.

After the victory of the Triumvirate in 41 B.C., Vergil's farm was part of the land confiscated by the State and partitioned among the disbanded soldiers. The governor of the province sent him to Rome with recommendations to Octavian. His farm was not restored to him, but he received compensation for it and in Rome he soon became one of the group of scholars and literary men that Maecenas drew about himself. Later he introduced the poet Horace into this same circle. Through the generosity of Maecenas and other patrons of men of letters, he was provided with financial means so that he was free to devote himself to his literary pursuits. His first works were the *Eclogues,* ten pastoral poems written between 43 and 37 B.C., in which he sings of the lives and loves of the shepherds and the country folk; modeled on the *Idylls* of the Greek Theocritus. These met with great appreciation from cultured Romans and established Vergil's reputation as a poet. The next seven years were spent in writing the *Georgics,* four books dealing with farming, vinegrowing, olive culture and pastoral life. These are considered the finest poems in the Latin language from the point of view of finish, and were said to have been written at the suggestion of Maecenas in the hope of stimulating interest in agricultural life and in the rehabilitation of farms which had been ruined during the civil wars.

But the book that was to immortalize the name of Vergil was still to be written. It was the emperor who urged him to tell in poetic form the story of Æneas, the Trojan who fled from the sack of Troy, sailed up the Tiber, settled in Rome and gradually established himself as the master of most of Italy, founder alike of the Roman nation and of the Julian family. Vergil's romantic Celtic imagination must have been fired by the theme and he spent eleven years in writing the *Æneid.* In 19 B.C. he embarked for a prolonged journey to Athens and Greece with the intention of spending a considerable time there in revising this manuscript. He was taken ill in Athens, took ship for Italy and reached Brundusium where he died on Sept. 21, 19 B.C. He was buried at Naples, on the road to Pozzuoli, as he had desired, and for several centuries his tomb was regarded as a sacred place.

Vergil's life apparently was one of calm enjoyment; his character such that the great minds of the era paid homage to him; the sweetness of his temper and the high moral quality of his life were in striking contrast to the licentiousness of the times. Horace paid tribute to him in his odes and epistles. He never married and his modesty was such that the recognition accorded to his genius during his lifetime was a source of genuine distress to him.

Despite the perfection of the *Georgics* and the more uneven versifying of the *Æneid,* the latter even in the unfinished state in which he left it ranks as his greatest work. This great historical epic shows a warmth of humanity, a fine range of poetic imagination fired by the high drama in many of the episodes treated that inspired the highest reaches of his genius. He was so far from satisfied with the work that shortly before his death he wished to have it destroyed, but was dissuaded from his purpose and the work was published with only such slight revision as was necessary.

AMERICUS VESPUCIUS   1452–1512

Americus Vespucius (věs pū′ shǐ ŭs), (Amerigo Vespucci) was an Italian navigator for whom America was named. He was born in Florence, Italy, on March 18, 1452 and acquired a practical knowledge of astronomy which made him eventually one of the greatest navigators of the times and the greatest expert in calculating longitude and latitude. While a clerk in a commercial office of the Medici in Florence, he studied geography, made a hobby of collecting globes, maps and charts, and became a skilled map draughtsman. In 1491 or earlier he was sent to Barcelona to represent the Medicis' important business interests in Spain and there he became connected in 1493 with the Seville commercial house of Juanoto Berardi who was employed by the Crown to fit out vessels for expeditions across the Atlantic. Berardi died in 1495 and it fell to Vespucius to complete a contract to supply twelve ships.

Our knowledge of the life of Vespucius from 1496 to 1504 is based on two of his letters, one written in 1503 to Lorenzo di Pier de' Medici;

the other in 1504 to Piero Soderini, gonfaloniere of Florence. The latter gives an account of four voyages in which he claimed to have taken part, two in the employ of Spain, two in that of Portugal. The first expedition sailed from Cadiz in May, 1497, and returned in October, 1498, evidently having explored the coast of South America. According to Vespucius' statement, he started on the second voyage in May, 1499, with three ships under Alonzo de Ojeda (Hojeda), sailed southwest and crossed the ocean in 44 days, finding land and returning to Cadiz in September, 1500.

Entering the service of Dom Manuel of Portugal, he then claims to have taken part in a third expedition which left Lisbon in May, 1501. He has given two accounts of this alleged voyage, differing in details, dates and distances. He apparently reached the American coast in August and returned to Portugal in September, 1502. His second Portuguese voyage, which was his last alleged trip to America, started from Lisbon in May, 1503, with six ships, reaching Brazil; he states that he built a fort and harbor and returned to Lisbon in June, 1504. In February of the next year he was again in Spain and met Christopher Columbus who in a letter to his son Diego speaks of him in the most friendly terms as "a very worthy man . . . determined to do all he can for me," which seems to refute the contention that Vespucius attempted to secure the credit which properly belonged to Columbus.

In April, 1505, Vespucius became a naturalized Spanish citizen; in 1508 he was appointed chief pilot of Spain, which office he filled until his death at Seville on Feb. 22, 1512.

It seems certain that he had explored a considerable part of the South American coast and perhaps sailed around the Gulf of Mexico and part way up the coast of North America, but investigators generally do not credit the voyage of 1497 and the portions of his accounts which have been preserved are so confused that it is difficult to arrive at exact knowledge of his voyages. The suggestion that the new world be named for Americus Vespucius was first made by the German geographer Martin Waldsenmüller who translated Vespucius' letter to Soderini and the name America was first given only to the South American continent, but gradually became applied to the whole of the western world.

QUEEN VICTORIA   1819–1901

ALEXANDRINA VICTORIA, who became queen of the United Kingdom of Great Britain and Ireland and Empress of India, was the only child of

Edward, Duke of Kent and fourth son of George III. She was born in Kensington Palace, May 24, 1819. Her mother was Victoria Maria Louisa, daughter of Francis, Duke of Saxe-Coburg. The Duke of Kent died in 1820, when the future queen was but eight months old. In addition to the usual education of a royal princess, Victoria was thoroughly instructed in the principles of the British government so that when she ascended the throne at the age of eighteen, following the death of her uncle, William IV, she was familiar with her duties and with the proper methods of royal procedure. She was crowned at Westminster Abbey on June 28, 1838 and reigned for sixty-three years. Her long reign (the longest in the history of the British Empire) covered a period of great prosperity and territorial expansion with development of Britain's colonies and dependencies and also of marked internal and legislative development. During those years England became a dominating industrial power, the Suez canal was opened and India came fully under British rule. Probably next to Elizabeth she was the greatest of England's queens and undoubtedly the best loved.

On Feb. 10, 1840 she married Albert, Prince of Saxe-Coburg and Gotha; a marriage not greatly to the liking of her advisers at the time but one which proved a most happy and successful union. Four sons and five daughters were born to the royal couple; the eldest son, Albert Edward, succeeded to the throne as Edward VII in 1901 and the Princess Royal, Victoria, married Frederick III of Germany. The Prince Consort, Albert, died in 1861 and although for several years thereafter the widowed queen seldom appeared in public, she did not neglect the duties of her high position.

She played a prominent part in the extension of the franchise (1865–68) which resulted in the Hyde Park riots, urging her new and conservative prime minister, Lord Derby, to obtain a settlement of the question. She had a horror of demonstrations of popular discontent, always fearing they might lead ultimately to republican demonstrations. Her insistence undoubtedly was effective in the passing of the final franchise bill, but not until Disraeli had ably piloted it through the House of Commons. She had little understanding of or sympathy for the Irish and regarded the demand for home rule as disloyal, refusing to establish a residence in Ireland or to have the Prince of Wales take up residence there, yet she appreciated the bravery of the Irish troops and one of her last public acts was a three weeks' visit to Dublin in 1900 as a recognition of their gallantry in the South African campaign. While she disapproved of Gladstone's policy of disestablishing and partially disendowing the Irish Protestant church as an encroachment on her own prerogatives and a concession to popery, she accepted it after it had been voted by the electorate.

Disraeli's short premiership in 1868 had won him royal favor, dispelling the dislike which she had formerly felt toward him. His vigorous foreign policy pleased her, as did his courtly homage. He acquired the Suez Canal for Britain and made Victoria Empress of India (1876). Among the many important events of her reign of national and international significance were the Opium War in China (1840–42); the Crimean War (1854–56); the Indian Mutiny of 1857–58 and the taking over of India by the government from the East India Company; the rebellion in Canada and the later establishment of the Canadian confederation (1867); the Transvaal War (1880); the establishment of British domination in Egypt (1882); the Australian federation (1900).

In her personal character and life Victoria was outstanding among British monarchs and exerted an enormous moral influence upon her subjects, as well as upon the larger policies of the government in bringing about harmonious relations and a spirit of unity between the home government and its various dependencies. Her own family life was most unostentatious and simple throughout.

The 60th year of her reign (1897) was observed as a Diamond Jubilee throughout the British dominions and a huge celebration was held in London. Honored and loved by her subjects, she died on Jan. 22, 1901 and was mourned by the entire world. The casket containing her remains was transported from the Isle of Wight between lines of warships and accompanied by a military procession from Windsor to London. She was buried in the Frogmore Mausoleum beside her consort.

FRANÇOIS VILLON   1431– circa 1463

FRANÇOIS VILLON (vē yon'), French poet, was born in 1431, probably in Paris. His real name was François de Montcorbier, but he was known throughout his life by the name of Villon, which he assumed out of gratitude to his "more than father," Guillaume de Villon, to whom he owed his education. He was sometimes known also as François de Loges. We have only meagre details of his life; his parents were poor and ignorant; his father died apparently while François was a young boy and from one of his ballads it appears that his mother was living when the poet was thirty. Guillaume de Villon, into whose home he was received, was chaplain in the collegiate church of Saint-Benoît-le-Bétourné and professor of canon law, and may have been a relative of the poet. François took the arts course at the University of Paris, received a bachelor degree in 1449 and his master's degree in 1452. He was evidently popular and lived the usual roistering life of students of that time. On June 5, 1455 in the rue Saint-Jacques, he became involved in a quarrel with a priest named Philippe Chermoye (or Sermaise) whom he stabbed, perhaps in self-defense. Upon the priest's death a short time later he went into hiding. A sentence of banishment was pronounced against him which was later remitted in January, 1456.

By the end of the year, however, he was embroiled in another difficulty, this time over a girl, Catherine de Vaucelles, mentioned frequently in his poems, and was so severely beaten that, fearing the ridicule of his companions, he fled to Angers where he had an uncle who was a monk. He had been involved also in the robbery of 500 gold crowns from the college of Navarre. The theft was discovered in March, 1457, and was traced to a band of student robbers, one of whose members, Guy Tabarie, arrested a year later, turned king's evidence and accused Villon of being their leader, intimating that he had gone to Angers to plan further robberies there. A sentence of banishment was again pronounced against the poet and he remained away from Paris for four years, wandering about the country, probably as one of a gang of thieves. He visited the court of the Duc d'Orléans at Blois; was imprisoned at Bourges and later found protection for a short time at Bourbonnais with the Duc de Bourbon. He wandered about Dauphiné, was imprisoned in Orléans, tortured and sentenced to death, but released on the passage through the town of the little Princess of Orléans. He was locked up in the bishop's prison at Meung during the summer of 1461, and was released with other prisoners upon the royal progress of Louis XI through the city.

Unedifying as this account is, he nevertheless won renown as one of the greatest lyric poets of the age. His *Petit Testament* (1456) was followed by the *Grand Testament,* a poem of 173 stanzas, which has made his fame immortal. It was written at about the age of 30 when the poet was suffering from torture, imprisonment and debauchery, with little to look forward to, and is a miscellany of cynical commentaries, ironic legacies to friends— all interwoven with many ballads and rondeaux. His style was picturesque and vivid and he paints a colorful and doubtless true picture of the sordid life of Paris of which he was a part. By the autumn of 1462 he was back in Paris determined to adopt a more orderly life, but in November he was imprisoned in the Châtelet on a charge of theft which was not proved and he was liberated on bail. Present at another street quarrel, from which he tried to escape, he was arrested, tortured and sentenced to be hanged.

After a year's imprisonment the punishment was changed to banishment from Paris.

Nothing further is known of François Villon's life. Aside from his two *Testaments* and a *Codicil*, his works consist chiefly of ballads and rondeaux mostly on the vanity of human life, pervaded by grim humor and a realism and frankness that is often revolting; but it is by the standards of his own times that he should be judged. Despite the many black pages of his life, he displayed a certain sincerity and patriotism, gratitude toward those who befriended him and above all sympathy for those who were in misery. He was always ready to acknowledge his sins and make a new start, but usually gave way to the first temptation.

VOLTAIRE   1694-1778

VOLTAIRE (vŏl'târ'), French writer and philosopher of whom it has been said that "his pen runs and laughs." His true name was François Marie Arouet. He was born in Paris, Nov. 21, 1694, the younger son of one François Arouet who was employed in the *Chambre des Comptes*. He was educated at the Jesuitical College Louis-le-Grand and showed himself a brilliant student. After a few years spent in the gay and somewhat dissipated life of the youth of the period, he went to Holland as a secretary in the suite of the ambassador, Marquis de Châteauneuf, but as the result of an intrigue he was dismissed and sent home, following which for a short time he studied in a lawyer's office in compliance with his father's wish.

He entered a poem in a contest for the Academy prize, lost it, lampooned his successful rival, and by that and other writings achieved a certain reputation as a wit. The Duc d'Orleans, who was Regent, banished him from Paris for a short time in 1716 because of an article supposedly directed at himself, and about a year later Voltaire wrote another accusing the Regent of horrible crimes, as a result of which and of certain other acts wrongly ascribed to him he was sent to the Bastille for eleven months. In 1718 his first tragedy, *Œdipe,* was performed with great success. At about this time he took the name of Voltaire. Several other plays were produced, but less successfully, and in the meantime he was working on his epic poem on Henry IV, in which he championed the cause of religious liberalism so well that he was prohibited from publishing it. In 1723 it was printed secretly at Rouen under the title of *La Ligue ou Henri le Grand*. Sent to the Bastille again in 1726 as the result of a quarrel with the Chevalier de Rohan-Chabot, he was released upon his promise to leave

France and he proceeded to England where he remained for some two years. He had already made the acquaintance of Lord Bolingbroke and through him he now met Pope, Chesterfield, and other intellectuals and, speedily learning the language, he became familiar with the works of the great English writers. He wrote in English an essay on epic poetry and one on the civil wars of France and republished his poem under the title of La Henriade, which brought him fame in England and throughout the Continent, despite the efforts of the French government to suppress it.

He was permitted to return to France about 1728, lived in Paris for four years and amassed a large fortune by speculating and participation in lotteries. He wrote several dramas, his *History of Charles XII,* and published one of his greatest works, *Letters Concerning the English Nation,* which were revolutionary in acquainting the French with many British institutions, notably its system of religious toleration; freedom of the individual and the press; its literature and the work of its scientists. In 1734 he formed an intimacy with Mme. du Châtelet, a woman of great intellectual attainments, at whose château he spent much time until her death in 1749. They were fruitful years. He wrote *Mérope, Mahomet, A Treatise on Metaphysics,* a treatise on Newton's philosophy. Stories, poems, dramas, novels, satires came from his pen. His English letters had brought him into disfavor at the court, but through the influence of the king's mistress, Mme. de Pompadour, he regained the royal favor, was made royal historiographer and gentleman-in-ordinary to the king, and was later elected to the Academy. After the death of Mme. de Châtelet, he established a home in Paris, but found himself unpopular and at odds with certain literary rivals and he yielded to the importunities of Frederick the Great, who had for some years been his admirer and flatterer, and had urged him to live at the Prussian court. In 1750 he went to Berlin where he was received with the greatest honor and affection. They soon quarreled, however, owing to Frederick's violent temper and to Voltaire's caustic ridicule of certain high personages, and within two years they parted. During his stay he had published his highly successful history, *Siècle de Louis XIV.*

In 1756–59 appeared his *Moeurs et l'Esprit de Nations,* an ambitious history of events from the time of Charlemagne to that of Louis XIV, which had engaged him for many years. *Candide* also appeared in 1759, followed by the tragedy *Tancrède.* Being again unwelcome at the French court, after four years in Geneva he bought an estate at Ferney where he spent his last twenty years, devoting himself largely to the writings of pamphlets and short articles which he distributed in defiance of the authorities. He was a shrewd business man and remained affluent throughout his life.

While his writings covered the field of drama, philosophy, romance, history, literary criticism, poetry, he is remembered chiefly for his keen satire and his attacks on religious intolerance and established Christian beliefs, although he has been erroneously described as an atheist. Whatever his subject, his style was always facile, gay and buoyant, carrying the reader along as a cork is carried on a hurrying brook. In 1778 he visited Paris to witness the production of his last tragedy, *Irene,* and was received with great acclaim. The fatigue and excitement proved too much for him and he died on May 30, 1778. In July, 1791, his body was transferred to the Pantheon.

RICHARD WAGNER   1813–1883

RICHARD WAGNER, German composer and creator of the music drama, was born May 22, 1813, at Leipzig, and educated in Dresden. He early showed an inclination for literature and music and had translated twelve books of the *Odyssey* when he was 13; a year later he wrote a tragedy. He was greatly influenced in his musical tastes by Beethoven and to a lesser extent by Weber. His first operatic composition was *Die Feen* which he began in 1833, but which was not performed until 1888, five years after his death. He was engaged for a time in musical activities in Königsberg, Heidelberg and Riga, but believing that he might find better opportunities in Paris he went to that city in 1839 and for three years made vain attempts to get his opera, *Rienzi,* performed, but eventually gave up hope and in 1843 returned to Dresden. There better fortune awaited him; *Rienzi* was performed with much success, and he was appointed kapellmeister that same year. He went to work on a new opera, *Der Fliegende Hollander,* which received a public hearing in 1844, but its reception was much less cordial than that accorded to *Rienzi*. The following year *Tannhäuser* was performed, meeting with even less success, and Wagner thereafter wrote several essays in which he undertook to explain his theory of music drama, in which the book, the music, the acting and the stage setting are of almost equal value in obtaining the effects aimed at.

Late in 1848 the Hungarian composer Liszt presented *Tannhäuser* more successfully at Weimar giving its author new hope and courage and the incident led to an abiding friendship between the two composers. Wagner had now completed *Lohengrin* and had written the poem, *Siegfrieds Tod,* but he was compelled to flee from Saxony before the opera received a production, owing to his sympathy with the revolutionary cause then agitating Germany. It was twelve years before he was allowed to return; years of hardship, poverty and bitterness, the latter finding expression in his polemical writings in which he showed his vein of sarcasm and invective. He worked intermittently on the poem of the *Nibelungen Ring,* which formed the books of the trilogy for which he later composed the music, completing it in 1852. He next set to work on *Rheingold,* an introduction to the trilogy, and by 1856 had completed *Die Walkurie,* which is Part I of his famous *Nibelungen Ring.* A year later the poem of *Tristan* had been written, and the two following years were devoted to composing the music.

He received permission to return to Germany in 1861, but failed to procure the production of his operas until King Ludwig of Bavaria invited him to Munich. There *Tristan und Isolde* was performed in 1865, and three years later his light opera, *Die Meistersinger.* The tide had at length turned and his career from then on was one of continuing triumph, although he was not without his detractors. Schopenhauer, who had been one of his early champions and had written much in favor of his theory of music drama, turned against him and denied the value of his music, but the public had found in his mythological operas something new, strange and beautiful, and they aroused more and more critical enthusiasm. *Siegfried,* Part II of his trilogy, was completed in 1869. In 1872 there was begun at Baireuth the building of a theater for the production of his operas which was completed in 1876, and the first of his works to be presented there was the *Nibelungen* trilogy, the last or third part of which, *Götterdämmerung,* he had finished two years earlier.

Parsifal had its first performance at Baireuth in 1882 and shortly thereafter Wagner went to Venice, where he died Feb. 13, 1883. He was buried in the garden of his home at Baireuth. He had married in 1836 but separated from his wife in 1861 and nine years later he married Cosima, daughter of the composer Liszt, and former wife of Von Bülow, who survived him until 1919. It was through her efforts after his death that the Baireuth festivals were successfully maintained.

WALLENSTEIN   1583–1634

ALBRECHT WENZEL EUSEBIUS VON WALLENSTEIN (or WALDSTEIN), famous Bohemian general of the Thirty Years' War, was born at Hermanic, Bohemia, Sept. 14, 1583, the son of a Czech Protestant noble who died while he was still a child. A Catholic uncle had the boy educated by the

Jesuits, and he became a staunch adherent of that faith. As a young man he fought in the Imperial army against the Turks in Hungary and served under the Archduke Ferdinand when the latter attacked Venice. He had in the meantime become one of the richest of Bohemia's noblemen through inheriting his uncle's estate and also that of a wealthy widow whom he had married and who died in 1614. When the Bohemians revolted against their emperor in 1618, he raised troops and fought for the emperor. Upon the defeat of the Bohemians he was rewarded for his zeal by grants of huge tracts of confiscated estates and in 1623 was made Prince of Friedland in Mecklenberg. Two years later he raised an army of 20,000 men which he equipped and offered to the emperor and in 1625 he was appointed to the high command of the imperial armies. With his troops, made up of adventurers from far and near, he proceeded against the forces of King Christian IV of Denmark who had taken up arms for the Protestants against the emperor and after a brilliant campaign in north Germany with the aid of Tilly he broke the power of Christian, defeated the Protestant princes of Jutland and Mecklenberg, winning those principalities for the emperor who sold him the dukedom of Sagan in Silesia, gave him the duchy of Mecklenberg and created Friedland a hereditary duchy. He made a number of unsuccessful attempts to capture Stralsund.

He was consumed by ambition; was arrogant and offensive to the princes of Germany and when Gustavus Adolphus brought an army into northern Germany to aid the Protestant cause, the princes were powerful enough to compel the emperor to dismiss Wallenstein in 1630. The following year, however, he was recalled to supreme command of the army and sent to check the advancing Swedish forces, after having driven the Saxons out of Bohemia. With a force of 40,000 well disciplined troops, he took up an entrenched position at Nuremberg and repulsed the efforts of Gustavus Adolphus to dislodge him. In 1632, however, he suffered a defeat by the Swedish troops at the great battle of Lutzen in which Gustavus Adolphus lost his life. Instead of making a further attempt to crush the Swedes, Wallenstein withdrew to Bohemia. Germany was distracted by the wars, the rivalries and jealousies of Protestant and Catholic princes, and Wallenstein took advantage of the unsettled state of affairs to attempt to forge a fortune and a dynasty for himself. He played Protestant noble against Catholic noble, deceiving both and deceiving the emperor who believed that his professed desire to restore peace to Germany was sincere. He carried on negotiations with France, Sweden, Saxony and Brandenburg.

His enemies were too strongly entrenched to be lightly thrust aside and they finally convinced Ferdinand that he was engaged in treasonable activities. In January, 1634, the emperor deposed him from his supreme command of the army and in February he was proclaimed a traitor. He still hoped to find a supporter among the German princes and made for Saxe-Weimar hoping to meet the Swedes under Duke Bernhard. He reached Eger but was there set upon and slain on Feb. 25, 1634 under the direction of a certain Col. Butler who had joined him by the way with instructions to seize his person. His estate were confiscated by the emperor who rewarded the murderers for their "act of justice." Wallenstein was buried at Gitschin and in 1732 his remains were reinterred in the castle chapel of Münchengrätz.

He was a statesman as well as a great soldier; tolerant and liberal toward those who differed with him in religion, on which he had no very deep convictions of his own, but he was unscrupulous and the victim of his own overpowering pride and ambition.

GEORGE WASHINGTON   1732–1799

GEORGE WASHINGTON, the "father of his country," commander-in-chief of the American forces in the war for independence, and first president of the United States, was born Feb. 22, 1732 at Bridges Creek, near Fredericksburg, Va., son of Augustine Washington, a well-to-do planter whose grandfather had emigrated from Sulgrave, Eng., in 1657. He attended school irregularly, rode about his father's six plantations, learned to raise tobacco and stock, and studied surveying. His father died when George was 11, leaving the boy to the guardianship of his half-brother, Lawrence, who died in 1752, making George his executor and heir. He became public surveyor of Fairfax County in 1749 and in 1752 was made adjutant of one of Virginia's four military districts. The next year Governor Dinwiddie sent him to warn the French from further encroachments in the Ohio Valley, later appointing him lieutenant-colonel of the provincial regiment in the French and Indian War. After defeating the French in a minor engagement he withdrew to the fort he had built at Great Meadows and was forced to surrender after a 9-hour siege. Promoted to a colonelcy, he served as aide to General Braddock against Fort Duquesne and when Braddock's army was ambushed and routed he brought up the reserves and thus effected the escape of the shattered army. In August, 1775, he was made commander of all the Virginia troops which he led for two years against the French and Indians. In 1758 he commanded the advance guard which finally captured Fort Duquesne.

Following his marriage on Jan. 6, 1759, to Martha Dandridge Custis, Virginia's richest widow, the care of her large estates was added to that of his own and he became one of the richest holders of tobacco plantations in the state. In May, 1774, he was a leading member of the first revolutionary legislature in Virginia, and was one of the state's seven delegates to the first Continental Congress in Philadelphia the following September. In November he took command of the Virginia volunteer companies, and soon after the first fighting was made commander-in-chief of the colonial army (June 15, 1775). On July 3, at Cambridge, Mass., he took command of the 16,000 poorly equipped men constituting the army and during the next several months, while keeping the British in Boston, he drilled and trained his men. When the British set sail for New York in March, 1776, he hurried thither by land and placed half of his army, under Gen. Israel Putnam, on Brooklyn Heights, where they were defeated on August 26 with a loss of 5000 men. While the British General Howe delayed in the attack, and under cover of a fog, Washington got the rest of his command across the river into New York City but was forced northward until the loss of two forts compelled him to cross the Hudson into New Jersey where he won brilliant engagements at Trenton and Princeton. Corwallis was sent to Trenton with 8000 men to capture him, but during the night Washington crossed the Delaware with his force to Morristown. After his defeat at Brandywine Creek, Sept. 11, 1777, and the loss of Philadelphia, he went into winter quarters at Valley Forge where his men endured the greatest hardships. His army was defeated at Monmouth through the treachery of Gen. Charles Lee who ruined Washington's attack by a sudden order to retreat. With the arrival of the French fleet in July, 1778, the British were held to New York and vicinity. The final decisive victory over the British under Cornwallis at Yorktown in October, 1781, was due to Washington's military genius.

Repelling all suggestions of founding a monarchy, Washington led his army into New York on Nov. 25, 1783, took leave of his men on Dec. 4, resigned his command, received the thanks of Congress and retired to his home at Mt. Vernon, Va. For four years he devoted himself to his affairs, repairing the losses sustained in the war and dispensing a lavish hospitality. He repeatedly urged an indissoluble union of the states; was one of Virginia's delegates to the Federal Convention in May, 1787 and for four months presided over the Constitutional Convention. In 1789 he was uanimously elected first president of the United States of America, was inaugurated in New York in April, 1790, and four years later was reelected. As an administrator he was able and methodical, giving close and careful attention to the organization of the various necessary departments and appointing able men to head them. He maintained a strictly non-partisan attitude and placed before the first session of congress an outline which became the basis of the new government.

When war broke out between England and France in 1793 he urged and enforced strict neutrality despite intense partisan feeling and bitter opposition from those who felt that gratitude should prompt the government to take the part of France. Resolved to safeguard the country from foreign entanglements, he unflinchingly withstood the attacks of those who accused him of favoring Great Britain, and sent John Jay to England to negotiate a commercial treaty which he signed on July 18, 1795. Among the many important events of his administration were the admission to the Union of Vermont, Kentucky and Tennessee; the chartering of the Bank of United States; the establishing of the national mint; the Whiskey Rebellion in Pennsylvania.

Refusing a third nomination, he retired in March, 1797, to Mt. Vernon, but the following year when war with France seemed likely he again accepted appointment as commander-in-chief of the army. Prolonged exposure in the winter weather brought on a severe attack of laryngitis and he died on Dec. 14, 1799. The passing of this great general and statesman was almost as deeply felt throughout Europe as in the nation which he had helped to form. He was buried at Mt. Vernon.

JAMES WATT   1736–1819

JAMES WATT, inventor of the modern condensing steam engine, was born at Greenock, Scotland, Jan. 19, 1736, the son of a small merchant who had ruined himself by speculation. Although prevented by ill health from regular attendance at school, he developed a love for reading and a taste for mathematics and spent much of his time in experimenting with ingenious mechanical devices. At the age of 19 he was apprenticed to an instrument maker in London and in 1756 sought to establish himself in Glasgow, but the city guilds would not recognize one whose apprenticeship had not been completed. He became mathematical instrument maker to the university until 1760 when he was able to establish himself independently. While at the university he had learned much from the professors and the students with whom he had discussed the problems of the steam engine and its improvement. The engine then in use was clumsy, consumed much fuel and was used chiefly for pumping water out of mines.

Watt began to experiment in 1761–62, but achieved no result of importance until 1764 when he was engaged to repair a model of New-comen's engine at the university. Its consumption of steam was so great that he set himself to find a means of diminishing it. He studied the properties of steam and by patient study and experimentation he found means to remedy the defects of the Newcomen engine and to make many improvements. He used all of his own resources and had financial assistance for a time from the founder of the Carron Iron Works, Dr. John Roebuck. In 1765 he built a small engine on the principle he had developed of an exterior condenser to prevent the loss of power which was a fault of the old type engine. He obtained patents on this and other innovations about 1767 and with Matthew Boulton, an enterprising manufacturer at Soho near Birmingham, he entered into the manufacture of engines on a considerable scale, supplying them to many industries on the Continent as well as in England.

He made a number of surveys for various canals and prepared plans for the harbors of Ayr, Port-Glasgow and Greenock, for deepening the Clyde, and for bridging it at Hamilton. He also invented a micrometer for measuring distances; devised the sun and planet gear wheels, the "parallel motion," applied the centrifugal governor to his engines, devised the double expansion principle for increasing power, invented a screw propeller, a copying press, a machine for reproducing sculpture and many other mechanical devices and processes, giving full play to his versatile inventive genius.

In 1800 he made over his share in the business at Soho to his two sons and retired to spend the rest of his life quietly at Heathfield Hall, near Birmingham, where he died on Aug. 19, 1819. He was twice married, first to his cousin Margaret Miller in 1763; and second to Anne McGregor in 1775. The University of Glasgow made him an LL.D. and he was the recipient of many other honors. A monument was erected to his memory in Westminster Abbey and a statue in Birmingham.

DANIEL WEBSTER   1782–1852

DANIEL WEBSTER, American orator and statesman, was born in Salisbury, N. H., Jan. 18, 1782, of New England farming stock. He had little early schooling, but through his passion for reading he gained an extensive knowledge of men and affairs and had a remarkable power of absorbing in a day what most minds would require a week to learn. He attended Phillips Academy, Exeter and then Dartmouth College where he became known as an orator and debater and gave the Fourth of July address when he was 18. He studied law in the office of Christopher Gore in Boston, was admitted to the bar in 1805 and two years later settled in Portsmouth where, with his imposing physique, his unusual eloquence and his ready grasp of commonsense, fundamental principles, he quickly gained distinction as a lawyer. His eloquence and ability carried him naturally into politics and from 1813 to 1817 he served in Congress where he opposed the war with England and a protective tariff on the ground that such a tariff would ruin the New England shipping interests. He made able speeches on the strengthening of the navy, on the currency and other matters.

At the expiration of his term he established a law practice at Boston and presently became one of the country's most prominent lawyers, appearing before the United States Supreme Court on several occasions in important cases. He became known also as a historical orator, especially with his 1820 bi-centennial oration celebrating the landing of the Pilgrims at Plymouth Rock, an address on the anniversary of the battle of Bunker Hill, and his Boston eulogy (Aug. 2, 1826) on John Adams and Thomas Jefferson, both of whom had died on July 4 of that year. In 1820 he had assisted in the revision of the constitution of Massachusetts. In 1823 he was reelected to the House and in 1827 to the Senate. While he believed that slavery was an evil thing, disastrous to the slave-holders and to the negroes alike, he held that as the Constitution recognized slavery it could not be abolished, but that its spread to additional sections of the country should be opposed by every constitutional means. He later advocated a protective tariff as an aid to the growing industrial and manufacturing activities of the north. His speech in 1830 in response to a southern attack upon New England was a considerable factor in the unification of the country. Many of his ideas on finance as indicated by his speeches during this period have since been incorporated into the Federal Reserve Banking System of the United States. He opposed Calhoun over nullification in 1833 and supported Andrew Jackson's stand, although not in sympathy with Jackson. He was one of the leaders of the Whig party upon its organization and there is little doubt that he hoped to succeed Jackson in the presidency in 1836, but Van Buren was elected and Webster turned his attention to his private affairs which were often in confusion for he was less successful in managing his own finances than in advising on those of the nation. Failing of appointment as ambassador to England in 1839, he visited Europe where he was received with many honors.

The election of 1840 returned Harrison to the presidency and Webster became his secretary of state, holding the office for a time after Tyler succeeded Harrison. During this period he was instrumental in settling the northeastern boundary controversy with Great Britain in 1842. After President Tyler's break with the Whigs, he resigned and returned to Boston but in 1845 was again in the Senate. With Clay and Calhoun, he opposed the war with Mexico (in which his son was killed) and devoted his energies to preventing the spread of slavery to the territory acquired by that war. He joined Clay in advocating the compromise measures of 1850, hoping thus to preserve peace between the North and the South. His last and one of his greatest speeches was that of March 7, 1850 in the Senate, in which he upheld his own position as to slavery and recommended concessions to the South in order to keep the Union intact. This brought a bitter attack from the anti-slavery party.

He became secretary of state for a second time under Fillmore in 1850 and in 1852, again disappointed in his hope of being nominated for presidency, he retired to his farm at Marshfield, Mass., where he died on Oct. 24, 1852 and was buried in the family plot. He had been twice married; in 1808 to Grace Fletcher and in 1829 to Caroline LeRoy.

NOAH WEBSTER   1758–1843

NOAH WEBSTER, American journalist, author and compiler of the famous *Webster's Dictionary,* was born at West Hartford, Conn., Oct. 16, 1758, a descendant of John Webster, governor of Connecticut, and, on his mother's side, of Governor William Bradford of Plymouth Colony. He spent his youth on his father's farm and prepared himself for Yale University from which he was graduated in 1778. He then taught in village schools for a time, studied law and was admitted to the bar at Hartford in 1781. Soon after this he began work on his *Grammatical Institute of the English Language* which was published in 1783–85 in three parts, a spelling-book, a grammar and a reader. It was a pioneer book in its field and was adopted by most of the schools in the United States, partly because of its patriotic nature, partly by reason of its simplification of English spelling. The sale is said to have reached more than 1,000,000 copies a year before 1861. He wrote a number of papers and essays of a political nature and himself regarded his *Sketches of American Policy,* issued in 1785, as the first proposals looking toward a United States Constitution.

He was for a short time at the head of an Episcopal school in Philadelphia and in 1788 removed to New York and started the *American Magazine* which he was able to keep going for only a year, after which he resumed the practice of law in Hartford. Five years later he was again in New York where he started a new publication, *The Minerva,* for the purpose of supporting Washington's administration and policies as against the designs of the French minister, Genet. *The Minerva* later became the *Commercial Advertiser,* which was absorbed by the *Globe.* He also issued a weekly edition of the *Herald,* which afterwards became the *New York Spéctator.* After his second New York venture he went to New Haven, Conn., published several books and articles on various subjects, was a member of the Connecticut House of Representatives for a time and held other public offices both in Connecticut and in Amherst, Mass., where he lived from 1812 to 1822; aided in forming Amherst College, and represented Amherst in the Massachusetts State legislature.

In 1806 he had published *A Compendious Dictionary of the English Language* which was somewhat in the nature of an encyclopedia, and in 1807 *A Philosophical and Practical Grammar of the English Language.* At about that time he began work on the great dictionary with which his name is associated. He devoted twenty years to the preparation of the book, spending nearly a year in England and Paris (1824–25), and completed it at the University of Cambridge. It was published in 1828 in two volumes. It contained 12,000 words and between 30,000 and 40,000 definitions that had not previously appeared in any dictionary of the English language. It was also published in England. He revised and enlarged the work, bringing out a second edition in 1840, and a few days before his death completed the revision of an appendix. New and revised editions continue to appear at intervals and many abridgements have been issued. Probably no other dictionary of the language has had so many editions or sold so widely.

Among his other works are *Dissertations on the English Language* (1789); *The Rights of Neutral Nations in Time of War* (1802); *A Collection of Papers on Political, Literary and Moral Subjects* (1843); and he prepared and edited for publication the *Journal* of Governor John Winthrop in 1790. He died in New Haven on May 28, 1843.

DUKE OF WELLINGTON 1769–1852

ARTHUR WELLESLEY, first Duke of Wellington, was a British statesman whose chief claim to fame was his defeat of Napoleon at Waterloo. He was born April 29, 1769, in Dublin, and was the son of the first Earl of Mornington. He was educated at Eton, Chelsea and a French military school at Angers. He was commissioned ensign in 1787 and rose rapidly until he reached the rank of colonel in 1796. He had served as aide to two viceroys in Ireland and had entered Parliament for Trim and in 1794–5 served with conspicuous bravery in Holland under the Duke of York. In 1797 he was sent to Calcutta, took a prominent part in the campaign of the British against the native Tippoo, Sultan of Mysore, and in other Indian troubles, and was later placed in charge of both the military and the civil administration of the conquered territory. In 1802 he was made a major-general and in 1803–5 at the head of the English forces in the south of India he broke the power of the Mahratta chiefs by his daring attacks.

He returned home in 1805 as Sir Arthur Wellesley, entered Parliament from Rye in 1806 and the following year was appointed Irish Secretary. During the same year he went to Copenhagen and drove the Danes out of Zealand. In 1808 he sailed with a British expedition to aid Portugal and Spain against Napoleon and for several years with brief intervals in England he was engaged in the Peninsular campaigns. His military genius was displayed in the campaign which ended in the expulsion of the French from Spain and the capture of Toulouse (1814). He was rewarded with a number of titles, among them Marquis Douro and Duke of Wellington (having been created Earl of Wellington, Marquis and Field-Marshal, the previous year), and was given a grant of 400,000 pounds. In July, 1814, he was named ambassador to France and the following year was sent to the Vienna Congress.

When news reached England that Napoleon had escaped from Elba, Wellington was given command of the British army in the Netherlands with the allied Belgian and Dutch forces. He had 150,000 men and Blücher, cooperating with him, had 116,000 Prussians. Napoleon defeated Blücher at Ligny and Wellington in turn defeated Ney at Quatre Bras. Wellington then fell back to Waterloo where he joined forces with Blücher and defeated Napoleon in the great battle of Waterloo on June 18, 1815. Wellington was created Prince of Waterloo and given an English estate at Strathfieldsaye. He commanded the joint army of occupation in France and in 1818, returning home, he became master-general of the ordnance in Lord Liverpool's cabinet. was made constable of the Tower and in 1827 commander-in-chief.

In January, 1828, he became prime minister. He introduced a bill for Catholic emancipation, believing it a necessary measure to prevent war with Ireland, but it was unpopular and he was accused of a design to introduce popery. In 1830 he declared against parliamentary reform, causing the downfall of his ministry, and he became so unpopular because of his antagonism to the reform bill that a mob hooted him on the anniversary of Waterloo and broke the windows of his residence, Apsley

House. In 1834 he became chancellor of the University of Oxford. William IV called upon him to form a new cabinet in that year but he recommended Peel for the post and himself became foreign secretary in Peel's cabinet. When Peel returned to power in 1841 Wellington again joined his cabinet and in 1842 again became commander-in-chief for life. He was president of the Privy Council in 1845; in 1846 supported Peel's corn-law measures and upon their defeat retired from public life.

In 1806 he had married the Hon. Catherine Pakenham, who bore him three sons and three daughters. Toward the close of his life he regained his place in the affections of the British nation and he died peacefully in his armchair at Walmer, Sept. 14, 1852 and was buried in St. Paul's Cathedral, London.

HERBERT GEORGE WELLS   1866–

H. G. WELLS, one of the most prominent, and certainly one of the most industrious and versatile of modern English writers, is perhaps most commonly thought of as a novelist whose fictions have usually been the vehicle for his scientific, ethical and socialistic thought. He was born, as he said himself, in the middle class, son of a storekeeper whose wife had been in domestic service. His birth occurred at Bromley, Kent, on Sept. 21, 1866. He was reared in conditions of poverty, his father adding to the very insufficient income from his store by engaging in professional cricket. As a youth he was apprenticed to a linen draper, an occupation so obnoxious to him that he broke away after two years and became a teacher of biology which he had studied under the famous Professor Huxley, the winning of scholarships having enabled him to supplement the meager education provided for boys of his class by a period of study at the Royal College of Science and at London University. His knowledge of biology was turned to account in his novel, *Ann Veronica,* published in 1909 and dealing with the subject of woman's emancipation from conventional restrictions. This book aroused a storm of more or less shocked discussion.

During and after his period of teaching he contributed articles to several leading English periodicals. In 1895 appeared *The Time Machine,* first of those fantastic fictions with a scientific flavor which he always delighted in, and which bespeak the influence of Jules Verne. But the mere analogy is hardly fair to Mr. Wells, for his glimpses into the imagined future are very much bound up with thoughts about developments in industrialism, social welfare, etc., which never troubled the inventive Frenchman. In the *War of the Worlds* (1898) the earth is invaded by the grotesque inhabitants of Mars who are graphically visualized, but the story is not as convincing as Poe's masterpiece, *Hans Pfaall*. Other works of the same general character are *When the Sleeper Wakes; The Food of the Gods; In the Days of the Comet; The Island of Dr. Moreau; The Invisible Man; Tales of Space and Time*. Notable among his novels is *Tono Bungay* (1909). Its title, the name given to a quack patent medicine, suggests the main theme of this splendid and scathing delineation of unprincipled methods of exploitation by which the gullible public is fooled; and the manufacturer of this useless nostrum is a fine example of the author's power of convincing characterization.

Other works include *Anticipations; A Modern Utopia; First and Last Things; The New Machiavelli; The Passionate Friends; The Wife of Sir Isaac Harman; The Research Magnificent; Love and Mr. Lewisham; Mankind in the Making; The Future of America; New Worlds for Old; Social Forces in England and America; The World Set Free; The Elements of Reconstruction; War and the Future; God, the Invisible King; The Soul of a Bishop; In the Fourth Year; Joan and Peter; Russia in the Shadows; The Salvaging of Civilization; The Secret Places of the Heart; Washington and the Hope of Peace; A Short History of the World; Men Like Gods*. He is the author also of many essays and short stories. His novel, *Mr. Britling Sees it Through* (1916) deals with the World War and produced a profound impression, not only as a splendid story but for its broad and humanitarian outlook. This, like *Ann Veronica* and several of his other novels, is drawn largely from his own experiences.

No list of the works of this prolific and inquisitive writer can be complete for there seems no abatement of his literary and intellectual energy. But particular mention should be made of his two-volume work (1920) *The Outline of History*, a new kind of general history, delightful to read and useful for ready reference. It spans the whole story of existence from the creation of the earth to the ending of the World War. This was followed by the two-volume *Science of Life* (1930) and in 1931 appeared *The Work, Wealth and Happiness of Mankind*, and in 1934 his *Experiment in Autobiography*, an exhaustive and remarkable account of his own life and work.

Mr. Wells' marriage to a cousin early in life proved so unsatisfactory that they separated and he later married Amy Catherine Robbins, who was herself a novelist. Although there existed between them marked antagonisms in literary as well as other matters, this union endured until her death, and in the preface to his *Outline of History* he pays high tribute to her valuable aid.

JOHN WESLEY

JOHN WESLEY, English clergyman and founder of Methodism, was born June 17, 1703 at Epworth, Lincolnshire, and was the 15th child of the rector, Rev. Samuel Wesley. He attended the Charterhouse School and in 1720 went to Christ Church, Oxford, which his brothers, Samuel and Charles, also attended. He was a conscientious student and lived an ascetic life, was ordained a deacon in 1725 and in 1726 became a fellow of Lincoln College and lecturer on Greek. The following year he left Oxford to help his father; was ordained a priest in 1728 and returned to Oxford the year following as a tutor. In 1735 he went to Georgia on a mission for a gospel society. He was a high churchman and intolerant of beliefs contrary to his own. An unfortunate love affair, in addition to his intolerance, brought about strife and he returned to England after three years. On his travels he had met some Moravian missionaries and was much impressed with their simple faith. After returning to London he was still more deeply interested through the preaching of one of their number, Peter Bohler, and was finally led to renounce many of the tenets of the Church of England.

With the pulpits of the established church therefore closed to him and his new doctrines and his denials of its teachings, he began to follow the practice of the evangelist, George Whitehead, and took to preaching in the open air, on street corners and in lanes. His congregations were the working people, miners, farmers, fishers, ironworkers, etc. On April 2, 1739 for the first time he preached an open-air sermon near Bristol. His reputation as a preacher and also for the uprightness of his life and the boldness of his doctrines, spread throughout the country and for the fifty years during which he continued to preach, crowds of from 10,000 to 30,000 persons would gather at a designated place and wait for him to put in an appearance. In July 1740 the first Methodist society was formed in London. He faced persecution and ostracism unflinchingly, his life was frequently in danger, but he could not be intimidated and lived to a ripe old age. He visited many countries in spreading Methodism, traveling more than a quarter of a million miles, and delivering more than 40,000 sermons. He made converts everywhere and his journeys in his later life were more like triumphal processions than the travels of a religious propagandist. He was aided in his work by his brother Charles and together the brothers wrote, it is said, some 6500 hymns, among them *Jesus, Lover of My Soul,* which was the work of Charles. The poetical works of the two fill 13 volumes in the edition prepared for the Wesleyan Conference

(1768–72). His work extended into every part of the British Isles and Methodism grew so rapidly that by 1790 he had over 500 preachers spreading his doctrines and more than 120,000 members in the societies.

He did a prodigious amount of literary work, most of it of an ecclesiastical and propagandist nature. He wrote short grammars of the English, French, Latin, Greek and Hebrew languages, a *Compendium of Logic,* translated extracts from Phaedrus, Ovid, Virgil, Horace, Juvenal, Persius and other Latin classic authors. He compiled an English dictionary, commentaries on the Old and New Testaments, a short *Roman History, A History of England* and *Ecclesiastical History,* a *Compendium of Social Philosophy,* and, in addition, fifty volumes of a *Christian Library* prepared for the itinerant preachers of the Methodist faith. He also edited many volumes, including the *Imitation of Christ,* the works of Bunyan, Baxter, Edwards, Law and others, including an abridged edition of Brooke's novel, *The Fool of Quality.* He prepared a *Compendium of Physic* and produced many collections of psalms, hymns, sermons, journals, and a monthly magazine which is still published.

He interested himself in many movements for the benefit of humanity, erected chapels, raising money for their support; aided in establishing Sunday schools and in other educational causes; founded an Orphans' Home at Newcastle, various charity schools in London, and a dispensary in Bristol. It has been said that no one man in his time "influenced so many minds, no single voice touched so many hearts." At the conference of 1770 he shocked good Calvinsts by introducing resolutions, which were adopted, declaring that the heathen who had never heard of Christ could be saved if they feared God and lived up to such light as they had. He died March 2, 1791 and was buried in a vault behind City Road Chapel in London.

JAMES ABBOTT McNEILL WHISTLER   1834–1903

JAMES ABBOTT McNEILL WHISTLER, one of the most eminent of American painters, was born at Lowell, Mass., on July 10, 1834. His father was a distinguished military engineer and his mother of a prominent southern family. He spent some time in his boyhood in St. Petersburg, Russia, where his father was building a railroad, and attended the Imperial Art Academy there, but at the age of 17 he returned home and entered West Point. Although he came of a family of soldiers, his own tastes were not military; his studies suffered, he was dismissed from the Academy, made an unsuccessful attempt to get into the Navy and then became a draughts-man in the Coast Survey Department at Washington. The tediousness of the work soon palled upon him and in 1854 he went to Paris where he studied painting for two years under Charles Gabriel Gleyre, a popular painter of the day in the Ingres tradition, whom he afterwards charac-terized as a "bourgeois Greek." That may have been one of the reasons for the Salon's refusal of a painting he submitted, which he then took to the Salon des Refusés where it was received with acclaim. In spite of this early success he won recognition but slowly. Arrogant, witty and satirical, he well knew the *Gentle Art of Making Enemies,* which was the title of a book he published in 1890. He delighted in puzzling and ridiculing the English painters, critics and public, and never hesitated to show his contempt for persons whom he disliked and for fashions that did not please him. He was something of a dandy in his dress and his lack of punctuality was a byword.

He eschewed the careful drawing, the minuteness of detail of the pre-Raphaelite movement; brilliant coloring was not to his taste; he com-posed rather color-poems in the soft, less assertive tones, emphasizing, as has been said, the "musical quality of color." His paintings did not "tell a story" nor were they noted for "sentiment." His work bore an approximation to the French impressionist school. Critics found him in-fluenced by Courbet, Velazquez, Puvis de Chavannes, Hogarth and Tin-toretto, but never at the expense of his own colorful individuality. He learned much from the Japanese and the influence of eastern art modified to occidental ideals is shown in "The Balcony," "La Princess du Pays de la Porcelaine," "The Golden Screen" and other works.

He devoted much time to lithography, which he brought to a high point of perfection and as an etcher he was second only to Rembrandt. It is estimated that he produced about 150 lithographs while the number of his etchings and drypoints is probably more than 400. Many of these were shown at the 1883 and 1886 exhibitions of the Fine Arts Society in London. In his paintings he delighted in neutral tones, his views of the Thames River shrouded in mist being among his most characteristic can-vases. His "nocturnes" display the same neutral tone values and are among his most popular works. He found and portrayed beauty in the London fogs and in the most commonplace and sordid places as well as in the most majestic scenes of nature. His best known single picture is his portrait of his mother. In 1886 he was elected president of the Royal Society of British Artists and upon failing to be reelected he remarked that "the artists had come out and the British had remained." He was the first president of the International Society. He excelled also as a decorator and devoted great care to the tones of the floor and walls of his studios, to the dresses worn by his sitters. The "Peacock Room" which he decorated in the home of F. R. Leyland at Knightsbridge, London, was transferred to the National Gallery, Washington. Of his many portraits, two of the most striking are his "Carlyle" and "Miss Alexander." He felt the analogy between music and color and described his pictures as symphonies, harmonies, nocturnes, arousing ridicule at the time, but his designations have since been accepted as true and natural.

His eccentricities and his exaggerated estimate of his own importance led him into many quarrels which he never hesitated to air in print as well as verbally. *The Baronet and the Butterfly* is his own published account of one of his most famous quarrels. These peculiarities doubtless had their part in delaying the full recognition of his genius until his later years. In 1888 he married a Mrs. Godwin who exerted a mellowing influence upon him, and in 1892 they settled in Paris where he for a time taught in the Academie Carmen, a school attended by many American students, which was later closed and in 1895 he returned to London because of his wife's health. Although much of his life was spent in England, he greatly desired that his works should pass into American hands; a desire fulfilled by the Freer collection in the National Gallery, Washington, which contains more than 50 examples of his work. He died in London, July 17, 1903.

WALT WHITMAN   1819–1892

WALT WHITMAN, American poet, was born at West Hills, near Huntington, L. I., on May 31, 1819, of mixed English, Dutch and Welsh stock. He attended the public schools of Brooklyn and New York, but his education was more largely derived from his wide reading and from contact with his fellow men. He learned carpentering and typesetting, spent some time in a lawyer's and a doctor's office and in 1838 was a country school teacher on Long Island, at the same time writing for newspapers and magazines. His next venture was the editing of a shortlived weekly newspaper, *The Long Islander,* at Huntington. In 1840 he was working as a printer in New York, and writing, and in 1846 became editor of the *Brooklyn Eagle,* in which newspaper he championed the idealistic reforms of the "transcendental" period of American history, the cause of American literature, drama and opera. He opposed the extension of slavery into new states of the Union with such fervor that the conservative *Eagle* felt it necessary to dispense with his editorial services. He then went to New Orleans and joined the staff of *The Crescent* (1848), later traveling in the South and Southwest and gratifying his intensely democratic instincts by mingling with all sorts and conditions of men and entering into their lives. He was fond of long walking tours and his wanderings had carried him into many parts of the West and into Canada when he returned north in 1850 and became editor of *The Freeman* in Brooklyn, which also was short-lived. For a few years he engaged in the business of building and selling houses.

His first volume of poetry was *Leaves of Grass,* published in 1855, a small quarto edition of 95 pages. His free, unrhymed, irregular verse was largely personal. He exalted the human body and its functions, saw beauty in all that was natural and sought to typify the general human personality in himself, his own body, soul, thoughts. It was understood by few and was not taken very seriously until Emerson gave it public praise and called it to the attention of thoughtful people, after which it became increasingly appreciated, was elaborated in new and larger editions until in 1860 it had grown to a volume of 456 pages, and had attracted attention abroad. Much of Whitman's later life was given to the elaboration of this work. He was strongly individualistic, with a hatred for conventionality and an intense ardor for naturalness. Thoreau, who visited him in Brooklyn, characterized him as "probably the greatest democrat that ever lived."

In 1862 he became a nurse in the hospitals of the Union army and for three years ministered to the wounded there and on the battlefields. His health suffered and in 1865 he was given an appointment in the Interior Department. A fourth edition of *Leaves of Grass,* incorporating his war poems, which had appeared under the title of *Drum-Taps,* was published in 1867 and a fifth followed four years later. Among the war poems was *When Lilacs Last in the Dooryard Bloom'd,* written on the death of Lincoln and considered one of his noblest poems. Perhaps his best known single poem is *O Captain, My Captain,* also written on the death of Lincoln. His hospital experience led him to sing of democracy in the mass in most of his later poems; he became a prophet of a world united in peace, something of a mystic, with a strong religious feeling. The utter frankness of some of the poems incorporated in his book gave offence and led to his dismissal from his government post. *The Good Gray Poet,* written by William Douglas O'Connor, castigated Secretary Harlan for the dismissal and incidentally fastened that name upon the poet, who was later given a clerkship in the Treasury Department and lived in Washington until 1873 when he was stricken with paralysis and thereafter made his home in Camden, N. J., where the remaining 18 years of his life were spent in poverty, but he remained cheerful and serene and his home became the Mecca of many literary folk from Europe as well as America. He continued to write but his later work lacked the vitality and imagination of his earlier years. He died March 27, 1892, and was buried in a tomb he had built for himself in Harleigh Cemetery, Camden. He had never married.

JOHN GREENLEAF WHITTIER   1807–1892

JOHN GREENLEAF WHITTIER, the "Quaker Poet," and abolitionist of America, was born on a farm in the Merrimack Valley near Haverhill, Mass., Dec. 17, 1807, of colonial Quaker stock in which Huguenot blood was mingled. He attended the primitive district school and first felt the call of poetry when a teacher loaned him a volume of Burns' poems. He was then 14 and soon began to try his own hand at verse, but nothing appeared in print until he was 18, when a sister sent one of his poems to the Newburyport *Free Press*. William Lloyd Garrison, editor of the paper, sought him out and there started an alliance between them which lasted until the abolition of slavery. Garrison and his friend, A. W. Thayer of the *Haverhill Gazette,* urged Whittier to continue his schooling and Thayer offered him a home while he attended the Haverhill Academy. He worked at slipper making and other things to pay his expenses and contributed verse to the newspapers, gaining some reputation thereby. He taught school for a time; in 1829 became editor of the Boston *American Manufacturer,* protectionist organ of Henry Clay, contributed to the *Philanthropist* and other publications, and became interested in humane reforms. Upon his father's death, after a lingering illness, he became the mainstay of his family. For six months in 1830 he edited the *Haverhill Gazette,* and then became editor of the *New England Review* in Hartford, Conn., a post which he resigned in 1837 because of ill health and returned to Haverhill to help his brother run the farm. He had meantime published *Legends of New England* (1831), a volume of poems and prose sketches.

This was the most unhappy period of his life, due to financial distress, a disappointment in love, overwork and thwarted ambition. The farm was sold in 1836 and the family moved to a cottage in Amesbury. Whittier now entered with passionate devotion into the crusade against slavery. He had been a delegate to the anti-slavery convention in Philadelphia in 1833; had published at his own expense an anti-slavery pamphlet on *Justice and Expediency;* and had served a term in the State Legislature in 1835, but illness prevented him from seeking reelection. He became widely known for his anti-slavery activities and many of his poems were written to arouse public sentiment in its behalf. For two years he edited the *Pennsylvania Freeman* in Philadelphia where his printing office was burned by a mob. His health, never robust, caused him to retire to Amesbury in 1840 and from that retreat he contributed reviews, editorials and poetry to the *National Era* in Washington, of which he was corresponding editor, and wrote many poems, most of which appeared in periodicals. A collection of anti-slavery poems, *Voices of Freedom,* was published in 1849 and during the Civil War appeared two volumes of patriotic verse—*In War Time* and *National Lyrics.*

From 1856 on he was a regular contributor to the *Atlantic Monthly,* founded in that year. *Snow-Bound,* issued in 1866, greatly increased his reputation and added to his income. This is probably his best known single poem, a long descriptive work portraying in simple phrase the homely life on the farm isolated by the winter snows. Each member of the household is described with a tenderness and a vividness which have endeared the poet to multitudes of readers. Later collections were *The Tent on the Beach, The Pennsylvania Pilgrim, Among the Hills, The Vision of Echard, The King's Missive* and a final volume, *At Sundown* (1890). Among the well known shorter poems most characteristic of his simple, sincere style are *Barbara Frietchie, Skipper Ireson's Ride, The Barefoot Boy, Maud Muller* and the beautiful psalm, *The Eternal Goodness.* He did much editing and compiling and published several prose volumes; *The Stranger in Lowell, The Supernaturalism of New England, Old Portraits and Modern Sketches.* He never married, died in Hampton Falls, N. H., Sept. 7, 1892 and was buried at Amesbury.

WILHELM II OF GERMANY 1859–

FRIEDRICH WILHELM VICTOR ALBERT, who became Emperor of Germany and King of Prussia as Wilhelm II, was born in Berlin, Jan. 27, 1859, and was the eldest son of Prince Friedrich Wilhelm of Prussia and Princess Victoria of England. He attended the Gymnasium at Cassel, spent six months with the First Regiment of Guards, and studied law and political economy at the University of Bonn for two years. After 1879 he spent several years in military training, chiefly at Potsdam, and in 1881 married Princess Auguste-Victoria of Schleswig-Holstein-Augustenburg, who bore him six sons and a daughter.

He succeeded to the throne of Germany on June 15, 1888, upon the death of his father, and was always jealous of his monarchic status and of Germany's international position. He soon came into conflict with Prince von Bismarck, the chief of his ministers, who had almost completely dominated the government, and in 1890 he demanded Bismarck's resignation and himself took entire control, calling to leading posts men relatively unfamiliar with the duties of their offices. He firmly believed that his own house of Hohenzollern was divinely appointed to rule over the German people and until the very end of his rule as Kaiser his imperial will was the guiding force in German policies, both foreign and domestic. He was himself an able soldier and from the beginning of his reign proclaimed his reliance on the army rather than on diplomacy and parliamentary decisions, and he built up a huge military organization. He maintained Bismarck's policy of the Triple Alliance with Italy and Austria, but abandoned efforts to establish a closer understanding with Russia. In his determination to secure Germany's "place in the sun," and convinced that the future of his country lay largely on the seas, he urged German colonization, commercial expansion, particularly in the East, and built up a powerful navy. At home he gave tremendous impetus to the establishing of educational institutions, scientific research and the development of industrialism.

Relations with England were disturbed by the clash of national interests in Africa and by Germany's taking the side of Russia and France in the Chinese-Japanese war of 1894. Germany's acquisition of a naval base in the Far East did not tend to heal misunderstandings. Wilhelm's policy of naval expansion increased the coldness between his country and Great Britain, which was still further intensified by his attitude in the Boer war, adding emphasis to the great divergence between German and English interests. (It must be borne in mind that Wilhelm was the grandson of Queen Victoria of England.) In 1908, while on a visit to England, in an ill-advised interview he commented so freely on relations between the two countries that violent protest was roused in Germany and a serious crisis threatened in his relations with his subjects. As a result he was compelled to promise his ministers that he would in the future undertake no political step without their advice and counsel. Bethmann-Hollweg, then chancellor, persuaded him to despatch the warship *Panther* to Morocco (1911) to bring pressure to bear on France to cede the French Congo to Germany in return for a free hand in Morocco, the result of which was further political isolation for Germany and the frustration of a new attempt at a *rapprochement* with Great Britain.

At the outbreak of the World War in 1914 he at first professed a desire for peace, insisting that England remain neutral and that Austria make her own settlement with Serbia for the assassination of the Austrian heir apparent. It was not long, however, before he joined forces with Austria, consented to the violation of Belgium's neutrality (stigmatizing the treaty which safeguarded it as a mere "scrap of paper"), and gave himself over to the furthering of war by every ruthless means for the aggrandizement of Germany and the complete annihilation of her foes. His fiery speeches inflamed and kept alive the bitter hatreds of the war, but he was kept away from the front and was himself never under fire. As the war progressed he became more and more a mere onlooker. He differed with von Tirpitz as to the use of the fleet and reluctantly he consented to the appointment of von Hindenburg to the supreme command. In 1918 a Crown Council under his presidency determined to start peace negotiations, but while the Kaiser hesitated in indecision, military matters took a fatal turn for Germany. Prince Max of Baden, who approved parliamentary methods which Wilhelm strongly opposed, became Imperial Chancellor in October, 1918. Woodrow Wilson's continued declarations that the Kaiser was an obstacle to peace negotiations were having their effect. Wilhelm's influence with his people had gradually decreased and the revolution of November, 1918, brought matters to a crisis with the demand for his abdication. On Nov. 9th he consented to abdicate his throne; the Crown Prince renounced his rights of succession; the socialists, who were in control, proclaimed a republic and Wilhelm fled to Holland where he later purchased Doorn Castle and settled down to a life of complete retirement.

After the death of the Empress in 1922 he married the widowed Princess Herminie of Schonaich-Carloath, born Princess of Reuss.

WILLIAM THE CONQUEROR   circa 1027–1087

WILLIAM I, king of England from 1066 to 1089, was born about 1027 in Normandy, the bastard son of Robert II of Normandy by Arletta, the daughter of a tanner at Falaise. In his early life he was known as William the Bastard and as Duke of Normandy he won the title of "The Conqueror" by his victory over the English king, Harold, at Hastings, thus gaining for himself the throne of England. Robert II had no legitimate son and when he started in 1034 for a pilgrimage to Jerusalem he named William as his successor and induced the Norman barons to accept him. Robert died the following year, on his pilgrimage, and the barons held to their promise. The boy's guardians were murdered during the following twelve years of rebellions and plottings and it was only because he was kept hidden by relatives that he escaped being taken captive.

When he was 20 a rebellion occurred with the object of putting his kinsman, Guy of Brionne, at the head of the Norman duchy. Henry I of France, William's overlord, helped him to suppress that insurrection at Val-dès-Dunes, in 1047, a victory which did not end the outbreaks against William but made his position more secure, and the following year he joined the French king in warring on their common enemy, Geoffrey Martel, Count of Anjou. He visited England in 1051 and is believed to have obtained a promise of the English succession from his kinsman, Edward the Confessor, who was then on the English throne. Two years later he married Matilda, daughter of Baldwin V of Flanders, who traced her descent from Alfred the Great. The papal council of Reims had forbidden the marriage and it was ten years before Pope Nicholas II granted a dispensation legalizing it, after which William and Matilda founded the abbeys of St. Stephen and the Holy Trinity at Caen. The political results of the marriage strengthened William's position, but brought him into conflict with the French king, who joined forces with their former enemy, Geoffrey Martel, to crush William. They invaded Normandy twice, but William checked the 1054 invasion by the victory of Mortemer, and that of 1058 by destroying the French rearguard at Varaville. He annexed Mayenne and after the death of Martel and Henry I he recovered Maine from the Angevins.

The English earl, Harold, visited Normandy about 1064 and is said to have promised his support of William's fancied claim to the English throne, but upon Edward's death Harold was crowned King of England. William, determined to make good his unlawful claim despite the perfidy of Harold, gathered a large army, obtained the Pope's sanction and invaded England. He landed at Pevensey on the southeast coast on Sept. 28, 1066 and on Oct. 14 met and defeated the English at Senlac, or Hastings, in the famous battle in which Harold was killed. He laid waste the country, forced his way into London and on Christmas Day was crowned at Westminster. For five years he continued his depredations, devastating the country, putting down many revolts, sacrificing many thousands of lives by slaughter and starvation and allotting to his own Norman barons the lands of those who fought against him. He returned to Normandy in 1067 to celebrate his triumph, but outbreaks in Northumbria, on the Welsh marshes, and in Kent, called him back in December. In 1069 the North declared for Edgar Atheling, won the support of Denmark and captured York, but William reduced that city, drove the Danes to their ships and bribed the fleet to leave. In 1072 he invaded Scotland

and forced into submission the Scottish king, Malcolm. For the next ten years he was occupied with wars on the Continent as well as with rebellions in England. He was compelled to fight against his own son, Robert, who took up arms against him; he put to death the powerful earl, Waltheof, after a particularly serious revolt in 1075, and kept in captivity for many years his own brother, Odo, whom he had left as regent in England during his absences. About 1086 he established in England the feudal system of Normandy.

He died at Rouen, Sept. 10, 1087, from injuries received while fighting against Philip I of France. He was the father of five daughters and four sons, two of whom, William and Henry, succeeded him on the throne of England. He was a man of great administrative powers, but unscrupulous and without mercy to his enemies, and he laid heavy burdens of taxation upon the people. His private life appears to have been blameless; he was religious and liberal to the church but insisted always upon his royal authority over its officials.

WILLIAM III OF ENGLAND   1650–1702

WILLIAM OF ORANGE, later William III, king of England from 1689 to 1702, was born at the Hague, Nov. 14, 1650, posthumous son of William II of Orange and Mary, the eldest daughter of Charles I of England. He was chosen Stadtholder (Viceroy) of the United Netherlands in 1672 when the Republic was in the midst of a protracted and seemingly vain war with Louis XIV of France. By his diplomatic skill he was able to bring the war to a close in 1678 with the treaty of Nimeguen which gave many advantages to the Dutch Republic. During the previous year he had married his cousin, the Princess Mary, eldest daughter of the Duke of York who became King James II of England in 1685.

The tyranny of James became insupportable to his subjects and a number of the nobles and other influential Englishmen united in inviting William of Orange to assume the English crown. He landed at Torbay with an army of 15,000 Dutch and English on Nov. 5, 1688. English leaders and English soldiers deserted James for the newcomer and in December the king fled to France and William entered London. The Convention Parliament declared the English throne vacant and on Feb. 13, 1689, William and Mary were proclaimed jointly king and queen of Great Britain. James and his adherents held out against the succession of his daughter and son-in-law, some of his followers taking refuge in

Scotland and some in Ireland, but the defeat of Dundee in July, 1689, and the surrender of Limerick in October, 1691, ended the struggle against William's accession two and a half years after he had been crowned.

He now turned his attention to the military campaigns in the Low Countries and with his joint English and Dutch forces took the field against Louis XIV, but was defeated by Marshal Luxembourg and the war came to a close in 1697 with the peace of Ryswick which he reluctantly signed. Despite the circumstances under which he had invaded England and despite his many excellent qualities, he never became popular with his British subjects; his health was not good, he was reserved in his bearing and he was a foreigner. With his Dutch bluntness of manner he was unable to establish a basis of sympathy and understanding with his people. Queen Mary's death on Sept. 28, 1694, rendered his position still more difficult. Parliament placed obstacles in the way of many of the measures he advocated; conspiracies against his life were formed by the still hopeful adherents of James, who remained throughout his life an exile at the French court, dependent upon the bounty of Louis XIV. The death of Charles II of Spain and the accession to the Spanish throne of Philip of Anjou was a further obstacle to William's purpose of uniting Europe against the French. He made an unsuccessful attempt to have the domain of the childless Charles II divided between England and France, but the whole of the heritage fell to France. He inflamed the English against Louis and war was declared in 1702, but William, long ailing, died on March 19, 1702, from the effects of a fall from his horse and a subsequent chill. He left no descendants.

During his reign many of the greatest political and financial reforms of England were instituted. The Bank of England was established and a new financial system was introduced; the standing army was transferred to the control of Parliament; liberty of the press was established; the British constitution was established on a firmer basis; and ministerial responsibility was recognized. Thus, besides delivering England from the bigotry and tyranny of James, William had done more for the country than had its native-born kings, and much that he accomplished was in spite of the opposition of Parliament and of many of the leading men of Great Britain; in spite also of misunderstandings caused by the barriers of his foreign birth and the coldness and reserve of his nature. It should be remembered that he labored under the discomforting knowledge that he was surrounded by treacherous or timid councillors, many of whom were always thinking of the possibility of a restoration and found it expedient to withhold the full spirit of loyalty and cooperation. Moreover, the fact that he had risen to power among an alien people and by the misfortune and flight of a near relative unquestionably colored his demeanor and gave him what in modern times would be called a complex of inadequacy to racial and national standards which were new and strange to him. Notwithstanding that he is alleged to have been unfaithful to the queen, he seems to have been for the most part a devoted husband. When he died a locket containing Mary's picture was discovered about his neck, bespeaking a touch of sentiment which was never manifest in his life.

ROGER WILLIAMS   circa 1604–1684

ROGER WILLIAMS, founder of the State of Rhode Island and pioneer of religious liberty, was born in London about 1604. It is quite probable that he was educated at the Charterhouse and at Pembroke College, Cambridge, under the patronage of Sir Edward Coke. He received his degree in 1627, studied theology, and in 1629 became chaplain to Sir William Macham of Otes, in Essex. He refused church advancement, became a Puritan, emigrated to Boston with his wife, Mary, in February, 1631, and a few months later became a teacher in the church at Salem. His views on religion were at variance with those of the churchmen at Boston and he left Salem for the Plymouth Colony where for two years he was assistant pastor, in the meantime studying the Indian languages. In 1633 he returned to Salem as a teacher but soon found himself again in conflict with the authorities of the Massachusetts Bay Colony. He asserted his belief that the civil authorities had no jurisdiction over the consciences and souls of men, and that the king's patent did not give rightful title to land in the new colony without adequate payment to the Indians for it.

These opinions and others caused him to be tried before the Massachusetts General Court in July, 1635, and upon his refusal to recant, a sentence of banishment from the colony was pronounced against him with a threat of sending him back to England in order that he might not spread his pernicious beliefs in the New World. He made his escape to Manton's Neck, which was within the jurisdiction of Plymouth Colony, and in June, 1636, at the instance of the Plymouth authorities, he moved entirely out of the Massachusetts colony and with a few followers founded the first white settlement in Rhode Island which he called Providence because of "God's merciful providence to him in his distress." He had learned the language of the Indians who lived on that part of the Atlantic Coast and bargained with them for the land upon which he now settled. The Indian sachems, Canonicus and Miantonomo, were friendly and gave him their confidence, for he was always just in his dealings with the Indian tribes.

A short time after he had settled in Providence the Pequot Indians rose against the Massachusetts Colony and sought to induce the Narragansett tribe to make common cause with them. Williams, through his influence with the two chiefs, was able to induce the Narragansetts to ally themselves with Massachusetts, thus rendering signal service to the colony which had exiled him. Complete religious freedom was established in the new settlement, which became a haven for many who were persecuted elsewhere for their faith. Williams established the first Baptist church in America, but very shortly lost his faith in the form of baptism by immersion upon which it was founded, and left the church to become a "Seeker" or "Independent." He visited England in 1643 and the following year obtained a charter for Providence, Newport and Portsmouth, under the title of "The Providence Plantations in Narragansett Bay." He lived in Providence from 1644 to 1646 when he removed to what is now Wickford, R. I. In 1651 he went to England a second time to procure a new and more explicit charter and during three years spent there he became the friend of Cromwell, Milton and other Puritan leaders. Returning to Rhode Island in 1654, he was elected president of the colony. He died in March, 1684, and was buried in a spot he had selected on his own land.

He wrote numerous tracts and pamphlets on religious subjects and entered into a controversy with the Quakers although he steadfastly refused to persecute them. His friendly relations with the Indians and his knowledge of their language enabled him to be of great service from time to time to the other New England colonies.

WOODROW WILSON   1856–1924

THOMAS WOODROW WILSON, President of the United States during the World War, was born in Staunton, Va., Dec. 28, 1856, of Scotch-Irish ancestry. His father was a Presbyterian clergyman. He attended Princeton University (1875–79), studied law at the University of Virginia, government and history at Johns Hopkins, and later became associate professor of history and political economy at Bryn Mawr. In 1888 he went to Wesleyan University in Connecticut in the same capacity and two years later to Princeton as professor of jurisprudence and political economy. He had already become widely known as a scholar and writer on political science and government. In 1902 he became president of Princeton University where he instituted many reforms and remained until he was elected governor of New Jersey in 1910, the first democrat to hold that office in 16 years. As governor he carried through a number of important laws, among them the direct primary law, corrupt practices act, employers' liability act; created a public utilities commission and obtained the passage of the so-called "Seven Sisters" acts to protect the public from exploitation by the trusts.

At the 1912 Democratic National Convention he was nominated on the 46th ballot and, largely by the support of William Jennings Bryan, was elected 28th president of the United States. Much progressive legislation was enacted during his administration and directly through his own efforts and leadership; the Underwood Tariff act, the adoption of a Federal income tax, the Federal Reserve act, Federal Trade Commission act, Clayton Anti-Trust act, and important measures affecting the Panama Canal tolls. He assumed a protectorate over Haiti, established a military government in Santo Domingo, refused to recognize the Huerta régime in Mexico, to which country he despatched General John J. Pershing in an inconclusive punitive expedition against the bandit, Francisco Villa. At the outbreak of the World War he insisted upon a policy of strict neutrality and opposed the extension of military preparedness, but protested at the sinking of neutral vessels by German submarines and exchanged many inconclusive notes with Germany on the matter. There followed the torpedoing of the *Lusitania* and the *Sussex* and after his reelection in 1916 diplomatic relations with Germany were broken off. His offer of mediation between the Allies and Germany had been rejected. He had emphasized the need of a league of nations, the limitation of armaments, the freedom of the seas, and had proclaimed the urgent necessity of a "peace without victory." Germany renewed submarine warfare on neutral shipping and in April, 1917, Wilson called a special session of Congress and a state of war was declared to exist.

He then proceeded to hand over the military policy to military experts; urged a selective service act and gave General Pershing command over the American expeditionary force, with full power. He encouraged the organization of the Council of National Defence, the creation of a Food and Fuel Administration, the taking over of the railroads by the government, and the creation of a War Industries Board. He continued to develop his ideas for a new international system and, laid down his famous "Fourteen Points," as a basis for a final peace settlement. Following the armistice of November, 1918, he attended the peace conference in Paris and succeeded in getting a League of Nations covenant incorporated into the peace treaty, but upon his return to the United States he found Congress hostile to him and entirely in control of the republicans, and he failed to induce them to ratify the treaty. He undertook a tour of the country to arouse popular support for the treaty and particularly for the League which had been his own proposal and which had been received with enthusiasm abroad. The strenuous speaking tour overtaxed his strength and he suffered a complete nervous collapse at Wichita, Kansas, followed by a paralytic stroke after his return to Washington, thus leaving the administration without a leader. He never entirely recovered but was able to take an interest in state affairs and at the election of 1920 he hoped for a "solemn referendum" in favor of the League of Nations. He was bitterly disappointed at the overwhelming victory of the republican candidate, Warren G. Harding, and although he lived to see the League firmly established, it was without the membership of the United States.

After the completion of his second presidential term he lived quietly in Washington until his death on Feb. 3, 1924. He was buried in the Bethlehem Chapel of the Washington Cathedral. He was a man of profound scholarly attainments and literary distinction. His style was forceful and captivating and he was the author of *A History of the American People* (1902), *Constitutional Government in the United States* (1908) and many other works. In December, 1920, he had been awarded the Nobel Peace Prize. His first wife, Ellen Louise Axson, the mother of his three daughters, died in the White House early in his first term and he later married Mrs. Edith Bolling Galt, who survived him.

JOHN WINTHROP   1588–1649

JOHN WINTHROP, the first governor of the Massachusetts Bay Colony, was born at Edwardston, Suffolk, England, on Jan. 12, 1588. He attended Trinity College, Cambridge, from 1602–04 and later took up the practice of law in which he appears to have been quite successful for about 1623 he was appointed an attorney in the court of wards and liveries, and was called upon frequently to draft parliamentary bills. For some reason he lost this lucrative appointment in 1629 and in August of that year he joined the so-called "Cambridge Agreement" by which he and others of the Puritans among whom he had a wide acquaintance and considerable influence, pledged themselves to emigrate to New England in consideration of the seat of government of the Massachusetts Colony being transferred to that colony. He separated entirely from the Church of England and threw in his lot with the Puritans. He was chosen governor of the Massachusetts Colony and sailed on the ship *Arbella* in March of 1630, arriving at Salem, Mass., in June in company with about 1000 others who hoped to find in America the religious freedom which England had denied to them.

For a brief time he lived in Charlestown but by the fall of the year he had settled in what later became Boston, and taken up the duties of his office. His life thereafter was closely connected with the history of Massachusetts. He was twelve times elected governor of the colony, serving from 1629 to 1634, from 1637 to 1640, from 1642 to 1644, and from 1646 until his death in 1649. When not actually in office as governor he was usually deputy governor, and always an assistant and close adviser. Not only did he devote his time and energy to the good of the colony, but he spent his own fortune in that cause. Of a conservative and aristocratic nature, he was just and usually magnanimous, although he was not free from the intolerance which characterized his fellow religionists and the age in which he lived; an intolerance which caused the banishment of Roger Williams from the colony. In 1636, while Sir Harry Vane was governor, there arose the Antinomian controversy, as a consequence of which Anne Hutchinson was also banished. Winthrop took a conservative attitude in this dispute and was more liberal than most of his fellow citizens.

In 1637 came the war with the Pequot Indians. In the same year a synod of the clergy at Boston listed 82 blasphemous, erroneous or unsafe opinions held in the colony. In 1643 a federation of the four colonies of Massachusetts, Connecticut, Plymouth and New Haven was brought about under the title of the United Colonies of New England, which was dominated by Massachusetts, and Winthrop became its first president. He was of the temper that later characterized the leaders of the Revolutionary War. In 1634–35 he was the leader in a movement to put the colony in a state of defence against possible coercion by the British government and again in 1645–46 he defended the colony against the threat of English interference. He was an able leader and much of the success of the colony was due to his ability and political wisdom. He died in Boston on March 26, 1649, and was interred in King's Chapel Burying Ground.

His "Journal," printed in full in Boston in 1825–26 is a valuable record of the early history of Massachusetts. In 1605 he married Mary Forth who bore him six children. The eldest, John Winthrop, was an assistant to his father during many years, founded the town of Agawam (now Ipswich, Mass.); was governor of Connecticut and a commissioner of the United Colonies of New England. His second wife died in childbirth; the third, Margaret Tyndal, followed him to the New World and bore him eight children, and after her death he married Mrs. Martha Coytmore who survived him and added one son to his family.

JAMES WOLFE   1727–1759

JAMES WOLFE, British general who, through his defeat of the French under Montcalm at Quebec, added Canada to the British possessions in North America, was born at Westerham, Kent, England, Jan. 2, 1727, elder son of Gen. Edward Wolfe who served with distinction under Marlborough. He was educated at private schools in Westerham and Greenwich and early became interested in a military career. In 1741 he received a commission in the marines, but was soon transferred into the line and sent to Flanders as an ensign in the 12th Foot in 1742, where he served until the close of the war of the Austrian Succession. He took part in the battles of Dettingen, Falkirk, Culloden and Laffeldt. In the latter engagement he was wounded. He proved a zealous, intelligent and gallant soldier and won the admiration of his superiors. His promotion was rapid and by 1749 he had risen to the rank of major and was named acting commander of the 20th Foot. The following year he became lieutenant-colonel of that regiment and served with it for eight years in Scotland and in the south of England.

He was appointed quartermaster-general in Ireland in 1757, but before he could assume his duties Pitt appointed him to the same office in the expedition against Rochefort. The campaign failed and Pitt and other influential persons believed that the failure was largely due to the refusal of the commander-in-chief to accept the plans for landing which Wolfe had suggested. This belief led to the selection of Wolfe to serve as brigadier under General Amherst (1758) in an expedition against the French fortified town of Louisburg on Cape Breton Island. This was to be the first step in a plan to drive the French out of Canada. Wolfe's brilliant conduct in this successful siege made him "the hero of Louisburg" and he was next placed in charge of an expedition which was to attempt the capture of Quebec. He was technically still under General Amherst, but was himself given full power to conduct operations as seemed best to him and was raised to the rank of major-general. He left England in February 1759 and in June landed his army of some 9000 men on the Isle of Orleans, a few miles below Quebec. He had first intended to land above the town and to attack it on the Heights of Abraham where the fortifications were weakest. Just why that plan was abandoned is not known, but he took possession of the heights on the south shore of the St. Lawrence, just opposite Quebec, from which position he could bombard the French army under Montcalm which was entrenched between the mouth of the Montmorenci river and the city of Quebec. He also established a position at the mouth of the Montmorenci. Montcalm remained inactive and at length, on July 31, Wolfe ordered an attack on the French position. It was repulsed at great cost to the British. Resolved upon a desperate course, he carefully reconnoitered and at a cove two miles above the city he discovered a zigzag path leading to the summit of the cliff on which the city stood. Before dawn on the morning of Sept. 13 he transported his troops across the river and scaled the precipitous Heights of Abraham. By daybreak 4500 men were drawn up in battle array, the French sentinels were surprised and Montcalm precipitately attacked, with a force which, while equal to the British in numbers, was not as well trained. The French troops could not withstand the excellent marksmanship of Wolfe's men at close quarters and after a few minutes' hot fire, the French broke and fled. Wolfe, wounded by a musket ball, died at the moment of victory. Five days later Quebec surrendered and Canada became a British possession. Montcalm also was fatally wounded in the battle.

Wolfe had evidently had a presentiment that he would not survive to reap the fruits of victory for during the day preceding the battle he gave to his friend (afterward Admiral Jarvis) a miniature which he carried of the lady whom he was to marry, to be returned to her if he fell in action. He had spent several weeks preceding the attack on a sickbed and during the crossing of the river in the gray dawn he sat thoughtfully repeating some lines from Gray's *Elegy,* "The paths of glory lead but to the grave," and it is said that he remarked, "I would rather be the author of that poem than to take Quebec."

CARDINAL WOLSEY   circa 1475–1530

THOMAS WOLSEY, English statesman and cardinal, was born about 1475 at Ipswich, the son of a humble butcher, grazier and woolen merchant. Of a studious turn of mind, he became a fellow of Magdalen College, Oxford, and was master of its school for 19 years. In 1500 he went to Limington, Somersetshire, where the Marquis of Dorset gave him a living. A year later he was appointed chaplain to Archbishop Dean and in 1506 became royal chaplain to King Henry VII. He was sent on embassies to Scotland and the Netherlands in 1508, and was made Dean of Lincoln.

He had made many friends at court and upon the accession of Henry VIII he was appointed king's almoner and a member of the king's council. He won the confidence of the monarch and his progress in clerical and state honors was rapid. His energy and ability, displayed in the war against France in 1513, won for him the bishopric of Tournai and the sees of Lincoln and York in the following year. Through his success in bringing about an amicable understanding between France and England later in the year he became one of the leading figures in Europe. He held successively the sees of Bath and Wells in 1518, of Durham in 1523, of Winchester in 1529, and the abbey of St. Albans.

Henry VIII appointed him Lord High Chancellor in 1515, and in the same year he was made a cardinal by Pope Leo X. Two years later he became the Pope's cardinal-legate, and upon the pontiff's death in 1521 he aspired to become pope, but his hopes were not fulfilled. He lost his popularity with the nobles and the common people of England because of his constant demands for money to supply the king's will which, to Wolsey, was the great motive power of the entire state. He tried to hold a balance between the power of the Emperor Charles and Francis I of France in order that England might recover the place in the comity of nations which she had lost during the Wars of the Roses. Between 1524 and 1529 he abolished some thirty monasteries, arousing tremendous opposition among the various religious orders affected.

When Henry wished to divorce Catherine of Aragon, he called upon Wolsey to obtain the necessary permission, but the cardinal was unsuccessful in his attempt to have Pope Clement VII declare the marriage void. He thus lost favor with the king, and his enemies used the occasion of his absence in France on a royal mission to still further undermine his prestige and alienate the king from him. Anne Boleyn, who had long been hostile to him, and who was determined to become Henry's queen, brought her influence to bear against Wolsey; Thomas Cranmer (later Archbishop of Canterbury) was gaining great influence; and in 1529 Wolsey was stripped of his offices. His descent from power and authority was even more swift than had been his rise. His enemies succeeded in having a charge of high treason placed against him and he was arrested by the Earl of Northumberland. Broken in body and spirit, he set out for London to answer to the charge, but was taken ill on the way and died at Leicester Abbey on Nov. 29, 1530.

The hatred on the part of the nobility and his unpopularity with the common people continued long after his death and it was not until state papers of that period were published that his character and reputation as a great statesman were rehabilitated. The vast estates which had been conferred upon him had given him an income far exceeding that of the king himself and he had adopted a magnificent style of living. He was ambitious, arrogant, greedy of power and lax in morals, but nevertheless he was devoted to the interests of his country and was a faithful and wise counselor to the king whose favor he so long enjoyed. He was a liberal patron of learning, and founded the college of Christ Church (which he intended to be called Cardinal College) at Oxford where he had spent so many years, besides another at Ipswich, his birthplace.

WILLIAM WORDSWORTH   1770–1850

WILLIAM WORDSWORTH, poet laureate of England, and notable among modern poets for the natural simplicity of manner and theme which characterizes his work, was born on April 7, 1770, at Cockermouth in Cumberland. He was the second son of John Wordsworth, attorney and agent on the estates of the first Earl of Lonsdale. He was sent to school at Penrith, where his parents lived, and after the death of his mother when he was eight years old he was transferred to Hawkshead, in Lancashire. In 1783 his father died, leaving his family in difficulties, and they were able to procure only a fraction of what was due them from Lord Lonsdale. At 17 the boy entered St. John's College, Cambridge, where he remained for four years, showing but slight interest in his regular studies, although his interest in poetry was intense. During his last year in college he made a walking tour in France with a fellow student, and thither he returned after taking his B.A. degree in 1791. He was deeply sympathetic with the aims of the French Revolution and seems to have cultivated the friendship of many of the Gironde party (the moderate republicans), a circumstance which might have been fraught with tragic consequences to himself had not his own depleted purse made necessary his return to England before his friends went to the guillotine.

At 23 he published two poems, *An Evening Walk, Addressed to a Young Lady* and *Descriptive Sketches, taken During a Pedestrian Tour Among the Alps,* which, although attracting slight attention from the public, greatly interested Samuel Coleridge, then a student at Cambridge, who later protested that he had discerned in them the seeds of undeveloped genius. It was evident to Wordsworth that his poetry, which would always be of a sort with these early efforts, could hardly be expected to furnish him a living, and he was in some perplexity as to how to replenish his means. Toward the church, which for some reason his friends thought a suitable career, he had at that time a strong aversion, and he was about to seek a solution of his problem by newspaper work in London when the death of a friend, who had a high regard for his genius, left him in possession of a considerable legacy. This money was bequeathed expressly to ease his path during the development of his genius, and it is an instance of the keen appreciation which the struggling poet enjoyed in the estimation of a small but discerning circle. Thenceforth his life was ideally that of a poet. With his only sister, Dorothy, who had the highest estimate of his powers and was always his devoted companion, he settled at Racedown Lodge in Dorsetshire, removing later to Alfoxden in Somersetshire in order to be near Coleridge who lived several miles distant at Nether Stowey.

Out of the intimacy thus begun came the famous *Lyrical Ballads,* published in 1798 as a joint enterprise of the two men. Its failure found Wordsworth serene; few poets have so completely found solace and satisfaction in expression. After a short tour in Germany he settled finally at Rydal Mount, the home with which his name is peculiarly associated and the beautiful surroundings of which his gentle life and genius have hallowed. The settlement of Lord Lonsdale's estate brought to him and his sister a considerable sum and in 1802 he married his cousin, Mary Hutchinson. In 1813 he was given a government post, requiring little of his time; a tribute to his genius rather than steady employment. In the following year he published his great poem, *The Excursion,* and at about that time republished *Lyrical Ballads* with much new matter and omitting the poems by Coleridge. *Poems, in Two Volumes,* appeared in 1807 and furnished occasion (although not good reason) for ridicule. The utter simplicity of his poems aroused much levity and the critics made merry at his choice of lowly and unpoetic themes, a kind of treatment which would have been quite as appropriate in the case of Robert Burns. Thus, the "lake school" came to be a sort of epithet, derived from the beautiful lake region in which he lived. But his real poetic genius triumphed over his own undoubted eccentricities, as well as over ridicule and critical abuse, and the gay tirades of his literary detractors did not produce the blighting effects which were so tragic in the case of the sensitive Keats. For Wordsworth the day of jeering passed and was followed by a rising tide of genuine appreciation. His last years were spent serenely, exemplifying the simple life, with the satisfaction of seeing himself acknowledged as one of the great poets of his country. In 1839, Oxford conferred on him the degree of D.C.L., a pension was given him and on the death of his friend, Southey, he succeeded as poet laureate. His life has been called priest-like and ought to satisfy those who have strangely deplored the shrewd business instinct of Shakespeare. He seems to fulfil all the ideal requirements of the true poet; he was pure, gentle and unworldly. He died peacefully among the surroundings which had come to be a very part of his life, on the 23rd of April, 1850.

Others of his works were *The White Doe of Rylstone, The Waggoner, Sonnets on the River Duddon, Ecclesiastical Sonnets, Yarrow Revisited, and other Poems,* and *Memorials of a Tour On the Continent.*

SIR CHRISTOPHER WREN   1632–1723

CHRISTOPHER WREN, English architect and scientist, was born at East Knoyle, Wiltshire, England, on Oct. 20, 1632, the son of Dr. Christopher Wren, Dean of Windsor, and nephew of Dr. Matthew Wren, Bishop of Hereford and later of Norwich and Ely. Young Christopher received his early education at Westminster and later went to Wadham College, Oxford, and became a fellow of All Souls. One of his early achievements was aiding in the perfecting of the barometer. He was professor of astronomy at Gresham College, London, for four years and then returned to Oxford as Savilian professor of astronomy. While living in London he had aided Boyle, Wilkins and others in forming the Royal Society. He had become widely known as a mathematician and scientist but his first work of an architectural nature seems to have been in 1663 when he was engaged to make a survey of St. Paul's Cathedral which was to be put under repair. The first building actually built from his plans was the chapel at Pembroke College, Cambridge, in 1663. Within the next three years he had drawn plans for the Sheldonian Theatre at Oxford, and for the library and other buildings of Trinity College, Cambridge. In 1665 he visited Paris.

It was the great London fire of 1666 that gave full scope to his genius as an architectural designer. Much of the city was destroyed and he was engaged to lay out plans for rebuilding it and to draw designs for its new public buildings. His plans called for wide streets, for fine quays, large parks, imposing public buildings, but unfortunately they were not carried out as he wished. He made the plans for the new St. Paul's cathedral and worked on the building, supervising its construction, from 1675 to 1710. This is the greatest single monument to his genius, although he designed more than fifty other London churches that had been destroyed. The Royal Exchange and the Custom House were built from his plans, as were Temple Bar, the College of Physicians, Greenwich Observatory, Chelsea Hospital, the Ashmolean Museum, Hampton Court, Greenwich Hospital, Buckingham House, Marlborough House and many other buildings. Never has an architect had such an opportunity as was his and he took full advantage of it. In recognition of his work in rebuilding the city he was knighted in 1673, but his plan for laying out the entire city with wide streets radiating from a central point was abandoned owing to opposition from owners of property which would have had to be sacrificed.

Among the churches which were rebuilt from his plans are St. Michael's in Cornhill, St. Bride's in Fleet Street, St. Mary-le-Bow in Cheapside, St. Stephen's in Walbrook and St. James', Piccadilly. He also drew plans for the north transept of Westminster Abbey and for its western towers. The towers were not built until several years after his death and whether or not his plans were used is a disputed point. He received the degree D.C.L., in 1660, and was elected president of the Royal Society in 1681. For many years he was a member of Parliament, representing Plymouth from 1685, Windsor from 1689, and Weymouth from 1700. For fifty years he was surveyor of the royal works, but was ousted from that post a few years before his death through some machinations. He died on Feb. 26, 1723 and was buried under the choir of St. Paul's Cathedral. A tablet on the inner north doorway bears the famous epitaph, *Si monumentum requiris, circumspice* (If thou seek his monument, look about thee). On the 200th anniversary of his death a memorial service was held in St. Paul's.

A history of the Wren family and particularly of Sir Christopher and his achievements was published in 1750 by his grandson under the title of *Parentalia*.

WILBUR AND ORVILLE WRIGHT   1867–1912   1871–

WILBUR AND ORVILLE WRIGHT, American pioneers in aviation, developed the first practicable airplane and made the first flights in a heavier than air machine. Their experiments began the science of aeronautics as we know it today.

Wilbur Wright was born near Millville, Ind., April 16, 1867 and his brother Orville at Dayton, Ohio, Aug. 19, 1871. They were the sons of Milton Wright, an editor and later Bishop of the United Brethren church. They attended public schools in Dayton, Richmond, Ind., and Cedar Rapids, Ia. An accident while playing ice hockey prevented Wilbur from entering college and from engaging in any active work for several years during which he cared for his invalid mother and aided his father in legal matters for the church. He later joined his brother Orville in a bicycle repairing business in Dayton and they became interested in the gliding experiments of the German, Otto Lilienthal, who died in an accident to his glider in 1896. The Wright brothers set out to develop a glider in which the center of gravity should remain constant while equilibrium was maintained by varying the air pressure on various parts of the mechanism through adjusting the angles of the wings and other parts— the system now known as aileron control.

From a sport, aeronautics soon became to them a scientific pursuit. They found existing data on the subject unreliable and undertook experiments from which to collect data of their own. In 1901 they built a wind tunnel in their workshop at Dayton and in it measured the lift and drag of different shaped airfoils at angles varying from zero to 45 degrees. They made measurements to determine the position of the center of pressure on cambered surfaces, the lift and drag when one surface was placed above another, or when it followed another. With the information thus gained and believing it possible to predict from their calculations the performance of a flying machine, they began to design an airplane which would require one-half or less motive power than had any of the earlier proposed planes. In October, 1902, they set to work on a machine to be propelled by a four-cylinder gasoline motor of 12 horse power. The weight of the machine and the pilot was to be 750 pounds. In December, 1903, they tested their first airplane at Kitty Hawk, N. C., where four free flights were made, the longest of which lasted 59 seconds and attained a speed of 30 miles an hour. Continuing their experiments, by September, 1905, they had learned how to avoid a "tail spin" when making short turns and thus were able to fly for greater distances. On Oct. 5th of that year, Wilbur flew for 38 minutes over a circular course, covering 24 miles.

The next several years were spent in attempting to find financial backing for the manufacture of their planes. Unsuccessful in America, Wilbur took the machine to France in 1908 where successful flights were made. The Michelin prize was awarded him after a flight of 56 miles and at Le Mans he covered 77 miles. Other flights followed in Rome and the attention of the entire world was attracted. The kings of Italy, Spain and England attended the demonstrations and the brothers received gold medals from the French Academy of Sciences and many honors in Europe and America. Returning to the United States, a spectacular flight was made over the Hudson River during the Hudson-Fulton Celebration of 1909, and the machine was demonstrated at Ft. Meyer, Va., for the United States government which thereafter purchased a plane for $30,000. It was later adopted by the U. S. Army and a government aviation school was established with Orville Wright as instructor. The Wright Company was later organized to take over the patents in the United States and both brothers were actively identified with the company until the death of Wilbur from typhoid fever at Dayton, Ohio, on May 30, 1912. Orville continued his work as director of the Wright Aeronautical Laboratory at Dayton. In 1915 he was appointed a member of the U. S. Naval Consulting Board and in that year the business of the Wright Company was taken over by New York interests with which he still continued his connection.

In December, 1928, the 25th anniversary of the first successful airplane flight was observed at Kitty Hawk, N. C., where the Wright brothers gave their first public demonstration of flying, and a tablet was erected commemorating their achievements. Neither of the brothers married.

JOHN WYCLIFFE   circa 1320–1384

John Wycliffe, English reformer and forerunner of the Reformation, was born about the year 1320 in Yorkshire, England, apparently of a well-to-do family. An excellent scholar, he won popularity as a teacher at Oxford and was made master of Balliol College in 1360, later becoming rector in successive nearby parishes. For a time he was warden of Canterbury Hall and held some small office at court, where he was employed to write pamphlets, constituting a sort of court propaganda. He had become known as an opponent of the encroachments of the Catholic Church, as represented by the Pope, into the affairs of the English clergy and the English government. Because of this attitude he was sent to Bruges in 1375 to meet with ambassadors from the Pope to confer on ecclesiastical abuses in England. He refused to abate his opposition and became widely popular among the citizens of London and with many of the influential nobles.

He offended the bishops of the church in England, however, by maintaining that the English secular power had the right of control over the clergy, and in 1377 he was summoned for a hearing before the Archbishop of St. Paul's. The council was disrupted by a quarrel between the Duke of Lancaster and the Bishop of London and the reformer continued on his course. The Pope now took a hand in the affair and addressed papal bulls to the king and the bishops of England and to the University of Oxford ordering them to arrest Wycliffe to answer for his course before the Archbishop and the Pope. Proceedings were finally taken against him, but without success in curbing his activities. The election of an anti-pope in 1378 threatened the supremacy of the church, and Wycliffe, who had hitherto aimed his attacks at the abuses of the church, now centered his efforts upon the very groundwork of the church itself. He boldly asserted that the Church would be better off without either pope or prelates; he denied the right of the priesthood to offer absolution of sins, its power to enforce confession, its authority for imposing penances, and its right to sell indulgences.

He abandoned the use of Latin in writing his appeals to the people and his attacks on the church, and began to write them in English, thus becoming the first of English prose writers. Besides continuing until his death the writing of his tracts, he gathered together a group of itinerant preachers whom he sent throughout the land to spread his doctrines and thus laid the foundation for the Reformation which followed. His list of the abuses of the church served as the keystone of later attacks upon it by Luther, Calvin, Knox, Zwingli and others, and his teachings formed the basis for the activities of the Bohemian reformer, John Huss.

Wycliffe made a complete translation of the Bible into English, and his work served as a basis for all later translations. In 1380 he assailed the Catholic dogma of transubstantiation, but his theses were condemned by a convocation of doctors at Oxford. He appealed to the king without success and in 1382 Archbishop Courtenay convoked a council which condemned Wycliffe's teachings. His followers were arrested and condemned, but he himself escaped that fate and withdrew from Oxford to Lutterworth, where he continued his writings of pamphlets against the church. He died Dec. 31, 1384 and thirty years later the Council of Constance condemned his doctrine as heretical and ordered his bones to be disinterred, burned and cast into the river Swift.

XENOPHON   circa 434 B.C.–circa 355 B.C.

XENOPHON (zĕn'ŏ fŏn), a Greek general and historian, was the son of one Gryllus, and was born near Athens about the year 434 B.C. He was a pupil and companion of Socrates, of whose life he has left some account in his *Memorabilia,* and was himself a cultivated gentleman whose versatile genius found expression in many ways and won him reputation as a philosopher and essayist as well as orator and soldier. He has given us many interesting and pleasing pictures of Greek life and much of the charm of his work lies in the simplicity of his style.

About the year 401 he joined an expedition which was organized by

Cyrus the Younger against his brother, Artaxerxes Mnemon, king of Persia. Cyrus was defeated and slain in the battle of Cunaxa, and the 10,000 Greek mercenaries who formed part of his army found themselves a thousand miles from home in a hostile country surrounded by enemies and betrayed by the treacherous Persians who killed most of their chief officers. Xenophon, by his own account, took command of the Greeks and led them on the adventurous five months' march back to the shore of the Black Sea and thence to the Bosporus. This march has become famous in history as the Retreat of the Ten Thousand. An account of the entire expedition is given in Xenophon's *Anabasis,* or Up-Country March, the work which has immortalized his name. The last six books of this famous work give an elaborate history of the homeward journey. It was written in the third person and in a pleasing, straightforward style, but was published some thirty years after the events which it recounts, and without other corroborative writings by which to check the accuracy of Xenophon's statements it is impossible to know how much the writer's recollections of events had been colored by the lapse of time, although the research of later scholars indicates the main events of the tale to be true.

It was doubtless due to his courage and skilful leadership that the Greek soldiers eventually reached the Hellespont (or Dardanelles) where they entered the service of the Spartans. Athens had passed a sentence of banishment against Xenophon, probably because of his participation in the Persian expedition, and for some years we find him identified with the Spartans, even to the extent of accompanying their king, Agesilaus, in 394 B.C., during the Corinthian War, when his own countrymen (the Athenians) were defeated at the battle of Coronea. After a few years at Sparta he settled on an estate given him by the Spartans near Olympia, in the province of Elis in southern Greece, where he lived for about 20 years, devoting himself to literature, hunting and agriculture. Here most of his works were written. He was at length driven from this home by the people of Elis after the defeat of the Spartans by the Thebans at Leuctra in 371, but although the Athenians had repealed the sentence of banishment, he apparently never returned to his native city. His two sons, however, were later in the Athenian army. He next took refuge in Corinth where he probably died about 355 B.C.

In his *Memorabilia* and *Symposium,* or *Banquet,* giving his recollections of Socrates' conversations and table talk, he presents the great philosopher in a human rather than a philosophic aspect. The *Memorabilia* was written to defend Socrates from charges which had been made against him of impiety and of corrupting the morals of the young and it is quite evident that the writer was more interested in the moral and practical aspect of Socrates' teachings than in his purely philosophical speculations. Other works are the *Æconomicus,* giving in dialogue form a picture of the home life of a young Greek couple; the history of Greece and the Peloponnesian War entitled *Hellenica; Cyropædia,* a romance based on the life of Cyrus the Elder, but which was made the vehicle for many of the writer's own views on training and education. A distinct moral purpose runs through the book, but strict adherence to the facts of Cyrus' life is often sacrificed. It was said to have been written in opposition to Plato's *Republic. Lacedæmonian Polity* is a biography of the Spartan general Agesilaus; and there are several treatises on *The Chase, Horsemanship, The Duties of a Cavalry Officer, Revenues of Athens* and other subjects.

XERXES I   circa 520 B.C.–465 B.C.

XERXES I (zĕrk'sēz) was one of the most famous kings of antiquity. He won his place in history by his almost complete conquest of the Greeks and his final overthrow at the naval battle of Salamis. He was the son of Darius I, King of Persia, and of Atossa, daughter of Cyrus the Great, and is believed to be the King Ahasuerus mentioned in the Bible. Babylonian documents of the period refer to him as "King of Persia and Media" or "King of Countries."

Upon his father's death he was able to supersede his three older brothers because of the fact that he had been born after his father's accession to the throne in 521 B.C. In October 485 B.C., soon after his accession to the throne, he invaded Egypt where a revolt had broken out the previous year. He put down the rebellion with a heavy hand and made his brother, Achaemenes, satrap along the Nile. Two years later he destroyed the "Kingdom of Babel," taking away the golden statue of the god Bel, or Marduk, and killing the priest who tried to prevent the seizure of the god. This led to other rebellions in Babylonia, probably in 484 and 479 B.C., which he was able to crush. About 483 he began to prepare for an expedition against the Greeks who had previously interfered in an Ionian rebellion against Persian authority and had defeated the Persians at Marathon in 490. His preparations were extensive. He caused a channel to be dug through the isthmus of the peninsula of Mount Athos, built two bridges across the Hellespont and had provisions stored at various places along the route he proposed to traverse. He formed an alliance with Carthage, which took from Greece the powerful support of Syracuse and Agrigentum, and a number of small Greek states deserted Athens and threw in their fortunes with the Persian invaders. Xerxes gathered a large fleet and set sail from Sardis in the spring of 480 B.C. He met with early successes. Coming into contact with the Greek fleet, which had been built up at the instigation of the Athenian, Themistocles, at Artemisium, the Greek triremes were defeated and forced to flee, but were not destroyed so that the Persian victory in that engagement was far from decisive. The pass of Thermopylae was stormed by the Persians despite the famous and heroic defence by the Spartan king, Leonidas, and 300 soldiers. Athens was conquered and laid waste, the Greeks driven back to the Isthmus of Corinth and the Bay of Salamis where the fleet was gathered.

By misleading messages from Themistocles, Xerxes was led to attack the Greek fleet at Salamis under conditions that were unfavorable to himself and correspondingly advantageous to the Greeks. The naval battle of Salamis was the decisive engagement of the Persian invasion and saved Greece from probable annihilation and enslavement. It was fought on Sept. 28, 480 B.C. Through the stratagem of Themistocles, the Greeks were enclosed in the narrow straits between the island of Salamis and the shores of Attica and Megaris. The enemy had rowed across the entrance to the east channel and detached a squadron to block the west channel. The Greeks could not retreat and the Persians could not utilize their superior numbers. As Xerxes' ships advanced into the narrow neck of the east strait they were attacked by the Greeks, thrown into confusion and after several hours' fighting were forced to retire with the loss of 200 ships and a corps of troops that had been landed. The Greeks lost 40 ships. Xerxes' communications by sea were cut off and he returned home.

Little is known of his later years. He was apparently never able to recover his power after the crushing defeat at Salamis. It is known that he sent out an expedition to attempt to sail around Africa and he built some palaces and left some inscriptions. He eventually became involved in harem intrigues and was murdered in 465 B.C. by his vizier, Artabanus.

BRIGHAM YOUNG 1801–1877

BRIGHAM YOUNG, a leader of the Mormon Church, was born at Whitingham, Vt., June 1, 1801, but while he was still very young the family moved to Mendon, N. Y., where he later became a painter, carpenter and glazier. In 1830 he was introduced to the *Book of Mormon* and two years later was converted to the new faith by a brother of Joseph Smith, the founder of the sect. Following his baptism in April, 1832, Young was appointed an elder of the church, met Joseph Smith at Kirtland, Ohio, and was sent on a proselyting mission to Canada where he met with considerable success, and was later sent to Missouri in the "Army of Zion." In 1835 he was elected as one of the original Quorum of Twelve, and was sent out to preach first to the Indians and then to the people of the eastern states. In 1838 he directed the moving of the Mormons (or Church of Jesus Christ of the Latter Day Saints) from Missouri to Illinois, and two years later he was sent to Liverpool to aid the apostles John Taylor and Wilford Woodruff in spreading the Mormon doctrines in England. Shortly after his return he was made president of the Quorum of Twelve (1844) and three years afterward was elected president of the church, although he had already been the real leader of the sect after the death in 1844 of Joseph Smith, the founder, at the hands of disaffected residents of Illinois. Young organized and directed the migration of his followers from Illinois to the unsettled West, leaving behind those who clung to the younger Joseph Smith, son of the founder, who never embraced polygamy and who vehemently denied that his father had sanctioned it.

In February, 1845, the first party of Mormons left Nauvoo, Ill., under Young's command. They wintered in camp on the Missouri River and he made his first and only "revelation" in his *Book of Doctrines and Covenants,* which gave detailed information as to the organizing of the "Camp of Israel," and the conduct of the long journey across the prairies. The company of "Saints" reached Salt Lake Valley in 1847. Young selected a site for the Temple and laid out the plans for a new city, after which the "State of Deseret" was organized and a legislature elected. He was chosen as first governor (1849) and applied to Congress for admission of the new "state" into the Union, instead of which the Territory of Utah was created, and President Fillmore appointed Young as governor, an office which he filled until the so-called Mormon War occurred in 1858. An attempt had been made the previous year to displace him as governor of the Territory, but he refused to relinquish the office. The people of Utah in the main supported him and there resulted what practically amounted to an insurrection. Federal officials and land officers were forced to leave the Territory and bands of Mormons known as Danites spread terror among the non-Mormons by their outrages. In the following spring President Buchanan issued a proclamation commanding that the Mormons submit to the federal authority, and sent out a new governor (Cumming) with a military force, to which Young and his followers submitted. Mormon accounts report that no hostility was shown to the soldiers when they arrived to put down the supposed rebellion, but that they were well received and made a favorable report to the government.

In 1851 Young had organized a public school system; he encouraged agriculture and manufactures, the building of roads and bridges, and carried out a contract to build 100 miles of the roadbed of the Union Pacific Railroad. Some years later he established a system of cooperative stores which still exist and form a large factor in the business of the state. In 1852 he declared polygamy to be an established tenet of the faith of the Latter Day Saints. He died on August 29, 1877 and left a fortune estimated at more than $1,000,000. His wives numbered seventeen or more and he was reputed to be the father of fifty-seven children.

ÉMILE ZOLA   1840–1902

ÉMILE ZOLA, a prolific realistic novelist of France, the son of an Italian engineer, was born in Paris, April 2, 1840. His first connection with the literary world was as a clerk in the publishing house of Hachette in Paris and it was not long before he was contributing articles, mostly of a political or critical nature, to the newspapers. He made small headway, however, in the newspaper world, nor were his attempts at writing for the stage much more successful. He found his true field in 1864 with the publication of a volume of short stories, *Contes à Ninon,* followed by *Nouveaux Contes à Ninon* (1874), *Le Capitaine Burle, Naïs Micoulin* and the *Attacque du Moulin* (1880), all of which met with a considerable degree of success. The so-called "naturalistic" school in French fiction was formed with Alphonse Daudet, Edmond de Goncourt and Ivan Turgenev, the famous Russian novelist then living in Paris, toward the close of Louis Napoleon's reign, and Zola's novel, *Thérèse Raquin* (1867) was his first contribution to this new method of writing fiction, a method which he was later to elaborate in the tremendous Rougon-Macquart series of twenty novels embracing social, military, political and commercial activities of his time in France. He termed this series a *Physiological History of a Family under the Second Empire* and members of the two families concerned figured in the entire twenty novels. He documented his material as carefully as a historian or a scientist and he carried his passion for realism to such lengths in the boldness of many of his descriptions that he aroused much disapproval against which he contended that he was introducing an entirely new "naturalistic" literary school. He worked on his series with indefatigable energy, amid attack and abuse, but lived to see himself become the greatest literary figure in France in the last quarter of the nineteenth century, with his novels selling in tremendous quantities.

The first of the great series was *La Fortune des Rougon*, followed by *La Curée* and *Son Excellence Eugène Rougon*, in which he faithfully depicted the social life in France at the end of the Second Empire; *La Faute de l'Abbé Mouret*, dealing with the evils of celibacy; *La Conquête de Plassans*, a study of provincial life; *Le Ventre de Paris*, and in 1876 appeared *L'Assommoir*, which is a dramatic picture of life in the working class of Paris and of the evils of drunkenness. The great success of this seventh volume was repeated in some of the later books of the series, notably in *Nana* and *Germinal*. The two final volumes were *La Débâcle* (1892) which is probably the best picture ever written of the Franco-German war, and *Le Docteur Pascal* (1893) which is a gathering together of the threads of the series. Zola next produced his novels of the three cities, *Lourdes, Rome* and *Paris*, the latter appearing in 1898. *Les Quatre Évangiles* next engaged his unflagging energy and he wrote in rapid succession *Fécondité, Travail* and *Verité,* three of the projected four evangels. *Justice,* the fourth, was unfinished when he died.

He was brought into international prominence in a political way when he threw himself passionately into the affair of Captain Alfred Dreyfus, a French artillery officer, who had been convicted and sentenced to life imprisonment for supplying military information to a foreign power. Believing that Dreyfus was innocent and also that he had been convicted by dishonest methods, Zola in 1898 wrote his famous document *J'Accuse,* which involved him with the military authorities. He was tried and adjudged guilty of libel and was himself sentenced to fine and imprisonment but he made his escape to England where he remained for some months until an amnesty was granted to all connected with the Dreyfus case. Upon his return to France, he was acclaimed by many as a great defender of human rights and his efforts finally resulted in a new trial and ultimate acquittal for Dreyfus. He was throwing his quenchless energies into new literary projects when he was accidentally suffocated by charcoal fumes in his home on Sept. 29, 1902. In 1908 his body was taken to the Pantheon in Paris.

ZOROASTER   circa 660 B.C.–583 B.C.

ZOROASTER (zō'rŏ ăs'tēr) or ZARATHUSTRA (zä rå thōōs'trå) was a prophet and a great religious teacher of Iran, or ancient Persia. Much uncertainty has existed as to his place in history and indeed for a considerable time he was regarded as a mythical rather than as an actual character, but scholars now generally agree that he actually lived, and probably about 600 B.C., although some believe that he flourished as much as 400 years earlier still. He was the son of one Pourushaspa and his wife, Dughedha, and is thought to have been born in Azerbaijan, to the west of the Caspian Sea, although much of his religious teaching was evidently carried on in the region farther to the east and south.

About his childhood we have only confused and legendary accounts, including some tales of miraculous happenings which accompanied his birth and early life. From about the age of 15 he seems to have lived mostly in retirement in preparation for the religious activity which was to follow. In his 30th year he is said to have received a revelation following which he emerged from his seclusion and went about opposing the superstitious beliefs which abounded in the religion of the day. During the following ten years he is said to have had seven celestial visions, in which the divine being and the seven archangels appeared to him and he then underwent a period of temptation by the archfiend, from which he emerged triumphant. His first convert, after his great temptation, appears to have been his cousin, Medyomah. The traditions which have clustered about his name indicate that he must have traveled widely through ancient Iran. At about his 42nd year, in obedience to divine command, he journeyed to the eastward and there, after first being cast into prison for a time, he made a convert of King Vishtaspa who ruled over the district to the east and south of the Caspian Sea. The queen, Hutaosa, followed her royal husband's lead in adopting the new religion, which presently gained adherents among the nobles of the court and eventually spread throughout Iran.

The tenets of his creed are preserved to us in the Zend Avesta and in other writings. The central idea was that of a supreme deity, Ormuzd, or Mazda (literally Lord Wisdom), the god of light, truth and goodness, the creator and ruler of the universe; and the bad god Ahriman, the god of the opposing forces of evil, who invaded the world and constantly causes disorder and conflict, but who will ultimately be overthrown and the kingdom of good established. Zoroaster taught the necessity of good thoughts, good words, good deeds, and prescribed careful religious rites for the safeguarding of the purity of body and soul. Agricultural pursuits and the care of useful animals were made a religious duty, and the elements of fire, earth and water were to be carefully protected from any defilement, especially through contact with any dead matter. Hence it was forbidden to either burn or bury the dead, whose bodies were therefore exposed on Dakhmas, or "Towers of Silence," to be consumed by vultures;

a custom which is religiously followed by the small groups of people who still adhere to Zoroastrianism, the Ghebers of Persia and the Parsees of India.

During an invasion of Iran by the Turanians, Zoroaster, then about 77 years of age, was slain, probably at Balkh or Bactria.

ULRICH ZWINGLI   1484–1531

ULRICH, OR HULDREICH, ZWINGLI (tsvĭng' lē) was a reformer and leader in the Reformation in Switzerland who lost his life fighting for the cause. He was born Jan. 1, 1484 at Wildhaus in St. Gall and was the son of a magistrate who gave the boy a good education. He pursued the customary studies leading to the priesthood, at Bern, Vienna and Basel, and was ordained a priest in 1506 at Glarus where he remained for 10 years during which time he taught himself the Greek language. At that time many of the young men of Switzerland were entering foreign military service and in 1512 and again in 1515 Zwingli accompanied them as field chaplain. He thereafter took a stand against this paid foreign service which he felt was detrimental to his countrymen and his opposition also to a suggested alliance with France led to his leaving Glarus and going to Einsiedeln where he first emerged into prominence as a reformer.

The Black Virgin of that town was believed capable of performing miracles of healing and a constant stream of pilgrims made offerings and pleaded for her intercession. Zwingli openly expressed his contempt for this practice which he termed mere superstition; and he was soon aroused to preach against the sale of indulgences which was then a common practice in the Catholic church. In 1518 he became preacher at the Zurich munster and was thus in a position of much greater influence which he used to arouse the people and the priesthood against the many abuses which had grown up in the church. He seems at this time to have had no thought of attacking the church of Rome itself but he urged a simple, commonsense interpretation of the Scriptures without the formalism which prevailed and he advocated many specific reforms, among them the renunciation of the institution of celibacy and the abolition of fasting. He gradually became bolder in his preaching of the Gospel and when a number of Swiss cantons made an alliance with France he was able to persuade the canton of Zurich to keep aloof from it. In 1523 he set forth his beliefs at a public meeting in Zurich in 67 theses. He renounced the supreme authority of the church and later in the year became embroiled in a dispute with the church authorities as to the efficacy of the mass and the use of images in the church. Zurich followed him in his new reforms and the mass and images were discarded.

The following year he was married to a Mrs. Anna Meyer. On Easter Sunday in 1525 he dispensed with the sacrament. He had become the greatest force in Switzerland for the Reformation and his doctrines were receiving widespread acceptance throughout the nation. Although on many points he was in accord with the doctrines which were being promulgated by Martin Luther in Germany, he became involved in a controversy with Luther growing out of Zwingli's views as to the Lord's Supper, which he first advanced publicly in 1524. The matter aroused much heated discussion and for a time split the reform movement into two camps and Protestantism itself seemed in danger of disintegration, especially when the Marburg Conference in 1529 failed to close the breach. Zwingli rejected the theories of the local or corporeal presence of Christ in the host; neither transubstantiation nor consubstantiation were acknowledged by him. The rapid progress that had been made by Protestantism in Switzerland aroused fierce hatreds and opposition from the good Catholics of the Forest Cantons and in 1528 five of the cantons formed an alliance which was joined by Archduke Ferdinand of Austria, and intolerance raged. A Protestant minister was burned at the stake. Zurich was aroused to frenzy and declared war against the Forest Cantons and the Archduke in 1529, and the shedding of blood in a religious war was averted only by the treaty of Kappel. Unrest, suspicion and hatred were not quenched, however, and 8000 men from the Forest Cantons set out for Zurich. They were met at Kappel by 2000 citizens of Zurich who after a fierce struggle were forced by superior numbers to flee, leaving many dead on the field of battle. Among them was Zwingli, who received his death thrust in the fray on Oct. 11, 1531.

This Swiss reformer antedated Luther by a year in preaching the reformed doctrines. He regarded the doctrine of original sin as a moral disease, believed in the salvation of unbaptized infants and held firmly to the doctrine of predestination.

INDEX

A

Abbey, **Edwin Austin, 1**
Abelard, Peter, 2
Abercromby, Gen. James, 479, 480
Aberdeen, Earl of, 252
Abolition and Abolitionists, 13, 71, 98, 259. (See also Slavery)
Abraham, Heights of, 480, 738, 739
Academy in Athens, 25, 538
" of Sciences, 153, 393
Acosta, Bert, 93
Adams, John, 4
" **John Quincy, 6**
" Maude, 589
Addison, Joseph, 7, 649, 650
Adolf, Archbishop, 262
Adrian I, Pope, 113
" IV, Pope, 289
Æschines, 161, 162
Æschylus, 9, 202, 642
Agamemnon of Æschylus, 10
Agassiz, Jean Louis Rodolphe, 10
Aguinaldo, Emilio, (Filipino Insurrectionist), 459
Aix-la-Chapelle, Treaty of, 425
Alaska Boundary, 585
Albert, Prince, 707
Alcott, Louisa M., 12, 281
Alexander V, Pope, 324
" The Great, 13, 26, 162, 552
Alfonso II, 673
Alfred The Great, 15
Allston, Washington, 486
American Academy of Arts and Letters, 92, 574
American Commission for Relief in Belgium, 310
American National Academy of Design, 486
Amherst, Gen. Jeffery, 742
Anaxagoras, 200, 523
Anderson, Hans Christian, 17
Anderson, Gen. Robert, 629
André, Major John, 388

Andrews, Samuel, 577
Andros, Sir Edmund, 453
Annapolis Convention, 268
Annandale, Marquis of, 322
Anne of Austria, 456, 530
" of Cleves, 147, 292
" Queen of England, 447
Annunzio, Gabriele d', 19, 183
Antietam, Battle of, 409, 458
Antigonus, 552
Antiochus, 270
Antony, Mark, 21, 124, 131
Appomattox, 258, 400, 409
Aquinas, Thomas, 22
Archias, 162
Aristarchus, 307
Aristides, 682
Aristophanes, 24, 201, 642
Aristotle, 14, 23, **25,** 278, 301, 538
Armada, Spanish, 177, 194, 531
Armistice, 215, 264, 300, 311
Armstrong Committee, 317
Arnold, Matthew, 27
Arthur, Chester A., 28, 240
" of Brittany, 355
Arundel, Earl of, 278
Aspasia, 523
Astor, John Jacob, 334
Atlantic Monthly, 281, 304, 429
Attic Aristocracy, 641
Audubon, John James, 30
Aurelius, Marcus, 31
Austrian Succession, War of, 479
Aztecs, 145, 146

B

Babington, Anthony, 452
Bacchylides, 9
Bach, Johann Sebastian, 33, 224
Bacon, Francis, 35, 432
" Sir Nicholas, 35
" **Roger, 37**
Balbo, Count Cesare, 107
Balchen, Bernt, 93, 94
Baliol, John of, 76
Balzac, Honoré de, 39, 244

Bancroft, George, 281, 545
Bandinelli, 108
Bank of England, 736
Banks, Sir Joseph, 349
    "   Gen. Nathaniel P., 340
Barbosa, Diego, 438
Bardi, Simone de, 155
"Barebones Parliament," 149
Barère, Bertrand, 432
Barlow, Joel, 233
Barnum, Phineas T., 40
Barometer, 747
Barrett, Elizabeth (See Brownings)
    "   Lawrence, 65, 605
Barrie, James M., 42, 462
Bastille, 427
Bavaria, Duke of, 164
Bayreuth Festivals, 413
Beaconsfield, Earl of (See Disraeli)
Beaton, Cardinal, 378
Beaumont, Francis, 44
Beauvais, Bishop of, 352
Becket, Thomas à, Archbishop of
    Canterbury, 45, 289
Becquerel, Henri, 152, 153
Beecher, Henry Ward, 47, 655, 656,
    662
Beethoven, Ludwig van, 49, 413
Belisarius, 365, 366
Bell, Alexander Graham, 50
    "   John, 277
Benedict XV, Pope, 352
Bennett, Arnold, 52, 178
    "   Floyd, 93
    "   James Gordon, 259, 646
Bentham, Jeremy, 468
    "   Sir Samuel, 468
Benton, Jesse, 338
    "   Thomas H., 338
Berkeley, Lord, 663
Bernard of Clairvaux, St., 155
    "   of Quintavalle, 221
Bernhardt, Sarah, 19, 53, 183, 184, 588
Berthollet, Claude L. (French chem-
    ist), 398
Bessemer, Sir Henry, 103
Bethmann-Hollweg, Theobald von,
    732
Beyle, Henri-Marie, (See Stendahl)
Bianchi, (Italian Political Party), 154
Bible, 147, 262
    "   translated into English, 751
Bigot, François, 479
Bismarck, Otto, Eduard Leopold, 55
Black Death (See Plague)
    "   Virgin, 759
Blaine, James G., 132, 240, 330, 458

Blair, Hugh, 633
Blake, William, 57
Blenheim, Battle of, 447
Blomfield, Sir Arthur, 272
Blood, Circulation of (See Harvey;
    also Servetus)
Blount, Charles, Earl of Devonshire,
    396
Blucher, Gen. Gebhard Leberecht,
    496, 722
Bobadilla, Nicholas, 329
Boccaccio, Giovanni, 58, 119, 529
Boleyn, Anne, 147, 193, 292, 744
Boer War, 263, 385, 416
Boileau, Despreaux, 555
Bolingbroke, Lord Henry St. John,
    711
Bolivar, Simon, 60
Bolsheviks, 400
Bonheur, Rosa, 61
Bon Homme Richard, Battle with
    Serapis, 360
Boniface VIII, Pope, 154, 422
Boone, Daniel, 63
Booth, Edwin, 64, 332, 409, 605
    "   John Wilkes, 65, 409
    "   Junius Brutus, 64
    "   William, 66
Boswell, James, 68, 242, 358
Bothwell, Earl of, 452
Borgia, Cesare, 402, 433
Bo Tree, 82
Boucicault, Dion, 345
Boulton, Matthew, 718
Bourbon, Duc de, 709
Boxer Uprising, 310
Boylston, Dr. Zabdiel, 453
Braddock, Gen. Edward, 715
Brahe, Tycho, 374
Braille System, 371
Bray, Charles, 150
Brever, Dr., 228
Bridgeman, Laura, 371
Bridgewater, Duke of, 233
Brill, Abraham Arden, 229
British Association for the Advance-
    ment of Science, 325, 412
Brodribb, John (See Sir Henry Irv-
    ing)
Brontë, Anne, 69, 70
    "   Charlotte and Emily, 69
Brook Farm, 281
Brown, Ford Madox, 587
    "   John, 70, 399, 686
Browne, Charles Farrar, 72, 129
    (Artemus Ward), 72, 129

Browning, Robert and Elizabeth Barrett, 73, 662
Bruce, Robert, 75
Bryan, William Jennings, 77, 459, 666, 739
Bryant, William Cullen, 79
Brutus, 21, 312, 365
Buccleuch, Duke of, 633
Buchanan, James, 80, 175, 227, 532, 755
Buckingham, Duke of, 115, 180, 396
Buddha, 82
Budget Bureau, 271
Buena Vista, 158
Bulgarians, 114
Bull Run, Battles of, 340, 341, 399, 409
Bulwer-Lytton, Sir Edward George Earle, 83
Bunyan, John, 85, 432
Burke, Edmund, 87, 280, 535, 564, 633
"   Thomas Henry, 512
Burleigh, William Cecil, Lord, 35
Burne-Jones, Sir Edward, 90, 485, 587
Burnett, David G., 314
Burns, Robert, 88, 101
Burr, Aaron, 268, 347, 675
Burroughs, John, 91
Burton, William E., 543
Byrd, Rear Admiral Richard E., 92
Byron, Lord George Gordon, 94, 370, 482, 651

C

Cabot, John, (Giovanni Caboto), 96
Caesar, Augustus, 21
"   Julius (See Julius Caesar)
Caesarion, 130, 364
Cailleaux, Joseph, 128
Calhoun, John C., 97, 158, 314, 339, 720
Caligula, 616
Calles, Plutarco E., (President of Mexico), 411
Calvin, John, 99, 378, 618, 619, 751
Canterbury, Archbishop of, 45, 146, 395
Canterbury Tales, 119
Carloman, (brother of Charlemagne), 113
Carlyle, Thomas, 100, 135, 195, 662
Carnegie, Andrew, 102
Carrier-Belleuse, 578
Carroll Lewis (See Charles Lutwidge Dodgson)
Carteret, John, 533

Caruso, Enrico, 104
Casimir IV, King of Poland, 335
Cass, Lewis, 532
Cassander, 552
Cassius, 21, 365
Castiglione, 558
Cataline's Conspiracy, 364
Catherine of Aragon, 193, 291, 744
"   The Great, 105, 360
Cathloic League, 261, 290
Cato, 364
Court of Claims, 532
Cavendish, Henry, (English chemist), 398
Cavour, Count Camillo Benso di, 107, 458
Cellini, Benvenuto, 108
Cervantes Saavedra, Miguel de, 110, 551
Chæronea, Battle of, 161
Chang Tso-ling, 660
Chana, 82
Chaplin, Charles Spencer, 112
Charcot, Jean Martin, 228
Charlemagne, 113
Charles I of England, 115, 148, 149, 150, 278, 396, 470, 471, 572, 699
Charles II of England, 86, 179, 180, 424, 471, 522, 659
Charles VII of France, 351, 352
"   VIII of France, 606
"   II of Spain, 425
"   V of Spain, 292, 293, 537
"   of Naples, 154
"   Albert of Sardinia, 457
Chase, Salmon P., 282
Chattanooga, Battle of, 258
Chatterton, Thomas, 117, 370
Chaucer, Geoffrey, 47, 119, 486
Chekhov, Anton, 120
Chemistry, Founding of, 397
Chesterfield, Lord Philip D.S., 711
Chinese Immigration, 29
"   Exclusion Act, 133
"   Republic, 659, 660
Chopin, Frédéric François, 121, 413
Christian IV of Denmark, 714
Christian Science, 185
Christians, Persecution of, 498, 541
Christina, Queen of Sweden, 165
Chronometer of Harrison, 500
Chryselephantine Technique in Greek Art, 529
Church of the New Jerusalem, 662
Churchill, Charles, (English poet), 303
Cibber, Colley, (English Actor), 243

Cicero, Marcus Tullius, 21, 123, 197, 201, 322
Cimon, 523
Circulation of Blood, (See Harvey; also Servetus)
Civil War, 165, 204, 210, 227, 239, 260, 283, 305, 409, 458
Clare, Richard de, Earl of Pembroke, 289
Clark, William, 347, 406, (See Meriweather Lewis)
Claudius I, 616
Clay, Henry, 125, 339, 545, 720
Clayton Anti-Trust Act, 739
Clémenceau, Georges, 127, 417
Clemens, Samuel Langhorne (Mark Twain) 73, 128
Clement IV, Pope, 38
" VII, Pope, 108, 461, 744
Cleomenes, 552
Cleon, 24
Cleopatra, 22, 130, 364
Cleveland, Grover, 132, 275
Cline, Henry, 350
Clinton, George, 5
Clive, Lord Robert, 279
Cobbett, William, 510
Cohan, George M., 507
Coleridge, Samuel Taylor, 134, 195, 284, 389, 662, 745, 746
Colet, Louise, 213
Columbus, Christopher, 96, 136, 205, 206, 706
Comédie Humaine (See Balzac)
Comeyn, John, 76
Commodus, 32
Communist International, 400, 401, 450, 494
Comte, Auguste, 602
Condé, Louis, (French General), 456
Confucius, 138
Constitutional Convention in N. Y., 585, 586
Constitutional Convention of Penn., 223
Conti, 456
Continental Congress, 268, 294, 343, 346
Coogan, Jackie, 113
Cook, Capt. James, 349
Coolidge, Calvin, 139, 311, 318
Cooper, James Fenimore, 141
Copernican Theory, 143, 164, 236
Copernicus, Nicholas, 143
Corday, Charlotte, 442
Cordova, Gonsalvo de, 205
Corn Laws, 252

Cornwallis, Gen. Charles, 716
Corot, Jean Baptiste Camille, 244
Cortes, Hernando, 144
Council of Constance, 751
Court of International Justice, 318
Courtenay, Archbishop, 751
Cousin, Victor, 668
Convent Garden Theatre, 243
Cox, James M., 271
Cranbrook, Earl of, 171
Cranmer, Thomas, Archbishop of Canterbury, 146, 378, 744
Crannon, Battle of, 162
Crassus, 123, 364, 545
Crimean War, 107, 170, 503
Cromwell, Oliver, 85, 101, 116, 148, 218, 396, 456
Cromwell, Thomas, 292
Crook, Gen. George, 458
Cross, Mary Ann Evans (George Eliot), 150, 272
Cross, John Walter, 151
Crusades, The, 567, 603
Cuba, 459, 532, 585, 666
Curie, Pierre and Marie, 152
Cyremaics, 539
Cyrus, The Elder, 752, 753
" The Younger, 752, 753
Czolgosz, Leon, 459

D

Danes, 16
Danites (See Mormons)
Dante, Alighieri, 119, 154, 527
Danton, George Jacques, 576
Darnley, Lord (Henry Stewart), 379 452
Darius, The Persian, 14, 753
Darwin, Charles Robert, 155, 326, 643, 644
Daudet, Alphonse, 213, 756
Daugherty, Harry M., 271
Davis, Jefferson, 157, 260, 409, 532
" John, 7
" Samuel, 294
Davy, Sir Humphrey, 202, 652
Dawes, Charles G., 271
Deane, Silas, 5, 387
Decimal System, 397
Declaration of Independence, 223, 343, 346
Defoe, Daniel, 159
De Kalb, Gen. Johann Baron, 387
de Medici (See Medici)
Demetrius, 552
Democritus, 301

Demosthenes, 161, 538
De Quincey, Thomas, 162
Derby, Lord Edward George V. S., 169, 707
Descartes, René, 164, 374
Desiderius, King of the Lombards, 113
De Soto, Hernando, 395
Dewey, Admiral George, 165
Dickens, Charles, 18, 166, 637
Dickinson, Charles, 338
Diderot, Denis, 591
Dingley Tariff Bill, 459
Diodorus, 10
Diogenes Laertius, 197
Disraeli, Benjamin, Lord Beaconsfield, 168, 252, 253, 404, 707, 708
Divine Comedy (See Dante; also Blake; also Dore; also Longfellow)
Dodgson, Charles Lutwidge (Lewis Carroll), 170, 250
Domitian, Roman Emperor, 367
Donatello, 171
Doré, Gustave, 173
Dostoyevsky, Fiodor Mikhailovitch, 693
Douglas, Stephen A., 174, 408, 532
Drake, Sir Francis, 176, 632
Dred Scott Case, 206
Dreiser, Theodore, 178
Drexel, Morgan & Co., 484
Dreyfus, Capt. Alfred, 127, 220, 757
"   Case, 127, 220, 757
Dritzehn, Andreas, 262
Drury Lane Theatre, 242, 627, 630
Dryden, John, 7, 179, 367, 615
Dudley, Joseph, (Governor of Massachusetts), 453
Dumas, Alexandre, 174, 181
Dunmore, Lord John Murray, Governor of Virginia, 294
Duse, Eleanora, 19, 183

E

Eaton, Mrs. John H. (See Peggy O'Neill)
Ebert, Friedrich (First President of Germany), 300
Eddy, Mary Baker G., 184
Edison, Thomas Alva, 186
Edward I of England, 75
"   II of England, 76
"   III of England, 76, 188
"   V of England, 569
"   VI of England, 147, 292, 378
"   VII of England, 67, 707

Edward, the Black Prince, 189, 231
"   the Confessor, 734
Edwards, Jonathan, 190
Egbert, King of England, 15
Einstein, Albert, 191
Eleanor of Aquitaine, 288, 289, 354
"Elia" (See Charles Lamb)
Eliot, George (See Mary Ann Evans Cross)
Elizabeth of Valois, 530
"   Queen of England, 35, 36, 147, 176, 193, 292 452, 530, 557
Ellis, Havelock, 449
Emancipation Proclamation, 409
Emerson, Ralph Waldo, 12, 91, 101, 195, 281, 428, 470, 477, 686
Ent, Dr. George, 278
Epicurus, 197
Erasistratus, 278
Erasmus, Desiderius, 198
Ericsson, Jacob, 261
Essex, Earl of (Robert Devereux), 35, 36, 194, 557
Ethelred, King of England, 16
Ethelwolf, 15
Euclid, 538
Eugenie, Empress of France, 62
Euripides, 200
Everett, Edward, 210
Evolution, 78, 155, 325, 643
Ewing, Thomas, 277

F

Fabian Society, 623
Fabius, the Delayer, 269
Fabricius, 278
Fairbanks, Douglas, 112
Fairfax, Gen. Thomas, 116, 149
Falero, Ruy, 438
Fall, Albert B., 271
Faraday, Michael, 202
Farmers—General, 398
Farragut, David, 165, 203, 599
Fascist Movement, 493
Faustina, 32
Federal Convention, 268
"   Power Commission, 311
"   Radio Commission, 311
"   Reserve Act, 739
"   Trade Commission, 739
"Federalist," The, 435
Feng Yü-hsiang, 660
Ferdinand V of Spain, 137, 205, 292, 460, 551
Ferenczi, 229
Ferrara, Duke of, 673

Field, Eugene, 206, 574
Fielding, Henry, 208, 571
Fillmore, Millard, 209
Finley, John, 63
Fisheries Dispute, 586
Fiske, John, 136
" Harrison Gray, 211
" Minnie Maddern, 184, 211, 272, 440
Flaminus, 269
Flamsteed, John, 500
Flaubert, Gustave, 213, 454, 692
Fletcher, John, 44
Fleury, Cardinal, 425
Florence, Republic of, 460
Foch, Ferdinand, 214, 264, 300, 525
Ford, Edsel B., 217
" Henry, 216
Ford's Theatre, 409
Fourcroy, Antoine, (French chemist), 398
Fox, Charles James, 280
" George, 217
France, Anatole, 219
Francis I, King of France, 109, 292, 403
" II King of Naples, 241
" of Assisi, 220
Franciscan Order, 38, 221, 222, 414, 553
Franco-Prussian War, 213, 242, 299, 353, 475
Franklin, Benjamin, 222, 232, 343, 346, 360, 509
Frederick III, Elector of Saxony, 430
Frederick, the Great, 34, 105, 224, 369, 432, 444, 592, 711
Free Silver, 77
Frémont, John C., 226
French Academy, 318, 354, 598, 668, 711, 749
French Institute, 551
" , Sir John, 263
" and Indian War, 225
" Revolution, 90, 388, 398, 441, 446
Freud, Sigmund, 228
Frick Committee, 274
Froebel, Friedrich Wilhelm August, 229,
Froebel, Karl, 230
Froissart, Jean, 231
Fronde (French Political organization), 456
Fugitive Slave Law. See Slavery.
Fuller, Sarah, 372

Fulton, Robert, 232
Fulvia, 22
Fust, Johann, 262

G

Gabrilowitsch, Ossip, 130
Gainsborough, Thomas, 234, 564
Galen, 278
Galileo, 164, 235, 374, 470
Galliéni, Gen. Joseph S., 353
Gama, Dom Vasco da, 237
Garfield, James A., 239, 275, 458
Garibaldi, Giuseppe, 181, 240, 457
Garrick, David, 242, 303, 358, 564, 630
Garrison, William Lloyd, 98, 730
Gaskell, Elizabeth, 70
Gates, Gen. Horatio, 381
Gaul (Now France), 21, 113, 364
Gaunt, John of, 119
Gautama Siddhattha (See Buddha)
Gautier, Théophile, 244
Geoffrey, Archbishop of York, 290
" of Nantes, 289
Geological Society, 325
George I of England, 448
" II of England, 533
" III of England, 303, 534
" , Prince of Denmark, 501, 649
George, Henry, 245, 622
Gettysburg, Battle of, 399, 409
Gibbon, Edward, 247, 633
Gilbert, Sir Humphrey, 556
" Sir William S., 249, 440
Girondists (French Political Party), 441, 442, 576
Gladstone, William Ewart, 169, 251, 331, 512, 590, 707
Globe Theatre, London, 621
Godolphin, Lord Sidney, 160
Goethals, Gen. George W., 666
Goethe, Johann Wolfgang von, 253, 320, 608, 612
Golden Horde, 336
Goldsmith, Oliver, 1, 242, 255, 564
Goncourt, Edmund de, 756
Konzago, Vincenzo, 592
"Good Gray Poet," 729
Gordon, Gen. Charles G., 252
Görgei, Arthur, 383
Grand Army of the Republic, 133
Grant, Ulysses S., 129, 204, 257, 260, 399, 409, 626
Gratian, Roman Emperor, 684
Gray, Lady Jane, 147
" Thomas, 118, 743
Great Northern System, 298

Greeley, Horace, 158, 258, **259**
Greene, Gen. Nathaniel, 267, 509
" Robert, 620
Gregory IX, Pope, 222
" XV, Pope, 330
Griffith, D. W., 112
Grimani, Cardinal, 199
Groot, Gerhard, 373
Grotius, Hugo (Dutch Scholar), 470
Guam, Island of, 459
Guelph (Italian Political Party), 154
Guettard, J. E., 397
Guggenheim, Daniel, Fund for the Promotion of Aeronautics, 410
Guiteau, Charles Jules, 240
Gustavus Adolphus, 260, 572, 714
Gutenberg, Johann, 261
Guthrun, the Dane, 16
Guy of Blois, 231
" of Brionne, 734

H

Hadrian, Roman Emperor, 31
Hague Conference, 276
" Court of Arbitration, 318, 586
Haig, Sir Douglas, 263
Hale, Nathan, 264
Halley, Edmund (Halley's Comet), 500
Hals, Frans, 266
Hamilton, Alexander, 267, 344, 347, 435
Hampden, Walter, 440, 589
Hancock, Gen. Winfield Scott, 240
Handel, George Frederick, 35
Hannibal, 269
Harding, Warren G., 140, **270,** 311, 318
Hardy, Gathorne, 171
" Thomas, 272
Harold, Last of Saxon Kings, 733, 734
Harpalus, 162
Harper's Ferry, 71, 340, 341, 399
Harriman, Edward H., 273, 298, 299, 484
Harrison, Benjamin, 133, **275,** 459
" John, 500
" William Henry, 259, 275, 276, 695
Harte, Bret, 129
Harvey, William, 277, 618
Hastings, Warren, 88, **279,** 432, 628
Hawaii, 133, 459
Hawkins, Sir John, 176
Hawthorne, Julian, 282

Hawthorne, Nathaniel, 12, 195, **280,** 428, 462, 531
Hay, John, 605
Haydon, Benjamin Robert, 370
Hayes, Rutherford B., 282, 429, 458
Hays, Will H., 271
Hazlitt, William, 163, **284,** 389
Hearn, Lafcadio, 285
Hearst, William Randolph, 317
Hegias (Athenian Sculptor), 528
Hegira, 472
Heights of Abraham, 480, 738, 739
Heilmann, Andreas, 262
" Anton, 262
Heine, Heinrich, 286
Heloise, 2
Hennell, Charles, 150
Hennepin, Father, 394
Henry II of England, 288, 354
" III of England, 421
" IV of England, 119
" VII of England, 96, 199, 291
" **VIII of England,** 47, 146, 199, 206, 222, **291,** 430, 744
Henry I of France, 734
" II of France, 451, 530
" III of France, 478
" **IV of France,** 290
Henry, O. (See **William Sydney Porter)**
Henry, Patrick, 293, 435, 476
Henslow, John S., 156
Herbert, Sidney, 503
Herculaneum and Pompeii, 540
Hermeias, 26
Herod Agrippa II, 363
Herodotus, 295, 306
Herophilus, 278
Herrick, Robert, 1, **296,** 486
Hieron, 9
Hildegarde (Wife of Charlemagne), 113
Hill, James J., 298, 484
Hindenberg Line, 215, 264, 300
Hindenberg, Paul von, 299, 733
Hippocrates, 300
Hippocratic Oath, 302
Hogarth, William, 302
Hogg, Thomas Jefferson, 624
Hohenzollern, House of, 732
Holmes, Dr. Oliver Wendell, 303
" **Justice Oliver Wendell, 305**
Holy Brotherhood, 205
" Grail, 2
" League, 205
Home Rule Bill, 252
Homer, 306, 529
Homery, Dr. Conrad, 262

Hood, Thomas, 84, 308
Hooker, Gen. Joseph, 341
Hoover, Herbert C., 271, 310, 318
Horace, 312, 704, 705
Houston, Sam, 313
Howard, Catherine, 293
"   Lord, 177
Howe, Gen. Richard, 265, 716
"   Dr. Samuel G., 371
Howells, William Dean, 211
Hudson, Henry, 315
Hughes, Charles Evans, 271, 316
Hugo, Victor, 213, 318, 579, 597
Huguenots, 572
Humboldt, Friedrich Heinrich Alexander, 11, 320
Hume, David, 321, 592, 604, 633
Hundred Years' War, 189
Huns, 114
Hunt, Holman, 587
"   Leigh, 370, 389, 624
Huss, John, 323, 430, 751
Hussite War, 324
Hutchinson, Anne, 741
Huxley, Thomas Henry, 325, 643, 644, 723
Hypatius, 365

I

Ibsen, Henrik, 183, 326
Ignatius of Loyola, St., 329
Iliad, 59, 80, 306, 307
Incas of Peru, 536, 537
Income Tax, 133, 141, 739
Ingersoll, Robert G., 330
Innocent III, Pope, 221, 355
"   VIII, Pope, 460
International Society of Sculptors, Painters and Engravers, 579
Inquisition, 531
Interstate Commerce Commission, 133
Irish Free States, 417
"   Land Question, etc., 246, 252, 535, 707, 708
Irving, Sir Henry, 332, 631, 679
"   Washington, 142, 333
Isabella, Queen of Spain, (See Ferdinand V), 137, 205, 292, 460, 551
Isocrates, 26
Ivan III of Russia, 335
"   IV of Russia, 336

J

Jackson, Andrew, 80, 98, 126, 313, 338, 695

Jackson, Sir Herbert, 581
"   , Thomas Jonathan, ("Stonewall" Jackson), 340
Jacobins, 510, 576
James I of England, 36, 115, 557, 699
"   II of England, 159, 447, 500, 520, 521, 735
James V of Scotland, 293, 451
"   VI of Scotland, 452
"   Henry, 282, 341
Janin, Louis, 310
Japan, 383, 532
Jay, John, 267, 343, 435
Jefferson, Joseph, 334, 344, 605
"   Thomas, 5, 6, 268, 346, 406, 435, 476
Jenghiz Khan, 348, 546
Jenner, Edward, 349
Jesuits, 56, 329, 330, 394, 673
Jewett, Sarah Orne, 656
Joan of Arc, 351
João, King of Portugal, 237, 238
Joffre, Joseph Jacques Césaire, 215, 263, 353
John, King of England, 289, 354
"   King of France, 189
"   II, King of Cyprus, 262
"   XXIII, Pope, 172
Johns Hopkins University, 326
Johnson, Andrew, 240, 356
"   Samuel, 9, 68, 242, 256, 357, 367, 432, 564, 631
Johnston, Gen. Joseph E., 340, 399
Joliet, Louis, 395
Jones, Ernest, 229
"   John Paul, 359
Jonson, Ben, 44, 360, 448, 619
Josephus, Flavius, 362
Julius II, Pope, 467, 558
Julius Caesar, 21, 124, 130, 312, 363, 548
Jung, Carl, 229
Justinian I, 365
Juvenal, Decimus Junius, 366

K

Kant, Immanuel, 368
Kaunitz, Wenzel Anton Dominik, Prince, 465
Kean, Edmund, 630
Kearney, Patrick, 178
Kearny, Gen. Stephen W., 227
Keats, John, 90, 369, 486, 746
Keene, Laura, 345
Keimer, Samuel, 223
Keith, William, Governor of Penn., 223

Keller, Helen, 51, 371
Kellogg-Briand Treaty, 311
Kelmscott Press, 486
Kempis, Thomas à, 372
Kepler, Johann, 373
Kerensky, Alexander F., 401
Khartoum, 252, 377
Kindergarten, 230
King's College, 267
Kipling, Rudyard, 375
Kitchener, Gen. Horatio Herbert, 263, 376, 417
"Know-Nothings," 210
Knox, John, 378, 751
Koch, Robert, 379
Königgratz, Battle of, 475
Koran, 472
Kosciuszko, Tadeusz, 381
Kossuth, Louis, 382
Kruger, Paul, 384
Kublai Khan, 385, 546

L

Ladysmith, 263
Lafayette, Marquis de, 387
Lamb, Charles, 163, 285, 308, 388
"   Mary, 389
Landseer, Sir Edwin Henry, 390
Langethal (educator), 229
Laynez, Diego, 329
Lanier, Sidney, 391
LaPlace, Pierre Simon, Marquis de, 393
La Salle, René Robert Cavelier, Sieur de, 394
Latini, Bruno, 154
Laud, William, Archbishop of Canterbury, 395
Laurens, John, 509
Lavoisier, Antoine Laurent, 397
Law, Bonar, 417
"   John, 425
League of Cambrai, 206
"   of Nations, 271, 318, 586, 739, 740
Lee, Gen. Charles, 716
"   Francis Lightfoot, 398
"   Richard Henry, 398
"   Gen. Robert E., 258, 340, 341, 398
Leeds Festival, 250
Lefevre, Pierre, 329
Legion of Honor, 62, 91, 94, 174, 215
Leibnitz, Gottfried Wilheim, 501
Leicester, Robert Dudley, Earl of, 194, 631
Leinster, Earl of, 289
Lenard, Philip, 581

Lenin, Nikolai, 400
Leo I, Pope, 467
"   III, Pope, 114
"   X, Pope, 199, 430, 460, 461, 558, 559, 744
Leo XIII, Pope, 666
Leonardo da Vinci, 402
Leonidas, 14
Lepidus, 21
Lesseps, Ferdinand de, 403
Lessing, Gotthold Ephraim, 405
Lewes, George Henry, 151, 643
Lewis, Meriweather, 347, 406
"   and Clark Centennial Exposition, 407
Liberator, The (See Simon Bolivar)
"Libertines," 99
Limitation of Armaments, Conference on, 271
Lincoln, Abraham, 65, 81, 158, 175, 227, 239, 259, 260, 356, 399, 408
Lind, Jenny, 41
Lindbergh, Charles A. 410
Lipton, Sir Thomas, 484
Lister, Joseph, 411
Liszt, Franz, 413, 712
Litchfield, Egbert, S., 298
Livingston, Robert R., 476
Livingstone, David, 414, 648
Lloyd-George, David, 416
Locke, John, 418
Logan (Indian Chief), 64
Lombards, 113
London, Founding of, 16
Long Parliament, 149, 297, 396
Longfellow, Henry Wadsworth, 419
Longsword, William, Earl of Salisbury, 290
Longueville, 456
Lorenzo the Magnificent, (See Medici)
Louis VIII of France, 420
"   IX of France, 420
"   XI of France, 422, 709
"   XII of France, 206, 403
"   XIII of France, 291, 456, 473, 572
Louis XIV of France, 395, 423, 456, 555, 736
Louis XV of France, 425
"   XVI of France, 360, 388, 426, 576
Louis, St., 420
Louisiana Lottery, 275
"   Purchase, 210, 347, 406, 476
Lowell, James Russell, 304, 428, 621
Loyola, St. Ignatius of, 329
Lucretius, 198

Lucy, Sir Thomas, 620
Ludendorff, Gen. Ehrich von, 299
Ludolphus of Saxony, 329
Ludwig of Bavaria, 713
Luther, Martin, 429, 751, 760
Lyautey, Gen. Louis H. G., 354
Lyceum, Origin of, 26
    "   Theatre, London, 332, 333
Lycurgus, 538
Lygdamis, 295
Lysimachus, 14, 552
Lyttelton, Lord, 209

M

Macaulay, Thomas Babington, 85, 180, 280, 431, 483
Machiavelli, Niccolò del, 432, 433
MacMillan Expedition, 93
Macy, Mrs. John (See Anne Sullivan)
Madison, "Dolly", 436
    "   James, 6, 268, 347, 434, 476
Maecenas, 312, 704
Maeterlinck, Maurice, 436
Magellan, Ferdinand, 176, 437
Magna Charta, 355
Magnifying Glass, invention of, 37, 38
Maillezais, Bishop, 553
Maintenon, Madame de, 424
Majuba Hill, 252
Mallet, David, Scottish Poet, 248
Malpighi, Marcello, 278
Manila Bay, Battle of, 165, 166
Mansfield, Richard, 439, 588, 623
Marat, Jean Paul, 441
Marconi, Guglielmo, 442
Marcus Aurelius, 31
Maria Theresa, of Austria, 225, 425, 444, 533
Maria Theresa, of Spain, 456
Marie Antoinette, 445, 445, 646
    "   Louise, 466
Marlborough, John Churchill, Duke of, 447
Marlowe, Christopher, 448
Marne, Battles of, 215, 216, 263, 353
Marquette, Father, 395
Martel, Charles, 113
    "   Geoffrey, Count of Anjou, 734
Martial (Roman Poet), 367
Marvel, Ik (See Donald G. Mitchell)
Marx, Karl, 400, 449, 623
Mary (Wife of William of Orange), 735
Mary Queen of England, 147, 176, 193, 293, 378, 530

Mary Queen of Scots, 194, 379, 451
Masefield, John, 462
Massacre of St. Bartholomew, 290
Mather, Cotton, 453
Maupassant, Guy de, 214, 454, 692
Maximilian (Emperor of Mexico), 626
Maximilian I, (Emperor of Germany), 292
Maximus, 684
Max of Baden, Prince, 733
Maxwell, James, 202
Mazarin Bible, 262
    "   Cardinal Jules, 262, 423, 424, 455
Mazzini, Giuseppe, 241, 457
McCarthy, Justin, 513
McClellan, Gen. George B., 340, 399, 409
McKinley Tariff Bill, 275, 458
    "   William, 77, 78, 458, 583, 584, 585, 666
Meade, Gen. George G., 409
Medici (family), 606, 607
    "   Catherine de', 451, 461
    "   Cosimo de', 109, 172, 460
    "   Giovanni de', 460
    "   Giuliano de', 460
    "   John de', 199
    "   Lorenzo de', 460, 466, 468, 606
    "   Marie de', 291
Mellon, Andrew, 271
Melville, Herman, 461
Mendelssohn, Moses, 462
Mendelssohn-Bartholdy, 462
Mensheviks, 400
Meredith, George, 272, 464, 665
    "   Hugh, 223
Metrodorus, 307
Metropolitan Museum of Art, N. Y. 484, 580
Metropolitan Opera Company, 104
Metternich, Prince, 465
Mexican War, 158, 174, 204, 399
Michelangelo, 109, 173, 259, 402, 460, 466, 558
Michelozzo, 172
Michelson, Albert, 192
Microscope, 236
Mill, James, 468
    "   , John Stuart, 127, 468, 644
Millerand, Alexandre, 353
Milner, Lord Alfred, 264
Miltiades, 682
Milton, John, 431, 469
Miranda, Francisco, 60
"Missouri Compromise," 126, 158, 175, 210, 314, 408, 476, 532, 695

Mitchell, Donald G., 656
" Dr. Samuel, 333
Mohammed, 471
Molière, (Jean-Baptiste Poquelin), 473, 555
Moltke, Helmuth Carl Bernhard von, 474
"Mona Lisa," 402
Monmouth, Duke of, 159, 418, 447
Monroe, James, 6, 97, 475
" Doctrine, 475, 476
Mons, Battle of, 263
Montaigne, Michel Eyquem de, 477
Montcalm, Louis Joseph, Marquis de, 479, 743
Monterey, 158
Montessori, Maria, 480
Montezuma, 145
Montojo, Admiral, 165
Montpensier, Duc de, 181
Moore, Thomas, 334, 370, 482, 628
Moors and Arabs in Spain, 114
More, Sir Thomas, 199, 292
Morgan, John Pierpont, 235, 274, 299, 483
Morillo, 61
Mormons, 133, 635, 636, 755, 756
Morris, Gouverneur, 346
" William, 90, 485, 587
Morrow, Dwight W., 411
Morse, Samuel F. B., 486
Morveau, Guyton de (French chemist), 398
Mount St. Agnes, 373
Mozart, Wolfgang Amadeus, 488
Murat, Joachim, 490
Murillo, Bartolomé Esteban, 491
Museum of Natural History, N. Y. 484, 518
Mussolini, Benito, 493
Mylius, Christlob, (German Journalist), 405

N

Nantes, Edict of, 291, 424
Napoleon III, 62, 107, 319, 457
Napoleon Bonaparte, 393, 466, 494, 615, 646, 669, 722
Narses, 365
Naseby, Battle of, 116, 149
National Institute of Arts and Letters, 574, 673
National Recovery Act (N.R.A.) 582, 583
National Society of Fine Arts (France), 579
Necker, M., 248, 427, 441, 633, 646

Nelson, Horatio, Lord, 496
Neri (Italian political party), 154
Nero, 366, 498, 539, 616, 617
Neuber, Caroline (German Actress), 405
Neuve Chapelle, 263
Newton, Sir Isaac, 192, 499, 664
Nicholas II, Pope, 734
" V, Pope, 262
Nicollet, John Nicholas, 226
Nietzsche, Friedrich Wilhelm, 501
Nightingale, Florence, 502
Nivelle, Gen. Robert G., 263, 354
Nobel Prize, 153, 192, 376, 381, 443, 584, 586, 740
Normand Jacques, 455
Norris, Frank, 178
North, Frederick, Lord, 87, 88
North Pole, 93, 518, 519
Northcote, James, 285
Northern Securities Co., 484
Noureddin, 603
Noville, George O., 93

O

O'Connell, Daniel, 504
O'Connor, William Douglass, 729
Octavia, 22, 131
Octavian, 21, 22, 124, 131, 312
Odyssey, 59, 80, 306, 307, 485
Olympias, 14
O'Neill, Eugene, 505
" Peggy, 696
Oregon Trail, 226
Orleans, Duc d', 181, 710
Orteig, Raymond, 410
Osbourne, Lloyd, 654
Ostend Manifesto, 532
Oudinot, Gen. Nicolas Charles Victor, 241
Owen, Ruth Bryan, 78
Oxenstierna, Axel, 261
Oxford University, Beginning of, 37, 45, 46; 745

P

Paderewski, Ignace Jan, 507
Paganini, Niccolo, Italian Violinist, 413
Paine, Thomas, 509
Palmer, John M., 77
Palmerston, Henry John Temple, Lord, 252
Panama, 133, 176, 403, 404, 584
" Canal, 666, 667, 739
Pan-American, Congress, 275, 318

Pan-American Exposition, 459, 586
Paoli, 68
Parkman, Francis, 510
Parker, Alton B., 78, 584
"   Sir Hyde, 497
Parnell, Charles Stewart, 512
Parr, Catherine, 293
Pasteur, Louis, 412, 513
Pazzi (Italian family), 460
Pater, Walter, 515
Patrick, St., 516
Paul III, Pope, 329
"   V, Pope, 330
Paulding, J. K., 333
Paulmier, Pierre, 618
Paulus, Lucius Æmilius, 269
Peace, Foundation for the Promo-
    tion of Industrial, 584
"Peace Ship", 217
Peary, Robert Edwin, 517
Peel, Sir Robert, 309
Peisistratos, 641
Penn, William, 519
Pepin the Short, 113
Pepys, Samuel, 521
Perdiccas, 552
Pericles, 522, 642
Perkins Institution for the Blind, 51,
    371
Permanent Court of Arbitration, 318,
    586
Perry, Commodore, 532
Pershing, Gen. John J., 524, 739
Perugia, Vincent, 403
Perugino, 558
Pestalozzi, Johann Heinrich, 229, 230
Pétain, Gen. Henri Philippe, 215, 263
Peter the Great, 525
"   of Catala, 221
Petition of Rights, 115
Petrarch, Francesco, 59, 119, **527**
Phidias, 523, **528**
Philip II of France, 289, 354, 355
"   VI, of France, 189
"   II of Spain, 177, 194, 290, **530**
"   III of Spain, 593
"   IV of Spain, 424, 593, 701
"   V of Spain, 425
Philip of Macedon, 13, 161
Philippa (wife of Edward III of
    England, 231, 232
Philippines, 166, 167, 437, 458, 666
Phillips, Dr. Wendell, 98
Phipps, Sir William, 453
Phoebus, Gaston, 231
Phoenix Park Murders, 252
Picard, Jean, 500

Pickering, Sir Gilbert, 179
Pickford, Mary, 112
Pierce, Franklin, 80, 158, 281, **531**
Pilgrim's Progress, 85, 86
Pinckney, Thomas, 5
Pindar, 9
Piso, Conspiracy of, 617
Pitt, William, Earl of Chatham, 432
    533
"   **William, 534**
Pizarro, Francisco, 536
Plague, 189, 422, 449, 607
Plancus, 21
Plato, 24, 25, 26, 301, **537,** 639
Players, The (Club), 65
Pliny The Elder, 539
"   The Younger, 539
Plutarch, 9, **541**
Pocahontas, 635
Poe, Edgar Allen, 428, **542,** 573
Poincaré, Raymond, 216
Polenta, Guido Novello da, 155
Polk, James Knox, 80, 126, 174, 227,
    544, 695
Pollio, 21
Polo, Marco, 386, **546**
Pompadour, Jeanne Antoinette Pois-
    son, Marquise de, 711
Pompeii and Herculaneum, 540
Pompey the Great, 364, **547**
Pomponius, 539
Pond, Captain Charles, 265
Pope, Gen. John, 283, 399
Porter, Capt. David, 203, 204
"   **William Sydney, (O. Henry)**
    549
Porto Rico, 458
Potomac, Army of, 258
Pre-Raphaelites, 90, 587, 596
Prescott, William Hickling, 550
Prester, John, 237
Priestly, Joseph, English physicist,
    398
Prodicus, 200
Prohibition, 583
"Protector, The" (See **Oliver Crom-
    well)**
Proust, Antonin, 579
Proxenus, 25
Prusias, King of Bithynia, 270
Psychoanalysis, 228, 229
Ptolemy I, 552
"   Auletes, 130
"   Dionysus, 130
Punic Wars, 269, 362
Puritans and Puritanism, 115, 148,
    396

Putnam, Gen. Israel, 716
Pythagoras, 144

Q

Quadruple Alliance, 466
Quakers, 217, 218, 219, 519, 520, 658
Quiller-Couch, A. T., 654
Quin, James, English Actor, 243
Quintilian, 367
Quixote, Don, 110, 637

R

Rabelais, François, 173, 553
"Race Suicide," 585
Rachel, French Actress, 630
Racine, Jean, 244, 473, 555
Radewyn, Florentius, 373
Radium, 152
"   Institute, 152, 153
Railway Strike, 133
Raleigh, Sir Walter, 449, 556
Randolph, John, 126
Raphael Santi, 558
Ravaillac, 291
Reade, Charles, 559, 679
Reconstruction Finance Corporation,
    311
"Red Week" Outbreak, 493
Reed, Thomas B., 458
Reformation, 99, 100, 378
Reign of Terror, 398, 576
Rembrandt Harmens van Rijn, 266,
    561
Renan, Ernest, 562
Restoration, 86, 179
Revolutionary War, (See War of In-
    dependence)
Reynolds, Sir Joshua, 564, 630, 633
Rhodes, Cecil John, 565
Richard I of England (Coeur de
    Lion), 289, 354, 355, 567, 603
Richard II of England, 232
"   III of England, 568
Richardson, Samuel, 208, 570
Richelieu, Armand Jean du Plessis,
    Duc de (Cardinal), 456, 571
Riley, James Whitcomb, 573
Rimski-Korsakov, Nicolas Andreie-
    vich, 574
Rizzio, David, 452
Robert of Naples, 58, 528
"   II of Normandy, 734
Roberts, Lord Frederick S., 263, 377
Robespierre, Maximilien de, 575
Rockefeller, John D., 577

Rockingham, Marquis of, 87, 88
Rocques, Gen. (French General), 353
Rodin, Auguste, 578
Rodriguez, Simon, 329
Roger de Coverly Papers (See Addi-
    son, also Steele)
Roncière de Noury, Admiral de la,
    404
Röntgen, Wilhelm Konrad von, 580
Roosevelt, Franklin Delano, 311, 581
"   Theodore, 78, 274, 306,
    477, 583, 586, 605
Root, Elihu, 585
Rosas, Manuel, 241
Rosecranse, Gen. William S., 399
Rosetti, Dante Gabriel, 90, 486, 515,
    587, 665
Rostand, Edmond, 588
Rothschild, Mayer Alselm, 589
"   Nathan Mayer, 589
Rough Riders, The, 584
Rousseau, Jean Jacques, 68, 576, 591
Rowley, Thomas (See Chatterton)
Roxana (Wife of Alexander The
    Great), 15
Royal Academy, 390, 391, 564, 605,
    693
Royal Geographical Society, 415, 648
"   Institute, 325
"   School of Mines, 325
"   Society, 192, 202, 325, 412, 500,
    521, 664, 747, 748
Royal Society of Berlin, 551
Rubens, Peter Paul, 592
Rubicon, 364
Rubinstein, Anton Grigorovich, 594,
    676
Rudolph II, Emperor of Germany,
    374
Rudolphine Tables, 374
"Rump Parliament," 149
Ruskin, John, 90, 587, 595
Russo-Japanese War, 401

S

Sabina, Cardinal, 38
Said Pasha, 403, 404
Saint-Beuve, Charles-Augustin, 597
St. Clair, Gen., 322
Saint-Gaudens, Augustus, 598
St. Paul's Cathedral, 250, 377, 391,
    497, 565, 606, 632, 694, 700, 722,
    747, 748
Saint-Saëns, Charles Camille, 600
Saint-Simon, Claude, 601
Saladin, 567, 603

Salisbury, Lord, 169
Salmeron, Alfonso, 329
Salvation Army (See William Booth)
Samoan Islands, Annexation of, 459
Sand, George, 122, 213, 693
Sandemanians, 203
Santa Anna, 314
Sappho, 197
Sardou, Victorien, 54
Sargent, John Singer, 342, 604
Savage, Richard, 358
Savonarola, Girolamo, 606
Savoye Theatre, 251
Saxons, 16, 114
Say, Jean Baptiste, 468
Schlegel, August Wilhelm, 201, 287, 647
Schiller, Johann von, 320, 607, 612
Schleswig-Holstein Question, 56
Schley, Gen. Winfield S., 166
Schöffer, Peter, 262
Schopenhauer, Arthur, 501, 609, 713
Schubert, Franz Peter, 611
Schumann, Robert, 612
Schurman Philippine Commission, 166
Schuyler, Gen. Philip J., 267
Scipio, Publius Cornelius, 269, 270
Scopes Trial, 78
Scott, Sir Walter, 142, 254, 334, 370, 391, 614, 664
Scott, Gen. Winfield, 257, 399, 532
Secession, 81, 158, 356, 399, 408, 409
Seleucus, 552
Selkirk, Alexander, 160
Seneca, Lucius Annæus, 197, 498, 616
"   M. Annæus, 616
Serapis, Battle with Bon Homme Richard, 360
Serrail, Gen., 353
Sertorius, 547
Servetus, Michael, 100, 617
Servilius, 269
Settle, Elkanah, 180
"Seven Sisters" Act, 739
Seven Weeks' War, 475
"   Years' War, 225, 425, 444, 533
Severn, Joseph, 371
Seward, William Henry, 260
Seymour, Horatio, 258
"   Jane, 193, 292
Sforza, Duke Lodovico, 402
Shaftesbury, Earl of, 180, 418
Shakespeare, William, 1, 111, 134, 135, 255, 361, 392, 449, 486, 608, 619, 702, 703
Shaw, George Bernard, 440, 622

Shelley, Percy Bysshe, 370, 486, 624
Sheridan, Gen. Philip Henry, 283, 625
"   Richard Brinsley, 280, 483, 535, 627
Sherman Anti-Trust Law, 578
"   John, 459
"   Gen. William T., 258, 275, 599, 628
Shiloh, Battle of, 257, 330
Siddons, Sarah T., 565, 630
Sidney, Sir Philip, 631
Sigismund, Emperor, 172, 324
Simone, Sculptor, 172
Simonides, 9
Simplified Spelling, 585
Single Tax, 246, 247
Sistine Chapel, 467, 468
Sixtus IV, Pope, 460, 461
Sklodowska, Ladislas, 152
Slavery, 7, 29, 80, 81, 98, 158, 175, 210, 227, 259, 346, 408, 409, 415, 520, 532, 655, 719
Sleepy Hollow Cemetery, 334
Smith, Adam, 632
"   Alfred E., 311, 582
"   Sir Donald A. (Lord Strathcona), 298
Smith, Capt. John, 315, 634
"   Joseph, 635, 755
"   Sydney, 431
Smollett, Tobias George, 637
Socialism, 449, 493, 601
Socrates, 25, 200, 201, 537, 638, 752
Soldiers' Bonus, 140
Solon, 640
Somers, Lord, 8
Somme, Battle of, 215, 263, 354
Sophist Philosophers, 638
Sophocles, 9, 201, 202, 529, 641
Sophroniscus, 638
Sorbonne, 153
South Pole, 94
Southampton, Earl of, 620
Southey, Robert, 134, 163
Soviet Republics, Founder of, 400
Spanish-American War, 166, 167, 459, 583
Spanish Armada, 177, 194, 531
Spartacus, 547
Spencer, Gabriel, 361
"   Herbert, 151, 643
Spenser, Edmund, 632
Spinoza, Benedictus de, 644
"Spirit of St. Louis", 410, 411
Staël, Madame de, 646, 651
"Stalwarts", 240
Stamp Act, 223, 534
Stanford, Leland, University, 310

Standard Oil Company, 577
Stanhope, Lord, *233*
Stanley, Henry M., 415, **647**
Stanton, Edwin M., 357
Star Chamber, 396
States-General in France, 427
States' Rights, 98, 158, 347, 476
Stead, William, 67
Steele, Sir Richard, 8, **649**
Stendahl, (Henri-Marie Beyle), **650**
Stephen of Blois, 288
"   George (Lord Mount Stephen), *298*
Stephenson, George, **652**
Stevenson, Robert Louis, 462, 465, 574, 599, **653**
Stewart, Henry (See Lord Darnley)
"   James, Duke of Richmond, 278
Stoddard, Charles W., 129
"   Richard Henry, 79
Story, Francis V., 259
Stowe, Harriet Beecher, **655**
Strauss, Richard, **656**
Stuart, Alexander, **199**
"   James, Earl of Mar and Moray, 452
Stuart, Mary, 293
Stuyvesant, Peter, **658**
Suez Canal, 169, 403, 404, 707, 708
Sullivan, Anne, 51, 371, (Mrs. John Macy)
Sullivan, Sir Arthur S., **249**
Sully, Maximilien de Bethune, 291
Sun Yat-Sen, **659**
Supreme Court, 133, 299, 305, 317, 484, 578, 582, 583
Supreme War Council, 264
Surgery, 411, 412
"Swede's Stone," 261
Swedenborg, Emanuel, **661**
Swift, Jonathan, 614, 659, **663**
Swinburne, Algernon Charles, 486, 588, **664**
Syme, Dr. James, 411
Syms, Dr. John, 297

T

Taft, William Howard, 78, 317, 318, 459, 584, **666**
Taine, Hippolyte Adolphe, **667**
Talleyrand, Due de, 646, **668**
Tamerlaine (Timŭr), **670**
Tariff Question, 98, 133, 545, 694, 739
Tarkington, Booth, **671**
Tasso, Torquato, **673**
Tatars (or Tartars), 335, 336, 337, 386

Taylor, John, 755
"   Zachary, 126, 158, 210, **675**
Tchaikovsky, Peter Ilyitch, **676**
"Teapot Dome" Scandals, 141, 271
Tecumseh, 276
Telegraph, Invention of, 486
Telephone, Invention of, 51
Telescope, 236, 374, 500
Temple, Sir William, 663
Tennessee, Army of, 257
Tennyson, Alfred, Lord, **678**
Terry, Ellen, 332, 623, 679
Texas, Annexation of, 98, 174
"   War for Independence, 314
Thackeray, William Makepeace, **638**, **680**
Thalberg, Sigismund, 413
Thames, Battle of, 277
Theagenes of Rhegium, 307
Themistocles, **682**, 752
Theocritus, 704
Theodora, Byzantine Queen, 366
Thedosius The Great, **683**
Theophrastus, 197
Thermometer, 236
Thicknesse, Philip, 234
Thirty Years' War, 261, 572, 608, 713, 714
Thoreau, Henry David, 12, 195, **685**, 729
Throgmorton, Elizabeth, 557
Thucydides, 683
Thumb, "Gen." Tom, 41
Tilden, Samuel J., 283
Tilton, Theodore, 48
Tirpitz, Alfred Friedrich von, Admiral, 733
Titian, **687**
Tolstoy, Count Leo, **688**
Trafalgar, Battle of, 497
Trial By Jury, Origin, 17
Trollope, Anthony, **690**
"Trusts," 584
Tuan Ch'-Jui, 660
Turenne, Gen. Henri, 456
Turgenev, Ivan Sergeyevich, 213, **691**, 756
Turner, Joseph Mallord William, 596, 693
Tuscany, Grand Duke of, 236, 237
Twain, Mark (See Samuel Langhorne Clemens)
Tyler, John, 98, **694**

U

"Uncle Tom's Cabin," 71
"Underground Railway," 71

Underwood Tariff Act, 739
Union Pacific "Corner," 274
United States Bank, 339
    "   Steel Corporation (See Car-
        negie)
Urban, Pope, 236

V

Vaccination, 349, 350, 453
Van Buren, Martin, 277, 339, 696
Vanderbilt, Cornelius, 697
Van Dyck, Anthony, 594, 699
Vane, Sir Harry, 741
Varro, Gaius Terentius, 269
Vasari, Architect and Writer, 173
Vatican City, 494
Vaudreuil, Marquis de, 479, 480
Velazquez, Diego, 266, 700
Venezuelan Question, 133
Vercingetorix, 364
Verdi, Giuseppe, 702
Verdun, 263, 354
Vergil, 155, 312, 313, 322, 703
Verrocchio, Andrea del, 402
Versailles, 417, 427
    "   Treaty of, 271, 300
Vespasian, 362, 539
Vespucius, Americus, 705
Vicksburg, Surrender of, 257
Victor Emmanuel, 242
Victoria, Queen of England, 169, 706
Villon, François, 708
Vinci, Leonardo da (See Leonardo)
Virgil (See Virgil)
Voetius, Gisbert, 164
Volstead Act, 271
Voltaire, François Marie Arouet, 8,
    68, 224, 225, 226, 406, 591, 710
Vortex Theory, 164, 374

W

Wagner, Richard, 413, 501, 712
Walker's Filibuster, 532
Wallace, Alfred R., 156
Wallenstein, Gen. Albrecht Wenzel
    Eusebius von, 713
Walpole, Hugh, 178
    "   Horace, 118, 533, 631, 650
War College, 585
    "   of Austrian Succession, 479
    "   of Independence, 476
    "   of the Rebellion (See Civil
        War)
War of 1812, 97, 203, 277, 339
Ward, Artemas (See Charles Farrar
    Browne)

Warner, Charles Dudley, 129
Warwick, Sir Philip, 148
Washington, George, 265, 267, 268,
    387, 388, 435, 510, 715
Watt, James, 717
Watts-Dunton, Theodore, 588, 665
Wayne, Gen. Anthony, 276, 406
Webster, Daniel, 277, 695, 718
    "   Noah, 720
Wedgewood, Josiah, 156
Weisse, C. F., (German Dramatist),
    405
Wellington, Arthur Wellesley, Duke
    of, 590, 721
Wells, Herbert George, 178, 723
Wenceslas, 231, 324
Wesley, John, 725
West, Benjamin, 233
West India Company, 658
Westminster Abbey, 44, 119, 150, 168,
    181, 252, 257, 273, 333, 359, 362,
    415, 448, 452, 501, 534, 536, 597,
    631, 679, 682, 707, 718, 748
West Point Military Academy, 399,
    524, 532
"Whiskey Insurrection," 406
Whistler, James Abbott McNeill, 580,
    726
Whitehead, George, 725
Whitman, Walt, 91, 728
Whittier, John Greenleaf, 428, 730
Wickersham Commission, 311
Wilderness, Battle of, 258
Wilhelm II of Germany, 731
Wilkes, John, 303
William I of England (The Con-
    queror), 75, 733
William III of England, 159, 520, 735,
    735
William of Champeaux, 2
    "   of Malmesbury, 17
    "   of Orange (See William III
        of England)
William the Lion, King of Scotland,
    289
Williams, Roger, 737
Willis N. P., 544
"Wilmot Proviso," 175
Wilson, Harry Leon, 672
    "   Woodrow, 78, 140, 271, 317,
        417, 581, 584, 586, 667, 733, 738
Winthrop, John, 740
Wireless Telegraphy, 442
Wishart, George, 378
Witchcraft (Salem), 454
Woffington, Peg, 243, 303
Wolf, Friedrich August, 307

Wolfe, Gen. James, 480, 742
Wolsey, Cardinal, 292, 743
Woman Suffrage, 259
Woodruff, Wilford, 755
Wordsworth, William, 134, 163, 389, 745
World Court, 586
World War, 214, 263, 299, 310, 342, 353, 377, 401, 443
Wren Sir Christopher, 747
Wright, Orville, 748
" Wilbur, 748
Wycliffe, John, 323, 750

X

X-Ray, 580
Xanthippe, 639
Xavier, St. Francis, 329
Xenocrates, 197

Xenophon, 639, 751
Xerxes, 683, 753
Ximenes, Cardinal, 206

Y

Yap, Island of, 271
Yorktown, 267
Young, Brigham, 754
" Italy Party, 457
Ypres, Battle of, 263
Yuan Shih-K'ai, 660

Z

Zend Avesta, 758
Zenodotus, 308
Zola, Émile, 213, 454, 756
Zoroaster, 757
Zwingli, Ulrich, 430, 751, 759